AF698472

2-7
23, 24
41-49
30-49
50-57
73-75
63, 65
ch 5 & 6
9
10
265-283
387-395
13

The Legal Environment of Business

Second Edition

Edward J. Conry
University of Colorado at Denver

Gerald R. Ferrera
Bentley College

Karla H. Fox
University of Connecticut

Allyn and Bacon
Boston London Sydney Toronto

Series Editor: Henry Reece
Senior Editorial Assistant: Katherine Grubbs
Cover Administrator: Linda Dickinson
Composition Buyer: Linda Cox
Manufacturing Buyer: Tamara Johnson
Editorial Production Service: York Production Services

Copyright © 1990, 1986 by Allyn and Bacon
A Division of Simon & Schuster
160 Gould Street, Needham Heights,
Massachusetts 02194

All rights reserved. No part of the material protected by this copyright notice may be reproduced or utilized in any form or by any means, electronic or mechanical, including photocopying, recording, or by any information storage and retrieval system, without written permission from the copyright owner.

Printed in the United States of America
10 9 8 7 6 5 4 3 2 95 94 93 92 91 90

Conry, Edward J.
The legal environment of business / Edward J. Conry, Gerald R. Ferrera, Karla H. Fox — 2nd ed.
p. cm.
Includes bibliographical references.
ISBN 0-205-12192-6
1. Industrial laws and legislation—United States. 2. Trade regulation—United States. 3. Commercial law—United States. I. Ferrera, Gerald R. II. Fox, Karla H. III. Title.
KF1600.C565 1990
343.73'07—dc20
[347.3037] 89-17847
CIP

Dedication

For Anne L. Conry — EJC

For my wife, Judith, and our son, David — GRF

For Scott McKee Pritchett — KHF

ACKNOWLEDGMENTS

We would like to thank the following reviewers for the valuable suggestions they offered while this book was being written: Wm. Dennis Ames, Indiana University of Pennsylvania; Renee D. Culverhouse, Auburn University at Montgomery; William J. Dunn, Loyola University of Chicago; Jack E. Karns, University of North Dakota; James E. McDonald, Weber State College; Irvin L. Tankersley, Memphis State University; and John W. Truslow, Georgia State University. Karla H. Fox wishes to acknowledge the invaluable assistance of her research assistant, Scott McKee Pritchett, and Gerald R. Ferrera wishes to acknowledge the invaluable assistance of Margo E. K. Reder of Bentley College, without whom their portions of the Second Edition would not have been written.

The Authors

EDWARD J. CONRY received a B.A. from California State University at Fullerton, an M.B.A. from the University of California at Berkeley, and a J.D. from the University of California at Davis. He is the author or co-author of over ten books on business law and/or business ethics, and is a co-author of the successful Allyn & Bacon text, *Business Law: Text and Cases, The Legal Environment*. Professor Conry is past president of the Rocky Mountain Business Law Association and has served as a reviewer and staff editor for the *American Business Law Journal*. He is the Founding Chair of the ABLA Section on Business Ethics. In addition, he has written a weekly column on Business Ethics for the past four years for *The Denver Post*. He is currently an associate professor of business law and ethics at the University of Colorado at Denver.

GERALD R. FERRERA received a B.S. from Boston College, an M.S. in taxation from Bentley College, and a J.D. from the New England School of Law. He, too, served as co-author of Allyn and Bacon's *Business Law: Text and Cases, The Legal Environment*. Professor Ferrera is a past president of the North Atlantic Business Law Association, a staff editor of the *North Atlantic Regional Business Law Journal,* a legal consultant to professional and business associations, and a member of the Massachusetts and Federal Bars. Professor Ferrera is currently a professor of business law and chair of the Law Department at Bentley College.

KARLA H. FOX received her B.A. and her J.D. from Duke University. She is past staff editor of the *American Business Law Journal,* past legal advisor to the Connecticut General Assembly, and is a member of the North Carolina and Connecticut Bars. Professor Fox is currently Associate Dean of the School of Business Administration at the University of Connecticut, where she is a Professor of Business Law.

Brief Contents

5 Business and Consumers 633

6 International Business Law 725

Expanded Contents

2 The Legal Environment of Business Transactions 171

19 Securities Regulations I 530

20 Securities Regulations II 549

21 Environmental Law 578

Cases

Preface

This book has several objectives, some traditional, some unique. The traditional objectives include describing the areas of law that seem to be of greatest importance to business managers. Thus, this book covers the legal environment topics that managers, particularly those in large organizations, may frequently deal with—topics such as contracts, insider trading, tying agreements, and relations with administrative agencies. This book also satisfies the AACSB requirement for "a background of the . . . legal environment . . . along with ethical, political and economic considerations . . . as they affect . . . business organizations" and covers international business transactions as well.

In addition the book attempts to accomplish a few fairly unique goals. First, it covers the basic core of business law topics: contracts, agency, property, and business organization. These are covered both because they are the legal issues that managers will most frequently encounter and because knowledge of these topics is often critical to an understanding of the legal environment topics. For example, students who understand the basics of contract law can digest the concept of employment-at-will more easily and with a greater appreciation of its import than can those without a background in contract law.

Coverage of these basic topics also reflects a sensitivity to the position of legal environment courses in today's curricula. Most legal environment courses are the student's first and only business law course. It is essential that these students have at least some exposure to basic business law before entering the business world. For those who take the legal environment course as an elective, usually after a basic business law course, the traditional coverage offers an opportunity to review the core topics and view them in light of legal environment issues. And, finally, surveys of managers and corporate counsel published by members of the American Business Law Association clearly indicate that the blending of basic business law topics with legal environment topics is the most appropriate coverage for the education of future managers. Studies of the perceptions of corporate counsel and practicing managers by Donnell (1968), Klayman-Nesser (1984), and Moore-Gillen (1984) support the conclusion that the blending of a few key traditional business law topics with the core of legal environment topics best suits the needs of today's managers.

Another feature of this text is its extensive integration of business ethics into the legal discussion, satisfying the AACSB requirements. In addition to an entire chapter devoted to law and business ethics, each chapter includes a discussion of ethical issues relevant to the chapter's theme. And ethical questions are presented at the end of each chapter, allowing students to explore and consider their personal beliefs in relation to potential business dilemmas. Thus the book represents a significant step toward the incorporation of ethics into the business school education.

Our motives for the focus on ethics are multiple. First, we view the law as perhaps the best curricular home for ethics. Lawyers are generally trained to balance competing social claims in their arguments and analysis, so they are usually comfortable dealing with ethical issues.

Further, the law is something more than a set of rules to be memorized. Business law is a "philosophical system," an articulation of this society's beliefs about right and wrong actions in business. Business law is a system that has been forced to confront and integrate the many philosophical, religious, and political belief systems in this country's pluralistic society. In this regard, it is a highly distinctive philosophical system—one that has been forced to *resolve the conflicts* among many of the other systems of basic thought. One who seeks maturity of insight into business ethics can wisely start with the study of business law.

Our most fundamental reason for exploring business ethics has been our concern for the students of business who now comprise about 20 percent of this nation's college graduates. These persons have for some years been educated with a nearly exclusive focus on the profitability of their conduct. The discipline's research suggests that business students are less morally mature than other students; further, business education fosters less moral growth than education in other majors. While our society needs efficient managers, it needs more managers who are *both* ethical and efficient. Thus our focus in the ethics portions of this book has been on the *personal level*. Students are asked repeatedly to decide what they believe to be right or wrong in a given situation. It is our hope that they will leave the course with a much clearer understanding of their own ethical views. We invite you to join us in this venture.

FEATURES OF THE NEW EDITION

New to this edition are the following features:

1. An additional chapter on Securities Regulations.
2. A new chapter on torts.
3. Expanded coverage of contracts.
4. Separate chapters on Property Law and Computer Law.
5. Vignettes discussing "Business Decisions and the Law"—every chapter opens with a vignette that gives a practical application of the themes to be discussed in that chapter.

CHAPTER ELEMENTS

Each chapter of the text begins with an opening quote relating to the ethical or philosophical dimension of the chapter theme. This is followed by a "business problem" that can be solved with the information in the chapter. Learning objectives familiarize students with the key concepts that should be mastered in the chapter and are followed by an introduction to the chapter.

An average of four cases per chapter illustrate relevant and current issues discussed within the chapter. Each case is followed by three case questions, one of which deals with an ethical consideration. These questions may be used for self-testing, self-exploration, or class discussion.

A section near the end of each chapter highlights ethical issues pertaining to the chapter's subject matter. Each chapter concludes with the following elements that can be used for review, study, or class discussion purposes: numbered summary of the chapter's key concepts; page-referenced key terms; legal questions; ethical questions; and suggested readings.

1 Introduction to the Legal Environment

1 Introduction to Law

"When I think then of the law, I see a princess mightier than she who once wrought at Bayeux [referring to a battle that united England into a single nation] eternally weaving into her web dim figures of the everlengthening past—figures too dim to be noticed by the idle, too symbolic to be interpreted except by her pupils, but to the discerning eye disclosing every painful step and every world-shaking contest by which mankind has worked and fought its way from savage isolation to organic social life."

—Oliver Wendell Holmes, Jr. (in steel letters on marble at Boalt Hall, Law School of the University of California, Berkeley)

■ LEARNING OBJECTIVES

After you have read this chapter, you should be able to:

1. Describe the reasons why potential business managers should study the legal environment of business.
2. Describe the major definitions of law offered by different schools of jurisprudence.
3. Define the major sources and categories of law affecting business.
4. Describe two basic philosophical concepts underpinning much of our law.

Business Decisions and the Law

Ability or Friendship?

As a manager, you will hire and fire people. That activity requires that you be familiar with a variety of the laws described in this book. The following fact pattern is presented to illustrate the kind of business decision that is influenced by the legal environment of business. All the chapters in this book begin with such a business decision. In the body of the chapter, the rule of law that influences the decision is described.

> Assume that you are the owner of a hamburger outlet that employs ten persons. You need to hire another employee and there are two applicants. One is a good friend from high school with whom you would enjoy working. The other is a minority woman who seems more talented at doing the work required by the job. As you think about the situation you decide that you would enjoy the company of your friend more than you would enjoy the extra profits generated by the more talented minority. Assuming that no state law affects your decision, is it legal for you to hire the friend instead of the minority woman?

Introduction

Across the country, students have expressed the following views on the study of the legal environment of business:

1. This course is more "real world" oriented than many other courses in the business curriculum. It communicates information that students consider essential to the successful practice of business after graduation.
2. Some students become excited about learning while taking this introductory law course. Often, persons who have been only mediocre students become intellectually alive during this course.
3. The course requires students to work harder than other courses do, but it is worth the additional effort.

Scholars and professors of the legal environment of business have identified a number of objectives for this course. The following objectives are among those most frequently mentioned.

1. Students need to know enough about the legal environment of business so that they will be able to spot legal problems when they encounter them during their careers.
2. As an obligation of citizenship, business students need to understand how the American legal system works and must be able to participate in it fully. They need to develop mature views about their duty to obey the law.
3. The study of law facilitates the liberal education of business students by exposing them to our civilization's most important ideas.
4. The study of law enables students to expand their ability to analyze, recall, evaluate, and synthesize information. This business topic, more than many others, strengthens these abilities in students.
5. The study of the legal environment of business allows students to form mature beliefs about what is morally right or wrong conduct in business.

This book is designed to help you accomplish all of these objectives. The authors believe that this course may be among the most important in your academic career.

Definitions of Law

Definitions of law are quite useful; they can help you figure out what motivates lawmakers when new law is made or when old law is changed.

Lay Definitions

There are a variety of definitions of the law. Most laypersons (those who are not lawyers) think of the law as something like "written rules of conduct enforced by the government." As an example, *Webster's New Collegiate Dictionary* defines law as "rules of conduct . . . enforced by a controlling authority." The law of Western nations is based in part on Roman legal concepts. One of these concepts is that individuals are held responsible only to *written* laws. This requirement is intended to protect the freedom and property of individuals from unfair attack.

Jurisprudential Definitions

If you wanted to be able to think more clearly and deeply about the function and meaning of the law, you would study **jurisprudence.** This is the study of the philosophy of law as distinguished from the study of only the rules of law. Jurisprudence is characterized by fairly well-defined schools of thought. Although these schools of thought agree on many points, they conflict on others. If you have a basic understanding of jurisprudence, you will be able to understand the law more easily, see the forces that shape new law, and predict the directions in which the law is likely to change.

Natural Law

The **natural law** theory of jurisprudence was the first one widely articulated. Many early Greek philosophers, such as Aristotle, might be characterized as natural law thinkers. The core idea of this school of thought is that there are truths about right law that humankind can come to know, usually by the use of the reasoning mind. The following are some examples of natural law conclusions:

1. Do good and avoid evil. (Aquinas)
2. Keep your promises. (Grotius)
3. Apply the law equally to all persons. (The Constitution of the United States)
4. Do not lie. (The Bible)
5. Repay those whom you have carelessly injured. (Grotius)

Natural law is universal. It exists independent of laws made by people and is superior to them. For example, there were in Nazi Germany many laws designed to persecute the Jews. Some persons who obeyed these laws were, after the Allied victory in World War II, convicted at the Nuremburg trials of violating natural law even though they obeyed the written laws of their country. Natural law is not necessarily written law.

One approach to natural law, used by Aristotle, is to *observe* the world, particularly humanity. Then we are able to see the "essence" of what it means to be, for example, a good worker or a good person. This essence is then the natural law goal for all persons. Other natural law thinkers apparently viewed the reasoning of a solitary mind as the path to knowing natural law. Thus, thinkers such as Thomas Aquinas viewed the reasoning process as a gift from God; therefore, reasoning is a process by which people come to know the will of God—that is, natural law.

A major criticism of natural law is that different persons reach different conclusions. Another criticism is that it encourages individuals to disobey written laws that they judge to be in conflict with natural law. For example, the television news program "60 Minutes" presented the story of a person with a doctorate from the Yale Divinity School who smuggled Mexican nationals across the American border (in violation of U.S. immigration laws) so they could find jobs and support their families. This person seemed to have a natural law perspective that made him feel so comfortable in violating written law that he was willing to make public his civil disobedience.

Historical School

The core idea of **historical jurisprudence** is that law is an expression of the historical "spirit of the people." That is, the unique history of each nation produces something similar to a consensus of the population, or ***Volksgeist,*** on what the law ought to be. Lawyers, legislators, and judges then simply give voice to this *Volksgeist* by creating law. Friedrich Karl von Savigny, a German who lived from 1779 to 1861, was the founder of this school of jurisprudential thought.

An example of laws reflecting the historical will of the people, this *Volksgeist,* might be the Eighteenth and the Twenty-First Amendments to the Constitution of the United States. After several decades of political activity by the temperance movement, which sought to outlaw the sale of "demon rum," the Eighteenth Amendment was adopted in 1918, prohibiting the sale or transportation of alcoholic beverages. By 1933, however, the widespread violation of Prohibition and the control of liquor sales by criminals produced a near consensus that the evils of demon rum were not as great as the evils of Prohibition. This *Volksgeist* resulted in the Twenty-First Amendment, which repealed the Eighteenth. The historical school of jurisprudence has been severely criticized on the grounds that it portrays persons and nations as mere pawns of the events of history.

Positive Law Jurisprudence

The core idea of **positive law jurisprudence** is that law is the end result of the lawmaking process of the legitimate governmental authority. In order to be legitimate, a law need only be the end product of the authorized process of the government in power. Positive law contrasts with natural law because almost all written law is legitimate positive law. This is not necessarily so for natural law. Positive law proponents must almost always obey the written law, unlike natural law proponents who may more easily justify not complying with evil laws. The positive law perspective promotes social stability. Unlike the historical school, positive law does not derive its legitimacy from a *Volksgeist* or historical will of the people of a nation. The next three paragraphs describe the history of positive law.

Thomas Hobbes, an English philosopher who lived from 1588 to 1679, is often described as the founder of the positive views of both law and government. The prevailing perspective on government before Hobbes' time was the feudal perspective. In this view God caused individuals to be born to *stations* such as that of the king. Thus the king's authority to rule and make laws was derived from God. In the feudal system it was the king's duty to determine the natural law, as God's will, and to implement it.

In 1533 King Henry VIII of England broke from the Catholic Church in order to divorce his wife Catherine of Aragon who bore him no sons. That separation from the Catholic Church caused the feudal legitimacy of the king to be undermined somewhat. The power of Parliment increased. The view of legitimacy based on consent of the governed then began to gain ground in England. In the early 1600s Hobbes was an advisor to King Charles I. Charles I was popular with the nobility but not necessarily with merchants, Parliament, or the army. A coalition of Puritan forces led by Oliver Cromwell rebelled against Charles, vested supreme governmental authority in Parliament, won a civil war against the king, and put Charles I to death in 1649. Clearly the death of Charles and the rise of Cromwell signaled a defeat for the English view of feudal legitimacy. The lack of popular support for the rebellion grew with the execution of the king. Accordingly, Cromwell's government was a blow to the idea of legitimacy based on the consent of the governed.

Hobbes had fled to Paris, where he surveyed his divided nation and the damage done by the civil war. Partly in reaction to this, he articulated his positivist view of law and government. It was not based on the will of God or the consent of the governed. In Hobbes' view, all established authority must be obeyed; stability and peace, he concluded, are the most important functions of the law.

The Jurisprudence of Legal Realism

The core idea of **legal realism** is that the American legal system is a good legal structure but that it can be corrupted when nonlegal factors influence legal decisions. In addition, some realists believe many legal decisions have such weak moral content, or the moral import of the decision is so hard to grasp, that nonlegal, nonmoral factors can dominate. This school believes that judges are easily and often influenced by the status, income, education, race, religion, and other nonlegal attributes of the people who participate in trials. According to legal realism, criticism of judges and juries can make them focus on the rules of law rather than the status of persons.

Comparing Jurisprudential Schools

There are other schools of jurisprudence. But the ones we have discussed fairly represent the range of thinking on this topic. Natural law and positive law are clearly the two major schools of Western thought and the ones most in conflict with each other. Natural law is most concerned with what *ought* to be written as law. Positive law focuses on what *is* written as law. Positive law prizes order and stability above all else, while natural law prizes fairness and justice at the expense of some disorder.

There are relations among schools of jurisprudence and the legal institutions in this country. Certainly legislators often view themselves as engaged in turning *Volksgeist* into written law. They are always likely to be defeated at the polls if they do not serve the people who elected them. Many people view the United States Constitution as the embodiment of a large number of natural law statements. Courts, especially when interpreting constitutions, often articulate natural law perspectives, but when interpreting statutes, they often seem historical or positivist.

Roots of the American Legal System in English Common Law

This country uses a legal system called the *common law system.* It is a common law country because of its historical ties to England. Since the original thirteen colonies were largely English, they adopted England's legal system as their own. When new states were admitted to the United States they also typically adopted "the common law of England" as their law. Other countries with historical ties to England tend to have common law systems. Thus Canada, Ireland, Australia, New Zealand, Nigeria, South Africa, and India are common law countries.

The other major legal system used by countries is called the *civil law system.* Civil law countries tend to model their legal systems after that of the Roman empire or France. Most of the world uses the civil law system. Italy, France, and West Germany are civil law countries. So are Spain, Mexico, Argentina, Poland, the Soviet Union, and China.

Two basic characteristics distinguish these systems. The first is the extent to which the systems rely on judge-made (i.e., court-made) law. Common law countries use this kind of law extensively, while civil law countries use a minimal amount of judge-made law. The second distinguishing feature is the amount of trust these two systems accord to government officials. Civil law countries place great trust in their government officials, while common law countries tend to rely much more on the "rule of law" than on the judgment of individual officials.

England's distrust of government officials arose from many causes. Perhaps the most pervasive cause was the frequency with which the country was ruled by someone with a different ancestry or religion than the native English. For example, the first king of England, William the Conqueror, was a Norman from the western part of France. In 1066 this foreigner defeated the combined forces of the kings of various English principalities. He and his ancestors left the English system of county or shire courts intact for some years. After the execution in about 1225 of *Magna Carta,* which generally limited the power of the king and emphasized the importance of the rule of law, London judges were sent to the county courts to ensure that law used throughout the country was uniform, or "common." Thus the words **common law** often mean the law of England after Magna Carta. These words also mean this English common law as refined after its transplantation to the United States.

Creation of Laws

Today, there are four basic ways to create laws in the United States:

1. Adoption of constitutions and constitutional amendments
2. Enactment of legislation
3. Creation of administrative regulations of governmental agencies
4. Decisions by appellate courts

These law creation processes occur on the federal, state, and local levels (see figure 1.1).

Constitutions

Law is created when people adopt constitutions or amend existing constitutions. Most citizens of the United States are governed by both the federal Constitution and the constitution of a particular state.

The Constitution of the United States of America was drafted at a constitutional convention and then submitted to the legislatures of the original states. When these state legislatures—acting on behalf of their people—ratified the Constitution, it became the fundamental federal law. Most states while still only territories submitted proposed constitutions to their voting citizens. Thus the people were, directly or indirectly, the source of the constitutions of this country.

Constitutions are generally the supreme sources of law. Thus no state legislation, administrative regulation, or court decision is valid if it conflicts with the state constitution. Similarly, no federal legislation, regulation, or court decision is valid if it conflicts with the Constitution of the United States. In addition, the federal Constitution is said to be "the supreme law of the land." This means that any state law—including a part of a state constitution—is void to the extent that it conflicts with the federal Constitution.

The Supreme Court of the United States is the final interpreter of the federal Constitution. The *state* supreme courts are the final authorities on the meaning of their state constitutions. In general, constitutions allocate governmental powers between people and governments, between the state and federal governments, and between the branches of government. Law that interprets the provisions of a constitution is called **constitutional law.**

Figure 1.1 Allocation of Lawmaking Powers

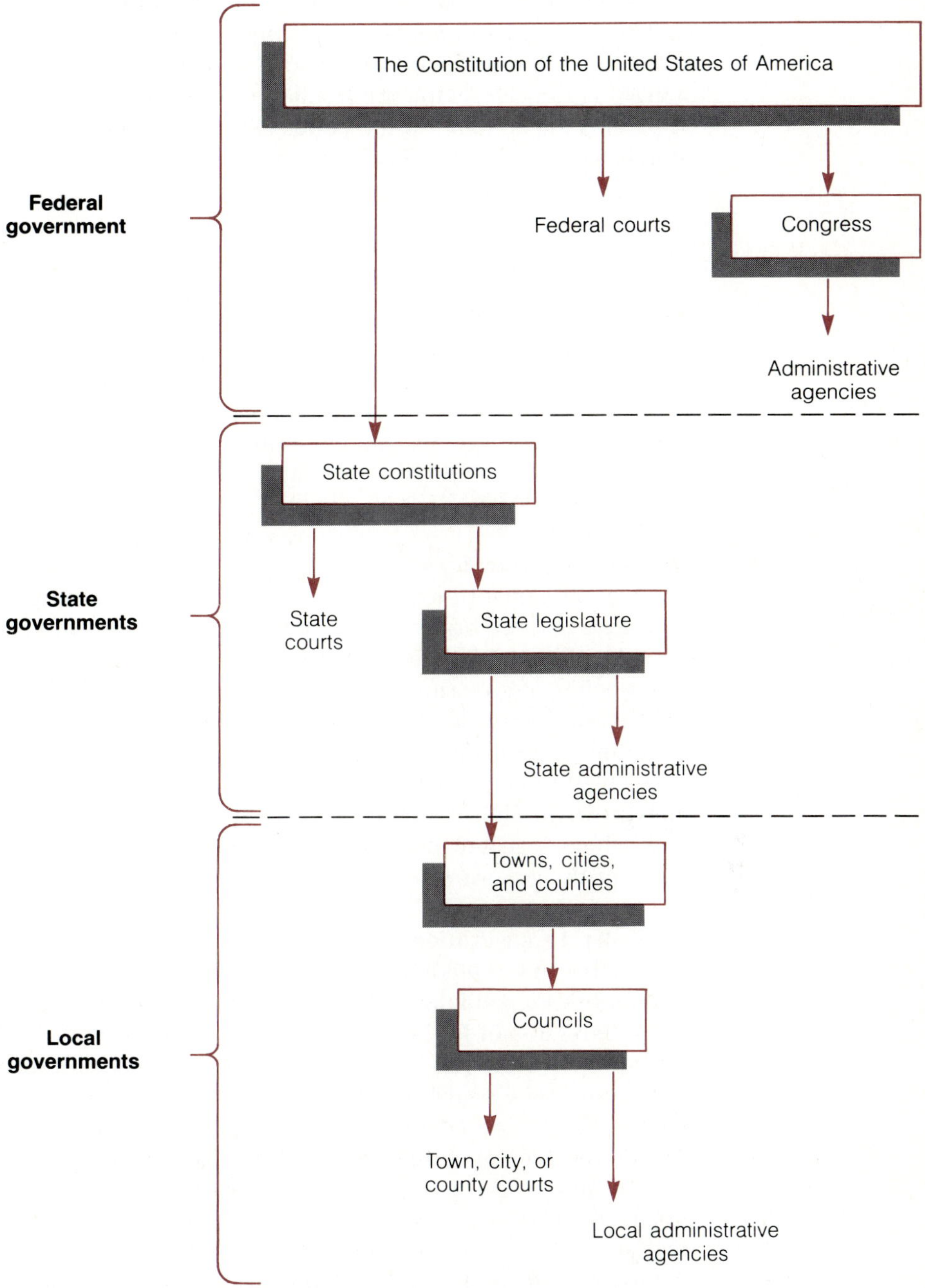

People versus Governments

The federal Constitution—particularly its first ten amendments, called the Bill of Rights—protects citizens from certain acts of government. Some of these limitations on governmental power apply only to the federal government, while others apply to both state and federal governments. The Bill of Rights is concerned, in general, with the freedoms of speech, press, and religion. It also constrains the conduct of the police and the courts. State constitutions usually contain similar provisions. Thus the constitutions allocate power and rights between the people and their government.

State Governments versus Federal Government

The federal Constitution allocates certain powers to the federal government and certain other powers to the state governments. For example, many governmental powers are divided between state governments and the federal government on the basis of interstate commerce. In general, the federal Constitution gives the federal government power to regulate interstate commerce. *Inter*state means between, or involving, two or more states. Regulation of *intra*state commerce is left to the states. Intrastate means that the commerce occurs only within one state.

Branches of Governments

The federal Constitution allocates the powers granted to the federal government among three branches of government: the executive, the legislative, and the judicial. State constitutions also allocate power, usually among three similar branches of government. And like the federal Constitution, state constitutions try to create a system of checks and balances among the branches to moderate governmental power.

Constitutional law affects business transactions in fundamental but often indirect ways. Thus constitutional law determines the extent to which any government can legislate in ways affecting business transactions, and it determines which of the governments, state or federal, are so empowered.

The Federal Constitution and Business

In 1776, the thirteen colonies broadcast their individual sovereignty in the Declaration of Independence. This declaration stated that the thirteen former colonies, "are, and of Right ought to be *Free and Independent* States" [emphasis added]. During the Revolutionary War, the colonies followed the leadership of a "Continental Congress." This body later proposed a national charter called the Articles of Confederation. While each of the states eventually adopted this charter, many states exercised their sovereignty by exempting themselves from some provisions. The Articles of Confederation thus created a very weak national government. The states retained the majority of the governmental powers.

As a result of the weak national government, problems developed with diplomacy, maintenance of armed forces, economic policy, and interstate commerce. Trade wars developed among the sovereign states as they tried to protect the economic position of their citizens. States enacted legislation banning the importation from other states of items like eggs, saddles, and tinware. They also imposed tariffs on products manufactured in other states. These trade policies became serious barriers to the growth of American business. Economic policies also varied dramatically from state to state. During the same period of economic slowdown, Massachusetts continued to support a "hard" money policy, while Rhode Island issued paper money that was basically worthless.

In response to the problems caused by a weak national government, a constitutional convention was called. It elected to discard the Articles of Confederation in favor of a new document, the Constitution of the United States. This Constitution created a much stronger federal government. It was ratified by all the states. The first new Congress assembled in 1789. As you can see, the business and economic realities of American life played a significant part in influencing the creation and character of our Constitution.

An abridged version of the Constitution follows. While only those articles, amendments, clauses, and sections that are very basic or directly important to business are presented, it still conveys the flavor of the whole document. As you read it, be particularly sensitive to whether it is the national government or the states to which specific sections apply. Also, watch for the use of the words *persons* and *citizens;* the Supreme Court has ruled that corporations and other business entities are persons within the meaning of the Constitution, but they are not citizens. The language of the Constitution incorporates the writing style of the time and may be a little new to you. Accordingly, you may find it helpful to read this short document two or three times in order to understand its basic ideas.

The Constitution of the United States of America

We the people of the United States, in Order to form a more perfect Union, establish Justice, insure domestic Tranquility, provide for the common defense, promote the general Welfare, and secure the Blessings of Liberty to ourselves and our Posterity, do ordain and establish this Constitution for the United States of America.

Article I

Section 1. All legislative Powers herein granted shall be vested in a Congress of the United States, which shall consist of a Senate and House of Representatives.

Section 7. [1] All Bills for raising Revenue shall originate in the House of Representatives; but the Senate may propose or concur with Amendments as on other Bills.

Section 8. The Congress shall have Power

1. To lay and collect Taxes, Duties, Imposts and Excises, to pay the Debts and provide for the common Defense and general Welfare of the United States; but all Duties, Imposts and Excises shall be uniform throughout the United States;
2. To borrow money on the credit of the United States;
3. To regulate Commerce with foreign Nations, and among the several States, and with the Indian Tribes;
4. To establish an uniform Rule of Naturalization, and uniform Laws on the subject of Bankruptcies throughout the United States;

5. To coin Money, regulate the Value thereof, and of foreign Coin, and fix the Standard of Weights and Measures;
8. To promote the Progress of Science and useful Arts, by securing for limited Times to Authors and Inventors the exclusive Right to their respective Writings and Discoveries;
18. To make all Laws which shall be necessary and proper for carrying into Execution the foregoing Powers, and all other Powers vested by this Constitution in the Government of the United States, or in any Department or Officer thereof.

Section 9. [5] No Tax or Duty shall be laid on Articles exported from any State.

6. No Preference shall be given by any Regulation of Commerce or Revenue to the Ports of one State over those of another: nor shall Vessels bound to, or from, one State be obliged to enter, clear, or pay Duties in another.

Section 10. [1] No State shall enter into any Treaty, Alliance, or Confederation; grant Letters of Marque and Reprisal; coin Money; emit Bills of Credit; make any Thing but gold and silver Coin a Tender in Payment of Debts; pass any Bill of Attainder, ex post facto Law, or Law impairing the Obligation of Contracts, or grant any Title of Nobility.

2. No State shall, without the Consent of the Congress, lay any Imposts or Duties on Imports or Exports, except what may be absolutely necessary for executing its inspection Laws; and the net Produce of all Duties and Imposts, laid by any State on Imports and Exports, shall be for the Use of the Treasury of the United States; and all such Laws shall be subject to the Revision and Control of the Congress.

Article II

Section 1. [1] The executive Power shall be vested in a President of the United States of America.

Article III

Section 1. The judicial Power of the United States, shall be vested in one supreme Court, and in such inferior Courts as the Congress may from time to time ordain and establish.

Article IV

Section 1. Full Faith and Credit shall be given in each State to the public Acts, Records, and judicial Proceedings of every other State.

Article V

The Congress, whenever two thirds of both Houses shall deem it necessary, shall propose Amendments to this Constitution.

Article VI

[2] This Constitution, and the Laws of the United States which shall be made in Pursuance thereof; and all Treaties made, or which shall be made, under the Authority of the United States, shall be the supreme Law of the Land; and the Judges in every State shall be bound thereby, and Any Thing in the Constitution or Laws of any State to the Contrary notwithstanding.

The Ratification of the Conventions of nine States shall be sufficient for the Establishment of this Constitution between the States so ratifying the Same.

ARTICLES IN ADDITION TO, AND AMENDMENT OF, THE CONSTITUTION OF THE UNITED STATES OF AMERICA, PROPOSED BY CONGRESS, AND RATIFIED BY THE LEGISLATURES OF THE SEVERAL STATES PURSUANT TO THE FIFTH ARTICLE OF THE ORIGINAL CONSTITUTION.

Amendment I [1791]

Congress shall make no law respecting an establishment of religion, or prohibiting the free exercise thereof; or abridging the freedom of speech, or of the press; or the right of the people peaceably to assembly, and to petition the Government for a redress of grievances.

Amendment IV [1791]

The right of the people to be secure in their persons, houses, papers, and effects, against unreasonable searches and seizures, shall not be violated, and no Warrants shall issue, but upon probable cause, supported by Oath or affirmation, and particularly describing the place to be searched, and the persons or things to be seized.

Amendment V [1791]

No person shall be deprived of life, liberty, or property, without due process of law; nor shall private property be taken for public use, without just compensation.

Amendment XIV [1868]

Section 1. No State shall make or enforce any law which shall abridge the privileges or immunities of citizens of the United States; nor shall any State deprive any person of life, liberty, or property, without due process of law; nor deny to any person within its jurisdiction the equal protection of the laws.

Amendment XVI [1870]

The Congress shall have power to lay and collect taxes on incomes, from whatever source derived, without apportionment among the several States, and without regard to any census or enumeration.

Amendment XVIII [1919]

Section 1. After one year from the ratification of this article the manufacture, sale, or transportation of intoxicating liquors within, the importation thereof into, or the exportation thereo United States and all territory subjec jurisdiction thereof for beverage pu hereby prohibited.

Amendment XXI [1933]

Section 1. The eighteenth article of amendment to the Constitution of the United States is hereby repealed.

Section 2. The transportation or importation into any State, Territory, or possession of the United States for delivery or use therein of intoxicating liquors, in violation of the laws thereof, is hereby prohibited.

Questions

1. Can the law created by a constitution be highly concrete and specified?
2. Can you see that this Constitution is very concerned with the governance of business and economic affairs?
3. Are there elements of this document, or characteristics of its history, that reflect particular schools of jurisprudence?

Statutory Law

The state constitutions and the Constitution of the United States created, respectively, the state legislatures and the Congress of the United States. These legislatures are composed of elected representatives of the people of a state and the nation. When they act as a body, the representatives of each legislature may enact new statutes.

A state legislature usually delegates some of its legislative authority to local governments. Thus towns, cities, and counties can legislate in those areas where the state has given them authority. Legislation is created by a city or town council or a county commission. This legislation is usually called an *ordinance* rather than a statute.

To be valid, the statute or ordinance must be constitutional. This means that it must not conflict with the provisions of the governing constitution or constitutions. The courts will determine whether or not a particular statute or ordinance is constitutional. You must be careful to distinguish the judicial activity of interpreting statutes from the activity of determining their constitutionality. Courts are the final authority on the constitutionality of statutes. On the other hand, when courts interpret the meaning of statutes, they are not, for practical purposes, the final authority; if a legislature does not approve of a judicial interpretation it can enact a law which, in effect, rewrites the statute.

One characteristic of a **statutory law** is that the creation process usually reflects the will of the people governed. Another characteristic is that legislatures can react rapidly to changes in society. A further characteristic is that legislatures can attack social problems with broad statutes that may significantly alter the legal environment of business. The following section presents a shortened version of a *federal* statue that has had such impact. As you read through the statute, pay particular attention to the clarity of the language used by the Congress.

Title VII of the Civil Rights Act of 1964 as amended by Equal Opportunity Act of 1972

Definitions

Section 701. For the purposes of this title—

(a) The term "person" includes one or more individuals, governments, governmental agencies, political subdivisions, labor unions, partnerships, associations, corporations. . . .

(g) The term "commerce" means trade, traffic, commerce, transportation, transmission, or communication among the several States; or between a State and any place outside thereof; . . . or between points in the same State but through a point outside thereof. . . .

(j) The term "religion" includes all aspects of religious observance and practice, as well as belief. . . .

Exemption

Section 702. This title shall not apply to . . . a religious corporation, with respect to the employment of individuals of a particular religion. . . .

Discrimination because of Race, Color, Religion, Sex, or National Origin

Section 703. (a) It shall be an unlawful employment practice for an employer—

1. to fail or refuse to hire or to discharge any individual or otherwise to discriminate against any individual with respect to his compensation, terms, conditions, or privileges of employment, because of such individual's race, color, religion, sex, or national origin; or
2. to limit, segregate, or classify his employees or applicants for employment in any way which would deprive or tend to deprive any individual of employment opportunities or otherwise adversely affect his status as an employee, because of such individual's race, color, religion, sex, or national origin. . . .

(c) It shall be an unlawful employment practice for a labor organization—

1. to exclude or to expel from its membership, or otherwise to discriminate against, any individual because of his race, color, religion, sex, or national origin; . . .
3. to cause or attempt to cause an employer to discriminate against an individual in violation of this section. . . .

(d) It shall be an unlawful employment practice for any employer, labor organization, or joint labor-management committee controlling apprenticeship or other training or retraining, including on-the-job training programs to discriminate against any individual because of his race, color, religion, sex, or national origin in admission to, or employment in, any program established to provide apprenticeship or other training. . . .

(h) Notwithstanding any other provision of this title, it shall not be an unlawful employment practice for an employer to apply different standards of compensation, or different terms, conditions, or privileges of employment pursuant to a bona fide seniority or merit system, or a system which measures earnings by quantity or quality of production or to employees who work in different locations, provided that such differences are not the result of an intention to discriminate because of race, color, religion, sex, or national origin; nor shall it be an unlawful employment practice for an employer to give and to act upon the results of any professionally developed ability test provided that such test, its administration or action upon the results is not designed, intended, or used to discriminate because of race, color, religion, sex, or national origin.

(j) Nothing contained in this title shall be interpreted to require any employer, employment agency, labor organization, or joint labor-management committee subject to this title to grant preferential treatment to any individual or to any group because of the race, color, religion, sex, or national origin of such individual or group on account of an imbalance which may exist with respect to the total number or percentage of persons of any race, color, religion, sex, or national origin employed by any employer . . . in comparison with the total number or percentage of persons of such race, color, religion, sex, or national origin in any community, State, section, or other area, or in the available work force in any community, State, section, or other area.

Questions

1. This statute defines the words *commerce* and *religion* in sections 701(g) and 701(j). Are these two definitions equally understandable? Can you determine which word is more likely to generate uncertainty about what this statute means?
2. This act allows employers to treat employees differently if *seniority* (length of time on the job) is the reason for this unequal treatment. Do you think this part of the statute is just?
3. Can you spot language in this statute that might need clarification before an employer would know exactly what conduct is legal or illegal?

Administrative Regulations

While legislatures can react quickly, they frequently lack the expertise needed to enact detailed statutes. In these cases the legislatures sometimes pass broad general statutes, such as Title VII, with the intention that the courts will later clarify that area of the law through the case law process. In other instances, when legislatures lack the expertise to legislate directly, they will create an administrative agency. For example, one part of Title VII (not reproduced here) created the Equal Employment Opportunity Commission (EEOC) and charged it with enforcing the statute.

Administrative agencies are created at all levels of government. The state, federal, and local legislatures often create administrative agencies. The Veterans Administration, the Social Security Administration, your state's driver's license division, and a city zoning commission are examples of administrative agencies. When creating agencies, legislative bodies will sometimes delegate part of their legislative powers to the agency. In these cases the agency is charged with developing expertise in a complex area and then issuing regulations or rules. Although they are created by legislatures, the agencies are usually operated by the executive branch of government. Thus the mayor, governor, or president will supervise the agency's activities.

The rules and regulations established by administrative agencies generally have the force of law; thus we call these **administrative laws.** Like statutes, the regulations can be reviewed by the courts to determine whether they are constitutional. In addition, the courts may invalidate a regulation if it is outside the scope of powers delegated by the legislature.

Case Law

Each state creates case law through its state courts. Similarly, federal courts establish federal case law. **Case law** is usually made after a trial has ended and one of the parties appeals the case. An appeal involves a review of parts of the trial by a higher court. Frequently, the appellate courts will review the trial judge's interpretation of the law. Occasionally, they will review the findings of fact. When the appellate court issues a written opinion on a case, that opinion constitutes case law.

The effectiveness of case law arises out of the doctrine of **stare decisis** (Latin for "to stand on decided cases"). This doctrine requires that once case law is established, it must be followed by lower courts in other similar cases. However, this doctrine does not strictly bind the court that rendered the appellate decision. Appellate courts can overturn their own earlier decisions.

The courts are the final authority on the interpretation of constitutions and the constitutionality of statutes and regulations. The courts also play a critical role in interpreting statutes passed by legislatures and rules made by agencies. Thus case law can be created when an appellate court is engaged in any one of the following judicial activities:

1. Interpreting a constitution
2. Determining the constitutionality of a statute
3. Interpreting a statute
4. Determining the constitutionality of an agency's rule or regulation
5. Determining the statutory authority for an agency's rule or regulation
6. Interpreting prior cases

The following case is a shortened version of an appellate court opinion. This opinion is in the same format as many others appearing in this book, so you will need to be able to interpret some of the special features of these cases. All appellate opinions are written and made public *after* a trial has ended and after the opposing parties have submitted oral and written arguments to the appellate court. Each opinion is written by one of the appellate judges. The following comments on title, citation, facts and holding, names, and disposition are intended to help you see the significance of these cases.

Title. The title of law cases is made up of the names of the parties to the lawsuit. In the following case Mr. Weber sued his employer, Kaiser Aluminum & Chemical Corporation, and his union, United Steelworkers of America. Kaiser's name was dropped when the case was assigned a title.

Citation. A citation to a case is designed to tell lawyers how to locate the particular case from among millions of cases usually found in a law library. In the citation 443 U.S. 193 (1979), the "U.S." is an abbreviation for a set of books called the *United States Reports*. This case appears within this set in volume 443. Within volume 443, this case begins on page 193. The citation also indicates that the decision was issued in 1979. All citations follow the same format of volume, set of books, page.

Facts and Opinion. The summary of the facts has been written by the authors of this text or adapted from the language of the judge to make it easier for readers to understand the case. The opinion is the language of the judge. It has been edited to make it easier for you to analyze and understand.

Names of the Parties. Court opinions use the word **plaintiff** to refer to the party who initiated the lawsuit. The word **defendant** refers to the party being sued by the plaintiff. Once the trial is concluded, the party who lost on an issue—it can be either the plaintiff or the defendant—may appeal to a higher court. Often appellate judges refer to the parties, not by their names, nor as plaintiff or defendant, but as **appellant** and **respondent.** An appellant is the one who initiated the appeal to overturn the lower court's decision. The respondent "responds" to the appeal and argues that the decision of the lower court was correct.

Disposition. In each appellate case the judge makes a decision about the next step in the process. This is usually a one- or two-word direction to a lower court such as "affirmed" or "reversed" or "remanded for a new trial." *Affirmed* means the lower court was correct in its view of the law or facts. *Reversed* means the lower court was incorrect. *Remanded for a new trial* means that additional facts must be determined during further trial proceedings. Other directions may also be given.

As you read through this case, try to compare the ways in which it is similar to, and different from, the Constitution and statute you have already read. Try to assess the extent of the problems addressed and the clarity (or ambiguity) of the language used.

United Steelworkers of America v. Weber

443 U.S. 193 (1979)

Facts

Brian Weber (plaintiff) brought this action against United Steelworkers of America (defendant) alleging discrimination on the basis of race in violation of Title VII of the Civil Rights Act of 1964.

The Steelworkers and Kaiser Aluminum & Chemical Corporation entered into a labor contract containing an affirmative action plan. The aim of the affirmative action plan was to eliminate racial imbalances among craft workers, who were then almost all white. The goal was to have the percentage of blacks in craft positions equal their percentage in the pool of local people qualified to do the work. The plan established an on-the-job training program and reserved 50 percent of the openings in these programs for blacks.

Weber brought suit against both the union and the employer, claiming that giving the craft training to blacks in preference to more senior white employees like himself was discrimination on the basis of race in violation of Title VII.

Opinion

Justice Brennan: We emphasize at the outset the narrowness of our inquiry. Since the Kaiser-USWA plan does not involve state action, this case does not present an alleged violation of the Equal Protection Clause of the Constitution. Further, since the Kaiser-USWA plan was adopted voluntarily, we are not concerned with what Title VII requires or with what a court might order to remedy a past proven violation of the Act. The only question before us is the narrow statutory issue of whether Title VII forbids private employers and unions from voluntarily agreeing upon bona fide affirmative action plans that accord racial preferences in the manner and for the purpose provided in the Kaiser-USWA plan.

Weber argues that Congress intended in Title VII to prohibit all race-conscious affirmative action plans. His argument rests upon a literal interpretation of §§703(a) and (d) of the Act. Those sections make it unlawful to "discriminate . . . because of . . . race" in hiring and in the selection of apprentices for training programs.

Weber's argument is not without force. But it overlooks the significance of the fact that the Kaiser-USWA plan is an affirmative action plan voluntarily adopted by private parties to eliminate traditional patterns of racial segregation. In this context Weber's reliance upon a literal construction of §703(a) . . . is misplaced. It is a "familiar rule, that a thing may be within the letter of the statute and yet not within the statute, because not within its spirit, nor within the intention of its makers." The prohibition against racial discrimination in §§703(a) and (d) of Title VII must therefore be read against the background of the legislative history of Title VII and the historical context from which the Act arose. Examination of those sources makes clear that an interpretation of the sections that forbade all race-conscious affirmative action would "bring about an end completely at variance with the purpose of the statute" and must be rejected.

[I]t was clear to Congress that "the crux of the problem [was] to open employment opportunities for Negroes in occupations which have been traditionally closed to them" (remarks of Sen. Humphrey), and it was to this problem that Title VII's prohibition against racial discrimination in employment was primarily addressed.

Given this legislative history, we cannot agree with Weber that Congress intended to prohibit the private sector from taking effective steps to accomplish the goal that Congress designed Title VII to achieve. . . . It would be ironic indeed if a law triggered by a nation's concern over centuries of racial injustice and intended to improve the lot of those who had "been excluded from the American dream for so long" (remarks of Sen. Humphrey), constituted the first legislative prohibition of all voluntary, private, race-conscious efforts to abolish traditional patterns of racial segregation and hierarchy.

We therefore hold that Title VII's prohibition in §§703(a) and (d) against racial discrimination does not condemn all private, voluntary, race-conscious affirmative action plans.

We need not today define in detail the line of demarcation between permissible and impermissible affirmative action plans. It suffices to hold that the challenged Kaiser-USWA affirmative action plan falls on the permissible side of the line. The purposes of the plan mirror those of the statute. Both were designed to break down old patterns of racial segregation and hierarchy.

At the same time the plan does not necessarily trammel the interests of the white employees. The plan does not require the discharge of white workers and their replacement with new black hires. Nor does the plan create an absolute bar to the advancement of white employees; half of those trained in the program will be white. Moreover, the plan is a temporary measure; it is not intended to maintain racial balance, but simply to eliminate a manifest racial imbalance. Preferential selection of craft trainees at the Gramercy plant will end as soon as the percentage of black skilled craft workers in the

Gramercy plant approximates the percentage of blacks in the local labor force.

Reversed. . . .

Case Questions

1. Is this case interpreting the Constitution, prior cases, or a statute?
2. Do you see any connection between this decision and the schools of jurisprudence discussed earlier in the chapter?
3. If the Congress disagreed with this interpretation of its statute by the United States Supreme Court, could it do anything to alter the impact of this decision?

Classification of Laws

Students must be familiar with certain legal terminology if they are to effectively study the legal environment of business. The most basic legal terminology deals with the classifications of laws.

Criminal and Civil Laws

Criminal Law

A violation of **criminal law** is called a crime. Most crimes are defined by statutes. The statutes typically say things like, "It shall be a [crime] within the State of New Hampshire to . . . [a statement of the prohibited act] . . . punishable by imprisonment for up to three years." The elements that generally must be proved in court to convict a person of a crime are (1) proof that the defendant's conduct violated a criminal statute, and (2) proof that the defendant intended to commit the act.

Criminal conduct is so serious that it is deemed to be an offense against society. Accordingly, certain agents of society—city police, county sheriffs, highway patrol officers, FBI agents, and prosecutors—will investigate potential criminal conduct and attempt to arrest and imprison those who commit criminal acts. A prosecutor will represent society in trying to convict the alleged criminal during a criminal trial. The defendant will be entitled to a trial by jury. Generally, each juror in a criminal trial must be convinced, beyond a reasonable doubt, that the evidence establishes the defendant's guilt, and all must vote to convict or the defendant goes free. If convicted, the criminal may be subjected to a fine, imprisonment, or even death.

Criminal law violations are generally classified as either misdemeanors or felonies. Misdemeanors are punishable by imprisonment for up to a year in jail. Felonies are punishable by imprisonment for periods longer than one year.

Civil Law

The words **civil law** as used here have a meaning entirely different from that associated with civil law systems, which were discussed earlier. In contrast to criminal conduct, a violation of a civil obligation usually subjects the party only to civil liability to the person injured. The elements that must be proved in court to establish civil liability are proof that (1) the defendant owed a duty to the plaintiff, (2) the defendant violated that duty, and (3) the defendant thereby caused injury to the plaintiff.

Civil offenses are considered less dangerous to society than crimes. Accordingly they are treated as an offense only against the party injured. Therefore the police and prosecutors usually will not become involved in civil disputes. And the injured party must hire her own attorney to prosecute the lawsuit. In civil cases the defendant is not always entitled to a trial by jury. The judge, or a majority of the jury, need only conclude that a "preponderance of the evidence" indicates that the defendant is liable. Civil defendants are usually not subject to being fined, imprisoned, or put to death. Usually they are only required to pay money. Occasionally they may be commanded to perform or commanded not to perform some act.

Civil laws are classified primarily by topic area. The topic areas of greatest importance to business are the ones discussed in this book.

Substantive and Procedural Laws

Substantive laws define that conduct which constitutes a civil or criminal offense. **Procedural laws** define the legal *process* that must be followed by the police, or the parties to a trial, or the judge, or the prison warden. Procedural laws also establish the penalties or remedies associated with violations of substantive laws. Remedies are the ways the courts will assist injured parties. Thus a statute stating, "No person shall drive a vehicle in the State of Colorado at a rate faster than 55 miles per hour," would be substantive. Case law that holds that certain "hearsay evidence is not admissible in court" would be procedural. The doctrine of stare decisis is procedural.

Frequently, laws are part substantive and part procedural. For example, if a federal statute stated, "receiving kickbacks in real estate transactions is a criminal offense punishable by a fine not to exceed $10,000," the part stating that kickbacks are illegal would be substantive, while the part defining the penalty would be procedural.

Law and Equity

In civil trials there are two different bodies of primarily procedural laws that might be used. They are called law and equity. These two systems arose in large part by historical accident.

The original civil courts in England were called *law courts*. Stare decisis influenced these courts to become very rigid and rulebound. As a consequence, law trials were conducted with great formality and great concern for minor technicalities. In addition, the only **remedies** (that is, the aid that a court gives the plaintiff who wins a lawsuit) were the award of money and the transfer of property from one party to another. These problems motivated some people to bring their problems before the king rather than the law courts.

The kings generally referred these matters to their spiritual advisors, the chancellors. As the number of these incidents grew, a new and separate system of courts called *chancery courts* or *equity courts* developed. This system was characterized by flexible rules and remedies. The equity courts gave their judges (or chancellors) great discretion in handling cases. Instead of relying on technicalities, the equity judges based their decisions on moral rights and natural justice. This flexibility was supported by the use of *maxims of equity* that guided equity judges in exercising their discretion. Two common maxims were: "He who seeks equity must do equity," and "He who comes to equity must do so with clean hands." Thus the equity courts would not grant a remedy if the plaintiff had treated the defendant unfairly (i.e., failed to "do equity") or had engaged in misconduct (i.e., had "unclean hands").

In addition to the remedies at law, the equity courts could also grant a decree of **specific performance.** That decree commanded a party to a lawsuit to perform some act, such as transferring title to realty. Further, equity courts could issue **injunctions.** Injunctions commanded persons to certain conduct. To minimize conflicts with law courts, the new equity courts adopted the rule that they would not grant their remedies if any remedy at law were adequate to solve the plaintiff's problems.

These separate court systems of law and equity flourished together for several hundred years in England. Most of the American states adopted this dual system of civil law. And most states have merged the courts so that one judge now hears both actions at law and suits in equity.

Figure 1.2 Classifications of Law

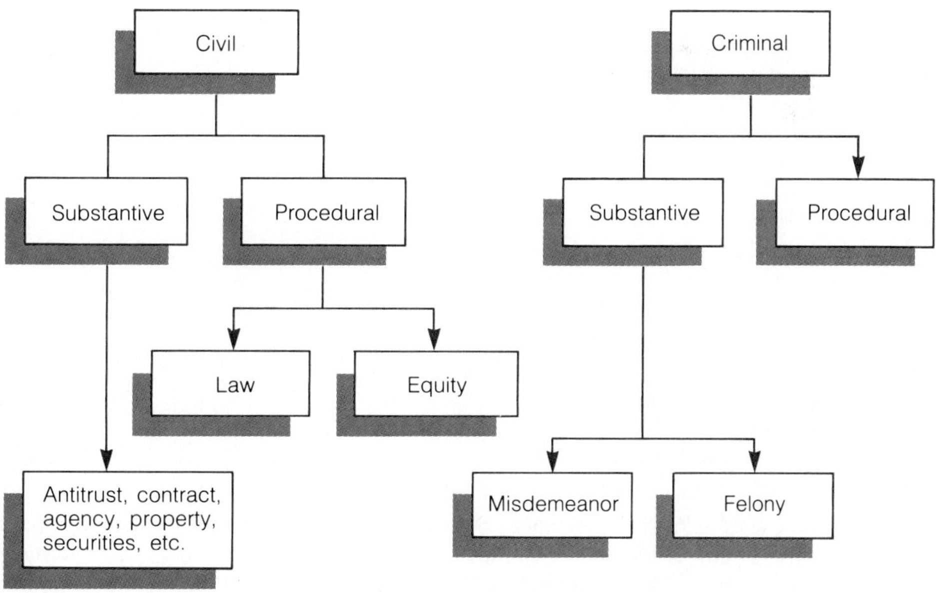

The distinctions between law procedure and equity procedure are still important in legal matters. Some states have separate systems. In states that have merged law and equity the distinctions still have important procedural significance. For example, defendants are generally entitled to a jury trial in actions at law but not in a suit in equity. Figure 1.2 presents a visual representation of many of the categories of law.

The following case discusses the modern federal view of the role of law and equity, along with such other issues as procedural law, constitutional law, and the right to a trial by jury in civil cases.

Memorex Corp. v. IBM Corp.

458 F. Supp. 423 (1978)

Facts

IBM was sued by ILC Peripherals and Memorex for monopolizing portions of the computer industry. The trial lasted five months. At its conclusion the jury was deadlocked and the judge therefore declared a mistrial. The trial court ordered that if the case should be retried, it should be before a judge alone and not before a jury.

Opinion

The trial lasted for five months and consumed ninety-six trial days. The parties called eighty-seven witnesses whose testimony filled more than 19,000 pages of transcript. More than 2,300 exhibits were admitted into evidence. After deliberating for nineteen days, the jury reported itself hopelessly deadlocked, and the court declared a mistrial.

The Seventh Amendment to the United States Constitution preserves the right of trial by jury "[i]n Suits at common law, where the value in controversy shall exceed twenty dollars." In England and in the federal courts in the United States until 1938, there was clear division between law and equity. This situation changed with the adoption of the Federal Rules of Civil Procedure. In *Ross* v. *Bernard,* 395 U.S. 531, 539–40 (1970), the Supreme Court said:

> Under the Rules there is only one action—a "civil action"—in which all claims may be joined and all remedies are available. . . . Under the Rules, law and equity are procedurally combined; nothing turns now upon the form of the action or the procedural devices by which the parties happen to come before the court.

The Court indicated that "[t]he Seventh Amendment question depends on the nature of the issue to be tried rather than the character of the overall action."

> As our cases indicate, the "legal" nature of an issue is determined by considering, first, the premerger custom with reference to such question; second, the remedy sought; and third, the practical abilities and limitations of juries.

The remedy sought by Memorex for IBM's alleged antitrust violations is damages, which has traditionally been regarded as a legal remedy. It is the third factor of the equation, the practical abilities and limitations of jurors, that causes the court to conclude that the issues in this case must be considered to be equitable.

Throughout the trial, the court felt that the jury was having trouble grasping the concepts that were being discussed by the expert witnesses, most of whom had doctorate degrees in their specialties. This perception was confirmed when the court questioned the jurors during the course of their deliberations and after they were discharged. When asked by the court whether a case of this type should be tried to a jury, the foreman of the jury said, "If you can find a jury that's both a computer technician, a lawyer, an economist, knows all about that stuff, yes, I think you could have a qualified jury, but we don't know anything about that." . . . When they were questioned after the trial, most of the jurors indicated that they thought a complex antitrust case like this one should be tried to the court.

The parties initially estimated that the trial of this case would last ten months. Because the hardship that such a long trial would impose on the jurors was obvious, a special pool of 175 prospective jurors was called in for this case. After excuses, there were only 29 candidates remaining from which to select 14 jurors. The 11 jurors to whom this case was submitted probably represented a random cross-section of people in the community who could afford to spend ten months serving on a jury, but it is open to question whether they were a true cross-section of the community. The six men and five women on the jury ranged in age from 32 years to 65 years, with the majority over 50. Several of the jurors were housewives, one was retired, and those who were employed worked at jobs where they could be replaced, but where neither their jobs nor their incomes were in jeopardy. Only one of the jurors had even limited technical education. While the court was appreciative of the effort they put into deciding the case, it is understandable that people with such backgrounds would have trouble applying concepts like cross-elasticity of supply and demand, market share and market power, reverse engineering, product interface, manipulation, discriminatory pricing, barriers to entry, exclusionary leasing, entrepreneurial subsidiaries, subordinated debentures, stock options, modeling, etc.

An additional consideration which the court feels warrants discussion is the burden that cases of this type impose upon the judicial system. Th trial of this case occupied the time of the court and its staff almost exclusively for seven months. . . . In addition, the jury expenses (borne by the government in this case) amounted to more than $32,000. All of this time and expense went for naught when the court was forced to declare a mistrial.

When a trial is by jury rather than to the court, there is the possibility that no decision will be made. In this case, a second trial by jury could very easily suffer the same fate as the first because the composition of the jury will not change significantly. . . .

For the reasons indicated above, the court hereby finds that the magnitude and complexity of the present lawsuit render it, as a whole, beyond the ability and competency of any jury to understand and decide rationally, and orders, in the event of a remand for retrial, that Memorex's jury demand be stricken. The jury was originally conceived as a protective shield between the litigants and the danger of an arbitrary decision by the sovereign. It would be a subversion of this ideal to insist upon submitting a case to a jury when there is a substantial risk that its decision will be arbitrary.

Case Questions

1. Does this case involve issues that are basically civil or criminal? Are these issues primarily substantive or procedural?
2. Is this suit one that sought a legal remedy, or an equitable remedy, or both?
3. Is this court basing its decision *primarily* on its interpretation of a constitution, of a statute or rule, or of prior cases?

Ethical Issues in Introduction to Law

Introduction

Almost all philosophers would agree that managers, and prospective managers like you, have a moral duty to learn the law so they can obey it. This may be a primary reason for you to work hard to master the material in this book. There are, however, other ethical reasons for studying the legal environment of business. One reason is simply that the law is based largely on ethics. Business laws are often statements about what is right and wrong conduct in business. Studying them will help you to strengthen your ability to decide what you believe is right and wrong business conduct.

An original objective of "education" was to help persons decide what they believed to be right or wrong. A "professional" is one who subscribes to a formal system of beliefs about what is right and wrong conduct in professional life. On nearly every list of character traits desired in managers, *integrity* is at or near the top. Frequently it is identified as the most important attribute for leadership in business. Accordingly, there are a variety of strong reasons why you should begin the process of deciding what you think is right or wrong behavior in business.

The following paragraphs discuss the two most basic philosophical concepts about ethics. They are presented here so that you might use them in formulating your own beliefs as you read this book, and so that you might understand the philosophical assumptions on which specific statutes and cases are based.

Overview of Basic Ethical Concepts

The two most fundamental ethical categories are teleology and deontology. **Teleology** judges the rightness or wrongness of conduct by weighing the consequences of the conduct. **Deontology,** in contrast, rejects the importance of consequences and holds that there is an ethical character to acts themselves that determines whether or not one should do them.

For example, you would assess lying differently using deontological and teleological analysis. The teleologist (consequentialist) views lying as morally neutral. If the consequences of a particular lie are good, then that act of lying is good. A deontologist would conclude that lying is inherently evil and cannot be justified by good consequences. This conflict between deontology and teleology is captured by the question, "Can the ends ever justify the means?" Deontologists answer no, while teleologists answer yes.

Laws sometimes have a deontological character. For instance, a law making it illegal to bribe foreign officials would be deontological. The bribing is condemned as wrong and cannot be justified by such good consequences as increased revenue, employment, or profits. In contrast, a law making illegal careless manufacturing of products that cause injury to consumers has somewhat of a teleological character. The negligent manufacturing is legally neutral, but when the consequences of this act are bad—consumer injury—the act becomes illegal.

Do you find one of these philosophical orientations more appealing than the other? Are you able to articulate reasons why you prefer one over the other?

The important concepts and terms in this chapter are listed below; page numbers have been provided for the key terms. By reading over each section you can assess your understanding of the chapter concepts and determine areas you may want to review.

Chapter Summary

1. The goals for students in this course are to develop:
   a. the ability to spot legal problems in business
   b. an understanding of how the American legal system operates
   c. familiarity with the key ideas that make our civilization work
   d. increased ability to think effectively
   e. more mature beliefs about what is right and wrong behavior in business
2. Natural law is discerned by human reason.
3. Positive law is law made by the government in power. Historical law reflects the will of the people.
4. According to legal realism jurisprudence, judges weigh many nonlegal factors when making decisions.
5. The federal Constitution is the supreme law of the United States. Constitutions allocate governmental power among levels and branches of government.
6. Statutory law is made at the federal, state, and local levels. Statutes are unenforceable if they conflict with a governing constitution.
7. An administrative agency's authority to make laws is derived from a statute enacted by a legislature. Administrative rules are invalid if they are unconstitutional or outside the scope of the administrative agency's statutory authority.
8. Case law is created when an appellate court issues an opinion. Stare decisis makes case law binding on lower courts.
9. Courts interpret and determine the constitutionality of statutes and rules. They also determine whether rules are within the scope of an agency's statutory power.
10. A crime is an offense against society. A civil wrong is an offense against the party injured.
11. Substantive laws define our civil and criminal rights and duties. Procedural law defines the process that must be followed by parties enforcing civil and criminal laws.
12. Law and equity are primarily procedural categories.
13. In the teleological system of ethical thought, consequences determine the moral character of an act. On the other hand, the deontological system judges the ethical character of an act by the nature of the act itself.

Key Terms

administrative laws 16
appellant 17
case law 16
civil law 19
common law 7
constitutional law 8

criminal law 19
defendant 17
deontology 24
historical jurisprudence 5
injunctions 21
jurisprudence 4
legal realism 6
natural law 4
plaintiff 17
positive law jurisprudence 5
procedural laws 20
remedies 20
respondent 17
specific performance 21
stare decisis 16
statutory law 13
substantive laws 20
teleology 24
Volksgeist 5

Questions on Ethics

Note to the student: The following problems present the kinds of ethical issues frequently confronted by today's managers. Unless you are unusually mature or have substantial work experience, you may not be able to reach firm conclusions about what you ought to do in response to these problems.

You may find the following suggestions from the authors useful as you try to analyze ethical issues:

1. Focus on what you *ought* to do.
2. Be particularly careful to base your beliefs on your thinking. Don't use your past conduct as a guide to what is right or wrong, and don't try to base your conclusions of what is right or wrong on forecasts of future behavior. Instead, concentrate on thinking about what you ought to do.
3. Try hard to be patient with yourself and to tolerate the initial uncertainty of your opinions.
4. Do not form very firm opinions until you have had adequate time to examine critically examine your beliefs about business ethics.
5. Do not try to change the facts in these problems to make your decision easier or to make the problem more realistic.

As you progress through this book and read the ethics problems at the end of each chapter, you will become more comfortable in dealing with them. But be patient, because this ability comes slowly for most people. At the conclusion of this course you should be more skilled in analyzing facts, have a clearer understanding of your basic beliefs about business ethics, and be better able to reason about these issues.

1. Suppose you owned a machine shop that generated monthly pretax profits of $4,000 for you. Assume that taxes would reduce the profits by half. Also assume that a dishonest bookkeeper has shown you a way to

avoid all taxes without any significant risk of being caught. Should you pay $2,000 per month to comply with the tax laws? Why or why not?

2. Suppose you were the owner of a company and needed to hire a production line worker. Also suppose the two best applicants included an old high school friend, but the other applicant was clearly better qualified for the job. You and your friend are the same sex, while the other applicant is a member of the other sex. Assume that you would rather have the good company of your friend than any increased profits created by selecting the best qualified applicant. You also know hiring your friend would violate Title VII. Should you violate this law in these circumstances? Why or why not?
3. The natural law and positive law schools of jurisprudence articulate perspectives that result in different conclusions in some situations about your moral obligation to obey written law. In business there are a wide variety of attitudes about compliance with the law. Some successful business persons are frank in admitting that they will only comply with the law when it is in their best interest to do so. If they know they can "get away with it," and to do so will be profitable, they will violate the law. What are your ethical views about compliance with the laws affecting business?
4. In the *Weber* case, Kaiser implemented a voluntary affirmative action program that the United States Supreme Court judged to be within the spirit of Title VII. In a sense, this company was assuming a duty not imposed upon it by the law. In contrast with Kaiser's conduct, many people believe that in business there is no moral obligation other than the obligation to obey the letter of the law. Will you recognize moral duties in business that extend beyond the duty to obey just the letter of the law?
5. A portion of Title VII, not reproduced in this text, describes which businesses are subject to the act. In general, this statute only applies to those firms engaged in interstate commerce that have fifteen or more employees. Suppose you were the owner of a computer store engaged in interstate commerce but with only ten employees. You would *not* be legally obligated to comply with the substantive provisions of this statute. Also assume that there was no state statute requiring nondiscriminatory treatment of employees. In such a situation should you recognize a duty not to discriminate? If you concluded that there is a duty not to discriminate, from where does that duty come?

Questions on Law

Note to the student: The following legal problems are typical of those found at the end of every chapter in this book. They are intended to give you an opportunity to *think* and *reason* about the legal concepts discussed in each chapter. It is very clear that the amount you learn depends on the effort you devote to studying. You will greatly increase your mastery of the material if, in addition to reading about the law, you also begin to reason about it.

1. A statute states, "The defendant may elect the form of execution, however such execution shall be by hanging, lethal injection, or by firing squad. Should the defendant fail to so elect, the sentencing judge shall specify one of the foregoing methods." Is such a statute substantive or procedural? Is it primarily related to civil or criminal matters?
2. Suppose a statute authorizes government inspections of work places to ensure compliance with safety regulations issued by a federal agency called the Occupational Safety and Health Administration. Is such a statute substantive or procedural? Is it civil or criminal?
3. Spannaus worked for Allied Structural Steel Co., which enrolled all of its employees, including Spannaus, in a pension plan. This plan created contractual rights for employees, allowing them to draw pension benefits once they reached age 65. The plan also allowed the company to cancel the plan at any time and for any reason.

   Spannaus worked at the company's plant in Minnesota. That state passed a law that had the effect of eliminating the company's right to cancel the pension plan for Spannaus. When the company closed its Minnesota operations it tried to cancel the plan, claiming that the "contract clause" in the federal Constitution stating, "No state shall . . . pass any . . . Law impairing the Obligation of Contracts" made the Minnesota statute unenforceable. Is this Minnesota statute valid? *Allied Structural Steel Co.* v. *Spannaus,* 98 S. Ct. 2716 (1978).
4. Congress created the Federal Communications Commission (FCC) and authorized it to regulate the broadcasting industries. Congress also enacted a statute called the Administrative Procedures Act (APA), which establishes standards for rulemaking by nearly all federal agencies. As part of its regulatory activities, the FCC developed rules that prohibited, among other things, the showing of more than a certain number of sporting events by cable TV companies. A cable TV company named Home Box Office challenged this administrative rule in court, claiming that the FCC had not complied with the APA. Can an administrative agency's rule be invalidated if it fails to comply with a congressional statute such as the APA? *Home Box Office, Inc.* v. *FCC,* 567 F.2d 9 (1977).
5. Suppose the city of New York and the state of New York engaged in a dispute over the imposition of a city sales tax, in addition to the state sales tax on goods sold within the city. Assume a majority of the voters in the city were in favor of the tax, while a majority of the voters in the state were opposed to such a tax. Which political entity, the city or the state, would have the final voice in determining whether or not such a tax could be implemented?

Suggested Readings

Callahan, D., and Bok, S. *Ethics Teaching in Higher Education*. New York: Plenum Press, 1980.

Conry and Nelson, ''Moral Growth and Business Law.'' 27 *American Business Law Journal* 1 (1989).

Hart, H. L. A. *Law, Liberty and Morality*. Stanford, Calif.: Stanford University Press, 1963.

2 Law and Business Ethics

Know thyself.

—Socrates

■ LEARNING OBJECTIVES

After you have read this chapter, you should be able to:

1. Define the roles of profits, the law, and ethics in managerial decision making.
2. Describe ethical attributes of the market and of the law as it regulates business.
3. Describe four ethics standards used in analyzing business problems.
4. Describe four areas of business life with common ethical characteristics.

Business Decisions and the Law

Ability or Need

Managers must make a variety of decisions based upon their knowledge of economics, the law, and ethics. The following fact pattern presents a dilemma that the information in this chapter may help you resolve. The dilemma is discussed in the body of the chapter at pages 44 to 49.

> Assume that you are the manager of production for the swing shift of a small firm. You supervise ten production line workers, but you have been told that one must be laid off. Nine of your workers are college men and women who are earning ex-

tra spending money while attending school. Three drive brand new cars: two Corvettes and one BMW. Several are saving money for trips to Europe and Asia. All of the college students achieve between 105 and 115 percent of their individual production goals.

The other worker is a 48-year-old divorced mother of four children. All of her salary is used to purchase such basic necessities as food, housing, and clothing for her family. She achieves only 85 percent of her production goal because she just isn't as physically coordinated as the younger workers. If the mother is fired, you forecast that she will be able to collect welfare support equal to about one-half her salary, and it will take her up to two years to find another job. If any of the college students are fired, you forecast that they will be able to find similar employment immediately. Who should you fire?

Introduction

Most scholars agree that a manager's most important function is decision making. If we were to ask experienced, mature business persons about the standards used in making business decisions, the list might look like this:

1. Is the proposed action profitable?
2. Is it legal?
3. Is it ethical?

Since good managers typically use all three standards, it is important for you to understand how they are related. In our experience, managers tend to apply the standards in order, asking first the profitability question, then the legal question, and last, the ethics question. And most frequently, any proposed course of action must meet all three standards. Figure 2.1 presents a simple visual description of this process, this search for actions that satisfy all three standards. It would be unrealistic to assume that all managers follow this procedure. Clearly, there are some who only apply the first and some who only apply the first and second standards.

Most courses on business focus on the first standard—(profitability) Thus, courses in economics, finance, marketing, and management typically share the common objective of identifying that conduct which is most profitable. This course on the legal environment of business focuses not on the profitability but on the legality of business conduct. This book is designed to equip you to spot legal difficulties and thus to apply the second standard on the list.

The purpose of this chapter is to help you begin deciding what you believe about the third standard—ethics. Our discussion illustrates a way to combine the study of the legal environment of business with the development of your personal beliefs about right and wrong conduct in business.

First, we describe the ethics implicit in decisions about the first two standards, profitability and legality.

Second, we explain a few philosophic ideas that you can use to assess the law and to assess your own values about business conduct.

Third, we describe areas in business where mature managers usually have fairly clear beliefs about what is ethical and where it is important for business students to begin developing such beliefs. This chapter, and the ethics content of the other chapters, give you the opportunity to develop your own values about business ethics. If you take up the challenge, you may significantly increase your ability and desire to apply the third standard.

It is clear that profits and the laws regulating business have ethical attributes. We are able, in most instances, to make some fairly firm statements about the ethical character of the conduct that produces profits in the free market. Similarly, the law as it regulates business does seek certain ethical objec-

Figure 2.1 Standards for Evaluating Business Conduct.

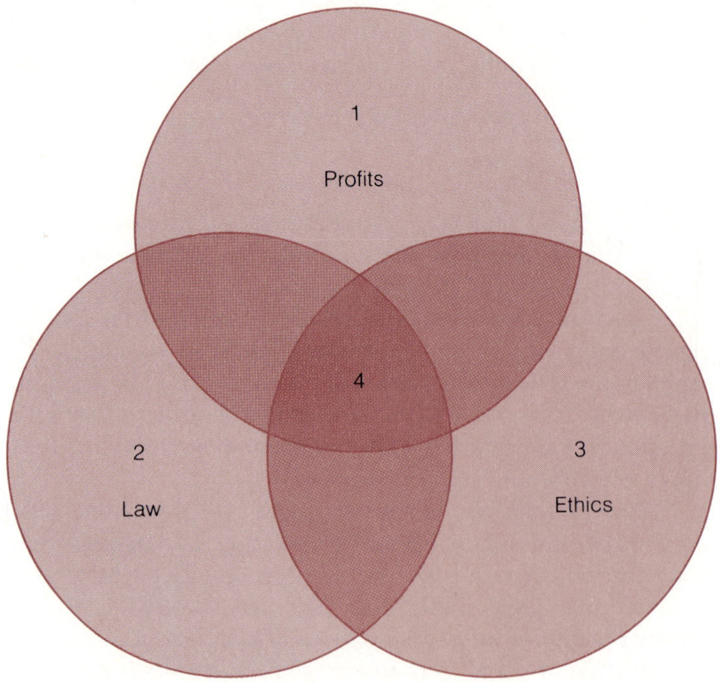

(1) This area represents conduct that is profitable but both illegal and unethical. Selling illicit drugs might be an example. (2) This area represents conduct that is legal but both unprofitable and unethical. An example of this conduct might occur if Montgomery Ward were to sell tires (at usual prices) that look normal but wear out after only 5,000 miles. (3) This area represents conduct that is ethical but both unprofitable and illegal. Hiring a needy, but untalented, Jew in Nazi Germany might have been an example of this conduct. (4) This area represents conduct that is profitable, legal, and ethical. Developing and selling an effective new medication might fall within this category. Most mature business persons try to find alternatives that fall within this category.

tives. Studying the ethical nature of profits and the ethical nature of the legal regulation of business is an effective way to learn to analyze business ethics problems.

The Market as a Mechanism Influencing the Ethical Character of Business Conduct

How the Market Works

In the view of Adam Smith, a Scottish moralist, the theory of the free market assumes that consumers select from the range of goods and services offered in the marketplace those things that each person most desires. All of the choices made by consumers end up telling producers (business), by the dollars spent, what consumers want.

Producers who are not sensitive to the needs and desires of their customers are likely to lose business to more sensitive competitors and perhaps even be driven out of business. On the other hand, those businesses that are highly skilled at serving consumer needs are likely to grow and generate significant profits.

Rivalry—competition for the business of consumers—is the driving force of the market. When there are many producers, the rivalry is intense; it often results in price reductions or product innovations. Rivalry may be substantially reduced if there are few producers.

Often, the marketplace—or as it is sometimes called, the free enterprise system—controls business behavior by making unethical conduct unprofitable. This is sometimes called the discipline of the market. If, for example, a tire manufacturer sold dangerous tires, its reputation among consumers would decline and sales would fall. Similarly, if Sears sold power lawnmowers that only lasted a single season, consumers would become upset and future sales of Sears lawnmowers, and perhaps other items, would decline.

It is clear that the market is a very potent force in directing business conduct in socially desirable directions. These socially desirable directions have been articulated in more concrete, more philosophical ways. The following are some of the ethical attributes of profits earned in the free market:

1. These profits are the product of a system that, because of its efficiency, advances the ethical objective of increasing the material well-being of society.
2. These profits are the product of a system that has the effect of maximizing personal liberty. Because the free market mechanism places economic decision making in the hands of many consumers and many producers, few have very great economic power over others.
3. These profits are justified by meritocracy. That is, because rewards are in proportion to social contribution, the profits are morally justified by the extent to which the individual or firm has contributed to society.

Imperfections in the Free Enterprise or Free Market System

While the market mechanism is quite powerful, it is widely acknowledged to be seriously imperfect. When the economic system is imperfect, some or all of its ethical attributes may not apply. Thus an imperfection may cause the profits earned to be out of proportion to one's social contribution. This in turn raises questions about whether one is entitled to such profits. One whole field of economics, industrial organization theory, carefully analyzes the causes of **market imperfections.** Among these imperfections are the following:

1. When there are either too few sellers or too few buyers, the market becomes imperfect. For example, if there were only a single seller of heating fuel in the country, it might become insensitive to consumer desires and yet not lose business. Consumers would not have other heating fuel businesses to turn to for better service. Thus the profits earned by the company would not be a measure of its social contributions. When businesses can afford to be insensitive to the needs of their customers they are said to have **market power.**
2. If there are **barriers to entry,** this creates either few sellers or few buyers and again causes the imperfection described in item 1. A barrier to entry is an artificial condition that prohibits or discourages new entrants into a field of business. Often the law creates barriers to entry. For example, in Utah, you must pay a fee and pass a test before you can install lawn sprinkling systems in residential yards. This law discourages entrants into this business and thus may be reducing rivalry, and perhaps it allows those fewer persons in the business to increase the prices for these services.
3. If either of the participants in the marketplace transaction *lacks perfect knowledge* about the market or the transaction, this can create an imperfection. This is called **imperfect information.** For example, if you bought a new car from your local Ford dealer when another dealer ten miles away would have sold you the car for $2,000 less, but you didn't know it, an imperfection would exist. You would suffer a $2,000 injury, the local dealer would have an inappropriately high profit, and the other dealer would have inappropriately low profits.
4. When **externalities** are associated with a marketplace transaction, there may be imperfections. An externality is a cost or benefit that is not properly accounted for in the transaction. That is, some cost or benefit goes to the wrong party. The most widely used example of an externality is pollution. If a factory dumps its waste into a local river, it saves money over what it would have paid to have the waste trucked to a nonpolluting waste disposal site. The cost of this pollution is borne, not by the manufacturer, but by the other users of the river. Tax money might even be spent to clean up the river. Thus, the profits of this firm are too high—they reflect the imperfection of this externality.
5. **Agency costs** arise when there is a separation of ownership and management. Thus in large corporations, ownership is held by vast

numbers of shareholders while the senior managers often own no stock. In these settings it is often tempting for the managers to act for their own benefit instead of the benefit of the owners of the corporation—the shareholders. When they engage in this conduct they produce the market imperfection of agency costs. Thus if the president of a corporation hires his son instead of a better qualified applicant, he helps his family at the expense of the corporation's owners. Actions that have been characterized as creating agency costs include nepotism, unjustified pay raises for friends, subcontracting with relatives ("sweetheart contracts"), "poison pills," and "golden parachutes." The most pervasive agency cost is promoting friends into high-paid, but unnecessary, jobs.

While there are other widely recognized imperfections, these examples illustrate the point that the ethics of the marketplace are potentially flawed. When these flaws are serious, then it is likely that one or several of the ethical objectives of the market may not be advanced by particular transactions. Accordingly, when we evaluate business transactions, the third standard of managerial decision making—ethics—is critically important.

The following case illustrates the way the market mechanism may fail to promote ethical business conduct. As you read through the case, try to assess how effectively the market was functioning before this case was decided. Also try to assess how effective the law made by this case would be in promoting ethical business conduct.

Jones v. Star Credit Corp.

298 N.Y. Supp. 2d 264 (1969)

Facts

On August 31, 1965, the plaintiffs, who were welfare recipients, agreed to purchase a home freezer unit for $900 as the result of a visit from a salesman representing Your Shop At Home Service, Inc. With the addition of the time credit charges, credit life insurance, credit property insurance, and sales tax, the purchase price totaled $1,234.80. The plaintiffs had paid $619.88 toward their purchase. The defendant claimed that with various added credit charges paid for an extension of time a balance of $819.81 was still due from the plaintiffs. The uncontroverted proof at the trial established that the freezer unit, when purchased, had a maximum retail value of approximately $300. The question is whether this transaction and the resulting contract could be considered unconscionable *[emphasis added] within the meaning of Section 2–302 of the Uniform Commercial Code, which provides in part:*

(1) If the court as a matter of law finds the contract or any clause of the contract to have been unconscionable at the time it was made the court may refuse to enforce the contract, or it may enforce the remainder of the contract without the unconscionable clause, or it may so limit the application of any unconscionabe clause as to avoid any unconscionable result.

Opinion

Justice Sol M. Wachtler: There was a time when the shield of "caveat emptor" would protect the most unscrupulous in the marketplace—a time when the law, in granting parties unbridled latitude to make their own contracts, allowed exploitive and callous practices which shocked the conscience of both legislative bodies and the courts.

The effort to eliminate these practices has continued to pose a difficult problem. On the one hand it is necessary to recognize the importance of preserving the integrity of agreements and the fundamental right of parties to deal, trade, bargain, and contract. On the other hand, there is the concern for the uneducated and often illiterate individual who is the victim of gross inequality of bargaining power, usually the poorest members of the community.

The law is beginning to fight back against those who once took advantage of the poor and illiterate without risk of either exposure or interference. From the common law doctrine of intrinsic fraud we have, over the years, developed common and statutory law which tells not only the buyer but also the seller to beware. This body of laws recognizes the importance of a free enterprise system but at the same time will provide the legal armor to protect and safeguard the prospective victim from the harshness of an unconscionable contract.

Section 2–302 of the Uniform Commercial Code enacts the moral sense of the community into the law of commercial transactions. . . .

It permits a court to accomplish directly what heretofore was often accomplished by construction of language, manipulations of fluid rules of contract law and determinations based upon a presumed public policy. . . .

There is no question about the necessity and even the desirability of installment sales and the extension of credit. Indeed, there are many, including welfare recipients, who would be deprived of even the most basic conveniences without the use of these devices. Similarly, the retail merchant selling on installment or extending credit is expected to establish a pricing factor which will afford a degree of protection commensurate with the risk of selling to those who might be default prone. However, neither of these accepted premises can clothe the sale of this refrigerator with respectability.

Support for the court's conclusion will be found in a number of other cases already decided. In *American Home Improvement, Inc.* v. *Mac-Iver,* the Supreme Court of New Hampshire held that a contract to install windows, a door, and paint, for the price of $2,568.60, of which $809.60 constituted interest and carrying charges and $800 was a salesman's commission was unconscionable as a matter of law. In . . . *Lefkowitz* v. *ITM, Inc.* . . . a deceptive and fraudulent scheme was involved, but standing alone, the court held that the sale of a vacuum cleaner . . . costing the defendant $140 and sold by it for $749 cash or $920.52 on time purchase was unconscionable as a matter of law. Finally, in *Frostifresh Corp.* v. *Reynoso* . . . the sale of a refrigerator costing the seller $348 for $900 plus credit charges of $245.88 was unconscionable as a matter of law. . . .

Having already paid more than $600 toward the purchase of this $300 freezer unit, it is apparent that the defendant has already been amply compensated. In accordance with the statute, the application of the payment provision should be limited to the amount already paid by the plaintiffs and the contract be reformed and amended by changing the payments called for therein to equal the amount of payment actually so paid by the plaintiffs.

Case Questions

1. Was the market mechanism, by itself, acting as an appropriate discipline on the conduct of the sellers described in this case? Which market imperfection do you think the plaintiff's behavior illustrates?
2. Do you believe the unconscionability section (UCC §2–302) helps judges promote ethical conduct in business? Can you point to language in this decision suggesting that judges might "bend the law" to achieve an ethical outcome? Should judges be allowed to do this?
3. Does the case law articulated by this judge support or curb the market process?

The Law as a Mechanism Influencing the Ethical Character of Business Conduct

Much of the legal environment of business is concerned with facilitating the operation of the marketplace. When you study legal topics such as property and contracts you will see that these areas of the law have evolved, in part, to allow the market to work. Both of these bodies of law try to clarify the rules about transferring ownership and possession of things in market transactions.

In other instances the law seeks not to facilitate the marketplace but to thwart its excesses. This type of law attempts to define the boundaries of socially acceptable marketplace activities. For example, criminal law forbids such profitable transactions as loan sharking (i.e., lending money at extremely high rates of interest).

Thus as the legal system regulates business, its chief purposes are (1) to aid the operation of the marketplace and (2) to define the boundaries outside which marketplace conduct is not allowed. When it helps the marketplace to operate, the law incorporates the principal ethical objectives of the market—*efficiency, liberty,* and *meritocracy*. When the law restricts market processes, it typically does so to advance the more traditional jurisprudential goals discussed in chapter 1—*order, advancing the popular will,* and *justice*.

The Law as a Cure for Market Imperfections

One common response to market imperfections is to enact laws to cure them. Indeed, your study of the legal environment of business will focus on many laws designed to minimize the impact of market imperfections. For example, labor law in large part attempts to redress the power that a small number of employers have when there are very many persons willing to do the work. In part, the chapters on antitrust law deal with artificial barriers to entry. Laws responding to the problem of imperfect information are described in the chapters on securities, consumer rights, and debtor/creditor relations; in many instances these laws require *full disclosure* as a cure for imperfect information. For example, the Truth-In-Lending Act requires disclosure of the actual interest rate on certain consumer loans. Externalities are, of course, the major focus of the chapter on environmental law. Product liability law can also be viewed as addressing the issue of human injury as an externality. Again, it is clear that the law is a powerful resource for minimizing the imperfections in the market process.

Imperfections in the Legal System

There was a period when all market imperfections were thought to be curable simply by passing another law. In fact, much of the law discussed in this text was created between 1930 and 1975 in attempts to "cure" market imperfections. After some experience with these laws, and the election of President Ronald Reagan in 1980, the emphasis on more legal regulation to cure marketplace imperfections diminished. In its place came an awareness that the law is not all-powerful and that the legal system is also characterized by imperfections.

Following are some of the principal reasons why the law sometimes fails to compel ethical conduct in business:

1. Often it is quite profitable to violate the law. This potential for illegal profits can create great pressures that many are unable to resist.
2. Frequently, the penalties for violating laws that regulate business are weak deterrents. Some studies have shown that fines are too small to motivate businesses to comply. And some observers note that for large businesses, the decision makers (corporate executives) are seldom the ones subject to punishment; more commonly, any fine merely reduces the money available for shareholders.
3. Enforcement of laws regulating business is often haphazard. In some areas, such as civil law, enforcement by injured private citizens may be too time-consuming or expensive. Administrative laws may not be adequately enforced because the governmental agency's budget is too small. And when a new political party takes office, enforcement policies for administrative laws may change.
4. Laws regulating business conduct are often much more complex than other laws, and this makes it difficult for some, particularly small businesses, to know what the law is.
5. The process of creating new laws or modifying existing laws can be influenced through campaign contributions and lobbying, so the law may not accomplish society's objectives.
6. Laws regulating business often lack the intuitive legitimacy of many other areas of the law. In contrast, laws regulating murder, theft, adoption, and inheritance seem to most persons clearly worthy of their support. Such laws have such a strong natural law component that the desired conduct might occur even in the absence of written laws. But many business laws appear to unsophisticated persons to lack visible legitimacy. For example, some may see nothing wrong when competing merchants agree to charge the same price. Business law condemns this and other conduct that is not, in the minds of the legally uneducated, obviously wrong.

The following case illustrates the way imperfections in the laws—such as the profitability of noncompliance, small penalties, and weak legitimacy—can influence business behavior. As you read through this case try to assess the way this company resolved the conflicts among profits, legality, and ethics.

United States v. Reader's Digest Association, Inc.

662 F.2d 955 (1981), cert. denied.

Facts

Reader's Digest *engaged in a series of sweepstakes promotional campaigns to encourage subscriptions to the magazine. A portion of the promotional mailer used simulated checks. In 1970 the Federal Trade Commission (FTC) concluded an investigation of these promotional practices, characterizing them as "unfair and deceptive" and therefore illegal. In 1971 the Digest agreed to accept a consent order that barred it from*

> *using or distributing simulated checks . . . or issuing or distributing any confusingly simulated item of value.*

This consent decree had the force of law in binding the Digest. *A federal statute provides that violators of an FTC consent decree can be fined up to $10,000 for* each *violation. In 1973 and 1975 the* Digest *engaged in promotional campaigns that used misleading "travel checks" and "cash convertible bonds." In response, the United States Justice Department filed an action seeking fines. The district court found* Reader's Digest *guilty of over seventeen million violations of the statute—one for each item mailed—and assessed a fine of $1,750,000.* Reader's Digest *appealed.*

Opinion

J. Hunter: The Digest challenges the district court's assessment of a $1,750,000 penalty for its violation of the consent order. The company's first assertion is that the trial court erroneously determined the number of violations of the order. It argues that each bulk mailing, and not, as the district court concluded, "each individual distribution of a Travel Check or Cash Convertible Bond," constituted a separate violation of the order. The Digest also maintains that the district court's calculation of the $1,750,000 penalty was based upon an improper analysis of the factors [previously] set forth by this court [to be used in setting fines]. . . . For the reasons given below, we disagree.

In determining the number of violations of the consent order, we must examine the applicable provisions of the statute, and the order itself. The statute provides, in pertinent part, that a violator of an FTC cease and desist order "shall forfeit and pay to the United States a civil penalty of not more than $10,000 for *each* violation" [emphasis added]. The statute further provides that "[e]ach separate violation of such an order shall be a separate offense." Turning to the applicable terms of the consent order, the Digest was prohibited from "[u]sing or distributing simulated checks, currency, 'new car certificates'; or using or distributing any confusingly simulated item of value." Juxtaposing the language of the statute and the order, we reach the same conclusion as the district court—the distribution of any simulated item of value comprised a violation of the order. Thus, each mailing of an individual travel check or cash convertible bond constituted a distinct violation of the consent order, punishable by a penalty not to exceed $10,000.

Our holding that each letter included as part of a mass mailing constitutes a separate violation is also predicated upon our belief that it is consistent with the legislative purpose underlying the penalty provision of the statute. As the Supreme Court held in *ITT Continental Baking,* "Congress was concerned with avoiding a situation in which the statutory penalty would be regarded by potential violators of FTC orders as nothing more than an acceptable cost of violation, rather than as a deterrence to violation." Adopting the Digest's position that one bulk mailing—no matter how large—comprises only one violation would . . . [eliminate] . . . any punitive or deterrent effect of FTC penalty proceedings.

In determining the size of the penalty to be assessed against the Digest, the district court took five factors into consideration: (1) the good or bad faith of the defendants; (2) the injury to the public; (3) the defendant's ability to pay; (4) the desire to eliminate the benefits derived by a violation; and

(5) the necessity of vindicating the authority of the FTC. The Digest does not challenge the district court's reliance on these factors; rather, it asserts that the court evaluated three of the factors improperly: good faith; public injury; and benefits derived by a violation. . . .

The record clearly supports the district court's conclusion that the Digest did not act in good faith when it disseminated the travel checks and cash convertible bonds. Although the FTC informed the Digest as early as April 13, 1973, that it considered the travel checks to be violative of the consent order, the Digest nonetheless proceeded to complete its promotional campaign by mailing millions of additional travel checks between April 13 and June 30, 1973. The Digest now maintains that these additional mailings simply reflected the lag time required by the logistics of bulk mailing. We reject this argument, and agree with the district court's conclusion that the course of conduct engaged in by the Digest between April 13 and June 30, 1973 "[did] not reflect a good faith effort to comply." . . .

Finally, with respect to the benefits derived by the violation, the district court concluded that the Digest received "substantial benefits from the violative distributions." We find ample support for the court's conclusion. The district court found that the Digest obtained more than $5,000,000 in gross subscription revenues from the travel check and cash convertible bond promotions. The travel check campaign ranked among the top three of all the company's promotions. Thus, the district court properly rejected the Digest's contention that it received no particular benefit from the violative mailings.

In sum, we conclude that the district court carefully considered the relevant factors prior to assessing the $1,750,000 penalty upon the Digest. We hold that there was no abuse of discretion by the district court. . . . Therefore, the judgement of the district court will be affirmed.

Case Questions

1. Who ends up really *paying* this fine, the subscribers, shareholders of the *Reader's Digest,* employees, or the managers who decided to go ahead and mail this promotional material? Which market imperfection do you think is illustrated by the *Digest*'s behavior?
2. What was motivating the *Reader's Digest* managers when they made this decision? Did these managers test their decision against all three standards—profitability, legality, and ethics?
3. What attitude about compliance with the law is indicated by the *Digest*'s conduct?

The Individual's Role in Influencing the Ethical Character of Business Conduct

As we have said, the managerial decision-making model involves determining whether a particular act is profitable, legal, and ethical. To this point we have focused on how answers to the profitability question and the legality question can help answer the ethics question. That is, if a business act is profitable, it is likely to have certain ethical attributes. Similarly, if a business act is legal, it is likely to have other ethical attributes. These assumptions break down, however, when the market or the law functions imperfectly. When imperfections exist, answering the third question of managerial decision making becomes more difficult.

Part of the difficulty arises because some people do not know what they believe about right or wrong conduct in business. Perhaps you can see that it is unrealistic to think that you can go into business and, without giving very serious thought to ethics, do the right thing. Psychologists have found that people who casually state as their beliefs "the views of their peer group" or "what they think most people believe" can be easily pressured into violating such beliefs. Beliefs like these that are not carefully thought through are often called **conventional wisdom.** Can you see that a manager of marketing at *Reader's Digest* might have expressed the conventional wisdom, "I believe in obeying the law"? However, when he was tempted by large profits, that shallow belief did not determine his conduct.

Research also indicates that those who deliberately adopt a belief after critically examining its strengths and weaknesses, its alternatives and its consequences, are much more likely to act in ways consistent with their beliefs. Perhaps if the manager at *Reader's Digest* had examined his beliefs about complying with the law, the company would have acted differently. This book tries merely to start you down the path of examining your beliefs about business ethics. The following section describes tools of ethical analysis that can help you develop your beliefs.

Tools of Ethical Analysis

Philosophy is the study of the basic issues of life; it is characterized by the clarity and logical consistency of the assumptions and reasoning used. Philosophy is extremely useful in making major decisions, such as those required to create values about the ethics of business conduct. The tools of ethical analysis described in this section will help you to analyze the issues of business ethics. These tools are epistemology, knowledge, and will.

Epistemology

Epistemology is the study of the way people obtain knowledge. If you think about something you know—for example, that you should not cheat on college exams—then you may be able to identify the *way* you obtained this item of knowledge. One way to obtain knowledge is by *revelation*. If someone or something tells you something, and you believe it, then you have obtained knowledge by revelation. If your parents or your professors told you that it is wrong to cheat on exams and you based your belief about cheating on their statements, then this belief is based on revelation. Similarly, if the Bible, or Koran, or the Bhagavad Gita told you cheating was wrong, or if the legal system told you and you based your beliefs on one of these authorities, your system of obtaining knowledge about not cheating on tests would be revelational. Most of our knowledge is, by necessity, revelational. Few people have the time to "know" everything in other ways.

Knowledge can also be obtained by *observation*. If you observed someone being caught and punished for cheating on an exam, you might conclude that cheating is dangerous, and that you should not do it because it can harm you. In this illustration, your system of acquiring knowledge is observational. Similarly, if you saw that sharp knives cut your finger, your knowledge of the danger of sharp knives would be observational. Experimentation is a way to acquire knowledge that is based primarily on observation.

Reason is another form of epistemology. Usually, reason is a way of expanding knowledge obtained by revelation or observation. For example, you might believe in the Ten Commandments and therefore believe that you should not lie. This belief would probably be revelational. Suppose you conclude by reasoning that cheating on an exam is quite similar to lying, and must therefore be wrong also. If this were so, your system of acquiring knowledge in this case is based, in part, on reason.

People have epistemological dispositions. Some rely only on revelation. Others reject revelation altogether. Some are only observational. Most people have knowledge or beliefs that combine elements of each epistemology. Often people fail to agree about ethical matters because their epistemological dispositions, the ways they normally acquire knowledge, are different.

Laws can be based on revelation, reason, or observation. Sometimes the legal system conducts experiments to see which laws work best. The doctrine of stare decisis implements an epistemology that is revelational. This doctrine requires judges to follow the law revealed to them by prior decisions. When interpreting statutory language, courts often employ observation—for example, by observing the plain meanings of words as they are commonly used. Sometimes judges, legislatures, and juries base their decisions on reports of scientific experiments. In one famous case, *Brown* v. *Board of Education of Topeka,* the United States Supreme Court based its decision partly on experimental studies that indicated that racial segregation in education injured segregated minorities.

As you read this book, particularly the cases, you will often be able to see the different epistemologies underlying various parts of the law. Often an epistemological difference between judges will cause them to reach different decisions. By learning to listen for this in legal arguments, you can better understand how the legal system works. And your thinking about business ethics is likely to be much clearer.

Knowledge

When a philosopher such as Socrates says "Know thyself," the words *know* and *self* have significantly different meanings from the modern understanding of these words. Knowledge for Socrates was an awareness of philosophical truth. You achieve this **Socratic knowledge** by the **Socratic dialog,** wherein you seek to make philosophical generalizations. These generalizations are examined, or tested, or subjected to intellectual scrutiny. By testing each of these generalizations against your other beliefs or observations you can come to know if the generalization is accurate, inaccurate, or even false. Thus you can by Socratic dialog come (in Socrates' view) to know philosophical truth.

Your instructor may engage in some Socratic dialog—perhaps using the problems at the end of the chapters or the cases. While this classroom technique has the probing, questioning style used by Socrates, it is unlikely to be used with the rigor, depth, and relentlessness employed by Socrates himself. Still, it may give you an impression of the power of learning from your own reasoning instead of from memorizing a lecture or a book. Note that the epistemology of memorizing lectures is primarily revelational, while the epistemology of the Socratic dialog is based primarily on reasoning.

Knowledge, for Socrates, means something similar to "right conviction." It is believed so firmly that it dictates your conduct. Thus if a person said "I believe it wrong to cheat on an exam" but later did cheat, Socrates would say that person did not really have "knowledge" about cheating.

There is an idea, related to the Socratic conception of knowledge, that true knowledge takes a lot of time to achieve. Therefore, you must be careful to seek that knowledge which is the most important. Since it is difficult to know everything (in a Socratic sense), we must select carefully those things about which we seek philosophic knowledge. For Socrates, and other highly regarded thinkers, the most important area of knowledge was ethics, particularly the ethics related to the major decisions in their lives. This is the concept already touched on in the idea of Socratic knowledge, that you are able to act on your beliefs. If you have strong enough **will,** you are able, in the face of temptation, to do what you think is right.

Will is especially important to business ethics for two reasons. First, the strength of temptation in business is often unusually high because the rewards for doing wrong can be great. Second, many of the ideas of business ethics are complicated. When ethical ideas become complicated, those who hold them become more vulnerable to temptation. For these reasons, your commitment to your values is unusually important. The ability to perceive epistemologies, to differentiate between conventional wisdom and philosophical knowledge, and to understand the role of will in human conduct can increase your capacity for ethical analysis.

Philosophical Beliefs about "The Good"

The good is the principal object toward which moral life is directed. It is the principal ethical standard for evaluating business conduct. While philosophers disagree about what the good ought to be, their conclusions and thinking can be quite useful to persons trying to sort out their own ethical values.

In chapter 1 you were introduced to the idea that ethical concepts can be characterized as teleological or deontological. Recall that teleology judges conduct by its consequences, while deontology attributes rightness or wrongness to each act without regard to consequences. Any good can be classified as teleological or deontological.

Another attribute of any good is its **perspective.** Perspective answers the question, whose good—that of the decision maker or that of others? If you were to conclude that pleasure were the good, then you would need to decide *whose* pleasure to maximize. One perspective is that of the *self.* This perspective would cause you to maximize your own pleasure. The second perspective is that of *others*. The other may be a group, perhaps a majority of the membership of a particular group, or it may be God, or anyone (or thing) other than the decision maker. Thus the good of pleasure could have another perspective if you sought to maximize the pleasure of the other members of your family.

It will help you to better understand the different definitions of the good if we are able to apply them to some concrete business decisions.

One business problem we can use is the situation discussed at the beginning of the chapter, of the needy, uncoordinated, 48-year-old divorced mother of four children who competes for her job against young, coordinated, college students. Recall that she uses her wages to buy food and shelter while the students buy new cars and vacations. The manager is required to decide whether to discharge her or one of the college students. We will refer to this dilemma as "the mother of four" problem.

In discussing the application of different philosophic goods to this dilemma, we will only try to communicate a basic flavor rather than present an exhaustive analysis. Sometimes this may mean making assumptions with which you do not agree. But once you see the rough outlines of the analysis associated with a particular good, you should be able to forecast the outcome of an analysis based on differing assumptions.

Egoism

One type of teleological thinking with a large business following is called **egoism.** This is a form of consequential ethics, and it is self-centered. These teleologists will judge conduct against the good of their self-interest. Often they engage in cost/benefit analyses to identify which alternatives help them most. Egoists claim that people are selfish, and philosophy, economics, and law must take this into account.

The most obvious form of egoism is **hedonistic egoism.** In this expression of egoism, individuals seek physical pleasures associated with their senses of sight, sound, touch, taste, and smell. Enjoying expensive good meals is an example of hedonistic egoism.

For the hedonistic egoist, the problem of the mother of four is easily resolved by ignoring the plight of the mother and her family and applying the standard of self-interested pleasure. Since firing the mother will increase the department's productivity, this is the path most likely to result in a pay raise. This pay raise can then be used to purchase material things and services that increase the physical pleasure of the decision maker.

A less obvious form of egoism is sometimes called **psychological egoism.** What the individual seeks here is not necessarily physical pleasure, but psychological comfort. Thus someone may buy a new BMW, not for the physical pleasure it generates, but for the psychological satisfaction flowing from the envy of others. Someone may earn a bachelor's degree because they want to be free from worry about unemployment. Often, persons with a conscience avoid evil, not because it is wrong, but because they don't want to feel guilty.

It is difficult to predict how a person acting out of psychological egoism would respond to the dilemma of the mother of four. Someone seeking peace of mind might fire a college student to avoid guilt about dismissing the mother of four. On the other hand, persons seeking respect from their bosses might identify the mother of four to be let go so their superiors will think of them as tough-minded.

Utilitarianism

Utilitarian theory is another form of consequential ethics. It has been important in philosophy since the nineteenth century, when its greatest proponents, Jeremy Bentham and John Stuart Mill, lived and wrote. The basic approach of **utilitarianism** is that an action is morally right if it produces the greatest amount of good for the greatest number of people affected by the act. Conversely, an action is wrong if it affects the majority adversely. Note that this focus is more on *whose* good than on *which* good. Utilitarian theory, like egoism, uses cost/benefit analyses. However, utilitarian analysis is based on calculation of how an action will affect others in the long run. A variety of goods can be the object of utilitarianism. For example, Bentham argued that the greatest pleasure for the greatest number is the best standard.

A major issue for utilitarians is the definition of who constitutes the "greatest number." Many who claim to be utilitarians only count the members of their family. Others only count the members of their company. Some count just the members of their neighborhood, city, state, or country. All of these forms of utilitarianism fall under the heading of **limited utilitarianism.** They seek to exclude some class of persons affected by their decisions from being counted in determining the "greatest number." **True utilitarianism counts everyone affected.**

Market systems are to a very large extent utilitarian. Our own capitalistic system provides a good example. In Adam Smith's view of capitalism, the self-interested behavior (egoism) of producers in the marketplace allocates scarce resources in ways that produce the greatest material benefit for the greatest number of consumers. The good inherent in this view is material well-being, which often means the same thing as pleasure. Here it is not the producer's but rather another, the consumer's. Thus capitalism is a distinctive system that, at least in Smith's theory, links the self-interested and other-interested perspectives.

A utilitarian who analyzes the problem of the mother of four children might try to assess costs and benefits separately and reason as follows: There is a *cost* to society in firing the mother. But there is little cost in firing one of the college students because the student will easily find another job. Therefore, on the cost side the greatest good for the greatest number probably occurs when a college student is dismissed. In reasoning about the benefit side, a utilitarian might conclude that the more productive workers will make the department and the company more profitable. The efficiency associated with keeping the most productive persons active in the workplace is likely to support economic growth, and perhaps lower prices. Thus the benefit side of the analysis suggests dismissing the mother may be the best strategy. In balancing the costs against the benefits for society, many utilitarians would be likely to conclude that dismissing the mother generates the best consequences for society.

Egoism and utilitarianism are two major teleological systems often motivating business behavior. There are also major systems of deontological ethics with great influence in business. Three are discussed next.

Deontology

Kant's Philosophy

Immanuel Kant (1724–1804) is commonly regarded as the father of modern deontology. He and other deontologists believe that consequences are difficult to forecast and that they often lead to ethically wrong conduct. **Kantian ethics** are based on the conclusion that persons are autonomous moral entities who, by practical reasoning, give to themselves moral law. From this base, Kant sought to discover the existence of an ultimate moral law that all persons should strive to obey.

Basically, Kant's philosophy states a test that may be used to determine whether an action, or principle of action, is moral. It can be paraphrased as follows: The conduct or principle must be *universalizable*. This means that for it to be moral, everyone must be able to follow a principle or mode of conduct without generating an inconsistent, self-defeating, or irrational situation. Thus if everyone is commanded to do an act, the performance by some must not preclude or interfere with the performance of the act by others. In Kant's words, "Act only according to that maxim by which you can at the same time will [i.e., intend] that it should become a universal law."

In his book, *Fundamental Principles of the Metaphysics of Morals,* Kant illustrates this idea by applying it to lying. He writes:

> The shortest but most infallible way to find the answer to the question as to whether a deceitful promise is consistent with duty is to ask myself: Would I be content that my maxim (of extricating myself from difficulty by a false promise) should hold as a universal law for myself as well as for others? And could I say to myself that everyone may make a false promise when he is in a difficulty from which he otherwise cannot escape? I immediately see that I could will (*i.e.,* intend) the lie but not a universal law to lie. For with such a universal law there would be no promises at all inasmuch as it would be . . . [useless] to make a . . . [promise]. Thus my maxim would destroy itself as soon as it was made a universal law.

The idea of testing one's conduct by universalizing it is the central idea of this philosophical good and can be looked at in three ways:

1. One ought never to act unless one is willing to have one's act, or the axiom on which it is based, become universal law.
2. One is obligated to treat every individual as an *end* and never exclusively as a *means*.
3. One must act as though one were a person who both makes the law and is bound by the law—one who is *both subject and sovereign*. That is, one must act in ways consistent with the way one desires others to act.

Formulations 1 and 3 are straightforward restatements of the universalizing idea, the idea that we must be consistent in demanding of ourselves what we demand of others, that we not treat ourselves as exceptions to the rules we desire others to follow. The second expression may not appear on the surface to be closely connected. Yet if we ask how we would like to be treated, we are likely to state the second expression. And to be consistent we must therefore accord to other persons this treatment. This duty to treat other persons as ends, not means, also rests on the observation that humans, as moral beings, must be treated with moral dignity. This would mean that I could not disregard your moral judgments or deprive you of the opportunity to exercise them.

A Kantian might analyze the problem of the mother of four children along the following lines: Is dismissing any of the workers treating them as means and not ends? While there is an element of using another as a means here, it is also true that no worker is being treated *exclusively* as a means. If we have not hidden from them this risk of employment and the likely rules for selecting those to be dismissed, then we have not treated them solely as means; their moral autonomy has not been impaired.

A Kantian might continue analyzing the problem with the following question: Would it be appropriate to make as a universal law this—that the least productive employee ought to be the one dismissed when layoffs are required? Since this law is likely to make the organization more efficient, it may therefore reduce the risks that additional layoffs will be required. Universalizing the alternative, laying off one of the most productive workers, probably is self-defeating, since that would make the firm more inefficient, thereby increasing the need for further layoffs, and eventually eliminating the firm. Since this is self-defeating, it fails Kant's test of universalizing. Accordingly, a Kantian may conclude that laying off the mother of four is ethical.

Rawls' Philosophy

John Rawls, a Harvard philosophy professor, has built on the work of Kant and substantially advanced our understanding of deontology. His book, *A Theory of Justice,* articulates the following ethical viewpoint.

Justice is grounded on consent, that is, on a social contract among everyone. However, in the real world, consent to social relations is very difficult to identify directly. Because we don't have direct consent from every individual, we must evaluate rules, laws, and principles of justice by a hypothetical test that would be acceptable to all rational persons.

Accordingly Rawls develops a mental test, similar to Kant's conception of being both sovereign and subject, to determine what is just. That test defines an imaginary "original position." In this position everyone acts in their rational self-interest and possesses equal liberty. But in the original position everyone is behind a "veil of ignorance." This means they do not know what their *status* would be on the other side of the veil, in the actual world. Thus they do not know their preferences, their conception of the good, or if they would be poor or rich, male or female, weak or strong, black or white, young or old, or talented or untalented.

From this original position they ask, what rules or principles would appear rationally just to everyone? The veil permits persons to evaluate social arrangements impartially, without regard to their own particular case.

Rawls concludes that in the original position people would reject Bentham's principle of utility. No one would be willing to accept a loss in return for a net increase in benefits for the whole group. Rawls *does* conclude that people would agree to two basic principles:

> First: each person is to have an *equal* right to the most extensive basic liberty (freedom of thought, speech, assembly, etc.) compatible with similar liberty for others.
>
> Second: social and economic *inequalities* (e.g., social status and wealth) are to be arranged so that they are both (a) reasonably expected to be to everyone's advantage, particularly for the least advantaged members of society, and (b) attached to positions and offices open to all under conditions of equality of opportunity.

The first principle is called the "liberty principle." It must be satisfied before the second principle—called the "difference principle"—can be invoked.

In analyzing the mother-of-four dilemma, Rawls might conclude that the "liberty principle" has been satisfied in this country. Therefore one may invoke the "difference principle." The question then becomes, does dismissing the mother of four help everyone, particularly the most poor?

It is reasonably clear that market economies increase the total wealth of society. Hiring the most talented (or, when necessary, firing the least talented) is an assumption of the market economy and means those working are able to produce more. Thus, "everyone" is improved, at least in the sense that the society has more to distribute to everyone.

On the other hand, the last part of the difference principle, the requirement that the social arrangement of firing the least talented must benefit the "least advantaged" members of society (probably the poorest) is not so clear cut. In order to satisfy this part of Rawls' difference principle, some of the wealth created by firing the least talented must be taxed and distributed through welfare to the least advantaged to increase their material well-being. Many serious scholars believe that democratic capitalism, combined with a strong welfare system, does satisfy Rawls' test for justice.

Judeo-Christian Ethics

While you can validly distinguish religious beliefs from philosophical topics such as ethics, for many business persons their religious views are the primary source of standards for judging rightness or wrongness. For this reason we need to consider the attributes of **Judeo-Christian ethics.** This is certainly the dominant ethics of this country. You can see the ethics content, rather than the religious content, of this belief system more clearly if you focus on those aspects that describe people's relationships with one another as opposed to those that describe their relationship with God. For example, the first three of the Ten Commandments deal with people's relationship with God, while the last seven deal with relations among persons.

The character of this ethic is largely deontological. It consistently imposes duties on believers that must be followed simply because of the inherent correctness of the duty. The command "Thou shalt not steal" is an example. On the other hand, some Judeo-Christian denominations interpret religious duties as almost exclusively means, steps on a path leading to eternal salvation.

The perspective of this ethic is primarily other oriented. Exhortations to "Honor thy father and mother," "Do unto others as you would have them do unto you," and the central command from Jesus to "Love one another as I have loved you" all display other orientations. Again, however, for some the focus on salvation evokes a self-oriented perspective.

Some of the Judeo-Christian precepts have direct application to business. For example, the commandment against lying has pervasive implications for nearly all business activities and particular importance for such functions as advertising.

To a large degree the Judeo-Christian ethic rejects materialism, particularly material excesses such as conspicuous consumption. This ethic accepts participation in the market economy if the motivating impulse is other-oriented service rather than greed. Even when profits are earned honestly and thus reflect the amount of service rendered, this ethic speaks to the use of this earned profit. Perhaps John Wesley, founder of Methodism, best captured this viewpoint about money with the directive to "Make all you can, save all you can, give all you can."

In applying the Judeo-Christian ethic to the problem of the mother of four children, many persons would conclude that we minimize injury—and therefore maximize love—by dismissing one of the college students who will find other work quite soon.

The ethical theories we have described cannot give you "the" answer to every moral dilemma that you or people in business face; mature persons must ultimately decide for themselves. However, ethical theory can prove quite helpful in defining the exact nature of the moral problems. And it offers insight into the manner in which philosophers who have given great thought to moral systems might solve a problem.

The following case illustrates at least two differing styles of ethical reasoning about a business problem. As you read this case, try to classify the reasoning of the defendant and that of the court.

Grimshaw v. Ford Motor Co.

174 Cal. Rptr. 348 (1981)

Facts

On May 28, 1972, Mrs. Gray, accompanied by 13-year-old Richard Grimshaw, set out in . . . [the family] Pinto from Anaheim for Barstow to meet Mr. Gray. The Pinto was then six months old and had been driven approximately 3,000 miles. Mrs. Gray stopped in San Bernadino for gasoline, got back onto the freeway (Interstate 15) and proceeded toward her destination at 60 to 65 miles per hour. As she approached the Route 30 off-ramp where traffic was congested, she moved from the outer fast lane to the middle lane of the freeway. Shortly after this lane change, the Pinto suddenly stalled and coasted to a halt in the middle lane. . . .

A car traveling immediately behind the Pinto was able to swerve and pass it but the driver of a 1962 Ford Galaxie was unable to avoid colliding with the Pinto. The Galaxie had been traveling from 50 to 55 miles per hour but before the impact had been braked to a speed of from 28 to 37 miles per hour.

At the moment of impact, the Pinto caught fire and its interior was engulfed in flames. According to plaintiff's expert, the impact of the Galaxie had driven the Pinto's gas tank forward and caused it to be punctured by the flange or one of the bolts on the differential housing so that fuel sprayed from the punctured tank and entered the passenger compartment. . . . By the time the Pinto came to rest after the collision, both occupants had sustained serious burns. When they emerged from the vehicle, their clothing was almost completely burned off. Mrs. Gray died a few days later of congestive heart failure as a result of the burns. Richard Grimshaw managed to survive but only through heroic medical measures. He underwent numerous and extensive surgeries and skin grafts and faced additional surgeries over the next ten years. He lost portions of several fingers on his left hand and portions of his left ear, while his face required many skin grafts from various portions of his body.

Opinion

DESIGN OF THE PINTO FUEL SYSTEM

In 1968, Ford began designing a new subcompact automobile that Ultimately became the Pinto. Mr. Iacocca, then a Ford vice-president, conceived the project and was its moving force. Ford's objective was to build a car at or below 2,000 pounds to sell for no more than $2,000.

Ordinarily marketing surveys and preliminary engineering studies precede the styling of a new automobile line. The Pinto, however, was a rush project, so that styling preceded engineering and dictated engineering design to a greater degree than usual. Among the engineering decisions dictated by styling was the placement of the fuel tank. The Pinto's styling . . . required the tank to be placed behind the rear axle, leaving only nine or ten inches of "crush space"—far less than in any other American automobile or Ford overseas subcompact. In addition, the Pinto was designed so that its bumper was little more than a chrome strip, less substantial than the bumper of any other American car produced then or later.

CRASH TESTS

[P]rototypes as well as two production Pintos were crash-tested by Ford to determine, among other things, the integrity of the fuel system in rear end accidents. . . .

[P]rototypes struck from the rear with a moving barrier at 21 miles per hour caused the fuel tank to be driven forward and punctured, causing fuel leakage. . . . A production Pinto crash tested at 21 miles per hour into a fixed barrier caused the fuel neck to be torn from the gas tank and the tank to be punctured by a bolt head on the differential housing.

Tests conducted by Ford on other vehicles, including . . . Pinto prototypes, proved safe at speeds at which the Pinto failed. Where rubber bladders had been installed in the tank, crash tests into fixed barriers at 21 miles per hour withstood leakage from punctures in the gas tank. . . .

Exhibit No. 125 was a report presented at a Ford production review meeting in April 1971, recommending action to be taken in anticipation of . . . federal standards on fuel system integrity. The report recommended, inter alia, deferral from 1974 to 1976 of the adoption of "flak suits" or "bladders" in all Ford cars, including the Pinto, in order to realize a savings of $20.9 million. The report stated that the cost of the flak suit or bladder would be $4 to $8 per car. The meeting at which the report was presented was chaired by Vice-President Harold MacDonald and attended by Vice-President Robert Alexander. . . . A reasonable inference may be drawn from the evidence that despite management's knowledge that the Pinto's fuel system could be made safe at a cost of but $4 to $8 per car, it decided to defer corrective measures to save money and enhance profits.

Ford contends that its motion for judgement notwithstanding the verdict should have been granted because the evidence was insufficient to support a finding of malice or corporate responsibility for such malice. The record fails to support the contention. . . .

Through the results of the crash tests Ford knew that the Pinto's fuel tank and rear structure would expose consumers to serious injury or death in a 20- to 30-mile-per-hour collision. There was evidence that Ford could have corrected the hazardous design defects at minimal cost but decided to defer correction of the shortcomings by engaging in a cost-benefit analysis balancing human lives and limbs against corporate profits. Ford's institutional mentality was shown to be one of callous indifference to public safety. . . .

There is substantial evidence that management was aware of the crash tests showing the vulnerability of the Pinto's fuel tank to rupture at low speed rear impacts with consequent significant risk of injury or death of the occupants by fire. There was testimony from several sources that the test results were forwarded up the chain of command; vice-president Robert Alexander admitted to Mr. Copp that he was aware of the test results; vice-president Harold MacDonald, who chaired the product review meetings, was present at one of those meetings at which a report on the crash tests was considered and a decision was made to defer corrective action; and it may be inferred that Mr. Alexander, a regular attender of the product review meetings, was also present at that meeting. MacDonald and Alexander were manifestly managerial employees possessing the discretion to make "decisions that will ultimately determine corporate policy."

DISPOSITION

The judgement in *Gray* v. *Ford Motor Co.* is affirmed.

Case Questions

1. Which ethical system, egoist, utilitarian, deontology, or Judeo-Christian, most reflects the thinking used by the defendant, Ford Motor Company, in this case?
2. Which ethical system, or systems, most reflect the thinking used by the court in this case?
3. Which ethical system do you think is most appropriate for the type of problem confronted by Ford?

Similarities and Differences between Law and Ethics

There are a variety of reasons why the legal environment of business is an excellent context in which to begin the process of articulating business ethics values. While ethics generally proscribes a much wider range of conduct than the law does, there is a natural and substantial alignment between legal and ethical issues in business. This overlap means that as you study these legal topics you are often studying statements quite similar to ethical statements. Yet it is important that you be able to distinguish between ethical principles and legal rules. While there are many differences, perhaps the two most important for students of management are that our law is created in a pluralistic society, by institutions that are, in part, political.

Legal rules often reflect the realities of legal institutions. For example, some laws are not enacted because they would burden the legal system with too many requests for aid. In other instances, laws are not created because the cost of enforcing them is too great.

Sometimes laws are created to protect or help a legal institution. For example, one common state statute requires that "contracts requiring more than one year to complete must be placed in writing and signed by the defendant . . ." in order to be enforceable. While on the surface this law seems designed to help those who contract, the original objective was to protect the reputation of the courts—to keep the courts from being tricked into enforcing a contract as part of a scheme to defraud someone. Again, institutional realities greatly influence the existence or the character of laws, and this is a major difference between laws and ethical principles.

Our nation is pluralistic. **Pluralism** means that people embrace a variety of political, social, philosophical, and religious beliefs. These varying perspectives find expression in our legal system.

Sometimes this causes major philosophical conflicts in parts of the law. For example, Title VII of the Civil Rights Act requires that employers not discriminate on the basis of sex, yet another federal statute requires some employers to give a preference to veterans—who are predominantly male. Partly because of our pluralistic nature and partly because modern life raises very difficult issues, the legal system often is forced to decide very hard questions. As a result, choosing among philosophical or religious systems is often required. The following case illustrates a clash between two opposing views. As you read through this case, try to weigh the merits of the side you instinctively oppose.

Schad v. Borough of Mount Ephraim

101 S. Ct. 2176 (1981)

Facts

In 1973, appellants began operating an adult bookstore in the commercial zone in the Borough of Mount Ephraim in Camden County, N.J. The store sold adult books, magazines, and films. Amusement licenses permitted the store to install coin-operated devices by virtue of which a customer could sit in a booth, insert a coin, and watch an adult film. In 1976, the store introduced an additional coin-operated mechanism permitting the customer to watch a live dancer, usually nude, performing behind a glass panel. Complaints were soon filed against the appellants charging that the bookstore's exhibition of live dancing violated §99–158 of Mount Ephraim's zoning ordinance. . . . Section 99–4 of the borough's code provided that "[a]ll uses not expressly permitted in this chapter be prohibited."

Appellants were found guilty in the municipal court and fines were imposed. . . . [Subsequent appeals affirmed the convictions.]

Opinion

J. White: Appellants appealed to this Court. Their principal claim is that the imposition of criminal penalties under an ordinance prohibiting all live entertainment, including nonobscene, nude dancing, violated their rights of free expression guaranteed by the First and Fourteenth Amendments of the United States Constitution. We . . . now set aside appellants' convictions.

As the Mount Ephraim code has been construed by the New Jersey courts—a construction that is binding upon us—"live entertainment," including nude dancing, is "not a permitted use in any establishment" in the Borough of Mount Ephraim. By excluding live entertainment throughout the Borough, the Mount Ephraim ordinance prohibits a wide range of expression that has long been held to be within the protections of the First and Fourteenth Amendments. Entertainment, as well as political and ideological speech, is protected . . . motion pictures, programs broadcast by radio and television and live entertainment, such as musical works, fall within the First Amendment guarantee. Nor may an entertainment program be prohibited solely because it displays the nude human figure. "Nudity alone" does not place otherwise protected material outside the mantle of the First Amendment. Furthermore, as the state courts in this case recognized, nude dancing is not without its First Amendment protections from official regulation.

Whatever First Amendment protection should be extended to nude dancing, live or on film, however, the Mount Ephraim ordinance prohibits all live entertainment in the Borough: no property in the Borough may be principally used for the commercial production of plays, concerts, musicals, dance or any other form of live entertainment. Because appellants' claims are rooted in the First Amendment, they are entitled to rely on the impact of the ordinance on the expressive activities of others as well as their own. . . .

The First Amendment requires that there be sufficient justification for the exclusion of a broad category of protected expression as one of the permitted commercial uses in the Borough. . . .

Where property interests are adversely affected by zoning, the courts generally have emphasized the breadth of municipal power to control land use and have sustained the regulation if it is rationally related to legitimate state concerns and does not deprive the owner of economically viable use of his property. But an ordinance may fail even under that limited standard of review.

Beyond that, as is true of other ordinances, when a zoning law infringes upon a protected liberty, it must be narrowly drawn and must further a sufficiently substantial government interest. . . .

In this case . . . Mount Ephraim has not adequately justified its substantial restriction of protected activity. . . .

Accordingly, the convictions of these appellants are . . . reversed.

[So ordered.]

Case Questions

1. Is this case really only about the interpretation of the Constitution?
2. What philosophic "good" is being advanced by this decision? Can you analyze the problem presented in this case by using the systems of ethics described in this chapter?
3. Can you articulate the ethical arguments that might be made on both sides of this case?

As you read this book, try to spend some of your time evaluating the law for its ethical content. You will find it useful in developing your personal beliefs about business conduct.

Values and the Study of the Legal Environment of Business

The Socratic dialog is a process of careful, precise, rational thought. Similarly, much of the law described in this book is the product of careful, deliberate, reasoned thinking. One drawback of this rational approach to practical ethics is that it is time-consuming and sometimes difficult to implement in high-pressure situations. Many managers are so busy they do not have time for the reflection characteristic of ethical discourse. So **values** often substitute for detailed rational thinking. Values are general beliefs, perhaps even philosophical principles, that you have internalized. This means you understand these ideas so well and believe them with such conviction that you do not need to think in detail about them to base decisions and actions on them. For example, many people have values about sportsmanship that guide them when they play competitive games. They don't carefully think through their responses to particular situations; instead, they react based on their values about sportsmanship.

Some thinkers have considered the range of ethical issues confronted by business managers and have attempted to identify frameworks for analyzing these problems. One framework attempts to identify key values that greatly influence large numbers of important business ethics issues. This is called the **categorical approach**, or categorical framework. It was developed by an interdisciplinary research group on business ethics at Yale University in 1982. This framework lends itself to the development of mature values about business ethics. In addition, it blends well with the study of the legal environment of business. The four value arenas described by this approach are:

1. Values about creation of, and compliance with, laws and social norms
2. Values about the legitimacy of various ways of participating in the economy
3. Values about your relationship with your employing organization
4. Values about your relations with co-workers—superiors, peers, and subordinates

This categorical approach also attempts to classify business ethics issues into categories of intellectual difficulty as well as into particular value arenas. The following paragraphs discuss the nature of these four categories.

Compliance with laws and social norms involves weighing the laws or social norms of society when making decisions. It also encompasses political activities designed to create, modify, or abolish laws. Thus, lobbying and campaign contributions by business fall within this value arena. Decisions to comply with the terms of a warranty agreement or to follow EEOC guidelines on advertising job openings incorporate an individual's values about compliance with laws. The conduct portrayed in the *Reader's Digest* case reflects one value system about compliance with the law.

Ethical decisions involving social norms might include giving reasonable advance notice of termination from a job, giving truthful descriptions of both career opportunities and pitfalls to job applicants, and maintaining plant facilities compatible with the surrounding neighborhood.

Participation in the economy concerns the ways in which people generate revenues in the marketplace. Thus practices such as selling radar detectors for car drivers fall within this arena. So would TV advertising that is legal but creates misimpressions about product characteristics, or tactics for "upgrading" customers from low-profit products to high-profit products. In a sense, this category of issues confronts questionable, but legal and certainly profitable, practices.

Values about participation in the marketplace are implicit in such conduct as knowingly selling a car with defective brakes or with a dangerous gas tank. Similarly, selling refrigerators for an extremely high price or selling pornographic material reflects values about participation in the economy. Treatment of suppliers, lenders, customers, shareholders, and other stakeholders also fall within this category.

Relations with employing organizations deal with an organization's internal issues. These may include generating profits by cutting costs, or altering the structure of an organization to make it more efficient or more responsive to the market. Such issues as bigger pay raises for friends and misrepresentation of one's job performance would fall within this category.

Relations with co-workers would include the problems of dealing with subordinates, peers, and superiors. Issues such as backstabbing, injury to a competitor's reputation, and exploitation of subordinates are within this category. Support for personal development or encouragement of mentoring (i.e., helpful coaching of subordinates) also raise this category of issue. The decision about whether or not to fire the mother of four children would probably fall within this category.

The chapters of this book can be related to these value arenas. Table 2.1 summarizes some of these relationships. Within each chapter, the text, cases, case questions, and ethics questions should help you probe and perhaps challenge your beliefs about right and wrong conduct in business. This repeated intellectual evaluation can be used to enhance your powers of moral reasoning and help you create business ethics values.

Ethical Issues in Law and Business Ethics

As citizens of this country, we need to understand the relationship between law and ethics. As potential business persons, we also need to understand the relationship between *business* law and *business* ethics. The following description of the events in the life of one man illustrates how important our understanding of both ethics and of law can be.

The man was charged with violating the law of his country. At his trial a jury sentenced him to death. The man and his friends believed that the law he was charged with violating was wrong, and that his trial had not been fair. Because of this, while the man was awaiting execution, his friends arranged an opportunity for him to escape. When told about this opportunity, the man turned to his personal ethics to decide whether it would be right or wrong, in

Table 2.1 Text Chapters and Business Ethics Categories

Category	Chapter
Values about creation of, and compliance with, laws and social norms.	1 Introduction to Law 2 Law and Business Ethics 3 Courts and Alternative Dispute Resolution 4 Constitutional Law and Business 5 and 6 Administrative Law 26 International Business Law
Values about participating in the economy.	7 Property Law 8 Computer Law 9 Contracts I 10 Contracts II 17 Antitrust I 18 Antitrust II 19 Securities Regulations I 20 Securities Regulations II 21 Environmental Law 22 Regulation of Advertising 23 Consumer Rights 24 Debtor/Creditor Relations 25 Product Liability
Values about relations with employing organizations.	13 Forms of Business Organizations 14 The Employment Relationship 16 Business and Labor Unions
Values about relations with co-workers.	11 Agency Relationships 15 Equal Employment Opportunity

his circumstances, to violate the law of his country and escape the unjust sentence. In reaching his decision he weighed three arguments. First he said, we should never harm others, and by escaping he would harm the state by violating its laws. Second, he reasoned, each citizen impliedly agrees to obey the laws of his or her country, and by escaping he would be breaking his promise—his implied agreement to obey the laws. A third reason was that one's country is like a teacher or parent and we ought therefore to obey our country and its laws as we obey parents. The man therefore concluded that it would be wrong for him to escape; accordingly, he declined the opportunity and was put to death.

The man was Socrates. One of the crimes for which he was convicted was corrupting the morals of the youth. Socrates tried to teach people to think for themselves, particularly about ethical matters. He believed that we should not rely solely on what other people think.

The knowledge or belief that Socrates possessed about law, in the framework of his personal ethics, became for him more important than his life. In this chapter we have tried to present tools that can help you define your personal ethics about that portion of your life that which will be expressed in the conduct of business.

The important concepts and terms in this chapter are listed below; page numbers have been provided for the key terms. By reading over each section you can assess your understanding of the chapter concepts and determine areas you may want to review.

Chapter Summary

1. Mature business persons test alternative courses of conduct against the standards of profits, legality, and ethics.
2. The market mechanism and the legal system pressure business persons, at least in theory, to behave ethically. But in practice both the economic and the legal systems are imperfect. Accordingly, individuals need to define for themselves what is right or wrong conduct in business.
3. Imperfections in the economic system include market power, barriers to entry, imperfect information, externalities, and agency costs.
4. Imperfections in the legal system include the following realities: violations can be very profitable, penalties are often weak deterrents, enforcement is often haphazard, laws are complex, and some laws are perceived as lacking legitimacy.
5. Epistemology, knowledge, and will are tools of philosophy useful in business ethics analysis.
6. "The good" can be viewed from the perspective of the self or the perspective of others.
7. Egoism, utilitarianism, deontology, and the Judeo-Christian ethic are major systems of ethics discussed in this chapter.
8. Ethics influences a broader range of behaviors than does the law. Law differs from ethics in part because the law is created by our pluralistic society and by institutions that are sometimes political.
9. Values are internalized beliefs. Categories of business values include:
   a. Values about creation of, and compliance with, laws and social norms.
   b. Values about the legitimacy of various ways of participating in the economy.
   c. Values about one's relationship with one's employing organization.
   d. Values about relations with co-workers—superiors, peers, and subordinates.

Key Terms

agency costs 34
barriers to entry 34
categorical approach 54
conventional wisdom 41
deontology 46
egoism 44
epistemology 41
externalities 34
the good 43
hedonistic egoism 44

imperfect information 34
Judeo-Christian ethics 49
Kantian ethics 46
limited utilitarianism 45
market imperfections 34
market power 34
perspective 44
pluralism 52
psychological egoism 45
Socratic dialog 42
Socratic knowledge 42
utilitarianism 45
values 54
will 43

Questions on Ethics

1. If you found a way to save $3,000 in income taxes by not disclosing certain income and you were certain there was no risk of detection, would you refuse to disclose? Why or why not?
2. If you learned that you could invest $10,000 in a company that manufactures radar detectors for use by speeding drivers and receive a 25 percent return on your investment each year, would you do so? Why or why not?
3. Suppose you are a new employee in the sales department of a large national organization. In your first week on the job you learn that the company has very clear policies about travel reimbursement. However, all the sales personnel "puff up" their travel expenses in violation of company policies and they pressure you to do it, too. The other salespersons feel that if you don't go along with them, the practice may come to light and injure them. Will you puff up your expenses? Why or why not?
4. Suppose you are in competition with a co-worker for a promotion. The person who is to make the decision is biased against members of the Democratic party. If you learned that your competitor was a Democrat, would you try to get that information to the decision maker? Why or why not?
5. Suppose you are the owner of a small furniture manufacturing company employing sixteen people. Assume that some of your equipment is old and does not meet the safety standards of the Occupational Safety and Health Administration (OSHA). Therefore, continued use of this equipment is illegal. However, you are convinced that the new equipment would not be any safer than the existing equipment. Also, you are absolutely certain OSHA will never discover your violation. Will you buy the new equipment if this would cause your income to fall from $75,000 to $55,000 in the year you made the purchase? Why or why not?

Note to the student: Legal questions have been omitted because this chapter does not discuss particular rules of law.

Suggested Readings

Bodenheimer, E. *Philosophy of Responsibility*. Littleton, Colo.: Rothman and Co., 1980.

Bowie, N. *Business Ethics*. Englewood Cliffs, N.J.: Prentice-Hall, 1982.

Callahan, D., and Bok, S. *Ethics Teaching in Higher Education*. New York: Plenum Press, 1980.

3 Courts and Alternative Dispute Resolution

The very essence of civil liberty certainly consists in the right of every individual to claim the protection of the laws, whenever he receives an injury.

—*Chief Justice Marshall,* Marbury *v.* Madison, *1 Cranch 137, 2 L. Ed. 60 (1803)*

■ LEARNING OBJECTIVES

After you have read this chapter, you should be able to:

1. Describe our legal system and the way it is used to ensure equal protection of the law and to enforce the legal rights of individuals.
2. Explain the procedure involved in the trial of a case and recognize its function of providing "due process of the law."
3. Describe the judicial system of the state and federal courts.
4. Explain arbitration as an alternative to a trial by jury and describe its use within our legal system.
5. Explain alternative dispute resolutions other than those of a judge or jury in a courtroom.
6. Explain the concept of jurisdiction as a territorial limitation on the power of the states.

Business Decisions and the Law

Alternatives to Trial

Business managers often represent their companies in disputes involving customers, employees, or with a government agency. Before lawyers are consulted, the managers may attempt to effect a resolution of the controversy. There are a variety of out-of-court alternative dispute resolutions discussed in this chapter. They include negotiations, mediation, and arbitration. As a business manager, you should know how to avoid litigation, as well as when to consult with a lawyer.

Assume you are the manager of a personnel placement firm. Your client has signed an agreement to pay your company 10 percent of her first year's salary as a commission, contingent upon finding her an appropriate job. Employment was secured, she worked for three months, left for a better paying job, and refused to pay your company the full commission. What are the legal remedies in and out of court to collect the commission? What would have been the effect of an arbitration clause in the contract? Would it be appropriate to negotiate a compromise settlement? Do you ethically think you have earned the full 10 percent commission even though she only worked three months? The material in this chapter will help you answer these questions.

Judges' Dilemma

The federal civil caseload has more than doubled recently but the resources with which to address this demand have not kept pace.

Litigants currently face a slow and expensive path to justice. In 1987, there were approximately twenty thousand federal cases more than three years old and the average time before a jury trial was five years. Moreover, litigants face rising attorneys' fees. Given these problems, how can justice be delivered efficiently?

Federal district court Judge Rya Zosel subjects the parties to a disciplined atmosphere that stops bickering and focuses attention on issues. Judge Richard Ensler relies on the **mock trial** technique. A six-member jury is chosen from the regular jury pool. The attorneys for the plaintiff and defendant present to the persons acting as a mock jury a summary of the case. The judge then explains the law to the "jury," whose nonbinding verdict is used as a basis for settlement discussion. In one complex case involving an aerospace firm allegedly causing environmental pollution, Judge Ensler estimated that a trial would take one and a half years to complete. So, the judge held a short mock trial. Almost unbelievably, the parties settled in just eight hours. Judge Sam Pointer streamlines his docket of cases by trying the issue of damages prior to trying the issue of liability in an attempt to determine if the stakes are too low for a full-scale trial. Parties thereby assess provable damages and usually settle out of court rather than spend comparable amounts on legal fees.

The United States Supreme Court recently announced its support for alternative dispute resolution in an effort to take cases out of the courts altogether. In *Shearson/American Express, Inc.* v. *McMahon,* to be discussed in this chapter, the Court endorsed arbitration of broker/customer securities disputes, concluding that the arbitration system is much improved and is a quick, economical method of resolving disputes.

While judges' attempts to manage their courtrooms efficiently are deserving of praise, justice must not be sacrificed in the process. Parties might reach hasty and ill-conceived settlements when responding to a judge's pressure to settle. Moreover, by settling a dispute rather than adjudicating it, parties surrender the right of appellate review, and the possibility of setting a legal precedent. A basic ethical problem for the legal system is conflict between the need for legal procedures that are fair *and* efficient.

The United States Constitution and the Declaration of Independence are the documents that breathe life into our legal system. Their tenets—that we hold certain "truths to be self-evident, that all men are created equal, that they are endowed by their Creator with certain unalienable rights, that among these are life, liberty, and the pursuit of happiness," and that "[no] State [shall] deprive any person of life, liberty, or property without due process of the law nor deny to any person within its jurisdiction the equal protection of the laws"—are the basis of our democratic history and a challenge to its future. As a participant in this democracy you will either enhance its vision or contribute to its deterioration. Are you willing to read a controversial Supreme Court decision or are you content to hear it summarized on the evening news? Have you formulated a value system built on solid ethical grounds that are tolerant and understanding of other points of view? Does your "pursuit of happiness" disregard the marginal and disenfranchised of our society? To what extent are you developing a "global vision" capable of implementing a Declaration of Interdependence?

An understanding of our legal system should not be reserved exclusively for lawyers. Since it is a part of American government, the judiciary and its procedures should be understood by all citizens, especially business managers. A business person must be familiar with the legal system and the procedures used to identify and resolve issues in dispute.

As you read this chapter try to envision your involvement in the legal process as a juror, a witness, or a business manager engaged in a company lawsuit assessing with your lawyer the merits of trying the case in court. Our discussion will be limited to civil proceedings as the legal environment in which most business disputes are resolved. The difference between civil and criminal matters was described in chapter 1.

Alternative Dispute Resolution (ADR)

There are a variety of dispute resolution techniques beyond that of a judge and jury determining liability or guilt. In fact, a trial is the exception. Of all cases filed in the courts, 90 to 95 percent are settled before a trial is concluded.

This statistic highlights the importance of ADR techniques in the American judicial system. Managers must begin to understand the various ADR methods and their legal effects. The following presents a brief description of each of the well-recognized methods:

1. *Negotiation*. This is communication in an effort to persuade the other side, and is the most widespread form of dispute resolution. It is a purely voluntary process in an effort to reach a mutually acceptable agreement. Any and all evidence is considered, as the process is unstructured; there is no third-party facilitator. Any agreement reached is private and may be enforceable as a contract.
2. *Mediation*. This encompasses all of the features of negotiation, except that a third party whom the disputants have agreed to facilitates the communication and negotiations. The third party usually has expertise in the subject matter, such as construction law and practice. The rationale of mediation is that an agreement is more likely to occur when an impartial third party referees the negotiation process.
3. *Arbitration*. This is more formal than the previous two methods. **Arbitration** is generally a voluntary process where the parties to a dispute agree that it will be submitted to a person called an arbitrator. They typically do so in an arbitration clause as part of a contract. The third-party arbitrator, selected by the disputants, is a decision maker in this method. The arbitrator allows each side to present evidence and arguments; any procedural rules or substantive laws to govern may be initially agreed to by the parties. Both parties agree in advance to be bound by the decision of the arbitrator. The results are private, but either party may seek judicial review. Courts will review an arbitral decision and will reverse it only if the results are clearly erroneous. Thus a private remedy may become public if a court review is sought. This method avoids the time-consuming and expensive court trial. There also exists court-annexed arbitration, whereby the court orders the parties to arbitrate some or all of their dispute. This type of arbitration is involuntary, nonbinding, and public.

The **Uniform Arbitration Act** establishes arbitration procedures. It has been adopted in twenty-three states and the District of Columbia. Other states have passed similar legislation providing for arbitration as a means of settling legal disputes. The **American Arbitration Association** maintains expert arbitrators who may be selected by the parties to resolve their controversy.

Note in the following case the United States Supreme Court's analysis leading to conclusions that securities fraud as well as civil racketeering charges are arbitrable, so that the parties do not need a traditional judicial forum in which to vindicate their claims.

Shearson/American Express, Inc., v. McMahon

107 S. Ct. 2332 (1987)

Facts

Julia and Eugene McMahon were customers of the brokerage firm Shearson/American Express. Mary Ann McNulty handled their accounts for Shearson. The McMahons signed the requisite brokerage agreement—a standard agreement requiring arbitration of all controversies. Later the McMahons filed suit in federal district court alleging that the defendants engaged in fraudulent excessive trading in violation of the Securities Exchange Act of 1934 (1934 Act) and the Racketeer Influenced and Corrupt Organizations Act (RICO).

The district court concluded that the parties' brokerage agreement mandated arbitration of 1934 Act claims, but that RICO claims were not arbitrable due to the strong policy favoring court enforcement of RICO violations. The court of appeals affirmed as to the RICO claim, but reversed as to the 1934 Act claim. It held that they, too, could not be arbitrated. The court of appeals cited Wilko v. Swann, *in which the United States Supreme Court held that claims arising under another securities act were not arbitrable. The Supreme Court granted certiorari to resolve a conflict among the circuits over the arbitrability of RICO and 1934 Act claims.*

Opinion

Justice O'Connor: The [Federal Arbitration] Act was intended to "revers[e] centuries of judicial hostility to arbitration agreement." The Arbitration Act accomplishes this purpose by providing that arbitration agreements "shall be valid, irrevocable, and enforceable. . . . The Act also provides that a court must stay [stop] its proceedings if it is satisfied that an issue before it is arbitrable under an agreement between the parties.

The Arbitration Act thus establishes a "federal policy favoring arbitration," . . . requiring that "we rigorously enforce agreements to arbitrate." Absent a well-founded claim that an arbitration agreement resulted from the sort of fraud or excessive economic power that "would provide grounds 'for the revocation of any contract,' " the Arbitration Act "provides no basis for disfavoring agreements to arbitrate. . . ."

To defeat application of the Arbitration Act . . . the McMahons must demonstrate that Congress intended to make an exception to the Arbitration Act for claims arising under RICO and the Exchange Act. . . .

When Congress enacted the Exchange Act in 1934, it did not specifically address the question of the arbitrability of 10(b) claims.

In *Scherk,* the Court upheld enforcement of a predispute agreement to arbitrate Exchange Act claims by parties to an international contract.

The other reason advanced by the McMahons . . . is that arbitration does "weaken their ability to recover under the [Exchange] Act." That is the heart of the Court's decision in *Wilko,* and respondents urge that we should follow its reasoning.

In *Mitsubishi,* for example, we recognized that arbitral tribunals are readily capable of handling the factual and legal complexities of antitrust claims. . . .

The suitability of arbitration as a means of enforcing Exchange Act rights is evident from our decision in *Scherk.*

In 1953 when *Wilko* was decided, the [Securities and Exchange] Commission had only limited authority. . . . Since the 1975 amendments to the Exchange Act, however, the Commission has had expansive power to ensure the adequacy of the arbitration procedures. . . .

We conclude that where, as in this case, the prescribed procedures are subject to the Commission's authority, an arbitration agreement does not affect a waiver of the protections of the Act. We refuse to extend *Wilko*'s reasoning to the Exchange Act in light of these intervening regulatory developments.

Accordingly, we hold the McMahons' agreements to arbitrate Exchange Act claims "enforce[able] . . . in accord with the explicit provisions of the Arbitration Act."

[T]here is nothing in the text of the RICO statute that evinces congressional intent to exclude civil RICO claims from the dictates of the Arbitration Act.

RICO's text and legislative history fail to reveal any intent to override the provision of the Arbitration Act. . . .

In sum, we find no basis for concluding that Congress intended to prevent enforcement of agreements to arbitrate RICO claims. The McMahons may effectively vindicate their RICO claim in an arbitral forum. . . .

Accordingly, the McMahons, "having made the bargain to arbitrate," will be held to their bargain.

Case Questions

1. Why did the Court hold the broker/customer agreement requiring arbitration extended to claims under the Securities and Exchange Act of 1934?
2. What was the Court's reasoning in allowing RICO claims to be resolved through the Arbitration Act?
3. Do you think it is ethical in securities fraud cases and civil racketeering charges to circumvent the traditional juridical forum by using arbitration?

Other ADR techniques include hybrid dispute resolution methods. They are so classified because they share characteristics of both traditional adjudication and the less formal methods discussed above.

1. **Summary Jury Trial.** Judges use this technique when there are many other cases typical of the current one, such as in resolving the myriad of asbestos suits. The court impanels a mock jury (i.e., a simulated jury that renders a verdict), each side presents evidence and arguments, and an advisory verdict is reached. The process is usually public and the results are nonbinding.
2. **Mini-Trial.** This is a voluntary, private process in an effort to reach an agreement, which is enforceable as a contract. It differs from the previous methods in that there are procedural rules, discovery, evidentiary rules, proofs, and arguments.
3. **Private Judging.** Also known as "Rent-a-Judge," this technique is more popular on the West Coast. Usually the decision maker is a former judge or attorney, and the process is private unless a party appeals to the courts. Each party presents proofs and arguments; the procedures are decided by the parties and the decision maker may make conclusions based on the findings of fact and conclusions of law.

Jurisdiction

The appropriate court must be selected if you and your lawyer decide to try the case. Do you have a case that can be tried in the federal court or must it be tried in a state court? If a federal or state court, which one of the many courts in the state and federal systems? The appropriate selection depends upon the court having *jurisdiction* (i.e., the power of a court to hear and decide a case) over the subject matter and the persons involved in the litigation.

Jurisdiction over the Subject Matter

A court must be authorized to hear the nature of the case being tried. For instance, on the state level there are criminal, probate, land, and housing courts. In some states if you were to bring a rent control dispute to the land court it would not have **jurisdiction over the subject matter;** you should properly be before the housing court. Both the federal and state legislatures establish various courts that have jurisdiction over diverse subject matters.

Jurisdiction over the Parties—State Courts

Having established jurisdiction over the subject matter, your lawyer must demonstrate that the court has **jurisdiction in personam,** jurisdiction over the person of the defendant. The plaintiff must show that he or she notified the defendant with **service of process,** which is the delivery of the complaint and summons to the defendant. Notice of the lawsuit is an essential part of "due process of the law" under the Fourteenth Amendment to the Constitution; notice must be given before a person can be deprived of "life, liberty, or property." If the defendant was properly served (notified) by being handed a copy of the **complaint** describing the nature of the case and a **summons** calling the defendant into the court, and the defendant does not appear in court to defend the suit, he or she will lose by **default judgment.**

In an old but famous 1877 U.S. Supreme Court case, *Pennoyer* v. *Neff,* the court held a state court had power to hear a case involving a nonresident defendant only if he could be personally served within the state or his property could be attached within the state. This became known as the *Rule of Presence Test,* meaning the physical presence of a defendant in the state, no matter how brief, is a sufficient basis for acquiring personal jurisdiction. A mobile society demanded a more flexible standard that was adopted in 1945 by the United States Supreme Court in the landmark *International Shoe Company* v. *State of Washington* case. The defendant, International Shoe Company, was incorporated in Delaware and had its principal place of business in Missouri. The company employed salesmen who sold shoes in the state of Washington, but did not maintain offices in Washington. The company "supplied its salesmen with a line of samples, each consisting of one shoe of a pair, which they displayed to prospective purchasers." Their authority was limited to exhibiting their samples and soliciting orders at prices and terms fixed by the company. The salesmen transmitted the orders to the home office in St. Louis for acceptance or rejection. The shoes were then shipped from points outside Washington to the purchasers within the state. The State of Washington assessed unemployment compensation taxes against the company based upon the compensation paid its salesmen. When the company refused to pay, Washington served a summons on one of the local sales agents. The company claimed its activities within the state were not sufficient to manifest its "presence" there. Hence the state court was without jurisdiction. The United States Supreme Court held the company's activities were neither irregular nor casual. Rather they were systematic and continuous throughout the years and resulted in a large volume of interstate business. The court stated: "It is evident that these operations establish sufficient contacts or ties with the state . . . to make it reasonable and just according to our traditional conception of fair play and substantial justice to permit the state to enforce the obligations which [the company] has incurred there." The doctrine allows a state to assert personal jurisdiction over nonresidents providing there are "sufficient contacts" with the state.

Long-Arm Statutes

The *International Shoe* decision's doctrine of expanded state court jurisdiction under the Due Process Clause inspired the state legislatures to enact jurisdictional statutes over nonresidents based upon various contacts within the state. They are called **long-arm statutes** and authorize the courts to claim jurisdiction over persons outside the state. They generally subject any person, whether or not a citizen or resident of the state, to the jurisdiction of the state court providing that person performs certain acts within the state, such as transacting business, committing a tort, owning or using property, or entering into a contract. For example, if a resident of Massachusetts were in a motor vehicle accident in Ft. Lauderdale, Florida, the long-arm statute in Florida could require you to have the case tried in Florida.

In the following 1987 Supreme Court case involving a long-arm statute, a Japanese corporation manufactured tire tube valves for motorcycles sold in the United States. The court had to resolve whether the tire valves in reaching California in the stream of commerce constituted "minimum contacts" between the defendant and California so that jurisdiction "does not offend traditional notions of fair play and substantial justice."

Asahi Metal Ind. Co., Ltd. v. *Superior Court*

107 S. Ct. 1026 (1987)

Facts

On September 23, 1978, on Interstate Highway 80 in Solano County, California, Gary Zurcher lost control of his Honda motorcycle and collided with a tractor. Zurcher was severely injured and his passenger and wife, Ruth Ann Moreno, was killed. In September 1979, Zurcher filed a product liability action in the Superior Court of the State of California. Zurcher alleged that the 1978 accident was caused by a sudden loss of air and an explosion in the rear tire of the motorcycle, and alleged that the motorcycle tire, tube, and sealant were defective. Zurcher sued Asahi Metal Industry Co., Ltd. (Asahi), the manufacturer of the tube's valve assembly. California's long-arm statute authorizes the exercise of jurisdiction "on any basis not inconsistent with the Constitution of this state or of the United States. Asahi argued that the State could not exert jurisdiction over it consistent with the Due Process Clause of the Fourteenth Amendment.

Opinion

Justice O'Connor: The Due Process Clause of the Fourteenth Amendment limits the power of a state court to exert personal jurisdiction over a nonresident defendant. "[T]he constitutional touchstone" of the determination whether an exercise of personal jurisdiction comports with due process "remains whether the defendant purposefully established 'minimum contacts' in the forum [court] State." Most recently we have reaffirmed the oft-quoted reasoning of *Hanson* v. *Denckla* that minimum contacts must have a basis in "some act by which the defendant purposefully avails itself of the privilege of conducting activities within the forum State, thus invoking the benefits and protections of its laws." "Jurisdiction is proper . . . where the contacts proximately result from actions by the defendant himself that create a 'substantial connection' with the forum State."

Applying the principle that minimum contacts must be based on an act of the defendant, the Court in *World-Wide Volkswagen Corp.* v. *Woodson* rejected the assertion that a *consumer's* [emphasis added] unilateral act of bringing the defendant's product into the forum State was a sufficient constitutional basis for personal jurisdiction over the defendant. It had been argued in *World-Wide Volkswagen* that because an automobile retailer and its wholesale distributor sold a product mobile by design and purpose, [an Audi automobile] they could foresee being haled into court in the distant States into which their customers might drive. The Court rejected this concept of foreseeability as an insufficient basis for jurisdiction under the Due Process Clause. The Court disclaimed, however, the idea that "foreseeability is wholly irrelevant" to personal jurisdiction, concluding that "[t]he forum State does not exceed its powers under the Due Process Clause if it asserts personal jurisdiction over a corporation that delivers its products into the stream of commerce with the expectation that they will be purchased by consumers in the forum State." The placement of a product into the stream of commerce, without more, is not an act of the defendant purposefully directed toward the forum State. Additional conduct of the defendant may indicate an intent or purpose to serve the market in the forum State, for example, designing the product for the market in the forum State, advertising in the forum State, establishing channels for providing regular advice to customers in the forum State, or marketing the product through a distributor who has agreed to serve as the sales agent in the forum State.

Assuming, that respondents have established Asahi's awareness that some of the valves sold . . . would be incorporated into tire tubes sold in California, respondents have not demonstrated any action by Asahi to purposefully avail itself of the California market. Asahi does not do business in California. It has no office, agents, employees or property in California. It does not advertise or otherwise solicit business in California. It did not create, control, or employ the distribution system that brought the valves to California. There is no evidence that Asahi designed its product in anticipation of sales in California. On the basis of these facts, the exertion of personal jurisdiction over Asahi by the Superior Court of California exceeds the limits of Due Process.

The judgment of the Supreme Court of California is reversed, and the case is remanded for further proceedings not inconsistent with this opinion.

Case Questions

1. Why did the Court decide that personal jurisdiction over Asahi by the Superior Court of California exceeds the limits of Due Process?
2. After *Asahi,* what incentive would a foreign manufacturer of components sold in the United States have to produce a safe product?
3. The Supreme Court of California argued the State had an interest in "protecting its consumers by ensuring that foreign manufacturers comply with the state's safety standards." Was the Supreme Court acting ethically in disregarding that state interest?

In Rem Jurisdiction

When the issue before the court involves property rights in an object (*in rem*—e.g., land, rather than a person), the land must be within the court's jurisdiction. This is called **in rem jurisdiction.** For example, the California state court has jurisdiction only over the land located within California.

Quasi In Rem Jurisdiction

A court may have *quasi in rem* jurisdiction over property within the state owned by a nonresident and may use that property to satisfy a debt owed to the plaintiff. For example, if a resident of Florida owns land in New York and owes a debt to a New York resident, the New York resident can sue her in New York and obtain a judgment up to the value of the New York property.

Venue

Although a court may have jurisdiction over the subject matter, person of the defendant, and property, it may not have proper venue. Once having established proper jurisdiction, the lawyer bringing the lawsuit must select the proper place for trial. **Venue** is a particular location (e.g., a county) within a judicial district where a lawsuit should be brought. Most states provide for venue in actions against residents, corporations, partnerships, and individuals doing business in the state.

Courts

State Court System

Although each of the fifty states and the District of Columbia can by legislation establish unique court systems, in most states there are (1) trial courts, including specialized courts such as the juvenile and small claims courts, (2) many intermediate appellate courts, and (3) one highest appellate court of the state. (See figure 3.1.) Your case must first be heard in the appropriate trial court, called a **court of original jurisdiction.** Here the opposing parties, plaintiff and defendant, give evidence on the facts and arguments on the law. If you were to lose the case at the trial level, either as the plaintiff or defendant, you may normally appeal to the intermediary **appellate court** to review the rulings of the trial court. An appeal from the intermediary appellate court may be heard by the highest appellate court of the state, often called the state supreme court. The *second* appeal is a limited right, as the state supreme court may select to hear only those cases it deems most important. A case may be appealed from the highest state court to the United States Supreme Court. However, most of these cases will not be heard unless four of the nine Supreme Court justices vote to do so.

Federal Court System

The United States Constitution provides in article III, section 1, "The judicial power of the United States, shall be vested in one Supreme Court, and in such inferior Courts as the Congress may from time to time ordain and establish." For the federal court to have jurisdiction, a case must involve violation of a

Figure 3.1 State Court System

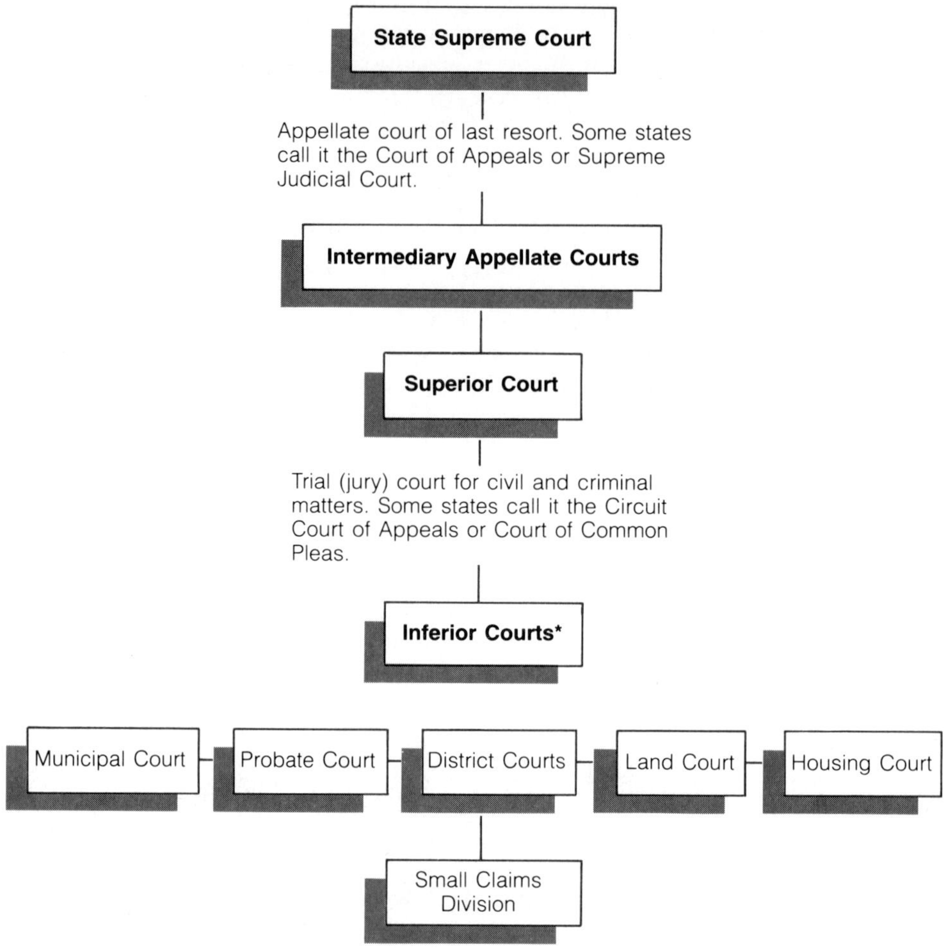

*Inferior courts of special jurisdiction vary from state to state and often use different names.

federal statute (e.g., a civil rights case), a claim in which the United States is either the plaintiff or defendant, or diversity of citizenship and minimum damages of $50,000. A state suing another state would also try the case in a federal court.

Federal courts have their own rules governing procedures called the **Federal Rules of Civil Procedure.** The federal court system (see figure 3.2) is composed of courts with original and appellate jurisdiction. **District courts** are trial courts that exercise original jurisdiction. District courts function in fifty states, Puerto Rico, the District of Columbia, the Virgin Islands, and Guam. The **court of appeals** is an appellate court, generally comprised of three judges, that exercises intermediate jurisdiction in various judicial circuits. (See figure 3.3.) If

Figure 3.2 Federal Court System

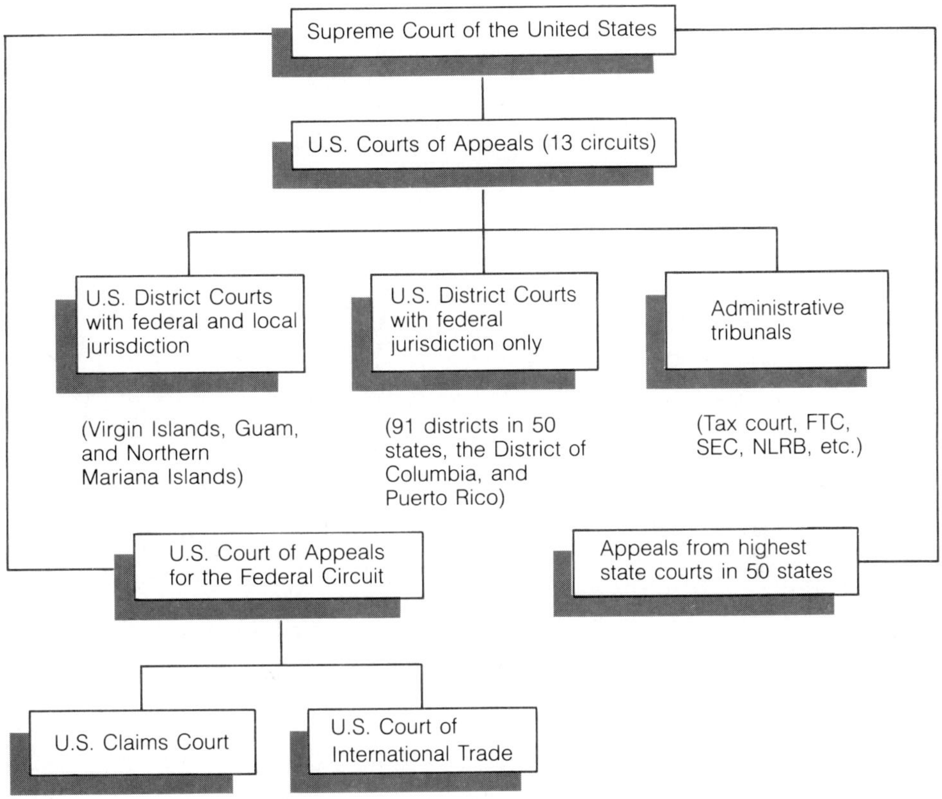

you lose a case in the federal district court, you may appeal to the court of appeals in your circuit. Appeals are usually made on questions of law as opposed to questions of fact. Appeals are also made from federal administrative agencies to the court of appeals. When administrative adjudications are reviewed at the appellate level, the court of appeals will also review the factual determinations made by the administrative law judge to ascertain whether the facts were supported by substantial evidence.

An appellate court will examine the record of the case on appeal and hear verbal arguments from the appellant (the person who appealed the case) and the appellee (the person against whom the appeal is taken). The court will then determine if the trial court committed prejudicial error and may reverse the decision, affirm it, or send it back to the trial court for further proceedings.

The **United States Supreme Court,** whose nine justices sit in Washington, D.C., is the nation's highest appellate court for federal and state cases. Section 2 of article III of the Constitution defines when the United States Supreme Court has original jurisdiction: "In all Cases affecting Ambassadors, other

Figure 3.3 The United States Judicial Circuits

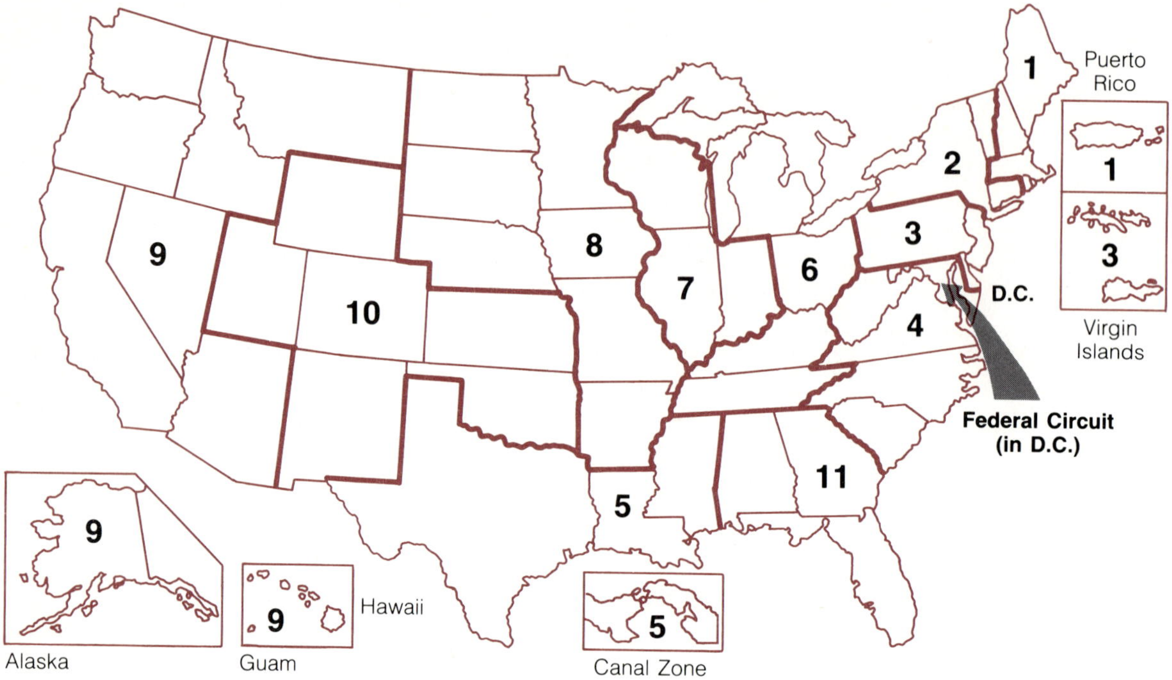

Public Ministers and Consuls, and those in which a State shall be a Party, the Supreme Court shall have original Jurisdiction." However, its most common function is appellate jurisdiction over decisions of the federal courts of appeals and the states' highest appellate courts.

Generally, if you wanted to appeal your case to the United States Supreme Court, your lawyer would submit a writ of certiorari, which requests the Court to hear your case. In this instance the Court is not required to hear your case and probably will not unless there is an important federal issue involved. In a few cases you have a right to appeal from the United States Court of Appeals if the Court decides a state statute is in violation of the Constitution or federal laws. You have a right to appeal from the highest appellate state court to the United States Supreme Court if the state court found a federal statute to be invalid or a state statute was in violation of the Constitution or federal laws.

There are also specialty courts such as the U.S. Tax Court, U.S. Bankruptcy Court, Court of Military Appeals, and the U.S. Claims Court and Contract Appeals.

Class Actions

The sixties saw a dramatic increase in such social movement litigation as environmental actions, sex and race discrimination, and mass tort claims. This trend is often attributed to Rule 23, of the *Federal Rules of Civil Procedure,* which allows federal courts to issue certification orders for a class action. A **class action** lawsuit is a legal action brought by a representative of a group of people who have the same questions of law and facts to be resolved. Damages awarded to the plaintiff/representative are then distributed to the class. The plaintiffs must convince the court by a **motion for class action certification** that the issues of the group are the same and that there are too many persons in the class to make them individually appear in court. The theory of a class action is that it is more effective to adjudicate claims in a single lawsuit than in numerous individual proceedings. Why should hundreds of trials with the same facts and legal issues regarding a defendant's liability be litigated over and over again? For instance, is it fair for a corporate defendant to put the same expert witnesses on the stand, in hundreds of trials, to testify on the same fact that its product was correctly designed? The class action was created to avoid multiple trials of common issues and facts and award multiple plaintiffs with adequate damages.

In the following case, which has been settled out of court, many Vietnam veterans and members of their families brought suit against numerous chemical companies for personal injuries caused by exposure to the herbicide Agent Orange. The plaintiffs (veterans and their families) brought a series of motions to be resolved, one of which was a motion for a class action under Rule 23 of the Federal Rules of Civil Procedure.

CLASS ACTION

In re Agent Orange Product Liability Litigation

506 F. Supp. 762 (1980)

Facts

Plaintiffs, Vietnam war veterans and members of their families claiming to have suffered damage as a result of the veterans' exposure to herbicides in Vietnam, commenced these actions against the defendant chemical companies (nineteen chemical companies were named as defendants)

There were four groups of plaintiffs: Vietnam veterans, their spouses, their parents, and their children. They asserted numerous theories of liability, including strict products liability, negligence, breach of warranty, intentional tort, and nuisance. Plaintiff veterans sought to recover for personal injuries caused by their exposure to Agent Orange. The family members sought to recover on various derivative claims; some of the children asserted claims in their own right for genetic injury and birth defects caused by their parents' exposure to Agent Orange and some of the veterans' wives sought to recover in their own right for miscarriages.

Opinion

District Judge George Pratt: Contending that many of the issues here presented are best determined by class action to avoid duplicitous litigation by the individual members of the proposed class, plaintiffs have moved for a conditional order pursuant to Federal Rules of Civil Procedure 23 permitting the suit to proceed as a class action on behalf of all persons exposed to Agent Orange and various members of their families.

THE PREREQUISITES OF RULE 23 (a)

1. Numerosity
   The members of the plaintiff class here are so numerous that joinder of all members of the class in the same action is impracticable. Indeed, if the only members of the class were the plaintiffs in the 167 actions now pending in this court, "numerosity" would be satisfied.
2. Commonality
   Rule 23(a) (2) states that a class action may only be maintained if "there are questions of law or fact common to the class." Here, the action raises numerous questions of law and fact common to the class. Whatever may be the individual questions relating to the manner and extent of each veteran's exposure to Agent Orange, and relating to the particular effects of Agent Orange on the veteran when considered along with his/her medical history, circumstances, lifestyle and other unique conditions, all of these claims share a common ground when proceeding through the many factual and legal issues relating to the government contract defense, negligence by the defendants, whether Agent Orange was a "defective product," and the many questions embodied in the concept of "general causation." In part, the requirement of commonality is one aimed at determining whether there is a need for combined treatment and a benefit to be derived therefrom. Here the need is compelling and the benefits are substantial.
3. Typicality
   Rule 23(a) (3) requires that in a class action "the claims or defenses of the representative parties [be] typical of the claims or defenses of the class." As already noted, plaintiffs' claims of negligence, products liability and general causation, as well as the defendants' government contract defense are not just "typical" of the entire class, they are identical. In a few areas such as the rules governing liability and the application of various statutes of limitations, the claims may fall into groups that are "typical," but even there the different groups' claims can be efficiently managed either on a subclass basis or directly by way of separately determining the issues. Although the named plaintiffs for purposes of the class action are yet to be designated, the court is satisfied that out of the extremely large pool available representative plaintiffs can be named who will present claims typical of those of the class. As already indicated, the issues of specific causation and damages will, of course, ultimately require individual consideration, but until that point in the litigation is reached, a class action appears to be the only practicable means for managing the lawsuit.
4. Adequacy
   Rule 23(a) (4) provides that a class action may only be maintained if "the representative parties will fairly and adequately protect the interests of the class." Adequacy of representation depends on the qualifications and interests of counsel for the class representatives, the absence of antagonism or conflicting interests and a sharing of interests between class representatives and absentees. Here the court will select from among the hundreds of plaintiffs representative persons who have a substantial stake in the litigation, who lack conflicts, antagonisms or reasons to be motivated by factors inconsistent with the motives of absentee members, and who will fairly and adequately protect the interests of the class. Further, the class will be represented by experienced, capable counsel, Yannacone and Associates, who have shown themselves willing to undertake the

considerable commitment of time, energy, and money necessary for the vigorous prosecution of the claims here asserted.

5. Additional Requirements
Courts have implied two additional prerequisites to class action certification that are not specifically mentioned in Rule 23: (1) there must be an identifiable class and (2) the class representatives must be members of the class. Here, the plaintiff class can be readily identified: they are persons who claim injury from exposure to Agent Orange and their spouses, children, and parents who claim direct or derivative injury therefrom.

(Plaintiffs' motion for class action was granted.)

Case Questions

1. Do you think a chemical company that manufactures a herbicide to be used in combat is ethically obligated to ensure its effects are harmless to humans?
2. What are the prerequisites for permitting a suit to proceed as a class action?
3. What are the plaintiffs' theories of liability to recover for personal injuries caused by their exposure to Agent Orange?

Civil Procedure

Introduction

This chapter has discussed various ways to resolve a business dispute outside of a civil lawsuit. The business manager must recognize settling the case out of court is not always possible. If you, or your company, become involved in a lawsuit it will be helpful to understand the procedural development of the case.

Pleadings

Documents filed with the court and the parties prior to the trial are called pleadings. A civil lawsuit is initiated by the plaintiff who files a *complaint* (sometimes called a *petition* or *declaration*) in court. The complaint is a document that states the names of the parties and briefly describes the facts on which the plaintiff's claim is based against the defendant and the granting of some relief. After the defendant has been served with the complaint she must file an **answer,** which responds to the allegations in the plaintiff's complaint. The answer may admit or deny each allegation in the complaint or state that the defendant does not have knowledge about the alleged truth of the plaintiff's allegations. The answer may include an **affirmative defense** that contains facts not stated in the complaint that would prevent the plaintiff from recovering. For example, the defendant was a minor at the time he signed a contract and was sued for breach of contract. If he demanded to get out of the contract during his minority, it would be an affirmative defense, which would enable the defendant to win the case. Affirmative defenses must be raised in the answer to notify the plaintiff of the issues to be raised at the trial. The answer may include a *counterclaim* by the defendant against the plaintiff. In a counterclaim the defendant states the facts of a new claim arising from the complaint and requests legal relief. Plaintiff is generally allowed to respond to a counterclaim or an affirmative defense by filing a *reply* that is a specific answer to the points raised in those pleadings. The purpose of the pleadings is to raise issues to be resolved during the trial. Allegations made in the pleadings will usually bind the parties and are not deemed in dispute. If the defendant believes that even if all the plaintiff's allegations in the complaint were true she would not have a case and hence not be entitled to a judgment, she may file a *motion to dismiss*. For instance, if a salesperson caused great stress and anxiety to a customer who decided to sue the store on that basis, the defendant/store's *motion to dismiss* would be allowed since there is no rule of law allowing recovery for hurt feelings. In some jurisdictions, after all the pleadings have been filed, the plaintiff or the defendant may make a *motion for judgment on the pleadings*. If allowed, this serves the same purpose as a motion to dismiss.

Discovery

The parties to a lawsuit want to learn all the relevant information about the case before the trial begins. Opposing counsel wants to prepare the case and interrogate the witnesses. Pretrial discovery procedures provide methods for obtaining these needs.

Depositions

If you or your company are involved in a lawsuit, the probability of its reaching the trial stage is remote, because most cases are settled out of court. However, the likelihood of your testifying out of court is fairly certain. A **deposition** is the pretrial process of testifying under oath. Depositions generally take place out of court, often in a lawyer's office, and may include the plaintiff, defendant, or any witness. Although your lawyer would assist you in preparing the testimony and reviewing the procedure, it is helpful to understand the use of a deposition and its function within the legal system. For example, if your company is sued in a product liability case for manufacturing a defective product that caused personal injury to a consumer, a corporate officer will probably be deposed in her lawyer's office. She will be expected to answer questions under oath concerning the safety considerations in designing and manufacturing the product. **Expert testimony** from an authority with special knowledge, known as an **expert witness,** perhaps an engineer or a physician, may also be taken by deposition.

Based on the disputed facts, admissions, and opinions of these witnesses, the lawyers on both sides will then evaluate the likelihood of a jury verdict for their client in an attempt to settle the case out of court. If the case is tried in court, the deposition is used to establish any inconsistencies between the testimony given in court and the statements made during the deposition. Remember that in our litigious society it is often as long as six years from the date a civil complaint is filed in court to the day of the jury trial. Because the deposition is generally taken while the facts are fresh on the mind of a witness, the jury will probably believe the testimony in the deposition if it contradicts the witness' trial testimony. A deposition is also important as a means of preserving testimony in the event the witness is unavailable for trial.

Other less formal methods used in the discovery process are *interrogatories* and *request to admit facts*. **Interrogatories** are a series of written questions (limited in number) seeking written answers to factual questions and signed under oath. A **request to admit facts** is a series of stated facts that the other party either admits or denies. A request to produce documents may request contracts, photographs, minutes of a meeting, or government records that are required to be maintained providing they are relevant to the issues at trial.

The business person and his or her attorney must comply with all discovery requests unless they are claimed to be irrelevant. In that instance the trial judge will rule on its relevancy and if he disagrees they must be provided.

Summary Judgment

After all the pleadings have been filed and the discovery process (sworn testimony taken outside of court to be discussed later in this chapter) is completed, either party may believe he or she is entitled to a judgment as a matter of law without the need for a trial. If the judge is convinced that no material fact remains to be decided she may grant a motion for **summary judgment.** The moving party must persuade the judge there is no issue of fact in dispute and the applicable law requires a judgment on his client's behalf. If the court grants the motion, the moving party wins the case without a trial; if denied, the case proceeds to trial.

Pretrial Conference

Judges often request a **pretrial conference** to narrow the issues and the areas of dispute between the parties in an attempt to reach a compromise settlement without a trial. Depositions may be used at a pretrial conference to ascertain disputed facts, because the plaintiff, defendant, or witnesses are not present. The trial judge may attempt to convince the parties to stipulate (agree to facts that do not require proof or on issues to expedite the trial). If the case cannot be settled at this stage it will proceed toward trial. Keep in mind that a case can be settled at any time if the plaintiff and defendant agree.

The Trial

The plaintiff has the burden of proving the case to the judge and jury. The **burden of proof** in a civil case has been defined as proof by a preponderance of the evidence. This means that the judge and jury must be persuaded that the plaintiff's presentation of the facts in evidence is more probable than not, and hence the plaintiff is entitled to prevail. Our adversarial system requires the lawyers to proceed in the trial by asking the appropriate questions of the witnesses. If a question is objected to by opposing counsel because it violates a **rule of evidence,** the trial judge will rule on its admissibility.

If you decide on a legal career and go to law school, you will take a course on evidence and study many rules that prohibit asking a witness certain questions. Common examples of questions that violate rules of evidence are leading questions that suggest an answer, irrelevant questions that are not related to the issues before the court, and questions that if answered would violate certain confidential relations, such as that between a husband and wife or a person and her minister. A few of these rules of evidence will be discussed to acquaint you with the court procedure involved.

Relevancy

Relevancy testimony will be objected to and excluded by the judge (''objection sustained'') unless it is logically connected to the issue sought to be proved. Suppose, for example, Harry is being sued for breach of a construction contract. If plaintiff's attorney called a witness to testify that Harry had been arrested for driving under the influence, that is not an issue in the case and it should be excluded.

Hearsay

Hearsay testimony is a question that asks a witness to repeat or describe an out-of-court statement, writing, or action by another person when that statement will be used to prove that fact. Such testimony if objected to is inadmissible. For example, suppose Harry's lawyer calls as a witness a fellow contractor to testify that a local union representative told him that ''Harry has often violated the collective bargaining agreement.'' Harry's lawyer would object because it violates the hearsay rule. It would be more satisfactory if the union representative were called to testify so that he could be examined and cross-examined.

Exceptions to the Hearsay Rule. A few common exceptions to the hearsay rule are:

1. *Admissions of a party*. Statements made by the plaintiff or defendant to a witness that is called to testify what they said are generally admissible. Suppose Harry said to a witness ''I have to cut corners on this job or I'll never finish on time.'' This relevant out-of-court statement is admissible since Harry is in court and can be questioned on the subject.
2. *Spontaneous statements*. Courts usually admit a hearsay statement made spontaneously under emotional stress. Suppose Harry was in an automobile accident and a police officer testified he heard a witness yell,

"You drunken bum, you killed that lady." Most judges would allow that spontaneous statement to be repeated by the witness on the basis the evidence may be relevant. Furthermore the statement is not admitted to prove the fact of Harry's sobriety.

3. *Written records kept in the usual course of business.* Suppose that an employee claimed he had been at work every day working on the construction project. The subcontractor that employed this worker was not in court; however, the records were introduced by the company accountant who kept the documents and cannot vouch for their accuracy. The records are statements of the job foreman and are hearsay. The judge would permit the introduction of these routine business records because they were made soon after the foreman's report was submitted to the accountant and there is no reason to suspect the reports are inaccurate.

Privilege

Suppose Harry, in seeking legal advice, informed his attorney that he was under time constraints and did not finish the construction job according to his agreement. May Harry's attorney be called by the plaintiff to testify as to this admission by his client? No. This is a statement made by a client to his attorney for the purpose of obtaining legal advice and is **privileged communication** that cannot be revealed without Harry's consent. In many jurisdictions there are privileged communications regarding statements between a patient and a medical doctor and confidential statements made by one spouse to another and by a parishioner to her clergyman.

Jury Selection

Chances are you will someday be selected for jury duty. As a member of a **jury,** usually twelve people, you may hear a civil or criminal case and be required to find facts and return a verdict to the trial judge. The trial judge and lawyer may ask you a few questions before the trial, called a **voir dire** examination, to identify any bias about the case. Lawyers representing either the plaintiff or the defendant may **challenge for cause,** and if there is a specific reason for a juror's rejection, that person may be excused from jury duty. For example, if you were related to the defendant, the plaintiff's lawyer would dismiss you for cause. The lawyers for both plaintiff and defendant are entitled to an unlimited number of "for cause" challenges.

Either lawyer may also dismiss you without a reason. This is called a **peremptory challenge.** State statutes vary on the number of peremptory challenges a lawyer may have.

The United States Supreme Court in the following case held that a juror's failure to respond to a question during *voir dire* did not entitle plaintiff to a new trial unless the juror's failure to disclose denied plaintiff the right to an impartial jury.

McDonough Power Equipment, Inc., v. Greenwood

464 U.S. 551 (1984)

Facts

Billy Greenwood, and his parents, sued McDonough Power Equipment, Inc., to recover damages sustained by Billy when his feet came in contact with the blades of a riding lawnmower manufactured by McDonough. The United States District Court entered judgment for McDonough upon a jury verdict and denied plaintiff's motion for a new trial. On appeal the Court of Appeals reversed the judgment of the District Court and ordered a new trial. It held that the failure of a juror to respond affirmatively to a question on **voir dire** *seeking to elicit information about previous injuries to members of the juror's immediate family had "prejudiced the Greenwoods' right to peremptory challenge," and that a new trial was necessary to cure this error. We granted certiorari and now hold that plaintiffs are not entitled to a new trial unless the juror's failure to disclose denied plaintiffs their right to an impartial jury. During the* **voir dire** *prior to the empaneling of the jury, Greenwoods' (plaintiff's) attorney asked prospective jurors the following question: "Now, how many of you have yourself or any members of your immediate family sustained any severe injury, not necessarily as severe as Billy, but sustained any injuries whether it was an accident at home, or on the farm or at work that resulted in any disability or prolonged pain and suffering, that is you or any members of your immediate family?"*

Ronald Payton, who eventually became a juror, did not respond to this question, which was addressed to the panel as a whole. After a trial which extended over a three-week period, the jury found for defendant McDonough. [It was later discovered that] . . . Payton's son had been injured in the explosion of a truck tire.

Opinion

Justice Rehnquist: This Court has long held that " '[a litigant] is entitled to a fair trial but not a perfect one, for there are no perfect trials." Trials are costly, not only for the parties, but also for the jurors performing their civic duty and for society which pays the judges and support personnel who manage the trials. It seems doubtful that our judicial system would have the resources to provide litigants with perfect trials, and still keep abreast of its constantly increasing caseload. Even this straightforward products liability suit extended over a three-week period. We have also come a long way from the time when all trial error was presumed prejudicial and reviewing courts were considered "citadels of technicality." One touchstone of a fair trial is an impartial trier of fact—"a jury capable and willing to decide the case solely on the evidence before it." **Voir dire** examination serves to protect that right by exposing possible biases, both known and unknown, on the part of potential jurors. Demonstrated bias in the responses to questions on **voir dire** may result in a juror's being excused for cause; hints of bias not sufficient to warrant challenge for cause may assist parties in exercising their peremptory challenges. To invalidate the result of a three-week trial because of a juror's mistaken, though honest, response to a question, is to insist on something closer to perfection than our judicial system can be expected to give. A trial represents an important investment of private and social resources, and it ill serves the important end of finality to wipe the slate clean simply to recreate the peremptory challenge process. We hold that to obtain a new trial in such a situation, a party must first demonstrate that a juror failed to answer honestly a material question on **voir dire,** and then further show that a correct response would have provided a valid basis for a challenge for cause.

The judgment of the Court of Appeals is reversed.

Case Questions

1. What was the Court's reason in not invalidating the three-week trial when a juror failed to answer a question on *voir dire?*
2. On what basis would the Court have allowed a new trial?
3. Was the Court ethically justified in stating "a litigant is entitled to a fair trial but not a perfect one, for there are no perfect trials"? What ethical theory would support that statement?

Once the jury has been selected, the plaintiff's lawyer makes an **opening statement,** which describes the nature of the case and how she intends to prove the allegations in the complaint. The defendant's lawyer will then describe how he intends to disprove the plaintiff's case. The lawyers then proceed by calling their witnesses to testify by asking them questions; this is called *direct examination*. Opposing counsel may then question the witness, referred to as *cross-examination*. After presenting all the evidence, lawyers for each side make a **summary statement** on the evidence introduced to the jury. It is a most important part of the trial and the lawyers' last chance to impress upon the jury their client's case. The trial judge then gives **instructions to the jury** on the law that must be applied to the facts found by the jury. The judge will also explain the plaintiff's burden of proof. Lawyers may submit in writing a **request for instructions** to the trial judge asking the judge to instruct the jury in a certain fashion. If the judge elects not to follow this request, which is also called a "request for rulings," it may be grounds for appeal. The jury is then taken to a separate room for **deliberation,** where it discusses the factual issues, the burden of proof, and the case in general. It then decides on the facts of the case and renders its **verdict** to the trial judge. A *general verdict* decides who won the case and the amount of a monetary award called **damages** (e.g., judgment for the plaintiff in the amount of $25,000).

A *special verdict* allows the jury to answer specific questions of fact; the trial judge will apply the law to these facts. If either party asserts that the evidence presented, even if believed by a jury, could not add up to a successful case, he or she may *motion for a directed verdict*. If allowed the trial judge would take the case out of the jury's hands and give judgment to the moving party. After the jury has reached a verdict the judge may enter judgment against the prevailing party if he allows a *motion for judgment notwithstanding the verdict* (this is also known as a judgment n.o.v.).

Ethical Issues in the Legal System

The foremost ethical question to be asked concerning our legal system is whether it provides a fair procedure capable of administering due process of the law to all of our citizens regardless of race, creed, color, or sex. If, with all its sophistication, the system is unfair, we must conclude it is unethical and immoral. However, misjudgments can occur in any system. The course of our legal system should be fixed on a heading consistent with our constitutional liberties. Even a slight variation from that heading demands immediate criticism and correction.

For instance, do the jurisdictional requirements over territory, persons, and property often needlessly delay resolving a legal controversy? Is such a delay necessary to ensure a fair trial? Do the rules of evidence prevent the court and jury from determining the truth? Or is the purpose of a trial not simply to determine the truth but to safeguard the constitutional rights of both plaintiff and defendant? Do large out-of-court settlements contribute to litigiousness? Is arbitration a fair substitute for a jury trial? Keep in mind as you answer these questions that "due process of the law" should provide people with a morally fair system capable of protecting their lives, liberty, and property.

The important concepts and terms in this chapter are listed below; page numbers have been provided for the key terms. By reading over each section you can assess your understanding of the chapter concepts and determine areas you may want to review.

Chapter Summary

1. A deposition is a pretrial discovery process of obtaining testimony under oath from the plaintiff, defendant, or any witness.
2. A pretrial conference is used by the judge and lawyers to narrow the issues in an attempt to reach a compromise settlement.
3. A question asked of a witness that violates a rule of evidence may be objected to by opposing counsel.
4. In voir dire examination, the judge and lawyers ask questions to determine a prospective juror's bias before the trial. Such a biased juror may be dismissed "for cause." A prospective juror may be dismissed for any reason by a peremptory challenge.
5. An opening statement is made by both the plaintiff's and the defendant's lawyers to explain how they intend to prove their case. The summation is the lawyers' review of the evidence at the end of the trial.
6. The trial judge instructs the jury by explaining to them the appropriate law to be applied to the facts found.
7. A court must have jurisdiction over the subject matter of the case, the plaintiff, and the defendants, as well as venue.
8. Long-arm statutes subject nonresidents to a court's jurisdiction.
9. State courts have trial courts with and without juries, intermediate appellate courts, and one highest appellate court.
10. Federal courts hear cases involving the violation of a federal statute, a claim in which the United States is either a plaintiff or defendant, a case

involving diversity of citizenship with minimum damages of $50,000, and suits by one state against another state.

11. Arbitration is a fact-finding process in which the parties to a dispute agree it will be resolved by a person called an arbitrator rather than by a court.
12. A class action is a lawsuit brought by a representative of a group of people with the same questions of law and fact to be resolved.
13. Alternative dispute resolutions include negotiations, mediation, arbitration, summary jury trial, mini-trial, and private judging.

Key Terms

affirmative defense 75
alternative dispute resolution 62
American Arbitration Association 63
answer 75
appellate court 69
arbitration 63
burden of proof 77
challenge for cause 79
class action 73
complaint 66
court of appeals 70
court of original jurisdiction 69
damages 81
default judgment 66
deliberation 81
deposition 76
district courts 70
expert testimony 76
expert witness 76
Federal Rules of Civil Procedure 70
hearsay 78
in rem jurisdiction 68
instructions to the jury 81
interrogatories 77
jurisdiction in personam 66
jurisdiction over the subject matter 65
jury 79
long-arm statutes 67
mini-trial 65
mock trial 61
motion for class action certification 73
opening statement 81
peremptory challenge 79
pretrial conference 77
private judging 65
privileged communication 79
relevancy 78
request for instructions 81
request to admit facts 77
rule of evidence 78
service of process 66
summary judgment 77
summary jury trial 65
summary statement 81
summons 66

Uniform Arbitration Act 63
United States Supreme Court 71
venue 69
verdict 81
voir dire 79

Questions on Ethics

1. In our legal system it is not unusual for a civil case to be delayed as long as six years from the date the complaint is filed in court to the day of the jury trial. What ethical problems do you see in a legal system that delays justice? What alternatives to a jury trial are available to those who have been deprived of their legal rights?
2. Our adversary system requires lawyers to proceed by asking appropriate questions of the witnesses. If opposing counsel objects to a question, and the trial judge sustains the objection, the witness will not be allowed to answer the question. Can you assess the moral value of a legal system that shields a witness from answering certain questions? Keep in mind that the witness may be eager to answer the question but will be prevented from doing so if it violates a rule of evidence. To what extent does such a system provide for due process of the law?
3. One of the grounds for allowing a case to be tried in a federal court is diversity of citizenship and minimum damages of $50,000. Do you think a legal system is morally justified in excluding citizens from a court based on the damages of the case? To what extent does this encourage plaintiffs to sue for more than the case is worth in order to gain admittance to the federal court?
4. A common complaint heard about our judicial system is that the traditional trial process takes so long. One reason given is that the number of federal court filings have increased from 35,000 to 180,000 between 1940 and 1981. States courts share the same problem. Because justice delayed is often justice denied, the threat of delay may create a pressure to settle on less than fair terms. To what extent do ADR techniques remedy this situation? Do you think it is good business judgment to have an arbitration clause included in your business contracts?
5. In the Agent Orange case, litigation was brought on behalf of a class of veterans exposed to Agent Orange in or near Vietnam, their children with birth defects, and their wives who had miscarriages. The case was finally settled for $180,000,000 against seven chemical companies. Should a chemical company that manufactures a herbicide to be used in combat be held to a higher ethical standard than a chemical company manufacturing a gas to be used in combat? or a company manufacturing bombs? To what extent will this settlement affect the judgments of the heads of corporations that are engaged in defense contracts?

Questions on Law

1. Suppose you are an officer in a company that is being sued for the negligent manufacture of a bicycle whose brakes failed, causing permanent physical injury to a consumer. Your lawyer has advised you that a deposition to be taken under oath will be used before the trial in an attempt to settle the case out of court. Your boss, the president of the company, has suggested you answer the questions in a way that will enhance the chances of a settlement. You know the answers suggested are not the absolute truth. What *legal obligation* do you have to respond truthfully to questions asked in a deposition?
2. Waldo Bailey has signed a contract with you containing an arbitration clause. Waldo has breached the contract and you are seeking relief by way of arbitration. Waldo objects on the basis that the arbitration clause violates his constitutional right to a jury trial and a loss of his right to the protection of the court system. Is Waldo correct?
3. Mindy Johnson, a resident of New Jersey, was in an automobile accident while on vacation in New Mexico. After returning home she received notice from the secretary of state of New Mexico that her case was to be tried in New Mexico. Mindy objects and wants the case tried in New Jersey, claiming that New Mexico does not have jurisdiction over a New Jersey resident. Is she correct?
4. Sanders, an investor in the Oppenheimer Fund, brought a class action on behalf of 120,000 other investors to recover the amount by which the fund artificially inflated the price they paid for shares in the fund. Sanders wanted to require the fund to compile a list of the names and addresses of the class from records kept by the fund so that individual notice required by law could be sent. In order to compile a list of the class members, the fund would have to sort manually through numerous records, keypunch 300,000 computer cards and create several new computer programs at a cost of over $16,000. Who must bear the expense of sending notice to all members of a class? *Oppenheimer Fund, Inc.* v. *Sanders,* 437 U.S. 340 (1978).
5. Charlotte Horowitz, a student at the University of Missouri Medical School, was dismissed by school officers during the final year of the study for failure to meet academic standards. Horowitz sued the medical school, alleging they had not accorded her procedural due process prior to her dismissal and deprived her of "liberty" and "property" within the meaning of the Fourteenth Amendment. In the spring of Horowitz's first year of study, several faculty members expressed dissatisfaction with her performance. Faculty dissatisfaction continued during the following year. Ten independent physicians were asked to recommend whether Horowitz should be allowed to graduate. Two recommended she graduate on schedule, five recommended she be immediately

dropped from the school, and three recommended that she not be allowed to graduate but continue on probation. In the middle of the year, she was informed that she would be dropped from the school. Was Horowitz legally entitled to a formal "due process" hearing where she could defend her academic ability and performance? *Board of Curators of the University of Missouri et al.* v. *Charlotte Horowitz,* 435 U.S. 78 (1977).

Suggested Readings

Boren, "Suits Against States in Federal Court: The Current Eleventh Amendment Controversy," 25 *American Business Law Journal* 4 (1988).

Fox, "Due Process and Student Academic Misconduct," 25 *American Business Law Journal* 4 (1988).

Shaw, "Due Process Constraints on Class Actions: Federal Rules of Civil Procedure 23," 14 *American Business Law Journal* 111 (1976).

"Special Issue on Alternative Dispute Resolution," 26 *American Business Law Journal 3* (1988).

4 Constitutional Law and Business

[A constitution is] [a] thing antecedent to a government, and a government is only the creature of a constitution. The constitution is not the act of its government, but the people constituting a government.

—Thomas Paine

■ LEARNING OBJECTIVES

After you have read this chapter, you should be able to:

1. Understand the role the courts play in the balance of power between the three branches of government.
2. Understand the principles courts use in deciding cases with constitutional questions.
3. Understand the relationship between the federal and state governments as outlined in the Constitution and how this relationship affects business.
4. Understand the constitutional basis of government's power to regulate business.

Business Decisions and the Law

The Case of the Maligned Minister

You are a nationally known fundamentalist Baptist minister, whose views on America's social and political structure are often reported in the national news media. One day, it is brought to your attention that you are the subject of a satirical advertising parody in a nationally distributed soft pornography magazine. Being that this parody depicts you and your mother as engaging in an alcohol-induced sexual encounter in an outhouse, you are (understandably) enraged. As a response, you file suit charging the publisher with defamation of character and intentional infliction of emotional distress. When your case lands in the Supreme Court of the United States of America, the Justices hand down a decision that says . . . (see *Falwell* v. *Hustler Magazine*).

Introduction

The supreme law of the United States is the Constitution. The Constitution establishes the form of the federal government and the relationship between the federal and state governments, and delineates the rights enjoyed by individuals and the states. Business, as a part of society, has rights under the Constitution and is subject to the actions of government, in accordance with these rights. In this chapter, we will introduce the constitutional framework of government. We will examine the extent of government's constitutional power to regulate business, as well as the constitutional rights enjoyed by business.

Introduction to the Constitution

History of the Constitution

From the founding of the United States in 1776 until 1789, the United States was governed under the Articles of Confederation, which established a weak central government. Unlike the central form of government we know today, under the Articles the central government could not collect taxes, make the states obey federal laws, or regulate interstate commerce. An example of the results include the bitter dispute between Connecticut and Pennsylvania over Connecticut's attempt to colonize portions of western Pennsylvania. At the same time, New Jersey was referred to as "the keg tapped at both ends," in light of tariffs on its products imposed by the surrounding states of Pennsylvania and New York. Such barriers against interstate economic trade fueled calls for a stronger central government.

In 1787, the Constitution of the United States was adopted, and it was ratified by the states by 1789. One reason it took so long to ratify the Constitution was that many people expressed fears that a strong central government would commit abuses of individual rights as the Crown had done before the Revolution. Therefore, some states agreed to ratify only on the condition that a specific Bill of Rights be written into the Constitution. A Bill of Rights, the first ten amendments to the Constitution, was adopted in 1791. We will study many of the specific provisions of the Bill of Rights affecting business in this chapter. At present, there are twenty-six amendments to the Constitution, including the Bill of Rights.

Interpretation of the Constitution

The United States Supreme Court is often called upon to interpret the meaning of constitutional provisions as they apply to specific cases. You should be aware that the Supreme Court has developed certain rules of interpretation to assist it in deciding cases involving constitutional questions, one of which is the **presumption of constitutionality.** Presumption of constitutionality states that a legislative statute or governmental action is presumed to be constitutional until proven otherwise. For example, if a person feels that Congress has passed a statute that violates some provision of the Constitution, the burden of proof is on the person challenging the statute to prove to the Court's satisfaction that the statute is in fact unconstitutional. The only exception to the principle of presumption of constitutionality occurs when a statute or governmental act is *unconstitutional on its face;* that is, it obviously violates a specific provision of the Constitution. Then the action will be presumed unconstitutional, and the burden of proof is on the government to show some extremely important national policy reason why the Court should uphold the governmental action.

In the following case, the Supreme Court is asked to rule on a local ordinance restricting the First Amendment right to free speech under the Constitution. The courts, recognizing that the government at times does have an interest in regulating the speech and activities of individuals, require that First Amendment restrictions be specifically related to furthering legitimate governmental interests.

Airport Commissioners of the City of Los Angeles vs. Jews for Jesus, Inc.

96 LEd2d 500 (1987)

Opinion

Justice O'Connor: Justice O'Connor delivered the opinion of the unanimous Court. The issue presented in this case is whether a resolution banning all "First Amendment activities" at Los Angeles International Airport (LAX) violates the First Amendment.

On July 13, 1983, the Board of Airport Commissioners (Board) adopted Resolution No. 13787, which provides in pertinent part:

> "NOW, THEREFORE, BE IT RESOLVED by the Board of Airport Commissioners that the Central Terminal Area at Los Angeles International Airport is not open for First Amendment activities by any individual and/or entity;
>
> . . . . .
>
> "BE IT FURTHER RESOLVED that after the effective date of this Resolution, if any individual and/or entity seeks to engage in First Amendment activities within the Central Terminal Area at Los Angeles International Airport, said individual and/or entity shall be deemed to be acting in contravention of the

stated policy of the Board of Airport Commissioners in reference to the uses permitted within the Central Terminal Area at Los Angeles International Airport; and

"BE IT FURTHER RESOLVED that if any individual or entity engages in First Amendment activities within the Central Terminal Area at Los Angeles International Airport, the City Attorney of the City of Los Angeles is directed to institute appropriate litigation against such individual and/or entity to ensure compliance with this Policy statement of the Board of Airport Commissioners. . . ."

Respondent Jews for Jesus, Inc., is a nonprofit religious corporation. On July 6, 1984, Alan Howard Snyder, a minister of the Gospel for Jews for Jesus, was stopped by a Department of Airports peace officer while distributing free religious literature on a pedestrian walkway in the Central Terminal Area at LAX. The officer showed Snyder a copy of the resolution, explained that Snyder's activities violated the resolution, and requested that Snyder leave LAX. The officer warned Snyder that the City would take legal action against him if he refused to leave as requested. Snyder stopped distributing the leaflets and left the airport terminal.

Jews for Jesus and Snyder then filed this action in the District Court for the Central District of California, challenging the constitutionality of the resolution under both the California and Federal Constitutions. First, respondents contended that the resolution was facially unconstitutional under Art. I, §2, of the California Constitution and the First Amendment to the United States Constitution because it bans all speech in a public forum. Second, they alleged that the resolution had been applied to Jews for Jesus in a discriminatory manner. Finally, respondents urged that the resolution was unconstitutionally vague and overbroad.

When the case came before the District Court for trial, the parties orally stipulated to the facts, and the District Court treated the trial briefs as cross-motions for summary judgment. The District Court held that the Central Terminal Area was a traditional public forum under federal law, and held that the resolution was facially unconstitutional under the United States Constitution.

The Court of Appeals concluded that an airport complex is a traditional public forum, and held that the resolution was unconstitutional on its face under the Federal Constitution. We granted certiorari and now affirm.

In balancing the government's interest in limiting the use of its property against the interests of those who wish to use the property for expressive activity, the Court has identified three types of fora: the traditional public forum, the public forum created by government designation, and the nonpublic forum. The proper First Amendment analysis differs depending on whether the area in question falls in one category rather than another. In a traditional public forum or a public forum by government designation, we have held that First Amendment protections are subject to heightened scrutiny. We have further held, however, that access to a nonpublic forum may be restricted by government regulation as long as the regulation is reasonable and not an effort to suppress expression merely because officials oppose the speaker's view.

The petitioners contend that LAX is neither a traditional public forum nor a public forum by government designation, and accordingly argue that the latter standard governing access to a nonpublic forum is appropriate. The respondents, in turn, argue that LAX is a public forum subject only to reasonable time, place or manner restrictions. Because we conclude that the resolution is facially unconstitutional under the First Amendment overbreadth doctrine regardless of the proper standard, we need not decide whether LAX is indeed a public forum, or what standard is applicable when access to a nonpublic forum is not restricted.

On its face, the resolution at issue in this case reaches the universe of expressive activity, and, by prohibiting *all* protected expression, purports to create a virtual "First Amendment Free Zone" at LAX. The resolution does not merely regulate expressive activity in the Central Terminal Area that might create problems such as congestion or the disruption of the activities of those who use LAX. Instead, the resolution expansively states that LAX "is not open for First Amendment activities by any individual and/or entity," and that "any individual and/or entity [who] seeks to engage in First Amendment activities within the Central Terminal Area . . . shall be deemed to be acting in contravention of the stated policy of the Board of Airport Commissioners." The resolution therefore does not merely reach the activity of respondents at LAX; it prohibits even talking and reading, or the wearing of campaign buttons or symbolic clothing. Under such a sweeping ban, virtually every individual who enters LAX may be found to violate the resolution by engaging in some "First Amendment activit[y]." We think it obvious that such a ban cannot be justified even if LAX were a nonpublic forum because no conceivable governmental interest would justify such an absolute prohibition of speech.

We conclude that the resolution is substantially overbroad. Accordingly, we hold that the resolution violates the First Amendment. The judgment of the Court of Appeals is affirmed.

Case Questions

1. Why was the resolution unconstitutional on its face?
2. Why was it irrelevant to the Court what type of forum was involved in the case?

A second rule of constitutional interpretation concerns statutes or governmental actions that are *unconstitutional as applied*. Sometimes a statute of governmental action will seem perfectly reasonable in the abstract, but will turn out to have an unconstitutional effect as administered. Because of the doctrine of presumption of constitutionality, the action is presumed to be constitutional, but a person may be able to prove to a court's satisfaction that the act in practice violates the Constitution. For example, suppose a city passes an ordinance requiring that all persons wishing to hold a parade within the city limits obtain a parade permit in advance. This type of requirement has been held to be constitutional in a number of court cases. Suppose, however, that it can be proven that the city is denying parade permits to members of a particular ethnic group, but allowing everyone else to get them. This discriminatory granting of permits is unconstitutional as applied because it is a denial of the Equal Protection Clause of the Fourteenth Amendment to the Constitution, which we will discuss later.

In this chapter and others throughout the book, you will read court cases that will use the principles of constitutional interpretation we have just discussed. You should keep these principles in mind, as they will assist in understanding court decisions.

The Constitutional Framework of Government

The Constitution establishes a delicate balance of power among the branches of the federal government, as well as between the federal and state governments. The functioning of business is often affected by the manner in which this governmental framework is set up. In this section, we will examine the constitutional framework of government.

The Relationship between the Branches of the Federal Government

The Constitution establishes three branches of federal government: the executive (the president), the legislative (the Congress), and the judicial (the Supreme Court). States also have constitutions that establish state governmental systems patterned after the federal system. The functioning of the federal government is based on the concept of *separation of powers,* the purpose of which is to insure that no branch can obtain total governmental power and, in effect, become dictatorial. To insure that each branch carries out its assigned functions and no others, the Constitution contains a number of checks on each branch's power, designed to balance off each branch's power against the others'. As an example, the president can veto statutes adopted by Congress (although it is possible for Congress to override the veto); Congress must approve the budget that funds the executive and judicial branches; and the Supreme Court can declare a statute or executive order unconstitutional and invalid.

Judicial Review of Federal Action

Although the authors of the Constitution went to great length to define the relationship among the branches of government, conflicts inevitably developed. One of the first problems that arose was over which branch of the government had the final word about interpretation of the Constitution. In *Marbury* v. *Madison,* decided in 1803, the United States Supreme Court held that it was the final arbiter of constitutional interpretation by stating that it had the power to order the executive branch to do something should the Court find that action was constitutionally required. This decision established the concept of **judicial review,** which states that the Supreme Court has final authority to decide on the constitutionality of statutes as well as legislative and executive actions.

A more recent case on substantially the same point is *United States* v. *Nixon,* decided in 1974. In that case, the Supreme Court held that it had the power to order the president to turn over certain tapes and documents to a court so that the court could determine whether the concept of "executive privilege" applied. The president had argued that, as the executive, only he had the power to determine whether the items were privileged. The Supreme Court, however, stated that the extent of executive privilege is a matter of constitutional and legal interpretation and that, quoting *Marbury* v. *Madison,* "It is emphatically the province and duty of the Supreme Court to say what the law is."

The Constitution does provide checks on the judicial branch of government, just as on the other branches: the legislative branch confirms the nomination of federal judges and appropriates the money the judicial branch needs to function, and the executive branch appoints federal judges and in theory could refuse to enforce judicial orders. However, it is firmly established that our nation is a nation under law, and that the judicial branch, through the process of judicial review, ultimately has the power to say what that law is.

The Relationship among Federal Government, State Government, and the Individual

The Bill of Rights

As we saw earlier, the Bill of Rights (the first ten amendments to the Constitution) was adopted to allay public fears that certain injustices practiced by the British might recur after independence. Therefore, the people insisted that certain guarantees of specific rights be written into the Constitution, which was accomplished by including **enumerated rights** in the first eight amendments.

Moreover, to insure absolutely that individual and/or states' rights would not be infringed upon by the federal government, two general preservation or catch-all rights were added in the Ninth and Tenth Amendments. The Ninth Amendment states. "The enumeration in the Constitution, of certain rights, shall not be construed to deny or disparage others retained by the people." The Tenth Amendment states, "The powers not delegated to the United States by the Constitution, nor prohibited by it to the States, are reserved to the States respectively, or to the people."

The wording of the Ninth and Tenth Amendments has been interpreted to protect certain types of rights not specifically set forth in the Constitution, such as the right to privacy, the right to travel, and freedom of association. These rights are referred to as **penumbral rights** (a penumbra being a shadow or umbrella). The theory of penumbral rights is that certain nonenumerated rights must be assumed to exist, and that they grow as a shadow from of the existence of the specific rights. For example, the Supreme Court has reasoned that if the First Amendment specifically guarantees individuals freedom of speech, religion, and assembly, it must mean that individuals can band together into groups to exercise these rights and, therefore, there exists a nonenumerated penumbral freedom of association.

Federal Judicial Review and State Action

It is often necessary for someone to examine whether federal laws, state laws, or other actions have priority under the Constitution. Very early in the life of the Republic, the question arose as to whether the Supreme Court had the power to declare unconstitutional a statute passed by a state legislature or to overturn a decision of a state court. In *Martin* v. *Hunter's Lessee,* decided in 1816, the Supreme Court held that it had the power to do both. Therefore, as we saw in chapter 3, an individual may appeal a decision of a state court (generally a state supreme court) to the United States Supreme Court or ask a federal court to declare a state statute to be in violation of the Constitution.

The Supremacy Clause and the Doctrine of Pre-emption

In order to preclude states' assertions that they, through their legislatures or their courts, could limit federal action, the Constitution included what has come to be known as the **Supremacy Clause,** which states, "This Constitution, and the Laws of the United States which shall be made in Pursuance thereof; and all Treaties made . . . shall be the Supreme Law of the Land; and the

Judges of every state shall be bound thereby. . . .'' The earliest interpretation of this clause was in *McCulloch* v. *Maryland,* decided in 1819. The Supreme Court held that the State of Maryland could not impose a tax on a federally chartered national bank, or otherwise regulate the way a federal bank did business.

From the Court's analysis of the Supremacy Clause in *McCulloch* v. *Maryland* evolved the doctrine of **pre-emption.** The doctrine of pre-emption, as it is now interpreted, means that a state cannot pass legislation that infringes on a constitutional power given to the federal government, either directly or by implication, if the federal government wishes to regulate an area exclusively. To illustrate, the Constitution specifically gives Congress the power to coin money. If a state began printing and distributing its own money, it would violate a specific section of the Constitution as well as the Supremacy Clause, and a court, using the doctrine of pre-emption, would declare the state action unconstitutional. You should keep in mind that the doctrine of pre-emption only prohibits a state from passing a law that *conflicts* with federal policies; it does not prohibit a state from enacting legislation that *complements* federal law. If the purposes of a state and a federal law are generally the same and the federal government has not stated unequivocally that it wishes to regulate in a particular area, courts will enforce both laws. So, for example, not only has the United States Congress adopted an Occupational Safety and Health Act and various other environmental protection measures, most states have also passed similar laws. As long as these state statutes complement the federal laws, even if they are more stringent than the federal laws, they are perfectly legal.

Notice in the following case how the Supreme Court uses the Supremacy Clause to decide an issue concerning entitlement programs.

Bennett v. *Arkansas*

99 LEd2d 455 (1988)

Per Curiam

This case involves an attempt by the State of Arkansas to attach certain federal benefits paid to individuals who are incarcerated in Arkansas prisons. In 1981, Arkansas adopted the State Prison Inmate Care and Custody Reimbursement Act, a statute that authorizes the State to seize a prisoner's property or "estate" in order to help defray the cost of maintaining its prison system. The Act specifically defines "estate" to include a prisoner's federal Social Security benefits, as well as other types of pension or retirement benefits. The State filed separate actions in state court seeking to attach Social Security benefits that had been paid to petitioner Bennett and Veterans' Administration (VA) disability pension benefits that were paid to another inmate, Shelton. In relevant part, the inmates responded by arguing that the Arkansas statute violates the Supremacy Clause of the Federal Constitution because it permits the State to attach funds that federal law exempts from legal process. In particular, petitioner pointed to 42 U. S. C. § 407(a) which provides that "none of the moneys paid or payable . . . under [the Social Security Act] shall be subject to execution, levy, attachment, garnishment, or other legal process." Similarly, Shelton contended that attachment of his VA benefits is inconsistent with 38 U. S. C. § 3101(a), which provides that such benefits "shall be exempt from the claim of creditors, and shall not be liable to attachment, levy, or seizure by or under any legal or equitable process whatever, either before or after receipt by the beneficiary."

The state trial court rejected the inmates' arguments and directed that a portion of each of their benefits be seized. The Supreme Court of Arkansas affirmed, with one justice dissenting. Briefly stated, the court found that there is no conflict between the federal and state statutes because "the federal statutes contain an implied exception to the exemption from legal process when the State provides for the care and maintenance of a beneficiary of social security or veterans' funds." We granted Bennett's petition for certiorari.

We think—contrary to the conclusion of the Supreme Court of Arkansas—that there is a clear inconsistency between the Arkansas statute and 42 U. S. C. § 407(a). Section 407(a) unambiguously rules out any attempt to attach Social Security benefits. The Arkansas statute just as unambiguously allows the State to attach those benefits. As we see it, this amounts to a "conflict" under the Supremacy Clause—a conflict that the State cannot win. We reject the State's attempt to avoid this conclusion by arguing that the federal statute contains an "implied exception" that would allow attachment of otherwise exempted federal payments simply because the State has provided the recipient with "care and maintenance." We declined to find such an exception in *Philpott* v. *Essex County Welfare Board* (1973), where we held that § 407 bars a State from attempting to attach Social Security benefits as reimbursement for state welfare assistance payments. *Philpott* may be factually distinguishable on the ground that there the State provided for only *part* of the needs of the Social Security recipient while here the State provides for *all* of the prisoners' needs. But we do not think that such a distinction carries the day given the express language of § 407 and the clear intent of Congress that Social Security benefits not be attachable.

Nor do we think that the State's "implied exception" argument is supported by our decision last Term in *Rose* v. *Rose.* There we held that 38 U. S. C. § 3101 did not bar a state court from holding a disabled veteran in contempt for failing to pay child support, even though the veteran's only means of paying his obligation was to use his VA disability benefits. But in that case we held that the benefits in question were designed by Congress to support not only the recipient of the benefits, but also his dependents. Accordingly, allowing the state court in that case to enforce a valid child support order was fully consistent with the underlying intent of § 3101, which was in part to " 'prevent the deprivation and depletion of the means of subsistence' " of the beneficiaries of the federal payments. Here, in contrast, the State cannot be said to be a "beneficiary" of petitioner's Social Security benefits.

The judgment of the Supreme Court of Arkansas is reversed.

Case Questions

1. What is the significance of the fact that this was a *per curium* opinion?
2. How do you distinguish this case from *Rose* v. *Rose,* which was discussed in the text?

The Privileges and Immunities Clause and State Legislation

Article IV of the Constitution contains a provision generally referred to as the **Privileges and Immunities Clause,** which provides, "The Citizens of each State shall be entitled to all Privileges and Immunities of Citizens in the several states." Additionally, the Fourteenth Amendment provides that no state shall abridge the privileges and immunities of citizens.

Through the years, cases involving the Privileges and Immunities Clause have been rather infrequent. However, in the past few years, migrations from state to state caused by economic conditions has brought the clause up as the subject of fairly extensive litigation. These cases have generally come up in the context of testing statutes that regulate hiring requirements, unemployment compensation, and other benefits at the state level.

A 1988 Supreme Court case considered a Virginia Supreme Court rule exempting permanent state residents from taking the Virginia bar examination, if they were already admitted to practice in another state. The Court held that the Virginia rule violated the Privileges and Immunities Clause of the Constitution because it discriminated against equally qualified applicants solely on the basis of citizenship or residency.

So far, we have been considering the general constitutional framework of government within which business must function. In the succeeding sections, we will examine government's power to regulate business and the constitutional rights enjoyed by business.

Government's Power to Regulate Business

The Commerce Clause

In order to alleviate the "trade wars" between states that existed under the Confederation, the framers of the Constitution included what has come to be known as the **Commerce Clause.** It provides that "the Congress shall have Power . . . To regulate Commerce . . . among the several States. . . ." You will notice that the clause gives the federal government the power to regulate *interstate* commerce (trade between different states); it does *not* give Congress the power to regulate *intrastate* commerce (trade solely within one state).

Until the twentieth century, Congress, following the prevailing laissez-faire attitude, did little to regulate commerce that was arguably intrastate. However, as you have already seen, in the twentieth century, government virtually exploded with business regulations, and Congress began to pass laws that regulated commercial enterprises that often seemed purely intrastate. In *Wickard* v. *Filburn,* decided in 1942, the Supreme Court held that a federal statute limiting wheat production was constitutional, even though this statute was used to limit the production of a farmer who grew a small amount of wheat for personal consumption on his own farm. The farmer had contended that this practice was purely intrastate commerce and, therefore, the Commerce Clause did not apply. However, the Supreme Court reasoned that Congress could use its commerce regulation powers, because even though the wheat itself would not be moved in interstate commerce, it had an *effect* on interstate commerce. With the *Wickard* criterion of possible effect on interstate commerce as the test for congressional regulation under the Commerce Clause, the amount of federal regulation of business, even that which is primarily local in character, increased dramatically. The courts have followed the *Wickard* "effect on commerce'' test, resulting in such decisions as the following by the United States Supreme Court: In 1964, in the case of *Katzenbach* v. *McClung,* it was held that federal antidiscrimination laws applied to a barbecue restaurant in Birmingham, Alabama, with an almost exclusively local clientele, primarily because 46 percent of its meat originated out-of-state; in 1980, in *McLain* v. *Real Estate Board of New Orleans,* it was held that the federal antitrust laws could extend to the activities of real estate firms doing business in one city only, because the transactions between buyers and sellers affected the demand for financial and title insurance, which are part of interstate commerce.

One issue the Supreme Court has examined is the extent to which the Tenth Amendment's guarantee of states' rights limits the power of the federal government to regulate state activities. In 1976, in *National League of Cities* v. *Usery,* the Court held that an attempt to extend a federal minimum wage requirement to state and local governments was unconstitutional. The Court determined that the Tenth Amendment granted states the right to determine their own minimum wage standards. However, in the following case, the Court reversed this position, stating that under the Commerce Clause, Congress *did* have the authority to extend to states the requirements of federal minimum wage standards.

Garcia v. San Antonio Metropolitan Transit Authority

471 U.S. 1049 (1985)

Facts

The San Antonio Metropolitan Transit Authority (SAMTA) received substantial federal financial assistance. Prior to the Supreme Court's 1976 decision in National League of Cities *v.* Usery, *the federal Wage and Hour Administration had ruled that the minimum wage and overtime requirements of the federal Fair Labor Standards Act (FLSA) applied to SAMTA. However, after Usery, which held that the FLSA did not apply to traditional governmental functions of state and local governments, SAMTA ceased compliance with the FLSA overtime requirements.*

Opinion

Justice Blackmun: We revisit in these cases an issue raised in *National League of Cities* v. *Usery* (1976). In that litigation, this Court, by a sharply divided vote, ruled that the Commerce Clause does not empower Congress to enforce the minimum-wage and overtime provisions of the Fair Labor Standards Act (FLSA) against the States "in areas of traditional governmental functions." Although *National League of Cities* supplied some examples of "traditional governmental functions," it did not offer a general explanation of how a "traditional" function is to be distinguished from a "nontraditional" one. Since then, federal and state courts have struggled with the task, thus imposed, of identifying a traditional function for purposes of state immunity under the Commerce Clause.

In the present cases, a Federal District Court concluded that municipal ownership and operation of a mass-transit system is a traditional governmental function and thus, under *National League of Cities,* is exempt from the obligations imposed by the FLSA. Faced with the identical question, three Federal Courts of Appeals and one state appellate court have reached the opposite conclusion.

Our examination of this "function" standard applied in these and other cases over the last eight years now persuades us that the attempt to draw the boundaries of state regulatory immunity in terms of "traditional governmental function" is not only unworkable but is inconsistent with established principles of federalism and, indeed, with those very federalism principles on which *National League of Cities* purported to rest. That case, accordingly, is overruled.

Appellees have not argued that SAMTA is immune from regulation under the FLSA on the ground that it is a local transit system engaged in intrastate commercial activity. In a practical sense, SAMTA's operations might well be characterized as "local." Nonetheless, it long has been settled that Congress' authority under the Commerce Clause extends to intrastate economic activities that affect interstate commerce. See, e.g., *Hodel* v. *Virginia Surface Mining & Recl. Assn.* (1981); *Heart of Atlanta Motel, Inc.* v. *United States* (1964); *Wickard* v. *Filburn* (1942). Were SAMTA a privately owned and operated enterprise, it could not credibly argue that Congress exceeded the bounds of its Commerce Clause powers in prescribing minimum wages and overtime rates for SAMTA's employees. Any constitutional exemption from the requirements of the FLSA therefore must rest on SAMTA's status as a governmental entity rather than on the "local" nature of its operations.

The prerequisites for governmental immunity under *National League of Cities* were summarized by this Court in *Hodel, supra.* Under that summary, four conditions must be satisfied before a state activity may be deemed immune from a particular federal regulation under the Commerce Clause. First, it is said that the federal statute at issue must regulate "the 'States as States.' " Second, the statute must "address matters that are indisputably 'attribute[s] of state sovereignty.' " Third, state compliance with the federal obligation must "directly impair [the States'] ability 'to structure integral operations in areas of traditional governmental functions.' " Finally, the relation of state and federal interests must not be such that "the nature of the federal interest . . . justifies state submission."

The controversy in the present cases has focused on the third *Hodel* requirement—that the challenged federal statute trench on "traditional governmental functions." The District Court voiced a common concern: "Despite the abundance of adjectives, identifying which particular state functions are immune remains difficult." 557 F. Supp., at 447. Just how troublesome the task has been is revealed by the results reached in other federal cases. Thus, courts have held that regulating ambulance services, licensing automobile drivers, operating a municipal airport performing solid waste disposal, and operating a highway authority are functions *protected* under *National League of Cities.* At the same time, courts have held that issuance of industrial development bonds, regulation of intrastate natural gas sales, regulation of traffic on public roads, regulation of air transportation, operation of a telephone system, leasing and sale of natural gas, operation of a mental health facility, and provision of in-house domestic services for the aged and handicapped are *not* entitled to immunity. We find it difficult, if not impossible, to identify an organizing principle that places each of the cases in the first group on one side of a line and each of the cases in the second group on the other side. The constitutional distinction between licensing drivers and regulating traffic, for example, or between operating a highway authority and operating a mental health facility, is elusive at best.

Thus far, this Court itself has made little headway in defining the scope of the governmental functions deemed protected under *National League of Cities.*

We therefore now reject, as unsound in principle and unworkable in practice, a rule of state immunity from federal regulation that turns on a judicial appraisal of whether a particular governmental function is "integral" or "traditional." Any such rule leads to inconsistent results at the same time that it disserves principles of democratic self-governance, and it breeds inconsistency precisely because it is divorced from those principles. If there are to be limits on the Federal Government's power to interfere with state functions—as undoubtedly there are—we must look elsewhere to find them. We accordingly return to the underlying issue that confronted this Court in *National League of Cities*—the manner in which the Constitution insulates States from the reach of Congress' power under the Commerce Clause.

The central theme of *National League of Cities*

was that the States occupy a special position in our constitutional system and that the scope of Congress' authority under the Commerce Clause must reflect that position. Of course, the Commerce Clause by its specific language does not provide any special limitation on Congress' actions with respect to the States. See *EEOC* v. *Wyoming* (concurring opinion). It is equally true, however, that the text of the Constitution provides the beginning rather than the final answer to every inquiry into questions of federalism, for "[b]ehind the words of the constitutional provisions are postulates which limit and control."

The sovereignty of the States is limited by the Constitution itself. A variety of sovereign powers, for example, are withdrawn from the States by Article I, § 10. The States unquestionably do retain a significant measure of sovereign authority. They do so, however, only to the extent that the Constitution has not divested them of their original powers and transferred those powers to the Federal Government. Apart from the limitation on federal authority inherent in the delegated nature of Congress' Article I powers, the principal means chosen by the Framers to ensure the role of the States in the federal system lies in the structure of the Federal Government itself. It is no novelty to observe that the composition of the Federal Government was designed in large part to protect the States from overreaching by Congress. The Framers thus gave the States a role in the selection both of the Executive and the Legislative Branches of the Federal Government. The effectiveness of the federal political process in preserving the States' interests is apparent even today in the course of federal legislation.

Insofar as the present cases are concerned, then, we need go no further than to state that we perceive nothing in the overtime and minimum-wage requirements of the FLSA, as applied to SAMTA, that is destructive of state sovereignty or violative of any constitutional provision. SAMTA faces nothing more than the same minimum-wage and overtime obligations that hundreds of thousands of other employers, public as well as private, have to meet.

This analysis makes clear that Congress' action in affording SAMTA employees the protections of the wage and hour provisions of the FLSA contravened no affirmative limit on Congress' power under the Commerce Clause. The judgment of the District Court therefore must be reversed.

Of course, we continue to recognize that the States occupy a special and specific position in our constitutional system and that the scope of Congress' authority under the Commerce Clause must reflect that position. But the principal and basic limit on the federal commerce power is that inherent in all congressional action—the built-in restraints that our system provides through state participation in federal governmental action. The political process ensures that laws that unduly burden the States will not be promulgated. In the factual setting of these cases the internal safeguards of the political process have performed as intended.

The Court in *National League of Cities* attempted to articulate affirmative limits on the Commerce Clause power in terms of core governmental functions and fundamental attributes of state sovereignty. But the model of democratic decisionmaking the Court there identified underestimated, in our view, the solicitude of the national political process for the continued vitality of the States. Attempts by other courts since then to draw guidance from this model have proved it both impracticable and doctrinally barren. In sum, in *National League of Cities* the Court tried to repair what did not need repair.

We do not lightly overrule recent precedent. We have not hesitated, however, when it has become apparent that a prior decision has departed from a proper understanding of congressional power under the Commerce Clause. Due respect for the reach of congressional power within the federal system mandates that we do so now.

National League of Cities v. *Usery* is overruled. The judgment of the District Court is reversed, and these cases are remanded to that court for further proceedings consistent with this opinion.

It is so ordered.

JUSTICE POWELL, with whom THE CHIEF JUSTICE, JUSTICE REHNQUIST, and JUSTICE O'CONNOR join, dissenting.

The Court today, in its 5–4 decision, overrules *National League of Cities* v. *Usery,* a case in which we held that Congress lacked authority to impose the requirements of the Fair Labor Standards Act on state and local governments. Because I believe this decision substantially alters the federal system embodied in the Constitution, I dissent.

There are, of course, numerous examples over the history of this Court in which prior decisions have been reconsidered and overruled. There have been few cases, however, in which the principle of *stare decisis* and the rationale of recent decisions were ignored as abruptly as we now witness.

More troubling than the logical infirmities in the Court's reasoning is the result of its holding, *i.e.,* that federal political officials, invoking the Commerce Clause, are the sole judges of the limits of their own power. This result is inconsistent with the fundamental principles of our constitutional system. Much of the initial opposition to the Constitution was rooted in the fear that the national government would be too powerful and eventually would eliminate the States as viable political entities. The Framers believed that the separate sphere of sovereignty reserved to the States would ensure that the States would serve as an effective "counterpoise" to the power of the federal government.

Thus, the harm to the States that results from federal overreaching under the Commerce Clause is not simply a matter of dollars and cents. Nor is it a matter of the wisdom or folly of certain policy choices. Rather, by usurping functions traditionally performed by the States, federal overreaching under the Commerce Clause undermines the constitutionally mandated balance of power between the States and the federal government, a balance designed to protect our fundamental liberties.

JUSTICE O'CONNOR, with whom JUSTICE POWELL and JUSTICE REHNQUIST join, dissenting.

The Court today surveys the battle scene of federalism and sounds a retreat. Like Justice Powell, I would prefer to hold the field and, at the very least, render a little aid to the wounded. I join Justice Powell's opinion. I also write separately to note my fundamental disagreement with the majority's views of federalism and the duty of this Court.

In my view, federalism cannot be reduced to the weak "essence" distilled by the majority today. There is more to federalism than the nature of the constraints that can be imposed on the States in "the realm of authority left open to them by the Constitution." The central issue of federalism, of course, is whether any realm *is* left open to the States by the Constitution—whether any area remains in which a State may act free of federal interference. "The issue . . . is whether the federal system has any *legal* substance, any core of constitutional right that courts will enforce." The true "essence" of federalism is that the States *as States* have legitimate interests which the National Government is bound to respect even though its laws are supreme. If federalism so conceived and so carefully cultivated by the Framers of our Constitution is to remain meaningful, this Court cannot abdicate its constitutional responsibility to oversee the Federal Government's compliance with its duty to respect the legitimate interests of the States.

Due to the emergence of an integrated and industrialized national economy, this Court has been required to examine and review a breathtaking expansion of the powers of Congress. In doing so the Court correctly perceived that the Framers of our Constitution intended Congress to have sufficient power to address national problems. But the Framers were not single-minded. The Constitution is animated by an array of intentions. Just as surely as the Framers envisioned a National Government capable of solving national problems, they also envisioned a republic whose vitality was assured by the diffusion of power not only among the branches of the Federal Government, but also between the Federal Government and the States. In the 18th century these intentions did not conflict because technology had not yet converted every local problem into a national one. A conflict has now emerged, and the Court today retreats rather than reconcile the Constitution's dual concerns for federalism and an effective commerce power.

In the decades since ratification of the Constitution, interstate economic activity has steadily expanded. Industrialization, coupled with advances in transportation and communications, has created a national economy in which virtually every activity occurring within the borders of a State plays a part. The expansion and integration of the national economy brought with it a coordinate expansion in the scope of national problems. This Court has been increasingly generous in its interpretation of the commerce power of Congress, primarily to assure that the National Government would be able to deal with national economic problems.

Subsequent decisions indicate that Congress, in order to regulate an activity, needs only a rational basis for a finding that the activity affects interstate commerce. Even if a particular individual's activity has no perceptible interstate effect, it can be reached by Congress through regulation of that class of activity in general as long as that *class,* considered as a whole, affects interstate commerce. Incidental to this expansion of the commerce power Congress has been given an ability it lacked prior to the emergence of an integrated national economy. Because virtually every *state* activity, like virtually every activity of a private individual, arguably "affects" interstate commerce, Congress can now supplant the States from the significant sphere of activities envisioned for them by the Framers.

The last two decades have seen an unprecedented growth of federal regulatory activity, as the majority itself acknowledges.

With the abandonment of *National League of Cities,* all that stands between the remaining essentials of state sovereignty and Congress is the latter's underdeveloped capacity for self-restraint.

The problems of federalism in an integrated national economy are capable of more responsible resolution than holding that the States as States retain no status apart from that which Congress chooses to let them retain. The proper resolution, I suggest, lies in weighing state autonomy as a factor in the balance when interpreting the means by which Congress can exercise its authority on the States as States. It is insufficient, in assessing the validity of congressional regulation of a State pursuant to the commerce power, to ask only whether the same regulation would be valid if enforced against a private party. That reasoning, embodied in the majority opinion, is inconsistent with the spirit of our Constitution. It remains relevant that a *State* is being regulated, as *National League of Cities* and every recent case have recognized. As far as the Constitution is concerned, a State should not be equated with any private litigant. Instead, the autonomy of a State is an essential component of federalism. If state autonomy is ignored in assessing the means by which Congress regulates matters affecting commerce, then federalism becomes irrelevant simply because the set of activities remaining beyond the reach of such a commerce power "may well be negligible."

I respectfully dissent.

Case Questions

1. How has the Commerce Clause come to affect the balance of power between the federal and state governments?
2. Will this case have a significant impact on states' rights?

The Contract Clause

One constitutional provision that has had a major impact on business operations is the **Contract Clause,** which provides, "No State shall . . . pass any . . . Law impairing the Obligation of Contracts." In the nineteenth century, this provision was often interpreted to forbid government regulation of contracts between businesses or between business people and their employees. In *Lochner* v. *New York,* decided in 1905, the Supreme Court held that the Contract Clause prohibited a state from enacting a maximum workweek law. (This case has now in effect been overruled, and states have passed such laws.)

Since the 1930s, the contract clause has been used increasingly less as a defense to governmental regulation, particularly regulation of business. However, the Contract Clause was used to limit government action in the case of *Allied Structural Steel Company* v. *Spannaus* (1978). The United States Supreme Court invalidated a Minnesota statute that assessed a "pension funding charge" against employers who ceased doing business in Minnesota, leaving what the state defined as inadequately funded pension plans for former employees. The Supreme Court stated, "If the Contract Clause is to retain any meaning at all, it must be understood to impose some limits upon the power of a State to abridge existing contractual relationships, even in the exercise of its otherwise legitimate police power."

The Taxing Power

One of the most long-standing governmental powers is the power to tax individuals and commercial enterprises. Today, as you know, all levels of government enjoy the power to tax, and few questions are even raised about this *power*. However, legal questions often arise regarding interpretation and implementation of tax laws. The courts have been careful to insure that government exercises its taxing power within appropriate constitutional constraints because, as has been aptly observed, the power to tax is ultimately the power to destroy. In one case, the United States Supreme Court held that the state of Hawaii could not impose a state tax on airlines' gross annual income in direct contradiction to the provisions of a federal statute (*Aloha Airlines, Inc.* v. *Director of Taxation of Hawaii* [1983]).

The Court also viewed the power to tax as inappropriately exercised in *Arkansas Writer's Project* v. *Charles G. Ragland* (1988) when an Arkansas tax statute was deemed unconstitutional. The Court held that a tax applying to some magazines published within the state and not to others was violative of the First Amendment.

The Doctrine of the Police Power

In our discussion of the contract clause, you will notice in the *Spannaus* case that the Supreme Court refers to an "exercise of . . . police power." The doctrine of the **police power** states that the government has the power to regulate (legislate) for the public health, welfare, safety, and morals. Although it is not mentioned specifically in the Constitution, the courts have implied the concept of a general police power from the specific powers given to government in the Constitution. As we discussed in chapter 1, laws are the embodiment of societal norms. In other words, when a statute is passed or a new common law doctrine is developed by the courts, a judgment has been made that it is in the best interests of the public as a whole that certain activities by individuals be forbidden or be carried out in certain ways. As illustration, consider the following examples of police power: to preserve public health, restaurant hygiene statutes and regulations have been enacted; to preserve public welfare, unemployment compensation statutes have been passed; to preserve public safety, traffic laws have been enacted; and to preserve public morals, anti-pornography and anti-prostitution laws have been adopted.

It is inevitable in application of government's police powers that individual rights at times will be curtailed in the interests of society. One perennial problem of the courts has been how to balance the public need for legitimate exercise of the police power against the rights of individuals. What the courts have done is look to the nature of the individual right being infringed upon by governmental actions. Generally, if the right is a specific right guaranteed under the Constitution, the individual right will prevail over the public interest; however, if the only individual right being infringed upon is some general property right, the police power will probably prevail over the individual's rights. Zoning laws are an excellent example of exercise of the police power. In zoning, the uses to which a piece of real property may be put are restricted on the theory that the public as a whole benefits from orderly and uniform land use. Suppose A buys a house in a residential area, intending to open up a woodworking business in his garage. A then discovers that the zoning laws prohibit any business use of his house. A may feel strongly that his property rights have been infringed upon because the house is not worth to him what he thought it would be had he been able to operate a business in it. However, if A sues to have the zoning laws invalidated as an infringement on his property rights, the court will uphold the zoning laws, because A's property rights are not regarded as substantial enough to outweigh the interests of the public as a whole. The earlier discussion of the *Spannaus* case illustrates how a specific constitutional right (the freedom to contract) can invalidate an otherwise legitimate exercise of the police power.

Much of the regulation of business that has occurred in the past fifty years has been justified as an exercise of the doctrine of the police power. We will discuss many instances of governmental action in which this doctrine has been applied, from passage of occupational safety and health acts to toxic waste control acts or securities trading regulation acts.

Business and Constitutional Rights

Our prior discussion about the governmental power to regulate business raises the issue of business' constitutional rights. There have been questions about the extent to which business, as a nonhuman legal entity, could claim certain constitutional rights. This section will examine selected constitutional rights that have applied to business.

Business and the First Amendment: Commercial Speech

The First Amendment guarantees freedom of speech. While the free speech rights of individuals have been carefully guarded throughout the history of the Republic, a concept evolved that **commercial speech,** speech by business, was not entitled to the same amount of protection as the speech of individuals. Therefore, it was reasoned that government could limit or prohibit commercial speech in such matters as advertising.

However, in 1976, in *Virginia State Board of Pharmacy* v. *Virginia Citizens Consumer Council,* the Supreme Court indicated that commercial speech was entitled to protection. In this case, which involved a state statute prohibiting licensed pharmacists from advertising prescription drug prices, the Court held that pure advertisement is protected by the First Amendment. The *Virginia Board of Pharmacy* case, however, has not been interpreted as meaning that business may say whatever it wants in advertising. Under the doctrine of the police power, the government may still regulate commercial speech to prevent deceptive advertising or communications that would violate some law, such as advertisements specifying the race or sex of job candidates. For example, the legal profession has been the subject of governmental exercise of police power in regulating advertising. In *Bates* v. *Arizona* (1977), the Supreme Court has held that a state bar association cannot flatly prohibit advertising by lawyers. Alternately, it also upheld suspension from the practice of law of an ''ambulance chasing'' attorney who claimed his right to solicit business from an automobile accident victim was protected by the First Amendment (*Ohralik* v. *Ohio State Bar Association* [1978]). However, the court's 1988 *Shapero* v. *Kentucky* decision upheld an attorney's right to advertise by direct mailings to persons facing specific legal problems.

Since the 1980 decision in *Central Hudson Gas and Electric Corporation* v. *Public Services Commission of New York,* which allowed advertising that promoted the use of electricity, the law seems well established that commercial speech advertising is protected by the First Amendment as long as it concerns lawful activity and is not misleading. However, the Supreme Court also upheld a statute instructing advertisement of casino gambling directed solely at citizens of Puerto Rico (*Posados de Puerto Rico Associates* v. *Tourism Company of Puerto Rico* [1986]). As you can see, the legal aspects surrounding the First Amendment relationship with commercial speech are complex, requiring extensive examination.

The legal and ethical aspects of this question extend to ''issue advertising,'' the right of business to take public positions on issues unrelated to their specific business activities. In the 1976 Supreme Court case of *First National Bank of Boston* v. *Bellotti,* a Massachusetts criminal statute was questioned regarding its prohibition on a corporation spending money for influencing public opinion on matters not specifically affecting that corporation's business. Citing the First Amendment, the Court held that businesses could publicize their views opposing a referendum to allow enactment of a graduated personal income tax. Similarly, in the 1980 case of *Consolidated Edison Company of New York, Inc.,* v. *Public Service Commission of New York,* the Supreme Court held that, because of the First Amendment, the New York Public Services Commission could not prohibit Consolidated Edison from inserting a brochure advocating nuclear power into customers' monthly electric bill statements.

The effect of the *Bellotti* and *Consolidated Edison* cases has been to encourage a large amount of "issue advertising," which, at times, has engendered controversy. For example, insurance companies have begun publicly campaigning to change the tort claims legal system.

Two objections to issue advertising are particularly common. First, some observers argue that business possesses so much economic power that it can "unfairly" influence legislators or influential segments of society, potentially to the detriment of society as a whole. (This objection was a factor in the *Bellotti* and *Consolidated Edison* cases.) Another objection raised within businesses themselves is that it is a waste of corporate monies to take positions on issues not directly affecting profits, especially since the public seems indifferent to businesses' positions on specific issues. Whatever objections may be raised to business issue advertising, it appears to be a trend that will remain and grow for the foreseeable future. You will see more coverage of legal and ethical issues in business advertising in chapter 22.

Another dimension to the relationship between business and the First Amendment is the extent to which the media (newspapers, magazines, television, and radio) is liable to individuals for the tort of defamation. Defamation is committed when one person knowingly utters an untrue and injurious statement about another person. Oral defamation is called slander, while printed defamation is known as libel.

Until 1964, a person who could prove that the media made an untrue statement about him could recover monetary damages. However, the Supreme Court decided in the 1964 case of *New York Times* v. *Sullivan,* that *public officials* could not recover for defamation from the media unless they could prove that the media made the defamatory statement with actual malice. Actual malice is defined as reckless disregard for truth or falsity, and generally means that the defamed person will have to prove that the media knew that the statement was probably false when it was made. The Supreme Court soon extended this "New York Times rule" to *public figures* as well as public officials. In 1974, the Supreme Court, in *Gertz* v. *Robert Welch, Inc.,* defined a public figure as someone having a pervasive involvement or a general notoriety in the community. After *Gertz,* private individuals could recover for defamation if they could prove that the media negligently made a false statement about them. The following case required that the Supreme Court weigh an individual's reputational rights against the media's right to publish satire.

Hustler Magazine v. Falwell

94 LEd2d 788 (1988)

Opinion

Justice Rehnquist: Petitioner Hustler Magazine, Inc., is a magazine of nationwide circulation. Respondent Jerry Falwell, a nationally known minister who has been active as a commentator on politics and public affairs, sued petitioner and its publisher, petitioner Larry Flynt, to recover damages for invasion of privacy, libel, and intentional infliction of emotional distress. The District Court directed a verdict against respondent on the privacy claim, and submitted the other two claims to a jury. The jury found for petitioners on the defamation claim, but found for respondent on the claim for intentional infliction of emotional distress and awarded damages. We now consider whether this award is consistent with the First and Fourteenth Amendments of the United States Constitution.

The inside front cover of the November 1983 issue of Hustler Magazine featured a "parody" of an advertisement for Campari Liqueur that contained the name and picture of respondent and was entitled "Jerry Falwell talks about his first time." This parody was modeled after actual Campari ads that included interviews with various celebrities about their "first times." Although it was apparent by the end of each interview that this meant the first time they sampled Campari, the ads clearly played on the sexual double entendre of the general subject of "first times." Copying the form and layout of these Campari ads, Hustler's editors chose respondent as the featured celebrity and drafted an alleged "interview" with him in which he states that his "first time" was during a drunken incestuous rendezvous with his mother in an outhouse. The Hustler parody portrays respondent and his mother as drunk and immoral, and suggests that respondent is a hypocrite who preaches only when he is drunk. In small print at the bottom of the page, the ad contains the disclaimer, "ad parody—not to be taken seriously." The magazine's table of contents also lists the ad as "Fiction; Ad and Personality Parody."

On appeal, the United States Court of Appeals for the Fourth Circuit affirmed the judgment against petitioners. The court rejected petitioners' argument that the "actual malice" standard of *New York Times Co.* v. *Sullivan,* must be met before respondent can recover for emotional distress. The court agreed that because respondent is concededly a public figure, petitioners are "entitled to the same level of first amendment protection in the claim for intentional infliction of emotional distress that they received in [respondent's] claim for libel." But this does not mean that a literal application of the actual malice rule is appropriate in the context of an emotional distress claim. In the court's view, the *New York Times* decision emphasized the constitutional importance not of the falsity of the statement or the defendant's disregard for the truth, but of the heightened level of culpability embodied in the requirement of "knowing . . . or reckless" conduct. Here, the *New York Times* standard is satisfied by the state-law requirement, and the jury's finding, that the defendants have acted intentionally or recklessly.

Respondent would have us find that a State's interest in protecting public figures from emotional distress is sufficient to deny First Amendment protection to speech that is patently offensive and is intended to inflict emotional injury, even when that speech could not reasonably have been interpreted as stating actual facts about the public figure involved. This we decline to do.

At the heart of the First Amendment is the recognition of the fundamental importance of the free flow of ideas and opinions on matters of public interest and concern. We have therefore been particularly vigilant to ensure that individual expressions of ideas remain free from governmentally imposed sanctions. The First Amendment recognizes no such thing as a "false" idea. *Gertz* v. *Robert Welch, Inc.,* 418 U. S. 323, 339 (1974). As Justice Holmes wrote, "[W]hen men have realized that time has upset many fighting faiths, they may come to believe even more than they believe the very foundations of their own conduct that the ultimate good desired is better reached by free trade in ideas—that the best test of truth is the power of the thought to get itself accepted in the competition of the market. . . ."

The sort of robust political debate encouraged by the First Amendment is bound to produce speech that is critical of those who hold public office or those public figures who are "intimately involved in the resolution of important public questions or, by reason of their fame, shape events in areas of concern to society at large."

Of course, this does not mean that *any* speech about a public figure is immune from sanction in the form of damages. Since *New York Times Co.* v. *Sullivan,* we have consistently ruled that a public figure may hold a speaker liable for the damage to reputation caused by publication of a defamatory falsehood, but only if the statement was made "with knowledge that it was false or with reckless disregard of whether it was false or not." False statements of fact are particularly valueless; they interfere with the truth-seeking function of the marketplace of ideas, and they cause damage to an individual's reputation that cannot easily be repaired by counterspeech, however persuasive or effective. But even though falsehoods have little value in and of themselves, they are "nevertheless inevitable in free debate," and a rule that would impose strict liability on a publisher for false factual assertions would have an undoubted "chilling" effect on speech relating to public figures that does have constitutional value. "Freedoms of expression require 'breathing space.' " This breathing space is provided by a constitutional rule that allows public figures to recover for libel or defamation only when they can prove *both* that the statement was false and that the statement was made with the requisite level of culpability. Thus while such a bad motive may be deemed controlling for purposes of tort liability in other areas of the law, we think the First Amendment prohibits such a result in the area of public debate about public figures.

Were we to hold otherwise, there can be little doubt that political cartoonists and satirists would be subjected to damages awards without any showing that their work falsely defamed its subject. The appeal of the political cartoon or caricature is often based on exploration of unfortunate physical traits or politically embarrassing events—an exploration often calculated to injure the feelings of the subject of the portrayal. The art of the cartoonist is often not reasoned or evenhanded, but slashing and one-sided. Despite their sometimes caustic nature, from the early cartoon portraying George Washington as an ass down to the present day, graphic depictions and satirical cartoons have played a prominent role in public and political debate. Respondent contends that the caricature in question here was so "outrageous" as to distinguish it from more traditional political cartoons. There is no doubt that the caricature of respondent and his mother published in Hustler is at best a distant cousin of the political cartoons described above, and a rather poor relation at that. An "outrageousness" standard thus runs afoul of our longstanding refusal to allow damages to be awarded because the speech in question may have an adverse emotional impact on the audience.

We conclude that public figures and public officials may not recover for the tort of intentional infliction of emotional distress by reason of publications such as the one here at issue without showing in addition that the publication contains a false statement of fact which was made with "actual malice," *i.e.,* with knowledge that the statement was false or with reckless disregard as to whether or not it was true. This is not merely a "blind application" of the *New York Times* standard, it reflects our considered judgment that such a standard is necessary to give adequate "breathing space" to the freedoms protected by the First Amendment. Here it is clear that respondent Falwell is a "public figure" for purposes of First Amendment law.

(Judgment in favor of Hustler Magazine and Larry Flynt.)

Case Questions

1. Is there any way for a cartoonist to be held liable for defamation or emotional distress after this decision?
2. Did this decision represent a change in the Supreme Court's prior stand on the First Amendment?

Business and the Fourth Amendment

The Fourth Amendment to the Constitution guarantees the right against unreasonable searches and seizures and provides that a search warrant shall not be issued unless it is supported by probable cause and particularly describes the place to be searched and the persons or things to be seized. There have been innumerable court cases through the years concerning what the Fourth Amendment means and when it applies. It is now established that the Fourth Amendment protects business establishments as well as private homes. Through judicial interpretation, certain exceptions to the Fourth Amendment have been found to exist. Two of the most important exceptions that may affect searches of businesses are the *"hot pursuit"* and *"plain view" exceptions.* As the "hot pursuit" name indicates, a law enforcement officer actively involved in chasing a suspected criminal would not have to stop and go to a magistrate to get a search warrant in order to search the premises if he saw that person run into a business establishment. Also, if an officer happens to be lawfully in a business establishment and sees evidence of criminal activity in plain view, he may seize the incriminating evidence without a search warrant. For example, if a police officer on foot patrol on a cold day enters a florist shop at the manager's invitation to "warm up," sees bookmaking slips and arrests the manager for illegal wagering, the evidence cannot be thrown out because it was seized in violation of the Fourth Amendment, since the evidence of illegal wagering was in plain view.

If an arrest, a search, or a seizure does violate the Fourth Amendment, evidence thereby obtained may not be used to convict an accused at trial. Admission of such evidence is prohibited by what is known as the **Exclusionary Rule.** Furthermore, any information obtained as a result of an unconstitutional arrest, search, or seizure is also generally excluded under the **fruit of the poisonous tree doctrine.** For example, in *Wong Sun* v. *United States,* the Supreme Court held that an arrest was illegal, and that therefore evidence seized as a result of a search conducted at the time of the arrest was illegal under the fruit of the poisonous tree doctrine.

However, within the "curtilage" of one's home, society is prepared to accept that occupants have a reasonable and legitimate expectation of privacy. *Curtilage* refers to an area so intimately tied to a home that it is covered under the home's "umbrella" of protection from warrantless searches under the Fourth Amendment. In the 1987 Supreme Court action in *United States* v. *Dunn,* open fields around a dwelling were not considered to be within the curtilage of that dwelling, under the "open field doctrine." Also, in the 1988 case of *California* v. *Greenwood,* the Supreme Court determined that a search of household garbage left outside for collection did not fall under the protection of the home's curtilage; thus, evidence seized in this search was admissible. Additionally, in *Dow Chemical Co.* v. *United States* (1986), the Supreme Court held that an administrative agency was entitled to obtain information about factory operations, without a warrant, through use of aerial photography from unrestricted air space. Although Dow asserted that such photography was a violation of the curtilage of its industrial complex, the Court held that the open areas of a factory, even the air space above that factory, are more appropriately judged as being an "open field" rather than a part of the curtilage of one's home. Therefore, the ruling held that any photographs taken were legally obtained and not subject to restriction under the Fourth Amendment.

While the legal principles regarding application of the Fourth Amendment are fairly well settled regarding searches of business premises, there have been a few very important cases in recent years regarding this subject. One very big problem for business resulted from a provision included in the original federal Occupational Safety and Health Act (OSHA), passed in 1970. This provision provided for "surprise" warrantless inspections (i.e., searches) of businesses to see if OSHA safety and health standards were being observed. In 1978, in *Marshall* v. *Barlow's Inc.,* the United States Supreme Court held that this OSHA provision violated the Fourth Amendment by allowing warrantless searches without a business owner's consent. However, the Supreme Court distinguished its *Barlow* ruling in the 1981 case of *Donovan* v. *Dewey,* in which the Court upheld warrantless searches of the mining industry. As a "closely regulated industry" with federal statute mandating an inspection program consisting of a minimum number of annual inspections, the Supreme Court reasoned that mine owners were "on notice" concerning searches of their property. Moreover, in *New York* v. *Burger* (1987), warrantless searches of the automobile junkyard industry were upheld under the same premise: that as a "closely regulated industry," the warrant requirement for searches could be eliminated in light of governmental interests.

The rights of employees within the workplace are also affected by warrantless searches. In *O'Connor* v. *Ortega* (1987), the Supreme Court observed that the search of an employee's desk was covered by Fourth Amendment protections, but that government searches to retrieve work-related materials or to investigate violations of workplace rules do not violate the Fourth Amendment. In determining the appropriate standard for a search conducted by a public employer in areas in which an employee has a reasonable expectation of privacy, a reasonable search is defined by the context within which the search takes place, and requires a balancing of the employee's legitimate expectation of privacy against the government's need for supervision, control, and the efficient operation of the workplace.

Business and the Fifth Amendment

The Fifth Amendment guarantees a number of specific rights to individuals, such as the right to due process and protection from criminal double jeopardy, which have also been interpreted as extending to business. One right guaranteed by the Fifth Amendment is the privilege against self-incrimination, which has been interpreted as applying to business in a limited fashion, depending on the manner in which the business function is being carried out. Basically, the privilege against self-incrimination has been interpreted as being *personal,* i.e., it applies to individual human beings. Therefore, courts have taken the position that while individuals engaged in a sole proprietorship or perhaps a very few people in a partnership can claim the privilege, large partnerships and corporations *cannot* claim it (nor can labor unions).

Of course, if an individual works for a corporation that has been engaging in illegal activities, that individual may personally "take the Fifth." However, if the corporation had records that would incriminate that individual, that person could *not* use his personal privilege to prevent turning over the records to a court or administrative agency. Courts have held that business records are not personal property and are not privileged.

Business and the Fourteenth Amendment

The Fourteenth Amendment to the Constitution, adopted following the Civil War, contains several provisions that have had a great impact on the laws of this country. The Fourteenth Amendment provides that, "No State shall make or enforce any law which shall abridge the privileges or immunities of citizens of the United States; nor shall any State deprive any person of life, liberty or property, without due process of law; nor deny to any person . . . equal protection of the laws." We have already discussed the concept of the Privileges and Immunities Clause earlier in this chapter, so this section will concentrate on the meaning and importance of the Due Process and Equal Protection Clauses.

Due Process Clause

There are two due process clauses in the Constitution: the one just noted in the Fourteenth Amendment, which applies to the states, and one in the Fifth Amendment, which applies to the federal government. The concept of **due process** is very complex, with both procedural and substantive dimensions. Cases concerning its meaning are probably more numerous than any other type of constitutional law cases.

Procedural due process concerns itself with whether governmental proceedings are conducted in a manner calculated to insure fundamental fairness; it focuses on the mechanisms of these proceedings. Alternately, substantive due process imposes a limit on governmental action, regardless of the procedures provided. For example, assume that a city, with no explanation, passes an ordinance requiring the closing of all gun shops. In this instance, gun shop owners could appeal the city's action as a violation of substantive due process, since they are deprived of their personal private property rights by a process that is fundamentally unfair. If the city had held a public meeting to discuss the potential gun shop closings, but allowed no input from the property owners, gun shop owners could also assert a violation of procedural due process.

Most of today's due process cases raise procedural questions, where procedures by which people's rights are affected are examined for "fundamental fairness." Some situations in which there might be procedural questions include welfare payment termination, the ability to get an abortion, being expelled from school, or being fired from a job. "Fundamental fairness," at the very least, means that people have the right to sufficient notice as well as to a meaningful hearing before government can affect their rights. Both administrative agencies and courts are governed by the Due Process Clause (due process in administrative agency procedures will be discussed in chapter 5). Additionally, criminal court cases require rigid adherence to due process. Criminal due process says that all of the specific rights guaranteed in the Constitution must be strictly observed in criminal proceedings.

Equal Protection Clause

Basically, **equal protection** means that a government cannot treat differently two or more people or businesses who are otherwise similarly situated. Two of the leading cases on equal protection, *Yick Wo* v. *Hopkins* (1886) and *Brown* v. *Board of Education* (1954), illustrate how the Equal Protection Clause is applied. In *Yick Wo,* the city of San Francisco passed an ordinance that all laundries operated in wooden buildings had to be licensed. The city building inspector granted licenses to Caucasian owners of wooden laundries, but denied licenses to almost all laundry operators of Chinese descent who applied. The Supreme Court ruled that the ordinance was unconstitutional as applied because it treated laundry operators of Caucasian and Chinese ancestry differently without an objectively valid justification. In *Brown* v. *Board of Education,* the Supreme Court declared unconstitutional racially segregated school systems, on the basis that "separate educational facilities are inherently unequal." It is interesting to note that the *Brown* decision repudiated an earlier decision, in *Plessy* v. *Ferguson,* which had held that racially separate facilities (railroad cars) were acceptable as long as they were roughly equal.

The courts rely upon three different standards of review in equal protection cases: the rational relation test, the heightened scrutiny test, and the strict scrutiny test. Should it appear that the government is engaging in actions resulting in unequal treatment, the rational relation test dictates that courts will uphold those actions provided that those actions further a legitimate state interest. For example, the ordinance in question in *Yick Wo* v. *Hopkins* required licensing only of laundries operated in wooden buildings, but not those in brick buildings. If the wood-brick dichotomy had been the only basis for denial of equal protection, the ordinance would probably not have violated the equal protection clause under the rational relation test, since it was passed in response to a disastrous fire that had destroyed great numbers of wooden buildings.

Unless a statute provokes "strict scrutiny" because it interferes with a fundamental right (for example, the right to privacy or the freedom of speech), or if that statute discriminates against a "suspect class" (i.e., a racial or religious group), the challenged classification will survive equal protection attacks provided that the statute is rationally related to a legitimate governmental purpose. The 1983 Supreme Court case of *Minneapolis Star* v. *Minnesota Commissioner of Revenue* involved an infringement on freedom of the press that was presumed to be unconstitutional under the strict scrutiny test. Cases involving allegations of racial and national origin discrimination (such as *Brown* v. *Board of Education*) are reviewed under the strict scrutiny test.

The heightened scrutiny standard of review is less rigorous than the strict scrutiny test, but more demanding than the rational relation test. Heightened scrutiny has generally been applied only in cases that involved discriminatory classifications based on sex or illegitimacy. In the case of *Plyler* v. *Doe* (1982), the Supreme Court applied a heightened scrutiny test in determining whether Texas could deny free public education to the children of illegal aliens and concluded that the state had failed to show that classifying children by parentage advanced a substantial state interest. In the 1988 Supreme Court case *Kadrmas* v. *Dickinson Public Schools,* the Court discussed all three standards of review before deciding the constitutionality of busing fees. Employing the rational relation test, the Court held that requiring parents to pay fees for school bus services was, in fact, constitutional.

Ethical Issues in Constitutional Law

As you have seen, the Constitution governs how institutions in the United States interact with each other. While some aspects of government's constitutional ability to regulate business have been settled for some time, new dimensions of the government-business relationship are constantly being revealed. It is our hope that this chapter's discussion on constitutional law and its relationship with the business environment will provide you with a framework for analysis of constitutional dimensions in business issues. Ethical considerations are equally as numerous as constitutional ones in today's business environment, and concepts such as substantive due process and penumbral rights can guide decision making in areas not clearly regulated by law.

Discussion has also arisen over the extent to which freedom of speech can conflict with the right to control and enjoy private property. In 1983, the Supreme Court of Connecticut upheld the right of owners of the West Farms Mall to prohibit the National Organization of Women from soliciting signatures from shoppers within the area of the mall. Additionally, the 1988 Supreme Court case of *Frisby* v. *Schultz* addressed how freedom of speech related to the right to picket private property. In this case, the Court maintained that the state's interest in protecting a "feeling of well-being, tranquility, and privacy" associated with a private residence outweighed the rights of an anti-abortion group to picket directly outside a physician's home.

Even in an area of the law as fundamental as constitutional law, with a written document to provide guidance in making legal decisions, the courts are increasingly being required to make judgments that inevitably influence societal norms and values. The development of substantive due process and penumbral rights issues necessitates complex Constitutional analyses as well as insight into American social policy. Only by being familiar with fundamental Constitutional precepts can one be aware of the far-reaching impacts of legal decisions.

The Ninth and Tenth Amendments' concept of penumbral, nonenumerated rights is based upon the idea that certain societal values exist and must be protected, even though these rights may not be provided for in the Constitution. Through penumbral rights, the Supreme Court has insured that a mechanism exists by which the evolution of societal norms can be inspected. Penumbral rights have been used to weigh such societal issues as the *Roe* v. *Wade* consideration of abortion. While the Supreme Court viewed penumbral rights as one medium that could assist in resolving this question, critics argued that the justices' declaration of the right to privacy was truly their attempt to impose their ethical standards upon society at large. Nonenumerated rights will play a part in the discussion of such issues as the societal impact of AIDS, drug testing in the workplace, and maintaining the integrity of computer information in light of the development of electronic piracy.

Ethical considerations in constitutional law do not fall exclusively under the domain of nonenumerated rights. In the 1988 Supreme Court case of *Lyng v. Northwest Indian Cemetery Protective Association,* the court held that the state's exercise of police power allowed the construction of a road through land held sacred to certain American Indians. Although the Indians maintained that the destruction of these religious sites violated the free exercise of religion clause of the Constitution, the government was not required to bring forward a compelling justification for its otherwise lawful actions.

Chapter Summary

1. Governmental actions are given a presumption of constitutionality unless they are *unconstitutional on their face;* that is, they obviously violate the Constitution.
2. Even if a governmental action is constitutional on its face, it may be *unconstitutional as applied.*
3. Under the concept of judicial review, it is within the power of the judicial system to say what the law is, even if this means declaring an action of the legislative or executive branch to be unconstitutional.
4. The first ten amendments to the Constitution are called the Bill of Rights; the first eight amendments contain enumerated specific rights, and the Ninth and Tenth Amendments contain general rights.
5. Certain penumbral (nonenumerated) rights such as the right to travel and freedom of association have been viewed by the courts as arising from the Ninth and Tenth Amendments.
6. The doctrine of pre-emption means that if an action by a state directly conflicts with federal statutes or policy, the federal action has legal priority over state action.
7. The Commerce Clause in the Constitution gives the federal government the power to regulate interstate commerce.
8. The doctrine of the police power means that government has the power to regulate for the public health, welfare, safety, and morals.
9. The First Amendment to the Constitution protects business' right of free speech, which is called "commercial speech."
10. The Fourth Amendment generally protects business from warrantless searches and seizures.
11. A person's or a business' personal or property rights may not be infringed upon without due process of law.

12. The Equal Protection Clause of the Fourteenth Amendment guarantees that a government cannot treat differently two or more business that are otherwise similarly situated.

Key Terms

Commerce Clause 96
commercial speech 103
Contract Clause 101
due process 110
enumerated rights 93
equal protection 111
Exclusionary Rule 108
fruit of the poisonous tree doctrine 108
judicial review 92
penumbral rights 93
police power 102
pre-emption 94
presumption of constitutionality 89
Privileges and Immunities Clause 95
Supremacy Clause 93

Questions on Ethics

1. Evidence indicates that exposure of workers to chemicals or other hazardous materials can cause birth defects in the workers' children. The possibility of dangerous exposure is especially acute for women. Some employers whose businesses require worker exposure to these hazardous substances have begun requiring women job applicants to divulge whether they plan to have children and/or whether they are sterile. Women job applicants have complained that such inquiries are an invasion of their right to privacy. (Note that, depending on the wording of these questions, they might also constitute a violation of Title VII of the 1964 Civil Rights Act.) Is it ethical for employers to ask job applicants such questions?
2. While the Constitution gives the legislative branch of government the power to pass laws and the judicial branch the power to decide law cases, some members of society may be unhappy with certain laws or court decisions. The 1960s saw the application of the concept of "civil disobedience," in which persons broke laws (in that case, racial segregation laws) that they considered to be morally wrong. This concept was also used by some persons protesting the Vietnam war. What are the moral arguments for and against civil disobedience? In what contexts has this concept come up recently?
3. It has been argued that the federal Social Security tax is unfair because it takes money from those who earn it and gives it to people who are no longer employed. Social Security, like many other governmental programs, in effect represents an income redistribution. What moral arguments can be advanced in favor of such social programs as Social

Security? Is a person who advocates abolition or cutting back of such programs taking an immoral position?

4. In recent years, United States businesses have come under pressure from some citizens either not to do business in South Africa or to abide by the Sullivan code. The South African government has officially adopted the practice of *apartheid,* a strict racial segregation. Such a practice has been interpreted by our courts to be unconstitutional and therefore forbidden in the United States. The Sullivan code, originally proposed by a black American clergyman, states that it is morally permissible for an American company to do business in South Africa, so long as the company does not abide by the *apartheid* rules, for example, by refusing to make promotions based on race or refusing to maintain racially segregated restrooms. Is it ethical for American companies to do business in South Africa? Is the Sullivan code, which in effect advocates breaking the law of South Africa, ethical?
5. In recent years, large corporations have attempted to cut their expenditures for employee health care plans by negotiating with hospitals and medical groups to get a reduced charge for their employees. Employees of the corporations are urged to utilize those hospitals and doctors giving a cut-rate fee. These medical providers are referred to as preferred provider organizations (PPOs). Traditionally, hospitals and medical groups have used the income generated by employed persons with insurance benefits to offset the costs of treating the indigent. Under pressure to become PPOs, these medical providers have in some cases begun to refuse to treat indigent persons. The poor may be denied life-saving treatments because hospitals can no longer finance their care by charging paying patients more. Is it ethical for large businesses to advocate such programs as PPOs?

Questions on Law

1. Virginia Supreme Court rules allowed qualified lawyers admitted to practice in another state to be admitted to the Virginia bar "on motion" (without taking the Virginia bar) if the applicant was a permanent resident of Virginia. A Maryland resident who practiced and maintained her residence in Virginia was denied admission to the Virginia bar because she was not a permanent resident of that state. Did the Virginia rule violate the Privileges and Immunities Clause of the Constitution? See *Supreme Court of Virginia* v. *Friedman,* 56 U.S.L.W. 4669 (June 21, 1988).
2. The state of Washington imposed a business and occupation (B&O) tax on engaging in business activities in the state, including manufacturing in the state and making wholesale sales in the state. The tax had a multiple activities exemption for local manufacturers. Was the multiple activities exemption a violation of the Constitution's Commerce Clause? *Tyler*

Pipe Industries v. *Washington Department of Revenue,* 55 U.S.L.W. 4978 (June 23, 1987).

3. A business closed its poultry packaging and processing plant and laid off most of its employees. Maine's director of the Bureau of Labor Standards filed suit to enforce the provisions of a state statute requiring employers, in the event of a plant closing, to provide a one-time severance pay. The employer contended that the state severance pay provision conflicted with the federal ERISA (Employee Retirement Income Security Act) and was therefore pre-empted by ERISA, because ERISA pre-empted any state employee benefit legislation on a topic covered by ERISA. Is the Maine statute constitutional? *Fort Halifax Packing Co.* v. *Coyne,* 55 U.S.L.W. 4699 (June 1, 1987).
4. Upon shouting at police in an attempt to divert their attention from his friend during a confrontation, Hill was arrested for violation of a municipal ordinance that made it illegal for anyone "to assault, strike or in any manner oppose, molest, abuse or interrupt any policeman in the execution of his duty." Was this ordinance constitutional? *City of Houston* v. *Hill,* 55 U.S.L.W. 4823 (June 16, 1987).
5. Ortega, a physician and psychiatrist, was an employee of a state hospital. Hospital officials became concerned about possible improprieties in his management of hospital programs. Therefore, while he was on administrative leave, hospital officials searched his office and seized personal items from his desk and file cabinets. Were these searches legal? *O'Connor* v. *Ortega,* 55 U.S.L.W. 4405 (March 31, 1987).

Suggested Readings

Hatano, "Should Corporations Exercise Their Freedom of Speech Rights?" 22 *American Business Law Journal* 167 (1984).

Liebman, "Introduction to the Special Issue: Business and the First Amendment," 23 *American Business Law Journal* 151 (1985).

Phillips, "The Life and Times of the Contract Clause," 20 *American Business Law Journal* 139 (1982).

5 Administrative Law: Procedures

Administrative agencies usually are created to deal with current crises or to redress serious social problems.

—*Ernest Gellhorn,* Administrative Law and Process in a Nutshell

■ LEARNING OBJECTIVES

After you have read this chapter, you should be able to:

1. Understand the legal relationship between administrative agencies and the three constitutionally established branches of government.
2. Understand the process of delegation.
3. Understand the administrative procedures of rulemaking and adjudication.
4. Understand the constitutional rights of individuals involved in rulemaking and adjudication procedures.

Business Decisions and the Law

A Bookie is Double Whammy

You are the sole proprietor of a very busy and rather profitable bookmaking operation. Knowing that state law has ruled your enterprise to be a criminal activity, you've maintained a low profile while steadily increasing your profits. However, one morning you receive notification that federal law will now require that you pay a 10 percent excise tax on all profits obtained from "wager-receiving." This immediately presents you with a classic no-win situation, with three apparent options:

1. Comply with federal law and risk prosecution under state law from admitting that you are engaged in an illegal activity.
2. Don't comply with federal law and risk prosecution from tax evasion.
3. Seek to have federal law overturned in court since compliance with the federal law would violate your Fifth Amendment right against self-incrimination.

You discretely consult your trusted legal advisor, who tells you that the case of *Marchetti* v. *U.S.* supplies all the precedent necessary to dictate your actions. You read *Marchetti* to discover . . .

Introduction

Today, everyone is affected in some way by the activities of administrative agencies, and business is regulated in many ways by a variety of agencies. In fact, one of the most common complaints of business is that compliance with agency regulations and orders consumes valuable time and increases the cost of doing business.

This chapter will examine how administrative agencies are created and how they function in our society. You will study the history of their creation and the nature of their power. Chapter 6 will also discuss administrative agencies but will focus on the role of the courts in reviewing their actions and the policy and ethical issues such actions raise.

Historical Background

The concept of an administrative agency wielding legal power is relatively new in the law. The Constitution of the United States, which established the basic legal and political framework of our political system, does not even mention them. In fact, the first federal administrative agency was not created until the Constitution was almost one hundred years old. Yet today, administrative agencies exercise enormous legal power. How did they come to have this power, which has led them to be referred to as "the fourth branch of government"?

The first federal agency established was the Interstate Commerce Commission (ICC), created in 1889, and the second was the Federal Trade Commission (FTC), created in 1914. It is important to discuss briefly the reasons for the creation of the early federal administrative agencies. They were established as a congressional response to dissatisfaction with business conditions as they existed in the United States at the turn of the century. The business practices at that time could be characterized by two concepts: **laissez-faire** capitalism and **caveat emptor** in buyer-seller relationships. The fundamental principle of laissez-faire capitalism is that government should not interfere in businesses' legal pursuit of profit maximization. *Caveat emptor* ("Let the Buyer Beware") means that if a buyer buys an unsatisfactory or defective product, it is the buyer, not the seller, who should sustain the loss—the buyer cannot return the product and get her money back or get monetary damages that would compensate for the lesser value of the defective product. The fundamental premise upon which caveat emptor is based is that when potential buyers and sellers are negotiating sales contracts they will have face-to-face negotiations of the sales terms. It is also assumed that the buyer will have the opportunity to examine adequately the goods and to reject them should they be defective. In other words, the concept of caveat emptor is based on the premise of *equality of bargaining power* between the parties. This basic premise of caveat emptor was not unreasonable when it originated in medieval England, for then business transactions were almost always directly between buyer and seller; buyers had a chance to examine goods, and other sellers of the same types of goods were generally available.

By the end of the nineteenth century in the United States, the Industrial Revolution and the invention of unique goods and services sold by few providers had created what many people viewed as failures in the concepts of caveat emptor and laissez-faire capitalism. Congress responded to these perceived flaws within the railroad industry by creating the Interstate Commerce Commission (ICC). The railroads, then owned by a few individuals who created monopolies in large geographic areas, had refused to deal with certain people and had charged discriminatory prices. The ICC was given the responsibility of ending such practices. Additionally, Congress created the Federal Trade Commission to "bust up" the oil industry, at that time controlled by one family.

The birth of the ICC and the FTC illustrates a common theme characteristic of the development of administrative law. When citizens perceive that an industry's actions injure the best interests of society, the need to circumscribe those activities becomes apparent. These citizens can bring pressure to bear upon a legislative body to create laws that would regulate the industry in a manner perceived to be more advantageous to society. Legislative bodies, however, usually do not have the time, structure, or the expertise to monitor industry activity; therefore, they often pass laws establishing an administrative agency to carry out the monitoring function. Since the establishment of the FTC and the ICC, thousands of administrative agencies have been established by all levels of government to regulate specific business activities. For example, the Internal Revenue Service is charged with collecting taxes and enforcing the federal tax laws; the Federal Occupational Safety and Health Administration is charged with insuring that employers comply with regulations to insure employee health and safety; and the federal and various state environmental protection agencies are responsible for insuring that businesses and others comply with antipollution laws. We will now examine how a governmental body creates an administrative agency.

Creation of Administrative Agencies

Perhaps one reason that administrative agencies were not created earlier was that, prior to the Supreme Court decision upholding the legality of the creation of the ICC, it was generally believed that no branch of government could delegate any of its powers to an entity not created by the Constitution. The legality of the ICC was upheld, however, on the theory that in creating the ICC, Congress was not delegating its power *to make* laws, but was only delegating its power *to act pursuant to the law*. With that as a guideline, Congress prescribed exactly what functions the ICC could perform, and the only activities that the ICC could engage in were those specifically designated by Congress.

All administrative agencies derive their power through the process of **delegation.** Delegation means that a governmental body is giving some limited part of its power to the agency. However, a governmental body can never give up *all* of its power to an agency. For example, Congress could never pass a law giving the Environmental Protection Agency complete power to enact legislation regarding toxic waste disposal. Moreover, certain types of governmental duties are completely *nondelegable:* an official whose office is established by the Constitution cannot turn over the power of that office to another person or any agency; an agency may not declare a tax; an agency may not declare an activity to be a crime, nor can an agency imprison anyone.

Aside from these broad and fundamental limitations on the power to delegate, there is a wide area in which delegation is possible. However, delegation can only occur for certain purposes and through certain procedures. An agency derives its power to act through the passage or adoption of **enabling legislation.** While it is possible for the executive or judicial branches of government to establish agencies through the issuance of orders, by far the most common method of delegation occurs through enabling legislation passed by a legislative body in the form of a statute. For example, the enabling legislation creating the Federal Trade Commission was the Federal Trade Commission Act; the enabling legislation that gives the federal Equal Employment Opportunity Commission the power to enforce antidiscrimination employment laws is Title VII of the 1964 Civil Rights Act.

Once an agency has been established, the only activities that the agency can carry out are those activities specially delegated to it in the enabling legislation. These delegated activities are commonly referred to as *standards*. If any agency fails to comply with the standards of its enabling legislation, such as by holding hearings when the enabling legislation did not give it power to hold hearings, the agency is said to have ''exceeded the scope of its enabling legislation.'' When an agency exceeds its scope, a court exercising judicial review can invalidate that illegal agency action.

A governmental body passing enabling legislation must have a legal purpose for doing so. The Bill of Rights in the United States Constitution applies to the enabling legislation of administrative agencies, and a governmental body that creates an agency cannot infringe upon an individual's constitutional or civil rights. The passage of enabling legislation must be for a public purpose, which will benefit society as a whole. When a governmental body legislates for the public health, safety, welfare, and morals, it is exercising the doctrine of **police power.** The creation of administrative agencies is an exercise of police power. Occasionally, a conflict arises between exercising police power and an individual's constitutional or civil rights.

Zoning law is an example of an area where exercise of the police power sometimes seems to conflict with individual rights. Zoning boards are administrative agencies created to protect the public welfare and safety by regulating land use within a given geographic area. A typical zoning provision restricts certain types of land uses in certain areas, for example, permitting only noncommercial businesses in an area designated residential only. However, a landowner who wishes to develop property in a residential zone may feel his property rights are infringed upon by a noncommercial use restriction. This individual's rights will then have to be balanced against the benefit of the public as a whole.

Generally, the less the public interest involved and the greater the individual rights at stake, the better the individual's chances are of prevailing. However, if an agency's exercise of its police power is alleged to infringe upon an individual's constitutional rights, a balancing of the interests involved must take place. The following case demonstrates such a balancing, when the Supreme Court considered the question of property rights versus Los Angeles County's interest in public health and safety.

First English Evangelical Lutheran Church v. *Los Angeles*

96 LEd2d 250 (1987)

Opinion

Chief Justice Rehnquist: In this case the California Court of Appeal held that a landowner who claims that his property has been "taken" by a land-use regulation may not recover damages for the time before it is finally determined that the regulation constitutes a "taking" of his property. We disagree, and conclude that in these circumstances the Fifth and Fourteenth Amendments to the United States Constitution would require compensation for that period.

In 1957, appellant First English Evangelical Lutheran Church purchased a 21-acre parcel of land in a canyon along the banks of the Middle Fork of Mill Creek in the Angeles National Forest. The Middle Fork is the natural drainage channel for a watershed area owned by the National Forest Service. The church operated on the site a campground, known as "Lutherglen," as a retreat center and a recreational area for handicapped children.

In July 1977, a forest fire denuded the hills upstream from Lutherglen, destroying approximately 3,860 acres of the watershed area and creating a serious flood hazard. Such flooding occurred on February 9 and 10, 1978, when a storm dropped 11 inches of rain in the watershed. The runoff from the storm overflowed the banks of the Mill Creek, flooding Lutherglen and destroying its buildings.

In response to the flooding of the canyon, appellee County of Los Angeles adopted Interim Ordinance No. 11,855 in January 1979, which provided that "[a] person shall not construct, reconstruct, place or enlarge any building or structure, any portion of which is, or will be, located within the outer boundary lines of the interim flood protection area located in Mill Creek Canyon." The ordinance was effective immediately because the county determined that it was "required for the immediate preservation of the public health and safety. . . ." The interim flood protection area described by the ordinance included the flat areas on either side of Mill Creek on which Lutherglen had stood.

The church filed a complaint in the Superior Court of California a little more than a month after the ordinance was adopted.

Appellant sought damages for loss of use of Lutherglen. The defendants moved to strike the portions of the complaint alleging that the county's ordinance denied all use of Lutherglen, on the view that the California Supreme Court's decision in *Agins* v. *Tiburon* decided that a landowner may not maintain an inverse condemnation suit in the courts of that State based upon a "regulatory" taking. In the court's view, maintenance of such a suit would allow a landowner to force the legislature to exercise its power of eminent domain. Under this decision, then, compensation is not required until the challenged regulation or ordinance has been held excessive in an action for declaratory relief or a writ of mandamus and the government has nevertheless decided to continue the regulation in effect. Based on this decision, the trial court in the present case granted the motion to strike the allegation that the church had been denied all use of Lutherglen.

On appeal, the California Court of Appeal too relied on the California Supreme Court's decision in *Agins* in rejecting the cause of action. The court found itself obligated to follow *Agins* "because the United States Supreme Court has not yet ruled on the question of whether a state may constitutionally limit the remedy for a taking to nonmonetary relief. . . ." It accordingly affirmed the trial court's decision to strike the allegations concerning appellee's ordinance. The Supreme Court of California denied review.

This appeal followed, and we noted probable jurisdiction. Appellant asks us to hold that the Supreme Court of California erred in *Agins* v. *Tiburon* in determining that the Fifth Amendment, as made applicable to the States through the Fourteenth Amendment, does not require compensation as a remedy for "temporary" regulatory takings—those regulatory takings which are ultimately invalidated by the courts. Four times this decade, we have considered similar claims and have found ourselves for one reason or another unable to consider the merits of the *Agins* rule. For the reasons explained below, however, we find the constitutional claim properly presented in this case, and hold that on these facts the California courts have decided the compensation question inconsistently with the requirements of the Fifth Amendment.

Appellant's complaint alleged that "Ordinance No. 11,855 denies [it] all use of Lutherglen," and sought damages for this deprivation. In affirming the decision to strike this allegation, the Court of Appeal assumed that the complaint sought "damages for the uncompensated *taking* of all use of Lutherglen by County Ordinance No. 11,855." It relied on the California Supreme Court's *Agins* decision for the conclusion that "the remedy for a *taking* [is limited] to nonmonetary relief. . . ." The disposition of the case on these grounds isolates the remedial question for our consideration. The rejection of appellant's allegations did not rest on the view that they were false. Nor did the court rely on the theory that regulatory measures such as Ordinance No. 11,855 may never constitute a taking in the constitutional sense. Instead, the claims were deemed irrelevant solely because of the California Supreme Court's decision in *Agins* that damages are unavailable to redress a "temporary" regulatory taking. The California Court of Appeal has thus held that regardless of the correctness of appellants' claim that the challenged ordinance denies it "all use of Lutherglen" appellant may not recover damages until the ordinance is finally declared unconstitutional, and then only for any period after that declaration for which the county seeks to enforce it. The constitutional question pretermitted in our earlier cases is therefore squarely presented here. We now turn to the question of whether the Just Compensation Clause requires the government to pay for "temporary" regulatory takings.

Consideration of the compensation question must begin with direct reference to the language of the Fifth Amendment, which provides in relevant part that "private property [shall not] be taken for public use, without just compensation." As its language indicates, and as the Court has frequently noted, this provision does not prohibit the taking of private property, but instead places a condition on the exercise of that power. This basic understanding of the Amendment makes clear that it is designed not to limit the governmental interference with property rights *per se,* but rather to secure *compensation* in the event of otherwise proper interference amounting to a taking. Thus, government action that works a taking of property rights necessarily implicates the "constitutional obligation to pay just compensation."

We have recognized that a landowner is entitled to bring an action in inverse condemnation as a result of " 'the self-executing character of the constitutional provision with respect to compensation . . .' The Court has frequently repeated the view that, in the event of taking, the compensation remedy is required by the Constitution. '[T]he general rule at least is, that while property may be regulated to a certain extent, if regulation goes too far it will be recognized as a taking.'

While the Supreme Court of California may not have actually disavowed this general rule in *Agins,* we believe that it has truncated the rule by disallowing damages that occurred prior to the ultimate invalidation of the challenged regulation."

"Temporary" takings which, as here, deny a landowner all use of his property, are not different in kind from permanent takings, for which the Constitution clearly requires compensation. It is axiomatic that the Fifth Amendment's just compensation provision is "designed to bar Government from forcing some people alone to bear public burdens which, in all fairness and justice, should be borne by the public as a whole." Where this burden results from governmental action that amounted to a taking, the Just Compensation Clause of the Fifth Amendment requires that the government pay the landowner for the value of the use of the land during this period. Invalidation of the ordinance or its successor ordinance after this period of time, though converting the taking into a "temporary" one, is not a sufficient remedy to meet the demands of the Just Compensation Clause.

Nothing we say today is intended to abrogate the principle that the decision to exercise the power of eminent domain is a legislative function, " 'for Congress and Congress alone to determine.' " Once a court determines that a taking has occurred, the government retains the whole range of options already available—amendment of the regulation, withdrawal of the invalidated regulation, or exercise of eminent domain. Thus we do not, as the Solicitor General suggests, "permit a court, at the behest of a private person, to require the . . . Government to exercise the power of eminent domain. . . ." We merely hold that where the government's activities have already worked a taking of all use of property, no subsequent action by the government can relieve it of the duty to provide compensation for the period during which the taking was effective.

Here we must assume that the Los Angeles County ordinances have denied appellant all use of its property for a considerable period of years, and we hold that invalidation of the ordinance without payment of fair value for the use of the property during this period of time would be a constitutionally insufficient remedy. The judgment of the California Court of Appeals is therefore reversed, and the case is remanded for further proceedings not inconsistent with this opinion.

Case Questions

1. Why did the administrative regulation amount to a "taking" in this case?
2. Why does the Constitution require just compensation for governmental taking of property?

Also in 1987, the United States Supreme Court held in *Nollan* v. *California Coastal Commission* that the Coastal Commission had the power to restrict Nollan's use of his land in order to advance some legitimate police-power purpose. The Commission also had the power to condition Nollan's use of his land upon a concession from him allowing the public to cross his property in order to get to the beach. However, the Commission had to acquire this property through *eminent domain,* paying just compensation for the legal right to use Nollan's private property "in the public interest."

The Relationship between Administrative Agencies and the Three Constitutionally Established Branches of Government

The executive, judicial, or legislative branch of government can establish an administrative agency; it is very rare, however, for the executive and judiciary branches to do so. When these two branches do create an agency, it is by issuance of an executive or judicial order, and the agency then functions solely as an internal support of the creating branch. The most common method of establishing an agency, however, is for the legislative branch to pass a statute.

Just as there are constitutional checks and balances among the three branches of government, there are checks and balances exercised in the operations of administrative agencies. Since almost all agencies are created by statute, the legislative branch generally retains the power to abolish the agency or to change by statute the standards that describe the activities an agency may carry out. The legislative branch also retains the "power of the purse" over the agency, since it passes the budget that contains the agency operating funds. Furthermore, some branch of the legislature is often required to confirm the appointment of high-ranking officials within an agency.

The executive branch can also exert control over an agency in a variety of ways, even if the agency is created by legislative statute. The enabling legislation often provides that the executive will appoint some of the agency personnel, usually those of the highest rank. Furthermore, in the federal and most state governments, the executive branch recommends the budget that is submitted to the legislature for approval. If the executive branch is unhappy with the performance of an agency, it may influence agency action through budgetary recommendations; for example, it might recommend a cut in money for investigatory personnel within an agency, resulting in the agency's decreased capacity to conduct as many investigations as it had done in the past.

The judicial branch of government also possesses an important check over agencies through the power of judicial review. The courts can declare an agency action unconstitutional or illegal and therefore not having the force of law. The courts can also insure that each of the other two branches of government is staying within its constitutional limits when interacting with an agency. You will study judicial review in chapter 6.

The following case details the extent to which the legislative branch has veto power over administrative agencies. Note that both houses of Congress must be in accord before a legislative veto of administrative agency action can be exercised.

Alaska Airlines, Inc., v. Brock

94 LEd2d 661 (1987)

Opinion

Justice Blackmun: Justice Blackmun delivered the (unanimous) opinion of the Court. In *INS* v. *Chadha,* 462 U. S. 919 (1983), this Court held unconstitutional the congressional-veto provision in § 244(c)(2) of the Immigration and Nationality Act, and found it severable from the remainder of that Act. Petitioners, 14 commercial airlines, in the present case contend that provisions protecting employees in the Airline Deregulation Act of 1978 (Act), 92 Stat. 1705 (codified at various sections of Title 49 U. S. C. App.), are ineffective because § 43(f)(3) of the Act, similarly subjects to a legislative veto implementing regulations issued by the Department of Labor (DOL). We granted certiorari to consider whether that legislative-veto provision is severable from the remainder of the Act.

After 40 years of extensive regulation of the commercial-airline industry by the Civil Aeronautics Board (CAB), Congress in 1978 decided to make "a major change and fundamental redirection as to the manner of regulation of interstate and overseas air transportation so as to place primary emphasis on competition." Congress abandoned the industry-wide fare structure gradually, altered the procedures by which airlines could enter new markets, and phased out the regulatory power of the CAB, eliminating the agency altogether in 1984.

Congress sought to ensure that the benefits to the public flowing from this deregulation would not be "paid for" by airline employees who had relied on the heavily regulated nature of the industry in deciding to accept and to retain positions with commercial air carriers. In order to assist employees dislocated as a result of deregulation, Congress enacted an Employee Protection Program (EPP) as § 43 of the Act, 49 U. S. C. App. § 1552. The EPP provides for benefits, in the event of workforce reductions, to "protected employees," who are defined as employees who had been employed by a certified carrier for at least four years as of October 24, 1978, the date the Act became effective.

The first part of the EPP establishes a monthly compensation program. If an airline is forced to make severe workforce reductions or to enter bankruptcy as a result of deregulation, furloughed or terminated eligible "protected employees" are entitled to federally provided monthly assistance payments.

The second portion of the EPP imposes on airlines certified under the prior regulatory system a "duty to hire" protected employees. If a protected employee is "furloughed or otherwise terminated," other than for cause, within 10 years of the enactment date of the statute, that employee has a "first right of hire, regardless of age, in his occupational specialty" with any carrier, covered by the section, who is "hiring additional employees." A hiring airline is permitted, however, first to recall any of its own previously furloughed employees.

The Secretary "may issue, amend, and repeal such rules and regulations as may be necessary for the administration of [the EPP]." Congress also included a "report and wait" provision, specifying that no final rule or regulation may be issued until 30 legislative days after it has been submitted to the Senate Committee on Commerce, Science, and Transportation and the House Committee on Public Works and Transportation. Finally, the EPP contains the legislative-veto provision which gave rise to this litigation. It declares that any final rule issued pursuant to § 43 shall be submitted to Congress and shall become effective after 60 legislative days, unless during that 60-day period either House of Congress adopts a resolution disapproving the rule.

Petitioners are certified carriers subject to the duty-to-hire provisions of the Act and to the regulations promulgated by the Secretary. They challenged the EPP in the United States District Court for the District of Columbia, contending that the legislative-veto provision in § 43 is unconstitutional under *Chadha,* and that the entire program must be invalidated because the veto provision is nonseverable from the rest of the EPP. Respondent employee unions intervened on behalf of the Secretary. The District Court granted summary judgment for petitioners, striking down the entire EPP, but leaving the remainder of the Act intact. It held the legislative-veto provision unconstitutional and ruled that it could not be severed from the EPP. Respondents appealed the finding of nonseverability. The United States Court of Appeals for the District of Columbia Circuit reversed, holding that the legislative-veto clause is severable from the remainder of the EPP program. We agree and affirm the judgment of the Court of Appeals.

"[A] court should refrain from invalidating more of the statute than is necessary. . . . '[W]henever an act of Congress contains unobjectionable provisions separable from those found to be unconstitutional, it is the duty of this court to so declare, and to maintain the act in so far as it is valid.' " The standard for determining the severability of an unconstitutional provision is well established: " 'Unless it is evident that the Legislature would not have enacted those provisions which are within its power, independently of that which is not, the invalid part may be dropped if what is left is fully operative as a law.' "

Congress could not have intended a constitutionally flawed provision to be severed from the remainder of the statute if the balance of the legislation is incapable of functioning independently. This is not a concern, however, when the invalid provision is a legislative veto, which by its very nature is separate from the operation of the substantive provisions of a statute. Indeed, when Congress enacted legislative-veto provisions, it contemplated that activity under the legislation would take place so long as Congress *refrained* from exercising that power. The independent operation of a statute in the absence of a legislative-veto provision thus could be said to indicate little about the intent of Congress regarding severability of the veto.

The more relevant inquiry in evaluating severability is whether the statute will function in a *manner* consistent with the intent of Congress. In considering this question in the context of a legislative veto, it is necessary to recognize that the absence of the veto necessarily alters the balance of powers between the Legislative and Executive Branches of the Federal Government. Thus, it is not only appropriate to evaluate the importance of the veto in the original legislative bargain, but also to consider the nature of the delegated authority that Congress made subject to a veto. Some delegations of power to the Executive or to an independent agency may have been so controversial or so broad that Congress would have been unwilling to make the delegation without a strong oversight mechanism. The final test, for legislative vetos as well as for other provisions, is the traditional one: the unconstitutional provision must be severed unless the statute created in its absence is legislation that Congress would not have enacted.

The inquiry is eased when Congress has explicitly provided for severance by including a severability clause in the statute. This Court has held that the inclusion of such a clause creates a presumption that Congress did not intend the validity of the statute in question to depend on the validity of the constitutionally offensive provision. See *INS* v. *Chadha.* In such a case, unless there is strong evidence that Congress intended otherwise, the objectionable provision can be excised from the remainder of the statute. In the absence of a severability clause, however, Congress' silence is just that—silence—and does not raise a presumption against severability.

In this case, the parties disagree as to whether there is a severability clause applicable to the EPP. There is abundant indication of a clear congressional intent of severability both in the language and structure of the Act and in its legislative history.

Congress' intent that the EPP's first-hire provisions should survive in the absence of the legislative-veto provision is suggested strongly by the affirmative duty the statute places directly on air carriers. The first-hire portion of the EPP establishes in detail an obligation to hire protected employees that scarcely needs the adoption of regulations by the Secretary, and thus leaves little of substance to be subject to a veto. . . .

The regulations eventually promulgated by DOL, 29 CFR § 220.01 *et seq.* (1986), support the conclusion that Congress itself elaborated most of the details necessary for the first-hire program.

Not only do the first-hire provisions stand on their own, independent of any need for extensive regulations, but, should Congress object to the regulations issued, it retains a mechanism for the expression of its disapproval that reduces any disruption of congressional oversight caused by severance of the veto provision. The EPP's "report and wait" provision in the statute requires the Secretary to forward regulations to the transportation committees of both chambers of Congress and to wait 30 days before issuing them as final regulations. § 43(f)(3). This interval gives Congress an opportunity to review the regulations and either to attempt to influence the agency's decision, or to enact legislation preventing the regulations from taking effect.

The legislative history of the EPP supports the conclusion that Congress would have enacted the duty-to-hire provisions even without a legislative-veto provision by revealing that Congress regarded labor protection as an important feature of the Act, while it paid scant attention to the legislative-veto provision.

The language and structure of the EPP and its legislative history provide an uncontradicted view of congressional intent with regard to severance of the legislative-veto provisions from the duty-to-hire program. This evidence leads to the conclusion that any concerns about the operation of the EPP related principally to the financial-assistance program. Even this concern was minimal. The emphasis during deliberations on the Act was placed overwhelmingly on the substantive provisions of the statute, with scant attention paid to any need for congressional oversight. In the almost total absence of any contrary refrain, we cannot conclude that Congress would have failed to enact the Airline Deregulation Act, including the EPP's first-hire program, if the legislative veto had not been included. Accordingly, we affirm the judgment of the Court of Appeals.

Case Questions

1. What criteria do courts use in determining whether an act's provisions are severable?
2. What happens if an act is unconstitutional and nonseverable?

In conclusion, all three branches of government assert some type of legal power over administrative agencies. The purpose of this system of checks and balances is to ensure that the agency acts in a constitutional manner and that it acts pursuant to law, by staying within the scope of its enabling legislation. In the next section, we will examine what functions an agency may be delegated to perform.

The Functions of Administrative Agencies

An administrative agency may carry out three types of functions: legislative, executive, and quasi-judicial. As the names of the categories indicate, these three functions closely parallel the types of functions carried out by the three constitutionally established branches of government. The functions or activities that a particular agency may carry out are determined by the standards contained in its enabling legislation. All agencies perform some types of executive functions; the extent to which legislative and quasi-judicial functions are delegated to the agency depends greatly on the nature of the particular administrative agency. For example, the federal Consumer Product Safety Commission can issue regulations about standards for product safety under its rulemaking function, but it cannot prosecute violations of these standards, because it was not given prosecutoral and quasi-judicial power in its enabling legislation.

Regarding the functions of administrative agencies, the **executive function** consists of an agency's internal operations; the legislative function is commonly referred to as the **rulemaking function,** while the **quasi-judicial function** is known as **adjudication.** Rulemaking is the process by which agencies issue administrative regulations which, when properly issued, have the force and effect of law. In adjudication, the agency functions like a court by holding hearings similar to court hearings, which is why adjudication is referred to as the *quasi*(like)-judicial function of agencies.

Executive Functions

The executive function of administrative agencies concerns how an agency operates internally, such as making decisions about office supplies or personnel promotion. Violations of an agency's enabling legislation can be investigated by that agency when investigatory power has been granted within its enabling legislation. For example, the enabling legislation for the Federal Trade Commission is the Federal Trade Commission Act. The FTC is given the power to investigate alleged violations of that Act's prohibition of unfair and deceptive trade practices. If, after engaging in its investigatory function, the FTC believes an unfair or deceptive trade practice has occurred, it has the power to enforce or prosecute these alleged violations through the use of its quasi-judicial power. It may then seek court enforcement of the FTCA. In addition to internal, investigative, and prosecutoral executive functions, an agency may be given the power to advise governmental officials on issues within the agency's particular field of expertise.

While the executive function of agencies is indispensable for the agency to function adequately, it is fairly unremarkable in a legal sense. The legislative (rulemaking) and quasi-judicial (adjudicatory) functions are much more complex and may have much greater impact on the public. We will now take a closer look at the rulemaking and adjudicatory functions of agencies.

Rulemaking

Whether a particular agency has rulemaking power and how this power may be carried out depends, again, on the terms of that agency's enabling legislation. Rulemaking and adjudicatory procedures of almost all federal agencies are determined by the **Administrative Procedure Act,** which describes in great detail how an agency must go about carrying out these functions. Most states have adopted state administrative procedure acts that closely parallel the federal APA to apply to the functioning of their state agencies.

The rulemaking process is very procedure oriented. In order for a regulation to be legal, it must be adopted in strict conformity with the procedures contained in the APA. There are, of course, exceptions to this rule, as well as a provision for emergency adoption of regulations, but generally, any deviation from the APA rulemaking procedure will result in a regulation being deemed illegal and ineffective. We will now examine the rulemaking process, which consists of three parts: (1) publication of a notice of intent to adopt a regulation;

(2) the holding of a rulemaking hearing, and (3) the publication of a final regulation.

Notice of Intent to Adopt a Regulation

An administrative regulation is like a legislative statute in that it is supposed to affect the public, not just one individual or small group. Therefore, in order to protect the public interest, there must be a public notice of intent to adopt the proposed regulation before a regulation can be adopted. The place of publication of the notice of intent to adopt will vary depending on the provisions of the applicable administrative procedure act. The federal APA requires publication of notice of intent to adopt in the *Federal Register,* a publication of the federal government. The notice of intent to adopt must contain the following information: the text of the proposed regulation or an accurate summary of the contents of that text, a citation to the statutory enabling legislation that allows the agency to adopt regulations, and a statement of the time, place, and date of the rulemaking hearing. There must be a *lag time,* or period of time between the date of the publication of the notice of intent to adopt and the actual date of the hearing; the duration of this lag time is determined by statute and is generally two to three weeks. The purpose of the lag time is to allow persons interested in presenting evidence at the rulemaking hearing to find out about the date of the hearing and gather any evidence they might wish to present.

In the following case, the United States Supreme Court ruled that a state must publish a general description of the basic structure of the Aid to Families with Dependent Children program, as well as its availability.

Gardebring v. Jenkins

99 LEd2d 515 (1988)

Opinion

Justice Stevens: In 1981 Congress amended the statute authorizing the Aid to Families with Dependent Children (AFDC) program to provide that a family receiving nonrecurring lump-sum income is ineligible for benefits for the number of months that the income would satisfy the family's standard of need. Section 2304 of the Omnibus Budget Reconciliation Act of 1981, as amended. In this case the United States Court of Appeals for the Eighth Circuit held that the Minnesota Department of Human Services (the Department) could not enforce that amendment against respondent, and the class she represents, because it had not given them the notice required by a regulation promulgated by the Secretary of Health and Human Services (the Secretary), 45 CFR § 206.10(a)(2)(i) (1987). We granted certiorari to review the Court of Appeals' interpretation of the Secretary's regulation as well as its remedial decision in favor of an injunction barring the Department from recouping payments made to respondent during her period of ineligibility. Because we conclude that the regulation was not violated, we do not reach the remedy question.

On October 31, 1983, respondent's husband received a retroactive Social Security disability payment of $5,752. Respondent used the entire lump sum to pay a $3,863.75 arrearage on the family's home mortgage, an overdue car repair bill of $1,366, and a legal fee of $150, and the remainder to purchase clothing for her children and on other bills. Within two days, the entire sum had been expended.

On November 2, 1983, respondent reported the receipt (and the expenditure) of the Social Security payment to her caseworker and was advised that under the 1981 amendment her family would be ineligible for benefits for the next several months. She immediately filed an administrative appeal and her family continued to receive benefits while the appeal was pending. The Appeals Referee decided that the benefits should not be terminated because the Jenkinses had not received any advance notice of the new lump-sum rule, but the Department's Deputy Commissioner reversed. While expressing disagreement with the policy implemented by the 1981 amendment, he concluded that the federal statute must be enforced even though the lack of advance notice had produced a "harsh result."

When the administrative review proceedings terminated in August, the Jenkins family was again eligible for benefits. The Department's decision, however, meant that benefits had been improperly paid for the period between October 1983 and May 1984. Accordingly, as required by the federal statute, in due course the Department ordered recoupment of the wrongfully paid benefits by deducting 1% from each future AFDC monthly payment, in accordance with state law.

Shortly after the conclusion of the state administrative proceedings, respondent intervened in an action already pending in Federal District Court challenging the Department's lump-sum policy on various grounds. In her complaint in intervention, respondent added an allegation that the Department's implementation of the new lump-sum rule without adequate notice to AFDC applicants and recipients violated the Secretary's regulation. The District Court certified a class and entered summary judgment in its favor on the notice issue.

The District Court awarded two forms of relief. First, it required the Department to prepare a written notice that adequately explained the lump-sum policy and to distribute it to all current AFDC recipients and all future applicants. Second, it ordered the Department to notify all class members who had been injured by the Department's violation that they might apply for corrective payments from their local welfare agencies. The court concluded that the Eleventh Amendment prevented it from ordering any repayment of benefits that had been improperly denied, *ibid.*, or from enjoining the Department from recouping overpayments to families like the Jenkinses.

A divided panel of the Court of Appeals affirmed the District Court's judgment insofar as it found a violation of the notice regulation and denied monetary relief to members of the class. It concluded, however, that the District Court should have enjoined the Department from recouping any amounts that were treated as "overpayments" under the post-1981 policy if they would have been proper under the pre-1981 lump-sum rule. In explaining its basic holding, the Court of Appeals pointed out that advance notice to lump-sum recipients was necessary to achieve the purposes of the 1981 amendment, and that to impose the new rule on a family that assumed that the old rule was still in effect "would be truly Kafkaesque." The dissenting judge did not believe that either the statute or the notice regulation conditioned the implementation of the new rule on advance notice to the small percentage of AFDC beneficiaries affected by it. He construed the regulation as simply requiring "the state to publicize generally in written form, and orally as appropriate, the AFDC program and its availability." Because of the significance of the Court of Appeals holding for States' administration of welfare laws, we granted certiorari.

The Secretary's notice regulation, which was first adopted in 1971 and later amended in 1978 and 1979, now provides:

> Applicants shall be informed about the eligibility requirements and their rights and obligations under the program. Under this requirement individuals are given information in written form, and orally as appropriate, about coverage, conditions of eligibility, scope of the program, and related services available, and the rights and responsibilities of applicants for and recipients of assistance. Specifically developed bulletins or pamphlets explaining the rules regarding eligibility and appeals in simple, understandable terms are publicized and available in quantity.

The question for us to decide is not whether advance written notice is desirable, or, indeed, whether such notice is necessary to accomplish the purposes of the 1981 statute. The question is whether the pre-existing regulation was intended to forestall the implementation of a congressionally mandated program change until the state agencies provided all AFDC recipients with notice of the change. Although such a rule might well represent sound policy, we do not believe that a fair reading of the text of § 206.10(a)(2)(i) conveys that message.

It is true that the regulation requires that individuals be given "information in written form, and orally as appropriate about . . . conditions of eligibility," but that is hardly how one would write a command stating that every such condition must be identified and explained before it may be enforced. The reference to "information" in both written and oral form "about" various aspects of the program seems to require instead merely a general descriptive statement regarding AFDC benefits. Thus, the plain language of the regulation does not require that information be disseminated regarding every specific change in eligibility requirements.

The Secretary, who is responsible for enforcing the regulation, does not agree with the strict interpretation adopted by the District Court. Rather, he believes that it is generally appropriate to rely on an oral explanation of the consequences of receiving a lump-sum payment when the recipient reports it to the family's caseworker. We recognize that the Secretary had not taken a position on this question until this litigation. However, when it is the Secretary's regulation that we are construing, and when there is no claim in this Court that the regulation violates any constitutional or statutory mandate, we are properly hesitant to substitute an alternative reading for the Secretary's unless that alternative reading is compelled by the regulation's plain language or by other indications of the Secretary's intent at the time of the regulation's promulgation.

Finally, respondent's emphasis on the harsh result in this particular case is actually, in large part, a criticism of the lump-sum rule itself. The record indicates that even if respondent had known about the rule, she would have been hard pressed not to use most of the $5,752 payment to avoid a foreclosure of the mortgage on the family home and to make promised payments to other creditors. Further, even though the rule, combined with the absence of advance notice, may have produced a "Kafkaesque" result for the Jenkins family, it is not irrational to assume that most needy families will realize that the receipt of a large lump sum may affect their future eligibility for benefits, and that it would be prudent to inform their caseworkers of the development before spending the money. Moreover, the harshness of the result is somewhat mitigated by the fact that the family's benefits continued during the administrative appeal and that the recoupment process only subtracts 1% of each monthly AFDC check, and the further fact that if AFDC benefits are actually terminated, a family may be immediately eligible for another form of public assistance, albeit a less generous one. In all events, since the regulation was written long before the lump-sum rule was enacted, it clearly was not designed to forestall the harsh consequences suffered by the Jenkinses.

In the final analysis, our decision rests on our agreement with the Secretary and the dissenting judge in the Court of Appeals that the regulation simply requires the State to publish a general description of the basic structure of the AFDC program and its availability. We would require a much more precise mandate to the States to permit courts to interfere with the workings of governmental benefits programs by ordering the taking of certain affirmative steps.

The judgment of the Court of Appeals is reversed, and the case is remanded for further proceedings consistent with this opinion.

It is so ordered.

Case Questions

1. Why did the Court rely so heavily on the Secretary's interpretation of the regulation, when the Secretary had not even taken a position on the notice issue until this litigation?
2. What does this case show about what "notice" means, legally speaking?

The Rulemaking Hearing

The rulemaking hearing is conducted by a *hearing examiner,* who is generally an employee of the agency proposing adoption of the regulation. Anyone can present written or documentary evidence to the hearing examiner. Oral evidence is allowed at the discretion of the hearing examiner; that is, she can decline to let some people testify at all, or she can limit the amount of time they have to speak. Very often, the agency will have persons who wish to testify sign a sheet stating their name, address, group that they represent (if any), and a brief description of the nature of their testimony. In controversial hearings, individuals may be allowed to sign a request to testify in advance of the hearing. Usually, anyone who wants to testify at a rulemaking hearing may do so, as long as their testimony is relevant and reasonable in length. Hearing examiners tend to let all persons who wish to testify orally do so, because the agency's duty is to get a sense of public sentiment on the proposed regulation. If a large number of people wish to testify orally, the hearing examiner will try to pick some representatives for each of the various viewpoints concerning the subject of the regulation. In any event, all persons have a right to submit written evidence at the hearing.

Publication of the Final Regulation

After agency personnel have considered all of the oral and written evidence presented at the rulemaking hearing, they have several options: (1) they can decide not to adopt any regulation at all, (2) they can adopt a regulation with the same or similar wording to the original proposed regulation, (3) theoretically, they can adopt a regulation very different from the text of the proposed regulation, or (4) they can propose a new, different regulation and hold a hearing on the new proposal. In no event does the final text of a regulation have to reflect the evidence presented at the rulemaking hearing.

Why does the agency have so many options regarding its final action on a proposed regulation and why does the hearing testimony seem to carry so little weight? Since the agency is supposed to represent the best interests of the public, if the agency concludes after conducting a rulemaking hearing that there is no public need for the proposed regulation, the agency does not have to adopt it. Suppose the agency holds a hearing and only a particular special interest group shows up to testify. It might not be fair to the public as a whole to adopt a regulation that reflected only the majority of evidence presented at the rulemaking hearing. Regarding alternatives 3 and 4, there are potential legal as well as public relations problems with adopting a regulation that has no relationship to the original proposal. So, if the rulemaking testimony indicates public sentiment for adopting a regulation entirely different from the one proposed, the agency will almost always choose alternative 4 and start the rulemaking procedure over again.

If an agency decides to adopt a regulation after the rulemaking hearing, it must then publish the regulation in its final form. This publication will be in the same place where the notice of intent to adopt was published—for example, federal agencies would publish in the *Federal Register*. Barring emergencies, there is a lag time of two to three weeks between the date of publication of the final regulation and its effective date. The reason for the lag time is to allow persons affected by the new regulation to conform their activities to its requirements, as well as to provide an opportunity for a person who believes the regulation is illegal to seek judicial review of the regulation before it goes into effect.

An exception to the prior discussion on the formal processes of rulemaking and publication concerns the "interpretive rule." An interpretive rule simply states what an administrative agency thinks an enabling statute means. An interpretive rule is not subject to the notice and comment procedures required by the Administrative Procedures Act.

Adjudication

The final function of an administrative agency, adjudication differs from rulemaking in that rulemaking affects the rights of the public, whereas adjudication only affects the rights of an individual or small group of individuals. It is not always easy to tell the difference between rulemaking and adjudication, but the following examples should serve as clarification. If a local zoning board issues a regulation declaring a certain area of town as residential only, they are exercising a rulemaking action, since all members of the public living in the area are affected. However, if the zoning board brings an administrative action against a particular homeowner for using his house for commerce in a residential area, this is adjudication, because his individual property rights are being affected.

When an agency performs its adjudicatory function, it acts like a court, since it affects a person's legal rights. As in the doctrine of the police power, there are constitutional and legal limits on how an agency can use its adjudicatory power. The agency must act within the scope of its enabling legislation and it cannot infringe on an individual's constitutional and civil rights. When the federal Administrative Procedure Act (and subsequent similar state acts) was first enacted, it was not clear whether due process under the Fifth and Fourteenth Amendments to the Constitution applied to administrative adjudicatory hearings. Questions concerning every rule of evidence as observed in a court of law remained unresolved. Over time, however, it has become clear that the adjudicatory process must comply with "fundamental due process." That means that it must be fundamentally fair to the person(s) whose rights are the subject of the hearing, it must comply with all the basic constitutional requirements protecting individual rights (such as the privilege against self-incrimination and the right to call witnesses on one's behalf), and it must comply with many of the rules of evidence used at trials.

Just as in rulemaking, there are three steps in adjudication: (1) publication of a notice of intent to hold an adjudicatory hearing, (2) conduct of an adjudicatory hearing, and (3) issuance of an adjudicatory order. There may be a fourth step in the adjudicatory process, depending on the enabling legislation of the individual agency: (4) the intra-agency appeals process.

Notice of Intent to Hold an Adjudicatory Hearing

The adjudicatory process primarily affects an individual's rights, but it is also of interest to members of the public. Therefore, both public and private notice are required at the beginning of the adjudicatory process. Private notice is sent to the individual whose rights would be affected by the proposed adjudicatory action. Public notice on the other hand, will be published in a forum designated in the enabling legislation. As in rulemaking, for example, federal adjudicatory actions are published in the *Federal Register*. The content of the adjudicatory notice is basically the same as the content of the rulemaking notice of intent to adopt a regulation: (1) a statement of the legal authority of the agency to hold an adjudicatory hearing, (2) a statement of the issues or charges that will be the subject of the hearing, and (3) a statement of the time, place, and date of the hearing. As is the case with rulemaking, there is almost always a lag time of some two to three weeks between the date of publication of the notice of intent and the date of the adjudicatory hearing. This allows the person whose rights are being adjudicated to prepare their case.

The Adjudicatory Hearing

Conduct of the Adjudicatory Hearing. Adjudicatory hearings can arise in myriad ways: a claimant may feel she has been illegally denied unemployment compensation benefits; a state board may wish to revoke an attorney's license to practice law due to alleged unethical conduct; the Securities and Exchange Commission may feel that the federal securities laws have been violated by an individual. The agency procedure used in each of these cases will be very similar. The adjudicatory hearing is conducted by a **hearing examiner** or administrative law judge, who is usually an agency employee. The conduct of an adjudicatory hearing is similar to the conduct of a court trial, although similarities will vary depending on the particular agency involved as well as the importance of the rights being adjudicated. As in a court of law, the parties to an adjudicatory proceeding must prove their case. For example, when considering disbarring a lawyer, the licensing board must present evidence that it is more likely than not that the lawyer behaved unethically. The lawyer, of course, will introduce evidence to prove that he is ethical and did not commit the unethical acts alleged by the agency. Evidence may include calling witnesses as well as presenting written and other documentary evidence. The Administrative Procedure Act requires a person whose rights are being adjudicated (such as the lawyer) the right to enforce the appearance of witnesses by **subpoena;** a witness may also be called by ***subpoena duces tecum,*** which requires them to appear at the hearing and to bring evidence.

After the witnesses of each party testify, they may be confronted or cross-examined by the other parties. Confrontation and cross-examination are not exactly the same thing. In confrontation, a party is allowed to present evidence to contradict the content of a witness' testimony, while in cross-examination, the opposing party can directly question the witness in an attempt to discredit her truthfulness. In most adjudicatory hearings, opposing parties have the right to cross-examine, rather than merely confront, witnesses.

In *Brock* v. *Roadway Express, Inc.*, the Supreme Court examines administrative hearing procedures concerning the reinstatement of a discharged employee. Hearings had already been conducted to determine the propriety of the discharge, and the Supreme Court was then asked to rule whether employers' interests were adequately protected without the right to confrontation and cross-examination. The following opinion explains that employer interests *are* adequately protected, as long as the employer has an opportunity to respond to the agency at some point.

Brock v. Roadway Express, Inc.

95 LEd2d 239 (1987)

Opinion

Justice Marshall: Section 405 of the Surface Transportation Assistance Act of 1982 protects employees in the commercial motor transportation industry from being discharged in retaliation for refusing to operate a motor vehicle that does not comply with applicable state and federal safety regulations or for filing complaints alleging such noncompliance. The statute provides for an initial investigation of an employee's discharge by the Secretary of Labor and, upon a finding of reasonable cause to believe that the employee was discharged in violation of the Act, requires the Secretary to issue an order directing the employer to reinstate the employee. The employer may then request an evidentiary hearing and a final decision from the Secretary, but this request does not operate to stay the preliminary order of reinstatement. The issue presented in this appeal is whether the failure of § 405 to provide for an evidentiary hearing before temporary reinstatement deprives the employer of procedural due process under the Fifth Amendment.

Appellee Roadway Express, Inc. (Roadway) is a large interstate trucking company engaged primarily in cargo transportation; it is subject to the requirements of § 405. On November 22, 1983, Roadway discharged one of its drivers, Jerry Hufstetler, alleging that he had disabled several lights on his assigned truck in order to obtain extra pay while waiting for repairs. Hufstetler filed a grievance, contending that he had not been discharged for an "act of dishonesty" as defined in the governing collective bargaining agreement, but rather had been discharged in retaliation for having previously complained of safety violations. The grievance was submitted to arbitration, which ultimately resulted in a ruling on January 30, 1984, that Hufstetler had been properly discharged.

On February 7, 1984, Hufstetler filed a complaint with the Department of Labor alleging that his discharge had violated § 405. The Occupational Safety and Health Administration notified Roadway of the complaint and began an investigation. An OSHA field investigator interviewed Hufstetler and other Roadwav employees and obtained statements substantiating Hufstetler's retaliatory discharge claim. Roadway was afforded an opportunity to meet with the investigator and submit a written statement detailing the basis for Hufstetler's discharge, but it was not provided with the names of the other witnesses or the substance of their statements. Roadway explained the discharge by reiterating that, as found by the arbitratrion board, Hufstetler had acted dishonestly in fabricating an equipment breakdown.

Following review of the evidence obtained by the field investigator, the Department of Labor Regional Administrator on January 21, 1985, issued a preliminary decision ordering Hufstetler's immediate reinstatement with backpay. Without detailing the evidence relied upon for this decision, the order stated that the Secretary of Labor had found reasonable cause to believe Hufstetler had been discharged in violation of § 405 for having previously complained about the safety of Roadway's trucks. The order characterized Roadway's asserted basis for the discharge as "conjecture."

Roadway then filed the present action in Federal District Court, seeking an injunction against enforcement of the Secretary's order and a declaratory judgment that § 405 was unconstitutional to the extent it empowered the Secretary to order temporary reinstatement without first conducting an evidentiary hearing. The District Court granted Roadway's motion for a preliminary injunction, and subsequently granted its motion for summary judgment.

The Secretary brought this direct appeal from the District Court's order granting Roadway summary judgment. We noted probable jurisdiction and now affirm in part, agreeing with the District Court that the Secretary's procedures unconstitutionally deprived Roadway of procedural due process by failing to provide Roadway with the substance of the evidence supporting Hufstetler's complaint, and reverse in part, rejecting the District Court's conclusion that § 405 is constitutionally infirm because it empowers the Secretary to order preliminary reinstatement without first conducting an evidentiary hearing and affording Roadway an opportunity to cross-examine witnesses.

Section 405 was enacted in 1983 to encourage employee reporting of noncompliance with safety regulations governing commercial motor vehicles. Congress recognized that employees in the transportation industry are often best able to detect safety violations and yet, because they may be threatened with discharge for cooperating with enforcement agencies, they need express protection against retaliation for reporting these violations. Section 405 protects employee "whistle-blowers" by forbidding discharge, discipline, or other forms of discrimination by the employer in response to an employee's complaining about or refusing to operate motor vehicles that do not meet the applicable safety standards.

Congress also recognized that the employee's protection against having to choose between operating an unsafe vehicle and losing his job would lack practical effectiveness if the employee could not be reinstated pending complete review. The longer a discharged employee remains unemployed, the more devastating are the consequences to his personal financial condition and prospects for re-employment.

The standard procedures which governed the investigation of Hufstetler's complaint against Roadway in this case required that Roadway be notified "of the complaint and of the substance of the allegation" and also that the field investigator consult with Roadway to obtain its explanation for the discharge before the Secretary made any findings and issued a preliminary reinstatement order. The current implementing rules provide for similar participation by the employer, including an opportunity to meet with the investigator and submit statements from witnesses supporting the employer's position. 51 Fed. Reg., at 42093 (proposed 29 CFR § 1978.103).

Neither set of procedures, however, requires that before ordering preliminary reinstatement the Secretary must hold an evidentiary hearing and allow the employer to cross-examine the witnesses from whom the investigator has obtained statements supporting the employee's complaint. Nor do the procedures require the Secretary to divulge the names of these individuals or the substance of their statements before the preliminary reinstatement order takes effect. Roadway claims that the lack of an evidentiary hearing and the confidentiality of the investigator's evidence operate to deny employers procedural due process under the Fifth Amendment.

"Once it is determined that due process applies, the question remains what process is due." Though the required procedures may vary according to the interests at stake in a particular context, *Boddie* v. *Connecticut,* 401 U. S. 371, 378 (1971), "[t]he fundamental requirement of due process is the opportunity to be heard 'at a meaningful time and in a meaningful manner.' " Depending on the circumstances, and the interests at stake, a fairly extensive evidentiary hearing may be constitutionally required before a legitimate claim of entitlement may be terminated. In other instances, however, the Court has upheld procedures affording less than a full evidentiary hearing if " 'some kind of a hearing' " ensuring an effective "initial check against mistaken decisions" is provided before the deprivation occurs, and a prompt opportunity for complete administrative and judicial review is available.

Determining the adequacy of predeprivation procedures requires consideration of the Government's interest in imposing the temporary deprivation, the private interests of those affected by the deprivation, the risk of erroneous deprivations through the challenged procedures, and the probable value of additional or substitute procedural safeguards. In the present case, the District Court assessed these factors and determined that § 405 was "unconstitutional and void to the extent that it empowers [the Secretary] to order reinstatement of discharged employees prior to conducting an evidentiary hearing which comports with the minimum requirements of due process." The court concluded that the employer must be given, "at a minimum, an opportunity to present his side and a chance to confront and cross examine witnesses." Our consideration of the relevant factors leads us to a different conclusion.

Reviewing this legislative balancing of interests, we conclude that the employer is sufficiently protected by procedures that do not include an evidentiary hearing before the discharged employee is temporarily reinstated. So long as the prereinstatement procedures establish a reliable "initial check against mistaken decisions," and complete and expeditious review is available, then the preliminary reinstatement provision of § 405 fairly balances the competing interests of the Government, the employer, and the employee, and a prior evidentiary hearing is not otherwise constitutionally required.

We conclude that minimum due process for the employer in this context requires notice of the employee's allegations, notice of the substance of the relevant supporting evidence, an opportunity to submit a written response, and an opportunity to meet with the investigator and present statements from rebuttal witnesses. The presentation of the employer's witnesses need not be formal, and cross-examination of the employee's witnesses need *not* be afforded at this stage of the proceedings.

The Secretary's current procedures allowing the employer to submit a written response, including affidavits and supporting documents, and to meet with the investigator to respond verbally to the employee's charges and present statements from the employer's witnesses satisfy the due process requirements for reliability. Except for the Secretary's failure to inform Roadway of the evidence supporting Hufstetler's complaint, similar procedures were followed in this case.

We conclude, however, that as a general rule the employer's interest is adequately protected without the right of confrontation and cross-examination, again so long as the employer is otherwise provided an opportunity to respond "at a meaningful time and in a meaningful manner." Providing the employer the relevant supporting evidence and a chance to meet informally with the investigator, to submit statements from witnesses and to argue its position orally, satisfies the constitutional requirement of due process for the temporary deprivation under § 405.

This is not to say, however, that the employer's interest in an expeditious resolution of the employee's complaint can never provide a basis for a due process violation. At some point, delay in holding postreinstatement evidentiary hearings may become a constitutional violation.

The District Court correctly held that the Secretary's preliminary reinstatement order was unconstitutionally imposed in this case because Roadway was not informed of the relevant evidence supporting Hufstetler's complaint and therefore was deprived of an opportunity to prepare a meaningful response. The court erred, however, in holding § 405 unconstitutional to the extent as interpreted by the Secretary it does not provide the employer an evidentiary hearing, complete with the right to confront and cross-examine witnesses, before the employee's temporary reinstatement can be ordered. Accordingly, the District Court's order of summary judgment is affirmed in part and reversed in part.

Case Questions

1. Did the fact that the Court was dealing with a "whistleblower" statute have any bearing on the outcome of the case?
2. What are the present rules regarding minimum due process for employers in cases such as this one?

During an adjudicatory hearing, the hearing examiner may be required to make rulings on questions of admissibility of evidence. Because a knowledge of administrative procedural law is necessary, hearing examiners are usually attorneys, although in many agencies they are not required to be. The hearing examiners of federal agencies are required to be attorneys.

Questions concerning adjudicatory hearing rules of evidence created controversy when the federal APA was being drafted. The authors of the APA provided for procedures that generally follow the court rules of evidence, although some technical requirements of court rules of evidence were deleted. Rules regarding admission of evidence and hearsay, which prohibits admission of statements made by persons not present in court, are examples of these deleted technical requirements.

Another important procedural difference between trial courts and adjudicatory hearings is that there is no jury in an adjudicatory hearing. The hearing examiner acts both as judge and jury, which is why he decides questions of law (such as whether a party should be allowed to cross-examine a witness) as well as questions of fact (such as whether a witness is lying or telling the truth).

Individual Constitutional Rights in Adjudicatory Hearings. The constitutional right to confrontation and cross-examination, as well as the right to obtain witnesses by subpoena, are granted to federal agencies under the Sixth Amendment of the Constitution and to state agencies under the Fourteenth. These are just two of the "fundamental" constitutional rights that apply in adjudicatory hearings. Two other very important rights that are applicable to a great extent in adjudicatory hearings are the Sixth Amendment right to counsel and the Fifth Amendment privilege against self-incrimination.

Administrative law right to counsel is not the same as the right to counsel that has become synonymous with the Miranda warnings in criminal law. "Counsel" in administrative law does not necessarily mean "attorney"; it can mean any trusted adviser. Adjudicatory hearings provide for the right to bring counsel to the hearing; however, unlike criminal proceedings, they do not provide for free counsel.

The Fifth Amendment privilege against self-incrimination also applies in administrative hearings. This right may be claimed by any individual in any type of administrative proceeding. Since this is a personal right, it may not be claimed by unions, corporations, or partnerships of over a few individuals.

The Supreme Court considered the Fifth Amendment in relation to corporate records in *Braswell* v. *United States,* which follows. The court held that since corporate records are not the property of any one individual, an individual could not assert the privilege against self-incrimination as justification for blocking the release of those papers. This holds true even if the release of those corporate papers does incriminate that individual.

Braswell v. United States

101 LEd2d 98 (1988)

Opinion

Chief Justice Rehnquist: This case presents the question whether the custodian of corporate records may resist a subpoena for such records on the ground that the act of production would incriminate him in violation of the Fifth Amendment. We conclude that he may not.

From 1965 to 1980, petitioner Randy Braswell operated his business—which comprises the sale and purchase of equipment, land, timber, and oil and gas interests—as a sole proprietorship. In 1980, he incorporated Worldwide Machinery Sales, Inc., a Mississippi corporation, and began conducting the business through that entity. In 1981, he formed a second Mississippi corporation, Worldwide Purchasing Inc., and funded that corporation with the 100 percent interest he held in Worldwide Machinery. Petitioner was and is the sole shareholder of Worldwide Purchasing, Inc.

Both companies are active corporations, maintaining their current status with the State of Mississippi, filing corporate tax returns, and keeping current corporate books and records. In compliance with Mississippi law, both corporations have three directors, petitioner, his wife, and his mother. Although his wife and mother are secretary-treasurer and vice-president of the corporations, respectively, neither has any authority over the business affairs of either corporation.

In August 1986, a federal grand jury issued a subpoena to "Randy Braswell, President Worldwide Machinery, Inc. [and] Worldwide Purchasing, Inc.," App. 6, requiring petitioner to produce the books and records of the two corporations. The subpoena provided that petitioner could deliver the records to the agent serving the subpoena, and did not require petitioner to testify. Petitioner moved to quash the subpoena, arguing that the act of producing the records would incriminate him in violation of his Fifth Amendment privilege against self-incrimination. The District Court denied the motion to quash, ruling that the "collective entity doctrine" prevented petitioner from asserting that his act of producing the corporations' records was protected by the Fifth Amendment. The court rejected petitioner's argument that the collective entity doctrine does not apply when a corporation is so small that it constitutes nothing more than the individual's alter ego.

The United States Court of Appeals for the Fifth Circuit affirmed, citing *Bellis* v. *United States* (1974) for the proposition that a corporation's records custodian may not claim a Fifth Amendment privilege no matter how small the corporation may be. The Court of Appeals declared that *Bellis* retained vitality following *United States* v. *Doe* (1984), and therefore, "Braswell, as custodian of corporate documents, has no act of production privilege under the fifth amendment regarding corporate documents." We granted certiorari to resolve a conflict among the Courts of Appeals. We now affirm.

There is no question but that the contents of the subpoenaed business records are not privileged. See *Doe, Fisher* v. *United States.* Similarly, petitioner asserts no self-incrimination claim on behalf of the corporations; it is well established that such artificial entities are not protected by the Fifth Amendment. *Bellis.* Petitioner instead relies solely upon the argument that his act of producing the documents has independent testimonial significance, which would incriminate him individually, and that the Fifth Amendment prohibits government compulsion of that act. The bases for this argument are extrapolated from the decisions of this Court in *Fisher* and *Doe.*

In *Fisher,* the Court was presented with the question whether an attorney may resist a subpoena demanding that he produce tax records which had been entrusted to him by his client. The records in question had been prepared by the client's accountants. In analyzing the Fifth Amendment claim forwarded by the attorney, the Court considered whether the client-taxpayer would have had a valid Fifth Amendment claim had he retained the records and the subpoena been issued to him. After explaining that the Fifth Amendment prohibits "compelling a person to give 'testimony' that incriminates him," the Court rejected the argument that the contents of the records were protected. The Court concluded that under the "facts and circumstances" there presented, the act of producing the accountants' papers would not "involve testimonial self-incrimination."

Eight years later, in *United States* v. *Doe,* the Court revisited the question, this time in the context of a claim by a sole proprietor that the compelled production of business records would run afoul of the Fifth Amendment. After rejecting the contention that the contents of the records were themselves protected, the Court proceeded to address whether respondent's act of producing the records would constitute protected testimonial incrimination. The Court concluded that respondent had established a valid Fifth Amendment claim. It deferred to the lower courts, which had found that enforcing the subpoenas at issue would provide the Government valuable information: By producing the records, respondent would admit that the records existed, were in his possession, and were authentic.

Had petitioner conducted his business as a sole proprietorship, *Doe* would require that he be provided the opportunity to show that his act of production would entail testimonial self-incrimination. But petitioner has operated his business through the corporate form, and we have long recognized that for purposes of the Fifth Amendment, corporations and other collective entities are treated differently from individuals. This doctrine—known as the collective entity rule—has a lengthy and distinguished pedigree.

The plain mandate of these decisions is that without regard to whether the subpoena is addressed to the corporation, or as here, to the individual in his capacity as a custodian, a corporate custodian such as petitioner may not resist a subpoena for corporate records on Fifth Amendment grounds.

To be sure, the holding in *Fisher*—later reaffirmed in *Doe*—embarked upon a new course of Fifth Amendment analysis. We cannot agree, however, that it rendered the collective entity rule obsolete. The agency rationale undergirding the collective entity decisions, in which custodians asserted that production of entity records would incriminate them personally, survives. The Court has consistently recognized that the custodian of corporate or entity records holds those documents in a representative rather than a personal capacity. Under those circumstances, the custodian's act of production is not deemed a personal act, but rather an act of the corporation. Any claim of Fifth Amendment privilege asserted by the agent would be tantamount to a claim of privilege by the corporation—which of course possesses no such privilege.

Indeed, the opinion in *Fisher*—upon which petitioner places primary reliance—indicates that the custodian of corporate records may not interpose a Fifth Amendment objection to the compelled production of corporate records, even though the act of production may prove personally incriminating.

We note further that recognizing a Fifth Amendment privilege on behalf of the records custodians of collective entities would have a detrimental impact on the Government's efforts to prosecute "white-collar crime," one of the most serious problems confronting law enforcement authorities. "The greater portion of evidence of wrongdoing by an organization or its representatives is usually found in the official records and documents of that organization. Were the cloak of the privilege to be thrown around these impersonal records and documents, effective enforcement of many federal and state laws would be impossible." If custodians could assert a privilege, authorities would be stymied not only in their enforcement efforts against those individuals but also in their prosecutions of organizations.

Although a corporate custodian is not entitled to resist a subpoena on the ground that his act of production will be personally incriminating, we do think certain consequences flow from the fact that the custodian's act of production is one in his representative rather than personal capacity. Because the custodian acts as a representative, the act is deemed one of the corporation and not the individual. Therefore, the Government concedes, as it must, that it may make no evidentiary use of the "individual act" against the individual.

Consistent with our precedent, the United States Court of Appeals for the Fifth Circuit ruled that petitioner could not resist the subpoena for corporate documents on the ground that the act of production might tend to incriminate him. The judgment is therefore affirmed.

Case Questions

1. Under what circumstances (if any) can an individual refuse to admit the existence of records?
2. What is the collective entity rule?

However, an individual may lose his right to claim the privilege against self-incrimination if he voluntarily waives it either by beginning to testify on a particular subject or if the public records doctrine applies. The **public records doctrine** provides that an individual cannot claim the privilege against self-incrimination for records that are required to be kept by law. There are, however, constitutional limits on the public records doctrine, as the case of *Marchetti* v. *United States* indicates. Federal tax statutes required that persons in the business of accepting wagers pay an excise tax of 10 percent on the gross amount of all wagers accepted. However, many states deemed accepting wagers as being a criminal act; therefore, compliance with federal tax statute by production of wagering records would automatically subject the owner of the wagering business to criminal prosecution under state anti-wagering statutes. Therefore, the Supreme Court invalidated that federal excise tax statute as violative of the Fifth Amendment.

Marchetti v. *United States*

390 U.S. 39 (1968)

Facts

Petitioner was convicted in the United States District Court for the District of Connecticut under two indictments which charged violations of the federal wagering tax statutes. The indictment averred that petitioner and others conspired to evade payment of the annual occupational tax imposed by 26 U.S.C. Sec. 4411.

After verdict, petitioner unsuccessfully sought to arrest judgment, in part on the basis that the statutory obligations to register and to pay the occupational tax violated his Fifth Amendment privilege against self-incrimination. The Court of Appeals for the Second Circuit affirmed.

Opinion

Justice Harlan: We granted certiorari to reexamine the constitutionality under the Fifth Amendment of the pertinent provisions of the wagering tax statutes. For reasons which follow we have concluded that these provisions may not be employed to punish criminally those persons who have defended a failure to comply with their requirements with a proper assertion of the privilege against self-incrimination. The judgment below is accordingly reversed.

The provisions in issue here are part of an interrelated statutory system for taxing wagers. Section 4401 of Title 26 imposes upon those engaged in the business of accepting wagers an excise tax of 10% on the gross amount of all wagers they accept, including the value of chances purchased in lotteries conducted for profit. Section 4411 imposes in addition an occupational tax of $50 annually but upon those subject to taxation under Sec. 4401 and upon those who receive wagers on their behalf. Sec. 4412 requires those liable for the occupational tax to register each year with the director of their local internal revenue district. The registrants must submit Internal Revenue Service Form 11-C, and upon it must provide their residence and business addresses, must indicate whether they are engaged in the business of accepting wagers, and must list the names and addresses of their agents and employees.

The issue before us is not whether the United States may tax activities which a State or Congress has declared unlawful. The Court has repeatedly indicated that the unlawfulness of an activity does not prevent its taxation, and nothing that follows is intended to limit or diminish the vitality of those cases. The issue is instead whether the methods employed by Congress in the federal wagering tax statutes are, in this situation, consistent with the limitations created by the privilege against self-incrimination guaranteed by the Fifth Amendment.

Wagering and its ancillary activities are very widely prohibited under both federal and state law. Information obtained as a consequence of the federal wagering tax laws is readily available to assist the efforts of state and federal authorities to enforce criminal penalties. Evidence of the possession of a federal wagering tax stamp, or of payment of the wagering taxes, has often been admitted at trial in state and federal prosecutions for gambling offenses; such evidence has doubtless proved useful even more frequently to lead prosecuting authorities to other evidence upon which convictions have subsequently been obtained.

In these circumstances, it can scarcely be denied that the obligations to register and to pay the occupational tax created for petitioner "real and appreciable," and not merely "imaginary and unsubstantial," hazards of self-incrimination. Petitioner was confronted by a comprehensive system of federal and state prohibitions against wagering activities; he was required, on pain of criminal prosecution, to provide information which he might reasonably suppose would be available to prosecuting authorities, and which would surely prove a significant "link in a chain" of evidence tending to establish his guilt. Every portion of these requirements had the direct and unmistakable consequence of incriminating petitioner; the application of the constitutional privilege to the entire registration procedure was in this instance neither "extreme" nor "extravagant." It would appear to follow that petitioner's assertion of the privilege as a defense to this prosecution was entirely proper, and accordingly should have sufficed to prevent his conviction.

We must next consider the relevance in this situation of the "required records" doctrine. Petitioner Marchetti was not, by the provisions now at issue, obliged to keep and preserve records "of the same kind as he has customarily kept"; he was required simply to provide information, unrelated to any records which he may have maintained, about his wagering activities. This requirement is not significantly different from a demand that he provide oral testimony. There are no public aspects to the information demanded from Marchetti. The Government's anxiety to obtain information known to a private individual does not without more render that information public; if it did, no room would remain for the application of the constitutional privilege.

We can only conclude, under the wagering tax system as presently written, that petitioner properly asserted the privilege against self-incrimination, and that his assertion should have provided a complete defense to this prosecution.

The judgment of the Court of Appeals is Reversed.

Case Questions

1. Why was the defendant able to claim the Fifth Amendment privilege against self-incrimination?
2. Why was the fact that the records required to be kept in this case had public aspects not sufficient to prevent use of the Fifth Amendment privilege against self-incrimination?
3. This case in effect represents a value judgment that it is more important to protect individual Fifth Amendment rights than it is to apprehend persons engaged in illegal gambling. What do you think are the reasons the Supreme Court made this judgment?

The Adjudicatory Order and Intra-Agency Appeals Process

Once the adjudicatory hearing is concluded, the hearing examiner must make a decision. Unlike rulemaking, adjudicatory due process requires that an adjudicatory order must be based only on the evidence presented at the adjudicatory hearing. The decision must be issued in writing, with supporting reasons.

The person whose rights have been adjudicated may have a right to appeal the decision within a certain period of time after receiving notice of it. The agency's enabling legislation determines how long the person has to appeal and to whom the appeal can be made. Most agencies allow for one appeal within the agency; in others, there may be as many as three or four levels (or tiers) of appeals. For example, suppose that the Federal Trade Commission brings an adjudicatory administrative action against Acme Enterprises, alleging that Acme has violated the Federal Trade Commission Act by using deceptive advertising. Further suppose a hearing examiner finds Acme did violate the act and orders that Acme be fined. If Acme feels that the hearing examiner made an error, Acme may use its right of intra-agency appeal and ask the agency's intra-agency appeals board, in this case the five FTC commissioners sitting as a group, to review the hearing examiner's decision. In reviewing the decision, any intra-agency appeals board is bound to consider all the evidence introduced at the original adjudicatory hearing. An intra-agency appeals board then has three options: it can uphold the decision of the hearing examiner, it can change the examiner's decision in some way, or it can send the case back to the hearing examiner in order for more evidence to be taken. Once a case has gone through all levels in the intra-agency appeals process, intra-agency appeals have been *exhausted*. Once exhaustion has occurred, judicial review of the agency decision is possible.

In chapter 6, you will learn about judicial review of agency action and you will be introduced to some statutes and legal doctrines that influence an agency's functioning within society.

Ethical Issues in Administrative Law Procedures

As you have seen, the primary purpose of administrative agencies is to redress social problems. Consequently, the passage of enabling legislation involves making value judgments as to how society should function, which, in effect, legislates morality. The creation of many administrative agencies has institutionalized certain value judgments. For example, the founding fathers stated, "We hold these truths to be self-evident, that all men are created equal. . . ." While this principle represents a basic assumption of our society, few laws were passed to enforce it until the 1960s. The antidiscrimination statutes of the 1960s and 1970s were passed to insure that persons of all races, colors, sexes, and ages were treated equally; an administrative agency, the Equal Employment Opportunity Commission, was established to enforce compliance with the law. Other examples of agency enabling legislation that institutionalized value judgments are the National Labor Relations Act (which formalized the principle that employees should be able to bargain with their employers concerning the terms and conditions of their employment) and the Occupational Safety and Health Act (which formalized the principle that employers should be required to insure their employees' workplace health and safety). Not everyone may agree with the premises that lead to the creation of an agency, and this disagreement may manifest itself as hostility to the agency.

Another ethical debate in administrative law centers around the conduct of administrative officials. For instance, while performing their duties, certain officials of the federal Environmental Protection Agency met for lunch on many occasions with representatives of businesses that the officials were supposed to be regulating. However, environmental groups such as the Sierra Club were not accorded the same attention; fewer opinions favored these groups than favored business interests. Given this scenario, is it ethical under any circumstances for administrative agency officials to meet "socially" with representatives of regulated businesses?

A great deal of enabling legislation for both federal and state agencies provides for the appointment of top agency officials by the executive branch of government. These appointments are often made as a matter of policy from persons in the same political party as the executive. Reports in 1983 concerning "political appointees at the federal Environmental Protection Agency alleged that decisions about toxic waste clean up were made on the basis of political considerations. Would it be ethical to base agency enforcement decisions on political considerations?

The subject of agency enforcement of its legislative mandate often engenders controversy and raises ethical dilemmas. Agencies such as the Federal Trade Commission have admitted that since they cannot enforce their enabling statutes against all violators, they "make examples" of certain violators in order to dissuade others from breaking the law. The violators singled out for enforcement procedures (through use of agency adjudication) object that it is not ethical for the agency to prosecute them when there are others who have violated the enabling statutes to the same or to a greater extent.

Another criticism of agencies is that they follow the letter of their enabling legislation and ignore their broader duty to the public or to the persons they are supposed to be protecting. For example, charges have been made that while the Occupational Safety and Health Administration may uncover workplace use of toxic chemicals that produce severe long-term hazards for workers, no effort has been made by OSHA to warn individual workers of the potential adverse impact on their health. OSHA has responded that it is not the agency's duty to warn these workers, but merely to prosecute the offending employers. What are the ethical issues involved in such a situation and what should the agency do?

The important concepts and terms in this chapter are listed below; page numbers have been provided for the key terms. By reading over each section you can assess your understanding of the chapter concepts and determine areas you may want to review.

Chapter Summary

1. Administrative agencies are created when one of the constitutionally established branches of government delegates part of its authority to the agency.
2. Delegation of authority to an agency is achieved through the adoption of enabling legislation, which sets up standards for agency action.
3. The executive function of an administrative agency concerns how the agency functions internally and may include investigatory functions.
4. Agency procedures are governed for the most part by the Administrative Procedure Act (APA) at the federal level and by similar acts in the states.
5. The legislative function of administrative agencies is called rulemaking.
6. The quasi-judicial function of administrative agencies is called adjudication.
7. An individual's rights under the Constitution are preserved in agency rulemaking and adjudication procedures.

Key Terms

adjudication 128
Administrative Procedure Act (APA) 128
caveat emptor 119
delegation 120
enabling legislation 120
executive function 127
hearing examiner 134
laissez-faire 118
police power 121
public records doctrine 141
quasi-judicial function 128
rulemaking function 128
subpoena 134
subpoena duces tecum 134

Questions on Ethics

1. Since administrative agency officials are not elected, is it ethical to give them so much control over individual rights?
2. Is it ethical to allow rulemaking regulations not to reflect the evidence presented at the rulemaking hearing?
3. Is it ethical to allow hearsay (statements alleged to have been made outside of the agency hearing) to be admitted in an agency hearing?
4. Is it ethical in the intra-agency appeals process to allow senior officials of the same agency employing a hearing examiner to review the legality of the examiner's decision?

Questions on Law

1. Can a federal district court require that interested parties in a rulemaking hearing be allowed to cross-examine witnesses? *Vermont Yankee Nuclear Power Corp.* v. *Natural Resources Defense Council,* 435 U.S. 519 (1978).
2. A worker's compensation hearing involved a question of whether adequate handholds had been provided for an injured worker. The administrative law judge hearing the case visited the scene of the accident and inspected the handholds. Did the judge act improperly? *Ethel D. Co.* v. *Industrial Accident Comm'n.,* 219 Cal. 699 (1934).
3. The Environmental Protection Agency issued a rule requiring car manufacturers to repair all vehicles of a recall class regardless of age or mileage at the time of repair. Was this an interpretive rule not subject to the notice and comment procedures of the Administrative Procedure Act? *General Motors Corporation* v. *Ruckelshaus,* 742 F. 2d 1561 (1984).
4. The Federal Communications Commission (FCC) considered issuing a regulation to regulate cable television. While considering issuance of the regulation, the FCC commissioners held private meetings with persons interested in the proposed regulation. Did the commissioners act properly? *Home Box Office, Inc.,* v. *FCC,* 567 F.2d 9 (D.C. Cir. 1977).
5. The property of a person alleged to have violated the federal tax laws was searched pursuant to a defective search warrant. The evidence seized in the search would not have been admissible in criminal proceedings. Are they admissible in civil tax proceedings? *United States* v. *Janis,* 428 U.S. 433 (1976).

Suggested Readings

Collins and Hurd, "Warrantless Administrative Searches: It Is Time to Be *Frank* Again," 22 *American Business Law Journal* 189 (1984).

Reed, "Must Quasi-Legislators, Like Caesar's Wife, Be Above Suspicion? Recusal of Rulemakers for Prejudice and Bias," 19 *American Business Law Journal* 1 (1981).

6 Administrative Law II: Judicial Review and Policy

The fundamental policy problem of the administrative process is how to design a system of checks which will minimize the risks of bureaucratic arbitrariness and overreaching, while preserving for the agencies the flexibility they need to act effectively.

—*Ernest Gellhorn,* Administrative Law and Process in a Nutshell

■ LEARNING OBJECTIVES

After you have read this chapter, you should be able to:

1. Understand at what point in time it is possible to appeal an agency action to a court.
2. Be familiar with the principles a court uses in deciding whether to overturn agency action.
3. Be familiar with various statutes and legal doctrines that affect the relationship between agencies and individuals.

Business Decisions and the Law

A Surprise Visit and Foreign Intrigue

Assibi Abudu, a native of Ghana living in the United States was in the process of appealing a deportation order from the Immigration and Naturalization Service (INS). He received a surprise visit from a former acquaintance who had become a high official in the Ghana government. The official invited Abudu to return to Ghana, but Abudu suspected that the invitation was a ruse to force him to disclose the whereabouts of his brother, who was an opponent of the regime in power in Ghana. Should the INS reopen Abudu's case to consider evidence of the surprise visit and other related developments? See *Immigration and Naturalization Service* v. *Abudu*.

Introduction

As you learned in chapter 5, the activities of administrative agencies have a great effect on the functioning of society. While agencies are desirable because they allow government to operate in areas that they might not otherwise have the time and expertise to deal with, the human tendency to "build an empire" might cause agencies to exceed their delegated authority if their power was unchecked. The legal check on agency power is judicial review. In this chapter, you will be introduced to the concept of judicial review and see how the agencies and the courts function vis à vis one another. You will also be introduced to certain statutes and legal doctrines that affect the relationship between agencies and individuals.

Judicial Review of Agency Action

One of the primary legal checks on agency action is **judicial review.** Through judicial review, courts can determine whether an agency is operating within the scope of its enabling legislation and is carrying out its legal duties properly.

While the existence of the possibility of judicial review is a check against agency abuses, it is not an automatic right of anyone who is unhappy with an agency decision. In order for persons to obtain judicial review, they must be proper petitioners for review and must state and prove a legal ground for relief from an agency decision. Furthermore, in determining whether a petitioner for judicial review is entitled to relief, a court will use certain legal doctrines that tend to restrict court intervention in agency action.

A Person Seeking Judicial Review Must Be a Proper Petitioner

In order for a person to obtain judicial review of agency action, the person must have *exhausted* all administrative remedies and must have *standing*, and the agency action appealed from must be *ripe*.

Exhaustion of Administrative Remedies

Before a court will hear a petitioner's case, the petitioner must prove **exhaustion of administrative remedies**—that is, that he has gone through any intra-agency appeals procedures contained in the agency's enabling legislation in a timely manner. There are several important policy reasons why courts generally insist that a petitioner first exhaust his administrative remedies before seeking judicial review: (1) it is more efficient to proceed through the agency hearing process because it is speedier and less costly than court proceedings;

(2) referring all similar cases to the agency allows the agency to use and preserve its expertise in a certain area; (3) constant bypassing of the agency process could weaken the agency and make it less autonomous than it should be; (4) use of the agency process permits full development of the facts prior to judicial review; and (5) the petitioner may be satisfied with the outcome of the administrative process, thereby obviating the need to use the court system at all.

For these reasons, a court will rarely hear the case of a petitioner who has not exhausted his remedies. However, there are some instances in which judicial review will be allowed without exhaustion. If a petitioner alleges that an agency is acting in an unconstitutional manner or in excess of the scope of its enabling legislation, or if exhaustion would be futile, the exhaustion requirement may be waived.

It is very important for a person who is unhappy with an initial agency decision to exhaust his administrative remedies within the time periods specified in the enabling legislation. If proper exhaustion does not occur, the person may not be able to get review from a court because of failure to exhaust, and it may be too late to use intra-agency appeals because such appeals were not filed in a timely fashion. Therefore, the person will be left with no legal remedy.

Standing

Any person who initiates an action in a court of law must have **standing,** and persons appealing from administrative decisions are no exception. Standing means that the person seeking court action must have a personal stake in the outcome of the case. This requirement grows out of a general constitutional requirement that courts hear only real cases and controversies. "A stake in the outcome" has generally been interpreted to mean that the plaintiffs must show some injury in fact to themselves.

In most cases involving judicial review, especially in cases of appeals from an adjudicatory order, it is no problem for petitioners to show that their personal rights are directly affected by the agency action. However, there are two important types of cases in which questions have arisen as to whether petitioners had standing to seek judicial review of agency action: (1) suits in which the petitioners base their standing solely on their status as taxpayers; and (2) suits brought by a group having a special interest in a particular agency's function.

Until the 1968 Supreme Court case of *Flast* v. *Cohen,* it seemed well established that a person could not challenge governmental action (including agency action) solely on the theory that he was a taxpayer and had legal questions about the manner in which taxpayer money was being spent. The *Flast* case held that in certain cases a taxpayer will have standing to bring a lawsuit based on his status as a taxpayer if he can meet a two-part test: the taxpayer must establish (1) that the challenged federal action is based on the government's power to tax and spend for the government's welfare; and (2) that the government's action is challenged as contrary to a specific constitutional limitation. In *Flast,* a taxpayer was held to have standing to challenge a federal program giving aid to parochial schools because federal money was being spent and the taxpayer alleged a violation of a specific part of the Constitution: the Establishment of Religion Clause in the First Amendment. The taxpayer standing principle established in *Flast* has been interpreted narrowly by the courts, and taxpayer suits since *Flast* have tended not to be successful.

A group of persons may have standing to challenge governmental action, but at least one member of the group must allege and prove a direct personal injury to himself. In the following case the Sierra Club was found not to have standing.

Sierra Club v. Morton

405 U.S. 727 (1972)

Facts

The Mineral King Valley is an area of great natural beauty nestled in the Sierra Nevada Mountains in Tulare County, California, adjacent to Sequoia National Park. It has been part of the Sequoia National Forest since 1926, and is designated as a national game refuge by special act of Congress. Though once the site of extensive mining activity, Mineral King is now used almost exclusively for recreational purposes.

Prodded by a rapidly increasing demand for skiing facilities, the United States Forest Service published a prospectus in 1965, inviting bids from private developers for the construction and operation of a ski resort that would also serve as a summer recreation area. The proposal of Walt Disney Enterprises, Inc., was chosen from those of six bidders, and Disney received a three-year permit to conduct surveys and explorations in the valley in connection with its preparation of a complete master plan for the resort.

The final Disney plan, approved by the Forest Service in January 1969, outlined a $35 million complex of motels, restaurants, swimming pools, parking lots, and other structures designed to accommodate 14,000 visitors daily. To provide access to the resort, the state of California proposed to construct a highway twenty miles in length. A section of this road would traverse Sequoia National Park, as would a proposed high-voltage power line needed to provide electricity for the resort.

In June 1969 the Sierra Club filed suit in the United States District Court for the Northern District of California, seeking a declaratory judgment that various aspects of the proposed development contravened federal laws and regulations governing the preservation of national parks, forests, and game refuges, and also seeking preliminary and permanent injunctions restraining the federal officials involved from granting their approval or issuing permits in connection with the Mineral King project. The petitioner Sierra Club sued as a membership corporation with "a special interest in the conservation and the sound maintenance of the national parks, game refuges and forests of the country," and invoked the judicial review provisions of the Administrative Procedure Act.

After two days of hearings, the district court granted the requested preliminary injunction. It rejected the respondents' challenge to the Sierra Club's standing to sue, and determined that the hearing had raised questions "concerning possible excess of statutory authority, sufficiently substantial and serious to justify a preliminary injunction. . . ." The respondents appealed, and the Court of Appeals for the Ninth Circuit reversed. With respect to the petitioner's standing, the court noted that there was "no allegation in the complaint that members of the Sierra Club would be affected by the actions of [the respondents] other than the fact that the actions are personally displeasing or distasteful to them."

Opinion

Justice Stewart: The first question presented is whether the Sierra Club has alleged facts that entitle it to obtain judicial review of the challenged action. Whether a party has a sufficient stake in an otherwise justiciable controversy to obtain judicial resolution of that controversy is what has traditionally been referred to as the question of standing to sue. Where the party does not rely on any specific statute authorizing invocation of the judicial process, the question of standing depends upon whether the party has alleged such a "personal stake in the outcome of the controversy," as to ensure that "the dispute sought to be adjudicated will be presented in an adversary context and in a form historically viewed as capable of judicial resolution."

The Sierra Club relies upon Sec. 10 of the Administrative Procedure Act (APA), which provides: "A person suffering legal wrong because of agency action or adversely affected or aggrieved by agency action within the meaning of a relevant statute, is entitled to judicial review thereof." In *Data Processing Service* v. *Camp,* and *Barlow* v. *Collins,* decided the same day, we held more broadly that persons had standing to obtain judicial review of federal agency action under Sec. 10 of APA where they had alleged that the challenged action had caused them "injury in fact," and where the alleged injury was to an interest "arguably within the zone of interests to be protected or regulated" by the statutes that the agency was claimed to have violated. The question, which has arisen with increasing frequency in federal courts in recent years, is what must be alleged by persons who claim injury of a noneconomic nature to interests that are widely shared.

The injury alleged by the Sierra Club will be incurred entirely by reason of the change in the uses to which Mineral King will be put, and the attendant change in the aesthetics and ecology of the area. Thus, in referring to the road to be built through Sequoia National Park, the complaint alleged that the development, "would destroy or otherwise adversely affect the scenery, natural and historic objects and wildlife of the park and would impair the enjoyment of the park for future generations." We do not question that this type of harm may amount to an "injury in fact" sufficient to lay the basis for standing under Sec. 10 of the APA. But the "injury in fact" test requires more than an injury to a cognizable interest. It requires that the party seeking review be himself among the injured.

The impact of the proposed changes in the environment of Mineral King will not fall indiscriminately upon every citizen. The alleged injury will be felt directly only by those who use Mineral King and Sequoia National Park, and for whom the aesthetic and recreational values of the area will be lessened by the highway and ski resort. The Sierra Club failed to allege that it or its members would be affected in any of their activities or pastimes by the Disney development.

Some courts have indicated a willingness to confer standing upon organizations that have demonstrated "an organization interest in the problem" of environmental or consumer protection. But a mere "interest in a problem," no matter how longstanding the interest and no matter how qualified the organization is in evaluating the problem, is not sufficient by itself to render the organization "adversely affected" or "aggrieved" within the meaning of the APA. The Sierra Club is a large and long-established organization, with a historic commitment to the cause of protecting our Nation's natural heritage from man's depredations. But if a "special interest" in this subject were enough to entitle the Sierra Club to commence this litigation, there would appear to be no objective basis upon which to disallow a suit by any other bona fide "special interest" organization, however small or short-lived. And if any group with a bona fide "special interest" could initiate such litigation, it is difficult to perceive why any individual citizen with the same bona fide special interest would not also be entitled to do so.

We conclude that the Court of Appeals was correct in its holding that the Sierra Club lacked standing to maintain this action. The judgment is affirmed.

Case Questions

1. Why was the interest in the agency action alleged by the Sierra Club not sufficient to give it standing?
2. What does the case indicate is necessary to give a plaintiff standing to bring a lawsuit questioning agency action?
3. Does this case (and the standing doctrine it represents) have the effect of preventing plaintiffs with a worthy point of view from being heard?

Class Action

A *class action* involves the filing of a court case seeking judicial review of agency action on behalf of a group of persons particularly affected by the agency action. For example, if the Food and Drug Administration issued a regulation mandating certain procedures to be used in manufacturing a new drug, a few pharmaceutical companies might file a lawsuit questioning the regulation on behalf of all pharmaceutical companies. Class action suits were once fairly common. However, their number has diminished because the Supreme Court now requires that substantially all members of the class be identified, notified of the action, and share in any monetary award received as a result of the lawsuit.

Ripeness for Judicial Review

Before a court will review the legality of agency action, the case must be ripe. **Ripeness** means that the facts of the controversy are settled and that agency action in the disputed matter is complete. Ripeness questions often arise when an agency has completed action but the agency regulation or order has not become effective. Since agency action generally is not regarded as final until it is effective, the case of a person who wishes to seek judicial review of the agency action before its effective date generally will be regarded as not being ripe.

There have been cases in which courts have allowed judicial review of agency action before the effective date of the action because (1) the facts of the case were well established and not likely to change and (2) hardship to the parties would result if the court withheld review.

The Person Seeking Judicial Review of Agency Action Must State Legal Ground for Review

There are four possible legal grounds for seeking review of agency action: (1) the agency action was unconstitutional, (2) the agency exceeded the scope of its enabling legislation, (3) the agency used improper procedures in carrying out its administrative functions (generally this means failure to comply with the provisions of the applicable administrative procedures act), and (4) the agency action was arbitrary, capricious, or an abuse of discretion. Proof of the first three of the four is generally straightforward: either the agency violated a specific provision of the Constitution or it did not; either the agency committed an act not allowed by its enabling legislation or it did not; either the agency complied with its APA in carrying out its functions or it did not. The last ground for judicial review, that an agency action was arbitrary, capricious, or an abuse of discretion, is the most amorphous of the four and, probably because of that fact, the most common.

Arbitrary, capricious, and *abuse of discretion* do not technically mean the same thing. However, they have been interpreted as being interchangeable and are usually referred to as **abuse of discretion.** An agency abuses its discretion when it makes a decision on the basis of inappropriate factors, or fails to consider all appropriate factors, or makes a clear error in judgment. For example, an agency decision to grant a license to a person who paid a bribe to an agency official would be an abuse of discretion. Decisions made on the basis of bias are always an abuse of discretion. As long as the agency considers only appropriate factors in arriving at its decision, a reviewing court will never substitute its own judgment for that of the agency; this is so because of a doctrine known as the substantial evidence rule, which will be discussed in the next section. The Supreme Court held in *Butz* v. *Glover Livestock Commission Company* (1973) that agency action must be upheld unless the action is without warrant in law or justification in fact. The following Supreme Court case discusses when the abuse of discretion standard will be used in judicial review of agency action.

Immigration and Naturalization Service v. Abudu

99 LEd2d 90 (1988)

Opinion

Justice Stevens: Regulations promulgated by the Attorney General authorize deportable aliens to file motions to reopen their deportation proceedings to request asylum on the basis of newly discovered evidence. Denials of such motions are subject to judicial review in the United States courts of appeals. The question in this case is whether those courts should review such Board of Immigration Appeals (BIA) denials under an abuse-of-discretion standard, as petitioner contends, or under the strict standard that would be applied when passing on a motion for summary judgment, as the Court of Appeals held. Consistently with our prior cases confirming the BIA's broad discretion in considering motions to reopen, we conclude that the abuse-of-discretion standard applies and therefore reverse the judgment of the Court of Appeals.

Respondent, Assibi Abudu, a native and citizen of Ghana, first entered the United States in 1965 as a student. While attending medical school in 1973, he spent his summer vacation in Ghana, and then reentered the United States on a student visa that authorized him to remain until 1976. After becoming a licensed physician, he married an American citizen and overstayed his visa. In 1981, he pleaded guilty to charges of attempting to obtain narcotic drugs (Demerol) by fraud. In due course, deportation proceedings were initiated, and respondent designated England as the country of deportation if necessary and expressly declined to seek asylum as a refugee. On July 1, 1982, the immigration judge ordered him deported, and on August 14, 1984, the BIA dismissed his appeal.

Respondent filed a petition for review in the Court of Appeals for the Ninth Circuit. While that petition was pending, on February 1, 1985, respondent filed a motion with the BIA requesting a reopening of his deportation proceeding to enable him to apply for asylum and a withholding of deportation. In that motion, which was supported by affidavits and other exhibits, respondent claimed that he had a well-founded fear that if England did not accept him and he was returned to Ghana, his life and freedom would be threatened by the regime in power. His fear was based largely on the facts that after the current government seized power in 1981, it had carried out a systematic campaign of persecution against its political enemies and that respondent's brother and certain close friends were among the targets of that campaign. Moreover, in 1984, respondent had received an unsolicited and surprise visit from a former acquaintance who had become a high official in the Ghana government. The visitor invited respondent to return to Ghana, ostensibly because qualified physicians are in short supply, but respondent concluded that his visitor actually wanted to entice him to return in order to force him to disclose the whereabouts of his brother and other enemies of the government.

(The BIA denied Abudu's motion to reopen his case. The Court of Appeals affirmed the deportation order, but reversed the order denying the motion to reopen and remanded for an evidentiary hearing on the asylum and withholding of deportation claims.)

We granted certiorari, not to decide the substantive issues of what constitutes a prima facie case for establishing eligibility for asylum on the basis of a well-founded fear of persecution, or of what standard of review applies, either initially or on motion to reopen, when the BIA rests its grant or denial of relief squarely on prima facie case grounds, but rather to determine the standard a Court of Appeals must apply when reviewing the BIA's conclusion that an alien has not reasonably explained his failure to assert his asylum claim at the outset.

There are at least three independent grounds on which the BIA may deny a motion to reopen. First, it may hold that the movant has not established a prima facie case for the underlying substantive relief sought. The standard of review of such a denial is not before us today. Second, the BIA may hold that the movant has not introduced previously unavailable, material evidence, or, in an asylum application case, that the movant has not reasonably explained his failure to apply for asylum initially. We decide today that the appropriate standard of review of such denials is abuse of discretion. Third, in cases in which the ultimate grant of relief is discretionary (asylum, suspension of deportation, and adjustment of status, but not withholding of deportation), the BIA may leap ahead, as it were, over the two threshold concerns (prima facie case and new evidence/reasonable explanation), and simply determine that even if they were met, the movant would not be entitled to the discretionary grant of relief. We have consistently held that denials on this third ground are subject to an abuse-of-discretion standard.

The BIA has discretion to deny a motion to reopen even if the alien has made out a prima facie case for relief; that is, our prior glosses on § 3.2 have served as support for an abuse-of-discretion standard of review for the third type of denial, where the BIA simply refuses to grant relief that is itself discretionary in nature, even if the alien has surmounted the requisite thresholds of prima facie case and new evidence/reasonable explanation.

But even before reaching the ultimate decision on an alien's application for discretionary relief from deportation, or before reaching the point at which mandatory relief is called for in a withholding of deportation case, the BIA's discretion may be called into play regarding the specific, evidentiary requirements of §§ 3.2 and 208.11. That is, in a given case the BIA may determine, either as a sufficient ground for denying relief or as a necessary step toward granting relief, whether the alien has produced previously unavailable, material evidence (§ 3.2), and, in asylum cases, whether the alien has reasonably explained his or her failure to request asylum initially (§ 208.11). We hold today that such decisions are subject to an abuse-of-discretion standard of review.

The reasons why motions to reopen are disfavored in deportation proceedings are comparable to those that apply to petitions for rehearing, and to motions for new trials on the basis of newly discovered evidence. There is a strong public interest in bringing litigation to a close as promptly as is consistent with the interest in giving the adversaries a fair opportunity to develop and present their respective cases.

As we have detailed above, the Court of Appeals in this case purported to decide "whether [respondent] presented a *prima facie* case for reopening." In so doing, the Court of Appeals set out a standard for BIA motions to reopen deportation proceedings that appears to have conflated the quite separate issues of whether the alien has presented a prima facie case for asylum with whether the alien has reasonably explained his failure to apply for asylum initially and has indeed offered previously unavailable, material evidence. To the extent that the reasoning of the Court of Appeals addresses the issue of reopening rather than the issue of prima facie case for asylum, it is not supported by our cases, and has been consistently rejected by other Circuits and by other panels in the Ninth Circuit. We have never suggested that all ambiguities in the factual averments must be resolved in the movant's favor, and we have never analogized such a motion to a motion for summary judgment. The appropriate analogy is a motion for a new trial in a criminal case on the basis of newly discovered evidence, as to which courts have uniformly held that the moving party bears a heavy burden. Moreover, this is the tenor of the Attorney General's regulations, which plainly disfavor motions to reopen. In sum, although all adjudications by administrative agencies are to some degree judicial and to some degree political—and therefore an abuse-of-discretion standard will often apply to agency adjudications not governed by specific statutory commands—INS officials must exercise especially sensitive political functions that implicate questions of foreign relations, and therefore the reasons for giving deference to agency decisions on petitions for reopening or reconsideration in other administrative contexts apply with even greater force in the INS context.

We have no doubt that if respondent had made a timely application for asylum, supported by the factual allegations and exhibits set forth in his motion to reopen, the immigration judge would have been required to grant him an evidentiary hearing. See 8 CFR §§ 280.6 (1987) (requiring appearance before immigration officer for asylum application) and 208.10(c) (permitting presentation of evidence in deportation proceedings). We are equally convinced, however, that an alien who has already been found deportable has a much heavier burden when he first advances his request for asylum in a motion to reopen. In passing on the sufficiency of such a motion, the BIA is entitled to attach significance to its untimeliness, both for the purpose of evaluating the probability that the movant can prove his allegations and for the purpose of determining whether the movant has complied with the regulation requiring a reasonable explanation for the failure to request asylum during the deportation proceeding.

In this case we have no hesitation in concluding that the BIA did not abuse its discretion when it held that respondent had not reasonably explained his failure to apply for asylum prior to the completion of the initial deportation proceeding. The surprise visit in 1984 was admittedly an event with uncertain meaning, but it was neither arbitrary nor unreasonable for the BIA to regard it as not providing any significant additional support for a claim that respondent had not previously considered strong enough to prompt him to assert that he had a well-founded fear of persecution.

(The BIA denial of the motion to reopen is affirmed).

Case Questions

1. Why is the abuse of discretion standard more favorable to the agency than using a summary judgment–type standard?
2. Did the fact that international and political issues were involved in this case have any effect on the Court's decision?

Judicial Principles Tending to Restrict Review of Agency Action

In deciding whether to grant a petition to review agency action, the courts use certain principles that have developed over the years regarding all types of appeals (not just appeals from agency action). These principles are the principles of *comity* and *abstention,* the doctrine of *primary jurisdiction,* and the *substantial evidence rule*. These four principles overlap to some extent, and their overall effect is to limit the circumstances under which a court will review or change agency action.

Comity and Abstention

The principles of comity and abstention are two sides of the same coin. **Comity,** ''friendly feeling,'' means that a court has respect for the functioning of other governmental bodies, such as administrative agencies or other courts. Growing out of this feeling of respect is the principle of **abstention,** which means that a court will not interfere with the functioning of an administrative agency or another court until that agency or court has completed its work. The principles of comity and abstention explain the reason for the doctrine of ripeness, discussed earlier, which generally does not allow court intervention in agency action until it is final. In the following case, which was one of the most newsworthy business law cases of its time, the Supreme Court discusses the concepts of comity and abstention.

Pennzoil Co. v. Texaco, Inc.

481 U.S. 1 (April 6, 1987)

Opinion

Justice Powell: The principal issue in this case is whether a federal district court lawfully may enjoin a plaintiff who has prevailed in a trial in state court from executing the judgment in its favor pending appeal of that judgment to a state appellate court.

Getty Oil Co. and appellant Pennzoil Co. negotiated an agreement under which Pennzoil was to purchase about three-sevenths of Getty's outstanding shares for $110 a share. Appellee Texaco, Inc. eventually purchased the shares for $128 a share. On February 8, 1984, Pennzoil filed a complaint against Texaco in the Harris County District Court, a state court located in Houston, Texas, the site of Pennzoil's corporate headquarters. The complaint alleged that Texaco tortiously had induced Getty to breach a contract to sell its shares to Pennzoil; Pennzoil sought actual damages of $7.53 billion and punitive damages in the same amount. On November 19, 1985, a jury returned a verdict in favor of Pennzoil, finding actual damages of $7.53 billion and punitive damages of $3 billion. The parties anticipated that the judgment, including prejudgment interest, would exceed $11 billion.

Although the parties disagree about the details, it was clear that the expected judgment would give Pennzoil significant rights under Texas law. By recording an abstract of a judgment in the real property records of any of the 254 counties in Texas, a judgment creditor can secure a lien on all of a judgment debtor's real property located in that county. If a judgment creditor wishes to have the judgment enforced by state officials so that it can take possession of any of the debtor's assets, it may secure a writ of execution from the clerk of the court that issued the judgment. But the judgment debtor "may suspend the execution of the judgment by filing a good and sufficient bond to be approved by the clerk." Rule 364(a). See Rule 368. For a money judgment, "the amount of the bond . . . shall be at least the amount of the judgment, interest, and costs." Rule 364(b).

Even before the trial court entered judgment, the jury's verdict cast a serious cloud on Texaco's financial situation. The amount of the bond required by Rule 364(b) would have been more than $13 billion. It is clear that Texaco would not have been able to post such a bond. Accordingly, "the business and financial community concluded that Pennzoil would be able, under the lien and bond provisions of Texas law, to commence enforcement of any judgment entered on the verdict before Texaco's appeals had been resolved." The effects on Texaco were substantial: the price of its stock dropped markedly; it had difficulty obtaining credit; the rating of its bonds was lowered; and its trade creditors refused to sell it crude oil on customary terms.

Texaco did not argue to the trial court that the judgment, or execution of the judgment, conflicted with federal law. Rather, on December 10, 1985—before the Texas court entered judgment—Texaco filed this action in the United States District Court for the Southern District of New York in White Plains, New York, the site of Texaco's corporate headquarters. Texaco alleged that the Texas proceedings violated rights secured to Texaco by the Constitution and various federal statutes. It asked the District Court to enjoin Pennzoil from taking any action to enforce the judgment. Pennzoil's response, and basic position, was that the District Court could not hear the case. First, it argued that the Anti-Injunction Act barred issuance of an injunction. It further contended that the court should abstain under the doctrine of *Younger* v.

Harris (1971). Third, it argued that the suit was in effect an appeal from the Texas trial court and that the District Court had no jurisdiction under the principles of *Rooker* v. *Fidelity Trust Co.* (1923), and *District of Columbia Court of Appeals* v. *Feldman* (1983).

The District Court rejected all of these arguments. It found the Anti-Injunction Act inapplicable because Texaco's complaint rested on 42 U. S. C. § 1983. It found *Younger* abstention unwarranted because it did not believe issuance of an injunction would "interfere with a state official's pursuit of a fundamental state interest." As to the *Rooker-Feldman* doctrine, the court noted only that it was not "attempting to sit as a final or intermediate appellate state court as to the merits of the Texas action. . . . Our only intention is to assure Texaco its constitutional right to raise claims that we view as having a good chance of success."

On appeal, the Court of Appeals for the Second Circuit affirmed. Pennzoil filed a jurisdictional statement in this Court. We noted probable jurisdiction. We reverse.

The courts below should have abstained under the principles of federalism enunciated in *Younger* v. *Harris* (1971). Both the District Court and the Court of Appeals failed to recognize the significant interests harmed by their unprecedented intrusion into the Texas judicial system. Similarly, neither of those courts applied the appropriate standard in determining whether adequate relief was available in the Texas courts.

The first ground for the *Younger* decision was "the basic doctrine of equity jurisprudence that courts of equity should not act, and particularly should not act to restrain a criminal prosecution, when the moving party has an adequate remedy at law," The Court also offered a second explanation for its decision:

> This underlying reason . . . is reinforced by an even more vital consideration, the notion of "comity," that is, a proper respect for state functions, a recognition of the fact that the entire country is made up of a Union of separate state governments, and a continuance of the belief that the National Government will fare best if the States and their institutions are left free to perform their separate functions in their separate ways. . . . The concept does not mean blind deference to "States" Rights' any more than it means centralization of control over every important issue in our National Government and its courts. The Framers rejected both these courses. What the concept does represent is a system in which there is sensitivity to the legitimate interests of both State and National Governments, and in which the National Government, anxious though it may be to vindicate and protect federal rights and federal interests, always endeavors to do so in ways that will not unduly interfere with the legitimate activities of the States.

This concern mandates application of *Younger* abstention not only when the pending state proceedings are criminal, but also when certain civil proceedings are pending, if the State's interests in the proceeding are so important that exercise of the federal judicial power would disregard the comity between the States and the National Government.

Another important reason for abstention is to avoid unwarranted determination of federal constitutional questions. When federal courts interpret state statutes in a way that raises federal constitutional questions, "a constitutional determination is predicated on a reading of the statute that is not binding on state courts and may be discredited at any time—thus essentially rendering the federal-court decision advisory and the litigation underlying it meaningless." This concern has special significance in this case. Because Texaco chose not to present to the Texas courts the constitutional claims asserted in this case, it is impossible to be certain that the governing Texas statutes and procedural rules actually raise these claims. Moreover, the Texas Constitution contains an "open courts" provision that appears to address Texaco's claims more specifically than the Due Process Clause of the Fourteenth Amendment. Thus, when this case was filed in Federal Court, it was entirely possible that the Texas courts would have resolved this case on state statutory or constitutional grounds, without reaching the federal constitutional questions Texaco raises in this case. As we have noted, *Younger* abstention in situations like this "offers the opportunity for narrowing constructions that might obviate the constitutional problem and intelligently mediate federal constitutional concerns and state interests."

Not only would federal injunctions interfere with the execution of state judgments, but they would do so on grounds that challenge the very process by which those judgments were obtained. So long as those challenges relate to pending state proceedings, proper respect for the ability of state courts to resolve federal questions presented in state court litigation mandates that the federal court stay its hand.

We express no opinion on the claims Texaco has raised in this case against the Texas bond and lien provisions, nor on the possibility that Texaco now could raise these claims in the Texas courts, see n. 16, *supra*. Today we decide only that it was inappropriate for the (New York) District Court to entertain these claims. If, and when, the Texas courts render a final decision on any federal issue presented by this litigation, review may be sought in this Court in the customary manner.

The judgment of the Court of Appeals is reversed. The case is remanded to the District Court with instructions to vacate its order and dismiss the complaint. The judgment of this Court shall issue forthwith.

It is so ordered.

Case Questions

1. What policy reasons did the Court cite for applying the doctrine of abstention?
2. How would you apply the doctrine of abstention in a case in which there is an appeal to a court of an on-going administrative agency case?

Primary Jurisdiction

The doctrine of **primary jurisdiction** states that if both a court and an administrative agency have jurisdiction over a case, the agency should hear the case first. Of course, once the agency's action on the matter is final, judicial review will then be available. The policy reasons for the doctrine of primary jurisdiction are generally the same as those supporting the doctrine of exhaustion of administrative remedies discussed previously: mainly, a desire not to undermine the authority of administrative agencies and to allow the agencies to maintain their expertise in a particular area. There are some instances, however, in which a court may decide to take original jurisdiction over a case: usually those in which the main question in a case is one of law and seems nontechnical (so there is no need for agency expertise).

Substantial Evidence Rule

Comity, abstention, and primary jurisdiction have the effect of preventing a court from hearing administrative cases. The last principle, the **substantial evidence rule,** concerns how a case that began in an administrative agency will be treated when a court reviews it. The substantial evidence rule states that a court will not set aside agency action if it is supported by substantial evidence on the record as a whole. The purpose of the substantial evidence rule is to guard against undermining agency authority. Therefore, on judicial review, the court examines the agency record (the transcripts of any agency hearings, any documentary evidence submitted, and any written decisions of the agency). If, after examining all the evidence on the record, both for and against the agency decision, the court determines that there is substantial evidence to support the agency's decision, the court will uphold that decision.

It is important to note the limited nature of the court's function in judicial review. The court will rarely conduct any type of a trial during judicial review, but will limit itself to consideration of a written record, usually supplemented by oral arguments and written briefs of the parties to the case regarding questions of law. If a court feels that it needs more facts to decide a case or that the reasons for the agency's decision are unclear, it will almost always **remand** (send back) the case to the agency, rather than hold a hearing itself. One example of a full hearing (called a **trial *de novo*** that might be held by a court would be the case of a petitioner who alleged that an agency was so biased against her that the agency would not give her a fair hearing if the case were remanded. The effect of the substantial evidence rule and the practice of not holding trials *de novo* in judicial review is that agency decisions tend to be upheld on appeal unless they are clearly irregular. Courts are hesitant to substitute their judgment for those of the "expert" agency. In an "ordinary" case in which substantial evidence supports both the agency's and the petitioner's positions, and the petitioner appeals on the ground that the agency's decision was an abuse of discretion, the court will almost always uphold the agency's decision.

It is very important to understand the effect of the substantial evidence rule on individual rights. Some persons who are unfamiliar with administrative law might feel that they can ignore agency rulemaking and adjudication procedures and then rely on courts to protect their rights or property interests through judicial review. However, as we have seen, once an agency has acted, the court will uphold the agency decision as long as there is substantial support for it (and as long as no specific constitutional rights have been infringed upon).

Through the process of judicial review, an administrative agency is tied into the constitutional government framework from which it deviated when it was established through a delegation of power from one of the three constitutionally established branches.

The Relationship of Administrative Agencies to Individuals and Society

The Administrative Agency and Individuals

As administrative agencies have assumed more power and importance, a feeling has grown that some agencies may be using their power to abuse individual rights. Statutes have been passed to safeguard individual rights against agency intrusion. Two such statutes are the federal *Freedom of Information Act* and the federal *Privacy Act*. Another development in the area of agencies' dealings with individuals is the reexamination by courts of the extent to which the common law concept of sovereign immunity applies to administrative officials.

Statutory Protections

The **Freedom of Information Act** (FOIA), which was amended into its present form in 1974, gives private parties the right to obtain information that is in the possession of the government. The purpose of the FOIA is to prevent "government in secret" by providing a mechanism for public disclosure of information in the possession of the government (including administrative agencies). The FOIA requires that each federal agency make available for public inspection and copying its opinions in decided cases, any statements of policy and interpretations not published in the *Federal Register,* and any administrative staff manuals that might affect the public. There are exceptions to the coverage of the FOIA, the reasons for most of which are obvious. Some of the most important of these exceptions are: materials concerning national defense or foreign policy; trade secrets and commercial or financial information that businesses have given to agencies to comply with statutes or administrative regulation; inter- or intra-agency memoranda that would not be available by law to a party in litigation with an agency; any information in medical, personnel, or other files, the disclosure of which would constitute an invasion of personal privacy; and law enforcement agency investigative files.

Records covered by the FOIA may be requested by the persons whom they concern, or by members of the public. In 1988, in *United States Department of Justice* v. *Julian,* the United States Supreme Court held that persons being considered for parole from federal prison could have access under the FOIA to their own presentence investigation reports. However, the Court noted that there was an exemption for information in the report that related to confidential sources, diagnostic opinions, and other information that might cause harm to third parties. The court expressed doubts as to whether third parties could gain access to the reports under the FOIA.

In conjunction with the 1974 amendments to the Freedom of Information Act, Congress also passed the federal **Privacy Act.** This act complements the FOIA by limiting how certain types of information obtained by the federal government (including agencies) can be used and limiting the number of persons who are entitled to receive confidential information in agency possession. The Privacy Act creates a legal tort action that may be brought by anyone who feels his rights under the act have been violated. This is a very important feature.

Immunity of Administrative Officials

As agencies' power has grown, so has the ability of administrative officials to affect people's lives. Courts have in recent years reexamined the question of whether these officials or their agencies may be sued and damages recovered by persons who feel the agencies have violated their legal rights. Generally, the doctrine of **sovereign immunity** applies to administrative officials and employees, which means that they cannot be liable for any damages caused by their decisions.

Therefore, the government has no Federal Tort Claims Act (FTCA) liability for injuries to members of the military service arising out of or in the course of activity incident to service. *United States* v. *Johnson* (1987). Also, federal officials whose decisions resulted in the improper denial of Social Security disability benefits could not be sued for damages for emotional distress and loss of necessities. *Schweiker* v. *Chilicky* (1988).

However, this absolute immunity only applies as long as the official is operating within the scope of his delegated authority and was not performing an otherwise illegal or unconstitutional act. In *Butz* v. *Economou* (1978), the Supreme Court held that a federal official may be liable if he knew or should have known that his actions violated statutory or constitutional law. Furthermore, although the court ruled in 1971 in *Bivens* v. *Six Unknown Narcotics Agents* that it is possible to recover money damages for injuries suffered as a result of federal agents' violation of the Fourth Amendment, cases since then have tended to extend immunity to law enforcement officials. In *Anderson* v. *Creighton* (1987), the Supreme Court ruled that an FBI agent would have qualified immunity from suit for violation of constitutional rights if he could establish as a matter of law that a reasonable officer could have believed that a search comported with the Fourth Amendment, even though it did not. The *Creighton* decision stated that whether an official is personally liable for an allegedly unlawful official action generally turns on the objective legal reasonableness of the action, assessed in light of the legal rules that were clearly established at the time the action was taken. Legal rules are clearly established if the contours of the right is sufficiently clear so that a reasonable official would understand that what he is doing violates that right.

The same rules regarding immunity of federal officials generally apply to state agency officials. However, it is possible for state officials to be liable under a particular federal civil rights statute that prohibits deprivation of civil rights under color of state law (42 U.S.C., Sec. 1983). State officials (agency official or otherwise) may be liable under this statute if they knew or had reason to know that their actions would violate an individual's basic constitutional rights. Some cases in which the Supreme Court indicated state or local officials might not have immunity from suit are *Wood* v. *Strickland,* in which members of a local school board allegedly violated a student's due process rights, and *Scheur* v. *Rhodes,* in which various university and state officials, including the governor, were sued.

Sovereign immunity from suit has also been generally extended to federal and state judicial officials. In the following case, which discusses the policy reasons for the immunity doctrine, the Supreme Court ruled that a state court judge does not have absolute immunity from a decision to demote and dismiss a court employee.

Forrester v. *White*

98 LEd2 555 (1988)

Opinion

Justice O'Connor: This case requires us to decide whether a state-court judge has absolute immunity from a suit for damages under 42 U.S.C. § 1983 for his decision to dismiss a subordinate court employee. The employee, who had been a probation officer, alleged that she was demoted and discharged on account of her sex, in violation of the Equal Protection Clause of the Fourteenth Amendment. We conclude that the judge's decisions were not judicial acts for which he should be held absolutely immune.

Respondent Howard Lee White served as Circuit Judge of the Seventh Judicial Circuit of the State of

Illinois and Presiding Judge of the Circuit Court in Jersey County. Under Illinois law, Judge White had the authority to hire adult probation officers, who were removable in his discretion. In addition, Judge White had the authority to appoint juvenile probation officers to serve at his pleasure.

In April 1977, Judge White hired petitioner Cynthia A. Forrester as an adult and juvenile probation officer. Forrester prepared presentence reports for Judge White in adult offender cases, and recommendations for disposition and placement in juvenile cases. She also supervised persons on probation and recommended revocation when necessary. In July 1979, Judge White appointed Forrester as Project Supervisor of the Jersey County Juvenile Court Intake and Referral Services Project, a position that carried increased supervisory responsibilities. Judge White demoted Forrester to a nonsupervisory position in the summer of 1980. He discharged her on October 1, 1980.

Forrester filed this lawsuit in the United States District Court for the Southern District of Illinois in July 1982. She alleged violations of Title VII of the Civil Rights Act of 1964, 42 U. S. C. § 1983. A jury found that Judge White had discriminated against Forrester on account of her sex, in violation of the Equal Protection Clause of the Fourteenth Amendment. The jury awarded her $81,818.80 in compensatory damages under § 1983. Forrester's other claims were dismissed in the course of the lawsuit.

After Judge White's motion for judgment notwithstanding the verdict was denied, he moved for a new trial. The District Court granted this motion, holding that the jury verdict was against the weight of the evidence. Judge White then moved for summary judgment on the ground that he was entitled to "judicial immunity" from a civil damages suit. This motion, too, was granted. Forrester appealed.

A divided panel of the Court of Appeals for the Seventh Circuit affirmed the grant of summary judgment. The majority reasoned that judges are immune for activities implicating the substance of their decisions in the cases before them, although they are not shielded "from the trials of life generally." Some members of a judge's staff aid in the performance of adjudicative functions, and the threat of suits by such persons could make a judge reluctant to replace them even after losing confidence in their work. Here, Forrester performed functions that were "inextricably tied to discretionary decisions that have consistently been considered judicial acts." Unless Judge White felt free to replace Forrester, the majority thought, the quality of his own decisions might decline. The Court of Appeals therefore held that Judge White was absolutely immune from Forrester's civil damages suit.

In dissent, Judge Posner argued that judicial immunity should protect only adjudicative functions, and that employment decisions are administrative functions for which judges should not be given absolute immunity.

In *Goodwin* v. *Circuit Court of St. Louis County, Mo.* (1984), the United States Court of Appeals for the Eighth Circuit held that a judge was not immune from civil damages for his decision to demote a hearing officer. We granted certiorari to resolve the conflict.

Suits for monetary damages are meant to compensate the victims of wrongful actions and to discourage conduct that may result in liability. Special problems arise, however, when government officials are exposed to liability for damages. To the extent that the threat of liability encourages these officials to carry out their duties in a lawful and appropriate manner, and to pay their victims when they do not, it accomplishes exactly what it should. By its nature, however, the threat of liability can create perverse incentives that operate to *inhibit* officials in the proper performance of their duties. In many contexts, government officials are expected to make decisions that are impartial or imaginative, and that above all are informed by considerations other than the personal interests of the decisionmaker. Because government officials are engaged by definition in governing, their decisions will often have adverse effects on other persons. When officials are threatened with personal liability for acts taken pursuant to their official duties, they may well be induced to act with an excess of caution or otherwise to skew their decisions in ways that result in less than full fidelity to the objective and independent criteria that ought to guide their conduct. In this way, exposing government officials to the same legal hazards faced by other citizens may detract from the rule of law instead of contributing to it.

Such considerations have led to the creation of various forms of immunity from suit for certain government officials. Aware of the salutary effects that the threat of liability can have, however, as well as the undeniable tension between official immunities and the ideal of the rule of law, this Court has been cautious in recognizing claims that government officials should be free of the obligation to answer for their acts in court. Running through our cases, with fair consistency, is a "functional" approach to immunity questions other than those that have been decided by express constitutional or statutory enactment. Under that approach, we examine the nature of the functions with which a particular official or class of officials has been lawfully entrusted, and we seek to evaluate the effect that exposure to particular forms of liability would likely have on the appropriate exercise of those functions. Officials who seek exemption from personal liability have the burden of showing that such an exemption is justified by overriding considerations of public policy, and the Court has recognized a category of "qualified" immunity that avoids unnecessarily extending the scope of the traditional concept of absolute immunity. See, *e.g.* *Scheuer* v. *Rhodes* (1974); *Butz* v. *Economou* (1978); *Harlow* v. *Fitzgerald* (1982).

This Court has generally been quite sparing in its recognition of claims to absolute official immunity. One species of such legal protection is beyond challenge: the legislative immunity created by the Speech or Debate Clause, U. S. Const., Art. I, § 6, cl. 1. Even here, however, the Court has been careful not to extend the scope of the protection further than its purposes require. Furthermore, on facts analogous to those in the case before us, the Court indicated that a United States Congressman would not be entitled to absolute immunity, in a sex-discrimination suit filed by a personal aide whom he had fired, unless such immunity was afforded by the Speech or Debate Clause. *Davis* v. *Passman* (1979).

Among executive officials, the President of the United States is absolutely immune from damages liability arising from official acts. *Nixon* v. *Fitzgerald* (1982). This immunity, however, is based on the President's "unique position in the constitutional scheme," and it does not extend indiscriminately to the President's personal aides, see *Harlow, supra,* or to cabinet level officers, *Mitchell* v. *Forsyth* (1985). Nor are the highest executive officials in the States protected by absolute immunity under federal law. See *Scheuer* v. *Rhodes, supra.*

As a class, judges have long enjoyed a comparatively sweeping form of immunity, though one not perfectly well-defined. Judicial immunity apparently originated, in medieval times, as a device for discouraging collateral attacks and thereby helping to establish appellate procedures as the standard system for correcting judicial error. Besides protecting the finality of judgments or discouraging inappropriate collateral attacks, judicial immunity also protects judicial independence by insulating judges from vexatious actions prosecuted by disgruntled litigants.

This Court has not been quick to find that federal legislation was meant to diminish the traditional common law protections extended to the judicial process. On the contrary, these protections have been held to extend to executive branch officials who perform quasi-judicial functions, see *Butz* v. *Economou, supra* or who perform prosecutorial functions that are "intimately associated with the judicial phase of the criminal process." The common law's rationale for these decisions—freeing the judicial process of harassment or intimidation—has been thought to require absolute immunity even for advocates and witnesses.

One can reasonably wonder whether judges, who have been primarily responsible for developing the law of official immunities, are not inevitably more sensitive to the ill effects that vexatious law suits can have on the judicial function than they are to similar dangers in other contexts.

The purposes served by judicial immunity from liability in damages have been variously described. The Court has emphasized that the nature of the adjudicative function requires a judge frequently to disappoint some of the most intense and ungovernable desires that people can have. As Judge Posner pointed out in his dissenting opinion below, this is the principal characteristic that adjudication has in common with legislation and with criminal prosecution, which are the two other areas in which absolute immunity has most generously been provided. If judges were personally liable for erroneous decisions, the resulting avalanche of suits, most of them frivolous but vexatious, would provide powerful incentives for judges to avoid rendering decisions likely to provoke such suits. The resulting timidity would be hard to detect or control, and it would manifestly detract from independent and impartial adjudication. Nor are suits against judges the only available means through which litigants can protect themselves from the consequences of judicial error. Most judicial mistakes or wrongs are open to correction through ordinary mechanisms of review, which are largely free of the harmful side-effects inevitably associated with exposing judges to personal liability.

When applied to the paradigmatic judicial acts involved in resolving disputes between parties who have invoked the jurisdiction of a court, the doctrine of absolute judicial immunity has not been particularly controversial. Difficulties have arisen primarily in attempting to draw the line between truly judicial acts, for which immunity is appropriate, and acts that simply happen to have been done by judges. Here, as in other contexts, immunity is justified and defined by the *functions* it protects and serves, not by the person to whom it attaches.

This Court has never undertaken to articulate a precise and general definition of the class of acts entitled to immunity. The decided cases, however, suggest an intelligible distinction between judicial acts and the administrative, legislative, or executive functions that judges may on occasion be assigned by law to perform.

Administrative decisions, even though they may be essential to the very functioning of the courts, have not been regarded as judicial acts. Likewise, judicial immunity has not been extended to judges acting to promulgate a code of conduct for attorneys. *Supreme Court of Virginia* v. *Consumers Union of United States, Inc.* (1980). Similarly, in the same case, we held that judges acting to enforce the Bar Code would be treated like prosecutors, and thus would be amenable to suit for injunctive and declaratory relief. Once again, it was the nature of the function performed, not the identity of the actor who performed it, that informed our immunity analysis.

In the case before us, we think it clear that Judge White was acting in an administrative capacity when he demoted and discharged Forrester. Those acts—like many others involved in supervising court employees and overseeing the efficient operation of a court—may have been quite important in providing the necessary conditions of a sound adjudicative system. The decisions at issue, however, were not themselves judicial or adjudicative. As Judge Posner pointed out below, a judge who hires or fires a probation officer cannot meaningfully be distinguished from a district attorney who hires and fires assistant district attorneys, or indeed from any other executive branch official who is responsible for making such employment decisions. Such decisions, like personnel decisions made by judges, are often crucial to the efficient operation of public institutions (some of which are at least as important as the courts), yet no one suggests that they give rise to absolute immunity from liability in damages under § 1983.

The majority below thought that the threat of vexatious lawsuits by disgruntled ex-employees could interfere with the quality of a judge's decisions. There is considerable force in this analysis, but it in no way serves to distinguish judges from other public officials who hire and fire subordinates. Indeed, to the extent that a judge is less free than most executive branch officials to delegate decisionmaking authority to subordinates, there may be somewhat less reason to cloak judges with absolute immunity from such suits than there would be to protect such other officials. This does not imply that qualified immunity, like that available to executive branch officials who make similar discretionary decisions, is unavailable to judges for their employment decisions. Absolute immunity, however, is "strong medicine, justified only when the danger of [officials' being] deflect[ed from the effective performance of their duties] is very great." The danger here is not great enough. Nor do we think it significant that, under Illinois law, only a judge can hire or fire probation officers. To conclude that, because a judge acts within the scope of his authority, such employment decisions are brought within the court's "jurisdiction," or converted into "judicial acts," would lift form above substance. Under Virginia law, only that State's judges could promulgate and enforce a Bar Code, but we nonetheless concluded that neither function was judicial in nature. See *Supreme Court of Virginia* v. *Consumers Union, supra.*

We conclude that Judge White was not entitled to absolute immunity for his decisions to demote and discharge Forrester. In so holding, we do not decide whether Judge White is entitled to a new trial, or whether he may be able to claim a qualified immunity for the acts complained of in Forrester's suit. The judgment of the Court of Appeals is reversed and the case is remanded for further proceedings consistent with this opinion.

It is so ordered.

Case Questions

1. What is the basis for the Court's decisions regarding which types of official acts will have absolute immunity and which will not?
2. Why didn't Judge White have absolute immunity in this case?

Ethical Issues in Administrative Law: Judicial Review and Policy

Today, administrative agencies wield an enormous amount of power. In recent years, there have been movements to curtail agency powers and to make them more responsive to the concerns of individuals and society.

The Freedom of Information Act and the Privacy Act are legislative attempts to meet the demand that agencies be more responsive to the public. Also in this category are the Government in the Sunshine Act, generally requiring agency meetings to be open to the public, and an executive order issued by President Jimmy Carter requiring that each federal regulation be written in plain English and signed by the person who drafted it.

"Deregulation," a tendency to cut back on the types of activities regulated by administrative agencies, began during the Carter administration and was greatly increased during the Reagan term. One example of deregulation is the abolition of an entire federal agency, the Civil Aeronautics Board (CAB). Deregulation represents a response to dissatisfaction with the extent to which administrative agencies have imposed burdens on society. The most common reasons for this dissatisfaction are the expense and time required to comply with government procedures. For example, compliance with Occupational Safety and Health Administration regulations has cost business millions of dollars; charges have been made that the procedures used by the Food and Drug Administration are so time-consuming and stringent that introduction of new life-saving drugs or procedures has been significantly delayed or prevented altogether. Proponents of deregulation have argued that the cost of administrative agency functioning is insufficiently offset by the benefits the agency confers on society.

Deregulation, however, is not universally regarded as a good thing. Opponents of deregulation cite the result of the deregulation of airline companies during the phase-out of the CAB: the major airlines "dumped" less profitable air routes, leaving many smaller cities with little or no air service, and they "bunched" their flight times, resulting in hours-long waits to take off and land at major airports during peak flying hours. The deregulation controversy has raised fundamental questions about the place and purpose of administrative agencies in society.

In addition to deregulation, federal budget cutbacks have reduced agency funding and in many instances have had the *de facto* effect of reducing agencies' power by decreasing their ability to operate. While some have applauded these cutbacks on the grounds that they free society from unnecessary expenses, others have complained that the cutbacks are dangerous, because they prevent such agencies as the Environmental Protection Agency and the Occupational Safety and Health Administration from adequately protecting people's health and safety.

Another area that has engendered controversy for almost as long as administrative agencies have existed is the relationship between the agencies and the industries they regulate. It is common for persons who work for an agency to leave it to go to work for a firm in the industry they were formerly regulating. For example, a former employee of the Environmental Protection Agency might get a job with a chemical company that produces toxic wastes. Some individuals develop a "revolving door" employment pattern: they switch back and forth between agency and private industry jobs. Opponents of close associations between agencies and business argue that they are unethical because the agencies will tend not to put the interests of the public first if they are too closely tied to business. Others argue that such associations may be helpful, because it gives the agencies a feel for the problems faced by the businesses.

The important concepts and terms in this chapter are listed below; page numbers have been provided for the key terms. By reading over each section you can assess your understanding of the chapter concepts and determine areas you may want to review.

Chapter Summary

1. Once an agency has taken final action, a court can review the agency action; this is called judicial review.
2. A person seeking judicial review must be a proper petitioner, which means that the petitioner must have exhausted all administrative remedies and must have standing, and the agency action must be ripe for judicial review.
3. A person seeking judicial review must state legal grounds for review and must show that the agency action was unconstitutional, or that the agency exceeded the scope of its enabling legislation, or that the agency used improper procedures in carrying out its administrative functions, or that the agency action was arbitrary, capricious, or an abuse of discretion.
4. Four legal doctrines that tend to restrict judicial review are comity, abstention, primary jurisdiction, and the substantial evidence rule.
5. Individual rights are protected by such federal statutes as the Freedom of Information Act, the Privacy Act, and the Government in the Sunshine Act.

6. The doctrine of sovereign immunity shields many administrative officials from lawsuits.

Key Terms

abstention 155
abuse of discretion 152
comity 155
exhaustion of administrative remedies 148
Freedom of Information Act 159
judicial review 148
primary jurisdiction 158
Privacy Act 160
remand 159
ripeness 152
sovereign immunity 160
standing 149
substantial evidence rule 158
trial *de novo* 159

Questions on Ethics

1. X formerly worked for Waste-Haulers, Inc., a company whose primary function consists of disposing of toxic wastes. X is appointed to a position in a state environmental protection agency, in a post where his primary duty will be regulating toxic waste disposers. Is it ethical to appoint X to such a position?
2. The effect of the substantial evidence rule is to ensure that administrative agencies almost always win court appeals of their actions. Is it ethical to have the law prejudiced in favor of the agency?
3. Taken together, the doctrines of comity, abstention, and exhaustion of remedies mean that, even if a person is being treated unfairly by an agency, that person cannot appeal to a court for help until the agency has finished acting. Are these doctrines ethical?
4. David Boyle, a Marine Corps helicopter pilot, drowned when his helicopter crashed into the sea. His estate sued Sikorsky Corporation, the manufacturer of the helicopter. In 1988, the United States Supreme Court held that, even though a jury found in favor of Boyle's estate on the question of defective design of the helicopter's escape hatch, the corporation was protected by the "military contractor defense," a kind of sovereign immunity. Even if it was legal for Sikorsky to escape liability on the grounds of immunity, was it ethical?
5. Stanley, a serviceman, volunteered for what was ostensibly a chemical warfare testing program, but which in fact was a test of the effects of the drug LSD. Due to taking LSD, Stanley underwent severe personality changes, resulting in his discharge from the Army and the breakup of his

marriage. In 1987, the Supreme Court held that, because of the doctrine of sovereign immunity, Stanley could not recover money damages for his injuries. Was it ethical for the Army to mislead Stanley about the true nature of the test he was volunteering for?

Questions on Law

1. Under United States law, any alien who has been deported and thereafter enters the United States is guilty of a felony. A group of Mexican nationals was arrested and deported after a group hearing at which they waived their rights to apply for suspension of deportation and to appeal. These same individuals were deported, but reentered the country and were arrested on felony charges. A court found that they had not knowingly waived their rights at the first deportation hearing. Could the Mexican nationals attack the legal validity of the original deportation proceedings? *United States* v. *Mendoza-Lopez,* 481 U.S. 828 (May 26, 1987).
2. "John Doe," a covert electronics technical for the CIA, was fired after he informed CIA officials that he was a homosexual. Federal law allows the director of the CIA to terminate any CIA employee whenever he deems such termination necessary or advisable in the interests of the United States. Doe sought judicial review of the CIA action. Should a court hear his case? *Webster* v. *Doe,* 56 U.S.L.W. 4568 (1988).
3. Consumer activist Ralph Nader was "bumped" from an Allegheny Airlines flight due to overbooking of the flight. Nader sued Allegheny for fraud in court. Allegheny responded by asserting that, under the doctrine of primary jurisdiction, Nader had to first ask for adjudication of the dispute by the Civil Aeronautics Board. What would be the result? *Nader* v. *Allegheny Airlines,* 426 U.S. 290 (1976).
4. The Food and Drug Administration (FDA) issued a regulation in final form requiring that the label of any drug contain both the proprietary name of the drug and its established (generic) name. Compliance with this regulation would cost the drug manufacturing companies millions of dollars. The drug companies felt that the FDA regulation was illegal, but it was questionable whether they could appeal the regulation before its effective date under the general rules of administrative law. If the companies did not appeal, they would be forced to spend millions to comply with an illegal regulation. What could the drug companies do? *Abbott Laboratories* v. *Gardner,* 387 U.S. 136 (1967).
5. The secretary of transportation decided to allow construction of a highway through a park. Opponents of the secretary's decision alleged that he had decided to allow construction because of pressures brought to bear on him by an influential member of a congressional committee. The opponents sued in court to overturn the secretary's decision. What would be the result? *D.C. Federation of Civic Associations* v. *Volpe,* 459 F.2d 1231 (D.C. Cir. 1972).

Suggested Readings

Ballam, ''The Occupational Safety and Health Act's Preemptive Effect on State Criminal Prosecutions of Employers for Workplace Deaths and Injurics,'' 26 *American Business Law Journal* 1 (1988).

Reed, ''The Sunshine Society and the Legal Regulation of Business Through Compulsory Disclosure,'' 16 *American Business Law Journal* 83 (1977).

Zollers, ''Rethinking the Government Contract Defense,'' 24 *American Business Law Journal* 404 (1986).

2 The Legal Environment of Business Transactions

7 Property Law

> *Law is the witness and external deposit of our moral life. Its history is the history of the moral development of the race.*
>
> *—Oliver Wendell Holmes, Jr.*

■ LEARNING OBJECTIVES

After you have read this chapter, you should be able to:

1. Distinguish between real, personal, and intellectual property.
2. Describe the major processes for transferring ownership of real property.
3. Describe the ways ownership of personal property can be acquired.
4. Describe the forms of legal protection for intellectual property.

The Law and Business Decisions

Commercial Tenants/Fixtures

You have just rented space in a small shopping center to operate a gourmet butcher shop. The lease says nothing about who will the things anything you attach to the rented property. You need to install refrigerated display counters. These are cemented to the floor, wired into the electrical system, and plumbed into the cold water line. Your concern is that a friend of yours installed a dishwasher in his apartment and at the end of the lease the landlord was able to prevent her from removing it. The dishwasher was only worth about $350 but your display counters are worth $9,000 each. Will the landlord own them at the end of the lease? The material in this chapter will help you answer this and similar questions.

Introduction

Generally, when you, as an individual, join a *group,* it is because your desires coincide with those of the group. Occasions often arise, however, when the desires of the individual differ from, or conflict with, those of the group.

This conflict between the individual and the group occurs frequently on several levels in all societies. The way it is resolved accounts for basic differences between economic systems such as capitalism and socialism, between political systems such as democracy and communism, between philosophical systems such as egoism and utilitarianism, and between styles of managing and interacting with others.

All societies try to advance "the common good"; that is, they try to improve the welfare of the society. While all societies share this goal, they differ dramatically on the extent to which they emphasize the individual good and the collective good as means for achieving the common good. In some societies, most decisions are made by asking whether the decision will directly advance the interests of the group or collective. In other societies, there is more of a willingness to see the individual as a *vehicle* for improving the welfare of the group. Thus, each society has a different conception of the rights of the individual and the rights of the group.

A nation's property law usually reflects its basic attitude about individual and group rights. For example, the property law of socialist countries is based on the idea that property should be held for the benefit of *all* citizens rather than for the benefit of particular individuals. In these countries, only the government can own the "means of production." In capitalist societies, however, the means of production are owned by individuals. Capitalists generally believe that the common good is advanced when individual self-interest is channeled, perhaps somewhat indirectly, toward the common good.

The most widely recognized justification for private ownership of property was articulated by John Locke. Locke makes an argument grounded on natural law. He wrote:

> Whether we consider natural reasons . . . or revelation . . . it is very clear that God . . . "has given the earth to the children of men," given it to mankind in common. Though the earth and all inferior creatures be common to all men, yet every man has a property in his own person; this nobody has any right to but himself. Whatsoever then he removes out of the state that nature has provided and left it in, he has mixed his labor with, and joined to it something that is his own, and thereby makes it his property.

A more modern—and clearly utilitarian—justification for private ownership has been articulated by Richard Poser. In his book, *Economic Analysis of Law,* he writes:

> Imagine a society in which all property rights have been abolished. A farmer plants corn, fertilizes it, and erects scarecrows, but when the corn is ripe his neighbor reaps it and sells it. The farmer has no legal remedy against his neighbor's conduct since he owns neither the land that he sowed nor the crop. After a few such incidents the cultivation of land will be abandoned and the society will shift to methods of subsistence (such as hunting) that involve less preparatory investment.
>
> This example suggests that the legal protection of property rights has an important economic function: to create incentives to use resources efficiently. . . .
>
> The creation of exclusive rights is a necessary rather than sufficient condition for the efficient use of resources. The rights must be transferable. Suppose the farmer in our example owns the land that he sows but is a bad farmer; his land would be more productive in someone else's hands. The maximization of value requires a mechanism by which the farmer can be induced to transfer rights in the property to someone who can work it more productively. A transferable right is such a mechanism. . . .
>
> The foregoing discussion suggests three criteria of an efficient system of property rights. The first is universality. Ideally, all resources should be owned, or ownable, by someone, except resources so plentiful that everybody can consume as much of them as he wants without reducing consumption by anyone else.
>
> The second criterion—is exclusivity. We have assumed so far that either the farmer can exclude no one or he can exclude everyone, but of course there are intermediate stages: the farmer may be entitled to exclude private individuals from reaping his crop, but not the government in time of war. It might appear that the more exclusive the property right, the greater the incentive to invest the right amount of resources in the development of the property.
>
> The third criterion of an efficient system of property rights is transferability. If a property right cannot be transferred, there is no way of shifting a resource from a less productive to a more productive use through voluntary exchange. The costs of transfer may be high to begin with; a legal prohibition against transferring may, depending on the penalties for violation, make the costs utterly prohibitive.

As you read through the material in this chapter, especially the law of intellectual property, you will see the way this nation's legal system balances the interest of "mankind in common" with that of the individual to achieve the common good.

Basic Categories of Property Law

The law of our country recognizes several classes of property. These classes generally determine which particular body of law will govern the ownership, transfer of ownership, taxation, and financing of the property. The major categories of property are real property, personal property, and intellectual property. For example, land is real property, cars are personal property, and a patent would be intellectual property. Differing rules of law are used to determine who is the owner of land, or cars, or patents.

Intellectual Property

Intellectual property is *intangible* (i.e., you can't touch it) and often created and defined by law. This chapter will discuss patents, trade secrets, copyrights, and trademarks. A patent protects inventions. The ballpoint pen is an invention that was protected by a patent. Trade secrets are items of information such as customer lists, formulae, even recipes, that are useful to a business and kept secret by the business. Thus the exact formula for making Coca Cola may be a trade secret. A copyright protects original works, such as books, advertisements, musical works, and radio or television shows. A trademark is a name used to distinguish some goods from others. For example, Coca Cola is a trademark.

Real Property

Land and things immovably attached to the land, such as buildings, are real property, or **realty.** The basic test for identifying real property is whether a tangible thing is moveable in a practical sense. A house can be moved, but because of the great effort required to do so, the law views it as immobile. Similarly, something permanently attached to a house, such as an under-the-counter dishwasher, is viewed as immobile and is therefore real property.

Personal Property

Generally, personal property, or personalty, is something that is tangible (i.e., something you can touch) and mobile. Cars, ships, airplanes, shoes, and blackboard chalk are personal property because they are tangible and mobile.

Many items of tangible property change legal status with differing uses. For example, wood is realty while a part of a tree still in the ground, personalty when cut into two-by-four studs, and realty when nailed into the frame of a house under construction. Because tangible property can shift status, the law has evolved other tests besides mobility to distinguish real and personal property in close cases.

Distinguishing Real from Personal Property

When the basic test of mobility is difficult to apply, we categorize things as real or personal using the more refined tests of annexation, adaptation, and intention. If a thing—like a built-in stove—that was once personal becomes real property, we call it a **fixture.**

The **annexation** test is a refinement of the basic test of mobility. If something tangible is permanently attached to realty, it is considered a part of the realty. If it is not permanently attached to the realty, then it is mobile and usually considered personalty. Structures or buildings are part of the real property only if they are permanently attached to the land. Thus, a house trailer sitting on its wheels is usually considered personal property. If, when a thing is removed from a structure, the removal damages the structure, the thing is probably realty. A free-standing stove is personalty, but a built-in stove is realty under the test of annexation.

The importance of a thing to the functioning of a structure may cause it to be treated as real property. Thus if a thing is essential to the operation of a building, it may be real property even though it is not permanently attached. This is the test of **adaptation.** For example, an electric forced-air furnace that merely sits on the floor, is plugged into an electrical outlet, and slides into a mating sheet metal duct is not permanently attached to the structure, but it is adapted because it is so essential to the functioning of the structure. Similarly, keys to the house are considered realty in several states under the test of adaptation.

The **intention** of the person attaching something to a structure may determine whether the thing is real or personal. If a landlord and tenant agree that a built-in dishwasher installed by the tenants can be removed at the end of the lease, then *with respect to these two parties* it will be treated as personalty. In the absence of such an agreement, the built-in dishwasher would be treated as realty.

The fixtures attached by business tenants are called **trade fixtures.** They are treated not as realty, but as personalty, because the courts presume the parties intend that they are not permanently attached. The refrigerated display counters installed by a tenant in the butcher business would be personal even if plumbed, wired, and bolted to the floor so that they would pass the test of annexation.

Introduction to Real Property Law

Components of Realty

Real property consists of both a bundle of *legal rights and duties* and certain *physical* components. The structures and fixtures we have discussed are physical components of realty. The other major components are:

Land. The basic physical element of realty is land. The basic legal right related to ownership of land is called a **surface right;** it is the right to occupy the surface of a land parcel.

Mineral rights. In addition, the earth beneath the surface is part of the realty. The right to dig or mine that earth is called a **mineral right.** One person may own the surface rights while another owns the mineral rights. In theory, the mineral rights extend to the center of the earth.

Air rights. The air space above the surface of the land, extending to the upper atmosphere, is also part of the realty. Ownership of that space is called the

right to air space. If the branch of a neighbor's tree grows into your air space, your right to air space would be violated and you would have the right to compel its removal.

Water rights. Water on the surface or under the ground is also part of the realty. Control of the water by a landowner is called a **water right.** Because water flows across and under land, the owner's control is not as absolute as his control of surface rights, mineral rights, and air space. An owner generally could not divert the path of a canal, ditch, or river and change its course through other property downstream.

Legal Components of Realty Freehold Estates

Every owner of realty possesses some ownership powers. But all owners do not have the same bundle of powers. For instance, some owners do not have the right to occupy their realty. The powers of ownership are determined by the **estate in land** that a new owner receives. The words used in the deed, lease, will, or other instrument transferring ownership determine which estate the new owner receives. (In legal terminology, the transfer of ownership is called a **conveyance.**) Each estate is composed of a distinct bundle of the ownership powers. Of course, one owner cannot convey to someone else an ownership power that he does not own.

One parcel of land usually supports only a single estate. Most owner-occupied homes, for example, involve just one estate. Occasionally, however, two or more estates exist in the same physical parcel. Thus, both the landlord and the tenant own estates in a rented apartment. The tenant's ownership rights include the right to occupy the property. The landlord's ownership rights include the power to collect the rent and regain possession at the end of the lease.

A **fee simple absolute** estate is an estate with all the ownership powers. The owner of this estate exercises all the power allowed by law, so there can be no other estate in the same land. Most buyers of homes and farms and commercial property purchase the fee simple absolute estate.

Conditional estates make ownership conditional on some act or event. For example, *A*, the owner of a fee simple absolute estate may sell and convey to *B*, "only so long as no barn is built on the premises." In this illustration, if a barn were built, ownership would revert back to *A*. Thus the seller retains some powers, and therefore the buyer receives less than fee simple absolute.

Whenever there is a conditional estate, or any estate less than fee simple absolute, there must be another corresponding estate. This second estate is usually retained by the party selling the conditional estate.

A **life estate** is ownership for a time limited by the length of a human life, so this owner exercises all the ownership powers except the right to convey permanent ownership. The length of the ownership period is generally measured by the life of the holder of the life estate. For example, a husband might convey, "to my wife Julia, for life." Julia's life estate will last as long as Julia is alive. On her death, it will revert back to her husband. Occasionally a life estate lasts for the life of one other than the owner.

Future interest estates usually grant the owner possession of the realty when a life or conditional estate terminates. In the previous example, Julia's husband owned a future interest during the time Julia owned the life estate. On Julia's death her life estate would *merge* with the husband's future interest so that the husband would then own fee simple absolute.

Legal Components of Realty: Leasehold Estates

The landlord-tenant relationship arises when the owner of a **freehold estate** (e.g., fee simple absolute, a conditional estate, or a life estate) transfers to another the right to temporarily possess the realty. Generally, the right of *possession* is given in exchange for the payment of *rent*. The temporary transfer of the right of possession is referred to as **demising** or **leasing** the property. Since the transfer of possession is temporary, the owner of the freehold will eventually regain possession. This power to regain possession is called the *right of reversion*. The owner of the freehold is called the *landlord* or *lessor*, and the party receiving the temporary right of possession is called the *tenant* or *lessee*. After transfer, the tenant is said to own a **leasehold estate.** (See figure 7.1.)

If a landlord-tenant relationship comes into being, the law will classify it as an estate at sufferance, an estate at will, a periodic estate, or an estate for years. The distinctions among the types of estates are important because the estates are terminated differently.

Figure 7.1 Creation and Termination of a One Year Leasehold Estate

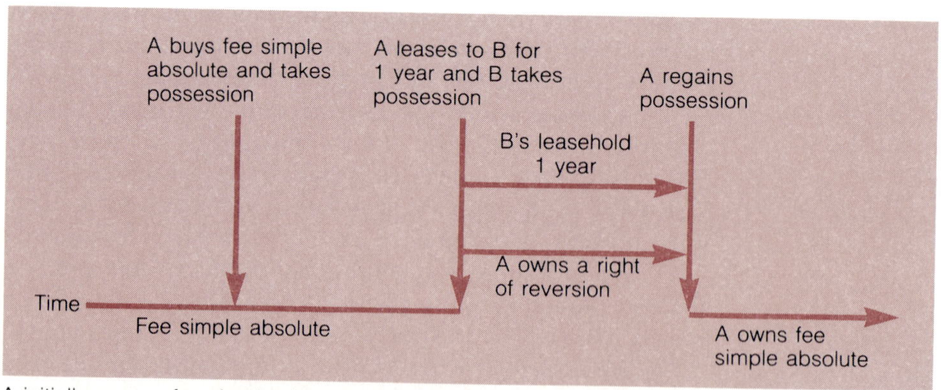

A initially owns a fee simple absolute; during the period of the lease A owns the reversion and is then referred to as the landlord or lessor.

B is the owner for one year of the leasehold estate and is the tenant or lessee.

The property is said to have been demised or leased or rented.

Estate at Sufferance. This **estate at sufferance** arises when one rightfully takes possession of property as a lessee, but then remains in possession *after* termination of the lease. A few states allow landlords to use self-help eviction if no force is used. But most states require notice of termination of an estate at sufferance and permit eviction only by a police officer after a lawsuit.

Estate at Will. When someone takes possession of the realty with the landlord's consent, but *without* entering into an oral or written lease, he or she owns an **estate at will.** This usually occurs when the parties agree that the prospective tenant can move in and that the lease will be negotiated later.

This landlord-tenant relationship can be terminated at any time by either party. Some states protect the lessee by requiring notice before eviction.

Periodic Estate. This relationship arises when the parties agree on the terms and conditions of lease but *do not specify its term (length).* For example, the parties may agree that the rent is "five dollars per day payable monthly in advance." There is a clear implication in this language that the lease is intended to run for longer than one month, yet the lease specifies no ending date. The law allows this tenant a **periodic estate.** In general, this estate continues for the *length of the payment period* and is automatically renewed unless one party gives adequate notice of termination. Often the notice of termination must equal the length of the payment period. Thus, where rent is paid every two months, most states would require a two-month notice to terminate.

The main characteristic of periodic leases is their flexibility. Since either the landlord or tenant can terminate, in most instances with a thirty-day notice, the terms of the lease are open to easy revision. For example, a landlord who wants to raise the rent 30 percent can submit a new lease to the tenant. For all practical purposes, the tenant must accept it or be forced to leave within about thirty days. On the other hand, the student who rented a periodic estate in the worst apartment in town on the first day of classes can easily move out in the middle of the semester when more attractive accommodations become available.

Estate for Years. This estate arises when the parties *agree on the beginning date and ending date for the lease*. The term ***estate for years*** is misleading because it can be for any length of time, such as one week, or two months, or 340 days, or five years. Because the parties know the date when the lease ends, no notice is required to terminate. Further, neither the landlord nor the tenant may terminate the lease without cause before the agreed termination date. Thus, if a student executed a nine-month lease and moved out after three months, he or she might be liable for six months' rent! That liability arises only when the landlord has used reasonable efforts to rerent but has not found a new tenant. If a new tenant rerents after a vacancy of three months, the original tenant will be liable for the amount of rent for the three months' vacancy. (See figure 7.2.)

Figure 7.2 Methods of Terminating Leasehold Estates

Estate	Self-Help Dispossession?	Notice Required to Terminate?	Termination on Death of Party?	Termination When Landlord Sells?
At sufferance	Yes*	No*	Yes	Yes
At will	No	No*	Yes	Yes
Periodic	No	Yes	No	No
Years	No	No	No	No

*Only in some states.

Holdover Tenants. Frequently tenants remain in possession after termination of the estate. When this occurs, the landlord generally has a choice of several remedies.

The holdover tenant can be **evicted**—that is, forceably removed from the property by the sheriff. Further, the tenant is liable for reasonable rent for the holdover period. In some states the landlord can collect double or triple rent for the holdover period.

If the tenant holds over, the landlord may elect to compel the tenant to remain. This is an alternative to eviction. In general, the tenant will thereby become liable for rent for a period equal to the length of the original term. Thus, if Harvey rented an apartment to Suzie for one year to terminate on January 1, and Suzie held over until January 3, Harvey could, in some states, treat her as his tenant for the remainder of the second year. If, however, Suzie had a month-to-month tenancy and held over, she would be liable for only one month's rent.

Co-Ownership

Co-ownership exists when an estate is owned by more than one party. Thus, two persons may buy a home together and become co-owners of the realty. There are several types of co-ownership, and each regulates the relations among the co-owners differently. But all methods of co-ownership have a common characteristic; all co-owners have equal rights to occupy all of the property. One co-owner may not exclude any other co-owner from any portion of their property. The major types of co-ownership for individuals are tenancy in common, joint tenancy, tenancy by entirety, and community property.

Tenancy in common regulates the relationship among the co-owners in a variety of ways. For example, if one tenant in common dies, her interest usually passes to the persons named in her will. Any number may co-own as tenants in common, and they may own unequal percentages. One may own 98 percent while two other co-owners each own 1 percent. Tenants in common may sell or mortgage their interest without the other co-owners' consent.

On the death of a **joint tenant,** his or her interest is evenly divided among the remaining joint tenants. This is called the **right of survivorship.** Any number may own as joint tenants, but each must have an equal interest. Thus, if there are four joint tenants, each must own 25 percent. Joint tenants, like tenants in common, may sell or mortgage their interest without the co-owners' consent.

Tenancy by entirety is only for married couples. If the couple is divorced or separated, tenancy by entirety is transformed into tenancy in common. Tenancy by entirety includes the right of survivorship. Each spouse must own a 50 percent interest. Aside from the requirement of marriage, tenancy by entirety is distinguished from joint tenancy only by the fact that each spouse must consent to any mortgaging or sale of the other spouse's interest.

Some western states recognize **community property** as a substitute for tenancy by entirety. Again, this method of co-ownership is only for married couples. In these states, property acquired during marriage is generally presumed to be community property. However, property owned by one spouse before marriage, or received during the marriage by gift or inheritance, is presumed to be that person's separate property.

Depending upon the laws of the particular community property state, a surviving spouse automatically receives either all or one-half of the deceased spouse's interest in the community property. Like joint tenants and tenants by entirety, each must own the same percentage. Often, both spouses must consent to any conveyance or mortgaging of community real property. Figure 7.3 summarizes the legal characteristics of these forms of co-ownership.

Figure 7.3 Legal Characteristics

Type of Co-ownership	Legal Characteristics					
	Right to occupy all the realty	Ownership interests must be equal	Consent required from co-owners for sale of interest	*All* interest passes to co-owners on death	Interest willable, but if not willed passes to co-owners on death	Only available to married couples
Tenants in common	✓					
Joint tenants	✓	✓		✓		
Tenants by entirety	✓	✓	✓	✓		✓
Community property	✓	✓	✓		✓	✓

The following case illustrates the way the law tries to prevent the right of survivorship from being abused.

In re Estate of Michael

218 A.2d 388 (Pa. 1966)

Facts

The owners of the King farm executed a deed transferring ownership to four persons (two married couples). The part of the deed which identified the persons receiving the farm and their form of co-ownership stated:

> *Harry L. Michael and Bertha M. Michael, his wife, tenants by the entireties and Ford W. Michael and Helen M. Michael, his wife, as tenants by the entireties, with right of survivorship.*

Harry and Bertha died, leaving their interests to a son, Robert. When Robert tried to assert ownership, he was sued by Ford and Helen. They claimed that as between the married persons, tenancy by the entirety existed. But between the couples, the form of co-ownership was joint tenancy. If it was joint tenancy, then all the ownership interest would be in Ford and Helen with Robert owning nothing. Robert responded by claiming that the form of co-ownership between the couples was tenancy in common. If it was tenancy in common, Robert would own a one-half interest in the farm. The trial court held for Ford and Helen and Robert appealed.

Opinion

Justice Jones: . . . At common law, joint tenancies were favored, and the doctrine of survivorship was a recognized incident to a joint estate. The courts of the United States have generally been opposed to the creation of such estates, the presumption being that all tenants hold . . . as tenants in common, unless a clear intention to the contrary is shown. . . .

In Pennsylvania, by the Act of 1812 [68 P.S. §110.], the incident of survivorship in joint tenancies was eliminated unless the instrument creating the estate expressly provided that such incident should exist. The Act . . . does not *forbid* creation of a joint tenancy if the language creating it *clearly* expresses that intent. . . .

[I]n order to engraft the right of survivorship on a co-tenancy which might otherwise be a tenancy in common, the intent to do so must be expressed with sufficient clarity to overcome the statutory presumption that survivorship is not intended . . . . Whether or not survivorship was intended is to be gathered from the instrument and its language . . ., but no particular form of words is required to manifest such intention. . . .

The phrase, "with right of survivorship," is capable, as appellant properly urges, of at least three possible interpretations: (1) explanatory of the one of the incidents of the estate, known as tenancy by the entirety; (2) explanatory of the one tenancy by the entirety, the creation of which it follows; or (3), as the appellee and the lower court contend, indicative of the creation of a right of survivorship as between the two sets of spouses. Any one of these interpretations is a *possibility* but deciding which was intended by the parties would involve nothing but a mere guess. Such ambiguous terminology falls far short of the *clear* expression of intent required to overcome the statutory presumption.

Nowhere in the deed is the term "joint tenants" employed. To create a right of survivorship the *normal* procedure is to employ the phrase "joint tenants, with a right of survivorship, and not as tenants in common" in describing the manner in which the grantees are to take or hold the property being conveyed or transferred. . . .

We cannot find within the four corners of this deed a *clearly* expressed intention to create a joint tenancy with the right of survivorship. Having failed to find a *clear* intention to overcome the statutory presumption against such estates, the Act of 1812 compels us to find that the deed of 1947 created a tenancy in common as between the two sets of married couples, each couple holding its undivided one-half interest as tenants by the entireties.

[Judgment reversed.]

Case Questions

1. What do you think was the true intent of the person who gave ownership to the Michaels? What evidence supports your belief?
2. Why do you think the legislature of Pennsylvania enacted a statute making it difficult to create joint tenancy? Can you see any way that this form of co-ownership could be used to cheat someone in the absence of such a statute?
3. Do you think it is ethical for the law to shift the focus away from the intent of the party executing the deed and to create a presumption against joint tenancy?

Others' Rights in the Owner's Realty

Someone who owns an estate in land that includes the right of possession may sometimes give some possessory right in the land to others. The following paragraphs discuss some of these powers that owners may give to others.

A theatre owner may grant someone the right to sit through one showing of a film. This kind of temporary written or oral right to come upon the realty of another is called a **license.** Store owners grant implied licenses to their customers to enter their stores to shop for goods. Dinner guests are on the host's property by right of a license. Generally, licenses are *revocable*. A student taking a class at a college is a licensee; if she is asked to leave, the student has her license revoked and must leave the realty of the college.

Easements are usually *irrevocable* rights to some limited use of another's realty. In contrast with licenses, easements are given for either substantial periods of time, say ten years, or permanently. To comply with the Statute of Frauds they must be in writing. Easements may be granted that allow another person to drive across the owner's land, bury a sewer line, hang power lines over the land, or make any other use that does not constitute exclusive possession.

Even when the owner of realty purchases fee simple absolute, she may still be prohibited from certain uses. This occurs when a **restrictive covenant** is created. A restrictive covenant is a promise by the owner, or by a former owner, that limits her use of the land in some way. It is frequently written into the deed. For example, if the buyer promises the seller, in the deed, that she will not graze sheep on the land, this becomes a restrictive covenant.

When a party other than the owner has a financial claim against the value of any estate, that party is said to have a **lien.** A lien generally allows the lien holder to cause the sale of the estate if the debt is not paid. Mortgages, trust deeds, and land sale contracts are voluntary liens against realty that owners usually grant in return for a loan to purchase the property. These are discussed in detail in chapter 23, "Debtor/Creditor Relations." Judgment liens, tax liens, and mechanic's liens are involuntary. They can arise when someone has a legal claim against an owner of an estate. If the claim is not voluntarily paid by the owner, it can be asserted involuntarily against the estate—usually after a trial.

The owner's use of realty can also be restricted by zoning ordinances. These ordinances may be adopted by cities or counties to regulate the location of residential, business, industrial, and agricultural districts. The purpose of zoning is to ensure fair use and orderly development of land within the community. The zoning power is very broad, and courts usually support the right of cities and counties to enforce community zoning goals at the expense of individual landowners. For example, a commercial area could be rezoned residential. If this zoning reduced the value of the owner's land, she would bear the loss and could not recover for the financial injury from the local government.

Transferring Ownership of Realty—The Deeding Process

The deed is the principal document used in transferring ownership of realty. Usually, a deed is a single piece of paper. Figure 7.4 presents a deed document. You may find it helpful to refer to it while reading the rest of this section. The law does not acknowledge a transfer of ownership simply because you process a deed; it only recognizes an ownership shift if the whole *deeding process* is completed. The elements of this process are execution, delivery, and acceptance.

Execution refers to the format, language, signing, and notarizing of the deed document. Notarizing involves marking signed documents in a way that indicates an official of the state has determined that the signatures are valid.

Delivery involves transferring possession of a properly executed deed to the buyer with the intention of shifting ownership. Thus, if a mother executed a deed in favor of a son, but left the deed in her safety deposit box until after her death, the deed would not transfer ownership because there was no transfer of possession. Further, if a deed were delivered only as security for a debt, ownership would not be transferred because there was no intention to shift ownership.

Acceptance means that the buyer indicates his willingness to assume ownership. Retaining the deed after delivery usually constitutes acceptance.

Types of Deeds

When the words of conveyance (see Figure 7.4, section two) in a deed state, "convey and warrant," this indicates that the grantor (the one giving up ownership) promises, or *warrants,* to the grantee (the one receiving ownership):

1. That the grantor owns and has the right to transfer the estate described in the deed, and will compensate the grantee if it turns out that the grantee does not receive all the ownership powers associated with that estate; and
2. That there are no liens, leases, easements, mortgages, or other claims against the property aside from those disclosed in the deed.

Deeds of this type are called **warranty deeds.** They are the kind most frequently used.

The other major type of deed is called the **quitclaim deed.** The word of

Figure 7.4 Warranty Deed

Warranty Deed

(1)

TERRY D. ALGER and KAYE L. ALGER, grantor(s) Husband and Wife of City and County of Denver, State of Colorado, hereby CONVEY and WARRANT to

(2) (3)

Edward J. Conry and Anne L. Conry, grantee husband and wife as joint tenants and not as tenants in common, with full rights of survivorship,

of **City of Blissfield, State of Michigan**

(4)

for the sum of Ten Dollars ($10.00) and other valuable consideration

the following described tract of land in Denver, Colorado:

(5) **Lot 14, Unit #8, HIDDEN VILLAGE Subdivision as shown by the official plat of said subdivision filed 4 April 1973 as Filing No. 372227 in the office of the Recorder of the county of Denver.**

(6) **Subject to all liens and encumbrances of record.**

(7) WITNESS, the hand of said grantor, this 11th day of July, A.D. 1989

Signed in the presence of

______________________ Terry D. Alger

______________________ Kaye L. Alger

______________________ ______________________

STATE OF UTAH,
ss.
County of Denver

On the **11th day of July, A.D. 1989,** personally appeared before me Terry D. Alger and Kaye L. Alger, Husband and Wife the signers of the within instrument, who duly acknowledged to me that they executed the same.

P Notary
Notary Public.
Residing in Denver, Colorado

My commission expires **4-8-90**

Key to Deed Sections

1. Grantors' Names
2. Words of Conveyance
3. Grantees' Names
4. Consideration Statement
5. Property Description
6. Habendum
7. Signatures and Certification

conveyance for it states simply "quitclaim." This deed merely transfers the grantor's ownership, if any. No promises or warranties are implied in the quitclaim deed. Thus if you gave someone a quitclaim deed to property you did not own, you would not be liable to her for breach of a warranty.

In the absence of other indications, the law usually presumes that the grantor and grantee intended the conveyance of the fee simple absolute estate. Conditional and life estates can usually be identified by examining the words of conveyance in the deed. For example, the words, "convey and warrant so long as no sheep are grazed on the land" would transfer a conditional estate. The words "quitclaim for life" would convey only a life estate.

Parts of the Deed

Aside from identifying the grantees, the deed identifies the form of co-ownership, if it exists, and each co-owner's percentage of ownership. Deeds usually describe only the physical boundaries of the parcel of land in legal terms. Street addresses and farm names generally do not qualify as legal descriptions. All the realty, but not the personal property, within the boundary of the legal description is transferred by the deeding process. So although the deed only describes land, the buildings and fixtures on the land are also conveyed.

An *encumbrance* is a financial or possessory claim against realty. A lien is one type of encumbrance. A lease is another type. In warranty deeds the grantor must identify all of the encumbrances that will affect the grantee's estate.

The deeding process is the most common way of transferring ownership of realty. Usually deeding occurs in the context of a sale. Deeds can also be used in transfers of ownership by gift, or by will. There are several other methods, used in unusual circumstances, for transferring ownership of realty. One of these is **condemnation**—where a government takes title from an owner involuntarily on payment of reasonable compensation. Another is **adverse possession,** which can transfer ownership when one publicly treats land as his own for a substantial period of time without opposition. The following case illustrates the way adverse possession cases arise and the way they are treated by the courts.

Ford v. Eckert

406 N.E.2d 1209 (Ind. Ct. App. 1980)

Facts

Two parcels of property in Birdseye, Indiana, were separated by a fence, but the fence was not on the property line. Rather it intruded into one property by a substantial distance. The Grants owned the property that was apparently increased in size because of the misplaced fence. They owned the property from 1938 to 1946. The Grants assumed the fence marked the true boundary and mowed and took care of all the property up to the fence. In 1946, the Grants sold the property to Ford. She continued to care for all the property up to the fence. Sometime before 1960 the fence was removed but Ford continued to care for the property up to the place where the fence had been. In 1960 Eckert bought the adjoining property that was reduced in size because of the misplaced fence. A survey was done. It revealed that the true boundary line was not where the fence had been. So Eckert claimed ownership of the strip of land between the true boundary and the old fence line. Ford responded by filing suit for adverse possession. The trial court found for Eckert and Ford appealed.

Opinion

Robertson, Presiding Judge: In order to establish title by adverse possession, Ford has to show her possession to be actual, visible, open and notorious, exclusive, under claim of ownership, hostile and continuous for the statutory period. ***

Prior to 1951, the applicable statute of limitations for adverse possession was 20 years, Since Eckert bought the property in 1960, and testified that she never acquiesced in ownership actions by Ford, Ford must show that the land was adversely possessed prior to Eckert's purchase of the property. It is clear that the statutory period need not be maintained by one person, but that successive periods may be tacked together to attain the necessary period. Here, Ford purchased the property in 1946. To prevail, she must present evidence as to the adverse possession of the same property by a prior owner. This is accomplished by tacking the eight years that the Grants were in possession, 1938–1946. From Grant's testimony, it is apparent that the Grants exercised the same control and ownership over the disputed area as did Ford. ***

A mere mistake in fact does not render the possession any less adverse. Here, Ford and her predecessors clearly intended to claim all the land up to the fence. They acted as if they were the sole owners of the property by maintaining it and using the land for its normal purpose. These facts evidence Ford and her predecessors' intent to claim title to the land. The fact that they believed the land to actually be theirs does not negate a conclusion that the possession was adverse. Consequently, we find the statutory requirements to be met.

We hold, therefore, that the facts presented show title to the land had passed to Ford prior to the acquisition of the property by Eckert.

Judgment reversed in favor of Ford.

Case Questions

1. Why should the law allow someone to acquire ownership of someone else's land by adverse possession? Can you think of a rational policy that justifies the doctrine of adverse possession?
2. The federal government has enacted a law that makes it impossible to adversely possess its land. Is it fair to treat the federal government in one way and the individuals another?
3. If you think about it you may be able to see ways to cheat neighboring absentee land owners out of their property by adversely possessing their property. If you saw a way to do this that would make $50,000 for you, do you believe it would be right? Would you do it?

Recording

Recording is the process of filing a document related to realty with the county clerk, or recorder, or commissioner of documents. Deeds, mortgages, land sales contracts, easements, and liens are among the many documents usually recorded. In general, recording influences **priority** and gives **notice.**

Priority determines the order in which claims against the realty are satisfied. Thus if there are two mortgages recorded against a property, and the owner defaults on the payments, the property can be sold but the first recorded mortgage will be paid completely before any funds are applied to the second. Also, if an owner gives two deeds for the same realty to different persons, the first grantee to record will, in most states, usually become the final owner. This is so even if he received the second deed.

Every buyer of realty is assumed by the law to have *notice* of all claims recorded against the property. This is true even though the buyer did not actually know of the claim and did not examine the public record. Thus, if an easement is recorded against a property later bought for development into a housing tract, the developer is bound by the easement even if it makes her development impossible.

Also, if a claim against property, such as a mortgage, is not recorded, and the property is sold, the buyer generally takes the property free of the claim.

The following case raises issues involving the definition of real and personal property, deeding, and recording.

Bailey v. Kruithoff

280 So. 2d 262 (1973)

Facts

Convie D. Bailey II brought this suit to recover the sum of $688.77 from defendant, Neal Kruithoff, for the alleged wrongful removal of 1,500 feet of barbed wire fence, with one hundred and fifty creosote posts from plaintiff's property.

The facts relating to the removal of the fence are undisputed. Defendant [Kruithoff] leased the seven and one-half acres of pasture land in Bossier Parish from Mrs. Sandy on November 27, 1970, for $15 per year. As part of their agreement, Mrs. Sandy, in a separate written instrument, gave defendant permission to remove, at the termination of the lease, a fence and hay shed he might construct on the property. This agreement was never recorded. *Defendant erected a four-strand barbed wire fence consisting of approximately one hundred fifty fence posts on the property and used the land to graze several head of cattle.*

On January 27, 1972, plaintiff [Bailey] purchased the seven and one-half acres from Mrs. Sandy. The deed contained no reservations and made no mention of the agreement between defendant and Mrs. Sandy concerning defendant's right to remove the fence. Plaintiff's uncontradicted testimony at the trial was that he had negotiated for some time by phone with Mrs. Sandy, who lived in El Paso, Texas, before the sale was finalized and at no time during these negotiations did she ever mention the agreement with the defendant concerning his right to remove the fence. He stated she merely told him of the lease to the defendant and that it was to terminate in December 1971.

Approximately three weeks after the sale, defendant came onto the property and physically removed the fence, except for about eight of the posts which he had to break off just above the ground because they were embedded in concrete. In addition, during this three-week period following the sale defendant continued to graze twelve to fifteen head of cattle on the property.

Opinion

The issue is whether defendant had the right to remove the fence. The decision depends on whether the fence is classified as a movable or an immovable.

Article 464 of the Louisiana Civil Code defines an immovable by nature as follows: "Land and buildings or other constructions, whether they have their foundations in the soil or not, are immovable by their nature."

The resolution of the issue . . . depends on the interpretation of the term "other constructions." . . . Some of the various objects which have been included within the definition of "other constructions" under Article 464 are: railroad trackage, . . . a brooder for beagle puppies 25 × 5 × 4 feet and a chicken brooder 10 × 5 × 4 feet, each set on 4 × 4 inch posts in the ground and a gas tank. . . .

Immovability by nature has been characterized as a creation of the law based on practical considerations and on inherent characteristics of the things concerned. What is a building or other construction qualifying as an immovable under

Article 464 is left for judicial determination according to prevailing notions in society. Two criteria that are often mentioned in decisions of the court are some degree of integration or attachment to the soil and some degree of permanency.

In this case, the fence was embedded in the ground—a few of the posts were in concrete—and thereby integrated with the soil. Pasture fences are generally regarded as permanent in nature.

The nature of a movable is generally such that its identity is not lost if it is moved from one location to another. Ordinarily, all that is necessary is to detach the object from its present location and move it elsewhere with no apparent diminution of its identification in the process. Certainly this is not true of a fence that has no identity as a fence until it has been *constructed.* Once constructed the fence becomes a component part of the land on which it is placed and as such must be regarded as an "other construction" and as an immovable by nature under Article 464. In order to move a fence it must be dismantled and its identity destroyed, which is inconsistent with any reasonable concept of a movable. . . .

We conclude that the fence involved in the case before us is an "other construction" under Article 464 and an immovable by nature. The fence was a "construction" under the ordinary, common sense meaning of that word. It was embedded in the soil, incorporated into the ground, and was a component part of the land. A fence is ordinarily regarded as having a degree of permanency—not to be readily moved about.

The agreement under which defendant retained the right to remove the fence was not recorded. The fence, together with the land, passed to plaintiff free and clear of defendant's unrecorded rights. Defendant had no right to come on the property after the sale to plaintiff and remove the fence, ownership of which was then vested in the plaintiff. Defendant is thus liable for the reasonable replacement cost of the fence he removed from plaintiff's property. The evidence shows this amount is $542.30.

Case Questions

1. How would you classify the fence using the tests of mobility or annexation? How would you classify the fence using the tests of intent or adaptation?
2. Would a different decision have been reached if the agreement about the fence had been recorded? Is the result of this decision fair? Does your answer to this last question depend upon your preference for natural or positive law?
3. If the deed only described the boundary of the land, would this also transfer a fence? Is there a conflict in the legal actions of Mrs. Sandy? Who will ultimately pay for the fence?

Introduction to Personal Property Law

Recall that personal property includes those tangible things that are mobile. Frequently this type of property is called a **chattel.** While some areas of personal property law are similar to the law of real property, others differ dramatically. The most significant difference is in the basic body of law that governs the sale of these classes of property. In general, real property sales are governed by the common law of contracts—a body of primarily state *case* laws. In contrast, sales of personal property are governed primarily by the Uniform Commercial Code—a body of state *statutory* law.

If a transaction involves primarily goods, rather than services or realty, then it is usually governed by the Uniform Commercial Code rather than by the common law of contracts. Many transactions involve both goods and services. An example would be a contract to paint a house, which includes charges for both labor and materials (the paint). These mixed transactions will be governed by the UCC if the goods are the dominant part of the sale, or by the common law of contracts if the services dominate. In this example, if the paint were billed at $450 and the labor at $750 for a total bill of $1,200, the whole transaction would be governed by the common law.

Acquiring Ownership of Personalty

Possession

You can obtain ownership of certain kinds of personalty merely by taking possession of the property. This can occur when the personal property is not owned by others. For example, *abandoned* property is available to the general public, and the first to take possession of the abandoned property will become its owner. Thus a Brittany Spaniel dog that has been truly abandoned can be acquired by taking possession. Similarly, when you go fishing and take possession of a rainbow trout, you acquire ownership because you have taken possession of property that no one owns.

Finding Property

If you find lost property, report the finding to certain public officials, and it is not claimed after a certain period of time, you will usually become the owner. There are two types of findings. Property is *mislaid* when its owner intentionally places it somewhere but later forgets the location. Suppose a student left her book on a shelf in the front of your bookstore while shopping, but forgot about it and walked out of the store. If you discovered the book, you would be finding mislaid property. The book would be mislaid because she intentionally placed it on the shelf. In contrast, goods are *lost* when they are accidentally (unknowingly) placed somewhere. Thus if the student unknowingly dropped a book while walking from class to her car the book would be lost, not mislaid. If you found this book you would be finding lost property. The owner who has lost or mislaid property is always entitled to possession over any finder. Thus she could recover her mislaid book from the bookstore or her lost book from anyone who found it in the parking lot.

The distinction between lost and mislaid goods becomes important when one person finds goods on the property of another person. This occurs very frequently in business. If the goods were lost, the *finder* is entitled to possession. If the goods were mislaid, the *owner* of the property is entitled to hold the goods until the true owner returns for them. This distinction exists because owners are much more likely to return to a place, often a place of business, looking for mislaid goods.

Purchase

Ownership of tangible personal property is referred to as **title.** One person may have title to goods even while they are in the possession of someone else. Title passes from a seller to a buyer when the parties intend it to pass. If there is a written contract, it will often specify the time or place at which title passes. If you want to generate evidence of the purchase of personalty, you might prepare a *bill of sale* to be signed by the parties.

Ownership of certain classes of personalty is registered with governmental agencies like a division of motor vehicles or the Federal Aviation Administration or the Maritime Administration. To transfer title to this type of personalty, the *certificate of title* is signed by the seller, delivered to the agency, and then reissued in the name of the buyer.

Gift

The thing that distinguishes a gift from a purchase is consideration. When you make a gift you usually do not get something (i.e., consideration) directly in return. Mere promises to make gifts are generally unenforceable. Three elements are required to make a gift irrevocable: delivery of possession, the intent to make a present gift, and acceptance.

Delivery can be actual or constructive. Actual delivery would occur if you gave a copy of this book to a needy student. If someone wanted to make a gift to you of a new freezer stocked with food, they might constructively deliver it by simply handing you the keys to the freezer.

Intent means that the party transferring possession (the donor) intends to make a present gift. This is called donative intent. Thus, lending a magazine to a classmate would not shift ownership, because donative intent is missing. Acceptance means simply that the person receiving the gift (the donee) must indicate a willingness to accept it.

The following case illustrates the gifting process and clarifies the idea of constructive delivery. The case involved a gift from a husband to his wife.

Matter of Cohn

176 N.Y.S. 225 (1919)

Facts

On his wife's birthday, Leopold Cohn wrote in the presence of his entire family the following:

> *West End, N.J., Sept. 20, 1911*
>
> *I give this day to my wife, Sara K. Cohn, as a present for her (46) forty-sixth birthday (500) five hundred shares of American Sumatra Tobacco Company common stock.*
>
> *Leopold Cohn*

That writing was immediately delivered to his wife. Six days later, Leopold died. At that time, Leopold owned 7,213 shares but the stock was in the name of and in the possession of his firm, A. Cohn & Co., in which he was a partner.

Opinion

Judge Shearn: There being no rights of creditors involved, no suggestion of fraud, the intention to make the birthday gift being conclusively established, the gift being evidenced by an instrument of gift executed and delivered to the donee on her birthday, and ever since retained by her, and the circumstances surrounding the making of the gift affording a reasonable and satisfactory excuse for not making actual delivery of the certificates at the time the gift was made, there was in my opinion a valid and effectual gift of the certificates mentioned in the instrument of gift.

There is no doubt that it has been held in a long line of cases in this State that delivery of the thing given is, as a general rule, one of the essential elements to constitute a valid gift. . . .

As the rule requiring delivery is clearly subject to exceptions, in order to apply it correctly in varying circumstances resort should be had to the reason for the rule. Under the civil law delivery was not requisite to a valid gift, but it was made a requisite by the common law as a matter of public policy. . . . The necessity of delivery where [oral] gifts . . . are asserted against the estates of decedents is obvious; but it is equally plain that there is no such impelling necessity when the gift is established by the execution and delivery of an instrument of gift. An examination of a large number of cases in this State discloses the significant facts that (1) in every case where the gift was not sustained, the gift rested upon . . . [oral] evidence; and (2) in every case of a gift evidenced by the delivery of an instrument of gift, the gift has been sustained. . . . It is interesting to note that in *Matson* v. *Abbey,* . . . sustaining a gift evidenced by an instrument of assignment without delivery of the property assigned, the court quotes with approval the statement of the English law in *Irons* v. *Smallpiece,* 2 Barn. & Ald. 551, 552, made by Abbott, C. J.: "I am of the opinion that by the law of England, in order to transfer property by gift, there must either be a deed or instrument of gift, or there must be an actual delivery of the thing to the donee." Based upon decisions in numerous other jurisdictions, it is stated . . . that: "The general rule is that a gift of property evidenced by a written instrument executed by the donor is valid without a manual delivery of the property." I am inclined to think that this is a broader statement than the New York cases would justify . . . for it does not assume a delivery of the instrument of gift. . . . It seems to me beyond serious question that the delivery of the instrument of gift in the instant case constituted a good symbolical delivery. . . .

Therefore, applying the rule of delivery in the light of the reasons which gave birth to it, and finding here no possibility of fraud of imposition, and no doubt whatever concerning the intention of the donor, and finding full support in . . . precedent . . . it is my opinion that there was a good constructive or symbolical delivery, consisting of the delivery of the instrument of gift, and that the gift should be sustained. . . .

Case Questions

1. What do you think are the reasons for requiring delivery or constructive delivery to create a valid gift?
2. Is any reason for requiring delivery not satisfied by the conduct of Leopold?
3. Can you identify the epistemologies that this judge uses in reaching this decision?

Co-Ownership of Personal Property

The law of co-ownership of personal property is essentially the same as for the co-ownership of real property. Thus personalty can be co-owned in tenancy in common, joint tenancy, tenancy by entirety, or as community property.

Financing Personal Property

Any creditor may establish financial rights in personal property, analogous to those of a lien holder in realty, by acquiring a **security interest** in the property. Most security interests in consumer goods are created when the consumer signs a document called a *security agreement*. For example, if you bought a new dining room set on credit from a furniture store, they would ask you to execute a contract promising to pay the purchase price. In addition, they would also ask you to sign a security agreement. When you take possession of the furniture after signing the security agreement, the store will have a security interest in the furniture. In transactions involving property other than consumer goods, such as business inventory or business equipment, the creditor must usually file a copy of the security agreement with the secretary of state.

The security interest gives the creditor the right, if the loan payments are not made as promised, to repossess the personal property, sell it, and use that money to pay the loan. Security interests are discussed in more detail in chapter 23, ''Debtor/Creditor Relations.''

Introduction to Intellectual Property Law

Generally, intellectual property is intangible and is created by intellectual (mental) effort as opposed to physical effort. Patents, copyrights, and trademarks are governed by federal law. Trade secrets are governed by state law.

Patents

The owner of a **patent** controls the right to *make, sell,* and *use* a *product* for a period of seventeen years or a *design* for fourteen years. It is the grant by the government of an *exclusive monopoly* as an incentive and reward for the creation of ideas that are novel and useful. Note the breadth of the patent power; an owner of a patent for a new airplane propeller can not only control its manufacture and sale but also its *use*. Thus aircraft owners using propellers that are manufactured by a competing firm, but that infringe the patent would be liable to the patent holder.

If you have an idea that might be patentable, the first step toward obtaining the patent right is to contact a patent attorney. This person is a specialized lawyer who is admitted to practice before the Patent Office and who usually has a technical undergraduate degree in a field such as engineering, chemistry, or physics as well as the Juris Doctor degree in law. After discussing the idea with the patent attorney, you would probably conduct a patent search to determine whether or not someone has already patented the idea. If the idea is new, then an application for a patent would be prepared by the patent attorney.

After the application has been filed with the Patent Office, it will be evaluated to determine whether the idea qualifies for a patent. In determining whether an idea or invention is patentable, the Patent Office evaluates several factors, but the most important are the following:

1. *Novelty*—is the idea new? If the idea is not new, or has been adequately described before, it is not patentable.
2. *Utility*—is the idea useful to society? If the idea or invention is not useful, it will not be patentable even if it is new.
3. *Nonobviousness*—is the idea or invention something that a person of ordinary skill in a particular field would not think of? If an idea or invention is obvious, it is not patentable even if it is new and useful.

If an idea or invention meets these three criteria, then a patent may be issued and the idea will thereby be disclosed to the general public. But even if the Patent Office grants the patent, this is not conclusive proof that the patent is valid. Frequently, federal courts decide during trials involving patents that the Patent Office was in error in issuing a patent.

Someone who manufacturers, sells, or uses a patented invention without authorization has probably committed **patent infringement.** The infringement exists even if the infringer did not know about the patent. Infringers can be liable for damages and may be enjoined from future infringement.

The party charged with patent infringement can escape liability in a variety of ways. One way is by proving that the challenged product or process is outside the scope of the patent. Another way is by proving that the patent is invalid because it fails to meet the criteria for patentability. A third way is to establish that the patent holder has misused the patent.

Misuse of a patent occurs when a patent holder uses the patent to achieve something illegal. The most common type of misuse occurs when the patent holder uses the patent to violate the antitrust laws. For example, suppose a company obtained a patent on a machine for very accurately dispensing salt into canned foods. If the company required that purchasers of the patented salt dispensing machine also purchase all their salt from the company, then this would constitute a violation of the antitrust prohibition against "tying agreements" and would also be a misuse of the patent. If the company sought to enforce the patent against an infringer, the infringer might avoid liability by proving this misuse.

Patents are issued to the person or persons who invent the product or process. However, these persons often *assign* their rights in the patent to others, such as their employers. Many corporations require scientific and technical employees to execute an assignment of patents agreement at the time of their employment. This type of agreement transfers the employee's patent rights to the corporation, but only if the patent is developed within the scope of the employment. Thus, if a scientist developed a patent unrelated to her job, the assignment of patent agreement would not transfer these patent rights.

Trade Secrets

Trade secrecy can be used to protect a wide range of information. The Restatement of Torts defines a **trade secret** as follows:

> A trade secret may consist of any formula, pattern, device or compilation of information which is used in one's business, and which gives him an opportunity to obtain an advantage over competitors who do not know or use it. . . . The subject matter of a trade secret must be secret.

Notice that two elements are required to qualify something as a trade secret. One, the information must have value to a business. Two, the information must be treated as a secret.

A distinctive manufacturing process and the list of a firm's customers are examples of things that can qualify as trade secrets because of their value to a business. If information is widely known within an industry, then that information cannot qualify as a trade secret even if it is valuable.

The secrecy of information is often difficult to establish. The steps taken to establish secrecy usually include labeling the information *Confidential* or *Secret*. Asking employees to sign an agreement not to disclose the firm's confidential information is also useful. While employees are under an implied obligation not to disclose such information, the written agreement lends weight to the claim that company information is a trade secret.

Unlike patents and copyrights, there is no time limit on the life of a trade secret; it is effective as long as the secrecy is maintained. The law protects trade secret from **wrongful appropriation.** This does not mean that a competitor cannot use the same manufacturing process. It only means that the competitor must arrive at the idea independently. If the competitor obtains the idea by bribing your employees or hiring away your employees and getting them to disclose the trade secret, that is wrongful appropriation.

Patents and trade secrecy can both protect ideas. Copyrights and trademarks, discussed next, protect only physical expressions of ideas.

Copyrights

A **copyright** protects the original work of authors, painters, sculptors, musicians, photographers, and others who produce works of artistic or intellectual merit. The copyright only protects the physical expression of the effort, not the idea. This book is copyrighted, so these sentences cannot be used by anyone without the consent of the copyright owner. However, anyone can take the ideas in this book and express them in different words.

A copyright is effective for the life of the creator plus an additional fifty years. If there is more than one creator, the copyright lasts for fifty years beyond the life of the longest surviving creator.

Anyone who creates an original work is protected by an automatic common law copyright. Thus, when the authors wrote a first draft of these chapters, that writing was protected by the common law copyright. That protection would be lost, however, if the chapter were widely distributed without statutory copyright protection. When material is widely published this way (without statutory copyright protection), it is said to be in the **public domain.** Material in the public domain may be used by anyone, without the consent of the creator.

To obtain statutory copyright protection, the material must be published (i.e., distributed) with the copyright notice. This notice takes the form of the word *copyright* or the abbreviation *copr.* or the symbol © followed by the year and the name of the copyright owner. The copyright for this book is on the back side of the title page. It someone violates the copyright created by the copyright notice, they may only be enjoined from future violations.

Copyrights may be registered. This occurs when forms are filed with the Register of Copyright and copies of the copyrighted material are provided for the Library of Congress. If someone violates a copyright created by registration, they may be liable for damages, fines, and imprisonment.

Creators and others who own a common law copyright, or a copyright created by publication or registration, can transfer their ownership to others. This is called *assignment*. For example, we authors have all signed contracts that assign some of our copyright powers to this publisher, Allyn & Bacon Publishing Co.

Trademarks

A **trademark** is some kind of a mark on goods that distinguishes the marked goods from competing goods. The mark may be a word, picture, or design.

Marks cannot be highly descriptive of the goods. Thus a valid mark probably could not be created for an off-road motorcycle named Dirt Bike II. Similarly, the mark cannot be exclusively generic. *Generic* means descriptive of a large category of goods, such as eggs. Thus, while "Kentucky Fried Chicken" may be acceptable, "Chicken" alone could not become a valid mark.

The Lanham Act establishes a system of federal registration for marks and makes unauthorized use of the marks of others illegal. For example, both "Pepsi" and "Coke" are registered marks. It is for this reason that most fast food restaurants serving Pepsi always respond to the question, "Can I have a Coke?" with, "Is Pepsi OK?"

Public perception plays a significant role in trademark law. If the public comes to perceive that a trademark is generic—that is, that the name refers to a category of products rather than a particular product—that name will lose its legal status as a trademark. For example, if the public comes to view the word *Coke* as generic, referring to the whole category of cola soft drinks, then the word becomes part of the public domain, available to all manufacturers, including Pepsi. Because of this, Xerox Corporation has bought ads in business publications trying to teach people to distinguish between "Xeroxing" and "photocopying." If the public believes *Xeroxing* refers to all types of photocopying, Xerox Corporation would lose this trademark.

Public perception can also create a legal right for an attribute of a product. If a product's shape or style or a feature is arbitrary and nonfunctional, and the general public comes to view it as associated with a particular product, it is said to have acquired a **secondary meaning.** This secondary meaning can be registered and protected. Thus the shape of the Coca Cola bottle has acquired secondary meaning and is registered. If Pepsi Cola Corporation started selling Pepsi Free in a bottle the same shape as the Coca Cola bottle, then Coca Cola could enjoin them from such conduct.

Ethical Issues in Property Law

This body of law, particularly intellectual property law, illustrates how this country tries to balance the interests of individuals against the interests of the collective to achieve the common good. There is a distinctly individualistic flavor to this law, which in many respects differs from that of other nations. It is, for example, common for some nations not to recognize the rights of individuals in patents and copyrights. In these countries, the common good is believed to be advanced by downplaying the role of the individual.

Clearly, the opposing opinions on this topic reflect differing views of the fundamental character of humankind. Capitalism tends to bet on the individual, and assumes that the individual has the will to intelligently exercise the freedom inherent in our system. In contrast, the socialist system tends not to trust individual decisions or value them highly. A paternalistic state, or central committee, makes the important decisions for most individuals. A belief that individuals really do not possess sufficient will to intelligently run their own lives is pervasive in these systems. The empirical evidence about individual will is mixed. What is your perception of this attribute of human character?

Can you see the way your view of the individual, and the individual's potential for contributing to the common good, can greatly influence your political, economic, managerial, and ethical views?

The important concepts and terms in this chapter are listed below; page numbers have been provided for the key terms. By reading over each section you can assess your understanding of the chapter concepts and determine areas you may want to review.

Chapter Summary

1. Real property is both a bundle of legal rights and certain physical objects. These include land, structures and fixtures, surface rights, mineral rights, air rights, and water rights.
2. Owners of realty do not all have the same ownership powers. For example, some owners cannot will away their ownership. Ownership powers are determined by the *estate in land* owned. The major *freehold estates* are fee simple absolute, conditional estates, life estates, and future interests. *Leasehold estates* include estates at sufferance, estates at will, periodic estates, and estates for years.
3. Co-ownership exists when more than one party owns the same estate. Particular forms of co-ownership regulate the legal relations among the co-owners differently. The major forms of co-ownership are tenancy in common, joint tenancy, tenancy by entirety, and community property.
4. Persons other than the owner frequently have some limited rights in realty. These include licenses, easements, restrictive covenants, and liens.
5. The deeding process is the most common method used to transfer ownership. The elements of the deeding process are *execution* of a deed, *delivery* of the deed, and *acceptance* of the deed.
6. In a warranty deed, the grantor promises that the grantee will receive the estate exactly as it is described in the deed. In a quitclaim deed the grantor makes no promises.
7. Recording real estate–related documents is a way to make public the fact that a particular transaction has occurred. Recording also establishes priority.

8. Title to most personalty is evidenced by possession. Sometimes a bill of sale is evidence of ownership. Other times ownership is indicated by a certificate of title.
9. Sales of personal property are governed by the UCC, while sales of real property are governed by the common law of contracts. The dominant component of a transaction, either goods or services and realty, determines whether the whole transaction is governed by the UCC or the common law of contracts.
10. A security interest in personalty is created with a security agreement and in some cases with a security agreement and filing. A security interest can give the secured party the right to repossess.
11. A patent is a governmental grant of monopoly as a reward for a new invention.
12. To be patentable, an idea must be *novel, useful,* and *nonobvious.* Patents are granted to persons. Persons may *assign* their ownership rights in the patent. If you *infringe* a patent, you may be liable to the patent owner. Many patents issued by the Patent Office are declared void when litigated in court.
13. Copyrights protect the physical expression of intellectual or artistic effort for the life of the creator plus fifty years. The copyright can be created by the common law, by publication with a copyright notice, and/or by registration with the Registrar of Copyrights.
14. Trademarks are used to distinguish the marked goods from competing goods. In order to qualify as a trademark, the mark must not be overly descriptive and it may not be generic.
15. If a nonfunctional, arbitrary attribute of a product develops *secondary meaning,* it may be protected by trademark registration.
16. Trade secrets must be kept secret. To qualify for protection, the secret must give the firm a competitive advantage.

Key Terms

license 183
lien 183
life estate 177
mineral right 176
notice 187
patent 193
patent infringement 194
periodic estate 179
priority 187
public domain 195
quitclaim deed 184
realty 175
recording 187
restrictive covenant 183
right of survivorship 181
right to air space 177
secondary meaning 196
security interest 192
surface right 176
tenancy by entirety 181
tenancy in common 180
title 190
trade fixtures 176
trademark 196
trade secret 194
warranty deed 184
water right 177
wrongful appropriation 195

Questions on Ethics

1. Frequently in business discussions, people toss out ideas to be evaluated by a group. Suppose you are brainstorming a problem with a group of your subordinates and one of them comes up with an idea that you judge to be quite useful to your company. Further assume that you could appropriate this idea as your own, in your discussions with your boss, without any risk of adverse consequences to yourself. If you think there might be a substantial benefit to you, perhaps a significant raise, should you do so? Why or why not? Do you think you would?
2. Suppose you had a elderly, but wealthy, aunt who was interested in doing business with you. The particular business was a tree harvesting operation. Your eighty-year-old aunt would put up $1.5 million to buy the land and you would be in charge of cutting the trees. In return profits would be split equally.

   At the time the deed to the property is being prepared, your aunt asks what form of co-ownership is appropriate. She knows little of legal technicalities and will follow your advice on the matter. She doesn't know the difference between tenancy in common and joint tenancy. She has three children who expect that they will inherit all of her money. Would it be right for you to suggest joint tenancy? Would you do it?
3. If you could see a way to intentionally use adverse possession to obtain the land of a neighbor, would it be right for you to do it? Would you do it?
4. If you found a gold Rolex watch with diamonds inset in it in a locker at a country club, would it be legal for you to keep it until the owner claimed it? Would it be ethical for you to keep it? Would you be tempted to conceal the finding if you could hock the watch for $7,000 in

another town? What do you think is the right thing and what do you think you would do?

5. Often in high technology companies the employees are required to sign statements in which they promise that they will not divulge the trade secrets of their employers to anyone during the period of employment or at any time in the future. Still, it is fairly common practice to hire technical persons such as programmers, engineers, and scientists, especially from smaller companies that lack legal resources, and get them to disclose the trade secrets. If you were a manager who could hire such a person to obtain a competitor's trade secrets, and you were sure the chance of adverse consequences were zero, should you do it? Why or why not?

Questions on Law

1. Smith owned a home in a suburban development and had been trying to sell it for over a year. His friend Alex expressed an interest in purchasing the property and the parties reached an agreement on the purchase price. They executed a contract that contained a legal description and described all the terms of the sale. This agreement only referred to a sale of the realty, and nothing was ever communicated between the parties about any of the personal property. Smith executed a warranty deed conveying fee simple absolute to Alex. At that point the parties realized that they had transferred title only to the realty, and they were uncertain about the legal status of many of the items in the home. These items included valuable throw rugs, drapes, a workbench bolted to the studs in the garage, a built-in dishwasher, a washer-dryer combination in the laundry room, a fireplace screen bolted to the stone fireplace, a matching fireplace set consisting of a shovel, tongs, and broom, garden hoses, and a garden shed resting on 2 × 4s in the back yard. Which of these items belong to Smith and which belong to Alex?
2. In 1957 Lober sold a parcel of real property to Brown. The conveyance was with a warranty deed. This deed described no encumbrances burdening the title received by Brown. In 1974 Brown executed a contract with Consolidated Coal Company in which Brown was to receive $6,000 and Consolidated was to receive the right to mine subsurface coal. After the contract was signed, Consolidated conducted a search of the title documents recorded against the property. They discovered that at the time of Lober's conveyance he only owned a one-third interest in the mineral rights. Accordingly, Consolidated paid Brown only $2,000. Brown then sued Lober for breach of the warranty. Has Lober breached a warranty? *Brown* v. *Lober,* 75 Ill. 2d. 549 (1979).
3. Bernice Paset went into the Old Orchard Bank to gain access to her safety deposit box. Once inside the vault she went into an examining booth, which contained a small table and a chair. The chair was partially

under the table. When Bernice pulled the chair out she discovered $6,325 in cash sitting on the seat of the chair. Is this property abandoned, lost, or mislaid? Who, between Bernice and the bank, is entitled to possession of the property? *Paset* v. *Old Orchard Bank,* 378 N.E.2d 1264 (1978).

4. E. I. duPont de Nemours & Co. (duPont) developed a new process for production of methanol and although it had not patented the process, it had taken steps to keep the process secret. In order to implement the discovery, duPont began construction of a refinery. During the construction process an aircraft was observed circling low above the construction site. When duPont traced the aircraft by its numbers they discovered that the occupants were photographers who had taken aerial pictures of the plant for an undisclosed client. duPont believed the photographs might communicate the nature of their trade secret. Accordingly they sued the photographers to obtain the identity of their client. duPont then planned to sue the client for misappropriation of a trade secret. Would duPont prevail in such a suit against the client? *duPont* v. *Christopher,* 621 F.2d 1012 (5th Cir. 1970).
5. Crown Handbags was in the business of manufacturing and selling handbags, purses, and pocketbooks. Vuitton Et Fils, S. A., a French firm, was also in this business. Vuitton had developed a seal, or crest, which it embossed upon all of its goods. This mark was registered on the Principal Trademark Register of the United States Patent Office in 1932. Since that time the mark of Vuitton had come to stand for high quality and prestige in the public mind. Crown sold six handbags bearing the Vuitton trademark. These handbags were superficially identical to those sold by Vuitton, although they were counterfeits manufactured using cheaper material and poorer workmanship. As it happened, these bags were sold to a private investigator hired by Vuitton. Vuitton then sued Crown, seeking a permanent injunction, damages, and attorney's fees. Will Vuitton prevail? *Vuitton* v. *Crown Handbags,* 492 F. Supp. 1071 (1979).

Suggested Readings

Ackerman, Bruce A. *Private Property and the Constitution,* New Haven: Yale University Press, 1977.

Grilliot and Yocum, "Tenancy by the Entirety: An Ancient Fiction Frustrates Modern Creditors," 17 *American Business Law Journal* 1 (1979).

Locke, John. *A Second Treatise of Government.* 1690.

8 Computer Law

The Judge: I suppose you are going to try to puzzle me with the question, "Can a corporation write?"

***

Sir Alister: But milord, there is the question of copyright.

The Judge: Copyright?

Sir Alister: Copyright. Milord, by the Act of 1911 the copyright in the literary works endures only for the author's lifetime and fifty years after his death; after which it becomes the property of the world.

The Judge: I know. A dammed shame.

Sir Alister: That is as it may be, milord. But, milord, a corporation *never dies—*

The Judge: True. I begin to see.

***

If a man builds a great house he can leave it to his son when he dies. And if his son lives for eighty years it will be his property when he dies; and he can leave it to his children and so on.

***

But the descendants of Charles Dickens . . . and Johann Strauss can only say, "These great works were once in our family, but now they are public property, and Tom Dick or Harry may do what they will with them and draw what profit they can.

—*Macintosh* v. *Haddock,* King's Bench, England

LEARNING OBJECTIVES

After reading this chapter you should be able to:

1. Describe the way several bodies of law regulate a single product.
2. Describe the way the law responds to rapid technological change.

3. Understand the role of copyright, patents, and trade secrets in protecting computer-related products.
4. Describe the way computer chips and computer programs are protected by the law.
5. Describe the consequences of copying software.

Ethical Dilemma Section To Come

Protecting Your Ideas

During your sophomore year in college you began to realize that the way you allocated your study time among courses greatly influenced your grade point average. Near the end of the term, you could shift study time from courses where you couldn't improve your grade to those where you could. And some courses could be *A*ce'd without much effort while others required great effort. In response to these observations, you developed a computer program to help you manage your study time to maximize your grade point average. When friends found out about your program, they offered to buy copies of it. Thinking that there might be big money in this, you decided to protect your program. How could you protect your computer program?

Introduction to Computer Law

By studying the development of computer law, you can observe the way the legal system adapts to changes in the business world. The growth of the computer industry has presented challenges to the legal system for a variety of primarily technical reasons. Most of the legal changes precipitated by computers have affected the law of property.

To understand computer law, you need to keep the elements of a computer purchase fixed clearly in your mind. A typical computer purchase includes three basic components: (1) the hardware, (2) the service contract, and (3) the software.

The computer **hardware** is the actual machine that you see advertised fairly often. The heart of every computer hardware system is a semiconductor **chip.** This is a small device, about half the size of a dime, manufactured from silicon. It reads and processes groups of electrical charges; this is the primary function performed by a computer. Most of the rest of the hardware is designed to aid in this function. A keyboard will create these charges to be sent to the chip to be processed in some fashion. The memory will store these groups of charges, and the printer will print letters on paper in response to the instructions expressed by the electrical charges. The machine, the chip, the keyboard, and the printer are part of the hardware.

A second element of most computer sales is a **service contract.** This often includes service and maintenance of the hardware.

A third element of the sale is the computer **software.** This includes the computer programs that interact with the hardware. Computer programs are stored, again as electrical charges, on a variety of media. They can be written out with paper and pencil, but they are much more often expressed with electrical charges on **floppy** or **hard disks** or embedded in a part of the memory of the computer.

In general, the legal system tried to treat computer problems in the same way as other property law problems, so computer-related transactions were viewed in the context of either real, personal, or intellectual property law. (For all practical purposes, real property law has had little influence in this field.) It was clear at the beginning of the computer revolution that some existing legal concepts accommodated the computer industry without difficulty: The physical equipment was clearly personal property and thus subject to the law of the Uniform Commercial Code. Similarly, maintenance contracts on the hardware were contracts for the sale of services and thus governed by the common law of contracts. And the traditional rule applied to transactions for the sale of hardware and services; the dominant component of the transaction determined which body of law would govern the whole transaction. Security interests in computer hardware gave the secured party the right to repossess. Thus, to a significant extent, the existing legal framework was able to accommodate many of the needs of this new industry. But the computer programs and heart of the computer, the chip, created critical problems.

The Problem of the Chip

The cost of research, design, and initial production of a chip can be enormous—up to $100 million. Firms need some assurance that the chip will be protected by the law from pirating (copying). This problem is significant, because existing chips can be copied for only about $1 million.

While the generic idea for the chip may have been patentable, the variants on this idea have not been not patentable, just as the invention of the automobile may have been patentable but modern models of an automobile are not patentable. Therefore, the most effective way to protect one's chip has been trade secrecy. While this works well during the research, design, and initial production phases, once the chip hits the market, it is very vulnerable. Competitors can "reverse engineer" the chip. This means that they can take it apart and figure out how it was designed and manufactured. After the "trade secreted" chip hits the market, it is only protected for the time required to reverse engineer, set up production facilities, and market a pirated chip. Firms manufacturing original chips frequently tried to manage this lead time by increasing the supply of the chip at a pace that drives down the price and thereby discourages copying. Still, the effect of weak legal protection of trade secracy was that chips had a relatively short economic life, and this discouraged firms from investing in the research needed to design chips for smaller markets.

As a consequence, the semiconductor industry lobbied Congress to modify the copyright law to allow chips to be copyrightable or patentable. The Semiconductor Chip Protection Act of 1984 provided a combination of patent and copyright protection for chips.

Legal Problems with Programs

Governing Law

The most troublesome area for the law was computer programming. Applications programs, such as Lotus 123, WordPerfect, or Wordstar, were often sold to the general public on floppy disks for prices of $300 at a time when the blank disk was worth only $3. Since each transaction involved the sale of both personal property (the disk) and the intangible product of labor (the program), there was initial confusion about whether the UCC or the common law of contracts governed the sales of these programs. At this time, the large majority of courts that have decided the issue have classified the program as a good, subject to the provisions of the UCC.

Program Licensing

In the early days of the industry, computer sales were very large transactions involving extensive sales effort and elaborate contracts. The strategy of computer companies like IBM was to try and protect their property right in a program by treating it as a trade secret. Thus it was common to require every buyer of a computer, and related programming, to sign a licensing agreement. This license would typically allow IBM to retain title to the program, state that the program was a trade secret, require the licensee to protect the secrecy of the program, and require that the licensee not make any copies of the program without the consent of the licensor.

As the computer industry matured, the volume of transactions increased and the character of the sales process changed. With the increase in sales of the PC (personal computer), the hardware cost declined, wholesalers and retailers became important parts of the chain of distribution, and the manufacturer had much less contact with the buyer. Licensing agreements to support trade secret strategies became less feasible. One attempt to solve this legal problem has been the development of "shrink wrap licensing." This involves a license printed on a box. By breaking open the shrink wrapper, the buyer agrees to be bound by the license agreement.

Patent Protection

In general, computer programs are not considered patentable because, by themselves, they fail to meet the tests of nonobviousness and novelty. Patent examiners and the courts believed that for any defined objective, there were lots of programmers who, given enough time, could write a program to achieve the objective. In 1968 the Patent Office took the position that, "computer programs per se . . . shall not be patentable.'' This position was significantly altered in 1981 when the Supreme Court recognized that a patent can be issued for a *process* that incorporates a computer program. This is called a **process patent.** The case establishing this law is presented below.

Diamond v. Diehr and Lutton

101 S. Ct. 1048 (1981)

Facts

Diehr and Lutton sought a patent for a process for curing rubber. The process involved a small computer and a computer program to monitor the time, temperature, and pressure of the curing process. Their application was denied on the grounds that a computer program was not patentable. They sued the Patent Office.

Opinion

Justice Rehnquist: The patent examiner rejected the Diehr and Lutton claims on the sole grounds that they were [not patentable] . . . under 35 U.S.C. §101. He determined that those steps in Diehr and Lutton's claims that are carried out by a computer under control of a stored program constituted nonstatutory subject matter. . . . The remaining step—installing rubber in the press and subsequent closing of the press—were "conventional in nature and cannot be the basis of patentability." The examiner concluded that Diehr and Lutton's claims defined and sought protection of a computer program for operating a rubber molding press.

. . . [A] process has historically enjoyed patent protection. . . . In defining the nature of a patentable process, the Court said:

> That a process may be patentable, irrespective of the particular form of the instrumentalities used, cannot be disputed. . . . A process is a mode of treatment of certain materials to produce a given result. It is an act, or a series of acts, performed upon the subject matter to be transformed and reduced to a different state or thing. If new and useful, it is just as patentable as is a piece of machinery. In the language of the patent law, it is an art. The machinery pointed out as suitable to perform the process may or may not be new or patentable; whilst the process itself may be altogether new, and produce an entirely new result. The process requires that certain things should be done with certain substances, and in a certain order; but the tools to be used in doing this may be of secondary consequence. (*Cochrane* v. *Deener* [1976].)

Recently, in *Gottschalk* v. *Benson* (1972), we repeated the above definition adding "Transformation and reduction of an article to a different state or thing is the clue to the patentability of a process claim. . . ." That Diehr and Lutton's claims involve the transformation of an article, in this case raw uncured synthetic rubber, into a different state or thing cannot be disputed. Diehr and Lutton's claims describe in detail a step-by-step method . . . beginning with the loading of a mold with raw uncured rubber and ending with the eventual opening of the press at the conclusion of the cure. Industrial processes such as this are the type which have historically been eligible to receive the protection of our patent laws.

Our conclusion regarding Diehr and Lutton's claims is not altered by the fact that in several steps of the process a mathematical equation and a programmed digital computer are used. This Court has undoubtedly recognized limits. . . . Excluded from such patent protection are laws of nature, physical phenomena and abstract ideas. . . .

Our recent holdings in *Gottschalk* v. *Benson,* and *Parker* v. *Flook,* both of which are computer-related, stand for not more than these long established principles. In *Benson,* we held unpatentable claims for an algorithm used to convert binary code decimal numbers to equivalent pure binary numbers. The sole practical application of the algorithm was in connection with the programming of a general purpose digital computer. We . . . concluded that such an algorithm, or mathematical formula, is like a law of nature, which cannot be the subject of a patent.

Parker v. *Flook* presented a similar situation. The claims were drawn to a method for computing an "alarm limit." An "alarm limit" is simply a number, and the Court concluded that the application sought to protect a formula for computing this number.

In contrast, Diehr and Lutton here do not seek to patent a mathematical formula. Instead, they seek patent protection for a process of curing synthetic rubber. Their process admittedly employs a well known mathematical equation, but they do not seek to pre-empt the use of that equation. Rather, they seek only to foreclose from others the use of that equation in conjunction with all of the other steps in their claimed process. These include installing rubber in a press, closing the mold, constantly determining the temperature of the mold, constantly recalculating the appropriate cure time through the use of the formula and a digital computer, and automatically opening the press at the proper time. Obviously, one does not need a "computer" to cure natural or synthetic rubber, but if the computer use incorporated in the process patent significantly lessens the possibility of "overcuring or undercuring," the process as a whole does not become unpatentable subject matter.

In this case, it may later be determined that the process is not deserving of patent protection because it fails to satisfy the statutory conditions of novelty under §102 or nonobviousness under §103. A rejection on either of these grounds does not affect the determination that Diehr and Lutton's claims recited [useful] subject matter which was eligible for patent protection under §101.

[Reversed for Diehr and Lutton.]

Case Questions

1. Are all computer programs patentable under this decision?
2. What are the attributes of patentable computer programs?
3. What are the attributes of nonpatentable computer programs?

In response to this decision, the Patent Office has begun encouraging applications for programming patents if the program "transforms or reduces an article to a different state of a thing." However, even when a program is included within a patent for a process, there is some doubt that copying just the program, as opposed to the whole process, would constitute patent infringement.

Copyright Protection

Evolution of Programs and Copyright Law

Copyright law also offered conceptual obstacles to those seeking to use the law to protect programs. Recall that copyright is available for the physical **expression** of an original work of intellectual merit, but copyright cannot be used to protect the idea. The physical expression requirement created a variety of problems. The main one was a Supreme Court decision which in 1909 held that the copyright protection only extends to "copies which were perceptible to humans—things written or printed . . . in intelligible notation." Interpretations of this decision caused some lower federal courts to conclude that programs were not qualified for copyright, because they were not expressed in a notation that the general public could understand. Other federal courts reached the opposite conclusion.

As the computer and programming industries expanded in the 1960s and 1970s, the economic importance of protecting programs grew. Congress, in 1974, appointed a National Commission of New Technological Uses of Copyright Works (CONTU). This commission was composed of legal experts on copyright law and technical experts on computers and programming. It performed as a quasi-administrative agency by bringing its expertise to bear on the problem of programs. CONTU then made recommendations to Congress on the ways the copyright law should be changed. These recommendations were implemented with the passage of the 1980 Computer Software Copyright Act. Among other things, this act made it clear that programs could be copyrighted. In addition, the act defined a *computer program* with the following language:

> A "computer program" is a set of statements or instructions to be used directly or indirectly in a computer to bring about a certain result.

Still the act did not resolve all of the issues associated with the copyright protection of programs.

How Programs Are Developed

In order to follow the legal battles over programs, you need to understand how programs are produced. The first step in the process is the definition of an objective for the program. Some programs, called **operating programs,** have the objective of running the internal machinery of the computer. These programs have names like CPM and DOS. Other programs, called **applications programs,** have the objective of manipulating words or numbers (data) supplied to the computer by an operator. Wordstar and SuperCalc are names of well-known computer applications programs.

After an objective has been clearly identified, a systems analyst may be asked to design a system to accomplish the objective. This system is sometimes described with a *flowchart*. This is a series of boxes, arrows, circles, and junction points that give a visual impression of the major steps that must be included within the program. It is somewhat similar to a blueprint. A flowchart is primarily a visual expression. It can be easily protected as a trade secret because it is not widely distributed. In computer programming, the flowchart describes the "structure, sequence, and organization" of a program.

Next, a programmer will be asked to write programming statements in a **high-level program language** to accomplish the tasks specified by the flowchart. BASIC, Pascal, and COBOL are examples of high-level languages. These are also sometimes called *source codes*. These languages are easy for programmers to work with because they are fairly easy to read. For example, a BASIC statement for adding two numbers might look like: LET A = B + C. Perhaps you can see that this is fairly easy to read and write. Computers, however, do not do their basic manipulations in these high-level languages. Instead, they compute using what is called a **machine language** or *object code*. The name of the nearly universal machine language is **binary.** The binary instruction to add, which was expressed in BASIC with simply a plus sign, is 01101001. Can you see that it is easier to program in high-level languages than in machine language?

Standard programs exist that, in effect, translate high-level languages into machine languages or object code. These translation programs are called *compilers* or *assemblers*. Both high-level and machine languages are generally acknowledged to be programs within the meaning of the current copyright law. Machine language is, in the language of the statute, "used directly . . . to bring about a certain result," while high-level languages are used "indirectly" because they must be compiled and/or assembled before the computer can follow the program directions.

Strategies for Protection of Ideas with Copyright

Programming firms are as interested in protecting the ideas behind programs as they are in protecting the physical expression of the ideas. In the absence of legislation to protect their ideas, these firms developed strategies to protect them within the changing legal frameworks.

Distribution in machine language. The distinction between machine and high-level languages is important, because high-level languages are easy to read, so copyrighting them in effect makes public the **idea,** or the flowchart, behind the program. Copies of the copyrighted material are made public by the Library of Congress when they are registered. To protect the idea behind a program, some firms do not copyright, but rather *distribute* the program in machine language. They hope that it cannot be easily analyzed and therefore it may still be a trade secret, although widely distributed.

Copyright of machine language. Another strategy involves *registering* the program in machine language. Because this is so difficult to translate, it in effect conceals the ideas behind the program. The Copyright Office, however, is reluctant to accept machine code because it is not capable of being readily understood. It does, however, accept such programs under its "rule of doubt," which resolves doubt in favor of allowing copyright protection. Still, there is uncertainty about the availability of remedies for violation of the copyrighted machine language.

Copyright of portions of programs. Another strategy employed to protect the idea behind a computer program is to copyright and register only a *portion* of the program expressed in a high-level language. The Copyright Office will register such programs if you provide the first 25 pages and the last 25 pages of programming. Since only a portion of the program is made public in a high-level language, the whole idea is not disclosed.

Copyright of whole programs. Some firms copyrighted their whole program in the hope that copyright law would protect everything associated with the program—perhaps even the idea. The following case illustrates the way one federal circuit court has responded to the problems confronted by programmers.

Whelan v. Jaslow

797 F.2d 1222 (3rd Cir. 1986)

Facts

***

*Jaslow Dental Laboratory, Inc. ("Jaslow Lab"), is . . . in the business of manufacturing dental prosthetics and devices. Appellant Dentcom, Inc. ("**Dentcom**") is . . . in the business of developing and marketing computer programs for use by dental laboratories.*

***

Jaslow Lab, like any other small- or medium-sized business of moderate complexity, has significant bookkeeping and administrative tasks. Each order for equipment must be registered and processed; inventory must be maintained; customer lists must be continually updated; invoicing, billing, and accounts receivable must be dealt with.

***

Although Rand Jaslow had not had extensive experience with computers, he believed that the business operations of Jaslow Lab could be made more efficient if they were computerized. In early 1978, he therefore bought a small personal computer and tried to teach himself how to program it so that it would be of use to Jaslow Lab. Although he wrote a program for the computer, he was ultimately not successful, limited by both his lack of expertise and the relatively small capacity of his particular computer.

A few months later, stymied by his own lack of success but still confident that Jaslow Lab would profit from computerization, Rand Jaslow hired the Strohl Systems Group, Inc. ("Strohl"), a small corporation that developed custom-made software to develop a program that would run on Jaslow Lab's new IBM Series One computer and take care of the Lab's business needs. Jaslow Lab and Strohl entered into an agreement providing that Strohl would design a system for Jaslow Lab's needs and that after Strohl had installed the system Strohl could market it to other dental laboratories. Jaslow Lab would receive a 10 percent royalty on all such sales. The person at Strohl responsible for the Jaslow Lab account was Elaine Whelan, an experienced programmer who was an officer and half-owner of Strohl.

*Ms. Whelan's first step was to visit Jaslow Lab and interview Rand Jaslow and others to learn how the laboratory worked and what its needs were. She also visited other dental laboratories and interviewed people there, so that she would better understand the layout, workflow, and administration of dental laboratories generally. After this education into the ways of dental laboratories, and Jaslow Lab in particular, Ms. Whelan wrote a program called **Dentalab** for Jaslow Lab. Dentalab was written in a computer language known as EDL (Event Driven Language), so that it would work with IBM Series One machines. The program was completed and was operative at Jaslow Lab around March 1979.*

Ms. Whelan left Strohl in November, 1979, to form her own business, Whelan Associates, Inc., which acquired Strohl's interest in the Dentalab program. Whelan Associates and Jaslow Lab entered into an agreement on July 30, 1980, according to which Jaslow Lab agreed to use its "best efforts and to act diligently in the marketing of the Dentalab package," and Whelan Associates agreed to "use its best efforts and to act diligently to improve and augment the previously successfully designed Dentalab package." The agreement stated that Jaslow Lab would receive 35 percent of the gross price of any programs sold and 5 percent of the price of any modifications to the programs. The agreement was for one year and was then terminable by either party on thirty days' notice.

*The parties' business relationship worked successfully for two years. During this time, as Rand Jaslow became more familiar with computer programming, he realized that because Dentalab was written in EDL it could not be used on computers that many of the smaller dental prosthetics firms were using, for which EDL had not been implemented. Sensing that there might be a market for a program that served essentially the same function as Dentalab but that could be used more widely, Rand Jaslow began in May or June of 1982 to develop in his spare time a program in the BASIC language for such computers. That program, when completed, became the alleged copyright infringer in this suit; it was called the Dentcom PC program ("**Dentcom** program").*

After approximately a year of work, on May 31, 1983, Jaslow's attorney sent a letter to Whelan Associates giving one month notice of termination of the agreement. . . . The letter stated that Jaslow Lab considered itself to be the exclusive marketer of the Dentalab program which, the letter stated, "contains valuable trade secrets of Jaslow Dental Laboratory." The letter concluded with a thinly veiled threat to Whelan Associates: "I . . . look for your immediate response confirming that you will respect the rights of Jaslow and not use or disclose to others the trade secrets of Jaslow."

Approximately two months later, on about August 1 . . . Rand Jaslow . . . formed defendant-appellant Dentcom to sell the Dentcom program. At about the same time, Rand Jaslow and Jaslow Lab employed a professional computer programmer, Jonathan Novak, to complete the Dentcom program . . . and Dentcom proceeded to sell it to dental prosthetics companies that had personal computers.

Despite Jaslow Lab's May 31 letter warning Whelan Associates not to sell the Dentalab program, Whelan Associates continued to market Dentalab. That precipitated the present litigation.

Opinion

The elements of a copyright infringement action— To prove that its copyright has been infringed, Whelan Associates must show two things: that it owned the copyright on Dentalab, and that Rand Jaslow copied Dentalab in making the Dentacom program. Although it was disputed below, the district court determined, and it is not challenged here, that Whelan Associates owned the copyright to the Dentalab program. We are thus concerned only with whether it has been shown that Rand Jaslow copied the Dentalab program.

As it is rarely possible to prove copying through direct evidence,

***

copying may be proved inferentially by showing that the defendant had access to the allegedly infringed copyrighted work and that the allegedly infringing work is substantially similar to the copyrighted work.

***

The district court found, and here it is uncontested, that Rand Jaslow had access to the Dentalab program, both because Dentalab was the program used in Jaslow Labs and because Rand Jaslow acted as a sales representative for Whelan Associates.

***

Thus, the sole question is whether there was substantial similarity between the Dentcom and Dentalab programs.

On appeal, the defendants attack . . . the district court's holding that there was sufficient evidence of substantial similarity. First, the defendants argue that because the district court did not find any similarity between the "literal" elements (source and object code) of the programs, but only similarity in their overall structures, its [the court's] finding of substantial similarity was incorrect, for the copyright covers only the literal elements of computer programs, not their overall structures.

***

It is well, though recently, established that copyright protection extends to a program's source and object codes.

***

In this case, however, the district court did not find any copying of the source or object codes, nor did the plaintiff allege such copying. Rather, the district court held that the Dentalab copyright was infringed because the *overall structure* of Dentcom was substantially similar to the overall structure of Dentalab. The question therefore arises whether mere similarity in the overall structure of programs can be the basis for a copyright infringement, or, put differently, whether a program's copyright protection covers the structure of the program or only the program's literal elements, i.e., its source and object codes.

Title 17 U.S.C. § 102(a)(1) extends copyright protection to "literary works," and computer programs are classified as literary works for the purposes of copyright. The copyrights of other literary works can be infringed even when there is no substantial similarity between the works' literal elements. One can violate the copyright of a play or book by copying its plot or plot devices. See, e.g., *Twentieth Century-Fox Film Corp.* v. *MCA, Inc.*, 715 F.2d 1327, 1329 (9th Cir. 1983) (13 alleged distinctive plot similarities between *Battlestar Galactica* and *Star Wars* may be basis for a finding of copyright violation).

***

By analogy to other literary works, it would thus appear that the copyrights of computer programs can be infringed even absent copying of the literal elements of the program.

***

A rule for distinguishing idea from expression in computer programs—It is frequently difficult to distinguish the idea from the expression thereof.

***

[T]he purpose or function of a utilitarian work would be the work's idea, and everything that is not necessary to that purpose or function would be part of the expression of the idea.

***

Although the economic implications of this rule are necessarily somewhat speculative, we nevertheless believe that the rule would advance the basic purpose underlying the idea/expression distinction, "the preservation of the balance between competition and protection reflected in the patent and copyright laws."

***

As we stated above, among the more significant costs in computer programming are those attributable to developing the structure and logic of the program. The rule proposed here, which allows copyright protection beyond the literal computer code, would provide the proper incentive for programmers by protecting their most valuable efforts, while not giving them a stranglehold over the development of new computer devices that accomplish the same end.

Application of the general rule to this case—The rule proposed here is certainly not problem-free. The rule has its greatest force in the analysis of utilitarian or "functional" works, for the purpose of such works is easily stated and identified. By contrast, in cases involving works of literature or "non-functional" visual representations, defining the purpose of the work may be difficult. Since it may be impossible to discuss the purpose or function of a novel, poem, sculpture or painting, the rule may have little or no application to cases involving such works. The present case presents no such difficulties, for it is clear that the purpose of the utilitarian Dentalab program was to aid in the business operations of a dental laboratory. . . . It is equally clear that the structure of the program was not essential to that task: there are other programs on the market, competitors of Dentalab and Dentcom, that perform the same functions but have different structures and designs.

This fact seems to have been dispositive for the district court.

***

We agree. The conclusion is thus inescapable that the detailed structure of the Dentalab program is part of the expression, not the idea, of that program.

***

We hold [therefore] that (1) copyright protection of computer programs may extend beyond the programs' literal code to their structure, sequence, and organization, and (2) the district court's finding of substantial similarity between the Dentalab and Dentcom programs was not clearly erroneous. The judgment of the district court will therefore be affirmed.

Case Questions

1. Do you agree with the Court? If you do, try to describe first the part of a computer program that constitutes the *idea* and second the part that constitutes the *expression.*
2. If structure were not protected, couldn't someone just rewrite any program in another language and thereby sidestep any copyright in a computer program?
3. Evaluate the conduct of Whelan and Jaslow in this factual situation. In a moral sense, who do you admire more?

Programs and Compatibles

As the PC market grew, most of the hardware used a fairly standard operating system called CPM. Programming firms developed and wrote applications programs such as Wordstar so they would operate on CPM systems. When Apple and IBM PCs appeared, they used distinctive operating systems instead of CPM. Since these particular hardware manufacturers captured very large shares of the market, many of the new programs were written for their machines. Some small hardware firms became quite profitable by marketing machines that were **"compatible"** with either IBM's or Apple's operating systems. For example, Franklin is "Apple compatible" and Compaq is "IBM compatible." In order to make their machines compatible, some manufacturers pirated copyrighted operating programs—particularly assembly and compiler programs. They claimed that these particular programs were not protected by the copyright because they were embedded in a permanent memory, called ROM, and that this did not qualify as a "physical expression." The following case involved such a lawsuit.

Apple Computer, Inc. v. Formula Intern., Inc.

725 F.2d 521 (1984)

Facts

Formula International, Inc. (Formula), appeals from the district court's grant of a preliminary injunction in favor of the plaintiff, Apple Computer, Inc. (Apple). The injunction prohibits Formula from copying computer programs having copyrights registered to Apple.

Formula is a wholesaler and retailer of electronic parts and electronic kits. In May 1982, Formula entered the computer market, selling a computer kit under the trademark "Pineapple." The computer was designed to be compatible with application software written for the home computer manufactured by Apple, the Apple II. Included within Formula's computer kit were two computer programs embodied in semiconductor devices called ROMs (Read Only Memory). Formula concedes for purposes of appeal that the two programs are substantially similar to two programs for which Apple has registered copyrights.

Opinion

Circuit Judge Ferguson: The computer programs involved in this lawsuit are operating programs, that is, programs that are designed to manage the computer system. For example, one program translates instructions written in a higher-level language that is more understandable to the computer user into lower-level object code [machine language] that the computer [itself] understands. . . .

Apple brought suit against Formula claiming copyright . . . infringement. . . . Formula counterclaimed for antitrust violations . . . and sought declaratory relief as to the validity of certain . . . copyrights. After a brief period of discovery, Apple moved for a preliminary injunction based on its copyright . . . claims. . . . The district court granted the motion. . . .

Formula asserts that the district court erred in granting the preliminary injunction by relying on the legal premise that the Copyright Act . . . extends protection to all computer programs regardless of the function which those programs perform. Formula contends that the computer programs involved in this lawsuit, because they control the internal operation of the computer are only "ideas" or "processes," and therefore, unlike application programs, they are not protected by copyright. *See* 17 U.S.C. & 102(b) ("In no case does copyright protection for an original work of authorship extend to any *idea, procedure, process, system, method of operation,* concept, principle, or discovery regardless of the form in which it is described, explained, illustrated, or embodied in such work.") [emphasis added]. Formula also points to the idea/expression dichotomy recognized in case law . . . and contends that a computer program is protected under the Copyright Act only if the program embodies expression *which is communicated to the user when the program is run on a computer.* . . .

Formula's reliance on the idea/expression dichotomy to argue that computer programs are copyrightable only if they provide expression to the computer user is misplaced. The distinction between ideas and expression is intended to prohibit the monopolization of an idea when there are a limited number of ways to express that idea:

> The "ideas-expression identity" exception provides that copyrighted language may be copied without infringing when there is but a limited number of ways to express a given idea. This rule is the logical extension of the fundamental principal that copyright cannot protect ideas. In the computer context this means that when specific instructions, even though previously copyrighted, are the only and essential means of accomplishing a given task, their later use by another will not amount to an infringement. . . . When other language *is* available, programmers are free to read copyrighted programs and use the ideas embodied in them in preparing their own works. CONTU Report at 20 . . . *See also Apple Computer, Inc.,* v. *Franklin Computer Corp.* 714 F.2d 1240 (3d Cir. 1983). . . .

As in *Franklin,* Apple "does not seek to copyright the method which instructs the computer to perform its operating functions but only the instructions themselves." . . . Apple introduced evidence that numerous methods exist for writing the programs involved here, and Formula does not contend to the contrary. . . . Thus, Apple seeks to copyright only its particular set of instructions, not the underlying computer process.

Further, Formula provides absolutely no authority for its contention that the "expression" required in order for a computer program to be eligible for copyright protection is expression that must be communicated to the computer user when the program is run on the computer. The Copyright Act extends protection to "original works of authorship fixed in any tangible medium of expression, now known or later developed, from which they can be perceived, reproduced, or otherwise communicated, either directly or with the aid of a machine or device." . . . The computer program when written embodies expression; never has the Copyright Act required that the expression be communicated to a particular audience. . . .

CONCLUSION

The district court did not abuse its discretion or rely on erroneous legal premises in issuing the preliminary injunction.

Case Questions

1. Is the Court entirely accurate in stating "never has the Copyright Act required that the expression be communicated to a particular audience"?
2. Do you think the outcome of this suit will have the effect of driving Formula out of business? Is that a good result for the consumers of computers? Does your answer to this last question depend on whether you look for good results in the long term or the short term?
3. Can you see that the uncertainties in this new area of the law made it difficult for Formula to determine whether particular business conduct would be legal or illegal?

Most of the computer problems and legal developments we have described are directed at controlling the conduct of competitors. Other problems arose when programs were distributed widely to consumers.

Consumer Duplication

When application programs such as Wordstar were mass-marketed, typically for about $300 per copy, many persons used their PCs to make extra copies of the program. Often they sold, or gave away, the duplicate copies to others. Because this violation of the copyright was so hard to detect, unauthorized duplication became very widespread. It is frequently estimated that between one-half and two-thirds of all copies of some popular programs are unauthorized duplicates.

One response to the problem was the development of techniques to **"copy protect"** or "lock" programs onto diskettes so they could not be duplicated. As soon as these copy-protected programs appeared on the market, some entrepreneurs, developed programs to **"unlock"** or "unblock" copy-protected floppy disks. These programs sold for $15 to $150 and allowed consumers to make as many copies of a copyrighted program as they might desire. Note that unauthorized duplication of a copyrighted program is clearly illegal, while the sale of the unlocking programs is not. Do you think selling the unlocking programs—which help people violate the copyright law—is ethical?

Criminal Law Recognition of Property Interests in Data

State Criminal Law

At common law, the definition of the simplest theft, larceny, was, "the unlawful taking and carrying away of the goods of another." Note that this language is directed at tangible personal property; the words "taking" and "goods" indicate this. Similarly, the common law definition of burglary was, "the breaking and entering of the premises of another with the intent to commit a felony therein." Notice that this language indicates a trespass upon the real property of another as an element of this crime.

Computer technology has created two major problems for the criminal law systems of the states. One arises from the fact that something of great value can now be present in an intangible form such as electrical impulses. The other is that computers can be easily linked together with a device called a **modem.** Many computer systems are set up so they can be connected to telephones with a modem. Thus, if you dialed the right number, and used your computer to send the right password to the other computer, you could gain access to all the information in that computer.

When people began stealing the information (data) in computers, states responded in one of two distinct ways. The first and most rapid response was to redefine the meaning of the words in existing statutes. The second way was to pass new statutes.

Often the meaning of the word *goods* was expanded to include *knowledge*. In states where the word *property* was used in the theft statutes, this was sometimes stretched to encompass computer program data and/or information. In other states, the courts had already defined the words *goods* or *property* in ways that made it impractical to broaden the meaning of these words. While these processes of adapting existing laws were underway, there was of course a great deal of uncertainty about the legality of taking the computer information of another.

Other obstacles existed for particular situations. One was that if your computer was accessed by a modem, and data was *duplicated* so that your computer retained all of its information but it was copied onto the intruder's computer, then there was no "taking" because you had all the property you did before the intrusion. Also, there was no burglary because there was no trespassing. Some states, such as California, responded to this dilemma by enacting a statute making the infringement of a trade secret a crime.

Other states enacted statutes that make nearly all forms of computer intrusion criminal. For example, Arizona has a statute that states that "accessing, altering, damaging, or destroying without authorization any computer, computer system, computer network, or any part of such computer system or network" is criminal conduct.

Federal Criminal Law

The federal government has responded to the problem by passing the 1984 Computer Fraud Act, which makes it a federal crime to use or access a computer, without authorization, if (1) the computer belongs to the federal government; (2) the data obtained relate to nuclear weapons, foreign relations, or national defense; or (3) the information relates to financial records or credit ratings of consumers.

While the scope of this legislation is very narrow, the federal law on **wire fraud** covers computer fraud that occurs in interstate commerce. The following case illustrates the application of this body of federal law.

United States v. *Seidlitz*

589 F.2d 152 (1978)

Facts

On January 1, 1975, defendant Seidlitz assumed the position of Deputy Project Director for Optimum Systems, Inc. (OSI), a computer service company which was under contract to install, maintain, and operate a computer facility at Rockville, Maryland, for use by the Federal Energy Administration (FEA). Under the arrangement between OSI and FEA, persons working for FEA in various parts of the country could use key boards at communications terminals in their offices to send instructions over telephone circuits to the large computers in Rockville, and the computers' responses would be returned and reflected on a CRT (cathode ray tube) terminal, which is a typewriter-like device with a keyboard and display screen similar to a television screen upon which the information is displayed as it is sent and received. Mr. Seidlitz helped to prepare the software which was installed at the Rockville facility as part of the project, and he was also responsible for the security of the central computer system. During his tenure, he had full access to the computers and to a software system known as "WYLBUR" which resided within them. In June, 1975, Seidlitz resigned this job and returned to work at his own computer firm in Alexandria, Virginia.

William Coakley, a computer specialist employed

by FEA, was assigned temporarily to the OSI facility. On December 30, 1975, in an attempt to locate a friend who might be using the OSI system, he had the computer display the initials of everyone who was then using the WYLBUR software. Among the initials displayed by the computer were those of his supervisor, who was standing nearby and who was not using the computer. Suspicious that an unauthorized "intruder" might be using these initials in order to gain access to the system, Coakley asked Mr. Ewing, an OSI employee, if Ewing could determine what was happening. He also asked Mr. Wack, an OSI supervisor, if he (Wack) could determine whether the mysterious user was at a remote terminal or at one of the terminals within the OSI complex which were directly wired to the computer and did not employ telephone circuits. Ewing instructed the computer to display for him the data it was about to transmit to the possible intruder, and it proved to be a portion of the "source code" of the WYLBUR software system. Using other data provided by the computer, Wack concluded that the connection was by telephone from outside the complex. At his request, the telephone company manually traced the call to the Alexandria office of the defendant. Wack was told that the trace was successful, but the telephone company informed him that it could not divulge the results of the trace except in response to a legal subpoena.

The following day, OSI activated a special feature of the WYLBUR system known as the "Milten Spy Function," which automatically recorded, after they had been received by the machinery at Rockville, any requests made of the computer by the intruder. The "spy" also recorded, before they were sent out to the intruder over the telephone lines, the computer's responses to such requests. Mr. Wack again asked the telephone company to trace the line when it was suspected that the unauthorized person, employing the same initials, was using the computer to receive portions of the WYLBUR source code. This manual trace on December 31 led once more to the defendant's office in Virginia, although OSI was not so informed.

Advised by OSI of the events of December 30 and 31, the FBI on January 3, 1976, secured a warrant to search the defendant's Alexandria office.

***

[T]he FBI executed the warrant to search Seidlitz' Alexandria office, seizing, among other items, a copy of the user's guide to the OSI system and some forty rolls of computer paper upon which were printed the WYLBUR source code. A warrant was then issued to search the Seidlitz residence in Lanham, where officers found a portable communications terminal which contained a teleprinter for receiving written messages from the computer, as well as a notebook containing information relating to access codes previously assigned to authorized users of the OSI computers.

The indictment handed down on February 3, 1976, charged that the defendant had, on December 30 and 31, transmitted telephone calls in interstate commerce as part of a scheme to defraud OSI of property consisting of information from the computer system. A motion to suppress the evidence seized from the office and the residence [was made].

***

Over defense objection, much of the challenged evidence was admitted at trial, and the telephone traces, as well as the operation of the "Milten Spy," were described to the jury. In the face of this evidence, the defendant conceded that he had retrieved the information from the computers, but claimed to have acted only out of concern for the security of the OSI system. In negation of fraudulent intent, Seidlitz testified that he acquired the data with the sole intention of presenting the printouts to OSI officials to prove to them that the steps taken to prevent unauthorized use of the computers were inadequate. Additionally, it was his position at trial that the WYLBUR software was not a trade secret or other property interest of OSI sufficient to qualify as "property" within the meaning of the wire fraud statute. On appeal he renews the "illegal surveillance" claims and also argues that the evidence before the jury was insufficient to establish either his fraudulent intent or that WYLBUR constituted "property."

***

Opinion

The language, the legislative history, and the Supreme Court's interpretation of the relevant provisions of Title III support the district court's conclusion that the telephone traces in this case were not the sort of "interceptions" of communications proscribed by the statute. "Intercept" is defined in 18 U.S.C. § 2510(4) to mean "the aural acquisition of the *contents* of any wire or oral communication through the use of any electronic, mechanical, or other device" (emphasis added); *** The evidence adduced at the suppression hearing conclusively shows that neither the manual traces conducted . . . [by the phone company] . . . entailed interference with or observation of the contents of the defendant's dialogues with the computers. That Congress intended to exempt such procedures from the coverage of the statute is borne out by the Senate Report which accompanied the legislation. . . .

***

[T]o the extent that the Milten Spy disclosed, *before* they were sent out over the telephone lines, the substance of the replies generated by the computer to the intruder's commands, the information was not a "wire communication" at the time of its retrieval, and its disclosure thus did not violate the statute. Under Title III, a "wire communication" is a communication made "in whole or in part" through the facilities of a common carrier, 18 U.S.C. § 2510(1), and the portion of the WYLBUR source code requested by Seidlitz was obtained by the "spy" before it had travelled through such facilities. While arguably this reasoning might not apply to the spy's duplication, after they had been received by the computer, of any of the instructions Seidlitz sent by telephone, it unquestionably legitimizes under the statute that portion of the retrievals which identified the outgoing information as the WYLBUR source code. Finally, Title III specifically authorizes the interception of a wire communication by a party to the communication or by a person acting with the consent of a party to the communication. 18 U.S.C. § 2511(2)(c), (d). In our opinion OSI, which leased, housed, programmed, and maintained the computers and subscribed to the relevant telephone numbers, was for all intents and purposes a party to the communications initiated by the defendant, since in a very real sense the company used the computers solely as a medium for imparting to customers, via telephone lines, its own expertise. Insofar as OSI installed on its line a computer which was capable of recording the messages exchanged in the course of responding to a remote user's requests, we consider this case analogous to those which recognize that a party may, consistent with Title III, use a device to capture and record both sides of his telephone conversation with another party.

We have carefully reviewed the other issues raised by the appellant and find them to be without merit. Viewed in the light most favorable to the government, *Glasser* v. *United States,* 315 U.S. 60, 62 S.Ct. 457, 86 L.Ed. 680 (1942), there was sufficient evidence from which the jury could find that the WYLBUR system was "property" as defined in the instruction given by the trial judge which is not contested on appeal. Even though software systems similar to OSI's WYLBUR were in use at non-OSI facilities, the evidence that OSI invested substantial sums to modify the system to suit its peculiar needs, that OSI enjoyed a multimillion dollar competitive advantage because of WYLBUR, and that OSI took steps to prevent persons other than clients and employees from using the system permitted a finding that the pilfered data was the property of OSI and not, as the defendant contends, property in the public domain subject to appropriation by persons such as himself. In a similar vein, the defendant disputes the sufficiency of the evidence to establish fraudulent intent, but in essence his argument is only that he feels the jury should not have discredited his own explanation of the purpose for which he acquired the WYLBUR data. It is of no consequence that Seidlitz was not shown by the government to have used the data retrieved from the OSI computers in his own business or to have attempted to sell it to others, see *United States* v. *Painter,* 314 F.2d 939 (4 Cir. 1963), *cert. denied,* 374 U.S. 831, 83 S.Ct. 1873, 10 L.Ed.2d 1054 (1963); *United States* v. *Bagdasian,* 291 F.2d 163 (4 Cir. 1961), *cert. denied,* 368 U.S. 834, 82 S.Ct. 60, 7 L.Ed.2d 36 (1961), and the circumstantial evidence in this case is ample to support a finding of the requisite intent.

Affirmed.

Case Questions

1. Do you think the legislators who drafted the wire fraud statute had any knowledge about modern computer technology?

2. Do you think the judge correctly applied Title III by holding that the "spy" intercepted the "content of the communication," but not while it was in interstate communication? Was the judge "stretching" the law to fit a new situation? Is it right for judges to do this?
3. What do you suppose happened to Mr. Seidlitz?

As you can see, technological advances present significant challenges to our existing legal structures. Generally, the law changes very slowly. It is clear, however, that the economic importance of an issue greatly influences the speed of response and amount of attention given the issue by the legal system. Because the computer revolution is such a major economic development, the law has been highly responsive.

Ethical Issues in Computer Law

This chapter has described a body of law which has changed quickly to address problems created by new technology. But notice that the lag in legal developments creates opportunities for individuals to act in ways that are legal at the moment but very likely to become illegal in the near future. Thus it was possible—for a while in many states—to steal computer information from others without committing a crime. That raises the basic issue of whether you believe the limits on your conduct are defined by just the law or by both the law and ethics?

Many persons believe, and act on the belief, that their only moral obligation in business is to not violate the law. They reject the view that there are nonlegal obligations, obligations arising out of ethics, which constrain them. The reasons advanced for the view include the following.

1. It is impossible to determine what one's ethical responsibilities in business are except by reference to the law. Ethics is too vague a topic to be a guide for business conduct.
2. Others will gain a competitive advantage by engaging in the so-called unethical conduct, so to stay competitive, I must also.
3. I'm in business for myself and I need to make a buck every way I can without getting arrested.

Can you articulate reasons on the other side of this issue? For you, is the law the only guide for your conduct? Or do you believe that your personal ethics also define what conduct is permissible?

The important concepts and terms in this chapter are listed below; page numbers have been provided for the key terms. By reading over each section you can assess your understanding of the chapter concepts and determine areas you may want to review.

Chapter Summary

1. Information about chips, hardware, and programs can be protected as trade secrets, as long as they are kept secret.
2. Copyright will clearly protect the source code and object code expressions of computer programs. Portions of programs may be copyrighted to protect the idea behind a program.
3. It *may* be that the structure, sequence, and organization of a computer program can be protected by copyright.
4. Duplication of floppy disks with copyrighted programs on them is illegal.
5. Computer programs can be patented as part of a process patent.
6. It is now a crime in nearly all states to access without authorization the computer of another.
7. It is wire fraud—a federal crime—to access without authorization the computer of another to obtain information when the activity occurs across state lines.

Key Terms

applications programs 208
binary 209
chip 203
compatible 213
copy protect 215
expression 207
floppy disk 204
hard disk 204
hardware 203
high-level program language 208
idea 209
machine language 209
modem 215
operating programs 208
process patent 206
service contract 204
software 204
unlock (copy protection) 215
wire fraud 216

Questions on Ethics

1. Frequently in business discussions, people toss out ideas to be evaluated by a group. Suppose you are brainstorming a problem with a group of your subordinates and one of them comes up with an idea that you judge to be quite useful to your company. Further assume that you could appropriate this idea as your own, in your discussions with your boss, without any risk of adverse consequences to yourself. If you think there might be a substantial benefit to you, perhaps a significant raise, should you do so? Why or why not? Do you think you would?

2. "Reverse engineering" is the process of examining a competitor's product to determine how it was produced. Computer programs expressed in a high-level language are very easy to reverse engineer to determine what the initial flowchart looked like. Machine code programs are much more difficult to reverse engineer, but with enough money it can be done. It is clear that reverse engineering to obtain a flowchart of a copyrighted program is legal. With this flowchart it's fairly inexpensive to have someone write a new computer program. This new program created by the reverse engineering is itself copyrightable. If it were profitable for your career—and your company—to engage in this type of reverse engineering, would you do so? Why or why not?
3. Many sellers of applications software attempt to copy protect or lock the program onto the floppy disk. They do this so that the program cannot be copied onto another disk and given away or sold. There are, however, firms in the programming industry that market programs to unlock these disks and thereby allow people to make as many copies of the programs as they desire. The practical reality is that a buyer of a locked program can unlock it and make copies with very little risk of being caught, although it is a clear violation of the copyright law. On the other hand, the creation and marketing of a program that unlocks the copy protection is not illegal. But the only purpose for such a program is to allow others to violate the law. If you were a smart computer programmer, should you write a program to break copy protection? Should you do it if someone offered to pay you $12,000 and it would take you about one month to do it? Why or why not? If you purchased an applications program, would you use an unlocking program to illegally copy it and then sell it to a friend to reduce your investment? Why or why not?
4. Often in high technology companies the employees are required to sign statements in which they promise that they will not divulge the trade secrets of their employers to anyone during the period of employment or at any time in the future. Still, it is fairly common practice to hire technical persons such as programmers, engineers, and scientists, especially from smaller companies that lack legal resources, and get them to disclose the trade secrets. If you were a manager who could hire such a person to obtain a competitor's trade secrets, and you were sure the chance of adverse consequences were zero, should you do it? Why or why not?
5. Assume that you were working in a state during the time when criminal laws didn't apply to the duplication of computer data. If you had the opportunity to earn an extra $7,500 simply by copying the computer data, would it, in your view, be ethical to do it? How tempted would you be? If you think it is wrong to do it, and you would be strongly tempted, what could you do in advance of the temptation to increase the chances that you would not yield?

Questions on Law

1. Suppose you contracted for two products. One is a standard word processing program, say, Wordstar. The other is a contract for the development of a custom program for managing your firm's production line. Which body of law—the UCC or the common law of contracts—applies to the Wordstar transaction and which to the production line management program?
2. Smith & Wesson had developed a proprietary program for allocating its advertising dollars among advertising outlets. It took precautions to conceal the structure, sequence, and organization of the program. Those with access to the program were required to sign a document saying that they would not reveal its contents. The documentation was labeled "CONFIDENTIAL" in red ink. When an advertising employee left Smith & Wesson for a competitor he took a copy of the program with him. What recourse does Smith & Wesson have against the ex-employee and the competing firm?
3. Salomon Bros. developed a system for identifying stocks which had a much higher than average potential for increasing in value within a one-month time frame. How should the firm protect this program? Should it try to patent it? Should it copyright the whole program? Should it copyright the machine code? Should it simply treat the program as a trade secret?
4. Shardy worked for the Internal Revenue Service. He knew the access for their program for selecting tax returns to be audited. In return for the promise of $50,000 he sat down at his PC in Maryland, used his modem to access the IRS computer, found the audit program, downloaded it to his program, and delivered it to the buyer. What federal laws have been violated by Shardy's conduct?
5. Assume that you were corporate counsel for a software development firm developing a new wordprocessing program. The firm's investment would be about $4.5 million. Describe the *legal* steps you would take to protect your firm's investment. Also describe the nonlegal steps you would take.

Suggested Readings

Samuels and Samuels, "The Semiconductor Chip Protection Act of 1984: An Analytical Commentary," 23 *American Business Law Journal* 601 (1986).

9 Contracts I: Offer, Acceptance, and Consideration

And though he promise to his loss,
He makes his promise good.

—Nahum Tate

LEARNING OBJECTIVES

After you have read this chapter, you should be able to:

1. Determine which rules of contract law are designed primarily to create justice between those contracting and which rules are designed primarily to facilitate the operation of the judicial system.
2. Utilize the vocabulary of contract law.
3. Determine whether or not particular actions cause an offer to be created.
4. Determine when an acceptance arises.
5. Identify consideration.

Business Decisions and the Law

The Kitchen Sink

Jerry owns a small business that installs the plumbing in new homes under construction. It depends on a variety of suppliers for many of the pipes and fixtures used. Accordingly, Jerry needs to know exactly when he can depend on the materials that have been promised. He knows that the courts will assist him if he has a contract with his suppliers but he's not exactly sure when a contract arises. The material in this chapter will help you understand when someone is legally bound to live up to their promise to business persons like Jerry.

Introduction

From an ethical perspective, contract law can be viewed as addressing the *duty of promise keeping*. Business persons vary greatly in their commitment to keeping promises. Some keep their promises only when it is in their best interest to do so. Others will sacrifice in order to "live up to their word." As you read this chapter on contract law, think about your personal philosophy on the duty of promise keeping.

Studying contract law can help you develop such a personal philosophy, because contract law represents judicial and legislative philosophies about valid promising and promise keeping. But it is easy to misunderstand these philosophies of lawmakers, because they are sometimes as concerned about making courts work well as they are about treating parties fairly.

As you read this chapter, ask yourself whether our lawmakers established a rule because they considered it just or because they considered it expedient. By focusing on the reasons for these legal rules (justice or expediency), you can get a feel for the moral character of this field of law. In addition, the focus may help you to distinguish between a moral duty and a legal obligation. In an ethically perfect world, all valid promises would be kept. In a world almost ethically perfect, all valid promises would be enforced by courts. But in the real world, many promises are broken, and many times courts will not enforce the broken promise.

The central legal issue of contract law is this: How will the courts assist one party when the other fails to live up to a promise? A very simplified answer is that only one type of assistance is available if there is no contract, while several types of assistance are available if the courts conclude that there is a contract.

The remedy when the parties attempt to contract but fail is called **restitution.** It permits a party to recover something, such as money, given to another party. This remedy places the parties in the same position they would have been in if they had never tried to contract.

The remedies available when there *is* a contract are designed to place the parties in the position they would have been in if both parties had performed as promised. These contractual remedies are called *damages* and *specific performance*. At its core, contract law focuses on the availability of the various remedies. Since access to remedies is largely determined by the existence or nonexistence of a contract, the first question of contract law is, "Is there a contract?" Offer, acceptance, and consideration are usually required to create a contract.

Overview of Contract Law

The following statements summarize contract law in a very general way:

1. Contracts are governed by the common law if they involve the sale of realty or services. If the contract involves **goods**—tangible personal property—it is governed by another body of law called the **Uniform Commercial Code (UCC).** When a transaction involves both categories, such as goods and services, the dominant component determines which laws govern the transaction.
2. In general, a contract is not, as is popularly believed, signed sheets of paper. Rather, the law defines a binding contract as the end product of a *process or series of events*. Tests are applied to each step in the process to determine whether the requirements of contract law have been met. Usually, if one step is legally defective, no contract exists even though all the other tests have been met.
3. The process of creating a contract begins when a legal offer to contract is made. If a legally effective acceptance is given in return, an **agreement** is created. If the agreement genuinely reflects the intentions of the parties, another test is passed. The agreement must usually include an exchange of acts or promises. This is called the test of **consideration.** A final test, one that applies only to some agreements, is that they must be placed in writing. If all of these events occur and all of the tests are met, courts will enforce the agreement.
4. If a contract exists, and one of the parties is a young person, or suffers from mental incapacity due to intoxication, insanity, or some other mental problem, then that person is said to "lack contractual capacity." This status gives the party special rights in the contract.
5. Parties to contracts generally have both **contractual rights** (such as the right to receive money) and **contractual duties** (such as the duty to paint a house). These rights and duties can often be transferred to others.
6. The law has special rules that determine when contractual duties have been performed or excused. If a contractual duty is owed, but not performed, then the contract is said to have been **breached.**
7. The specific assistance—or remedies—that courts grant a party who is injured when a contract is breached vary greatly from transaction to transaction. The basic remedies are restitution (where you get back something you have given the other party), **money damages** (where you collect money for a financial injury caused by the breach), and **specific performance** (where the court directs the breaching party to perform the act promised in the contract).

The Nature of Contract Law

Before the end of the fifteenth century, contract law evolved in England primarily as a mechanism for enforcing promises. In this country, when states became a part of the Union, they typically adopted the "common law of England" as a part of their state law. In that fashion they incorporated England's contract law as a part of state law. The states then began the processes of clarifying and modifying the common law. As this occurred, the contract law of the various states became different. That made doing business between different states awkward and expensive because two different bodies of law had to be consulted. Partly in response to this problem, lawyers, judges, and law professors gathered to write a Uniform Commercial Code (UCC). That document articulated in statutory language many of the common law contract rules. Eventually, the UCC was adopted by all the states except Louisiana, which enacted only a part of it.

For contract law purposes, the UCC applies only to "contracts for the sale of goods." The key word in that language is "goods." Under the UCC, goods are tangible (touchable), movable, personal property. That means the UCC does *not* apply to transactions for *services* or *realty*. These contracts are still governed by the common law of contracts.

The UCC differs from the common law of contracts in some important ways. The following case illustrates the way these differences can influence the outcome of litigation. The case concerns the "statute of limitations," a rule that determines how soon one must file suit after a legal duty has been breached. In the case, this time limit is four years under the UCC and six years under the common law of contracts.

Consolidated Edison v. Westinghouse

567 F. Supp. 358 (1983)

Facts

Westinghouse contracted to furnish an operable nuclear power plant for Consolidated Edison (Con Ed). The plant was built in Buchanan, New York. About a year after completion, defects in the plant became apparent. Westinghouse and Con Ed entered into negotiations over who was responsible for the defects. These negotiations took a long time. Because they were in part unsuccessful, Con Ed filed suit for, among other things, breach of contract. Westinghouse defended, in part, by claiming that the suit was barred by the statute of limitations.

Opinion

District Judge Lasker: Under New York law, a four-year statute of limitations applies to causes of action based on contracts for the sale of goods, which are governed by the Uniform Commercial Code [2–725], while a six-year statute of limitations applies to causes of action based on service or construction contracts, which are governed by the common law. *** [T]he timeliness of its contract claims with respect to the steam turbines and other equipment depends upon whether the IP 2 Agreement is "in essence" a contract for the sale of goods under the UCC, or whether instead it is a service contract. . . .

Westinghouse argues, in favor of the applicability of the UCC, that the primary object of the Agreement was the purchase by Con Ed of Westinghouse-manufactured and -designed component parts—the steam generators, turbines, and other components of the IP 2 Plant. ***

In answer Con Ed points out that the IP 2 Agreement is a contract not simply for the sale of specific items of power plant equipment, but for the construction of a complete nuclear power plant. The

Agreement, Con Ed argues, not only required Westinghouse to provide all architectural and engineering services necessary to the construction of the plant, along with the labor required for its construction, but also provided that Westinghouse would take all necessary steps to assure that the plant would be granted an operating license under the requirements established by the United States Atomic Energy Commission. Con Ed contends that the scope of Westinghouse's responsibilities under the Agreement, which continued throughout several years of design, construction, testing and licensing, differentiates the Agreement from typical "goods" contracts involving the one-time installation of a specific item of equipment. ***

The New York cases exploring the distinction between sales and services contracts provide no clear answer to the proper classification of the IP 2 Agreement. In several instances New York courts have held that contracts as to which "service predominates and the transfer of title to personal property is an incidental feature of the transaction" are outside the scope of the UCC. In the present case, however, on the record as it stands, neither the goods nor the services aspect of the Agreement can reasonably be characterized as "incidental." Just as Con Ed plainly could not have considered the power generating equipment to be an incidental feature of its contract with Westinghouse, so also the architectural, engineering and testing services provided by Westinghouse, and the labor necessary to carry them out, were crucial to the Agreement's objective. ***

Where, as here, the question is closely balanced, factual development is necessary before the issue is resolved. The pleadings do not reveal the allocation of contract price as between construction and equipment costs, . . . or other matters that may contribute to a proper resolution of the question. It may be, as Westinghouse argues, that the "essential" nature of the contract will not be significantly clearer following development of the record, but the accuracy of this prediction cannot be determined in advance of obtaining the facts.

Westinghouse motion to dismiss denied.

Case Questions

1. Do you think a contract for a nuclear power plant is one primarily for goods or services?
2. Can you think of a reason why there should be two different statutes of limitations depending upon whether a transaction is governed by the UCC or the common law of contracts?
3. Should Con Ed's ability to sue here turn on a rule, such as the statute of limitations? As an alternative, a judge could determine how the passage of time has reduced the ability of Westinghouse to defend itself effectively. Can you see that a uniform rule is very efficient for the judicial system? Case-by-case determinations are expensive but perhaps more just. Which approach is more morally appealing?

Creating a Contract

In general, a contract comes into being when there is a genuine offer and acceptance, consideration, and in some cases a writing. If one of these tests is not met, there is usually no contract.

Offers

Overview of Offers

The party who makes an **offer** is called an *offeror*. The party to whom the offer is made is called the *offeree*. A legally satisfactory offer may be simple or complex, depending on the nature of the proposed transaction. There are, however, certain minimum requirements for a sufficient offer. These requirements are:

1. The proposal must manifest an *intent* to contract.
2. The proposal must contain the *essential and definite* terms.
3. The proposed activity must be *legal.*
4. The proposal must be *communicated* to the offeree.

If an offer exists, then one of the obstacles to the creation of a contract has been hurdled. Equally important, a legally valid offer gives the offeree power to bind the offeror into a contract by accepting the offer. If the other tests are met, then once acceptance occurs, the contract exists and the offeror cannot withdraw from the agreement without the offeree's consent. For example, suppose you made a valid offer to sell your car for $450, and there was a valid acceptance. You could not withdraw from the transaction without the buyer's consent, if the other requirements of the contract had been met. If you were to learn after the acceptance that the true value of the car was $1,000, you still could not get out of the contract without the buyer's agreement.

Manifesting a Present Intent to Contract

The party making an offer must appear to intend to contract. Some proposals clearly indicate a lack of intention to enter into a binding agreement. Statements that are mere inquiries, or preliminary questions, or invitations to make offers, or words spoken in obvious jest or anger do not create offers.

The law judges the intent of the offeror from the appearance of his or her conduct. The offeror's actual intention does not govern. The standard used by most courts is whether or not a "reasonable man" would interpret the offeror's words and acts, in the context of all the facts and circumstances, as indicating an intention to enter into a binding contract. Suppose, for example, you invested $150,000 in developing a computer program to calculate the income tax liability of small businesses. Further assume that in a fit of pride and out of an offbeat sense of humor, you wrote IBM describing the program in detail and offering to sell it for $10,000 (a price that seems laughably low to you). If IBM wrote back accepting, would there be a contract? In a trial, the judge or jury would decide; they would apply the **test of the reasonable man.** In effect, they would ask whether or not a reasonable person would interpret your letter as serious or as a joke. If a reasonable person would see it as a joke, there would be no offer and thus no contract. On the other hand, if a reasonable person would interpret your letter as a serious offer, there would be a contract at the $10,000 price.

Essential, Definite, and Legal Terms

The offer must contain enough information so that a court could determine the rights and duties of the parties to a resulting contract.

The offer must contain the essential terms. This means there is a minimum amount of information that must be communicated by the offer. The amount of required information depends upon the complexity of the transaction. For example, a consumer's offer to buy fresh apples from a farmer would be sufficient if the offeror specified just the quantity and the price. This offer is sufficient because of the simple nature of the transaction. In contrast, an offer to purchase a home must be more detailed, because the transaction is complex. Essential terms for this offer include the identities of the parties, the terms of payment, the date when the buyer is to take possession, the quality of the title to be conveyed, and a description of the property.

While the UCC generally follows the common law of contracts with regard to essential and definite offers, it does make important changes. One is that the offer under the UCC need not be definite about price. Thus if an offer for the sale of goods fails to state a price, and the courts could determine a *reasonable price,* there will still be a valid offer. Price is generally essential under the common law but not the UCC.

Courts usually impose more stringent requirements in determining whether advertisements contain all of the essential terms. This is because advertising would be discouraged if ads were easily construed as legally binding offers. If terms are omitted from ads, they are treated as invitations to the public to make offers and not as offers themselves.

The essential terms must be definite. This means the terms are able to be identified or measured by the parties and by the courts. For example, an offer to purchase a home for "no more than $125,000" would not be definite. On the other hand, an offer to purchase for "a price to be equal to appraised value established by Mr. J. Appraiser, M.A.I." would be definite. Although the amount is not known at the time the contract is executed, it can be determined later by the parties or by the courts. If an essential term is not definite, there is generally no offer and no contract.

The following case illustrates the way courts view the requirement that offers be definite and certain.

Rivers v. Beadle

7 Cal. Rptr. 170 (1960)

Facts

This case is based on the following agreement executed by the plaintiff and the defendants:

March 3, 1955

In consideration of Vera Rivers Realty handling my purchase of three lots located at Center Avenue, corner K Street, San Rafael, without brokerage, as evidenced by attached copy of deposit receipt, I hereby agree as follows:

1. To build on each of said three lots a speculative home, which is to be placed on the market immediately for sale on completion of same.

2. To give Vera Rivers Realty the exclusive right to sell each of such houses and pay a 3 percent commission of selling price, this exclusive right to sell to be effective immediately and to continue to effect for a period of one year from date of completion of each of such houses.

/s/ Philander B. Beadle

/s/ Eva May Beadle

/s/ Vera Rivers

Later, the Beadles refused to build. Vera Rivers sued and at trial won a judgment for damages of $1800. The Beadles appealed, asserting that the *agreement was too indefinite to constitute a contract.*

Opinion

[L]et us examine the contract.

(a) It clearly sets forth each party to the contract. The parties are the defendants on the one hand, and Vera Rivers on the other.

(b) The subject matter is that in consideration of the waiving of a commission by Vera Rivers for her handling defendants' purchase of the described three lots, defendants agree to build on each lot "a speculative home" to be placed on the market for sale immediately on completion.

(c) The agreement also clearly shows "the terms and conditions of all the promises constituting the contract and by whom and to whom the promises are made." These are, first, that defendants agree to build the homes (although the time is not stated, such an agreement imports an understanding that it must be built within a reasonable time); secondly, that defendants will place the homes for sale on the market immediately upon completion, and that Vera Rivers has the exclusive right . . . to sell them, and defendants agree that on such sale Vera Rivers will receive a commission of 3 percent of the sale price. While the selling price is not fixed in the agreement (it could not be until the homes were built and their cost obtained), implied in the agreement, and well understood by the parties, is that the defendants would fix the selling price to return a profit to them. Vera Rivers was not concerned with the selling price. She was given the right to sell, if possible, the houses for whatever price defendants might place the houses on the market. There was nothing indefinite in this term of the contract.

"Speculative home" as here used is not indefinite or vague. It had a definite meaning to the parties. The evidence showed that this is a term well known in real estate circles and to defendants, as meaning simply a home built with expectation of selling it at cost plus a profit and of the type and price of homes being then generally built and sold in the area. Applicable here is *Betterment* v. *Gilroy Theatre Co., Inc.,* 261 P.2d 351, where this court held that an agreement " '. . . to errect [sic] a *First class Theatre*' " [emphasis added] was sufficiently definite and certain to create and impose a contractual obligation. . . .

It is true that some explanation [i.e., testimony] has to be made of what the parties meant by a "speculative home," just as in *Betterment, supra,* explanation was required as to what the parties had in mind by " '*First class Theatre.*' " In considering this question applicable here is the following from *Avalon Products Inc.* v. *Lentini,* 219 P.2d 485: "The law leans against the destruction of contracts because of uncertainty and favors an interpretation which will carry into effect the reasonable intention of the parties if it can be ascertained. The description of the subject matter of an agreement may be indefinite but if it is capable of being identified and rendered definite and certain by evidence *aliunde* [from elsewhere], the contract is enforceable." A "speculative home" appears from the evidence to be sufficiently definite and certain to enable the defendants to know what they had undertaken to do.

The Facts of our case differ greatly from those in *Ferrara* v. *Silver, supra,* 292 P.2d 251, where the contract provided that a "banquet room building' " was to be built, and we held that that expression was so vague that the contract could not be enforced. There the parties, at the time of entering into the agreement, did not have in mind any particular type, size or price of building. As the court there said, the parties did not have "in mind as a form or standard" any building, such as the parties in *Bettancourt, supra,* did. In our case the parties did have in mind a norm or standard. It was the type, materials and range of price of speculative homes in the general area. In determining the sufficiency of [a] contract, the purpose of the contract must be borne in mind. Its basic purpose was to enable the real estate broker to obtain a commission on the sale of the houses, to make up for the waiver of a commission then due for the purchase by defendants of the lots. *While the description might be considered too vague were this a contract of purchase of a house or houses, it is not too vague for the purpose intended* [emphasis added]. The type, materials and price (within the norm or standard above mentioned) was left to the discretion of defendants, but they were to build the houses and the broker was to be permitted to sell them on commission. . . .

Judgment affirmed.

Case Questions

1. Which terms were the most indefinite in this contract—"three lots," "3 percent" or "speculative home"?
2. Would this judge have enforced the agreement if it recited just "a commission" instead of "a 3 percent commission"?
3. Does the legal requirement of essential and definite terms exist because it is just, or expedient, or both? Assume you were Philander Beadle and the court had found that the agreement was not sufficiently definite, so no contract existed. Would you still pay the commission to Vera Rivers?

Offers must propose transactions that are legal. For example, a proposal to enter into a gambling agreement would seldom constitute an offer because gambling is usually illegal. If the proposal is for an illegal purpose, there is no offer and, therefore, no contract.

Communication of the Offer

The offer must be communicated to the offeree. In general, no one other than the offeree may accept an offer, and an offer is not effective until the intended communication occurs. For example, suppose you are negotiating for the sale of a purebred horse, and the prospective buyer walks into your empty office during the lunch hour and finds a copy of a written, signed offer addressed to him. If the prospective buyer signs the document and takes a copy, this would not create a contract; this is because you were deprived of the last opportunity to change your mind before mailing the offer. Therefore, there was no intentional communication, and thus no offer, and thus no contract.

In summary, the offer exists only when there has been conduct or words indicating an intent to contract, the essential terms are described in a definite manner, the activities proposed are legal, and the proposal has been intentionally communicated to the offeree.

Unilateral and Bilateral Offers

All offers are either bilateral or unilateral. A **unilateral offer** is one that indicates that the offeree should accept by the performance of the *act* requested. It is a promise exchanged for an act. In contrast, a **bilateral offer** allows an acceptance in the form of a promise. Bilateral offers propose the exchange of a *promise* for a *promise*.

The words used in the offer determine whether it is unilateral or bilateral. A unilateral offer might state, "I'll pay you $10 to mow my lawn. You can accept this offer by mowing the lawn next Saturday." A bilateral offer might state, "I promise to pay you $10 if you promise to mow my lawn next Saturday." When the words are not clearly unilateral or bilateral, the courts will resolve the ambiguity by finding that the offer is bilateral. The distinction between a unilateral offer and a bilateral offer is important in determining when and if a contract comes into being. For example, if you respond to the bilateral offer with the words, "I accept," a contract exists. If you respond to the unilateral offer with the words, "I accept," a contract does *not* exist. Figure 9.1 presents a diagram illustrating unilateral and bilateral offers.

Figure 9.1 Unilateral and Bilateral Contracts

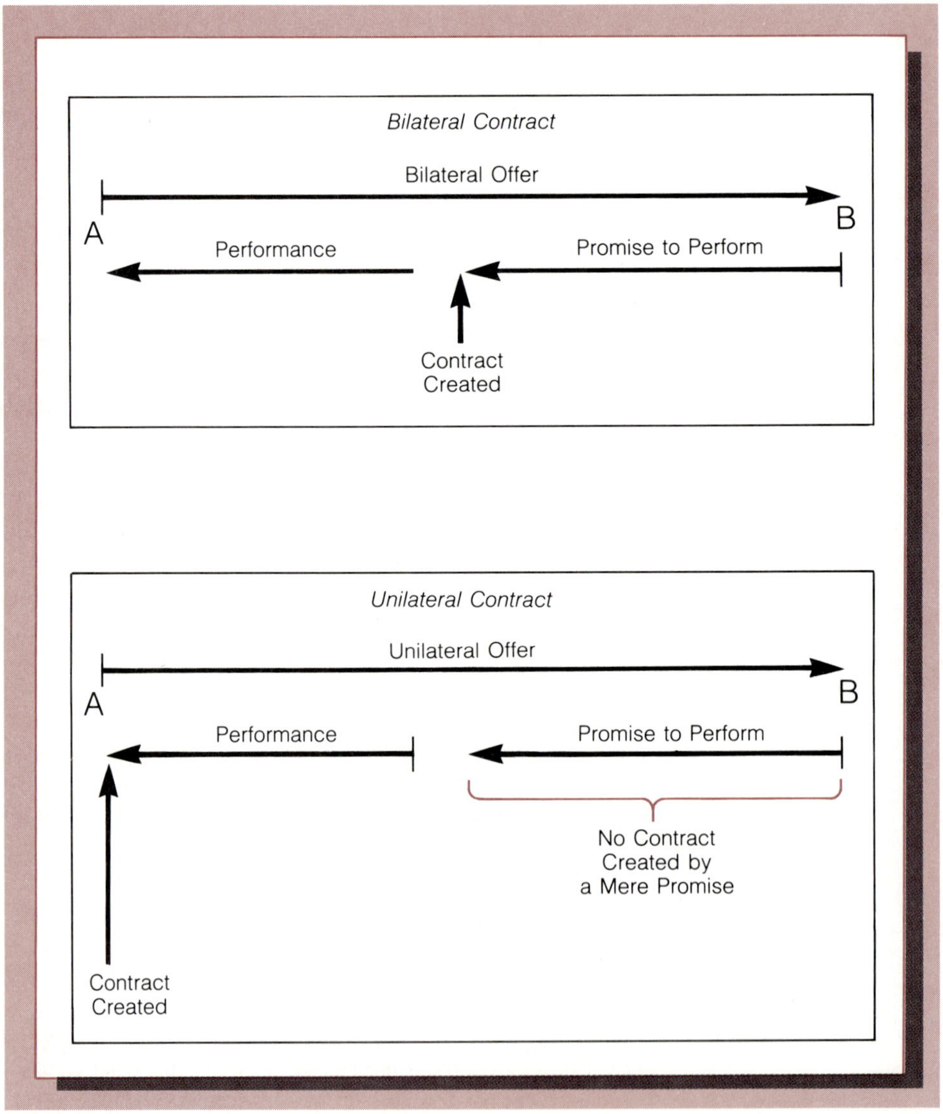

Termination of Offers

If an offer is made, a variety of events can cause its termination. One way to terminate an offer is by **revocation.** The offeror has the power to revoke (i.e., withdraw) the offer any time before the acceptance occurs. An offeror might revoke by stating the following: "I know I offered to pay you $10 to mow my lawn, but I've changed my mind and I'm going to have someone else do it."

Promises Not to Revoke. Sometimes the offeror will promise not to revoke for a certain period of time. For example, he or she may write in an offer:

> I offer to sell the above described accounting services for the indicated price and terms and I hereby agree to leave this offer open until ten days from this date.

The common law generally treats this as a mere promise not supported by consideration, and thus the offeror is not bound to leave the offer open, since the promise does not create a contract. It may be revoked at any time. If the offer were for goods, and thus governed by the UCC, a written, signed promise by a merchant to leave an offer open would bind the merchant. The merchant would only be bound for a maximum of three months. This is sometimes called a **firm offer.**

Options. In order to create an irrevocable offer, the parties frequently create an option contract. An **option** contract will exist when money or other consideration is given in return for the promise to leave the offer open for a definite period of time. Option contracts must meet all the tests required of any other type of contract. Thus the following language in an offer would probably create an option:

> I offer to sell the above described oil refinery for the indicated price and terms. Further, in exchange for $250, receipt of which is hereby acknowledged, I agree to leave this offer open for ten days from this date.

Consequence of Revocation. Once revocation occurs, the offeree no longer has the power to bind the offeror with an acceptance. A new offer is needed if the parties are to agree and contract.

Life of an Offer. Offerors frequently specify the length of time during which the offeree may accept. This time period is called the **life of an offer.** If the offeree attempts to accept after the time period has expired, no contract is created because the offer is no longer alive.

If the offer is **silent** about the length of its life, then it will exist for a reasonable time. The facts and circumstances surrounding each offer determine what will be a reasonable time for the life of that offer. Thus, an offer to buy stock traded on a national exchange would have a very short life—perhaps one or two days—because stock prices can change in a short period of time. An offer to purchase a carload of bananas would have a relatively short life—perhaps ten to twenty hours—because bananas spoil rapidly. An offer to sell land, when the offer is silent about the length of its life, may be in effect for a few months, depending upon the facts and circumstances surrounding the offer. Because it is difficult to determine what is a reasonable time, the offeror should specify the length of the offer's life.

Destruction of the Subject Matter. Offers can be terminated by the destruction of the subject matter of the offer. Thus if an offer is made by a buyer in Texas to purchase a warehouse in Alabama, and the warehouse burns down, the seller could not create a contract by accepting after the fire. The offer terminated when the fire destroyed the subject matter of the offer.

Death or Insanity. The law automatically terminates an offer if either the offeror or offeree dies or becomes insane. Thus if I offered to sell you my thirty-two-foot-long pet boa constrictor for $12,000, then I mysteriously died before you accepted, your acceptance after my death would not create a contract. Offers die when the offeror or offeree dies.

Similarly, if the offer becomes illegal before an acceptance, the offer is terminated.

Rejection, Counteroffers, and Solicitation of Additional Offers

If an offer is made, it creates a series of legal alternatives that may be voluntarily exercised by the offeror or the offeree. As we have said, the offeror may end the offer by *revoking* it. The offeree may *reject* the offer, or suggest different terms with a *counteroffer,* or ask the offeror to make an *additional offer,* or *accept*.

A **rejection** is a refusal, by words or conduct, to accept an offer. Thus, if an offeror states, "I will sell you this book for $45," and the offeree merely shakes her head from side to side, she has rejected. A rejection ends the offer. Thus if an offeree rejects, a later attempted acceptance would not create a contract. For example, the following dialog would not create a contract:

A: *I offer to sell you this book for $45. (An offer)*
B: *No thanks. (A rejection)*
B: *I've changed my mind, and I accept your offer. (An ineffective attempted acceptance)*

Counteroffers arise when the offeree tells the offeror that he or she wants to contract but on terms different from those in the offer. Counteroffers contain an implied rejection of the terms of the original offer. The law, therefore, treats a counteroffer as both a *rejection* and a *new offer*. The new offer flows from the original offeree to the original offeror. Since the original offer has been rejected, it cannot be accepted later. Thus the following dialog would not create a contract:

A: *I offer to sell you this book for $49.95. (An offer)*
B: *I'll give you a flat $45! (A counteroffer)*

A: *No, that's not enough! (A rejection of the counteroffer)*
B: *Well, after thinking it over, I've decided to accept your offer at $49.95. (An ineffective attempted acceptance)*

Many counteroffers are unintentional. An offeree who attempts to accept but in some way modifies the terms of the offer, under the common law, has created not an acceptance, but a counteroffer.

There are only two alternatives open to the offeree that do not terminate the offer: solicitation of an additional offer and acceptance. **Solicitation of an additional offer** is basically a negotiating ploy. It involves delaying the response to the offer while encouraging the offeror to make a second offer on different, perhaps more favorable, terms. The following dialog illustrates the solicitation of an additional offer:

A: *I offer to sell you this HP 12C calculator for $70. (An offer)*
B: *Gee, let me give that some thought, OK?*
A: *OK.*
B: *By the way, I wonder if you might offer it for a lower price. If you could come down $15 or $20, I could accept right now. (Solicitation of an additional offer)*
A: *I'll sell it for $50. (The additional offer)*

Courts generally view solicitations of additional offers with disfavor. They will often try to interpret the offeree's language and conduct as indicating either a rejection or a counteroffer. Figure 9.2 illustrates the alternatives available after an offer has been made.

Acceptance

Acceptance of an offer creates a contract. There are four major requirements for an **acceptance:** intent, mirroring the offer, performance of acceptance, and communication.

1. The test of intent for acceptance is similar to the test of intent for the offer. That is, would a "reasonable man" interpret the offeree's words and conduct, in light of all the facts and circumstances, as indicating an intention to accept?
2. The acceptance must match, or mirror, the terms and conditions contained in the offer. If the acceptance materially varies those terms, a counteroffer is created rather than an acceptance. Under the UCC, however, some variation in the acceptance is permitted. Thus, in a contract for the sale of goods, an acceptance can include "additional terms." When this occurs, a contract arises. Its terms include only the terms contained in both the offer and acceptance. Generally the additional terms are treated as proposals for modifying the contract. The offeror can accept or reject the proposed additional terms.
3. The acceptance must satisfy any requirements stipulated in the offer that

Figure 9.2 Post Offer Alternatives and Events

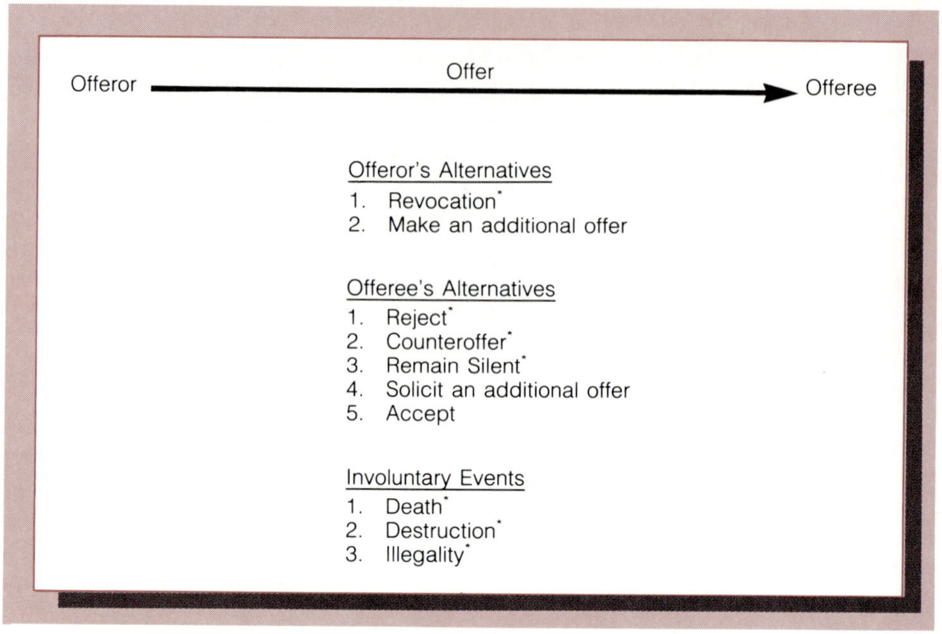

*The offer is extinguished by this alternative or event.

are related to the manner of acceptance. Thus, if the offer specifies a time for acceptance, or a manner of acceptance (such as by telegram), or an act required for acceptance (such as the delivery of a cashier's check for $5,000), these terms must be satisfied or there is no acceptance. When a unilateral offer is made, it must be accepted by the performance of the act requested—the giving of a promise is not acceptance.

4. An acceptance is not effective until it is communicated. And the offeror has the right to revoke any time before the acceptance is effective.

The following case discusses the law precisely when an acceptance is effective.

Morrison v. Thoelke

155 So.2d 889 (Fla. 1963)

Facts

Defendants signed an offer for the purchase of the plaintiffs' real property. Then the offer was mailed to the plaintiffs. Plaintiffs signed and mailed the contract back to the defendants. Before the contract arrived, plaintiffs called defendants on the phone and repudiated the signed document. After the document arrived, the defendants recorded it. Defendants filed suit to determine whether a contract existed. The lower court found for the plaintiff.

Opinion

J. Allen: The question is whether a contract is complete and binding when a letter of acceptance is mailed, thus barring repudiation prior to delivery to the offeror, or when the letter of acceptance is received, thus permitting repudiation prior to receipt. Appellants, of course, argue that posting the acceptance creates the contract; appellees contend that only receipt of the acceptance bars repudiation.

The appellant, in arguing that the lower court erred in giving effect to the repudiation of the mailed acceptance, contends that this case is controlled by the general rule that insofar as the mail is an acceptable medium of communication, a contract is complete and binding upon posting of the letter of acceptance . . . . Appellees, on the other hand, argue that the right to recall mail makes the Post Office Department the agent of the sender, and that such right coupled with communication of a renunciation prior to receipt of the acceptance voids the acceptance. In short, appellees argue that acceptance is complete only upon receipt of the mail acceptance . . . .

Turning first to the general rule relied upon by appellant some insight may be gained by reference to the statement of the rule in leading encyclopedias and treatises . . . .

A leading treatise on the law of contracts, Corbin, Contracts 78 and 80 (1950 Supp. 1961), also devotes some discussion to the "rule" urged by appellants. Corbin writes:

> Where the parties are negotiating at a distance from each other, the most common method of making an offer is by sending it by mail; and more often than not the offeror has specified no particular mode of acceptance. In such a case, it is now the prevailing rule that the offeree has power to accept and close the contract by mailing a letter of acceptance, properly stamped and addressed, within a reasonable time. The contract is regarded as made at the time and place that the letter of acceptance is put into the possession of the post office department.

Like the editor of Williston, Corbin negates the effect of the offeree's power to recall his letter:

***

> In view of common practices, in view of the difficulties involved in the process of interception of a letter, and in view of the decisions and printed discussions dealing with acceptance by post, it is believed that the fact that a letter can be lawfully intercepted by the sender should not prevent the acceptance from being operative on mailing. If the offer was made under such circumstances that the offeror should know that the offeree might reasonably regard this as a proper method of closing the deal, and the offeree does so regard it, and makes use of it, the contract is consummated even though the letter of acceptance is intercepted and not delivered.

***

The rule that a contract is complete upon deposit of the acceptance in the mails, herein before referred to as "deposited acceptance rule". . . had its origin, insofar as the common law is concerned, in *Adams* v. *Lindsell* 1 Barn. & Ald. 681, 106 Eng. Rep. 250 (K.B. 1818).

Examination of the decision in *Adams* v. *Lindsell* reveals three distinct factors deserving consideration. The first and most significant is the court's obvious concern with the necessity of drawing a line, with establishing some point at which a contract is deemed complete. . . . A second factor, again a practical one, was the court's apparent desire to limit but not overrule the decision in *Cooke* v. *Oxley,* . . . that an offer was revocable at any time prior to the acceptance.

***

Finally, having effectively circumvented the inequities of *Cooke* v. *Oxley,* the court, apparently constrained to offer some theoretical justification for its decision, designated a mailed offer as "continuing" and found a meeting of the minds upon the instant of posting assent. Significantly, the factor of the offeree's loss of control of his acceptance is not mentioned.

In short, both advocates and critics muster persuasive arguments. As Corbin indicated, there must be a choice made, and such choice may, by the nature of things, seem unjust in some cases. Weighing the arguments with reference not to specific cases but toward a rule of general application and recognizing the general and traditional acceptance of the rule as well as the modern changes in effective long-distance communication, it would seem that the balance tips, whether heavily or near imperceptively [sic], to continued adherence to the "Rule in *Adams* v. *Lindsell.*"

In the instant case, an unqualified offer was accepted and the acceptance made manifest. Later, the offerees sought to repudiate their initial assent. [A]dopting the view that the acceptance was effective when the letter of acceptance was deposited in the mails, the repudiation was equally invalid and cannot alone support the summary decree for appellees (plaintiffs). The summary decree, for the plaintiffs, is reversed and the case remanded for further proceedings.

Case Questions

1. Notice that the changes in the postal regulations created legal uncertainty about when an acceptance is effective. Can you justify injuring one party in this case because they guessed wrong about the way the courts would react to the change in postal regulations?
2. Can fairness in an individual case be ignored because doing so produces fairness in one hundred other cases?
3. Is it more important to have a clear rule here than to have a completely logical rule?

The Genuineness of the Offer and Acceptance

Even if there is intent, mirroring of the offer, performance of acceptance, and communication of acceptance, the courts may still conclude that there is no contract if there has been a mutual mistake of fact, fraud, duress, or undue influence.

Mutual mistake of fact occurs when both parties enter into an agreement based upon a common belief about a fact later discovered to be wrong. Thus, if both parties to a contract believed that a property contained forty acres when it really only contained twenty-five acres, the courts would probably conclude that no contract existed.

In general, if only one party is mistaken about a material fact, the agreement is enforceable. However, where one party is reasonably mistaken about the *identity* of the subject matter of the agreement, this error is usually treated as a mutual mistake of fact.

If both parties make a **mistake of law**—that is, they are mistaken as to the law that applies to their transaction—the agreement will be enforced on the assumption that "ignorance of the law is no excuse." However, when one party makes an inaccurate representation about the law, and he or she is a lawyer, accountant, real estate broker, banker, or someone else with special legal expertise, the courts will not enforce the agreement against the nonexpert. Courts generally will enforce the agreement when the misstatement of law is made by a nonexpert.

Misrepresentation occurs when one party misleads another about a material fact on which the other party justifiably relies. Misrepresentation often occurs when the offending party acted mistakenly, but honestly and without an intent to deceive. The remedy for misrepresentation is generally limited to restitution, that is, treating the contract as void and restoring the parties to their pre-contract positions. Suppose you advertised a six-month-old VW for sale, found a buyer, told her that the new car warranty could be transferred to her, that the warranty was good for another six months, and concluded the sale for $7,500. If you were innocently mistaken about the transferability of the warranty, the buyer could sue for misrepresentation and force you to take back the VW and to return the $7,500.

In general, **fraud** occurs when one party *intentionally* misrepresents a material fact that the other party reasonably relies on to his or her injury. The statement must be made with the intent to deceive. The author or speaker of the statement must know it is false or must communicate the fact with reckless disregard for its truth. The fact must be material, that is, important to the transaction. And the party to whom the statement is made must reasonably rely on the statement and be injured because of the statement.

Suppose in the middle of a dry summer a potential buyer of your $95,000 home asked about the roof and you, the seller, replied, "The roof doesn't leak." The buyer could probably withdraw from the agreement if it turned out that the roof leaked, you knew that, and its repair would cost $3,000. Your conduct likely constitutes fraud. The remedies for fraud, as for misrepresentation, include restitution. But in addition, the victim of fraud can recover damages and in some cases **punitive damages.** Punitive damages are awards unrelated to the victim's injuries that are designed to punish the wrongdoer.

Figure 9.3 Elements of Offer and Acceptance

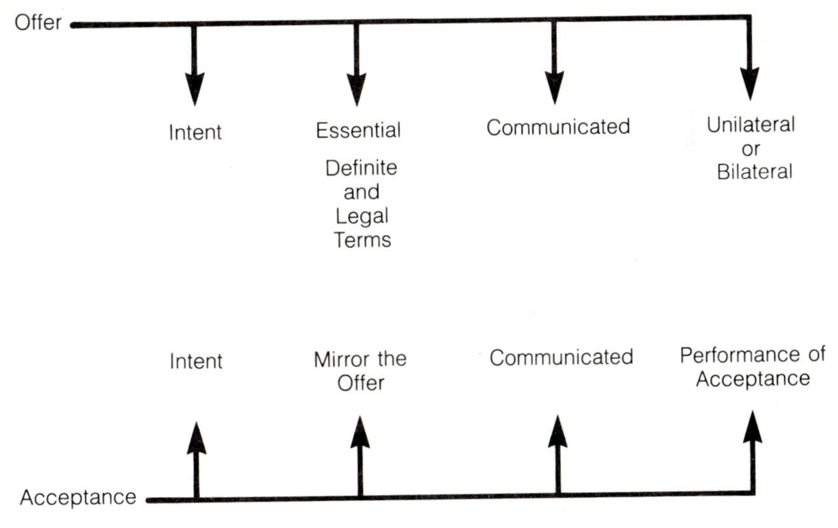

Similar tests are used to determine whether offers and acceptances exist.

Duress is the creation of fear, through the threat of force or another illegal or wrongful act, to win the assent of one of the parties. The victim of the force or threat is not bound by the purported agreement. The threat of a legal act generally does not constitute duress. Thus an agreement executed by a seller because the buyer threatened to set fire to the seller's building would not bind the seller. On the other hand, a threat to sue the owner over an unrelated matter unless the owner contracted to sell would *not* constitute duress, because the act threatened would be legal and not wrongful. The remedy for duress is restitution.

Undue influence usually involves an abuse of a special relationship whereby a dominant party achieves an unfair advantage over a subordinate party. Special relationships would include those of doctor/patient, lawyer/client, accountant/client, parent/child, and mature child/elder parent. The remedy for undue influence is the same as that for duress—restitution.

Consideration

Consideration is the factor that transforms an agreement into a binding contract. Without consideration, a party is limited to the remedy of restitution. Recall that restitution involves being placed back in the position one was in before reaching the agreement. If consideration does exist, then either party may, if there is a breach by the other side, obtain money damages or perhaps specific performance.

Consideration Defined

Consideration has two elements. First, there must be an exchange of promises or acts for which the parties have negotiated. This is called a *bargained-for exchange*. Second, there must be a change in legal position because of each party's act or promise. This is called the *test of legal sufficiency*.

The bargained-for exchange element requires that acts or promises be traded one for another. Thus, the act of paying the purchase price of a book must be traded for the delivery, or the promise of delivery, of the book. If one party makes a gift of the book, and the other party later promises to make a gift of money, an exchange occurs, but it has not been "bargained for." Similarly, if a woman fixes a man's flat tire, and the man in gratitude promises to mow her lawn, no contract is created. Although there is an exchange, it did not involve the bargaining or trading of the two things.

Legal sufficiency means that there is a change in the legal position of the party making the promise or performing the act. Suppose a builder contracted to construct a house in return for the payment of $85,000, then after receiving the money and building half the house, he refused to finish construction. If the owner promised payment of an extra $5,000 in exchange for the builder's promise to finish, there would be no legal sufficiency, because the builder was already legally obligated to complete the house. Therefore his promise to finish construction did not change his legal position. Accordingly, if the builder finished the house and sued for the extra $5,000, he could not collect. Since there was no consideration for the promise to pay the $5,000, there is no contractual duty to pay it.

Many promises and acts do not have legal value. The promise of a minor not to purchase beer until age 18 has no legal value if the minor is already obligated by law not to purchase beer. Similarly, if a police officer arrests a bank robber after a reward has been offered, she cannot collect the reward, since her act had no legal value. She was under a legal duty to make the arrest before the reward was offered.

Each act or promise exchanged must have legal sufficiency. Consequently, if one party's promise or act has legal sufficiency, but the other party's does not, there is no contract. Promises have legal sufficiency if the acts underlying them have legal value. Suppose you promise to help a local auto repair shop set up a computerized accounting system in return for their promise to pay you $3,500. Your promise has legal value because the act underlying it—setting up the accounting system—has legal value.

Adequacy of Consideration

Adequacy, or fairness, of consideration is not required to create a contract under the common law. If there is a bargained-for exchange of acts or promises that have legal value, then consideration exists, and the agreement is enforceable as a contract. Thus, the courts would probably enforce a contract for the sale of a lake shore cabin for $35,000 even if its appraised value were $75,000. The courts assume that the parties will protect their own interests.

The UCC makes *unconscionable* contracts unenforceable. So the adequacy of consideration may in effect be questioned in some situations where there is a sale of goods. Thus, if a retailer sold a refrigerator worth $400. for $2,100. to a recent immigrant who did not understand English well, the contract would probably be unconscionable.

Promissory Estoppel

If the test of consideration we have described is not met, courts may still enforce an agreement if they find that **promissory estoppel** occurred. Thus, promissory estoppel is a substitute for consideration. Promissory estoppel occurs when:

1. A promise is made, and
2. The promisor could reasonably foresee that the promisee would rely on the promise, and
3. The promisee did in fact rely on the promise, and
4. The promisee would suffer a substantial injury unless the promise is enforced.

For example, assume that a father felt sympathy for one son with a large family who did not own a home. Therefore, the father promised to give the son a deed to a building lot within three years (the promise) and told him he could begin construction immediately (reasonably foreseeable reliance). The son built a home on the lot (reliance in fact). Now the father refuses to deed the property to his son. Since the son would lose the value of the home (the substantial injury), courts will generally enforce the father's promise under the doctrine of promissory estoppel. Note that the son promised the father nothing, and therefore there was no consideration, so that without promissory estoppel the son would suffer a very unfair injury. The following case illustrates how the courts apply these concepts of consideration and promissory estoppel.

Timko's Estate v. Oral Roberts Evangelistic Assoc.

51 Mich. App. 662 (1974)

Facts

The decedent, Nicholas Timko, was a member of the board of trustees of the Oral Roberts Evangelistic Association (hereinafter referred to as the Association). In January 1964 at a meeting of the board of trustees in Tulsa, Oklahoma, Mr. Timko proposed that the board buy a building in Detroit. He explained that with a down payment of $25,000 the building could be purchased for $145,000. He further stated that in the event the Association purchased the building on these terms and made payments at the rate of $1,000 per month for five years, he would pay the unpaid balance at the end of the five years.

Opinion

Judge T. M. Burns: The minutes of the board of trustees' meeting relating to this proposal read in pertinent part as follows:

> Mr. Timko called attention to a building in Detroit, Michigan, known as 7030 East Seven Mile Road, and stated that it was being offered for sale for $155,000, but that he thought he might be able to buy it for the Association for $145,000. Mr. Timko proposed that if arrangements could be made whereby the Association could purchase the building for $145,000 upon a down payment of $25,000 cash, $1,000 per month for five years, and the remaining balance at the end of five years, it would be his intention to make contributions to the Association which would match the deferred payments of the purchase price. It was thereupon moved by Mr. Shakarian, seconded by Carl Wilson and unanimously carried that the Association purchase the said building at a purchase price of $145,000, $25,000 down payment, $120,000 to be paid by the Association at the rate of $1,000 per month for five years, and the remaining balance to be paid at the end of the five years with interest on the unpaid balance of the purchase price at the rate of 6% per annum.

After the trustees' meeting, the minutes were signed by all the members of the board including the decedent, Mr. Timko. Subsequently, in February 1964, the building was purchased by the Association. Mr. Timko dealt with the owners of the property on behalf of the Association, arranged for a bank loan, attended to other closing details, and paid closing costs in excess of $5,000.

In December 1964, Mr. Timko wrote a letter to the president of the Association indicating that he expected to donate the full amount of the building sometime in February of 1965 and that this donation would "clear off all debts." The letter reads in its entirety:

> Dec. 17, 1964
>
> Dear Bro. Moore:
> Received your letter of Nov. 19 in regard to the bldg. in Det. I appreciate the information by Stanfield & O'Dell. I expect to donate the full amount of bldg. sometime in Feb. of 65 which will clear off all debts. May Christmas find you and sister Moore in good health.
>
> In His Service
> /s/ N. Timko

After Mr. Timko paid the closing costs, he made no additional payments to the Association toward the purchase of the building after the letter of December 17. . . .

Mr. Timko died in January 1969. The Association filed a claim against his estate for the amount of the unpaid balance on the purchase price of the building. After a hearing on the claim before a probate referee, the Association's claim was denied. The decision was later affirmed by both the Macomb County Probate Court and the Macomb County Circuit Court.

On appeal, the Association asserts that Mr. Timko's promise to pay the unpaid balance of the cost of the building constituted a valid enforceable claim against his estate under either the doctrine of . . . [consideration] or in the alternative under the concept of promissory estoppel. However, from the record it is clear that there were in fact no other promises upon which Mr. Timko relied as consideration for his promise regarding the building. Therefore, it is patent that the Association's claim must rise or fall on the applicability of the promissory estoppel doctrine.

In order for a promise to be enforceable under the concept of promissory estoppel, there must be a (1) promise that the promisor should reasonably have expected to induce action of a definite and substantial character on the part of the promisee, (2) which in fact produced reliance or forbearance of that nature, (3) in circumstances such that the promise must be enforced if injustice is to be avoided.

Mr. Timko made a promise to pay the unpaid balance on the building in question. This promise, particularly in view of his position on the board of trustees, was one in which he should have reasonably expected "to induce action or forbearance of a definite and substantial character on the part of the promisee." The record in this case clearly establishes that the building was purchased by the Association solely on the basis of Mr. Timko's promise to pay the unpaid balance after five years. Moreover, Mr. Timko personally attended to the closing details and arranged for a bank loan on behalf of the Association. Under these circumstances we see no alternative other than enforcing Mr. Timko's promise if injustice is to be avoided. Accordingly, the Association's claim against Mr. Timko's estate should have been allowed.

Reversed and remanded for proceedings not inconsistent with this opinion.

Case Questions

1. Why isn't this agreement supported by consideration?
2. In this case, would the Association really suffer an injury, aside from the loss of Timko's money, if his promise were not enforced?
3. If you made a promise not supported by consideration or promissory estoppel, would you conclude, based on your own beliefs, that it would be ethical for you to break the promise?

Ethical Issues in Offer, Acceptance, and Consideration

As you can see, contract law represents ethical views on the duty of promise keeping. Can you also see, however, the way in which expediency—the need to operate courts with reasonable efficiency and integrity—influences the law of contracts? For example, the statute of frauds is in large part concerned with protecting courts from being used to enforce a contract where none existed. To accomplish this, the statute of frauds denies aid, rather arbitrarily, to some parties. Thus the law is, in effect, balancing equitable treatment of individuals with the need to operate courts expediently. It is forced to do so because human institutions such as the courts are imperfect. Would you feel comfortable backing out of a promise because it did not satisfy the statute of frauds? Do you recognize a duty that is broader than your legal obligations?

The important concepts and terms in this chapter are listed below; page numbers have been provided for the key terms. By reading over each section you can assess your understanding of the chapter concepts and determine areas you may want to review.

Chapter Summary

1. The remedies of damages and specific performance are usually only available when a contract is found to exist.
2. The elements of an offer are: contractual intent, essential, definite, and legal terms, and communication.
3. If an offer has been made, the offeror can revoke, while the offeree can reject, counteroffer, solicit an additional offer, remain silent, or accept.
4. A valid acceptance must manifest contractual intent, must mirror the offer, must satisfy the requirements of the offer concerning acceptance, and must be communicated.
5. There is no genuine offer and acceptance if there has been a mutual mistake of fact, misrepresentation, fraud, duress, or undue influence.
6. Consideration exists when there has been a bargained-for exchange of acts or promises that have legal value. Promissory estoppel is a substitute for consideration.

Key Terms

acceptance 235
agreement 225
bilateral offer 231
breach (of contract) 225
consideration 225
contractual duties 225
contractual rights 225
counteroffers 234
duress 240
firm offer 233
fraud 239
goods 225
life of an offer 233
misrepresentation 238
mistake of law 238
money damages 225
mutual mistake of fact 238
offer 227
option 233
promissory estoppel 241
punitive damages 239
rejection 234
restitution 224
revocation 233
solicitation of an additional offer 235
specific performance 225
test of the reasonable man 228
undue influence 240
Uniform Commercial Code 225
unilateral offer 231

Questions on Ethics

1. Suppose you promised to help a friend study for a final exam. Later you were offered a chance to earn $50 doing odd jobs, but that would mean that you could not help your friend. Further, your friend would not have time to find someone else to help.

   Do you believe you created a moral duty for yourself when you promised to help? Do you believe you would be justified in violating that duty? Why or why not? Would you give up the $50 to help your friend? Why or why not?
2. Suppose you made a unilateral offer to sell a work of art for $5,000. In response, a stranger *promised* to pay the money within three days. In reaction to this bilateral acceptance, you said nothing and the stranger mistakenly assumed that there was an contract between the two of you. Later someone offered you $5,250 for the painting. Would you utilize your legal rights to ignore the stranger and collect the extra $250? Why or why not? Is it all right to use technical legal knowledge to gain an advantage over someone less familiar with the law?
3. Suppose you have made a noncontractual social promise. Perhaps you have promised a friend to take her to lunch. But the person to whom you have made the promise has a slightly different interpretation of what the agreement is. She believes you intended to take her to dinner. In the law, such a difference can mean that there is no contract. There was no valid offer and acceptance. Do you feel comfortable treating social promises in the same way the law treats commercial promises? Would you feel justified in saying that you had no obligation whatsoever? Is the law morally justified in its approach to promise keeping in commercial contexts?
4. Is the law's requirement of consideration ethically justified? Why shouldn't promises lacking consideration be enforced? Isn't the law encouraging promise-breaking by not enforcing these promises? Would you feel less of a moral obligation because you made a promise, but it wasn't supported by consideration?
5. Try to state the rules you would use in determining whether you had made a noncontractual social promise which you feel would be binding.

Questions on Law

1. Smith and Jones were neighboring farmers and friends. Smith had been trying for several years to buy Jones's 160-acre farm. Smith had made several offers ranging from $85,000 to $110,000. Jones always rejected, claiming that the farm was worth at least $250,000. One night, after playing poker until 1:00 A.M. and sharing a six-pack of beer, Smith said, "Well Jimmy my friend, I'll give you $95,000 for this lousy farm of yours!" Jones replied, "Sure Sam, sure." Smith then wrote out a ten-

sentence contract of sale, which they both signed. When Smith tried to enforce the agreement, Jones claimed that he was only joking. What issues will be litigated in this case? Who prevails?

2. CLOCK magazine placed a return postcard in all copies of its magazines. The front of the card was addressed to CLOCK. On the back of the card were the following words:

   > Please send me 30 weeks of CLOCK for only $7.50 and bill me later. (You pay only 25 cents a week. CLOCK is 75 cents a week on newstands, 35 cents a week at the basic subscription rate.)
   > Mr./Ms. ______________________
   > Address ______________________
   > Signature ______________________

   Is this ad an offer? If it were an offer, who would be the offeror? Would the offer be unilateral or bilateral? Would this transaction fall within the Statute of Frauds? If a minor entered into the contract, could he disaffirm? If an adult sent in the postcard, but didn't pay the bill, what remedies would CLOCK have?
3. Jerry made a written offer to Sam for the purchase of a small apartment house for $290,000. This offer contained all the essential and definite terms. Sam wrote on the document these words, "I accept at $245,000" and Sam then signed the document and returned it to Jerry. Is there a contract? Is there an offer that is alive at this point in the negotiations? If an offer is alive, who is the offeror?
4. Patricia offered in writing to sell her car to Sally for $6,250. Sally responded in writing saying, "I'll only pay $6,000 cash for the following described automobile. . . ." Patricia wrote back, "No, the least I'll take is $6,100. . . ." How many offers have been made by Patricia? How many offers have been made by Sally? Who has rejected an offer? Has any offer been revoked?
5. Richard Foster wanted to take dancing lessons. Dean Taylor owned a dancing studio that used a standard form contract for the sale of lessons. One of Taylor's employees, Juliet, filled out the form, signed it, and presented it to Richard. Richard looked at the form and saw that the total price was $1,200. He scratched out that amount and wrote above it "$850," then signed the form, tore off his copy, and walked away. Is there a contract? Was there an offer and if there was, who made it? Was there a rejection? A counteroffer?

Suggested Readings

Fuller, Lon. *The Morality of the Law*. Rev. ed. New Haven: Yale University Press, 1964.

Kant, Immanuel. *Foundations of the Metaphysics of Morals*. Translated by Lewis White Beck. Indianapolis: Bobbs-Merrill, 1959.

Manning, Frank V. *Managerial Dilemmas and Executive Growth*. Reston, Va.: Reston, 1981.

10 Contracts II: Writing, Capacity, Assignment, and Remedies

A sense of duty pursues us ever. It is omnipresent, like the Deity. If we take to ourselves the wings of the morning, and dwell in the uttermost parts of the sea, duty performed or duty violated is still with us for our happiness or our misery. If we say the darkness shall cover us, in the darkness as in the light our obligations are yet with us.

—Daniel Webster

LEARNING OBJECTIVES

After reading this chapter, you should be able to:

1. Describe those agreements that must be placed in writing and signed before they are enforceable by a court.
2. Describe the rights that minors, the intoxicated, and the mentally incapacitated have in the contracts they execute.
3. Describe the legal consequences of assigning and delegating contractual rights and duties.
4. Describe the rules used by courts to interpret contractual language.
5. Describe the ways courts will aid those injured by the breach of a promise contained in a contract.

Business Decisions and the Law

An "Up-Tick" in Share Price

Diane had an contract with Sophie whereby Sophie promised to sell 100 shares of stock in a small business for $15,000. Before the money had been paid or the stock delivered, its market value went from $150 per share to $225. Because of the increase in value, Sophie refused to accept the money or deliver the stock. How will courts assist people in situations such as Diane's? This chapter will answer that question.

Introduction

This chapter continues the theme of "promise keeping" that was introduced in chapter 9, "Contracts I." But the concern here is not so much with what constitutes a valid promise. Rather, the focus shifts to "what is a valid excuse for breaking a promise?" Three kinds of "excuses" recognized by the law are presented in this chapter. One is the excuse that although there may have been a promise, it won't be enforced because it wasn't placed in writing. This isn't an excuse related so much to promise keeping as it is related to the fair operation of the courts. But still it raises the question of one's commitment to stand by a promise when not forced to do so.

A second excuse addressed by the law is that one party to the promise wasn't able to take care of their own interests. So since that party wasn't able to negotiate on equal footing, she or he should be given the opportunity to back out of the promise. In many situations, this body of law gives persons the opportunity to back out even when they were, in fact, able to look out for their best interests. So, again, these persons have the opportunity to determine whether their *promise*, by itself, is sufficient to bind them.

A third class of excuses might be labeled "changed circumstances." This legal excuse says that, in many situations, as long as you are willing to pay for the injury you cause the other party, you can avoid your promise. As you read through this chapter, make an attempt to evaluate your own beliefs about when, if ever, one is justified in failing to live up to a promise.

Contracts That Should Be Written

All important contracts should be placed in writing. But the **Statute of Frauds** requires that certain classes of contracts be placed in writing to be always enforceable. In general, these are:

1. Contracts for the sale of an interest in real property
2. Contracts that require more than one year to perform
3. Contracts for the sale of goods (but not services) for $500 or more

Other more technical categories exist, so it is always wise to place important contracts in writing.

The amount of written information required by the Statute of Frauds varies. Contracts under the common law, such as those for the sale of services or realty, must have all the material terms in writing and must be signed by the party from whom damages or specific performance is sought. If the transaction is for the sale of goods, and thus governed by the UCC, the writing need only indicate that a sale occurred and be signed by the party from whom damages or specific performance is sought. If the amount of the writing is not sufficient, the courts will treat the agreement as if it were completely oral.

If the Statute of Frauds requires that the contract be placed in writing, and it is not, the courts will only sometimes refuse to enforce it. The extent to which the oral contract has been performed determines its enforceability. When none of the acts promised have been performed, the contract is called completely executory, or an **executory contract.** When some, but not all, acts have been performed, it is a **partially executed contract.** When all the acts have been performed, it is completely executed, or an **executed contract.** Parties to contracts that violate the Statute of Frauds and are either completely executory or completely executed will not receive judicial aid. Courts will not grant damages or specific performance in these cases. When an oral contract is partially executed, the courts may enforce the contract, but only if the acts that have been performed clearly indicate the existence of the contract.

To illustrate, suppose a seller makes an oral agreement to sell a refrigerator for $650 to a buyer, and neither party has performed. This oral, completely executory contract is not enforceable in court. If all the money has been paid and the buyer has taken possession of the refrigerator, neither party can back out of this completely executed transaction. If the buyer has taken possession and paid $100, then the seller might be able to enforce this partially executed oral contract.

The following case illustrates the way courts apply the Statute of Frauds.

Cohen Salvage Corp. v. Eastern Electric Sales Co.

206 A.2d 331 (1965)

Facts

In the latter part of June 1963, plaintiff, located in Bladensburg, Maryland, and defendant, located in Philadelphia, . . . had a telephone conversation in which plaintiff advised defendant that it had a quantity of electric cable for sale. Arrangements were made for defendant to send one of its employees to Bladensburg, Maryland, to examine the cable. After this employee examined the cable and returned to Philadelphia, another oral conversation transpired, as a result of which plaintiff shipped the cable, weighing 36,440 pounds, to defendant in Philadelphia. The cable was run off plaintiff's reels to defendant's reels, and was taken by defendant's employees and placed in defendant's warehouse.

Opinion

Judge Ethan Allen Doty: The plaintiff brought this action . . . for the cable allegedly sold and delivered. The defendant's position at trial was . . . [that] even if there was a contract it is unenforceable because of the Statute of Frauds. . . .

Defendant's reliance on the Statute of Frauds to vitiate this contract is misplaced. Section 2–201(1) of the Uniform Commercial Code provides that a contract for the sale of goods in excess of $500 is not enforceable:

> Unless there is some writing sufficient to indicate that a contract for sale has been made between the parties and signed by the party against whom enforcement is sought, or by his authorized agent or broker.

In this case plaintiff introduced into evidence a written sales order which contained plaintiff's name, the notation, "SOLD TO: Eastern Electric," the date, the name of the shipper, the quantity and description of the goods, and the weight of the goods, as well as the notation, "Your Order

Number," and "Our Sales Number." This form was admittedly signed by an authorized agent of the defendant's company. . . .

This writing clearly afforded a basis for believing that the oral evidence rests on a real transaction. The fact that price was omitted (and it was the only relevant term omitted) is not fatal since "A writing is not insufficient because it omits . . . a term agreed upon. . . .

There is another reason why the Statute of Frauds does not preclude a verdict for plaintiff in this case. Section 2–201(3)(c) of the Code provides:

> A contract which does not satisfy the requirements of subsection (1) but which is valid in other respects is enforceable with respect to goods which have been received and accepted.

That the cable was received there can be no doubt. After it was received by defendant it was run from one reel to another by several of the defendant's employees who admitted they inspected it at that time. It was then tagged and placed in the defendant's warehouse, where it remains. . . .

[Judgement for plaintiff.]

Case Questions

1. Would there have been a different outcome to this case if the transaction had involved accounting advice instead of wire?
2. Was this rule of law established because it is just, or expedient, or both?
3. As a general rule, do you think it is moral to assert the Statute of Frauds as a defense to a valid charge of breach of contract? Why or why not?

In summary, a contract exists if the processes of offer and acceptance have occurred and the tests of genuineness, consideration, and a writing are met. The rest of this chapter discusses issues that come up when it is assumed that a contract has been created.

Contracts with Special Parties

Certain parties to contracts are assumed by the law to lack the maturity, experience, intelligence, or other mental abilities needed to protect their own self-interest. Accordingly, the law grants these parties special contractual rights designed to ensure that they are not cheated. The special parties are minors and the mentally incapacitated. There are two basic types of protections granted to both of these parties.

When protected parties purchase things classified as **necessaries**—things needed to maintain life and lifestyle—the special parties need only pay the fair market value rather than the contracted price.

When these parties purchase **nonnecessaries,** things that for them are relative luxuries, they must pay the contracted price, but they have the option to *disaffirm* the contract. **Disaffirmance** involves the return of the consideration by both parties. Special parties may disaffirm during the time of their minority or incapacity and within a reasonable time after attaining capacity or adult status. Note that only the special party may disaffirm. The other parties to these contracts do not have the option to disaffirm. Thus, if a special party leased, for one year, a luxury condominium by paying two months' rent and a cleaning deposit, he or she could disaffirm a week later by giving possession back to the landlord, and recover the payments. The landlord, however, could not withdraw from the agreement without the consent of the special party.

In most states, persons under the age of eighteen are legally "infants." In other states the age of majority is twenty-one. Minors may disaffirm contracts for nonnecessaries during their minority. They may also disaffirm for a reasonable length of time after achieving their majority. After reaching majority, the power to disaffirm is immediately cut off if they *ratify* the contract. **Ratification** is acting toward the contract as though one intends to be bound by it. The following case discusses the issue of ratification.

Jones v. *Dressel*

582 P.2d 1057 (Colo. App. 1978)

Facts

While a minor, the plaintiff signed a contract with Free Flight Sport Aviation for services associated with parachute jumping. A clause in the contract stated that Free Flight would not be liable for its own negligence. After achieving majority, plaintiff was injured when a Free Flight aircraft crashed while he was on board. He sued, claiming that the contract clause was invalid because it was signed while he was a minor.

Opinion

C. J. Silverstein: Plaintiff sued to recover damages for personal injuries suffered in an airplane crash. He alleged that defendants were guilty of negligence and of malicious, oppressive, wilful and wanton misconduct. Defendants moved for a summary judgment of dismissal. The trial court granted the motion as to the negligence claim only, determined there was no just reason for delay, and directed entry of a judgment dismissing the negligence claim pursuant to C.R.C.P. 54(b). Plaintiff appeals from that judgment. We affirm.

The facts pertinent to this appeal are not in dispute. Plaintiff, then seventeen years old, entered into a contract with defendant, Free Flight Sport Aviation, Inc., under which Free Flight provided facilities for free-flight, or parachute jumping. Ten months after plaintiff's eighteenth birthday, a plane furnished by Free Flight crashed while carrying plaintiff and others preparatory to a parachute jump, causing the injuries to the plaintiff. The other defendants were owners or operators of the plane, acting as agents or employees of Free Flight Sport Aviation, Inc.

In granting the summary judgment the court relied on provisions of the contract, under which plaintiff exempted and released Free Flight, "its owners, officers, agents, servants, employees, and lessors from any and all liability [resulting from negligence and] . . . arising out of any damage, loss or injury to [plaintiff] . . . while upon the . . . aircraft of [Free Flight] or while participating in any of the activities contemplated by this agreement. . . ." The contract also contained a covenant not to sue for such injuries.

Plaintiff contends the trial court erred because the contract is void. . . .

It is well settled in Colorado that a contract entered into by a minor is not void but only voidable by the minor. *Fellows* v. *Cantrell,* 143 Colo. 126, 352 P.2d 289 (1960). Affirmance is not merely a matter of intent; it may be determined by the actions of a minor who accepts the benefits of a contract after reaching the age of majority, or by his silence or acquiescence in the contract for a considerable length of time. *Fellows* v. *Cantrell, supra.* Furthermore, § 13–22–101(1), C.R.S. 1973, states that "every person, otherwise competent, shall be deemed to be of full age at the age of eighteen years or older for the following specific purposes:

(a) To enter into any legal contractual obligation and to be legally bound thereby to the full extent as any other adult person. . . ."

Thus, on reaching the age of eighteen plaintiff was required either to disaffirm the contract within a reasonable time, or be bound thereby. And, the undisputed facts establish that, after turning eighteen, plaintiff not only did not disaffirm the contract, but instead ratified it by accepting the benefits thereof. Hence, his being a minor when he entered the contract is without significance as to its present enforceability against him.

[Judgment for defendants affirmed.]

Case Questions

1. Exactly what action by the plaintiff would this court require to constitute disaffirmance of this contract?
2. Exactly what action constituted the ratification by the plaintiff?
3. Do you think it is possible to justify morally a rule of law that says that the minor who every day accepts the benefits of a contract can still disaffirm on the last day of her seventeenth year but not on the first day of her eighteenth year? Is there a moral justification for drawing such a sharp legal distinction when that distinction doesn't exist in factual reality?

Insanity is much less precisely defined than minority. It applies in general to those who do not understand the consequences of their contractual acts. Thus, the psychotic, the senile, and the mentally retarded are protected in essentially the same manner as minors. If a person is adjudicated as insane, his or her contracts for nonnecessaries are void rather than voidable.

Severely intoxicated or drugged persons will be granted the same special contractual protection as minors and the insane. In general, the special rights are only granted when the mental impairment is so severe that the special party did not realize he or she was contracting. Figure 10.1 depicts the way special parties are treated in contracts for nonnecessaries.

Transfers of Contract Rights and Duties

Contract law allows the parties to a contract to transfer their **rights** and **duties** in the contract to others. For example, in a simple real estate transaction, the buyer has the right to receive the deed and the duty to pay the money. The seller, on the other hand, has the right to receive the money and the duty to deliver the deed. When the rights in a contract are transferred, this is called an **assignment.** When the duties are transferred, it is called a **delegation.**

Satisfaction of Duties

The most common way of extinguishing or satisfying a contractual duty is by performance of the duty created by the contract. In addition, a duty may be extinguished by events other than performance. Figure 10.2 illustrates this process.

If it becomes impossible for a party to perform a contractual obligation,

Figure 10.1 Rights of Minors and the Mentally Incapacitated in Contracts for *Non-necessaries*

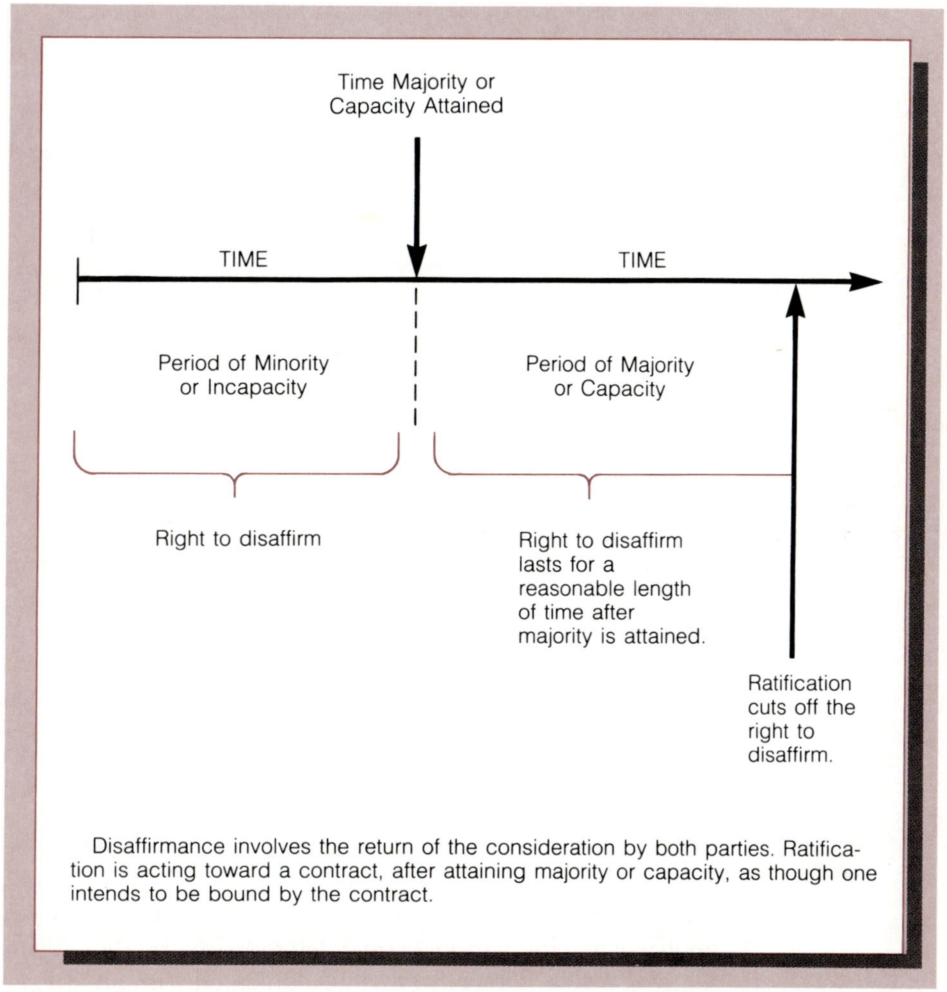

then the contract can be set aside. The impossibility must, however, be objective. This means that it must be impossible for anyone to perform, rather than merely impossible for a particular person. For example, if parties contract for the painting of an apartment house, and it burns down, it is then impossible to perform the contract. Impossibility is the standard applied to contracts governed by the common law—those for the sale of realty and the sale of services.

Some contracts may be set aside if they become impracticable. Generally, the party seeking this relief must show that an unforeseen circumstance arose that imposed a risk or expense that was disproportionate to the contract. A contract is not impractical just because one of the parties made a bad deal.

Figure 10.2 Contract Rights and Duties

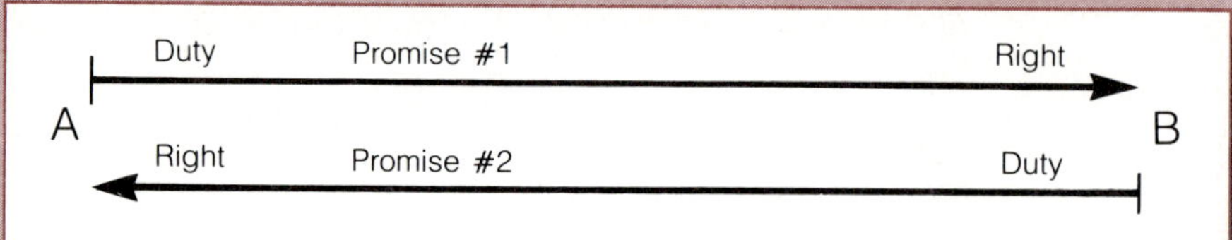

Contract *rights* flow to a party and duties flow *from* a party.

Impracticability is the standard usually applied to contracts governed by the UCC—those for the sale of goods.

Interpretation of Contracts

In order for an agreement to be enforceable, it must contain the essential and definite terms. The meanings of these terms can greatly influence the rights of the parties to the contract. All human communications leave a great deal of room for varying interpretation. The courts have, therefore, developed guides to assist in interpreting contracts. Managers need to be familiar with these guidelines because managers frequently draft the contracts that courts may attempt to interpret.

The Parol Evidence Rule

This rule of law guides courts in interpreting certain *written* contracts. The rule applies when the writing is intended to be the *final and complete expression of the agreement*. This is sometimes indicated with an *integration clause* similar to the following:

> It is agreed that the terms written here constitute the entire contract between the parties.

The length and detail of the document might also indicate that the parties intend the writing to be the *complete agreement.*

The consequence of indicating such an intent is that oral or written negotiations or agreements made by the parties before or while executing the written agreement, if they vary, or add to, the final complete written agreement, are *not* admissible in court. These inadmissible statements are called *parol statements* or *parol evidence*. Thus if a complete written agreement for the sale of a house is signed, a court will not admit oral testimony showing that the seller agreed to paint the exterior before vacating. Of course the testimony would be admissible if the written contract indicated that the agreement was partly oral and partly written.

Even when there is a complete written agreement, the parol evidence may be admissible if it shows any of the following:

1. The written contract was not intended to be a complete agreement.
2. The contract never came into existence.
3. Fraud or forgery occurred.
4. The parties created another oral contract *after* executing the written contract.
5. Parol evidence is always admissible to clarify *ambiguities* in the written agreement.

Rules of Contractual Construction

Courts are often required to determine what the written and oral communications mean. In these situations courts use rules of construction, to help arrive at their decisions.

General Rules of Construction

The plain and normal meaning of words will be used to determine the meaning of the contract. Where the words are ambiguous, they will be given the meaning that the parties *intended*. Further, if an agreement can be interpreted in two ways, the courts will choose the way that renders the agreement a contract. Lastly, courts will interpret ambiguities against the party writing or speaking.

Specific Rules of Construction

If, as in most real estate transactions, the parties use a typeset *form,* and there is a conflict between the print and something typewritten or handwritten, the writing, not the conflicting print, determines the contract's meaning. Similarly a typewritten agreement that includes a conflicting handwritten statement or clause will be interpreted in favor of the handwritten portion.

When contracts refer to amounts of money, they often describe the amount with arabic numerals, like *10,* and with words like *ten.* If there is a conflict between the number and the word, and one is ambiguous, then the unambiguous expression will prevail. For example, "Two twenty-five dollars ($2.25)" will be interpreted by reliance on the arabic numbers. When both the writing and the numbers are unambiguous, then the writing prevails. For example, "Two hundred twenty-five and 00/100 ($235.00)" will be interpreted in reliance on the words.

Major and Minor Promises

Contracts can contain two classes of promises—major promises and minor promises. A minor promise can be breached and the injured party must still perform his or her duties under the contract. In contrast, major promises are so important to the transaction that their breach relieves the injured party of the duty to perform. Promises are usually classified as major or minor based on their *materiality*. The more important the promise is to the contract, the more likely it is to be classed as major. For example suppose a buyer promises in a contract for the purchase of a $75,000 home, to pay "$250 when sellers approve the sale, $65,000 on delivery of deed which shall be on or before January 15th next." The promise to pay the $250 is a minor promise, while the promise to pay the $65,000 is a major promise. The duty to deliver the deed is not extinguished by the failure to pay the $250. It is extinguished by the failure to pay the $65,000.

In some cases the language of the contract indicates the status of the promise. For example the statement, "as a condition of this lease, the tenant promises not to keep pets on the premises," is probably a major promise, violation of which terminates the lessor's duty to rent to the tenant. Use of words, like *condition* and *subject to,* generally create major promises. When the language is ambiguous, the courts prefer to find a minor promise.

Promises about performance by a certain date or time are presumed to be minor. If the act is not completed on the date stated, only a minor promise is breached. When the act is not performed within a *reasonable* length of time after the date, then a major promise may have been breached, if the act is material. If the contract states that "Time is of the essence of this agreement," then each timed event must be strictly satisfied or a breach of a major promise occurs.

The following case illustrates the way one court interprets contract language.

Grove v. Charbonneau Buick-Pontiac, Inc.

240 N.W.2d 853 (N.D. Sup. Ct. 1976)

Facts

At a golf course Lloyd Grove saw and read a poster that advertised a Labor Day Golf Tournament at the Dickenson Golf Course. The poster stated that Charbonneau Buick-Pontiac would give a 1974 automobile to the "first entry who shoots a hole-in-one on hole No. 8."

The Dickenson course has only nine holes but is laid out so that it can be played as though there were eighteen holes simply by going around twice. To facilitate this, there are two tees for each hole, in slightly different locations. Thus the tee area marked "8" and the tee area marked "17" are both played to the same hole. However, the 17th tee was about sixty yards further from the hole.

On the first day of the tournament, Grove shot a hole-in-one into the 8th hole, but while playing from the seventeenth tee. Then he claimed the prize. Charbonneau refused to award the prize because, "Grove got the hole-in-one while playing the 17th hole, not the 8th." Grove sued and prevailed in the trial court. Charbonneau appealed.

Opinion

Judge Sand: The sole dispute between Grove and Charbonneau relates to the interpretation of the words and phrases used in the offer. When good arguments can be made for either of two contrary positions as to the meaning of a term in a document, an ambiguity exists. Where a contract contains ambiguous terms which are in dispute, it is the duty of the court to construe them. The ambiguous terms of a contract will be interpreted most strongly against the party who caused the ambiguity.

In *Schreiner* v. *Weil Furniture Co.,* the court stated that a document must be interpreted against the one who has prepared it, and applied such a rule to an offer of a prize made to the public. The court held that it was the duty of the defendant to explain the contest so that the public would not be misled. We believe the rule on ambiguous contracts applies to this case, and therefore, any language of this contract which is not clear must be interpreted most strongly against Charbonneau. The offer does not contain any qualifications or limitations as to what is meant by the phrase "on hole No. 8." Neither does the award or offer make any statement restricting or qualifying that the hole-in-one on hole No. 8 may be accomplished only from tee No. 8. If Charbonneau had in mind to impose limitations, he could have made this in the offer so that a person of ordinary intelligence would have been fully apprised of the offer in every respect.

If this rule of law on ambiguous contracts were not applied, it would permit the promoter who is so inclined to keep adding requirements or conditions which were not stated in the offer. By interpreting and construing the ambiguous provisions of the offer most strongly against the party who caused them, we construe [the contract] to mean that an entrant in the tournament who drives the ball in one stroke into hole No. 8 from either the 8th or the 17th tee has met the conditions of the offer and is entitled to the award.

Judgment for Grove affirmed.

Case Questions

1. What arguments can be made to support Charbonneau's position about the meaning of the sign?
2. What arguments can be made to support Grove's position about the meaning of the sign?
3. Aside from the legal rule requiring that ambiguity be construed against the author, which of the above arguments is strongest? How much ambiguity do you think a court would require before it would use this rule?

Breach of Contract and Remedies

As discussed above, the law divides breaches of contract into **major** (or material) **breaches** and **minor breaches.** Different remedies are granted for injuries caused by minor and major breaches.

The significance of any breach, and therefore its classification as major or minor, is an issue of fact. A judge or a jury will try to determine whether a reasonable person would, in light of the particular facts and circumstances, view the breach as major or minor. There are, however, guidelines that help in classifying. The primary guideline is the significance of the breach in relation to the entire contract. For example, if a contractor built a twelve-room home for you but failed to paint four of the rooms, this would probably be a minor breach; the cost of painting the rooms is quite minor in comparison to the cost of building a house. On the other hand, if a painting contractor agreed to paint the inside of your twelve-room house but failed to paint four of the rooms, this would probably be a major breach.

There are other, less weighty, guidelines. If the breach is willful, occurs at the beginning of the performance period, or is impossible to correct, it is more likely to be major. If the breach can be easily corrected, then it is more likely to be considered minor. If the injured party is a merchant or business person, the breach is more likely to be classified as minor.

The party injured by *either* a major or minor breach has the obligation to:

1. Notify the defaulting party promptly;
2. Not hinder the defaulting party's attempts to perform;
3. **Mitigate** injury (minimize the extent of the injury), for example, by immediately rerenting an apartment when a tenant vacates early.

Minor Breach

The only remedy generally available for a minor breach is money damages. Thus, if a buyer paid cash to have a new home built and upon moving in discovered that four rooms were not painted, the buyer could sue and recover the cost of painting the rooms. If the purchase price had not been paid, the buyer could recover damages through *off-set*. That is, the buyer could deduct the cost of the painting from money to be paid for the house.

Parties injured by a minor breach must continue to perform their contractual obligations.

Major Breach

If the breach is classified as a major breach, then the injured party can choose among the remedies of restitution, compensatory money damages, consequential money damages, liquidated money damages, and specific performance.

Restitution

Restitution permits the injured party to recover money or property given to the defaulting party. It is intended to place the parties in the same legal position they were in before contracting. Thus, if a seller of realty committed a major breach by failing to deliver the deed, the buyer could sue for restitution and recover any money paid for the property. When restitution is granted, all the contractual obligations of the parties are extinguished.

This remedy is also usually available when the parties have attempted to contract, but failed, and in the process one party has delivered something of value to the other.

Money Damages

An award of **compensatory money damages** seeks to place injured parties in the same financial position they would have been in if there had been no breach. Specifically, the remedy grants the "benefit of the bargain." For example, if a homeowner contracted to sell at $65,000, when the fair market value of the property was $75,000, the buyer would be receiving a $10,000 "bargain." If the seller then committed a material breach, the buyer could recover the amount of her "bargain," $10,000, as compensatory money damages.

In awarding **consequential money damages,** the court again tries to place the injured party in the same financial position he would have been in if the contract had been performed. This remedy grants money for the foreseeable injuries caused by the breach. Consequential damages are generally foreseeble when a reasonable person would know that the breach would cause the injury. For example, suppose you contracted for the purchase of a new set of *Encyclopaedia Britannica* at the unusually low price of $300. If you breached by not paying the money, there would probably be no compensatory damages available to the seller, because there was no bargain for the seller. However, because the lost profits and contribution to overhead are generally foreseeable, you would probably be liable for these amounts.

Consequential damages are specifically foreseeable if the defaulting party has been told that breach will cause the injury. For example, suppose a buyer tells the seller that she needs to take possession of her commercial property on or before January 1 because eight boxcars of ski boots will be arriving then, and must be stored on the property. If the seller delays giving possession so the buyer is forced to rent storage space, the seller will be liable for the rent. The buyer's injury (rent payments) is specifically foreseeable, and therefore consequential damages will be awarded. Consequential damages may be granted for both major and minor breaches.

Parties to a contract sometimes agree that a certain amount of money will be paid if a certain breach occurs. This is called **liquidated money damages.** Such a clause might state:

> In the event the purchaser fails to pay the balance of said purchase price for said IBM 360 computer, the amounts already paid hereon shall be retained by the seller as liquidated damages.

Not all liquidated damages clauses are enforceable. When the amount of the liquidated damages is **punitive,** the clause will not be enforced. When the liquidated damages clause is not enforceable, the injured party can only collect damages by proving compensatory or consequential damages. For example, suppose a contract clause provided that the seller must pay a daily rental rate of $1,000 for every day of delay in delivering a $30,000 used truck to the buyer. This clause clearly would not be enforced because it attempts to penalize the seller. A liquidated damages clause will only be enforced when it stipulates an amount reflecting a reasonable attempt to forecast the damages that would result from the breach. If it does reflect a reasonable forecast, it will be enforced even when no damages are actually suffered.

Specific Performance

This remedy seeks to place the injured party in the actual position he or she would have occupied if the contract had been performed. It grants to the injured party the thing—like a deed, or a painting or heirloom—for which the injured party contracted. For example, suppose a person contracted for the purchase of a duplex and the seller refused to execute the deed. The buyer then could sue and win a decree of specific performance directing the seller to execute the deed. If the seller refused, the court could issue a decree vesting title in the buyer.

Specific performance is the most difficult remedy to obtain. In general, the thing sought must be unique, and money damages must be an inadequate remedy for the injured party. This means that the decree would not be available to a buyer of sixteen place settings of Corning Ware dishes. This is because Corning Ware dishes can be purchased from others and actual money damages will protect the plaintiff's financial position. On the other hand, a contract to purchase a 1932 Rolls Royce is specifically enforceable because money damages will not satisfy the purchaser's real desire—possession of that particular antique auto. In general, realty is always considered unique, so contracts for the sale of realty are specifically enforceable.

In addition, the court must be capable of supervising the specific performance. It is almost impossible for a court to supervise personal service contracts, and therefore these contracts are usually not specifically enforceable. Courts will not specifically enforce a contract in which terms are vague or ambiguous. Finally, because specific performance is an equitable remedy, a court will not award the remedy unless the party seeking it is blameless and has acted reasonably and fairly throughout the transaction. This is often called "clean hands." The following case about specific performance illustrates the concept of an inadequate remedy at law and the doctrine of clean hands.

Campbell Soup Co. v. Wentz

172 F.2d 80 (3rd Cir., 1948)

Facts

Campbell Soup Company contracted with Wentz for the purchase of all the Chantenay red carrots he could grow on his fifteen-acre farm. The contract price was $30 per ton.

One clause in the contract allowed Campbell to refuse the carrots and at the same time prohibit Wentz from selling them to others. After execution of the contract, the market price of Chantenay carrots rose to $90 per ton, and a shortage developed.

When Wentz harvested the carrots he began selling them to others at the high price and refused to deliver his crop to Campbell at the contract price. Campbell sued for specific performance to obtain Wentz's carrots at the contract price. The trial court declined to grant the decree, holding that carrots were not unique, therefore the remedy at law (damages) was adequate.

Opinion

Circuit Judge Goodrich: The trial court denied equitable relief. We agree with the result reached, but on a different ground from that relied upon by the District Court. . . .

We think that on the question of adequacy of the legal remedy the case is one appropriate for specific performance. It was expressly found that at the time of the trial it was "virtually impossible to obtain Chantenay carrots in the open market." This Chantenay carrot is one which the plaintiff uses in large quantities furnishing the seed to the growers with whom it makes contracts. It was not claimed that in nutritive value it is any better than other types of carrots. Its blunt shape makes it easier to handle in processing, and its color and texture differ from other varieties. The color is brighter than other carrots . . . It also appeared that it uses these Chantenay carrots diced in some . . . [soups] . . . and that the appearance is uniform. The preservation of uniformity in appearance in a food article marketed throughout the country and sold under the manufacturer's name is a matter of considerable commercial significance and one which is properly considered in determining whether a substitute ingredient is just as good as the original. . . .

Judged by the general standards applicable in determining the adequacy of the legal remedy we think that on this point the case is a proper one for equitable relief. There is considerable authority, old and new, showing liberality in the granting of an equitable remedy. We see no reason why a court should be reluctant to grant specific . . . [performance] . . . when it can be given without supervision of the court or other time-consuming processes against one who has deliberately broken his agreement. Here the goods of the special type contracted for were unavailable on the open market, the plaintiff had contracted for them long ahead in anticipation of its needs, and had built up a general reputation for its products as part of which reputation uniform appearance was important. We think if this were all that was involved in the case specific performance should have been granted. . . .

We are not suggesting that the contract is illegal. Nor are we suggesting any excuse for the grower in this case who has deliberately broken an agreement entered into with Campbell. We do think, however, that a party who has offered and succeeded in getting an agreement as tough as this one, should not come to [the] chancellor and ask [the] court [for] help in the enforcement of its terms. That equity does not enforce unconscionable bargains is too well established to require elaborate citation.

Case Questions

1. Exactly what part of this contract does the court find "unconscionable?" Is it the low price? Is it the ability of Campbell to prohibit Wentz from selling the carrots to others? Do you find anything objectionable?
2. Would the judge have reached a different conclusion if Chantenay carrots were available in the marketplace, but at the price of $600 per ton?
3. What do you think of the ethical character of Wentz's and Campbell's conduct in this situation?

Ethical Issues in Writing, Capacity, Assigments, and Remedies

Many people use their knowledge of contract law to gain an advantage over others. Young people familiar with the law of capacity might use their knowledge to benefit themselves legally while doing injury to others. If you were in a position to take advantage of one of these imperfections for your own benefit, would you do so? Do you look upon the law as the final statement about what is right and wrong for you to do in business?

Some persons do not look to the law as the exclusive determinant of what is right or wrong. Instead, they also rely on a sense of justice. This kind of person might honor a commitment even when there is no enforceable legal obligation. Which category do you think you want to belong to—the group that exploits imperfections in the legal system, or the group that acts on the basis of a sense of justice?

The important concepts and terms in this chapter are listed below; page numbers have been provided for the key terms. By reading over each section you can assess your understanding of the chapter concepts and determine areas you may want to review.

Chapter Summary

1. The remedies of damages and specific performance are usually only available when a contract is found to exist.
2. The Statute of Frauds requires that only certain contracts be placed in

writing. Unwritten contracts within the statute of frauds will be enforced if there has been "part performance."

3. Those who lack contractual capacity may disaffirm contracts for the purchase of nonnecessaries during their incapacity and for a reasonable length of time after gaining capacity. They are only bound to pay fair market value for any necessaries purchased.
4. Contract rights may be assigned and contract duties may be delegated.
5. In interpreting contracts, courts follow the parol evidence rule and classify promises as major and minor.
6. The remedies for breach of contract include restitution, money damages, and specific performance.

Key Terms

Questions on Ethics

1. Suppose you entered into a contract at age 16 for the purchase of a motorcycle for $3,200. After you used it for one year its value fell to $1,600. At that point you learned that you have the legal right, in your state, to disaffirm and get back the whole $3,200.

   Assuming that the seller had treated you very fairly, do you think it would be morally wrong to disaffirm? Why or why not? If you said you would not disaffirm, would you really sacrifice the $1,600 to do what you think is right? What is the moral justification for the law of capacity?
2. Suppose you entered into an oral agreement for the purchase of one hundred cattle at $450 per head. This amount was fair at the time it was agreed upon. Later, but before the cattle were delivered, the price fell to $350 per head.

Assume that you can avoid this contract by asserting the Statute of Frauds. Do you think that you have a moral duty to live up to this agreement? Do you believe that there is a justification for violating the duty in this situation? Does this body of law treat individuals fairly? What is the moral purpose of the Statute of Frauds?

3. Suppose you are a painting subcontractor in the construction industry. Assume you entered into a contract to buy a year's supply of paint base—about four thousand gallons—for $4.80 per gallon. That wholesale price represents the fair market value for that volume of that quality of paint. Later you learn of a pending bankruptcy sale of similar paint that you think might be available for $2.00 per gallon. After talking with the wholesaler you learn that his profit on the existing contract is about 50 cents per gallon. You also learn that this is a relatively big transaction for him and that he has made the decision to add another employee to his staff in partial reliance on your contract. Your lawyer informs you that the liability for breach of this particular contract is limited to the supplier's profit and overhead—$2,000.00. By breaching the contract, paying the damages, and buying the bankruptcy paint, you can save about $9,200.00.

   Do you think you have a moral duty to live up to your agreement? Do you think there is a valid justification for violating any duty present here? Why or why not?
4. Suppose you contracted for the purchase of a unique product, forty pints of a relatively rare type of blood plasma, to be delivered within thirty days. You intend to use the blood to do research on a disease that affects beef cattle. After contracting, the hospital calls, asking to be relieved of its obligation, claiming that the blood is needed to save the life of a young child who is a hemophiliac. After consulting with your lawyer, you learn that the contract is specifically enforceable. You estimate the loss to your company from a breach to be about $20,000. The annual profits of your company are about $2,000,000. The hospital is unwilling to pay your firm the $20,000 for a breach and is asking that you waive your rights under the contract. Also, you are unable to obtain any other information about the young child but you do judge that there is a life at risk. How do you analyze the ethical and legal issues in this situation? What would you do and why?
5. Setting aside legal considerations, what circumstances do you think justify breaking your promise?

Questions on Law

1. Wicks advertised a used Hewlett-Packard 86 personal computer in the newspaper for $1,500. Zonka came over and inspected the machine, stating that he once owned an Osborne-I and still had lots of CP/M type software. Zonka asked, "Will my CP/M software work on this Hewlett-Packard?" Wicks, who was not very familiar with computers, but

honestly believed that the Hewlett-Packard would run CP/M, replied, "Sure." After purchasing the machine, Zonka discovered that an adaptor card was required to allow the machine to run CP/M. It cost $249. Zonka sued Wicks. Who will prevail? Can Zonka return the Hewlett-Packard 86 and recover his $1,500? Can Zonka keep the Hewlett-Packard 86 and collect the $249?

2. Dan Rather bought a 1980 Buick for $3,000. The odometer showed that the car only had 30,000 miles on it at the time of purchase. After encountering lots of mechanical problems, Dan checked with the previous owners of the car and concluded that the dealer who sold him the car had changed the odometer from 80,000 miles to 30,000. Can Dan collect the difference in the value of the car associated with the extra 50,000 miles? Could Dan return the car and get back his $3,000? Could Dan recover punitive damages from the dealer?
3. Mark Hershey entered into a contract to buy a new IBM computer system complete with a laser printer. To total price for the system was $9,000. As part of the contract, the seller agreed to give Mark a copy of GRAMATIK. That is a program which analyzes writing to identify long sentences or awkward sentences, grammatical errors, and writing level. The market value of the program was $75. Thirty days after delivery of the system, Mark realized that he hadn't received the program. Is this breach by the seller major or minor? Can Mark return the computer system and get back his purchase price because of this breach? Can Mark collect money damages?
4. Marilyn Sergant read an ad in the newspaper which offered, "$10,000 for information leading to the arrest of the person who murdered my brother." While jogging, Marilyn later discovered a pistol in the weeds by the side of the road. She called the police. They determined that the pistol had been used in the murder. Also, the police found fingerprints on the pistol which led to the arrest and trial of an ex-convict. But the ex-convict was acquitted. Will Marilyn be able to collect the reward?
5. Ted was in the wholesale office supply business. He contracted to sell nearly $5,000 worth of standard folding chairs to a customer at $38 each. Another more important customer later offered to buy the chairs for $42 each. Ted accepted and delivered his entire inventory. Now the first customer sues. What remedies are available?

Suggested Readings

Bickel, Alexander. *The Morality of Consent*. New Haven: Yale University Press, 1973

Fried, Charles. *Contract as Promise*. Cambridge: Harvard University Press, 1981.

Kronman, A., and Posner, R. *The Economics of Contract Law*. Chicago: University of Chicago Press, 1979.

11 Agency Relationships

Thurst ivrybody, but cut th' ca-ards.

—Finley Peter Dunne (Mr. Dooley)

■ LEARNING OBJECTIVES

After you have read this chapter, you should be able to:

1. Identify situations in which one party is acting as the agent of another party in business transactions.
2. Determine whether or not the acts of an agent bind the party whom the agent represents.
3. Describe the duties that agents owe to the parties they represent.
4. Describe the legal claims that might be asserted against each of the parties to an agency transaction.

Business Decisions and the Law

Split Milk

Assume that you are the owner of a large regional dairy who hires persons to make home deliveries of dairy products. These persons own their own milk trucks, set their own hours, schedule their own deliveries, are assigned a territory, and receive as pay a percentage of the sales within their territory. When investigating liability insurance for these persons you learn that rates for milk truck drivers who are "employees" are fifty times higher than for drivers who are classified by the law as "independent contractors."

Are your drivers independent contractors so that your firm qualifies for the much lower rate? The answer is found on page 279 of the text.

Introduction

The business ethics issue most closely associated with the law of agency is that of trusting co-workers. Agency law creates a legal system that allows one party to trust wisely certain other parties in business transactions. The basis for this trust is the force of law; if parties who are by law supposed to be trustworthy are not, they can be legally liable for their untrustworthy conduct.

As you read this chapter, you will see a contrast between the way in which the law defines normal business relationships and the way it defines these relationships of trust. By examining the differing aspects of these two kinds of relationships, you can decide which provides the better guide for development of your business character. Agency law describes in detail what is required of one in whom trust is placed. As you read, try to decide exactly what duties you will assume when someone begins trusting you. Will you go as far as the law does?

Most commercial relationships are said to be at **arm's length.** This means that the law assumes that the parties will look out for their own self-interest. Thus, for example, a used car dealer might sell a five-year-old Volkswagen for 25 percent more than its fair market value. As long as there has been no misrepresentation or deception the courts will enforce the agreement because the parties must look out for their own self-interest.

Arm's length relationships are often commercially impractical. Unless a contract is extremely detailed and comprehensive, it often does not accommodate conditions that might change later. Further, arm's length relationships put parties to a contract in the role of adversaries; these relationships are often not suitable where there is a need for trust between parties. To fill the commercial need, the courts have created an alternative relationship characterized by flexibility and trust—the **fiduciary relationship.** In contrast to arm's length transactions, the law in fiduciary transactions requires one party to suppress his self-interest for the benefit of the other party. The most common fiduciary relationship is agency.

The Core Structure of Agency

Grant of Authority

In general, agency relationships are created when one party gives authority to another to act for her, usually to alter, or help to alter, legal relations. This transfer, or *grant of authority,* is the core characteristic of agency relationships. Thus, an agency relationship would arise if one party authorized another to represent her in buying a diamond or purchasing a computer or running a business. These activities involve altering or helping to alter legal relations. The party who gives this authority is called the **principal;** the party who receives it is called the **agent.** A party dealing with a principal, when the principal is represented by an agent, is called a **third party.**

Scope of Authority

If the agent does what the principal requests, the agent is said to be acting within her **scope of authority.** If the agent does something that the principal has not authorized, the agent is said to have acted *outside* the scope of authority. If the agent acts within the scope of authority and, for example, negotiates a contract for the principal, the principal will be bound by the contract. However, if the agent acted outside the scope of authority in negotiating the contract, the contract will not bind the principal.

Usually, agents are not personally liable in the transactions they negotiate on behalf of their principals. However, agents who act outside the scope of their authority may become liable. If the third party suffers an injury because the agent acted outside the scope of his authority and thus the contract cannot be enforced against the principal, the third party can recover from the agent. Suppose, for example, a homeowner (the principal) confers agency authority on a real estate broker (the agent) *only to find a buyer* for the home. If the broker goes beyond this scope of authority and executes a deed on behalf of the homeowner, then the homeowner will not be bound by the deed. Further, the agent may be liable to the purported buyer (the third party) for injury flowing from the agent's unauthorized acts.

Fiduciary Duties

The existence of the agency relationship imposes certain unique obligations upon the agent. Recall that in normal contract law the parties to the contract should be able to identify all the terms and conditions of their agreement merely by reflecting on their conduct and the communications they have had with each other. However, there are certain terms and conditions that the parties to agency agreements could not normally perceive. These terms and conditions are the **fiduciary duties.** In essence, fiduciary duties require the agent to act skillfully and to place the interests of the principal above the interests of all others. (See figure 11.1.)

Creation of Agency

Agency relationships arise in a wide variety of settings. The relationship often exists between an employer and an employee. For example, a clerk in a shoe store is an agent because he assists in altering the principal's legal relations by accepting the money paid for the shoes. On the other hand, the janitor of the

Figure 11.1 Major Agency Roles and Issues

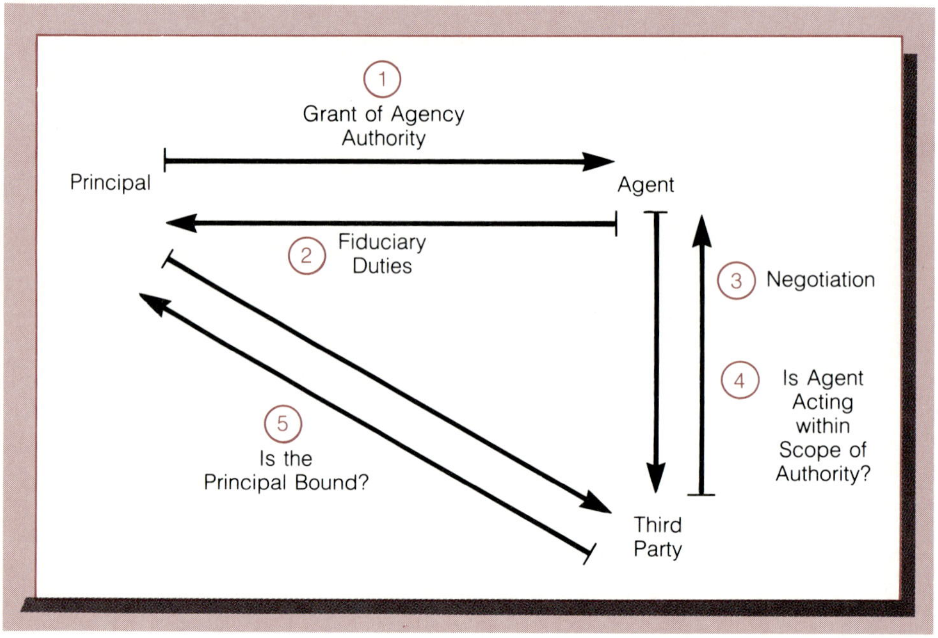

same store would not be an agent, because the janitor merely cleans and does nothing directly to assist in altering the employer's legal relations with others. A secretary may or may not be an agent. If the employer authorizes the secretary to contract or assist in contracting, then the secretary will be an agent. To illustrate: A secretary who is authorized to purchase office supplies and charge them to the firm's account is an agent. But a secretary who merely types letters, takes dictation, maintains files, and files reports about the productivity of the sales force is not an agent. So some employees are agents, while others are not.

Many agency relationships arise in the context of a contract. A corporation might use a forty-page contract to employ a new president. However, a contract is not always needed between a principal and an agent. Thus a homeowner might ask a neighbor to pick up some paint at the local hardware store and charge it to the homeowner's account there. Even though there is no contract between the neighbor and the homeowner, the agency relationship exists. Agency exists because the homeowner authorized the neighbor to alter a legal relationship with the hardware store. The homeowner would be bound by the contract with the hardware store to pay for the paint, and the neighbor would be bound as the fiduciary of the homeowner. When the agency relationship is not based on a contract, the agent is called a *gratuitous agent*.

Methods of Creation

Grant and Acceptance of Authority

When a principal tells a prospective agent to assist in altering a legal relationship, and the agent agrees, then agency has been created by the process called the **grant and acceptance of authority.** The communication of the agency authority may be by spoken words, written words, or even by the mere conduct of the principal toward the agent. If a banker gave a gasoline credit card to her secretary, then this conduct would probably indicate that the secretary had agency authority to fill the company car with gasoline.

An acceptance of the agency authority may occur by a formal acceptance, such as the signing of an agreement, or it may occur informally, simply by the performance of the act requested by the principal. The prospective agent is not bound by the fiduciary duties until he or she has accepted the grant of authority. Grant and acceptance of authority is the process by which the vast majority of agency relationships are created.

Ratification

Ratification not only creates an agency relationship, but it also is a mechanism for curing many of the problems that arise when an agent acts outside the scope of authority. In general, ratification occurs when a person accepts the benefit of an act done by a self-appointed agent or an agent acting outside the scope of his authority. Thus if the agent then goes to the principal and discloses all the material facts about the transaction, and the principal *accepts and retains* the benefits of the transaction, the principal is bound by the transaction. This is so even though the agent lacked authority at the time of the negotiations.

For example, suppose a company manufacturing fire hydrants authorized a new salesperson *only to solicit orders* and not to contract on behalf of the company. Further, assume that a city, anxious to conclude a transaction quickly, got the salesperson to sign a contract on behalf of the company for the sale of one hundred hydrants for $25,000. At this point neither the company nor the city would be bound, because the salesperson acted outside the scope of authority. But if the salesperson took the contract and the $25,000 back to the company, and the company accepted and retained the money, both the city and the company would become bound under the doctrine of ratification. In fact, the contract would bind the parties even if the salesperson had never been employed by the company.

Grant of Apparent Authority

When the principal acts toward a third party in a way that leads the third party to believe that someone possesses agency authority, then the law will hold that principal bound by a contract negotiated under this **apparent authority.** Of course, the transaction must be within the scope of the agent's apparent authority.

Apparent authority is usually valid even when the principal and agent have agreed either orally or in writing that the agent will not represent the principal in such transactions. This is because the principal's conduct toward the third party creates the authority, and the law will hold the principal responsible for such representations. Of course, if the third party learns of the agreement limiting the agent's authority, the apparent authority is eliminated. Similarly, if the third party sees, or should have seen, that the apparent agent is not really acting in the best interests of the principal, then again the apparent authority is eliminated. The following case illustrates the doctrines of ratification and apparent authority.

Bruton v. Automatic Welding & Supply

513 P.2d 1122 (Alaska, 1973)

Facts

Jerry Bruton loaned a D8 Caterpillar bulldozer to David Ekvall rent free. They agreed that Ekvall would be responsible for minor repairs. When Ekvall began using the D8 Cat to clear land, it broke down. After several attempts to fix it on the site, Ekvall took the D8 Cat to a repair shop called AWS. After AWS made major repairs costing about $2,300, Bruton, the owner of the Cat, happened into the shop and authorized AWS to do other unrelated work on the Cat. Once repaired, the D8 Cat was returned to Ekvall, who used it finish clearing the land. AWS billed Bruton for all the work on his Cat. When Bruton didn't pay, AWS sued both Bruton and Ekvall. The trial court, in finding for AWS, concluded that Ekvall had apparent authority to authorize the repairs and further that Bruton had ratified Ekvall's acts.

Opinion

Justice Boochever: Apparent authority . . . involves a representation by the principal either by words or conduct to a *third person,* "which reasonably interpreted, causes the third person to believe that the principal consents to have the act done on his behalf by the person purporting to act for him."

[H]ere there were no words or conduct of Bruton which could have caused AWS to believe that Bruton consented to have the repairs made on his behalf. There was no testimony to the effect that Bruton made any representation to AWS that Ekvall was authorized to order repairs on his behalf. The mere fact that Bruton permitted Ekvall to use the Cat did not constitute any representation to AWS that Ekvall was authorized to make repairs to it on Bruton's behalf. . . . To conclude from the record that Ekvall had apparent authority was clearly erroneous. . . .

As with apparent authority, ratification is an agency doctrine. It was created by common law courts to deal with a situation where, after a transaction is entered into by a second party purporting to act for a principal, the principal manifests an intent to be bound by the acts of the second party. Thus, ratification is unnecessary where a person acts with a principal's authority or apparent authority. . . .

But ratification was wrongly applied in the instant case. As stated in *Pullen* v. *Dale,* 109 F.2d 538, 539, "It is sufficient to say that for the doctrine of ratification to apply, it is a requisite that the act sought to be ratified be done by someone who held himself out to the third party as an agent."

No evidence was presented below that Ekvall purported to be acting for Bruton when he authorized the Cat to be brought into the AWS shop. In fact, the testimony of Roetman [an employee of AWS] indicated that Ekvall, who up until that time had explicitly authorized all repair bills for the D8 Cat, had the major repairs done on his own account. Roetman testified:

> I explained to him what we were trying to do, and that in the event this didn't work, it would then become a major repair job, and have to go to the

shop, and he said well, we don't want to put any more money into it . . . than we have to, but we've got to repair it, so do whatever you see fit. . . .

But even if Ekvall had purported to act for Bruton in authorizing the major repairs, there was no ratification for yet another reason. Neither through conduct nor speech did Bruton affirm any responsibility to pay for repairs authorized by Ekvall.

AWS . . . argues that by receiving or by retaining the benefit of the work done on the Cat without protest, Bruton impliedly affirmed his liability for the repairs.

[The legal test of] receipt of benefits and retention of benefits were . . . inappropriately applied [by the trial court]. Both rest on the notion that the acquiescence of the principal through acceptance of the benefits of an unauthorized transaction may reasonably be assumed to be authorization. But Bruton never realized that he was considered responsible for the cost of repairs until after he received the bill from AWS. After the major repair, the Cat was returned to Ekvall, who continued to use it for some length of time. When it was finally returned to Bruton there was no way for him to have the repairs undone. . . .

Reversed in part.

Case Questions

1. Do you think giving someone possession of a D8 Cat constitutes "acting toward others" as if the possessor had authority to repair the equipment at the owner's expense?
2. Why is AWS suing both Ekvall and Bruton?
3. If one assumes that Ekvall is not very strong financially, then who should bear the loss caused by Ekvall: AWS, who dealt with Ekvall about the repairs, or Bruton, who gave Ekvall possession of this very expensive piece of machinery?

Agency Agreements Required to Be in Writing

The Statute of Frauds applies to agency transactions in the same way it does to nonagency transactions. For example, if an agent were hired for an eighteen-month period, the agreement should be placed in writing and signed because it is a contract requiring more than one year to complete.

One provision of the Statute of Frauds deals specifically with agency transactions. It applies to agency agreements that authorize the agent to execute documents required by law to be in writing. If the document must be in writing, then the agency agreement authorizing another to execute it must also be in writing. This is called the **equal dignity rule.** Thus, if one party wanted to authorize another to execute a contract for the sale of a painting for $25,000 (a contract for the sale of goods for $500 or more), the agency agreement must be in writing. There are also instances in which the equal dignity rule requires more than just a writing. When execution of an instrument requires notarization or witnesses, then the agency authority to execute the instrument must also be notarized or witnessed.

Capacity and Agency

In general, the principal and third party in agency relationships have the same contractual capacity protection that is given to any party who contracts. Thus a principal or third party who is a special party may be bound to pay only the fair market value for necessaries rather than the contracted price. Similarly, they may have the power to disaffirm a contract for nonnecessaries.

Because third parties are often not in direct contact with principals, the laws in many states protect third parties by creating an *agent's warranty of the principal's capacity*. Then if an agent represents a party without contractual capacity, and that party invokes any special rights to the detriment of the third party, the third party can recover the amount of the loss from the agent. This is an exception to the general rule that an agent is not liable for contracts negotiated within the scope of his authority.

Agent's Capacity

The rule on an agent's capacity is that the agent need merely possess sufficient mental ability to understand the transaction. For example, a six-year-old girl can probably act as the agent of her parents in purchasing a quart of milk. Neither the parents nor the grocer would have any special rights because this agent is a minor. However, this young girl would probably not have sufficient mental maturity to represent the parents in purchasing a new car. She clearly would not have the agency capacity to represent them in purchasing a home. The agent's capacity is assessed by matching the mind of the agent with the complexity of the transaction. If the agent lacks the mental capacity to represent the principal, then neither the principal nor the third party will be bound. Note that the standard for capacity to act as an agent differs significantly from the standard for capacity to contract.

Almost any act that persons can perform for themselves can be performed for them by an agent. An agent can represent a principal in selling real estate, purchasing a $4 million diamond, managing a Fortune 500 corporation, or marrying a California belly dancer. There are, however, some acts that cannot be performed through an agent. An agent cannot, on behalf of another, serve a prison sentence, fulfill a Selective Service obligation, vote, or execute a will. Aside from these fairly obvious limitations, agents can represent their principals in altering or establishing nearly any legal relationship.

In certain instances, state or federal law requires that persons be licensed to act as agents. Stockbrokers, real estate brokers, accountants, lawyers, and others must be certified as competent to represent principals in their technically complex fields. Lawyers were the first agents to be recognized by the law. Lawyers are also called attorneys-at-law—the word *attorney* is Old French for agent. That is why a written authorization to act as the agent of another is called a **power of attorney.** Persons operating under a power of attorney are called attorneys-in-fact.

Scope of Authority

The authority that the principal transfers to the agent can take several forms. When the principal tells the agent what his authority is, in written or spoken words, this is called **express authority.** Another kind of authority, *implied au-*

thority, contains three subcategories: incidental, customary, and apparent authority.

When someone has express authority, there are often related tasks that must be performed before an agent can exercise express authority. For example, one expressly authorized to record a deed usually needs to pay a small recording fee. If the express authority to pay the fee does not exist, the law will imply from the express authority to record the deed an **incidental authority** to pay the fee.

Some agency relationships, such as real estate sales agency agreements, occur frequently without much express and incidental authority being given. In such cases the law will supplement these forms of authority with **customary authority,** to reflect the way the parties understand that these transactions are customarily handled. For example, parties who enter into real estate sales agency agreements often do not mention that the agent is authorized to place FOR SALE signs on the property. Still, if the parties know that this is customary, the law will probably include it within the scope of the agent's authority.

Apparent authority is created when the principal, not the agent, causes the third party to believe that a party is an agent or has certain agency authority.

Interpretation of Authority

In normal contract law, courts interpret instruments and agreements by trying to determine what the parties intended at the time the contract was created. Agency law requires that agency authority be interpreted not only in light of what the parties intended when they created the agency relationship, but also in light of the agent's knowledge of what should be in the best interests of the principal. The fiduciary duties that agents owe principals cause the agency rule of interpretation to differ from the normal contract rule. Agents must modify their scope of authority to serve the best interests of the principal.

Third Party's Duty to Determine Authority

The law requires that the third party bear the responsibility for determining the scope of the agent's authority from sources other than the agent. If it turns out that the agent has misrepresented his authority, the principal is not bound, and the third party can only look to the agent to recover any loss. If, however, the agent has apparent authority, the third party may rely on it. But remember that apparent authority flows from the principal to the third party, not from the agent to the third party.

A third party who learns that there is a written agency agreement will be bound by any of the limitations in that agreement, even if he did not read it. Of course, in these instances the third party can recover from the agent who has acted outside the scope of his or her authority. The following case illustrates several forms of agency authority.

Pailet v. Guillory

315 S.2d 893 (Ct. App., Louisiana 1975)

Facts

Rae Abramson and Ruth Pailet were sisters who together owned a parcel of real property. They desired to lease the property. Dr. Albert Abramson, Rae's husband, helped them rent it. Dr. Abramson assisted them in leasing the property to Cenla Equipment Company, Inc., for five years. After about three years, Cenla stopped paying rent. Thereafter, Cenla approached Dr. Abramson with a request that the lease be terminated. After checking with the sisters, he informed Cenla that the termination was acceptable and no further rent would be owed. When the rental income stopped, Ruth Pailet (plaintiff) filed suit against Cenla (defendant), stating that she did not agree to the termination of the lease.

Opinion

Judge Fruge: The present action was instituted by Ruth Pailet, one of the lessors, for her half of the rents due under the lease since December 1, 1973. She claims that no rent has been paid since that time and under an acceleration clause in the lease, defendants are indebted to her to the extent of one-half of 24 months rent at the rate of $82.50 per month, or a total of $1,980.

Defendants admit that no rent was paid after November of 1973. They contend, however, that the lease was cancelled and they are under no obligation to pay any rentals.

All matters concerning the leased property . . . [were] . . . handled for the lessors by Dr. Albert Abramson, who was the husband of Rae Abramson at the time the lease was entered into. The record shows that the defendants contacted Dr. Abramson about leasing the property, that they paid rent checks to Dr. Abramson (made out to the sisters) and that Dr. Abramson handled minor repairs on behalf of the lessors on his own authority. The defendants have never had any direct contact with the lessors concerning the property. Their only contact was through Dr. Abramson.

Dr. Abramson made it clear to the defendants that he did not own the leased property and that on certain matters he could act only with the permission of the lessors. For instance, Dr. Abramson made it clear that he did not have authority to lease the premises. The lease was made only upon approval of the terms by the lessors and they signed the lease themselves.

In March of 1973, [Cenla] approached Dr. Abramson and asked that the lease be cancelled. Dr. Abramson informed him that he would have to check with the lessors, Mrs. Abramson and Mrs. Pailet, as he did not have the authority to cancel. A few days later Dr. Abramson notified the lessee that the lessors had agreed to cancel the lease.

At trial, Mrs. Pailet denied that she had ever been contacted by Dr. Abramson about cancelling the lease. She testified that had she been so contacted she would not have agreed to the cancellation because she needed the income from the rent. Dr. Abramson testified that he contacted Mrs. Pailet and thought she had agreed to the cancellation. He admitted that there had apparently been a misunderstanding.

The trial court clearly found that Mrs. Pailet did not agree to cancelling the lease. . . . Appellants contend that even if Mrs. Pailet did not agree to cancellation of the lease, she is bound by the act of Dr. Abramson who was vested with the *implied authority* [emphasis added] to cancel the lease.

In this case, Dr. Abramson's agency authority included collecting the rent and making minor repairs. Certainly the authority to cancel the lease is not incidental or necessary to his authority to collect rent and make minor repairs. No such authority can be inferred in these circumstances, particularly where the authority to lease . . . was not given.

We turn now to the issue of *apparent authority.* [Emphasis added.] The concern here is whether the principal did anything to clothe the agent with apparent authority to perform the act. . . . Because third persons are not privy to the actual terms of the agency agreement, they may rely upon the indicia of authority with which the agent is vested. . . .

We do not find that the lessors in this case clothed Dr. Abramson with the apparent authority to cancel the lease. Dr. Abramson himself denied that he had any authority to do so. The lease agreement . . . was signed by the lessors and not by Dr. Abramson. Thus, all the indications were that Dr. Abramson did not have authority to cancel.

Appellants rely on the fact that all of their communications with the lessors concerning the leased property were through Dr. Abramson. This alone is not enough. The fact that Dr. Abramson failed to secure cancellation of the lease from Mrs. Pailet is not imputable to her, but rather to the appellants since they relied on Dr. Abramson to secure cancellation.

For the reasons assigned the judgment of the trial court is affirmed. Costs are assessed to defendants—appellants.

Case Questions

1. Who in this situation has acted most unreasonably, Ruth Pailet, Dr. Abramson, or the lessee?
2. Has a lack of knowledge of business law injured any party in this situation?
3. If you were Dr. Abramson, would you conclude that you owed an ethical duty to either Ruth Pailet or the lessee in this situation? If you owed an ethical obligation, what would it be?

Agent's Fiduciary Duties

Agents owe the fiduciary duty to their principals. The courts have identified four elements of the fiduciary duty: the duty of loyalty and obedience, the duty of reasonable care and skill, the duty of confidentiality, and the duty of accounting.

Duty of Loyalty and Obedience

The **duty of loyalty and obedience** is the core fiduciary duty. It requires simply that the agent place the interests of the principal above the interests of everyone else. It also obligates the agent to obey the reasonable instructions of the principal.

Secret profits violate the duty of loyalty. If the agent is being compensated by the principal, the law requires that this compensation be the sole profit that the agent earns from a transaction; any other profit earned in the transaction by the agent belongs to the principal. For example, if a corporate treasurer receives money on behalf of the corporation and places it in a savings account where it earns interest, the interest belongs to the corporation. Failure to disclose or pay over the interest would be a breach of this fiduciary duty. Even if the agent earns the profit in a way that does not injure the principal, the profit belongs to the principal.

Biased advice will violate the duty of loyalty. Thus, the agent must place the principal's interests above his interests in collecting a sales commission or in reducing a clerical obligation. To illustrate: Suppose a law firm has received two offers at the same price and under slightly different terms for the sale of a corporation that the firm's client owns. Further assume that the offer most attractive to the client is also the one that would mean the least profit for the law firm. The fiduciary duty of loyalty requires that the law firm place the interests of the client above its own interests. In this case, then, the firm must recommend acceptance of the offer most attractive to the client.

The agent must place the interests of the principal not only above her own interests, but also above those of the third party. **Dual agency** exists when an agent represents both parties to a transaction. Thus a broker representing both the seller and the buyer of realty would be a dual agent. Although very knowledgeable agents, such as lawyers with expertise in agency law, act occasionally as dual agents in relatively simple transactions, most wise agents consider dual agency legally risky. A dual agent owes all fiduciary duties to both parties. If either party suffers financial injury without its full knowledge and informed consent, that party will probably be able to recover damages from the dual agent.

Duty of Reasonable Care and Skill

Agents are obligated by law to perform their authorized acts with *reasonable care and skill*. The standard of skill varies with the occupation of the agent; a lawyer must perform with the skill of a reasonable lawyer, and a corporate president must perform with the skill of a reasonable corporate president. Agents who purport to represent others are obligated to exert some minimal effort to advance the interests of their clients. So a lawyer who represents a client on a risky contingency fee basis must work for that client in the same way as if he were receiving a more attractive hourly rate.

The communication of all material facts about a transaction is an essential part of the **duty of reasonable care and skill.** If the agent is aware of any fact that might affect the conduct of the principal in the transaction, then that information must always be communicated.

Even if the agent performs numerous services for the client, he may still breach this duty if the services are not performed with sufficient skill. For example, an accountant who carelessly prepares an income tax return in a way that subjects his client to tax penalties may have violated the fiduciary duty of reasonable care and skill.

Duty of Confidentiality

The **duty of confidentiality** forbids the agent to disclose any information about the principal that the principal wants to keep confidential. The information must be kept secret during the life of the agency relationship and also *after* the agency relationship has terminated. For example, suppose that a toy manufacturing company authorized its marketing manager to negotiate certain patent rights necessary to produce a new product. If the company asked the marketing manager to treat this transaction confidentially, he would, as an agent, be legally bound to do so. If he later resigned his position, he would still be bound by this duty of confidentiality.

Duty of Accounting

The **duty of accounting** requires the agent to disclose to the principal the sources and use of all the principal's money that the agent has controlled. Part of the duty of accounting—and one with an ancient history—is the obligation not to *commingle*. **Commingling** means mixing the principal's money with the agent's money. The concern of the law is that if the principal's money is not treated as separate from the agent's money, the agent will be tempted to start using the principal's money for her own purposes, and then will be unable to deliver the money owed when it is due. Since that would discredit the agent's profession and all agency relationships, the courts and the professions themselves have dealt harshly with those who commingle.

Principal's Consent to Adverse Acts

Many specific duties that the agent owes the principal can be waived if, after being informed of the consequences of the waiver, the principal consents. For example, an auctioneer can avoid liability on the fiduciary duties of loyalty and confidentiality when advertising property as "for sale by a distressed seller" by obtaining the seller's consent to advertise in this manner.

Principal's Remedies for Breach of Fiduciary Duties

When an agent fails to perform the fiduciary duties and thereby injures the principal, the courts tend to treat the conduct as a major breach of the agency agreement, so the principal may treat the contract as terminated. Often courts also conclude that the agent who commits a material breach of a fiduciary duty is not entitled to an agent's compensation. And if an agent's breach of a fiduciary duty causes financial injury to the principal, the agent will be liable for the amount of the injury.

Principal's Duty to the Agent

Principals owe agents all the duties expressly promised to the agent in the agency agreement or grant of authority. In addition, they owe certain duties that are implied in most contracts. Thus, the principal must cooperate in good faith with the agent. Similarly, the principal may not interfere with the agent's performance of her duties.

Principals generally owe their agents a **duty of reimbursement.** This requires that the principal repay the agent for the expenses that the agent incurs in carrying out the principal's instructions. For example, if a corporation retains an attorney in an industrial accident case, and the attorney hires a private investigator to examine the scene of the accident, the corporation (the principal) must reimburse the attorney (the agent) for the cost of the investigator.

Agent's Duties to Third Parties

Classical agency law makes the agent the representative only of the principal. The agent deals with the principal as a fiduciary. On the other hand, agency law obligates the agent to deal with third parties at arm's length. In general, the agent will not be liable on a contract between the principal and the third party, even if the principal breaches it.

In some instances, however, the agent's conduct can make him liable. If an agent intentionally participates in fraud or misrepresentation, or negligently communicates a material misrepresentation, he can thereby become liable to the third party. The following case illustrates the way courts view the liability of the agent for misrepresentations made to a third party.

Cameron v. Terrell & Garrett, Inc.

599 S.W.2d 680 (Ct. Civ. Apls. Tex. 1980)

Facts

Jerry and JoAnn Cameron sought to purchase a home. They contacted a real estate salesperson, who showed them several homes. In the process of showing homes to the Camerons, this agent allowed them to look at a multiple listing book that contained a description of the property they ultimately bought. That description stated that the home contained 2,400 square feet of space. After the purchase, the Camerons learned that in fact it contained only 2,245 square feet. The Camerons filed suit against Terrell & Garrett, the real estate agents of the seller, who had submitted the information for the multiple listing book. Terrell & Garrett had obtained the square footage information from the seller.

Opinion

Justice Hughes: Although an agent is generally not liable for contracts made by him for the benefit of his principal, the agent can be held personally liable to a third person for damages arising out of intentional deceit in procuring such contracts under certain circumstances.

. . . [A]n agent will not be personally liable for damages for deceit if he honestly believes that the representations made to him [which] induce the third party purchaser to contract were true. It is clear that an agent is entitled to rely in good faith upon the information supplied to him by a principal concerning something which the principal seeks to sell. If any misrepresentations about the item to be sold are made by the seller to his agent, and the agent is unaware of these misrepresentations, he is liable to an injured third party only (1) if he is put on actual notice of the misrepresentations; (2) if in the exercise of attempting to verify the representations of the seller the agent determines that the representations are false and continues to make such representations with knowledge of the falsity of them; or (3) if the agent undertakes to verify the accuracy of the principal's representations and because of negligence on his own part fails to uncover some evidence of misrepresentation which he either would have discovered had he completed his investigation or which, under the same or similar circumstances, a reasonable person acting as an agent would discover.

Affirmed for Terrell & Garrett, Inc.

Case Questions

1. Would Terrell & Garrett have been liable if the home had been 1,700 square feet in size instead of 2,225 square feet?
2. Would Terrell & Garrett have been liable if it were customary for agents to actually measure the size of the listed home?
3. Does the statement, "if the agent undertakes to verify the accuracy of the principal's representations and fails to uncover . . . [the] misrepresentation . . . [he will be liable]" suggest that it would be wise *not* to attempt to verify the principal's representations in some situations? Is such a strategy for avoiding legal risk consistent with your ethical standards?

Principal's Liability for Agent's Acts

Liability for Agent's Misrepresentation

If an agent engages in fraud or deceit that injures the third party, then of course the third party will be able to sue the agent and recover damages. Frequently, however, the third party will seek to hold the principal liable for these acts of the agent. In these situations, the courts ask whether the principal directed the agent to engage in the specific conduct or supplied the incorrect information. If the principal directed the conduct, she is liable to the third party as though she had acted directly. Even if the principal is unaware of the agent's conduct, in some states, the principal will be liable if the agent was acting within the scope of authority when the deceit or fraud occurred.

Liability for Agent's Torts

The liability of the principal for torts of the agent hinges upon the control exercised by the principal over the agent. Usually when the principal has great control over the agent, the principal is liable for the agent's torts. And of course the reverse is true; the principal is generally not liable when she does not control the agent. The degree of control also determines which agents are employees. In general, an **employee** is one who is subject to the supervision and control of an employer. Since employers control employees, employers are generally liable for the torts of their employees. This is true whether or not the employee is an agent. For example, if a dairy hired someone to make home deliveries of milk and gave instructions on how and when the deliveries were to be made, the driver would be under the control of the dairy—that is, he would be its employee. Thus, the dairy would be liable for the driver's torts. If the driver negligently ran over a pedestrian, both the driver and the dairy would be liable.

Sometimes persons are hired to accomplish an objective but are not subject to control over how to accomplish it. If you hired a lawyer to give you legal advice, you would not tell him how to research the law or write a legal memorandum. You would agree to pay for the result—the advice—and would not control the means used to achieve the result. This type of person or organization is an **independent contractor,** not an employee. Since independent contractors are not subject to control over how they accomplish the objective, those who hire independent contractors are generally *not* liable for their torts.

Suppose a dairy hired a milk truck operator, had the operator buy the truck, agreed to refer all delivery requests to him, assigned him a territory, and agreed to pay him a set percentage of sales. If the driver could set his own hours and delivery schedule, he would probably be an independent contractor. If, while working, he negligently ran over a pedestrian, only the driver would be liable, not the dairy.

Of course, employers cannot control all the conduct of their employees. Accordingly, employers are only liable when those whom they control are acting "within the scope of their employment." This means that the employee is either following the employer's directions or is trying to advance the employer's business. Suppose a milk truck driver who was an employee disobeyed specific directions and exceeded the speed limit, causing an accident while making deliveries. The driver was acting within the scope of his employment because he was advancing the business of his employer. Therefore both the driver and the dairy would be liable. If, on the other hand, the driver drove one hundred miles to the next town to visit a girlfriend and caused an accident there, he would not have been acting within the scope of employment. Therefore only the driver would be liable.

In summary, principals will be liable for the torts of their agents when the agents are subject to the principals' control—that is, when they are employees acting within the scope of their employment. Principals are generally not liable when the agent is an independent contractor.

Agent's Liability When the Principal Is Undisclosed or Partially Disclosed

Usually when an agent contracts on behalf of a principal, the principal is bound and the agent is not. This rule changes, however, when the principal is *undisclosed* or *partially disclosed*.

Undisclosed Principal

An **undisclosed principal** exists when the third party is unaware of both the identity of the principal and the existence of the agency. In these situations the third party believes that the transaction is only between the agent and the third party.

Undisclosed principals can enforce the contract against the third party. To do this, the principal must often file suit, and of course in this process the principal's identity is disclosed. But note that this disclosure occurs after the contract is created.

The third party can enforce the contract against the agent. This is most likely to occur when the principal breaches for some reason. If, after a breach, the third party learns of the previously undisclosed principal, an election is required. That is, the third party must choose to recover from either the principal or the agent; she cannot recover from both.

Partially Disclosed Principal

A **partially disclosed principal** exists when the third party is aware of the agency but not the identity of the principal. As with the undisclosed principal, this principal can enforce the contract. The agent will be liable to the third party if the principal breaches. And again, the third party must elect between recovering from the principal or the agent.

Undisclosed and partially disclosed principals are used in situations where secrecy is desired. For example, if a land developer were trying to buy all the residences on a city block for development into a commercial site, she might fear that the last owner of a residence there would learn of the plan and refuse to sell except at an extremely high price. To avoid this risk, she might purchase each residence through a different agent and remain undisclosed until all the properties were purchased. Assuming that the principal was disclosed, do you think it would be ethical for the last property owner to take advantage of the principal's vulnerability and charge the highest possible price? Do you think it is unethical for the principal to avoid this risk by being undisclosed?

Assignment and Delegation

The law views agency relationships as personal. Therefore, in most cases agency rights may not be assigned and agency duties may not be delegated. If, however, the agent's responsibilities include some acts that are *ministerial*—i.e., acts not requiring the exercise of significant professional judgment—these responsibilities may be delegated. For example, typing, filing, and recording documents would probably be ministerial acts that an agent could delegate.

Termination of Agency

Agency relationships are so personal they are said to be *consensual*. This means that the principal and agent must consent to the relationship's continued existence. Agency differs from other types of contracts, which will be enforced after they are created, regardless of the wishes of one of the parties. In effect, both the principal and the agent have the power to terminate an agency relationship at any time. Neither the principal nor the agent will be subject to a decree of specific performance.

On the other hand, while the law grants the power to terminate, it does not always grant the right. This means that while the agency authority can be terminated (the power), liability in damages may arise (lack of the right) from the termination. Suppose a college football player authorized a firm to represent him in negotiations with National Football League teams and promised to pay the firm 10 percent of his salary for the first three years of his football career. If midway through the negotiations the football player became dissatisfied with the firm representing him, he would have the power to terminate the firm's agency authority. Upon his telling the firm and the NFL that the authority was revoked, the firm would lose the legal ability to bind him. However, the firm might still collect its 10 percent. This is because the football player had the power but not the right to terminate.

There is an exception to the general rule we have just stated. It is that the principal loses the power to terminate an agency relationship when she grants an **agency coupled with an interest.** This arises in situations in which the agent has a legal or equitable interest in the thing that is the subject matter of the agency. For example, a woman who owed money to a real estate broker for investment advice might agree to satisfy her obligation by giving the broker title to 10 percent of certain property, along with a listing on her 90 percent. This would create an agency coupled with an interest, and the owner would have neither the power nor the right to terminate this agency agreement.

Since agency is so personal, the death or incapacity of either the principal or the agent automatically ends the agency relationship. If, however, there is an agency coupled with an interest, the agent's rights will survive the death or incapacity of the principal.

Of course, agency authority will end at the time specified by the agency agreement. Even an agency coupled with an interest expires at the agreed-upon time. The following case discusses termination of agency authority.

Sarokhan v. Fair Lawn Memorial Hospital, Inc.

199 A.2d 52 (N.J. 1964)

Facts

Dr. Sarokhan entered into an agreement with Fair Lawn Memorial Hospital whereby he agreed to act as the hospital's medical director for a period of ten years. The agreement stated that "[this agreement] may not be revoked or altered by the hospital during that [ten-year] period." After six months, the hospital became dissatisfied with Dr. Sarokhan's services and notified him that his relationship with the hospital was terminated. Dr. Sarokhan filed suit and raised, among other issues, the termination of his employment and agency status.

Opinion

Defendants feel that they have just cause to terminate plaintiff's services; and, *even if just cause were lacking* [emphasis added], they have the power to terminate the agency or employment relationship, subject only to an action for damages if, in so doing, there is a wrongful breach of contract. Plaintiff's position is that defendants created an *agency coupled with an interest* [emphasis added] and have neither the right nor the power to terminate it during the ten-year term.

The mere fact that the appointment recites that it will be irrevocable during the term of the appointment does not preclude the principal from exercising the power to revoke it. This does not mean that the principal may breach such a contract with impunity. For a wrongful breach, the agent may sue at law and recover money damages.

The law has recognized, as an exception to the general rule, that "an agency coupled with an interest" can not be revoked by the principal during the term fixed for its existence.

Defendants concede that, if the contract herein created an agency coupled with an interest . . . in the subject matter . . . [the agency could not be revoked]. . . . The power conferred by defendant hospital was not one "coupled with an interest." Accordingly, it is not irrevocable, despite the terminology used by the parties.

We conclude that the contract in issue did not create an agency coupled with an interest and that defendants had the power to terminate it. . . . We make no determination as to whether defendants breached any contractual right of plaintiff in terminating his relationship with the hospital.

The order under review is reversed.

Case Questions

1. Do you think a hospital should be required to keep a director of medical services for ten years if it does not feel comfortable with him?
2. If you were the owner of the hospital, would you have broken your word to Dr. Sarokhan? Why or why not?
3. Should our legal system encourage persons to break their word, as it does with the concept of "power without the right"?

Ethical Issues in Agency Relationships

You can think about arm's length and fiduciary relations from an ethical perspective. In an arm's length transaction, the law tolerates conduct that most people would consider unethical—as, for example, when a used car salesperson sells a junker to a young adult for substantially more than it is worth. In contrast, fiduciary relations hold one party, the agent, to a very high ethical standard of trustworthiness—but only toward the principal. So people often find themselves operating in radically different legal and ethical settings in business.

Another way to look at arm's length and fiduciary relations is from the perspectives of self-interest and other-interest. One view has it that the relationship itself will determine how parties behave—arm's length relations are self-interested, while fiduciary relations are other-oriented. Another view, which focuses on the individual, says that circumstances force business people to be either predominantly self-oriented or predominantly other-oriented. Strongly self-oriented persons in business are commonly called "wolves," and some organizations actively seek to employ them. Other-oriented persons are often called "shepherds," and some organizations prefer to hire this type of person. There are also "wolves in shepherds' clothing." Which style of business person do you find most appealing? Which would you want to work with? Do you think that if you had to compete with "wolves" for a new customer or a promotion, you might be pressured to act in ways that conflict with your values?

The important concepts and terms in this chapter are listed below; page numbers have been provided for the key terms. By reading over each section you can assess your understanding of the chapter concepts and determine areas you may want to review.

Chapter Summary

1. Agency is created when principals authorize agents to alter the principals' legal relations.
2. The agent only binds the principal when acting within the scope of authority.
3. Agents are not liable on the contracts they negotiate for their principals unless they have acted outside the scope of their authority.
4. Agents owe the fiduciary duties to their principals.
5. Agency relationships can be created by contracts or they can be gratuitous. Only some employees are agents of their employers.
6. Agency can be created when authority is granted by the principal and accepted by the agent. Agency can also be created when the principal accepts and retains the benefits of a purported agent's unauthorized acts. This process is called ratification. Finally, agency can be created

when the principal's direct or indirect conduct leads third parties to believe that someone has that principal's agency authority. This is called apparent authority.

7. The equal dignity rule requires that agency authority to execute a document must be created with the same degree of formality as is required to execute the document itself.
8. Agents warrant to third parties the capacity of their principals. Agents need not possess contractual capacity in order for the contract between the principal and third party to be fully enforceable.
9. The principal's words generally create express authority. Incidental and customary authority can expand the scope of an agent's express authority. Apparent authority flows from the principal to the third party.
10. The duty of loyalty requires that the agent place the interests of the principal above the interests of all others. Secret profits violate the duty of loyalty, and dual agency raises enormous risks of a breach of the duty of loyalty.
11. The duty of reasonable care and skill requires that agents perform competently. They must communicate all material facts to their principals, or they breach the duty of reasonable care and skill.
12. Agents owe the duty of confidentiality to the principal both during the life of the agency agreement and after its termination.
13. Agents cannot mix their own money with their clients' money, or the duty of accounting is breached. Agents must also tell their clients what has happened to all of the clients' money that has come into their possession.
14. The fiduciary duties are not breached when the principal has consented to the agent's apparently adverse conduct.
15. If an agent breaches a fiduciary duty, the principal can terminate the agency, recover the agent's compensation, and collect damages.
16. The principal must perform the duties specified in the agency agreement, and in addition the principal must cooperate with the agent.
17. Principals will be liable for their agents' injurious acts when these acts are specifically authorized by the principal or the agent was acting within the scope of employment.
18. Both the principal and the agent have the power, but not the right, to terminate the agency relationship. But an agency coupled with an interest cannot be terminated by the principal.
19. Death or incapacity of the principal or agent generally revokes agency authority.

Key Terms

agency coupled with an interest 281

agent 267

apparent authority 269

arm's length relationship 266

biased advice 275
commingling 276
customary authority 272
dual agency 275
duty of accounting 276
duty of confidentiality 276
duty of loyalty and obedience 275
duty of reasonable care and skill 276
duty of reimbursement 277
employee 279
equal dignity rule 271
express authority 272
fiduciary duties 267
fiduciary relationship 266
grant and acceptance of authority 269
incidental authority 272
independent contractor 279
partially disclosed principal 280
power of attorney 272
principal 267
ratification 269
scope of authority 267
secret profits 275
third party 267
undisclosed principal 280

Questions on Ethics

1. Assume that you are the personnel manager for your firm. Your new hires are instructed not to discuss their salaries with other employees. ("Pay secrecy" is, in fact, a reality of organizational life.) Assume you have interviewed a great candidate for the unique position of sales representative. The market salary for this position is $18,000. However, this applicant, when asked about her salary expectations, said, "I'd feel good if I could land a job at $13,500." You know you could pay her this amount without violating any equal employment opportunity laws because there is only one position like this in the organization. Also, you know that you are the agent of the firm, you are dealing with the applicant at arms's length, and you have been instructed to hire people at the lowest possible salary. What will you do and why?
2. Every organization has what management scholars call a culture. This culture is made up of the shared values of key people in the organization. Every major organization has an ethical component to its culture. For instance, in some organizations, all employees are treated with great dignity, while in other organizations employees are viewed exclusively as economic entities and the way they are treated depends upon how much they contribute to the organization. New employees are usually indoctrinated into the culture, including its ethical component. Most new graduates of business schools quickly embrace the culture of their employing organizations. Is that what you will do? How do you feel about letting a company determine your ethical values? Would you ever be willing to quit your job if your personal ethical values conflicted with those of your company? Can you perceive the ethical values of any

of the organizations with which you have contact? Would you try to determine the ethical culture of an organization before agreeing to work for it?

3. Our legal system acknowledges two or perhaps three basic types of relationships, each with a different ethical character. Do you think there is a justification for treating different categories of people in ethically different ways? Why does our legal system do this? Would you as a manager treat superiors, subordinates, and peers in ethically different ways? As you respond to the last question, think about: the power your boss (a superior) has over your material well-being; the competition that often exists between peers; and the opportunities you might have to exploit subordinates to your own advantage.
4. A subordinate of yours is doing an outstanding job and making you look like an excellent manager, but your boss doesn't know about this superstar. Suppose that your boss indicates that one of your peers—a manager on the same level as you—is leaving and that your boss is looking for a replacement. Also, your boss expects to be promoted within the next year. Would you recommend your superstar for the other management position? Would you recommend the superstar if you thought that with her departure your department's performance would decline just when you might have an opportunity for a promotion? Would you recommend her if you believed she could easily outperform you and be promoted instead of you? In other words, will you relate to her as a fiduciary or at arm's length?
5. Assume that you are the northeastern regional sales manager for your company. Suppose your boss, the national sales manager, quit recently. His boss, the president, has announced that he will pick one of the six regional sales managers for promotion. You judge that it will be a close race, but only between you and the southwestern regional manager, Kirk. You are aware that the president has very strict sexual standards, while Kirk has been living with three girlfriends at different periods over the last year. Will you weave this information into your conversation with the president if you think it will help you win the promotion?

Questions on Law

1. Mrs. Terry, dealing with Alice, a clerk in Peters Department Store, sees a cashmere sweater she likes, but she notices it is slightly soiled. Alice, pushing for a sale, agrees to mark it down from twenty-five dollars to fifteen dollars, which she has no authority to do. Mrs. Terry says, "Fine," asks that the sweater be delivered, and promises to pay C.O.D. The manager of Peters sees the item being wrapped, corrects the bill, and sends it out to Mrs. Terry. On seeing her sweater accompanied by a bill for twenty-five dollars, Mrs. Terry calls and is told by Peters that Alice had no authority to mark down the price. Mrs. Terry is told that

she should either pay the bill or return the sweater. Is Mrs. Terry entitled to her bargain? Why or why not? From Mearns, "Vicarious Liability for Agency Contracts," 48 *Va. L. Rev.* 76 (1962).

2. ABC hired Agnes as its president. After a few years of hard work, Agnes was successful in making ABC profitable. Agnes asked for substantial salary increases and his relationship with the company deteriorated. He then copied customer lists and recruited an ABC vice-president to help him start a new company to engage in the same business as ABC. ABC filed suit against Agnes. Will it prevail? *ABC Trans., etc.* v. *Aeronautics Forwarders, Inc.* 379 N.E.2d 1228 (1978).
3. Snort was the purchasing agent for Cile Corporation. One of his major purchases each year was the auto fleet for the company's sales representatives. The firm that won the supply contract the previous year approached Snort two months before the usual bidding process began and proposed that it again supply the thirty cars but for 7 percent less than the amount charged the previous year. In addition, the car company offered to give Snort a 50 percent personal discount from the suggested retail price for any car on its lot. Both of these terms were conditioned on the contract being awarded directly—without going through the bidding process. Snort judged that the bidding process would not reduce the purchase price of cars, and, in addition, sidestepping the bidding process would significantly reduce the department's operating costs. Based solely on these considerations, he went forward with the transaction, saving the company about $24,000 and himself about $5,000. What are the legal rights of Cile Corporation, Snort, and the car company?
4. Lowe Realty had a twelve-month listing on a $180,000 home owned by Mr. Calvin. The listing contract provided that the realty company could collect a 6 percent commission on the sale price if it found a buyer willing to purchase on terms acceptable to Mr. Calvin. After showing the home to prospective buyers for three months, the realty company began telling potential buyers that Mr. Calvin would be willing to accept an offer of $155,000. The statement is true; Mr. Calvin did say that to the listing agent, but he did not consent to the disclosure of the information to anyone else. Because of the real estate agent's disclosure, an offer of $155,000 was made and Mr. Calvin accepted. Lowe Realty collected its commission. The fair market value of the home was $175,000 at the time of the sale. Later, Mr. Calvin learned of the agent's statement and filed suit. What is the likely outcome of the case and why? Assume that Mr. Calvin can prevail; how much money could he collect?
5. Mario developed plans for the construction of a large office building at an attractive location in Boston. When he applied for construction loans, he was turned down by several lenders because he lacked both construction and office management experience. Finally he approached a private investor, who made the loan but required that she be allowed to

act as Mario's agent for collecting the rents to insure that she would be repaid. Mario agreed, appointed her as his agent, and the building was a financial success. Six years later Mario died. Under his will, his wife, Alice, received the building. She now claims the investor's agency authority was terminated by Mario's death and that she, Alice, was entitled to collect the rents. Did the agency relation terminate on Mario's death?

Suggested Readings

Danley, John R. "Corporate Moral Agency." In *Action and Responsibility,* vol. 2. Ed. Michael Bradie and Myles Brand. Bowling Green, Ohio: Bowling Green State University Department of Philosophy, 1980.

Dunfee, "Business Ethics and the Business School Curriculum," 17 *American Business Law Review* 120 (1979).

Holmes, "The History of Agency Law," 5 *Har. L. Rev.* 1 (1892).

12 The Law of Torts

"The law of torts is concerned with the allocation of losses arising out of human activities. The purpose of the law of torts is to adjust these losses, and to afford compensation for injuries sustained by one person as the result of the conduct of another."

—*William L. Prosser,* Law of Torts

■ LEARNING OBJECTIVES

After you have read this chapter, you should be able to:

1. Describe what an intentional tort is, and identify different types of intentional torts.
2. Describe what constitutes the tort of negligence.
3. Discuss the concept of strict liability in tort.
4. Identify recent issues involving "tort reform."

Business Decisions and the Law

How Private are Store Dressing Rooms

Lewis was an undercover police officer who carried a concealed weapon. When Lewis went into a fitting room in a department store, he was observed by a security guard who had climbed a ladder located in a storeroom behind the fitting rooms. When the guard saw Lewis' gun, he called the police. Upon emerging from the fitting room, Lewis was confronted by a uniformed officer who pointed a gun at him. After a short detention while Lewis identified himself, he was released. Lewis sued the store for invasion of privacy, false imprisonment, and intentional infliction of emotional distress. Will he win? See *Lewis* v. *Dayton Hudson Corporation*.

Introduction

One of the earliest fields of law was torts. Tort law is a form of civil law where private parties use the legal system to resolve disputes among themselves. Persons who feel that someone else has committed a personal wrong against them can sue for monetary damages. Resolution of tort cases has always involved making societal risk allocation decisions. For example, in one of the oldest types of torts, negligence, a judge (often in conjunction with a jury) would be asked to decide who should pay damages if a farmer's lack of attention to driving his cart resulted in a horse-and-carriage accident. Who should bear the risk of loss in this case, the careless farmer, or the driver of the carriage? Many types of tort law are hundreds of years old, and so most people in our society take for granted the policies embodied in this law (such as assuming that the careless farmer should be responsible for his negligence). Other types of torts, such as strict liability in tort in product liability law, are relatively new, and the risk allocation decisions that they represent have excited much comment and controversy.

The field of law that seeks to compensate those who have suffered an injury to themselves or their property as the result of a wrong committed by another is known as **tort.** Tort law covers a large number of different causes of action. In this chapter a number of the more common torts will be discussed.

In today's complex society, persons seem increasingly to be subject to suit based on tort claims. Businesses are also subject to claims that have their basis in tort. Tort claims arise from activities ranging from the simple situation in which a customer slips and falls on the business premises to extremely expensive litigation when a multitude of persons are injured by a product that is defectively designed or mismanufactured. There are many other acts that a business or individual may commit that could result in potential tort liability.

A tort is a civil action based on the violation of a standard of behavior established by society. Liability for the commission of a tort results in the obligation to compensate the injured party.

The question arises as to what types of behavior that cause injury should result in the compensation of the victim for his loss. One useful method of classifying these various types of behavior is to visualize them as covering a spectrum of activity ranging from *intentional acts* at one extreme to *accidents* at the other. In between are those types of acts that are not intentional but that result from behaving in an unreasonable manner characterized as *negligent* acts.

The law has long imposed liability on those who injure others as a result of their *intentional acts*. Thus, if one individual strikes another intentionally, he could be sued for the tort of battery. On the other hand, the law in most cases does not impose liability on those involved in an accident where reasonable care was being used. There is no requirement that liability be imposed on someone simply because an accident occurs. Society has decreed that the parties are not responsible for any damages other than their own when the accident is unavoidable. Of course, in most cases, accidents are avoidable. At an early time in the development of the law, however, even though an injury resulted from an individual's behaving in an unreasonable manner, no liability was imposed unless there was an intent to injure. Later the tort of *negligence* was developed, which allows one to recover for those injuries resulting from acts that may not be perpetrated with the intent to cause injury but that are performed in a negligent manner.

More recently the law has imposed liability without regard to fault on individuals engaged in dangerous activities as well as in what have become known as *products-liability* cases. This concept is known as *strict liability*. Thus, if one engages in blasting rock and takes all reasonable precautions when doing so, he is still liable in most states for damages that occur as a result of any concussion from the blasting. In another type of case discussed in chapter 25, a manufacturer of a product may be liable for injuries received from a product manufactured by him if it is inherently dangerous and defective. This liability is imposed without regard to any negligence in the production of the good by the manufacturer. Now let us examine very briefly some of the more common torts for purposes of illustration.

Intentional Torts

You remember that an **intentional tort** results when one person purposefully injures another in some manner. The examples of intentional torts that are discussed in this section may be categorized into three parts. One category concerns torts where the injury is primarily against the individual's *economic interest*. Another category of torts is committed against the *person,* that is, an individual is either injured in his or her person or reputation. A third category of intentional torts concerns those that are committed against the *property* of the individual.

Torts against Economic and Business Interests

Interference with Contractual Relations

Most of the important law concerning the tortious **interference with contractual relations** has arisen since the start of the twentieth century, although the tort originated earlier. The tort was the basis of a well-known 1853 British case, *Lumley* v. *Gye,* in which Miss Johanna Wagner, a famous opera singer, was under contract to sing exclusively to Lumley for a definite term. Gye, knowing of this contract, "enticed and procured" Miss Wagner to refuse to carry out her agreement and sing for Gye instead. The court held that it constituted a tort to entice Miss Wagner to break her contract with Lumley.

The courts have found defendants guilty of this tort even when the contract is terminable at will by the third party. It is, however, necessary that the plaintiff prove that the defendant interfered with the contractual relationship, not that he merely reaped the benefits of a broken contract. It is also often stated that an additional requirement of this tort is malice. This may be confusing unless one understands that the term *malice* as used here may mean anything from intending an act, knowing of the plaintiff's contractual interests that will interfere with those interests, to interfering for the express purpose of doing harm to the plaintiff for its own sake.

The case of *Harsha* v. *State Savings Bank,* which is presented later in the discussion of the tort of intentional infliction of mental distress, illustrates the development of a new tort theory that may be described as "interference with business relationships." This concept, which began to be raised in the 1980s, is often referred to as "lender liability." Most of these cases have involved situations similar to the *Harsha* case, where a lending institution allegedly made and then rescinded a promise to loan money. Other fact situations creating "lender liability" include lending more money than the borrower could reasonably be expected to repay, calling in a loan or refusing to lend further when such an act would obviously financially ruin the borrower, and using the lender's economic power to meddle in the internal operations of the borrower. While some of these cases obviously involve the application of contract law principles, they are primarily based on the law of intentional torts and represent a new appraisal of the dynamics of risk allocation in our society.

Slander of Title and Disparagement of Goods

Clearly related to defamation, but distinct from it, are a series of injuries that may result from false statements that may be made about one's product or business or title to property. Any type of property interest that may be legally protected may be the subject of disparagement. The disparagement may consist of a falsehood about land, leases, patents, or literary property, or statements that reflect on the character of a business or a product. It is necessary that the plaintiff prove actual damages as a result of the disparagement, generally that a third person has refrained from dealing with the plaintiff as a result of the disparagement.

Theft and Misappropriation of Trade Secrets

The most important asset of some businesses may be classified as a trade secret. A **trade secret** may be a process, tool, formula, mechanism, compound, or even a customer list that is known only to the owner or certain employees of a business. In order to be protected, the information must be truly a secret. If the information is revealed to the public or in some way becomes public knowledge, then it is no longer a secret and no longer subject to protection. For example, if an application for a patent is filed with the U.S. Patent Office, the trade secret will be lost because of the public disclosure of the information necessary in order to obtain the patent.

Trade secrets may be protected under a number of theories. For instance, an employee may sign a contract with the employer agreeing not to reveal certain trade secrets. An employee also owes his employer a duty of loyalty and may be liable for the misuse of trade secrets as a result of breaching this duty of loyalty. Trade secrets may be stolen, either by employees or by others outside the company. In all these cases the person who has wrongfully obtained the trade secret may be liable for damages and in some cases subject to an injunction—a court order—prohibiting use or further communication of the trade secret.

When an employee leaves his employer, he may take with him and use the general skill and knowledge that he obtained while on the job. However, he cannot disclose trade secret information such as secret formulas or processes or disclose the customer list of his former employer.

Infringement of Trademarks and Tradenames

A *trademark* is a sign or mark that is used to identify articles that are produced by a particular person and to distinguish them from articles produced by others. A *tradename* serves a similar purpose but is used to identify a person's business, products, or services in order to establish goodwill.

The right to own a trademark or tradename is recognized by the common law. Since the purpose of a trademark is to identify the origin of articles, the trademark must be of the type that may be used exclusively by one person. Then if another person uses the trademark, the owner of it will have an action for trademark infringement against the person who has wrongfully appropriated it. The wrongful use of a trademark or tradename owned by another person would lead to confusion as to the origin of the goods.

There are limits on the words or symbols that can be used as a trademark. Generally, a trademark cannot be a term that is merely descriptive of the product, a personal name, or the name of geographic areas. The mark or words must generally be unusual or fanciful. The reason for the requirement is so that the term is exclusively associated with the origin of the goods. However, if words that would not normally qualify for trademark or tradename protection are used in an unusual way or with an unusual mark or photograph, they may qualify for trademark protection. Examples are Gibraltar Belts, Panama Hats, and English Leather Aftershave. Examples of words that are clearly unusual or fanciful are Kodak and Xerox.

It is possible to lose the right to a trademark or a tradename. This can happen if a company's trademark becomes so popular that it no longer identifies the origin of a particular product or process, but is used in the generic sense. For instance, the following words have lost their distinctiveness over the years and as a result are no longer subject to trademark protection: aspirin, cola, linoleum, cellophane, and yo-yo. Can you think of some names that might be in jeopardy today? One example is Xerox.

In addition to obtaining protection of a trademark under the common law, a person may also register his trademark and tradename under the Lanham Act, which gives federal protection to trademarks that are properly registered. It is not necessary to register a trademark or tradename under the Lanham Act in order to obtain common law protection of the trademark or tradename. There are some advantages to registering under the Lanham Act, such as gaining access to the federal courts, the presumption that the public is aware of the trademark or tradename as a result of the registration, and the more liberal remedies that are available under the Act to those who are successful in suing for trademark and tradename infringement.

Infringement of Patents

A *patent* is an exclusive right granted by the federal government to make, use, or sell an invention for a period of seventeen years. If the patent is granted for a design, the period of exclusive use cannot exceed fourteen years.

The purpose of the patent laws is to advance the arts and science and not specifically to reward individuals for their inventions. If an inventor does not have the exclusive right to exploit his invention for a period of time, there might be some hesitation in sharing its development with the public. So in order to encourage inventors to reveal the products of their efforts, the patent laws allow them a period of time to exclusively make, use, or sell the invention. They may also profit from this government-granted monopoly, but that is not the primary objective of the patent law.

A patent will not be granted for abstract ideas or principles. The invention must be a new and useful process, machine, composition of material, or method of manufacture. A patent may be granted a new or useful improvement. In general, the person seeking the patent must be the first to invent the subject of the patent. In addition the statute states as a test of patentability that the invention must be novel, have usefulness, and not be obvious.

Direct or contributory patent infringement is a tort. It occurs when some right of the patent holder is invaded. Direct patent infringement occurs when a nonpatent holder makes, uses, or sells a patented device. Contributory infringement occurs when a party induces someone else to infringe a patent. A patent cannot be infringed unless it is valid. So one defense to the claim of patent infringement is that it is not valid. The fact that the U.S. Patent Office issues a patent is not conclusive as to its validity. A court may declare it invalid. This fate befalls about two-thirds of the patents that are actually challenged in the courts.

Litigation over the claims of patent infringement can be expensive, time consuming, and risky. Often patent owners will license others to make use of their patents for a fee in order to avoid this expense.

Infringement of Copyright

A *copyright* is the exclusive right of the author or owner of a copyright to print, publish, and sell the subject of the copyright. It is important to note that the protection extended by the Copyright Act is to the expression itself but not to the uniqueness of the thoughts in the expression. In other words, if one describes an idea in a book, the form of the expression of the idea is protected but not the actual idea itself.

In 1976 Congress passed the first general revision of the copyright laws since 1909, incorporating several major changes in the new Act. For example, the period of copyright protection under the 1909 Act was for twenty-eight years and was renewable. Under the 1976 Act, the copyright protection generally extends through the period of the life of the author plus fifty years. In addition, the old law required that a work had to be *published* in order to be protected. This requirement was changed by the 1976 Act so that the protection of the copyright statute begins from the date the work is "fixed in any tangible medium of expression" from which it may be perceived or reproduced. Thus the writing of a manuscript, videotaping a television program, or placing a computer program on a magnetic disk results in the required *fixation*.

If a substantial portion of a copyrighted work is copied, then an infringement occurs. Just as with a patent, one may be liable as a contributory infringement if he participates in the copying of the copyrighted work.

One defense to a charge of copyright infringement is the doctrine of *fair use*. The doctrine allows the limited reproduction of portions of a copyrighted work for purposes such as criticism, comment, news reporting, teaching, scholarship, or research. So if one is writing a criticism of a book, it would be permissible to copy certain parts of the book in order to demonstrate what the critic is saying.

Torts against the Person

Assault and Battery

Although frequently mentioned together, these are two separate torts, the tort of assault and the tort of battery. *Battery* may be defined simply as an unpermitted touching. The obvious question raised in many cases involves whether the touching is permitted or not. One walking through a narrow store door in a crowd of holiday shoppers, for instance, may be touched, but the person gives implied permission to the touching, hence there is no battery. On the other hand, the store detective who pushes a customer without cause may have committed a battery.

The tort of assault occurs when one's action creates in another a reasonable apprehension of bodily harm. Assault consists of an act that causes an individual to apprehend a battery. For instance, pointing a gun at an individual under circumstances giving rise to a reasonable apprehension of bodily harm would constitute an assault. A battery may never occur, yet it is not required for the tort of assault. On the other hand, it is not necessary that there be any assault preceding a battery. For instance, one who is struck from behind with a lead pipe has been the victim of a battery, but he has not been the victim of an assault since the tort requires an apprehension of harm. In this case the victim would not be aware of the impending blow until it occurred.

There are a number of defenses to the tort of battery. In addition to the defense that the touching was done with consent, one may defend on the ground of *self-defense*. Basically, an individual may use a reasonable amount of force to defend himself against the attack of another. In many jurisdictions there is no requirement that one first attempt to retreat from the attack.

Defamation

Defamation consists of a false communication that tends to injure one's reputation by lessening his esteem, respect, or goodwill in the community. Most often the statement tends to hold one up to ridicule or contempt. A requirement of defamation is that the statement must be published, which simply means that it be made to a third party.

Defamation consists of the torts of *libel* and *slander,* libel being written defamation and slander being oral defamation. A frequent problem that arises in defamation cases is whether the plaintiff must prove actual or special damages. When the communication is libelous, the existence of damages is presumed from the publication and need not be proved. Defamation by slander is more complicated. The courts long ago determined that some types of slanderous statements were so likely to cause monetary loss that it was unnecessary actually to prove specific *(special)* damages. These statements are lumped into a category known as *slander per se*. They consist of the imputation of a crime or of a loathesome disease and of those statements affecting the plaintiff in his business, trade, profession, office, or calling. Later the courts or legislatures added the imputation of unchastity to a woman. All other slanderous statements require proof of special damages regardless of how derogatory the statement may be. This latter category is often called *slander per quod*. In some states the distinction between slander per quod and per se has been eliminated. The effect of eliminating the distinction is that actual damages must be proved in all slander cases.

There are circumstances in which an individual is protected against liability for published false statements because of *privilege*. Statements made in judicial proceedings, legislative proceedings, and certain executive communications, for instance, are protected by *absolute privilege*. The purpose of these exceptions is so that these functions may proceed unencumbered by the fear that any statement made may later be submitted to the scrutiny of a jury. This protection is necessary in a free society if our government institutions are to operate freely and openly.

Other statements are made with a *qualified privilege*. The qualification is that the statement must be made in a reasonable manner and for a proper purpose. It is a communication that is "fairly made by a person in the discharge of some public or private duty, whether legal or moral, or in the conduct of his own affairs, in matters where his interest is concerned." Thus any statement reasonably necessary to protect one's reputation against defamatory statements or to protect the mismanagement of a business in which one has an interest is protected by a qualified privilege. A statement by a client to his attorney that may be false is protected.

Since the 1960s, the courts have treated the law of libel somewhat differently in cases that involve either the media as a defendant or where the plaintiff qualifies as a public figure or a public official. The media as a defendant in a lawsuit includes newspapers, magazines, and similar publications. A *public figure* is someone who is newsworthy or concerned with a matter of public interest. Examples would be politicians who are not holding governmental office, sports figures, and movie, television, and radio personalities. A public figure may also be a less well-known person, if he or she is very well known in the local community. For example, a local high school football coach might qualify as a public figure for purposes of libel law. A *public official* is a person who holds public office or, in many cases, is an employee of the government. A number of courts have ruled that a police officer may qualify as a public official.

The law of libel in cases involving the media or public figures reflects an attempt to resolve the conflict between the right of a person not to have his or her reputation unjustly damaged and the need in an open society to protect the freedom to discuss and report on issues involving public officials or figures. Initially the Supreme Court in the well-known case of *New York Times* v. *Sullivan* (1964), held that a public official could not recover for a defamatory falsehood that related to his official conduct unless he could demonstrate that the statement was made with *actual malice*. Later this rule was extended to include public figures who were not public officials. *Curtis Publishing Co.* v. *Butts* (1967). The courts have defined malice to include false statements made by a media defendant either with knowledge of their falsity or with reckless disregard of the truth.

The question remains as to what standard should be applied when a media defendant is sued by a private plaintiff, that is, a plaintiff who is not a public figure or a public official. As the following case indicates, the U.S. Supreme Court has left the determination of the standard to be applied up to the states. The one restriction on the states is that a state may not create a *no fault* standard in the case of a suit by a private plaintiff against a media defendant. Courts in many states have held that a private plaintiff may recover against a newspaper or other media defendant upon showing that the false statement was published negligently. Some states have held that the standard of malice should be applied in suits by private plaintiffs as well as in suits by public figures when the defendant is a newspaper or other member of the media. Note the importance in many jurisdictions of determining whether a defendant in a libel suit is a public figure. In those jurisdictions that distinguish between a test for private plaintiffs and public figures it is much more difficult for a public figure or public official to recover for alleged libel by a newspaper because the test is more difficult. The plaintiff who is a public figure must prove that the false statement was made with malice whereas the private individual in many jurisdictions need only prove that the false statement was made negligently. A majority of the states appear to distinguish between private plaintiffs and public figures or officials when the defendant is a member of the media. For a further discussion of the tort of defamation see Chapter 4, "Constitutional Law and Business" for a discussion regarding the First Amendment.

Right of Privacy

One of the more recently created torts developed in the 1960s is the **right of privacy.** It is defined as a right to be free from an unwarranted use of taking advantage of an individual's personality, or the wrongful intrusion into one's private affairs in which the public has no concern. The tort also includes a wrongful intrusion into one's activities in such a manner as would seem outrageous or cause mental suffering or humiliation to a person of ordinary sensibilities. One of the primary reasons for its creation is the complexity of our society with its attendant sophisticated means of giving publicity to events as well as the actions of persons. Among acts that may give rise to a right of action for invasion of privacy are illegal wiretaps or the unauthorized use of a person's photograph for advertising purposes. Privacy is the right to be left alone. That right must be balanced against other rights, such as freedom of the press.

The right of privacy is different from the tort of defamation in one important respect: truth is no defense. Thus, if one publishes a statement about an individual that is true, there is no libel or slander. However, if the true statement is published in such a manner as to constitute an unwarranted invasion in the affairs of another, the publishers would be liable. Whether the statement happened to be true or not would probably have an impact on the damages that might be awarded to the victim.

One of the keys to an understanding of the right of privacy is that the publication of information must be unwarranted. Therefore if the information is newsworthy, the fact that an individual has not been a well-known figure or celebrity prior to the publication would not give him an action for invasion of the right of privacy. Likewise, an individual may waive the right either by expressly giving his consent or impliedly by his actions. The right of privacy is designed primarily to protect the feelings and sensibilities of persons in this complex society and is not applicable to corporations.

In the following case, a court had to decide the extent to which a department store customer has a reasonable expectation of privacy in a fitting room.

Lewis v. *Dayton Hudson Corporation*

128 Mich. App. 165, 339 N.W. 2nd. 857 (1983)

Opinion

Chief Judge Danhof: Plaintiff appeals as of right from an order of the trial court dismissing his invasion of privacy claim pursuant to GCR 1963, 117.2(3).

The pertinent facts involved in this case are not in dispute. Plaintiff was shopping in the men's clothing department of one of defendant's stores. Plaintiff was employed as an undercover police officer and was required to carry a firearm concealed on his person at all times. While he was shopping at defendant's store, one of defendant's security officers became suspicious that plaintiff might be a shoplifter. When plaintiff took some clothing into one of the store's fitting rooms, the security officer followed him.

Two mirrors were located in the fitting rooms. On each mirror was a sticker which informed customers: "This area under surveillance by Hudson's personnel." The fitting rooms were equipped with louvred doors which did not lock and which did not extend all the way to the floor. In addition, there was a grille located in the ceiling from which persons in the fitting rooms could be observed. Access to the observation area was by a ladder located in a storeroom behind the fitting rooms.

When plaintiff entered the fitting room, the

security officer watched him from the overhead observation area where he saw plaintiff remove his firearm and place it on a chair. The security officer contacted another employee who called the police.

By the time the police arrived, plaintiff had returned to the main area of the store where a police officer pointed a gun at plaintiff and told him not to move. The officer did not at first accept plaintiff's explanation that he was an undercover police officer. It was not until other police officers arrived that plaintiff was removed to a non-public area of the store where his identification was examined and he was permitted to leave.

Plaintiff commenced this action alleging invasion of privacy, false imprisonment and intentional infliction of emotional distress. The trial court granted defendant's motion for summary judgment with respect to the invasion of privacy claim. The remaining two claims were voluntarily dismissed with prejudice.

The tort of invasion of privacy has been divided into four separate types of claims. See Prosser, *Torts* (4th ed.). The four are: (1) intrusion upon plaintiff's seclusion or solitude, or into his private affairs; (2) public disclosure of embarrassing private facts about the plaintiff; (3) publicity which places the plaintiff in a false light in the public eye; and, (4) appropriation, for the defendant's advantage, of the plaintiff's name or likeness.

The only form of these four which is involved in this case is intrusion upon plaintiff's seclusion. It has been held that this type of invasion of privacy is analogous to a trespass. However, it is unnecessary to show physical invasion onto a person's property. Eavesdropping upon private conversations by wiretaps or spying into windows of a private home have been held to be actionable.

In Michigan, this tort has been discussed in *Earp* v. *Detroit* (1969). In *Earp,* plaintiff claimed that defendant, his employer, intruded upon his seclusion when it sought information from the police about plaintiff which led to plaintiff's discharge. The Court held that in order to maintain an action for this type of tort, plaintiff must show that there was: (1) an intrusion by defendant; (2) into a matter which plaintiff has a right to keep private; (3) by the use of a method which is objectionable to the reasonable person. Although the Court in *Earp, supra,* recognized the existence of this form of tort, it noted that the right to be free from intrusion is not absolute. It held that such a right does not extend so far as to subvert those rights which spring from social conditions, including business relations.

Turning to the facts of the present case, we are in agreement with plaintiff that there are many circumstances in which conduct of the kind defendant was involved in would constitute an unwarranted invasion of privacy. For example, in *People* v. *Abate* (1981), the Court held that defendant's installation of a two-way mirror over the women's restroom of his roller skating rink constituted an unwarranted intrusion into an area where defendant's customers had a legitimate expectation of privacy. However, in spite of the foregoing, we do not believe that under the circumstances of this case the conduct of defendant's security officer constituted an unwarranted invasion of plaintiff's privacy.

It has been recognized that retailers in this country face a shoplifting epidemic of dynamic proportions. Fitting rooms which retailers provide for their customers are particularly suited to concealment of stolen property. In *In re Deborah C* (1981), the California Supreme Court was faced with a similar claim in the context of a criminal case involving a claim of illegal search and seizure. The court held that it was not unreasonable for store security personnel to view patrons in fitting rooms from an adjacent corridor through which customers and salesclerks frequently passed. The court noted that there were large gaps above and below the fitting room doors which provided an obvious view into each fitting room. In holding that no reasonable expectation of privacy existed, the court stated the following:

"Though designed perhaps to give minimal protection to modesty, the doors hardly could promote any reasonable feeling that all actions and objects behind them were insulated from public observation.

. . . .

"One who uses a dressing room is entitled to the modicum of privacy it appears to afford."

Although it is conceded that the nature of the surveillance involved in this case was more intrusive than that which was involved in *In re Deborah C, supra,* it must be kept in mind that, unlike the situation presented in that case and in

People v. *Abate, supra,* in the present case signs were posted in the fitting rooms informing customers that the area was under surveillance. Although plaintiff claims that he cannot recall whether he saw the signs, he does not dispute defendant's claim that the signs were prominently located and plain to see.

The only case which we were able to locate which discussed the expectation of privacy a store customer is legitimately entitled to where such signs are located in a fitting room was *Gillett* v. *State,* Tex.Cr.App., 1979. *Gillett* involved a criminal prosecution for shoplifting. Defendant was observed entering a fitting room with a sweater. There were signs posted on the mirror of the fitting room similar to those involved in this case. A store security guard was able to observe defendant place the sweater in her purse by getting down on her hands and knees and looking under the door. In rejecting defendant's claim that the intrusion was unreasonable, the court stated the following:

> What people seek to preserve as private, even areas accessible to the public, may be constitutionally protected by the Fourth Amendment. *Katz* v. *United States,* 389 U.S. 347 (1967). Further, areas such as public toilet stalls are private to the extent they are offered to the public for private, although temporary, use. Such constitutional protection, however, extends only to the limits that the design, purpose and plan of the public facility affords so that, when the design is such that there is no right to expect absolute privacy, there can be no invasion of privacy.
>
> In the present case, the posted sign on the mirror which would under nearly all circumstances be looked at by female occupants of a fitting room was notice that one could not expect privacy. This room was for use by the public on conditions established by the business. If appellant did not want to use the fitting room under the posted conditions, she was not compelled to do so.

The conclusion reached in *Gillett, supra,* is consistent with federal court decisions holding that a person's expectation of privacy is diminished significantly where signs posted at airports notify passengers that they and their baggage are subject to search.

We agree with *Gillett, supra,* that by posting these signs defendant placed plaintiff on notice that he was subject to the type of observation which was conducted by defendant's employee. Whatever expectation of privacy he may have had in the absence of such signs was removed by the placement of the signs in the fitting room. Therefore, we hold that the conduct of defendant's security guard was not objectionable. When plaintiff placed the gun on the chair inside the fitting room the fact that he possessed such a weapon was no longer a private matter. Plaintiff had no claim for this type of invasion of privacy.

We do not mean to suggest by the foregoing that by merely placing signs such as those involved here in fitting rooms merchants are absolutely immune from claims of invasion of privacy. On the contrary, had the observation in this case been conducted by persons not authorized to perform such surveillance, or by a member of the opposite sex, our decision might well have been different. We may also have reached a different conclusion if defendant's security guard, rather than simply relaying this information to the police, had utilized the information in an objectionable fashion. However, we hold that where, as here, signs are clearly posted notifying customers that they are under surveillance while inside the fitting room of a retail establishment, the "modicum of privacy" the fitting room appears to afford does not include freedom from overhead observation by a store security guard who is of the same sex as the customer.

Our disposition of the foregoing renders moot plaintiff's remaining claim.

The decision of the trial court is affirmed. Costs to appellee.

Case Questions

1. Was the court here saying that customers in dressing rooms have no reasonable expectation of privacy?
2. Might there have been a different result in this case if the surveillance had been of a restroom?

False Imprisonment

False imprisonment consists of the intentional unprivileged detention of a person without his consent. It is not limited to the concept of an unlawful arrest without a warrant. False imprisonment may consist of a store manager's detaining a customer on grounds of shoplifting when there is no probable cause for believing that the customer engaged in the shoplifting, or it may consist of an official arrest by a police officer without legal justification.

The essence of the tort is the unlawful detention, but this does not mean that the plaintiff must be locked up by physical force; it may be accomplished by threats of force that result in the plaintiff's detention against his will. On the other hand, if the plaintiff consents to the detention, there is no false imprisonment. Many states have passed statutes specifically granting shopkeepers the right to temporary detention of suspected shoplifters. There is no liability when a customer agrees to remain in a store to clear himself of suspicion of a theft. Of course, a shopkeeper may detain a suspect when he reasonably believes that the person detained is engaged in shoplifting. Many cases often revolve around the question of whether the shopkeeper was reasonable in his belief.

Notice that in the preceding (Lewis) case, the plaintiff customer was detained in the store while an investigation of suspected shoplifting was made. The plaintiff's false imprisonment charge was dismissed by the court, presumably on the grounds that the store had a limited privilege of detention under state law.

Deceit or Fraud

The tort of deceit, otherwise known as **fraud,** consists of a false representation when it is made with knowledge of the falsity, when it is made with the intention of inducing the plaintiff to rely on the statement, and when the plaintiff justifiably relies on the statement and an injury results. Fraud may also be used as a defense in a breach-of-contract action.

Intentional Infliction of Mental Distress

The law has been slow to allow a party to recover against one who has committed a wrong against him or her when the only injury suffered is mental distress. It is only comparatively recently that a cause of action based solely on the infliction of mental distress has been recognized. The reason for the hesitancy of the courts to allow compensation for the infliction of mental distress is the notion that it is intangible and subjective. That is, it cannot be observed, such as in the case of a broken bone. So the courts worried that allowing a person to recover solely for mental distress might open the door for fictitious and frivolous claims.

At first, the courts required some physical injury to the person before allowing damages for emotional distress. For example, if the plaintiff suffered even a very slight injury then he or she would be able to recover additional damages for the infliction of mental distress. Some physical injury is still required if the act causing the mental distress was negligent.

More recently, courts have allowed recovery where a person has suffered mental distress as the result of the intentional act of the defendant even though there has been no physical injury. Generally, the conduct must have been outrageous. Another way of stating the requirement is to say that the conduct of the defendant is substantially certain to cause mental distress. The trend of the law has also been toward allowing the recovery of mental distress for acts directed at another individual. An example would be the case of a mother who sees her child shot and killed. Thus far the courts have limited the right to recover in most cases to those situations where the act takes place in the physical proximity of the person seeking to recover for emotional distress. The courts have also often required that there be some relationship between the person suffering the physical injury and the person seeking to recover for emotional distress.

In the following case, the court had to decide whether a bank's decision not to give a customer a loan could give rise to a cause for action for intentional infliction of mental distress.

Harsha v. State Savings Bank

346 N.W. 2d 791 (Iowa 1984)

Opinion

Uhlenhopp, Presiding Justice: This appeal presents questions that arose from an alleged oral agreement by the State Savings Bank of Baxter, Iowa (bank), through its president, Jack E. Edge, to lend money to David G. Harsha and Richard L. Perry to open and operate a livestock feed sales business to be known as Baxter Feed Center, Inc. (Baxter Feed).

The following issues were submitted to the jury at trial: (1) whether the bank made and subsequently breached a contract to lend $25,000 to Baxter Feed on a long-term basis; (2) whether acts by the bank and Edge tortiously interfered with prospective business relationships of Baxter Feed; and (3) whether the bank and Edge intentionally inflicted severe emotional distress upon Harsha. The jury returned the following verdicts: for Baxter Feed and against the bank in the sum of $126,000 for breach of contract; for Baxter Feed and against the bank and Edge in the sums of $104,864 compensatory and $85,000 punitive damages for tortious interference with prospective business relationships; and for Harsha and against the bank and Edge in the sums of $50,000 compensatory and $15,000 punitive damages for intentional infliction of severe emotional distress. The trial court found that the contract and tortious interference verdicts were duplicative, but otherwise upheld the verdicts.

The bank and Edge appealed and Harsha and Baxter Feed cross appealed. The bank and Edge argue on appeal that no contract to lend money existed because of lack of consideration and that substantial evidence was not introduced in support of the two tort claims. Baxter Feed argues on cross appeal that the ruling regarding duplicative damages was erroneous.

Viewing the evidence in the light most favorable to the verdicts, the jury could find the facts substantially as follows. In the spring of 1971, Harsha and Perry discussed the possibility of opening their own livestock feed sales business. The two included Edge in some of their conversations as they were interested in obtaining a long-term bank loan guaranteed by the Small Business Administration (SBA). Various loan amounts were considered. Edge testified the loan was to be for $15,000. Harsha and Perry, however, sought and obtained an SBA guarantee of $25,000, and Edge made the note for that amount.

Harsha and Perry then prepared to open the business. They acquired a place to operate, made arrangements with a producer to obtain feed to sell, contributed $2500 each to the business, and incorporated as Baxter Feed Center, Inc. They opened for business in September 1971.

During the first year several events occurred: (1) Baxter Feed lost $2549, a sum more than $2000 less than the first-year loss of $4560 originally projected; (2) Perry became displeased, left the business, and was replaced by Harsha's mother, Zelda L. Harsha; (3) Baxter Feed executed a promissory note to the bank for $25,000, and the bank disbursed $5000 of that amount on each of three dates: November 2 and December 10, 1971, and June 9, 1972; and (4) Baxter Feed began to repay the long-term loan at a monthly rate of $397 in principal and interest.

Edge testified he became displeased with Harsha's management: running up large accounts receivable instead of selling on feed contracts, and failing to collect accounts vigorously. In June 1972, the bank informed SBA by letter that it would lend no more long-term money than $15,000 already disbursed and asked that the monthly payment figure be reduced accordingly. On December 29 Baxter Feed owed $3000 plus $24 interest on the short-term note as well as $233.80 on the long-term note, instead of $397 which would have been owed if $25,000 in long-term money had been provided.

Harsha continued to operate with the short-term loans but the business began losing more money.

By the fall of 1975 Baxter Feed was in very poor financial condition. Harsha consulted Edge, who suggested bankruptcy. Harsha closed the business at the end of November 1975, and filed for bankruptcy in October 1976.

Harsha claims that Edge calculated to destroy Baxter Feed and succeeded in doing so, and that Edge's motive was the purchase of a competing feed sales business, the Country Farm Store of Baxter, owned by Charlotte L. McCormick.

We turn to the parties' arguments.

CONTRACT CLAIM

The bank argues that the claimed agreement to lend $25,000 lacked consideration. Alternatively, it argues that the trial court submitted a wrong measure of damages to the jury and that a proper foundation was not laid for expert testimony as to damages and causation, but it does not address the causation issue in the event the expert testimony is in fact admissible. It also argues that the trial court erred in an instruction on acquiescence.

Initially, the bank attempts to draw a distinction between a promise to lend money and an actual loan of money. It argues that more consideration than a promise to repay is required to support a promise to lend money.

The jury could find the basic facts on this issue to be that the bank initially promised to lend Baxter Feed $25,000 at interest, subject to SBA approval which was obtained. The record will not support a finding that Baxter Feed expressly promised to borrow the money; we need not decide whether a finding could reasonably be made of a promise implied in fact to borrow the money. But the record shows without question that Baxter Feed did give the bank its note for $25,000 in response to the bank's promise to lend.

The bank's promise to lend may be considered an offer to be accepted by performance—an offer to lend in return for Baxter Feed's giving its note for the loan. Under such circumstances, an offer and an acceptance both existed when the bank promised to lend and Baxter Feed performed by giving its note.

The bank is correct that for its promise to lend to be enforceable, consideration for the promise was essential. The consideration might consist of a return promise by Baxter Feed to borrow at interest, or of a bargained-for performance by Baxter Feed in actually giving its note at interest. The conclusion is reasonable under the evidence that the bank bargained for Baxter Feed's giving its note at interest, which Baxter Feed did, and that consideration for the bank's offer to lend existed in that performance by Baxter Feed.

TORTIOUS INTERFERENCE

Interference with prospective business relationships is an intentional tort which requires a showing that the actor had a purpose to "injure or destroy" the plaintiff's business. If a defendant acts for two or more purposes, his improper purpose must predominate in order to create liability. W. Prosser, *Handbook of the Law of Torts* § 129 (4th ed. 1971). The tort may also be committed by improper means. Deliberate breach of a contract is generally not considered to be improper means, as the law remedies such breaches with damages calculated to give the injured party the benefit of the bargain; generally no need thus exists for additional tort remedies. See *R.E.T. Corp.* v. *Frank Paxton Co.* (Iowa 1983) (distinguishing tort and contract damages). Where however a party breaches a contract with the immediate purpose of injuring or destroying prospective business relationships the means may be considered improper. *Buxbom* v. *Smith* (Cal. 1944) (breach of contract was intended as means of injuring plaintiff and "constitutes an unfair method of interference with advantageous relations"); *Schisgall* v. *Fairchild Publications, Inc.* (N.Y. 1955) (for a party to breach a contract and pay damages is one case but if the party goes further and "act[s] with intent to inflict injury beyond that contemplated as a result of the mere breach of a contract . . . the contract does not grant the defaulter immunity from tort liability"); *Cherberg* v. *People's National Bank of Washington* (Wash. 1977) ("[where] the conduct of the breaching party indicates a motive to destroy some interest of the adverse party, a tort action may lie and items of damage not available in contract actions will be allowed").

For Baxter Feed to succeed on its claim for tortious interference with prospective business relations, the record must contain substantial evidence showing that Edge acted with a predominately improper purpose or by improper means. To sustain this burden Baxter Feed relies on circumstantial evidence. Circumstantial and direct evidence are equally probative, but the substantial evidence rule requires that the circumstances have "sufficient probative force to constitute the basis for a legal inference, and not for mere speculation. . . ." ("Circumstantial evidence must do more than raise a suspicion; it must amount to proof. It is necessary that there be some reasonable connection between the facts proved and the fact at issue."). Circumstances are not sufficient when the conclusion in question is based on surmise, speculation, or conjecture.

Baxter Feed claims that by refusing in the summer of 1972 to advance the final $10,000 of long-term money, Edge set forces in motion which ultimately destroyed it and prevented it from having future business relationships, and that Edge refused to advance the final $10,000 with an improper objective—to eliminate Baxter Feed as a competitor after Edge eventually acquired the McCormick property (a competing business).

Substantial evidence of a connection between Edge's refusing further long-term credit and the later McCormick transaction does not appear. Any relationship is simply too attenuated. This tort basis of liability should not have been submitted for jury consideration.

SEVERE EMOTIONAL DISTRESS

The bank claims that Harsha did not introduce substantial evidence of the tort of severe emotional distress.

The elements of this tort are

1. Outrageous conduct by the defendant;
2. The defendant's intentional causing, or reckless disregard of the probability of causing emotional distress;
3. Plaintiff suffering severe or extreme emotional distress; and
4. Actual and proximate causation of the emotional distress by the defendant's outrageous conduct.

W. Prosser, *The Law of Torts* § 12 (4th ed. 1971). We consider two of the elements here—outrageous conduct and severe or extreme emotional distress.

For conduct to be "outrageous" it must be "so extreme in degree, as to go beyond all possible bounds of decency, and to be regarded as atrocious, and utterly intolerable in a civilized community." Restatement (Second) of Torts § 46, Comment *d* (1965). Here the jury found the bank, through Edge, breached a contract. We do not condone such conduct but it does not approach the requisite standard of outrageousness which is necessary to create liability. The evidence of a nexus between Edge's refusal to extend more long-term credit and the McCormick transaction (a transaction with a competing business) is not substantial and cannot provide a foundation for a finding of outrageousness.

The evidence pertaining to Harsha's emotional distress was also insubstantial. It showed he was bothered by creditors at night, he made enemies out of friends by trying to collect accounts receivable before they were due, he was degraded by having to go into bankruptcy, his credit was destroyed, and he had to give up plans to remodel his childhood schoolhouse into his home. His mother, Zelda Harsha, testified that he "wasn't as interested, or he was downhearted more or less" and "depressed" when the business began to go downhill.

This evidence is similar to that in cases where evidence of severe or extreme emotion distress was held to be insufficient. *Poulsen* v. *Russell* (plaintiff was "very, very down," "feeling super badly," and feeling as if he had "lost everything"); *Vicnire* v. *Ford Motor Co.* (Me. 1979) (plaintiff felt "kind of down," "mad," and "nervous for about a month"); *Harris* v. *Jones* (Md. 1977) (plaintiff was "shaken up" and "felt like going into a hole and hide"); *Hubbard* v. *United Press International* (Minn. 1983) (plaintiff was "depressed" and became "physically ill in terms of throwing up"). The present evidence does not measure up to the proof of the distress in the cases allowing recovery. *Randa* v. *U.S. Homes, Inc.* (evidence of substantial defects in new home costing $160,000 caused near nervous breakdown); *Ford* v. *Hutson* (S.C. 1981) (plaintiff diagnosed as suffering from depression after suffering attack of shaking, nauseau, cramps, and hysteria).

This basis of tort liability should not have been submitted to the jury for decision.

CROSS APPEAL

As we have held the two tort bases of recovery are without merit, we have no occasion to consider the question in the cross appeal as to whether the tortious interference recovery duplicates the contract recovery.

We uphold the contract recovery, overturn the tort recoveries, and return the case to district court to vacate the original judgment and enter judgment in favor of Baxter Feed and against the bank in the sum of $126,000 together with interest and costs. We assess the costs in this court against the bank.

Affirmed in part, reversed in part, and remanded.

Case Questions

1. What factors prompted the finding of liability on the breach of contract claim?
2. Why did the court hold that Baxter Feed could not recover for emotional distress?

Torts against Property

Trespass to Land

Trespass to land is an intentional or negligent entry onto the land of another without permission or where the entry is not privileged. A person may also commit a trespass to land if he causes something to enter onto the land of another such as by throwing stones or debris. The tort of trespass to land does not require proof of actual damages or injury. However, if there is no proof of injury or damage, then the plaintiff would only be entitled to receive nominal damages, that is, the decision would be in favor of the plaintiff but only for a token amount of money.

Questions often arise as to whether persons entering onto land are trespassers, or whether they have at least an initial privilege to enter. At common law, and still today in most states, entrants onto land were categorized into three groups: trespassers, licensees, and invitees. The duties owed to these entrants by the occupiers of land vary according to the category into which they fall.

A *trespasser* is a person who has no privilege, even an initial one, to enter onto land. Today, most persons who enter onto land are not presumed to be trespassers unless *no trespassing* signs have been posted, or circumstances clearly indicate that they would not be welcomed by the occupier (for example, a burglar). The only duty owed under the common law to a trespasser is the duty not to set traps. Examples of impermissible traps are shotguns rigged with trip wires set to go off if a window is raised, or large, unbarricaded excavations.

Licensees are persons with a limited privilege to enter land for a specific purpose. Classic examples of licensees are letter carriers, meter readers, and delivery personnel. Today, there is usually a presumption that entrants are licensees and not trespassers. Social guests are licensees. The duty owed by an occupier of land to a licensee is to warn of nonobvious hazards that are known to the occupier. Notice that the occupier is not necessarily under a duty to inspect his premises to discover hazards, and if he knows of hazards that are not obvious (for example, a loose step), his only duty is to warn of their existence, not remedy them.

Invitees are business guests, that is, potential customers of a business. A person who enters a grocery store with the intent to shop is an invitee. Occupiers of land owe invitees a duty to take reasonable efforts to seek out and remedy hazards. Therefore, a shopkeeper is under a duty to keep his sidewalk free from ice in winter. In recent years, a number of states have discarded the common-law approach of categorizing entrants onto land and then deciding, based on their classification, what duty was owed to them. Instead, these courts have asked, "How would one reasonably expect an occupier to treat such an entrant under the circumstances?"

There is also a right to the vertical airspace above the land. Therefore, a trespass may be committed by running wires above another's land. The question of how high above the ground one's right to the land extends has arisen since the advent of air travel. The more modern cases hold that flights above the land are privileged so long as they do not interfere with the use of the land. The problem is to balance the interests of the land owner against the necessity of using the air space above the land for flight that is of importance to the public.

Trespass to Personal Property

Trespass to personal property is a tort that allows the plaintiff to recover damages against a defendant who interferes with the plaintiff's possession of personal property. The tort does not require that the person who interferes with the right to possession of the goods intend to damage them. So if a person hides the personal property of another as a joke and the goods are damaged, a trespass to personal property has occurred. The plaintiff would be entitled to recover the goods and compensation for the damage caused to them.

Conversion

Conversion is related to trespass to personal property. The difference is that conversion involves a more serious interference with the right to possess and control personal property. Dean Prosser, in his book the *Law of Torts,* has said that trespass to personal property is a little brother of conversion. So, if the interference with the right to possession and control of goods is so significant that the wrongdoer must pay the full value of the goods, it is a conversion.

The tort of conversion consists of any wrongful act that interferes with one's right to possession of personal property. The act is wrongful when it is without proper permission and without just cause. The act does not have to be a conscious wrongdoing. For instance, a refusal to deliver property to one who is entitled to it constitutes a conversion. Transferring property from one place to another may also constitute conversion. If goods are left with another for safekeeping or for transfer to another, delivery to the wrong person may constitute a conversion by the one to whom the goods are entrusted.

Nuisance

Nuisance results from a substantial interference with a right or an interest of another person, most often the right to enjoy and use his property. The classes of wrongs that are lumped under the category of nuisance are innumerable. The standard—as stated in the *Restatement of Torts,* which is used to determine what sort of behavior constitutes a nuisance—is that of offensiveness, inconvenience, or annoyance to the normal person in the community. Obviously what constitutes a nuisance today may not be considered a nuisance in other times. The use of one's property to create excessive noise, pollution, or smoke may constitute a nuisance although it may otherwise be legal. On the other hand, every use of one's property that may cause others an inconvenience does not necessarily constitute a nuisance. It often depends upon whether one's use of his property is reasonable or not, and the courts are frequently placed in the position of balancing one party's interests against another's. In reality, nuisance is not so much a tort, as a way of stating a type of damage to one's property interest.

Negligence

The tort of **negligence** covers types of behavior that result in injuries for which the perpetrator of the act may be liable. It is behavior that is not intended to injure anyone but that involves a failure to exercise due care. Typical negligence cases involve automobile accidents and medical and legal malpractice. There are four elements that must be proved in order to establish the tort of negligence: the existence of a duty, the breach of that duty, causation, and injury to the plaintiff.

Duty

In order to recover for the tort of negligence, the plaintiff must prove that the person who is accused of committing the tort owed a *duty of care* to the plaintiff. For instance, one has a duty of care to fellow motorists to drive on the highways in a prudent and reasonable manner. On the other hand, if one is sitting on the beach, he has no duty to rescue a fellow swimmer who is in trouble, even though he has the means to do so.

Perhaps a better example would be to examine the duty owed to persons who come on one's property, a subject discussed earlier in this chapter. Let us assume the case of a storekeeper. Three classes of persons may come into the store: *invitees, licensees,* and *trespassers*. The storekeeper's duty of care to each of these three classes varies. An invitee is one who comes on the premises for the benefit of the property owner. In this example, a customer would be an invitee. The storekeeper's duty toward an invitee is to make the premises safe not only against those dangers of which he is aware, but also against those dangers that he might discover with reasonable care. A licensee is one who, for his own benefit, comes on one's premises with permission from the owner. In our example, a salesman from a wholesaler would be a licensee. The storekeeper's duty to a licensee is to refrain from any active negligence, but he has no duty to make the premises safe, as for example, by inspection. A trespasser, of course, is one who is on the premises without permission, and the owner of the land—our shopkeeper, in this instance—merely must refrain from willfully and intentionally injuring him. There are some exceptions to this rule, the best known being that condition known as *attractive nuisance,* which applies to children. If one maintains a condition on his property that might be dangerous to and reasonably expected to be a lure to children—a swimming pool, for example—he has a duty to exercise reasonable care to protect them, even though technically they may be trespassers. This doctrine has been adopted by a majority, but not all states.

In the following case, the United States Supreme Court had to decide whether the United States government could be held liable for negligence for allowing an intoxicated off-duty serviceman to carry a firearm.

Sheridan v. United States

108 S. Ct. 707 (1988)

Opinion

Justice Stevens: On February 6, 1982, an obviously intoxicated off-duty serviceman named Carr fired several rifle shots into an automobile being driven by petitioners on a public street near the Bethesda Naval Hospital. Petitioners brought suit against the United States alleging that their injuries were caused by the Government's negligence in allowing Carr to leave the hospital with a loaded rifle in his possession. The District Court dismissed the action—and the Court of Appeals affirmed—on the ground that the claim is barred by the intentional tort exception to the Federal Tort Claims Act (FTCA). The question we granted certiorari to decide is whether petitioners' claim is one "arising out of" an assault or battery within the meaning of 28 U.S.C. § 2680(h).

When it granted the Government's motion to dismiss, the District Court accepted the petitioners' version of the facts as alleged in their complaint and as supplemented by discovery. That version may be briefly stated. After finishing his shift as a naval medical aide at the hospital, Carr consumed a large quantity of wine, rum, and other alcoholic beverages. He then packed some of his belongings, including a rifle and ammunition, into a uniform bag and left his quarters. Some time later, three naval corpsmen found him lying face down in a drunken stupor on the concrete floor of a hospital building. They attempted to take him to the emergency room, but he broke away, grabbing the bag and revealing the barrel of the rifle. At the sight of the rifle barrel, the corpsmen fled. They neither took further action to subdue Carr, nor alerted the appropriate authorities that he was heavily intoxicated and brandishing a weapon. Later that evening, Carr fired the shots that caused physical injury to one of the petitioners and property damage to their car.

The District Court began its legal analysis by noting the general rule that the Government is not liable for the intentional torts of its employees. The petitioners argued that the general rule was inapplicable because they were relying, not on the fact that Carr was a Government employee when he assaulted them, but rather on the negligence of other Government employees who failed to prevent his use of the rifle. The District Court assumed that the alleged negligence would have made the defendant liable under the law of Maryland, and also assumed that the Government would have been liable if Carr had not been a Government employee. Nevertheless, although stating that it was "sympathetic" to petitioners' claim, it concluded that Fourth Circuit precedents required dismissal because Carr "happens to be a government employee rather than a private citizen."

The Court of Appeals affirmed. Like the District Court, it concluded that the Circuit's prior decisions foreclosed the argument advanced by the petitioners. We granted certiorari.

The Federal Tort Claims Act gives Federal District Courts jurisdiction over claims against the United States for money damages "for injury or loss of property, or personal injury or death caused by the negligent or wrongful act or omission of any employee of the Government while acting within the scope of his office or employment, under circumstances where the United States, if a private person, would be liable to the claimant in accordance with the law of the place where the act or omission occurred." However, among other limitations, the Act also provides that this broad grant of jurisdiction "shall not apply to . . . [a]ny claim arising out of assault, battery" or other specified intentional torts.

The words "any claim arising out of" an assault or battery are unquestionably broad enough to bar all claims based *entirely* on an assault or battery. The import of these words is less clear, however, when they are applied to a claim arising out of two tortious acts, one of which is an assault or battery and the other of which is a mere act of negligence. Nonetheless, it is both settled and undisputed that in at least some situations the fact that an injury was directly caused by an assault or battery will not preclude liability against the Government for negligently allowing the assault to occur. Thus, in *United States* v. *Muniz* (1963), we held that a prisoner who was assaulted by other inmates could recover damages from the United States because prison officials were negligent in failing to prevent the assault that caused his injury.

In describing the coverage of the FTCA in *Panella* v. *United States* (2d Circuit 1954), Judge (later Justice) Harlan emphasized the statutory language that was critical to his analysis. As he explained, the Act covers actions for personal injuries "caused by the negligent or wrongful act or omission *of any employee of the Government* while acting within the scope of his office or employment . . . (Italics supplied)." We need only move the emphasis to the next phrase—"while acting within the scope of his office or employment"—to apply his analysis to the assault and battery committed by the off-duty, inebriated enlisted man in this case. If nothing more was involved here than the conduct of Carr at the time he shot at petitioners, there would be no basis for imposing liability on the Government. The tortious conduct of an off-duty serviceman, not acting within the scope of his office or employment, does not in itself give rise to Government liability whether that conduct is intentional or merely negligent.

As alleged in this case, however, the negligence

of other Government employees who allowed a foreseeable assault and battery to occur may furnish a basis for Government liability that is entirely independent of Carr's employment status. By voluntarily adopting regulations that prohibit the possession of firearms on the naval base and that require all personnel to report the presence of any such firearm, and by further voluntarily undertaking to provide care to a person who was visibly drunk and visibly armed, the Government assumed responsibility to "perform [its] 'good Samaritan' task in a careful manner." The District Court and the Court of Appeals both assumed that petitioners' version of the facts would support recovery under Maryland law on a negligence theory if the naval hospital had been owned and operated by a private person. Although the Government now disputes this assumption, it is not our practice to reexamine a question of state law of that kind or, without good reason, to pass upon it in the first instance. On this assumption, it seems perfectly clear that the mere fact that Carr happened to be an off-duty federal employee should not provide a basis for protecting the Government from liability that would attach if Carr had been an unemployed civilian patient or visitor in the hospital. Indeed, in a case in which the employment status of the assailant has nothing to do with the basis for imposing liability on the Government, it would seem perverse to exonerate the Government because of the happenstance that Carr was on a federal payroll.

In a case of this kind, the fact that Carr's behavior is characterized as an intentional assault rather than a negligent act is also quite irrelevant. If the Government has a duty to prevent a foreseeably dangerous individual from wandering about unattended, it would be odd to assume that Congress intended a breach of that duty to give rise to liability when the dangerous human instrument was merely negligent but not when he or she was malicious. In fact, the human characteristics of the dangerous instrument are also beside the point. For the theory of liability in this case is analogous to cases in which a person assumes control of a vicious animal, or perhaps an explosive device. Cf. *Palsgraf* v. *Long Island R. Co.* (1928). Because neither Carr's employment status nor his state of mind has any bearing on the basis for petitioners' claim for money damages, the intentional tort exception to the FTCA is not applicable in this case.

The judgment of the Court of Appeals is reversed and the case is remanded for further proceedings consistent with this opinion.

It is so ordered.

Case Questions

1. What was the basis for finding the government negligent?
2. Why did the Court say that whether Carr's behavior was characterized as an intentional assault rather than a negligent act was irrelevant?

Breach of Duty: The Reasonable Man

The second element that must be proved is that the duty of care was *breached*. In the determination of whether an act is negligent, an *objective standard*—the *reasonable man*—is used. Under this concept, the basic question is "How would a reasonable man have behaved under the circumstances?" The issue is not how a juror would behave or how the judge or defendant would behave, but how the reasonable man, the objective standard, would behave under the circumstances. For instance, although the speed limit on a road is 55 miles per hour, the reasonable man might not drive that fast because of circumstances affecting driving conditions, such as fog or ice. If the reasonable man would not drive 55 miles per hour, then the defendant has breached his duty of care by driving that fast, regardless of whether he thought that speed was safe or not.

Breach of Duty: Negligence Per Se

While a plaintiff has always had to prove breach of an existing duty in order to recover for negligence, over time the concept of **negligence per se** has developed to assist the plaintiff in carrying his burden of proof. Generally, negligence per se exists when the defendant breaches his duty of care by violating a statute. An example of negligence per se could be violation of state dram shop acts. Dram shop acts usually prohibit licensed purveyors of alcoholic beverages from selling these products to minors or intoxicated persons. Many states presume that such a sale violates the statutory duty, but also constitutes a prima facie case for the existence of negligence. Thus, once an injured plaintiff can show that a seller violated a dram shop act, the seller is presumed to be liable, and the burden of proof shifts to the seller to show otherwise. In recent years, some states have passed statutes expanding liability for serving intoxicants to cover social hosts. This development in the area of negligence represents a new frontier in many respects regarding legal regulation of personal relationships.

Causation and Injury

It is not enough to show that the defendant behaved in a negligent manner. It must also be shown that the negligent behavior caused the injury in question. The question of *causation* is not difficult in rather simple cases, as, for example, when a pedestrian is struck by a negligently driven car. Causation is more difficult to establish in other cases, however. For instance, it would be negligence for a physician to remove a patient's right leg instead of the left one. But suppose that the patient dies while on the operating table as the operation is being completed. The important question is whether the physician's negligence caused the patient's death or whether he died from some other cause.

Even where a plaintiff acts in an unreasonable manner, if the act does not have a causal relation to the injury, then neither the doctrine of contributory negligence nor the comparative negligence approach is applicable. The plaintiff's recovery based upon the defendant's negligence would not be reduced or denied if the plaintiff's unreasonable conduct did not contribute to causing the injury.

For example, suppose that Homeowner decides to dig a large excavation in his front yard and erects no fence or other barricade to prevent someone from falling into the hole. While Homeowner is digging in the excavation, Dan drives by. Just as he passes Homeowner's property, Dan drops a map he has been reading. While still driving the car, Dan leans down into the floorboard to retrieve the map, causing his car to swerve off the road and run into the excavation. Homeowner is severely injured and sues Dan for negligence. Even if Homeowner had erected a makeshift barrier sufficient to warn passerby of the existence of the excavation, that barricade would not have prevented Dan's car from crashing into the hole. Therefore, even though Homeowner may have acted in an unreasonable manner in not erecting a barrier, that act had no causal relationship to his injury, and he can recover from Dan. Dan's action in driving a car without looking where he was going was the proximate cause (the cause in fact) of Homeowner's injury.

Causation and the Doctrine of Res Ipsa Loquitur

As was pointed out earlier, one problem that can prevent an injured plaintiff from recovering in a product liability case is the requirement that the plaintiff prove the exact cause of his injury. Often the product that causes the injury is destroyed or changed in character by the event in which the plaintiff is hurt. For example, a plaintiff might be injured in a car crash that he alleges was caused by improperly manufactured brakes. Suppose the brakes were twisted and consumed by fire in the crash. The plaintiff can testify that when he put his foot on the brake pedal, the brakes did not hold, but at common law he would be required to prove specifically what aspect of the braking system failed, which he could not do in this situation.

Especially since the 1940s, a legal doctrine has developed that assists plaintiffs in proving negligence. This doctrine is known as ***res ipsa loquitur*** (RIL), "the thing speaks for itself." The basic premise of RIL is that some events just do not occur except in the presence of negligence, and that it may sometimes be appropriate to waive to a certain extent the requirement that a plaintiff prove the exact cause of an injury. The only purpose of *res ipsa loquitur* is to allow a plaintiff to "get to a jury" on the question of the existence of negligence on the part of the defendant. In the past, if a plaintiff could not prove the exact cause of an injury, a judge would often direct a verdict in favor of the defendant, and the plaintiff would not even get a chance to let the jury decide whether negligence was present. (For a discussion of directed verdicts, see chapter 3.)

The doctrine of *res ipsa loquitur* states that a plaintiff who proves all of the following three elements will be legally entitled to have a jury decide whether a defendant was negligent: (1) the event that injured the plaintiff ordinarily does not occur except when negligence is present, (2) the instrumentality that caused the accident was under the sole control of the defendant, and (3) the plaintiff was not contributorily negligent. To use the same example discussed a moment ago, the plaintiff could get to the jury in the case of the allegedly defective brakes by showing: (1) ordinarily brakes work to slow a car when pressure is applied to the brake pedal, (2) the brakes had not been adjusted or undergone any change since leaving the control of the manufacturer and/or retailer, and (3) the plaintiff had not engaged in any activity that would make the brakes defective (like tampering or improper maintenance). The jury could then decide whether the defendant was negligent and whether the plaintiff was entitled to a recovery. Due to its nature, increased use of RIL has not meant that more plaintiffs recover in negligence cases, but it has meant that more plaintiffs have a chance of recovering.

Defenses to Negligence

A common defense in a negligence action is **contributory negligence.** Contributory negligence occurs when the plaintiff is guilty himself of some negligence that contributes to his injury. Thus a pedestrian crossing against a red light will not be able to recover for the injuries received when struck by a speeding car. In many states, contributory negligence is a complete defense. Occasionally a case may arise in which a plaintiff may still recover, even though guilty of contributory negligence. This occurs when the defendant, once negligent, has a chance to resume exercising due car and does not. This most often is known as the doctrine of *last clear chance*.

Another frequently used defense in a negligence suit is **assumption of risk.** If one knowingly enters an area of danger, he cannot recover as the result of another's negligence. Thus if one sits along the third-base foul line in a baseball park which has no protective screen, he assumes the risk of being hit by a foul ball.

In recent years the doctrine of contributory negligence has been criticized because it is an all-or-nothing approach. For example, if an accident is primarily the fault of one party, but the other party is even slightly at fault, the party whose fault is less will receive nothing. His contributory negligence is a complete bar to any recovery.

The **comparative negligence** approach has been adopted by a large number of states because of the criticism of the defense of contributory negligence. In those jurisdictions where comparative negligence has been adopted, a plaintiff may often recover even though he or she is also at fault. Under this approach, the amount of the plaintiff's recovery may be reduced by the amount of the fact-finder, often the jury, finds that he is at fault. For example, suppose the jury determines that a plaintiff has incurred damages in the amount of $100,000. However, it also determines that the fault of the defendant was 80 percent of the cause of the accident and that the fault of the plaintiff was 20 percent. In those jurisdictions adopting the comparative negligence approach, the plaintiff's recovery would be reduced to $80,000. Where the doctrine of contributory negligence is still applied, the plaintiff would recover nothing.

Most of the states that have adopted the comparative negligence doctrine have done so by statute. Some jurisdictions have adopted what may be termed the equal-to-or-greater-than rule. In these jurisdictions, if the defendant's negligence is "equal to or greater than" the plaintiff's, then the plaintiff will recover damages reduced by the amount his negligence contributed to his injury. On the other hand, if the plaintiff's negligence exceeds that of the defendant, he will recover nothing. Other jurisdictions have adopted a "pure" comparative negligence approach that allows the plaintiff to recover even when his negligence exceeds that of the defendant.

Strict Liability

Up to this point, we have discussed tort liability based on fault, either because of an intentional act or the negligence of an individual. There are some situations in which courts have held that a person was liable for injuries to another even when he was not *at fault* as that term is generally understood in the law. The reason for certain exceptions to the fault requirement is that some activities, although legal, pose such a danger to the community that, if someone is hurt as a result of the activity, liability should be imposed upon the actor without regard to fault. Storage of explosives and keeping wild animals or dangerous domestic animals are examples of activities that have been held to be abnormally dangerous so that the doctrine of **strict liability** may be imposed. Other activities would include spraying with chemicals and engaging in blasting operations.

Recently a great deal of attention has been given to the field of **products liability.** When applied in this area, the doctrine of strict liability holds one liable for injuries caused by a defective, unreasonably dangerous product that he has placed on the market. In recent years, a number of states have passed products liability legislation. Many of the statutes alter to some extent the doctrine of strict liability when applied to manufacturers and limit its application in the case of retailers and wholesalers. This subject is discussed thoroughly in chapter 25.

Since the doctrine of strict liability is not based on fault, the defense of contributory negligence is not usually available to a defendant sued on this theory. However, if a person knowingly places himself in a place of danger or engages in a dangerous activity, then a defendant may raise as a defense the fact that the plaintiff has assumed the risk of injury. Of course, the plaintiff who sues on the theory of strict liability must show that the activity subject to the doctrine has a causal relationship to his injury.

Recent Developments in Tort Law

In recent years, courts have begun hearing cases involving new theories of tort liability, and legislatures have become more involved in the method of litigation of tort cases and the kinds of damages that can be recovered in these cases. This section will discuss these new developments in tort law.

Two new theories that are fundamentally based on tort law are the concept of *lender liability* and the duty of employers to provide a safe work environment. **Lender liability,** embodying the concept that financial institutions can be civilly liable for their business decisions that produce harm, is discussed above.

The duty to provide a safe work environment is a civil action, based on tort concepts, that complements statutory duties imposed under Occupational Safety and Health Acts. These statutes are discussed in chapter 14, "The Employment Relationship." The idea that employers are under a duty to provide a safe and healthful work environment represents yet another expansion of tort concepts into the legal regulation of interpersonal relationships. In the following case, an employee sought an injunction to prevent his employer from exposing him to tobacco in the workplace.

Smith v. Western Electric Co.

643 S.W. 2d 10 (Mo. App. 1983)

Opinion

Dowd, Presiding Judge: Plaintiff appeals from an order dismissing his petition on the ground that it fails to state a claim upon which relief can be granted.

The petition seeks an injunction to prevent plaintiff's employer from exposing him to tobacco smoke in the workplace and from affecting his pay or employment conditions because of his medical reaction to tobacco smoke. The petition alleges that by allowing smoking in the work area, defendant permits its employees to be exposed to a health hazard and thereby breaches its duty to provide a safe place in which to work.

Plaintiff contends the trial court erred in dismissing his petition in that it invokes legal principles entitling him to relief and shows that injunctive relief is appropriate. Plaintiff further contends that federal law does not preempt state common law in this case.

In reviewing the dismissal of this petition for failure to state a claim, we grant the petition its broadest intendment and liberally construe its averments. We accept as true all factual allegations and their favorable inferences. If the averments thus viewed invoke principles of substantive law upon which relief can be granted to plaintiff, the petition is not subject to dismissal. Any reasonable doubt with regard to the petition's sufficiency is resolved in favor of plaintiff.

The petition includes the following allegations. Plaintiff has been employed by defendant since 1950 and has worked in defendant's Missouri branch since 1967. He is a nonsmoker sharing an open office area with other employees, many of whom smoke tobacco products as they work. In 1975 plaintiff began to experience serious respiratory tract discomfort as a result of inhaling tobacco smoke in the workplace. A subsequent medical evaluation determined that plaintiff suffers a severe adverse reaction to tobacco smoke. His symptoms include sore throat, nausea, dizziness, headache, blackouts, loss of memory, difficulty in concentration, aches and pains in joints, sensitivity to noise and light, cold sweat, gagging, choking sensations, and lightheadedness. After a sufficient period of non-exposure to smoke, plaintiff's symptoms abate somewhat. The symptoms have become increasingly severe over the years, however. Doctors evaluating and treating plaintiff have advised him to avoid contact with tobacco smoke whenever possible.

The petition further alleges that plaintiff first complained to defendant about the tobacco smoke in the workplace in 1975. Defendant thereafter moved plaintiff to different locations within the plant, but no improvement resulted because each location contained significant amounts of tobacco smoke. In 1978 plaintiff was informed that he should no longer submit complaints about the smoke through defendant's anonymous complaint procedure since defendant would not process them. In response to recommendations of the National Institute for Occupational Safety and Health, defendant adopted a smoking policy in April 1980. The declared policy was to protect the rights of both smokers and nonsmokers by providing accommodations for both groups and by making a reasonable effort to separate the groups in work areas. Because defendant has failed to implement its policy by making such a reasonable effort, improvement of the air in the workplace has not resulted.

According to the petition, in August 1980 plaintiff filed with defendant a Handicapped Declaration Statement that he was handicapped by his susceptibility to tobacco smoke. Refusing to segregate smokers or to limit smoking to non-work areas, defendant informed plaintiff he could either continue to work in the same location and wear a respirator or apply for a job in the computer room (where smoking is prohibited). The latter option would entail a pay decrease of about $300 per month. Defendant thereafter provided plaintiff with a respirator that has proven ineffective in protecting plaintiff from tobacco smoke.

The petition states that plaintiff has exhausted all avenues of relief through defendant, he has no adequate remedy at law; he is suffering and will continue to suffer irreparable physical injuries and financial losses unless defendant improves working conditions. The petition alleges that defendant is breaching its common law duty as an employer to provide plaintiff a safe place to work, and that defendant has available reasonable alternatives to avoid the continuing breach of duty, as demonstrated by defendant's ability to protect its computer equipment from tobacco smoke. The petition further states that, although "second-hand smoke" is harmful to the health of all employees, defendant is permitting them to be exposed in the workplace to this health hazard which is neither related to nor a necessary by-product of defendant's business.

Construing these allegations favorably to plaintiff, we must determine whether they invoke principles of law entitling him to relief.

It is well-settled in Missouri that an employer owes a duty to the employee to use all reasonable care to provide a reasonably safe workplace, e.g., *Todd* v. *Watson* (Mo. 1973); *Hightower* v. *Edwards* (Mo. 1969), and to protect the employee from avoidable perils. *Moles* v. *Kansas City Stock Yards Co. of Maine* (Mo.App. 1968). Whether the employer has fulfilled its duty depends upon the facts of each case. For example, in *McDaniel* v. *Kerr* (Mo. 1953), the employer had failed to provide a safe workplace where the employee's inhalation of dust on the job caused damage requiring removal of his lung. In *DeMarco* v. *United States,* (E.D.N.Y. 1962), the court found a negligent failure to provide a safe working environment where the plaintiff was injured when he fainted and fell after complaining about gasoline fumes in an unventilated work area.

The allegations of the instant case, taken as true, show that the tobacco smoke of co-workers smoking in the work area is hazardous to the health of employees in general and plaintiff in particular. The allegations also show that defendant knows the tobacco smoke is harmful to plaintiff's health and that defendant has the authority, ability, and reasonable means to control smoking in areas requiring a smoke-free environment. Therefore, by failing to exercise its control and assume its responsibility to eliminate the hazardous condition caused by tobacco smoke, defendant has breached and is breaching its duty to provide a reasonably safe workplace. See *Shimp* v. *New Jersey Bell Telephone Co.* (1976). As stated in *Thompson* v. *Kroeger* (Mo. 1964):

> The exercise of due care requires precautions which a reasonably prudent employer would have taken in given circumstances, even though other employers may not have taken such commensurate precautions. What usually is done may be evidence of what ought to be done, but what ought to be done is fixed by a standard of reasonable prudence, whether it usually is complied with or not.

If plaintiff's petition establishes defendant's failure to provide a safe place for plaintiff to work, we must next consider whether injunctive relief would be an appropriate remedy. An injunction may issue to prevent the doing of any legal wrong whatever, whenever in the opinion of the court an adequate remedy cannot be afforded by an action for damages. Injunctive relief is unavailable unless irreparable harm is otherwise likely to result, and plaintiff has no adequate remedy at law.

The petition alleges that plaintiff's continuing exposure to smoke in the workplace is increasingly deleterious to his health and is causing irreparable harm. Assuming the allegations and reasonable inferences therefrom to be true, we think it is fair to characterize deterioration of plaintiff's health as "irreparable" and as a harm for which money damages cannot adequately compensate. This is particularly true where the harm has not yet resulted in full-blown disease or injury. Money damages, even though inadequate, are the best possible remedy once physical damage is done, but they are certainly inadequate to compensate permanent injury which could have been prevented. Plaintiff should not be required to await the harm's fruition before he is entitled to seek an inadequate remedy. Moreover, the nature of plaintiff's unsafe work environment represents a recurrent risk of harm that would necessitate a multiplicity of lawsuits. Finally, the petition states that plaintiff has no adequate remedy at law and alleges facts indicating that prior to this action plaintiff unsuccessfully pursued relief, both through his employer's in-house channels and through administrative agencies. Viewing the petition favorably, as we must to determine its sufficiency, we find that injunction would be an appropriate remedy.

Defendant contends the trial court lacks jurisdiction to provide relief, and therefore the petition fails to state a claim upon which relief can be granted, because the subject matter of this case is preempted by the federal Occupational Safety and Health Act (OSHA). The Act specifically states, however, that it does not affect the common law regarding "injuries, diseases, or death of employees arising out of . . . employment." The Act also declares that it does not prevent a state court from asserting jurisdiction over an occupational safety or health issue for which no OSHA standard is in effect. We are unpersuaded by defendant's argument that § 653(b)(4) refers only to the common law pertaining to workers' compensation laws. In addition, defendant has not directed our attention to any OSHA standard figured in the opinions of other courts considering OSHA and tobacco smoke. Furthermore, defendant conceded in oral argument that a court may retain jurisdiction in the absence of an OSHA standard.

We conclude that plaintiff has stated a claim upon which relief can be granted and that the trial court therefore erred in dismissing the petition. Plaintiff should be allowed the opportunity to prove his allegations.

The judgment is reversed and the cause remanded.

Case Questions

1. Why was tobacco smoke "unsafe" for the plaintiff in this case?
2. Why could the plaintiff sue under state law, instead of having to make his complaint under the Occupational Safety and Health Act?

A trend in the law, primarily fostered by business activity, began to occur in the 1980s with the inception of the **tort reform** movement. During the 1970s, for a variety of reasons, the amount of business insurance premiums escalated dramatically, often quadrupuling within a few years. In addition, some businesses found it difficult to obtain insurance coverage anywhere. The insurance companies and many business organizations identified as the primary factor in these events a dramatic increase in both the number of lawsuits (mostly for tort claims) and the size of the judgments collected by successful plaintiffs in these lawsuits. Chapter 25, "Product Liability," contains a lengthy discussion of these issues in the context of litigation of product liability cases, which are usually tort cases. To address the problem precipitated by the insurance "crisis," business groups in the various states began to advocate the concept of "tort reform," and as of 1990, a number of states had passed some sort of statute regulating the outcome of tort cases. While state tort reform statutes vary widely, a common theme in all of them is an attempt to limit the amount and type of monetary damages a successful plaintiff can recover in a tort case.

One common component of these statutes is a limitation on the collection of nonactual damages. Actual damages might be thought of as "out-of-pocket expenses" and include such monetary losses as medical bills, lost wages, property losses, and payment for domestic or nursing assistance. In tort cases under the common law, in addition to the collection of actual damages, juries have been able to award damages for pain and suffering caused by the commission of a tort. The amount of these nonactual damages, often referred to as "exemplary damages," in many cases exceeded the amount of the plaintiff's actual damages. The tort reform movement to cap recovery of exemplary damages, usually by limiting them to some percentage of actual damages, has proven successful in legislative initiatives, and, in early challenges of these statutes, courts have tended to uphold their legality. Business-initiated changes in tort law represent a significant shift in traditional policies of risk allocation, and thus provide an important example of the complex dynamics of the interactions between business, the law, and society in general.

Ethical Issues in Tort Law

Since tort law is so well-established, many issues that might be regarded as "ethical" have been formalized by the law, and until recently, basic ethical questions about this area of the law have seldom been raised. However, three areas where there has been significant debate in recent years on ethical issues in tort law involve adoption of the concept of comparative negligence, the creation of the concept of strict liability in tort in product liability, and the emergence of the tort reform movement.

As indicated in the discussion above, at common law such defenses to the tort of negligence as contributory negligence and assumption of the risk were a complete defense to recovery by a plaintiff, even if the fault for the injury rested primarily with the defendant. The passage of comparative negligence statutes, which apportions damages by reducing the amount of the plaintiff's recovery by the degree of his fault for the injury, represents a policy decision that it is unethical and inequitable for a basically innocent victim to be denied any recovery for torts committed against him.

The creation of the concept of strict liability in tort in product liability, with its policy that a seller of goods whose product is defective and unreasonably dangerous should be liable without specific proof of how an injury occurred, is a significant development that has expanded seller liability tremendously. In effect, a plaintiff injured by a product has a much lower burden of proof to sustain now than in the past. The development of this concept represents a policy decision that it is more ethical to place the monetary responsibility for injuries caused by products on the seller than on product users.

The tort reform movement has precipitated a firestorm of debate on ethical issues. Is it ethical for businesses to make attempts to change laws that allow innocent injured parties to recover damages? If it is ethical for businesses to become involved in these issues, is it ethical for them to advocate limitation on the amount of recovery for suffering that a plaintiff can make? Is it ethical for business in effect to insert its views into the judicial process? The answers to these questions are not clearcut, but raising them illustrates the many situations in which law and ethics overlap.

The important concepts and terms in this chapter are listed below; page numbers have been provided for the key terms. By reading over each section you can assess your understanding of the chapter concepts and determine areas you may want to review.

Chapter Summary

1. A *tort* consists of a violation of a standard of behavior established by society. Some torts may be classified as intentional. These may be further classified as torts against the person, torts against property, and torts against business and economic interests.
2. Torts against the *person* include: assault, battery, right of privacy, abuse of process, malicious prosecution, false imprisonment, deceit, intentional infliction of mental distress, and defamation. Defamation may be broken down into slander, which is the oral statement, and libel, which is the written statement. Slander may be either per se or per quod. An individual may be protected against suits for libel or slander because of privilege. The privilege may either be qualified or absolute. In order to recover for defamation, a public figure may have to prove that the publication was made with malice or reckless disregard for the truth.
3. Intentional torts against *property* include trespass to land, trespass to personal property, and conversion. Although the tort of conversion is related to the tort of trespass to personal property, it involves a more serious interference with the right to possess and control personal property. Nuisance results from a substantial interference with a right to enjoy the use of property.
4. The group of torts classified as being against one's economic or business interest include: interference with contractual relations, slander of title and disparagement of goods, theft and misappropriation of trade secrets, and infringement of trademarks, tradenames, patents, and copyrights.
5. Another type of tort is negligence. The elements of negligence are the existence of a duty of care, a breach of the duty, causation, and injury. Those who own real property owe a duty to three classes of persons, invitees, licensees, and trespassers. A duty may be owed to trespassing children because of the doctrine of attractive nuisance. An objective standard, the reasonable man, is used to determine if one has breached his duty of care.
6. One common defense to a charge of negligence is the negligence of the plaintiff known as *contributory negligence*. Sometimes the plaintiff may overcome this defense by the doctrine of *last clear chance*. Another

defense to a negligence charge is that the plaintiff *assumed the risk* by knowingly placing himself in a position of danger.

7. In a large number of jurisdictions, a *comparative negligence* approach has replaced the doctrine of contributory negligence.
8. This chapter discussed a class of cases to which the doctrine of *strict liability* or liability without fault applies. Among those types of cases to which the doctrine applies are those involving injuries caused by animals, explosives, or the spraying of chemicals. Most of the activities to which strict liability applies are those involving an abnormal threat to the community. One particular class of cases to which the doctrine of strict liability applies are *products liability* cases.

Key Terms

assault and battery 295
assumption of risk 313
comparative negligence 313
contributory negligence 313
defamation 296
disparagement of goods 292
false imprisonment 301
fraud 301
infringement of patents 294
intentional infliction of mental distress 301
intentional tort 291
interference with contractual relations 291
lender liability 314
negligence 307
negligence per se 311
products liability 314
res ipsa loquitur 312
right of privacy 297
strict liability 314
tort 290
tort reform 317
trade secrets 292
trespass 305

Questions on Ethics

1. California has enacted a statute that limits the amount of damages a plaintiff in a tort case can recover for pain and suffering to a percentage of recovery of actual damages. Assuming that this law is legal, is it ethical?
2. Ned is trying to peel an apple with a knife. The knife blade breaks off from the handle, and Ned cuts himself. If Ned sues the manufacturer of the knife, he will probably recover under the theory of strict liability in tort. However, it is possible that the defect in the knife did not originate during the manufacturing process. Is it ethical to hold the manufacturer liable when it may not have been at fault for the defect?

3. Should social hosts be liable for accidents caused by their inebriated guests?
4. Would it be ethical to spy on customers in dressing rooms if signs were not posted stating that surveillance might take place?
5. Is it ethical for a financial institution to lend money to a borrower who the lender thinks may very well not be able to repay the loan?

Questions on Law

1. A couple in New Jersey sold their home without telling the purchasers that their well water was contaminated by gasoline. Will they be liable for money damages to the buyers, who became ill from drinking the water?
2. Can a plaintiff recover for emotional distress, as well as for physical illness, for injury caused by ingestion of toxic chemicals?
3. Putney was eleven years old. While sitting in school one day he reached across the aisle and slightly kicked one of his schoolmates, Vosburg, in the shin. Vosburg hardly felt the kick, but a few minutes later felt a violent pain. The leg later became infected and Vosburg lost full use of the leg. Vosburg had previously suffered an injury to the same part of his leg kicked by Putney. At trial the jury found that Putney did not intend to injure Vosburg. Putney contended on appeal that he was not liable. Is he correct? [*Vosburg* v. *Putney,* 80 Wisc. 523, 50 N.W. 403 (1891).]
4. Lucille Hawkins entered the H. E. Butt Grocery store. She took one or two steps off a mat that was located inside the door. She slipped and fell in some rain water that had accumulated there. Lucille suffered injuries as a result of the fall and sued the H. E. Butt Company. The store manager testified that water had accumulated at the spot where Hawkins had fallen during previous rain storms when the wind came from the North. He testified that the area had been mopped four or five times during the hour before Hawkins fell. No warning sign was placed at the spot. What defenses would you raise for H. E. Butt? Do you think you would be successful? To what class of persons who might enter the H. E. Butt store does Lucille belong? What duty is owed to her by H. E. Butt? [*H. E. Butt Grocery Co.* v. *Hawkins,* 594 S.W.2d 187 (Tex. App. 1980).]
5. Mills appeared before the city council of Des Moines. During the meeting, the Mayor stated to him: "Mills, you know that our hands are tied by the courts. You are guilty of dereliction of duty as an attorney towards your client inasmuch as you seemingly advised her that the City Council could take any action which would or could result in the resumption of bus service. . . . You have appeared here only as a publicity stunt." A local newspaper printed the story, and Mills sued the Mayor. What defense may the Mayor raise? Do you think it will be successful? [*Mills* v. *Denny,* 63 N.W.2d 222 (Iowa 1954).]

Suggested Readings

F. Gibson & E. Klayman, ''Landlord Liability: a New Dimension,'' 25 *Amer. Bus. L. J.* 1 (1987).

D. Ballam, ''Intentional Torts in the Workplace: Expanding Employee Remedies, 25 *Amer. Bus. L. J.* 63 (1987).

R. Prentice & B. Winslett, ''Employee References: Will a 'No Comment' Policy Protect Employers Against Liability for Defamation?'' 25 *Amer. Bus. L. J.* (1987).

13 Forms of Business Organizations

If incorporated business is to become professionalized, it is to the managers, not to the owners, that we must look for the accomplishment of this result. . . . If the social responsibility of business means merely a more enlightened view as to the ultimate advantage of the stockholder/owners, then obviously corporate managers may accept such social responsibility without any departure from the traditional view that their function is to seek to obtain the maximum amount of profits for their stockholders.

—Dodd, "For Whom Are Corporate Managers Trustees?" 45 Harv. L. Rev. *1145 (1932)*

■ LEARNING OBJECTIVES

After you have read this chapter, you should be able to:

1. Recognize and explain the legal and ethical obligations of corporate directors and officers.
2. Explain the various types of business organizations and understand their advantages and disadvantages.
3. Explain the social effects of corporate officers and directors being indemnified for wrongful conduct.
4. Explain the function of the audit committee and its effect on corporate accountability.
5. Explain the business judgment rule and understand its use in corporate governance.
6. Explain the rights of a stockholder

Business Decisions and the Law

Partnerships Become a Way of Life for Corning Glass Works

Corning has come a long way since it helped Thomas Edison develop the light bulb. The well-known manufacturer of fine crystal and housewares is also a highly respected partner in joint ventures ranging from the production of glass fiber to blood and wine analyzers.

In a typical Corning venture it engages in a lengthy courtship, for example, with the Japanese Asaki Company, the world's largest manufacturer of glass bulbs. This resulted in the formation of Corning Asaki Video Products, whose products will include large-sized and advanced high-resolution glass bulbs for TVs and computer terminals. Corning will manage the venture, and Asaki will contribute money. Corning presently owns 67% of the venture, with Asaki eventually increasing its ownership share to 49%.

Commentators attribute Corning's success in ventures to, among other things its humble corporate culture and ability to let its partner assume control. Chairman James Houghton suggests his company's success with ventures depends upon trust between partners and the ability of management to share. He cautioned that ventures are ill-fated if each partner has to look over its shoulder at the other. In response to the query of "why involve your company in a venture with another company?" Houghton and others explain that a start-up venture is usually more costly. Also, ventures are a form of leverage in a world too complicated for firms to enter new markets and form new businesses on their own.

This chapter will acquaint you with the different kinds of business organizations. We will first discuss opposing points of view regarding corporate social responsibility. Liability exposure of the business venture, its managers, and owners becomes the central theme of the chapter.

Corporate Social Responsibility

In 1932 Professor E. Merrick Dodd of Harvard University challenged corporate America to a new standard of professional management, demanding corporate social responsibility beyond the maximization of profits. Since then, in no other area of the law has ethics become more relevant than in the operation of business organizations. It is within these organizations that American life and culture are nurtured and developed. In some business you will spend your working hours delivering a product or a service to the community.

We depend upon business organizations for food, clothing, shelter, transportation, technology, insurance, education, and health care. The traditional long-term goal of profit maximization as the business organization's sole objective has been criticized in recent years. Profit maximization is the position of

Professor Milton Friedman, who stated, "There is one and only one social responsibility of business—to use the resources and engage in activities designed to increase its profits so long as it stays within the rules of the game, which is to say, engages in open and free competition without deception or fraud" (*Capitalism and Freedom* [Chicago: University of Chicago Press, 1962], 133). You should keep in mind as you read this chapter that businesses function within a complex legal environment. In addition to profits, businesses have to deal with consumer rights, employer/employee relationships, and government regulations that make them accountable to the public. Within this environment there are moral and ethical business relationships that management must account for, such as the company's pollution of our air and water, conservation of our natural resources, workplace safety, decent wages, and equal opportunity for all of its employees. Accordingly, some would agree with Professor Harvey J. Goldschmid, who wrote, "The corporation responsibilities which most concern us as a society are not those running to shareholders but to other segments of the public and to society as a whole" ("The Greening of the Board Room: Reflections on Corporate Responsibility," 10 *Colum. J.L.S.P.* 36–37 [1973]).

There is often tension between the two positions of profit maximization and responsibility to society. Business decisions must achieve both economic and societal objectives. This requires a professionally managed company fully accountable to its owners, to its employees, and to the community in which it functions. This chapter will acquaint you with types of business organizations and will identify certain legal, social, and ethical responsibilities of business.

Selection of a Business Organization

Once you decide to enter a business venture on your own or with others, your first decision will be to select an appropriate business organization. You can do business as (1) a sole proprietorship, (2) a general partnership, (3) a limited partnership, (4) a business trust, or (5) a corporation. (See figure 13.1, Comparison of Business Organizations.) Your lawyer and accountant will assist you in selecting and organizing the business and maintaining the proper legal and financial records. It is not unusual for a sole proprietorship to be converted to a partnership or a corporation as the business develops. This chapter will examine the various kinds of business organizations and the legal environment in which they operate.

Sole Proprietorship

The most common type of business organization is the **sole proprietorship,** in which the owner manages the business for a profit and is personally liable for any legal claims brought against the business. Although there is only one owner

Figure 13.1 Comparison of Business Organizations

	General Partnership	Limited Partnership	Business Trust	Corporation
Creation	By agreement per U.P.A.	In writing per R.L.P.A.	Filing Business Trust certificate per statute	Filing articles of organization per statute
Liability	Unlimited liability with respect to torts and contracts for all partners	Unlimited liability for general partners, limited partners are generally not liable for business torts and contracts	Trust beneficiaries may be personally liable if they have power to control the trust management; trustees may be held liable for business obligations	Shareholders are generally not liable for corporate obligations
Management	Unless changed by the Partnership Agreement, each partner has an equal vote per U.P.A.	General partners manage with equal vote, unless changed by agreement—limited partners do not manage the business	Trustees manage the trust business in accordance with the trust agreement	Officers carry out the management policy determined and authorized by the board of directors
Agency	Each partner is an agent of the partnership for partnership business per U.P.A.	General partners are agents, limited partners are not	Trustees are agents for business trust purposes, beneficiaries are not	Officers are agents, directors and shareholders are not
Taxation	Not a taxable entity but files an information return	Taxed similar to a general partnership, limited partners have limited liability and are taxed as partners	Taxable entity, may be taxed as a corporation due to corporate attributes	Taxable entity—may qualify as an S corporation and avoid double taxation

in a sole proprietorship, it may have as many employees as necessary to carry out its business purpose. In such an instance the sole proprietor creates the relationship of master and servant or principal and agent with his employees. Because the sole proprietor is the only owner, the business profits and losses are reported on his individual state and federal income tax returns.

Sole proprietorships are the most popular kind of business enterprise because of their organizational and operational convenience. Upon making your first sale you are a sole proprietor—you do not need to file any documents with the government or contract with co-owners. However, if you are engaged in business under a fictitious name (e.g., Reliable Used Cars), your name and address must generally be registered in a **business certificate** filed in the local city hall. This is required so that business creditors can easily determine your name and address in the event of a lawsuit. Retailers must acquire a sales tax license, and service proprietors such as electricians are obligated to obtain a state occupational license.

The most glaring disadvantage of a sole proprietorship is the personal liability of the owner in the event of a lawsuit. For example, if the proprietor of a retail business sells a product that injures a person, the victim can bring a product liability suit against the retailer, whose business and personal assets can both be liquidated to satisfy the claim. The occupational or professional sole proprietor may be sued for *malpractice* for the negligent performance of a duty. Both product liability and malpractice insurance may be purchased to underwrite this potential liability.

So long as the sole proprietor's personal assets are held in trust, or are held jointly with another person who was not part of the business venture *before* the claim occurred, such assets are legally beyond the reach of business creditors in most cases. In spite of its limitations, the sole proprietorship is the most common form of business organization in the United States because its primary advantages are managerial control and legal simplicity. *Managerial control* means operational control of the business by one person who makes all decisions.

General Partnership

For any number of reasons it may be appropriate to enter your business venture with others as co-owners who will share in the profits and losses. In such a case you are doing business as a *general partnership,* and your organization is governed by the Uniform Partnership Act (UPA). A **general partnership** is a contractual agreement between competent parties to combine their capital and/or services in a business and to share in the profits and losses.

If you and your associates verbally agree to form a partnership, there can be a legal partnership, because the UPA does not require a written partnership agreement. Of course, months or years later there may be a misunderstanding of your original agreement, so a written partnership document, known as the **articles of partnership,** is always advisable (see figure 13.2). Depending on the business venture, the agreement may be brief and simple, or it may require a complex legal document such as that found in a law, accounting, or medical partnership.

The fact that you and your associates agree to run the business as a partnership is not in itself conclusive evidence of a partnership. The courts are concerned with a sharing in the net profits as the co-owners carry on the business for a profit, and they may either find a partnership or deny partnership status depending on the facts of each case. There must be more than one business transaction entered into for a profit. The UPA lists certain instances in

Figure 13.2 General Partnership Agreement (Short Form)

GENERAL PARTNERSHIP AGREEMENT (Short Form)

Agreement, made this ______ day of __________, 19____, by and between John Doe, of __________________, and Richard Roe, of __________________.

Whereas, Richard Roe has acquired an undivided one-half interest in the real estate and insurance business heretofore owned and conducted by John Doe, with office and place of business located at ______________________________;

It is agreed as follows:

1. **Name and Duration.** The parties hereby agree to continue the operation of said business as partners under the name of ______________________, the partnership to continue for an indefinite time and until terminated as herein provided or as may be mutually agreed upon.

2. **Capital.** The amount of capital contributed to the partnership by the parties is hereby agreed to be the sum of $__________ each, and is represented by the following personal property: [*here describe*].

3. **Reserve Fund.** An additional sum of ________ dollars ($________) shall be set up and reserved from the profits of the partnership business, and shall become and be a part of the invested capital, it being agreed that not less than ____% of the net earnings shall be so reserved until said amount is accumulated.

4. **Banking.** The funds of the partnership shall be deposited in its name in the ________ Bank of __________, and all trust funds shall be deposited in such bank in a separate account. All such funds, partnership or trust, shall be subject to withdrawal only by check made in the name of the partnership and signed by either partner.

5. **Duties.** Each partner shall devote all his time and attention to the business of the partnership, and shall not, directly or indirectly, engage in any other business without the consent of the other partner.

6. **Books.** Full and accurate accounts of the transactions of the partnership shall be kept in proper books, and each partner shall cause to be entered therein full and accurate accounts of all his transactions in behalf of the partnership. Such books shall be kept at the place of business of the partnership, and each party shall at all times have access to and may inspect and copy any of them.

7. **Drawings.** Each party shall be entitled to withdraw such amounts and at such times, from the partnership earnings, as shall from time to time be fixed and agreed upon.

8. **Profits and Losses.** At the end of each calendar year, a full and accurate inventory shall be prepared, and the assets, liabilities, and income, both gross and net, shall be ascertained, and the net profits or net losses of the partnership shall be fixed and determined. The net profits or net losses shall be divided equally between the parties, and the account of each shall be credited or debited with his proportionate share thereof.

9. **Limitations.** Neither party shall, without the written consent of the other, make, execute, deliver, indorse or guaranty any commercial paper, nor agree to answer for, or indemnify against, any act, debt, default or miscarriage of any person, partnership, association or corporation, other than that of the parties hereto.

10. **Termination.** The partnership may be terminated by either party upon giving 60 days notice to the other party of his desire to withdraw, in which event an accounting shall be had and a division of the partnership assets made, provided, however, that the party to whom notice is given shall have the right to acquire the whole interest of the partnership at a price not to exceed the book value thereof, on such terms as may be agreed upon, and to continue the partnership business under the same name.

In Witness Whereof, the parties have signed this agreement.

______________________________ ______________________________

[Signatures]

Reprinted with permission from Edmund O. Belsheim's *Modern Legal Forms*. Copyright © 1971 by West Publishing Co.

which the sharing of profits does not infer a partnership: (1) when profits are received in payment of a debt; (2) when profits are received as wages of an employee, or rent to a landlord; (3) when profits are received as an annuity to a widow of a deceased partner; (4) when profits are received as interest on a loan; and (5) when profits are received as the consideration for the sale of the goodwill of a business. The critical thing to remember in each of these cases is that if the recipient of the profits also has a right to participate in the management of the business, then there is a co-ownership and a resulting partnership.

In the following case, a family partnership brought suit alleging an "oral" partnership with a previous partner of their family firm. The court found that the oral partnership was not proved by "clear, unequivocal and decisive evidence." Notice that the money received by the previous partner was viewed as investments in the partnership rather than as a sharing in the net profits.

Singer v. Singer

634 P.2d 766 (1981)

Facts

The Singer family formed an oil production partnership in the late 1930s. The original partnership was called Josaline Production Co. and was made up of the following partners: Joseph B. Singer, Joe L. Singer, Alex Singer, the Trachtnberg Brothers, and the Singer Bros. In 1947 the partnership was dissolved and the Trachtnberg Brothers received 17 percent of the assets. The Singer family continued to operate as a partnership after the Trachtnbergs were excluded. In 1962 a revised partnership contract was executed between the Singer family members. The new partnership consisted of essentially the same partners, except for the Trachtnbergs.

After 1947 the Trachtnbergs continued to hold a 17 percent undivided co-ownership in the oil and gas properties that had been distributed when they were dismissed from the partnership. Josaline continued to do business. As opportunities arose, in many cases, the Trachtnbergs were permitted to invest in Josaline projects to the same extent (17 percent) as their original holdings. It is important to note that profit from each of the oil and gas properties was distributed to the Trachtnbergs as royalty owners, or as working interest co-owners, and not as distributions from the Josaline partnership. In other words, since 1947, the Trachtnbergs were treated as co-tenants and participating investors in most of the projects in which the Josaline partnership was involved.

The suit was brought on behalf of Josaline and its partners. The case was tried on the theory that the Josaline partners had been simultaneously engaged in an "oral" partnership within the Josaline partnership. This "oral" partnership included the Trachtnbergs and affected the partners' business dealings.

Opinion

Judge Boydston: Partnership is a creature of voluntary agreement. A partnership relationship can be created by oral agreement but proof of the fact of partnership and its terms must be established, by "clear, unequivocal and decisive" evidence. Oral testimony offered to prove these facts is not given much weight. Therefore, the question presented here is whether the terms and fact of the alleged oral partnership have been proven by clear, unequivocal and decisive evidence. We find the judgment is clearly against the weight of the evidence.

We observe the manner of dealing between these highly sophisticated investors, partners and family members completely belies a casual business relationship. It is noted that the various businesses owned by the parties all were family partnerships and each was carefully reduced to writing. It is inconsistent that men of such sound business tradition would be party to an oral business relationship as extensive and pervasive as that claimed by plaintiffs without also reducing it to writing.

For their common profit and convenience, they did business together. All such business was conducted through the Josaline partnership. However, outside the Josaline partnership, any interest offered to outsiders was treated as an *ad hoc* co-investment opportunity. These outside investors included the Trachtnbergs, who retained the privilege of whether to accept or reject the investment opportunity. In other words, the parties outside Josaline were simply investors with a common area of interest. Investment in oil and gas leases as co-tenants or co-owners gives no presumption of the existence of partnership. It is well settled that the relationship of co-tenancy is not a [partnership] relationship.

Case Questions

1. The court stated ". . . It is inconsistent that men of such sound business tradition would be party to an oral business relationship as extensive and pervasive as that claimed by plaintiff without also reducing it to writing." The Uniform Partnership Act does not require (or mention) that a partnership agreement be in writing. Should the court require a writing, as in this case, because of the parties' "sound business tradition"?
2. Did the Josaline partners have an ethical obligation to obtain a written agreement concerning their relationship with the Trachtnberg brothers? Do you think parties to any substantial transaction have a moral duty to each other to reduce their verbal agreement to writing?
3. Should the Uniform Partnership Act require all partnership agreements to be in writing? Would such a provision diminish the number of partnership lawsuits?

Partnership by Estoppel

You may work for a partnership as a mere employee but be held out to the general public as a partner. For instance, your name may be listed on firm stationery or in firm catalogues as a partner. If the firm, with your consent, listed you as a partner on an application for a bank loan, and the bank extended credit in reasonable reliance on that fact, you would be estopped from denying your partnership status and could be held liable with the partners on the loan. In such a case it would not be necessary for you to sign the promissory note with the partners, so long as the loan was used for business purposes. This **partnership by estoppel** doctrine exists so that your firm cannot lead a creditor to believe that you are a partner and then later attempt to deny that you are a partner.

Partnership Management

Each partner, unless there is an agreement to the contrary, is entitled to one vote on the internal management of partnership affairs. A majority vote will decide normal and customary business affairs; a unanimous vote is needed to enact extraordinary business that would require a change in the partnership agreement. For example, if you and your partners in an accounting firm vote on a proposal to extend the office lease for another five years, the majority will rule, because this is a normal and customary business decision. However, a proposal to move the firm from one city to another will necessitate unanimous approval, as this is a change in the partnership agreement and is therefore extraordinary business.

Authority of Partners

The UPA states that each partner is an *agent* of the partnership for the purpose of carrying on, in the usual way, the partnership business. The legal environment in which partnerships function is governed by the law of agency; partners are agents, the partnership is the principal, and its customers are the third parties. Partners must act within the express authority of the partnership agreement and the implied authority customarily found in a business or professional partnership. You may wish to review chapter 11, because agency law is the foundation of the Uniform Partnership Act. All of the partners have *actual authority* to bind the firm, as well as *apparent authority* to carry on partnership business with customers and creditors who reasonably rely on such authority.

For example, let us say that you are the managing partner of a hardware store, which is a trading partnership organized to buy and sell inventory. You have express authority to purchase inventory on credit and bind the firm even though your other partners are not aware of the transaction. You have *implied authority* to borrow money and sign promissory notes in the firm name, to hire and fire personnel, to pay partnership creditors with partnership funds, to settle and compromise a partnership claim, to make representations that may bind the firm, and to receive notice on any matter relating to partnership affairs. However, a partner in a *nontrading* partnership—that is, one that only provides a service—does not have implied authority to borrow money and execute promissory notes in the partnership name, unless an emergency requires it or it is customary in that business to do so.

In the following case, the defendant contends that since he did not authorize his copartner in writing to enter into a real estate contract, the contract was binding only on his copartner and not on the partnership. Notice how the court applies the law of agency to the facts of the case.

Ball v. Carlson

641 P.2d 303 (1981)

Facts

Kenneth C. Ball and Theresa A. Ball brought this action against defendants Dennis Carlson, Charles Edward Ishmael, and Stephen M. Teegardin, individually and doing business as C.I.T. Construction Company (C.I.T.) to recover damages resulting from the alleged breach of a contract for the sale of a lot and the construction of a home thereon.

C.I.T., a partnership consisting of Teegardin, Carlson, and Ishmael, was engaged in the development and sale of real estate. C.I.T. was in the process of acquiring and developing a parcel of land in El Paso County at the time that Carlson and the Balls negotiated and signed the contract in February 1978. The contract called for a closing date of May 10, 1978, and specified that time was of the essence and that the contract was "contingent upon approval of subdivision by county commissioners."

At the time the contract was signed, C.I.T. had not yet obtained approval for its subdivision from the county commissioners. As the closing date approached, the subdivision still had not been approved, but Carlson assured the Balls that it probably would be approved at the next meeting of the commissioners. The Balls agreed to wait for closing until the plans were approved. C.I.T.'s subdivision plans were approved by the commissioners in July 1978 and, as found by the trial court, were in substantially the same form as originally submitted by C.I.T. in February 1978.

In June 1978, Teegardin and Carlson met with the Balls. Although nothing was said about rescission, Teegardin informed them that it would cost between $7,000 and $8,000 more to build their house than the price specified in the contract. On August 1, 1978, the listing agent for C.I.T., Real Estate Specialists, by its broker, defendant Teegardin, informed the Balls that C.I.T. considered the contract to be terminated, and returned the earnest money to them.

The Balls commenced this action for damages, alleging that C.I.T. had breached its contractual duty to construct and sell the house.

Teegardin contended that since he did not authorize Carlson in writing to enter into the real estate contract, the contract was only binding on Carlson individually.

The district court entered judgment for the plaintiffs. One of the defendants, Teegardin, appealed.

Opinion

Judge Van Cise: Every partner is an agent of the partnership for the purpose of its business, and the act of every partner, including the execution in the partnership name of any instrument for apparently carrying on in the usual way the business of the partnership of which he is a member, binds the partnership. The status of a partner, as both principal and agent of the partnership, serves as complete authority with respect to acts which are apparently within the usual course of the partnership's particular business, unless the other party knows that he has no such authority. This obviates the necessity of a specific written authorization from the other partners. Thus, the act of a partner in selling real estate, when in the apparent scope of the partnership, is binding upon the partnership and the other partners without obtaining their written consent, notwithstanding the statute of frauds requirement, that the authority of an agent to sell real estate must be in writing.

C.I.T. was engaged in the business of real estate development and sale. Therefore, Carlson bound each partner by signing the contract in C.I.T.'s name. Hence, the trial court did not err in entering judgment against Teegardin.

Judgment affirmed.

Case Questions

1. The court found the entire partnership liable for breach of the sales contract. What theory of partnership law led to this decision?
2. Do you think that Carlson had an ethical duty, although not a legal one, to obtain written consent from his copartners to enter into the real estate contract?
3. Were the Balls acting reasonably in assuming that the partnership authorized the sales contract?

Rights of a Partner

The UPA grants to you as a partner, unless otherwise agreed in the articles of partnership, the following statutory rights:

1. To share equally in the profits and losses, regardless of the amount of capital each partner has contributed;
2. To share equally in the management of the firm regardless of capital contribution;

3. To be paid interest on a loan you make to the partnership and to be repaid the principal when the loan is due;
4. To receive interest on a capital contribution you make to the partnership from the date when repayment should be made;
5. To inspect and copy partnership books and records;
6. To vote on the admission of new partners;
7. To be reimbursed for payments made and reasonable personal debts incurred in properly carrying on the partnership business; and
8. To be indemnified for damage to your personal property while it is used in the partnership business.

Notice how the court in the following case resolved the issue of whether the *goodwill* of a partnership (the reputation of the company expressed as a value over and above its assets) is an asset subject to a retired partner's claim. The case involves the conversion of a partnership into a corporation and the subsequent continuation of the same business.

Swann v. *Mitchell*

408 So.2d 681 (1982)

Facts

In 1966 William Alfred Swann, Sr., entered into a partnership agreement with the Mitchells. The agreement provided that Swann would receive a 5 percent profit share although he made no capital contribution. The Mitchells provided the capital in varying shares. Swann was to manage the business of the partnership, an automobile dealership. This agreement essentially continued a relationship between the parties that had been in existence for twelve years. In 1967, Swann retired as business manager and ceased all activities in the business and partnership affairs. However, he continued to receive payments representing his profit share, although paid to him in the form of salary or wages, until 1979. In that year, the partnership was dissolved by the remaining partners, and all assets were transferred to a corporation whose capital stock was issued to certain partners who continued with the business. Swann was not notified or consulted concerning the partnership dissolution and conversion of the business to the corporate form until early in 1980, at which time he received a final payment from the business. Swann came to the conclusion that the dissolution without his consent was wrongful, and that the distribution made to him failed to fully take account of all undistributed profits. He then filed suit, seeking a share of the value of the partnership's goodwill.

Opinion

Per curiam: We have examined the UPA and find nothing there to alter the accepted definition of profit. The labeling of various partnership assets for bookkeeping convenience cannot alter their nature as profits due to Swann.

An issue is presented whether the goodwill of the partnership is an asset subject to evaluation and partial distribution as claimed in Swann's behalf. While the goodwill of the partnership business is a valuable commodity, its value is virtually impossible of determination without an actual sale of the ongoing business. No "sale" as such has occurred here, since it is clear that the partners remaining after Swann's retirement continued the business for some twelve years and then simply transferred partnership assets to a corporation and continued the business under the corporate name. The remaining partners clearly reserved the right, under the partnership agreement, to modify, amend or change the agreement. They could have elected at any time to terminate the partnership, since it was not to exist for any fixed period of time, or they could have elected, which they did, to continue the business. We determine that these aspects of the partnership agreement, coupled with the limitation of Swann's interest to profits only, would preclude a finding that the partnership goodwill is subject to any claim by Swann. Accordingly, in determining the extent of Swann's unpaid partnership interest, if any, the value of the goodwill should not be considered.

Case Questions

1. Why did the court conclude that the value of the partnership's goodwill should not be considered in determining the extent of Swann's unpaid partnership interest?
2. The court stated, "While the goodwill of the partnership business is a valuable commodity, its value is virtually impossible of determination without an actual sale of the ongoing business." Can you devise a way to determine the value of goodwill without a sale of the business?
3. Was it ethical for the Mitchells to pay Swann his profit distribution as a partner in the form of salary or wages as a retired business manager? Was it ethical for Swann to accept such payments as wages from 1967 to 1979? Can you see how attempting to mislabel profits created costly litigation to both parties?

Partner as a Fiduciary

Keep in mind that partners, as agents, must act on behalf of the partnership. In that capacity they incur the common law duties of *fiduciaries*. In addition to compliance with the terms of the partnership agreement, a partner must act within the fiduciary duties of loyalty and reasonable care. A partner who violates a fiduciary duty can be sued by the other partners. Even if the fiduciary duties are not mentioned in the articles of partnership, they are implied by law.

A partner is not liable for an honest business judgment that may cause a financial loss to the firm. However, a partner is personally liable to the partnership for a loss caused by his negligence. For example, if the manager of a construction firm, after consulting with an insurance agent, decides to reduce the firm's insurance coverage and a lawsuit is later brought whose damages exceed the amount paid by the insurance policy, the partner is not liable. However, he would be held personally liable if he dropped all insurance coverage, because that would clearly be a careless business judgment.

Partners must act with good faith and complete loyalty to the firm. Unless the copartners agree, a partner cannot compete with the partnership. A partner is personally liable to his copartners for any profits made in a competing business.

Liability of Partners

As a partner, you can be sued for breach of contract by the other partners if you violate the partnership agreement, or you can be sued in tort if you breach a fiduciary duty. Suits among partners will generally dissolve the partnership. A partner who is unable to settle a dispute with other partners can petition a court of equity for an accounting.

Customers may also sue the firm and hold the partners jointly liable for contracts that the partnership has made. Partners are *jointly and severally* liable—that is, liable both as individuals and as a partnership—for loss or injury to any outsider for torts committed in the ordinary course of the partnership business. All partners will be held liable to an injured party for negligent acts performed by the partnership, even if all partners did not participate in the acts. This unlimited *personal liability exposure* for each partner for both contracts and torts is considered a disadvantage to the partnership form of business organization. Adequate liability and/or malpractice insurance should be considered a cost of doing business as a partnership. As in the case of a sole proprietorship, in the absence of fraud, personal assets of a partner that are jointly held or placed in trust before the claim occurs cannot be reached by partnership creditors.

The following case illustrates the joint and several liability of partners in a medical partnership for a malpractice claim.

Zuckerman v. Antenucci

478 N.Y.S. 2d 578 (1984)

Facts

Daniel Zuckerman, an infant, by his mother and natural guardian, Elaine Zuckerman, and Elaine Zuckerman, individually, brought a medical malpractice action against Dr. Joseph Antenucci and Dr. José Pena. Both had treated the mother during pregnancy. Although the summons did not state that the two defendants were partners, the undisputed, unopposed, and uncontradicted evidence at the trial established that relationship and that the alleged acts of malpractice were done in the course of partnership business. The jury returned a verdict finding that defendant Pena was guilty of malpractice, but defendant Antenucci was not guilty of malpractice. The amount of the verdict totalled $4 million dollars ($4,000,000.00).

Opinion

Judge Leviss: The issue is whether this court has jurisdiction to render a judgment against defendant Antenucci on the basis of a tort committed by his partner, even though the summons served did not designate defendant Antenucci as a partner. A party may be sued individually and directly for the tort of his partner. A partnership is liable for the tortious act of a partner, and a partner is jointly and severally liable for tortious acts chargeable to the partnership. "Thus if a partner while acting in the course of the partnership business injures a third person, such third person would have the right to sue all of the partners together in one lawsuit, or any one or all of the partners individually, including even one who did not cause the injury***." (Beane, *The Essentials of Partnership Law,* p. 63) It may thus be seen that the plaintiffs herein did not have to sue a partnership entity and did not have to write "Joseph Antenucci, a partner" on the summons in order to hold him liable on a partnership theory for the act of defendant Pena. Jurisdiction over defendant Antenucci individually is sufficient for a judgment against him based on a tort committed by his partner. Therefore, even though the jury found that defendant Antenucci was not guilty of any malpractice in his treatment of the patient, but that defendant Pena (his partner) was guilty of malpractice in his treatment of the patient, they were then both jointly and severally liable for the malpractice committed by defendant Pena by operation of law. Accordingly, plaintiff's motion is granted and plaintiffs are entitled to judgment against defendant Joseph Antenucci and José Pena in the amount of Four Million ($4,000,000,00) Dollars as a matter of law.

Case Questions

1. Why did the court hold Dr. Antenucci guilty of malpractice when the tort was committed by his partner, Dr. Pena?
2. Do you think it can be ethically justified to hold a person legally responsible for another's negligence?
3. What could a partner do to protect himself from a result similar to this case?

Taxation of a Partnership

A partnership is not a separate taxable entity, although it must file an information tax return (Form 1065) stating the amount of each partner's *distributive share* (i.e., the partner's portion of the profits and surplus) of the partnership's income and expenses. Each member of the partnership must pay income tax on her distributive share of the partnership income, whether it is distributed or not.

Partnership Property

The distinction between partnership property and a partner's personal property is significant when the partnership is being sued or dissolved. Business creditors can generally reach partnership assets and the personal assets of the individual partners. **Partnership property** is defined by the UPA as "all property originally brought into the partnership . . . or subsequently acquired by purchase or otherwise. . . ." Equipment and inventory used by the partnership are examples of *partnership personal property,* and the land and building where it is located is *partnership real property* if owned by the partnership. The Uniform Partnership Act allows the partnership to hold personal and real property in its own name. For example, the partnership deed could be recorded in the local registry of deeds in the partnership name. In order to satisfy a claim against the partnership, a partnership's creditor could liquidate the land and building owned by the partnership. To avoid this, partners often have their land and building held in trust *before* any liability occurs. In the absence of fraud, the law will recognize the building trust as a separate entity from the partnership and will prevent creditors from selling the land and building to satisfy their claim.

A distinct statutory method of holding partnership property, both real and personal, is by **tenancy in partnership.** The following statutory characteristics apply to partnership property held as tenancy in partnership unless there is an agreement to the contrary between the partners:

1. the partners have an equal right to use partnership property for partnership purposes;

2. partnership property cannot be sold, assigned, or mortgaged without the unanimous consent of the partners;
3. a partner's personal creditors cannot reach and attach specific partnership property, although this property can be reached by business creditors;
4. upon the death of a partner, her interest in specific partnership property vests in the surviving partners and not in the spouse or heirs at law;
5. a deceased partner's right in partnership property is not subject to any interest of her surviving spouse.

Tenancy in partnership is a unique way of owning partnership property that gives ownership preference to the partners rather than to the partners' personal creditors or a deceased partner's spouse.

Dissolution, Winding up, and Termination

Partners often leave their firms for another job or because of retirement, disability, or death. Any one of these, as well as a court decree of a partner's inability to carry on partnership business, can cause a dissolution of the partnership. The UPA defines a **dissolution** as "a change in the relation of the partners caused by any partner ceasing to be associated in the carrying on . . . of the business." Upon dissolution, a partner, or a deceased partner's spouse, is entitled to his or her partnership interest and distributive share of the profits.

The **winding-up** process begins when dissolution is caused by a change in the partner's relationship with the firm. (However, a partner who wrongfully dissolves a partnership—for example, in violation of the partnership agreement—is not entitled to demand that the dissolved partnership be wound up.) Winding up is the orderly liquidation of partnership assets and the distribution of proceeds, first to partnership creditors and then to the partners themselves. Unless the partners provided for a "buy and sell agreement" with a method to evaluate, fund, and pay off a partner's interest in the event of dissolution, the partnership will be liquidated and the assets distributed. Keep in mind that the partnership must first pay off its liabilities to creditors; if the partnership is insolvent, a deceased partner's estate is liable for the deceased partner's share of the partnership debts.

A partnership is not terminated upon dissolution, but rather continues until the winding up of partnership affairs is completed. Any expenses generated by the delay in winding up the partnership must be shared by the partners.

The sequence of events leading to a partnership **termination** is dissolution caused by a partner ceasing to be associated with the firm, followed by the winding up, which consists of paying out to the partner or the deceased partner's spouse his or her share of the partnership profits. If the partnership agreement provides for and funds this pay-out, the firm will not be terminated. But if the partnership cannot pay off the partner's interest and the distributive share, the partnership is terminated and its assets must be distributed in accordance with the UPA: first the firm's creditors are paid, then a partner's advances (loans) to the firm must be repaid, followed by a refund of a partner's capital contribution. Then, unless otherwise agreed by the partners, any remaining assets must be distributed equally as profits.

The primary advantage of organizing a business as a partnership is that it can be formed even without a written agreement. Permission to do business is not required in the state of organization or any other state where the partnership may engage in transactions. Its predominant disadvantage is the unlimited liability of the partners for claims against the partnership. If a partnership is found liable for wrongdoing and is incapable of paying the damages from company assets, the personal assets of all partners may be reached to satisfy the business claim, even if some did not sign the contract or commit the tort that led to the lawsuit.

Limited Partnership

Many investors seek tax shelters in such ventures as oil drilling, real estate development, and motion picture production. As an investor, you probably would not want managerial responsibility or liability for more than you invest. The **limited partnership** is a partnership formed by two or more persons that has one or more limited partners with limited liability. Limited partners have the same tax advantages as full partners—for instance, losses may be deducted against their other income—but limited partners enjoy limited liability for claims against the partnership. Limited partnerships are a state statutory business organization governed by the Uniform Limited Partnership Act (ULPA) and in a few states by the Revised Uniform Limited Partnership Act of 1976. Current tax reform has restricted the use of tax shelters, including the limited partnership.

Formation

The ULPA defines a limited partnership as "a partnership formed by two or more persons . . . having as members one or more limited partners." Unlike a general partnership, the formation of a limited partnership requires a written certificate signed by all of the partners (see figure 13.3). This certificate is usually filed in the registry of deeds in the county where the principal business of the firm is carried on; the certificate is open to public inspection.

Liability of Partners

The firm is divided into general and limited partners. The general partners conduct the business affairs and are personally liable to partnership creditors. Limited partners are not personally liable provided they do not participate in management. The statutory policy is that at least one general partner should be personally liable for business obligations, and the limited partners are exempt from personal liability so long as they do not take part in the control of the

Figure 13.3 Form of Limited Partnership Certificate

FORM OF LIMITED PARTNERSHIP CERTIFICATE

We, the undersigned, for the purpose of forming a limited partnership pursuant to the Uniform Limited Partnership Act as set forth in Sections ________ of the ________ Code, hereby certify:

1. Name. The name of the partnership is ____.

2. Character of Business. The character of the business to be carried on is to engage in the business of ________.

3. Place of Business. The location of the principal place of business of the partnership is ____________________.

4. General Partners. The name and place of residence of each general partner are:

____________________ ____________________

____________________ ____________________

Limited Partners. The name and place of residence of each limited partner are:

____________________ ____________________

____________________ ____________________

5. Term. The term for which the partnership is to exist is indefinite [*or* from ________, 19___, to the close of business on ________, 19___, and thereafter from year to year].

6. Initial Contribution of Each Limited Partner. The amount of cash and a description of and the agreed value of the other property contributed by each limited partner are:

Name	Cash	Description of Other Property	Agreed Value of Other Property
________	________	________	________
________	________	________	________

7. Additional Contributions of Each Limited Partner. Each limited partner may (but shall not be obliged to) make such additional contributions to the capital of the partnership as may from time to time be agreed upon by the general partners.

8. Return of Contribution to Each Limited Partner. The contribution of each limited partner is to be returned to him as may from time to time be agreed upon by the general partners.

9. Profit Shares of Each Limited Partner. The share of the profits or other compensation by way of income which each limited partner shall receive by reason of his contribution is:

____________________ ____________________ %

____________________ ____________________ %

10. Assignment of Limited Partner's Interest. Each limited partner is given the right to substitute an assignee as contributor in his place, provided that the assignment is approved by all the general partners.

11. Admission of Additional Limited Partners. The general partners are given the right to admit additional limited partners, provided that the admissions are approved by all the general partners, but in no event other than upon a cash contribution to the partnership and upon the same terms as herein expressed.

12. Death, Retirement or Insanity of General Partner. In the event of the death, retirement or insanity of a general partner, the remaining general partners shall have the right to continue the business of the partnership under the same name by themselves or in conjunction with any other person or persons they may select.

13. Right of Limited Partner to Receive Property Other Than Cash. Each limited partner is given the right to demand and receive property other than cash in return for his contribution, and the value of such property shall be that shown on the books of the partnership.

Signed the ____________ day of ________, 19___.

[*Signatures of general and limited partners*]

Subscribed and sworn to before me this ________ day of ____________________, 19___.

____

Notary Public

Reprinted with permission from Edmund O. Belsheim's *Modern Legal Forms*. Copyright © 1971 by West Publishing Co.

business. Courts have held that sales managers who sign partnership checks as limited partners but who do not have authority to hire or fire or set sale prices are not liable as general partners. A repair shop foreman who discussed business decisions with the general partner but who had no decision-making authority was held to be not liable as a general partner. However, a limited partner could be held liable as a general partner if she held herself out to the public as a general partner. Limited partners must make a capital contribution to the firm, not just services as in the case of a general partner.

A limited partner may inspect the partnership books and records, have his or her contribution returned in accordance with the certificate of limited partnership, and share in the profits of a solvent firm upon dissolution.

After the dissolution of a limited partnership, payments are made in the following order, according to the ULPA: first, payment to partnership creditors; second, payment to limited partners in respect to their share of the profits and other income earned on their contribution; third, payment to limited partners in respect to their capital contribution; fourth, payment to general partners other than for capital contribution and profits; fifth, payment to general partners for profits; and sixth, payment to general partners for their capital contribution.

In order to allow general partners to have limited liability, some states permit the general partners to incorporate. In such an instance, the general partners are employees and stockholders of the general partner corporation and are exempt from personal liability. The firm's creditors can reach only its business assets. The partners still want the tax shelter advantages of a limited partnership—the ability to deduct partnership losses, expenses, and depreciation allowances from their other income—so their lawyers obtain an advance ruling from the Internal Revenue Service to insure the tax benefits of a partnership. The Treasury has proposed taxing a limited partnership with more than thirty-five partners as if it were a corporation. In effect, that proposal would prevent large publicly offered partnerships from passing on tax writeoffs to limited partners for use in offsetting their income.

Keep in mind as you read the following case that not all states allow a corporation to be a general partner of a limited partnership. Pay attention to the court's reasoning in placing the burden on Frigidaire to obtain personal guarantees from the stockholders of the general partner corporation in order to hold them personally liable.

Frigidaire Sales Corp. v. Union Properties, Inc.

562 P.2d 244 (1977)

Facts

Frigidaire Sales Corp. entered into a contract with Commercial Investors (Commercial), a limited partnership. Leonard Mannon and Raleigh Baxter were limited partners of Commercial and were also officers, directors, and shareholders of Union Properties, Inc., the only general partner of Commercial. Mannon and Baxter controlled Union

Properties, and through their control of Union Properties they exercised the day-to-day control and management of Commercial. Commercial breached the contract with Frigidaire Sales Corp., and Frigidaire brought suit against Union Properties and against Mannon and Baxter individually.

Frigidaire Sales Corp. did not contend that Mannon and Baxter acted improperly by setting up the limited partnership with a corporation as the general partner.

Frigidaire's sole contention was that Mannon and Baxter should incur general liability for the limited partnership's obligations because they exercised the day-to-day control and management of Commercial. Mannon and Baxter, on the other hand, argued that Commercial was controlled by Union Properties, a separate legal entity, and not by them in their individual capacities.

Opinion

Associate Justice Hamilton: When the shareholders of a corporation, who are also the corporation's officers and directors, conscientiously keep the affairs of the corporation separate from their personal affairs, and no fraud or manifest injustice is perpetrated upon third persons who deal with the corporation, the corporation's separate entity should be respected.

For us to find that Mannon and Baxter incurred general liability for the limited partnership's obligations would require us to apply a literal interpretation of the statute and totally ignore the corporate entity of Union Properties, when petitioner knew it was dealing with that corporate entity. There can be no doubt that Mannon and Baxter, in fact, controlled the corporation. However, they did so only in their capacities as agents for their principal, the corporate general partner. Although the corporation was a separate entity, it could act only through its board of directors, officers, and agents. Frigidaire Sales Corp., entered into the contract with Commercial. Mannon and Baxter signed the contract in their capacities as president and secretary/treasurer of Union Properties, the general partner of Commercial. In the eyes of the law it was Union Properties, as a separate corporate entity, which entered into the contract with petitioner and controlled the limited partnership.

Further because Mannon and Baxter scrupulously separated their actions on behalf of the corporation from their personal actions, Frigidaire never mistakenly assumed that Mannon and Baxter were general partners with general liability. Frigidaire knew Union Properties was the sole general partner and did not rely on Mannon and Baxter's control by assuming that they were also general partners. If Frigidaire had not wished to rely on the solvency of Union Properties as the only general partner, it could have insisted that Mannon and Baxter personally guarantee contractual performance. Because Frigidaire Sales entered into the contract knowing that Union Properties was the only party with general liability, and because in the eyes of the law it was Union Properties, a separate entity, which controlled the limited partnership, there is no reason for us to find that Mannon and Baxter incurred general liability for their acts done as officers of the corporate general partner.

Case Questions

1. Section 1 of the Uniform Limited Partnership Act states, "A limited partnership is a partnership formed by two or more persons having as members one or more general partners and one or more limited partners." In this case Union Properties, Inc., was the sole general partner of the limited partnership, Commercial Investors, and its stockholders, Mannon and Baxter, were not personally liable for the contract with Frigidaire Sales Corp. Do you think it is ethically fair for general partners to incorporate, even though legally allowed to do so, for the sole purpose of avoiding personal liability?
2. What was the court's reasoning for holding against the plaintiff, Frigidaire Sales Corp.? Do you agree?
3. Give a legal reason why Mannon and Baxter did not simply form one corporation rather than a limited partnership with a corporation as the general partner.

Notice how the court in an earlier case in a different jurisdiction with a similar set of facts as *Frigidaire* reaches a contrary result.

Delaney v. Fidelity Lease Limited et al.

526 S. W. 2d 543 (1975)

Facts

Fidelity Lease Limited is a limited partnership organized under the Texas Uniform Limited Partnership Act to lease restaurant locations. It is composed of twenty-two individual partners, and a corporate general partner, Interlease Corporation. Interlease's officers, directors and shareholders were W. S. Crombie, Jr., Alan Kahn, and William D. Sanders, who were also limited partners of Fidelity. Plaintiff Delaney entered into an agreement with the limited partnership, Fidelity, acting by and through its corporate general partner, Interlease, to lease a fast-food restaurant to the partnership. In accordance therewith, plaintiff built the restaurant, but Fidelity failed to take possession or pay rent. Plaintiff brought suit for damages for breach of the lease agreement, naming as defendants the limited partnership of Fidelity Lease Limited, its corporate general partner Interlease Corporation, and all of its limited partners.

Opinion

Judge Daniel: Pertinent portions of the Texas Uniform Limited Partnership Act, Article 6132a, provide: "Sec. 8. A limited partner shall not become liable as a general partner unless, in addition to the exercise of his rights and powers as a limited partner, he takes part in the control of the business." It was alleged by the plainitff that the three limited partners controlled the business of the limited partnership, albeit through the corporate entity. The defendant limited partners argue that they acted only through the corporation and that the corporation actually controlled the business of the limited partnership. The defendant limited partners also contend that the "control" test enumerated in §8 of Article 6132a for the purpose of inflicting personal liability should be coupled with a determination of whether the plaintiff relied upon the limited partners as holding themselves out as general partners. Thus, they argue that, before personal liability attaches to limited partners, two elements must coincide: (1) the limited partner must take part in the control of the business; and (2) the limited partner must have held himself out as being a general partner having personal liability to an extent that the third party, or plaintiff, relied upon the limited partners' personal liability. They observe that there is no question in this case but that the plaintiff was in no way misled into believing that these three limited partners were personally liable on the lease, because the lease provided that the plaintiff was entering into the lease with Fidelity Lease, Ltd., a limited partnership acting by and through Interlease Corporation, General Partner. We disagree with this contention. Section 8 of Article 6132a simply provides that a limited partner who takes part in the control of the business subjects himself to personal liability as a general partner. The statute makes no mention of any requirement of reliance on the part of the party attempting to hold the limited partner personally liable. Crombie, Kahn, and Sanders argue that, since their only control of Fidelity's business was as officers, of the alleged corporate general partner, they are insulated from personal liability arising from their activities or those of the corporation. This is a general rule of corporate law, but one of several exceptions in which the courts will disregard the corporate fiction is where it is used to circumvent a statute. That is precisely the result here, for it is undisputed that the corporation was organized to manage and control the limited partnership. Strict compliance with the statute is required if a limited partner is to avoid liability as a general partner. In no event should they be permitted to escape the statutory liability which would have devolved upon them if there had been no attempted interposition of the corporate shield against personal liability. Otherwise, the statutory requirement of at least one general partner with liability in a limited partnership can be circumvented or vitiated by limited partners operating the partnership through a corporation with minimum capitalization and therefore minimum liability.

Case Questions

1. What was the argument of the three limited partners, Crombie, Kahn, and Sanders that they were insulated from personal liability under the lease?
2. Why did the court disregard the corporation, Interlease?
3. What ethical reasoning did the court use in disregarding the corporate entity?

Business Trust

In our discussion of sole proprietorships and partnerships, you will recall that the common disadvantage was the personal liability of the owners as either proprietors or general partners. We said that the land and building where the business operates are often held in trust to exclude the property from a business claim. Although the owners of the trust are usually the proprietor or partners in the business, creditors of the proprietorship or partnership cannot reach the business trust in an attempt to satisfy a claim against the business, because the trust is a separate legal entity from the business.

Similar to common law trust, a **business trust,** sometimes called a Massachusetts trust, is a legal device by which title to the trust property is held by trustees on behalf of trust beneficiaries. The trustees hold legal title to the property and administer and manage the trust for the beneficiaries, who hold transferable trust certificates and equitable interest in the trust, which means that the property is to be administered in accordance with the trust instrument solely for their benefit. The written trust instrument, called a **declaration of trust** (see figure 13.4), is generally recorded in the registry of deeds where the land is located.

The trustees must have the right to manage and control the trust without being controlled by the beneficiaries. For example, as the beneficiary/owner of a trust, you could carry on your partnership business in the building managed by the trustees but co-owned by you, your partners, and perhaps other investors. The partnership would pay rent to the trust, and the building would be managed by the trustees. You could sell your trust certificate to your partners in the event you decided to leave the firm. Tort or contract claims by creditors directly against the trust allow the plaintiff to recover both from the trust property and from the personal assets of the beneficiaries if they have the right to control the trust management, unless the beneficiaries have an agreement with the creditors to the contrary. This risk to a trust is often covered by an adequate liability insurance policy. Because trusts may have the corporate attributes of centralized management, transferability of shares, and limited liability of the owners, they are usually taxed as corporations. Hence, the ability of partners to deduct their proportionate share of expenses and losses from their taxes is not available to the beneficiaries of a trust. This can be a serious

Figure 13.4 Declaration of Trust

BUSINESS TRUST

1. *Declaration of Trust.* Made on ________, 19____ by ______________________________ [*insert names of five individuals*] as Trustees and __________________ (stockholders).

2. *Purpose.* The purpose of this Trust is that the Trustees shall acquire and manage properly the earnings, the proceeds of which will be divided into shares whose certificates are to be held by the shareholders.

3. *Name.* This Trust is to be named ______________ Company Unincorporated. It shall conduct all business under this name.

4. *Term of Office.* Of the five Trustees ________________, ________________, and ________________ will hold office until the first annual meeting of stockholders. ________________ and ________________ will hold office until the second annual meeting of stockholders.

Should a Trustee prove unable to fulfill his term of office, the remaining Trustees shall fill the vacancy for the unexpired term.

5. *Election of Trustees.* The Trustees are to be elected by the stockholders. Three are to be elected at the first annual meeting and two are to be elected at the second annual meeting. The election of Trustees shall follow this same pattern in alternative years thereafter.

6. *Trust Property.* Trust property is to be held by the Trustees in joint tenancy, with survivorship among the remaining Trustees upon the death, resignation, or removal of any of them.

The Trustees hold legal title to all property belonging to the Trust and have absolute control thereof.

7. *Powers.* The Trustees may engage in any business, including sale, exportation, manufacture, production purchase, or transportation of ______________________________ [*describe nature of Business Trust*]. The Trustees may enter into any contracts necessary to conduct the business, loan and borrow money, indemnify each other, and employ counsel and initiate suits at law, equity, or arbitration. ____________________ [*List other powers.*]

8. *Officers.* The Trustees will elect annually a President, Vice-President, Treasurer, and Secretary from their ranks. These Officers will have the authority and perform the duties usually incident to officers in a corporation. The Secretary shall keep a record of all stockholder, Trustee, and Officer's meetings.

9. *Certificates.* The beneficial interest in the Business Trust shall be held by the shareholders in the form of Certificates having a par value of $______ (dollars). These are to be considered personal property, to be passed on in such manner upon the death of a stockholder.

10. *Duration.* This Trust shall continue for a term of ________________ years, at which time the then Trustees shall wind up its affairs, liquidate its assets, and distribute them among the stockholders.

11. *Compensation.* The Trustees are to be compensated as follows: ____________________
____
____

12. *Amendments.* The stockholders may amend this Declaration of Trust by a two-thirds vote, at an annual or special meeting. However, the fact that Trustees, Officers, employees and stockholders are exempt from personal liability may not be amended.

____
____
____
____

Signatures of Trustees

Reprinted by permission from *Basic Legal Forms* by Marvin Hyman, 1981. Copyright © 1981, Warren, Gorham and Lamont, Inc., 210 South Street, Boston, Mass. All Rights Reserved.

disadvantage, because it deprives property owners of depreciation deductions that they would be allowed to take if the property were not held in trust.

In the following leading case, the United States Supreme Court explains the nature of a business trust. The trustees brought suit in the Federal District Court to recover damages for breach of a promissory note held in their name as trustees. The defendant, Navarro Savings Association, was a Texas firm. Some of the trust's beneficial shareholders were also Texas residents. Because federal court jurisdiction is based on diversity of citizenship the District Court dismissed the action for want of subject matter jurisdiction and claimed a business trust is a citizen of every State in which its shareholders reside. The U.S. Court of Appeals reversed and the trustees appealed to the U.S. Supreme Court. Notice how the court examines the written trust instrument to determine the trustees' powers and their authority over the trust property.

Navarro Savings Assn. v. Lee et al.

446 U.S. 458 (1980)

Facts

Respondents are eight individual trustees of Fidelity Mortgage Investors, a business trust organized under Massachusetts law. They hold title to real estate investments in trust for the benefit of Fidelity's shareholders. The declaration of trust gives the trustees exclusive authority over this property "free from any power and control of the Shareholders, to the same extent as if the Trustees were the sole owners of the Trust Estate in their own right." Trustees have power to transact Fidelity's business, execute documents, and "sue and be sued in the name of the Trust or in their names as Trustees of the Trust." They may invest the funds of the trust, lend money, and initiate or compromise lawsuits relating to the trust's affairs. In 1971 trustees lent $850,000 to a Texas firm in return for a promissory note payable to themselves as trustees. The note was secured by a commitment letter in which petitioner, Navarro Savings Association, agreed to lend the Texas firm $850,000 to cover its obligation to the Trustees. In 1973, the trustees called upon Navarro to make the "takeout" loan. Navarro refused, and this action followed.

Opinion

Judge Powell: Navarro contends that Fidelity's trust form masks an unincorporated association of individuals who make joint real estate investments. Navarro observes that certain features of the trust's operations also characterize the operations of an association; centralized management, continuity of enterprise, and unlimited duration. Arguing that this trust is in substance an association, Navarro reasons that the real parties to the lawsuit are Fidelity's beneficial shareholders. We need not reject the argument that Fidelity shares some attributes of an association. In certain respects, a business trust also resembles a corporation. But this case involves neither an association nor a corporation. Fidelity is an express trust, and the question is whether its trustees are real parties to this controversy for purposes of a federal court's diversity jurisdiction. A trustee is a real party to the controversy for purposes of diversity jurisdiction when he possesses certain customary powers to hold, manage, and dispose of assets for the benefit of others. The trustees in this case have such powers. At all relevant times, Fidelity operated under a declaration of trust that authorized the trustees to take legal title to trust assets, to invest those assets for the benefit of the shareholders, and to sue and be sued in their capacity as trustees. Trustees filed this lawsuit in that capacity. They seek damages for breach of an obligation running to the holder of a promissory note held in their own names. Fidelity's 9,500 beneficial shareholders had no voice in the initial investment decision. We conclude that these trustees are active trustees whose control over the assets held in their names is real and substantial. Nor does Fidelity's resemblance to a business enterprise alter the distinctive rights and duties of the trustees. There is no allegation of sham or collusion. The respondents are not "naked trustees" who act as "mere conduits" for a remedy flowing to others. They have legal title; they manage the assets; they control the litigation. In short, they are real parties to the controversy. For more than 150 years, the law has permitted trustees who meet this standard to sue in their own right without regard to the citizenship of the trust beneficiaries. The judgment of the Court of Appeals is affirmed.

Case Questions

1. Why did the Supreme Court conclude that although Fidelity resembled a business enterprise it was, in fact, a business trust?
2. The District Court claimed a business trust is a citizen of every state in which its shareholders (i.e., beneficiaries) reside. There were 9,500 shareholders of this trust. Why did the Supreme Court permit the trustees to sue in their own right without regard to the citizenship of the trust shareholders?
3. Is it ethical for a trust, similar to Fidelity Trust, to sue in its own name without the consent of its shareholders?

Corporation

If you and several associates were to start a retail business, your lawyer would probably recommend the *corporation* as the most appropriate form of business organization. The primary reason for this is that the corporation is a distinct legal entity, separate from the owner/shareholders. You could be a corporate officer, director, shareholder, and employee of the corporation and still enjoy limited liability. Your personal assets (home, bank accounts, car, etc.) would be exempt from liability in a claim against the business. Although there are some exceptions to this rule, from a liability viewpoint you and the co-workers in a corporation are in a far better position than proprietors or partners, who can be held *personally* liable to business creditors. You can also sell shares of stock without having the new stock owners participate in the direct management of the business. The ability to raise large sums of money by selling stock to the public, whose risk is limited to the amount of the investment, makes the corporation the best form of business organization for larger industry.

A **corporation** is a legal entity created by statute authorizing its officers and directors to carry on an enterprise; it has corporate powers to make contracts, own property, issue securities (stocks and bonds), and bring a lawsuit or be sued in its own name. The organization of a corporation requires compliance with state statutory law. The application for incorporation, called the **articles of organization** (see figure 13.5), is generally filed in the secretary of state's office.

Although we are primarily concerned with *business* organizations in this chapter, you will no doubt encounter a variety of different types of corporate

Figure 13.5 Structure of the Corporation

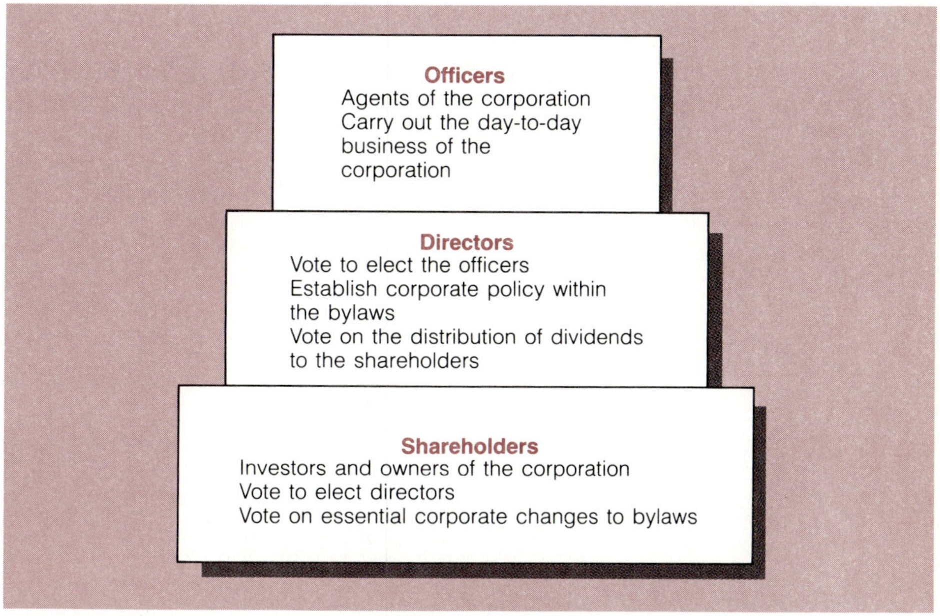

structures throughout your career. For instance, the college providing you with your education is an example of a *nonprofit corporation*. You may receive medical services from a *professional corporation* that is co-owned by your doctor and other licensed physicians. Hospital procedures are provided by the hospital as a nonprofit corporation. The company you work for may very well be a *private corporation* organized to conduct a business for profit. Finally, the city where you live may be a *public corporation*. Special state statutory laws govern the organization and operation of the various kinds of corporations. Corporate America is a suitable description of an economy that primarily uses the corporation to develop and transmit goods and services to its citizens.

Organization of a Corporation

The formation of a corporation occurs upon the filing of the articles of organization with the secretary of state's office, which grants authorization to incorporate (see figure 13.6). An **organizational meeting** is then held. At this meeting the bylaws (the rules governing the internal management of the corporation) are adopted, the stockholders elect directors, the directors elect officers, the issuance of stock and the form of stock certificates are authorized, a bank is selected to hold the corporate checking account, and the corporate seal is approved.

Figure 13.6 Example of Articles of Organization

The Commonwealth of Massachusetts

OFFICE OF THE MASSACHUSETTS SECRETARY OF STATE

MICHAEL JOSEPH CONNOLLY, Secretary

ONE ASHBURTON PLACE, BOSTON, MASS. 02108

ARTICLES OF ORGANIZATION

(Under G.L. Ch. 156B)

Incorporators

NAME **POST OFFICE ADDRESS**

Include given name in full in case of natural persons; in case of a corporation, give state of incorporation.

The above-named incorporator(s) do hereby associate (themselves) with the intention of forming a corporation under the provisions of General Laws, Chapter 156B and hereby state(s):

1. The name by which the corporation shall be known is:

2. The purpose for which the corporation is formed is as follows:

3. The total number of shares and the par value, if any, of each class of stock within the corporation is authorized as follows:

CLASS OF STOCK	WITHOUT PAR VALUE	WITH PAR VALUE		
	NUMBER OF SHARES	NUMBER OF SHARES	PAR VALUE	AMOUNT
Preferred				$
Common				

*4. If more than one class is authorized, a description of each of the different classes of stock with, if any, the preferences, voting powers, qualifications, special or relative rights or privileges as to each class thereof and any series now established:

*5. The restrictions, if any, imposed by the Articles of Organization upon the transfer of shares of stock of any class are as follows:

*6. Other lawful provisions, if any, for the conduct and regulation of business and affairs of the corporation, fc · its voluntary dissolution,or for limiting, defining, or regulating the powers of the corporation, or of its directors or stockholders, or of any class of stockholders:

Courtesy of Michael J. Connolly, Secretary. Office of the Massachusetts Secretary of State, Boston, MA.

Figure 13.6 *Continued*

7. By-laws of the corporation have been duly adopted and the initial directors, president, treasurer and clerk, whose names are set out below, have been duly elected.

8. The effective date of organization of the corporation shall be the date of filing with the Secretary of the Commonwealth or if later date is desired, specify date. (not more than 30 days after the date of filing.)

9. The following information shall not for any purpose be treated as a permanent part of the Articles of Organization of the corporation.

   a. The post office address of the initial principal office of the corporation of Massachusetts is:

   b. The name, residence, and post office address of each of the initial directors and following officers of the corporation are as follows:

	NAME	RESIDENCE	POST OFFICE ADDRESS
President:			
Treasurer:			
Clerk:			
Directors:			

   c. The date initially adopted on which the corporation's fiscal year ends is:

   d. The date initially fixed in the by-laws for the annual meeting of stockholders of the corporation is:

   e. The name and business address of the resident agent, if any, of the corporation is:

IN WITNESS WHEREOF and under the penalties of perjury the INCORPORATOR(S) sign(s) these Articles of Organization this day of 19

Corporation as a Legal Person

Once the articles of organization are filed, the corporation exists as a distinct legal person endowed with its own powers. The property owned by the corporation is not the property of the stockholders, its managers, or its directors, but is owned by the corporation in the corporate name. This separate and distinct legal entity status provides the stockholders with limited liability. Providing the officers and directors act within the state corporate law, the law of agency, and their fiduciary standards of behavior, they cannot be held personally liable for business claims.

Taxation of a Corporation

Unlike the sole proprietorship and partnerships, the corporation is a taxable entity and must pay state and federal corporate income taxes. (An exception will be discussed in the next paragraph.) The federal tax imposed for each taxable year on the corporation's income beginning after June 30, 1987, is 15 percent from 1 to $50,000, 25 percent from $50,001 to $75,000, 34 percent over $75,000, from $100,000 to $335,000 the tax rate is 5%. As a shareholder, you are required to pay personal income tax on any dividends you receive at your personal income tax rate. This double taxation, once at the corporate level and again at the shareholder level, is considered a disadvantage of the corporate form of business organization.

An **S corporation** is taxed differently. The Internal Revenue Code allows small, closely held corporations to be taxed in a manner similar to partnerships, and thereby to avoid paying any *federal* corporate income tax. For a corporation to be eligible for S corporation treatment under the Subchapter S Revision Act of 1982, (1) the number of permitted stockholders must not exceed thirty-five; (2) only one class of stock (e.g., voting as well as nonvoting common stock) is allowed; the corporation cannot issue both common and preferred stock; (3) all shareholders must consent to the election as an S corporation; and (4) corporations with royalty or rental income qualify only as long as they do not have accumulated earnings and profit at the close of the taxable year. Many small, closely held companies elect the Subchapter S treatment because of its federal tax benefits, although there may be state tax consequences.

Liability of Officers and Directors

Upon accepting a position as a corporate officer or director, you assume various legal duties and responsibilities; noncompliance with these could result in civil or criminal liability, or both. Remember that you can be held liable even without personal knowledge of a wrongdoing or an intent to violate the law.

Directors and officers must act within the common law fiduciary duties of due care and loyalty.

Directors can be sued by the corporation or, if it refuses to bring suit, by the stockholders in a derivative shareholders' action. A *derivative shareholders' action* is a lawsuit against the directors and officers for breach of their managerial duties resulting in a depletion of corporate assets. The Securities and Exchange Commission, other federal agencies, and the state attorney general's office may also sue the directors for wrongdoing, and may prosecute them for criminal conduct with resulting fines or imprisonment. Members of the board of directors may not act contrary to the articles of organization or the bylaws of the corporation. In some instances stockholders must ratify board actions, such as votes to increase the amount of authorized stock or to approve a corporate merger. Judgments on the declaration of dividends and appointing corporate officers are primary duties of the board. Because directors are exposed to so much liability by the common law, state law, administrative regulations, and federal statutes, many are obtaining liability insurance to indemnify their conduct. (See figure 13.7, Corporate Management.)

Common Law Duties of Officers and Directors as Fiduciaries

Officers and directors are fiduciaries of their corporation. Although they exercise independent business judgments, they owe their corporation the common law fiduciary duties of due care and loyalty. Statutory corporate laws generally define the duty of care as that which "an ordinary prudent person in a like position would exercise under similar circumstances; and when exercising a business judgment, with the belief, premised on a rational basis, that the decision is in the best interest of the corporation." The courts refer to this duty of care as the **business judgment rule.** Under this rule, an officer or director will not be held personally liable for an honest and rationally informed business judgment that turns out to be wrong. Many state statutes provide a "safe harbor" for officers and directors who make an *informed rational decision* based on a *reasonable inquiry* with respect to the business judgment and who acted in *good faith* without a *disabling conflict of interest*.

Directors, as a matter of sound economic and social policy, must be encouraged to be independent and to engage in innovative risk-taking ventures that will occasionally be contrary to the stockholders' desires. In the following case, the stockholders brought suit against the directors of the Chicago National League Ball Club, Inc., the owners of the Chicago Cubs. The stockholders alleged that the directors were negligent in not installing lights at Wrigley Field, which was owned by the corporation. This, the stockholders said, caused financial losses due to inadequate attendance at the Cubs' home games because of an absence of scheduled night baseball games. The directors agreed with the opinion of Mr. Wrigley, the corporate president, "that baseball is a daytime sport," and therefore they refused to install lights. When you read this case, make special note of the court's reason for applying the "business judgment rule" and its decision not to interfere with the board's decision.

Figure 13.7 Corporate Management

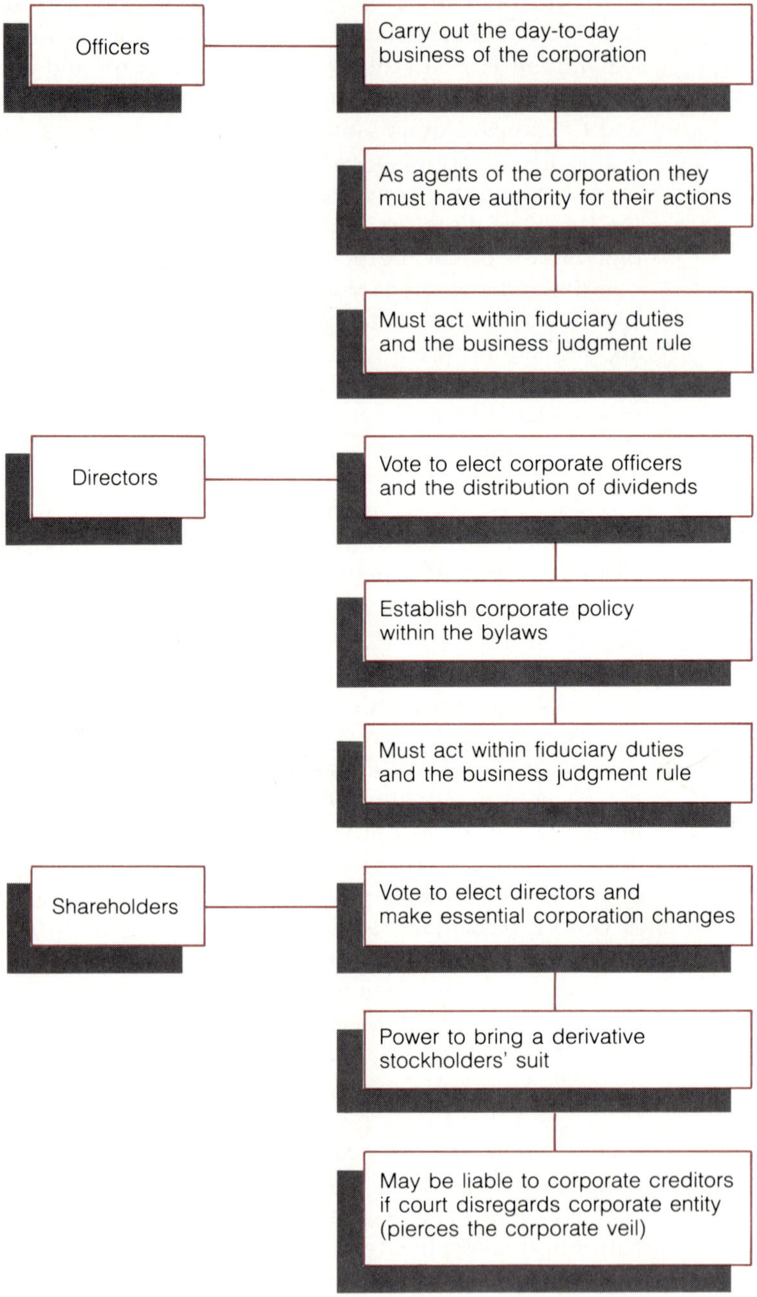

Shlensky v. Wrigley

237 N.E.2d 776 (1968)

Facts

Plaintiff was a minority stockholder of defendant corporation, Chicago National League Ball Club (Inc.). Defendant corporation owned and operated the major league professional baseball team known as the Chicago Cubs. The corporation also engaged in the operation of Wrigley Field, the Cubs' home park. The individual defendants were directors of the Cubs and had served for varying periods of years. Defendant Philip K. Wrigley was also president of the corporation and owner of approximately 80 percent of the stock therein.

Opinion

Justice Sullivan: Plaintiff alleges that since night baseball was first played in 1935, nineteen of the twenty major league teams have scheduled night games. In 1966, out of a total of 1,620 games in the major leagues, 932 were played at night. Plaintiff alleges that every member of the major leagues, other than the Cubs, scheduled substantially all of its home games in 1966 at night, exclusive of opening days, Saturdays, Sundays, holidays, and days prohibited by league rules. Allegedly this has been done for the specific purpose of maximizing attendance and thereby maximizing revenue and income.

The Cubs, in the years 1961–65, sustained operating losses from its direct baseball operations. Plaintiff attributes those losses to inadequate attendance at Cubs' home games. He concluded that if the directors continue to refuse to install lights at Wrigley Field and schedule night baseball games, the Cubs will continue to sustain comparable losses and their financial condition would continue to deteriorate.

Plaintiff alleges that, except for the year 1963, attendance at Cubs' home games has been substantially below that at their road games, many of which were played at night.

Plaintiff further alleges that defendant Wrigley has refused to install lights not because of interest in the welfare of the corporation but because of his personal opinions "that baseball is a 'daytime sport' and that the installation of lights and night baseball games will have a deteriorating effect upon the surrounding neighborhood." It is alleged that he has admitted that he is not interested in whether the Cubs would benefit financially from such action because of his concern for the neighborhood, and that he would be willing for the team to play night games if a new stadium were built in Chicago.

Plaintiff alleges that the other defendant directors, with full knowledge of the foregoing matters, have acquiesced in the policy laid down by Wrigley and permitted him to dominate the board of directors in matters involving the installation of lights and scheduling of night games, even though they knew he was not motivated by a good faith concern as to the best interests of defendant corporation, but solely by his personal views set forth above.

It is charged that the directors are acting for a reason or reasons contrary and wholly unrelated to the business interests of the corporation; that such arbitrary and capricious acts constitute mismanagement and waste of corporate assets, and that the directors have been negligent in failing to exercise reasonable care and prudence in the management of the corporate affairs.

This is an appeal from a dismissal of plaintiff's complaint on motion of the defendants. Plaintiff sought damages and an order that defendants cause the installation of lights in Wrigley Field and the scheduling of night baseball games.

We do not agree with plaintiff's contention that failure to follow the example of the other major league clubs in scheduling night games constituted negligence. Plaintiff made no allegation that these teams' night schedules were profitable or that the purpose for which night baseball had been undertaken was fulfilled. Furthermore, it cannot be said that directors, even those of corporations that are losing money, must follow the lead of the other corporations in the field. Directors are elected for their business capabilities and judgment and the courts cannot require them to forego their judgment because of the decisions of directors of other companies. Courts may not decide these questions in the absence of a clear showing of dereliction of duty on the part of the specific directors and mere failure to "follow the crowd" is not such a dereliction.

For the foregoing reasons the order of dismissal entered by the trial court is affirmed.

Case Questions

1. Is it ethical for the directors of a corporation that is losing money to continue an existing policy because of the insistence of a majority shareholder/director? Do you think Mr. Wrigley was giving preference to a social objective by refusing to install lights for night baseball games because of its "deteriorating effect upon the surrounding neighborhood"?
2. What was the court's reason for affirming the trial court's dismissal of plaintiff's complaint? Do you agree?
3. What kind of proof would be necessary to show that the directors engaged in a "clear dereliction of duty" by not installing lights in Wrigley Field? Was such evidence available to the plaintiff? If not, can this case be ethically justified?

This case approaches a judgment by the directors based on their perception of a social good, namely, concern for the neighborhood, in not installing lights. But the court avoided holding that directors may implement social welfare at shareholders' expense. It seems reasonable to argue that shareholders invest in a company to realize a return on their investment and may have a different point of view regarding social welfare. In any event, in 1988 Wrigley Field saw the light.

Within the tension caused by the directors' accountability to the stockholders and their obligation to make independent business judgments they are required to comply with a special duty of care and the business judgment rule. The Supreme Court of Delaware, a leader in corporate law, decided the following case that illustrates how the directors are presumed to have acted on an informed basis and in good faith with the honest belief that their decision was in the best interest of the corporation. This presumption of compliance with the business judgment rule was rebutted by the plaintiffs who proved the directors failed to inform themselves of all material information reasonably available to them. In this case involving a corporate merger, the directors never reviewed the merger documents, never had an outside valuation study made of the merger, and approved the merger at a quickly called meeting based on a twenty-minute oral presentation by the chairman of the board. This violated their duty to being informed and constituted gross negligence thereby rebutting compliance with the business judgment rule.

Directors are in a special position and owe a fiduciary duty to the corporation. Therefore they have an affirmative duty to protect the corporation's financial interests and a responsibility to view critically all transactions affecting the corporation. The mere absence of bad faith or fraud does not absolve directors of liability. The directors are liable, concluded the court, since their conduct amounted to at least gross negligence notwithstanding the profit they made. The court will not protect those whose judgment is unintelligent or unadvised.

Smith v. Van Gorkom

488 A. 2d 858 (Del. 1985)

Facts

This suit arises out of a class action brought by shareholders of a corporation seeking rescission of the merger, or alternatively, damages. The defendant, Jerome W. Van Gorkom (chairman and CEO of TUC) devised a scheme for a merger of TUC into a company with a high capital income, disclosing this to only a few senior TUC personnel. Donald Romans, TUC's chief financial officer, performed a "very brief bit of work" on this scheme and merely "ran the numbers" based upon rough calculations to determine feasibility.

Van Gorkom seized upon the figure of $55 per share as the sole measure of TUC's valuation. In fact, this merely represented the averages of rough calculations Romans made when figuring the cash flow needed for a leveraged buy-out, rather than a fair price for the company. It is notable that Van Gorkom was about to retire, and personally stood to gain over $4 million based upon a sale of stock at $55 per share.

Van Gorkom met with Jay A. Pritzker, a well-known corporate takeover specialist, regarding the possibility of Pritzker acquiring TUC. Van Gorkom's actions relating to a fundamental corporate change took place without consulting the board of directors. Pritzker became interested in the merger proposal and moved swiftly. Van Gorkom failed to apprise TUC's legal staff of the merger proposal. He finally reported the negotiations to senior management, whose reaction was completely negative. Later, Van Gorkom presided over a special meeting of the board of directors. He provided no reports ahead of time, nor had he given advance notice to all members of the board as to the subject of the meeting. Van Gorkom did not invite Salomon Brothers, TUC's investment bankers, or TUC's Chicago-based partner.

At the special meeting, Van Gorkom announced Pritzker's interest in a merger agreement and the terms, but supplied neither a copy of the agreement nor the methodology used to compute the price. Further, he failed to disclose that he actually proposed the price to Pritzker. The board took only two hours to approve the proposed merger, based upon oral presentations, although the board claimed to have attached conditions to its acceptance. Van Gorkom signed the merger agreement at a formal social event, even though neither he nor any director read the agreement prior to its signing.

Subsequently, senior management's dissension forced Pritzker to accept modifications of the merger agreement. Again the TUC board approved of the modified agreement, sight unseen. The plaintiff shareholders commenced suit seeking to block the proposed merger; however, the board voted to proceed with it.

Opinion

Judge Horsey: We turn to the issue of the application of the business judgment rule to the meeting of the Board. Under Delaware law, the business judgment rule is the offspring of the fundamental principle . . . that the business and affairs of a . . . corporation are managed by or under its board of directors.

[D]irectors are charged with an unyielding fiduciary duty to the corporation and its shareholders. The rule itself "is a presumption that in making a business decision, the directors of a corporation acted on an informed basis, in good faith and in the honest belief that the action taken was in the best interests of the company. Thus, the party attacking a board decision as uninformed must rebut the presumption that its business judgment was an informed one.

Under the business judgment rule there is no protection for directors who have made "an unintelligent or unadvised judgment." A director's duty to inform himself in preparation for a decision derives from the fiduciary capacity in which he serves the corporation and its stockholders. [H]e must execute that duty with the recognition that he acts on behalf of others. Such obligation does not tolerate faithlessness or self-dealing. But fulfillment of the fiduciary function requires more than the mere absence of bad faith or fraud. Representation of the financial interests of others imposes on a director an affirmative duty to protect those interests and to proceed with a critical eye in assessing information of the type and under the circumstances present here.

Thus, a director's duty to exercise an informed business judgment is in the nature of a duty of care, as distinguished from a duty of loyalty.

[D]irector liability is predicated upon concepts of gross negligence.

We think the concept of gross negligence is also the proper standard for determining whether a business judgment reached by a board of directors was an informed one.

In the specific context of a proposed merger of domestic corporations, a director has a duty . . . to act in an informed and deliberate manner in determining whether to approve an agreement of merger before submitting the proposal to the stockholders.

It is against those standards that the conduct of the directors of Trans Union must be tested. . . .

On the record before us, we must conclude that the Board of Directors did not reach an informed business judgment . . . in voting to "sell" the Company for $55 per share pursuant to the Pritzker merger proposal. Our reasons, in summary, are as follows:

The directors (1) did not adequately inform themselves as to Van Gorkom's role in forcing the "sale" of the Company and in establishing the per share purchase price; (2) were uninformed as to the intrinsic value of the Company; and (3) given these circumstances, at a minimum, were grossly negligent in approving the "sale" of the Company upon two hours' consideration, without prior notice, and without the exigency of a crisis or emergency.

For the foregoing reasons, we conclude that the director defendants breached their fiduciary duty of candor by their failure to make true and correct disclosures of all information they had, or should have had, material to the transaction submitted for stockholder approval.

Case Questions

1. The court stated "director liability is predicated upon concepts of gross negligence." Why did the court find that the corporate board was grossly negligent and hence not protected by the business judgment rule?
2. Would the corporate board be protected, with the same set of facts, by the Delaware Statute in figure 13.8?
3. Is it ethical for a state to allow a provision in the certificate of incorporation that eliminates the personal liability of a director for breach of a fiduciary duty? What are the social effects of this type of statute?

Reaction to the *Van Gorkom* case was generally not favorable. Directors have always had the security of knowing the business judgment rule would shield them from liability for honest errors made in carrying out their official corporate duties. The *Van Gorkom* decision has destroyed the traditional legal shield protecting the board since they can now be held liable for acts of gross negligence. Many directors fear their personal assets are at risk especially with the prohibitive cost of directors' and officers' liability insurance. The following is a typical comment by the corporate bar.

> The Delaware Supreme Court in *Van Gorkom* exploded a bomb: Stated minimally, the court there pierced the business judgment rule and imposed individual liability on independent (even eminent) outside directors of Trans Union Corporation because (roughly) the court thought they had not been careful enough, and had not enquired enough, before deciding to accept and recommend to Trans Union's shareholders a cashout merger at a per-share price that was less than the "intrinsic

value" of the shares. The corporate bar generally views the decision as atrocious. Commentators predict dire consequences as directors come to realize how exposed they have become.

[Bayless Manning, *The Business Lawyer,* vol. 41 (Nov. 1985)]

Many States have enacted legislation similar to the Delaware Code (see figure 13.8, Del. Code Ann. S102 (b) (7) allowing limited liability of directors) to eliminate or limit the personal liability of the corporate directors for breach of a fiduciary duty as a director.

Indemnification of Corporate Board

Because of board members' exposure to personal liability for their acts, many companies are providing indemnification for any costs incurred by directors exercising their duties. State laws commonly provide authorization for corporate indemnification. For instance, the Delaware statute, sec. 145 (a), states in part that a director may be indemnified who "acted in good faith and in a manner he reasonably believed to be in or not opposed to the best interests of the corporation, and with respect to any criminal action or proceeding, had no reasonable cause to believe his conduct was unlawful." A company will often purchase directors' insurance coverage from a third party insurance carrier to fund this indemnification.

A **conflict of interest** can arise when a director makes an individual contract with the corporation with which he serves, or when he is a member of interlocking boards—that is, he sits on two or more corporate boards and approves transactions between those corporations. State laws generally allow such a contract if it is fair and reasonable to the corporation and if the "conflicting" relationship is disclosed to the corporate board and to stockholders if they must

Figure 13.8 Delaware Law Allowing the Elimination of Directors' Liability

DEL. CODE ANN. § 102(b)(7) (1983 & Supp. 1986). In addition to the matters required to be set forth in the certificate of incorporation . . . the certificate of incorporation may also contain any or all of the following matters . . . a provision eliminating or limiting the personal liability of a director to the corporation or its stockholders for monetary damages for breach of fiduciary duty as a director, provided that such provision shall not eliminate or limit the liability of a director (i) for any breach of the director's duty of loyalty to the corporation or its stockholders, (ii) for acts or omissions not in good faith or which involve intentional misconduct or a knowing violation of law, (iii) under section 174 of the Title, or (iv) for any transaction from which the director derived an improper personal benefit. No such provision shall eliminate or limit the liability of a director for any act or omission occurring prior to the date when such provision becomes effective. All references in this subsection to a director shall also be deemed to refer to a member of the governing body of a corporation which is not authorized to issue capital stock.
The statute became effective on August 1, 1986.

approve the contract. Courts place the burden on the director to prove that the contract was fair and reasonable and that adequate disclosure was made to the appropriate parties.

The **corporate opportunity doctrine** prohibits directors from using their positions of trust with the stockholders to make a profit for themselves. The fiduciary duty of loyalty requires directors to make a full disclosure to the board and/or to stockholders and to obtain their approval before seizing a self-serving corporate opportunity. Failure to do so will result in the director's being held liable to the corporation and/or to the stockholders for any profits made from taking advantage of the corporate opportunity. For example, a director of a real estate company may not purchase for herself a piece of property that the board is considering as an investment unless she receives the board's approval.

Federal Statutory Duties of Directors

Employee Retirement Income Security Act of 1974. ERISA extends the common law fiduciary duties of a director to employees of a corporation and to the beneficiaries of the employees' pension plans. Although the board can assign to a committee the administration of the plan, it cannot delegate the responsibility of reviewing the committee's findings to ensure that the plan is administered in a reasonable manner. Directors must become adequately informed about the administrative policies of employee plans and must carefully review their periodic reports. The Department of Labor, the plan employees, and the employees' beneficiaries may sue the directors for violating their fiduciary duties as defined by the statute.

Securities Exchange Act of 1934. The SEA includes a corporate director within its definition of an "insider" who may have access to confidential corporate information that could allow him or her to make a profit by the purchase or sale of the corporate securities. If the company has securities registered with the Securities and Exchange Commission (SEC), the directors must file a report with the SEC at the end of any month when they purchase or sell the corporate securities. The corporation or its shareholders may sue the directors as "insiders" to recover *short-swing* profits—profits made by an insider on the sale of a security that was held for less than six months.

Foreign Corrupt Practices Act. The FCPA requires corporations that report to the SEC to comply with specific accounting provisions; it also prohibits any interstate business association, including those not subject to the act, from engaging in corrupt practices with foreign officials. The antibribery section of the act applies to directors of any corporation engaged in interstate commerce who corruptly pay any official of a foreign government for the purpose of influencing any decision in order to obtain or retain business. Violation of the act may subject a director to civil as well as criminal liability. Conviction for a willful violation of the act could mean a fine of up to $100,000 and/or imprisonment for up to five years. For more detailed discussion of the FCPA, see page 571.

Audit Committee. Any company with a listing on the New York Stock Exchange must maintain "an Audit Committee comprised solely of directors independent of management. . . . Directors who are affiliates of the company or officers or employees of the company or its subsidiaries would not be qualified for Audit Committee membership." The **audit committee** should recommend to management the accounting firm to be employed as the independent auditor. The committee's primary responsibility is to review the corporation's annual and quarterly financial statements that are filed with the SEC or other regulatory bodies, and to review those statements issued to shareholders and creditors. Failure of a corporate board whose company is listed on the New York Stock Exchange to install an audit committee would subject it to liability for violation of its duty of care if the corporation suffered a loss that might have been prevented had there been an audit committee. The board may, in discharging its duties, rely on committee information and reports, providing the directors reasonably believe the committee is "reliable, competent, and disinterested."

Shareholders

Shareholders purchase stock in a corporation and acquire certain rights that generally include: (1) the right to vote for directors at shareholders' meetings; (2) the right to receive a dividend if one is declared; (3) the right to inspect corporate books; (4) the right to transfer the stock; (5) the right to sue the corporation for improper action; and (6) the right to share in the profits upon dissolution.

Right to Vote

Shareholders have the right to vote for the directors and on other appropriate matters at their annual meeting or at any duly called special stockholders' meeting. The right to vote may be denied to any class of stock in the articles of incorporation, in which event a stockholder has *nonvoting shares*. Changes in the articles of incorporation require directors' and stockholders' approval and the amended articles to be filed at the office of the Secretary of State. For example, a corporate name change or recapitalization generally requires approval by a majority of the stockholders

Dividends

If you were to invest in a corporation as a stockholder, you would expect a return on your investment by way of a **dividend** and an increase in the market value of the stock. A dividend is a portion of the corporate net profits or *surplus* set aside for distribution to the shareholders. It is within the discretion of the directors to declare a dividend, but it is not to be declared when the corporation is insolvent. *Until a dividend is declared by the board of directors, the stockholders have no right to receive one.* If the directors refuse to declare a dividend and have clearly abused their discretion by continuously voting against a "declaration," a court may require the payment of a dividend.

Right to Inspect Corporate Books

The common law granted to a shareholder the right to inspect the corporate books and records at reasonable times for a proper purpose. It is the "proper purpose" aspect of this right that frequently causes a problem. For example, may a public interest group, such as the environmentalists, purchase a block of stock (100 shares) in a corporation and demand the right to review the minute book of the board of directors and shareholders? Generally no, because a shareholder does not demonstrate a "proper purpose" by disapproving of a corporate activity such as a manufacturing company causing a high rate of pollution.

Financial Statements

An inspection of the corporate books may include the minutes of the directors' and stockholders' meetings, the stock transfer books, and the books of account. Due to their personal nature, we have seen most states require a "proper purpose" to inspect. There is generally no such limitation to the shareholders' right to receive financial statements showing the corporation's assets, liabilities, and operations.

Transfer of Shares

The rights and duties of corporations and stockholders to transfer stock is governed by Article 8 of the Uniform Commercial Code. Article 8 was revised in 1977 to include a security investment not represented by a written certificate defined as an "uncertificated security." The issuance of an "uncertificated security" is *registered* upon the security transfer book maintained by the corporation. An *initial transaction statement* is then sent to the shareholder. The Official Comment to the Uniform Commercial Code, section 8–101 states: "This Article does not purport to determine whether a particular issue of securities should be represented by certificates, in whole or in part. That determination is left to the parties involved, subject to federal and state law."

Transfer of Uncertificated Securities. An uncertificated security is transferred by the transferor (seller) instructing the corporation to issue a *transaction statement* to the new owner (or pledgee) and register the transaction on its transfer ledger. *Within two business days after the registration of a transferred uncertificated security,* the corporation must send the new registered owner (or registered pledgee) and the transferor a *transaction statement*. The transaction statement serves as registration notice to the new owner and a reduction of interest notice to the transferor-seller.

A *periodic statement* must be sent at least annually to the registered owners describing the issuance of which the uncertificated security is a part.

Transfer of Certificated Securities. To effect a proper transfer of a certificated security (stock certificate), the transferor-seller must deliver the certificate and if necessary endorse it over to the purchaser. If the transfer is of a temporary nature (e.g., a pledge of the stock as security for a bank loan), the owner may make the assignment on a separate instrument which requires delivery of both the separate document pledging the stock and the stock certificate.

Restrictions on Transfer. The incorporators of a closely held corporation may decide to issue its stock to select shareholders. For instance, a family business may desire to keep control of its ownership and management. The articles of incorporation and the bylaws may state a restriction allowing the corporation or its shareholders the right to purchase the stock before it is offered to outsiders. The selling price may be established in accordance with a specified formula stated in the text of the restriction or it may be the current market price. Restrictions on the transfer of stock are generally valid if they are conspicuous and reasonable. Because a purchaser is generally not aware of restrictions in the articles of incorporation or bylaws, the stock certificate must conspicuously note the restriction, unless the buyer has actual knowledge of it, in order for it to be effective.

Stockholders' Derivative Suit. As a shareholder you may individually, or with other minority shareholders, bring an action on behalf of the corporation against the directors and officers on the basis of breach of their managerial fiduciary duties resulting in a depletion of corporate assets. You must procedurally first prove that, on proper demand, the corporation refused to bring suit against the officers and/or directors for mismanagement. This means you must first exhaust your internal corporate remedies. You do this by first requesting the board of directors to take proper action, unless it would be futile to do so (e.g., a majority of the board are involved in the wrong, or are prejudiced). If such a request is unsuccessful or futile, then you must request the shareholders at a corporate meeting to take proper action, unless it would be futile to do so (e.g., a majority are involved in the wrong, or a majority are biased). You may also bring an action on behalf of the corporation against an outside person if the corporation wrongfully refuses to do so. Such actions are called "derivative" actions. In both instances the right to sue and damages awarded belong to the corporation.

Stockholders' Direct Suit. If as a shareholder you were deprived of a rightful incident of share ownership (e.g., the right to vote, a claim to compel dividends wrongfully withheld, a claim that a corporate action is *ultra vires*, an action to inspect corporate books and records) you would have a direct action claim against the corporation. Damages are awarded to you as an individual in a direct action suit. If such a wrong were perpetrated upon other shareholders as well as yourself, you could bring an action on behalf of yourself and the other shareholders against the corporation. This is called a "class" or "representative" action.

An Ethical Perspective on Forms of Business Organizations

While nobody would deny that business organizations are in business to make a profit, the methods used to meet that objective will always be subjected to ethical examination. In this chapter we have discussed certain legal constraints in the organizational and operational makeup of various forms of business organizations. We emphasized in the introduction that business organizations function in relationships that involve the entire community. It is these relationships that create moral and ethical obligations, because it is people who comprise, operate, and are affected by business organizations. Legal standards for business often establish only minimum levels of responsibility—hence the need for managers to acquire a sense of social responsibility that complements their legal obligations.

An area of both ethical and legal concern is government regulation of business that, some argue, can make it impossible for companies to generate needed capital. Has government overregulated business? Or is more regulation necessary? This topic will be discussed in more detail in part 4. Do state corporation statutes grant to corporate boards greater power than necessary without effective accountability to the stockholders, consumers, and the community? This will be discussed in part 5. The 1983 Revised Model Business Corporation Act, sec. 8.30, *General Standards for Directors,* states, "A director shall discharge his duties . . . in good faith [and] with the care an ordinarily prudent person in a like position would exercise under similar circumstances, and when exercising his business judgment, with the belief, premised on a rational basis, that his decision is in the best interests of the corporation." Does this codification of the business judgment rule protect directors who refuse to recognize a corporate social responsibility? Does the "best interest of the corporation" support Professor Friedman's thesis of increased profits being the only social responsibility of business? To what extent, if any, does our legal system discourage a more responsible managerial attitude toward social issues? As you read this text, try to understand the legal environment of business as one of relationships with moral and ethical obligations going beyond the organizational structure.

The important concepts and terms in this chapter are listed below; page numbers have been provided for the key terms. By reading over each section you can assess your understanding of the chapter concepts and determine areas you may want to review.

Chapter Summary

1. The most common types of business organizations are (a) the sole proprietorship, (b) the general partnership, (c) the limited partnership, (d) the business trust, and (e) the corporation.
2. In a sole proprietorship, the individual owner manages the business for a profit and is personally liable for any legal claims brought against the

business. Its primary advantages are complete managerial control and legal simplicity in its operation. However, the primary disadvantage is that the owner is personally liable for claims brought against the business.

3. A general partnership is a contractual agreement between competent parties to combine their capital and/or services in a business and to share in the profits and losses. The owners, as partners, must have the right to participate in the management of the business as well as share in the net profits.
4. In addition to compliance with the terms of the articles of partnership, a partner must act within the implied fiduciary duties of loyalty and reasonable care.
5. Partners incur unlimited personal liability for business contracts and torts committed in the ordinary course of partnership business. This is generally considered a disadvantage of doing business as a partnership.
6. A partnership may own personal and real property as tenancy in partnership with distinct statutory consequences. In general, such ownership gives ownership preference to the partners rather than to the partners' personal creditors or a deceased partner's spouse.
7. A partnership dissolution is "a change in the relation of the partners caused by any partner ceasing to be associated in the carrying on . . . of business." The winding-up process begins upon a dissolution that entitles a partner or a deceased partner's spouse to his partnership interest and distributive share of the profits.
8. A limited partnership is formed in writing by two or more persons, and has as members one or more general and one or more limited partners. The general partners conduct the business affairs and are personally liable to partnership creditors. Limited partners are not personally liable provided they do not participate in the firm's management.
9. A business trust is a legal device that enables title to the trust property to be held by trustees on behalf of trust beneficiaries. The trustees hold legal title to the property and administer and manage the trust for the beneficiaries, who hold transferable trust certificates and equitable title to the trust.
10. A corporation is a legal entity created by statute authorizing its officers and directors to carry on an enterprise with corporate powers.
11. A Subchapter S corporation is a tax election by a small corporation (thirty-five or fewer shareholders) to be taxed in a similar manner to a partnership and thereby to avoid paying any federal corporate income tax.
12. Corporate directors are not liable for damages when their honest business judgments cause financial loss to the corporation. They can be held liable for negligence or for taking advantage of a corporate opportunity.
13. State law often authorizes corporations to indemnify directors and officers for any costs they incur in exercising their corporate duties,

providing they acted in good faith and in a manner they reasonably believed to be in the best interest of the corporation.

14. Shareholders have rights that generally include a right to vote, to receive dividends if declared, to inspect corporate books, to sell their stock, to sue the corporation and its board of directors for improper behavior, and to share in the profits upon dissolution.

Key Terms

articles of organization 346
articles of partnership 327
audit committee 359
business certificate 327
business judgment rule 351
business trust 343
conflict of interest 357
corporate opportunity doctrine 358
corporation 346
declaration of trust 343
dissolution 337
dividend 359
general partnership 327
limited partnership 338
organizational meeting 347
partnership by estoppel 333
partnership property 336
S corporation 350
sole proprietorship 325
tenancy in partnership 336
termination 337
winding up 337

Questions on Ethics

1. You are one of three partners in a computer consulting firm. Each of you has signed a written partnership agreement. One of your associates enjoys working weekends and casually mentioned to you that she expects to be paid a bonus at the end of the year. Your lawyer has informed you that partners are not entitled to extra compensation beyond what their agreement provides and a sharing in the profits. Would you feel ethically obliged to inform your partner that she will not be paid a bonus for the extra work?
2. You have just joined a CPA tax accounting firm as a new partner. Prior to joining the firm you had a successful accounting practice. You would like to continue working with your own clients during evenings and weekends. Would you feel ethically obliged to inform the tax accounting partnership of your private tax practice if nobody asked you about it? Do you see a relationship between your fiduciary duties as a partner and an ethical duty to your associates?
3. Assume you are a director in a corporation that has an opportunity to obtain a $500,000 contract with a foreign government. An agent of the foreign government has informed you that to place the contract he will

require $10,000 in cash. Your lawyer has informed you that this would violate the antibribery section of the Foreign Corrupt Practices Act. You think the $10,000 is a commission and not a bribe. Give an ethical argument distinguishing a bribe from a commission. Do you have an ethical obligation to follow the advice of the attorney who explained that the transaction would be considered a bribe under the Foreign Corrupt Practices Act?

4. Is it ethical for the Delaware statute to authorize corporate indemnity for a director for *criminal action* so long as the director "had no reasonable cause to believe his conduct was unlawful?"
5. Do you think it is ethical for a business person to put her property in trust to avoid paying *potential* creditors? Do you think it is ethical to place property in trust to avoid paying *actual* creditors? Does the law allow a person to do so in either or both situations?

Questions on Law

1. The directors of Unity Savings Association referred its customers who needed insurance to an insurance agency in the bank's office building that was organized and owned by the directors. Kerrigan, a shareholder of Unity Savings, brought suit, alleging the wrongful use of a corporate opportunity without first offering it to the corporation. May directors take advantage of a corporate opportunity for themselves without first offering it to the corporation? Support your decision with the legal theory regarding a corporate opportunity. What, if anything, could the directors have done to avoid liability? Establish an ethical argument for or against the directors' conduct. *Kerrigan* v. *Unity Savings Assn.*, 58 Ill. 2d 20 (1974).
2. Several AT&T shareholders brought suit against the directors for breach of their fiduciary duty in not attempting to collect a $1.5 million corporate debt owed AT&T by the Democratic National Convention. Forgiveness of the debt was an illegal campaign contribution under federal law. The directors alleged they made a valid business decision under the business judgment rule. Decide. Your answer should include an ethical argument for or against the legal theory of the business judgment rule. *Miller* v. *American Telephone & Telegraph Co.* 507 F.2d 759 (1974).
3. Mary Epic is one of ten shareholders of a corporation organized and operated as a retail sporting goods store. All of the stock is common, but five of the ten shareholders own nonvoting Class B common stock. Corporate income consists of sales from inventory and some rental income from a small portion of the store that is sublet. Mary has heard of an S corporation and asks you what it is and does she qualify for S corporation status? Advise.

4. Steve Larner is a partner in Larner, O'Tool and Epic, an accounting firm located in Boston. Steve has notified the firm of his intention to leave and join a local college as a full-time accounting professor. What is the legal effect of this incident? What, if anything, is Steve entitled to upon leaving the partnership? Assume there is no "buy-and-sell agreement" among the partners.
5. Betty Mitchell and Harry Willard were partners in a dental practice. They signed a partnership agreement providing, among other things, that each partner would contribute equally to the capital of the firm in the form of dental equipment, that compensation would be paid as agreed annually, that all debts and obligations of the partnership would be shared equally, and that all profits would be distributed equally. Betty filed suit for the dissolution and an accounting of the partnership. Betty claimed she was entitled to extra compensation for working evenings and giving up her summer vacation. Is Betty entitled to be paid for her extra time spent in performing partnership business?

Suggested Readings

Epstein. "The Corporate Social Policy Process and the Process of Corporate Governance," 25 *American Business Law Journal* 3 (1987)

Kempin. "The Problem of Control in Limited Partnership Law: An Analysis and Recommendation," 22 *American Business Law Journal* 443 (1985).

Rodewald. "The Corporate Social Responsibility Debate: Unanswered Questions about the Consequences of Moral Reform," 25 *American Business Law Journal* 3 (1987)

3 The Legal Environment of Employer-Employee Relations

14 The Employment Relationship

"A fair day's-wages for a fair day's-work": it is as just a demand as governed men ever made of governing. It is the everlasting right of man.

—Thomas Carlyle

LEARNING OBJECTIVES

After you have read this chapter, you should be able to:

1. Understand how workers' compensation acts function.
2. Be familiar with these federal statutory programs that regulate certain aspects of the employment relationship: the Fair Labor Standards Act, unemployment compensation, Social Security, ERISA, and the Occupational Safety and Health Act.
3. Be able to understand how the traditional view of "employment at will" has continued to be the dominant attitude toward the employment relationship.
4. Be able to appreciate some of the ethical questions that maintenance of a laissez-faire attitude toward the employment relationship has created.

Business Decisions and the Law

The Fate of a Whistle Blower

Sheets was a quality control manager for Teddy's Frosted Foods, Inc., a producer of frozen food items. While doing his job, Sheets became aware that Teddy's was violating various provisions of the state food act. When Sheets complained about the violations, he was fired. Sheets sued for monetary damages, claiming that he had been wrongfully discharged. Will he win? See *Sheets* v. *Teddy's Frosted Foods*.

Introduction

One hundred years ago, employees in the United States often worked fourteen-hour days, with no health or retirement benefits, and if they were injured on the job, they were often fired. Today, maximum hour and minimum wage laws protect workers from exploitation, and a system of workers' compensation guarantees that injured workers will obtain financial support. In the nineteenth century, employer-employee relationships were viewed as a private affair, in which the government should not intervene. The practical result of this view was that the workers were at a great disadvantage when they negotiated with management over their terms and conditions of employment. The workers did not have equality of bargaining power with management, because labor was so plentiful that management could always find new workers. An oversupply of labor resulted in wages, salaries, and terms of employment that were unfavorable to workers.

The passage of state and federal laws has changed the employer-employee relationship from a purely private matter to one in which employees have certain guaranteed rights. You should note that while the laws that we will discuss guarantee workers certain rights, the employer-employee relationship is still regarded primarily as a private affair in our country. This chapter deals mainly with two topics: statutory regulation of employment relations in certain areas, and areas of ethical concern where there is no legal regulation. Several other chapters in this book treat specific aspects of the employment relationship completely or in part. Those chapters that you have already studied are Contracts and Business Transactions (chapters 9 and 10) and Agency Relationships (chapter 11). Two succeeding chapters that concern specific aspects of the employment relationship are Equal Employment Opportunity (chapter 15) and Business and Labor Unions (chapter 16).

The Legal Regulation of the Employment Relationship

Workers' Compensation Laws

One of the most striking aspects of the nineteenth-century attitude toward employer-employee relations concerned the rights of an employee injured on the job. An injured employee had a right to sue the employer under the common law and to recover damages if he could prove that the employer had committed a legal wrong against him. The legal theory most often used by employees was the tort theory of negligence, which was based on the idea that the employer had breached a duty of care he owed to his employees, for example, by using unsafe equipment. (A discussion of the tort of negligence is contained in chapter 25 on product liability.)

The problems that an injured worker faced in recovering damages for job injuries were almost insurmountable. First of all, the worker had to hire a lawyer to sue the employer in court. Usually, the injured worker did not have the money to hire a lawyer, so he could not sue the employer. If the worker did secure a lawyer, the burden of proof was on him to prove in court that the employer was negligent. For example, suppose that the worker lost an arm when he fell into a piece of machinery that was not protected by a guard rail. He would have to prove that the employer was negligent in exposing him to an unreasonable risk of harm by not protecting against a foreseeable danger. Even if the employee could prove the employer was negligent, the employer had three defenses he could use to avoid liability: **contributory negligence, assumption of the risk,** and the **fellow servant doctrine.** Any one of these defenses was a complete bar to the employee's recovery of damages. Thus, in this example, even if the employee could prove that the employer was negligent, the employee could not recover any money damages from the employer if the employer could prove one of the following: (1) the employee was not looking where he was going when he slipped and fell into the machine (*contributory negligence*); (2) the employee knew that working around that machinery was dangerous because he had witnessed similar injuries to others, but he continued to work around the machinery anyway (*assumption of the risk*); or (3) the worker was injured because another employee accidentally knocked him into the machine (*fellow servant doctrine*). As you can imagine, use of these defenses usually resulted in employers' winning lawsuits brought by injured workers and discouraged other workers from suing.

Public dissatisfaction with the perceived unfairness of preventing injured workers from recovering for their work-related injuries resulted in the states' passing **workers' compensation** acts. While the provisions of these acts vary from state to state, they all have similar characteristics. The most important aspect of these acts is that they guarantee recovery for job-related injuries and they abolish the three common law employer defenses just discussed. Today, any worker injured on the job can recover under workers' compensation if she can prove that her injury was work-related. There is a growing trend today to allow recovery for mental illness caused by working conditions, even if the illness does not have physical manifestations. Indeed, about the only "defense" an employer now has available is that the employee was not injured while carrying out his employment duties. In the following case, a court had to decide whether a worker on an employer's premises before the workday commenced was entitled to workers' compensation benefits.

Richard A. McNamara v. *Town of Hamden et al.*

176 Conn. 547 (1979)

Facts

This appeal presents a question under the Workmen's Compensation Act: whether an injury sustained while the plaintiff was engaged in a customary and permitted game of ping-pong on his employer's premises before the start of the work day, using equipment purchased by the employees, arose out of and in the course of his employment so that it was error to deny him compensation.

The compensation commissioner's finding and award disclosed the following facts: On April 15, 1975, the plaintiff was employed by the public works department of the defendant town of Hamden. The work day was from 8:00 A.M. to 4:30 P.M. Some of the work force of about eighty employees were in the habit of assembling in the department's garage about a half hour before 8:00 A.M. They drank coffee, talked, and generally passed the time until they went "on the clock" at 8:00 A.M. and received the day's assignments from their supervisors. A few months prior to April 15, about ten or twelve of the "early birds" obtained permission from the "director or the assistant director" of the department to purchase a ping-pong table and accessories at their own expense and to install the table near their lockers located in a corner of the garage.

The playing space was about twenty-five feet by twenty-five feet. The employer limited the playing time as follows: from about 7:30 A.M. to 8:00 A.M.; from noon to 12:30 P.M., which was lunch time; and from about 4:00 P.M., as the employees gathered toward the end of the work day, until 4:30 P.M., when they went "off the clock." Eventually about twenty of the department's eighty employees used the table. A superintendent sometimes played.

On April 15, 1975, at 7:55 A.M., the plaintiff tripped and fell while playing ping-pong, severely injuring his right ankle. As a consequence he lost time from work and incurred medical and hospital expenses for which he claimed workmen's compensation benefits.

From these subordinate facts the commissioner concluded that no benefit accrued to the employer from the employees' playing ping-pong; that the table was for the exclusive use and benefit of the players; and that, therefore, ping-pong was not an incident of the plaintiff's employment or connected with it in any manner so as to require the employer to pay compensation. The commissioner dismissed the plaintiff's claim and an appeal was taken to the Court of Common Pleas, where the trial court found that the plaintiff had failed to meet his burden of proof and dismissed the appeal. In denying compensation both the commissioner and the trial court seized upon the lack of benefit to the employer. The plaintiff appealed to this court from the judgment rendered.

Opinion

Judge Speziale: The issue before us is whether the commissioner properly concluded that the plaintiff's injury was one not "arising out of and in the course of his employment" within the meaning of the Workmen's Compensation Act.

It is an axiom of workmen's compensation law that awards are determined by a two-part test. The employee has the burden of proving that the injury claimed arose out of the employment and occurred in the course of the employment. There must be a conjunction of the two requirements, in the course of the employment and out of the employment to permit compensation. The former relates to the time, place and circumstance of the accident, while the latter refers to the origin and cause of the accident. While easily stated, this test has been confused over the years. This confusion has developed as a result of a half century of factual variations on the legal rule. We take this opportunity to reaffirm the basic analysis to be applied in workmen's compensation cases, and to set forth a new and expanded test for cases like the present one.

On the record before us, it appears that the parties, the commissioner, and the court have implicitly treated the injury sustained as one "arising out of" the employment, and their focus on this appeal has been on the "in the course of" employment aspect of the test. Thus, we will confine our discussion and review to that element in deciding this case.

In order to come within the course of the employment, an injury must occur (a) within the period of the employment; (b) at a place the employee may reasonably be; and (c) while the employee is reasonably fulfilling the duties of the employment or doing something incidental to it. In the present case the employee was not fulfilling an employment duty, and therefore the proper inquiry under part (c) of the test will be whether the activity, playing ping-pong, was incidental to his employment.

First, the plaintiff was clearly at a place he could reasonably be, on the premises just before he "clocked in." And he was, according to the definition developed in workmen's compensation law, within the period of employment, regardless of the fact that it was five minutes prior to the commencement of the official work day. The exact time is not significant, so long as the employee is on the premises reasonably close to the start or finish of the work day. Moreover, even when an employee is still in the process of coming to or going from work, once he or she is on the premises, whether arriving a little early, or leaving a little late, this court has found the employee to be within the period of the employment. Therefore, a distinction based on an activity's occurring five minutes before work, as opposed to at lunch or during the last half hour of the work day, would be unwarranted especially because both the early gathering and the recreation involved here were together designated by the employer as permissible activities.

The crux of this case rests, therefore, on the proper application of the second portion of part (c) of the course of employment test: whether the injury sustained occurred when the employee was doing something "incidental to the employment." It is this inquiry that has been most subject to distortion from one type of case to another. The "going and coming" cases, in which the employee is injured traveling to or from work; "personal comfort" cases, in which the employee is attending to some personal need when injured; and "horseplay" cases, in which an employee is injured while wrestling have become special categories in the law.

For example, in the going and coming cases, it is necessary for the commissioner to find a benefit to the employer before compensation will be awarded. As a result, in going and coming cases that have also involved recreational or social aspects, as when an employee is on the way to a union-sponsored picnic, the benefit test has been applied. There is a crucial difference between the going and coming cases (whether or not they also involve the element of recreation) and other types, because in the going and coming cases the injury has not occurred on the premises of the employer. Therefore, the need arose to reach out for the additional element of employer benefit to make up for the fact that employees going to or coming from work do not satisfy both of the first two course-of-employment requirements, place and period of employment. If the recreational activity takes place on some distant vacant lot, several hours after the day's work has ceased, some independently convincing association with the employment must be built up to overcome the initial presumption of disassociation with the employment established by the time and place factors.

When an employee is *on the premises* and is *within the period of employment,* however, it should not be necessary to satisfy the additional test of employer benefit. Rather, the basic test should be remembered and applied: Is this activity incidental to the employment? The meaning of the term "incidental" need not be defined as compulsion by or benefit to the employer in all cases. For example, other activities such as those typical of the personal comfort and horseplay cases fulfill the requirements of place and time, without being of benefit to the employer; and yet compensation may be awarded in such instances, because the injury had occurred on the premises as the result of a customary activity sanctioned by the employer through approval or acquiescence. It would be anomalous indeed for courts to assert that smoking is an ordinary personal need whereas exercise is not, or that shoving, tripping or punching a fellow employee is inevitable horseplay, simply indulging a natural human tendency, whereas engaging in a planned recreational activity like ping-pong is not. How can one realistically evaluate the actual benefit an employer receives from permitting on-premises recreational activities? The obvious difficulty in drawing such distinctions or weighing such intangibles is sufficient reason to adopt a new rule which will avoid arbitrary and unjust results.

This case clearly illustrates the need for a consistent approach to the question of whether certain types of injuries are work related. Experts in the field of workmen's compensation law have pointed out the inconsistency of using the employer benefit test in situations such as recreation, personal comfort, and horseplay cases where an employer-sanctioned activity regularly occurs on the premises. Both Professor Larson and Professor Davis advocate a test of employer acquiescence or approval in such cases, whether they be recreation, personal comfort, or horseplay situations.

The ping-pong game was found by the commissioner not to be of benefit to the employer, a finding we cannot and need not disturb. The commissioner did, however, find employer permission and regularity of activity. The employer sanctioned the games by regulating the permitted playing times, by allowing the equipment on the premises, and by setting aside actual work hours in the afternoon for the activity. The games occurred regularly on the premises of the employer. Those facts constitute a sufficient basis on which to conclude that the games were an incident of the employment under the test we now adopt.

In conclusion, we restate the rule to be applied in workmen's compensation cases generally: In order to be compensable, an injury must (1) arise out of the employment; and (2) occur in the course of the employment. To occur in the course of the employment, the injury must take place (a) within the period of the employment, (b) at a place where the employee may reasonably be, and (c) while the employee is reasonably fulfilling the duties of the employment or doing something incidental to it.

We now go a step further and hold that when determining whether the activity is incidental to the employment, the following rule should be applied: If the activity is regularly engaged in on the employer's premises within the period of the employment, with the employer's approval or acquiescence, an injury occurring under those conditions shall be found to be compensable.

There is error, the judgment is set aside and the case is remanded to the Superior Court with direction to sustain the appeal and to remand the cause to the workmen's compensation commissioner to render an award in favor of the plaintiff.

Case Questions

1. What are the general requirements an employee must meet in order to be able to recover for workers' compensation?
2. When will an employee be able to recover for injuries sustained while carrying out activities incidental to employment?
3. Does it seem fair to make an employer bear the cost of an injury that happened while an employee was playing a game before working hours?

If a worker is injured on the job, the amount of her monetary recovery is determined by a "schedule of benefits." This is a detailed document that assigns recovery of monetary awards based on the type and severity of the worker's injury. Generally, the amount of a worker's recovery is based on a percentage of the salary she was earning at the time of her injury, although there may be an absolute maximum on the amount of money she can collect. For example, for an injury classified as a permanent, total disability, such as becoming blind or losing an arm, the worker might be entitled to receive, indefinitely, two-thirds of the amount she was earning when the injury occurred. Employers are required to carry workers' compensation insurance (unless they are approved by a state agency to be self-insured), so usually the worker collects her benefits from an insurance company, and not from the employer directly.

The passage of workers' compensation laws was the first instance in which a public law was used to alter the employer-employee relationship. Although workers' compensation laws have been in effect in most states for at least fifty years, there are some criticisms of them today from both employers and employees. Employers today accept payment of unemployment compensation premiums as a cost of doing business. However, some employers are unhappy with the complete abolition of the common law defenses to workers' claims, because courts have tended to define the term *work-related* very broadly, and workers engaging in questionable activities that might constitute contributory negligence have been allowed to recover. Employees have been more vocal in their criticism of workers' compensation laws, primarily on the grounds that the schedule of benefits payments is inadequate. Suppose a student studying to be a draftsman is working in a manufacturing plant part-time for the minimum wage, and that in an accident he loses a hand due to improperly maintained equipment, which significantly interferes with his career plans. Under the workers' compensation schedule, he will probably receive much less than he would have received if he had sued the employer in court for negligence and won, because in court the effect of the accident on his future earnings would be considered, but this factor would not affect his workers' compensation payments. Since workers' compensation is an *exclusive remedy,* the student cannot sue in court and may well collect much less under workers' compensation than he would have gotten if he had lost his hand in some other way, such as an automobile accident.

Federal Regulation of the Employer-Employee Relationship

With the exception of the passage of workers' compensation acts, which are state laws, most of the statutes that now regulate the employer-employee relationship are federal. For many years, it was felt that the constitutional guarantee against infringement of the freedom of contract (discussed in chapter 3 on constitutional law) prevented Congress from regulating in any area of private employer-employee relations. However, it is now well established that Congress can pass laws that do this. Two of the oldest important federal laws regulating employer-employee relations are the *National Labor Relations Act,* passed in 1935, and the **Fair Labor Standards Act,** enacted in 1938. The National Labor Relations Act, which guarantees the rights of workers to form unions and to bargain collectively, is discussed in chapter 16. The Fair Labor Standards Act will be discussed here, along with certain other important federal statutory programs that directly regulate various aspects of employer-employee relations, including the Social Security and unemployment compensation programs and *the Employee Retirement Income Security Act.* One important federal statute that significantly affects the employer-employee relationship without directly regulating it is the *Occupational Safety and Health Act (OSHA),* which will be discussed in a subsequent section.

The Fair Labor Standards Act (FLSA)

The *Fair Labor Standards Act (FLSA)* was passed in 1938 as an exercise of Congress' Commerce Clause power. The FLSA applies to workers whose jobs make them engage in interstate commerce and to workers employed by a company producing goods for interstate commerce. The act establishes minimum wages that an employer may pay and the maximum hours an employee may be required to work. An employee who works over the standard work week of forty hours is entitled to overtime pay. The FLSA also regulates the employment of persons under the age of eighteen, generally prohibiting completely the employment of children under the age of thirteen and restricting the types of employment of persons between the ages of thirteen and eighteen. The FLSA is enforced by the Wage and Hour Division of the Department of Labor.

There are exemptions from the minimum wage and overtime provisions of the FLSA. Some of the most important exemptions are for executive, administrative, and professional employees, including teachers. In 1985, in *Garcia* v. *San Antonio Metropolitan Transit Authority,* the Supreme Court held that the FLSA did apply to state and local governments. Most states have minimum wage laws that often cover employees exempted from the federal act. One important "semi-exemption" from the FLSA concerns employees who earn part of their income (over twenty dollars a month) from tips; their employers can credit an employee's tips for up to 50 percent of the minimum wage and thereby reduce the amount they have to pay the employee. More recent amendments to the FLSA have also exempted full-time students who work in retail or service establishments, agriculture, or institutions of higher learning.

Unemployment Compensation

The concept of **unemployment compensation** payments was created with the passage of the federal Social Security Act in 1935. Today, the individual states administer unemployment compensation programs, which are financed through a tax imposed on employers doing business within the state. Employers are generally liable to pay a tax of about 3 percent of an employee's first $6,000 of wages. The amount of tax an employer actually has to pay depends on its "experience rating"—an employer with a low employee turnover rate will pay less tax than an employer with a high turnover rate. Any employer that has one or more employees who worked a total of twenty weeks a year or who received a minimum of $1,500 in a calendar quarter is required to pay the tax.

In order for an employee of a covered employer to be eligible for benefits, certain state statutory requirements must be met. While these requirements vary among states, generally they include the following: (1) the employee must have worked a certain period of time (usually about a year), (2) the employee must have earned a specific average income during the period, and (3) the employee cannot have quit or been fired for misconduct. Former employees must apply to a state agency for benefits, and after a specified statutory waiting period, they will receive compensation benefits within a range fixed by state statute, based on a percentage of the salary they were receiving before being laid off. All states require persons receiving unemployment compensation benefits to seek employment actively. These persons are only required to seek suitable work compatible with their training and work experience, however. All states provide for payment of unemployment compensation benefits for a minimum of twenty-six weeks. Federal law provides for extension of these benefits under certain economic conditions, such as a prolonged period of national unemployment above a certain percentage level.

One question regarding unemployment compensation is whether strikers should be allowed to recover unemployment compensation benefits. Most states do not allow them to do so because, just as with workers who resign their jobs, the strikers voluntarily brought about their unemployment. Another issue that the United States Supreme Court addressed in the late 1980s is the extent to which persons who are discharged for reasons having to do with their religious observances can be refused unemployment compensation benefits. In 1987, in *Hobbie* v. *Unemployment Appeals Commission of Florida,* the court held that an employee who refused to work on Saturdays and Friday evenings because of religious beliefs could not be denied unemployment compensation benefits on the grounds of that her actions constituted "misconduct." This principle was reaffirmed in 1988 in *Employment Division of Oregon* v. *Smith.*

Social Security

The federal **Social Security** program was created in 1935 by the Social Security Act. The original, and still primary, purpose of the Social Security program was to provide for payments to retired workers who worked and contributed to the program for a minimum number of quarters during their working lives. The Social Security program is financed by taxes paid by most wage earners.

Besides providing for a retirement program for covered employees, the present Social Security system also provides payments to children of deceased covered workers and funds the Medicare system, which pays most of the medical expenses of the elderly.

Due to the large numbers of retired persons and the increase in medical costs and longevity, the cost of the Social Security system has increased dramatically. It is not uncommon today for a worker to pay more in Social Security taxes than he does in federal income tax.

Although Social Security was established as a public sector pension program, some commentators argue today that it is in fact a welfare program, and ought to be viewed as such.

Employee Retirement Income Security Act (ERISA)

It is common for employers to offer pension plans as an employee benefit. In 1974, Congress enacted the **Employee Retirement Income Security Act (ERISA)** to regulate the administration of private employer pension plans. All pension plans in effect on ERISA's effective date and any started thereafter are covered by the act.

Among the most important provisions of ERISA are its requirements that pension plan managers must make prudent investments, keep records, and publish an annual report that has been reviewed by an independent actuary and certified public accountant. Another significant feature of ERISA is that it created the Pension Benefit Guaranty Corporation to pay retirement benefits if the pension plan funds fail or are inadequate. One of the desirable provisions of ERISA from the employee's point of view is the requirement of vesting of pension rights. While certain options are available to employers regarding when pension rights vest, i.e., become legally enforceable by the employee, under ERISA, after a certain period of time (usually ten years), the employer cannot terminate the employee's pension rights for any reason. Furthermore, an employee who has gained vested rights can collect them even if he transfers from one job to another. Employers are not required to establish general employee pension plans, but ERISA provides that an employer can contribute directly into an employee's individual retirement account (IRA) set up at a financial institution.

ERISA has been criticized because its provisions are so complex that it is hard to understand and hard to comply with. Employers, especially small businesses, often have difficulty meeting all of its costly and time-consuming requirements. On the other hand, it certainly seems to be of benefit to employees and has eliminated the former occasional practice of eliminating pension rights by firing workers just before their retirement, often after twenty or more years of service. One problem that may develop with ERISA in the future is the "time bomb" potential of the Pension Benefit Guaranty Corporation provision. If a large number of employers go out of business leaving inadequately funded pension plans, the federal government might have to step in with funds to keep the plans operating, and that might in turn necessitate federal tax increases.

Occupational Safety and Health Acts (OSHAs)

So far in this chapter, we have discussed laws that were passed to directly affect the employment relationship. In 1970, Congress enacted the **Occupational Safety and Health Act (OSHA),** which regulates the condition of the physical premises of a business. The purpose of the law, as its name indicates, is to protect employees' safety and health, and to prevent injuries or illnesses from occurring in the workplace. In a sense, OSHA is a kind of "environmental protection" statute. It carries further the concept initiated by the passage of workers' compensation laws by seeking to prevent employee injuries from occurring, rather than by compensating the worker after the injury has happened. Since the passage of the federal OSHA in 1970, many states have passed OSHA laws that complement the federal statute. We will only examine the federal OSHA, because state OSHAs are very similar.

Federal OSHA Provisions and Enforcement

The Occupational Safety and Health Act is enforced by the Occupational Safety and Health Administration in the Department of Labor. You should note that both the Occupational Safety and Health *Act* and the Occupational Safety and Health *Administration* are often referred to as OSHA. The federal OSH Act delegates much authority to the OSH Administration. The act contains a "general duty" clause requiring employers to maintain a workplace free from recognized hazards that might cause death or serious physical harm to employees. Violations of this clause might include maintaining frayed electrical wiring in an office or keeping a drum of toxic chemicals uncovered. The main substantive provision of the act, however, gives the OSH Administration power to set detailed standards for each type of industry. Over a period of years, the OSHA has developed extensive and detailed standards for all types of industries (ranging from manufacturing plants to offices) and all types of potential hazards. Originally, most of OSHA's safety regulations were "consensus standards" voluntarily adopted by industry in 1968 before OSHA's enactment. In 1989, OSHA adopted sweeping new standards, setting exposure limits for nearly 400 hazardous materials. These regulations tightened standards on 212 hazardous substances and added 164 substances not previously regulated. While it seemed that the result of the adoption of the 1989 standards would be a reduction in exposure-related deaths, illnesses, and lost workdays, such government action almost inevitably drives business costs up. The OSH Act established a National Institute of Occupational Safety and Health (NIOSH) to study workplace health and determine what industrial practices may constitute health or safety risks (for example, how much noise does it take to cause worker hearing impairment).

Almost all private employers whose working conditions are not regulated by another federal law are covered by OSHA, and so is the federal government. OSHA is enforced by inspections by OSHA inspectors. The original OSHA law allowed surprise inspections by OSHA officials who had not obtained a search warrant. In the 1976 case of *Marshall* v. *Barlow's, Inc.*, the Supreme Court held that an employer could require an OSHA inspector to obtain a search warrant before inspecting a workplace. The right to request a warrant has been little used since the *Barlow's* case. Requesting a search warrant is merely a delaying tactic, since the *Barlow's* opinion made it easy for an inspector to get a search warrant by providing that the inspector does not have to show any reason to believe there is any specific violation of OSHA standards, but only that the inspection is to be conducted subject to a general plan of inspection of that type of business in the area.

Business and OSHA

Many businesses have expressed dissatisfaction with the OSHA law, not because of disapproval of the basic goal of preventing worker injury, but because the act is costly to comply with. OSHA standards are very detailed and even good faith efforts to meet all of them may be difficult. Furthermore, attempts to meet the standards may require the acquisition of very costly new machinery or modification of a physical plant. In the following case, the Supreme Court addressed the argument that a "cost/benefit analysis" approach should be used in determining whether it is necessary for an industry to comply with all OSHA regulations. You should note that this case was decided in the year following *Industrial Union Department* v. *American Petroleum Institute* (the "benzene" case), in which the Supreme Court held that, where worker exposure to probable cancer-causing agents existed, OSHA was not required to support its exposure standards by proving scientific certainty of ill effects but could risk error on the side of over-protection rather than under-protection.

American Textile Manufacturers v. Donovan

(Cotton Dust Case) 452 U.S. 490 (1981)

Facts

The air in cotton mills ordinarily contains substantial amounts of cotton dust. Cotton dust has been defined as "dust present in the air during the handling or processing of cotton, which may contain a mixture of many substances, including ground-up plant matter, fiber, bacteria, fungi, soil, pesticides, noncotton plant matter, and other contaminants which may have accumulated with the cotton during the growing, harvesting, and subsequent processing or storage periods."

The inhaling of cotton dust for a prolonged period of time can cause byssinosis, often called "brown lung" disease. In its mildest form, byssinosis produces chest tightness, shortness of breath, coughing, and wheezing. In its most serious form, it is a chronic, irreversible, and completely disabling lung disease. The advanced stage of byssinosis is clinically similar to severe emphysema or asthma and can cause sudden death from heart failure as a result of strain on the cardiovascular system. The disease sometimes advances through different stages, but in many cases the advanced stage will suddenly appear. Studies showed that at least 25 percent of cotton mill workers suffered some form of byssinosis.

In 1968, two years before OSHA's enactment, the Labor Department had limited cotton dust at mills doing government contract work to 1.0 milligrams per cubic meter of air (1.0 mg/m^3) averaged over an eight-hour day. Shortly after the enactment of OSHA, the department, acting through its Occupational Safety and Health Administration, adopted this exposure limit as a temporary OSHA standard for all cotton mills. After extensive research and study, the National Institute for Occupational Safety and Health in 1974 adopted a new measurement unit of "respirable" (particles small enough to enter the lungs) rather than total dust, and recommended that worker exposure be limited to 0.2 mg/m^3 of respirable dust.

In 1978, the department promulgated a final cotton dust standard. This standard limited worker exposure to respirable cotton dust, averaged over an eight-hour period, to 0.2 mg/m^3 in yarn manufacturing, 0.75 mg/m^3 in slashing and weaving operations, and 0.5 mg/m^3 in all other cotton industry processes. The Department chose an implementation strategy for the standard that depended primarily on a mix of engineering controls, such as installation of ventilation systems, and work practice controls, such as special floor sweeping procedures. Full compliance was required within four years, except to the extent that employers could establish that the engineering and work practice controls were infeasible. During this compliance period, and at certain other times, the standard required employers to provide respirators to employees. Other requirements included *monitoring cotton dust exposure, medical surveillance of all employees, annual medical examinations, employee education and training programs, and posting of warning signs. Another provision required employers to transfer employees unable to wear respirators to another position, if available, having a dust level at or below the required limits, with "no loss of earnings or other employment rights or benefits as a result of the transfer."*

The American Textile Manufacturers Institute and others representing the cotton industry challenged the validity of the standard in a U.S. Court of Appeals. The basis for this challenge was that the Labor Department's Occupational Safety and Health Administration (officially acting under the name of Donovan, the Secretary of Labor) had not engaged in "cost-benefit analysis" prior to adopting the standard. A U.S. Court of Appeals upheld the standard, and the textile manufacturers appealed to the U.S. Supreme Court.

Opinion

Justice Brennan: . . . The principal question presented in this case is whether the Occupational Safety and Health Act requires the [Labor Department], in promulgating a standard pursuant to Section 6(b)(5) of the Act, to determine that the costs of the standard bear a reasonable relationship to its benefits. [The manufacturers] urge not only that [the Department] must show that a standard addresses a significant risk of material health impairment, but also that [it] must demonstrate that the reduction in risk of material health impairment is significant in light of the costs of attaining that reduction. [The Department contends] on the other hand that the Act requires [it] to promulgate standards that eliminate or reduce such risks "to the extent such protection is technologically and economically feasible."

The starting point of our analysis is the language of the statute itself. Section 6(b)(5) of the Act provides:

> The Secretary, in promulgating standards dealing with toxic materials or harmful agents under this subsection, shall set the standard which most adequately assures, *to the extent feasible,* on the basis of the best available evidence, that no employee will suffer material impairment of health or functional capacity even if such employee has regular exposure to the hazard dealt with by such standard for the period of his working life. [Emphasis added.]

Although their interpretations differ, all parties agree that the phrase "to the extent feasible" contains the critical language in Section 6(b)(5) for purposes of this case.

The plain meaning of the word "feasible" supports [the Department's] interpretation of the statute. According to Webster's Third New International Dictionary of the English Language, "feasible" means "capable of being done, executed, or effected." Thus, Section 6(b)(5) directs the [Labor Department] to issue the standard that "most adequately assures . . . that no employee will suffer material impairment of health," limited only by the extent to which this is "capable of being done." In effect then, as the Court of Appeals held, Congress itself defined the basic relationship between costs and benefits, by placing the "benefit" of worker health above all other considerations [except] those making attainment of this "benefit" unachievable. Any standard based on a balancing of costs and benefits by the [Labor Department] that strikes a different balance than that struck by Congress would be inconsistent with the command set forth in Section 6(b)(5). Thus, cost-benefit analysis by OSHA is not required by the statute because feasibility analysis is.

Not only does the legislative history confirm that Congress meant "feasible" rather than "cost-benefit" when it used the former term, but it also shows that Congress understood that the Act would create substantial costs for employers, yet intended to impose such costs when necessary to create a safe and healthful working environment. Congress viewed the costs of health and safety as a cost of doing business. Senator Yarborough, a cosponsor of the bill, stated: "We know the costs would be put into consumer goods but that is the price we should pay for the 80 million workers in America." He asked:

> One may well ask too expensive for whom? Is it too expensive for the company who for lack of proper safety equipment loses the services of its skilled employees? Is it too expensive for the employee who loses his hand or leg or

eyesight? Is it too expensive for the widow trying to raise her children on a meager allowance under workman's compensation and social security? And what about the man—a good hardworking man—tied to a wheel chair or hospital bed for the rest of his life? That is what we are dealing with when we talk about industrial safety. . . . We are talking about people's lives, not the indifference of some cost accountants.

Senator Eagleton commented that "the costs that will be incurred by employers in meeting the standards of health and safety to be established under this bill are, in my view, *reasonable and necessary costs of doing business.*"

Other members of Congress voiced similar views. Nowhere is there any indication that Congress contemplated a different balancing by OSHA of the benefits of worker health and safety against the costs of achieving them. Indeed Congress thought that the *financial costs* of health and safety problems in the workplace were as large or larger than the *financial costs* of eliminating these problems. In its statement of findings and declaration of purpose encompassed in the Act itself, Congress announced that "personal injuries and illnesses arising out of work situations impose a substantial burden upon, and are a hindrance to, interstate commerce in terms of lost production, wage loss, medical expenses, and disability compensation payment."

The judgment of the Court of Appeals is affirmed.

Case Questions

1. As a result of the *Cotton Dust* decision, does OSHA have to consider cost of compliance in deciding whether to promulgate regulations?
2. What should the owner of a mill that produces cotton dust residue do if the workers refuse to wear respirators, as required by OSHA regulations?
3. One possible result of implementation of expensive OSHA regulations that was not discussed by the Supreme Court is that a plant doing business in the United States will close and move to another country with less stringent health apparatus requirements. Should the courts take this possible effect into account in making their decisions?

The court interpretation of the policy of the OSH Act is to side with worker safety as opposed to cost, and there can be no question that compliance with OSHA standards has cost American industry billions of dollars. While the primary thrust of OSHA has been to emphasize worker concerns, in recent years there has been some movement to make OSHA compliance easier for business by repealing some of the more trivial regulations and by reducing the number of OSHA inspectors (and, therefore, the number of inspections). The cost of compliance with OSHA is one reason cited by some United States–owned companies for deciding to relocate outside the country. Thus, OSHA may have hidden costs that may not have been fully appreciated by those who enacted it.

Worker Rights and Statutory and Other Protections

An interesting question that has arisen since the passage of OSHA is whether the Act confers on employees the legal right to refuse to carry out an employer directive that would violate OSHA regulations. In 1980, the United States Supreme Court indicated that OSHA does confer such a right, in the limited circumstances in which an employee is not able to report the illegal directive to OSHA authorities. Here is how the Court analyzed this question:

Whirlpool Corporation v. Marshall

445 U.S. 1 (1980)

Facts

Two employees in a Whirlpool plant in Marion, Ohio, refused to perform maintenance work on a wire-mesh screen that they considered unsafe. Their pay was docked and written reprimands were placed in their files. The Secretary of Labor filed suit, alleging violation of an OSHA regulation allowing employees to refuse to work under certain hazardous circumstances and seeking an injunction ordering the expunging of the reprimand and payment of the lost wages. The District Court refused the injunction: It found the OSHA regulation invalid because it was inconsistent with the provisions of the 1970 Act. The Court of Appeals reversed.

Opinion

Held, affirmed, the regulation is valid and relief should be granted to the two workers.

Judge Stewart: The petitioner company maintains a manufacturing plant in Marion, Ohio, for the production of household appliances. Overhead conveyors transport appliance components throughout the plant. To protect employees from objects that occasionally fall from these conveyors, the petitioner has installed a horizontal wire-mesh guard screen approximately 20 feet above the plant floor. This mesh screen is welded to angle-iron frames suspended from the building's structural steel skeleton.

Maintenance employees of the petitioner spend several hours each week removing objects from the screen, replacing paper spread on the screen to catch grease drippings from the material on the conveyors, and performing occasional maintenance work on the conveyors themselves. To perform these duties, maintenance employees usually are able to stand on the iron frames, but sometimes find it necessary to step onto the steel mesh screen itself.

In 1973, the company began to install heavier wire in the screen because its safety had been drawn into question. Several employees had fallen partly through the old screen, and on one occasion an employee had fallen completely through to the plant floor below but had survived. A number of maintenance employees had reacted to these incidents by bringing the unsafe screen conditions to the attention of their foremen. The petitioner company's contemporaneous safety instructions admonished employees to step only on the angle-iron frames.

On June 28, 1974, a maintenance employee fell to his death through the guard screen in an area where the newer, stronger mesh had not yet been installed. . . .

. . . Following this incident, the petitioner effectuated some repairs and issued an order strictly forbidding maintenance employees from stepping on either the screens or the angle-iron supporting structure. An alternative but somewhat more cumbersome and less satisfactory method was developed for removing objects from the screen. This procedure required employees to stand on power-raised mobile platforms and use hooks to recover material.

On July 7, 1974, two of the petitioner's maintenance employees, Virgil Deemer and Thomas Cornwell, met with the plant maintenance superintendent to voice their concern about the safety of the screen. The superintendent disagreed with their view, but permitted the two men to inspect the screen with their foreman and to point out dangerous areas needing repair. Unsatisfied with the petitioner's response to the results of this inspection, Deemer and Cornwell met on July 9 with the plant safety director. At that meeting, they requested the name, address, and telephone number of a representative of the local office of the Occupational Safety and Health Administration (OSHA). Although the safety director told the men that they "had better stop and think about what [they] were doing," he furnished the men with the information they requested. Later that same day, Deemer contacted an official of the regional OSHA office and discussed the guard screen. . . .

The next day, Deemer and Cornwell reported for the night shift at 10:45 P.M. Their foreman, after himself walking on some of the angle-iron frames, directed the two men to perform their usual maintenance duties on a section of the old screen. Claiming that the screen was unsafe, they refused to carry out this directive. The foreman then sent them to the personnel office, where they were ordered to punch out without working or being paid for the remaining six hours of the shift. The two men subsequently received written reprimands, which were placed in their employment files.

A little over a month later, the Secretary filed suit in the United States District Court for the Northern District of Ohio, alleging that the petitioner's actions against Deemer and Cornwell constituted discrimination in violation of Section 11(c)(1) of the Act. As relief, the complaint prayed, *inter alia,* that the petitioner be ordered to expunge from its personnel files all references to the reprimands issued to the two employees, and for a permanent injunction requiring the petitioner to compensate the two employees for the six hours of pay they had lost by reason of their disciplinary suspensions.

Following a bench trial, the District Court found that the regulation in question justified Deemer's and Cornwell's refusals to obey their foreman's order on July 10, 1974. The court found that the two employees had "refused to perform the cleaning operation because of a genuine fear of death or serious bodily harm," that the danger presented had been "real and not something which [had] existed only in the minds of the employees," that the employees had acted in good faith, . . . and that no reasonable alternative had realistically been open to them other than to refuse to work. The District Court nevertheless denied relief, holding that the Secretary's regulation was inconsistent with the Act and therefore invalid. . . .

. . . The Court of Appeals for the Sixth Circuit reversed the District Court's judgment. . . .

We granted certiorari, . . . because the decision of the Court of Appeals in this case conflicts with those of two other Courts of Appeals on the important question in issue. . . . That question, as stated at the outset of this opinion, is whether the Secretary's regulation authorizing employee "self-help" in some circumstances . . . is permissible under the Act.

. . . The Act itself creates an express mechanism for protecting workers from employment conditions believed to pose an emergent threat of death or serious injury. Upon receipt of an employee inspection request stating reasonable grounds to believe that an imminent danger is present in a workplace, . . . OSHA must conduct an inspection. . . . In the event his inspection reveals workplace conditions or practices that "could reasonably be expected to cause death or serious physical harm immediately or before the imminence of such danger can be eliminated through the enforcement procedures otherwise provided by" the Act, . . . the OSHA inspector must inform the affected employees and the employer of the danger and notify them that he is recommending to the Secretary that injunctive relief be sought. . . . At this juncture, the Secretary can petition a federal court to restrain the conditions or practices giving rise to the imminent danger. By means of a temporary restraining order or preliminary injunction, the court may then require the employer to avoid, correct, or remove the danger or to prohibit employees from working in the area. . . .

. . . In the light of this detailed statutory scheme, the Secretary is obviously correct when he acknowledges in his regulation that, "as a general matter, there is no right afforded by the Act which would entitle employees to walk off the job because of potential unsafe conditions at the workplace." By providing for prompt notice to the employer of an inspector's intention to seek an injunction against an imminently dangerous condition, the legislation obviously contemplates that the employer will normally respond by voluntarily and speedily eliminating the danger. And in the few instances where this does not occur, the legislative provisions authorizing prompt judicial action are designed to give employees full protection in most situations from the risk of injury or death resulting from an imminently dangerous condition at the worksite.

As this case illustrates, however, circumstances may sometimes exist in which the employee justifiably believes that the express statutory arrangement does not sufficiently protect him from death or serious injury. Such circumstances will probably not often occur, but such a situation may arise when (1) the employee is ordered by his employer to work under conditions that the employee reasonably believes pose an imminent risk of death or serious bodily injury, and (2) the employee has reason to believe that there is not sufficient time . . . or opportunity either to seek effective redress from his employer or to apprise OSHA of the danger.

Nothing in the Act suggests that those few employees who have to face this dilemma must rely exclusively on the remedies expressly set forth in the Act at the risk of their own safety. But nothing in the Act explicitly provides otherwise. Against this background of legislative silence, the Secretary has exercised his rulemaking power . . . and has determined that, when an employee in good faith finds himself in such a predicament, he may refuse to expose himself to the dangerous condition, without being subjected to "subsequent discrimination" by the employer.

. . . The question before us is whether this interpretative regulation constitutes a permissible gloss on the Act by the Secretary, in light of the Act's language, structure, and legislative history. Our inquiry is informed by an awareness that the regulation is entitled to deference unless it can be said not to be a reasoned and supportable interpretation of the Act. . . .

The regulation clearly conforms to the fundamental objective of the Act—to prevent occupational deaths and serious injuries. . . .

To accomplish this basic purpose, the legislation's remedial orientation is prophylactic in nature. . . . The Act does not wait for an employee to die or become injured. It authorizes the promulgation of health and safety standards and the issuance of citations in the hope that these will act to prevent deaths or injuries from ever occurring. It would seem anomalous to construe an Act so directed and constructed as prohibiting an employee, with no other reasonable alternative, the freedom to withdraw from a workplace environment that he reasonably believes is highly dangerous.

Moreover, the Secretary's regulation can be viewed as an appropriate aid to the full effectuation of the Act's "general duty" clause. That clause provides that "[e]ach employer . . . shall furnish to each of his employees employment and a place of employment which are free from recognized hazards that are causing or are likely to cause death or serious physical harm to his employees." . . . As the legislative history of this provision reflects, it was intended itself to deter the occurrence of occupational deaths and serious injuries by placing on employers a mandatory obligation independent of the specific health and safety standards to be promulgated by the Secretary. Since OSHA inspectors cannot be present around the clock in every workplace, the Secretary's regulation ensures that employees will in all circumstances enjoy the rights afforded them by the "general duty" clause.

. . . The regulation thus on its face appears to further the overriding purpose of the Act, and rationally to complement its remedial scheme. In the absence of some contrary indication in the legislative history, the Secretary's regulation must, therefore, be upheld, particularly when it is remembered that safety legislation is to be liberally construed to effectuate the congressional purpose. . . .

. . . Accordingly, the judgment of the Court of Appeals is affirmed.

Case Questions

1. When can a worker refuse to comply with a work order?
2. Do you think the fact that a worker had recently been killed due to unsafe netting had an effect on the Court's decision?
3. Could the results of this case mean that workers could use OSHA regulations as an excuse not to perform work that was actually not dangerous?

In 1988, Congress enacted a statute significantly curtailing the use of polygraph (lie-detector) tests by employers. Prior to the passage of this law, use of such tests was almost routine in some lines of business as part of the hiring or promotion process, or in situations where employee wrongdoing was suspected. Under the new law, prehiring screening and random testing are prohibited, and tests can only be administered if the company has evidence of theft or other wrongdoing that causes loss or injury, as well as evidence that the employee to be tested may have been involved. Furthermore, before the test can be given, the employee must be given a statement describing the reasonable suspicion of the employer that justifies the test. Certain types of firms, such as ones that provide security guards or pharmaceutical companies, are exempt from the new act. At the time of its passage, the new law was heralded as a big step forward in the protection of workers' rights to privacy.

In another action that was seen, especially by labor, as increasing employee rights, in 1988, as part of trade reform legislation, Congress mandated that large companies give sixty days notice of large plant closings or long layoffs. This provision was seen as providing a better possibility that groups of employees or a locality of a plant could take steps to persuade the employer to remain, or make better provision for laid-off workers.

In a response to concerns about drug use in the workplace, in late 1988, Congress enacted the Drug-Free Workplace Act of 1988, which took effect in March 1989. This law requires that contractors receiving federal funds certify to the contracting agency that they will provide a drug-free workplace. The contractor must inform employees of its written policy, which details penalties to be exacted for drug use by employees who are directly engaged in performing work related to a government contract. The Act does not require the contractor to do drug screening or drug testing, or to provide drug counseling. The Act is a strong policy statement against employee drug use. States have also begun to pass statutes regarding employee drug use and drug testing by employers, but the state laws are widely divergent, with some limiting the use of drug testing in the workplace, while others establish procedures to be followed if the employer elects to do drug testing. Such federal and state legislation represents a significant incursion into the traditionally private employer-employee relationship.

For many years, employers faced a legal and ethical dilemma caused by their hiring of workers who were not legally residing in the United States. Prior to 1986, the law attempted to deal with the problem of illegal alien residents taking jobs (presumably from Americans) by authorizing the federal Immigration and Naturalization Service (INS) to detain and deport such workers. However, in 1986, Congress instituted a new approach to the problem of illegal aliens by requiring employers to take steps to insure that only legal residents of the United States were hired. Under the terms of the Immigration Reform and Control Act of 1986, also known as the Simpson-Rodino Act, employers are required to verify the citizenship status of all new employees when they are hired and to maintain records of that verification. This verification procedure, which applies even to small businesses with as few as four employees, involves filling out a government form known as the I-9. Failure to verify legal resident status or to keep proper records can result in the imposition of civil fines ranging from $100 to $1,000 for each violation. Knowingly hiring an illegal worker could bring a fine of up to $10,000 for repeat offenders. The Simpson-Rodino Act did not take full effect until June of 1988, but the Immigration and Naturalization Service has been aggressive in enforcing it. The passage of this legislation, like other federal acts passed in the mid- to late 1980s, has the effect of increasing governmental incursion into the employer-employee relationship, and of exhibiting how an issue (whether to hire undocumented workers) which was once regarded as primarily ethical in nature is now being addressed through the mechanism of the law.

Employer Liability for Tortious and Criminal Behavior

During the 1980s, courts began to hear more cases brought by workers claiming that their employers had committed intentional torts against them, and there was a significant increase in criminal prosecutions of employers for injuries caused by their business decisions and practices.

In perhaps the most famous civil case involving unsafe working conditions, the Supreme Court ruled that an employer may have civil tort liability, which includes liability for punitive damages. In 1984, in *Silkwood* v. *Kerr-McGee,* the family of Karen Silkwood was allowed to recover $505,000 in compensatory damages and $10 million in punitive damages. Silkwood, who died in a 1974 auto accident, had been exposed to nuclear radiation when her employer ignored Nuclear Regulatory Commission safety procedures. She was exposed to so much radiation that her clothes at home were contaminated and had to be burned. The *Silkwood* case may have set a precedent for other suits by injured workers. Examples of the types of intentional actions by employers alleged to give rise to rights to damages include knowing exposure to noxious chemicals, intentional removal of safety devices from equipment, using employees as test subjects for radiation exposure without informing the employees the tests were being done, failure of the employer to ascertain the risks of employee electrocution, and failure to provide a smoke-free workplace. One unresolved question regarding the filing of intentional tort suits against employers is the extent to which these suits are barred by workers' compensation acts. Some state courts have made an exception to the general rule that workers' compensation is the exclusive remedy that an employee has against an employer in the case of commission of intentional torts. The issue is a complex one, which the courts, and presumably the legislative branch, will have to examine.

Traditionally, business managers have been immune from criminal liability for business decisions they made that resulted in injury to workers. However, in 1985, three businessmen were found guilty of the crime of murder for requiring their employees to work under deadly conditions in violation of OSHA regulations. The workers had been required to work, without special apparatus, around open vats containing cyanide poison. This case set a new precedent concerning employer responsibility for worker safety. Since 1985, there have been a number of criminal prosecutions brought on the basis of violation of criminal statutes. For example, in Texas in 1987, a construction official was charged with criminal negligence in the deaths of two workers killed when the walls of a trench they were digging caved in. On the other hand, some courts have refused to apply criminal statutes to business executives, usually on the theory that such prosecutions are outside the scope of criminal law jurisdiction, and/or can only be pursued by charges brought under federal or state Occupational Safety and Health Acts. The idea that business officers could end up going to jail because of the results of their management decisions represents a significant expansion of the concept of the duties that employers owe to employees.

Job Security and Worker Termination

Historically, the employment relationship in the United States has been adversarial in nature. There can be little doubt that many workers in the nineteenth century were exploited by having to work long hours for low pay under poor conditions. These nineteenth-century employment practices created a resentment and mistrust of employers by employees that often still exists today.

Overall, the development of the law in the area of employer-employee relations in the twentieth century has emphasized the rights of workers. The reason for this policy was to attempt to readjust the balance of bargaining power between employers and employees that was perceived as having been tipped almost completely towards the side of the employers in the nineteenth century. You should keep in mind that, even with the establishment of certain worker protection statutes and the growth of labor unions, the United States still has a capitalistic economy based on the concept of freedom of contract between employer and employee. Thus, a private employer can generally fire an employee at will, and an employee is similarly free to quit at any time, assuming the parties have not entered into an employment contract for a specified period of time. The American employment relationship is still all too often adversarial; employees are often viewed as expendable commodities whom it is not necessary to bring into the business decision-making process, and employers are viewed as cold-hearted technocrats, only interested in the "bottom line" and not in worker welfare.

By contrast, in socialist states and countries such as Japan, workers are guaranteed job security. This guarantee is generally not available in our country, unless an employee works for the government civil service or is covered by a union contract containing dismissal and layoff provisions. Of course, a worker who can prove that a firing or a failure to hire violated civil rights or anti-discrimination laws may be able to obtain and/or retain a job. Some commentators argue that worker productivity would increase if the average American worker had greater job security, while others argue that just the opposite would happen.

In recent years, some discharged employees have won court cases based on the argument that their employers made contracts with the employees when they were hired that prohibited them from being fired except under certain circumstances. These employees have relied on alleged express contracts, often consisting of statements in employee handbooks. Such express promises might consist of statements that an employee would always have a job with the employer as long as his work was satisfactory. Another ground for breach of contract liability is implied contract, which interprets employer statements and actions as indicating that the employee has job security unless "just cause" for firing the employee is demonstrated by the employer.

In addition to bringing an action for breach of contract, many courts have recognized the right of fired employees to maintain a tort action, usually referred to as the tort of "wrongful discharge." The two most common grounds for alleging wrongful discharge are breach of public policy, a theory now recognized by a majority of the states, or breach of an employer duty of good faith and fair dealing. Discharges in violation of public policy have often been found in so-called whistleblower cases, where an employee complains about illegal or unethical employer practices, or in cases where employees were fired for attempting to assert their legitimate legal rights. Breach of the duty of good faith and fair dealing has been found to exist in situations where an employee was fired to avoid paying him commissions to which he was legitimately entitled, or where dismissal of an employee who had been with the company for eighteen years occurred based on unsubstantiated and uninvestigated allegations of misconduct.

The law regarding the erosion of the at-will employment doctrine is presently in a state of flux. The two cases that follow were decided by the same state Supreme Court seven years apart. In *Sheets* v. *Teddy's Frosted Foods, Inc.*, the court held that an employee had stated a cause of action for wrongful discharge. In *Finley* v. *Aetna Life and Casualty Company,* a discharged employee did not recover in a suit alleging breach of contract, promissory estoppel, and breach of the implied covenant of good faith. As you read these two cases, try to differentiate the facts that resulted in the employee winning in one case and losing in the other one. Comparison of these two cases provides guidance as to what factors must be present before courts are willing to abrogate the general principle of at-will employment.

Emard H. Sheets v. Teddy's Frosted Foods, Inc.

179 Conn. 471, 427 A.2d 385 (1980)

Facts

The issue in this case is whether an employer has a completely unlimited right to terminate the services of an employee whom it has hired for an indefinite term. The plaintiff, Emard H. Sheets, filed a complaint that as amended alleged that he had been wrongfully discharged from his employment as quality control director and operations manager of the defendant, Teddy's Frosted Foods, Inc. The defendant responded with a motion to strike the complaint as legally insufficient. The plaintiff declined to plead further when that motion was granted. From the consequent rendering of judgment for the defendant, the plaintiff appealed to this court.

Opinion

Justice Peters: Since this appeal is before us pursuant to a motion to strike, we must take the facts to be those alleged in the plaintiff's complaint as amended, and must construe the complaint in the manner most favorable to the pleader. The complaint alleges that for a four-year period, from November 1973 to November 1977, the plaintiff was employed by the defendant, as its quality control director and subsequently also as operations manager. In the course of his employment, the plaintiff received periodic raises and bonuses. In his capacity as quality control director and operations manager, the plaintiff began to notice deviations from the specifications contained in the defendant's standards and labels, in that some vegetables were substandard and some meat components underweight. These deviations meant that the defendant's products violated the express representations contained in the defendant's labeling; false or misleading labels in turn violate the provisions of the Connecticut Uniform Food, Drug and Cosmetic Act. In May of 1977, the plaintiff communicated in writing to the defendant concerning the use of substandard raw materials and underweight components in the defendant's finished products. His recommendations for more selective purchasing and conforming components were ignored. On November 3, 1977, his employment with the defendant was terminated. Although the stated reason for his discharge was unsatisfactory performance of his duties, he was actually dismissed in retaliation for his efforts to ensure that the defendant's products would comply with the applicable law relating to labeling and licensing.

The plaintiff's complaint alleges that his dismissal by his employer was wrongful in three respects. He claims that there was a violation of an implied contract of employment, a violation of public policy, and a malicious discharge. On this appeal, the claim of malice has not been separately pursued, and we are asked to consider only whether he has stated a cause of action for breach of contract or for intentionally tortious conduct. On oral argument, it was the tort claim that was most vigorously pressed, and it is upon the basis of tort that we have concluded that the motion to strike was granted in error.

The issue before us is whether to recognize an exception to the traditional rules governing employment at will so as to permit a cause of action for wrongful discharge where the discharge contravenes a clear mandate of public policy. In addressing that claim, we must clarify what is not at stake in this litigation. The plaintiff does not challenge the general proposition that contracts of permanent employment, or for an indefinite term, are terminable at will. Nor does he argue that contracts terminable at will permit termination only upon a showing of just cause for dismissal. Some statutes, such as the Connecticut Franchise Act, do impose limitations of just cause upon the power to terminate some contracts; but the legislature has recently refused to interpolate such a requirement into contracts of employment. There is a significant distinction between a criterion of just cause and what the plaintiff is seeking. "Just cause" substantially limits employer discretion to terminate, by requiring the employer, in all instances, to proffer a proper reason for dismissal, by forbidding the employer to act arbitrarily or capriciously. By contrast, the plaintiff asks only that the employer be responsible in damages if the former employee can prove a demonstrably *improper* reason for dismissal, a reason whose impropriety is derived from some important violation of public policy.

The argument that contract rights which are inherently legitimate may yet give rise to liability in tort if they are exercised improperly is not a novel one. Although private persons have the right not to enter into contracts, failure to contract under circumstances in which others are seriously misled gives rise to a variety of claims sounding in tort. The development of liability in contract for action induced by reliance upon a promise, despite the absence of common-law consideration normally required to bind a promisor rests upon principles derived at least in part from the law of tort. By way of analogy, we have long recognized abuse of process as a cause of action in tort whose gravamen in the misuse or misapplication of process, its use in an improper manner or to accomplish a purpose for which it was not designed.

It would be difficult to maintain that the right to discharge an employee hired at will is so fundamentally different from other contract rights that its exercise is never subject to judicial scrutiny regardless of how outrageous, how violative of public policy, the employer's conduct may be. The defendant does not seriously contest the propriety of cases in other jurisdictions that have found wrongful and actionable a discharge in retaliation for the exercise of an employee's right to: (1) refuse to commit perjury [citations omitted]; (2) file a workmen's compensation claim [citations omitted]; (3) engage in union activity [citations omitted]. While it may be true that these cases are supported by mandates of public policy derived directly from the applicable state statutes and constitutions, it is equally true that they serve at a minimum to establish the principle that public policy imposes some limits on unbridled discretion to terminate the employment of someone hired at will. No case has been called to our attention in which, despite egregiously outrageous circumstances, the employer's contract rights have been permitted to override competing claims of public policy, although there are numerous cases in which the facts were found not to support the employee's claim [citations omitted].

The issue then becomes the familiar common-law problem of deciding where and how to draw the line between claims that genuinely involve the mandates of public policy and are actionable, and ordinary disputes between employee and employer that are not. We are mindful that courts should not lightly intervene to impair the exercise of managerial discretion or to foment unwarranted litigation. We are, however, equally mindful that the myriad of employees without the bargaining power to command employment contracts for a definite term are entitled to a modicum of judicial protection when their conduct as good citizens is punished by their employers.

The central allegation of the plaintiff's complaint is that he was discharged because of his conduct in calling to his employer's attention repeated violations of the Connecticut Uniform Food, Drug and Cosmetic Act. This act prohibits the sale of mislabeled food. The act imposes criminal penalties upon anyone who violates section 19–213; subsection (b) of section 19–215 makes it clear that criminal sanctions do not depend upon proof of intent to defraud or mislead, since special sanctions are imposed for intentional misconduct. The plaintiff's position as quality control director and operations manager might have exposed him to the possibility of criminal prosecution under this act. The act was intended to safeguard the public health and promote the public welfare by protecting the consuming public from injury by product use and the purchasing public from injury by merchandising deceit.

It is useful to compare the factual allegations of this complaint with those of other recent cases in which recovery was sought for retaliatory discharge. In *Geary* v. *United States Steel Corporation,* in which the plaintiff had disputed the safety of tubular steel casings, he was denied recovery because, as a company salesman, he had neither the expertise nor the corporate responsibility to "exercise independent, expert judgment in matters of product safety." By contrast, this plaintiff unless his title is meaningless, did have responsibility for product quality control. Three other recent cases in which the plaintiff's claim survived demurrer closely approximate the claim before us. In *Trombetta* v. *Detroit, Toledo & Ironton R. Co.* (Michigan), a cause of action was stated when an employee alleged that he had been discharged in retaliation for his refusal to manipulate and alter sampling results for pollution control reports required by Michigan law. There as here falsified reports would have violated state law. In *Harless* v. *First National Bank in Fairmont* (W. Va. 1978), an employee stated a cause of action when he alleged that he had been discharged in retaliation for his efforts to ensure his employer's compliance with state and federal consumer credit protection laws. There as here the legislature had established a public policy of consumer protection. In *Pierce* v. *Ortho Pharmaceutical Corporation* (N.J. 1979), the plaintiff was entitled to a trial to determine whether she had been wrongfully discharged for refusing to pursue clinical testing of a new drug containing a high level of saccharin; the court noted that the plaintiff's status as a physician entitled her to invoke the Hippocratic Oath as well as state statutory provisions governing the licensing and the conduct of physicians. There as here the case might have been dismissed as a conflict in judgment.

In light of these recent cases, which evidence a growing judicial receptivity to the recognition of a tort claim for wrongful discharge, the trial court was in error in granting the defendant's motion to strike. The plaintiff alleged that he had been dismissed in retaliation for his insistence that the defendant comply with the requirements of a state statute, the Food, Drug and Cosmetic Act. We need not decide whether violation of a state statute is invariably a prerequisite to the conclusion that a challenged discharge violates public policy. Certainly when there is a relevant state statute we should not ignore the statement of public policy that it represents. For today, it is enough to decide that an employee should not be put to an election whether to risk criminal sanction or to jeopardize his continued employment. Remanded for further proceedings.

Case Questions

1. Why did the Court find that Sheets could sue for wrongful discharge?
2. How important was it that Sheets felt he had knowledge of violation of a criminal statute?
3. If the legislative branches of federal and state governments have refused to pass laws to protect employees in cases like this one, should the courts step in and do it?

Finley v. Aetna Life and Casualty Company

202 Conn. 190, 520A.2d 208 (1987)

C. J. Peters: This appeal involves claims of an employee that he was wrongfully discharged despite assurances of lifelong employment so long as his performance remained satisfactory. The plaintiff, Thomas P. Finley, brought an action in three counts against the defendant, Aetna Life & Casualty Company, alleging that the defendant's termination of his employment was wrongful because of: (1) breach of express contract; (2) promissory estoppel; and (3) breach of an implied covenant of good faith. Following a jury trial, the trial court, *Missal, J.,* granted the defendant's motion for directed verdicts on the second and third counts of the complaint, and submitted the first count, alleging breach of express contract, to the jury. The jury rendered a general verdict for the defendant. The plaintiff appealed to the Appellate Court, which found error and ordered a new trial on the first and second counts of the complaint. We granted the defendant's petition for certification and now reverse the judgment of the Appellate Court.

This case arises out of the defendant's decision to terminate the employment of the plaintiff on April 12, 1976. The plaintiff, who had been employed by the defendant for twenty-four years, was a manager in the defendant's Medicare department, part B, at the time of his discharge. The jury might reasonably have found that the defendant, through its agents and its personnel manual,[1] made representations to him that his employment would not be terminated so long as his performance was satisfactory. Furthermore, the plaintiff at trial introduced into evidence written performance appraisals made during his employment with the defendant, as well as the oral statements of one of his former supervisors, to show that his job performance had been satisfactory. From the defendant's evidence, however, the jury might also reasonably have found that for some time before the plaintiff's discharge, he and his immediate supervisor had been involved

[1]The manual provided, in a section subtitled "Involuntary Terminations (Dismissals)," that "[i]t is Company policy to terminate any employee who cannot perform satisfactorily, whose attendance is poor, or who is otherwise unsuited to his job."

in a divisive and acrimonious departmental dispute. Both men ultimately were discharged because of their inability to resolve their differences.

The plaintiff's amended complaint alleged, in the first count, the breach of an express contract arising out of the defendant's assurances that the plaintiff would remain employed so long as his job performance was satisfactory. Despite the defendant's motion for a directed verdict on this count, the trial court permitted this claim to go to the jury. The jury found for the defendant.

The plaintiff's second count, sounding in promissory estoppel, alleged that the plaintiff had relied to his detriment on the defendant's representations of continued employment. His third count alleged that the defendant violated an implied covenant of good faith by wrongfully terminating his employment. As to these two counts, the trial court granted the defendant's motion for a directed verdict. After the adverse jury verdict on count one, the plaintiff moved to set aside the verdict and for a new trial on these latter counts only. This motion was denied by the trial court.

The defendant correctly asserts that it is not "settled" law in Connecticut that statements in an employer's personnel manual may form the basis of a contract between employer and employee. This court, however, has never held, as the trial court instructed the jury, that such statements cannot form the basis for such a contract. To the contrary, we have stated only recently that such representations, under appropriate circumstances, may give rise to an express or implied contract between employer and employee. *Magnan* v. *Anaconda Industries, Inc.* (1984); see generally *Dolak* v. *Sullivan* (1958) (statements in written retirement plan gave rise to employer-employee contract); *Tilbert* v. *Eagle Lock Co.* (1933) (assurances in employee benefit plan constituted enforceable promise to pay benefits in accordance with plan).

In the present case, statements in the defendant's personnel manual were of critical relevance to the issue of whether an express contract existed between the defendant and the plaintiff. " 'The intention of the parties manifested by their words and acts is essential to determine whether a contract was entered into and what its terms were. . . .' " The relevant statements in the defendant's personnel manual certainly could have been interpreted as noncontractual. In the absence of "definitive contract language," however, "the determination of what the parties intended to encompass in their contractual commitments is a question of the intention of the parties, and an inference of fact." In this case, therefore, whether the defendant's personnel manual gave rise to an express contract between the parties was a question of fact properly to be determined by the jury.

We agree with the defendant that the general verdict rule applies in the present case, and that the verdict for the defendant comprises an "implicit finding" that the plaintiff was terminated for his failure to perform his job satisfactorily. The plaintiff concedes that even if the jury had found that the parties entered into a contract, it reasonably could have found that the plaintiff was terminated for failing to perform his job satisfactorily.

Our conclusion that the general verdict rule requires the sustaining of the defendant's verdict on the first count makes it unnecessary for us to reach the merits of the defendant's fourth and final claim. That claim is that the Appellate Court erroneously reversed the directed verdict for the defendant on the second count of the plaintiff's complaint, which alleged a cause of action in promissory estoppel. Under a promissory estoppel theory, a party may maintain a claim for damages based upon a promise which induces the party's action or forbearance, if such action or forbearance is undertaken in reasonable reliance upon the promise. *Sheets* v. *Teddy's Frosted Foods, Inc.* (1980).

In the present case, the plaintiff based his cause of action in the second count upon the defendant's alleged promise not to terminate him so long as he performed his job satisfactorily. As discussed above, we presume that the jury's general verdict on the first count of the complaint encompassed a finding that the defendant's termination of the plaintiff was justified by his unsatisfactory job performance. The verdict stands as a final determination of that factual issue.

The judgment of the Appellate Court is reversed and the case is remanded with direction to render judgment for the defendant.

Case Questions

1. Under the reasoning in this case, would it be possible for an employee to win a case based on a theory of breach of implied contract?
2. What factors distinguish this case from the *Sheets* case?

A developing issue in wrongful discharge cases is the amount of damages a winning plaintiff can recover. In a significant 1989 California Supreme Court case, wrongful discharge cases were characterized as "fundamentally contractual." The court therefore limited the plaintiff's recovery to lost pay and related economic losses, but refused to allow such tort-based damages as recovery for emotional distress and punitive damages. It will be some time before it becomes apparent whether other states will follow California's lead regarding the measure of damages in wrongful termination cases.

Covenants Not to Compete

An old legal mechanism for regulating the employer-employee relationship that has increased in use in recent years is the **covenant not to compete.** These covenants are contracts that provide that employees will not compete with their employers in certain ways if the employment relationship ends. The early common law attitude toward these covenants was that they were against public policy, since they infringed on freedom of contract. However, the prevailing modern legal position is that such contracts are enforceable as long as they are reasonably limited in *duration, geographic area,* and *scope*. It is very common for local media personalities to sign such contracts. For example, a news announcer for a television station might sign a contract stipulating that she would not become a news announcer for a competing television station for a year after she terminates her position with her original employer. This contract would probably be upheld by a court because it was limited in duration (one year), geographic area (only the broadcast area of the original employer), and scope (it only applied to being a news announcer, and not, for example, a local talk-show host). A court will not enforce such a covenant if it is overly broad (such as, in the preceding example, prohibiting the former employee from working for another television station in any capacity).

Today, many businesses rely on **trade secrets** to safeguard their manufacturing processes: that is, they decide not to patent their ideas, but to keep them a secret from their competitors. It is a tort to steal trade secrets. In addition to taking security precautions, these firms usually require the employees who develop the secret processes to sign covenants not to compete. In these covenants, the employees promise that if they do go to work for a competitor, they will not divulge any information that the original employer is trying to protect. Use of these covenants is commonplace in high-technology fields. When the legality of these contracts is called into question, courts have to balance the rights of businesses to protect their property against the freedom of individuals to choose their employers. The use of trade secrets is widespread and growing, so it seems likely that legal questions concerning the validity of specific covenants are likely to continue for some time.

Ethical Issues in the Employment Relationship

The employment relationship is one area where the nineteenth-century laissez-faire attitude still prevails in the law. Perhaps for this reason, there are many areas of controversy regarding what the nature of the employer-employee relationship should be.

One controversial topic in employer-employee relations today concerns the problem of when an employee should publicly reveal that his employer has been engaging in an illegal or morally questionable activity. It seems clear that traditional religious and ethical teachings would indicate that an employee has a moral obligation to reveal employer practices that might result in physical harm to third parties. What about the case of an employee who reveals information of public importance that does not involve illegal actions, such as an employee who reveals waste in the performance of government contracts? When these issues have been raised in the past, it was often the employees who suffered from their **whistle blowing** by losing their jobs. The case of *Sheets* v. *Teddy's Frosted Foods, Inc.,* which you have just read, illustrates the fate of many whistleblowers. When an employee is ethically compelled to reveal his employer's practices publicly must be considered on a case-by-case basis. The courts must necessarily balance the gravity of the potential harm of the employer's practice against the likelihood that the revelation will abate the potential harm and will not injure the whistleblower too severely. Some states have enacted "whistleblower statutes" to protect the whistleblowers and encourage employee disclosures of questionable business practices. However, these statutes have not been used a great deal, possibly because of the doubts employees have about how effective they are.

Another ethical question that arises often is whether a business owes any duty to a community in which it is operating if the business decides to relocate. Since this is a free country, business has a legal and constitutional right to relocate either within the country or to a foreign country. As you have seen, federal law now requires that large companies give sixty-day notice of large plant closings or long layoffs. However, the view has often been expressed that business has a moral duty to employees who do not move with the business and to the town in which the abandoned facility is located. Many businesses have voluntarily tried to ease the effect of their relocation on their former employees and communities. One approach is to sell the business facility to the employees or a community group instead of dismantling it.

A controversy that has gained considerable public attention in recent years centers on executive salaries and bonuses. Million-dollar bonuses have been given to high-ranking executives of large corporations that were in economic trouble only a few years before. The federal government helped some of these corporations by restraining foreign competition to keep the domestic companies viable. The government's rationale for assisting the companies was to keep workers employed and to help consumers. However, some of these same corporations raised their prices, thereby adversely affecting consumers, and gave their workers small increases in salary while the executives got huge bonuses. Criticism of the bonuses is based on the rationale that without the bonuses, prices could have been kept lower, the average employee could have gotten a bigger raise, or the shareholders could have gotten a bigger dividend, or some combination of the three. The executives countered that it was primarily their hard work and managerial strategy that pulled the companies out of their tailspins and that they needed the incentives of bonuses. Is there an ethical dilemma over the issue of executive bonuses?

The tendency toward increased governmental regulation of the employment relationship seems to have been ameliorated to some extent in recent years by the general desire to stop government intrusion into private matters. Furthermore, government intrusion is expensive, and apprehension has grown with the realization that, instead of complying with costly government regulation, business may opt to go abroad. However, recent federal legislation has in some areas expanded governmental intrusion. It is difficult to predict whether the latest governmental actions regarding such issues as drug testing and use of lie-detectors represent the end of governmental involvement in the employer-employee relationship.

The important concepts and terms in this chapter are listed below; page numbers have been provided for the key terms. By reading over each section you can assess your understanding of the chapter concepts and determine areas you may want to review.

Chapter Summary

1. The common law regards the employment relation as an "at-will" contract, which either the employer or the employee could terminate at any time.
2. Workers' compensation laws were passed to provide financial benefits to employees who are injured while performing activities within the scope of their employ.
3. Workers' compensation statutes reject the three common law employer's defenses of contributory negligence, assumption of the risk, and the fellow servant doctrine.
4. The Fair Labor Standards Act sets minimum wages and maximum hours for most workers.
5. Unemployment compensation payments are administered by the states. To be eligible for payments, an applicant must meet certain state requirements, such as having worked a certain period of time.

6. The federal Social Security Act provides for public pension payments for the retired, as well as Medicare medical payments.
7. The federal Employee Retirement Income Security Act (ERISA) regulates the administration of private employer pension plans.
8. Federal and state occupational safety and health acts aim to prevent worker injuries by providing for the issuance of administrative regulations to set safety and health standards in the workplace.
9. Inspectors for the Occupational Safety and Health Administration may be required to get a search warrant to inspect business premises.
10. The traditional attitude of the employment relationship as being "at will" has been modified in some states by courts who found that the employer breached a contract or committed the tort of wrongful discharge.
11. Many employees sign contracts called covenants not to compete, in which they promise not to compete with former employers.

Key Terms

assumption of the risk 370
contributory negligence 370
covenant not to compete 393
Employee Retirement Income Security Act 376
Fair Labor Standards Act 374
fellow servant doctrine 370
Occupational Safety and Health Act 377
Social Security 376
trade secret 393
unemployment compensation 375
whistle blowing 394
workers' compensation 370

Questions on Ethics

1. The federal government at one point announced that it was immediately terminating federal disability payments to a large number of citizens. These persons' cases would then be reviewed and if it was found that they were eligible, their payments would be reactivated. Terminated recipients were supposed to report in person to reapply for benefits. Some terminated recipients were bedridden and could not report to reapply. Did the government act ethically in terminating these persons' benefits without ascertaining first whether they were eligible?
2. Should strikers be able to obtain unemployment benefits?
3. Is it ethical to pass a law such as ERISA, which might ultimately obligate the taxpayers to fund not only the federal Social Security systems but also private pension funds that have gone bankrupt?

4. Social Security Medicare requests for payments from hospitals and doctors are now based on a DRG (diagnosis-related group) schedule, whereby Medicare does not pay the actual cost of a particular procedure (e.g., a hip operation), but instead pays what the government has determined is the average cost of that procedure. If the DRG payment is insufficient, the patient (or if the patient is indigent, the hospital or the doctor) has to make up the difference. The result of the DRG program seems to be that the government is not paying as much for Medicare, but Medicare patients are not receiving the same level of care as before. It is conceivable that the lower level of care (e.g., sending a patient home earlier than would have formerly been the case) could result in patient deaths. What are the ethical issues involved in the DRG program?
5. Unlike pension rights, which are usually vested under ERISA, retiree health benefits through employers are generally regarded as terminable at the will of the employer. Assuming that it is legal for employers to terminate retiree health benefits, is it ethical?

Questions on Law

1. Weiner was hired by McGraw-Hill, Inc. When he applied for his job, he signed a job application stating that his employment would be subject to the handbook on personnel policies and procedures. This handbook stated that the company would discharge employees "for just and sufficient cause only." Later, Weiner was fired. He sued McGraw-Hill, alleging he was fired without just cause. Will he win? *Weiner* v. *McGraw-Hill, Inc.*, 443 N.E.2d 441 (N.Y. 1982).
2. Frampton was ordered to report for jury duty, and when he did so, he was fired. He sued his employer. Will he recover? *Frampton* v. *Central Indiana Gas Co.*, 297 N.E.2d 425 (Ind. 1973).
3. Segler worked in a manufacturing plant. Near his work station was a conveyor belt which, when working, brought flasks attached to the conveyor belt into an industrial oven, so that the contents of the flasks could be "cooked." While the conveyor belt was not working, but the oven was still warm, Segler placed a frozen pot pie into the oven, crossing the conveyor belt to do so. When he went to retrieve the pie, the belt started up and he was pinned between the oven and a flask, causing him severe injuries. Can he recover under workers' compensation? *Segler* v. *The Industrial Commission*, 406 N.E.2d 542 (Ill. 1980).
4. Two years after Praprotnik, a management-level employee in a city of St. Louis governmental agency, successfully appealed a temporary suspension to the city Civil Service Commission, he was transferred to a clerical position in another city agency, from which he was laid off the

next year. Praprotnik sued, alleging violation of his civil rights on the theory that his First Amendment rights had been violated through retaliatory actions taken in response to his suspension appeal. Is the city liable for its treatment of Praprotnik? *City of St. Louis* v. *Praprotnik,* 56 U.S.L.W. 4201 (March 2, 1988).

5. In order to assist coal miners who may be eligible for black lung benefits, the Secretary of Labor issued regulations describing five ways in which a claimant might prove that he is entitled to an interim presumption of eligibility. In order to prove eligibility under the regulations, must an applicant prove a single item of qualifying evidence, or must he show more? *Mullins Coal Company* v. *Department of Labor,* 56 U.S.L.W. 4044 (Dec. 14, 1987).

Suggested Readings

Prentice and Winslett, "Employee References: Will a "No Comment" Policy Protect Employers against Liability for Defamation?" 25 *American Business Law Journal* 206 (1987).

Dworkin and Near, "Whistleblowing Statutes: Are They Working?" 25 *American Business Law Journal* 240 (1987).

Bible, "Screening Workers for Drugs: The Constitutional Implications of Urine Testing in Public Employment," 24 *American Business Law Journal* 309 (1986).

15 Equal Employment Opportunity

I have a dream that my four little children will one day live in a nation where they will not be judged by the color of their skin, but by the content of their character.

—Martin Luther King, Jr., speech at the civil rights march on Washington, D.C., 28 August 1963

■ LEARNING OBJECTIVES

After you have read this chapter, you should:

1. Be familiar with federal and state statutes that have been passed to help ensure equal employment opportunity.
2. Be familar with the functions of the Equal Employment Opportunity Commission.
3. Be familiar with the concept of affirmative action plans.
4. Be familiar with such current issues as reverse discrimination and comparable worth.

Business Decisions and the Law

Are Contract Awards for Minorities Legal

The city of Richmond, Virginia, adopted a plan requiring general contractors awarded city construction contracts to subcontract at least 30 percent of the dollar amount of each contract to one or more Minority Business Enterprises, consisting of at least 51 percent ownership by black, Spanish-speaking, Oriental, Indian, Eskimo, or Aleut citizens. Is this minority set-aside program constitutional? See *City of Richmond* v. *Croson Company*.

Introduction

As late as the 1950s, the doctrine of laissez-faire applied to employers in the area of hiring, promoting, and firing workers. This meant that there were no laws to prevent employers from discriminating on the basis of race, sex, religion, national origin, or any other category. Racial segregation was common in many areas of the country, with members of certain racial and ethnic groups being automatically disqualified from consideration for many types of jobs. It was standard practice to use employment advertisements that categorized job openings according to "Help Wanted—Male" and "Help Wanted—Female."

Today, it is illegal for an employer to discriminate in hiring, promotion, or firing on the basis of any of the following: race, color, religion, sex, national origin, age, handicap, or pregnancy. How did this change come about? As we have pointed out before, society may become dissatisfied with the actions of some of its members because it perceives that these individuals are not acting in the best interests of the general public. Therefore, a law will be passed to bring the individuals' activities more into line with societal expectations. This phenomenon is exactly what occurred in the 1960s and 1970s in the area of employment discrimination. People began to feel it was unfair not even to consider individuals for some employment positions simply because they were members of certain groups. Therefore, over a period of time, a number of laws were passed and other governmental action was taken to prevent employment discrimination based on the categories we have mentioned.

In this chapter, we will discuss the statutes that forbid certain types of discrimination in employment, as well as governmental activities that have been carried out for the same purpose. Throughout the chapter, and especially in the concluding sections, you will be presented with various employment discrimination issues that are unresolved and require the balancing of societal and individual interests.

Equal Employment Opportunity Statutes

Title VII of the 1964 Civil Rights Act

Introduction and Coverage of the Act

As the introduction pointed out, a number of federal antidiscrimination statutes have been passed. **Title VII of the 1964 Civil Rights Act** is the single most important equal employment opportunity statute, because it has produced the most litigation and established the enforcement mechanisms that are used in most other antidiscrimination statutes. Part of Title VII is contained in chapter 1.

Title VII was passed as part of the 1964 Civil Rights Act, a comprehensive civil rights act designed to combat various types of discrimination in such areas as housing, public accommodations, and educational institutions. Title VII (as amended in 1972) prohibits employers with fifteen or more employees, as well as labor unions, employment agencies, and state and local governments, from discriminating on the basis of race, color, religion, sex, or national origin in hiring, firing, compensation, or in terms or conditions of employment. The majority of the cases brought under Title VII have been against employers, rather than unions, employment agencies, or governmental units, so for convenience our discussion will refer to enforcement against employers. Those who feel their rights under Title VII have been violated may sue under the act. Title VII may also be enforced by the Equal Employment Opportunity Commission (EEOC), a federal administrative agency.

Enforcement Procedures under Title VII—The Equal Employment Opportunity Commission

Congress created a new federal administrative agency, the **Equal Employment Opportunity Commission (EEOC),** to enforce the provisions of Title VII. Today, the EEOC also enforces the Equal Pay Act, the Age Discrimination in Employment Act, and the Pregnancy Discrimination Act under the procedures outlined in Title VII.

The main mechanism for enforcing Title VII is investigation of individual complaints. Normally, a complaint must be filed within 180 days of an alleged violation of one of the antidiscrimination statutes. The EEOC will then begin an investigation of the complaint, unless the state or locality where the alleged discriminatory act occurred has established its own agency to investigate such charges. In this case, the EEOC must allow the other agency sixty days to act before it begins its investigation. Title VII requires that the EEOC attempt conciliation with an employer before starting a lawsuit in federal court. However, the EEOC, after conciliation attempts, may bring a lawsuit alleging violation of Title VII. Sometimes the EEOC does not start a lawsuit itself but gives a *right to sue* letter to the charging party, allowing the alleged victim of discrimination to sue.

Another method of enforcing Title VII is through what is known as **pattern and practices suits.** In this type of lawsuit, the EEOC may initiate a lawsuit without an individual complaint if it determines after investigation that an employer is engaging in systematic discrimination. Probably the most famous patterns and practices suit was the one filed by the EEOC against American Telephone and Telegraph (AT&T), which was settled by a court consent decree in 1979, and which resulted in dramatic changes in AT&T's hiring and promotion policies.

To help it identify potential patterns and practices cases, the EEOC requires that all employers of one hundred employees or more who have government contracts of $50,000 or more file annual reports regarding the composition of their work force.

Types of Discrimination Prohibited by Title VII

Title VII prohibits discrimination on the basis of race, color, sex, religion, and national origin. We will now examine what constitutes discrimination on each of these bases.

Race and Color. The single most important reason for the passage of Title VII was to put an end to the policies of racial segregation in employment. When the act was passed, it was customary to divide employment opportunities into "whites only" and "blacks only." Title VII made this discriminatory practice illegal and thus, in effect, ended overt racial or color-based discrimination. In recent years, overt racial discrimination has become virtually nonexistent. Plaintiffs have still managed to recover under Title VII by showing intent to discriminate through circumstantial evidence. For example, if a qualified black person applied for a job and was turned down while the position remained unfilled, a presumption would arise that the applicant had been discriminated against on the basis of race, and the burden of proof would be on the employer to prove that there was some other legitimate, nondiscriminatory reason for not hiring that particular candidate.

One of the most controversial aspects of equal employment opportunity law in the past few years has been the development of charges that enforcement of antidiscrimination provisions create "reverse discrimination," particularly against white males. This subject will be discussed later in the chapter.

Sex. When Title VII first became effective, sex discrimination became one of the major subjects of litigation under the act. This development stemmed not only from the general practice of sex discrimination in employment through the 1960s, but also from confusion over what constituted "sex discrimination." The prohibition against sex discrimination was put into Title VII in an attempt to prevent passage of the entire 1964 Civil Rights Act. As a consequence, there was practically no congressional debate to shed light on the nature of this type of discrimination, and the EEOC and the courts were generally left to develop their own interpretations. The EEOC quickly adopted guidelines stating what type of activities it regarded as constituting sex discrimination, and these guidelines have been amended several times. Courts have generally followed the EEOC guidelines fairly closely, even though the guidelines are not binding on them, because of the judicial doctrine of deference to administrative agencies (discussed in the chapter on administrative agencies), and because, due to lack of proof of congressional intent, the guidelines represent the best source for interpreting the meaning of the sex discrimination provision other than judges' intuition.

Two early cases that present a sample of the kinds of sex discrimination cases initially faced by the courts under Title VII are *Diaz* v. *Pan American World Airways, Inc.*, and *Phillips* v. *Martin Marietta*. In *Diaz*, a 1971 case decided by the federal Fifth Circuit Court of Appeals, a male was denied a job as a flight attendant due to an airline's "female only" policy for that type of position. The court held that the policy constituted sex discrimination, since the female-only requirement was not reasonably necessary to the successful carrying out of the job. The court rejected the notion that the preferences of passengers for one sex over another should be controlling. In the 1971 *Phillips* case, the first Title VII case to be heard by the United States Supreme Court, that Court struck down a lower court theory that an employer could discriminate on the basis of sex plus another objective categorization (the so-called sex plus test). The "plus" category in *Phillips* was the status of being a mother (a dissent in the Court of Appeals had noted that being a mother appeared sex-related).

In recent years, many practices have come under analysis to determine whether they constitute sex discrimination. The areas of salary, insurance benefits, and maternity benefits are just a few that have been examined. Many of these present areas of concern will be discussed later in the chapter.

National Origin. The most obvious purpose of Title VII's prohibition of discrimination because of national origin was to prevent employers from refusing to consider hiring job applicants who were born in a foreign country or maintained an ethnic identity as persons descended from ancestors who came from a foreign country. For example, under Title VII, refusal to consider hiring persons of Hispanic or Japanese background simply because of their national origin would be clearly illegal.

Overt discrimination based on national origin appears to be largely a thing of the past. However, questions have been raised in recent years regarding the extent to which enforcement of language requirements and citizenship requirements may constitute discrimination based on national origin. Whether an employer can discriminate against a job applicant due to the applicant's inability to speak English depends on application of a **business necessity test:** If the applicant's lack of English language skills will prevent him from properly carrying out his duties (such as communicating with customers or reading instructions), the employer *may* discriminate. However, a ban on workers ever speaking any language other than English while on the job, even in casual conversations, would be discriminatory. In 1973, in *Espinoza* v. *Farah Manufacturing Company,* the United States Supreme Court held that a company *could* discriminate against non-American citizens. The Court limited its holding by stating that an employer could not use a "citizens only" hiring policy to veil discrimination against a particular ethnic group. In *Espinoza,* the plaintiff alleged that she had not been hired because of her Mexican citizenship and claimed that the employer was discriminating against persons of Mexican lineage. However, the evidence showed that some 96 percent of all employees in the plant in question were of Mexican descent, so the Court held that claims of general national origin discrimination were unfounded.

Religion. Title VII was intended to prevent discrimination based on an employee's or job applicant's religious preferences. For example, an employer would be prohibited under Title VII from discriminating against a job application because he was Catholic or Jewish. You should note, however, that Title VII contains a provision that exempts religious organizations from the prohibition against religious discrimination in employment. In 1987, the Supreme Court held that this Title VII exemption did not violate the Establishment of Religion Clause of the First Amendment. Therefore, religious organizations could discriminate by hiring members of their religion, even if they were performing secular activities.

Questions have arisen concerning the extent of an employer's rights when the exercise of an employee's religion requires changes in the employer's normal methods of business operations. Title VII provides that, as a defense to a charge of religious discrimination, an employer may demonstrate that he is unable reasonably to accommodate an employee's or prospective employee's religious observance without undue hardship on the conduct of the employer's business. The United States Supreme Court considered this question of religious accommodation in the 1977 case of *Trans World Airlines, Inc.*, v. *Hardison.* Hardison was a member of a religious group that prohibited working on Saturdays. Due to the business necessity of round-the-clock staffing and the terms of a collective bargaining agreement that guaranteed workers vacation time, TWA was eventually put into a position where it had to fire Hardison, break the collective bargaining agreement, or make supervisory personnel take over Hardison's job. The Court held under these circumstances that TWA could fire Hardison because of undue hardship caused by his religious observances.

In 1986, the Supreme Court addressed the question of the extent to which an employer must accommodate an employee's religious beliefs if dismissal is not an issue (as it was in *Hardison*). Philbrook, a school teacher in Connecticut, was allowed only three days of paid leave for observance of religious holidays, but said he needed six. The teachers' collective bargaining contract allowed three additional days for "necessary personal business," but specifically stated they could not be used for religious observances. Philbrook requested that the school board allow the three necessary personal business days be allowed to be used for religious observances, but the board refused. He then sued the board for religious discrimination under Title VII, citing the Title VII provision that employers should reasonably accommodate an employee's religious beliefs if this can be done without undue hardship on the conduct of the employer's business. The federal Court of Appeals ruled in Philbrook's favor, stating that where both the employer and the employee each propose a reasonable accommodation to the employee's religious beliefs, the employer must accept the employee's proposal unless that accommodation causes undue hardship to the conduct of the employer's business. The Supreme Court held that an employer meets its obligation under Title VII when it demonstrates that it has offered a reasonable accommodation to the employee, and that the employer need not further show that each of the employee's alternative accommodations would result in undue hardship. Undue hardship is an issue only where the employer claims that it is unable to offer any reasonable accommodation without hardship (as was the case in *Hardison*). In *Philbrook,* the court remanded the case to the district court for a determination of whether the school board's leave policy constituted a reasonable accommodation of religious beliefs, but the court did observe that requiring unpaid leave for religious observances did not appear to be a reasonable accommodation when paid leave was provided for all purposes except religious ones.

Proof of Discrimination under Title VII

The earliest Title VII cases often involved instances of overt discrimination in which an employer denied that discrimination occurred or relied on the main exception of Title VII, the bona fide occupational qualification exception. Later cases began to deal with more subtle forms of discrimination in which a plaintiff alleged that the employer was discriminating or was producing the effect of discriminating against a group as a whole. In this section, we will examine the limits of the bona fide occupational qualification exception to Title VII and the two most common legal theories used to attack "subtle" discrimination; disparate treatment and disparate impact.

Bona Fide Occupational Qualification. Title VII does allow a "defense" to a charge of discrimination if an employer can show that sex, religion, or national origin (but not race or color) is a **bona fide occupational qualification (BFOQ)** reasonably necessary to the normal operation of that particular business or enterprise. When Title VII first became effective, many employers sought to raise the BFOQ exception as a defense to most charges of discrimination, particularly on the basis of sex. One of the earliest of these cases was *Diaz* v. *Pan American World Airways, Inc.*, discussed previously in the section on sex discrimination, which held an airline's female-only flight attendant policy illegal. The courts have tended to follow very closely the EEOC guidelines, which state that the BFOQ exception is to be construed very narrowly, and very few cases have accepted an employer's BFOQ defense. One Supreme Court case that did allow a BFOQ defense, however, is *Dothard* v. *Rawlinson* (1977). *Dothard* upheld the state of Alabama's policy that prison guards at the state's maximum security prison had to be male, based on the strong proven state need for security in prison operation.

A very interesting current issue that has not been decided by the Supreme Court is the application of the BFOQ exception to national origin employment requirements. The specific question involved is whether companies operating in the United States but owned by foreign nationals can discriminate in favor of citizens of the owner countries. The few early court cases dealing with the issue indicated that the company cannot so discriminate unless a treaty between the United States and the company's home country allows it. In 1982 in *Avagliano* v. *Sumitomo Shoji America, Inc.*, the United States Supreme Court ruled that the United States–Japanese treaty signed at the end of World War II did not exempt Japanese companies doing business in the United States from the provisions of Title VII. *Avagliano* only concerned whether the treaty prevented filing a lawsuit under Title VII, and the Court specifically refused to rule on whether the Japanese-owned company could use a BFOQ or business necessity defense. The plaintiffs in *Avagliano* had also raised questions of sex discrimination, to which the defendants had asserted BFOQ defenses. Thus, it is still unclear to what extent a foreign-owned company may favor its country's citizens and enforce its country's customs even if they violate Title VII. However, it appears that foreign companies will be held by the courts to be subject to Title VII. In *Wickes* v. *Olympic Airways* (1984), the Sixth Circuit Court of Appeals held that a 1951 treaty with Greece allowed Olympic Airlines to discriminate on the basis of national origin in hiring for managerial and technical positions, but not for other purposes.

Discrimination Based on Disparate Treatment. The concept of a lawsuit based on disparate treatment was developed to deal with a situation in which a plaintiff cannot show any specific proof that an employer refused to hire a worker based on discriminatory motives. In *McDonnell Douglas Corporation* v. *Green,* the United States Supreme Court stated how a prospective employee can prove illegal discrimination without discriminatory intent. The plaintiff must prove that he or she (1) is in a class protected by Title VII, (2) applied for a job for which the employer was seeking applicants, (3) was qualified to perform the job, (4) was denied the job, and (5) the employer continued to seek applicants for the position. A plaintiff who has established these facts has proven illegal discrimination unless the prospective employer can show a legitimate, nondiscriminatory reason for rejecting the plaintiff's application. Such legitimate reasons could include poor performance on aptitude tests, a poor work record, and questionable letters of recommendation.

Discrimination Based on Disparate Impact. It is possible that an employer might adopt policies or procedures that, while appearing neutral and nondiscriminatory, would have the impact of reduced hiring or promotion of members of certain groups. The earliest United States Supreme Court case to consider this probem was *Griggs* v. *Duke Power Co.* (1971). In *Griggs,* the court invalidated the use of intelligence and mechanical comprehension tests administered by the Duke Power Company to select employees for departments that, prior to the enactment of Title VII, had been staffed only by whites. Far more whites than blacks passed the test, with the result that the departments stayed largely white. The court said, "[Title VII] proscribes not only overt discrimination but also practices which are fair in form, but discriminatory in operation. The touchstone is business necessity. If an employment practice which operates to exclude Negroes cannot be shown to be related to job performance, the practice is prohibited."

In the following case, the Supreme Court discussed proof of actionable disparate impact, as well as disparate treatment, and ruled that bias in subjective employment decisions may be proven by statistical evidence showing that an employer's practices have a discriminatory effect.

Watson v. Fort Worth Bank and Trust

108 S. Ct. 2777 (1988)

Opinion

Justice O'Connor: This case requires us to decide what evidentiary standards should be applied under Title VII of the Civil Rights Act of 1964 in determining whether an employer's practice of committing promotion decisions to the subjective discretion of supervisory employees has led to illegal discrimination.

Petitioner Clara Watson, who is black, was hired by respondent Fort Worth Bank and Trust (the Bank) as a proof operator in August 1973. In January 1976, Watson was promoted to a position as teller in the Bank's drive-in facility. In February 1980, she sought to become supervisor of the tellers in the main lobby; a white male, however, was selected for this job. Watson then sought a position as supervisor of the drive-in bank, but this position was given to a white female. In February 1981, after Watson had served for about a year as a commercial teller in the Bank's main lobby, and informally as assistant to the supervisor of tellers, the man holding that position was promoted. Watson applied for the vacancy, but the white female who was the supervisor of the drive-in bank was selected instead. Watson then applied for the vacancy created at the drive-in; a white male was selected for that job. The Bank, which has about 80 employees, had not developed precise and formal criteria for evaluating candidates for the positions for which Watson unsuccessfully applied. It relied instead on the subjective judgment of supervisors who were acquainted with the candidates and with the nature of the jobs to be filled. All the supervisors involved in denying Watson the four promotions at issue were white.

Watson filed a discrimination charge with the Equal Employment Opportunity Commission. After exhausting her administrative remedies, she filed this lawsuit in the United States District Court for the Northern District of Texas. She alleged that the Bank had unlawfully discriminated against blacks in hiring, compensation, initial placement, promotions, terminations, and other terms and conditions of employment.

The District Court concluded that Watson had failed to establish a prima facie case of racial discrimination in hiring: the percentage of blacks in the Bank's work force approximated the percentage of blacks in the metropolitan area where the Bank is located.

The District Court addressed Watson's individual claims under the evidentiary standards that apply in a discriminatory treatment case. See *McDonnell Douglas Corp.* v. *Green* (1973). It concluded, on the evidence presented at trial, that Watson had established a prima facie case of employment discrimination, but that the Bank had met its rebuttal burden by presenting legitimate and nondiscriminatory reasons for each of the challenged promotion decisions. The court also concluded that Watson had failed to show that these reasons were pretexts for racial discrimination. Accordingly, the action was dismissed.

A divided panel of the United States Court of Appeals for the Fifth Circuit affirmed the District Court's conclusion that Watson had failed to prove her claim of racial discrimination under the standards set out in *McDonnell Douglas.*

Watson argued that the District Court had erred in failing to apply "disparate impact" analysis to her claims of discrimination in promotion. Relying on Fifth Circuit precedent, the majority of the Court of Appeals panel held that "a Title VII challenge to an allegedly discretionary promotion system is properly analyzed under the disparate treatment model rather than the disparate impact model." Other Courts of Appeals have held that disparate impact analysis may be applied to hiring or promotion systems that involve the use of "discretionary" or "subjective" criteria. We granted certiorari to resolve the conflict.

Several of our decisions have dealt with the evidentiary standards that apply when an individual alleges that an employer has treated that particular person less favorably than others because of the plaintiff's race, color, religion, sex, or national origin. In such "disparate treatment" cases, which involve "the most easily understood type of discrimination," *Teamsters* v. *United States* (1977), the plaintiff is required to prove that the defendant had a discriminatory intent or motive. In order to facilitate the orderly consideration of relevant evidence, we have devised a series of shifting evidentiary burdens that are "intended progressively to sharpen the inquiry into the elusive factual question of intentional discrimination." *Texas Department of Community Affairs* v. *Burdine* (1981). Under that scheme, a prima facie case is ordinarily established by proof that the employer, after having rejected the plaintiff's application for a job or promotion, continued to seek applicants with qualifications similar to the plaintiff's. The burden of proving a prima facie case is "not onerous," and the employer in turn may rebut it simply by producing some evidence that it had legitimate, nondiscriminatory reasons for the decision. If the defendant carries this burden of production, the plaintiff must prove by a preponderance of all the evidence in the case that the legitimate reasons offered by the defendant were a pretext for discrimination. We have cautioned that these shifting burdens are meant only to aid courts and litigants in arranging the presentation of evidence: "The ultimate burden of persuading the trier of fact that the defendant intentionally discriminated against the plaintiff remains at all times with the plaintiff."

In *Griggs* v. *Duke Power Co.* (1971), this Court held that a plaintiff need not necessarily prove intentional discrimination in order to establish that an employer has violated § 703. In certain cases, facially neutral employment practices that have significant adverse effects on protected groups have been held to violate the Act without proof that the employer adopted those practices with a discriminatory intent. The factual issues and the character of the evidence are inevitably somewhat different when the plaintiff is exempted from the need to prove intentional discrimination. The evidence in these "disparate impact" cases usually focuses on statistical disparities, rather than specific incidents, and on competing explanations for those disparities.

The distinguishing features of the factual issues that typically dominate in disparate impact cases do not imply that the ultimate legal issue is different than in cases where disparate treatment analysis is used. Nor do we think it is appropriate to hold a defendant liable for unintentional discrimination on the basis of less evidence than is required to prove intentional discrimination. Rather, the necessary premise of the disparate impact approach is that some employment practices, adopted without a deliberately discriminatory motive, may in operation be functionally equivalent to intentional discrimination.

Perhaps the most obvious examples of such functional equivalence have been found where facially neutral job requirements necessarily operated to perpetuate the effects of intentional discrimination that occurred before Title VII was enacted. In *Griggs* itself, for example, the employer had a history of overt racial discrimination that predated the enactment of the Civil Rights Act of 1964. Such conduct had apparently ceased thereafter, but the employer continued to follow employment policies that had "a markedly disproportionate" adverse effect on blacks. The *Griggs* Court found that these policies, which involved the use of general aptitude tests and a high school diploma requirement, were not demonstrably related to the jobs for which they were used. Believing that diplomas and tests could become "masters of reality," which would perpetuate the effects of pre-Act discrimination, the Court concluded that such practices could not be defended simply on the basis of their facial neutrality or on the basis of the employer's lack of discriminatory intent.

This Court has repeatedly reaffirmed the principle that some facially neutral employment practices may violate Title VII even in the absence of a demonstrated discriminatory intent. We have not limited this principle in cases in which the challenged practice served to perpetuate the effects of pre-Act intentional discrimination. Each of our subsequent decisions, however, like *Griggs* itself, involved standardized employment tests or criteria. See, e.g., *Albemarle Paper Co.* v. *Moody* (1975) (written aptitude tests); *Washington* v. *Davis* (written test of verbal skills); *Dothard* v. *Rawlinson* (1977) (height and weight requirements); *New York City Transit Authority* v. *Beazer* (1979) (rule against employing drug addicts); *Connecticut* v. *Teal* (1982) (written examination). In contrast, we have consistently used conventional disparate-treatment theory, in which proof of intent to discriminate is required, to review hiring and promotion decisions that were based on the exercise of personal judgment or the application of inherently subjective criteria. See, e.g., *McDonnell Douglas Corp.* v. *Green* (discretionary decision not to rehire individual who engaged in criminal acts against employer while laid off); *Furnco Construction Corp.* v. *Waters* (1978) (hiring decisions based on personal knowledge of candidates and recommendations); *Texas Dept. of Community Affairs* v. *Burdine* (1981) (discretionary decision to fire individual who was said not to get along with co-workers); *United States Postal Service Bd. of Governors* v. *Aikens* (discretionary promotion decision).

Our decisions have not addressed the question whether disparate impact analysis may be applied to cases in which subjective criteria are used to make employment decisions. As noted above, the

Courts of Appeals are in conflict on the issue. In order to resolve this conflict, we must determine whether the reasons that support the use of disparate impact analysis apply to subjective employment practices, and whether such analysis can be applied in this new context under workable evidentiary standards.

The parties present us with stark and uninviting alternatives. Petitioner contends that subjective selection methods are at least as likely to have discriminatory effects as are the kind of objective tests at issue in *Griggs* and our other disparate impact cases. Furthermore, she argues, if disparate impact analysis is confined to objective tests, employers will be able to substitute subjective criteria having substantially identical effects, and *Griggs* will become a dead letter. Respondent and the United States (appearing as *amicus curiae*) argue that conventional disparate treatment analysis is adequate to accomplish Congress' purpose in enacting Title VII. They also argue that subjective selection practices would be so impossibly difficult to defend under disparate impact analysis that employers would be forced to adopt numerical quotas in order to avoid liability.

We are persuaded that our decisions in *Griggs* and succeeding cases could largely be nullified if disparate impact analysis were applied only to standardized selection practices. However one might distinguish "subjective" from "objective" criteria. it is apparent that selection systems that combine both types would generally have to be considered subjective in nature. Thus, for example, if the employer in *Griggs* had consistently preferred applicants who had a high school diploma and who passed the company's general aptitude test, its selection system could nonetheless have been considered "subjective" if it also included brief interviews with the candidates. So long as an employer refrained from making standardized criteria absolutely determinative, it would remain free to give such tests almost as much weight as it chose without risking a disparate impact challenge. If we announced a rule that allowed employers so easily to insulate themselves from liability under *Griggs,* disparate impact analysis might effectively be abolished.

We are also persuaded that disparate impact analysis is in principle no less applicable to subjective employment criteria than to objective or standardized tests. In either case, a facially neutral practice, adopted without discriminatory intent, may have effects that are indistinguishable from intentionally discriminatory practices. It is true, to be sure, that an employer's policy of leaving promotion decisions to the unchecked discretion of lower level supervisors should itself raise no inference of discriminatory conduct. Especially in relatively small businesses like respondent's, it may be customary and quite reasonable simply to delegate employment decisions to those employees who are most familiar with the jobs to be filled and with the candidates for those jobs. It does not follow, however, that the particular supervisors to whom this discretion is delegated always act without discriminatory intent. Furthermore, even if one assumed that any such discrimination can be adequately policed through disparate treatment analysis, the problem of subconscious stereotypes and prejudice would remain. In this case, for example, petitioner was apparently told at one point that the teller position was a big responsibility with "a lot of money . . . for blacks to have to count." Such remarks may not prove discriminatory intent, but they do suggest a lingering form of the problem that Title VII was enacted to combat. If an employer's undisciplined system of subjective decisionmaking has precisely the same effects as a system pervaded by impermissible intentional discrimination, it is difficult to see why Title VII's proscription against discriminatory actions should not apply. In both circumstances, the employer's practices may be said to "adversely affect [an individual's] status as an employee, because of such individual's race, color, religion, sex, or national origin." We conclude, accordingly, that subjective or discretionary employment practices may be analyzed under the disparate impact approach in appropriate cases.

Having decided that disparate impact analysis may in principle be applied to subjective as well as to objective practices, we turn to the evidentiary standards that should apply in such cases. It is here that the concerns raised by respondent have their greatest force. Respondent contends that a plaintiff may establish a prima facie case of disparate impact through the use of bare statistics, and that the defendant can rebut this statistical showing only by justifying the challenged practice in terms of "business necessity," or "job relatedness."

Standardized tests and criteria, like those at issue in our previous disparate impact cases, can often be justified through formal "validation studies," which seek to determine whether discrete selection criteria predict actual on-the-job performance. Respondent warns, however, that "validating" subjective selection criteria in this way is impracticable. Some qualities—for example, common sense, good judgment, originality, ambition, loyalty, and tact—cannot be measured accurately through standardized testing techniques. Moreover, success at many jobs in which such qualities are crucial cannot itself be measured directly. Opinions often differ when managers and supervisors are evaluated, and the same can be said for many jobs that involve close cooperation with one's co-workers or complex and subtle tasks like the provision of professional services or personal counseling. Because of these difficulties, we are told, employers will find it impossible to eliminate subjective selection criteria and impossibly expensive to defend such practices in litigation. Respondent insists, and the United States agrees, that employers' only alternative will be to adopt surreptitious quota systems in order to ensure that no plaintiff can establish a statistical prima facie case.

We agree that the inevitable focus on statistics in disparate impact cases could put undue pressure on employers to adopt inappropriate prophylactic measures. It is completely unrealistic to assume that unlawful discrimination is the sole cause of people failing to gravitate to jobs and employers in accord with the laws of chance. It would be equally unrealistic to suppose that employers can eliminate, or discover and explain, the myriad of innocent causes that may lead to statistical imbalances in the composition of their work forces. Congress has specifically provided that employers are *not* required to avoid "disparate impact" as such:

> Nothing contained in [Title VII] shall be interpreted to require any employer . . . to grant preferential treatment to any individual or to any group because of the race, color, religion, sex, or national origin of such individual or group on account of an imbalance which may exist with respect to the total number or percentage of persons of any race, color, religion, sex, or national origin employed by any employer . . . in comparison with the total number or percentage of persons of such race, color, religion, sex, or national origin in any community, State, section, or other area, or in the available work force in any community, State, section, or other area.

Preferential treatment and the use of quotas by public employers subject to Title VII can violate the Constitution. Respondent and the United States are thus correct when they argue that extending disparate impact analysis to subjective employment practices has the potential to create a Hobson's choice for employers and thus to lead in practice to perverse results. If quotas and preferential treatment become the only cost-effective means of avoiding expensive litigation and potentially catastrophic liability, such measures will be widely adopted. The prudent employer will be careful to ensure that its programs are discussed in euphemistic terms, but will be equally careful to ensure that the quotas are met. Allowing the evolution of disparate impact analysis to lead to this result would be contrary to Congress' clearly expressed intent, and it should not be the effect of our decision today.

We do not believe that disparate impact theory need have any chilling effect on legitimate business practices. We recognize, however, that today's extension of that theory into the context of subjective selection practices could increase the risk that employers will be given incentives to adopt quotas or to engage in preferential treatment. Because Congress has so clearly and emphatically expressed its intent that Title VII not lead to this result, we think it imperative to explain in some detail why the evidentiary standards that apply in these cases should serve as adequate safeguards against the danger that Congress recognized. Our previous decisions offer guidance, but today's extension of disparate impact analysis calls for a fresh and somewhat closer examination of the constraints that operate to keep that analysis within its proper bounds.

First, we note that the plaintiff's burden in establishing a prima facie case goes beyond the need to show that there are statistical disparities in the employer's work force. The plaintiff must begin by identifying the specific employment practice that is challenged. Although this has been relatively easy to do in challenges to standardized tests, it may sometimes be more difficult when subjective selection criteria are at issue. Especially in cases where an employer combines subjective criteria with the use of more rigid standardized rules or tests, the plaintiff is in our view responsible for isolating and identifying the specific employment practices that are allegedly responsible for any observed statistical disparities.

Once the employment practice at issue has been identified, causation must be proved; that is, the plaintiff must offer statistical evidence of a kind and degree sufficient to show that the practice in question has caused the exclusion of applicants for jobs or promotions because of their membership in a protected group. Our formulations, which have never been framed in terms of any rigid mathematical formula, have consistently stressed that statistical disparities must be sufficiently substantial that they raise such an inference of causation.

Nor are courts or defendants obliged to assume that plaintiffs' statistical evidence is reliable. They may endeavor to impeach the reliability of the statistical evidence, they may offer rebutting evidence, or they may disparage in arguments or in briefs the probative weight which the plaintiffs' evidence should be accorded. Without attempting to catalogue all the weaknesses that may be found in such evidence, we may note that typical examples include small or incomplete data sets and inadequate statistical techniques. Similarly, statistics based on an applicant pool containing individuals lacking minimal qualifications for the job would be of little probative value.

A second constraint on the application of disparate impact theory lies in the nature of the "business necessity" or "job relatedness" defense. Although we have said that an employer has "the burden of showing that any given requirement must have a manifest relationship in the employment in question," such a formulation should not be interpreted as implying that the ultimate burden of proof can be shifted to the defendant. On the contrary, the ultimate burden of proving that discrimination against a protected group has been caused by a specific employment practice remains with the plaintiff at all times. Thus, when a plaintiff has made out a prima facie case of disparate impact, and when the defendant has met its burden of producing evidence that its employment practices are based on legitimate business reasons, the plaintiff must "show that other tests or selection devices, without a similarly undesirable racial effect would also serve the employer's legitimate interest in efficient and trustworthy workmanship." Factors such as the cost or other burdens of proposed alternative selection devices are relevant in determining whether they would be equally as effective as the challenged practice in serving the employer's legitimate business goals. The same factors would also be relevant in determining whether the challenged practice has operated as the functional equivalent of a pretext for discriminatory treatment.

Our cases make it clear that employers are not required, even when defending standardized or objective tests, to introduce formal "validation studies" showing that particular criteria predict actual on-the-job performance.

In the context of subjective or discretionary employment decisions, the employer will often find it easier than in the case of standardized tests to produce evidence of a "manifest relationship to the employment in question." It is self-evident that many jobs, for example those involving managerial responsibilities, require personal qualities that have never been considered amenable to standardized testing. In evaluating claims that discretionary employment practices are insufficiently related to legitimate business purposes, it must be borne in mind that "[c]ourts are generally less competent than employers to restructure business practices, and unless mandated to do so by Congress they should not attempt it."

In sum, the high standards of proof in disparate impact cases are sufficient in our view to avoid giving employers incentives to modify any normal and legitimate practices by introducing quotas or preferential treatment.

We granted certiorari to determine whether the court below properly held disparate impact analysis inapplicable to a subjective or discretionary promotion system, and we now hold that such analysis may be applied.

Case Questions

1. What is the difference between disparate treatment and disparate impact analysis?
2. What policy reasons did the Court give to extending disparate impact analysis to subjective employment decisions?

In 1989, the Supreme Court once again considered the proof necessary to make out a successful disparate impact case and affirmed its approach in *Watson*. In *Wards Cove Packing Company* v. *Atonio,* the court was faced with the issue of what constitutes the proper reference group for determining whether a disparate impact exists. This case concerned employment at a cannery in Alaska, where the employees were divided into two groups: cannery workers who were production workers, and noncannery workers, who were predominantly supervisory or skilled labor. The majority of the cannery workers were nonwhite, but most noncannery workers were white. The primary question in the case was the appropriate reference group to use to determine the relevant workforce in order to ascertain whether there was a disparate impact in hiring based on race. The court held that the proper reference group in these cases is the pool of qualified job applicants or the qualified population in the labor force. The court rejected the notion that the relevant workforce for determining disparate impact was the composition of the company's overall work force, and refused to require that any employer who has a segment of his work force that is racially imbalanced must run the risk of being "hauled into court and forced to engage in the expensive and time-consuming task of defending the 'business necessity' of the methods used to select the other members of his work force." The court noted that if employers were required to carry this burden, "The only practicable option for many employers will be to adopt racial quotas, ensuring that no portion of his work force deviates in racial composition from the other portions thereof; this is a result that Congress expressly rejected in drafting Title VII." Thus, the court reaffirmed its commitment to determining disparate impact using a frame of reference of qualified workers for particular positions, not all employees of a company, or the composition of the population as a whole.

Other Federal Antidiscrimination Statutes

While Title VII of the 1964 Civil Rights Act is the most used antidiscrimination statute, other federal statutes prohibit specific types of discrimination in employment. They are the Equal Pay Act, the Age Discrimination in Employment Act, the Rehabilitation Act, the Pregnancy Discrimination Act, and the 1866 Civil Rights Act.

The Equal Pay Act

The **Equal Pay Act** was passed in 1963 as an amendment to the Fair Labor Standards Act of 1938. The Equal Pay Act prohibits differences in pay between the sexes for employees whose work requires "equal skill, effort and responsibility" and is "performed under similar working conditions." Originally administered by the Wage and Hour Division of the Department of Labor, the Equal Pay Act is now enforced by the EEOC. The main issues of litigation under the Equal Pay Act have been what constitutes "equal" work and "similar working conditions." The main criterion for application of the act seems to be substantial similarity of job requirements. An employer may not tailor job descriptions for performance of essentially the same tasks in order to avoid paying equal pay for equal work.

When the Equal Pay Act first took effect, many employers had to develop job classifications with accompanying job descriptions in order to be able to determine whether similar jobs involved "equal work." This classification often represented the first time employers had attempted an objective evaluation of the activities performed by their workers. As the use of objective job classifications has become widespread, the number of Equal Pay Act cases filed has tended to go down. However, a new issue called "comparable worth," involving the monetary value assigned to different types of work, has arisen in recent years. Comparable worth is discussed in the section entitled "Current Issues in Discrimination Law."

Age Discrimination in Employment Act

The **Age Discrimination in Employment Act (ADEA),** originally passed in 1967 and amended in 1978 and 1986, prohibits discrimination on the basis of age against persons between the ages of forty and seventy. The act applies to private employers with twenty or more employees and to employment agencies, the federal government, and almost all employees of state and local governments. The ADEA, which is administered by the EEOC, prohibits mandatory retirement for most covered employees and outlaws mandatory retirement based on age for federal employees.

Some of the types of cases in which employees have won lawsuits filed under the ADEA have included incidents of laying off older, higher-paid workers first in order to save more money than would be saved by dismissing younger workers, and reassigning older workers into unfamiliar or more physically demanding positions within a company in order to harrass them into early retirement. A good illustration of the type of actions to which the ADEA applies is *Houghton* v. *McDonnell Douglas,* a case decided by the Eighth Circuit Court of Appeals in 1977. This case involved a test pilot, Houghton, who was removed from active flying status when his employer decided to reduce its test pilot staff. Ultimately, Houghton was fired due to his refusal to be transferred to another department. When Houghton sued his former employer, alleging age discrimination, the employer's main defense was that age was a bona fide occupational qualification. Houghton won his case, mainly because he was able to show that he was in perfect health and that a test pilot's performance actually tended to improve with age, due to an increase in experience that led to fewer flight accidents.

In 1985, the United States Supreme Court decided its first case regarding the effect of the ADEA on company mandatory retirement laws. In *Western Airlines* v. *Criswell,* the Court ruled unanimously that before employers can institute a mandatory blanket retirement rule, they must show that the stated retirement age is a bona fide occupational qualification, which means that all persons over the mandatory retirement age would present a safety risk, or that it is "highly impractical" to make individual judgments about the employees' health. The *Criswell* case was similar to *Houghton,* in that it involved the mandatory retirement of airline flight engineers. The Supreme Court did note that there was a significant difference between the jobs of flight engineers (such as Criswell), who only read instruments, and pilots such as Houghton. These cases are interesting because their outcome points up one of the fundamental principles of antidiscrimination law: that an employer cannot make personnel decisions based on stereotyped characterizations of a group (for instance, that everyone's physical abilities automatically decline when they reach a certain age), but must look at the qualifications of the individual.

In 1989, the Supreme Court had to interpret a provision of the ADEA which exempts from the Act the terms of any bona fide employee benefit plan (such as a retirement, pension, or insurance plan) which is not a subterfuge to evade the purposes of the ADEA. In *Public Employees Retirement System of Ohio* v. *Betts,* the court held that an employee seeking to challenge an employee benefit plan provision as a subterfuge for violation of the ADEA bears the burden of proving that the discriminatory plan provision actually was intended to serve the purpose of discriminating in some nonfringe-benefit aspect of the employment relationship. The court noted that Congress left the employee benefit battle for another day, and legislated only as to hiring and firing, wages and salaries, and other nonfringe-benefit terms and conditions of employment.

Rehabilitation Act

The Vocational Rehabilitation Act, passed in 1973 and amended in 1978 and 1986, prohibits discrimination against *qualified* handicapped persons. The act is enforced by the Department of Labor and applies whenever federal funding is used. The purpose of the act is to insure that a handicapped person be given a fair chance of getting a job if he or she can do the work, and to prevent an employer from assuming that handicapped people are automatically incapable of adequate performance. The 1978 amendment to the act made clear that it is not necessarily a violation of the act to discriminate against a person who is addicted to drugs or alcohol.

Much of the litigation under the Rehabilitation Act has centered around the question of what constitutes a handicapped individual, and when such an individual is "qualified" to perform a job. The Rehabilitation Act defines a handicapped individual as one who has a physical or mental impairment that substantially limits one or more of a person's major life activities, or has a record of such an impairment, or is regarded as having such an impairment. In 1987 in *School Board* v. *Arline,* the United States Supreme Court considered the question of whether a person with a contagious disease could qualify as a handicapped person for purposes of the antidiscrimination provisions of the Rehabilitation Act. The court held that such a person might be qualified for employment, and therefore protected from discrimination, under certain circumstances. The decision about job qualification should be made on an individualized basis, considering the following factors: the nature of the risk (e.g., how the disease is transmitted); the duration of the risk (how long the carrier is infectious); the severity of the risk (what the potential harm is to third parties); and the probabilities the disease will be transmitted and will cause varying degrees of harm. In *Arline,* the plaintiff had tuberculosis; the very important issue in this area which the Supreme Court has yet to address is the question of the extent to which the Rehabilitation Act protects individuals with AIDS.

Another difficult question considered by the Supreme Court in 1988 was the extent to which alcoholism is a disease. As mentioned above, the Rehabilitation Act has an exemption for individuals who are alcoholic or drug abusers whose current use of alcohol or drugs prevents such individuals from performing the duties of the job or whose employment would constitute a direct threat to property or the safety of others. *Traynor* v. *Turnage* concerned the validity of a law that required former servicemen to use their G.I. Bill educational benefits within ten years after their military service, or lose them. The Veterans Administration could extend the time limit beyond ten years if the veteran had been prevented from using the benefits by a physical or mental disorder that was not the result of willful misconduct. The Veterans Administration refused to extend some veterans benefits because they were incapacitated due to alcoholism, which was characterized as "willful misconduct." The veterans sued the Administration, under the theory that the refusal of benefits was discrimination on the basis of handicap under the Rehabilitation Act. The Court held that the Rehabilitation Act did not repeal the earlier veterans' benefit statute, and that therefore Congress must have intended for the Veterans Administration to have the power to interpret alcoholism as willful misconduct. The court concluded that there was no inconsistency between the Rehabilitation Act and a presumption that alcoholism not motivated by mental illness is "willful."

Pregnancy Discrimination Act

The **Pregnancy Discrimination Act** was passed in 1978 as an amendment in Title VII of the 1964 Civil Rights Act. Since the act is an amendment to Title VII, it is administered by the EEOC under Title VII procedures. The act prohibits discrimination on the basis of pregnancy, childbirth, or related medical conditions in employment, including receipt of benefits under fringe benefit programs.

Prior to the passage of this act, courts had differed on whether treating pregnant workers differently than other workers constituted sex discrimination. The act makes clear that discrimination against pregnant wommen is forbidden. Therefore, employers cannot fire, demote, or refuse to promote a woman when she becomes pregnant, and they cannot carry insurance that covers all physical conditions except pregnancy. In 1983, the United States Supreme Court decided the following case brought under the Pregnancy Discrimination Act which considered the act's effect on rights of spouses of male workers.

Newport News Shipbuilding and Dry Dock Company, Petitioner v. *EEOC*

462 U.S. 669 (1983)

Facts

In 1978 Congress amended Title VII of the Civil Rights Act of 1964 to prohibit sex discrimination on the basis of pregnancy. On the effective date of the act, Newport News Shipbuilding Company amended its health insurance plan to provide its female employees with hospitalization benefits for pregnancy-related conditions to the same extent as for other medical conditions. The plan continued, however, to provide less favorable pregnancy benefits for spouses of male employees. The question presented is whether the amended plan complies with the amended statute.

Opinion

Justice Stevens: Section 703(a) makes it an unlawful employment practice for an employer to "discriminate against any individual with respect to his compensation terms, conditions, or privileges of employment, because of such individual's race, color, religion, sex, or national origin." Health insurance and other fringe benefits are "compensation, terms, conditions, or privileges of employment." Male as well as female employees are protected against discrimination. Thus, if a private employer were to provide complete health insurance coverage for the dependents of its female employees, and no coverage at all for the dependents of its male employees, it would violate Title VII. Such a practice would not pass the simple test of Title VII discrimination that we enunciated in *Los Angeles Department of Water and Power* v. *Manhart,* for it would treat a male employee with dependents "in a manner which but for that person's sex would be different." The same result would be reached even if the magnitude of the discrimination were smaller. For example, a plan that provided complete hospitalization coverage for the spouses of female employees but did not cover spouses of male employees when they had broken bones would violate Title VII by discriminating against male employees.

Petitioner's practice is just as unlawful. Its plan provides limited pregnancy-related benefits for employees' wives, and affords more extensive coverage for employees' spouses for all other medical conditions requiring hospitalization. Thus the husbands of female employees receive a specified level of hospitalization coverage for all conditions; the wives of male employees receive such coverage except for pregnancy-related conditions. The 1978 Act makes clear that it is discriminatory to treat pregnancy-related conditions less favorably than other medical conditions. Thus petitioner's plan unlawfully gives married male employees a benefit package for their dependents that is less inclusive than the dependency coverage provided to married female employees.

There is no merit to petitioner's argument that the prohibitions of Title VII do not extend to discrimination against pregnant spouses because the statute applies only to discrimination in employment. A two-step analysis demonstrates the fallacy in this contention. The Pregnancy Discrimination Act has now made clear that, for all Title VII purposes, discrimination based on a woman's pregnancy is, on its face, discrimination because of her sex. And since the sex of the spouse is always the opposite of the sex of the employee, it follows inexorably that discrimination against female spouses in the provision of fringe benefits is also discrimination against male employees. By making clear that an employer could not discriminate on the basis of an employee's pregnancy, Congress did not erase the original prohibition against discrimination on the basis of an employee's sex. The pregnancy limitation in this case violates Title VII by discriminating against male employees. The judgment of the Court of Appeals is affirmed.

Case Questions

1. Why was paying the wives of male employees less pregnancy-related benefits than those paid female employees held to be discrimination?
2. What does this case point out as being the relationship between the general antidiscrimination provisions of the Pregnancy Discrimination Act?
3. The more medical benefits an employer provides to its employees, the higher its insurance premiums. The result of this case is that the employer's insurance premiums are going to go up, and (presumably) so are the employees' premiums. Is it ethical to charge workers more for insurance premiums so that the spouses of some workers can have greater benefits?

Since the *Newport News* case, the Supreme Court has considered the relationship between the Pregnancy Discrimination Act and various types of state statutes. Two cases decided in 1987 dealt with the validity of a California statute that required employers to provide leave and reinstatement to employees disabled by pregnancy, and with a Missouri statute concerning eligibility for unemployment compensation. In both cases, the Supreme Court upheld the state statutes, but in one case the woman plaintiff got the relief she wanted, and in the other, she did not. The Supreme Court upheld the California statute giving limited job security to women, on the basis that it did not conflict with Title VII of the federal 1964 Civil Rights Act, and instead the two statutes shared the common goal of achieving equality of employment opportunities. On the other hand, the Supreme Court allowed to stand a Missouri decision that denied unemployment compensation benefits to women who quit their jobs due to pregnancy. A Missouri statute denied unemployment compensation benefits to anyone who left work voluntarily without good cause attributable to his work or to his employer. The court held that this statute did not unfairly discriminate against women who voluntarily quit their jobs due to pregnancy, because the statute applied to the general population and did not single out pregnancy for unfavorable treatment. The court noted that the purpose of the Pregnancy Discrimination Act was not to mandate preferential treatment.

Civil Rights Act of 1866

Following the Civil War, at the time the Thirteenth, Fourteenth, and Fifteenth Amendments were added to the Constitution. Congress passed certain civil rights acts, including the **Civil Rights Act of 1866.** One of the most important aspects, legally speaking, of this act is that it does not require *government action*. If a person sues under the Fourteenth Amendment, alleging violation of the Equal Protection Clause, he has to prove that his rights were infringed upon by some public action (actions by state or local governments). The Civil Rights Act of 1866 prohibits both public and private actions that discriminate, and therefore allows a victim of discrimination to sue an alleged discriminator (such as a private employer) even if no government action is involved.

In the area of employment discrimination, the 1866 act may complement Title VII of the 1964 Civil Rights Act. You should note that a plaintiff who sues under the 1866 act is not bound by technical requirements of Title VII of the 1964 Civil Rights Act, such as the requirement to file a complaint with the EEOC within 180 days of the incident.

Various provisions of the 1866 act have been used to challenge alleged instances of employment discrimination. Section 1981 of the act provides that all persons within the United States shall have the same right to full and equal benefit of all laws as is enjoyed by white citizens. Prior to 1987, the Supreme Court had construed that language to forbid all "racial" discrimination in the making of private as well as public contracts. In 1987, in *Saint Francis College* v. *Al-Khazraji,* the court held that persons of Arabian ancestry may be protected from "racial" discrimination under section 1981. The court reasoned that the legislative history of 1981 indicates that Congress intended to protect identifiable classes of persons who are subjected to intentional discrimination solely because of their ancestry or ethnic characteristics.

In 1989, in *Patterson* v. *McLean Credit Union,* the Supreme Court considered the question of whether racial harassment relating to the conditions of employment is actionable under section 1981, and held that it is not. The court reaffirmed its earlier decision in the case of *Runyon* v. *McCrary* that section 1981 prohibits racial discrimination in the making and enforcement of contracts, but reasoned that it does not apply to conduct which occurs after the formation of a contract and which does not interfere with the right to enforce established contract obligations. Patterson, a black woman, had sued under section 1981, charging that her employer had harassed and failed to promote her, and had ultimately fired her, on account of her race. The court left open the possibility that a person who was already employed might be able to state a valid claim under section 1981 if the employer failed to promote the employee to a position entailing a level of opportunity for a new and distinct relation between the employer and employee.

Another provision of the 1866 Civil Rights Act that is often used in civil rights cases, some of which may involve employment discrimination issues, is section 1983. Section 1983 prohibits deprivation of civil (including Constitutional) rights under color of state law. In *Rankin* v. *McPherson,* a 1987 case, the Supreme Court held that a discharged employee could sue under section 1983 when the reason she was fired was exercise of her First Amendment rights of free speech.

State Equal Opportunity Statutes

Many state and local governments have passed their own equal opportunity in employment statutes. These statutes generally complement Title VII of the 1964 Civil Rights Act. Remember that Title VII provides that if a state or local government has adopted a statutory antidiscrimination agency procedure, the EEOC must defer to that agency for a period of time.

Affirmative Action Plans and Executive Order 11246

Ever since President Truman issued an order ending racial segregation in the armed forces, United States presidents have used their power to issue executive orders to combat discrimination by the federal government and by persons doing business with the federal government. The most important such executive order is **Executive Order (EO) 11246,** issued by President Johnson in 1965. As amended, EO 11246 prohibits discrimination on the basis of race, creed, color, national origin, and sex by all employers having contracts with the federal government. The most unique feature of EO 11246 is its requirement that all such employers file **affirmative action plans (AAPs)** with the Office of Federal Contract Compliance Programs (OFCCP) in the federal Department of Labor.

The concept of affirmative action as embodied in EO 11246 is different from the concept of antidiscrimination statutes. The goal of the typical antidiscrimination statute is to give a person a legal remedy after she has suffered discrimination; the goal of affirmative action is to remedy the effects of past discrimination by giving members of formerly disadvantaged groups preference in hiring and promotion.

Every federal contractor must file an initial AAP with the OFCCP and then submit yearly updates. The OFCCP has issued detailed guidelines as to the contents of AAPs to be filed by contractors doing $50,000 or more business with the federal government and employing fifty or more workers. The first step in compiling an AAP consists of obtaining a statistical analysis of the composition of the employer's work force and comparing that composition with a statistical analysis of the relevant population. The composition of the employer's work force will then be compared to the composition of the relevant general work force to see if discrepancies exist that suggest the existence of discrimination. The population to which the employer's work force will be compared will vary by job description. For example, since accountants are often recruited nationally or regionally, in determining whether the employer has adequate representation of minorities in its accounting department, national or regional statistics on the number of minority accountants will be used. On the other hand, secretaries are almost always recruited locally, so that the relevant statistics to use to determine adequate representation of minorities in secretarial positions are population figures for the geographic area near the employer's place of business.

The second step in compiling an AAP is to determine whether there is minority underrepresentation in the employer's work force, and, if there is, to establish goals for eliminating that underrepresentation. For example, if 30 percent of the population in the location of a contractor's manufacturing plant was black, but the contractor had only 10 percent black assembly line workers, the contractor would set a goal to increase the percentage of black assembly line workers to around 30 percent.

An AAP goal is not supposed to be a quota. A quota is an absolute requirement that an employer hire a specific number of persons who are members of a particular class. Actual quotas have generally been imposed through court orders or through collective bargaining agreements, or in compliance with state or federal law. For example, a court might issue an order telling a city that the next twenty firemen it hired would have to be black or Hispanic. AAP goals are not quotas because there exist what might be called "defenses" for a contractor's failure to meet his AAP goals. The main defenses are: no minority members applied, no qualified minority members applied, and qualified minority members were offered a job but turned it down. The first two defenses are only valid if the contractor can prove that he took affirmative steps to solicit minorities, including such activities as going out to schools and colleges and actively trying to recruit applicants and/or setting up job training programs. If a contractor does not meet his AAP goals and cannot satisfactorily explain his failure to do so, the OFCCP may terminate his federal contract.

The avowed purpose of AAPs is to give preference to minorities in order to make up for past discrimination. Implicit in affirmative action procedures is the possibility of "reverse discrimination," that is, discrimination against "majority" groups such as white males. We will discuss the legal problems caused by reverse discrimination in the next section.

Current Issues in Discrimination Law

As you have seen, the equal employment opportunity laws have two goals: to prevent discrimination in employment against minorities from occurring, and to compensate for past discrimination. These dual purposes are illustrated by the differences between antidiscrimination statutes such as Title VII, which give after-the-fact legal relief to individual victims of discrimination, and Executive Order 11246 affirmative action plans, which require special efforts to recruit minorities. As early as the middle 1970s, tension was apparent between these two antidiscrimination approaches. Furthermore, it has also become apparent that the antidiscrimination statutes and the affirmative action plan requirement may produce wide-ranging social consequences that may not have been foreseen by their originators. In this section, we will discuss some of the current areas of concern created by these antidiscrimination mechanisms. You should note that most of these current areas of concern have important ethical as well as legal aspects.

Reverse Discrimination

Perhaps the single issue that has created the most controversy over antidiscrimination laws during the past few years is the problem of so-called **reverse discrimination.** Reverse discrimination occurs when the goal of remedying past discrimination clashes with the goal of avoiding all discrimination. For example, suppose that an employer is faced with the dilemma of choosing between two equally qualified candidates for a position; one candidate is a white male; the other is a black female. If that employer is a government contractor eager to meet his affirmative action goals, he will almost certainly choose the black female for the position. In choosing the woman candidate, however, he will implicitly have discriminated against the white male on the basis of race and/or sex. Thus, in order to meet AAP requirements and further the goal of remedying past discrimination, he may have frustrated the goal of nondiscrimination.

The United States Supreme Court considered the problem of reverse discrimination in 1979 in the case of *United States Steelworkers of America* v. *Weber,* which is contained in chapter 1. This case involved interpretation of the terms of a collective bargaining agreement between a union and Kaiser Aluminum Company, in which Kaiser agreed that 50 percent of the positions in its crafts training program would be reserved for black employees. Weber was a white Kaiser employee who would normally have been chosen for the training program if 50 percent of the positions had not been reserved for blacks. Weber sued Kaiser under Title VII, alleging that he was the victim of racial discrimination. The Supreme Court held that the collective bargaining agreement was legal and that "Title VII's prohibition against racial discrimination does not condemn all private, voluntary, race-conscious affirmative action plans."

The year after *Weber,* in *Fullilove* v. *Klutznick,* the Supreme Court held that a federal statute requiring that 10 percent of federal funds used in local public works projects be used to procure services or supplies from minority-owned businesses was not an unconstitutional denial of equal protection. Note that this statute set a quota (an absolute target that must be complied with), whereas the goal under an affirmative plan does not necessarily have to be reached (as was discussed in the section on AAPs). Nevertheless, the Court held that the quotas set by the statute were enforceable, even though they created implicit racial discrimination, because the congressional objective of preventing perpetuation of construction industry discrimination was valid and the quota system was a valid method to achieve the objective.

In 1989, the Supreme Court once again addressed the problem of reverse discrimination in *City of Richmond* v. *Croson Company*. The *City of Richmond* case was similar to *Fullilove* in many respects, in that it involved certain "set-aside" requirements for minority-owned businesses. In *City of Richmond,* however, the court held that the minority contractor set-aside requirement was a denial of equal protection because it discriminated on the basis of race. As you read the *Richmond* case, which follows, try to discern the basis for what may appear to be different results in similar cases.

City of Richmond v. *Croson Company*

109 S. Ct. 706 (1989)

Opinion

Justice O'Connor: In this case, we confront once again the tension between the Fourteenth Amendment's guarantee of equal treatment to all citizens, and the use of race-based measures to ameliorate the effects of past discrimination on the opportunities enjoyed by members of minority groups in our society. In *Fullilove* v. *Klutznick,* (1980), we held that a congressional program requiring that 10% of certain federal construction grants be awarded to minority contractors did not violate the equal protection principles embodied in the Due Process Clause of the Fifth Amendment. Relying largely on our decision in *Fullilove,* some lower federal courts have applied a similar standard of review in assessing the constitutionality of state and local minority set-aside provisions under the Equal Protection Clause of the Fourteenth Amendment. Since our decision two Terms ago in *Wygant* v. *Jackson Board of Education* (1986), the lower federal courts have attempted to apply its standards in evaluating the constitutionality of state and local programs which allocate a portion of public contracting opportunities exclusively to minority-owned businesses. We noted probable jurisdiction in this case to consider the applicability of our decision in *Wygant* to a minority set-aside program adopted by the city of Richmond, Virginia.

On April 11, 1983, the Richmond City Council adopted the Minority Business Utilization Plan (the Plan). The Plan required prime contractors to whom the city awarded construction contracts to subcontract at least 30% of the dollar amount of the contract to one or more Minority Business Enterprises (MBEs). The 30% set-aside did not apply to city contracts awarded to minority-owned prime contractors.

The Plan defined an MBE as "[a] business at least fifty-one (51) percent of which is owned and controlled . . . by minority group members." "Minority group members" were defined as "[c]itizens of the United States who are Blacks, Spanish-speaking, Orientals, Indians, Eskimos, or Aleuts." There was no geographic limit to the Plan; an otherwise qualified MBE from anywhere in the United States could avail itself of the 30% set-aside. The Plan declared that it was "remedial" in nature, and enacted "for the purpose of promoting wider participation by minority business enterprises in the construction of public projects." The Plan expired on June 30, 1988, and was in effect for approximately five years.

The Plan authorized the Director of the Department of General Services to promulgate rules which "shall allow waivers in those individual situations where a contractor can prove to the satisfaction of the director that the requirements herein cannot be achieved."

There was no direct evidence of race discrimination on the part of the city in letting contracts or any evidence that the city's prime contracts had discriminated against minority-owned subcontractors.

[Croson Company was the low bidder for a city project, but could not get a waiver of the MBE requirement, and ultimately lost the project.]

Shortly thereafter Croson brought this action under 42 U. S. C. § 1983 in the Federal District Court for the Eastern District of Virginia, arguing that the Richmond ordinance was unconstitutional on its face and as applied in this case.

The District Court upheld the Plan in all respects. In its original opinion, a divided panel of the Fourth Circuit Court of Appeals affirmed. Both courts applied a test derived from "the common concerns articulated by the various Supreme Court opinions" in *Fullilove* v. *Klutznick* (1980), and *University of California Regents* v. *Bakke* (1978). Relying on the great deference which this Court accorded Congress' findings of past discrimination in *Fullilove,* the panel majority indicated its view that the same standard should be applied to the Richmond City Council, stating:

> Unlike the review we make of a lower court decision, our task is not to determine if there was sufficient evidence to sustain the council majority's position in any traditional sense of

weighing the evidence. Rather, it is to determine whether "the legislative history . . . demonstrates that [the council] reasonably concluded that . . . private and governmental discrimination had contributed to the negligible percentage of public contracts awarded minority contractors."

Croson sought certiorari from this Court. We granted the writ, vacated the opinion of the Court of Appeals, and remanded the case for further consideration in light of our intervening decision in *Wygant* v. *Jackson Board of Education* (1986).

On remand, a divided panel of the Court of Appeals struck down the Richmond set-aside program as violating both prongs of strict scrutiny under the Equal Protection Clause of the Fourteenth Amendment. The majority found that the "core" of this Court's holding in *Wygant* was that, "[t]o show that a plan is justified by a compelling governmental interest, a municipality that wishes to employ a racial preference cannot rest on broad-brush assumptions of historical discrimination." As the court read this requirement, "[f]indings of *societal* discrimination will not suffice; the findings must concern 'prior discrimination *by the government unit involved.*' "

In this case, the debate at the city council meeting "revealed no record of prior discrimination by the city in awarding public contracts. . . ." Moreover, the statistics comparing the minority population of Richmond to the percentage of *prime* contracts awarded to minority firms had little or no probative value in establishing prior discrimination in the relevant market, and actually suggested "more of a political than a remedial basis for the racial preference." The court concluded that, "[i]f this plan is supported by a compelling governmental interest, so is every other plan that has been enacted in the past or that will be enacted in the future."

The Court of Appeals went on to hold that even if the city had demonstrated a compelling interest in the use of a race-based quota, the 30% set-aside was not narrowly tailored to accomplish a remedial purpose. The court found that the 30% figure was "chosen arbitrarily" and was not tied to the number of minority subcontractors in Richmond or to any other relevant number. The dissenting judge argued that the majority had "misconstrue[d] and misapplie[d]" our decision in *Wygant.* We noted probable jurisdiction of the city's appeal, and we now affirm the judgment.

The parties and their supporting *amici* fight an initial battle over the scope of the city's power to adopt legislation designed to address the effects of past discrimination. Relying on our decision in *Wygant,* appellee argues that the city must limit any race-based remedial efforts to eradicating the effects of its own prior discrimination. This is essentially the position taken by the Court of Appeals below. Appellant argues that our decision in *Fullilove* is controlling, and that as a result the city of Richmond enjoys sweeping legislative power to define and attack the effects of prior discrimination in its local construction industry. We find that neither of these two rather stark alternatives can withstand analysis.

In *Fullilove,* we upheld the minority set-aside contained in § 103(f)(2) of the Public Works Employment Act of 1977 (the Act) against a challenged based on the equal protection component of the Due Process Clause.

The Act contained the following requirement: "Except to the extent the Secretary determines otherwise, no grant shall be made under this Act . . . unless the applicant gives satisfactory assurance to the Secretary that at least 10 per centum of the amount of each grant shall be expended for minority business enterprises." *Fullilove* (quoting 91 Stat. 116, 42 U. S. C. § 6705(f)(2)). MBEs were defined as businesses effectively controlled by "citizens of the United States who are Negroes, Spanish-speaking, Orientals, Indians, Eskimos, and Aleuts."

The principal opinion in *Fullilove,* written by Chief Justice Burger, did not employ "strict scrutiny" or any other traditional standard of equal protection review. The Chief Justice noted at the outset that although racial classifications call for close examination, the Court was at the same time, "bound to approach [its] task with appropriate deference to the Congress, a co-equal branch charged by the Constitution with the power to 'provide for the . . . general Welfare of the United States' and 'to enforce by appropriate legislation,' the equal protection guarantees of the Fourteenth Amendment." The principal opinion asked two questions: first, were the objectives of the legislation within the power of Congress? Second, was the limited use of racial and ethnic criteria a permissible means for Congress to carry out its objectives within the constraints of the Due Process Clause?

On the issue of congressional power, the Chief Justice found that Congress' commerce power was sufficiently broad to allow it to reach the practices of prime contractors on federally funded local construction projects. Congress could mandate state and local government compliance with the set-aside program under its § 5 power to enforce the Fourteenth Amendment.

The Chief Justice next turned to the constraints on Congress' power to employ race-conscious remedial relief. His opinion stressed two factors in upholding the MBE set-aside. First was the unique remedial powers of Congress under § 5 of the Fourteenth Amendment:

> Here we deal . . . not with the limited remedial powers of a federal court, for example, but with the broad remedial powers of Congress. It is fundamental that *in no organ of government, state or federal, does there repose a more comprehensive remedial power than in the Congress,* expressly charged by the Constitution with competence and authority to enforce equal protection guarantees.

Because of these unique powers, the Chief Justice concluded that "Congress not only may induce voluntary action to assure compliance with existing federal statutory or constitutional antidiscrimination provisions, but also, where Congress has authority to *declare certain conduct unlawful,* it may, as here, authorize and induce state action to avoid such conduct."

In reviewing the legislative history behind the Act, the principal opinion focused on the evidence before Congress that a nationwide history of past discrimination had reduced minority participation in federal construction grants. The second factor emphasized by the principal opinion in *Fullilove* was the flexible nature of the 10% set-aside.

Appellant and its supporting *amici* rely heavily on *Fullilove* for the proposition that a city council, like Congress, need not make specific findings of discrimination to engage in race-conscious relief.

What appellant ignores is that Congress, unlike any State or political subdivision, has a specific constitutional mandate to enforce the dictates of the Fourteenth Amendment.

That Congress may identify and redress the effects of society-wide discrimination does not mean that the States and their political subdivisions are free to decide that such remedies are appropriate. Section I of the Fourteenth Amendment is an explicit *constraint* on state power, and the States must undertake any remedial efforts in accordance with that provision. To hold otherwise would be to cede control over the content of the Equal Protection Clause to the 50 state legislatures and their myriad political subdivisions. The mere recitation of a benign or compensatory purpose for the use of a racial classification would essentially entitle the States to exercise the full power of Congress under § 5 of the Fourteenth Amendment and insulate any racial classification from judicial scrutiny under § 1. We believe that such a result would be contrary to the intentions of the Framers of the Fourteenth Amendment, who desired to place clear limits on the States' use of race as a criterion for legislative action, and to have the federal courts enforce those limitations.

We do not, as Justice Marshall's dissent suggests, find in § 5 of the Fourteenth Amendment some form of federal pre-emption in matters of race. We simply note what should be apparent to all—§ 1 of the Fourteenth Amendment stemmed from a distrust of state legislative enactments based on race; § 5 is, as the dissent notes, " 'a *positive* grant of legislative power' " to Congress. Thus, our treatment of an exercise of congressional power in *Fullilove* cannot be dispositive here.

If the city could show that it had essentially become a "passive participant" in a system of racial exclusion practiced by elements of the local construction industry, we think it clear that the city could take affirmative steps to dismantle such a system. It is beyond dispute that any public entity, state or federal, has a compelling interest in assuring that public dollars, drawn from the tax contributions of all citizens, do not serve to finance the evil of private prejudice.

The Equal Protection Clause of the Fourteenth

Amendment provides that "[N]o State shall . . . deny to *any person* within its jurisdiction the equal protection of the laws" (emphasis added). As this Court has noted in the past, the "rights created by the first section of the Fourteenth Amendment are, by its terms, guaranteed to the individual. The rights established are personal rights." The Richmond Plan denies certain citizens the opportunity to compete for a fixed percentage of public contracts based solely upon their race. To whatever racial group these citizens belong, their "personal rights" to be treated with equal dignity and respect are implicated by a rigid rule erecting race as the sole criterion in an aspect of public decisionmaking.

Absent searching judicial inquiry into the justification for such race-based measures, there is simply no way of determining what classifications are "benign" or "remedial" and what classifications are in fact motivated by illegitimate notions of racial inferiority or simple racial politics. Indeed, the purpose of strict scrutiny is to "smoke out" illegitimate uses of race by assuring that the legislative body is pursuing a goal important enough to warrant use of a highly suspect tool. The test also ensures that the means chosen "fit" this compelling goal so closely that there is little or no possibility that the motive for the classification was illegitimate racial prejudice or stereotype.

Classifications based on race carry a danger of stigmatic harm. Unless they are strictly reserved for remedial settings, they may in fact promote notions of racial inferiority and lead to a politics of racial hostility. We thus reaffirm the view expressed by the plurality in *Wygant* that the standard of review under the Equal Protection Clause is not dependent on the race of those burdened or benefited by a particular classification.

Our continued adherence to the standard of review employed in *Wygant,* does not indicate that we view "racial discrimination as largely a phenomenon of the past" or that "government bodies need no longer preoccupy themselves with rectifying racial injustice." As we indicate below, States and their local subdivisions have many legislative weapons at their disposal both to punish and prevent present discrimination and to remove arbitrary barriers to minority advancement. Rather, our interpretation of § 1 stems from our agreement with the view expressed by Justice Powell in *Bakke,* that "[t]he guarantee of equal protection cannot mean one thing when applied to one individual and something else when applied to a person of another color."

Even were we to accept a reading of the guarantee of equal protection under which the level of scrutiny varies according to the ability of different groups to defend their interests in the representative process, heightened scrutiny would still be appropriate in the circumstances of this case. One of the central arguments for applying a less exacting standard to "benign" racial classifications is that such measures essentially involve a choice made by dominant racial groups to disadvantage themselves. If one aspect of the judiciary's role under the Equal Protection Clause is to protect "discrete and insular minorities" from majoritarian prejudice or indifference, some maintain that these concerns are not implicated when the "white majority" places burdens upon itself.

In this case, blacks comprise approximately 50% of the population of the city of Richmond. Five of the nine seats on the City Council are held by blacks. The concern that a political majority will more easily act to the disadvantage of a minority based on unwarranted assumptions or incomplete facts would seem to militate for, not against, the application of heightened judicial scrutiny in this case.

We think it clear that the factual predicate offered in support of the Richmond Plan suffers from the same two defects identified as fatal in *Wygant.* The District Court found the city council's "findings sufficient to ensure that, in adopting the Plan, it was remedying the present effects of past discrimination in the *construction industry.*" Like the "role model" theory employed in *Wygant,* a generalized assertion that there has been past discrimination in an entire industry provides no guidance for a legislative body to determine the precise scope of the injury it seeks to remedy. It "has no logical stopping point." "Relief" for such an ill-defined wrong could extend until the percentage of public contracts awarded to MBEs in Richmond mirrored the percentage of minorities in the population as a whole.

Appellant argues that it is attempting to remedy various forms of past discrimination that are alleged to be responsible for the small number of minority businesses in the local contracting industry. Among these the city cites the exclusion of blacks from skilled construction trade unions and training programs. This past discrimination has prevented them "from following the traditional path from laborer to entrepreneur." The city also lists a host of nonracial factors which would seem to face a member of any racial group attempting to establish a new business enterprise, such as deficiencies in working capital, inability to meet bonding requirements, unfamiliarity with bidding procedures, and disability caused by an inadequate track record.

While there is no doubt that the sorry history of both private and public discrimination in this country has contributed to a lack of opportunities for black entrepreneurs, this observation, standing alone, cannot justify a rigid racial quota in the awarding of public contracts in Richmond, Virginia. Like the claim that discrimination in primary and secondary schooling justifies a rigid racial preference to medical school admissions, an amorphous claim that there has been past discrimination in a particular industry cannot justify the use of an unyielding racial quota.

It is sheer speculation how many minority firms there would be in Richmond absent past societal discrimination, just as it was sheer speculation how many minority medical students would have been admitted to the medical school at Davis absent past discrimination in educational opportunities. Defining these sorts of injuries as "identified discrimination" would give local requirements license to create a patchwork of racial preferences based on statistical generalizations about any particular field of endeavor.

These defects are readily apparent in this case. The 30% quota cannot in any realistic sense be tied to any injury suffered by anyone. There is nothing approaching a prima facie case of a constitutional or statutory violation by *anyone* in the Richmond construction industry.

The District Court accorded great weight to the fact that the city council designated the Plan as "remedial." But the mere recitation of a "benign" or legitimate purpose for a racial classification, is entitled to little or no weight.

Reliance on the disparity between the number of prime contracts awarded to minority firms and the minority population of the city of Richmond is similarly misplaced. There is no doubt that "[w]here gross statistical disparities can be shown, they alone in a proper case may constitute prima facie proof of a pattern or practice of discrimination" under Title VII. But it is equally clear that "[w]hen special qualifications are required to fill particular jobs, comparisons to the general population (rather than to the smaller group of individuals who possess the necessary qualifications) may have little probative value."

In the employment context, we have recognized that for certain entry level positions or positions requiring minimal training, statistical comparisons of the racial composition of an employer's workforce to the racial composition of the relevant population may be probative of a pattern of discrimination. See *Teamsters* v. *United States* (statistical comparison between minority truck drivers and relevant population probative of discriminatory exclusion). But where special qualifications are necessary, the relevant statistical pool for purposes of demonstrating discriminatory exclusion must be the number of minorities qualified to undertake the particular task.

In this case, the city does not even know how many MBEs in the relevant market are qualified to undertake prime or subcontracting work in public construction projects. Compare *Ohio Contractors Assn.* v. *Keip* (713 F. 2d) (relying on percentage of minority *businesses* in the State compared to percentage of state purchasing contracts awarded to minority firms in upholding set-aside). Nor does the city know what percentage of total city construction dollars minority firms now receive as subcontractors on prime contracts let by the city.

Finally, the city and the District Court relied on Congress' finding in connection with the set-aside approved in *Fullilove* that there had been nationwide discrimination in the construction industry. The probative value of these findings for demonstrating the existence of discrimination in Richmond is extremely limited.

In sum, none of the evidence presented by the

city points to any identified discrimination in the Richmond construction industry. We, therefore, hold that the city has failed to demonstrate a compelling interest in apportioning public contracting opportunities on the basis of race. To accept Richmond's claim that past societal discrimination alone can serve as the basis for rigid racial preferences would be to open the door to competing claims for "remedial relief" for every disadvantaged group. The dream of a Nation of equal citizens in a society where race is irrelevant to personal opportunity and achievement would be lost in a mosaic of shifting preferences based on inherently unmeasurable claims of past wrongs. "Courts would be asked to evaluate the extent of the prejudice and consequent harm suffered by various minority groups. Those whose societal injury is thought to exceed some arbitrary level of tolerability then would be entitled to preferential classifications. . . ." Bakke, 438 U. S., at 296–297 (Powell, J.). We think such a result would be contrary to both the letter and spirit of a constitutional provision whose central command is equality.

The foregoing analysis applies only to the inclusion of blacks within the Richmond set-aside program. There is *absolutely no evidence* of past discrimination against Spanish-speaking, Oriental, Indian, Eskimo, or Aleut persons in any aspect of the Richmond construction industry. The District Court took judicial notice of the fact that the vast majority of "minority" persons in Richmond were black. It may well be that Richmond has never had an Aleut or Eskimo citizen. The random inclusion of racial groups that, as a practical matter, may never have suffered from discrimination in the construction industry in Richmond, suggests that perhaps the city's purpose was not in fact to remedy past discrimination.

If a 30% set-aside was "narrowly tailored" to compensate black contractors for past discrimination, one may legitimately ask why they are forced to share this "remedial relief" with an Aleut citizen who moves to Richmond tomorrow? The gross overinclusiveness of Richmond's racial preference strongly impugns the city's claim of remedial motivation.

First, there does not appear to have been any consideration of the use of race-neutral means to increase minority business participation in city contracting. See *United States* v. *Paradise* (1987) ("In determining whether race-conscious remedies are appropriate, we look to several factors, including the efficacy of alternative remedies"). Many of the barriers to minority participation in the construction industry relied upon by the city to justify a racial classification appear to be race neutral. If MBEs disproportionately lack capital or cannot meet bonding requirements, a race-neutral program of city financing for small firms would lead to greater minority participation. The principal opinion in *Fullilove* found that Congress had carefully examined and rejected race-neutral alternatives before enacting the MBE set-aside. There is no evidence in this record that the Richmond City Council has considered any alternatives to a race-based quota.

Second, the 30% quota cannot be said to be narrowly tailored to any goal, except perhaps outright racial balancing. It rests upon the "completely unrealistic" assumption that minorities will choose a particular trade in lockstep proportion to their representation in the local population.

Nothing we say today precludes a state or local entity from taking action to rectify the effects of identified discrimination within its jurisdictions. If the city of Richmond had evidence before it that nonminority contractors were systematically excluding minority businesses from subcontracting opportunities it could take action to end the discriminatory exclusion. Where there is a significant statistical disparity between the number of qualified minority contractors willing and able to perform a particular service and the number of such contractors actually engaged by the locality or the locality's prime contractors, an inference of discriminatory exclusion could arise. Under such circumstances, the city could act to dismantle the closed business system by taking appropriate measures against those who discriminate on the basis of race or other illegitimate criteria. See e.g., *New York State Club Assn.* v. *New York City* (1988). In the extreme case, some form of narrowly tailored racial preference might be necessary to break down patterns of deliberate exclusion.

Even in the absence of evidence of discrimination, the city has at its disposal a whole array of race-neutral devices to increase the accessibility of city contracting opportunities to small entrepreneurs of all races. Simplification of bidding procedures, relaxation of bonding requirements, and training and financial aid for disadvantaged entrepreneurs for all races would open the public contracting market to all those who have suffered the effects of past societal discrimination or neglect.

Because the city of Richmond has failed to identify the need for remedial action in the awarding of its public construction contracts, its treatment of its citizens on a racial basis violates the dictates of the Equal Protection Clause. Accordingly, the judgment of the Court of Appeals for the Fourth Circuit is affirmed.

Case Questions

1. What factors did the Court consider in distinguishing *Fullilove* from this case?
2. Is the fact that *Fullilove* involved a federal statute and this case involved a city ordinance the main determining factor in the outcome of the case? Should it be?

In the *City of Richmond* case, the Supreme Court seemed to recognize that preferential treatment for certain "protected classes" can produce a discriminatory impact against other groups, who may in fact be the majority of the population. The court has now made a strong statement in favor of employing race-neutral devices whenever possible to avoid offending the Equal Protection Clause, while at the same time acknowledging that preferential treatment for previously disadvantaged groups may sometimes be necessary in order to alleviate the impact of past discrimination. The fact that the Court has not rejected race-conscious plans when they are deemed necessary to remedy the effects of past discrimination is illustrated by the 1987 case of *United States* v. *Paradise,* a case cited favorably in *City of Richmond*. In *Paradise,* the Supreme Court upheld a federal district court order requiring the Alabama state troopers to promote one black for every white promoted. The Court reasoned that the court order was narrowly tailored to serve the purpose of promoting blacks into the upper echelons, and was necessary to eliminate the effects of the troopers' "long-term, open and pervasive discrimination, including the absolute exclusion of blacks in the upper ranks."

Collective Bargaining Agreements and Discrimination

An exception to the provision of Title VII provides that "it shall not be unlawful for an employer to apply different standards of compensation, or different terms, conditions or privileges of employment pursuant to a bona fide seniority or merit system provided that such differences are not the result of an intention to discriminate because of race, color, religion, sex or national origin." Over the years, this "collective bargaining agreement" section has been raised as a defense to allegations of Title VII discrimination.

One of the main areas of conflict regarding the extent of this Title VII exception concerns the discriminatory impact of the many collective bargaining agreements that tie wage scales and employment privileges to seniority. The most obvious problem centers on collective bargaining layoff provisions, which invariably tie the order of layoff to the amount of seniority under the "last to be hired, first to be fired" rationale. The United States Supreme Court has consistently upheld bona fide collective bargaining provisions, even if they have discriminatory effect. Thus, in *International Brotherhood of Teamsters* v. *United States* (1977), the court upheld a seniority system, created through collective bargaining before Title VII was passed, that had the effect of allowing white workers with more seniority as line (long distance) drivers to be considered first for the highest-paying work and to be retained the longest if layoffs occurred. In 1982, in *American Tobacco Company* v. *Patterson,* the Supreme Court held that the collective bargaining exception to Title VII applies even to agreements with discriminatory impact that were passed after Title VII took effect.

In 1983, in *W. R. Grace and Company* v. *Local Union 759, International Union of the United Rubber, Cork, Linoleum and Plastic Workers of America,* the Supreme Court considered the legal effect of a conflict between a collective bargaining agreement and an EEOC conciliation agreement signed by an employer, and held that the collective bargaining agreement would take priority. In the following case, the Supreme Court considered the legal effect of a conflict between a collective bargaining agreement and a court consent decree.

The following year (1984), in *Firefighters Local Union No. 1784* v. *Stotts,* the Supreme Court considered the legal effect of a conflict between a collective bargaining agreement and a court consent decree. The City of Memphis had a collective bargaining agreement with a firefighters union which contained a common "last hired, first fired" layoff provision. The city had also entered into a court consent decree providing for promotion of black firefighters until the proportion of minority representation in each job classification in the fire department equaled the proportion of blacks in the local population. When the city experienced financial difficulties and had to lay off firefighters, the conflict between the collective bargaining agreement, which favored job security for more senior, white employees, and the court consent decree, which favored promotion of blacks, became apparent. The Supreme Court, following the reasoning of the *W. R. Grace* case, gave priority to the collective bargaining agreement. Thus, the Supreme Court's policy of giving priority to collective bargaining agreements seems unchanged.

Discrimination in Pension Plans

It is a statistical fact that women live longer on the average than men. This fact is of extreme importance in determining rates for retirement pensions. Pensions for workers upon their retirement have become a standard fringe benefit provided by employers. Many of these pension plans take into account the greater longevity of women and pay retired women workers a smaller monthly pension than that paid to men, on the theory that since the average woman lives longer than the average man, ultimately men and women will collect the same amount in pension payments. In *Los Angeles Department of Water and Power* v. *Manhart* (1981), the United States Supreme Court invalidated as violating Title VII an employer requirement that female employees pay more in monthly premiums than males. In 1983, in a unanimous opinion in *Arizona* v. *Norris,* the Supreme Court reviewed the legality of the disparate treatment of the sexes resulting from paying women a lower monthly retirement benefit than men, and found that the practice violated Title VII, since it discriminated in the terms of employment on the basis of sex.

After *Arizona* v. *Norris,* most employers and insurers switched pension funds to sex-blind actuarial tables. However, sex-based disparities continued under most plans for payments to people who retired before 1983. In 1988, in *Florida* v. *Long,* the Supreme Court considered the legality of these continuing discriminatory payments. The court ruled that the Norris decision barring sex bias in pension benefits was not retroactive, and that liability could not be imposed for pre-*Norris* discriminatory conduct. The court reasoned that retroactive awards were not necessary to further Title VII's purposes and to insure compliance with the *Manhart* and *Norris* decisions. Further, the imposition of retroactive liability on the states, local governments, and other employers that offered sex-based pension plans to their employees would be inequitable, since it would impose financial costs that would threaten the security of both the plans and their beneficiaries.

Comparable Worth in Salaries

An issue currently exciting much controversy is the concept of **comparable worth** in salaries. You will remember that the federal Equal Pay Act requires equal pay for equal work. In order for a plaintiff to prove a case under the Equal Pay Act, therefore, he or she had to prove that males and females were being paid different salaries for substantially similar work. What are the consequences if job descriptions require the same educational qualifications and the same amount of physical exertion (that is, the jobs are of *comparable worth*), but the amount of the compensation is different? For example, a city might require its water meter readers (most of whom were men) and its parking meter readers (most of whom were women) to have a high school diploma and engage in the same amount of physical exertion, and yet it might pay water meter readers more than parking meter readers. Unless the two jobs were found to be substantially similar, a female parking meter reader could not sue under the Equal Pay Act, even though she could show that the meter reading jobs were comparable.

In 1981, the United States Supreme Court examined one aspect of this comparable worth compensation issue. In *County of Washington* v. *Gunther,* the court held that Equal Pay Act restrictions do not apply to Title VII and that a claim of discriminatory undercompensation under Title VII was not barred merely because the plaintiffs (female guards for the female section of a county jail) were not performing work equal to that of male prison guards.

(The Supreme Court accepted a trial court's findings that the guards' work was unequal because the male guards guarded ten times as many prisoners as the female guards.) At the conclusion of the *Gunther* case, the Supreme Court stated, "We do not decide in this case the precise contours of lawsuits challenging sex discrimination in compensation under Title VII." Thus, the Supreme Court indicated that comparable worth lawsuits were possible, but did not give any guidelines as to how they might be decided.

Since *Gunther,* a number of comparable worth lawsuits have been filed. In 1983, the United States Federal District Court for the State of Washington held that the concept of comparable worth required reexamination of the entire state employee compensation system. But in 1985 the Appeals Court reversed that decision. The concept of comparable worth requires re-evaluation of the nature of how society compensates individuals for their function in society and is possibly the most profound issue addressed by the antidiscrimination laws thus far.

Partnerships and Discrimination

In the past, most lawsuits brought against employers have been filed against corporations. As you saw in chapter 13 on forms of business organizations, a partnership maintains many of the legal attributes of the individual partners, unlike a corporation, which takes on a completely separate legal character. While partnerships have been sued for alleged illegal discrimination in the past, these suits did not involve the questions of how the decision to choose an individual to be a partner should be made. Indeed, it was widely assumed that partnership decisions were exempt from the antidiscrimination laws, especially Title VII of the 1964 Civil Rights Act.

Many of the most influential partnerships in our society are composed of professionals, such as doctors, lawyers, and accountants. In 1984, in the case of *Hishon* v. *King & Spaulding,* the Supreme Court held that partnerships are not exempt from the coverage of Title VII. This case represented a significant departure from the former view that partnership decisions will not be reviewed by the courts. *Hishon* left unanswered the question of what a person must show to prove that they have been discriminated against in a partnership decision. In the following case, decided five years after *Hishon,* the Supreme Court addressed the question of what a plaintiff has to show to prove sex discrimination under Title VII in a partnership decision case.

Price Waterhouse v. Hopkins

109 S. Ct. 1775 (1989)

Ann Hopkins was a senior manager in an office of Price Waterhouse when she was proposed for partnership in 1982. She was neither offered nor denied admission to the partnership; instead, her candidacy was held for reconsideration the following year. When the partners in her office later refused to repropose her for partnership, she sued Price Waterhouse under Title VII of the Civil Rights Act of 1964, charging that the firm had discriminated against her on the basis of sex in its decisions regarding partnership. Judge Gesell in the District Court for the District of Columbia ruled in her favor on the question of liability, and the Court of Appeals for the District of Columbia Circuit affirmed. We granted certiorari to resolve a conflict among the Courts of Appeals concerning the respective burdens of proof of a defendant and plaintiff in a suit under Title VII when it has been shown that an employment decision resulted from a mixture of legitimate and illegitimate motives.

At Price Waterhouse, a nationwide professional accounting partnership, a senior manager becomes a candidate for partnership when the partners in her local office submit her name as a candidate. All of the other partners in the firm are then invited to submit written comments on each candidate—either on a "long" or a "short" form, depending on the partner's degree of exposure.

Ann Hopkins had worked at Price Waterhouse's Office of Government Services in Washington, D. C., for five years when the partners in that office proposed her as a candidate for partnership. Of the 662 partners at the firm at that time, 7 were women. Of the 88 persons proposed for partnership that year, only 1—Hopkins—was a woman. Forty-seven of these candidates were admitted to the partnership, 21 were rejected, and 20—including Hopkins—were "held" for reconsideration the following year. Thirteen of the 32 partners who had submitted comments on Hopkins supported her bid for partnership. Three partners recommended that her candidacy be placed on hold, eight stated that they did not have an informed opinion about her, and eight recommended that she be denied partnership.

In a jointly prepared statement supporting her candidacy, the partners in Hopkins' office showcased her successful 2-year effort to secure a $25 million contract with the Department of State, labeling it "an outstanding performance" and one that Hopkins carried out "virtually at the partner level." Despite Price Waterhouse's attempt at trial to minimize her contribution to this project, Judge Gesell specifically found that Hopkins had "played a key role in Price Waterhouse's successful effort to win a multi-million dollar contract with the Department of State." Indeed, he went on, "[n]one of the other partnership candidates at Price Waterhouse that year had a comparable record in terms of successfully securing major contracts for the partnership."

The partners in Hopkins' office praised her character as well as her accomplishments, describing her in their joint statement as "an outstanding professional" who had a "deft touch," a "strong character, independence and integrity." Clients appear to have agreed with these assessments. A high ranking official praised Hopkins' decisiveness, broadmindedness, and "intellectual clarity"; she was, in his words, "a stimulating conversationalist." Evaluations such as these led Judge Gesell to conclude that Hopkins "had no difficulty dealing with clients and her clients appear to have been very pleased with her work" and that she "was generally viewed as a highly competent project leader who worked long hours, pushed vigorously to meet deadlines and demanded much from the multidisciplinary staffs with which she worked."

On too many occasions, however, Hopkins' aggressiveness apparently spilled over into abrasiveness. Staff members seem to have borne the brunt of Hopkins' brusqueness. Long before her bid for partnership, partners evaluating her work had counseled her to improve her relations with staff members. Although later evaluations indicate an improvement, Hopkins' perceived shortcomings in this important area eventually doomed her bid for partnership. Virtually all of the partners' negative remarks about Hopkins—even those of partners supporting her—had to do with her "interpersonal skills." Both "[s]upporters and opponents of her candidacy," stressed Judge Gesell, "indicated that she was sometimes overly aggressive, unduly harsh, difficult to work with and impatient with staff."

There were clear signs, though, that some of the partners reacted negatively to Hopkins' personality because she was a woman. One partner described her as "macho"; another suggested that she "overcompensated for being a woman"; a third advised her to take "a course at charm school." Several partners criticized her use of profanity; in response, one partner suggested that those partners objected to her swearing only "because it[']s a lady using foul language." Another supporter explained that Hopkins "ha[d] matured from a tough-talking somewhat masculine hard-nosed mgr to an authoritative, formidable, but much more appealing lady ptr candidate." But it was the man who, as Judge Gesell found, bore responsibility for explaining to Hopkins the reasons for the Policy Board's decision to place her candidacy on hold who delivered the coup de grace: in order to improve her chances for partnership, Thomas Beyer advised, Hopkins should "walk more femininely, talk more femininely, dress more femininely, wear make-up, have her hair styled, and wear jewelry."

In previous years, other female candidates for partnership also had been evaluated in sex-based terms. As a general matter, Judge Gesell concluded, "[c]andidates were viewed favorably if partners believed they maintained their femin[in]ity while becoming effective professional managers"; in this environment, "[t]o be identified as a 'women's lib[b]er' was regarded as [a] negative comment."

Judge Gesell found that Price Waterhouse legitimately emphasized interpersonal skills in its partnership decisions, and also found that the firm had not fabricated its complaints about Hopkins' interpersonal skills as a pretext for discrimination. Moreover, he concluded, the firm did not give decisive emphasis to such traits only because Hopkins was a woman; although there were male candidates who lacked these skills but who were admitted to partnership, the judge found that these candidates possessed other, positive traits that Hopkins lacked.

The judge went on to decide, however, that some of the partners' remarks about Hopkins stemmed from an impermissibly cabined view of the proper behavior of women, and that Price Waterhouse had done nothing to disavow reliance on such comments. He held that Price Waterhouse had unlawfully discriminated against Hopkins on the basis of sex by consciously giving credence and effect to partners' comments that resulted from sex stereotyping. Noting that Price Waterhouse could avoid equitable relief by proving by clear and convincing evidence that it would have placed Hopkins' candidacy on hold even absent this discrimination, the judge decided that the firm had not carried this heavy burden.

The Court of Appeals affirmed the District court's ultimate conclusion, but departed from its analysis in one particular: it held that even if a plaintiff proves that discrimination played a role in an employment decision, the defendant will not be found liable if it proves, by clear and convincing evidence, that it would have made the same decision in the absence of discrimination. Under this approach, an employer is not deemed to have violated Title VII if it proves that it would have made the same decision in the absence of an impermissible motive, whereas under the District Court's approach, the employer's proof in that respect only avoids equitable relief. We decide today that the Court of Appeals had the better approach, but that both courts erred in requiring the employer to make its proof by clear and convincing evidence.

The specification of the standard of causation under Title VII is a decision about the kind of conduct that violates that statute. According to Price Waterhouse, an employer violates Title VII only if it gives decisive consideration to an employee's gender, race, national origin, or religion in making a decision that affects that employee. On Price Waterhouse's theory, even if a plaintiff shows that her gender played a part in an employment decision, it is still her burden to show that the decision would have been different if the employer had not discriminated. In Hopkins' view, on the other hand, an employer violates the statute whenever it allows one of these attributes to play any part in an employment decision. Once a plaintiff shows that this occurred, according to Hopkins, the employer's proof that it would have made the same decision in the absence of discrimination can serve to limit equitable relief but not to avoid a finding of liability. We conclude that, as often happens, the truth lies somewhere in-between.

In passing Title VII, Congress made the simple but momentous announcement that sex, race, religion, and national origin are not relevant to the selection, evaluation, or compensation of employees. Yet, the statute does not purport to limit the other qualities and characteristics that employers may take into account in making employment decisions. The converse, therefore, of "for cause" legislation, Title VII eliminates certain bases for distinguishing among employees while otherwise preserving employers' freedom of choice. The balance between employee rights and employer prerogatives turns out to be decisive in the case before us.

Congress' intent to forbid employers to take gender into account in making employment decisions appears on the face of the statute. In now-familiar language, the statute forbids an employer to "fail or refuse to hire or to discharge any individual, or otherwise to discriminate with respect to his compensation, terms, conditions, or privileges of employment," or to "limit, segregate, or classify his employees or applicants for employment in any way which would deprive or tend to deprive any individual of employment opportunities or otherwise adversely affect his status as an employee, because of such individual's . . . sex." We take these words to mean that gender must be irrelevant to employment decisions. To construe the words "because of" as colloquial shorthand for "but-for causation," as does Price Waterhouse, is to misunderstand them.

When, therefore, an employer considers both gender and legitimate factors at the time of making a decision, that decision was "because of" sex and the other, legitimate considerations—even if we may say later, in the context of litigation, that the decision would have been the same if gender had not been taken into account.

To attribute this meaning to the words "because of" does not, as the dissent asserts, divest them of causal significance. A simple example illustrates the point. Suppose two physical forces act upon and move an object, and suppose that either force acting alone would have moved the object. As the dissent would have it, neither physical force was a "cause" of the motion unless we can show that but for one or both of them, the object would not have moved; to use the dissent's terminology, both forces were simply "in the air" unless we can identify at least one of them as a but-for cause of the object's movement. Events that are causally overdetermined, in other words, may not have any "cause" at all. This cannot be so.

We need not leave our commonsense at the doorstep when we interpret a statute. It is difficult for us to imagine that, in the simple words "because of," Congress meant to obligate a plaintiff to identify the precise causal role played by legitimate and illegitimate motivations in the employment decision she challenges. We conclude, instead, that Congress meant to obligate her to prove that the employer relied upon sex-based considerations in coming to its decision.

To say that an employer may not take gender into account is not, however, the end of the matter, for that describes only one aspect of Title VII. The other important aspect of the statute is its preservation of an employer's remaining freedom of choice. We conclude that the preservation of this freedom means that an employer shall not be liable if it can prove that, even if it had not taken gender into account, it would have come to the same decision regarding a particular person. The statute's maintenance of employer prerogatives is evident from the statute itself and from its history, both in Congress and in this Court.

To begin with, the existence of the BFOQ exception shows Congress' unwillingness to require employers to change the very nature of their operations in response to the statute. And our emphasis on "business necessity" in disparate-impact cases, and on "legitimate, nondiscriminatory reason[s]" in disparate-treatment cases, results from our awareness of Title VII's balance between employee rights and employer prerogatives.

The central point is this: while an employer may not take gender into account in making an employment decision (except in those very narrow circumstances in which gender is a BFOQ), it is free to decide against a woman for other reasons. We think these principles require that, once a plaintiff in a Title VII case shows that gender played a motivating part in an employment decision, the defendant may avoid a finding of liability only by proving that it would have made the same decision even if it had not allowed gender to play such a role. This balance of burdens is the direct result of Title VII's balance of rights.

In deciding as we do today, we do not traverse

new ground. We have in the past confronted Title VII cases in which an employer has used an illegitimate criterion to distinguish among employees, and have held that it is the employer's burden to justify decisions resulting from that practice. When an employer has asserted that gender is a bona fide occupational qualification within the meaning of § 703(e), for example, we have assumed that it is the employer who must show why it must use gender as a criterion in employment. In a related context, although the Equal Pay Act expressly permits employers to pay different wages to women where disparate pay is the result of a "factor other than sex," we have decided that it is the employer, not the employee, who must prove that the actual disparity is not sex-linked. Finally, some courts have held that under Title VII as amended by the Pregnancy Discrimination Act, it is the employer who has the burden of showing that its limitations on the work that it allows a pregnant woman to perform are necessary in light of her pregnancy. As these examples demonstrate, our assumption always has been that if an employer allows gender to affect its decisionmaking process, then it must carry the burden of justifying its ultimate decision. We have not in the past required women whose gender has proved relevant to an employment decision to establish the negative proposition that they would not have been subject to that decision had they been men, and we do not do so today.

We have, in short, been here before. Each time, we have concluded that the plaintiff who shows that an impermissible motive played a motivating part in an adverse employment decision has thereby placed upon the defendant the burden to show that it would have made the same decision in the absence of the unlawful motive. Our decision today treads this well-worn path.

In saying that gender played a motivating part in an employment decision, we mean that, if we asked the employer at the moment of the decision what its reasons were and if we received a truthful response, one of those reasons would be that the applicant or employee was a woman. In the specific context of sex stereotyping, an employer who acts on the basis of a belief that a woman cannot be aggressive, or that she must not be, has acted on the basis of gender.

Although the parties do not overtly dispute this last proposition, the placement by Price Waterhouse of "sex stereotyping" in quotation marks throughout its brief seems to us an insinuation either that such stereotyping was not present in this case or that it lacks legal relevance. We reject both possibilities. As to the existence of sex stereotyping in this case, we are not inclined to quarrel with the District Court's conclusion that a number of the partners' comments showed sex stereotyping at work. As for the legal relevance of sex stereotyping, we are beyond the day when an employer could evaluate employees by assuming or insisting that they matched the stereotype associated with their group, for " '[i]n forbidding employers to discriminate against individuals because of their sex, Congress intended to strike at the entire spectrum of disparate treatment of men and women resulting from sex stereotypes.' " *Los Angeles Dept. of Water & Power* v. *Manhart,* 435 U. S. 702, 707, n. 13 (1978), quoting *Sprogis* v. *United Air Lines, Inc.,* 444 F. 2d 1194, 1198 (CA7 1971). As employer who objects to aggressiveness in women but whose positions require this trait places women in an intolerable and impermissible Catch-22: out of a job if they behave aggressively and out of a job if they don't. Title VII lifts women out of this bind.

Remarks at work that are based on sex stereotypes do not inevitably prove that gender played a part in a particular employment decision. The plaintiff must show that the employer actually relied on her gender in making its decision. In making this showing, stereotyped remarks can certainly be evidence that gender played a part. In any event, the stereotyping in this case did not simply consist of stray remarks. On the contrary, Hopkins proved that Price Waterhouse invited partners to submit comments; that some of the comments stemmed from sex stereotypes; that an important part of the Policy Board's decision on Hopkins was an assessment of the submitted comments; and that Price Waterhouse in no way disclaimed reliance on the sex-linked evaluations. This is not, as Price Waterhouse suggests, "discrimination in the air"; rather, it is, as Hopkins puts it, "discrimination brought to ground and visited upon" an employee. By focusing on

Hopkins' specific proof, however, we do not suggest a limitation on the possible ways of proving that stereotyping played a motivating role in an employment decision, and we refrain from deciding here which specific facts, "standing alone," would or would not establish a plaintiff's case, since such a decision is unnecessary in this case.

As to the employer's proof, in most cases, the employer should be able to present some objective evidence as to its probable decision in the absence of an impermissible motive. Moreover, proving "that the same decision would have been justified . . . is not the same as proving that the same decision would have been made." An employer may not, in other words, prevail in a mixed-motives case by offering a legitimate and sufficient reason for its decision if that reason did not motivate it at the time of the decision. Finally, an employer may not meet its burden in such a case by merely showing that at the time of the decision it was motivated only in part by a legitimate reason. The very premise of a mixed-motives case is that a legitimate reason was present, and in deed, in this case, Price Waterhouse already has made this showing by convincing Judge Gesell that Hopkins' interpersonal problems were a legitimate concern. The employer instead must show that its legitimate reason, standing alone, would have induced it to make the same decision.

The courts below held that an employer who has allowed a discriminatory impulse to play a motivating part in an employment decision must prove by clear and convincing evidence that it would have made the same decision in the absence of discrimination. We are persuaded that the better rule is that the employer must make this showing by a preponderance of the evidence.

Although Price Waterhouse does not concretely tell us how its proof was preponderant even if it was not clear and convincing, this general claim is implicit in its request for the less stringent standard. Since the lower courts required Price Waterhouse to make its proof by clear and convincing evidence, they did not determine whether Price Waterhouse had proved by a *preponderance of the evidence* that it would have place Hopkins' candidacy on hold even if it had not permitted sex-linked evaluations to play a part in the decisionmaking process. Thus, we shall remand this case so that that determination can be made.

We hold that when a plaintiff in a Title VII case proves that her gender played a motivating part in an employment decision, the defendant may avoid a finding of liability only by proving by a preponderance of the evidence that it would have made the same decision even if it had not taken the plaintiff's gender into account. Because the courts below erred by deciding that the defendant must make this proof by clear and convincing evidence, we reverse the Court of Appeals' judgment against Price Waterhouse on liability and remand the case to that court for further proceedings.

It is so ordered.

Case Questions

1. Is an employer liable for violation of Title VII if it can prove that, even if it had not taken gender into account, it would have not made a person a partner?
2. What must a plaintiff in a partnership discrimination case prove to win?
3. Do remarks at work that are based on sex stereotypes prove that gender played a part in a particular employment decision?

The *Hishon* and *Hopkins* cases have put partners on notice that their partnership admissions decisions will be subject to court scrutiny. The reaction of various partnerships will vary, but it seems safe to say that they will probably begin using a more formal and objective set of criteria in making their partnership decisions.

Private Clubs and Organizations

A continuing source of controversy from the time of the passage of the 1964 Civil Rights Act has been the extent to which private clubs and organizations can discriminate against members of certain groups. Even after the passage of the 1964 act, purely private groups were often able to discriminate on the basis of such characteristics as race, religion, and sex. Aside from the basic civil rights issues involved in such exclusionary policies, this form of discrimination has been viewed by the excluded group as causing employment or economic discrimination, because business is often transacted at clubs or organization meetings, thereby disadvantaging the excluded groups. During the middle 1980s, the Supreme Court decided several cases that had the effect of "opening up" such formerly private clubs and organizations. In the first of a series of cases, the Supreme Court held that the United States Jaycees, a nonprofit national educational and charitable organization, could not force its Minnesota chapters to discriminate against women in violation of the Minnesota Human Rights Act (*Roberts* v. *United States Jaycees,* 1984). The court specifically rejected the Jaycees' argument that forcing Jaycee chapters to accept women as regular members would violate the male members' constitutional rights of free speech and association.

In 1987, the Supreme Court considered whether another private organization, Rotary International, could prohibit women from becoming members. Members were admitted to local Rotary clubs based on their business, professional, and institutional activity in the community. Rotary International terminated a California chapter when it admitted women. The chapter sued for reinstatement. The court held that Rotary International's male-only membership rule violated a California statute that entitled all persons, regardless of sex, to full and equal accommodations, advantages, facilities, privileges, and services in all business establishments in the state. The court noted that business concerns were motivating factors in joining local clubs, and that admitting women would not interfere unduly with the club members' freedom of private association. The court pointed out that the relationship between Rotary Club members was not the kind of intimate or private relation that warranted constitutional protection, thus leaving open the possibility that a more "exclusive" club might be able to exclude certain groups.

A year after the *Rotary Club* case, in 1988, the Supreme Court decided yet another private club case, *New York State Club Association, Inc.,* v. *City of New York.* New York City's Human Rights Law prohibited discrimination in places of public accommodation, resort, or amusement, but exempted institutions or clubs distinctly private in nature unless they had more than four hundred members, provided regular meal service, and regularly received payment from nonmembers for furtherance of trade or business. Benevolent orders and religious corporations were exempted from the law. An association of New York clubs sued to have the ordinance declared unconstitutional as a violation of the First and Fourteenth Amendments. The court, citing the *Jaycees* and

Rotary Clubs cases, held that the law was not unconstitutional, since the law assumed some sort of business activity or relationship in the club activities, and since it had to be assumed that many of the large clubs could advance their desired viewpoints without limiting their membership to only certain groups. After the *City of New York* case, the status of the law seems to be that, while it is possible for a purely private, exclusive club whose purpose is not primarily the carrying out of business to discriminate against certain groups, it is very difficult to prove a constitutional right to discriminate. The ability to discriminate is especially suspect if there is a state or local statute that prohibits such practices.

Sexual Harassment

Another topic that has created controversy is the question of **sexual harassment** on the job. Discussion of the subject of sexual harassment in the workplace only became widespread around 1980. One widely used definition of sexual harassment was formulated by the federal Office of Personnel Management: "deliberate or repeated unsolicited verbal comments, gestures or physical contact of a sexual nature which are unwelcome." Sexual harassment can include conditioning hiring, firing, or promotion on sexual conduct. It can also include such activities as a male supervisor asking a female employee to look at what a court characterized as "girlie" magazines and tell him if any of the models looked like her. It is difficult to determine the extent of sexual harassment in employment because the field has not been well researched, and because the determination of when an activity constitutes sexual harassment is often subjective. One survey of federal employees, published in 1980, found that 42 percent of the women surveyed and 15 percent of the men felt that they had been sexually harassed at work during the period between May 1978 and May 1980.

The EEOC has issued guidelines that declare sexual harassment to be a form of sex discrimination. These guidelines are contained in appendix C of this book. Among their many provisions, the guidelines specifically state that requiring sexual conduct as a condition for employment or promotion is illegal. Recently, sexual harassment cases have begun to be heard by courts, who have tended to follow the provisions of the EEOC guidelines carefully. Notice that the sexual harassment procedures apply equally to women and men, and there have been a few cases in which male employees have alleged sexual harassment by female supervisors.

Ethical Issues in Equal Employment Opportunity

Many of the issues discussed in the previous section on current issues involve questions with ethical as well as legal aspects. Some argue that enforcement of equal employment opportunity laws is a waste of time and money, because the only effect of the law is to change the nature of discrimination from overt to covert. This argument ignores the efficacy of the law as a statement of ethics. It would be possible to use several different ethical theories and arrive at the conclusion that making assumptions about a person based on her membership in a group instead of knowledge of her as an individual is unethical. It is often helpful to use the device of assessing how a person would view society and individuals' places in it if she did not know what her place in society would be. You should examine closely such issues as unisex pension plans and partnership choice, discussed in preceding sections, to determine ethical aspects of the problems.

Perhaps the most vexing current issue in employment discrimination law concerns the various aspects of "reverse discrimination." Is it fair and morally desirable that the existence of discrimination against certain groups in the past should be used as a reason to discriminate against other groups now? Perhaps nowhere is the difficulty of applying ethical theories through the law more clearly drawn than in the problem of reverse discrimination. The difficulty, of course, is that it is often necessary to make choices that will hurt someone. A good illustration of the problem is the *Weber* case, which was discussed in this chapter and in chapter 1. The courts have followed the course of leaving ethical decisions to individuals, or at least to legislative bodies, and have tended to sidestep direct confrontation with the ethical dilemma created by the fact that discrimination in favor of one group may inherently involve discrimination against another group.

Another major issue that is probably the most controversial issue in this area at present is the "comparable worth" concept. One of the fundamental economic concepts of our society is the doctrine of supply and demand. Many argue that the concept of comparable worth as it has been interpreted by the courts negates the premise that the marketplace should set salary levels for types of jobs. Is it desirable to change the doctrine of supply and demand, or will the concept of comparable worth indeed do that?

Equal employment opportunity is a very controversial area because the questions raised by the concept have affected many people. It is an area in which there is a large overlap between law and ethics, and it raises questions with which society will have to grapple in the future.

The important concepts and terms in this chapter are listed below; page numbers have been provided for the key terms. By reading over each section you can assess your understanding of the chapter concepts and determine areas you may want to review.

Chapter Summary

1. The most used equal employment opportunity statute is Title VII of the 1964 Civil Rights Act, which prohibits discrimination by most employers in hiring, firing, promotion, and other terms and conditions of employment on the basis of race, color, sex, religion, and national origin.

2. Other federal equal employment opportunity statutes are the Equal Pay Act, the Age Discrimination in Employment Act, the Rehabilitation Act, the Pregnancy Discrimination Act, and the Civil Rights Act of 1866.
3. Federal Executive Order 11246 mandates that all federal contractors formulate affirmative action plans (AAPs) and attempt to meet the goals contained in these AAPs.
4. Current areas in which legal and ethical issues overlap are reverse discrimination, unisex pension plans, partnership choices, and sexual harassment.

Key Terms

affirmative action plans 419
Age Discrimination in Employment Act 413
bona fide occupational qualification 405
business necessity test 403
Civil Rights Act of 1866 418
comparable worth 430
Equal Employment Opportunity Commission 401
Equal Pay Act 413
Executive Order 11246 419
pattern and practices suits 401
Pregnancy Discrimination Act 415
reverse discrimination 421
sexual harassment 438
Title VII of the 1964 Civil Rights Act 400

Questions on Ethics

1. Is it ethical for a (nongovernment contractor) employer who has a job opening to hire a relative or the relative of a friend—who is of the same ethnic background as the employer—rather than to advertise the position and select the best candidate?
2. "Reverse discrimination" is legal, at least in certain cases; is it ethical?
3. If pension plans provide for different rates of pay-out based on statistical differences between the sexes, is it ethical to attempt to produce a system that pays everyone the same benefit after years of charging them the same premium?
4. Should fathers as well as mothers be entitled to maternity leave?
5. Is it ethical to prohibit married couples from doing the same type of job for the same employer?

Questions on Law

1. Lois applies for a promotion, but is passed over. Lois feels that she was passed over because of her ethnic background. What are her rights under Title VII of the 1964 Civil Rights Act?

2. Fred is denied admission to a bar because of his race. What are his rights under the Civil Rights Act of 1866?
3. John is being harassed by co-workers because of his race. Is the employer legally liable to John if it fails to take corrective action? *Lucero* v. *Beth Israel Hospital,* 479 F. Supp. 452 (D. Colo. 1979).
4. Molly was upset when she found that her co-workers had drawn cartoons about her that accentuated certain characteristics of her appearance. Was she being sexually harassed? *Kyriazi* v. *Western Electric Company,* 486 F. Supp. 894 (D. N.J. 1978).
5. Three ironworkers with years of experience and outstanding work records asked on a number of occasions to be promoted to foreman, but were always denied. Two of the workers were black and one was Puerto Rican. The foreman jobs always went to whites. The three could not prove a specific intent to discriminate against them. Could they recover under Title VII of the 1964 Civil Rights Act? *Grant* v. *Bethlehem Steel Corp.,* 635 F.2d 1007 (2d Cir. 1980).

Suggested Readings

Hiller, "Civil Rights Enforcement and Japanese Subsidiaries," 21 *American Business Law Journal* 463 (1984).

Hurd, Murray, Shaw, "Comparable Worth: A Legal and Ethical Analysis," 22 *American Business Law Journal* 406 (1984).

Stevens, "The Cruel 'Trilemma': Sexual Harassment Under Title VII and the Tangible Job Benefit—*Bundy* v. *Jackson,*" 20 *American Business Law Journal* 109 (1982).

16 Business and Labor Unions

I am fully aware that in this era of automation and onrushing technological change, no problems in the domestic economy are of greater concern than those involving job security and employment stability. . . . Congress may eventually decide to give organized labor or government a far heavier hand in controlling what until now have been considered the prerogatives of private business management. That path would mark a sharp departure from the traditional principles of a free enterprise economy.

—*Justice Potter Stewart,* Fibreboard Corp. *v.* Labor Board *379 U.S. 203 (1964)*

■ LEARNING OBJECTIVES

After you have read this chapter, you should be able to:

1. Discuss early problems with union formation in the United States, focusing on pre-1935 legislation that attempted to correct those problems.
2. Identify both management and union unfair labor practices.
3. Know the functions and duties of the National Labor Relations Board.
4. Describe the collective bargaining process.

Business Decisions and the law

The Case of the Drug Car

Misco, Inc., had an employment rule that listed as cause for discharge the possession or use of controlled substances on company property. Isiah

Cooper, an employee who operated a hazardous machine, was arrested by the police in the backseat of someone else's car, which was parked on Misco property and which was filled with marijuana smoke and contained a marijuana cigarette in the frontseat ashtray. When Cooper was discharged because of the incident, his case proceeded to binding arbitration under the terms of a collective bargaining contract, and the arbitrator found in Cooper's favor and ordered reinstatement. Will Cooper's reinstatement award be upheld in court? See *United Paperworkers International Union, AFL-CIO* v. *Misco, Inc.*

Introduction

The concepts evoked by the word *labor* can be considered from many points of view. Some view it simply as a production factor that is combined with capital and other expenditures to produce goods and services that are consumed by the public. Others view it as people who are both helped and harmed by the union movement. Labor has been much in the news with such events as the firing of government-employed air traffic controllers after a strike in 1981, the influx of Japanese imports, and unions' often well-publicized collective bargaining with management.

The focus of this chapter will be the major federal statutes that deal with the organization of unions and collective bargaining and their effects on business. Before we can understand those effects, however, we must take a brief look backward at the beginnings of the labor movement in this country.

Workers did not begin to organize until the 1800s in the United States. The first attempts were made by skilled workers who wanted to gain higher wages, but such attempts were in no way favored by the law. When the skilled workers threatened or conducted strikes or boycotts, their employers took them to court, alleging breach of contract or criminal conspiracy under the common law.

Under the law of contracts, the courts held that workers were engaged, by their own choosing, in an employment contract for a specified wage with the employer. Demands for higher wages, when supported by work stoppages or boycotts, were a breach of that contract. This theory assumed equal bargaining power between employers and employees. In reality, contract terms were dictated by the employers in a labor market saturated with large numbers of immigrants seeking work.

Using the criminal conspiracy doctrine of the common law, employers alleged that by joining together to receive higher wages workers were entering into illegal combinations. Such illegal combinations, it was then thought, injured society as a whole, because their purpose was to benefit those who joined and to punish those who would not join the group. This view changed somewhat during the nineteenth century, when it was held in 1842 that unless the group's aims or activities were unlawful, their acting in concert was not criminal conspiracy (*Commonwealth* v. *Hunt,* 4 Metcalf 111, 38 Am. Dec. 346).

With the powerful weapon of criminal conspiracy taken away, and with courts viewing labor unions as legal organizations in the mid-1800s, employers resorted to other means to stop unionization. They found help in the Sherman Antitrust Act, which was passed by Congress in 1890. The act prohibited unlawful combinations in restraint of trade. Although its purpose was to stop anticompetitive activities by business firms, employers were successful in convincing courts that unions were in violation of the act because they were combining to restrain trade. This was a major setback to organized labor.

The worst blow of all, however, was dealt by the use of injunctions in labor disputes. An employer faced with strikes or boycotts needed a tool that would prohibit such activities and force the workers back on the job. This could be accomplished by the use of an **ex parte injunction,** with which a court ordered the employees back to work after hearing only the employer's side of the dispute. A trial could be held later, but based on the employer's claim that a continued strike would cause irreparable harm to his business, the striking employees were ordered to cease disruption of such business. To disobey such an injunction meant jail for contempt of court.

As you can see, interpretation of the law by the judiciary worked in favor of the employers. Courts recognized the employers' ownership interests in the property of their businesses and thus interpreted statutes and the common law to curb union activity.

Federal Legislation Prior to 1935

As we have seen, neither courts nor legislatures in the late nineteenth and early twentieth centuries encouraged the growth of labor unions in the United States. Yet organized labor continued to grow, both in numbers and in power. The Great Depression of the 1930s forced Congress to take a closer look at our economic system to determine where, if at all, organized labor should have a place. That look resulted in the federal laws discussed next.

Clayton Act

In 1914, Congress passed the first federal statute of importance to the labor movement. It is essentially an antitrust law, prohibiting mergers and other anticompetitive business practices. Section 6, however, exempts labor unions from the antitrust laws, so long as the unions or their members are lawfully carrying out their legitimate objectives. The exemption does not apply if a labor union joins with someone outside of organized labor (an employer) for the purpose of restraining trade. Another section of the act ostensibly prohibits federal courts from using injunctions in such labor activities as strikes and picketing when those disputes concern terms or conditions of employment.

Railway Labor Act

Congress enacted the Railway Labor Act in 1926. This statute encourages collective bargaining in the railroad industry for the resolution of labor disputes that would otherwise disrupt transportation. It is still the basic governing statute for labor-management relations in this industry. It has since been extended to cover air transportation. Under the Railway Labor Act, the National Mediation Board was established to designate the bargaining representatives for employees in the covered industries, as well as to mediate disputes concerning rates of pay or working conditions. Certain unfair labor practices, such as the refusal to bargain collectively, were outlawed by the act.

Norris-LaGuardia Act

The 1932 *Norris-LaGuardia Act* legitimized labor unions by making unenforceable those employment agreements that forbid union membership, the so-called **yellow-dog contracts.** That provision of the act is still in effect today. Further, Norris-LaGuardia stripped the federal courts of their power to issue injunctions against most union activities. However, illegal strikes, such as those by public employees, or unlawful acts that would cause substantial and irreparable damage may be restrained. Procedural safeguards for issuance of injunctions in such disputes were added. The act does *not* limit the power of *state* courts to issue labor injunctions.

Federal Legislation since 1935

The federal courts had been ordered by Norris-LaGuardia to exercise judicial nonintervention, staying out of peaceful labor disputes and allowing economics to determine the winner. During the Great Depression of the 1930s, this policy was injurious to the economy. Strikes crippled the country, and President Franklin Roosevelt was urged by business to take corrective action. The legislation that followed is discussed next.

National Labor Relations Act

The first federal statute to lay down comprehensively the structure for our present labor law was passed by Congress in 1935. It is sometimes referred to as the *Wagner Act*. The act set forth as its policy the protection by law of the right of employees to organize and bargain collectively—that is, to be represented by a union in negotiations with an employer over an employment contract. The act recognizes the right to bargain collectively as fundamental. Section 7 provides:

> Employees shall have the right to self organization, to form, join, or assist labor organizations, to bargain collectively through representatives of their own choosing, and to engage in concerted activities for the purpose of collective bargaining or other mutual aid or protection.

After recognizing the fundamental right of **collective bargaining,** Congress set about the task of putting together the machinery to practice that right. Several new aspects were added by the act to our system of labor relations, including the creation of the National Labor Relations Board and the identification of *unfair labor practices*.

National Labor Relations Board

Section 9 of the Wagner Act spells out the procedures by which employees select their representatives. It also charges the *National Labor Relations Board (NLRB),* which administers the act, to determine the "appropriate bargaining unit" that will represent the employees. When a majority of the workers in such a unit choose a union, then all workers in that unit will be represented by that union. This process of exclusive representation prevents an employer from having to deal with more than one union in order to come to an agreement with one group of employees. The NLRB also handles charges filed against an employer by issuing a complaint and then conducting a hearing before an administrative law judge. The structure and organization of the NLRB are covered in detail later in this chapter.

Unfair Labor Practices (ULPs) by Employers

Under the act, certain employer practices that are neither criminal nor civil offenses are forbidden when they hamper the fundamental right of an employee to bargain collectively. These **unfair labor practices** (ULPs) include: interference with employees' efforts to form, join, or assist labor organizations; domination of a labor organization ("company union"); discrimination in hiring or tenure of employees because of union affiliation; discrimination against employees who file charges with the NLRB or who give testimony in proceedings of the board; and failure and/or refusal to bargain collectively with the designated employee representative. Employer ULPs will be covered more extensively in a subsequent section.

The Wagner Act contributed to the growth of the union movement by increasing its strength and influence. By 1946, however, many employers who had traditionally had the upper hand felt that the unions were now calling the shots. They complained loudly that the labor organizations had unequal bargaining power, with their ability to call strikes that effectively crippled the nation. In 1946, a wave of strikes rocked the United States, setting a record high for the number of work days lost. The public reaction was overwhelmingly negative, and Congress responded in an effort to public opinion.

Labor-Management Relations Act

Congress overrode a veto by then-President Harry Truman to pass the *Taft-Hartley Act,* as the *Labor-Management Relations Act* is more commonly known, in June 1947. It served as an amendment to the Wagner Act, adding new sections to be enforced. Work stoppages had the effect of burdening commerce, and this amendment was designed to ease some of that burden. The most important provisions of the act are the Federal Mediation and Conciliation Service, unfair labor practices, the right to work, freedom of speech, and a cooling-off period.

Federal Mediation and Conciliation Service. Charged with the responsibility of trying to persuade both sides in a labor dispute to settle it by helping them to see a common ground, the service was designed to minimize the chances of a strike.

Unfair labor practices (ULPs). Until the passage of this act, only employers could be guilty of unfair labor practices, and that produced some very one-sided results. The act recognized six unfair labor practices that could be committed by a union and that were illegal: (a) coercing an employee to join a union or coercing an employer to choose a bargaining representative; (b) discriminating against an employee who is not a member of the union; (c) refusing to bargain in good faith with the employer; (d) strikes, pickets, or **secondary boycotts** (organized refusal to deal with a secondary employer in order to force such an employer to stop dealing with another business, the primary target of the union) for illegal purposes; (e) excess initiation fees with an intent to discriminate against certain applicants; and (f) **featherbedding** (causing an employer to pay for services that have not and will not be performed). More detailed information on the interpretation of these ULPs is provided later in this chapter.

Right to work. The *closed shop* was outlawed, but the *union shop* was permitted in those states that did not forbid it by passing *right-to-work-laws*. Each state was given the right to decide for itself whether or not it would permit union shop agreements. In a **closed shop** contract, the employer agrees not to hire an employee who is not a member of a particular union. The **union shop** contract only requires membership in the union after the employee has been hired, such being a condition of continued employment. This requirement can only be imposed after the thirtieth day of employment. **Right-to-work laws** prohibit employer agreements that require union membership as a condition of employment. This is probably the most disliked aspect of the Taft-Hartley law among unions; about twenty states have right-to-work laws.

Freedom of speech. Because employers had complained that the Wagner Act violated their First Amendment rights, Congress inserted the following provision:

> 8(c) The expressing of any views, argument, or opinion, or the dissemination thereof, whether in written, printed, graphic, or visual form, shall not constitute or be evidence of an unfair labor practice under any of the provisions of this Act, if such expression contains no threat of reprisal or force or promise of benefit.

This right applies to both labor unions and employers, but neither side is allowed to make election speeches on company time to large groups of employees the day before an election.

Cooling-off period. The President of the United States was given the power to handle situations in which he believes that a threatened or actual strike that affects an entire industry or a substantial part thereof will endanger national safety or health if allowed to continue or to occur. In the event of such a national emergency strike, the President is empowered to appoint a board of inquiry to study the strike and to report back to the President its findings and recommendations. The President, through the attorney general, then may seek an injunction in federal court, ordering the striking or soon-to-strike employees back to work for an eighty-day **cooling-off period.** If a settlement has not been reached at the end of that period, the employees are then free to strike again for an indefinite length of time. A national emergency strike is one that involves national defense or major industries, or that has a substantial effect on the national economy.

In the following case, the Supreme Court had to decide whether a union could distribute handbills to customers at a shopping mall.

DeBartolo v. Florida Gulf Coast Building and Construction Trades Council

56 S.S.L.W. 4329 (April 20, 1988)

Opinion

Justice White: This case centers around the respondent union's peaceful handbilling of the businesses operating in a shopping mall in Tampa, Florida, owned by petitioner, the Edward J. DeBartolo Corporation (DeBartolo). The union's primary labor dispute was with H. J. High Construction Company (High) over alleged substandard wages and fringe benefits. High was retained by the H. J. Wilson Company (Wilson) to construct a department store in the mall, and neither DeBartolo nor any of the other 85 or so mall tenants had any contractual right to influence the selection of contractors.

The union, however, sought to obtain their influence upon Wilson and High by distributing handbills asking mall customers not to shop at any of the stores in the mall "until the Mall's owner publicly promises that all construction at the Mall will be done using contractors who pay their employees fair wages and fringe benefits." The handbills' message was that "[t]he payment of substandard wages not only diminishes the working person's ability to purchase with earned, rather than borrowed, dollars, but it also undercuts the wage standard of the entire community." The handbills made clear that the union was seeking only a consumer boycott against the other mall tenants, not a secondary strike by their employees. At all four entrances to the mall for about three weeks in

December 1979, the union peacefully distributed the handbills without any accompanying picketing or patrolling.

After DeBartolo failed to convince the union to alter the language of the handbills to state that its dispute did not involve DeBartolo or the mall lessees other than Wilson and to limit its distribution to the immediate vicinity of Wilson's construction site, it filed a complaint with the National Labor Relations Board (Board), charging the union with engaging in unfair labor practices under § 8(b)(4) of the National Labor Relations Act (NLRA), as amended. The Board's General Counsel issued a complaint, but the Board eventually dismissed it, concluding that the handbilling was protected by the publicity proviso of § 8(b)(4). The Court of Appeals for the Fourth Circuit affirmed the Board (1981), but this Court reversed in *Edward J. DeBartolo Corp.* v. *NLRB* (1983). There, we concluded that the handbilling did not fall within the proviso's limited scope of exempting "publicity intended to inform the public that the primary employer's product is 'distributed by' the secondary employer" because DeBartolo and the other tenants, as opposed to Wilson, did not distribute products of High. Since there had not been a determination below whether the union's handbilling fell within the prohibition of § 8(b)(4), and, if so, whether it was protected by the First Amendment, we remanded the case.

On remand, the Board held that the union's handbilling was proscribed by § 8(b)(4)(ii)(B). It stated that under its prior cases "handbilling and other activity urging a consumer boycott constituted coercion." The Board reasoned that "[a]ppealing to the public not to patronize secondary employers is an attempt to inflict economic harm on the secondary employers by causing them to lose business," and "such appeals constitute 'economic retaliation' and are therefore a form of coercion."

The Court of Appeals for the Eleventh Circuit denied enforcement of the Board's order. Because there would be serious doubts about whether § 8(b)(4) could constitutionally ban peaceful handbilling not involving nonspeech elements, such as patrolling, the court applied our decision in *NLRB* v. *Catholic Bishop of Chicago* (1979), to determine if there was a clear congressional intent to proscribe such handbilling. The language of the section, the court held, revealed no such intent, and the legislative history indicated that Congress, by using the phrase "threaten, coerce, or restrain," was concerned with secondary picketing and strikes rather than appeals to consumers not involving picketing. The court went on to construe the section as not prohibiting consumer publicity; DeBartolo petitioned for certiorari. Because this case presents important questions of federal constitutional and labor law, we granted the petition, and now affirm.

Another rule of statutory construction, however, is pertinent here: where an otherwise acceptable construction of a statute would raise serious constitutional problems, the Court will construe the statute to avoid such problems unless such construction is plainly contrary to the intent of Congress.

We agree with the Court of Appeals and respondents that this case calls for the invocation of the *Catholic Bishop* rule, for the Board's construction of the statute, as applied in this case, poses serious questions of the validity of § 8(b)(4) under the First Amendment. The handbills involved here truthfully revealed the existence of a labor dispute and urged potential customers of the mall to follow a wholly legal course of action, namely, not to patronize the retailers doing business in the mall. The handbilling was peaceful. No picketing or patrolling was involved. On its face, this was expressive activity arguing that substandard wages should be opposed by abstaining from shopping in a mall where such wages were paid. Had the union simply been leafletting the public generally, including those entering every shopping mall in town, pursuant to an annual educational effort against substandard pay, there is little doubt that legislative proscription of such leaflets would pose a substantial issue of validity under the First Amendment. The same may well be true in this case, although here the handbills called attention to a specific situation in the mall allegedly involving the payment of unacceptably low wages by a construction contractor.

The case turns on whether handbilling such as involved here must be held to "threaten, coerce, or restrain any person" to cease doing business with another, within the meaning of § 8(b)(4)(ii)(B). We note first that "induc[ing] or encourag[ing]" employees of the secondary employer to strike is proscribed by § 8(b)(4)(i). But more than mere persuasion is necessary to prove a violation of § 8(b)(4)(ii): that section requires a showing of threats, coercion, or restraints. There is no suggestion that the leaflets had any coercive effect on customers of the mall. There was no violence, picketing, or patrolling and only an attempt to persuade customers not to shop in the mall.

Our decision in *Tree Fruits* (*NLRB* v. *Fruit Packers*), however, makes untenable the notion that *any* kind of handbilling, picketing, or other appeals to a secondary employer to cease doing business with the employer involved in the labor dispute is "coercion" within the meaning of § 8(b)(4)(ii)(B) if it has some economic impact on the neutral. In that case, the union picketed a secondary employer, a retailer, asking the public not to buy a product produced by the primary employer. We held that the impact of this picketing was not coercion within the meaning of § 8(b)(4) even though, if the appeal succeeded, the retailer would lose revenue.

The Board's reading of § 8(b)(4) would make an unfair labor practice out of any kind of publicity or communication to the public urging a consumer boycott of employers other than those the proviso specifically deals with. On the facts of this case, newspaper, radio, and television appeals not to patronize the mall would be prohibited; and it would be an unfair labor practice for unions in their own meetings to urge their members not to shop in the mall. Nor could a union's handbills simply urge not shopping at a department store because it is using a nonunion contractor, although the union could safely ask the store's customers not to buy there because it is selling mattresses not carrying the union label. It is difficult, to say the least, to fathom why Congress would consider appeals urging a boycott of a distributor of a nonunion product to be more deserving of protection than nonpicketing persuasion of customers of other neutral employers such as that involved in this case.

Neither do we find any clear indication in the relevant legislative history that Congress intended § 8(b)(4)(ii) to proscribe peaceful handbilling, unaccompanied by picketing, urging a consumer boycott of a neutral employer.

In our view, interpreting § 8(b)(4) as not reaching the handbilling involved in this case is not foreclosed either by the language of the section or its legislative history. That construction makes unnecessary passing on the serious constitutional questions that would be raised by the Board's understanding of the statute. Accordingly, the judgment of the Court of Appeals is affirmed.

Case Questions

1. What type of union activity might constitute illegal coercion?
2. Did the fact that a First Amendment freedom of speech issue was involved here make a difference?

Labor-Management Reporting and Disclosure Act

This congressional legislation, more familiarly known as the *Landrum-Griffin Act,* was passed in 1959 in reaction to evidence of violence, corruption, and undemocratic procedures practiced by some unions. Such practices became known to the general public as a result of congressional hearings conducted prior to passage of the act. The new statute amended the National Labor Relations Act.

Under the Landrum-Griffin Act, union members received a "bill of rights," which had not been recognized before. These rights are in addition to rights they may have under other laws or under union bylaws or constitutions. They include: the right to nominate candidates, to vote in elections, to attend meetings of the membership, and to speak about business dealings of the union; the right to freely express themselves at meetings; the right to vote on increases in dues or fees; the right to sue the union and to testify against it; the right to be accorded due process in connection with any charges brought against them by the union; and the right to receive a copy of the collective bargaining agreement. The statute allows a civil suit for damages and an injunction for violation of the stated rights.

The Landrum-Griffin Act went even further in attempting to "clean up" union activities, with extensive requirements for public financial disclosure by unions and union leaders and with procedures for regulating the election of union officials by the membership. The following Supreme Court case considers the question of whether a union could use members' fees to engage in such activities as lobbying and organizing the employees of other employers.

Communications Workers of America v. *Beck*

56 U.S.L.W. 4857 (June 29, 1988)

Opinion

Justice Brennan: Section 8(a)(3) of the National Labor Relations Act of 1935 (NLRA) permits an employer and an exclusive bargaining representative to enter into an agreement requiring all employees in the bargaining unit to pay periodic union dues and initiation fees as a condition of continued employment, whether or not the employees otherwise wish to become union members. Today we must decide whether this provision also permits a union, over the objections of dues-paying nonmember employees, to expend funds so collected on activities unrelated to collective bargaining, contract administration, or grievance adjustment, and, if so, whether such expenditures violate the union's duty of fair representation or the objecting employees' First Amendment rights.

In accordance with § 9 of the NLRA, a majority of the employees of American Telephone and Telegraph Company and several of its subsidiaries selected petitioner Communications Workers of America (CWA) as their exclusive bargaining representative. As such, the union is empowered to bargain collectively with the employer on behalf of all employees in the bargaining unit over wages, hours, and other terms and conditions of employment, § 9(a), and it accordingly enjoys "broad authority . . . in the negotiation and administration of [the] collective bargaining contract." This broad authority, however, is tempered by the union's "statutory obligation to serve the interests of all members without hostility or discrimination toward any," a duty that extends not only to the negotiation of the collective bargaining agreement itself but also to the subsequent enforcement of that agreement, including the administration of any grievance procedure the agreement may establish. CWA chartered several local unions, co-petitioners in this case, to assist it in discharging these statutory duties. In addition, at least in part to help defray the considerable costs it incurs in performing these tasks, CWA negotiated a union security clause in the collective bargaining agreement under which all represented employees, including those who do not wish to become union members, must pay the union "agency fees" in "amounts equal to the periodic dues" paid by union members. Under the clause, failure to tender the required fee may be grounds for discharge.

In June 1976, respondents, 20 employees who chose not to become union members, initiated this suit challenging CWA's use of their agency fees for purposes other than collective bargaining, contract administration, or grievance adjustment (hereinafter "collective bargaining" or "representational" activities). Specifically, respondents alleged that the union's expenditure of their fees on activities such as organizing the employees of other employers, lobbying for labor legislation, and participating in social, charitable, and political events violated petitioners' duty of fair representation, § 8(a)(3) of the NLRA, the First Amendment, and various common law fiduciary duties. In addition to declaratory relief, respondents sought an injunction barring petitioners from exacting fees above those necessary to finance collective bargaining activities, as well as damages for the past collection of such excess fees.

The District Court concluded that the union's collection and disbursement of agency fees for purposes other than bargaining unit representation violated the associational and free speech rights of objecting nonmembers, and therefore enjoined their future collection.

A divided panel of the United States Court of Appeals for the Fourth Circuit agreed that respondents stated a valid claim for relief under the First Amendment, but, preferring to rest its judgment on a ground other than the Constitution, concluded that the collection of nonmembers' fees for purposes unrelated to collective bargaining violated § 8(a)(3). Turning to the specific activities challenged, the majority found that for certain categories of expenditures, such as lobbying, organizing employees in other companies, and funding various community services, the error was harmless inasmuch as the activities were indisputably unrelated to bargaining unit representation. The majority remanded the case for reconsideration of the remaining expenditures, which the union claimed were made in connection with valid collective bargaining activities.

On rehearing, the en banc court vacated the panel opinion and by a six-to-four vote again affirmed in part, reversed in part, and remanded for further proceedings.

The decision below directly conflicts with that of the United States Court of Appeals for the Second Circuit. We granted certiorari to resolve the important question concerning the validity of such agreements, and now affirm.

Added as part of the 1947 Labor Management Relations Act, or Taft-Hartley Act, § 8(a)(3) makes it an unfair labor practice for an employer "by discrimination in regard to hire or tenure of employment . . . to encourage or discourage membership in any labor organization." Taken as a whole, § 8(a)(3) permits an employer and a union to enter into an agreement requiring all employees to become union members as a condition of continued employment, but the "membership" that may be so required has been "whittled down to its financial core." The statutory question presented in this case, then, is whether this "financial core" includes the obligation to support union activities beyond those germane to collective bargaining, contract administration, and grievance adjustment. We think it does not.

Both the structure and purpose of § 8(a)(3) are best understood in light of the statute's historical origins. Prior to the enactment of the Taft-Hartley Act of 1947, § 8(3) of the Wagner Act of 1935 (NLRA) permitted majority unions to negotiate "closed shop" agreements requiring employers to hire only persons who were already union members. By 1947, such agreements had come under increasing attack, and after extensive hearings Congress determined that the closed shop and the abuses associated with it "create[d] too great a barrier to free employment to be longer tolerated." The 1947 Congress was equally concerned, however, that without such agreements, many employees would reap the benefits that unions negotiated on their behalf without in any way contributing financial support to those efforts. As Senator Taft, one of the authors of the 1947 legislation, explained, "the argument . . . against abolishing the closed shop . . . is that if there is not a closed shop those not in the union will get a free ride, that the union does the work, gets the wages raised, then the man who does not pay dues rides along freely without any expense to himself." Thus, the Taft-Hartley Act was

> intended to accomplish twin purposes. On the one hand, the most serious abuses of compulsory unionism were eliminated by abolishing the closed shop. On the other hand, Congress recognized that in the absence of a union-security provision "many employees sharing the benefits of what unions are able to accomplish by collective bargaining will refuse to pay their share of the cost."

The legislative solution embodied in § 8(a)(3) allows employers to enter into agreements requiring all the employees in a given bargaining unit to become members 30 days after being hired as long as such membership is available to all workers on a nondiscriminatory basis, but it prohibits the mandatory discharge of an employee who is expelled from the union for any reason other than his or her failure to pay initiation fees or dues. As we have previously observed, Congress carefully tailored this solution to the evils at which it was aimed:

> Th[e] legislative history clearly indicates that Congress intended to prevent utilization of union security agreements for any purpose other than to compel payment of union dues and fees. Thus Congress recognized the validity of unions' concerns about "free riders," i.e., employees who receive the benefits of union representation but are unwilling to contribute their *fair share* of financial support to such union, and gave unions the power to contract to meet *that problem* while withholding from unions the power to cause the discharge of employees for any other reason [emphasis added].

Indeed, "Congress' decision to allow union-security agreements *at all* reflects its concern that . . . the parties to a collective bargaining agreement be allowed to provide that there be no employees who are getting the benefits of union representation without paying for them."

In *Machinists* v. *Street,* we concluded that the Railway Labor Act (RLA) contemplated "compulsory unionism to force employees to share the costs of negotiating and administering collective agreements, and the costs of the adjustment and settlement of disputes," but that Congress did not intend "to provide the unions with a means for forcing employees, over their objection, to support political causes which they oppose." Construing the statute in light of this legislative history and purpose, we held that although the RLA on its face authorizes the collection from nonmembers of "periodic dues, initiation fees, and assessments . . . *uniformly required* as a condition of acquiring or retaining membership" in a union (emphasis added), this authorization did not "ves[t] the unions with unlimited power to spend exacted money." We have since reaffirmed that "Congress' essential justification for authorizing the union shop" limits the expenditures that may properly be charged to nonmembers under the RLA to those "necessarily or reasonably incurred for the purpose of performing the duties of an exclusive [bargaining] representative." Given the parallel purpose, structure, and language of § 8(a)(3), we must interpret that provision in the same manner.

We conclude that § 8(a)(3) authorizes the exaction of only those fees and dues necessary to "performing the duties of an exclusive representative of the employees in dealing with the employer on labor-management issues." Accordingly, the judgment of the Court of Appeals is affirmed.

Case Questions

1. Why did Congress decide to allow mandatory agency fee collection?
2. Why did the Supreme Court hold that agency fees could not be used for organizing other employers or for lobbying?

As was discussed previously, a major provision of the National Labor Relations Act was the establishment of a mechanism that would allow unions to practice the right to bargain collectively with employers. That mechanism is the National Labor Relations Board, which is described in the following section.

National Labor Relations Board

Enforcement and administration of the National Labor Relations Act are carried out by the *National Labor Relations Board (NLRB).* Under the direction of the act, the board is responsible for preventing unfair labor practices and for settling questions of representation. The board cannot initiate action on its own, but any employer or union may file proceedings. The five members of the board are appointed by the president for terms of five years each. A general counsel is also appointed by the president, and that term of office is four years. The board and the general counsel work together in carrying out the functions outlined in the act. The general counsel does most of the work assigned to its division through regional field offices throughout the United States. Each of the thirty-one regional field offices is headed by a regional director.

Cases Heard

Cases involving charges of unfair labor practices—called *complaint cases*—can be filed by an employer, an employee, or a union. The regional director conducts an investigation; if the charge is found to have merit, the regional director files a formal complaint, and a hearing is conducted before an administrative law judge of the board. The board will then review the findings of the administrative law judge regarding the facts of the case, the applicable law, and the remedy ordered. If the board finds that an unfair labor practice has indeed occurred, an administrative order will be issued, requiring the party charged to correct the unfair labor practice. The decision of the board can be reviewed on appeal by a U.S. court of appeals. If the court of appeals affirms the decision of the board, it will order compliance. The penalty for failure to comply with such an order may be a fine, a jail sentence for contempt, or both. The appeals court decision can only be reviewed by the Supreme Court upon the granting of a petition for a writ of certiorari.

Representation questions—called *representation cases*—involve the selection of the appropriate bargaining unit to represent the union and to deal with the employer. If an employer refuses to recognize voluntarily the right of its employees to be represented by a particular union and refuses to bargain with the union, a majority of employees in a unit may select the union. Such elections are conducted by secret ballot and are supervised by the board, after a petition is filed to request an election. The board will investigate the facts alleged in the petition; allegations such as employer refusal to recognize employees' right to union representation or refusal to bargain with a union. These allegations must be supported by recitations of specific instances with dates and the parties involved. Then, if the board finds reasonable cause, it convenes a hearing on the question of whether or not representation exists. If the hearing proves the existence of such a question, a representation election is held, and the results are certified by the board.

Once a particular union has been certified by the NLRB as the official collective bargaining representative for a particular unit, that union has the right to represent all of the employees in the unit, even if some of the employees belong to another union. In *Landers* v. *National Railroad Passengers Corporation,* a 1988 case, the United States Supreme Court held that under the

Railway Labor Act, an employee is not entitled to be represented at company-level grievance or disciplinary proceedings by any union except his official collective bargaining representative. The Railway Labor Act is very similar to the National Labor Relations Act, but applies only to railroads. The court pointed out that the employee could be represented by the union of his choice at the appellate level, but that Congress had mandated official bargaining agent representation at the company-level hearing phase.

Jurisdiction

Congress gave the National Labor Relations Board jurisdiction over any business that affects commerce, with certain exceptions. It has exclusive jurisdiction over unfair labor practices that relate to interstate commerce. However, inadequate budgets and staff shortages at the NLRB have effectively limited the board's pursuit of unfair labor practices in interstate commerce to large business concerns, such as the following:

1. Wholesalers and other nonretail operations with an interstate flow (flow of trade between states) of at least $50,000
2. Retail enterprises with annual sales of at least $500,000
3. Businesses running office buildings with gross revenues of at least $100,000 per year
4. Interstate transportation businesses
5. Local transit systems grossing at least $250,000 annually
6. Public utilities having a local annual gross of $250,000, or interstate business of $50,000 per year
7. Newspapers that have interstate contacts and gross at least $250,000 per year
8. Communication businesses with a gross annual revenue of at least $100,000
9. Businesses having a substantial impact on national defense
10. Hotels and motels serving transient customers and grossing at least $500,000 per year
11. Nonprofit health care facilities
12. Private postsecondary schools

As we mentioned, some employers are not subject to coverage under the National Labor Relations Act. These include federal, state, and municipal governments. Also, certain occupations do not fall under the umbrella of the act. They are agricultural, supervisory, managerial, and domestic workers, as well as independent contractors, persons who work for parents or spouses, and workers covered by the Railway Labor Act.

The establishment by federal law of unfair labor practices on the part of both unions and employers did much to further the cause of collective bargaining. Further discussion of unfair labor practices follows.

Unfair Labor Practices

As we have noted, both unions and employers may commit unfair labor practices (ULPs). Such practices are defined in the National Labor Relations Act (Wagner Act) as being legal wrongs for which a cause of action is allowed. Before the Wagner Act was passed, these practices had never been recognized as being subject to legal redress. The Wagner Act only addressed ULPs attributable to employers. In 1947 the Labor-Management Relations (Taft-Hartley) Act recognized that unions could also be guilty of ULPs. By making certain acts on the part of both unions and employers illegal, Congress was attempting to encourage collective bargaining by forcing both sides to "play fair." Neither side is allowed to abuse its power or position.

Employer ULPs

The Wagner Act, as amended later by Landrum-Griffin, recognized six specific unfair labor practices that employers might commit. They are:

1. Interference with, restraint of, or coercion of employees in their efforts to form, join, or assist labor organizations
2. Domination of or interference with formation or administration of a labor organization, or supporting such organization financially or otherwise
3. Discrimination in hiring, tenure, or any term or condition of employment because of union affiliation
4. Discrimination by discharge or other action due to testimony given or charges filed under the act
5. Refusal to bargain collectively in good faith with a duly designated union representative
6. Agreeing with a labor organization to engage in a secondary boycott

Union ULPs

Because the Wagner Act did not contain any provisions concerning unfair labor practices by labor unions, it was perceived to be one-sided and unbalanced. This inequity was remedied by the Taft-Hartley Act and later the Landrum-Griffin Act, which specified eight union unfair labor practices. They are:

1. Constraining or coercing an employee to form, select, join, or assist a labor union
2. Causing or attempting to cause an employer to discriminate against an employee who is not a union member
3. Refusing to bargain with an employer
4. Engaging in a secondary boycott, or striking or picketing for illegal purposes
5. Charging discriminatory or excessive membership fees

6. Causing an employer to pay for work not actually performed (featherbedding)
7. Picketing an employer to require it to recognize or bargain with an uncertified union
8. Agreeing with an employer to engage in a secondary boycott

Federal law has also specified the procedure to be followed by both parties or against both parties in filing charges of unfair labor practices.

Procedures for Filing ULP Charges

Charges of unfair labor practices, as stated earlier, can be filed against an employer, a union, or both by contacting the National Labor Relations Board. The charge must be filed within six months after the alleged unfair labor practice occurred, and the defendant must actually be served with the complaint before the time period expires. Cases involving secondary boycotts, hot cargo contracts, organizational and recognition picketing, and discrimination against individual employees are given priority by the NLRB. Hot cargo contracts are contracts stating that workers will not be required to handle materials produced by nonunion workers or by a company with which a union has a dispute. Organizational and recognition picketing involves picketing activities conducted for the purpose of forcing an employer to realize that employees want to organize as union members and to recognize the employees' chosen union.

An individual filing a ULP charge may have the case handled before a complaint is ever issued. The charge may be settled by an *adjustment,* by which a formal or informal agreement between plaintiff and defendant is reached. If the charge has no merit, it will be *dismissed.* Such a dismissal may be appealed to the general counsel, who would then issue the final decision. And the individual in some cases may decide to *withdraw* the complaint.

In the event that none of these three situations occurs, the NLRB issues a complaint, which the accused party answers. The administrative law judge then conducts a hearing at which the party filing the charge presents her evidence of unfair labor practices, the defendant presents his side of the story, and in some cases the general counsel of the NLRB participates. The administrative law judge then makes recommendations in an intermediate report. The parties in the case are allowed to file exceptions to the report; the NLRB will consider both the report and the filed exceptions. If no exceptions to the report are filed, the NLRB will adopt the intermediate report as its decision. Remedies available for unfair labor practices include injunctions and money damages. Figure 16.1 illustrates the steps in the process.

Process of Collective Bargaining

Selection of a union as a bargaining representative is only the first step in the long and often arduous process of bargaining with the employer to make a

Figure 16.1 Basic Steps in Unfair Labor Practices Cases

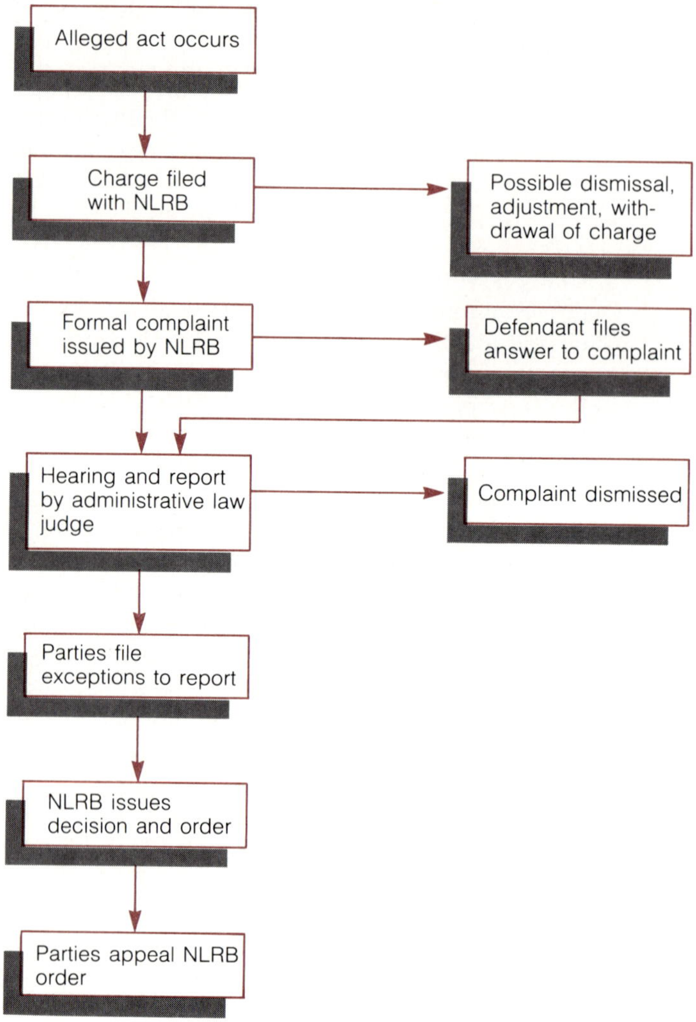

contract or agreement. Such an agreement will cover all aspects of the employment relationship. Collective bargaining is the negotiation of that agreement by the employer and the union.

Nowhere is the concept of majority rule more apparent than in collective bargaining. After a particular group of employees has been recognized as an appropriate bargaining unit, a majority of those employees will choose a particular union as their representative. That union will represent *all* employees in the unit; even those who did not vote in favor of that particular union will be bound by the collective bargaining agreement that will come about between the union and the employer. Such is the case even for employees who do not belong to the union. The employer will only bargain with the designated union representative of the employee unit.

Good Faith Bargaining

Under Section 8(d) of the Wagner Act, Congress defined the duty to bargain collectively as the "performance of the mutual obligation" of the parties "to meet and confer in good faith with respect to wages, hours, and other terms and conditions of employment." It is an unfair labor practice for either a union or an employer to refuse to bargain in good faith. This duty requires each party to participate actively in attempting to reach an agreement by setting forth honest and reasonable proposals. They must each listen to the arguments and propositions of the other side and look for some common ground. There is no legal duty to *make* an agreement, but an honest attempt is required.

While good or bad faith is obviously a question of subjective intent, judgments can only be made on the outward manifestations of that intent. When the question arises whether someone is bargaining in good faith, the NLRB examines all of the circumstances to decide from the employer's or the union's conduct whether there was no intention of reaching an agreement or whether it was simply not possible to arrive at a mutually satisfactory agreement. If bad faith is found, the NLRB does not have the power to insert a disputed clause into the collective bargaining agreement. The board is limited to issuance of a cease and desist order to the offending party.

Subjects of the Agreement

Also in Section 8(d) of the Wagner Act, Congress required employer and union to bargain collectively on the mandatory subjects of "wages, hours, and other terms and conditions of employment." These mandatory subjects include wage rates or any form of monetary compensation, working time and paid nonworking time, discharge and discipline provisions, promotion and transfer policies, seniority rules, and safety rules. As you can imagine, what constitutes a term or condition of employment has been the subject of much courtroom discussion. Table 16.1 presents a list of issues that are likely to appear in a collective bargaining agreement.

Once a subject has been determined to be mandatory, an employer is forbidden from making a change in that term without first bargaining over the issue. A union can only lawfully strike over a mandatory term and will be liable for any damages caused by an unlawful strike. An item that would ordinarily be considered mandatory may not be so in a situation where an employer has done something in a certain way for a long period of time without objection from the union or insistence by the union upon bargaining about it. Bargaining in that instance would only be required if a change from the existing practice is proposed.

Some items can never be the subject of collective bargaining. Some of these illegal subjects include unreasonable and discriminatory membership rules and secondary boycott provisions. The ban on unreasonable membership rules refers to the practice of including in the agreement a closed shop clause, which requires individuals to be union members before they can be hired by the employer. This constitutes discrimination on the basis of union membership and is an unfair labor practice. Secondary boycotts are used by the union to draw innocent third parties into the dispute with an employer. Hot cargo agreements are forms of secondary boycotts by which the employer agrees not to do business with a third party because of the union's dispute with that third party.

The middle ground between mandatory subjects and illegal subjects is occupied by *permissive* subjects, those that can be negotiated and included in the agreement if the parties so desire, but neither party has the right to insist that such topics be included in the agreement. These matters usually involve company policy not directly affecting either the employment relationship or internal union matters. Of great concern to the union are decisions that will not directly involve the employment relationship but will affect the employees. Plant closings and relocations are decisions normally made by the employer without consultation with employees. The ramifications of these decisions, however, are of great interest to employees, since retraining, severance pay, new assignments and such are mandatory subjects of collective bargaining. Union interests in management decisions are illustrated by the next case.

Table 16.1 Issues Likely to Appear in a Collective Bargaining Agreement

Ability to do the job—Definition
Absences—How to report, authorized and unauthorized
Arbitration—Description of the process used
Bargaining unit—Definition
Contract—Length, expiration date
Discipline—Reasons for discharge
Employee benefits—Insurance, clothing allowances, vacation, sick leave
Grievances—General procedures
Handicapped employees—Definition, equality of
Holidays—Compensated, uncompensated
Hours of work—Shifts, full day's work
Insurance—Company paid, optional employee paid
Layoffs—Procedure, recall, seniority
Overtime—Frequency, distribution of
Pension—Description, eligibility
Rates of pay—Hiring, seniority, overtime
Seniority—Bidding, definition, layoffs, use of
Strikes—General procedures
Suspension—Reasons for
Transfers—Pay changes, new bargaining unit
Union—Officials, stewards, recognition of
Vacation—Duration, length of service

In order to do a good job of representing its members, the union may need access to information it does not possess, but which is in the hands of the employer. As a general rule, the union is entitled to receive the information upon request. It is entitled, however, only to information that is considered to be necessary or relevant to the collective bargaining process. There is no hard and fast rule concerning what is relevant or necessary, and the courts handle the determination on a case-by-case basis. If the NLRB determines that the union is entitled to a disclosure order, it will tailor the order so that it takes into account the legitimate business concerns of the employer. The employer will not ordinarily be required to disclose more information than is necessary for the union to know in order to fairly represent the employees.

An interesting issue that the Supreme Court has addressed is the relationship between subjects covered by collective bargaining contracts and events that may give rise to rights to sue under state or federal laws. Section 301 of the Labor Management Relations Act (LMRA) provides that suits for violation of collective bargaining contracts may be brought in federal courts. But what if the alleged violation of the contract may also constitute a tort or a violation of a statute, such as an antidiscrimination statute? The Supreme Court considered this question in three cases in the mid to late 1980s. In *Allis-Chalmers Corporation* v. *Lueck* (1985), the court held that a Wisconsin tort remedy for bad-faith handling of an insurance claim could be applied to the prosecution of a claim for disability benefits that was authorized by a collective bargaining agreement, but that section 301 LMRA prevented such a tort action, and that the only remedy of the plaintiff was a suit in federal court under the LMRA. The court stated the basic principle that it uses in cases of this kind: if resolution of a state law claim depends on interpretation of the meaning of a collective bargaining agreement, the aggrieved party's only remedy is a lawsuit under section 301 LMRA in federal court. The policy embodied in this principle is to maintain uniform judicial rules for interpretation of collective baraining contracts. In 1987, in *International Brotherhood of Electrical Workers* v. *Hechler*, the court followed the rationale of the *Allis-Chalmers* case and held a union member could not maintain an action in a Florida state court for breach of an alleged duty on the part of the union to insure her a safe workplace. The court reasoned that any duty the union might have to insure safe working conditions would arise primarily out of the terms of its collective bargaining agreement with the employer. Since determining whether such a duty existed would necessarily involve interpretation of the terms of the collective bargaining agreement, the plaintiff's only remedy would be a lawsuit brought under section 301 LMRA in federal court. In 1988, however, in *Lingle* v. *Norge, Inc.*, the court held that a union member could bring a retaliatory discharge action alleging violation of state law in an Illinois court, even while arbitration was proceeding under the terms of a collective bargaining agreement. The court distinguished the *Allis-Chalmers* and *Hechler* cases on the grounds that, in this case, the state court could decide the retaliatory discharge tort claim without having to interpret the terms of the collective bargaining agreement. Therefore, section

301 LMRA did not prevent maintenance of the state tort action. Based on these Supreme Court decisions, it appears that whether a union member covered by a collective bargaining contract can sue an employer depends on the extent to which state courts will be required to interpret the terms of the contract in order to decide the case.

Grievance and Arbitration

While the terms and conditions of collective bargaining agreements vary greatly among employers and unions, there is almost universal use of grievance-arbitration clauses to resolve disputes. These mechanisms insure that someone who feels aggrieved by the employer will receive attention and a hearing on the problem within a relatively short period of time.

The usual grievance procedure begins when an employee files a written charge or complaint (a **grievance**) with either the local union office or the designated union representative. The charge is then taken by the union to the employer, who is then required to consult with the union in an attempt to resolve the dispute. The first consultation usually occurs between lower-echelon management personnel and the union steward. If they are unable to resolve the conflict, the charge will proceed to higher-level representatives within the company.

When no solution is reached at any level, the problem will proceed to the last step in the resolution process: binding **arbitration.** Arbitration consists of submitting a dispute to a neutral third party for a binding decision. Since arbitration is the result of a consensual arrangement, the parties can tailor the process used to suit their individual needs. There may be only one arbitrator, or the agreement may call for three. The hearing process itself may be spelled out in detail, or it may be left to the discretion of the arbitrators. At any rate, the hearing conducted on the grievance will be much less formal than a trial in court, with no formal rules of evidence being used. Each party is allowed to present evidence to substantiate his or her version of the facts. The arbitrator then issues a written opinion, which sets forth the basic findings of fact and the decision. This is called an *award*. The following case presents a typical grievance (though not a typical fact situation) and the procedures followed and circumstances considered by the arbitrator when making an award.

When a grievance has proceeded through arbitration and one party is dissatisfied with the decision rendered, his right to appeal that decision is much more limited than it would be in a court proceeding. As a general rule, an arbitrator's decision will not be overturned in the absence of bad faith. Arbitrators are not bound by precedent and are able to tailor remedies to fit each individual situation. If one party refuses to abide by the decision of the arbitrator, the other party may go to court to obtain an enforcement of the award. The following Supreme Court case illustrates the great extent to which courts will go to uphold an arbitration decision.

United Paperworkers International Union v. *Misco*

484 U.S. 29 (1987)

Opinion

Justice White: The issue for decision involves several aspects of when a federal court may refuse to enforce an arbitration award rendered under a collective-bargaining agreement.

Misco, Inc. (Misco, or the Company), operates a paper converting plant in Monroe, Louisiana. The Company is a party to a collective-bargaining agreement with the United Paperworkers International Union, AFL-CIO, and its union local (the Union); the agreement covers the production and maintenance employees at the plant. Under the agreement, the Company or the Union may submit to arbitration any grievance that arises from the interpretation or application of its terms, and the arbitrator's decision is final and binding upon the parties. The arbitrator's authority is limited to interpretation and application of the terms contained in the agreement itself. The agreement reserves to management the right to establish, amend, and enforce "rules and regulations regulating the discipline or discharge of employees" and the procedures for imposing discipline. Such rules were to be posted and were to be in effect "until ruled on by grievance and arbitration procedures as to fairness and necessity." For about a decade, the Company's rules had listed as causes for discharge the bringing of intoxicants, narcotics, or controlled substances on to plant property or consuming any of them there, as well as reporting for work under the influence of such substances. At the time of the events involved in this case, the Company was very concerned about the use of drugs at the plant, especially among employees on the night shift.

Isiah Cooper, who worked on the night shift for Misco, was one of the employees covered by the collective-bargaining agreement. He operated a slitter-rewinder machine, which uses sharp blades to cut rolling coils of paper. The arbitrator found that this machine is hazardous and had caused numerous injuries in recent years. Cooper had been reprimanded twice in a few months for deficient performance. On January 21, 1983, one day after the second reprimand, the police searched Cooper's house pursuant to a warrant, and a substantial amount of marijuana was found. Contemporaneously, a police officer was detailed to keep Cooper's car under observation at the Company's parking lot. At about 6:30 P.M., Cooper was seen walking in the parking lot during work hours with two other men. The three men entered Cooper's car momentarily, then walked to another car, a white Cutlass, and entered it. After the other two men later returned to the plant, Cooper was apprehended by police in the backseat of this car with marijuana smoke in the air and a lighted marijuana cigarette in the frontseat ashtray. The police also searched Cooper's car and found a plastic scales case and marijuana gleanings. Cooper was arrested and charged with marijuana possession.

On January 24, Cooper told the Company that he had been arrested for possession of marijuana at his home; the Company did not learn of the marijuana cigarette in the white Cutlass until January 27. It then investigated and on February 7 discharged Cooper, asserting that in the circumstances, his presence in the Cutlass violated the rule against having drugs on the plant premises. Cooper filed a grievance protesting his discharge the same day, and the matter proceeded to arbitration. The Company was not aware until September 21, five days before the hearing before the arbitrator was scheduled, that marijuana had been found in Cooper's car. That fact did not become known to the Union until the hearing began. At the hearing it was stipulated that the issue was whether the Company had "just cause to discharge the Grievant under Rule II.1" and, "[i]f not, what if any should be the remedy."

The arbitrator upheld the grievance and ordered the Company to reinstate Cooper with backpay and full seniority. The arbitrator based his finding that there was not just cause for the discharge on his consideration of seven criteria. In particular, the arbitrator found that the Company failed to prove that the employee had possessed or used marijuana on company property: finding Cooper in the backseat of a car and a burning cigarette in the front-seat ashtray was insufficient proof that Cooper was using or possessed marijuana on company property. The arbitrator refused to accept into evidence the fact that marijuana had been found in Cooper's car on company premises because the Company did not know of this fact when Cooper was discharged and therefore did not rely on it as a basis for the discharge.

The Company filed suit in District Court, seeking to vacate the arbitration award on several grounds, one of which was that ordering reinstatement of Cooper, who had allegedly possessed marijuana on the plant premises, was contrary to public policy. The District Court agreed that the award must be set aside as contrary to public policy because it ran counter to general safety concerns that arise from the operation of dangerous machinery while under the influence of drugs, as well as to state criminal laws against drug possession. The Court of Appeals affirmed, with one judge dissenting. The court ruled that reinstatement would violate the public policy "against the operation of dangerous machinery by persons under the influence of drugs or alcohol." The arbitrator had found that Cooper was apprehended on company premises in an atmosphere of marijuana smoke in another's car and that marijuana was found in his own car on the company lot. These facts established that Cooper had violated the Company's rules and gave the company just cause to discharge him. The arbitrator did not reach this conclusion because of a "narrow focus on Cooper's procedural rights" that led him to ignore what he "knew was in fact true: that Cooper *did* bring marijuana onto his employer's premises." Even if the arbitrator had not known of this fact at the time he entered his award, "it is doubtful that the award should be enforced today in light of what is now known."

Because the Courts of Appeals are divided on the question of when courts may set aside arbitration awards as contravening public policy, we granted the Union's petition for a writ of certiorari and now reverse the judgment of the Court of Appeals.

The Union asserts that an arbitral award may not be set aside on public policy grounds unless the award orders conduct that violates the positive law, which is not the case here. But in the alternative, it submits that even if it is wrong in this regard, the Court of Appeals otherwise exceeded the limited authority that it had to review an arbitrator's award entered pursuant to a collective-bargaining agreement. Respondent, on the other hand, defends the public policy decision of the Court of Appeals but alternatively argues that the judgment below should be affirmed because of erroneous findings by the arbitrator. We deal first with the opposing alternative arguments.

Collective-bargaining agreements commonly provide grievance procedures to settle disputes between union and employer with respect to the interpretation and application of the agreement and require binding arbitration for unsettled grievances. In such cases, and this is such a case, the Court made clear almost 30 years ago that the courts play only a limited role when asked to review the decision of an arbitrator. The courts are not authorized to reconsider the merits of an award even though the parties may allege that the award rests on errors of fact or on misinterpretation of the contract. "The refusal of courts to review the merits of an arbitration award is the proper approach to arbitration under collective bargaining agreements. The federal policy of settling labor disputes by arbitration would be undermined if courts had the final say on the merits of the awards." As long as the arbitrator's award "draws its essence from the collective bargaining agreements," and is not merely "his own brand of industrial justice," the award is legitimate.

> The function of the court is very limited when the parties have agreed to submit all questions of contract interpretation to the arbitrator. It is confined to ascertaining whether the party seeking arbitration is making a claim which on its face is governed by the contract. Whether the moving party is right or wrong is a question of contract interpretation for the arbitrator. In these circumstances the moving party should not be deprived of the arbitrator's judgment, when it was his judgment and all that it connotes that was bargained for.
>
> The courts, therefore, have no business weighing the merits of the grievance, considering whether there is equity in a particular claim, or determining whether there is particular language in the written instrument which will support the claim.

The reasons for insulating arbitral decisions

from judicial review are grounded in the federal statutes regulating labor-management relations. These statutes reflect a decided preference for private settlement of labor disputes without the intervention of government. The courts have jurisdiction to enforce collective-bargaining contracts; but where the contract provides grievance and arbitration procedures, those procedures must first be exhausted and courts must order resort to the private settlement mechanisms without dealing with the merits of the dispute. Because the parties have contracted to have disputes settled by an arbitrator chosen by them rather than by a judge, it is the arbitrator's view of the facts and of the meaning of the contract that they have agreed to accept. Courts thus do not sit to hear claims of factual or legal error by an arbitrator as an appellate court does in reviewing decisions of lower courts. To resolve disputes about the application of a collective-bargaining agreement, an arbitrator must find facts and a court may not reject those findings simply because it disagrees with them. The same is true of the arbitrator's interpretation of the contract. The arbitrator may not ignore the plain language of the contract; but the parties having authorized the arbitrator to give meaning to the language of the agreement, a court should not reject an award on the ground that the arbitrator misread the contract. So, too, where it is contemplated that the arbitrator will determine remedies for contract violations that he finds, courts have no authority to disagree with his honest judgment in that respect. If the courts were free to intervene on these grounds, the speedy resolution of grievances by private mechanisms would be greatly undermined. Furthermore, it must be remembered that grievance and arbitration procedures are part and parcel of the ongoing process of collective bargaining. It is through these processes that the supplementary rules of the plant are established. As the Court has said, the arbitrator's award settling a dispute with respect to the interpretation or application of a labor agreement must draw its essence from the contract and cannot simply reflect the arbitrator's own notions of industrial justice. But as long as the arbitrator is even arguably construing or applying the contract and acting within the scope of his authority, that a court is convinced he committed serious error does not suffice to overturn his decision. Of course, decisions procured by the parties through fraud or through the arbitrator's dishonesty need not be enforced. But there is nothing of that sort involved in this case.

The Company's position, simply put, is that the arbitrator committed grievous error in finding that the evidence was insufficient to prove that Cooper had possessed or used marijuana on company property. But the Court of Appeals, although it took a distinctly jaundiced view of the arbitrator's decision in this regard, was not free to refuse enforcement because it considered Cooper's presence in the white Cutlass, in the circumstances, to be ample proof that Rule II.1 was violated, No dishonesty is alleged; only improvident, even silly, factfinding is claimed. This is hardly sufficient basis for disregarding what the agent appointed by the parties determined to be the historical facts.

Nor was it open to the Court of Appeals to refuse to enforce the award because the arbitrator, in deciding whether there was just cause to discharge, refused to consider evidence unknown to the Company at the time Cooper was fired. The parties bargained for arbitration to settle disputes and were free to set the procedural rules for arbitrators to follow if they chose. Section VI of the agreement, entitled "Arbitration Procedure," did set some ground rules for the arbitration process. It forbade the arbitrator to consider hearsay evidence, for example, but evidentiary matters were otherwise left to the arbitrator. Here the arbitrator ruled that in determining whether Cooper had violated Rule II.1, he should not consider evidence not relied on by the employer in ordering the discharge, particularly in a case like this where there was no notice to the employee or the Union prior to the hearing that the Company would attempt to rely on after-discovered evidence. This, in effect, was a construction of what the contract required when deciding discharge cases: an arbitrator was to look only at the evidence before the employer at the time of discharge. As the arbitrator noted, this approach was consistent with the practice followed by other arbitrators. And it was consistent with our observation in *John Wiley & Sons, Inc.* v. *Livingston,* that when the subject matter of a dispute is arbitrable, "procedural" questions which grow out of the dispute and bear on its final disposition are to be left to the arbitrator.

Under the Arbitration Act, the federal courts are empowered to set aside arbitration awards on such grounds only when "the arbitrators were guilty of misconduct . . . in refusing to hear evidence pertinent and material to the controversy." If we apply that same standard here and assume that the arbitrator erred in refusing to consider the disputed evidence, his error was not in bad faith or so gross as to amount to affirmative misconduct.

To conclude from the fact that marijuana had been found in Cooper's car that Cooper had ever been or would be under the influence of marijuana while he was on the job and operating dangerous machinery is an exercise in factfinding about Cooper's use of drugs and his amenability to discipline, a task that exceeds the authority of a court asked to overturn an arbitration award. The parties did not bargain for the facts to be found by a court, but by an arbitrator chosen by them who had more opportunity to observe Cooper and to be familiar with the plant and its problems. Nor does the fact that it is inquiring into a possible violation of public policy excuse a court for doing the arbitrator's task. If additional facts were to be found, the arbitrator should find them in the course of any further effort the Company might have made to discharge Cooper for having had marijuana in his car on company premises. Had the arbitrator found that Cooper had possessed drugs on the property, yet imposed discipline short of discharge because he found as a factual matter that Cooper could be trusted not to use them on the job, the Court of Appeals could not upset the award because of its own view that public policy about plant safety was threatened. In this connection it should also be noted that the award ordered Cooper to be reinstated in his old job or in an equivalent one for which he was qualified. It is by no means clear from the record that Cooper would pose a serious threat to the asserted public policy in every job for which he was qualified.

The judgment of the Court of Appeals is reversed. So ordered.

Case Questions

1. Why has the Supreme Court adopted such a strong policy in favor of upholding arbitrator's decisions?
2. Do you think the Justices thought Cooper was smoking marijuana?

Decertification

Employees who have decided that they are no longer happy with the union have an opportunity to be rid of it. They may hold a **decertification** election. A decertification petition must be filed with the NLRB, indicating that at least 30 percent of the employees want to oust the union. A secret ballot decertification election is then conducted by the NLRB, and if a majority of employees vote to decertify the union, it will no longer be the collective bargaining agent for that unit. The petition may only be filed by employees or persons or unions acting on behalf of the employees. It may *not* be filed by the employer. If the employer even encourages or helps his employees to file such a petition, he is guilty of an unfair labor practice.

Labor Law and the Public Sector

To this point, our discussion of labor law and labor relations has focused on employees in the private sector. As we all know, or have read, the number of workers employed by government is growing rapidly. Those employees are excluded from coverage by the National Labor Relations Act. Public employees thus have the constitutional right to join a union, but there is no such right to engage in collective bargaining or to strike.

The policy of the federal government toward its employees' labor rights was not established until 1962 by President John Kennedy. His Executive Order 10988 set up a labor relations program for federal employees, but it limited collective bargaining. No central agency was established to handle labor relations, and individual cabinet heads determined appropriate bargaining units and unfair labor practices. President Richard Nixon's Executive Order 11491 changed this procedure in 1969 by setting up one structure to handle federal labor relations, but he did little else for federal employees with respect to the scope of bargaining.

In 1970, postal employees engaged in an unlawful strike, which was met by Congress with the Postal Reorganization Act. The U.S. Postal Service was declared a public corporation, and its labor relations fell under the authority of the National Labor Relations Board. The right to strike, however, was not extended to postal employees.

President Jimmy Carter created the Federal Labor Relations Authority, vesting it with the power to determine collective bargaining units for federal employees, to certify and to decertify unions, and to hear charges of unfair labor practices. Employees were given the right to bargain collectively with respect to wages and benefits. Again, government employees were not given the right to strike.

Public employers, on the federal level especially, have emphatically resisted attempts by workers to strike. In August 1981, for example, air traffic controllers, members of the Professional Air Traffic Controllers Organization (PATCO), called for a strike, seeking, among other things, a shortened work week. All workers who engaged in that strike were permanently discharged. PATCO was then decertified by the Federal Labor Relations Authority.

The public often equates labor unions with strikes. The feeling is strong that if public employees are allowed to be members of unions and to bargain collectively, they will strike if their demands are not met. There has been a reluctance to give the power to strike to a group of individuals who could effectively shut down the country. Thus, public sector employees retain the right to join a union but not the right to strike.

Unions and the Duty of Fair Representation

Over time, by judicial interpretation of the labor statutes, the courts have imposed on unions a "duty of fair representation." This concept, discussed earlier, means, among other things, that unions must collectively bargain in the best interests of *all* of their members, that they must represent every member of the unit in disciplinary or like proceedings, and that they cannot be negligent in safeguarding their members' rights. In addition to the labor relations chapter that we have discussed in this chapter, Title VII of the 1964 Civil Rights Act makes it illegal for labor unions to discriminate on the basis of sex, race, religion, national origin, or color. In the following case decided in 1987, the Supreme Court held that a union could be liable for violating the 1964 and 1866 Civil Rights Acts by failing to assert claims of racial discrimination by an employer. The Lukens Steel Company could be regarded as an expansion of the duty of fair representation, even though the Supreme Court declined to discuss that issue directly.

Goodman v. Lukens Steel Company

482 U.S. 656 (1987)

Opinion

Justice White: In 1973, individual employees of Lukens Steel Company (Lukens) brought this suit on behalf of themselves and others, asserting racial discrimination claims under Title VII of the Civil Rights Act of 1964, and 42 U. S. C. § 1981 [part of the 1866 Civil Rights Act which gives all persons the full and equal benefit of the laws as those enjoyed by white persons] against their employer and their collective-bargaining agents, the United Steelworkers of America and two of its local unions (Unions). After a bench trial, the District Court specified the periods for which Title VII claims could be litigated; it also reaffirmed a pretrial order that the Pennsylvania 6-year statute of limitations governing claims on contracts, replevin and trespass applied to the § 1981 claims and that claims with respect to the period after July 14, 1967, were accordingly not barred. On the merits, the District Court found that Lukens had discriminated in certain respects, but that in others plaintiffs had not made out a case. The District Court concluded that the Unions were also guilty of discriminatory practices, specifically in failing to challenge discriminatory discharges of probationary employees, failing and refusing to assert instances of racial discrimination as grievances, and in tolerating and tacitly encouraging racial harassment. The District Court entered separate injunctive orders against Lukens and the Unions, reserving damages issues for further proceedings. Lukens and the Unions appealed, challenging the District Court's liability conclusions as well as its decision that the Pennsylvania 6-year statute of limitations, rather than the 2-year statute applicable to personal injuries, would measure the period of liability under § 1981.

The Court of Appeals, differing with the District Court, held that the 2-year statute of limitations controlled but affirmed the liability judgment against the Unions. The employees' petition for certiorari in No. 85-1626 challenged the Court of Appeals' choice of the § 1981 limitations period. The Unions' petition in No. 85-2010 claimed error in finding them liable under Title VII and § 1981. We granted both petitions (1986). [The Court then concluded that a two-year statute of limitations applied.]

This case was tried for 32 days in 1980. One-hundred fifty-seven witnesses testified and over 2,000 exhibits were introduced. On February 13, 1984, the District Court filed its findings and conclusions. In an introductory section discussing the relevant legal principles, the trial judge discussed, among other things, the nature of "disparate treatment" and "disparate impact" cases under Title VII, recognizing that in the former the plaintiff must prove not only disparate treatment, but trace its cause to intentional racial discrimination, an unnecessary element in disparate impact cases. The District Court also emphasized that proof of discriminatory intent is crucial in § 1981 cases and that such intent cannot be made out by showing only facially neutral conduct that burdens one race more than another.

The District Court proceeded to find that the company had violated Title VII in several significant respects, including the discharge of employees during their probationary period, the toleration of racial harassment by employees, initial job assignments, promotions, and decisions on incentive pay. The court also found that in these identical ways the company had also violated § 1981, a finding the court could not have made without concluding that the company had intentionally discriminated on a racial basis in these respects.

Similarly, the Unions were found to have discriminated on racial grounds in violation of both Title VII and § 1981 in certain ways: failing to challenge discriminatory discharges of probationary employees; failure and refusal to assert racial discrimination as a ground for grievances; and toleration and tacit encouragement of racial harassment.

What the conduct of the Unions had been and whether they had treated blacks and whites differently were questions of historical fact that Federal Rule of Civil Procedure 52(a) enjoins appellate courts to accept unless clearly erroneous. So is the issue of whether the Unions intended to discriminate based on race. Unless there are one or more errors of law inhering in the judgment below, as the Unions claim there are, we should affirm it.

The Unions contend that the judgment against them rests on the erroneous legal premise that Title VII and § 1981 are violated if a Union passively sits by and does not affirmatively oppose the employer's racially discriminatory employment practices. It is true that the District Court declared that mere Union passivity in the face of employer discrimination renders the Union liable under Title VII and, if racial animus is properly inferrable, under § 1981 as well. We need not discuss this rather abstract observation, for the court went on to say that the evidence proves "far more" than mere passivity. As found by the court, the facts were that since 1965, the collective-bargaining contract contained an express clause binding both the employer and the Unions not to discriminate on racial grounds; that the employer was discriminating against blacks in discharging probationary employees, which the Unions were aware of but refused to to do anything about by way of filing proferred grievances or otherwise; that the Unions had ignored grievances based on instances of harassment which were indisputably racial in nature; and that the Unions had regularly refused to include assertions of racial discrimination in grievances that also asserted other contract violations.

In affirming the District Court's findings against the Unions, the Court of Appeals also appeared to hold that the Unions had an affirmative duty to combat employer discrimination in the workplace. But it, too, held that the case against the Unions was much stronger than one of mere acquiescence in that the Unions deliberately chose not to assert claims of racial discrimination by the employer. It was the Court of Appeals' view that these intentional and knowing refusals discriminated against the victims who were entitled to have their grievances heard.

The Unions submit that the only basis for any liability in this case under Title VII is § 703(c)(3), which provides that a Union may not "cause or attempt to cause an employer to discriminate against an individual in violation of this section," and that nothing the District Court found and the Court of Appeals accepted justifies liability under this prohibition. We need not differ with the Unions on the reach of § 703(c)(3), for § 703(c)(1) makes it an unlawful practice for a Union to "exclude or to expel from its membership, *or otherwise to discriminate against,* any individual because of his race, color, religion, sex, or national origin." (Emphasis added.) Both courts below found that the Unions had indeed discriminated on the basis of race by the way in which they represented the workers, and the Court of Appeals expressly held that "[t]he deliberate choice not to process grievances also violated § 703(c)(1) of Title VII." The plain language of the statute supports this conclusion.

The Court of Appeals is also faulted for stating that the Unions had violated their duty of fair representation, which the Unions assert has no relevance to this case. But we do not understand the Court of Appeals to have rested its affirmance on this ground, for as indicated above, it held that the Unions had violated § 703.

The Unions insist that it was error to hold them liable for not including racial discrimination claims in grievances claiming other violations of the contract. The Unions followed this practice, it was urged, because these grievances could be resolved without making racial allegations and because the employer would "get its back up" if racial bias was charged, thereby making it much more difficult to prevail. The trial judge, although initially impressed by this seemingly neutral reason for failing to press race discrimination claims, ultimately found the explanation "unacceptable" because the Unions also ignored grievances which involved racial harassment violating the contract covenant against racial discrimination but which did not also violate another provision. The judge also noted that the Unions had refused to complain about racially based terminations of probationary employees, even though the express undertaking not to discriminate protected this group of employees, as well as others, and even though, as the District Court found, the Unions knew that blacks were being discharged at a disproportionately higher rate than whites. In the judgment of the District Court, the virtual failure by the Unions to file any race-bias grievances until after this lawsuit started, knowing that the employer was practicing what the contract prevented, rendered the Unions' explanation for their conduct unconvincing.

As we understand it, there was no suggestion below that the Unions held any racial animus against or denigrated blacks generally. Rather, it was held that a collective-bargaining agent could not, without violating Title VII and § 1981, follow a policy of refusing to file grievable racial discrimination claims however strong they might be and however sure the agent was that the employer was discriminating against blacks. The Unions, in effect, categorized racial grievances as unworthy of pursuit and, while pursuing thousands of other legitimate grievances, ignored racial discrimination claims on behalf of blacks, knowing that the employer was discriminating in violation of the contract. Such conduct, the courts below concluded, intentionally discriminated against blacks seeking a remedy for disparate treatment based on their race and violated both Title VII and § 1981. As the District Court said, "A union which intentionally avoids asserting discrimination claims, either so as not to antagonize the employer and thus improve its chances of success on other issues, or in deference to the perceived desires of its white membership, is liable under both Title [VII] and § 1981, regardless of whether, as a subjective matter, its leaders were favorably disposed toward minorities."

The courts below, in our view, properly construed and applied Title VII and § 1981. Those provisions do not permit a union to refuse to file any and all grievances presented by a black person on the ground that the employer looks with disfavor on and resents such grievances. It is no less violative of these laws for a union to pursue a policy of rejecting disparate treatment grievances presented by blacks solely because the claims assert racial bias and would be very troublesome to process.

In both Nos. 85-1626 and 85-2010, the judgment of the Court of Appeals is affirmed.

It is so ordered.

Case Questions

1. How did the unions violate Title VII of the 1964 Civil Rights Act?
2. How could it be argued that the unions violated a duty of fair representation?

An Ethical Perspective on Business and Labor Unions

An interesting development with important economic ramifications is the demand by workers and their unions for more and different fringe benefits. We are all familiar with paid vacations, medical, hospital, and life insurance policies, pension plans, and paid sick leave. Some unions are now receiving for their members more sophisticated benefits, such as prepaid legal plans and investment counseling. In some cases, employers are not able to increase their work force, not for lack of work, but because of their inability to pay for the fringe benefits they would be required to furnish. Such action will have a direct effect on the output of companies, reducing productivity and the amount of goods and services moving into the stream of commerce. That affects consumers, in that fewer goods and services are available, and consumers must pay a premium for those.

Also coming into question is the manner in which unions have traditionally approached collective bargaining with employers. In the past, it was solely an adversarial relationship, where unions tended to assume that management was "out to get them," and they did not always believe or trust the employer at the bargaining table. Some studies have recently shown, however, that most employers are genuinely concerned about the welfare of their workers, and that they are attempting to make jobs more palatable to employees by giving them a voice. Such devices as quality circles, job rotation, and job flexibility have gone a long way to make workers view their employer's business as a cooperative venture. Some companies have even gone so far as to put members of the work force or union on the board of directors, with direct input to the policy-making process.

With workers being able to participate more in the actual management process and with employers becoming more concerned about the quality of life on the job, more and more people see the function of the union changing. The spirit of cooperation between labor and management has altered the traditional combative form of bargaining, with less antagonism on both sides. Even in industries where the old hostilities still exist, the subjects for collective bargaining have changed. No longer worried about a fair wage for a day's work, the modern union member is concerned about job security. Will there be jobs for the workers when they are replaced by robots? Can they legitimately expect to be retrained by the company, at its expense? What will happen during hard economic times? Should the company be forced to guarantee workers a paycheck? Such issues have changed the scope and focus of collective bargaining in today's society.

The important concepts and terms in this chapter are listed on the following page; page numbers have been provided for the key terms. By reading over each section you can assess your understanding of the chapter concepts and determine areas you may want to review.

Chapter Summary

1. Early union organizers faced criminal prosecution for conspiracy to form illegal combinations, as well as suits for breach of an employment contract and violations of antitrust laws. Injunctions were widely used to halt strikes.
2. Prior to 1935, the Clayton Act, Railway Labor Act, and Norris-LaGuardia Act aided the development of labor unions by exempting

them from antitrust provisions, encouraging collective bargaining for railway employees, and outlawing the use of yellow-dog employment contracts.

3. In 1935, the Wagner Act (National Labor Relations Act) recognized the right of employees to unionization and collective bargaining. It established the National Labor Relations Board to administer and enforce the act. Election procedures for union representation and employer unfair labor practices were described.
4. The Taft-Hartley Act (Labor-Management Relations Act) of 1947 amended the Wagner Act. It created the Federal Mediation and Conciliation Service, gave the president the power to issue an eighty-day injunction for national emergencies, and recognized that unions could also be guilty of unfair labor practices.
5. The Wagner Act was again amended in 1959 by the Landrum-Griffin Act (Labor-Management Reporting and Disclosure Act), which gave union members a bill of rights, regulated the internal affairs of unions, and prohibited secondary boycotts.
6. The National Labor Relations Board enforces and administers the Wagner Act by ruling on unfair labor practices and conducting certification elections for representation of a bargaining unit.
7. Both unions and employers may be guilty of unfair labor practices and are subject to injunctions and money damages for committing such practices.
8. The process of collective bargaining is central to representation by a union. It requires both the union and the employer to bargain in good faith. Disagreements over interpretation or enforcement of specific provisions of the agreement are usually handled by the process of grievance and arbitration, and not spelled out in the collective bargaining agreement itself.
9. Employees who become dissatisfied with a union have the right to conduct a decertification election to attempt to oust that union as their bargaining representative.

Key Terms

arbitration 462
closed shop 447
collective bargaining 446
cooling-off period 448
decertification 466
ex parte injunction 444
featherbedding 447
grievance 462
right-to-work laws 447
secondary boycotts 447
unfair labor practices 446
union shop 447
yellow-dog contract 445

Questions on Ethics

1. The employees of General Electric were negotiating a new contract through their union representatives. The union contended that certain jobs were classified at wage rates below what other major companies in the industry were paying. The negotiator for the employer assured the union representatives that the company had received an industry salary survey indicating that the wage rates of General Electric were comparable to those of the industry. The union was refused permission to review the salary survey on the grounds that it was confidential. Should the union be entitled to see this information? *NLRB* v. *General Electric Co.*, 414 F.2d 918 (4th Cir. 1969), *cert. denied,* 396 U.S. 1005 (1970).
2. A certification election was held at Lou Viola Industries, and a union was selected to be the bargaining agent of the employees. The union representative contacted Lou and suggested that they make arrangements to begin the collective bargaining process. Lou informed the union representative that he was about to leave the country on a buying expedition and that he would return in approximately one month. The union representative repeated his call after the expiration of the month. Lou informed the representative that he was extremely busy, but he set up a time to meet the following month. On the day of the meeting, the union representative received a call from Lou, informing him that something important had come up and he would be unable to meet. When another date was suggested, the union representative was informed that Lou was extremely busy for the next three weeks, but that he would meet with the union the following month. The union representative chastised Lou and reminded him of his duty to bargain in good faith. Lou informed the representative that the company was small, that the demands on his time were great, and that he would not be able to sit down at the bargaining table until things calmed down a little. The union filed a charge with the NLRB. Is there a better way to handle this impasse?
3. John Lob decided that a good way to improve morale among his employees was to offer an employee stock ownership plan, whereby employees were allowed to purchase up to a specified amount of nonvoting company stock. John also thought that this might be a good way to do away with talk of forming a union within the company. How would union officials feel about such a plan? Why?
4. Franklin Flyer owned a small, unionized company that manufactured certain airplane parts. The competition in that industry had recently become very intense, with new companies springing up everywhere. Franklin had trouble maintaining his profit percentage, because the new companies were nonunion, paying lower wages. Franklin notified his employees that he was filing a petition under Chapter 11 of the Federal

Bankruptcy Act, asking for a reorganization of his company, and asking to be excused from the recently negotiated collective bargaining agreement. Is Franklin's action ethical? Why or why not?

5. If a union has agreed to a salary cut because the employer was experiencing economic difficulty, is the employer under any ethical duty to reinstate the former wage rate if its financial picture improves?

Questions on Law

1. Section 109 of the federal Omnibus Budget reconciliation Act of 1981 provides that no household may become eligible to participate in the food stamp program while any of its members is on strike, or receive an increase in the allotment of food stamps it is already receiving because the income of the striking member has decreased. Various unions brought a lawsuit to have this law declared unconstitutional as a violation of First Amendment associational and expressive rights. Is the act constitutional? *Lyng* v. *International Union,* 56 U.S.L.W. 4268 (March 23, 1988).
2. Does a new employer, succeeding to another's business, have an obligation to bargain with the union representing the predecessor's employees? *Fall River Dyeing and Finishing Corp*. v. *NLRB,* 55 U.S.L.W. 4706 (June 1, 1987).
3. Safeway Stores had always ended the week for pay purposes on Wednesday, and checks were issued to employees on Thursday. After some consultation and deliberation, the company decided that the pay period would change. The pay week would end on Friday, and checks would be issued on Tuesday following. Thus, the first checks issued under the new system covered work performed on Thursday and Friday. The union in a grievance charged that the collective bargaining agreement guaranteed pay for forty hours each week and that the new payment policy was in violation of that agreement. The arbitrator agreed with the union, ordering the employer to pay the employees for an additional twenty-four hours of work, even though that work had not been performed. Safeway refused to abide by the award, and the union went to court for enforcement. Should the court order enforcement of the award? Can the award be set aside if the court disagrees with the findings of the arbitrator? *Safeway Stores* v. *Bakery Workers, Local 111,* 390 F.2d 79 (5th Cir. 1968).
4. The registered nurses at Brunswick Hospital Center held a representation election and chose the National Union of Hospital and Health Care Employees as their bargaining representative. Negotiations did not proceed well, and several months later an agreement still had not been reached with the hospital. Many supervisors expected a strike and asked the nurses whether or not they would participate. The nurses were told that they would be fired for striking. A strike did occur, and

most of the nurses participated. The hospital hired replacements for the striking nurses and took photographs of the picket line. Several nurses who continued to work and picketed on their days off were fired. The union filed charges of unfair labor practices against the hospital. Will the union be successful? If it is, to what remedies is it entitled? *Brunswick Hospital Center, Inc.*, NLRB Case No. 29-CA-8165 (Sept. 25, 1981).

5. A union was involved with a supplier of building stone in a labor dispute, which resulted in a strike. The company, which usually delivered stone to construction companies on its own trucks, found that the same construction companies had made arrangements with independent trucking companies for delivery of the stone. These construction companies deducted the cost of delivery from the price they paid for the stone. The striking employees picketed both the stone supplier and the construction companies. The stone supplier filed an unfair labor practice charge against the union. What would the charge have been? Would the company be successful? *Laborers Local 859* v. *NLRB* (Thomas S. Byrne, Inc.), 446 F.2d 1319 (D.C. Cir. 1971).

Suggested Readings

Brankey, ''Prohibited Discrimination in the Replacement and Reinstatement of Strikers Under Section 8(a)(3) of the National Labor Relations Act,'' 23 *American Business Law Journal* 583 (1986).

Rasnic, ''Labor's Return from ''Waterloo'': Congressional Response to *NLRB* v. *Bildisco,*'' 23 *American Business Law Journal* 632 (1986).

Wines, ''*Pattern Makers* v. *NLRB:* Loss of the Right to Discipline Members Who Quit,'' 25 *American Business Law Journal* 652 (1988).

4

Government Regulation of Business

17 Antitrust I—Monopolizing and Horizontal Restraints of Trade

In dealing with the big corporations we call trusts we must . . . proceed by evolution and not by revolution. . . . We can do nothing of good in the way of regulating and supervising these corporations until we fix clearly in our minds that we are not attacking these corporations, but endeavoring to do away with the evil in them.

—Theodore Roosevelt (1902)

■ LEARNING OBJECTIVES

After you have read this chapter, you should be able to:

1. See the way the law evolves over time in new areas.
2. Understand the concept of *market power*.
3. Identify situations in which business behavior may be illegal because it may constitute *monopolization*.
4. Identify business conduct that is probably illegal because it constitutes a horizontal restraint of trade.

Business Decisions and the Law

Cost Saving Competitors

Gil owns an auto parts store which he purchased three years after completing a marketing degree in college. In Gil's small community, there is another auto parts store owned by Sara. While the community is large enough to support both stores, the constant competition for customers causes Sara and Gil to run frequent *specials* designed to increase market share by offering a widely used part—such as spark plugs—for 30 to 40 percent less than normal retail. After Gil and Sara got to know each other socially, they began discussing the elimination of these costly promotional strategies. After a little checking they both concluded that their profits would increase by about 10 percent if they agreed to quit cutting prices. Would Sara and Gil be violating the law if they implemented this plan?

Introduction

How Markets Work

Recall the discussion in chapter 2 on the market, law, and business ethics. There we described the operation of free markets in some detail and described **markets** as mechanisms that channel the conduct of persons with varying philosophical perspectives into serving the material needs of society. You may find it helpful to review that discussion.

In his 1776 treatise on economics entitled *The Wealth of Nations,* Adam Smith originated the now well-known phrase "the invisible hand" to describe the moral character of the free markets. In his words:

> As every individual . . . endeavours as much as he can both to employ his capital in the support of domestic industry, and so to direct industry that its produce may be of greatest value; every individual necessarily labors to render the annual revenue of the society as great as he can. He generally, indeed, neither intends to promote the public interest, nor knows how much he is promoting it . . . he intends only his own gain, and he is in this, as in many other cases, led by an invisible hand to promote an end which was no part of his intention.

Smith's ideas can be stated as follows: Market competition, among individuals pursuing self-interest, yields a socially optimal allocation of society's scarce resources. The marketplace exists when independent parties, acting freely, buy and sell from one another. If you sold this book to another student, the transaction would be viewed as occurring in a marketplace—the one for used books.

Persons with different philosophical perspectives have differing views of the role of marketplaces. However, it is reasonably clear that the marketplaces are primarily utilitarian in character. They are *means* to some end. While we may not all agree on what that end is, or ought to be, most people in this country agree that the marketplace achieves some ends that they find desirable. To a large extent, business persons define their moral character by the marketplace ends that they elect to emphasize.

One such end is self-interested personal pleasure. The market offers persons who are *producers* the opportunity to get rich. These riches can then be used to purchase those things that give the producers the most pleasure, such as large homes and cars and expensive vacations. On the other hand, the market can also be a means of achieving pleasure for *consumers*. Since consumers individually decide how to spend their money in the marketplace, producers often try to offer those things that consumers find most pleasurable. The marketplace offers fine food and beverages, entertainment, the symbols of status and power, and nearly every sensual satisfaction. In a sense then, the marketplace can be viewed as an arena where you can attempt to maximize your self-interested pleasure.

Another utilitarian end for the marketplace is *personal liberty*. Because decisions are made in the marketplace by large numbers of producers and consumers acting independently, no person or organization gains very much power over anyone else. This contrasts with, for example, the communistic approach, in which the means of production are owned by the government. Note that under communism not only is economic power concentrated, it is concentrated in the hands of the same organization (the government) that controls social and political life.

A third end or objective for the marketplace is *service* in the spiritual or religious sense. This viewpoint considers the main function of the market to be serving the material needs of society. This was the opinion of Adam Smith, the English moralist who was influential in arguing that a free market and Christianity are morally compatible. Smith argued that as producers sought their own self-interest in the marketplace they would use society's scarce resources in ways that satisfied the material interests of others. In a sense this view of the marketplace as a vehicle for service links the self-interest of the individual with, in Smith's view, the good of the group as a whole. Riches obtained in the marketplace *may* then constitute a sign of the extent to which one has rendered service to one's society.

There is a fourth view of the most appropriate end for the market; it is *efficiency* and the economic growth that is associated with it. Since society has access to only a limited quantity of resources at any time, there must be some mechanism used to decide how those resources are to be distributed. In communistic systems the government decides. In competitive systems, the marketplace sends signals—in the form of revenues and profits—that tell producers how best to use those resources they control. There are often many producers competing with each other. The ones who survive are those who are most innovative and most sensitive to their customers' needs, and who therefore produce products of higher quality or lower cost. Thus the rivalry among producers stimulates efficiency and, one would hope, economic growth.

These four views of the appropriate end of the marketplace—self-interested pleasure, dilution of power to increase individual liberty, service to society, and efficiency (or growth)—are often compatible with each other. They are not always inconsistent or even distinct.

As we said in chapter 2, when markets work perfectly, they often cause persons with differing philosophical perspectives to behave in the marketplace in about the same way. On the other hand, when markets work imperfectly, they often force persons to elect one of the competing philosophical perspectives over the others. Accordingly, it is important that every business person know clearly what his personal philosophical perspective is and that he be able to determine when markets are operating imperfectly.

In chapter 2 we identified the following imperfections:

1. *Too few sellers or too few buyers;*
2. *Barriers to entry,* which keep either new buyers or new sellers from entering a particular market;
3. *Imperfect knowledge* by either a buyer or a seller;
4. *Externalities,* that is, costs such as pollution, which are not borne by the appropriate seller or buyer.

These imperfections can also be classified as those that create market power and those that create externalities. The first three imperfections cause one party in a marketplace transaction to have *market power.*

Market Power

Market power exists when someone operating in the marketplace has, because of imperfections in a particular market, more power than she would have in a perfectly functioning marketplace. When market power exists, one party—buyer or seller—has more influence over the terms of the transaction than the other party. An extreme example of market power can be easily seen in a situation in which there is a single firm selling a product that cures cancer. Even if the firm's cost of research, production, marketing, and distribution were only $1.00 per unit, it could set a much higher price. If, however, there were ten firms selling this product, the competition among them would drive down the price. Thus with one firm, its *market power* allows it to control the price, while with ten firms the *marketplace* determines price.

An individual who achieves market power must decide whether or not to exercise it. If one views personal pleasure as the basic goal of the marketplace, then it is logical to use the market power to enhance your wealth and pleasure. Suppose, for example, that you owned the only electrical generator for sale in a small town affected by a power outage. This creates an imperfection because there is only one seller and many potential buyers. You might—if pleasure were your basic goal—auction off the generator to the highest cash bidder; perhaps the wealthiest person in town.

If your view of the market is that its basic function is the reduction of power of people over each other, and the associated increase in *individual liberty,* you might decline to auction the generator and perhaps allow the group to draw lots to determine how to use it.

If your view of the market is that its basic function is material *service to society,* you might logically decline to auction off the generator out of a sensitivity to the fact that the imperfection in this situation—one seller—prevents the market mechanism from maximizing service to society. You might, in trying to maximize service, make a *gift* of the generator to the local hospital.

If you consider the market's greatest goal to be economic efficiency or growth, you might again recognize the imperfections in the marketplace and *negotiate* a fair sale of the generator, instead of auctioning it, to the largest employer in the community so jobs would be preserved.

This chapter on antitrust law deals with marketplace imperfections. As you read, try to decide what you believe to be the most important function of the marketplace. Is it your personal pleasure, individual freedom, service to society, or economic growth?

Evolution of Antitrust Law and Analysis

The development of antitrust laws illustrates a common type of interplay among *statutory* law, *case* law, and *administrative* law. Antitrust laws also highlight the way the legal process evolves, even gropes forward, in new legal areas. These laws also illustrate the way law sometimes relies heavily on an academic discipline such as economics.

In 1890 Congress enacted the Sherman Act, which states:

> Section 1. Every contract, combination in the form of trust or otherwise, or conspiracy, in restraint of trade or commerce among the several States, or with foreign nations, is hereby declared to be illegal. . . . Every person who shall make any contract, or engage in any combination or conspiracy hereby declared to be illegal shall be deemed guilty of a misdemeanor. . . .
>
> Section 2. Every person who shall monopolize, or attempt to monopolize, or combine or conspire with any other person or persons, to monopolize any part of the trade or commerce among the several States, or with foreign nations, shall be deemed guilty of a misdemeanor. . . .

Note that the critical language of the statute is highly ambiguous. Key terms such as "restraint of trade" and "attempt to monopolize" are not clear and are not defined in the statute. Congress very likely intended that the courts should clarify the Sherman Act by determining the meaning and application of the statutory language. Today a very large percentage of the meaning of the Sherman Act is established by the decided cases and only a small percentage is determined by the language of the actual statute.

The Sherman Act provided several remedies for its violation. First, the act made violation a crime, punishable by fine and imprisonment. Second, it authorized courts to issue injunctions that prohibit future illegal conduct. Third, those injured by violation are allowed to sue for **treble damages.** This means that they can collect, in a civil suit, three times the amount of their actual financial injury. In addition, if the suit is won, the plaintiff can recover reasonable attorneys' fees. The Sherman Act is unusual in the range and severity of penalties that may be imposed on those who violate it.

A substantial amount of litigation and many appeals helped to clarify the meaning of the Sherman Act. The initial judicial interpretation of section 1 focused on the language "Every contract, combination . . . or conspiracy in restraint of trade." Responding to the word "Every," courts held all agreements in restraint of trade to be illegal. However, as time passed it became clear that all contracts restrain trade to some extent. Thus, a contract to purchase from one supplier all the plumbing material to build one house automatically excludes other plumbing suppliers from that very small market. Accordingly, later cases overruled the literal view, and in effect, modified the language of the statute by declaring illegal only "*unreasonable* restraints of trade." This view has come to be known as the *rule of reason*.

Later, Congress examined the case law developments in the antitrust field and judged some as desirable and others as undesirable. Some applications of the rule of reason offended Congress. An example is the judicial decision that labor unions were an unreasonable restraint of trade, and therefore illegal. Many other judicial decisions were supported by Congress. The business community, however, felt quite uncomfortable with the vagueness of the rule of reason test and with the great power it gave to the courts. As a result, Congress enacted the Federal Trade Commission Act in 1914, establishing the FTC and authorizing it to deal—administratively—with "unfair methods of competition." The motive was to use the administrative agency to clarify the *very* vague statute and *fairly* vague case law so that business persons would have a clearer understanding of the distinction between legal and illegal activities in the antitrust field.

Also in 1914, Congress passed the Clayton Act. This statute in part overruled previous case decisions. For example, the statute made labor unions largely exempt from the antitrust laws. It also clarified the prior statutory and case law and represented, because of its concreteness, a giant step forward in making antitrust law clear and predictable. The Clayton Act made illegal:

1. Price discrimination—when selling to parties who compete with each other or when it unfairly injures a competitor.
2. Exclusive dealings agreements—for example, an agreement between a manufacturer and a retailer whereby the retailer promises not to sell any products that compete with those of the manufacturer.
3. Corporate mergers that involve the purchase of the stock of a competing firm when the effect of the merger is to lessen competition substantially.
4. Interlocking corporate directorates among competing firms—that is, situations in which members of a corporate board also serve as directors for the firm's competitors.

Later, in 1936, Congress again tried to clarify antitrust legislation by enacting the Robinson-Patman Act. This amended the Clayton Act by describing the major forms of price discrimination and providing detailed descriptions of defenses to charges of price discrimination. The single paragraph on price discrimination in the original (1914 version) Clayton Act was expanded by Robinson-Patman to six paragraphs.

Attempts to control mergers with the Clayton Act turned out to be ineffectual for two major reasons. First, the Clayton Act prohibited only those mergers involving the purchase of stock; accordingly, many anticompetitive mergers were implemented by the purchase of *assets* instead of *stock*. Second, the Clayton Act prohibited only stock mergers between firms that were in direct competition with one another. It did not prohibit vertical mergers (e.g., between a manufacturer and one of its retailers) or conglomerate mergers (between large firms that do not compete with each other or supply goods or services to one another). In response to these problems, Congress in 1950 enacted the Celler-Kefauver Amendment to the Clayton Act. This amendment addressed each of these merger areas.

In 1976 Congress enacted the *Hart-Scott-Rodino Antitrust Improvements Act*. This legislation requires that large firms notify the Justice Department thirty days in advance of a merger. The act also gives *state* attorney generals the power to sue violators of the antitrust laws when the violation injures state citizens.

At the same time the law was evolving in the antitrust area, economics was also evolving. This academic discipline made major strides forward in understanding the way competitive markets act. Theoretical advances and the introduction of empirical (data-based) validation of theory gave the discipline of economics substantial influence in the antitrust field. This is illustrated by the fact that the professional staff at the FTC's Bureau of Competition evolved from being almost all lawyers to the point where it is now about half lawyers and half economists. Also, as you read the cases in this chapter you will notice references to "the academic literature." This means that the courts are looking not just at prior cases, but also at the research of economists.

One consequence of the economists' influence is the modern tendency to analyze antitrust problems in economic categories rather than in legal categories. Thus, modern discussion focuses less on "violation of Section 1 or 2" than on the economist's terms *horizontal restraint* and *vertical restraint*. An antitrust offense often violates several laws but only a single economic principle. So it is usually easier to understand the basic economic framework than it is to memorize the language of all the statutes.

We have organized the two antitrust chapters in this book according to economic categories. This, the first chapter, deals only with the economic category *horizontal restraints*—conduct that affects relations between competitors. The second chapter looks exclusively at *vertical restraints*—conduct that affects relations between, for example, a manufacturer and its wholesaler or between a wholesaler and its retailers.

The history of antitrust law is highly evolutionary, a process of trial and error with dynamic interaction between case, statutory, and administrative law. It depicts the legal system as perhaps engaged in experimentation to refine the rules of competition. It also illustrates the law borrowing ideas and concepts from a sister discipline.

Coverage of the Antitrust Laws

Exemptions

Not all economic activities are subject to the antitrust laws. In general, when an industry is exempted from antitrust laws, government regulation is used as a substitute for the discipline of a competitive marketplace. Sometimes government regulation is substituted because competition is too costly. For example, some argue that if there were two electrical supply companies in your area, the total cost of electricity might double, since each would need to invest in extremely expensive power poles and lines, land, and generators. The very high proportion of fixed costs for these operations would force price increases more than competition would reduce them.

In some instances political power is used to take an industry out of the marketplace and place it in the category of a regulated industry. For example, the insurance industry lobbied Congress and won the passage of the McCarran-Ferguson Act in 1945. This statute exempts the industry from the majority of the antitrust laws and leaves regulation in the hands of state regulatory agencies. Insurance companies usually have more influence with the generally understaffed, and less sophisticated, state insurance commissions than with the FTC or the Department of Justice. Accordingly, the McCarran-Ferguson Act gives the industry greater control over its legal environment.

The following is a list of the major exempted industries, the nature of their exemption from antitrust laws, and their regulatory agencies.

1. *Agricultural and fishing organizations*. These businesses may combine in the sale of their agricultural or fishing products. They are regulated respectively by the Department of Agriculture and the Department of Interior.
2. *Labor unions*. Workers may unite in their negotiations with employers. Unions are regulated primarily by the Department of Labor.
3. *Export associations*. Domestic firms may combine for the sole purpose of engaging in foreign trade as long as their activities do not injure domestic competitors or domestic consumers. Generally, the FTC regulates these export associations.
4. *Broadcasting industries*. Radio and TV industries obtain government grants of a monopoly right to broadcast with a certain power over a certain frequency. They are regulated by the Federal Communications Commission (FCC).
5. *Transportation industries*. Railroads, truckers, airlines, and maritime companies have historically been exempted from some provisions of the antitrust laws. Usually the entry of potential competitors has been restricted by supervising administrative agencies. Prices have often been regulated. Recently, the trucking and airline industries have been substantially deregulated. The Interstate Commerce Commission (ICC) supervises railroads and truckers, and the Maritime Administration supervises American-registered oceangoing vessels. The Civil Aeronautics Board (CAB), no longer in existence, used to supervise airline competition.
6. *Financial institutions*. Banks and savings and loans have historically been granted protection from potential competitors. They are regulated by state agencies if chartered by the state or by the Federal Reserve Board or Federal Home Loan Bank Board if they are nationally chartered banks or nationally chartered savings and loans. Banking

institutions have recently been substantially deregulated. Stock exchanges allow buyers and sellers to combine and agree on how sales will occur. They are regulated by the Securities and Exchange Commission (SEC). Insurance companies also are exempted from some aspects of the antitrust laws and are regulated by state insurance commissioners.

7. *Baseball.* This sport is exempt.

Requirement of Interstate Commerce

As with all federal law, antitrust laws must have a constitutional basis. And like much federal legislation, the basis for antitrust law is section 8, clause 3: "The Congress shall have the power . . . to regulate commerce . . . among the several states. . . ." Thus, it is clear that if an activity constitutes **interstate commerce**—that is, exchange of goods that involves parties or goods located in different states—Congress has the power to regulate the transaction. Judicial interpretation of this clause has expanded the initial meaning so that the Constitution now tolerates federal power over transactions involving (1) goods or services (2) where there is some effect on interstate commerce or (3) the mere use of *instrumentalities* of interstate commerce.

Thus the modern congressional power probably extends to nearly every commercial transaction. However, Congress did not elect to extend the coverage of the antitrust laws both to transactions affecting interstate commerce and to those using an instrumentality of interstate commerce. Instead, the reach of these laws is limited to transactions *affecting* interstate commerce. A recent articulation of federal antitrust coverage appeared in the case of *McClain* v. *New Orleans Board of Realtors*. There, real estate brokers, all located within a single state, had agreed to charge the same sales commission. The properties and the parties with whom the brokers dealt were also located in the same state. However, the Court held that these transactions *did affect* interstate commerce because the mortgage money often came from out of state and the loans were often federally insured. Thus the federal antitrust laws apply to almost every important business transaction.

Monopolization

Section 2 of the Sherman Act states, "Every person who shall monopolize, or attempt to monopolize, or conspire with any other person or persons to monopolize . . . shall be deemed guilty. . . ." The definition of **monopolization** is somewhat difficult because ambiguity remains a hallmark of this area of the law. It is clear, however, that two basic elements must be established before a firm will be found guilty of monopolization: *monopoly power* and *monopolizing conduct*.

Monopoly Power

In order to determine whether a firm has monopoly power, courts must evaluate the extent of the firm's *geographic market* and the extent of the firm's *market power.*

The geographic scope of a market varies from industry to industry. Thus Ford and General Motors compete in national or even international markets. In contrast, grocery chains typically compete in regional markets of three to ten states. Individuals who own gasoline stations probably compete in a market of a single town or neighborhood.

Market power exists when a firm ceases being a slave to the forces in its geographic marketplace. Instead of reacting to the dictates of the market, a firm with market power is able to influence the market in some way. Compare the economic positions of a wheat farmer operating in a free national market with that of the only surgeon in your region of the country able to perform a particular life-saving procedure. The farmer has little influence over the terms of sale. He cannot influence price or the conduct of other farmers. In contrast, the surgeon has a great deal of control over the price she will charge for her services. The surgeon has market power while the farmer does not.

Almost all firms do have some degree of market power. For example, General Motors acted for a time as the *price leader* for domestically manufactured autos. It would announce the annual price increases and then Ford, Chrysler, and American Motors would follow General Motors' lead with quite similar increases. General Motors was exercising market power. When a firm acquires sufficient market power in a particular market so that it exercises control over price or is able to exclude competition, then the firm is exercising so much market power that it has **monopoly power.**

Market share has come to be a sign of the presence or absence of monopoly power. If a firm has a small market share, say 5 percent, there is a presumption that it does not have monopoly power. In contrast, if a firm has a very large market share, say 70 to 100 percent, then the courts become concerned about whether the market share indicates monopoly power. Clearly, there may be some difficulty in computing the market share for particular firms. The main difficulty is in determining which products are in the same market. For example, are short-sleeve Izod shirts in the same market with short-sleeve polo shirts, with T-shirts, with undershirts, with long-sleeve button-down-collar dress shirts, or with all of these?

In a sense, all goods compete with each other; for example, when the price of housing increases, some consumers purchase fewer new cars. Thus, all goods are in the same market for consumers' dollars. To find the defendant's total market, or in legal terms, the **relevant market,** the courts examine the **cross elasticity of demand,** or substitutability, between the defendant's product and other products. Cross elasticity of demand measures the way price changes for one product affect sales volume of another. For example, if a seller of dental floss reduced its price 50 percent, that might significantly reduce sales by other sellers of dental floss. Thus we could conclude that these products are in the same relevant market. It may even be that the price reduction would decrease somewhat the sale of certain mouthwashes, and perhaps even Dentyne chewing gum. In the case of *United States* v. *du Pont & Co.,* 351 U.S. 377 (1956), the Supreme Court defined the relevant market for *cellophane,* an inexpensive, transparent, light, flexible packaging material. The government charged that du Pont had monopolized the market and that the relevant market was the "cellophane market." du Pont's defense was that its relevant market included butcher paper, wax paper, and similar "flexible wrapping materials." Under the government's definition of the relevant market, du Pont would probably have a very large market share and would thus have monopoly power. Under du Pont's definition, its market share would only be about 18 percent. The following language from the *du Pont* case illustrates the way courts determine the size of the relevant market:

> Determination of the competitive market . . . depends upon how different . . . are the . . . commodities. . . .
>
> In considering what is the relevant market . . . no more definite rule can be declared than that commodities be reasonably interchangeable by consumers for the same purposes. . . .
>
> . . . If a slight decrease in the price of cellophane causes a considerable number of customers of other flexible wrappings to switch to cellophane it would be an indication that a high cross-elasticity of demand exists between them; the products compete in the same [relevant] market. The Court below held that "[g]reat sensitivity of customers in the flexible packaging markets to price or quality changes" prevented du Pont from possessing monopoly control over price. The record sustains these findings.

Monopolizing Conduct

Monopoly power generally is not a sufficient basis for concluding that a firm has monopolized. It must also have engaged in **monopolizing conduct.** If the monopoly power arises because of the firm's "skill, efficiency and foresight," then, without monopolizing conduct, the defendant is not guilty of monopolizing. Monopolizing conduct usually involves illegal conduct that injures either competition or competitors.

The following case is the landmark opinion in the area of monopolization. It discusses the issues of market share, relevant market, and monopolizing conduct.

United States v. Aluminum Co. of America

148 F.2d 416 (2d Cir. 1945)

Facts

In 1889 a fellow by the name of Hall obtained a patent to extract the metal aluminum from the ore bauxite. Hall assigned the patent to the Aluminum Company of America (Alcoa). Alcoa maintained its legal monopoly with this and related patents until 1906.

In order to protect its position, Alcoa entered into

agreements with its suppliers of electricity whereby the suppliers promised not to sell electricity to anyone else for the manufacture of aluminum. In addition, Alcoa entered into agreements with foreign manufacturers of aluminum that fixed prices and restricted aluminum imports into the United States.

Opinion

Before L. Hand, Swan, and Augustus N. Hand, Circuit Judges.

Circuit Judge L. Hand: . . . The action was brought under §4 [title 15], praying the district court to adjudge that the defendant, Aluminum Company of America, was monopolizing interstate and foreign commerce, particularly in the manufacture and sale of "virgin" aluminum ingot, and that it be dissolved. . . .

From 1902 onward until 1928 "Alcoa" was making ingot in Canada through a wholly owned subsidiary; so much of this as it imported into the United States it is proper to include with what it produced here. In the year 1912 the sum of these two items represented nearly ninety-one percent of the total amount of "virgin" ingot available for sale in this country. This percentage varied year by year up to and including 1938: in 1913 it was about seventy-two percent; in 1921 about sixty-eight percent; in 1922 about seventy-two; with these exceptions it was always over eighty percent of the total and for the last five years 1934–1938 inclusive it averaged over ninety percent. . . .

There are various ways of computing "Alcoa's" control of the aluminum market—as distinct from its production—depending upon what one regards as competing in that market. The [trial] judge figured its share—during the years 1929–1938, inclusive—as only about thirty-three percent; to do so he included "secondary [ingot]" and excluded that part of "Alcoa's" own production which it fabricated and did not therefore sell as ingot. . . . The percentage we have already mentioned—over ninety—results only if we both include all "Alcoa's" production and exclude "secondary." That percentage is enough to constitute a monopoly; it is doubtful whether sixty or sixty-four percent would be enough; and certainly thirty-three percent is not. . . . All ingot–with trifling exceptions—is used to fabricate intermediate, or end, products; and therefore all intermediate, or end, products which "Alcoa" fabricated and sells, . . . reduce the demand for ingot itself. . . . We cannot therefore agree that the computation of the percentage of "Alcoa's" control over the ingot market should not include the whole of its ingot production. . . .

It is entirely consistent with the evidence that it was the threat of greater foreign imports which kept "Alcoa's" prices where they were, and prevented it from exploiting its advantage as sole domestic producer; indeed, it is hard to resist the conclusion that potential imports did put a "ceiling" upon those prices. Nevertheless, within the limits afforded by the tariff and the cost of transportation, "Alcoa" was free to raise its prices as it chose, since it was free from domestic competition, save as it drew other metals into the market as substitutes. Was this a monopoly within the meaning of §2? The judge found that, over the whole half century of its existence, "Alcoa's" profits upon capital invested, after payment of income taxes, had been only about ten percent, and, although the plaintiff puts this figure a little higher, the difference is negligible. . . .

A profit of ten percent, so conditioned, could hardly be considered extortionate. . . .

But the whole issue is irrelevant anyway, for it is no excuse for "monopolizing" a market that the monopoly has not been used to extract from the consumer more than a "fair" profit. . . .

It does not follow because "Alcoa" had such a monopoly, that it "monopolized" the ingot market: it may not have achieved monopoly; monopoly may have been thrust upon it. . . .

The courts have at least kept in reserve the possibility that the origin of monopoly may be critical in determining its legality. . . .

This notion has usually been expressed by saying that size does not determine guilt; that there must be some "exclusion" of competitors. . . . What engendered these compunctions is reasonably plain; persons may unwittingly find themselves in possession of a monopoly, automatically so to say: that is, without having intended either to put an end to existing competition, or to prevent competition from arising when none had existed; they may become monopolists by force of accident. . . .

It would completely misconstrue "Alcoa's" position in 1940 to hold that it was the passive beneficiary of a monopoly, following upon an involuntary elimination of competitors by automatically operative economic forces. . . . There were at least one or two abortive attempts to enter the industry, but "Alcoa" effectively anticipated and forestalled all competition, and succeeded in holding the field alone. . . . The only question is whether it falls within the exception, established in favor of those who do not seek but cannot avoid, the control of a market. . . . "Alcoa" meant to keep, and did keep, that complete and exclusive hold upon the ingot market with which it started. That was to "monopolize" that market, however innocently it otherwise proceeded. So far as the judgement held that it was not within §2, it must be reversed.

Case Questions

1. How large a market share is required before this court will infer monopoly power?
2. What products are within the relevant market in this case?
3. Do you think it would be morally wrong for one firm to control 95 percent of a relevant market if it achieved that share without "monopolizing conduct"? Does the answer to this question depend upon your philosophical perspective toward marketplace activities?

Attempts to Monopolize

The cases that deal with the clause in Section 2 of the Sherman Act prohibiting **"attempts to monopolize"** tend to focus on specific anticompetitive *conduct*, as opposed to market *structure* (e.g., a 90 percent share of the relevant market). Generally there must be some market power that the defendant attempts to use to suppress competition. For example, in *Lorain Journal Co.* v. *United States*, 342 U.S. 143 (1951), the Supreme Court found an attempt to monopolize where the *Journal*, a newspaper with a practical monopoly over advertising in the city of Lorain, informed its advertisers that those who advertised on a newly established radio station, WEOL, would not be permitted to continue advertising through the *Journal*. The *Journal*'s market power came from the fact that consumers in Lorain were accustomed to obtaining almost all product information solely through the *Journal*. Advertisers would suffer a significant loss of business if they were limited to ads only on WEOL. Accordingly, the *Journal*'s conduct was held to be an *attempt to monopolize*.

Collaboration among Competitors

If you can see that monopoly power is injurious to the competitive process, then perhaps you can also see that combining the market powers of supposedly competing firms might also injure competition in the same way. For example, if all the modern aluminum manufacturers—Kaiser, Alcoa, and Reynolds—agreed among themselves on the price to be charged for virgin ingot, they by collaboration would achieve the same result that Alcoa had achieved by monopolization.

Not all relations among competitors are illegal. Only relations that injure competition are illegal under the antitrust laws. But like many other areas of the law, there are *degrees* of injury. And sometimes a small injury is offset by a large benefit to society. Because of these realities, the courts have adopted two categories of antitrust violations: those which fall under a *rule of reason* and those which are *per se* illegal.

Rule of Reason

This is a balancing test that weighs an injury to competition against the benefits of a relationship among competitors. The United States Supreme Court has articulated the rule of reason in *Chicago Board of Trade* v. *United States* with the following language:

> Every statement concerning trade, every regulation of trade, restrains. To bind, to restrain, is of their very essence. The true test of legality is whether the restraint imposed is such as merely regulates and perhaps *promotes* competition or whether it is such as may *suppress or even destroy* competition. [Emphasis added.]

Per Se Illegality

After the courts had heard a variety of collaboration cases under the rule of reason—particularly those cases involving price fixing—the United States Supreme Court articulated a second test intended to be an alternative to the rule of reason test. This alternative is called **per se illegality.** For certain classes of restraints of trade, the courts were not to examine the justification for, or the reasonableness of, or the effect of the restraint. Rather, the courts were to find the charged party liable if that party restrained trade and the restraint was the type considered illegal per se.

Price Fixing

Price fixing was the first type of collaboration declared to be illegal per se. Price fixing occurs when competitors agree, expressly or impliedly, to charge the same price for a product or service. The following case illustrates the way the courts think about price fixing.

United States v. Trenton Potteries Co.

273 U.S. 392 (1927)

Opinion

Justice Stone: There is no contention here that the verdict was not supported by sufficient evidence that respondents, controlling some 82 percent of the business of manufacturing and distributing in the United States vitreous pottery [for use in bathrooms and lavatories] combined to fix prices and to limit sales in interstate commerce. . . .

The question . . . to be considered here is whether the trial judge correctly withdrew from the jury the consideration of the reasonableness of the particular restraints charged.

That only those restraints upon interstate commerce which are unreasonable are prohibited by the Sherman Law was the rule laid down by the opinions of this Court in the Standard Oil and Tobacco cases. [Citations Omitted.] But it does not follow that agreements to fix or maintain prices are reasonable restraints and therefore permitted by the statute, merely because the prices themselves are reasonable. Reasonableness is not a concept of definite and unchanging content. Its meaning necessarily varies in the different fields of the law, because it is used as a convenient summary of the dominant considerations which control in the application of legal doctrines. Our view of what is a reasonable restraint of commerce is controlled by the recognized purpose of the Sherman Law itself. Whether this type of restraint is reasonable or not must be judged in part at least, in the light of its effect on competition, for whatever difference of opinion there may be among economists as to the social and economic desirability of an unrestrained competitive system, it cannot be doubted that the Sherman Law and the judicial decisions interpreting it are based upon the assumption that the public interest is best protected from the evils of monopoly and price control by the maintenance of competition. . . .

The aim and result of *every* price-fixing agreement, if effective, is the elimination of one form of competition. [Emphasis added.] The power to fix prices, whether reasonably exercised or not, involves power to control the market and to fix arbitrary and unreasonable prices. The reasonable price fixed today may through economic and business changes become the unreasonable price of tomorrow. Once established, it may be maintained unchanged because of the absence of competition secured by the agreement for a price reasonable when fixed. *Agreements which create such potential power may well be held to be in themselves unreasonable or unlawful restraints, without the necessity of minute inquiry whether a particular price is reasonable or unreasonable as fixed* and without placing on the government in enforcing the Sherman Law the burden of ascertaining from day to day whether it has become *unreasonable* through the mere variation of economic conditions [emphasis added]. Moreover, in the absence of express legislation requiring it, we should hesitate to adopt a construction making the difference between legal and illegal conduct in the field of business relations depend upon so uncertain a test as whether prices are reasonable—a determination which can be satisfactorily made only after a complete survey of our economic organization and a choice between rival philosophies. . . .

That such was the view of this court in deciding the Standard Oil and Tobacco cases, and that such is the effect of its decisions both before and after those cases, does not seem fairly open to question. . . . [U]niform price-fixing by those controlling in any substantial manner a trade or business in interstate commerce is prohibited by the Sherman Law, despite the reasonableness of the particular prices agreed upon. . . .

It follows that the judgement of the Circuit Court of Appeals must be reversed and the judgement of the District Court reinstated.

Reversed.

Case Questions

1. What economic motivation might cause members of an industry to collaborate and establish "reasonable" prices as opposed to "unreasonable" prices?
2. Isn't the court saying that even "reasonable" price fixing will not be tolerated, in major part because the courts have a hard time determining what is a reasonable or unreasonable price?
3. If "reasonable" price fixing is illegal simply because it is hard for courts to deal with it, does this make such laws less ethically legitimate in your mind?

Since the *Trenton Potteries* case, there have been numerous applications of the concept of per se illegality to price-fixing cases. The most famous case involved General Electric and Westinghouse Corporations. They and other manufacturers of turbine generators used by electrical utilities engaged in price fixing. As a consequence, forty-five executives were found guilty of criminal violations, seven served jail sentences, the companies paid $1.9 million in criminal fines and—because of the treble damage clause—they also paid $405 million to settle the civil suits.

Price-fixing attempts have been widely prosecuted. Per se convictions have occurred in national and local industries ranging from manufacturers of watches, eyeglasses, typewriters, and stainless steel to Utah egg dealers and small travel agencies. In 1976 the Sherman Act was amended to increase the penalties. Now criminal violations can be punished by imprisonment for up to three years; fines are now $100,000 per count for individuals and $1,000,000 per count for corporations.

Conscious Parallelism

Sometimes price fixing is proved with the written documents used by the parties to communicate the pricing agreement. In other cases, circumstantial evidence may strongly indicate price fixing. For example, when officials of competing organizations meet to discuss price-related issues and end up charging the same price for their competing products, courts may infer price fixing. The following case illustrates this approach to proving the conspiracy.

Esco Corporation v. United States

340 F.2d 1000 (9th Cir. 1965)

Facts

This is an appeal from a jury verdict convicting appellant corporation of violating Section 1 of the Sherman Act by means of its participation in an alleged price-fixing conspiracy, admittedly a per se violation of the act.

Opinion

The "central criminal design" charged herein was the restraint of trade by fixing prices on stainless steel pipe and tubing within the described market area. But, it is contended, Esco's "relationship" to the two . . . [Los Angeles] meetings and the Salt Lake City meeting of the competitors was "perfectly legal. . . ." [Defendant's] counsel [argues] "there is a compelled inference" that Tubesales, the biggest competitor, called the meeting "not to ask for agreement, but simply to announce" its own pricing plans. Were we triers of fact, we might well ask if this were so, what purpose was to be served by a meeting of competitors?

Nor are we so naive as to believe that a formal signed-and-sealed contract or written resolution would conceivably be adopted at a meeting of price-fixing conspirators in this day and age. In fact, the typical price-fixing agreement is usually accomplished in a contrary manner.

While particularly true of price-fixing conspiracies, it is a well recognized law that any conspiracy can ordinarily only be proved by inferences drawn from relevant and competent circumstantial evidence, including the conduct of the defendants charged. . . . A knowing wink can mean more than words. Let us suppose five competitors meet on several occasions, discuss their problems, and one finally states—"I won't fix prices with any of you, but here is what I am going to do—put the price of my gidget at X dollars, now you all do what you want." He then leaves the meeting. Competitor number two says—"I don't care whether number one does what he says he's going to do or not; nor do I care what the rest of you do, but I am going to price my gidget at X dollars." Number three makes a similar statement—"My price is X dollars." Number four says not a word. All leave and fix "their" prices at "X" dollars.

We do not say the foregoing illustration compels an inference in this case that the competitors' conduct constituted a price-fixing conspiracy, including an agreement to so conspire, but neither can we say, as a matter of law, that an inference of no agreement is compelled. As in so many other instances, it remains a question for the trier of fact to consider and determine what inference appeals to it [the jury] as most logical and persuasive after it has heard all the evidence as to what these competitors had done before such meetings, and what actions they took thereafter, or what actions they did not take.

An accidental or incidental price uniformity, or even "pure" conscious parallelism of prices is, standing alone, not unlawful. Nor is an individual competitor's sole decision to follow a price leadership standing alone, a violation of law. But we do not find that factual situation here.

It is not necessary to find an express agreement, either oral or written, in order to find a conspiracy, but it is sufficient that a concert of action be contemplated and that defendants conform to the arrangement. . . . Mutual consent need not be bottomed on express agreement, for any conformance to an agreed or contemplated pattern of conduct will warrant in inference of conspiracy. . . . An exchange of words is not required. . . . Thus not only action, but even a lack of action, may be enough from which to infer a combination or conspiracy. . . .

Applying these rules to the facts at hand, the jury came to an opposite conclusion from that which [Esco] urges, and the fact that Esco's involvement was in but two of ten allegedly conspiratorial situations does not absolve Esco from participation in the entire conspiracy if its involvement in the two was unlawful and knowingly and purposely performed. We hold that sufficient evidence existed for the jury to find participation in a price-fixing conspiracy.

Case Questions

1. Does this case deal with substantive or procedural law?
2. Can you describe some market situations in which price fixing agreements will not be adhered to by some collaborators?
3. What facts would need to be proved in court to convict someone of price fixing?

Conscious parallelism means that a firm consciously decides to copy the behavior of another firm. Thus Ford may decide to copy the pricing policies of General Motors. As the *Esco* decision indicates, this is legal if Ford's decision is truly independent. However, when the parallel behavior is combined with other evidence of conspiracy, then it may be classified as illegal conscious parallelism.

Territorial Allocations

Business persons often see benefits for themselves in dividing geographic markets among competitors. Alcoa, for example, entered into agreements with European manufacturers of aluminum whereby the Europeans agreed not to sell to the U.S. market and Alcoa agreed not to try to sell aluminum in Europe. By making such **territorial allocations,** firms can often reduce advertising and transportation expenses. Sometimes they can achieve other economies. Still, the courts view this activity as a conspiracy in restraint of trade. The net economic effect of a territorial allocation is, of course, a reduction of the number of competitors in each territory. Certainly it is easy to imagine situations in which allocation of territories might allow some firms to amass enough market power so that, within their exclusive territories, they achieve monopoly power. Territorial allocations among competitors are generally illegal per se.

Concerted Refusals to Deal (Boycotts)

Competitors may want to avoid the powerful winds of competition on issues other than price or territory. Often, competitors see good reasons for agreeing among themselves about standard, or uniform, ways to handle particular problems or transactions. Typically, a **concerted refusal to deal** arises when a group of businesses promise each other that they will refuse to deal, with either customers or suppliers, except in a particular way. Stated another way, the competitors try to enforce *agreed terms* on the customers or suppliers by refusing to deal in any other way. Concerted refusals to deal are often illegal per se; accordingly there is no justification that business can offer to defend the conduct.

In the classic boycott case, Fashion Originators Guild of America, a trade association of manufacturers of designer dresses, sought to restrict its members from selling to retailers who also carried legal copies of the fashion designs. This activity was held illegal per se. It involved members of an industry agreeing to treat their customers in the same way—a way that reduced competition between designer dresses and their legal copies.

The following case illustrates the more modern approach, one that does not rely exclusively on per se analysis, to judge a concerted refusal to deal.

Northwest Wholesale Stationers v. *Pacific Stationers*

105 S. Ct. 2613 (1985)

Opinion

Justice Brennan: This case . . . turns . . . on whether the decision to expel Pacific is properly viewed as a group boycott or concerted refusal to deal mandating per se invalidation. "Group boycotts" are often listed among the classes of economic activity that merit per se invalidation under § 1. Exactly what types of activity fall within the forbidden category is, however, far from certain. . . . Some care is therefore necessary in defining the category of concerted refusals to deal that mandate per se condemnation.

Cases to which this Court has applied the per se approach have generally involved joint efforts by a firm or firms to disadvantage competitors by "either directly denying or persuading or coercing suppliers or customers to deny relationships the competitors need in the competitive struggle." In these cases, the boycott often cuts off access to a supply, facility, or markets necessary to enable the boycotted firm to compete, and frequently the boycotting firms possessed a dominant position in the relevant market. In addition, the practices were generally not justified by plausible arguments that they were intended to enhance overall efficiency and make markets more competitive. Under such circumstances the likelihood of anticompetitive effects is clear and the possibility of countervailing procompetitive effects is remote.

Although a concerted refusal to deal need not necessarily possess all of these traits to merit per se treatment, not every cooperative activity involving a restraint or exclusion will share with the per se forbidden boycotts the likelihood of predominantly anticompetitive consequences. . . .

Wholesale purchasing cooperatives such as Northwest are not a form of concerted activity characteristically likely to result in predominantly anticompetitive effects. Rather, such cooperative arrangements would seem to be "designed to increase economic efficiency and render markets more, rather than less, competitive." The arrangement permits the participating retailers to achieve economies of scale in both the purchase and warehousing of wholesale supplies, and also ensures ready access to a stock of goods that might otherwise be unavailable on short notice. The cost savings and order-filling guarantees enables smaller retailers to reduce prices and maintain their retail stock so as to compete more effectively with larger retailers.

Pacific, of course, does not object to the existence of the cooperative arrangement, but rather raises an antitrust challenge to Northwest's decision to bar Pacific from continued membership. It is therefore the action of expulsion that must be evaluated to determine whether per se treatment is appropriate. The act of expulsion from a wholesale cooperative does not necessarily imply anticompetitive animus and thereby raise a probability of anticompetitive effect. Wholesale purchasing cooperatives must establish and enforce reasonable rules in order to function effectively. Disclosure rules, such as the one on which Northwest relies, may well provide the cooperative with a needed means for monitoring the credit worthiness of its members. Nor would the expulsion characteristically be likely to result in predominantly anticompetitive effects, at least in the type of situation this case presents. Unless the cooperative possesses market power or exclusive access to an element essential to effective competition, the conclusion that expulsion is virtually always likely to have an anticompetitive effect is not warranted. Absent such a showing with respect to a cooperative buying arrangement, courts should apply a rule-of-reason analysis. At no time has Pacific made a threshold showing that these structural characteristics are present in this case.

Case Questions

1. How does the action of the wholesale purchasing cooperative differ from than of Fashion Originators Guild?
2. Has the Court stated that the definition of a concerted refusal to deal is one which meets the test of the rule of reason? That is, is the Court here saying that one must engage in a rule of reason analysis to determine whether per se illegality exists?
3. Might some members of the cooperative want to exclude other members if by doing so they run up their competitors' cost of goods? What do you think is the motivation for excluding Pacific Stationers from the cooperative?

If the goal of the boycott is noncommercial, it will definitely be tested under the rule of reason rather than per se. For example the National Organization of Women (NOW) asked its members and others to boycott the convention facilities of states that did not ratify the proposed Equal Rights Amendment. Missouri was one of those states and it sued NOW for violation of the antitrust laws because its convention business suffered. But Missouri lost because NOW's goal was political, not economic. *Missouri* v. *NOW, Inc.*, 620 F.2d

1301 (1981). Further, businesses may engage in concerted political activity, such as lobbying. Even if the goal is economic, the fact that the businesses are engaging in political action exempts them from antitrust liability.

Variations on the Basic Violations

Since antitrust law rests—in very large part—upon economic theory, collaboration among competitors that merely *resembles* price fixing, territorial allocations, or concerted refusals to deal are very likely to be illegal per se. Thus, of course, a division of customers, instead of territories, is illegal per se. Similarly agreements to limit production output, to restrict product innovation, or to limit improvements in quality are likely to be treated in the same fashion as the other per se violations. In general, the criminal penalties of the antitrust laws are most likely to be invoked when a party has committed a per se violation.

Horizontal Mergers

If you can see the injury to competition caused by monopoly or collaboration among competitors, then you can probably understand why mergers between competitors can be illegal; these **horizontal mergers** reduce the number of firms competing and therefore perhaps reduce the intensity of the rivalry.

Not all mergers among competitors are illegal, however. Section 7 of the Clayton Act provides:

> That no person engaged in commerce . . . shall acquire, directly or indirectly, the whole or any part of the stock or other share capital [or] . . . the whole or any part of the assets of another person engaged also in commerce where in any line of commerce in any section of the country, the effect of such acquisition may be *substantially to lessen competition,* or to tend to create a monopoly. [Emphasis added.]

A merger between two firms, each with 1 percent of the market, would probably not "substantially lessen competition" if these were the smallest firms in the industry. Because the number of firms and the market share of each firm in an industry will influence the effect of any merger on competition, the Department of Justice has issued *Merger Guidelines*. These guidelines define—in terms of the number and market shares of firms in an industry—when a horizontal merger will be challenged.

Ethical Issues in Monopolizing and Horizontal Restraints of Trade

Many important moralists have given substantial thought to the practices of business persons and the operations of markets. For example Aristotle, Aquinas, and Luther all wrote on this topic. In general, their major concern has been with "extortion" and "exploitation" of poor or powerless persons in the marketplace. For some time this concern was expressed in the condemnation of usury, the charging of interest on money lent. This condemnation occurred before people realized that there is a *time value* associated with the possession of money—that one dollar today is worth more to almost everyone than one dollar twenty-five years from today. Because these moralists did not clearly perceive this time value concept, they viewed the charging of interest as a manifestation of market power in which the party with money to lend was able to "unjustly extort" interest from a desperate borrower. Careful reading of their works reveals that it was the exercise of market power that they condemned rather than simply the collection of interest.

For modern business persons it is fairly easy to perceive the presence of market power in many transactions. Often, business persons make decisions about market power with the following formula:

1. Is the transaction illegal? If so, I won't do it.
2. If it is legal, is there still present so much market power that I judge it to be legal but morally wrong? If so, I won't do it.

Note that the second element is quite similar to the rule of reason test used by the law; it balances the inherent good of the transaction against the exercise of market power.

Many business persons criticize this "ethical rule of reason" approach as slow, awkward, and inconsistent with the philosophy of the free market. These persons often advocate ignoring the idea of market power altogether. Their test of morality is simply, "Is it legal?" Of course, the criticism of this approach is that it ignores the imperfections of the law as a moral system. The end-of-chapter problems on ethics allow you to think through *your* position on the use of market power in business transactions.

The important concepts and terms in this chapter are listed below; page numbers have been provided for the key terms. By reading over each section you can assess your understanding of the chapter concepts and determine areas you may want to review.

Chapter Summary

1. Markets exist when buyers and sellers freely negotiate sales.
2. Competitive markets can achieve a variety of philosophical ends. These include personal pleasure, personal liberty, material service, and efficiency.
3. Market power exists when one party to a transaction has more influence over the terms of the transaction than the other party.
4. The Sherman Act was the first major antitrust statute. It made monopolization and agreements in restraint of trade illegal.
5. The Federal Trade Commission Act established the FTC and authorized it to deal administratively with "unfair methods of competition."
6. The Clayton Act prohibits price discrimination, exclusive dealing agreements, anticompetitive mergers, and interlocking corporate directorships among competitors.

7. The Robinson-Patman Act describes the major forms of price discrimination and the valid defenses to a charge of price discrimination.
8. As time passes, the antitrust laws become more concrete. Thus, defining illegal behavior becomes easier for business.
9. The federal antitrust statutes generally regulate transactions "affecting interstate commerce."
10. Monopolization is the presence of monopoly power and the use of monopolizing conduct within a firm's geographic market. Monopoly power exists when a firm can exercise control over price or exclude competition.
11. Monopoly power can be inferred when one firm has a very large share of a *relevant market*. Cross elasticity of demand is a measure of product substitutability. It is the primary tool used to define a relevant market. Cross elasticity of demand measures the way a change in the price of one product will affect the sales volume of another product.
12. *Attempts to monopolize* usually involve the use of anticompetitive conduct by a firm with substantial market power.
13. By collaborating, competitors can achieve the same position as a single firm with monopoly power.
14. Under the rule of reason, a restraint of trade is legal if it merely promotes competition, but it is illegal if it destroys competition. Under the per se test, certain classes of conduct are illegal even when there is no proof of an injury to competition.
15. Price fixing by competitors is illegal per se.
16. Price fixing can sometimes be proven with circumstantial evidence.
17. Territorial allocation by competitors is illegal per se.
18. Boycotts by a group of competitors are called *concerted refusals to deal*.
19. Horizontal mergers are illegal if they are likely to lessen competition.
20. The criminal penalties for violation of the antitrust laws are most likely to be imposed on those who commit per se violations.

Key Terms

attempts to monopolize 490
concerted refusal to deal 495
conscious parallelism 494
cross elasticity of demand 487
horizontal merger 497
interstate commerce 486
markets 479
market power 481
monopolization 486
monopolizing conduct 488
monopoly power 487
per se illegality 491
price fixing 491
relevant market 487
rule of reason 491
territorial allocations 495
treble damages 482

Questions on Ethics

1. Suppose you owned one of three gasoline stations in a small rural town located more than fifty miles away from the nearest competition. Further assume that the other two stations owners had agreed to raise prices fifteen cents per gallon. They approached you and asked you to join them. After a very careful analysis, you concluded that if you participated your income would double. You and your family definitely need the money for things like college educations for your children. Assume that there is absolutely no risk that you would be caught. If you believe that such conduct is wrong, would you be willing to give up the additional income? If you *do* believe the conduct is wrong, do you think the greater wrong is violating the law or causing someone an economic injury?
2. Suppose you owned the *only* gasoline station in the rural town discussed in question number 1. Since there is only one station, you have substantial market power. Assume that many residents would gladly pay an additional fifteen cents per gallon rather than drive the fifty miles to the next town. After consulting an antitrust attorney you become convinced that such a price increase is perfectly legal. Would you raise your price as high as you possibly, and profitably, could or would you decline to completely exploit your market power? What reasons influence your decision?
3. Assume that you are the managing partner of a regional CPA firm. One of the firm's major clients—a local company—is being sold to new owners. The new owners have announced that they will be using the services of another accounting firm and you believe that there is absolutely no chance that they will ever use your firm in the future. The contract of sale for the business requires that a comprehensive, complex accounting evaluation of the firm occur before the new owners take title to the business. The contract also requires that this accounting work be awarded to the lowest bidder in a sealed bidding procedure. You know that all other bids for this work will be based on the cost of doing the work. In addition, you are aware that your firm's prior experience with the company will allow you to do the work for about 85 percent less than the cost of any other accounting firm. There are two bidding strategies open to you: you can bid $7,500 if you base your bid, as the other accounting firms will, on your cost to do the job, or you can bid $49,000 if you base your bid on your estimate of the lowest amount needed to win the job. Both bids will probably win the work for your firm. Note that your prior experience working with the company gives your organization a type of market power in this particular bidding situation. By exercising this power you can earn extra revenue of about $41,500. Will you do so? Why or why not?
4. Suppose you are the chief purchasing agent for a large aerospace firm.

One of your responsibilities is arranging for the janitorial services for the firm's local offices. The firm currently doing the work is going out of business. Three other local firms do janitorial work. After receiving sealed bids from these firms, you have the opportunity to "whipsaw" the firms, playing one against the other in the bidding process. You could call one firm and disclose the amount of the lowest bid and ask if it would be willing to do the work for at least 10 percent less than that bid. If that firm says yes, you could call the second firm and ask if it will go even lower. This process can be continued in some situations until you have driven almost all of the profit (often much of the overhead) out of the supplying firms' bids. Will you accept the first bids or will you "whipsaw"? Why or why not?

5. Suppose you are the marketing manager of a profit-making firm that has discovered a way to collect whole blood, process it into plasma, and store it for long periods of time. As a result the firm always has on hand a large inventory of blood plasma. The market for plasma is usually very stable because the rate of consumption is—most of the time—relatively uniform across the country. Occasionally there is a major disaster, such as an earthquake or hurricane, which dramatically increases the demand by hospitals for plasma. If, as marketing manager, you carefully price your product to reflect market conditions, charging one normal price and another much higher price during emergencies, you can substantially influence the profitability of the firm. Would you recommend to your firm that it use such pricing policies? Why or why not?

Questions on Law

1. Efco Corporation developed a product that had unique thermal characteristics. It is a liquid that will freeze into a solid chunk of ice rapidly and melt slowly. Because of these characteristics, the product has a variety of industrial and consumer applications. One consumer application is "ice bags," the product that people use to keep portable ice chests cool. The ice bag is frozen at home and then placed in the ice chest immediately before a trip. Efco elected not to patent its product but rather relied on treating the chemical formulation as a trade secret. When the product was introduced it captured about 95 percent of the market, primarily because there were no competitors. Efco was able to maintain this market share for nearly four years. Eventually its competitors learned the details about the trade secret and as a result market share fell to about 15 percent. Did Efco have market power during the four-year time period? Did Efco have monopoly power during the four-year time period? Did Efco engage in monopolizing conduct? Could consumers collect treble damages in a suit charging Efco with monopolizing?

2. The Fairfax County Bar Association, concerned about the quality of legal service that its members provided, published a "minimum fee schedule" that all member lawyers were advised to follow. Failure to follow the schedule was grounds for disciplinary action by the bar association. The purpose of the schedule was not to increase the profitability of practicing law but to ensure that cutthroat competition would not drive down prices to a level where the lawyers could not afford to spend the time needed to do a professional, high-quality job. Does the bar association's conduct violate any provision of the antitrust laws? Which test, rule of reason or per se illegality, is used to evaluate this conduct? *Goldfarb* v. *Virginia State Bar,* 421 U.S. 773 (1975).
3. American Linseed Oil Co. entered into agreements with other firms in its industry whereby they would share information about pricing and customers. Each member was required to publish a list of its prices, to be distributed to all the participating firms, and to treat those prices as minimum prices. Failure to abide by your published price list subjected you to a "fine" by the members of the organization. Does this conduct violate any provision of the antitrust laws? If everyone in the industry ended up charging the same price for their products, could the government prove price fixing? What type of proof could be used to suggest the price fixing? *United States* v. *American Linseed Oil Co.,* 262 U.S. 371 (1923).
4. Two competing companies were located in separate states, one in Montana and the other in Idaho, both near the Montana-Idaho border. Most of their business came from the state governments—for road repaving during the spring, summer, and fall seasons. Since they were engaged in the same business, the owners became friends, eating lunch together about twice a week. After about three years each firm stopped bidding on jobs in the other firm's state. As a result, the profits of each firm increased significantly. Is there any chance that these owners will serve time in jail because of their business conduct? What law may have been violated and how could the violation be proved?
5. Chevrolet dealers in the Los Angeles area were all members of the same trade associations. One of the problems encountered by the dealers was the development of "discount houses," nondealers who advertised discount prices on the sale of new cars. A discount house would enter into an agreement with a consumer for the sale of a car with particular features. The discount house would next approach an authorized dealer with whom it had an established relationship and buy the car through the dealer for about eighty-five dollars over cost.

   Sales through these discount houses undermined the profitability of the dealers either by lost sales or by lower margins. Accordingly, some dealers sought to eliminate the discount houses from the market. These dealers tried to do this by persuading General Motors Corp. (GM), the manufacturer of Chevrolet automobiles, to require all dealers to agree not to deal with discount houses. GM did pressure the appropriate dealers to force them to stop working with the discount houses. Did this conduct violate any antitrust laws? If you conclude that it did violate such laws, was it illegal per se or illegal under the rule of reason? *United States* v. *General Motors Corp.,* 385 U.S. 127 (1966).

Suggested Readings

Areeda, Phillip. *Antitrust Analysis*. Chapters 1, 2, and 3. Boston: Little Brown, 1967.

Bork, R. *The Antitrust Paradox* (1978).

Rawls, John A. *A Theory of Justice*. Cambridge, Mass.: Harvard University Press, 1971.

18 Antitrust II—Vertical Relations

"The life of the law has not been logic, it has been experience."

—Oliver Wendell Holmes

LEARNING OBJECTIVES

After you have read this chapter, you should be able to:

1. Describe pricing policies that are illegal.
2. Describe how manufacturers illegally restrict a retailer's sales to particular territories and particular customers.
3. Describe when a manufacturer's control over a retailer's mix of products is illegal.

Business Decisions and the Law

Marketing Strategy

Bif owns a small corner grocery store in Atlantic City. He caters to people in the local neighborhood. His most recent problem is that a national chain just built a large supermarket about 6 blocks from his store. Because the supermarket receives quantity discounts from the sellers of items such as milk, it charges consistently lower prices for many goods than Bif does. Bif wants to maintain customer loyalty, so he plans to offer an item each week which is "HALF-OFF." This means he must often sell the product for substantially less than he paid for it. Are Bif's actions legal, or must he devise a different strategy for reacting to the new competition?

Introduction

Chapter 2 discussed the idea of epistemology, which refers to the ways one can obtain knowledge. There we identified revelation, observation (including experimentation), and reasoning as the principal epistemologies. This chapter describes a body of law that is distinguished by its instability. Even though antitrust law has enormous economic impact, it has often vacillated so sharply, over such short periods of time, that some observers have concluded that experiments are being conducted to determine the best law. As you read through this chapter, and particularly the cases, listen for the epistemology of the judges and try to classify their perspectives. Do they rely on statutory interpretation or stare decisis (revelation), or on academic literature (revelation), or on trial and error (observation), or on reasoning?

Also, you may find it useful to think about how your beliefs about compliance with the law are affected by the *legal uncertainty* described in this chapter. If the law is volatile, changing, or uncertain, does this change your obligation to follow it? If you embrace a positive law perspective, then changes are not so important in determining your conduct. If you adopt a natural law perspective, then continued change might undermine your view of the legitimacy of the written law. If, as a believer in natural law, you concluded that a law lacks legitimacy, then under what conditions would it be ethical for you to violate such a law? Could a believer in natural law violate an illegitimate law in secret? Or would there be an obligation to make the violation public? As you read through the balance of this chapter, try to decide what you *ought* to do when you believe the law is wrong.

Horizontal Relations

The distribution of goods or services can occur in a variety of ways in the marketplace. The ways in which this distribution occurs influence the antitrust laws that regulate the distribution process.

Chapter 17 discussed a variety of **horizontal relations.** *Horizontal* means that the firms are in direct competition with one another. For example, the Ford dealer and the Chrysler dealer in the same town are horizontal competitors. Recall that it is generally illegal per se for horizontal competitors to fix prices, allocate territories, or engage in group boycotts.

The principal concern of the law in regulating horizontal relationships is the preservation of **interbrand competition.** Interbrand competition is competition between two different brands of the *same* product. For example, the antitrust law described in chapter 17 ensures that competition is preserved between the local Hertz and Avis car rental agencies. This is the most fundamental objective of the antitrust laws.

Vertical Relations

In contrast with horizontal relations, there are **vertical relations.** These are relations between businesses that are engaged in the distribution of the same product down a chain that usually leads to the consumer. For example, there is a vertical relationship between Chrysler Corporation and a local Chrysler dealer in South Bend, Indiana. Chrysler Corporation manufacturers the cars, then sells them to the South Bend dealer, who resells them to consumers. Vertical relationships often involve a manufacturer, a wholesaler, and a retailer. Antitrust law regulates horizontal and vertical relations differently. It is for this reason that chapter 17 discussed horizontal relations while this chapter discusses vertical relations. You should be aware, however, that many antitrust lawsuits involve both horizontal and vertical issues.

Preservation of **intrabrand competition** is the main concern in antitrust control of vertical relations. Intrabrand competition occurs when two sellers compete to sell the same brand of product. For example, when two supermarkets in the same neighborhood try to increase sales of a single produce, such as Coke, by cutting prices, they are engaged in *intrabrand* competition. Intrabrand competition most often occurs between wholesalers or between retailers. Preserving intrabrand competition is only sometimes a goal of the antitrust laws.

In some situations a manufacturer may elect to distribute the product through *multiple* channels. When this occurs, the manufacturer must carefully balance inter- and intrabrand competition. For example, IBM might distribute its personal computers through company-owned retail stores and, in addition, through independent retailers such as Sears. In this situation, IBM's policies in dealing with Sears will influence its own total volume of sales and the allocation of this volume between its own retail operations and that of Sears. Thus IBM must choose between being very generous with Sears and increasing its own total sales (and intrabrand competition), or treating Sears more restrictively and increasing the percentage of sales through its own retail outlets, which may generate more profit per sale (and reduce intrabrand competition). If you have a solid understanding of interbrand and intrabrand competition and their impact on firms in the chain of distribution, you will be able to grasp the antitrust law governing vertical relations quite easily. Reread these last three paragraphs if you do not clearly understand the distinction between intrabrand and interbrand competition.

Pricing and Vertical Relations

Antitrust regulation of *price* is a very important topic for every potential manager because so many business persons are actively engaged in developing pricing strategies.

Sales below Cost

Financially strong businesses want to sell products for less than their cost when they face financial weak competitors. For example, a local hardware store owned by a millionaire would be tempted to temporarily cut prices below cost if its only competitor were owned by someone worth only $20,000. After both stores had lost $20,000 because of the low prices, the financially weak store would be bankrupt, while the millionaire's store would be the only one left in town. As the only store in town, the millionaire's store could easily raise prices to a point higher than those that prevailed before the price war. Since this of course would injure consumers, such **sales below cost** are illegal under both state and federal laws.

Resale Price Maintenance

Manufacturers are often motivated to influence the price at which wholesalers and retailers resell the goods. In some situations, manufacturers want to keep the retail price low. For example, manufacturers of generic grocery products would want retailers to keep their prices as low as possible to increase the product's appeal to shoppers who are very concerned with price. In contrast, a manufacturer of perfume might want its product to be resold at a higher price so that its image as an exclusive, expensive, high-quality product would be reinforced. In other instances, a manufacturer might want a high retail price for its product so that it would be a sufficiently profitable item for retailers to want to continue carrying it or want to display it prominently in their stores.

The economic problem with resale price maintenance is that it produces, with respect to a single product, the same result as horizontal price fixing. In the language of the Supreme Court.

> such vertical control destroys horizontal competition as effectively as if wholesalers formed a combination and endeavored to establish the same restrictions . . . by agreement with each other.[1]

Thus (intrabrand) competition is reduced or eliminated.

Historically, three principal mechanisms have been used by firms to control resale prices. These are fair trade laws, refusal to deal tactics, and consignments.

Fair Trade Laws

In 1911 the United States Supreme Court ruled in the *Dr. Miles* case that *contracts* to establish resale prices were illegal per se under section 1 of the Sherman Act. By 1935, wholesalers had begun convincing state legislatures that contracts creating **resale price maintenance** were socially desirable because interbrand price rivalry would protect the interests of consumers even if there were no intrabrand price rivalry. That is, these lobbyists argued that the inter-

1. *California Retail Liquor Dealers Association* v. *Midcal Aluminum* 445 U.S. 97 (1970).

brand rivalry between Maytag and Whirlpool would lower prices even if all Maytag dealers were required—by a resale price maintenance contract—to sell the Maytags at the same price. States responded to this argument by enacting statutes called **fair trade laws,** which allowed *intrastate* sales agreements to implement resale price maintenance. Thus Maytag could require all retailers in California to sell for no less than $600 per unit. By 1937, the lobbying efforts resulted in passage by Congress of the Miller-Tydings Act which, as amended, legalized resale maintenance in *interstate* commerce and in effect invalidated the *Dr. Miles* decision.

Some retailers sought to take advantage of the vacuum created by uniform high prices for many branded products. One tactic used by high volume retailers was to simply ignore the contract, lower prices, and assume that the supplier would not risk losing the high volume retailer as an outlet for its products. In many instances this proved to be both effective and quite profitable. In effect these retailers used market power to evade liability for breaching a contract. What do you think of such tactics?

Eventually, because of this and similar tactics, only a small percentage of products being sold remained fair-traded items. This, and the realization that intrabrand competition generates significant benefits to consumers, caused Congress to repeal Miller-Tydings. As a result, nearly all resale price maintenance contracts were eliminated. Thus, the *Dr. Miles* decision again became (and is now) the federal law. Many states also repealed their fair trade laws.

Refusals to Deal

Resale price maintenance must involve an agreement or contract—for example, between a manufacturer and a retailer—establishing resale prices. As we have stated, *Dr. Miles* made that illegal. However, in the absence of a resale price maintenance *contract* or agreement, a manufacturer can tell retailers that there will be no future sales if the product is sold below a suggested price. This is called **refusal to deal.** The major refusal to deal case, *United States* v. *Colgate,* was decided in 1919. The Colgate Company sent to dealers of its products letters and telegrams showing uniform prices and giving notice that future sales would be suspended for those failing to adhere to the prices. The United States Supreme Court ruled that such a plan did not violate the Sherman Act.

Later, in *Beach Nut,* the Court ruled that, without the existence of a contract, the Sherman Act was violated when the manufacturer went beyond mere announcements and refusals to deal. Like Colgate, Beach Nut refused to sell to wholesalers who sold to retailers violating the announced pricing policy. But in addition Beach Nut would reinstate an offending retailer if the retailer gave assurances of compliance with the policy. The effect of these policies was, in the Court's view, the same as a contract, and thus the conduct was declared illegal. Today, if a manufacturer, in its relationship with a retailer or wholesaler, "steps over the line" established by *Colgate,* then resale price maintenance occurs.

The *Colgate* line can be stepped over when a manufacturer either acts alone or in concert with some of its wholesalers or retailers. Alone, a manufacturer can illegally compel a retailer to *agree* to allow the manufacturer to set the price. A *conspiracy or combination* between a manufacturer and some of its retailers can arise for example when they conspire to terminate a price cutting retailer. The following case describes such a situation.

Monsanto v. Spray-Rite

465 U.S. 752 (1984)

Facts

Monsanto manufactures a variety of chemicals used by farmers to protect their crops from insects. Spray-Rite, a wholesaler, bought these products from Monsanto and resold them to retailers. Spray-Rite charged lower prices that some of Monsanto's other wholesalers. Because of this, the other wholesalers complained to Monsanto about Spray-Rite's pricing. Shortly after the complaints, Monsanto terminated Spray-Rite as a distributor. Spray-Rite sued Monsanto, alleging that it was terminated because it refused to participate in a conspiracy, among Monsanto and its wholesalers, to set prices, in violation of Section 1 of the Sherman Act.

Opinion

Justice Powell: This Court has drawn two important distinctions that are at the center of this and any other distributor-termination case. First, there is the basic distinction between concerted and independent action—a distinction not always clearly drawn by parties and courts. Section 1 of the Sherman Act requires that there be a "contract, combination . . . or conspiracy" between the manufacturer and other distributors in order to establish a violation. Independent action is not proscribed. A manufacturer of course generally has a right to deal, or refuse to deal, with whomever it likes, as long as it does so independently. *United States* v. *Colgate & Co.* Under *Colgate,* the manufacturer can announce its resale prices in advance and refuse to deal with those who fail to comply. And a distributor is free to acquiesce in the manufacturer's demand in order to avoid termination.

The second important distinction in distributor-termination cases is that between concerted action to set prices and concerted action on nonprice restrictions. The former have been *per se* illegal since the early years of national antitrust enforcement. The latter are judged under the rule of reason, which requires a weighing of the relevant circumstances of a case to decide whether a restrictive practice constitutes an unreasonable restraint on competition. See *Continental T.V., Inc.* v. *GTE Sylvania, Inc.*

While these distinctions in theory are reasonably clear, often they are difficult to apply in practice. . . . [T]he legality of arguably anticompetitive conduct should be judged primarily by its "market impact." But the economic effect of all of the conduct described above—unilateral and concerted vertical price-setting, agreements on price and nonprice restrictions—is, in many, but not all, cases similar or identical. And judged from a distance, the conduct of the parties in the various situations can be indistinguishable. For example, the fact that a manufacturer and its distributors are in constant communication about prices and marketing strategy does not alone show that the distributors are not making independent pricing decisions. A manufacturer and its distributors have legitimate reasons to exchange information about the prices and the reception of their products in the market. Moreover, it is precisely in cases in which the manufacturer attempts to further a particular marketing strategy by means of agreements on often costly nonprice restrictions that it will have the most interest in the distributors' resale prices. The manufacturer often will want to ensure that its distributors earn sufficient profit to pay for programs such as hiring and training additional salesmen or demonstrating the technical features of the product, and will want to see that "free-riders" do not interfere. Thus, the manufacturer's strongly felt concern about resale prices does not necessarily mean that it has done more than the *Colgate* doctrine allows.

Nevertheless, it is of considerable importance that independent action by the manufacturer, and concerted action on nonprice restrictions, be distinguished from price-fixing agreements, since under present law the latter are subject to *per se* treatment and treble damages. On a claim of concerted price-fixing, the antitrust plaintiff must present evidence sufficient to carry its burden of proving that there was such an agreement. If an inference of such an agreement may be drawn from highly ambiguous evidence, there is a considerable danger that the doctrines enunciated in *Sylvania* and *Colgate* will be seriously eroded.

The flaw in the evidentiary standard adopted by the Court of Appeals in this case is that it disregards this danger. Permitting an agreement to be inferred merely from the existence of complaints, or even from the fact that termination came about "in response to" complaints, could deter or penalize perfectly legitimate conduct. As Monsanto points out, complaints about price-cutters "are natural—and from the manufacturer's perspective, unavoidable—reactions by distributors to the activities of their rivals." Such complaints, particularly where the manufacturer has imposed a costly set of nonprice restrictions, "arise in the normal course of business and do not indicate illegal concerted action." Moreover, distributors are an important source of information for manufacturers. In order to assure an efficient distribution system, manufacturers and distributors constantly must coordinate their activities to assure that their product will reach the consumer persuasively and efficiently. To bar a manufacturer from acting solely because the information upon which it acts originated as a price complaint would create an irrational dislocation in the market. In sum, "[t]o permit the inference of concerted action on the basis of receiving complaints alone and thus to expose the defendant to treble damage liability would both inhibit management's exercise of independent business judgment and emasculate the terms of the statute."

Thus, something more than evidence of complaints is needed. There must be evidence that tends to exclude the possibility that the manufacturer and nonterminated distributors were acting independently. [T]he antitrust plaintiff should present direct or circumstantial evidence that reasonably tends to prove that the manufacturer and others "had a conscious commitment to a common scheme designed to achieve an unlawful objective."

***

Applying this standard to the facts of this case, we believe that there was sufficient evidence for the jury reasonably to have concluded that Monsanto and some of its distributors were parties to an "agreement" or "conspiracy" to maintain resale prices and terminate price-cutters. In fact there was substantial *direct* evidence of agreements to maintain prices. There was testimony from a Monsanto district manager, for example, that Monsanto on at least two occasions in early 1969, about five months after Spray-Rite was terminated, approached price-cutting distributors and advised that if they did not maintain the suggested resale price, they would not receive adequate supplies of Monsanto's new corn herbicide. When one of the distributors did not assent, this information was referred to the Monsanto regional office, and it complained to the distributor's parent company. There was evidence that the parent instructed its subsidiary to comply, and the distributor informed Monsanto that it would charge the suggested price. Evidence of this kind plainly is relevant and persuasive as to a meeting of minds.

***

If, as the courts below reasonably could have found, there was evidence of an agreement with one or more distributors to maintain prices, the remaining question is whether the termination of Spray-Rite was part of or pursuant to that agreement. It would be reasonable to find that it was, since it is necessary for competing distributors contemplating compliance with suggested prices to know that those who do not comply will be terminated. Moreover, there is some circumstantial evidence of such a link. Following the termination, there was a meeting between Spray-Rite's president and a Monsanto official. There was testimony that the first thing the official mentioned was the many complaints Monsanto had received about Spray-Rite's prices. In addition, there was reliable testimony that Monsanto never discussed with Spray-Rite prior to the termination the distributorship criteria that were the alleged basis for the action. By contrast, a former Monsanto salesman for Spray-Rite's area testified that Monsanto representatives on several occasions . . . approached Spray-Rite, informed the distributor of complaints from other distributors—including one major and influential one—and requested that prices be maintained. Later that same year, Spray-Rite's president testified, Monsanto officials made explicit threats to terminate Spray-Rite unless it raised its prices.

We conclude that the Court of Appeals applied an incorrect standard to the evidence in this case. The correct standard is that there must be evidence that tends to exclude the possibility of independent action by the manufacturer and distributor. That is, there must be direct or circumstantial evidence that reasonably tends to prove that the manufacturer and others had a conscious commitment to a common scheme designed to achieve an unlawful objective. ***

Affirmed.

Case Questions

1. Exactly what conduct by Monsanto caused its actions to become illegal?
2. Would the termination by Monsanto without the complaints have been illegal?
3. How do you judge the moral character of Monsanto's actions in dismissing Spray-Rite simply because competitors of Spray-Rite objected to its pricing policies? What marketplace goal is displayed by Monsanto: material well-being for itself, for society, service, or personal liberty? What goal motivated the other retailers?

Consignment

A *consignment* occurs when someone such as a manufacturer gives possession, *but not ownership,* of a product to another (such as a retailer) with the intent that the retailer will act as an agent in causing the sale. Since the manufacturer owns the goods, it seems logical that he should be able to specify the price at which they may be sold. While this may be logical, the United States Supreme Court ruled in *Simpson* v. *Union Oil Co.* (1964) that the *form* of such a transaction ought not to be allowed to disguise its *substance*. That substance is resale price maintenance, and thus it is illegal per se when conducted on a large scale.

Price Discrimination

In 1914 Congress passed the Clayton Act, which, among other things, made **price discrimination** illegal. The relevant language is:

> Section 2. (a) . . . it shall be unlawful for any person engaged in commerce . . . to discriminate in price between different purchasers of commodities of like grade and quality . . . where the effect of such discrimination may be substantially to lessen competition.

Congress enacted clarifying legislation in 1936 called the Robinson-Patman Act. This amended the Clayton Act by describing the major forms of price discrimination and giving detailed descriptions of the defenses to charges of price discrimination. The single paragraph on price discrimination in the original 1914 version of the Clayton Act was expanded by Robinson-Patman to six paragraphs dealing with the following concepts:

1. Price discrimination is illegal when it lessens competition.
2. It is illegal to implement price discrimination disguised as any of the following:
   a. Commissions or discounts
   b. Contracts for services and facilities
   c. Preferential methods of payment
3. After a showing of different prices, the burden of proof shifts to the defendant to show that the different prices are justified on the basis of the costs of manufacture, sale, or delivery.
4. It is unlawful to induce knowingly or receive discriminatory prices.
5. Price discrimination between geographic areas where the purpose is to destroy competition is illegal.
6. Selling at unreasonably low prices to destroy competition is illegal.

Part of the motivation for passing Robinson-Patman was that some firms were concealing their price discrimination by granting a commission to one subsidiary for sales to another subsidiary of the same company. Fictitious payments for services were also used in this fashion in an attempt to sidestep the Clayton Act.

Subsequent case law has made it clear that there are two major types of price discrimination and two defenses that make certain forms of price discrimination legal. The two types of discrimination, which we will describe in detail, are called *primary line injury* and *secondary line injury*. The two defenses are *cost justification* and the *meeting competition* justification.

Primary Line Injury

In some instances, it is profitable for a strong business to sell its products to different customers at different prices to drive weak competitors out of a market. Like sales below cost, this strategy is based on the reality that in a long price war, the rich competitor can outlast the poor competitor. For example, a wealthy national brewery might try to penetrate a regional market by reducing its prices in that region below the prices it charges in the rest of the country. If this drove local brewers out of business, thereby reducing the number of competitors in that market, the national brewer's volume of sales would probably increase. In effect, the national brewery might have used its high prices in the national market to subsidize its low prices in the regional market. This does great injury to the local competitors and is called **primary line injury.**

The elements of primary line injury are:

1. Charging different prices to different customers . . .
2. . . . when the prices vary from one market or geographic region to another . . .
3. . . . with the result that your competitors in some markets or geographic areas are injured by the discriminatory prices.

Figure 18.1 Primary and Secondary Line Injury

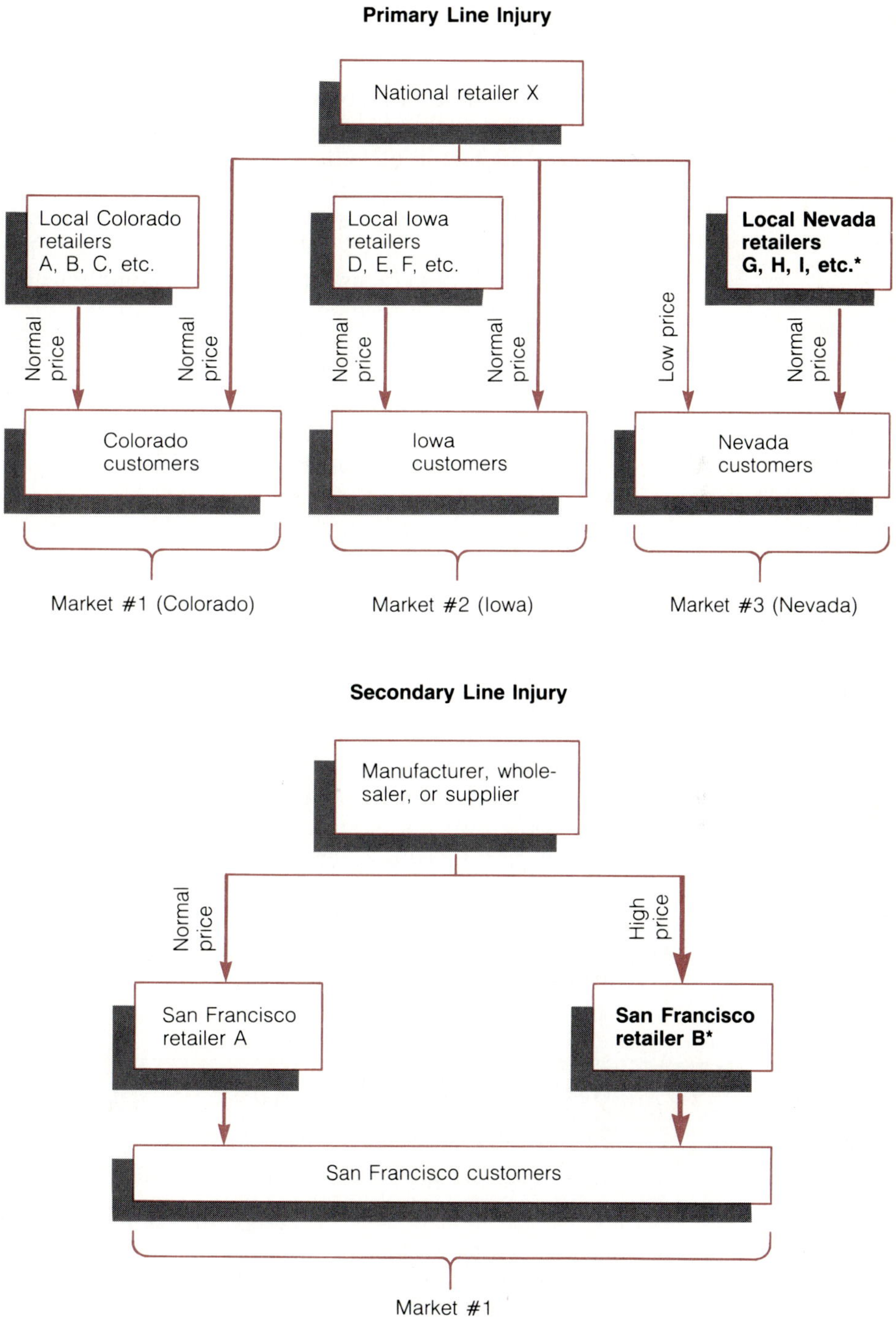

*These are the parties most immediately injured by the price discrimination.

Primary line injury is illegal because it is a tactic by which a wealthy competitor tries to destroy competition by *temporarily* reducing prices.

Secondary Line Injury

Often, businesses such as large retailers try to use their market power, or their influence with wholesalers or manufacturers, to achieve an advantage over smaller competing retailers. For example, a chain of auto repair shops, such as Firestone, might approach the suppliers of a brand name of sparkplugs, such as Champion, and ask them to charge higher prices to those few independent auto repair businesses located near Firestone's shops in a particular city. Since Firestone probably purchases substantially more sparkplugs than the independents, Champion would be under pressure to comply with Firestone's request. If it failed to respond, Firestone might shift to Autolite sparkplugs. If Firestone charged different prices it would cause **secondary line injury.**

The problem with allowing such secondary line injury is that it gives the large, powerful retailer a competitive advantage based on market power rather than on the quality of its service to consumers.

The elements of secondary line injury are:

1. Charging different prices to different customers . . .
2. . . . when the prices vary *within* one market so that customers in competition with each other pay different prices for your product . . .
3. . . . with the result that one of your *customers* is injured.

In primary line injury, your price discrimination injures your *competitor,* while in secondary line injury, the price discrimination injures one of your *customers*. Figure 18.1 presents a visual representation of the differences between primary and secondary line injury.

Note that both primary and secondary price discrimination are only illegal if their effect is "to lessen competition." It is clear that driving one of your regional competitors out of business lessens competition. Similarly, if your discriminatory prices drive a weak customer out of business, the competition among your customers is lessened. But, as the following case illustrates, this *degree* of injury is not necessary. As you read through the case, try to think about the economic motives of the defendants. Their conduct portrays a fairly typical pattern of price discrimination.

Utah Pie Co. v. ***Continental Baking Co.***

386 U.S. 685 (1967)

Facts

This suit for treble damages was brought by Utah Pie Company against Continental Baking Company, Carnation Company, and Pet Milk Company. The complaint charged violations of section 2(a) of the Clayton Act as amended by the Robinson-Patman Act. The jury found for Utah Pie on the price discrimination charge.

The product involved is frozen dessert pies. The period covered by the suit comprised the years 1958, 1959, and 1960 and the first eight months of 1961. Petitioner is a Utah corporation which for thirty years had been baking pies in its plant in Salt Lake City and selling them in Utah and surrounding states. It entered the frozen pie business in late 1957. Utah Pie's share of this market in those years was 66.5%, 34.3%, 45.5% and 45.3%, respectively, its sales volume steadily increasing over the four years. Its financial position also improved. Petitioner is not, however, a large company.

Each of the defendants is a large company and each of them is a major factor in the frozen pie market in one or more regions of the country. Each entered the Salt Lake City frozen pie market before petitioner began freezing dessert pies. None of them had a plant in Utah. They sold primarily on a delivered price basis.

The major competitive weapon in the Utah market was price. The location of petitioner's plant gave it natural advantages in the Salt Lake City marketing area and it entered the market at a price below the then going prices for defendant's comparable pies. For most of the period involved here, Utah Pie's prices were the lowest in the Salt Lake City market. It was, however, challenged by each of the defendants at one time or another and for varying periods. There was ample evidence to show that each of the defendants contributed to what proved to be a deteriorating price structure over the period covered by this suit, and each of the defendants in the course of the ongoing price competition sold frozen pies in the Salt Lake market at prices lower than it sold pies of like grade and quality in other markets considerably closer to its plants.

Opinion

Justice White: Petitioner's case against Continental is not complicated. . . . Effective for the last two weeks of June it offered its 22-ounce frozen apple pies in the Utah area at $2.85 per dozen. It was then selling the same pies at substantially higher prices in other markets. The Salt Lake City price was less than its direct cost plus an allocation for overhead. . . . Utah's going price at the time . . . was $3.40 per dozen.

The Court of Appeals concluded that Continental's conduct had had only minimal effect, that it had not injured or weakened Utah Pie as a competitor, that it had not substantially lessened competition and that there was no reasonable possibility that it would do so in the future.

We differ with the Court of Appeals. Its opinion that Utah [Pie] was not damaged as a competitive force apparently rested on the fact that . . . [Utah Pie's] sales volume continued to climb in 1961. . . . But this retrospective assessment fails to note that Continental's discriminatory below-cost price caused Utah Pie to reduce its price to $2.75. The jury was entitled to consider the potential impact of Continental's price reduction absent any responsive price cut by Utah Pie. . . . The jury could rationally have concluded that had Utah not lowered its price, Continental, which repeated its offer once, would have continued it. . . . It could also have reasonably concluded that a competitor who is forced to reduce his price to a new all-time low in a market of declining prices will in time feel the financial pinch and will be a less effective competitive force. . . .

Section 2(a) does not forbid [all] price competition. . . . But Congress has established some ground rules for the game. Sellers may not sell like goods to different purchasers at different prices if the result may be to injure competition in either the sellers' [primary line] or the buyers' [secondary line] market unless such discriminations are justified as permitted by the Act. This case concerns the sellers' market. In the context, the Court of Appeals placed heavy emphasis on the fact that Utah Pie constantly increased its sales volume and continued to make a profit. But we disagree with its apparent view that there is no reasonably possible injury to competition as long as the volume of sales in a particular market is expanding and at least some of the competitors in the market continue to operate at a profit. Nor do we think that the Act only comes into play to regulate the conduct of price discriminators when their discriminatory prices consistently undercut other competitors. It is true that many of the primary line cases that have reached the courts have involved blatant predatory price discriminations employed with the hope of immediate destruction of a particular competitor. On the question of injury to competition such cases present courts with no difficulty, for such pricing is clearly within the heart of the proscription of the Act. Courts and commentators alike have noted that the existence of predatory intent might bear on the likelihood of injury to competition. In this case there was some evidence of predatory intent with respect to each of these [defendants]. There was also other evidence upon which the jury could rationally find the requisite injury to competition. . . . We believe that the Act reaches price discrimination that erodes competition as much as it does price discrimination that is intended to have immediate destructive impact. In this case, the evidence shows a drastically declining price structure which the jury could rationally attribute to continued or sporadic price discrimination. The jury was entitled to conclude that "the effect of such discrimination," by each of these [defendants], "may be substantially to lessen competition . . . or to injure, destroy, or prevent competition with any person who either grants or knowingly receives the benefit of such discrimination. . . ."

Case Questions

1. Could Continental be liable for anything besides price discrimination?
2. In what way does Continental's behavior injure consumers?
3. In what other ways could Continental compete with Utah Pie?

Defenses to Price Discrimination

If a difference in price is caused by differences in the cost of delivery, or the cost of sale, or the cost to manufacture a product, then the resulting discriminatory prices are not illegal. For example, a refiner might sell gasoline for a low price to gas stations located near the refinery and for a much higher price to gas stations located farther away. If the difference in price is caused by the difference in the cost of shipping, it will be legal. Similarly, a woodworking shop might charge significantly different prices for custom-manufactured doors depending upon the quantity ordered. A builder ordering 20 doors might be legally charged double the unit price charged a competing builder who orders 150 similar doors. But the price difference must be caused by the difference in the *unit cost* of manufacturing 20 as opposed to 150 doors. Thus if the unit cost of the 20 doors were $125 each and the unit cost of 150 doors were $75 each, a price difference of $50 could be justified.

If a difference in price is caused by a good faith response to a competitor's price, it is not illegal. This is called **meeting competition.** Thus a national retailer could charge $3.00 per dozen for frozen pies in Colorado and Nevada and $2.50 per dozen in Utah *if* the lower price was set because a Utah competitor was charging $2.50. This would not, however, justify any price lower than $2.50.

Vertical Control of Customers and Territories

Just as manufacturers or wholesalers sometimes desire to control price, they also sometimes desire to control the retailer's territory or the customers to whom retailers can sell. By limiting the territories of retailers, the manufacturer can reduce intrabrand competition, perhaps allowing retailers to charge higher prices. This may cause the retailers to try harder to sell manufacturer's product. Customer restrictions are most frequently imposed when the manufacturer desires to sell directly to certain customers, such as governmental agencies or big industrial users because of their large-volume purchases.

Like fair trade laws, the history of vertical control of customers and territory has been inconsistent. At first, vertical nonprice restrictions were tested under the rule of reason. In *United States* v. *Schwinn* (1967), however, the Supreme Court ruled that vertical restrictions on customers and territories were illegal per se. Schwinn sold its bicycles through independent retail outlets. It contracted with these dealers to restrict the territories in which the dealers could sell. The Court concluded in *Schwinn* that these policies injured consumers by eliminating intrabrand competition. Ten years later, the Court again reversed itself with the landmark decision *Continental* v. *GTE Sylvania* (1977), which follows. In this case the Court weighed and described the interaction between intrabrand competition and interbrand competition. As you read through the case, try to grasp the economic motives behind Sylvania's treatment of its retailers. Also try to assess the ultimate impact of this conduct on consumers.

Continental T.V., Inc. v. GTE Sylvania, Inc.

433 U.S. 36 (1977)

Facts

Respondent GTE Sylvania, Inc. (Sylvania) manufactures and sells television sets through its Home Entertainment Products Division. Prior to 1962, like most other television manufacturers, Sylvania sold its televisions to independent or company-owned distributors [wholesalers] who in turn resold to a large and diverse group of retailers. Prompted by a decline in its market share to a relatively insignificant 1 to 2 percent of national television sales, Sylvania conducted an intensive reassessment of its marketing strategy, and in 1962 adopted the franchise plan challenged here. Sylvania phased out its wholesale distributors and began to sell its televisions directly to a smaller and more select group of franchised retailers. An acknowledged purpose of the change was to decrease the number of competing Sylvania retailers in the hope of attracting the more aggressive and competent retailers thought necessary to the improvement of the company's market position. To this end, Sylvania limited the number of franchises granted for any given area and required each franchisee to sell his Sylvania products only from the location or locations at which he was franchised. A franchise did not constitute an exclusive territory, and Sylvania retained sole discretion to increase the number of retailers in an area in light of the success or failure of existing retailers in developing their market. The revised marketing strategy appears to have been successful during the period at issue here, for by 1965 Sylvania's share of national television sales had increased to approximately 5 percent, and the company ranked as the nation's eighth largest manufacturer of color television sets.

Opinion

Justice Powell: This suit is the result of the rupture of a franchiser-franchisee relationship that had previously prospered under the revised Sylvania plan.

Most important for our purposes was the claim that Sylvania had violated §1 of the Sherman Act by entering into and enforcing franchise agreements that prohibited the sale of Sylvania products other than from specified locations. . . .

In answers to special interrogatories, the jury

found that Sylvania had engaged "in a contract, combination or conspiracy in restraint of trade in violation of the antitrust laws with respect to location restrictions alone," and assessed Continental's damages at $591,505, which was trebled . . . to produce an award of $1,774,515.

On appeal, the Court of Appeals for the Ninth Circuit . . . reversed. . . . The court acknowledged that there is language in *Schwinn* that could be read to support the District Court's instruction but concluded that *Schwinn* was distinguishable on several grounds. Contrasting the nature of the restrictions, their competitive impact, and the market shares of the franchisers in the two cases, the court concluded that Sylvania's location restriction had less potential for competitive harm than the restrictions invalidated in *Schwinn* and thus should be judged under the "rule of reason" rather than the per se rule stated in *Schwinn.*

Both Schwinn and Sylvania sought to reduce but not to eliminate competition among their respective retailers through the adoption of a franchise system. . . . These restrictions allowed Schwinn and Sylvania to regulate the amount of competition among their retailers [intrabrand competition by preventing a franchisee from selling franchised products from outlets other than the one covered by the franchise agreement.

Since its announcement, *Schwinn* has been the subject of continuing controversy and confusion, both in the scholarly journals and in the federal courts. The great weight of scholarly opinion has been critical of the decision, and a number of the federal courts confronted with analogous vertical restrictions have sought to limit its reach.

. . . The traditional framework of analysis under § 1 of the Sherman Act is familiar and does not require extended discussion. Section 1 prohibits "[e]very contract, combination . . . or conspiracy, in restraint of trade or commerce." Since the early years of this century a judicial gloss on this statutory language has established the "rule of reason" as the prevailing standard of analysis. *Standard Oil Co.* v. *United States,* 221 U.S. 1 (1911). Under this rule, the factfinder weighs all of the circumstances of a case in deciding whether a restrictive practice should be prohibited as imposing an unreasonable restraint on competition. *Per se* rules of illegality are appropriate only when they relate to conduct that is manifestly anticompetitive. . . .

The market impact of vertical restrictions is complex because of their potential for a simultaneous *reduction* of intrabrand competition and *stimulation* of intrabrand competition [emphasis added]. . . .

Vertical restrictions reduce intrabrand competition by limiting the number of sellers of a particular product competing for the business of a given group of buyers. Location restrictions have this effect because of practical constraints on the effective marketing area of retail outlets. Although intrabrand competition may be reduced, the ability of retailers to exploit the resulting market may be limited both by the ability of consumers to travel to other franchised locations, and, perhaps more importantly, to purchase the competing products of other manufacturers.

Vertical restrictions promote interbrand competition by allowing the manufacturer to achieve certain efficiencies in the distribution of his products. These "redeeming virtues" are implicit in every decision sustaining vertical restrictions under the rule of reason. Economists have identified a number of ways in which manufacturers can use such restrictions to compete more effectively against other manufacturers. For example, new manufacturers and manufacturers entering new markets can use the restrictions in order to induce competent and aggressive retailers to make the kind of investment of capital and labor that is often required in the distribution of products unknown to the consumer. Established manufacturers can use them to induce retailers to engage in promotional activities or to provide service and repair facilities necessary to the efficient marketing of their products. Service and repair are vital for many products, such as automobiles and major household appliances. The availability and quality of such services affect a manufacturer's goodwill and the competitiveness of his product.

Economists also have argued that manufacturers have an economic interest in maintaining as much intrabrand competition as is consistent with the efficient distribution of their products.

The question remains whether the *per se* rule stated in *Schwinn* should be . . . abandoned in favor of a return to the rule of reason . . . widely used in our free market economy. Certainly, there has been no showing in this case, either generally or with respect to Sylvania's agreements, that vertical restrictions have a "pernicious effect on competition" or that they "lack . . . any redeeming virtue." Accordingly, we conclude that the *per se* rule stated in *Schwinn* must be overruled. . . .

In sum, . . . the . . . decision is to return to the rule of reason that governed vertical restrictions prior to *Schwinn.*

Case Questions

1. What ultimate impact will Sylvania's conduct have on consumers of color televisions?
2. Do Sylvania's policies injure Continental? Which group is more important in antitrust decisions—consumers, or retailers such as Continental?
3. Given the legal uncertainty surrounding nonprice vertical restrictions, was it unethical for Sylvania to engage in this conduct? Note that at the time in question *Schwinn* was the law enunciated by the United States Supreme Court, and under *Schwinn* Sylvania's conduct was illegal per se.

Vertical Control of Products

Manufacturers often desire to compel their retailers to handle the manufacturer's other products. For example, IBM would undoubtedly like to compel those who purchase its computers to also buy its typewriters. If it were able to do this it would have what is called a *tying agreement.* In other instances, manufacturers want retailers to carry only their brand of a product and not to carry competing brands. Thus Coke might like to compel grocery stores to carry only Coke and not Pepsi. More realistically, RCA might try to pressure small TV stores into carrying RCA exclusively. If successful, this would establish an *exclusive dealings arrangement.*

Tying Agreements

In general, a **tying agreement** exists when you refuse to sell one product except on the condition that the buyer also purchase another product. In a classic tying agreement case, International Salt Company developed and patented machines for dispensing salt into the tin cans used for food products such as tomato soup. When it leased the patented machines it required that its salt be used in the machines. The United States Supreme Court ruled this tying agreement to be illegal per se. It concluded that International Salt was using the tying agreement to extend the competitive advantage of its machine patents into a competitive advantage in the salt business.

Today the court still views tying agreements as highly suspect. While the language of per se illegality is frequently used in tying cases, an action appears to be illegal per se only when some type of market power—perhaps flowing from a patent or large market share—is associated with one of the products. The requirements for finding a per se tying agreement are the following.

1. *Two separate products must be tied.* Whether products are separate is sometimes difficult to decide. Thus a new car includes many features that some consumers may not desire, such as air conditioning or tinted

windows. One guide used by courts in determining whether products are separate is whether they are offered separately by others in the market. So the tinted windows would probably not be considered a separate product.

2. *The seller must have market power.* Suppose a local grocery store required that you buy a gallon of milk in order to purchase bread at a low sale price. Clearly these are separate products. But this would not be per se illegal because the grocery stores typically have no market power. They don't have a patent or large market share and you can buy bread and milk in many other places.

Tying agreements which do not meet these tests can be evaluated under the rule of reason test.

The Technology Defense

The courts will allow a tying agreement when its purpose is clearly to preserve technical performance. For example, if International Salt's salt had been substantially purer, and use of competing salt would injure the patented machines, perhaps the Court would have allowed the tying agreement.

Tying and Franchise

A **franchise** is a contract in which a franchisor gives a franchisee the right to use a trademark and a system of doing business. Burger King and Wendy's are examples of franchises. Each store is operated by a local investor using the trademark and business system provided by the franchisor. Frequently the franchise contract requires the franchisee to buy certain products from the franchisor. Accordingly, franchise agreements typically involve tying. In partial response to the franchise movement, Congress enacted the federal trademark law, called the Lanham Act. In part, the act sought to encourage franchises by requiring that franchisors exercise control over the quality of trademarked goods. This statutory obligation in the trademark law opens the legal door for franchisors to tie products to their trademarks. Thus franchise agreements tend to occupy a special place in antitrust law.

The following case illustrates the way tying agreements are analyzed in the context of franchising. As you read through the case, draw on your own knowledge and experience, and try to determine whether challenged conduct by McDonald's is ultimately good or bad for the consuming public.

Principe v. McDonald's Corp.

631 F.2d 303 (1980)

Facts

This appeal presents the question of whether a fast food franchise that requires its licensees to operate their franchises in premises leased from the franchisor is guilty of an illegal tying arrangement in violation of Section 1 of the Sherman Act.

Opinion

The . . . Principes . . . are franchisees of McDonald's hamburger restaurant[s] in Hopewell, Virginia, . . . [and] in Colonial Heights. . . .

They filed this action . . . alleging . . . McDonald's violated federal antitrust laws by tying store leases and $15,000 security deposit notes to the franchise rights at the Hopewell and Colonial Heights stores. . . .

McDonald's is not primarily a fast food retailer. While it does operate over a thousand stores itself, the vast majority of the stores in its system are operated by franchisees. Nor does McDonald's sell equipment or supplies to its licensees. Instead its primary business is developing and collecting royalties from limited menu fast food restaurants operated by independent business people.

McDonald's develops new restaurants according to master plans . . . and . . . uses demographic data generated by the most recent census and its own research in evaluating potential sites. . . .

After the specifics of each proposed new restaurant are approved, McDonald's decides whether the store will be company operated or franchised. If the decision is to franchise the store, McDonald's begins the process of locating a franchisee. . . .

McDonald's acquires the land, either by purchase or long-term lease, and constructs the store. Acquisition and development costs averaged over $450,000 per store in 1978. All McDonald restaurants bear the same distinctive features with a few exceptions due to architectural restrictions: the golden arches motif, the brick and glass construction and the distinctive roofline. According to the defendants, these features identify the stores as a McDonald's even where zoning restrictions preclude other advertising or signs.

As constructed, McDonald's restaurants are finished shells; they contain no kitchen or dining room equipment. Furnishing store equipment is the responsibility of the operator. . . .

Having acquired the land, begun construction of the store, and selected an operator, McDonald's enters into two contracts with the franchisee. Under the first, the franchise agreement, McDonald's grants the franchisee the rights to use McDonald's food preparation system and to sell food products under the McDonald's name. The franchisee pays a $12,500 franchise fee and agrees to remit three percent of his gross sales as a royalty in return. Under the second contract, the lease, McDonald's grants the franchisee the right to use the particular store premises to which his franchise pertains. In return, the franchisee pays a $15,000 refundable security deposit (as evidence of which he receives a twenty-year non-negotiable non-interest-bearing note) and agrees to pay eight and one half percent of his gross sales as rent.

The Principes argue McDonald's is selling not one but three distinct products, the franchise, the lease, and the security deposit note. The alleged antitrust violation stems from the fact that a prospective franchisee must buy all three in order to obtain the franchise.

As evidence that this is an illegal tying arrangement, the Principes point to the unfavorable terms on which the franchisees are required to lease their stores. Not only are franchisees denied the opportunity to build equity and depreciate their property, but they must maintain the building, pay for improvements and taxes, and remit 8.5 percent of their gross sales as rents. In 1978 the gross sales of the Hopewell store generated about $52,000 in rent. That figure nearly equalled McDonald's original cost for the site and corresponds to more than a fourth of the original cost of the entire Hopewell restaurant complex. At that rate of return, the Principes argue, McDonald's will have recouped its entire investment in four years and the remainder of the lease payments will be pure profit. The Principes contend that the fact the store rents are so high proves that McDonald's cannot sell the leaseholds on their own merits.

A separate tied product is the note that evidences the lessee's $15,000 security deposit, according to the appellants.

McDonald's responds that it is not in the business of licensing use of its name, improving real estate for lease, or selling long-term notes. Its only business is developing a system of hamburger restaurants and collecting royalties from their sales. The allegedly tied products are but parts of the overall bundle of franchise benefits and obligations. According to McDonald's the appellants are asking the court to invalidate the way McDonald's does business and to require it to adopt the licensing procedures of its less successful competitors. Federal antitrust laws do not compel such a result, McDonald's contends. . . .

As support for their position, the Principes rely primarily on the decision of the Ninth Circuit in *Siegel* v. *Chicken Delight, Inc.,* one of the first cases to address the problem of franchise tie-ins. Chicken Delight was what McDonald's characterizes as a "rent a name" franchisor: it licensed franchisees to sell chicken under the Chicken Delight name but did not own store premises or fixtures. The company did not even charge franchise fees or royalties. Instead, it required its franchises to purchase a specified number of cookers and fryers and to purchase certain packaging supplies and mixes exclusively from Chicken Delight. These supplies were priced higher than comparable goods of competing sellers. A class composed of franchisees challenged the tying arrangements as a violation of the Sherman Act. The district court held for the franchisees and Chicken Delight appealed.

In addressing Chicken Delight's argument that the allegedly tied products all were essential components of the franchise system, the Ninth Circuit looked to the "function of the aggregation." Viewing the essence of a Chicken Delight franchise as the franchisor's trademark, the court sought to determine whether requiring franchisees to purchase common supplies from Chicken Delight was necessary to ensure that their operations lived up to the quality standards the trademark represented. In the court's view, Chicken Delight had attempted to "extend trademark protection to common articles (which the public does not and has no reason to connect with the trademark)," a classic kind of illegal tying arrangement.

The Principes urge this court to apply the *Chicken Delight* reasoning to invalidate the McDonald's franchise lease note aggregation. They urge that McDonald's can protect the integrity of its trademarks by specifying how its franchisees shall operate, where they may locate their restaurants and what types of buildings they may erect. Customers do not and have no reason to connect the building's owner with the McDonald's operation conducted therein. Since company ownership of store premises is not an essential element of the trademark's goodwill, the Principes argue, the franchise, lease and note are separable products tied together in violation of the antitrust laws. In *Philips* v. *Crown Central Petroleum Corporation,* this court . . . noted that "the very essence of a franchise is the purchase of several related products in a single competitively attractive package." Franchising has come a long way since the decision in *Chicken Delight.*

Without disagreeing with the result in *Chicken Delight,* we conclude that the Court's emphasis in that case upon the trademark as the essence of a franchise is too restrictive. Far from merely licensing franchisees to sell products under its trade name, a modern franchisor such as McDonald's offers its franchisees a complete method of doing business. It is often unrealistic to view a franchise agreement as little more than a trademark license.

Given the realities of modern franchising, we think the proper inquiry is not whether the allegedly tied products are associated in the public mind with the franchisor's trademark, but whether they are integral components of the business method being franchised. Where the challenged aggregation is an essential ingredient of the franchised system's formula for success, there is but a single product and no tie-in exists as a matter of law.

First, because it approaches the problem of restaurant site selection systematically, McDonald's is able to obtain better sites than franchisees could select. Armed with its demographic information, guided by its staff of experts and unencumbered by preferences of individual franchisees, McDonald's can wield its economic might to acquire sites where new restaurants will prosper without undercutting existing franchisees' business or limiting future expansion.

Second, McDonald's policy of owning all of its own restaurants assures that the stores remain part of the McDonald's system. McDonald's franchise arrangements are not static: franchisees retire or die; occasionally they do not live up to their franchise obligations and must be replaced; even if no such contingency intervenes, the agreements normally expire by their own terms after twenty years. If franchisees owned their own stores, any of these events could disrupt McDonald's business and have a negative effect on the system's goodwill. Buildings whose architecture identified them as former McDonald's stores would sit idle or be used for other purposes. Replacement franchisees would have to acquire new and perhaps less desirable sites, a much more difficult and expensive process after the surrounding business area has matured. By owning its own stores, McDonald's assures its continued presence on the site, maintains the store's patronage even during management changes and avoids the negative publicity of having former McDonald's stores used for other purposes. By preserving the goodwill of the system in established markets, company store ownership produces attendant benefits for franchisees.

Finally, because both McDonald's and the franchisee have a substantial financial stake in the success of the restaurant, their relationship becomes a sort of partnership that might be impossible under other circumstances. McDonald's spends close to half a million dollars on each new store it establishes. Each franchisee invests over $100,000 to make the store operational. Neither can afford to ignore the other's problems, complaints or ideas. Because its investment is on the line, the Company cannot allow its franchisees to lose money. This being so, McDonald's works with its franchisees to build their business, occasionally financing improvements at favorable rates or even accepting reduced royalty payments in order to provide franchisees more working capital.

All of these factors contribute significantly to the overall success of the McDonald's system. The formula that produced systemwide success, the formula that promises to make each new McDonald's store successful, that formula is what McDonald's sells its franchisees. To characterize the franchise as an unnecessary aggregation of separate products tied to the McDonald's name is to miss the point entirely. Among would-be franchisees, the McDonald's name has come to stand for the formula, including all that it entails. We decline to find that it is an illegal tie-in.

Case Questions

1. Has McDonald's engaged in tying?
2. Has this tying helped or hurt the consuming public?
3. What is motivating the Principes to bring this suit?

Exclusive Dealings Arrangements

In general, an individual manufacturer would prefer that retailers who carry its product not carry competing products. Thus Toro, the lawnmower manufacturer, might desire that retailers who carry its line not carry Honda lawnmowers. This benefits Toro in several ways. First, it causes the retailer to focus intently on displaying, advertising, selling, and servicing Toro products. Second, it denies Honda and other lawnmower manufacturers access to some retail outlets. This is likely to increase Toro's market share and to decrease the shares of its competitors. Such **exclusive dealings arrangements** are only workable when the manufacturer has some substantial market power. Thus if a very small local lawnmower manufacturer, which does not advertise its product, asked its retailers not to carry competing products, they would probably decline; stocking only one unknown brand would diminish the retailer's appeal to the consuming public. Exclusive dealings arrangements tend to benefit large, well-known firms and to injure new, small firms.

In 1985 the Department of Justice issued guidelines that indicate when it, but not necessarily the courts, will find that there has been an illegal exclusive dealings agreement. The factors weighed by the Department of Justice include the following.

1. The seller's market is concentrated, i.e., there are few firms in the industry, and the leading firms use exclusive dealings contracts.
2. Those buyers, subject to the exclusive dealings arrangement, control a large portion of their market.
3. Entry into the buyers' or sellers' market is difficult.

The presence of these factors indicates that an exclusive dealings contract will be challenged by the Department.

In response to exclusive dealings arrangements, Congress passed section 3 of the Clayton Act, which makes it illegal to:

> lease or make a sale . . . of . . . commodities, whether patented or unpatented . . . on the condition, agreement or understanding that the lessee or purchaser thereof shall not use or deal in the . . . commodities of a competitor . . . of the lessor or seller, where the effect of such . . . [arrangement] may be to substantially lessen competition or tend to create monopoly in any line of commerce.

The language of the act makes the conduct illegal only when the consequence is to "substantially lessen competition." The courts have ruled that this occurs when the manufacturer has a large market share.

After initially establishing *de facto* per se illegality for exclusive dealings contracts for those with substantial market power, the Court retreated to its current position, which treats these cases in ways more similar to the rule of reason case-by-case examination.

Refusal to Sell

Recall that the *Colgate* decision allows a firm to announce a price list and refuse to deal with those who fail to follow it. Similarly, firms can announce a policy of selling only to those retailers who carry its product exclusively and can refuse to sell to those who violate the policy. As long as the firm doesn't step over the line established by *Colgate,* this tactic allows a large market share firm to accomplish the same end that is illegal when achieved by direct contractual agreement. Should, in your opinion, the *means* used to accomplish the end—that is, an exclusive dealings arrangement—determine whether the end is legal or illegal?

Vertical Mergers

When one organization in the chain of distribution acquires another firm in the chain that handles the same product or product line, then a vertical merger has occurred. For example, if Schwinn purchased a chain of retail bicycle shops, this would be a forward vertical merger. Similarly, if Sears purchased a furniture manufacturer, this would be a backward vertical merger.

Section 7 of the Clayton Act makes illegal anticompetitive vertical mergers. Whether or not a particular vertical merger is anticompetitive depends upon a number of factors. The major factor considered by the courts is the degree of *foreclosure*. This refers to the amount of the geographic and product markets that are controlled by the merged companies. Thus if Schwinn, by the purchase of one hundred retail shops in Florida, were able to thereby control 70 percent of all retail sales of bicycles in that market, this would undoubtedly violate section 7 because it would allow Schwinn to "foreclose" other bicycle manufacturers from selling as effectively in the Florida retail market. On the other hand, if Schwinn were only able to control 5 percent of the retail market, this would in all likelihood not violate section 7.

The courts recognize a legitimate business interest in securing outlets for products or services by vertical merger. They also acknowledge a legitimate business interest in securing certain supplies, such as furniture for Sears, via vertical merger. But when the degree of foreclosure is large, the anticompetitive effects are considered to outweigh the legitimate business interests, so the merger is illegal.

Ethical Issues in Antitrust—Vertical Relations

In this chapter we have described a very important but very volatile area of the law. The changes that characterize this field make it difficult for business persons to be certain that they know the law and can forecast the direction of its evolution. The rule of reason test adds to this uncertainty, at least in comparison to the per se test. And note that the most recent trend has been to reduce the applications of per se illegality and expand the application of the rule of reason. Should this uncertainty, and the frequent changes, affect how you comply with antitrust laws? How do you assess the conduct of Sylvania? During at least part of the time they operated their distribution system, the law of this land, as articulated in *Schwinn,* made that system illegal. Yet when they fought their case all the way to the United States Supreme Court, they won. And they changed the law. Were they wise or just lucky? Was their conduct ethical?

The important concepts and terms in this chapter are listed below; page numbers have been provided for the key terms. By reading over each section you can assess your understanding of the chapter concepts and determine areas you may want to review.

Chapter Summary

1. Antitrust laws regulate both horizontal and vertical relations. Horizontal relations exist between competitors, while vertical relations exist between sellers and buyers of the same product, such as manufacturers, wholesalers, and consumers.

2. *Inter*brand competition occurs between different brands. *Intra*brand competition occurs between sellers of the same brand.
3. Sales below cost violate both state and federal laws.
4. Resale price maintenance in interstate commerce is illegal unless it is implemented simply by a refusal to deal.
5. Price discrimination causes primary line injury when it injures your competitors. It violates section 2 of the Clayton Act.
6. Price discrimination causes secondary line injury when it injures one of your customers. It also violates section 2 of the Clayton Act.
7. Price discrimination is legal if it is justified by either the cost defense or the meeting competition defense.
8. The rule of reason is used to test the legality of vertical control of customers or territory.
9. Tying agreements by those with substantial market power are illegal per se.
10. *Contracts* for goods that create exclusive dealing arrangements may violate section 3 of the Clayton Act.
11. Exclusive dealings arrangements can be legal if they are implemented simply by a refusal to deal.
12. The history of antitrust law's control of vertical relations is full of trial-and-error approaches to creating law.

Key Terms

exclusive dealings arrangement 523
fair trade law 508
franchise 520
horizontal relations 505
interbrand competition 505
intrabrand competition 506
meeting competition 516
price discrimination 511
primary line injury 512
refusal to deal 508
resale price maintenance 507
sales below cost 507
secondary line injury 514
tying agreement 519
vertical relations 506

Questions on Ethics

1. Suppose you earn spare money in college by operating a service that pays some students to take notes in classes so other students, who pay for the notes, can concentrate completely on the lectures. Assume you built the business to the point where it generated $500 per month for you. At that point another student started a competing service. Suppose you know that the student had to generate a profit in the first month or

quit and take a job as a bus boy in a restaurant. Assuming it is legal and profitable, would it be ethical for you to reduce your price to drive this competitor out of business? Why or why not? Would consumers be better or worse off if you engaged in this type of price competition? Would it make a difference how much you reduced your price?

2. Suppose your company decided to implement a legal resale price maintenance plan by using refusal to deal. Your supervisor explained the plan to you and assured you of its legality. Suppose that he also described to you ways to implement the plan by "crossing the line" established by *Colgate,* but without generating evidence of the illegal conduct. If this action were discretionary—you would earn an extra $15,000 per year if you did it but would suffer no career injury if you declined—should you do it? Why or why not?
3. Assume that you are an influential member of a city council and the owner of a profitable drycleaning store in a small town. If someone owns property and is considering building a competing drycleaning store on the site, should you use your influence to change the zoning for the site from commercial to residential if that would eliminate your competitor? Why or why not?
4. Suppose your firm operates in a country where black persons are denied basic civil rights. Assume that you are your firm's sales manager for the country. If that country had a law that required you to treat your black employees unfairly, would you do so? If you decided to violate the law, would you do so in secret or publicly? Why or why not?
5. Suppose the United States enacted a law that required you to discriminate against members of the opposite sex in making hiring decisions. Would it be right for you to comply with this law? Why or why not? If you elected to violate the law, would it be ethical for you do so in public or in private?

Questions on Law

1. Suppose you own a small convenience grocery store. Your principal competitor is located two blocks away. This competitor consistently advertises certain staples, such as bread and milk, at prices lower than the price you have paid for these items. A local bakery and a dairy supply the items and you suspect they are charging your competitor the same price they charge you. Your competitor simply elects to take a loss on these items to draw customers to his store. Is his conduct illegal?
2. Parke Davis sold pharmaceutical drugs to five wholesalers who resold to about 360 drugstores in the Washington, D.C., and Richmond, Virginia, areas. The Parke Davis Catalog, distributed to both wholesalers and retailers, announced a resale price maintenance policy. One spring,

several druggists started advertising Parke Davis vitamins at prices below the suggested minimum retail price. Thereafter, the branch manager for Parke Davis put into effect a program for promoting observance of the suggested minimum retail prices by the retailers involved. In order to insure that retailers who did not comply would be cut off from sources of supply, representatives of Parke Davis visited the wholesalers and told them, in effect, that not only would Parke Davis refuse to sell to wholesalers who did not adhere to the policy announced in its catalog, but also that it would refuse to sell to wholesalers who sold Parke Davis products to retailers who did not observe the suggested minimum retail prices. Each wholesaler was interviewed individually, but each was informed that his competitors were also being apprised of this. The wholesalers without exception indicated a willingness to go along.

At the same time, representatives called upon the retailers involved, individually, and told each of them that if they did not observe the suggested minimum retail prices, Parke Davis would refuse to deal with them, and that furthermore they would be unable to purchase any Parke Davis products from the wholesalers. Each of the retailers was also told that his competitors were being similarly informed.

Is the conduct of Parke Davis legal? *United States* v. *Parke Davis and Co.,* 363 U.S. 29 (1960).

3. Klor's, Inc., was a small appliance store in downtown San Francisco. It was located next door to a Broadway-Hale store, part of a large chain of department stores. The two stores competed in the sales of radios, television sets, refrigerators, and other household appliances. However, General Electric, RCA, Admiral, Zenith, Emerson, and other manufacturers conspired among themselves and with Broadway-Hale either not to sell to Klor's or to sell only at prices higher than those charged Broadway-Hale. Does any conduct described here violate the antitrust laws? Which conduct violates which law? *Klor's, Inc.* v. *Broadway-Hale Stores,* 359 U.S. 207 (1959).
4. Anheuser-Busch is a beer producer with national sales. In the St. Louis, Missouri, market it competes with local brewers such as Falstaff and Greesedieck Brothers Brewing Company. Generally, Anheuser-Busch charged a higher price than its regional competitors, traditionally about 58 cents more per case of beer. However, it began cutting its price in the St. Louis market to the point where its price was lower there than in any other market. While Anheuser-Busch did substantially reduce its price, the price never fell below that charged by the regional competitors. Has Anheuser-Busch engaged in price discrimination? What type—primary or secondary? Are there any defenses available to Anheuser-Busch? *F.T.C.* v. *Anheuser-Busch, Inc.,* 363 U.S. 536 (1960).
5. Assume that you own a motorcycle shop selling motorcycles priced from \$600 to \$8,000. A local manufacturer has developed a cheap, bottom-of-

the-line cycle that would sell for $600. It would compete with Honda and Kawasaki. This manufacturer has asked you to sell and service his bike. It is appealing because the profit margin on the local bikes is about three times as great as those of established lines. The local manufacturer does not yet have even 1 percent of the market for motorcycles in that price range. To ensure that you fully promote and service the new motorcycle, the manufacturer wants you to sign a contract promising not to carry competing motorcycles in that price category. Does this contract violate the antitrust laws?

Suggested Readings

Blair, Roger D., and Kaserman, David L. *Antitrust Economics*. Homewood, Ill.: Richard D. Irwin, 1985.

Posner, Richard A. *Economic Analysis of Law*. Boston: Little, Brown, 1977.

Schwartz, Louis B., Flynn, John J., and First, Harry. *Free Enterprise and Economic Organization: Antitrust*. St. Paul: Foundation Press, 1985.

19 Securities Regulations I

[N]either this Court nor Congress has ever suggested that investor protection was the sole purpose of the Securities Act. . . . Prevention of frauds against investors was surely a key part of that program, but so was the effort to achieve a high standard of business ethics . . . in every facet of the securities industry.

—United States *v.* Naftalin, *99 U.S. 2077 (1979)*

■ LEARNING OBJECTIVES

After you have read this chapter, you should be able to:

1. Define securities and understand when their issuance is regulated by the federal government or the states.
2. Explain the procedures involved in public and private securities offerings.
3. Understand securities regulations as an attempt by the government to insure high standards of business ethics in the securities industry.
4. Understand when an investment contract is a security.

Business Decisions and the Law

Is the Offering to Sell a Condominium a Security within the Federal Security Law?

Could a Hawaiian resort condominium be a security so as to subject it to the registration and other requirements of the Securities Act of 1933?

Gerald Hocking of Las Vegas, Nevada, decided after a trip to Hawaii, to purchase a condominium there as an investment. He found an acceptable condominium in a complex developed by Aetna Life Insurance Company. Upon purchasing the unit, Hocking made an agreement whereby an agent managed the condominium. His profits were pooled with those of the other unit owners and then he shared pro rata in the pool's income and expenses.

The buyer, Gerald Hocking, did indeed find himself the owner of a security. Simple real estate transactions are generally not considered securities transactions. However, in this instance there was an added expectation of profits from a common enterprise. The Securities and Exchange Commission is acutely aware of the expanding resort condominium market and takes the view that a condominium is *automatically* a security if offered in connection with a rental pool agreement. (See page 534 for the court's decision of the Hocking case.)

This chapter will assist you in understanding when an "investment contract" is a security and will explain the laws that regulate securities exchanges like the New York Stock Exchange. The United States Supreme Court has stated that securities regulation is an effort by the government to achieve a high standard of business ethics in every facet of the securities industry. This chapter will explore various aspects of the securities industry as the business environment in which corporations and their investors operate.

As a citizen of corporate America, you will probably be a security owner. A **security** may be a stock, bond, or other document showing an interest in the company that is owned by an investor. Perhaps you will inherit stocks from your parents or you may work for a large corporation and own securities in the company pension plan that will provide for your retirement. Many corporations offer employee stock option plans that will permit you to purchase company stock at favorable rates. You may decide to "play the market" and follow the prices of stock in the *Wall Street Journal* or on a daily cable TV stock market broadcast. Part of your financial planning will include a life insurance policy whose premiums will be invested by the company in the securities market. The college providing you with your education and degree, although a nonprofit organization, is very likely an investor in the securities market. No wonder the United States Supreme Court insists upon a high standard of business ethics for the securities industry!

Why do you think the Supreme Court is concerned with a high standard of business ethics? Let's examine a security—for instance, a share of common stock—as a thing of value. Suppose you incorporated a business to sell computer software. In the articles of incorporation that you file with the secretary of state's office, you would indicate the amount of stock you will be authorized to issue. For example, if in your articles of incorporation you state ten thousand shares, you will be authorized to sell up to ten thousand shares of common stock representing equal units of ownership in the company. The value of that stock depends upon your persuasive powers to convince investors of the company's potential profitability; value also depends on the stock's voting rights and the value of the company's assets upon liquidation. The unusual thing about a stock security is that it represents value in something other than itself, namely, the profitability of the issuing company. So you can easily imagine the temptation to exaggerate, and indeed misrepresent, the value of the computer software stock that you are offering for sale to a potential investor.

Unlike securities, most items that you purchase are not resold but rather are used until they are obsolete or defective. But securities in publicly owned corporations are resold *(traded)* so often that it was necessary to create exchanges, such as the New York Stock Exchange (NYSE) and the over-the-counter (OTC) market, to handle the number and volume of old and newly created securities. Federal statutes regulate the *interstate* sale of Securities.

The state securities laws, known as **blue sky laws,** regulate *intrastate* security transactions so long as the state laws do not contradict federal securities law. They are called blue sky laws because an early Supreme Court decision described their purpose as "laws to prevent speculative schemes which have no more basis than so many feet of blue sky." Federal securities acts specifically allow the states to regulate securities. Hence, securities transactions may be subject to state blue sky laws as well as federal securities laws. State securities laws commonly provide for the registration of broker/dealers and the registration of securities to be offered for sale in the state. In an attempt to standardize state securities laws, thirty states have adopted the Uniform Securities Act of 1956.

History of Securities Laws

Securities laws, the Securities and Exchange Commission, and the Federal Reserve Bank work together to control stock speculation and set margin requirements on the purchase of stock to prevent a recurrence of the stock market crash of October 29, 1929, known as Black Tuesday.

The Prohibition days of the 1920s were not lacking for social and financial excitement. The airplane industry, brought to the forefront by the publicity that accompanied Charles Lindbergh's first trans-Atlantic flight, was rapidly developing. Radios and other household utilities were becoming a booming industry. The government assumed a passive role in this era of plentiful money. An easy money policy was encouraged by the Federal Reserve Bank, which allowed member banks to borrow money at 5 percent and lend in the market at 12 percent. President Calvin Coolidge left office in 1929 without predicting any economic problems. About 3 percent of our population had annual incomes over \$10,000 and were considered wealthy. Most American families had no savings, and incomes between \$3,000 and \$10,000 were considered adequate. Many who had money to invest purchased stock with only 10 percent down; by using the stock as collateral, the investors could borrow the balance from their brokers, who would obtain loans from commercial banks. If the investor defaulted on the loan and the stock *decreased* in value, the broker might be forced to default on his loan from the bank.

Within this environment, speculators in the stock market could make fortunes with unethical conduct. The bubble burst on October 29, 1929, followed by the worst market decline in 1931 and 1932. After the 1929 crash many banks failed as brokers defaulted on their bank loans. A national panic developed as people rushed to the banks to withdraw their savings, resulting in additional bank failures. Deposits were not insured, and many people lost their lifetime savings. The Dow Jones industrials hit a record low of 42 on July 8, 1932, and the country was ready when Congress reacted with strong remedial legislation, the Securities Act of 1933 and the Securities Exchange Act of 1934.

Definition of a Security

A **security** is given a very broad definition under section 2(1) of the 1933 act.

> The term "security" means any note, stock, treasury stock, bond, debenture, evidence of indebtedness certificate of interest or participation in any profit-sharing agreement, collateral trust certificate or subscription, transferable share, investment contract, voting-trust certificate, certificate of deposit for a security, fractional undivided interest in oil, gas, or other mineral rights, or, in general, any interest or instrument commonly known as a "security," or any certificate of interest or participation in, temporary or interim certificate for, receipt for, guaranty of, or warrant or right to subscribe to or purchase, any of the foregoing.

Although you may think of a security as a share of stock or a bond, the statutory definition indicates a much broader perspective.

As you can see from a careful reading of the act's definition, the language includes various types of financial instruments. Since the act's adoption the courts have liberally construed the term *security* to include such investments as franchises and condominiums. A leading United States Supreme Court case, *SEC* v. *Howey,* 328 U.S. 293 (1946), established the criteria for the existence of an "investment contract." Howey, the defendant company, owned large tracts of citrus acreage in Florida. It offered half of the citrus groves to out-of-state investors by way of a land sales contract and a service contract to cultivate the groves. Howey was given authority to cultivate, harvest, and market the crops for the investor and allocated the profits on their behalf. The Supreme Court found all the elements of a profit-seeking business venture and the presence of a "security" as an investment contract. The court stated "The investors provide the capital and share in the earnings and profits; the promoters manage, control and operate the enterprise. . . . The test is whether the scheme involves an investment in money in a common enterprise with profits to come solely from the efforts of others."

In the following case the court applied the *Howey* criteria to an offer to sell a condominium unit with an option to participate in a rental pool agreement in order to determine if it constituted an "investment contract" under the security laws.

Hocking v. Dubois

839 F. 2d 560 (9th Cir. 1988)

Facts

Gerald Hocking visited Hawaii and became interested in buying a condominium there as an investment. When he returned to his home in Las Vegas, he made this known to a co-worker whose wife, Maylee Dubois, was a licensed real estate agent in Hawaii. A meeting was arranged between Hocking and Dubois. Subsequently, Dubois agreed to help Hocking find a suitable unit. Dubois found a condominium unit owned by Tovik and Yaacov Liberman that was for sale. The unit was located in a resort complex developed by Aetna Life Insurance Company ("Aetna"). As a part of the original development, Aetna had offered purchasers an opportunity to participate in a rental pool arrangement ("RPA"). In arranging the sale of the Libermans' condominium, Dubois advised Hocking of the availability of the rental pool arrangement. Hocking purchased the condominium unit . . . [and] . . . entered into a rental management agreement with Hotel Corporation of the Pacific ("HCP") and a rental pool agreement. It appears that HCP performed management services at the option of the condominium purchasers. Hocking subsequently filed suit alleging violations of the antifraud provisions of the Securities Exchange Act of 1934. We also review de novo *the district court's determination whether a transaction is a security.*

Opinion

Circuit Judge Reinhardt: The term "security" is defined in section 2 of the Securities Act of 1933, and in section 3 of the Securities Exchange Act of 1934. The sections, which are substantially identical, define a security to include any "investment contract." However, the definition is not a static one. Congress cast it "in sufficiently broad and general terms so as to include within that definition the many types of instruments that in our commercial world fall within the ordinary concept of a security." It embodies a flexible principle "capable of adaptation to meet the countless and variable schemes devised by those who seek the use of the money of others on the promise of profits." Generally, simple transactions in real estate, without more, do not satisfy the [*SRC* v. *Howey*] criteria. When a purchaser is motivated exclusively by a desire to occupy or develop the land personally, no security is involved. Real estate transactions may involve an offer to securities when an investor is offered both an interest in real estate and a collateral expectation of profits. However, drawing the line between the offering of land sales contracts and investment contracts has not been easy. To resolve this difficulty, at least in the area of condominiums, the Securities and Exchange Commission issued guidelines in 1973 on the applicability of federal securities laws to the burgeoning resort condominium market. In Release 5347, the Commission states unequivocally that it will view a condominium as a security if it is *offered* with the "offering of participation in a rental pool arrangement." . . . The offering of a condominium with an RPA *automatically* makes the investment a security. Even apart from the guidelines, we find that under the three *Howey* criteria an offer of a condominium with an RPA constitutes an offer of an investment contract.

1. *Investment of Money.* Hocking invested money in the condominium.
2. *Common Enterprise.* We define common enterprise as a venture in which the "fortunes of the investor are interwoven with and dependent upon the efforts and success of those seeking the investment of third parties." Horizontal commonality describes a common enterprise among several investors, while vertical commonality describes a common enterprise between the investor and the seller, promoter or some other party. A rental pool arrangement creates horizontal commonality with other parties involved in the RPA. If Dubois' offer to sell the condominium did not include the option of joining the RPA, then Hocking's investment in the condominium would be his alone and not an investment in a common venture. In

the absence of other investors, there would be no horizontal commonality and it would be proper to move on to an examination of the vertical relationship involved. But, as we have noted earlier, we assume for purposes of this opinion that the offer of a condominium to Hocking did include an offer of an option to enter an RPA. Accordingly, horizontal commonality exists. It is readily apparent that an RPA for condominiums is a common enterprise. Each investor buys one share—a condominium—in a common venture that pools the rents from all of the units. The success of each participant's individual investment clearly depends on the entire RPA's success.

3. *Expectation of Profits Produced by Others' Efforts.* We conclude that this requisite is met whenever a condominium is sold with an RPA option. This is what the Commission has done in its guidelines for condominiums. The SEC and its advisory committee recognized the wisdom of having a rule that would make the sale of all the condominiums in a particular condominium development subject to the securities laws or would exclude the sale of all those units—regardless of the fortuity of the individual economic expectations of the particular buyer. A rule correctly notes that, under some circumstances, a real estate offering can constitute an "investment contract" and thus a "security" within the meaning of the federal security laws.

Case Questions

1. The issue in this case is whether an "investment contract" was offered to Hocking. Why did the court hold the three *Howey* criteria were satisfied?
2. The Securities and Exchange Commission guidelines on the applicability of federal securities laws to condominiums views its offerings as securities if accompanied by a rental pool agreement. What is the legal theory supporting that position?
3. Is it ethical to find an investment contract when the buyers purchased a parcel of real estate with an option to enroll in the developers' rental pool?

Securities and Exchange Commission

The SEC was created under the authority of the Securities Exchange Act of 1934. Any company that issues securities (the *issuer*) and makes a public interstate offer must file with the SEC a **registration statement** that consists of a prospectus and other financial/managerial information. It is unlawful to sell the securities in interstate commerce until the SEC approves the registration statement, unless there is a statutory exemption from the requirement to file. By accepting the registration statement, the SEC neither approves the offering nor guarantees that the disclosures made by the issuing company are accurate. It is the investor who must make an informed evaluation of the value of the security and the risks involved. But false information filed with the SEC subjects the issuing company, its directors and officers, and others who sign the registration statement to a fine, imprisonment, or both.

National securities exchanges, utility holding companies, investment trusts, and investment advisors must also register with the SEC. Brokers and dealers of over-the-counter securities must also register with the SEC. The SEC is located in Washington, D.C., and has nine regional offices.

Securities Act of 1933 and Initial Public Offerings

The Securities Act of 1933 requires that *all* securities, unless exempted by statute, be registered before being sold to the public so that investors can obtain certain information, which can be found in the registration statement (see figure 19.1). For example, if you want to sell stock in a new computer company, you must provide a **prospectus** that has been approved by the SEC. A prospectus will provide the following information:

1. certified financial statements by a public accounting firm,
2. a history of the company,
3. the experience of the managerial team, and
4. the use and purpose of the offering.

Other information and financial exhibits about the corporation need not be furnished in the prospectus but are available for public inspection at the Securities and Exchange Commission offices.

Once the buyer reviews the prospectus and evaluates its merit, an intelligent decision can be made about the risks of the investment. Keep in mind that approval of the prospectus by the SEC is not an indication that the security is a good investment.

Filing Process

"Going public" is an expensive undertaking. If you are the owner of a small business that wants to sell its stock to the public, you will hire a securities lawyer and a certified public accountant (CPA) to prepare the registration statement and an **underwriter** who will sell your stock to a **dealer** before it is sold to the public. An underwriter is a person or organization that will purchase securities from your company with a view to offering or selling them on your behalf. A dealer is a person who buys and sells securities for his own account. Depending upon the offering amount, the fees can easily run over $100,000.

The **filing process** consists of (1) the pre-filing period, (2) the waiting period, and (3) the post-effective period. Certain legal prohibitions attach to each period. For example, after your securities lawyer and CPA have completed the registration statement, it is signed by the corporate president, a majority of the board of directors, and the chief financial and accounting officer. The document is then filed with the SEC in Washington, D.C., and unless rejected, it becomes effective twenty days after filing.

Pre-Filing Period

During the **pre-filing period,** that is, the time before the registration statement is filed, you may negotiate with an underwriter regarding the underwriter's purchase of your stock. The stock may not be offered to dealers during the pre-filing period.

Figure 19.1 Form S-1 Registration Statement (Front Page)

SECURITIES AND EXCHANGE COMMISSION
Washington, D.C. 20549

FORM S-1
REGISTRATION STATEMENT
Under
THE SECURITIES ACT OF 1933

CONSOLIDATED COMPANY
(Exact name of registrant as specified in its charter)

New Jersey	0400 2010	04-1234567
(State or other jurisdiction of incorporation or organization)	(Primary Standard Industrial Classification Code Numbers)	(I.R.S. Employer Identification Number)

123 Berry Boulevard
New York, N.Y. 10020
(212) 555-2000
(Address, including zip code, and telephone number, including area code, of registrant's principal executive offices)

CLARK CARAWAY, ESQ.
Vice President, General Counsel and Secretary
Consolidated Company
123 Berry Boulevard
New York, N.Y. 10020
(212) 555-2106
(Name, address, including zip code, and telephone number, including area code, of agent for service)

Copies to:

LARRY LAW, ESQ.	TOM TEMPLAR, ESQ.
Attorney & Law	Templar & Templar
30 Legal Circle	80 Barrister Boulevard
New York, New York 10112	New York, New York 10005

Approximate date of commencement of proposed sale to the public: As soon as practicable after the effectiveness of this Registration Statement.

If any of the securities on this Form are to be offered on a delayed or continuous basis pursuant to Rule 415 under the Securities Act of 1933 check the following box. ☐

CALCULATION OF REGISTRATION FEE

Title of each class of securities to be registered	Amount to be registered	Proposed maximum offering price per unit	Proposed maximum aggregate offering price	Amount of registration fee
% Senior Subordinated Debentures due January 15, 1999.	$75,000,000	$1,000	$75,000,000	$15,000

The Registrant hereby amends this Registration Statement on such date or dates as may be necessary to delay its effective date until the Registrant shall file a further amendment which specifically states that this Registration Statement shall thereafter become effective in accordance with Section 8(a) of the Securities Act of 1933 or until this Registration Statement shall become effective on such date as the Commission, acting pursuant to said Section 8(a), may determine.

From Weinstein, Stanley, Daniel Schaechtman, and Michael A. Walter, *SEC Compliance—Financial Reporting Forms,* Vol. 3. © 1984 Mann/Judd/Landau. Reprinted by permission of Prentice-Hall, Inc.

Waiting Period and the Preliminary Prospectus

The stock of your issuing company may be verbally offered to the public, but not sold, during the **waiting period,** the time between the filing of a registration statement with the SEC and its effective date. However, an advance notice of the stock sale as commonly found in the *Wall Street Journal* is allowed. This is referred to as a **tombstone ad** (see figure 19.2).

If the offering price of the stock and other information is omitted in a notice of the stock offering prior to the effective date, a legend must be printed in red on the preliminary prospectus. This legend is referred to as a **red herring notice.** The waiting period has special importance, because the SEC will require a written statement from the underwriter that all prospective purchasers have been mailed a **preliminary prospectus,** which is a prospectus made available in advance of the offering. A preliminary prospectus must also be provided to all salespersons by their dealers and to any customer upon written request.

Post-Effective Period

Your registration statement will automatically become effective twenty days after filing with the SEC, unless delayed or rejected by the commission. At that time your underwriters may sell the **registered securities** to the dealers who will probably resell them to the public. Generally, a prospectus must be given to each buyer in every initial interstate security sale.

Exemptions from the Securities Act of 1933

The Securities Act of 1933, in certain restricted circumstances, allows exemptions from the formal registration process. The act exempts certain kinds of *transactions* and certain kinds of *securities*. In view of the time and expense involved in "going public," it is important to recognize the more common exemptions.

Exempt Transactions

Intrastate Offerings. SEC Rule 147 provides that the offering will be considered "intrastate" if no resales are made to nonresidents of the state for a period of at least nine months after the completed sale. The issuing company must be a resident doing business within the state where the securities are sold and the buyers must be residents within that state. This exemption presumes that state securities laws are sufficient to protect the investors.

Regulation D. The SEC in 1982 adopted **Regulation D,** which consists of Rules 501 to 506 exempting some private stock offerings from the formal registration process. For example under Rule 504 a issuer may sell up to $500,000 worth of stock in any twelve-month period without providing any information to the buyers. Keep in mind that state securities laws may require state registration and may require that a disclosure document be given to the buyer. Under Rule 505 you may sell up to $5 million worth of stocks in any twelve-month period

Figure 19.2 Announcement of a Stock Offering by Underwriters

This is neither an offer to sell nor a solicitation of an offer to buy these securities. The offer is made only by the Prospectus and the related Prospectus Supplement.

NEW ISSUE

January 11, 1985

800,000 Shares

IPALCO Enterprises, Inc.

Common Stock

(without par value)

Price $33 per Share

Copies of the Prospectus and the related Prospectus Supplement may be obtained in any State in which this announcement is circulated only from such of the underwriters as may lawfully offer these securities in such State.

Kidder, Peabody & Co. Incorporated

Lehman Brothers Shearson Lehman/American Express Inc.

Merrill Lynch Capital Markets

Bear, Stearns & Co. — The First Boston Corporation — Alex. Brown & Sons Incorporated
Dillon, Read & Co. Inc. — Donaldson, Lufkin & Jenrette Securities Corporation — Drexel Burnham Lambert Incorporated
Goldman, Sachs & Co. — E. F. Hutton & Company Inc. — Lazard Frères & Co.
Morgan Stanley & Co. Incorporated — PaineWebber Incorporated — Prudential-Bache Securities
L. F. Rothschild, Unterberg, Towbin — Salomon Brothers Inc — Smith Barney, Harris Upham & Co. Incorporated
Thomson McKinnon Securities Inc. — Wertheim & Co., Inc. — Dean Witter Reynolds Inc.
A. G. Edwards & Sons, Inc. — Advest, Inc. — Robert W. Baird & Co. Incorporated — Blunt Ellis & Loewi Incorporated
K. J. Brown & Company, Inc. — City Securities Corporation — Collett & Company, Inc.
J. J. B. Hilliard, W. L. Lyons, Inc. — Ladenburg, Thalmann & Co. Inc. — McDonald & Company Securities, Inc.
Moseley, Hallgarten, Estabrook & Weeden Inc. — Prescott, Ball & Turben, Inc.
Raffensperger, Hughes & Co. Incorporated — Traub and Company, Inc. — Tucker, Anthony & R. L. Day, Inc.
Boettcher & Company, Inc. — J. C. Bradford & Co. Incorporated — Dain Bosworth Incorporated — R. G. Dickinson & Co.
Doft & Co., Inc. — First of Michigan Corporation — Gruntal & Co., Incorporated
Headford & Company Incorporated — Janney Montgomery Scott Inc. — Jesup & Lamont Securities Co., Inc.
Edward D. Jones & Co. — Josephthal & Co. Incorporated — Legg Mason Wood Walker Incorporated
Moore & Schley Capital Corporation — Newhard, Cook & Co. Incorporated — David A. Noyes & Company
The Ohio Company — Parker/Hunter Incorporated — Piper, Jaffray & Hopwood Incorporated — Roney & Co.
Scherck, Stein & Franc, Inc. — Stifel, Nicolaus & Company Incorporated — Wheat, First Securities, Inc.

to as many as thirty-five nonaccredited investors and an unlimited number of **accredited investors,** and your offering will still be considered private. Rule 501 defines *accredited investor* as any bank, insurance company, investment company, pension plan, charitable or educational institution, director, officer, or general partner of the issuer, a person who purchases at least 150,000 of the securities offered, or an investor with a net worth of more than $1 million or an annual income of more than $200,000. You can see that the SEC is taking a public policy position protecting only the casual investor from a stock sale that does not go through the formal registration process. It is understood that institutions and individuals defined as accredited investors are in a financial position to afford their own professional advisors who will assist them in evaluating the investment risks.

If there are *any* nonaccredited investors, generally the information provided in the formal registration statement must be furnished to all the investors.

Under Rule 506 you could sell an unlimited amount of stock to any number of accredited investors and up to thirty-five nonaccredited investors, so long as the nonaccredited purchaser is a knowledgeable or experienced business person capable of evaluating the investment risk.

Regulation A. The so-called **Regulation A** offering is very popular with the small-business segment of our economy as an exemption for public offerings. It is a simplified version of registration for smaller offerings. If your company's sales of its securities during any twelve-month period did not exceed $1.5 million, it would qualify for the Regulation A exemption. Your first step would be to file with the SEC regional office closest to your company an **offering statement,** also called an offering circular, at least 10 days before the offering. The offering statement may be unaudited, but it must contain financial statements and other information found in the ordinary registration statement's prospectus. Once you have received and responded to any SEC comments on the offering statement, the stock may be offered for sale. The offering statement must be furnished to investors with the written stock offer. The issuer is liable for any misstatements or omissions in the offering statement.

Private Offering. A private offering is defined in section 4(2) of the Securities Act as a "transaction by an issuer not involving any public offering." Private offerings often consist of large blocks of stocks sold to institutional investors, such as insurance companies or pension funds. The rationale behind this exemption is that institutional purchasers have the power and resources to insist upon information far more extensive than that commonly found within a registration statement. Other examples of private placements exempt from registration are stock offerings to key employees and offers made to stockholders in an attempt to acquire the stock of small corporations. General advertisement of the offered securities is not allowed, and the corporation will often place a sales restriction on the face of the security prohibiting its resale as the investors agree to hold them for investment purposes and not for the purposes of resale.

In the following case, the court resolved the question of whether a company made a private or a public offering.

Hill York Corporation v. American International Franchises, Inc.

448 F.2d 680 (1971)

Facts

Plaintiffs, Hill York Corporation, purchased stock from the defendant, American International Franchises, Inc., promoters of a nationwide franchise operation. Defendant never filed a registration statement with the SEC with respect to this offering (sale) of securities. Plaintiffs sued the defendants to have the stock sales rescinded as a violation of section 5, and to obtain recovery under sections 12(1) and 12(2) of the Securities Act of 1933. The defendant alleged that this was not a public offering but, rather, a private offering and that it was made to sophisticated business persons and lawyers who planned to do business with the firm. The plaintiffs alleged that this was a public offering, and that, while they were sophisticated in business affairs, they did not have the information required to be disclosed to them by the act and, therefore, were not sophisticated buyers.

Opinion

Justice Clark: Judgment for the plaintiffs. This was a public offering that required registration with the SEC.

To determine if there was a public offering the following factors are relevant:

1. The number of offerees and their relationship to each other and to the issuer. The more offerees, the more likelihood that the offering is public. If the offerees know the issuer and have special knowledge as to its business affairs, then the offering is apt to be private.
2. The number of units offered. Although there is no magic fixed number, the smaller the number of units offered, the greater likelihood the offering will be considered private.
3. The size of the offering. The smaller the size of the offering the more probability it is private.
4. The manner of offering. A private offering is more likely to arise when the offer is made directly to the offerees rather than through the facilities of public distribution such as investment bankers or the security exchanges. Public advertising is incompatible with the claim of a private offering.

The plaintiffs did not possess the information required for a registration statement and hence could not bring their sophisticated knowledge of business affairs to bear in deciding whether or not to invest in the franchise sales center. The record contains no evidence as to the number of offerees. The fact that there were only thirteen actual purchasers is irrelevant. The plaintiffs had never met nor in any way communicated with the defendants prior to purchasing their stock.

Case Questions

1. What reason did the court give for holding that this was a public offering requiring the filing of a registration statement, although the offering was made to sophisticated business persons and lawyers?
2. The court enumerated four relevant factors for determining whether there was a public offering. Explain the significance of each to this case.
3. What ethical purpose is served by requiring a registration statement to be filed when a public offering is made? Why should there be a distinction between a public and a private offering?

Exempt Securities

Government Securities. Municipalities and states do not register the sale of their securities. For example, a city that issues tax-exempt bonds need not file with the SEC.

Short-Term Commercial Paper. Promissory notes, drafts, and bills of exchange are exempt from registration with the SEC, provided the issuance arises out of a current business transaction and has a maturity date of not more than nine months.

Nonprofit Organizations. Corporations organized for educational, health, recreational, or charitable purposes are also exempt from federal registration. For example, a college that issues tax-exempt bonds need not file with the SEC.

Regulation of Trading Markets

Securities Exchange Act of 1934

In order to sell your stock on a stock exchange or in the over-the-counter market, you must register by filing the necessary forms with the stock exchange and the SEC under the Securities Exchange Act of 1934 unless exempted. A company that has more than five hundred shareholders and more that $1 million in assets, even though it is not listed on a national securities exchange, must file a detailed statement about the company, and must file annual reports (form 10-K) and quarterly reports (form 10-Q) to shareholders (see figures 19.3 and 19.4).

One of the unethical practices of the 1920s was the manipulation of the stock market by large groups of investors acting together to distort the market price of a security. The Securities Exchange Act of 1934 contains certain antifraud provisions that prohibit such manipulative schemes. One of the most important provisions is **Rule 10b-5,** which makes it unlawful ". . . to engage in any act, practice, or course of business which operates or would operate as a fraud or deceit upon any person in connection with the purchase or sale of any security." The rule applies to both registered and nonregistered securities and to any security without exception. It is discussed in detail in Chapter 20, Securities Regulation II on page 560.

An Ethical Perspective on Securities Regulations

Securities regulations are laws that protect the relationship between businesses and their investors. The courts, Congress, and the SEC are concerned with the prevention of fraudulent transactions in the securities industry. The entire securities regulations area is replete with business ethics standards regarding the business/investor relationship.

On of the primary objectives of the securities laws is to provide investors

Figure 19.3 Annual Report Form 10-K

SECURITIES AND EXCHANGE COMMISSION
Washington, D.C. 20549
FORM 10-Q

QUARTERLY REPORT UNDER SECTION 13 OR 15(d) OF THE SECURITIES EXCHANGE ACT of 1934

For Quarter Ended March 31, 1981 — Commission File Number 1-2345

FORGE INDUSTRIES CORPORATION
(Exact name of registrant as specified in its charter)

DELAWARE	**12-3456789**
(State or other jurisdiction of incorporation or organization)	(I.R.S. Employer Identification No.)

FORGE BUILDING, HEAVY DRIVE, ANYTOWN, DELAWARE 99999
(address of principal executive offices and zip code)

Registrant's telephone number, including area code (777) 555–0000

Indicate by check mark whether the registrant (1) has filed all reports required to be filed by Section 13 or 15(d) of the Securities Exchange Act of 1934 during the preceding 12 months (or for such shorter period that the registrant was required to file such reports), and (2) has been subject to such filing requirements for the past 90 days. Yes X No ______

Indicate the number of shares outstanding of each of the issuer's classes of common stock, as of the latest practicable date.

Class	Outstanding at April 30, 1981
Common Stock, par value 66-2/3¢ per share	7,020,531

FORGE INDUSTRIES CORPORATION
INDEX

Source: Securities and Exchange Commission, Washington, DC 20549.

Figure 19.4 Quarterly Report Form 10-Q

SECURITIES AND EXCHANGE COMMISSION
Washington, D.C. 20549

FORM 10-K

ANNUAL REPORT

PURSUANT TO SECTION 13 OR 15(d) OF THE SECURITIES EXCHANGE ACT OF 1934

For the fiscal year ended June 30, 1982 — Commission file number 1-9999

CHANDLERS, INC.
(Exact name of registrant as specified in its charter)

Delaware	**13-1234567**
(State or other jurisdiction of incorporation or organization)	(I.R.S. Employer Identification Number)
4444 Fourth Street, New York, N.Y.	10099
(Address of principal executive offices)	(Zip Code)

(212) 555–4444
(Registrant's telephone number)

Securities registered pursuant to Section 12(b) of the Act:

Title of each class	Name of each exchange on which registered
Common Stock—Par Value $1 Per Share	New York Stock Exchange Pacific Coast Stock Exchange

Securities registered pursuant to Section 12(g) of the Act:

4% Convertible Subordinated Debentures due November 1, 1990
(Title of class)

9½% Sinking Fund Debentures originally due November 15, 1995
(Title of class)

Indicate by check mark whether the registrant (1) has filed all reports required to be filed by Section 13 or 15(d) of the Securities Exchange Act of 1934 during the preceding 12 months and (2) has been subject to such filing requirements for the past 90 days.

Yes X   No —

Indicate by check mark whether the registrant has filed all documents and reports required to be filed by Sections 12, 13 or 15(d) of the Securities Exchange Act of 1934 subsequent to the distribution of securities under a plan confirmed by a court.

Yes X   No —

The aggregate market value of Common Stock, Par Value $1 Per Share, held by non-affiliates (based upon the closing sale price of the New York Stock Exchange) on August 13, 1982 was approximately $38,998,000.

As of August 31, 1982, there were 7,799,584 shares of Common Stock, Par Value $1 Per Share, outstanding.

DOCUMENTS INCORPORATED BY REFERENCE

Portions of the definitive Proxy Statement for the Annual Meeting of Stockholders on November 12, 1982 are incorporated by reference into Part III.

Source: Securities and Exchange Commission, Washington, DC 20549.

in public offerings with enough accurate information to make rational decisions about the purchase of securities. The SEC does not approve or disapprove the public offering. The stock offered, in fact, may be worthless. Do you think it is ethical for a corporation to file a registration statement based solely upon its prospective earning potential? To what extent is the investor capable of determining the risks involved from a prospectus? Is our free enterprise system best served by placing that risk solely on the investor?

Chapter Summary

1. Securities regulations are an effort by the government to achieve a high standard of business ethics in every facet of the securities industry.
2. Stock is created by a corporation where it issues part or all of the authorized amount of stock stated in its articles of organization.
3. Stock represents "value" in the profitability of the issuing company.
4. Securities laws are concerned with assuring the investing public that corporate reports are accurate. These laws represent a governmental policy of insisting upon ethical behavior in the securities industry.
5. The securities markets are regulated by the Securities Exchange Act of 1934.
6. Federal statutes and state "blue sky" laws regulate the sale of securities by the issuing corporation and its agents.
7. A security is a stock, bond, note, treasury stock, profit-sharing agreement, trust certificate, preorganization trust subscription, voting-trust certificate, interest in a limited partnership, savings and loan investment, or other investment contract.
8. The stock market crash of 1929 led to the enactment of the Securities Act of 1933 and the Securities Exchange Act of 1934.
9. The Securities and Exchange Commission is responsible for implementing the regulations mandated by the Securities Act of 1933 and the Securities Exchange Act of 1934.
10. The Securities Exchange Act of 1934 requires that all securities, unless exempt, be registered with the SEC before being sold to the general public in interstate commerce.
11. The SEA of 1934 has a formal filing process that must be followed by the issuing company.
12. Exempt from normal registration requirements are private placements (Regulation D) and small business (Regulation A) offerings.
13. Regulation D allows a company to offer to sell up to $500,000 in securities during any twelve-month period without providing the buyer with specific information (Rule 503). Regulation D also allows a company to sell up to $5 million in securities during any twelve-month period if there are no more than thirty-five non-accredited investors (Rule 505).

14. Rule 501 of Regulation D defines an accredited investor as:
    a. a bank
    b. an insurance company
    c. a pension plan
    d. a charitable or educational institution
    e. a director, officer, or general partner of the issuer
    f. any person who purchased at least 150,000 of the securities offered
    g. any person with a net worth of more than $1 million
    h. any person with an annual income of more than $200,000
15. A Regulation A exemption is available to a company that sells no more than $1.5 million worth of securities to the public during a twelve-month period. At least ten days before the offer, an offering circular must be filed with the regional SEC office.
16. The Securities Exchange Act of 1934 requires registration with the SEC of any company with more than five hundred public shareholders and more than $1 million in assets, even though not listed on a national securities exchange.

Key Terms

accredited investors 540
blue sky law 532
dealer 536
filing process 536
offering statement 540
pre-filing period 536
preliminary prospectus 538
prospectus 536
red herring notice 538
registered securities 538
registration statement 535
Regulation A 540
Regulation D 538
Rule 10b-5 542
security 531
tombstone ad 538
underwriter 536
waiting period 538

Questions on Ethics

1. Harry Slade is a corporate comptroller for a corporation with a public listing of securities. He is reviewing the corporation's books and records with the auditor, Nancy Wilson. Harry's company trades with third world countries that often require "front money" before a contract is signed. The company maintains a "slush fund" for such payments. When questioned by Nancy about the nature of the payments, Harry has equated them to a commission. Nancy insists they are bribes. How would you characterize the nature of the front money payments that are required before any contracts are executed? Would you find it an ethical practice to provide front money in order to be awarded a contract?

Would the fact that this is a customary practice in some foreign countries affect your answer?

2. The directors of Tax Disk Co., a computer software corporation, want to make a private placement of $400,000 worth of common stock by offering it for sale throughout the country. The corporate attorney has informed them that the company qualifies for a Regulation D filing with the SEC, which means that it need not file a registration statement. Thus no information need be provided to the buyers unless required by state securities laws. Is a private placement exemption from filing a registration statement an ethical practice? Why should a buyer who pays $5,000 for stock be given no information because the corporation qualifies for a statutory exemption in making a private offering?
3. Bill Slade was offered and purchased a condominium unit and was given an option to purchase a management rental agreement. Bill never exercised the option. Is it ethical for the SEC to make this transaction automatically an investment security subject to SEC registration?
4. Is it ethical for Congress to exempt from SEC registration municipal tax-exempt bonds? What ethical theory may justify that exemption?
5. Hi Tech, Inc., a Florida corporation, offered stock only to its residents to raise $1 million. Under SEC Rule 147 the offering qualified as an exempt intrastate offering. What ethical theory would justify that exemption?

Questions on Law

1. Ernst and Ernst, an accounting firm, was retained by First Securities Company of Chicago, a brokerage firm and member of the Midwest Stock Exchange, to perform audits of the firm's books and records. In connection therewith, Ernst and Ernst prepared for filing with the SEC the annual reports required. Plaintiff, Hochfelder, was a customer of First Securities who innocently invested in a fraudulent securities scheme perpetrated by Lester B. Noy, the president and owner of 92 percent of First Securities Company stock. In 1968 Noy committed suicide, leaving a note that described First Securities as bankrupt. Plaintiff filed this negligence action against Ernst and Ernst, contending that they failed to utilize appropriate auditing procedures and thus failed to discover internal practices of the firm, and that they were in violation of section 10(b) and Rule 10b-5. Does violation of section 10(b) and Rule 10b-5 require intentional misconduct? *Ernst and Ernst* v. *Hochfelder,* 425 U.S. 185 (1976).
2. Accounting Procedures, Inc., is an accounting consulting firm specializing in computer applications for small companies. It has decided to raise $250,000 in six months by selling its common stock. The directors of Accounting Procedures have asked you if it is possible to

sell the stock without filing a registration statement with the SEC and/or within the state where the securities will be sold. Explain.

3. Maria Ferris is a general partner in a limited partnership that owns a large shopping center/hotel complex in Boston. Limited partnership shares are about to be sold to the general public to raise $1 million. Maria has asked you if a limited partnership share could be a security, and if so, would a limited partnership selling shares interstate be subject to SEC regulations?
4. Barbara Dean was recently promoted to president and chief executive officer of Aerotech Industries, Inc., a multinational corporation with stock traded on the New York Stock Exchange. Part of her compensation includes 15 percent common stock ownership in the company. Barbara sold 5 percent of her stock within five months of its purchase and realized a short-term capital gain of $20,000. How does the securities law characterize Barbara's status? What, if any, SEC legal requirement must she comply with? What legal remedy, if any, do the shareholders of Aerotech Industries have against Barbara?
5. Harry Johnson, a New York resident, purchased a condominium unit in Vermont as a vacation home and for rental income. Harry was offered and signed a rental pool agreement with the condominium trustees. Harry now claims he did not receive sufficient information about the transaction and that there is a violation of the antifraud provisions of the Securities Exchange Act. Was the offer to sell the condominium an investment contract and hence subject to the Securities Exchange Act?

Suggested Readings

Loss, Louis, *Fundamentals of Securities Regulations*. Boston: Little, Brown, 1984.

Ratner, David L. *Securities Regulation in a Nutshell*. 2d ed. Nutshell Series. St. Paul: West, 1982.

20 Securities Regulations II

The 1934 Act was designed to protect investors against manipulation of stock prices. Underlying the adoption of extensive disclosure requirements was a legislative philosophy: "There cannot be honest mistakes without honest publicity. Manipulation and dishonest practices of the market place thrive upon mystery and secrecy." This Court repeatedly has described the "fundamental purpose" of the Act as implementing a "philosophy of full disclosure."

—*Justice Blackmun,* Basic Inc. *v.* Levinson *108 S. Ct. 978 (1988)*

■ LEARNING OBJECTIVES

After you have read this chapter you should be able to:

1. Explain a tender offer and understand the purpose and use of the Williams Act.
2. Explain "insider trading" and the types of transactions that violate Rule 10b-5.
3. Understand and explain the function of the Foreign Corrupt Practices Act.
4. Explain and understand the rules governing a dissident shareholder's proposal to a proxy.
5. Explain what constitutes liability for "short-swing" profits.
6. Appreciate the legal and ethical problems of a takeover bid.

Business Decisions and the Law

What Constitutes Insider Trading?

What could possibly happen when a Merrill Lynch broker starts scheming with *Business Week* magazine's print room employees? A lot, discovered former U.S. Attorney Rudolph W. Guiliani, as he revealed the plan whereby broker William Dillon paid printers $20 to $30 per issue for advance copies of *Business Week*. It is alleged that upon obtaining that week's issue, Dillon purchased and sold securities prior to the magazine's distribution to the public, based upon information from the "Inside Wall Street" column.

It is reported that Dillon earned net profits of approximately $94,000 during the two-year period of the scheme. This highly publicized case of trading on nonpublic information has created a stir in the financial community. R. R. Donnelly & Sons Company, the printer of *Business Week*, has fired seven workers in connection with the scheme. Meanwhile, at least nineteen people at Merrill Lynch are being questioned about this case. Mr. Dillon is fighting the criminal charges and, if convicted, faces imprisonment for up to five years, and fines of up to $250,000.

Receiving information regarding publicly traded securities and acting on it prior to its distribution to the public is illegal insider trading. Some cases, such as this one, are clear violations under the rule announced by the United States Supreme Court in *Carpenter* v. *United States*, to be discussed in this chapter, upholding the conviction of a *Wall Street Journal* columnist who tipped a stock broker on the contents of his column prior to its publication.

Still other cases of insider trading fall in a gray area. These include overheard conversations and inadvertent disclosure of material information by a third party. Distinguishing between tips so as to stay within the law is a difficult task for both individual and corporate investors.

This chapter will explain the major provisions and leading cases under the 1934 Securities Exchange Act, in such areas as tender offers, insider trading, Rule 10b-5, proxy regulation, and dissident shareholder proposals.

Tender Offer

A **tender offer** occurs when an offeror or bidder (a corporation, an individual, or a group of persons) makes an offer directly to the shareholders of the target corporation to purchase its shares, usually at a price above the market price. The offer, called a **takeover bid,** invites the shareholders to tender their shares of stock to the offeror at a premium price. The offeror may offer the target shareholders cash, securities, or a combination of both in exchange for their stock. However, cash tender offers are the most common. If the incumbent management of the target corporation approves the tender offer and the bidder and management negotiate a price for the stock acceptable to the shareholders, the arrangement is referred to as a **"friendly" takeover.** Often, however, the incumbent management resists the offer by employing antitakeover defenses and the hostile bidder is then referred to as a corporate "raider" or a "shark." Our discussion will focus on the hostile takeover attempt to acquire a company by means of a tender offer. If successful, the acquiring company generally will replace management of the target company with their own people.

To illustrate, suppose you owned stock in a company that had a market price on the New York Stock Exchange of $21 per share. The *Wall Street Journal* advertised that an offer was made to all the shareholders of the company to purchase the stock for $28 per share, providing 51 percent of the target company stock was tendered to the bidder within ten days of the offer. You may wish to "tender" your stock by having your broker forward the stock to a depository bank acting as an agent for the bidder. The $7 premium per share would certainly induce you to tender into the hostile bid.

We are assuming that a "friendly" takeover could not be arranged with your target company's board of directors. Since the corporate board voted to disallow the acquisition by a merger or a sale of all its assets and decided not to submit the offer to the stockholders, the now hostile bidder has to make the offer directly to the stockholders. You may ask, how could the incumbent board of directors of the target company, who act as fiduciaries with a duty of loyalty owed to the stockholders, turn down such an enticing offer? In a 1985 case, *Moran* v. *Household International Inc.*, 500 S.2d 1346, the Delaware Supreme Court said,

> While we conclude . . . that the . . . directors are protected by the business judgment rule . . . the ultimate response to an actual takeover bid must be judged by the director's action at that time, and nothing relieves them of their fundamental duties to the corporation and its stockholders.

The corporate board must show it had reasonable grounds to oppose the tender offer; the directors have a right to oppose the tender offer if they reasonably deem it to be in the shareholders' best interest. Often the shareholders or the bidder sue the directors for interfering with a tender offer.

The economics of a takeover struggle and its effect on free enterprise are extremely controversial. Should the management of corporate America live in fear of being a target in a tender offer? Some would argue that shareholders should not be denied the opportunity to maximize the return on their investment at the expense of an unaccountable corporate board functioning at a suboptimal performance. Assume in our earlier example, you earned $7 on each share sold to the hostile bidder who replaced the target company's top management with its own corporate board of directors. Subsequently, the directors upgraded the operation resulting in a stock increase in the market value from $21 to $45 per share. The stockholders and the economy in general have benefited from the acquisition. Others would argue that hostile takeovers destroy jobs and force plants to close and relocate at the expense of the employees and local community.

Within this legal environment, what is the role of the courts in reviewing the defensive tactics of incumbent management of a target company to determine if they are acting in the best interest of the shareholders? In a 1984 decision, *Norlin Corp*. v. *Rooney Pace, Inc.*, the United States Court of Appeals, Second Circuit, said,

> When these battles for corporate dominance spawn legal controversies, the judicial role is neither to displace the judgment of the participants nor to predetermine the

> outcome. Rather, the responsibility of the court is to insure that rules designed to safeguard the fairness of the takeover process be enforced.

The following section will discuss these rules.

The Williams Act

During the early 1960s, there were few state or federal laws regulating the tender offer. Stockholders were often in a position where they could only make hasty, ill-informed judgments on whether to sell their stock to an offeror. In 1968 Congress passed the **Williams Act,** which amended the Securities Exchange Act of 1934 by adding Sections 13(d)-(e) and 14(d)-(e) to the Exchange Act. The Williams Act is not a substantive regulatory statute. Its purpose is to provide an adequate flow of information to the target-company shareholders and management from the offeror/bidder and to create a "level playing field" between incumbent management and the bidder so that neither can manipulate the shareholders' judgment.

Section 13(d)—Disclosure by 5 Percent Owners

The Act provides a disclosure requirement whenever a person or group acquires more than 5 percent of the voting stock of a public company. If the buyer acquires control of the company, he must send information regarding the business plan he has for the company to the SEC on Schedule 13-D (Figure 20.1) within ten days of the purchase. Copies must be sent to the issuer of the security and to the exchanges on which the security is traded.

Since bidders often initially accumulate target stock through the open market, this disclosure requirement will alert management of a potential tender offer. In a 1975 United States Supreme Court case, *Rondeau v. Mosiner Paper Corp.,* Chief Justice Burger stated,

> The purpose of the Williams Act is to insure that public shareholders who are confronted by a case tender offer for their stock will not be required to respond without adequate information regarding the qualifications and intentions of the offering party. By requiring disclosure of information to the target company as well as the SEC, Congress intended to do no more than give incumbent management an opportunity to express and explain its position . . . [to the shareholders]. . . . [T]he Act's draftsmen commented upon the "extreme care" which was taken "to avoid tipping the balance of regulation either in favor of management or in favor of the person making the takeover bid."

Section 14(e)—Anti-Fraud Provision

Incumbent management of the target corporation may negotiate with the offeror attractive compensation arrangements that guarantee them continued employment and large cash payments (referred to as "golden parachute" agreements) in the event of a buy out by the takeover company. Must the details of

Figure 20.1 Securities and Exchange Commission

SECURITIES AND EXCHANGE COMMISSION
Washington, D.C. 20549

SCHEDULE 13D

Under the Securities Exchange Act of 1934
(Amendment No. ....)*

....
(Name of Issuer)

....
(Title of Class of Securities)

....
(CUSIP Number)

....
(Name, Address and Telephone Number
of Person Authorized to Receive
Notices and Communications)

....
(Date of Event which Requires Filing
of this Statement)

---

1) Names of Reporting Persons S. S. or I. R. S. Identification Nos. of Above Persons
....

2) Check the Appropriate Box if a Member of a Group (See Instructions) ....
(a) ....
(b) ....

3) SEC Use Only ....

4) Source of Funds (See Instructions) ....

5) Check if Disclosure of Legal Proceedings is Required Pursuant to Items 2(d) or 2(e) ....
....

6) Citizenship or Place of Organization ....

Number of Shares Beneficially Owned by Each Reporting Person With	
	(7) Sole Voting Power ....
	(8) Shared Voting Power ....
	(9) Sole Dispositive Power ....
	(10) Shared Dispositive Power ....

11) Aggregate Amount Beneficially Owned by Each Reporting Person ....

12) Check if the Aggregate Amount in Row (11) Excludes Certain Shares (See Instructions) ....
....

13) Percent of Class Reported by Amount in Row (11) ....

14) Type of Reporting Person (See Instructions) ....
....
....

such an arrangement be disclosed to the target company's stockholders if a tender offer has been made? Or consider the target company buying the shares already obtained by the hostile bidder over its cost if he will stop the takeover attempt. Is this defensive antitakeover tactic, referred to as "greenmail," a violation of the antifraud provisions of section 14(e)?

Section 14(e) provides, in part:

> It shall be unlawful for any person to make any untrue statement of a material fact or omit to state any material fact necessary in order to make the statement made . . . not misleading, or to engage in any fraudulent, deceptive, or manipulative acts or practices, in connection with any tender offer

As target management creates various forms of antitakeover defenses, they must be sure the tactics are not in violation of section 14(e). The shareholders to whom a tender offer has been made may sue the target management and/or the hostile bidder under section 14(e) alleging untrue statements or omissions of a material fact or fraudulent, deceptive, or manipulative acts regarding an invitation to purchase the stock.

In the following United States Supreme Court case, the plaintiff shareholders alleged the takeover/bidder and target company management violated section 14(e)'s prohibition of manipulative practices by withdrawing a tender offer and, after agreements with management, substituting a new tender offer. The court had to resolve whether or not the conduct of the parties was manipulative within section 14(e). Note that a target corporation and its shareholders may sue a takeover bidder under section 14(e) for damages and may also assert a claim for injunctive relief.

Schreiber v. Burlington Northern, Inc.

472 U.S. 1 (1985)

Facts

The United States Supreme Court interpreted section 14(e) of the Securities Act of 1934 to determine the meaning of manipulative practices within the context of a tender offer to public shareholders.

Petitioner Barbara Schreiber owned shares of El Paso Gas Company, which became the target of a takeover by Respondent. The shareholders fully subscribed to Burlington-Northern's tender offer. Burlington-Northern, however, refused these tendered shares, and following further negotiations announced to the El Paso Gas Company shareholders a new takeover agreement. Burlington-Northern succeeded in this takeover attempt as well.

Petitioner was among those who had tendered their shares pursuant to the first offer, which was rescinded. When Burlington-Northern superceded this offer with the second one, it thereby caused the initially tendering shareholders to receive diminished payments for their shares. Schreiber filed suit, arguing that the substitution of tender offers was a manipulative act within section 14(e), which prohibits "fraudulent, deceptive or manipulative acts or practices . . . in connection with any tender offer."

Opinion

Chief Justice Burger: We are asked in this case to interpret §14(e) of the Securities Exchange Act.

The starting point is the language of the statute. Section 14(e) provides:

> It shall be unlawful for any person to make any untrue statement of a material fact or omit to state any material fact necessary in order to make the statements made, in the light of the circumstances under which they are made, not misleading, or to engage in any fraudulent, deceptive, or manipulative acts or practices, in connection with any tender offer or request or invitation for tenders, or any solicitation of security holders in opposition to or in favor of any such offer, request, or invitation.

Section 14(e) was originally added to the Securities Exchange Act as part of the Williams Act . . . to insure that public shareholders who are confronted by a cash tender offer for their stock will not be required to respond without adequate information. It is clear that Congress relied primarily on disclosure to implement to purpose of the Williams Act.

Petitioner relies on a construction of the phrase, "fraudulent, deceptive, or manipulative acts or practices." Petitioner reads the phrase . . . to include acts which, although fully disclosed, "artificially" affect the price of the takeover target's stock. Petitioner's interpretation relies on the belief that §14(e) is directed at purposes broader than providing full and true information to investors. [This] reading . . . conflicts with the normal meaning. . . .

[I]t is a familiar principle of statutory construction that words grouped in a list should be given related meaning. [F]raudulent, deceptive, or manipulative . . . are directed at failures to disclose. The use of the term "manipulative" provides emphasis and guidance. . . . [I]t does not suggest a deviation from the section's facial and primary concern with disclosure. . . .

Our [unanimous] conclusion that "manipulative" acts under §14(e) require misrepresentation or nondisclosure is buttressed by the purpose and legislative history of the provision. [The term "manipulative"] connotes 'conduct designed to deceive or defraud investors.' . . . Nowhere in the legislative history is there the slightest suggestion that §14(e) serves any purpose other than disclosure, or that the term "manipulative" should be read as an invitation to the courts to oversee the substantive fairness of tender offers; the quality of any offer is a matter for the marketplace. [W]e hold that the actions of respondents were not manipulative. The amended complaint fails to allege that the cancellation of the first tender offer was accompanied by any misrepresentation, nondisclosure, or deception.

Case Questions

1. What argument did the Court submit in its holding that the actions of the tender offeror were not manipulative under section 14(e) of the Securities Act of 1934?
2. Why was section 14(e) added to the Securities Exchange Act?
3. Do you think the Court's statement, "the quality of any offer is a matter for the marketplace" is an ethical statement?

Insider Trading

Insider trading occurs when a company **"insider"** (i.e., a director, officer, controlling stockholder, or any others who by virtue of their relationship to the company have acquired a duty of confidentiality) buys or sells that company's securities on the basis of "material" nonpublic inside information. The business-ethics issue relates to the advantage the insider has trading on information not yet available to the investing public. A person inside the corporation who has knowledge of a material new development, that if known to the investing public would influence the market value of the stock or the investor's decision to buy or sell, has an unfair advantage. The purchase or sale of the stock by the insider based on the undisclosed good or bad corporate development could profit the insider at the expense of the investing public.

For instance, if an insider knew her company had just discovered a drug that would cure AIDS but that information was not yet released, and she purchased more stock before the news was public and the market increased in value, the insider would make a profit. You can easily understand that the corporation may not want to publicize the information until it can legally protect its interest by obtaining the appropriate patents and administrative clearance for sale of the drug. So long as the insider does not *trade* the security, she need not disclose the information until the corporation decides it is ripe for disclosure to the general public.

Common Law and Insider Trading

The common law generally takes the position that officers and directors owe a fiduciary obligation to their corporation and its stockholders regarding corporate dealings but *not as individuals* trading in the corporations' securities, providing there is no misrepresentation, half-truths or active concealments in the transaction. Many commentators subscribed to the theory that abuse of inside information under the common law contributed to the 1929 stock market crash. Congress responded by passing remedial legislation with the Securities Exchange Act of 1934 section 16(a) and (b) and section 10(b) and 10(b)(5).

Short-Swing Profits

16(a) and 16(b)

Section 16(a)

Insiders must file with SEC. [See Fig. 20.2.]

Every person who is directly or indirectly the beneficial owner of more than 10 per centum of any class of any equity security . . . which is registered . . . or is an officer or director of the issuer of such security, shall file . . . within 10 days after he becomes such beneficial owner, director, or officer, a statement with the [SEC] . . . of the amount of all securities . . . and within 10 days after the close of each calendar month thereafter, if there has been a change in such ownership shall file with the [SEC] his ownership and such change . . . as have occurred during the . . . month.

Section 16(b)

"Short-swing" profits made by insiders recoverable by the corporation.

For the purpose of preventing the unfair use of information which may have been obtained by . . . [insider] . . . any profit realized by him from any purchase and sale . . . of any equity . . . within any period of less than six months . . . shall . . . be recoverable by the issuer, irrespective of any intention on the part of such owner, director, or officer.

Figure 20.2 Statement of Change in Beneficial Ownership of Securities

FORM 4

U.S. SECURITIES & EXCHANGE COMMISSION
Washington, D.C. 20549

Statement of Changes in Beneficial Ownership of Securities

Filed pursuant to Section 16(a) of the Securities Exchange Act of 1934, Section 17(e) of the Public Utility Holding Company Act of 1935 or Section 30(f) of the Investment Company Act of 1940.

(Please print or type.)

1. NAME AND BUSINESS ADDRESS OF REPORTING PERSON	2. STATE OF INCORPORATION	3. IF AN AMENDMENT GIVE DATE OF STATEMENT AMENDED	4. NAME OF COMPANY
LAST FIRST MIDDLE		MO. DAY YR.	
(ZIP CODE)	5. IRS OR SS IDENTIFYING NUMBER OF REPORTING PERSON	6. STATEMENT FOR CALENDAR MONTH OF MONTH YEAR	7. DATE OF LAST PREVIOUS STATEMENT MO. DAY YR.
			8. RELATIONSHIP OF REPORTING PERSON TO COMPANY *(Instruction 4)*

TABLE I. Securities Bought, Sold or Otherwise Acquired or Disposed of

Furnish the information required by the following table as to securities of the company bought or sold or otherwise acquired or disposed of by the reporting person during the month for which this statement is filed *(See Instruction 5)* and as to securities of the company beneficially owned, directly or indirectly, at the end of the month. However, transaction involving the acquisition or disposition of puts, calls, options or other rights or obligations to buy or sell securities of the company shall be reported in Table II.

1. TITLE OF SECURITIES *(Instruction 8)*	2. *(FOR SEC USE ONLY)*	3. DATE OF TRANS-ACTION *(Instruction 9)*	4. AMOUNT OF SECURITIES ACQUIRED *(Instruction 10)*	5. AMOUNT OF SECURITIES DISPOSED OF *(Instruction 10)*	6. CHARACTER OF TRANSACTION REPORTED *(Instruction 12)*	7. PURCHASE OR SALE PRICE PER SHARE OR OTHER UNIT *(Instruction 13)*	8. AMOUNT OWNED AT END OF MONTH *(Instruction 10)*	9. NATURE OF OWNERSHIP OF SECURITIES OWNED AT END OF MONTH *(Instruction 11)*

SEC 1474 (2-87) REMEMBER: THREE COPIES ARE REQUIRED. ONE SHOULD BE MANUALLY SIGNED AND SUITABLE FOR REPRODUCTION *(OVER)*

Section 16(b) applies to directors and officers of publicly held corporations and to all 10-percent beneficial owners of publicly held equity securities.

Suit to recover **short-swing profits** must be brought in federal courts by the corporation or a derivative stockholders suit on its behalf. Recovery of the profits will be paid to the corporation.

Automatic Liability for Short-Swing Profits

An insider (director, officer, or beneficial owner of 10 percent of the stock) is automatically liable for his short-swing profits *whether or not he had inside information*. Consider the problems that result from section 16(b). If you were a corporate officer and purchased company stock on the basis of an undisclosed beneficial development and held the stock for more than six months, you are not liable under 16(b), no matter how significant the undisclosed inside information was, since you did not sell your stock in less than six months. *There must be a stock trade purchase and a sale or a sale and a purchase for section 16(b) to apply*. However, if you sold the stock and made a profit within the six-month period you would be *automatically liable* under section 16(b), no matter how little information you possessed or how honest your intentions were.

In the following case, the federal court found the insider liable despite the lack of inside information.

Texas International Airlines v. National Airlines, Inc.

714 F.2d 533 (5th Cir. 1983)

Facts

TIA, in an action to gain control of National Airlines (NA), purchased 121,000 shares of NA stock. On this date, March 14, 1979, TIA owned more than 10 percent of NA's common stock. Earlier, NA had entered into a merger agreement with Pan American World Airways, Inc. (Pan Am), which provided for the merger of NA into Pan Am. Within six months of the March 14 purchase, TIA and Pan Am entered into a stock purchase agreement whereby TIA agreed to sell 790,700 shares of NA common stock to Pan Am. TIA knew of NA's merger plan, but inexplicably decided to sell its NA common stock prior to the merger.

The closing day was held on July 30, 1979. Under the section 16(b) rules, the stock sale is deemed to include the 121,000 shares purchased only four months before. It was not until after this closing date that NA was merged into Pan Am.

TIA sought declaratory relief that it was not liable for profits on its deal with Pan Am. NA counterclaimed, seeking recovery of the profits and moved for summary judgment. The district court found TIA's actions violative of section 16(b), rejecting its arguments that its actions were excepted from the general rule of liability. NA was awarded $1,149,195, representing TIA's profits from the purchase and sale, less brokerage commissions and transfer taxes.

Opinion

Judge Johnson: Texas International (TI) appeals the grant of summary judgment for National Airlines (National) holding TI liable to National under section 16(b) of the Securities Exchange Act of 1934 (the Exchange Act) for the "short swing profits" made on the sale of 121,000 shares of National common stock.

The three factors which trigger section 16(b) liability were all present—TI was a ten percent beneficial owner of National that purchased and sold National stock within a six-month period.

TI urges this Court to create an exception to automatic section 16(b) liability in cases where a defendant can prove that, notwithstanding its ownership of over ten percent of the stock of the issuer, the defendant had no access to inside information concerning the issuer.

Application of section 16(b) in this type of case, argues TI, does not serve congressional goals. . . .

TI's argument is unsupported by the legislative history of section 16(b). Although the abuse Congress sought to curb was speculation by stockholders with inside information, "the only method Congress deemed effective to curb the evils of insider trading was a *flat rule* taking the profits out of a *class of transactions* in which the possibility of abuse was believed to be intolerably great." In explaining the necessity for a "crude rule of thumb" to Congress, Thomas Corcoran, a principal draftsman of the Act, stated: "You have to have a general rule. In particular transactions it might work a hardship, but those transactions that are a hardship represent the sacrifice to the necessity of having a general rule."

It is apparent that Congress selected such a broad, harsh mechanism because it recognized that in no other way could the purpose of the statute be fully implemented. . . .

The Court is in agreement with the statements of legislative purpose. . . . [T]he mechanical application of section 16(b) to the specified class of transactions is necessary in order to guarantee that the abuse at which the statute is aimed will be effectively curbed.

In *Kern County* the Supreme Court approved an extremely narrow exception to the objective standard of section 16(b). The Court held that when a transaction is "unorthodox" or "borderline," the courts should adopt a pragmatic approach in imposing section 16(b) liability which considers the opportunity for speculative abuse, i.e., whether the statutory "insider" had or was likely to have access to inside information.

The Supreme Court clearly distinguished the unorthodox transaction—a conversion of securities—before it, from the traditional cash-for-stock transaction in the instant case: "traditional cash-for-stock transactions . . . are clearly within the purview of §16(b)."

In the instant case, TI voluntarily entered into the stock purchase agreement with Pan Am before the National–Pan Am merger was effectuated. Despite the alleged lack of access to inside information and therefore the possibility of speculative abuse, the volitional character of the exchange is sufficient reason to trigger applicability of the language of section 16(b).

CALCULATION OF SHORT SWING PROFITS

On appeal, TI complains of the district court's disallowance of the various other expenses by which it sought to reduce the amount of its profit. TI also sought deductions for various legal, investment banking, and other consulting fees.

In considering the calculation of profit under section 16(b) the need has been recognized to "squeeze every possible penny of profit out of such transactions" in order to effectuate the remedial purpose of the statute.

Indeed, the method of computing profit within section 16(b) can result in a "profit," albeit a theoretical one, even though the short swing trader has suffered a net loss from his trading during the period.

In the instant case, the district court disallowed what has been characterized as "takeover expense deductions" and permitted TI to deduct only those expenses truly incidental to the transaction—brokerage commissions and transfer taxes.

CONCLUSION

The judgment of the district court is affirmed.

Case Questions

1. What were the factors in this case that triggered section 16(b)?

2. What was TIA's argument that it was not liable for profits on its deal with Pan Am?
3. Do you agree with the ethics of a rule, as stated by Mr. Corcoran, the draftsman of section 16(b) of the Securities Exchange Act, "In particular transactions it might work a hardship, but those transactions that are a hardship represent the sacrifice to the necessity of having a general rule"?

Rule 10b-5: Anti-fraud and Manipulation

Section 10(b) of the 1934 Act states,

> It shall be unlawful for any person . . . to use . . . any manipulative or deceptive device . . . in contravention of such rules and regulations as the . . . [SEC] may proscribe.

In 1942 the SEC adopted the following Rule 10b-5:

> It shall be unlawful for any person, directly or indirectly, by use of any means or instrumentality of interstate commerce, or of the mails, or of any facility of any national exchange, (1) to employ any device, scheme or artifice to defraud, (2) to make any untrue statement of a material fact or to omit to state a material fact necessary in order to make the statements made, in the light of the circumstances under which they were made, not misleading, or (3) to engage in any act, practice or course of business which operates or would operate as a fraud or deceit upon any person in connection with the purchase or sale of any security.

"Standing" to Sue under Rule 10b-5

A private party may bring a civil action under **Rule 10b-5.** The United States Supreme Court in a 1983 case, *Herman and Moe Learn* v. *Huddleston* (459 U.S. 375) allowed the buyers of registered securities to bring a Rule 10b-5 action alleging they were defrauded by misrepresentation in a registration statement. The Supreme Court held in a 1975 case, *Blue Chip Stamps* v. *Manor Drug Stores,* that to bring suit under Rule 10b-5 the plaintiff must be a buyer or seller of securities. Of course the SEC on its own behalf can institute administrative proceedings against any person who violates Rule 10b-5 and seek an injunction in the federal courts or refer the matter to the Department of Justice for possible criminal prosecution.

Duties Imposed by Rule 10b-5

Misrepresentations and Omissions

At the outset it is important to note that Rule 10b-5 applies to any company, public or private, whether or not it is listed on a public stock exchange. As long as the transaction is in connection with interstate commerce, the federal statute will apply. Use of the mails or even a local telephone call will establish this jurisdictional interstate requirement.

Preliminary Merger Negotiations. Companies that engage in preliminary merger negotiations create special problems as to when such "merger talk" should be disclosed to the general public. At what point is there a duty under Rule 10b-5 to make affirmative disclosure of material information to the shareholders regarding a potential merger?

Under the "bright-line" test, "merger talk" is not material and need not be disclosed until there is *agreement* on the price and structure of the merger. The theory of the "bright-line" test is that premature disclosure may be harmful to the stockholders' interest as rumors of a merger may cause the stock to fluctuate in value. In the following 1988 Supreme Court case, the Court rejected this bright-line test and held that materiality depends on the facts and is to be determined on a case-by-case basis.

Basic, Incorporated, et al. v. *Max L. Levinson, et al.*

108 S. Ct. 978 (1988)

Facts

Basic, Incorporated (Basic) was a publicly traded company that manufactured chemical refractions for the steel industry. Combustion Engineering, Inc. (CEI), a producer of refractories, expressed an interest in acquiring Basic. It prepared a strategic plan to this end, planning to purchase Basic for $30 million.

Beginning in 1976, CEI met with and telephoned Basic officers, directors, and shareholders concerning its goal. During the following two years, 1977 and 1978, Basic stated on three occasions public denials of the existence of merger negotiations.

On December 18, 1978, Basic requested that the New York Stock Exchange suspend trading of its shares, and then issued a public statement that it has been pursued by a corporate suitor. On December 19, 1978, Basic enclosed CEI's offer and, on December 20, 1978, publicly announced its approval of the offer.

The plaintiffs comprise a class of former Basic shareholders who sold their stock after Basic's first public announcement but before the December 18 suspension of trade. They asserted that Basic issued three false or misleading public statements violative of section 10(b) and Rule 10b-5, and alleged damages from their sale of shares.

The district court held that the statements were immaterial since the merger agreement was not necessarily certain. The Court of Appeals found Basic's public statements misleading, and that merger negotiations could be material. It then adopted a rebuttable presumption of reliance by shareholders on material misrepresentations.

We granted certiorari, . . . to resolve the split . . . among the Court of Appeals as to the standard of materiality applicable to preliminary merger discussions.

Opinion

Justice Blackmun: This Court "repeatedly has described the 'fundamental purpose' of the Act as implementing a 'philosophy of full disclosure.' "

[A] private cause of action exists for a violation of § 10(b) and Rule 10b-5, and constitutes an essential tool for enforcement of the 1934 Act's requirements.

The Court previously has addressed various positive and common-law requirements for a violation of § 10(b) or of Rule 10b-5.

The Court also explicitly has defined a standard of materiality under the securities laws . . . concluding in the proxy-solicitation context that "[a]n omitted fact is material if there is a substantial likelihood that a reasonable shareholder would consider it important in deciding how to vote."

[T]he Court was careful not to set too low a standard of materiality; it was concerned that a minimal standard might bring an overabundance of information within its reach, and lead management "simply to bury the shareholders in an avalanche of trivial information—a result that is hardly conducive to informed decisionmaking."

Petitioners argue that, preliminary merger discussions do not become material until "agreement-in-principle" as to the price and structure of the transaction has been reached between the would-be merger partners.

A bright-line rule indeed is easier to follow than a standard that requires the exercise of judgment in the light of all the circumstances. But ease of application alone is not an excuse for ignoring the purposes of the securities acts and Congress' policy decisions.

[T]he Second Circuit had explained the role of the materiality requirement of Rule 10b-5, with respect to contingent or speculative information or events, in a manner that gave that term meaning. . . . Under such circumstances, materiality "will depend at any given time upon a balancing of both the indicated probability that the event will occur and the anticipated magnitude of the event in light of the totality of the company activity."

Generally, in order to assess the probability that the event will occur, a factfinder will need to look to indicia of interest in the transaction at the highest corporate levels. Without attempting to catalog all such possible factors, we note by way of example that board resolutions, instructions to investment bankers, and actual negotiations between principals or their intermediaries may serve as indicia of interest. To assess the magnitude of the transaction to the issuer of the securities allegedly manipulated, a factfinder will need to consider such facts as the size of the two corporate entities and of the potential premiums over market value.

As we clarify today, materiality depends on the significance the reasonable investor would place on the withheld or misrepresented information. The fact-specific inquiry we endorse here is consistent with the approach a number of courts have taken in assessing the materiality of merger negotiations. Because the standard of materiality we have adopted differs from that used by both courts . . . we remand the case for reconsideration of the question.

Case Questions

1. How did the Court define the materiality requirement of Rule 10b-5 with respect to speculative information such as preliminary merger negotiations?
2. What material should a factfinder review to assess the probability that an event will occur at the highest corporate level that would create a duty to disclose preliminary merger talk?
3. The Court defined materiality as the "significance a reasonable investor would place on the withheld or misrepresented information" in determining whether merger negotiation is material. What ethical standard is the Court suggesting by relying upon the "reasonable investor" to determine materiality?

The Court, by requiring a case-by-case review for materiality, creates a flexible and realistic rule. It appears a *duty to disclose* preliminary merger talk occurs only when it would not hurt business prospects. Disclosure of even material information is premature and not ripe when it may harm corporate and shareholder interest.

Antifraud Provisions: Insider Trading on Material Nonpublic Inside Information

The statutory duty imposed by Rule 10b-5 prohibits all persons from engaging in any act, practice, or course of business that operates or would operate as a fraud or deceit upon any person, in connection with the purchase or sale of any security.

The federal courts have held a wide variety of persons liable under this section of Rule 10b-5.

1. *Conventional Insiders.* The classic case of insider trading involves a breach of a fiduciary duty owed by officers, directors, majority shareholders, and high-level employees to the corporation and stockholders. This group of conventional insiders must disclose material nonpublic inside information before trading in the security or abstain from trading until the information is made public. This is known as their duty to "disclose or abstain" from trading.
2. *Constructive Insiders.* Some outside individuals will have a working arrangement with a company that establishes a corporate expectation that disclosed nonpublic information be kept confidential. In footnote 14 of the important Supreme Court case of *Dirks* v. *SEC,* 463 U.S. 646 (1983), the court stated,

   > Under certain circumstances, such as where corporate information is revealed legitimately to an underwriter, accountant, lawyer or consultant working for the corporation, these outsiders may become fiduciaries of the shareholders. The basis for recognizing this fiduciary duty is . . . that they have entered into a special confidential relationship . . . and are given access to information solely for corporate purposes.

   In order to be a **constructive insider** you must be employed by the company and be given confidential information for corporate purposes. In this capacity you may not trade the stock before the information is made public.
3. *Noninsiders.* Simply trading on material nonpublic information is not a violation of Rule 10b-5 if the trader had no fiduciary relationship or similar duty with the corporation. In the 1980 Supreme Court case, *Chiarella* v. *United States,* the Department of Justice brought a criminal action alleging intentional violation of Rule 10b-5 against a printer who handled documents that announced a tender offer and bought stock in the target company. Chiarella was a printer who, in 1975 and 1976, worked as a "markup man" in the New York composing room of the Pandick Press, a financial printer. Among various documents that Chiarella handled were five announcements of corporate takeover bids. Chiarella was able to deduce from the documents the names of the target companies to be purchased. Without disclosing his knowledge, he purchased stock in the target companies and immediately sold the shares after the takeover attempts were made public, realizing a gain of more than $30,000 in the course of fourteen months. Chiarella was indicted for violating section 10(b) and SEC Rule 10b-5. Did Chiarella have a duty to disclose the information he obtained? No duty could arise from Chiarella's relationship with the sellers of the target company's securities, for Chiarella had no prior dealings with them. He was not their agent, he was not a fiduciary, he was not a person in whom the sellers had placed their trust and confidence. He was, in fact, a complete stranger who dealt with the sellers only through impersonal market transactions.

Shortly after *Chiarella* was decided, the SEC issued *Rule 14e-3* that states in part:

> If any person has taken a substantial step to commence . . . a tender offer, it shall constitute a fraudulent, deceptive or manipulative act . . . for any person . . . in possession of [such] material information . . . which he knows is nonpublic and . . . which has been acquired directly or indirectly from (1) the offering person, (2) the issuer of the securities, or (3) any person, director, officer, partner, or employee or any other person acting on behalf of the offering person or such issuer, to purchase or sell [the securities], unless within a reasonable time prior to any purchase or sale such information and its source are publicly disclosed by press release or otherwise.

4. *Wrongful "Tippee" Trader.* A **tippee** receives nonpublic material information from an inside tipper. A tippee has no independent fiduciary duty to the corporation or its shareholders and hence his liability derives from the tipper violating a duty to disclose that is passed onto the tippee. In order to be a wrongful tipper, there must be a breach of the fiduciary duty by the tipper passed on to the tippee.

The following landmark Supreme Court case involved an officer of a broker/dealer firm who specialized in investment analysis of insurance company securities. A former officer of a life insurance corporation informed him that the corporation's assets were fraudulently overstated and asked him to verify the fraud and disclose it publicly. Such inside material information given from one party to another creates a "tipper/tippee" relationship. Although neither the broker/dealer nor his firm owned or traded in the insurance company stock, throughout his investigation he openly discussed the information he obtained with a number of his clients and investors, some of whom sold their holdings to avoid a loss. As you read the case, carefully note the reasons why the tippee, the investment analyst, was not under a duty to abstain from using the inside information.

Dirks v. SEC

463 U.S. 646 (1983)

Facts

In 1973, Dirks was an officer of a New York broker/dealer firm who specialized in providing investment analysis of insurance company securities to institutional investors. On March 6, Dirks received information from Ronald Secrist, a former officer of Equity Funding of America. Secrist alleged that the assets of Equity Funding, a diversified corporation primarily engaged in selling life insurance and mutual funds, were vastly overstated as the result of fraudulent corporate practices. Secrist also stated that various regulatory agencies had failed to act on similar charges made by Equity Funding employees. He urged Dirks to verify the fraud and disclose it publicly.

Dirks decided to investigate the allegations. The senior management denied any wrongdoing, but certain corporation employees corroborated the charges of fraud. Neither Dirks nor his firm owned or traded any equity funding stock, but throughout his investigation he openly discussed the information he had obtained with a number of *clients and investors. Some of these persons sold their holdings of Equity Funding securities, including five investment advisers who liquidated holdings of more than $16 million.*

During the two-week period in which Dirks pursued his investigation and spread word of Secrist's charges, the price of Equity Funding stock fell from $26 per share to less than $15 per share. This led the New York Stock Exchange to halt trading on March 27.

The SEC began an investigation into Dirks' role in the exposure of the fraud. The SEC concluded: "Where 'tippees'—regardless of their motivation or occupation—come into possession of material information that they know is confidential and know or should know came from a corporate insider, they must either publicly disclose that information or refrain from trading." Recognizing, however, that Dirks "played an important role in bringing [Equity Funding's] massive fraud to light," the SEC only censured him.

Opinion

Justice Powell: We were explicit in *Chiarella* in saying that there can be no duty to disclose where the person who has traded on inside information "was not [the corporation's] agent, . . . was not a fiduciary, [or] was not a person in whom the sellers [of the securities] had placed their trust and confidence."

Imposing a duty to disclose or abstain solely because a person knowingly receives material nonpublic information from an insider and trades on it could have an inhibiting influence on the role of market analysts, which the SEC itself recognizes is necessary to the preservation of a healthy market.

The conclusion that recipients of inside information do not invariably acquire a duty to disclose or abstain does not mean that such tippees always are free to trade on the information. The need for a ban on some tippee trading is clear. Not only are insiders forbidden by their fiduciary relationship from personally using undisclosed corporate information to their advantage, but they may not give such information to an outsider for the same improper purpose of exploiting the information for their personal gain. Similarly, the transactions of those who knowingly participate with the fiduciary in such a breach are "as forbidden" as transactions "on behalf of the trustee himself."

Thus, some tippees must assume an insider's duty to the shareholders not because they receive inside information, but rather because it has been made available to them improperly. Thus, a tippee assumes a fiduciary duty to the shareholders of a corporation not to trade on material nonpublic information only when the insider has breached his fiduciary duty to the shareholders by disclosing the information to the tippee and the tippee knows or should know that there has been a breach.

In determining whether a tippee is under an obligation to disclose or abstain, it thus is necessary to determine whether the insider's "tip"constituted a breach of the insider's fiduciary duty. All disclosures of confidential corporate information are not inconsistent with the duty insiders owe to shareholders. In contrast to the extraordinary facts of this case, the more typical situation in which there will be a question whether disclosure violates the insider's *Cady, Roberts* duty is when insiders disclose information to analysts. In some situations, the insider will act consistently with his fiduciary duty to shareholders, and yet release of the information may affect the market. For example, it may not be clear—either to the corporate insider or to the recipient analyst—whether the information will be viewed as material nonpublic information. Corporate officials may mistakenly think the information already has been disclosed or that it is not material enough to affect the market. Whether disclosure is a breach of duty therefore depends in large part on the purpose of the disclosure. Thus, the test is whether the insider personally will benefit, directly or indirectly, from his disclosure. Absent some personal gain, there has been no breach of duty to stockholders. And absent a breach by the insider, there is no derivative breach.

Under the inside-trading and tipping rules set forth above, we find that there was no actionable violation by Dirks. It is undisputed that Dirks himself was a stranger to Equity Funding, with no preexisting fiduciary duty to its shareholders. He took no action, directly or indirectly, that induced the shareholders or officers of Equity Funding to repose trust or confidence in him. There was no expectation by Dirk's sources that he would keep their information in confidence. Nor did Dirks misappropriate or illegally obtain the information about Equity Funding.

The tippers received no monetary or personal

benefit for revealing Equity Funding's secrets, nor was their purpose to make a gift of valuable information to Dirks. As the facts of this case clearly indicate, the tippers were motivated by a desire to expose the fraud. In the absence of a breach of duty to shareholders by the insiders, there was no derivative breach by Dirks.

We conclude that Dirks, in the circumstances of this case, had no duty to abstain from use of the inside information that he obtained.

Case Questions

1. What is the test, established by the *Dirks* case, to determine whether a tippee is under an obligation to disclose an insider's tip?
2. How did the Court apply the tippee test to Dirks in this case?
3. Give an ethical argument for the legal position of the SEC requiring that tippees who ". . . come into possession of material information that they know is confidential and know or should know came from a corporate insider must either publicly disclose that information or refrain from trading." Can you see a moral obligation for the tippee to disclose?

---

5. *Misappropriation Theory*. A recent development under Rule 10b-5 involves an employee having access to confidential information and a consequent duty not to misappropriate the information for his own use. Chief Justice Burger, dissenting in the *Chiarella* case, stated, "I would read Rule 10b-5 to encompass and build on this principle: to mean that a person who has misappropriated nonpublic information has an absolute duty to disclose that information or to refrain from trading." Justice Burger would allow Rule 10b-5 to reach *any* person engaged in *any* fraudulent scheme and not just corporate insiders.

In the following 1987 Supreme Court case, this **misappropriation theory** was used to affirm the conviction of a *Wall Street Journal*'s author of an investment column "Heard on the Street." The author, aware of the *Journal*'s rule that the column's contents were its property until publication, misappropriated the information and gave advanced leaks to others who bought and sold securities based on the leaked information, and shared the profits with him.

Carpenter v. U.S.

108 S.Ct. 316 (1987)

Facts

This case arises out of a scheme by the three petitioners, Kenneth Felis, R. Foster Winans, and David Carpenter, to misappropriate the Wall Street Journal*'s confidential information for their personal monetary benefit. The* Wall Street Journal *employed Winans, who periodically wrote for a column discussing stocks and their prospects. The perceived integrity of this column was formed to directly impact financial markets. Although Winans knew of the* Journal*'s policy of confidentiality prior to publication, he leaked advance information to two Kidder Peabody employees. The conspirators shared in profits made through their prepublication* *trades of the stocks later appearing as subjects in Winans' columns. The Court of Appeals for the Second Circuit agreed with the district court convictions of Felis and Winans for violations of: (1) § 10 (b) of the Securities Exchange Act of 1934 and Rule 10b-5; (2) the federal mail and wire fraud statutes; and (3) conspiracy. The other petitioner, Carpenter, was convicted for aiding and abetting the conspiracy. The United States Supreme Court granted certiorari.*

Opinion

Justice White: The Court is evenly divided with respect to the convictions under the securities laws and . . . affirms the judgment below. . . . [Petitioners] knowingly breached a duty of confidentiality by misappropriating prepublication information regarding the timing and contents of the "Heard" columns . . . [which] was a fraud and deceit on the *Journal* [in violation of §10(b) and Rule 10b-5]. [The court considered this] to be "in connection with" a purchase or sale of securities within the meaning of the statute and the rule . . . [since] the scheme's sole purpose was to buy and sell securities at a profit based on advance information of the column's contents.

[The Court next considered Petitioners' convictions under the federal mail and wire fraud statutes. The Court unanimously affirmed petitioners' convictions. Here, the object of the scheme was to take the *Journal*'s confidential business information. . . .] Both courts below expressly referred to the *Journal*'s interest in the confidentiality of the contents and timing the "Heard" column as a property right . . . and [the Court agrees] with that conclusion. [T]he publication schedule and contents of the "Heard" column—and its intangible nature does not make it any less "property" protected by the mail and wire fraud statutes. The confidential information was generated from the business and the business had the right to decide how to use it. . . . [An actionable mail and wire fraud claim does not require monetary loss because] it is sufficient that the *Journal* has been deprived of its right to exclusive use. . . . [The Court rejected] petitioners' further argument that Winans' conduct in revealing prepublication information was no more than a violation of work place rules . . . [rather than a violation of both the federal wire] and mail fraud statute[s]. [Since the statutes reach any scheme to deprive another of money or property by means of false or fraudulent pretenses, the Court stated that] even in the absence of a written contract, an employee has a fiduciary obligation to protect confidential information obtained. . . . [The Court had] little trouble in holding that the conspiracy here to trade on the *Journal*'s confidential information is not outside the reach of the mail and wire fraud statutes provided the other elements of the offenses are satisfied. [T]he District Court's conclusion that each of the petitioners acted with the required specific intent to defraud is strongly supported by the evidence—lastly, we reject the submission that using the wires and the mail to print and send the *Journal* to its customers did not satisfy the requirement that those mediums be used to execute the scheme. . . . [The] circulation of the "Heard" column was not only anticipated but an essential part of the scheme.

Case Questions

1. How did the court resolve the problem that Winans had no written contract to protect confidential information of the *Wall Street Journal?*
2. How did the Court use the misappropriations theory to establish liability under section 10(b) and Rule 10b-5?
3. How would you assess Winans' ethics in this case?

The Insider Trading Sanctions Act of 1984

On August 10, 1984, President Reagan signed the **Insider Trading Sanctions Act,** Public Law 93–376, whose provisions increase the sanctions against unlawful insider trading in publicly held securities by people possessing material nonpublic information. Before this law was passed, the SEC could bring an injunction against an inside trader, and the defendant insider had to turn over any profits made from the illegal transaction. Under the act, a district court may now impose a civil penalty of up to three times the profit gained by any person who has violated the 1934 Securities Exchange Act by purchasing or selling a security while in possession of material nonpublic information. A criminal fine for violation of the Securities Exchange Act is increased under the statute from $10,000 to $100,000. The Insider Trading Sanctions Act authorizes the SEC to bring administrative proceedings against "any person who was a cause of the failure" to comply with the statute by "aiding and abetting" the wrongdoer's offense. This language will allow the SEC to bring administrative proceedings against nontrading "tippers." That can include brokers and dealers who knew of the inside information or passed it on to a customer.

Proxies

You recall from the chapter on business organizations that the board of directors is elected by the stockholders at the annual meeting. Stockholders also vote on other essential business matters that would change the nature of the business or its ownership. A change in the purpose of the business, a change in its authorized stock, or its merging with another company all require stockholder approval. For each share of stock owned you have one vote. However, most shareholders of large corporations do not attend annual meetings; instead, they give their votes in writing to management in advance of the meeting. This is called a **proxy.** With a sufficient number of votes, management can ensure control of the corporate board by electing or re-electing its selected representatives.

In an attempt to protect the investing public, the SEC has established rules that regulate the proxy form and the information it provides to the stockholders. The rules pertain only to those corporations that have registered securities with the SEC. Under the rules, prior to a stockholders' annual meeting, each shareholder must be furnished a **proxy statement** accompanied by an annual report containing financial information for at least the past two years. A proxy statement is a document providing sufficient information to allow stockholders to authorize others intelligently to vote on their behalf.

Any company that distributes to its shareholders a proxy statement that contains misleading information may be liable in damages to a stockholder who sold or purchased the company's securities in reliance on the misleading information in the proxy statement.

What Constitutes Solicitation

In a 1966 Second Circuit case, *Studebaker Corporation* v. *Gittlin* (360 F. 2d 692), a stockholder, Gittlin, of Studebaker Corporation wanted to change the board of directors and desired to solicit proxies from the shareholders for the annual meeting. He brought suit when Studebaker refused to give him a list of the company shareholders. Studebaker then filed suit contending that Gittlin, the stockholder, gathered written authorization of forty-two shareholders, which constitutes a "solicitation." The court held the authorizations were proxy statements within the meaning of Section 14(a), and Rule 14a-3 was violated since he did not make the required filings within the SEC or give the forty-two shareholders the written proxy statements. Justice Friendly explained his rationale for this broad application for solicitation when he stated: "[T]he very fact that a copy of the stockholders list is a valuable instrument to a person seeking to gain control is a good reason for insuring that shareholders have full information before they aid its procurement."

Dissident Shareholder Proposals

Recent proxy proposals are concerned not so much with the traditional stockholders' interest in controlling management but rather with corporate social and political activities such as doing business in South Africa, pollution, and equal employment. As a shareholder of a corporation with registered securities, you have the right under **Rule 14a-8** to present a proposal to be voted upon at a stockholders' meeting. Management must include your proposal in its proxy statement and allow other shareholders to vote on it in their proxy. If management opposes your proposal, it must include in the proxy statement your written proposal in not more than two hundred words. To avoid complaints of any nature from interfering with the stockholders' meeting, management may omit your proposal if it (1) relates to a personal grievance, (2) is deemed by state corporate law to be an improper proposal, (3) is a nomination for a personal candidate to the board of directors, (4) relates to ordinary business conduct within the function of the corporate management, (5) is not related to the company's business, or (6) is similar to a previous proposal submitted and defeated during the past five years. However, if the proposal receives 3 percent of the votes cast, it can be resubmitted the following year. *Rule 14a-8(c)(5)* allows management to omit a shareholder's proposal if it is not *significantly related* to the issuer's business. The SEC allows a proposal to be omitted if it relates to operations of *less than* 5 percent of the issuer's total assets and *less than* 5 percent of its net earnings and gross sales if the proposal is *not otherwise significantly related* to the issuer's business.

In the following case, management refused to include plaintiff's proposal to investigate a company procedure used to forcefeed geese in its proxy, claiming it was not significantly related to its business.

Lovenheim v. Iroquois Brands, Ltd.

618 F. Supp. 554 (D.D.C. 1985)

Facts

Peter C. Lovenheim, owner of two hundred shares of Iroquois Brands, Ltd. (IBL), seeks to prevent IBL from excluding his proposed resolution from the proxy materials prepared for a shareholders' meeting. Lovenheim's proposal relates to procedures used to forcefeed geese, and calls upon IBL to research the problem and report to the shareholders its findings. Lovenheim contends that the production methods amount to cruelty to animals and brought suit under section 14(a) of the Securities Exchange Act of 1934 and the Securities Exchange Commission Rule 14a-8. IBL, relying on an exception to the general rule of proposal inclusion, contends that its position is legally justified. IBL argued that, as a securities issuer, it may omit such shareholder proposals since the proposal relates to operations accounting for less than 5 percent of total assets, net earnings, and gross sales. Indeed, IBL lost money the year before on its paté sales. Lovenheim contends that his proposal is includable notwithstanding its failure to reach the 5 percent threshold. Therefore, Lovenheim submitted a motion for a preliminary injunction seeking to bar IBL from excluding his proposal from the corporation's proxy materials.

Opinion

Judge Gasch: The likelihood of plaintiff's prevailing in this litigation turns primarily on the applicability to plaintiff's proposal of the exception to the shareholder proposal rule contained in Rule 14a-8(c)(5).

None of the company's net earnings and less than .05 percent of its assets are implicated by plaintiff's proposal.

Plaintiff does not contest that his proposed resolution relates to a matter of little economic significance to Iroquois/Delaware. Nevertheless he contends that the Rule 14a-8(c)(5) exception is not applicable. . . .

Iroquois/Delaware challenges plaintiff's view that ethical and social proposals cannot be excluded even if they do not meet the economic or five percent test. Instead Iroquois/Delaware views the exception solely in economic terms as permitting omission of any proposals relating to a de minimis share or assets and profits. Iroquois/Delaware asserts that since corporations are economic entities, only an economic test is appropriate.

The Court would note that the applicability of the Rule 14a-8(c)(5) exception to Mr. Lovenheim's proposal represents a close question given the lack of clarity in the exception itself. Because of the apparent ambiguity of the rule, the Court considers the history of the shareholder proposal rule in determining the proper interpretation of the most recent version of the rule.

The Commission stated in 1976 that it did "not believe that subparagraph (c)(5) should be hinged solely on the economic relativity of a proposal." Thus the Commission required inclusion . . . "where the proposal has raised policy questions important enough to be considered 'significantly related' to the issuer's business."

As indicated above, the 1983 revision adopted the five percent test of economic significance in an effort to create a more objective standard. Nevertheless, in adopting this standard, the Commission stated that proposals will be includable notwithstanding their "failure to reach the specified economic thresholds if a significant relationship to the issuer's business is demonstrated.". . .

The Court cannot ignore the history of the rule which reveals no decision by the Commission to limit the determination to the economic criteria relied on by Iroquois/Delaware. The Court therefore holds that in light of the ethical and social significance of plaintiff's proposal and the fact that it implicates significant levels of sales, plaintiff has shown a likelihood of prevailing on the merits. . . .

CONCLUSION

For the reasons discussed above, the Court concludes that plaintiff's motion for preliminary injunction should be granted.

Case Questions

1. According to the court, when should a shareholder's proposal be included in a proxy that does not meet the specified economic thresholds. (i.e., the 5 percent test)?
2. Why did the court grant plaintiff's motion for a preliminary injunction that will allow the shareholder's proposal into the corporation's proxy material?
3. Do you agree with the court's holding that this case has an ethical and social significance? What ethical theory would justify the company's practice of forcefeeding geese?

Foreign Corrupt Practices Act of 1977

Congress passed the **Foreign Corrupt Practices Act (FCPA)** in response to the unethical practice of bribing foreign officials to obtain a contract in a foreign country. The act amends section 13(b) of the Securities Exchange Act of 1934 and requires corporations that report to the SEC to comply with specific accounting standards; it also prohibits any interstate business association, including those not subject to the Securities Exchange Act, from engaging in corrupt practices with foreign officials.

Accounting Standards

Under the FCPA, if your company had securities registered under the Securities Exchange Act of 1934 it would have to "make and keep books, records and accounts, which in reasonable detail, accurately and fairly reflect the transactions and dispositions of the assets of the issuer." In addition, various internal accounting controls must be maintained. Accountants generally audit financial documents on behalf of corporations. Often, corporate directors or officers make false, misleading, or incomplete statements to accountants. **Rule 13B2–2** provides that "no director or officer shall make a materially false or misleading statement, or omit to state, or cause another person to omit to state, any material fact necessary in order to make the statements made not misleading to an accountant in connection with any required audit or any preparation of a required document or report." Managers who communicate with auditors must make detailed and accurate statements or be held liable under the rule. Consider the potential strain this rule could place on a manager who is being questioned by an auditor. The manager knows that he can be held liable for any misleading or incomplete statement, even if it is unintentionally so. Do you think this is conducive to open and honest communication between corporations and their auditors? Keep in mind that violation of the act may subject the executive to criminal as well as civil liability. The accounting provisions of the FCPA apply to all corporations that have registered their securities with the SEC, even if they are not engaged in foreign business. Registered corporations must utilize detailed accounting controls and independent auditors at great expense. Under the FCPA, the SEC now requires that a more detailed account of financial information be given to present stockholders and potential investors.

Internal accounting controls are required to ensure that "(i) transactions are executed in accordance with management's general or specific authorization; (ii) transactions are recorded as necessary (I) to permit preparation of financial statements in conformity with generally accepted accounting principles or any other criteria applicable to such statements, and (II) to maintain accountability for assets; (iii) access to assets is permitted only in accordance with management's general or specific authorization; and (iv) the recorded accountability for assets is compared with the existing assets at reasonable intervals and appropriate action is taken with respect to any differences."

Off-the-books "slush funds" that were used to bribe foreign officials are made illegal by the act.

Foreign Corrupt Practices

The antibribery section of the FCPA applies to reporting corporations subject to the SEC, their officers, directors, employees, agents, and stockholders, and nonreporting corporations engaged in interstate commerce, that corruptly pay any official of a foreign government or a foreign political party for the purpose of influencing any decision in order to obtain or retain business. When there is doubt about the nature of payments to a foreign official, the Justice Department will review the material facts and will inform the corporation of its decision on the legality of the transaction.

Amendments of 1988

In 1988 the Foreign Corrupt Practices Act was amended. The amendments allow facilitating payments to a foreign official, political party, or party official to expedite or secure the performance of a routine governmental action. It is a prohibited foreign trade practice to use the mails (or any instrumentality of interstate commerce) to offer, pay, or promise to pay money to a foreign official or foreign political party in order to obtain or retain business. Violation under the amended Act permits a corporation fine of not more than $2,000,000, a civil fine of not more than $10,000, and a criminal fine of not more than $100,000 and/or imprisonment of not more than five years against an officer, director, or stockholder acting on behalf of a corporation.

The FCPA has been criticized for a variety of reasons. Some foreign countries have centuries-old traditions that often conflict with American concepts of ethical behavior. An example of this is the paying of money to officials to obtain a business contract. When American companies compete in foreign markets where bribery is a standard practice, do we place ourselves at a competitive disadvantage by not engaging in bribery? The public policy position established by the FCPA is clearly that bribery is an unacceptable way of transacting business, regardless of the economic benefit that may result.

An Ethical Perspective on Securities Regulations

Rule 10b-5 makes is unlawful to defraud or make a statement that would be misleading regarding the purchase or sale of a security. This rule is a perfect example of how the law can codify an ethical obligation between the buyer and seller of a security. The seller may take the unethical position that his primary purpose in the transaction is to persuade rather than inform the investor. Rule 10b-5 allows persuasion, providing that it is not misleading. An investor's freedom of choice is violated if she purchases a security based on information that is fraudulent, untrue, or misleading.

Another example of business ethics in the securities laws is the liability of a tippee who uses inside material information about a business that would affect the value of its securities without first disclosing that information to the investing public. Is it unethical for a corporate insider who has access to such information to keep it quiet for his own profit-making purposes? Can it be ethically argued that one of the benefits of being a corporate executive is the availability of insider information to be used for private profit?

The important concepts and terms in this chapter are listed on the following page; page numbers have been provided for the key terms. By reading over each section you can assess your understanding of the chapter concepts and determine areas you may want to review.

Chapter Summary

1. Rule 10b-5 makes it unlawful "to engage in any act, practice, or course of business which operates as a fraud or deceit upon any person in connection with the purchase or sale of any security." The rule applies to registered and nonregistered securities.
2. A tender offer is an offer made by an acquiring company to the shareholders of a company targeted for acquisition to purchase their stock. Generally, an information statement about the terms of the tender offer must be filed with the SEC and each stockholder to whom the offer is made.
3. Insiders who purchase securities are required to hold them for six months or be held liable for short-swing profits.
4. Dissident shareholders have a right to present a proposal to management for inclusion in the proxy statement; unless excluded under SEA rules, the proposal must be voted upon at a stockholders' meeting.
5. The Foreign Corrupt Practices Act requires corporations that have registered securities with the SEC to comply with specific accounting standards and prohibits any business association engaging in interstate commerce from engaging in corrupt practices with foreign officials.
6. A tippee is a person who acquires material inside information, and in breach of his or her fiduciary duty, trades securities without first disclosing that information to the public.
7. The Williams Act (section 13d of the Securities Exchange Act of 1934) provides a disclosure requirement whenever a person or group acquires more than 5 percent of the voting stock of a public company.
8. A private party may bring a civil action under Rule 10b-5 alleging misrepresentation in a registration statement.
9. A person who has misappropriated nonpublic information has an absolute duty to disclose that information under Rule 10b-5 or refrain from trading his stock.
10. The SEC allows a dissident shareholder proposal to be omitted if it relates to operations of *less than* 5 percent of the issuer's total assets

and *less than* 5 percent of its net earnings and gross sales if the proposal is *not otherwise significantly related* to the issuer's business.

Key Terms

constructive insider 563
Foreign Corrupt Practices Act (FCPA) 571
"friendly" takeover 550
Insider Trading Sanctions Act 567
insider 555
misappropriation theory 566
proxy 568
proxy statement 568
Rule 10b-5 560
Rule 13B2–2 571
Rule 14 a-8 569
short-swing profits 558
takeover bid 550
tender offer 550
tippee 564
Williams Act 552

Questions on Ethics

1. Harry Slade is a corporate comptroller for a corporation with a public listing of securities. He is reviewing the corporation's books and records with the auditor, Nancy Wilson. Harry's company trades with third world countries that often require "front money" before a contract is signed. The company maintains a "slush fund" for such payments. When questioned by Nancy about the nature of the payments, Harry has equated them to a commission. Nancy insists they are bribes. How would you characterize the nature of the front money payments that are required before any contracts are executed? Would you find it an ethical practice to provide front money in order to be awarded a contract? Would the fact that this is a customary practice in some foreign countries affect your answer?
2. Mary Cummings is a shareholder who is deeply distressed with her company's methods of marketing of infant formula in third world countries. She feels ethically obligated to express her concern in a proxy statement and allow other shareholders to vote on her proposal demanding that the company stop marketing the infant formula in some countries. Her lawyer has informed her that under SEC Rule 14a-8, management may omit her proposal because it relates to a personal grievance and such a marketing decision is within the sole function of corporate management. Do you agree with her lawyer's judgment? Are ethical grievances within the province of a stockholder's proxy

proposal? Do you think a stockholders' meeting is the proper forum to discuss ethical issues? Explain.

3. David Johnson is a director of Air Industries, Inc., a publicly owned corporation that recently signed a $5 million contract with the Department of Defense to produce air conditioning systems for nuclear-powered submarines. Before the news was published, anticipating a substantial increase in the company stock, he purchased an additional ten thousand shares. Johnson feels that acquiring inside information is one of the benefits of being a director and that there is nothing wrong with his conduct. Do you agree?
4. Fast Delivery Company has submitted a proposal of purchase to the directors of one of its competitors, Fly Package, Inc., to buy its entire stock. The proposal was refused by the directors of Fly Package, and Fast Delivery has proceeded to effect a deal directly with the shareholders of Fly Package by making an attractive tender offer to purchase their stock. The motive for purchasing Fly Package is to eliminate the competition and acquire its aircraft. Is it ethical for an acquiring company whose proposal to purchase was refused by the directors of the target company to make a tender offer to the target company's shareholders in order to effect a merger and eliminate the target company's competition?
5. Harry Peterson is a marketing vice-president for DIPCO, Inc. He purchased ten thousand shares of DIPCO stock based on inside information that the company was about to enter into a joint venture with a Chinese company. The potential sales in the People's Republic of China could exceed a million dollars. Harry held the stock for seven months, then sold the stock and made a substantial profit. Under the short-swing profit rule, Harry is not liable because he held onto the stock for more than six months. What is the underlying ethical theory that supports a rule of this nature where a person can use inside information to his own advantage providing he holds the stock for six months? Was Harry acting ethically by holding his stock for seven months before selling to make a profit?

Questions on Law

1. Mosinee Paper Corporation had 800,000 shares outstanding. Rondeau made large purchases of Mosinee stock in the over-the-counter market and eventually owned 40,413 shares of Mosinee stock. Rondeau never filed a Schedule 13D and accumulated 60,000 total shares. He was notified by the chairman of the board of Mosinee of a securities law violation. He then filed a Schedule 13D indicating that his original purchases had been made with an investment intent but he was currently considering obtaining control of Mosinee through a tender offer.

Mosinee sent a letter to its shareholders informing them of Rondeau's late filing of his Schedule 13D and filed suit in the federal district court alleging a 13D violation and seeking an injunction prohibiting Rondeau from voting his stock or acquiring additional stock. Decide. *Rondeau* v. *Mosinee Paper Corp.*, 422 U.S. 49 (1975).

2. Merrill Lynch was the managing underwriter for a proposed debenture offering of Douglas Aircraft Co., who informed Merrill Lynch that its projected earnings would be much lower than it previously indicated in its public statements. Several of Merrill Lynch's employees disclosed this confidential information to a number of institutional investors who were customers of Merrill Lynch. They then sold more than 165,000 shares of Douglas stock. The information on the decreased earnings of Douglas was not made public until later. Plaintiff brought a class action, on behalf of all persons who purchased Douglas stock before the information on decreased earnings was made public, against Merrill Lynch and its employees who tipped the institutional investors. Merrill Lynch claims the "disclose or abstain" rule is not applicable here because the transactions involved were not face-to-face sales to plaintiffs. Decide. *Shapiro* v. *Merrill Lynch, Pierce, Fenner & Smith*, 495 F.2d 288 (2d Cir. 1974).
3. A shareholders' proposal would prohibit abortions in Hospital Corporation of America's facilities, other than emergency procedures necessary to prevent the imminent death of a pregnant woman. The company sought to omit the proposal based on Rule 14a-8(c) permitting exclusion of proposals on matters relating to the conduct of ordinary business operations. Decide. *Hospital Corp. of America* v. *SEC* (February 12, 1986).
4. Baird, an investment banking firm, employed Gaspar, who counseled DKM Corporation in an acquisition of Clark Oil and Refining Corporation. Gaspar informed Schreck, a registered representative of a broker dealer, of the potential takeover before this information was known to the public. Schreck then purchased Clark stock before the information became public. Gaspar, however, did not trade any shares of Clark Oil. The SEC brought a section 10(b) action against Gaspar. Discuss the liability, if any, of Gaspar. *SEC* v. *Gaspar*, Federal Securities Law Reports (CCH), S. 92, 004 (S.D. N.Y. 1985).
5. Barbara Dean was recently promoted to president and chief executive officer of Aerotech Industries, Inc., a multinational corporation with stock traded on the New York Stock Exchange. Part of her compensation includes 14 percent common stock ownership in the company. Barbara sold 5 percent of her stock within five months of its purchase and realized a short-term capital gain of $20,000. How does the securities law characterize Barbara's status? What, if any, SEC legal requirement must she comply with? What legal remedy, if any, do the shareholders of Aerotech Industries have against Barbara?

Suggested Readings

Bagby, "The Evolving Controversy over Insider Trading," 24 *American Business Law Journal* 4 (1987).

Fox, "SEC Rule 10b-5: Tippee Liability Revisited," 22 *American Business Law Journal* 3 (1984).

Hurd, "Insider Trading and Foreign Bank Secrecy," 24 *American Business Law Journal* 1 (1986).

Huss and Leete, "Insider Trading Regulations: A Comparison of Judicial and Statutory Sanctions," 25 *American Business Law Journal* 2 (1987).

Wang, "*Dirks* v. *Securities and Exchange Commission:* An Outsider's Guide to Insider Trading Liability Under Rule 10b-5," 22 *American Business Law Journal* 4 (1985).

21 Environmental Law

> *There was a time when the seas seemed endless and the skies vast enough to swallow any of the mistakes and errors of man. The world used to be big and men could afford to be small. Now the world is small and men must be big.*
>
> *—Elliot Lee Richardson*

LEARNING OBJECTIVES

After you have read this chapter, you should be able to:

1. Explain the traditional "common fund" view regarding use of the environment.
2. Be familiar with how common law legal theories and zoning laws are used to regulate use of the environment.
3. Understand the federal laws that have been passed in an attempt to protect the environment.
4. Appreciate the legal and ethical problems that may arise when society's interest in cleaning up the environment conflicts with individual property rights and the ability of some individuals to make a living.

Business Decisions and the Law

Meeting the Future Head-On

You have assumed the responsibilities of chief executive officer at a large plant that manufactures heavy-duty motor vehicles. Your company's research and development department informs you that your company has the technical capability to achieve a particular level of emission control in your engines, but no more. However, an Environmental Protection Agency representative informs you that you will have to conform to emission control guidelines the agency states can be achieved. Your company's chief engineer in charge of product development flatly states that the EPA standards cannot be achieved with the technology available today. When your legal department advises you that suit in federal court is the avenue by which you can have the question resolved, you file suit to learn . . . (see *Natural Resources Defense Council* v. *Thomas*).

Introduction

Throughout most of the history of the common law, the environment was regarded as a "common fund" that everyone could use in any way they saw fit, as long as another person's specific property rights were not violated. There was no legal liability for indirect damage to the environment. For example, a person who owned a piece of forested property on a hill could cut down all of the timber, even if the result was soil erosion that damaged fields at the bottom of the hill. The landowner could not, of course, cut wood on the property of another. This attitude was in keeping with the theory of laissez-faire (let them do what they will), which was prevalent at the time.

As the years passed, especially with the advent of the Industrial Revolution, it became obvious that a laissez-faire attitude toward use of the environment was having an adverse impact on everyone. Untreated wastes of all types were being discharged into waterways; the burning of coal created severe air pollution, particularly in manufacturing areas; and chemical or toxic wastes were dumped in any convenient place. The result of these practices was often undrinkable water in which fish could not live, air that caused respiratory ailments, and physical injury caused by exposure to chemical wastes. An example of the last-mentioned problem was the so-called Mad Hatter syndrome. The problem occurred during the nineteenth century among workers who made hats (which were treated with lead and mercury). The bizarre behavior that resulted from their exposure to these chemicals led to the creation of the stereotype of the "mad hatter."

By the late nineteenth century, misuse of the environment by business and others had become bad enough that the first "environmentalist" movement began, and Congress began to pass laws to deal with some of the problems. The establishment of the United States National Parks system, which generally prohibited business use of national park lands, was a first step in limiting laissez-faire ideas of environmental use. In 1890, Congress passed the first specific environmental law, the Rivers and Harbors Act, which is still used today to alleviate water pollution problems.

As you will see in the following discussion, most of the legal regulation of the environment is the result of laws passed since the 1960s. The passage of these laws coincided with an era of legal activism in such other areas as consumer protection and employer-employee relationships. This activism was fostered by a societal decision that private individuals and business had failed to serve the best interests of society in their interactions with the environment, and that, therefore, the passage of laws was necessary to protect the environment for the good of the public. In this chapter, we will examine the use of the common law to alleviate environmental pollution, and we will concentrate on the federal statutes that have become effective since 1970 and form the backbone of environmental law today.

Common Law Legal Theories and Zoning Laws

The common law (judge-made or case law) has not played an extremely important part in regulating the effects of human activity on the environment. However, four common law theories that might be used in environmental cases are trespass, strict liability, riparian rights, and nuisance, with nuisance being the only theory that has been used frequently.

An action for *trespass* can be maintained when one person uses or interferes with another person's property rights. *Strict liability in tort* may come into play if a person or business engages in an extremely hazardous activity, such as blasting with explosives, which injures another person or his property. Under the theory of *riparian rights,* in all parts of the country except certain states in the West, an upstream landowner cannot change the course of flow or significantly change the volume of flow of a waterway.

The tort of **nuisance** dates back to the Middle Ages. Nuisance consists of an unreasonable interference with either a person's use or enjoyment of his real property or with the well-being of the public. Nuisance and trespass differ in that trespass requires a physical intrusion onto someone's property, while nuisance does not. Some examples of nuisance include maintenance of unhealthy conditions that allow vermin to breed and overrun adjoining property; construction of a fly-infested, smelly livestock feed lot in a hot climate directly adjacent to an apartment complex; burning refuse in a location that allows smoke to billow onto a public road. If a plaintiff can prove that a condition constitutes an illegal nuisance, the usual remedy is issuance of an injunction, although it is possible to receive an award of monetary damages.

Nuisance cases often require courts to determine whether it is more appropriate to grant a plaintiff a remedy of injunction or monetary damages, as shown in a case involving the Reserve Mining Company of Minnesota. The courts determined that it was in the best interest of society to let Reserve continue to operate as it paid monetary damages and began to "clean up its act," rather than issue a shut-down injunction. On the other hand, the 1981 federal court case of *Twitty* v. *North Carolina* resulted in the courts denying both injunctive and monetary relief to private citizens bringing action against the state of North Carolina and the Environmental Protection Agency. The suit sought an injunction denying the state of North Carolina the right to use a landfill approved by the state legislature as a disposal site for toxic PCBs, asserting such usage would constitute a nuisance. However, the court refused to enjoin as a nuisance an action authorized by valid legislative authority; it also determined that the federal Toxic Substances Control Act automatically pre-empted any state or local ordinances that the landowners raised.

Local **zoning** ordinances can also be used to deal with environmental pollution. Municipalities have state statutory authorization to control land use through zoning ordinances. The typical zoning ordinance divides a municipality into areas (zones) and designates the types of land use allowed in each area. For example, an apartment building cannot be built in an area designated single-family residence only. Zoning ordinances can be used to prohibit or limit certain types of land use that might have a damaging effect on the environment. For example, they might restrict industrial use to certain areas, so as to minimize exposure of the residents to fumes or smoke. Whether zoning laws exist and the extent to which they have an effect on pollution sources varies by locality.

Federal Regulation of Use of the Environment

Environmental law, which limits the types of effects individuals and businesses may have on the environment, is almost overwhelmingly federal statutory law. In this section you will study the most important federal environmental statutes. You should note that most states have passed various types of environmental protection laws that complement the federal statutes and have created state agencies that carry out activities similar to those of the federal Environmental Protection Agency.

Although a large number of federal statutes deal with protection of the environment, the ones with the greatest impact are the National Environmental Policy Act, the Clean Air Act, the Clean Water Act, the Solid Waste Disposal Act, the Toxic Substances Control Act, and the Comprehensive Environmental Response, Compensation and Liability Act (Superfund). We will study each of these acts and analyze both their provisions and the problems that have occurred in their administration.

The National Environmental Policy Act

The **National Environmental Policy Act (NEPA),** which went into effect in 1970, is the "granddaddy" of federal environmental statutes. This act does not contain a large number of provisions that regulate specific activities affecting the environment, but instead makes a general policy statement that the government is committed to assessing and regulating the impact of individual activities on the environment. The NEPA established a Council on Environmental Quality (CEQ), which is required to gather information concerning the environment, to review and evaluate existing federal environmental policies and recommend new ones if needed, and to make annual reports on the condition of the environment.

Perhaps the most legally significant provision of the NEPA is its requirements for submission of **environmental impact statements (EISs).** The NEPA requires that before the occurrence of any major proposed federal action that significantly affects the quality of the human environment (including actions by federal agencies and by others, including states, who act using federal funds), an environmental impact statement must be submitted. The CEQ has issued guidelines concerning the preparation of EISs (including a requirement that the EIS generally be no longer that 150 pages). The NEPA requires an EIS to contain a detailed statement of (1) the environmental impact of a proposed action, (2) any adverse environmental effect that cannot be avoided should the proposal be implemented, (3) alternatives to the proposed action, (4) the relationship between local short-term uses of the environment and the maintenance and enhancement of long-term productivity, and (5) any irreversible and irretrievable commitments of resources that would be involved in the proposed action should it be implemented.

Almost all litigation concerning the NEPA has centered on the EIS requirement and interpretation of such phrases in the requirement as "major action," "federal action," "a significant effect," and "quality of the human environment." There have been so many cases covering such a great number of specific issues that it is difficult to make any meaningful generalizations about the interpretation of these phrases. However, as examples, the following would require filing of an EIS: building fairly long lengths of state roads using federal funds, building missile silos, and leasing federal lands for mining purposes. The following would not require the filing of an EIS: a decision by the Army to eliminate an Army base, or a decision by a federal agency to reduce its workforce due to budgetary cutbacks. While there has been a decrease in the number of NEPA lawsuits filed since the middle 1970s, a number of environmental groups, property owners, and business associations continue to insist that the NEPA's EIS provisions be enforced.

Metropolitan Edison Company v. People Against Nuclear Energy

103 S. Ct. 1556 (1983)

Facts

The issue in these cases was whether petitioner Nuclear Regulatory Commission (NRC) complied with the National Environmental Policy Act (NEPA) when it decided to permit petitioner Metropolitan Edison Co. to resume operation of the Three Mile Island Unit 1 nuclear power plant (TMI-1). The Court of Appeals for the District of Columbia Circuit held that the NRC improperly failed to consider whether the risk of an accident at TMI-1 might cause harm to the psychological health and community well-being of residents of the surrounding area. The Supreme Court reversed.

Metropolitan owns two nuclear power plants at Three Mile Island near Harrisburg, Pennsylvania. Both of these plants were licensed by the NRC after extensive proceedings, which included preparation of environmental impact statements (EIS). On March 28, 1979, TMI-1 was not operating; it had been shut down for refueling. TMI-2 was operating, and it suffered a serious accident that damaged the reactor. Although, as it turned out, no dangerous radiation was released, the accident caused widespread concern.

After the accident, the NRC ordered Metropolitan to keep TMI-1 shut down until it had an opportunity to determine whether the plant could be operated safely. The NRC then published a notice of hearing specifying several safety related issues for consideration. The notice stated that the commission had not determined whether to consider psychological harm or other indirect effects of the accident or of renewed operation of TMI-1. It invited interested parties to submit briefs on this issue.

Petitioner, People Against Nuclear Energy (PANE), intervened and responded to this invitation. PANE is an association of residents of the Harrisburg area who are opposed to further operation of either TMI reactor. PANE contended that restarting TMI-1 would cause both severe psychological health damage to persons living in the vicinity, and serious damage to the stability, cohesiveness, and well-being of the neighboring communities.

The NRC decided not to take evidence concerning PANE's contentions. PANE filed a petition for review in the Court of Appeals, contending that both NEPA and the Atomic Energy Act required the NRC to address its contentions. Metropolitan intervened on the side of the NRC.

The Court of Appeals concluded that the Atomic Energy Act does not require the NRC to address PANE's contentions. It did find, however, that NEPA requires the NRC to evaluate "the potential psychological health effects of operating" TMI-1 that have arisen since the original EIS was prepared. It also held that, if the NRC finds that significant new circumstances or information exist on this subject, it shall prepare a "supplemental [EIS] which considers not only the effects on psychological health but also effects on the well-being of the communities surrounding Three Mile Island." The Supreme Court granted certiorari.

Opinion

Justice Rehnquist: All the parties agree that effects on human health can be cognizable under NEPA, and that human health may include psychological health. The Court of Appeals thought these propositions were enough to complete a syllogism that disposes of the case: NEPA requires agencies to consider effects on health. An effect on psychological health is an effect on health. Therefore, NEPA requires agencies to consider the effects on psychological health asserted by PANE. PANE, using similar reasoning, contends that because the psychological health damage to its members would be caused by a change in the environment (renewed operation of TMI-1), NEPA requires the NRC to consider that damage. Although these arguments are appealing at first glance, we believe they skip over an essential step in the analysis. They do not consider the closeness of the relationship between the change in the environment and the "effect" at issue.

To paraphrase the statutory language (of NEPA) in light of the facts of this case, where an agency action significantly effects the quality of the human environment, the agency must evaluate the "environmental impact" and any unavoidable adverse environmental effects of its proposal. The theme of 102 is sounded by the adjective "environmental": NEPA does not require the agency to assess *every* impact or effect of its proposed action, but only the impact or effect on the environment. If we were to seize the word "environmental" out of its context and give it the broadest possible definition, the words "adverse environmental effects" might embrace virtually any consequence of a governmental action that someone thought "adverse." But we think the context of the statute shows that Congress was talking about the physical environment—the world around us, so to speak. NEPA was designed to promote human welfare by alerting governmental actors to the effect of their proposed actions on the physical environment.

The federal action that affects the environment in this case is permitting renewed operation of TMI-1. The direct effects on the environment of this action include release of low-level radiation, increased fog in the Harrisburg area (caused by operation of the plant's cooling towers), and the release of warm water into the Susquehanna River. The NRC has considered each of these effects in its EIS. Another effect of renewed operation is a risk of a nuclear accident. The NRC has also considered this effect.

PANE argues that the psychological health damage it alleges "will flow directly from the risk of [a nuclear] accident." But a *risk* of an accident is not an effect on the physical environment. A risk is, by definition, unrealized in the physical world. In a causal chain from renewed operation at TMI-1 to psychological health damage, the element of risk and its perception by PANE's members are necessary middle links. We believe that the element of risk lengthens the causal chain beyond the reach of NEPA.

Risk is a pervasive element of modern life; to say more would belabor the obvious. Many of the risks we face are generated by modern technology, which brings both the possibility of major accidents and opportunities for tremendous achievements. Medical experts apparently agree that risk can generate stress in human beings, which in turn may rise to the level of serious health damage. For this reason among many others, the question whether the gains from any technological advance are worth its attendant risks may be an important public policy issue. Nonetheless, it is quite different from the question whether the same gains are worth a given level of alteration of our physical environment or depletion of our natural resources. The latter question rather than the former is the central concern of NEPA.

The Court of Appeals thought the harm alleged by PANE is far more severe than the harm alleged in other cases. It thought the severity of the harm is relevant to whether NEPA requires consideration of an effect. This cannot be the case. NEPA addresses environmental effects of federal actions. The gravity of harm does not change its character. If a harm does not have a sufficiently close connection to the physical environment, NEPA does not apply.

For these reasons, we hold that the NRC need not consider PANE's contentions. NEPA does not require agencies to evaluate the effects of risk, *qua* risk. The judgment of the Court of Appeals is reversed, and the case is remanded with instructions to dismiss the petition for review.

It is so ordered.

Case Questions

1. According to the Court, what type of impact on the environment must be discussed in an environmental impact statement (EIS)?
2. Does the Court accept impact on psychological health as a proper subject for an EIS?
3. As the Court points out, mounting medical evidence indicates that psychological stress can cause illness in human beings. Is it ethical then to discount the stress caused to persons living near an atomic energy plant?

The Environmental Protection Agency

The **Environmental Protection Agency (EPA)** was established by Reorganization Plan Number 3 in 1970 to consolidate the activities of various federal agencies regulating use of the environment as well as to enforce federal environmental laws. Although the number of lawsuits under the NEPA have declined over recent years, actions under such EPA-monitored legislation as the Clean Water Act (CWA), the Resource Conservation and Recovery Act (RCRA), and the Comprehensive Environmental Response, Compensation and Liability Act (CERCLA) have steadily risen since 1978. Courts are increasingly finding violators liable under all three of these acts; for example, an Alabama court determined that an electroplating company's CWA, RCRA, and CERCLA violations in illegal disposal of liquid electroplating wastes justified a \$200,000 fine as well as a prison sentence for the owner of the electroplating firm, while the company was liable for the estimated \$1.3 million cleanup cost of those wastes. One side effect of the EPA enforcement actions has been the birth of the "environmental-services industry," which exhibited a 30 to 40 percent growth rate in 1988.

The EPA is centered in Washington, D.C., and is headed by an administrator who also oversees the nation's ten regional EPA offices. This dispersion of monitoring responsibilities reflects the nature of the EPA enforcement task, which often requires on-site inspections.

The Clean Air Act

The **Clean Air Act (CAA),** which was originally enacted in 1955, amended into its basic form in 1970 and into its present form in 1977, strives to deal with the problem of air pollution in a number of ways. Its main functions are to allow the creation (by the EPA administrator) of air quality and air emissions standards and to provide for state implementation of EPA standards.

The EPA has devised different categories of standards to deal with various types of air pollution. General standards that outdoor air must meet to protect the public health are called **primary air quality standards,** while **secondary air quality standards** are designed to protect the public interest in other areas, such as vegetation and private property. The EPA requires that stationary (such as factories) and mobile (such as motor vehicles) sources of pollution reduce their emissions to the level of the primary and secondary air quality standards of the surrounding geographic area. Any new source of pollution whose emissions might endanger the public welfare must meet certain performance standards, which may be more restrictive than the standards for existing sources of pollution. Moreover, the most stringent pollution standards are reserved for those pollution sources that emit hazardous substances such as mercury or asbestos. Congress also extended the CAA's coverage with a 1986 amendment authorizing a research program concerning radon gas and indoor air quality.

One of the major criticisms of the CAA is that sources of pollution (both stationary and mobile) are supposed to meet air quality standards according to a timetable, and yet the technology to meet the standards may not exist at the time specified as a compliance deadline. Another criticism is that insufficient consideration is given under the CAA to the cost of compliance, especially the cost of achieving marginal maximum compliance (for example, the cost of meeting 100 percent of standards as opposed to 97 percent). It should be noted that the EPA can grant waivers and variances from its standards if they are unattainable or if compliance will create energy-related or economic (e.g., severe unemployment) emergencies.

The primary compliance mechanism of the CAA is the requirement that each state submit for the EPA's approval a state implementation plan (SIP). EPA approval of a state SIP is contingent upon the state's presenting both a plan and a timetable in which all areas of the state would meet EPA air quality standards. This requirement has created problems, particularly for areas that are already industrially developed, since strict enforcement of air quality standards could mean that no new plants could be built in a location that was already not in compliance with the standards. However, in the landmark CAA Supreme Court case of *Union Electric* v. *EPA* (1976), the Court held that compliance with an EPA-approved state implementation plan was mandatory, stating that technological infeasibility or economic considerations could not provide exemptions to the SIP mandate.

The following federal Court of Appeals case raised the question of whether EPA standards should be based on the technological capability of an industry leader, or whether the EPA had the authority to determine what standards an industry could become capable of meeting over a period of time.

Natural Resources Defense Council v. *Thomas*

805 F.2d 410 (D.C. Cir. 1986)

Opinion

Chief Judge Wald: The Clean Air Act Amendments of 1977 mandated for the first time emissions reduction for heavy duty motor vehicles. Congress required the Environmental Protection Agency to set standards for both gaseous and particulate matter emissions. After years of delay, and pursuant to an order of the District Court for the District of Columbia, the agency issued a notice of proposed rulemaking in 1984, and, finally, promulgated regulations to reduce heavy duty motor vehicle emissions in 1985. Raising a variety of substantive and procedural challenges, the Natural Resources Defense Council (NRDC) and the Engine Manufacturers Association petitioned this court for review of those regulations, the former arguing, essentially, that the standards were too lenient, the latter maintaining, predictably, that the standards were too stringent. We find that the agency has in the main acted reasonably in interpreting the substantive mandate of the law, but find that in two instances the agency failed to follow the appropriate statutory procedure. Therefore, we affirm in part, and reverse and remand in part.

The regulations under attack in this case represent one aspect of a twenty year old quest by Congress for effective motor vehicle emissions reduction. Responding to a national outcry for air pollution control, the Clean Air Act Amendments of 1965 first authorized the Environmental Protection Agency (agency or EPA) to regulate heavy duty vehicle (HDV) emissions. By the mid-1970s little had been done, however, and in 1977 Congress enacted a detailed, mandatory set of standards (Clean Air Act Amendments of 1977 or 1977 amendments) to effect emissions reduction from HDVs.

At issue here are the provisions requiring emissions reduction of oxides of nitrogen (NOx) and of particulate matter (PM). Along with carbon monoxide and hydrocarbons, oxides of nitrogen are a type of gaseous emission that Congress set out to reduce.

The NRDC's main argument is that the EPA failed to set HDV emissions standards at levels based on the capability of the technological leader in the industry, thereby running afoul of congressional intent. In reviewing an administrative agency's construction of its own enabling statute, we must follow the now familiar dictates of *Chevron U.S.A Inc.* v. *Natural Resources Defense Council, Inc.,* That case set forth a two-step procedure for judicial review of agency statutory construction. First, always, is the question whether Congress has directly spoken to the precise question at issue. If the intent of Congress is clear, that is the end of the matter.

If, however, "the statute is silent or ambiguous with respect to the specific issue, the question for the court is whether the agency's answer is based on a permissible construction of the statute.

Accordingly, we may reverse the agency's interpretation only if it is either contrary to a clear congressional mandate or if it is an unreasonable construction of that mandate.

The NRDC maintains that the statutory language for both NOx and PM emissions reduction mandates that the agency set standards based not on what the engine manufacturing industry as a *whole* can meet, but rather on what the *most advanced engine,* i.e., the technological leader, is capable of achieving. The NOx and PM emissions reduction provisions that the NRDC relies on read, respectively, as follows:

> In revising any [NOx] standard . . ., the Administrator shall determine the maximum degree of emission reduction which can be

achieved by means reasonably expected to be available for production of such period and shall prescribe a revised emission standard in accordance with such determination. . . .

[PM] regulations shall contain standards which reflect the greatest degree of emission reduction achievable through the application of technology which the Administrator determines will be available for the model year to which such standards apply, giving appropriate consideration to the cost of applying such technology within the period of time available to manufacturers and to noise, energy, and safety factors associated with the application of such technology.

The NRDC contends that by using the words "maximum" and "greatest" before the phrase "degree of emission reduction," in the NOx revised standards provision and the PM standards provision, respectively, Congress expressly indicated its intention that HDV emissions reduction standards be set at the performance level of the engine capable of achieving the "maximum" or "greatest" emissions reduction, i.e., the technological leader.

The NRDC agrees that a balance must take place, but maintains that it must occur within the confines of the technological leader. That is, the NRDC believes that the statute requires the agency to determine which engine can achieve the greatest emissions reduction, ascertain what level of emissions would result from the reduction, and then ratchet the standard back up to account for cost and other factors as they affect that leading engine. We find, however, nothing in the language of the provisions quoted above to indicate that Congress mandated such a leader-specific balancing of all the relevant factors in emissions reduction. Since the law was obviously meant to affect the whole industry, the more natural reading of the provisions as a whole is that Congress intended the balancing of emissions reduction capability versus cost and other factors to be done on an industry-wide basis, taking into account the broad spectrum of technological capabilities as well as cost and other factors. To read these provisions as mandating a standard that balances all the relevant statutory factors only within the framework of one engine rather than on an industry-wide basis would be a sufficiently novel interpretation as to require laser-like clarity on the part of Congress. Under basic statutory construction principles of clear statement, we certainly cannot imply such an interpretation from the language cited above.

A congressional scheme for complex regulation, like the Clean Air Act, ultimately requires much adjusting and finetuning. Its numerous mandates are rarely specific enough to be put in place automatically or followed mechanically. More often its purposes must be implemented through means and compromises chosen by the agency. So long as the main thrust of agency implementation appears to advance the congressional purpose, courts should be wary of interfering. Where congressional intent as to means is not clear, our role is merely to ensure that the agency's means are reasonable ones.

In this case, petitioners have offered a number of theories, often plausible, of how Congress intended the Clean Air Act Amendments of 1977 to be carried out. Because in most instances, however, where their claims were cognizable by the Court, the EPA was able to adduce an equally reasonable interpretation of the law it was assigned to execute, we must defer to the agency. Accordingly, the petitions for review are denied.

Case Questions

1. Did the court impose an impossible standard on the motor vehicle industry?
2. How important to the decision in this case were the rules of statutory construction regarding deference to agency action?

In addition to the debates surrounding technological feasibility and economic consideration of CAA compliance, the EPA had to address the problem of **nonattainment areas,** which are areas within a state not in compliance with federal EPA standards. The EPA has the final approval on designation of an area as attainment or nonattainment. In the federal Court of Appeals case of *Ohio* v. *Ruckelshaus* (1985), a Ohio county was designated as a nonattainment area, even though the air quality within the county met the EPA's required standards. The court upheld the EPA's refusal to redesignate the county as an attainment area, since evidence showed that county emissions contributed to ozone concentrations in urban "nonattainment" areas.

It is possible to build or add on to a facility in a nonattainment area if a permit is obtained in advance. A builder can obtain a permit if he shows that (1) the facility will use technology that achieves the lowest emissions possible, (2) all of that builder's other facilities in the state are meeting the air emissions standards of the state implementation plan, and (3) the builder **offsets** pollution from the new facility by reducing the same type of pollutants from other plants in the area. The concept of offsets is a mechanism by which the EPA balances economic growth with the mandates of the CAA.

In addition to creating provisions for allowing new construction in nonattainment areas, the CAA includes provisions for *prevention of significant deterioration* (PSD) in areas whose air quality was better than that prescribed by EPA standards. Persons wanting to build in a PSD area must install the best available control technology and must be able to show that the operation of the facility will not cause air quality to deteriorate. The state carries out a review before construction begins, and the preconstruction review procedures are included in the revised SIP that the state must submit to the EPA.

The EPA **"bubble concept"** allows any changes in equipment that either lower or maintain existing emissions rates to be exempt from preconstruction review requirements in PSD areas. In addition, a facility's compliance rate is calculated on the overall amount of pollution generated, not the amount generated by each pollution source—for example, each smokestack.

While the offset and bubble concepts were designed in the knowledge that compliance with the CAA can be very expensive for business, the CAA, as amended in 1977, did gain some new teeth for enforcement. Businesses that fail to comply with EPA air quality standards may now be assessed a penalty equal to the economic cost of compliance. This provision was designed to close a loophole in the CAA 1970 amendments, under which businesses found it less expensive to pay permanent damages than to take the measures necessary to attain applicable air quality standards.

The Clean Water Act

As noted in the chapter introduction, the federal government began regulation of discharges into waterways with the passage of the Rivers and Harbors Act of 1890. The evolution of water pollution control laws brought us the modern standard for regulation, the Water Pollution Prevention and Control Act of 1970. Although hailed as a landmark that would insure the quality of lakes, rivers, and streams, the 1970 act was amended by the **Clean Water Act** of 1977 (CWA), and was further amended by the Water Quality Act of 1987.

Unlike the Clean Air Act, the Clean Water Act regulates pollution by requiring all dischargers of waste into water from any point source (any specific place where waste is discharged) to obtain a permit, whether or not the discharge existed before passage of the Water Pollution Prevention and Control Act. Like the Clean Air Act, the CWA relies primarily on state enforcement. Any discharger must obtain a state (or EPA) permit, which will only be granted it the discharger meets *effluent limitations*—that is, limitations placed on the amount and type of wastes discharged into water.

Under the Water Pollution Prevention and Control Act, as amended by the CWA, and the Water Quality Act, two standards for water pollution control were established: preexisting dischargers had to install "the **best practicable control technology (BPT)** then available" by 1977; and by 1987 all dischargers must use "the **best available technology economically achievable (BAT).**" However, the amending 1987 Water Quality Act extended the industry's BPT deadline to March of 1989, while the BAT deadline was set at no later than two years after the BPT deadline (1991). In the following case, the Supreme Court discusses the possibility of obtaining a variance from 1977 BPT and BAT requirements although, as noted, amendments have since changed the compliance deadlines.

Environmental Protection Agency v. National Crushed Stone Association

449 U.S. 64 (1980)

Facts

In April and July 1977, the Environmental Protection Agency (EPA), acting under the Federal Water Pollution Control Act (Act), as amended, promulgated pollution discharge limitations for the coal mining industry comprising the crushed-stone, construction-sand, and gravel categories. Although the act does not expressly authorize or require variances from the 1977 limitation, each set of regulations contained a variance provision. Respondents sought review of the regulations in various courts of appeals, challenging both the substantive standards and the variance clause. In National Crushed Stone Assn. *v.* EPA, *and in* Consolidation Coal Co. *v.* Costle, *the court of appeals set aside the variance provision as "unduly restrictive" and remanded the provision to EPA for reconsideration.*

To obtain a variance from the 1977 uniform discharge limitations a discharger must demonstrate that the "factors relating to the equipment or facilities involved, the process applied, or other such factors relating to such discharger are fundamentally different from the factors considered in the establishment of the guidelines." Although a greater than normal cost of implementation will be considered in acting on a request for a variance, economic ability to meet the costs will not be considered. A variance, therefore, will not be granted on the basis of the applicant's economic inability to meet the costs of implementing the uniform standard.

The Court of Appeals for the Fourth Circuit rejected this position. It required EPA to "take into consideration, among other things, the statutory factors set out in 301 (c)," which authorizes variances from the more restrictive pollution limitations to become effective in 1987 and which specifies economic capability as a major factor to be taken into account.

Opinion

Justice White: We granted certiorari to resolve the conflict between the decisions below the *Weyerhaeuser Co.* v. *Costle,* in which the variance provision was upheld.

We shall first briefly outline the basic structure of the Act, which translates Congress' broad goal of eliminating "the discharge of pollutants into the navigable waters," into specific requirements that must be met by individual point sources.

Section 301 (b) of the Act authorizes the Administrator to set effluent limitations for categories of point sources. With respect to existing point sources, the section provides for implementation of increasingly stringent effluent limitations in two steps. The first step to be accomplished by July 1, 1977, requires all point sources to meet standards based on "the application of the best practicable control technology currently available [BPT] as defined by the Administrator. . . ." The second step, to be accomplished by July 1, 1987, requires all point sources to meet standards based on application of the "best available technology economically achievable [BAT] for such category or class. . . ." Both sets of limitations—BPTs followed within 10 years by BATs—are to be based upon regulatory guidelines established under 304 (b).

Section 402 authorizes the establishment of the National Pollutant Discharge Elimination System (NPDES), under which every discharger of pollutants is required to obtain a permit. The permit requires the discharger to meet all the applicable requirements specified in the regulations issued under 301. Permits are issued by either the Administrator or state agencies that have been approved by the Administrator.

Section 301 (c) of the Act explicitly provides for modifying the 1987 (BAT) effluent limitations with respect to individual point sources. A variance under 301 (c) may be obtained upon showing "that such modified requirements (1) will represent the maximum use of technology within the economic capability of the owner or operator; and (2) will result in reasonable further progress toward the elimination of the discharge of pollutants." Thus, the economic ability of the individual operator to meet the costs of effluent reductions may in some circumstances justify granting a variance from the 1987 limitations.

No such explicit variance provision exists with respect to BPT standards, but in *E. I. du Pont de Nemours & Co.* v. *Train,* we indicated that a variance provision was a necessary aspect of BPT limitations applicable by regulations to classes and categories of point sources. The issue in this case is whether the BPT variance provision must allow consideration of the economic capability of an individual discharger to afford the costs of the BPT limitation. For the reasons that follow, our answer is in the negative.

The plain language of the statute does not support the position taken by the Court of Appeals. Section 301 (c) is limited on its face to modifications of the 1987 BAT limitations. It says nothing about relief from the 1977 BPT requirements. Nor does the language of the Act support the position that although 301 (c) is not itself applicable to BPT standards, it requires that the affordability of the prescribed 1977 technology be considered in BPT variance decisions. This would be a logical reading of the statute only if the factors listed in 301 (c) bore a substantial relationship to the considerations underlying the 1977 limitations as they do those controlling the 1987 regulations. This is not the case.

To allow a variance based on the maximum technology affordable by the point source, even if that technology fails to meet BPT effluent limitations, would undercut the purpose and function of BPT limitations. Rather than the 1987 requirement of the best measures economically and technologically feasible, the statutory provisions for 1977 contemplate regulations prohibiting discharges from any point source in excess of the effluent produced by the best practicable technology currently available in the industry. Necessarily, if pollution is to be diminished, limitations based on BPT must forbid the level of effluent produced by the most pollution-prone segment of the industry, that segment not measuring up to "the average of the best existing performance." So understood, the statute contemplated regulations that would require a substantial number of point sources with the poorest performances either to conform to BPT standards or to cease production. To allow a variance based on economic capability and not to require adherence to the prescribed minimum technology would permit the employment of the very practices that the Administrator had rejected in establishing the best practicable technology currently in use in the industry.

The Administrator's present interpretation of the language of the statute is amply supported by the legislative history which persuades us that Congress understood that the economic capability provision of 301 (c) was limited to BAT variances; that Congress foresaw and accepted the economic hardship, including the closing of some plants, that effluent limitations would cause; and that Congress took certain steps to alleviate this hardship, steps which did not include allowing a BPT variance based on economic capability.

Congress did not respond to this foreseen economic impact by making room for variances based on economic impact. In fact, this possibility was specifically considered and rejected. Instead of economic variances, Congress specifically added two other provisions to address the problem of economic hardship.

First, provision was made for low-cost loans to small businesses to help them meet the cost of technological improvements. Second, an employee protection provision was added, giving EPA authority to investigate any plant's claim that it must cut back production or close down because of pollution control regulations.

In rejecting EPA's interpretation of the BPT variance provision, the Court of Appeals relied on a mistaken conception of the relation between BPT and BAT standards. The court erroneously believed that since BAT limitations are to be more stringent than BPT limitations, the variance provision for the latter must be at least as flexible as that for the former with respect to affordability. The variances permitted by 301 (c) from the 1987 limitations, however, can reasonably be understood to represent a cost in decreased effluent reductions that can only be afforded once the minimal standard expressed in the BPT limitation has been reached.

We conclude, therefore, that the Court of Appeals erred in not accepting EPA's interpretation of the Act. EPA is not required by the Act to consider economic capability in granting variances from its uniform BPT regulations.

The judgments of the Court of Appeals are reversed.

Case Questions

1. What is the difference between BPT (the best practicable control technology then available) and BAT (the best available technology economically achievable)?
2. Why did the Supreme Court refuse to allow economic hardship to be a defense to meeting the BPT standards?
3. The Supreme Court acknowledged in its decision that some businesses might be forced to close as a result of its decision. Is it ethical to force some companies out of business in order to meet some arbitrary water pollution standards?

The Supreme Court underscored the EPA's jurisdiction over CWA violations in the 1985 Supreme Court case of *Chemical Manufacturers Association* v. *Natural Resources Defense Council, Inc.* A challenge to the EPA's FDF variance (fundamentally different factor) was initiated under the CWA clause that states that the EPA may not "modify" any effluent limitation requirement concerning discharge of toxic materials. Although a lower court interpreted this clause as preventing the EPA from granting FDF variances, the Supreme Court disagreed, stating that the EPA action was rational and, therefore, subject to the Court's deference.

Since there are no bubble concept or emission offset exceptions in the CWA as there are in the CAA, judicial as well as legislative attention has been given to when the standards of the Clean Water Act might be relaxed. Under the CWA, Congress established the National Pollutant Discharge Elimination System (NPDES), which gave the EPA administrator the power to grant variances to CWA restrictions. The EPA administrator can grant an NPDES variance by issuing a permit authorizing the discharge of pollutants in accordance with specified conditions. The 1987 Supreme Court case of *Gwaltney* v. *Chesapeake Bay Foundation* was initiated by private citizens against a company that had a history of NPDES permit violations, but had since taken measures to bring its actions into compliance with NPDES stipulations. The Court held that past violations could not be the basis for a lawsuit if there was no evidence that the discharger's actions were either currently or could foreseeably be in violation of the CWA.

The Solid Waste Disposal Act, the Resource Conservation and Recovery Act, and the Hazardous and Solid Waste Amendments of 1984 Act

So far in this section on federal statutes, we have discussed pollution of the air and water. We will now discuss what might be called "land pollution," pollution of the earth caused by use or disposal of solid wastes, which might be toxic or radioactive.

The first federal statute specifically regulating the disposal of solid waste was the **Solid Waste Disposal Act (SWDA),** originally passed in 1965 and amended by the Resource Recovery Act of 1970. The primary purpose of these acts is to assist states and cities in dealing with problems of solid waste disposal by giving grants to study waste disposal problems and to construct waste disposal projects (such as facilities that turn solid waste into energy).

The Solid Waste Disposal Act establishes nonbinding guidelines that recipients of federal grants can follow in establishing solid waste disposal programs. The original SWDA as amended in 1970 did not, however, *mandate* the method for disposing of waste. In the middle 1970s, a series of events, most notably the revelations of contamination of a residential community in Love Canal, New York, and worker and environmental injury caused by improper manufacturing and disposal of Kephone insecticide in Virginia, focused attention on the need for more specific regulation of the use and disposal of certain types of hazardous wastes. Therefore, in 1976, Congress passed the **Resource Conservation and Recovery Act (RCRA),** which amended the Solid Waste Disposal Act, and the *Toxic Substances Control Act (TSCA),* which will be discussed in the next section. Generators, transporters, and storers of hazardous waste are all liable for violation of the act. As amended in 1986, the act now includes the disposal of used motor oil as a category of hazardous waste. The 1986 amendment states that if a person knowingly violates RCRA, and that violation puts someone else in danger of death or bodily harm, then the violator is subject to a criminal fine of up to $250,000, as well as up to fifteen years in prison. If the violator is an organization, they shall not be liable for a fine greater than $1,000,000. Moreover, noncompliance with an EPA corrective action order can subject the violator to civil penalties of up to $25,000 per day.

The following 1986 federal Court of Appeals case extended liability for RCRA violations to include corporate officers as well as company stockholders. The court determined that shareholders and officers of a corporation who were personally involved in or directly responsible for corporate acts that violated RCRA were individually liable for contributing to "imminent and substantial endangerment" to health and environment.

United States v. Northeastern Pharmaceutical & Chemical Co.

810 F.2d 726 (8th Cir. 1986)

Opinion

Circuit Judge McMillian: Northeastern Pharmaceutical & Chemical Co. (NEPACCO), Edwin Michaels and John W. Lee appeal from a final judgment entered in the District Court for the Western District of Missouri finding them and Ronald Mills jointly and severally liable for response costs incurred by the government after December 11, 1980, and all future response costs relative to the cleanup of the Denney farm site that are not inconsistent with the national contingency plan (NCP) pursuant to §§ 104, 107 of the Comprehensive Environmental Response, Compensation, and Liability Act of 1980 (CERCLA). For reversal, appellants argue the district court erred in applying CERCLA retroactively, finding Michaels and Lee individually liable, failing to dismiss NEPACCO as a party defendant, and awarding response costs absent affirmative proof that the response costs were consistent with the NCP.

The United States cross-appeals from that part of the district court judgment denying recovery of response costs incurred before December 11, 1980, and finding appellants and Mills were not liable for response costs pursuant to § 7003(a) of the Resource Conservation and Recovery Act of 1976 (RCRA) (also known as the Solid Waste Disposal Act).

For reversal the government argues the district court erred in (1) finding the government could not recover response costs incurred before the effective date of CERCLA, December 11, 1980, and (2) finding appellants and Mills were not liable for response costs under RCRA § 7003(a).

Michaels formed NEPACCO, was a major shareholder, and was its president. Lee was NEPACCO's vice-president, the supervisor of its manufacturing plant located in Verona, Missouri, and also a shareholder. Mills was employed as shift supervisor at NEPACCO's Verona plant.

From April 1970 to January 1972 NEPACCO manufactured the disinfectant hexachlorophene at its Verona plant. Michaels and Lee knew that NEPACCO's manufacturing process produced various hazardous and toxic byproducts, including 2,4,5-trichlorophenol (TCP), 2,3,7,8-tetrachlorodibenzo-p-dioxin (TCDD or dioxin), and toluene. The waste byproducts were pumped into a holding tank which was periodically emptied by waste haulers. Occasionally, however, excess waste byproducts were sealed in 55-gallon drums and then stored at the plant.

In July 1971 Mills approached NEPACCO plant manager Bill Ray with a proposal to dispose of the waste-filled 55-gallon drums on a farm owned by James Denney located about seven miles south of Verona. Ray visited the Denney farm and discussed the proposal with Lee; Lee approved the use of Mills' services and the Denney farm as a disposal site. In mid-July 1971 Mills and Gerald Lechner dumped approximately 85 of the 55-gallon drums into a large trench on the Denney farm (Denney farm site) that had been excavated by Leon Vaughn. Vaughn then filled in the trench. Only NEPACCO drums were disposed of at the Denney farm site.

In October 1979 the Environmental Protection Agency (EPA) received an anonymous tip that hazardous wastes had been disposed of at the Denney farm. Subsequent EPA investigation confirmed that hazardous wastes had in fact been disposed of at the Denney farm and that the site was not geologically suitably for the disposal of hazardous wastes. Between January and April 1980 the EPA prepared a plan for the cleanup of the Denney farm site and constructed an access road and a security fence. During April 1980 the EPA conducted an on-site investigation, exposed and sampled 13 of the 55-gallon drums, which were found to be badly deteriorated, and took water and soil samples. The samples were found to contain "alarmingly" high concentrations of dioxin, TCP and toluene.

In July 1980 the EPA installed a temporary cap over the trench to prevent the entry and run-off of surface water and to minimize contamination of the surrounding soil and groundwater. The EPA also contracted with Ecology & Environment, Inc., for the preparation of a feasibility study for the cleanup of the Denney farm site. Additional on-site testing was conducted. In August 1980 the government filed its initial complaint against NEPACCO, the generator of the hazardous substances; Michaels and Lee, the corporate officers responsible for arranging for the disposal of the hazardous substances; Mills, the transporter of the hazardous substances; and Syntex, the owner and lessor of the Verona plant, seeking injunctive relief and reimbursement of response costs pursuant to RCRA § 7003, 42 U.S.C. § 6973 (count I). In September 1983 the feasibility study was completed.

The district court held that RCRA § 7003(a) requires a finding of negligence in order to hold past off-site generators and transporters liable for response costs, and thus RCRA did not apply to past non-negligent off-site generators and transporters of hazardous substances.

CERCLA § 104 authorizes the EPA to take direct "response" actions, which can include either short-term "removal" actions or long-term "remedial" actions or both, pursuant to the NCP, with funds from the "Superfund," and to seek recovery of response costs from responsible parties pursuant to CERCLA § 107, in order to replenish the Superfund. The EPA can also use CERCLA § 106, to seek injunctions to compel responsible parties to clean up hazardous waste sites that constitute an "imminent and substantial endangerment" to health and the environment. In the present case, count II sought injunctive relief pursuant to CERCLA § 106, and count III sought recovery of the government's past and future response costs pursuant to CERCLA §§ 104, 107.

The district court applied CERCLA retroactively, but held the government could not recover response costs incurred before the effective date of CERCLA, December 11, 1980. The district court also held CERCLA imposes a standard of strict liability, and that responsible parties can be held jointly and severally liable.

The district court also found NEPACCO liable as an "owner or operator" pursuant to CERCLA § 107(a)(1). With respect to the individual defendants, the district court found Mills liable as a "person who . . . accepted any hazardous substances for transport to disposal . . . sites selected by such person," pursuant to CERCLA. The district court also found Lee liable as an "owner or operator" pursuant to CERCLA § 107(a)(1), and as a "person who by contract, agreement, or otherwise . . . arranged with a transporter for transport for disposal . . . of hazardous substances," pursuant to CERCLA. The district court found Michaels liable as a person who arranged for the transport and disposal of hazardous substances pursuant to CERCLA. The liability of NEPACCO, Lee, Michaels, and Mills was joint and several.

The district court further found the government's right to recovery of response costs was very broad and included litigation costs, attorney's fees, future response costs, and prejudgment interest, and that the defendants in an action by the government for recovery of response costs had the burden of proving that the government's response costs were inconsistent with the NCP.

Although CERCLA does not expressly provide for retroactivity, it is manifestly clear that Congress intended CERCLA to have retroactive effect. The language used in the key liability provision, CERCLA § 107, refers to actions and conditions in the past tense: "any person who at the time of disposal of any hazardous substances owned or operated," CERCLA § 107(a)(2).

Further, the statutory scheme itself is overwhelmingly remedial and retroactive. CERCLA authorizes the EPA to force responsible parties to clean up inactive or abandoned hazardous substance sites, CERCLA § 106, and authorizes federal, state and local governments and private parties to clean up such sites and then seek recovery of their response costs from responsible parties, CERCLA §§ 104, 107. In order to be effective, CERCLA must reach past conduct. CERCLA's backward-looking focus is confirmed by the legislative history. Congress intended CERCLA "to initiate and establish a comprehensive response and financing mechanism to abate and control the vast problems associated with abandoned and inactive hazardous waste disposal sites."

Related to the question of CERCLA's application to pre-1980 acts is the question whether the government can recover response costs incurred prior to CERCLA's effective date.

CERCLA § 107(a)(4)(A)–(C) sets forth three types of liability: (A) response costs incurred by the United States or a state that are not inconsistent with the NCP, (B) any other necessary response costs incurred by any other person that are consistent with the NCP, and (C) natural resource damages. By separately considering the place of each type of liability in the statutory scheme, we can discern Congressional intent with respect to recovery of pre-enactment response costs.

In summary, we hold the district court erred in finding that CERCLA does not authorize recovery of pre-enactment response costs. That part of the district court judgment holding that pre-enactment response costs cannot be recovered is reversed.

As an alternative basis for recovery of the response costs incurred before December 11, 1980, the government argues on cross-appeal that it can also recover its response costs pursuant to RCRA § 7003(a). The district court did not reach the recovery issue because it held that under RCRA § 7003(a) (prior to 1984 amendments discussed below), proof of fault or negligence was required in order to impose liability upon past off-site generators and transporters. Because the government did not allege or prove negligence, the district court found no liability under RCRA § 7003(a) (prior to 1984 amendments). The government argues that the standard of liability under RCRA § 7003(a), as initially enacted and as amended in 1984, is strict liability, not negligence, and that liability under RCRA can be imposed even though the acts of disposal occurred before RCRA became effective in 1976. We agree.

As amended in 1984, RCRA § 7003(a), 42 U.S.C.A. § 6973(a) (West Supp.1986) (new language italicized; deleted language in brackets), now provides in pertinent part:

> Notwithstanding any other provision of this chapter, upon receipt of evidence that the *past or present* handling, storage, treatment, transportation or disposal of any solid waste or hazardous waste may present an imminent and substantial endangerment to health or the environment, the Administrator may bring suit on behalf of the United States in the appropriate district court [to immediately restrain any person] *against any person (including any past or present generator, past or present transporter, or past or present owner or operator of a treatment, storage, or disposal facility) who has contributed or who is* contributing to such handling, storage, treatment, transportation or disposal [to stop] *to restrain such person from* such handling, storage, treatment, transportation, or disposal [or to take such other action as may be necessary], *to order such person to take such other action as may be necessary, or both.*

As amended, RCRA § 7003(a) specifically applies to *past* generators and transporters.

The House Conference Report stated:

Section 7003 focuses on the abatement of conditions threatening health and the environment and not particularly human activity. Therefore, it has *always reached those persons who have contributed in the past or are presently contributing to the endangerment, including but not limited to generators, regardless of fault or negligence.* Thus, for example, *non-negligent generators whose wastes are no longer being deposited or dumped at a particular site may be ordered to abate the hazard to health or the environment posed by the leaking of the wastes they once generated and which have been deposited on the site.* The amendment reflects the long-standing view that generators and other persons involved in the handling, storage, treatment, transportation or disposal of hazardous wastes must share in the responsibility for the abatement of the hazards arising from their activities. The section was intended and is intended to abate conditions resulting from past activities.

Thus, following the 1984 amendments, past off-site generators and transporters are within the scope of RCRA § 7003(a). From the legislative history of the 1984 amendments, it is clear that

Congress intended RCRA § 7003(a), as initially enacted and as amended, to impose liability without fault or negligence and to apply to the present conditions resulting from past activities. In other words, RCRA § 7003(a), as initially enacted and as amended, applies to past non-negligent off-site generators like NEPACCO and to non-negligent past transporters like Mills.

In summary, we hold that RCRA § 7003(a), as initially enacted and as clarified by the 1984 amendments, imposes strict liability upon past off-site generators of hazardous waste and upon past transporters of hazardous waste. We reverse that part of the district court judgment holding that RCRA does not apply to past non-negligent off-site generators and transporters.

Appellants concede NEPACCO is liable under CERCLA § 107(a)(3), for arranging for the transportation and disposal of hazardous substances at the Denney farm site. Because NEPACCO's assets have already been liquidated and distributed to its shareholders, however, it is unlikely that the government will be able to recover anything from NEPACCO.

CERCLA § 107(a)(3) imposes strict liability upon "any person" who arranged for the disposal or transportation for disposal of hazardous substances. As defined by statute, the term "person" includes both individuals and corporations and does not exclude corporate officers or employees.

We hold Lee and Michaels are individually liable as "contributors" under RCRA § 7003(a). Lee actually participated in the conduct that violated RCRA; he personally arranged for the transportation and disposal of hazardous substances that presented an imminent and substantial endangerment to health and the environment. Unlike Lee, Michaels was not personally involved in the actual decision to transport and dispose of the hazardous substances. As NEPACCO's corporate president and as a major NEPACCO shareholder, however, Michaels was the individual in charge of and directly responsible for all of NEPACCO's operations, including those at the Verona plant, and he had the ultimate authority to control the disposal of NEPACCO's hazardous substances.

In summary, we hold Lee individually liable for arranging for the transportation and disposal of hazardous substances in violation of CERCLA § 107(a)(3), and Lee and Michaels individually liable for contributing to an imminent and substantial endangerment to health and the environment in violation of RCRA § 7003(a).

In conclusion, we hold CERCLA applies retroactively, the government can recover its pre-enactment response costs under CERCLA, RCRA imposes strict liability upon past off-site generators and transporters of hazardous substances, and Lee and Michaels can be held individually liable.

Case Questions

1. Was it ethical for Congress to impose strict liability on past generators of hazardous waste who may not have had anything to do with the waste for years?
2. Why were Michaels and Lee held liable for violations of RCRA?

The basis of RCRA is a federal permit system for the use and disposal of *hazardous waste*—that is, waste that might cause serious injury or illness to human beings exposed to it. The primary enforcement mechanism of RCRA is a special type of permit system called a **manifest system.** All businesses that use, transport, or store hazardous waste are covered by the manifest system. Businesses that create hazardous wastes are called *generators*. Whenever they create such wastes, they must label them with a document *(manifest)* that states the nature and quantity of the waste. Generators must file an annual report with the EPA. If the generator's wastes are transported, the transporters, which have been issued an EPA identifying number, must make entries on the manifests and must deliver the wastes (and manifests) to EPA-approved operators of hazardous waste disposal facilities that have been designated by the generators. Generators, transporters, and storers of hazardous wastes are all liable for violation of the act, which has criminal penalties of up to one year in jail and civil penalties of up to $25,000 per day.

In November 1984, Congress passed the **Hazardous and Solid Waste Amendments of 1984 Act (HASWA),** which amended RCRA. HASWA's purpose is to strengthen regulation of the disposal of solid and hazardous waste and to increase the EPA's powers to regulate in this area. The two main purposes of the HASWA are to regulate previously exempt small waste generators and to curtail drastically the land disposal of hazardous wastes. Under RCRA, generators of up to 1,000 kilograms of hazardous waste per month were exempt from coverage, but HASWA extends coverage to these businesses, which were estimated by Congress to number about 100,000. These small waste generators are required to use some form of the RCRA manifest system, with land disposal of hazardous waste, particularly in landfills or surface impoundments, being the least favored method. HASWA contains a four-year timetable for progressively banning land disposal of certain designated types of wastes based on their degree of hazardousness. For example, the disposal of bulk liquid hazardous wastes in landfills is prohibited as of 1986. By 1987, the EPA was required to determine whether land disposal of any particular identified hazardous waste should be permitted.

In addition to expanding preexisting statutory authority, HASWA contains new provisions. It mandates that new landfills and surface impoundments, as well as replacement units and lateral expansions of existing facilities, are required to use such devices as double liners, leachate collection systems, and groundwater and air emissions monitoring systems. HASWA provides that every hazardous waste treatment storage or disposal facility must be inspected at least every two years. For the first time, HASWA establishes a regulatory program for underground storage tanks, and it mandates that the EPA look into the hazardous effects of burning or recycling used oil. It also creates a National Groundwater Commission to evaluate the adequacy of the nation's groundwater (water within the earth that supplies wells and springs) and to consider the adequacy of existing hazardous waste regulations for their ability to protect groundwater. One unique aspect of HASWA is that it expands the right of individuals to sue to enforce RCRA or HASWA if an imminent hazard exists and the EPA is not prosecuting an action.

The HASWA is an interesting statute because Congress drafted it by going into great detail, instead of drafting it in broad terms and leaving the details to the EPA, as it did with other environmental protection statutes. EPA discretion was reduced because revelations that surfaced in the early 1980s indicated that the EPA was not enforcing the environmental protection statutes to the degree Congress had expected. Since statistics indicate that America's annual hazardous waste output in 1988 was approximately 275 million tons, with a $6 billion annual handling cost expected to double by 1991, it is evident that the societal cost of such business practices will come under increasingly close scrutiny.

Toxic Substances Control Act

The **Toxic Substances Control Act (TSCA),** passed in 1976, has two purposes: to compile information about what chemical substances exist in the environment and to allow the EPA to regulate the manufacture and sale of chemicals with adverse effects on humans. The initial requirement of TSCA was to direct the EPA to make a comprehensive list of all chemicals being manufactured (the EPA issued regulations requiring the submission of such information). Once the list was compiled, the EPA could issue regulations concerning the manufacturing process or the dissemination of classes of chemicals (such as PCBs) that presented unreasonable risks of harm to humans.

The TSCA requires manufacturers to notify the EPA before they begin to manufacture a new chemical. If the EPA determines through testing that the chemical is hazardous, it may issue an order prohibiting manufacture. Manufacturers of existing chemicals are required to give the EPA any information regarding harmful effects of the substances.

The Comprehensive Environmental Response, Compensation and Liability Act (Superfund)

Up until 1980, although Congress had taken steps to limit pollution of the environment and improper disposal of various types of wastes, little had been done to remedy the effects of past pollution or inadequate disposal of wastes. Many revelations, including the Love Canal case in which toxic wastes improperly disposed of in the early 1950s began to cause physical injuries in the 1970s, generated concern about the effect of pre-to-mid–1970s "dumping" or inadequate disposal of dangerous wastes. To address these concerns, in 1980, Congress passed the **Comprehensive Environmental Response, Compensation and Liability Act,** with the dual purpose of first identifying and then cleaning up sites of past inadequate waste disposal. This act is commonly referred to as the *Superfund Act,* because its main provision establishes a $1.6 billion fund to be used to identify and clean up dangerous hazardous waste disposal sites. A large part of the fund's money comes from taxes levied on manufacturers who create designated chemical and petroleum products such as mercury and methane.

In 1986, Congress passed the Superfund Amendments and Reauthorization Act (SARA), which strengthened and clarified CERCLA. Congress increased the EPA's authority to designate sites for priority cleanup action, and the EPA extended its enforcement actions to include "backyard" manufacturing dumping sites and sanitary landfills that received little attention prior to SARA. SARA established cleanup standards more stringent than those imposed by CERCLA, bringing about a dramatic increase in the financial liability of CERCLA violators. The EPA has repeatedly maintained a "hard line" on adherence to its regulations, often rejecting less expensive but comparable remedies developed independently of the agency's procedures.

SARA also granted the EPA the authority to require disclosure of a company's general financial data so that it could determine the business's ability to pay for hazardous waste cleanup. EPA personnel are now able to enter business offices to inspect and copy records, to conduct plant inspections, or to take samples of possible hazardous wastes. If a company fails to respond to a request for information by the EPA, it could be liable for up to $25,000 a day in penalties.

One of the most interesting provisions of the Superfund Act is that it imposed strict as well as joint and several liability on generators, transporters, and disposers of hazardous wastes. Essentially, strict liability means that any party involved in the generation or disposal of hazardous waste may be liable for the cleanup costs of those wastes without regard to "fault," that is, regardless of their knowledge of or participation in improper disposal of hazardous wastes. Further, any of these parties can be liable for the entire cleanup cost under the theory of "joint and several" liability. Joint and several liability states that any participation by a party that contributes to improper disposal of hazardous wastes subjects that party to either partial or total liability for cleanup costs. SARA also clarified that any party held solely liable for cleanup costs could obtain partial reimbursement from other potentially responsible parties. Subsequent court rulings have, however, held that primary product manufacturers (who supply raw materials) are not responsible parties under the act.

Besides being responsible for cleanup and proper disposal of hazardous wastes, parties liable under Superfund have also been ordered to pay the expenses of medical testing, relocations, and litigation. For example, in 1988, the Atlantic Richfield Company agreed to pay $1 million in past EPA costs to relocate seven families from Mill Creek, Montana, where its Anaconda Copper Company smelting plant contaminated area land with high levels of arsenic, cadmium, and lead. However, this agreement did not determine the extent of ARCO's liability for a comprehensive cleanup of the Mill Creek area.

Although the early years of EPA enforcement of the Superfund Act were marked by allegations of mismanagement, Superfund expenditures were projected to increase from the 1987 level of $800 million to $1 billion in 1988 and to $1.5 billion in 1989. As government increases its hazardous waste enforcement actions and industry becomes more cautious about hazardous waste liability, the effectiveness of Superfund will be a topic of even greater discussion. Predictions that Superfund spending of $1.2 billion in 1988 and $1.5 billion in 1989 have been prompted by increased government enforcement and industry's fears of liability suits.

Other Federal Environmental Protection Statutes

Although this chapter discusses the most far-reaching statutes dealing with regulation of the environment, there are many that we will not discuss at all. However, two statutes that deserve specific mention are the 1972 Environmental Pesticides Control Act (an amended form of the 1947 Federal Insecticide, Fungicide, and Rodenticide Act), and the Occupational Safety and Health Act (OSHA).

The **Federal Pesticides Control Act** of 1972, administered by the EPA, requires the registration of all pesticides manufactured in the United States into either general use or restricted use categories. Federal and state registration requirements also extend to any person selling, distributing, producing, or applying those pesticides. The act provides for civil penalties of up to $5,000 for each violation, while criminal penalties extend to a $25,000 fine and a year's prison sentence. Most recently, litigation has examined the improper application of pesticides, as well as the duty to warn of potential health hazards associated with their use through proper labeling.

The **Occupational Safety and Health Act (OSHA)** is not an "environmental protection" statute in the usual sense at all, but is generally regarded as a statute regulating various aspects of the employment relationship, which is why it is discussed in Chapter 15 of this book. However, it is important to note that by placing limits on employees' exposure to toxic substances in the workplace, the Occupational Safety and Health Administration is protecting the "environment" of workers and indirectly limiting the amount of unhealthy substances discharged into the outside atmosphere.

Environmental Law as a Societal Policy Statement

As we discussed at the beginning of this chapter, the traditional view in our society was that damage to the environment was not a cost that business had to consider. This environmental cost could be referred to as "external" to the the price of a polluter's goods or services. The basic thrust of the environmental protection laws has been to "internalize" these formerly external costs. For example, by legally requiring that "scrubbers" be placed on smokestacks to reduce discharge of pollutants into the air, the discharger is now directly bearing the costs of its polluting activities. It should be noted, however, that even if the polluter is required to internalize pollution costs, ultimately it is society that bears the cost. Before the environmental laws were passed, society often bore the costs of pollution through ill health or property damage caused by pollution. Now, the environment may be healthier than it was previously, but society is paying more for many goods and services, since former polluters did not absorb the costs of complying with the environmental laws, but passed them along to consumers. The decision to enact and implement environmental protection laws can thus be viewed as a societal application of "cost/benefit" analysis, with the basic premise being that increased health and beauty in the environment is worth the extra expense needed to achieve that goal.

One important problem that has developed as environmental laws have been implemented is that pollution control requirements have raised the cost of American goods, and those goods have become less competitive with foreign goods. Many foreign competitors do not have to comply with antipollution statutes similar to those in the United States, or their governments absorb more of the cost of antipollution activities. Thus, it has been argued that compliance with federal antipollution statutes has put American industry at a competitive disadvantage to their foreign counterparts, with results that could include the closing of American factories and increased American labor layoffs.

Many environmental protection statutes such as the federal Clean Air and Clean Water Acts and local zoning statutes depend on enforcement by state or local officials. These officials may be subject to pressure from other government officials who are more interested in keeping or attracting industry to their areas than in enforcing the environmental protection laws. Thus, the very persons in charge of pollution control may find themselves in an ethical dilemma, torn between not performing their duty and (possibly) losing their jobs.

Although the EPA's budget suffered cutbacks in the early 1980s, Congressional enactment of SARA significantly enhanced government's chances of enforcing compliance with environmental protection statutes. One dilemma created by enforcement of environmental protection laws is that if enforcement appears too lax, government is argued to be shirking its responsibility to protect the health and welfare of American society. However, if enforcement should significantly increase, then it can be argued that government has adopted a "get business" mentality. The true challenge to American government, industry, and society is to strike a balance between healthy growth and competition in foreign markets while preserving the American environment both outdoors and in the workplace.

Ethical Issues in Environmental Law

Environmental issues are some of the most complex faced by our society today, resulting in part from our earlier manner of facing them by ignoring them. America is now having to reckon with the unconsidered consequences of earlier environmental practices, with ramifications including birth defects, chronic illnesses, and death. The following are a few of the many ethical problems (with accompanying legal aspects) that have arisen in the past few years.

In 1988, beachgoers off the coast of New York were forbidden to enter the waters as a result of the discovery that used hypodermics, vials of blood (some of which tested positive for hepatitis B as well as the AIDS antibody), stained surgical bandages, and drug paraphernalia had washed ashore. Although these items had no readily identifiable source, it was alleged that in trying to keep operating costs down, hospitals might have contracted with hazardous waste dumping services that used improper disposal methods. It appears that this hospital waste was dumped into the waters surrounding New York in violation of federal environmental statutes. Given that America's economic system thrives on cost competition, what steps should American society take to insure both safe public waters and affordable hospital care?

In the 1980s, the EPA approved dumping of wet sludge from New York and New Jersey sewage-treatment centers 106 nautical miles from the entrance to New York Harbor; soon, local fishermen raised questions about the health of their catches, citing lesions and deformities on the fish that they believed to be caused by the authorized waste disposal. What ethical questions are at issue if the fishermen sold their catches to distributors, who, knowing of the health questions, sold these same fish to retailers who then made these products available to the public?

"Acid rain" has resulted in adverse effects on vegetation in certain areas of North America, notably the northeastern corner of the United States as well as Canada. It now seems well established that the primary sources of acid rain are "high-stack" smokestacks built by manufacturing and energy-producing plants in the Midwest to comply with the Clean Air Act. Many lobbyists in the Midwest have worked against more stringent legal steps aimed at the acid rain generators. Given that these pollution control methods have been questioned not only in respect to their impact on America, but on an American ally, what ethical issues would you consider were you an elected American official charged with resolution of this situation?

The important concepts and terms in this chapter are listed below; page numbers have been provided for the key terms. By reading over each section you can assess your understanding of the chapter concepts and determine areas you may want to review.

Chapter Summary

1. Until the twentieth century, the environment was regarded as a "common fund" that anyone could use or affect without regard for the long-term consequences.
2. Prior to the passage of specific environmental protection statutes, the common law theories that could be used to sue for deleterious effects on the environment were nuisance, strict liability, riparian rights, and trespass.
3. Local zoning laws can be used to regulate use of and effect on the environment.
4. The federal Environmental Protection Agency was created in 1970 to oversee the enforcement of various federal antipollution laws.
5. The National Environmental Protection Act (NEPA), passed in 1970, established a Council on Environmental Quality (CEQ) and requires that before the occurrence of any major proposed federal action that significantly affects the quality of the human environment, an environmental impact statement must be submitted.
6. The federal Clean Air Act provides for creation of air quality and emissions standards by the EPA and for state implementation of EPA standards.
7. The federal Clean Water Act requires all businesses discharging waste into water systems to obtain a state permit to discharge. These dischargers must meet federal standards for discharge content in order to obtain the state permit.

8. The federal Solid Waste Disposal Act, as amended by the Resource Conservation and Recovery Act, provides for disposal of hazardous waste by use of a manifest system that traces the transportation of such waste from generators to storers.
9. The federal Toxic Substances Control Act empowered the Environmental Protection Agency to compile information about what chemical substances now exist in the environment and to allow the EPA to regulate the manufacture and sale of chemicals with adverse effects on humans.
10. The federal Comprehensive Environmental Response, Compensation and Liability Act (Superfund Act) was passed in order to identify and then clean up sites of past inadequate waste disposal.

Key Terms

best available technology economically achievable 589

best practicable control technology 589

bubble concept 588

Clean Air Act 585

Clean Water Act 589

Comprehensive Environmental Response, Compensation and Liability Act (Superfund) 598

environmental impact statement (EIS) 582

Environmental Protection Agency (EPA) 584

Federal Pesticides Control Act 600

Hazardous and Solid Waste Amendments of 1984 Act 597

manifest system 596

National Environmental Policy Act 581

nonattainment areas 587

nuisance 580

Occupational Safety and Health Act 600

offsets 588

primary air quality standards 585

Resource Conservation and Recovery Act 592

secondary air quality standards 585

Solid Waste Disposal Act 592

Toxic Substances Control Act 598

zoning 581

Questions on Ethics

1. Acme Chemical Company creates a new chemical compound that is not on a list of toxic substances that was compiled by the Environmental Protection Agency under the authority of the Toxic Substances Control Act. Events at Acme convince Acme management that special expensive

processes will be needed to manufacture, transport, and dispose of the chemical. Acme notifies the EPA that it wishes to manufacture the chemical, and the EPA approves manufacture with less stringent requirements for manufacturing and distribution than Acme suspects are necessary. The EPA officials were overworked when they granted the approval, and Acme feels they failed to grasp all of the implications of the data Acme sent them on its approval application. Is Acme ethically required to use more stringent manufacturing and distribution processes than those specified by the EPA?

2. J. P. Smith, president of Smith Industries, fires Waste Haulers, Inc., as his agent for disposing of Smith's toxic wastes when Smith learns that Waste Haulers has been falsifying manifests for hazardous waste disposals and has been illegally dumping wastes. Smith suspects that Waste Haulers has criminal connections. Is Smith ethically required to notify state and federal officials of his suspicions regarding Waste Haulers' activities?
3. If it could be shown scientifically that high smokestack pollution in the Midwest was causing acid rain in New England, is it the ethical duty of the midwestern polluters to take the steps necessary to prevent acid rain?
4. In 1986, Ashland Oil Company decided to relocate a four-million-gallon oil tank from Cleveland to Pittsburgh. An investigation of the company's movement of the tank concluded that Ashland "displayed a pervasive pattern of neglect at virtually every step" in relocating the tank. In January 1988, during severe frigid weather, the tank burst, creating a massive oil spill in the Monongahela and Ohio rivers. Did Ashland breach an ethical duty by not being more careful about the method in which it moved and re-erected the oil tank?
5. In June 1988, W. R. Grace & Co. pleaded guilty to a charge of lying to federal authorities investigating the contamination of drinking wells in Woburn, Massachusetts. It was alleged that Grace's corporate dumping practices contaminated wells, which caused six leukemia deaths, illnesses, and birth defects. Grace settled this lawsuit for $9 million in 1986. What do you feel is Grace's ethical responsibility to the people of Woburn?

Questions on Law

1. Is it legally required that an environmental impact statement be prepared when budgetary cutbacks to the federal National Wildlife Refuge System are proposed? *Andrus* v. *Sierra Club,* 422 U.S. 347 (1979).
2. A group of ocean fishermen sued various governmental bodies and officials of New York, New Jersey, and the United States, claiming that these governmental bodies failed to enforce environmental protection laws, to the group's damage. May the fishermen sue the governments

using such a theory? *Middlesex County Sewerage Authority* v. *National Sea Clammers Assn.,* 453 U.S. 1 (1981).

3. Tumin abandoned three drums of ethyl ether in a residential neighborhood of Rockaway, New York. Ethyl ether has an extremely low flashpoint and when mixed with air is extremely volatile; any spark whatsoever can result in an explosion. Did Tumin violate the "knowing endangerment" provision of the Resource Conservation and Recovery Act?
4. United States Steel Corporation sued the Environmental Protection Agency after the EPA ordered U.S. Steel to lower the pollution content of its air emissions because it was in a designated nonattainment area. U.S. Steel introduced evidence that indicated that its operations were not the primary source of pollution in the area. Must U.S. Steel follow the EPA's order? *United States Steel Corporation* v. *EPA,* 605 F.2d 283 (1979).
5. More than a thousand residents of the town of Times Beach, Missouri, sued Syntex Corporations, alleging that Syntex's dumping of the dangerous chemical dioxin forced them to abandon their homes. Syntex maintained that it was not responsible for the dioxin dumping. Will Syntex pay the legal expenses of litigating this case, or will they settle out of court?

Suggested Readings

Fisher, "A Survey of Selected Federal Environmental Laws in the United States," 17 *American Business Law Journal* 121 (1979).

Karp, "Judicial Review of Environmental Impact Statement Contents," 16 *American Business Law Journal* 127 (1978).

Marcus, "Landowner Liability under CERCLA and SARA." *Temple Environmental Law and Technology Journal* 117 (1987).

22 Regulation of Advertising

He said likewise
That a lie which is half a truth is ever the blackest of lies,
That a lie which is all a lie may be met and fought with outright,
But a lie which is part a truth is a harder matter to fight.

—Alfred, Lord Tennyson

■ LEARNING OBJECTIVES

After you have read this chapter, you should be able to:

1. Describe the way federal agencies regulate advertising.
2. Describe the legal rights that your competitors can use to control your advertising.
3. Describe the legal rights that consumers can use to control your advertising.

Business Decisions and the Law

Effective Ads

Jeff wants to place an ad about his newly designed lawn mower in a trade publication. He believes that the mower operates more efficiently than any machine on the market and will also last longer. The more specific he gets in the ad, the more business he will attract. But he is concerned that he may be sued by competitors if he does not have proof of his claims. Is his concern valid? This chapter will answer this and similar questions.

Introduction

Advertising law raises a fundamental ethical issue: *truthtelling*. Two of the components of truthtelling are discussed in this introduction. The first is the definition of truthfulness. People's definitions vary significantly. Some believe they have lied when they intentionally misstate something very important and thereby cause injury to another. Others believe they have lied whenever they have merely *allowed* someone to misunderstand. The second component discussed in this introduction is the *justification,* if there is any, for lying in one's business dealings.

Definitions of Lying and Truthtelling

Exactly when is it that we have failed to tell the truth? Obviously when we state as true something that is untrue, we have lied. Suppose you say to me, "Please sign this lease document right now because I'm in a hurry to get home; the rental amount in the lease is $295 per month." If the rental amount stated in the lease is actually $395 and you know it and intend to deceive, then clearly you have *lied* (and probably committed fraud). However, once we depart from this type of clearcut situation, truthtelling and/or lying becomes more difficult to identify.

Would it be lying for you to ask the prospective tenant to sign the lease after stating the true monthly rent, but without disclosing that the lease agreement gave the landlord (you) the right to keep the cleaning deposit even if the apartment were left spotless at the end of the lease? In other words, is it a lie if you leave out of your description important information about the transaction? The courts sometimes call this a *material omission.*

Suppose I ask you, "How much will the utilities for the apartment cost?" If you don't know, would it be a lie for you to say, "They are about average for an apartment this size"? Or suppose you *do* know that the utility expenses are unusually high; is it a lie for you to give an *evasive* answer such as, "Utilities in this part of the state are about the same as in the rest of the state, and incidentally, did you get a good look at the size of closets in the main bedroom?"

Further, there are truthtelling issues associated with using broad, flowery terms such as, "It is a *wonderful* place for a student to live!" If you know that noises, distractions, price, and distance to campus make this statement untrue, is it still OK because the term "wonderful" is vague? The courts use the word *puffing* to refer to terms such as *wonderful.*

If someone clearly misunderstands reality, would you be obligated to correct their perception? Suppose I said to you, "I like the apartment because it is only twenty-five minutes from campus." If you knew that during most times of the day the actual travel time in congested traffic was sixty-five minutes, would you be lying if you remained silent? If you did tell the true travel time, the courts would call that an *affirmative disclosure.*

Justifications for Lying

Do you think everyone is always entitled to receive truthful information from you? Suppose the owner of a competing apartment building asked you for information about the rental rates in your building. Do you think he has a right to that information? If you conclude that he does not have a right to the information, would you therefore be justified in giving him wrong information?

Another problem is associated with your *reason* for lying. Suppose I say, "I'm sure I will meet lots of members of the opposite sex in this apartment complex whom I can date, don't you think so?" If you think I will not because I am an extremely unappealing person, should you tell me so? Would it be wrong to lie to me by agreeing with my statement? Would it make a difference if your reason, or motive, for lying were to rent the apartment rather than to protect my feelings?

One last justification needs to be raised: profits. In business, this is the most frequent "justification" offered for lying. Perhaps you can see that if you did not understand your own definition of lying, you might be more easily pressured into lying by the lure of profits. And even when you have a clear personal definition, you might still lie if there were enough money at stake. Or could you withstand the temptation?

Styles of Moral Reasoning about Truthtelling

Some persons view truthtelling from a teleological or consequential perspective. For them, whether or not one may lie is based on the *results* of lying. If these people are purely self-interested, then they may lie only if there is a benefit to them, such as additional rental income. But they may refuse to lie if they fear that a reputation for lying will cause them injury.

Other persons embrace certain things as "good" in and of themselves, without regard for the consequences. Their orientation is *deontological*. Truthtelling is one of the things these people (and religious writings such as the Bible, the Koran, and the Gita) usually consider a *good* irrespective of its consequences. Thus, many deontologists will be strongly committed to truthtelling for its own sake.

Note that business is basically a consequential mode of thinking: "Advertising is good if it increases sales," or, "He's a good man if he contributes to the profitability of the firm." The consequentialist may have an easier time than the deontologist deciding when to tell the truth in business life. The deontologist would be required to switch mental modes, to shift from the normal consequential style of day-to-day business decision making to the differing mode of deontology when making decisions about truthtelling.

As you read through the material in this chapter, give some thought to the nature of your beliefs about truthtelling. Try to articulate your definition of the truth and what your reason is—consequential or deontological—for being truthful. Don't focus so much on what you have done in the past as on what you think you *ought* to do in the future.

The Nature of Advertising Law

This chapter is distinctive because it describes the legal environment of a very common business function rather than one category of legal rules. Unlike chapters such as those on contract law, constitutional law, and agency law, which describe intimately related bodies of legal rules, this chapter describes the way one business function is influenced by a variety of often unrelated federal, state, and local laws. This chapter should give business students a feel for the way business functions are usually regulated.

The body of law with the greatest impact on advertising is federal law—particularly that portion associated with the Federal Trade Commission. Next in importance is the law associated with the Food and Drug Administration. Federal and state laws on warranties and state contract law also are major influences on advertising. This chapter examines the law of advertising first from the perspective of *federal agencies,* then from the perspective of the *competitors* of an advertiser, and lastly from the perspectives of *consumers.*

Federal Regulation of Advertising

The Federal Trade Commission

As we noted in chapter 5, the Federal Trade Commission (FTC) was created by the Federal Trade Commission Act (1914). That statute authorized the FTC to stop **unfair methods of competition.** Thus it was primarily designed to protect businesses from those forms of competition by other businesses that are unfair. Untruthful advertising can certainly be a form of unfair competition. In 1938 the United States Congress amended the Federal Trade Commission Act with the Wheeler-Lea Act. This amendment gave the FTC the power to stop "unfair or deceptive acts or practices." Thus the FTC's authority was expanded to protect *consumers* as well as businesses. The vast majority of FTC decisions on advertising are based on the statutory language prohibiting "unfair or deceptive . . . practices."

The legal definition of *deception* is somewhat vague. However, there appear to be two major types of FTC and court actions directed against **deceptive advertising.** One type of decision develops a general framework for identifying deception. The second type addresses specific promotional practices.

Deception

Advertising is illegal when it is deceptive. Historically, the courts and the FTC have evolved very broad definitions of deception. As a consequence of this, many ads were vulnerable to legal attack while at the same time business persons were uncertain about the exact definition of deception. When Ronald Reagan won the presidency in 1980, he began appointing new commissioners to the FTC. These new appointees shared the new president's views favoring a more limited role for government in the regulation of business. This view was manifest in their concern over the breadth of the FTC's definition of deception. Once in control of the chairmanship and with a majority of the commissioners, the Reagan appointees attempted to narrow this definition. This political strategy for altering business and consumer conduct caused the law to become somewhat uncertain in this area, with the FTC advancing a position which, at this writing, has not been sanctioned by the courts. The following two sections discuss, first, the historical definition of deception and then, second, the definition advanced by the Reagan administration appointees.

The Historical Definition of Deception. In the past, the FTC examined ads to determine whether an ad's total impression had the *capacity* to deceive *some* consumers. The capacity to deceive has generally been grounded on a finding of either a *misrepresentation* or an *omission*. A few of the cases are rather clear-cut, as when a mail-order advertiser offered a "sure-fire" insect killer, "guaranteed to kill insects every time." What the consumer received was two blocks of wood marked "A" and "B" with the instructions, "place insect on block A and hit with block B." The total impression of this ad had the capacity to deceive many consumers.

In order to determine whether deception exists, it is necessary to identify the group of consumers who may be deceived. The ad need not deceive all, or even a majority of consumers. The capacity to deceive the average consumer has *not* been the test. Generally the FTC and the courts have sought to use the group of consumers toward whom the advertising is directed in order to assess deception. This test encompasses, in some instances, the "ignorant, the unthinking and the credulous."

Even when an ad appears on the surface to be deceptive, it may be legal if a *defense* is available. The most common defense is **puffing** or "sales talk." These are expressions of personal opinion about intangible qualities of the product. For example, a claim that a certain toothpaste would "beautify the smile" was held by the FTC to be mere puffing and not deceptive. Similarly, endorsements by Santa Claus or the portrayal of a "tiger in your [gas] tank" have been considered puffing.

While puffing can be a defense, **literal truth** (the idea that all of the statements made are technically true) is not always a defense. The **total impression deception** may exist even when each individual statement is true. For example, the FTC issued a cease-and-desist order against P. Lorillard Company for advertising that its Old Gold cigarettes were, according to an article published in *Reader's Digest,* the lowest in nicotine of seven brands tested. The statement, though literally true, created a *total impression*—that Old Golds were low in nicotine—that was deceptive, because Old Golds were not significantly lower in nicotine than other cigarettes.

The FTC does not always win total impression cases. In a DuPont ad for Zerex antifreeze, a scene showed a hole being punched in a can of Zerex. Antifreeze poured out for a moment, then dribbled to a stop, showing the leak-stopping capabilities of Zerex. The ad was challenged as deceptive on the grounds that the contents of the can were not under pressure, as is the liquid in a radiator. DuPont, however, was able to show that Zerex worked the same way in a radiator as it did in the can. Thus the ad was not deceptive.

The following case illustrates the way the courts have handled cases involving such issues as the puffing defense, literal truth, total impression, and the particular group of consumers deceived.

Firestone Tire & Rubber Company v. Federal Trade Commission

6th Cir., 1973

Facts

Firestone sought review of an order of the Federal Trade Commission. The FTC had found Firestone guilty of unfair and deceptive advertising in relation to two particular advertisements. One of them may be characterized as the "Safe Tire" ad.

As to this series of advertisements, the parties stipulated as follows:

I. Duration of Advertising Program

1. *Beginning on December 25, 1967, and continuing through May 18, 1968, the following text, or a text substantially similar to it, was used in certain Firestone advertisements:*

THE SAFE TIRE. FIRESTONE

When you buy a Firestone tire—no matter how much or how little you pay—you get a safe tire, Firestone tires are custom-built one by one. By skilled craftsmen. And they're personally inspected for an extra margin of safety. If these tires don't pass all of the exacting Firestone inspections, they don't get out.

Every new Firestone design goes through rugged tests of safety and strength far exceeding any driving condition you'll ever encounter. We prove them in our test lab. On our test track. And in rigorous day-to-day driving conditions. All Firestone tires meet or exceed the new Federal Government testing requirements. (They have for some time.)

Firestone—The Safe Tire. At 60,000 Firestone Safe Tire Centers. At no more cost than ordinary tires.

II. Firestone's Design and Manufacturing Testing and Quality Control Procedures

1. *The state of tire manufacturing technology is such that use of the best manufacturing procedures and tests and quality control techniques known to the industry cannot insure that each tire produced by a manufacturer is absolutely free from any defects in materials or workmanship.*
2. *During the period of the advertisements set forth above, Firestone exercised due care and used its best efforts to employ the best manufacturing procedures and tests and quality control techniques known to the industry to design and manufacture tires free from defects in materials and workmanship.*

Opinion

Circuit Judge Edwards: As to this issue the Commission's opinion says:

> We conclude that respondent's absolute representation that its tires are "safe" is false and deceptive on its own admission that tires cannot under today's technology be assured of being free of defects. In view of this technological impossibility, it is an unfair and deceptive act and practice for respondent to make the unqualified assertion of safety which it made in this case. . . .
>
> While it is clear from the face of the advertisement that respondent makes no explicit claim that its tires are safe under all conditions of use, we believe it does so *implicitly*. [Emphasis added.] Respondent's advertisement asserts flatly that the Firestone tire is "The Safe Tire" and describes the exacting rugged tests ("far exceeding any driving conditions" consumers will ever encounter) which the tires are put through to assure this safety. Respondent's advertisement gives no indication that there is any limit to the safely of this tire or what such limits might be.

Firestone, on the other hand, emphasizes the stipulation recited above as to its employing the language, "the best manufacturing procedures and tests and quality control techniques known to the industry" and interprets the "Safe Tire" ad as "assuring average tire consumers that Firestone did everything humanly and technically possible to sell tires free of defects." Firestone also emphasizes that a large majority of persons interviewed concerning the "Safe Tire" ad thought that it meant something less than a guarantee of absolute safety.

In approaching the decision of this issue, this court is limited by statute and case law as to its proper function. The statute which provides for our review also provides that "the findings of the Commission as to the facts if supported by evidence, shall be conclusive." . . . This court has described such findings as "entitled to be given great weight," and has noted that "the Commission is permitted to draw reasonable inferences from the evidence. . . ."

Even more to the point and worth quoting at length is the following description of our function in the words of a leading Supreme Court opinion:

> In reviewing the substantive issues in the case, it is well to remember the respective roles of the Commission and the courts in the administration of the Federal Trade Commission Act. When the Commission was created by Congress in 1914, it was directed by §5 to prevent "[u]nfair methods of competition in commerce." Congress amended the Act in 1938 to extend the Commission's jurisdiction to include "unfair or deceptive acts or practices in commerce"—a significant amendment showing Congress' concern for consumers as well as for competitors. It is important to note the generality of these standards of illegality; the proscriptions in §5 are flexible, "to be defined with particularity by the myriad of cases from the field of business."
>
> This statutory scheme necessarily gives the Commission an influential role in interpreting §5 and in applying it to the facts of particular cases arising out of unprecedented situations. Moreover, as an administrative agency which deals continually with cases in the area, the Commission is often in a better position than are courts to determine when a practice is "deceptive" within the meaning of the Act. This Court has frequently stated that the Commission's judgment is to be given great weight by reviewing courts. This admonition is especially true with respect to allegedly deceptive advertising since the finding of a §5 violation in this field rests so heavily on inference and pragmatic judgment. *Nevertheless, while informed judicial determination is dependent upon enlightenment gained from administrative experience, in the last analysis the words "deceptive practices" set forth a legal standard and they must get their final meaning from judicial construction. . . .* [Emphasis added]

Employing these standards, we affirm the findings of the FTC on the "Safe Tire" issue and enforce its order.

There is, of course, no question but that the ad indulges in some puffing. [But puffing about safety will not be recognized as a defense in this case.]

When the statement is compared to the stipulation previously quoted, its deficiencies are obvious:

> 1. The state of tire manufacturing technology is such that use of the best manufacturing procedures and tests and quality control techniques known to the industry cannot insure that each tire produced by a manufacturer is absolutely free from any defects in material or workmanship.

This stipulation, in effect, concedes that defective Firestone tires can and do reach the consumer.

We deal, of course, with a statutory ban on "unfair or deceptive acts or practices." If no one were misled, we might reexamine our own conclusions vis-à-vis the Commission's inferences about this ad in considerably more detail. Here, however, Firestone's own consumer survey demonstrated that 15.3% of a scientifically selected sample of tire purchasers thought the "Safe Tire" and meant:

> (d) "Every Firestone tire is absolutely safe no matter how it is used and regardless of the tire inflation pressure and load of the car"; or

"Every single Firestone tire will be absolutely free from any defects."

We find it hard to overturn the deception findings of the Commission if the ad thus misled 15% (or 10%) of the buying public.

We find no overbreadth or deficiency in the remedial order of the Commission, and as to it we affirm and grant enforcement.

The Commission order to cease and desist is affirmed. . . .

Case Questions

1. Which body, the FTC or the courts, is better able to determine when an ad is "deceptive"? Why?
2. As a marketing manager, how would you go about deciding for yourself whether or not an ad is deceptive by the standards articulated by this case?
3. Why do the courts tolerate "false puffing" in many instances, yet reject it in this case? Is "false puffing" always morally wrong? If you think it is, why isn't it always legally wrong?

Recent Developments. In *Cliffdale Associates, Inc., et al.,* the FTC sharply altered its definition of deception. It articulated in that case a significantly narrower definition. There it wrote:

> Consistent with its Policy Statement on Deception, issued on October 14, 1983, the Commission will find an act or practice deceptive if,
> first, there is a representation, omission or practice that,
> second, is likely to mislead consumers acting reasonably under the circumstances, and
> third, the representation, omission or practice is material.

Note that this definition of deception changes the standard from "having the capacity or tendency to deceive" to "likely to mislead." In addition, the group to whom the standard is applied changes from the "ignorant, the unthinking and the credulous" to "consumers acting reasonably under the circumstances." These standards have the effect of reducing the number of ads that can be held to be deceptive.

While the FTC's position on deception is now reasonably clear, there is still substantial uncertainty about the way the courts will react to this new definition by the administrative agency. Recall the language in the *Firestone* case, in which the court stated that the definition of deception is ultimately a judicial determination. Perhaps the outcome will depend upon which judges review future FTC proceedings—those appointed by President Reagan or those appointed before his presidency.

Regulation of Specific Promotional Practices

This line of decisions encompasses price advertising, demonstrations, and surveys. Detailed FTC regulations exist to ensure that such statements as "one-half of regular price" or "75-cent discount" are literally true. Similarly, statements such as "a $25 retail value" must be true.

Demonstrations of a product's performance must be literally true. Lever

Brothers once used a commercial showing a man with an ink-stained shirt standing before the camera telling how All detergent would get the stain out. The room filled with water, the man poured in the All, wiggled a bit, the water receded, and presto, the stain was gone! The FTC contended that that amount of detergent in that much water with that much agitation would never get the shirt clean. The ad was changed to a cutaway of a washing machine with the words "simulated washing sequence" displayed on the screen. When the camera came back, the shirt was clean. Needless to say, the commercial lost most of its creative appeal.

Another example was the well-known Campbell Soup case that dealt with ads in which glass marbles were placed in the bottom of a bowl of soup to elevate the vegetables to the top. Campbell defended the action by saying that the soup shown in the ad had the standard amount of vegetables that would be found in any can on the shelf. The advertising problem was that viewers of the ad would not be able to see the vegetables because they naturally sink to the bottom of the bowl. This defense was fruitless, as the FTC pointed out that consumers know that vegetables sink, and if they can be seen on top, the assumption is that there are more vegetables underneath, not marbles.

The following case illustrates the way the United States Supreme Court and the FTC respond to one type of promotional strategy.

FTC v. Colgate-Palmolive Co.

380 U.S. 374 (1965)

Facts

The basic question before the Court was whether it is a deceptive trade practice, prohibited by section 5 of the Federal Trade Commission Act, to represent falsely that a televised test, experiment, or demonstration provides a viewer with visual proof of a product claim, regardless of whether the product claim is itself true.

The case arose out of an attempt by respondent Colgate Palmolive Company to prove to the television public that its shaving cream, Rapid Shave, "outshaves them all." Respondent Ted Bates & Company, Inc., an advertising agency, prepared for Colgate three one-minute commercials designed to show that Rapid Shave could soften even the toughness of sandpaper. Each of the commercials contained the same "sandpaper test." The announcer informed the audience that "to prove Rapid Shave's super-moisturizing power, we put it right from the can onto this tough, dry sandpaper. It was apply . . . soak . . . and off in a stroke." While the announcer was speaking, Rapid Shave was applied to a substance that appeared to be sandpaper, and immediately thereafter a razor was shown shaving the substance clean.

Opinion

Chief Justice Warren: The Federal Trade Commission issued a complaint against respondents Colgate and Bates charging that the commercials were false and deceptive. The evidence disclosed that sandpaper of the type depicted in the commercials could not be shaved immediately following the application of Rapid Shave, but required a substantial soaking period of approximately 80 minutes. The evidence also showed that the substance resembling sandpaper was in fact a simulated prop, or "mock-up," made of plexiglass, to which sand had been applied.

However, the examiner found that Rapid Shave could shave sandpaper, even though not in the short time represented by the commercials, and that if real sandpaper had been used in the commercials, the inadequacies of television transmission would have made it appear to viewers to be nothing more than plain, colored paper.

The [Federal Trade] Commission . . . found that since Rapid Shave could not shave sandpaper within the time depicted in the commercials, respondents had misrepresented the product's moisturizing power. Moreover, the Commission found that the undisclosed use of a plexiglass substitute for sandpaper was an additional material misrepresentation that was a deceptive act separate and distinct from the misrepresentation concerning Rapid Shave's underlying qualities. Even if the sandpaper could be shaved just as depicted in the commercials, the Commission found that viewers had been misled into believing they had seen it done with their own eyes. As a result of these findings the Commission entered a cease-and-desist order against the respondents. . . .

We are not concerned in this case with the clear misrepresentation in the commercials concerning the speed with which Rapid Shave could shave sandpaper, since the Court of Appeals uphold the Commission's finding on that matter and the respondents have not challenged the finding here. We granted certiorari to consider the Commission's conclusion that even if an advertiser has himself conducted a test, experiment or demonstration which he honestly believes will prove a certain product claim, he may not convey to television viewers the false impression that they are seeing the test, experiment or demonstration for themselves, when they are not because of the undisclosed use of mock-ups.

We accept the Commission's determination that the commercials involved in this case contained three representations to the public: (1) that sandpaper could be shaved by Rapid Shave; (2) that an experiment had been conducted which verified this claim; and (3) that the viewer was seeing this experiment for himself. Respondents admit that the first two representations were made, but deny that the third was. The Commission, however, found to the contrary, and, since this is a matter of fact resting on an inference that could reasonably be drawn from the commercials themselves, the Commission's finding should be sustained. For the purposes of our review, we can assume that the first two representations were true; the focus of our consideration is on the third which was clearly false. The parties agree that §5 prohibits the intentional misrepresentation of any fact which would constitute a material factor in a purchaser's decision whether to buy. They differ, however, in their conception of what "facts" constitute a "material factor" in a purchaser's decision to buy. Respondents submit, in effect, that the only material facts are those which deal with the substantive qualities of a product, The Commission, on the other hand, submits that the misrepresentation of any fact so long as it materially induces a purchaser's decision to buy is a deception prohibited by §5. . . .

Respondents claim that all . . . [the cases cited by the FTC] . . . are irrelevant to our decision because they involve misrepresentations related to the product itself and not merely to the manner in which an advertising message is communicated. This distinction misses the mark for two reasons. In the first place, the present case is not concerned with a mode of communication, but with a misrepresentation that viewers have objective proof of a seller's product claim over and above the seller's word. . . .

[Affirmed.]

Case Questions

1. Did Chief Justice Warren ground this decision on a deontological or consequential basis? Was the ad illegal because it created a false impression alone, or because the false impression would increase sales, or both?
2. Do you think the tangible (physical) props (the glass and sand) made it easier for the FTC to attack this misrepresentation? Do you think it would be more difficult to prove an *intangible* misrepresentation, such as an inference that drinking a diet cola will increase your sex appeal?
3. Is section 5, as described in this case, more deontological or consequential?

The Unfairness Doctrine

The Wheeler-Lea Act of 1938 gave the FTC the power to protect consumers from "unfair trade practices" in the same way that businesses had been protected up to that time from dishonest competitors.

The Magnuson-Moss Warranty Act (1975) gave the FTC the authority to establish trade regulation rules that prohibit certain "unfair" practices. Since 1972, the FTC has invoked the **unfairness doctrine** several times. In general, there have been two major types of decisions under the unfairness doctrine. The first includes the literal truth and total impression types of deceptive advertising. Thus most of the ads that are deceptive are also unfair to consumers.

Advertisements to children make up the second type controlled by this unfairness concept. For example, Hudson Pharmaceutical Corp. agreed to limit the use of "Spider Man" in its vitamin ads because children might be induced to take too many vitamins. Similarly, General Foods was not allowed to continue showing Ewell Gibbons in Grape Nuts ads picking and eating wild plants and stating that the plant is edible or good tasting, because some plants could be harmful if eaten. In another ad, a very young girl was seated next to a bathroom sink filled with water washing the hair on her doll. Her mother came in and gave her a hair dryer. The mother then left, and the little girl dried the doll's hair. The FTC directed the company to discontinue this commercial on the grounds that it might induce or encourage unsafe behavior by children. AMF also discontinued the showing of what were considered to be unsafe bicycle and tricycle riding in its ads.

In 1978 the FTC proposed, on the basis of the unfairness doctrine, a trade regulation rule that would ban all advertising directed at children under 8 and ban the advertising of sugared food items to those under 12. The rule also required that dental health and nutritional ads be paid for by the food industry. Partly in response to the proposed ban, the unfairness doctrine was strongly criticized by business as a violation of the First Amendment, as an unlawful delegation of legislative powers, as lacking in due process, and as lacking any meaningful criteria for determining unfairness. This contributed to the passage of the FTC Improvement Act in 1980, which limits and restricts the FTC's use of the unfairness doctrine. Although the unfairness doctrine can still be applied on a *case-by-case* basis, the FTC is prohibited from promulgating any *rule* that "prohibits or otherwise regulates any commercial advertising on the basis that such commercial advertising constitutes an unfair act or practice in or affecting commerce" for the fiscal years 1980, 1981, and 1982. By mid-1984 the FTC had informally agreed not to constrain advertising with trade regulation rules based on the unfairness doctrine.

Substantiation

Advertising substantiation has become a major issue in recent years. The FTC began to require in 1971 that advertisers, at the request of the FTC, furnish tests, studies, or other data to support any claims made about product safety, performance, efficiency, quality, or comparative price. Since that time, the FTC has implemented the substantiation program in two ways: first, by the use of industry-wide disclosures, in which all companies in a selected industry are required to submit substantiation for advertising claims; and second, on a case-by-case basis. Between 1971 and 1981, the FTC initiated twenty-nine industry-wide rounds, and numerous individual cases were pursued in response to competitor and consumer complaints.

The FTC takes the position that advertisers are obligated to substantiate advertising claims before they are made. The commission contends that it is unfair to make a claim without having a "reasonable basis" for the claim. This may be true even if the claim is true or if the product performs as advertised.

Remedies

Advertising complaints may be directed to the FTC by competitors, by consumers, or they may be initiated by one of the FTC's agents. The complaint is then investigated by field agents, and a report is prepared by the FTC's Bureau of Consumer Protection, Division of National Advertising. If the bureau decides that the complaint is justified, the case goes to the commission itself. The sanctions imposed by the FTC depend on the willingness of the offender to cooperate, the offender's past history of compliance with trade regulation laws, and the seriousness of the alleged offense. After a complaint is issued, the challenged firm has thirty days to respond.

The FTC has several alternatives when a firm is found guilty of illegal advertising:

1. The firm can voluntarily agree to refrain from making the offending claim in the future. This can be done with either a written assurance of voluntary compliance or a signed consent decree. In neither case does the action constitute can admission of guilt by the advertiser.
2. The FTC can issue a **cease-and-desist order;** which is a type of injunction requiring that the claim no longer be made. Under provisions of the FTC Improvement Act of 1975, the FTC can hold all firms in an industry to a cease-and-desist order even if only one firm actually signed the order.
3. An offending firm can be fined up to $10,000 for each day it knowingly violates a cease-and-desist order.
4. The FTC can seek restitution for consumers.
5. The FTC can require corrective advertising or affirmative disclosure.

Corrective advertising and **affirmative disclosure** have been used as remedies when advertisements are judged to be deceptive or misleading. Corrective advertising is used to change or correct existing erroneous beliefs, while the objective of affirmative disclosure is to instill new beliefs. The concept of corrective advertising originated with a group of law students—Students Opposed to Unfair Practices (SOUP)—in the FTC suit against Campbell Soup Company mentioned earlier. While corrective advertising was not required in that case, the FTC observed that deceptive claims could continue to influence consumers after the offending ad was discontinued. The commission suggested that a corrective message has three basic objectives:

1. To dispel the residual effects of deceptive advertisements.
2. To help restore competition to the stage that prevailed before unfair practices or deceptions influenced the market.
3. To deprive firms of unfairly obtained gains to which deceptive advertising may have contributed.

Implementation of the corrective advertising remedy may simply involve requiring a company to disclose in future ads some fact not previously revealed. On the other hand, a firm can be required to devote a percentage of its advertising budget to communicating a message admitting that previous claims were false. The first corrective advertising order ever made by the FTC required ITT Continental Baking Company to devote 25 percent of its media budget for one year to FTC-approved corrective advertisements stating that Profile bread had no effect in weight reduction. Profile had been advertised as a weight-loss aid, but the reason Profile had fewer calories than other types of bread was that it was sliced thinner. The company estimated that the corrective ads led to a 20 to 25 percent sales decline.

The following case illustrates the way the FTC and the courts view corrective advertising.

Warner-Lambert Company v. Federal Trade Commission

(C.A. D.C., 1977)

Facts

The Warner-Lambert Company petitioned for review of an order of the Federal Trade Commission requiring it to cease and desist from advertising that its product, Listerine antiseptic mouthwash, prevents, cures, or alleviates the common cold. The FTC order further required Warner-Lambert to disclose in future Listerine advertisements that: "Contrary to prior advertising, Listerine will not help prevent colds or sore throats or lessen their severity." The circuit court affirmed, but modified the order to delete from the required disclosure the phrase "Contrary to prior advertising."

Opinion

Circuit Judge J. Skelly Wright: The order under review represents the culmination of a proceeding begun in 1972, when the FTC issued a complaint charging petitioner with violation of Section 5(a)(1) of the Federal Trade Commission Act by misrepresenting the . . . [effectiveness] of Listerine against the common cold.

Listerine has been on the market since 1879. Its formula has never changed. Ever since its introduction it has been represented as being beneficial in certain respects for colds, cold symptoms, and sore throats. Direct advertising to the consumer, including the cold claims as well as others, began in 1921.

Following the 1972 complaint, hearings were held before an administrative law judge (ALJ). The hearings consumed over four months and produced an evidentiary record consisting of approximately 4,000 pages of documentary exhibits and the testimony of 46 witnesses. In 1974 the ALJ issued an initial decision sustaining the allegations of the complaint. Petitioner appealed this decision to the Commission. On December 9, 1975 the Commission issued its decision essentially affirming the ALJ's findings. It concluded that petitioner had made the challenged representations that Listerine will ameliorate, prevent, and cure colds and sore throats, and that these representations were false. Therefore the Commission ordered petitioner to:

(1) cease and desist from representing that Listerine will cure colds or sore throats, prevent colds or sore throats, or that users of Listerine will have fewer colds than non-users;

(2) cease and desist from representing that Listerine is a treatment for, or will lessen the severity of, colds or sore throats; that it will have any significant beneficial effect on the symptoms of sore throats or any beneficial effect on symptoms of colds; or that the ability of Listerine to kill germs is of medical significance in the treatment of colds or sore throats or their symptoms;

(3) cease and desist from disseminating any advertisement for Listerine unless it is clearly and conspicuously disclosed in each such advertisement, in the exact language below, that; "Contrary to prior advertising, Listerine will not help prevent colds or sore throats or lessen their severity." This requirement extends only to the next ten million dollars of Listerine advertising.

Petitioner seeks review of this order. The American Advertising Federation and the Association of National Advertisers have filed briefs as amici curiae.

The first issue on appeal is whether the Commission's conclusion that Listerine is not beneficial for colds or sore throats is supported by the evidence. The Commission's findings must be sustained if they are supported by substantial evidence on the record viewed as a whole. We conclude that they are.

Both the ALJ and the Commission carefully analyzed the evidence. They gave full consideration to the studies submitted by petitioner. The ultimate conclusion that Listerine is not an effective cold remedy was based on . . . the following . . . specific findings of fact.

First, the Commission found that the ingredients of Listerine are not present in sufficient quantities to have any therapeutic effect. . . .

Second, the Commission found that in the process of gargling it is impossible for Listerine to reach the critical areas of the body in medically significant concentration. . . .

Third, the Commission found that even if significant quantities of the active ingredients of Listerine were to reach the critical sites where cold viruses enter and infect the body, they would not interfere with the activities of the virus because they [the ingredients] could not penetrate the tissue cells.

Fourth, the Commission discounted the results of a clinical study conducted by petitioner on which petitioner heavily relies. Petitioner contends that in a four year study schoolchildren who gargled with Listerine had fewer colds and cold symptoms than those who did not gargle with Listerine. The Commission found that the design and execution of the "St. Barnabas study" made its results unreliable. For the first two years of the four-year test no placebo was given to the control group. For the last two years the placebo was inadequate: The control group was given colored water which did not resemble Listerine in smell or taste. There was also evidence that the physician who examined the test subjects was not blinded from knowing which children were using Listerine and which were not. . . .

Fifth, the Commission found that the ability of Listerine to kill germs by millions on contact is of no medical significance in the treatment of colds or sore throats. Expert testimony showed that bacteria in the oral cavity, the "germs" which Listerine purports to kill, do not cause colds and play no role in cold symptoms. Colds are caused by viruses. . . .

Sixth, the Commission found that Listerine has no significant beneficial effect on the symptoms of sore throat. . . .

Petitioner and amici further contend that corrective advertising is not a permissible remedy because it trenches on the First Amendment. Petitioner is correct that this triggers a special responsibility on the Commission to order corrective advertising only if the restriction inherent in its order is no greater than necessary to serve the interest involved. . . . Amici curiae go further, arguing that, since the Supreme Court has recently extended First Amendment protection to commercial advertising, mandatory corrective advertising is unconstitutional.

A careful reading of Virginia State Board of Pharmacy v. Virginia Citizens Consumer Council compels rejection of this argument. For the Supreme Court expressly noted that the First Amendment presents "no obstacle" to government regulation of false or misleading advertising. The First Amendment, the Court said,

> as we construe it today, does not prohibit the State from insuring that the stream of commercial information flow[s] clearly as well as freely.

In a footnote the Court went on to delineate several differences between commercial speech and other forms which may suggest that a different degree of protection is necessary ***. For example, the Court said, they may

> make it appropriate to require that a commercial message appear in such a form, or include such additional information, warnings, and disclaimers, as are necessary to prevent its being deceptive.

Affirmative disclosure has also been required when an advertisement although not misleading if taken alone, becomes misleading considered in light of past advertisements. For example, for 60 years Royal Baking Powder Company had stressed in its advertising that its product was superior because it was made with cream of tarter, not phosphate. But, faced with rising costs of cream of tartar, the time came when it changed its ingredients and became a phosphate baking powder. It carefully removed from all labels and advertisements any reference to cream of tartar and corrected the list of ingredients. But the new labels used the familiar arrangement of lettering . . . and design, so that they looked exactly like the old ones. A new advertising campaign stressed the new low cost of the product and dropped all reference to cream of tartar. But the advertisements were also silent on the subject of phosphate and did not disclose the change in the product.

The Commission held, and the Second Circuit agreed, that the new advertisements were deceptive, since they did not advise consumers that their reasons for buying the powder in the past no longer applied. The court held that it was proper to require the company to take affirmative steps to advise the public. . . .

In another case the Waltham Watch Company of Massachusetts had become renowned for the manufacture of fine clocks since 1849. Soon after it stopped manufacturing clocks in the 1950's, it transferred its trademarks, good will, and the trade name "Waltham" to a successor corporation, which began importing clocks from Europe for resale in the United States. The imported clocks were advertised as "product of Waltham Watch Company since 1850," "a famous 150-year-old company."

The Commission found that the advertisements caused consumers to believe they were buying the same fine Massachusetts clocks of which they had heard for many years. To correct this impression the Commission ordered the company to disclose in all advertisements and on the product that the clock was not made by the old Waltham company and that it was imported. The Seventh Circuit affirmed, relying on "the well established general principle that the Commission may require affirmative disclosure for the purpose of preventing future deception."

It appears to us that the orders in Royal and Waltham were the same kind of remedy the Commission has ordered here. Like Royal and Waltham, Listerine has built up over a period of many years a widespread reputation. When it was ascertained that reputation no longer applied to the product, it was necessary to take action to correct it. Here, as in Royal and Waltham, it is the accumulated impact of past advertising that necessitates disclosure in future advertising. To allow consumers to continue to buy the product on the strength of the impression built up by prior advertising—an impression which is now known to be false—would be unfair and deceptive. . . .

Having established that the Commission does have the power to order corrective advertising in appropriate cases, it remains to consider whether use of the remedy against Listerine is warranted and equitable. We have concluded that part 3 of the order should be modified to delete the phrase "Contrary to prior advertising." With that modification, we approve the order. . . .

Case Questions

1. Is it your belief that the conduct of the Royal Baking Powder Company, in failing to disclose the change in ingredients, was morally wrong? Why or why not?

2. *Assume* Listerine had been advertised solely as a mouthwash that stops bad breath, when in fact it did not stop bad breath. Is the FTC as likely to require corrective advertising for this claim as for the "cures colds" claim? Why or why not?
3. Which legal standard, literal truth or total impression, is used to condemn the Listerine ads?

Other Federal Regulation of Advertising

The Food and Drug Administration

There are a number of other federal laws that affect advertising strategy. The Food and Drug Administration (FDA) was created in 1906 to monitor the safety and labeling of food items. Today, the FDA has jurisdiction over labeling, packaging, and sale of food, drugs, and cosmetics.

Food is regulated in several ways. Advertising statements must accurately describe food products. Thus, hot dogs cannot be advertised as "all-beef weiners" unless the content is in reality nearly "all beef." Safety levels are set by the FDA for additives. Additives that cause cancer in animals or humans at any level of concentration are generally banned. The FDA also administers both voluntary and mandatory nutrition labeling programs. **Nutrition labeling** is required when nutrients are added to food. Kellogg's Special K is an example of a food to which nutrients (in this case vitamins) have been added. Mandatory labeling is also required when labels contain claims of nutritional quality. Coor's Lite makes claims of nutritional quality by describing itself as a low-calorie beer.

Drugs are the most highly regulated product in our society. In general, the FDA is charged with determining whether a drug is safe. Thalidomide, a sedative that causes severe birth defects when used by some pregnant women, cannot be sold because it is not safe. Also, new drugs must be effective for the purpose sold. If new drugs meet these two requirements—safe and effective—the FDA will determine whether they will be sold over the counter or only by prescription.

United States Postal Service

Federal law makes it a crime, punishable by a fine of up to $1,000 or five years in prison, or both, to engage in **mail fraud.** The definition of mail fraud is broader than that of ordinary fraud. Mail fraud exists when two elements are present. The first is a scheme to defraud others. This scheme has been described as an attempt to gain undue advantage by means of a representation known to be false. Thus, the misrepresentation must be intentional. In deciding whether or not there is a representation known to be false, the courts carefully weigh overt misrepresentations, omissions, concealment, and half-truths.

The second element of mail fraud is use of the United States Postal Service in the execution of the fraudulent scheme. Sending intentionally false ads through the mail would be mail fraud. If one printed a coupon and distributed it door to door along with instructions that it be clipped and mailed, then *receipt* of the coupon would be use of the mails.

Other Regulations

Several laws regulate packaging and labeling. These include the Wool Products Labeling Act (1939), the Fur Product Labeling Act (1951), the Textile Fiber Products Identification Act (1958), the Hazardous Substances Labeling Act (1960), the Fair Packaging and Labeling Act (1966), and the Cigarette Labeling Act (1966).

The Robinson-Patman Act of 1936 requires that advertising allowances provided to business buyers generally must be given to all business buyers on the same basis. Trademarks are granted under provisions of the Lanham Act (1946), and the Court of Customs and Patent Appeals oversees trademark protection and litigation. The Consumer Credit Protection Act, also called the Truth-in-Lending Act, was passed in 1968 and requires that finance charges be accurately and completely communicated when mentioned in advertising.

The Communications Act of 1934 gave the Federal Communications Commission (FCC) power to regulate and license broadcasters. It imposes restrictions on the advertising of certain products and on advertising message content. Although it does not prohibit such advertising, the FCC has historically opposed the advertising on TV or radio of physicians, clergy, and marriage counselors, contraceptives, and liquor containing more than 14 percent alcohol. In the late 1960s and early 1970s, the FCC required television stations to air antismoking advertisements.

The Securities and Exchange Commission (SEC) controls all advertising of public offerings of stocks and bonds. The Alcohol Tax Unit of the U.S. Treasury Department oversees the sale, packaging, labeling, and advertising of alcoholic beverages.

Competitors' Remedies

Up to this point in the chapter, we have discussed the power of the federal government, not competitors or consumers, to attack illegal ads. This section discusses the remedies available to *competitors* injured by illegal advertising. This area of the law is also changing quite rapidly. Accordingly, there is a great deal of uncertainty in many areas of the law related to competitors' remedies.

Palming Off

A suit for **palming off** is the oldest of the competitor remedies. It is available when one party creates an impression—by use of a trademark, trade name, container label, package, or other distinctive feature—that its goods are the goods of a competitor. For example, if Pepsi began packaging its drinks in a bottle shaped just like the famous Coca Cola bottle, Coke could prevail in a suit for palming off. Palming off is a tort, and the victim can recover damages and obtain an injunction.

Disparagement

Disparagement is often called **trade disparagement.** It occurs when someone makes a *false statement* about *someone else's* business or product. In addition to having to prove the falsity of statements, the plaintiff must also be able to establish that the disparagement caused a loss of business and/or profits. Thus, for example, it was held an actionable trade disparagement for agents of Magnaflux Corp. to state to the customers and potential customers of its competitor, Testing Systems Inc., that the U.S. government had found Testing System's equipment only 40 percent as effective as that of Magnaflux, when that statement was untrue.

False advertising

False advertising exists when you make untrue statements about *your product or business*. Until the 1940s, competitors were not permitted to sue someone engaged in false advertising; only the government—or perhaps consumers—had the legal ability to stop false advertising. In 1946, Congress enacted the Lanham Act. While this act was generally aimed at clarifying trademark law, section 43(a) prohibited "any false description or representation of goods." Since the statute was signed into law, there have been many suits in different parts of the country in which one company sues another, claiming the defendant has made untrue advertising claims about its products. Some federal district and circuit courts have rejected competitors' suits on the grounds that the false description or representation must involve a trademark or conduct similar to trademark infringements. Other federal district and circuit courts, in fact a majority of them, have read the same statute and reached a different conclusion. In those jurisdictions competitors can recover from those who falsely represent characteristics of their own products in advertisements. As you can see, this area of the law is currently unclear. It could be clarified by a congressional amendment to the statute or by an opinion by the United States Supreme Court interpreting the existing statute.

The following case illustrates one court's treatment of a false advertising claim under section 43(a) and illustrates the way the doctrine of stare decisis (discussed in chapter 3) controls judicial conduct.

American Consumers, Inc. v. The Kroger Company

416 F. Supp. 1210 (E.D. Tenn. 1976)

Facts

The Kroger Company (defendant) engaged in an advertising campaign known as the Price Patrol Report. American Consumers, Inc., contended that the advertising was false in various respects and therefore violated the Lanham Act.

Opinion

District Judge Wilson: The plaintiff contends that section 43(a) of the Lanham Act is sufficiently broad in its language and scope as to include false price advertising as allegedly engaged in by Kroger in its grocery merchandising. The defendant, upon the other hand, contends the that section 43(a) is but a part of the trademark laws of the United States and is limited in its scope and intent to merchandising practices equivalent to the misuse of trademarks, that is the passing or "palming off" of one's goods as those of a competitor.

Section 43(a) provides in relevant part:

> Any person who shall . . . use in connection with any goods or services . . . any false description or representation . . . tending falsely to describe or represent the same . . . shall be liable to a civil action by any person . . . who believes that he is or is likely to be damaged by the use of any such false description or representation.

. . . [F]ollowing the passage of the Lanham Act in 1946, the courts did not initially construe that Act as widening the scope of unfair competition claims beyond the . . . common law precedents. Although some courts continue to interpret section 43(a) as being confined to situations where there had been a "palming off" of goods of the defendant for those of the plaintiff, with the passage of time, a "checkerboard . . . of apparently conflicting decisions" developed in the federal courts in regard to the interpretation to be placed upon section 43(a).

More recent cases have generally recognized that section 43(a) did not simply reenact the common law tort of "palming off," but rather created a new federal statutory tort rendering actionable any false description or misrepresentation by a defendant of his merchandise where that merchandise moves in interstate commerce.

It must be acknowledged that a review of the case law . . . reveals that most of the false descriptions or representations complained of by a plaintiff have been false descriptions or representations concerning the ingredients or qualities inherent to the defendant's product. This is in contrast to the instant case where the false statements allegedly made by the defendant do not pertain to the inherent ingredients or qualities of the defendant's goods, but rather pertain to the pricing of those goods in relation to the plaintiff's pricing of similar or identical goods. The question thus presented to the court is whether section 43(a) of the Lanham Act extends to those situations where the alleged false statements are made by a defendant with regard to the prices of its goods in comparison with the prices of the plaintiff's goods.

Focusing on the words of section 43(a) which would be relevant here, it can be seen that the Lanham Act applies to "any false description or representation" used "in connection with any goods" which tends "falsely to describe or represent the same." . . . [I]t would appear to this Court that the price of a particular item would be as much a "false representation" of the item as any representation concerning the goods' inherent ingredients or qualities. This would be especially true where, as here, the only real and material difference between two competitors' goods are their prices and the only real area of competition is price competition. It can hardly be argued in a case such as this that false representations concerning the comparative prices of similar or identical grocery items would be any less damaging to the business of a plaintiff-competitor than false representations made by a defendant concerning the inherent qualities or ingredients of its groceries. Thus it would appear that . . . falsity in price advertising is equally as unfair and damaging as falsity in the designation of the inherent qualities or ingredients of the goods. It would further appear that false price advertising would equally tend to "falsely . . . represent" the goods as would falsity in the description of the inherent qualities or ingredients of the goods.

However, the foregoing reasoning and conclusion in regard to the interpretation of section 43(a) of the Lanham Act would appear to be precluded in this Circuit by the decision in the case of Federal-Mogul-Bower Bearings, Inc. v. Azoff. Although that case was decided in 1963, it appears to be the most recent, if not the only, decision in this Circuit upon the issue now before the Court. In that case the Court, quoting with approval the following language from Sampson Crane Co. v. Union National Sales, Inc., stated:

> The intent of congress in passing the Act is set forth in the final paragraph of Section 1127. Only one phrase of that paragraph fails to use the word "mark." And that phrase ("to protect persons engaged in such commerce against unfair competition") must in such a context be

construed to refer not to any competitive practice which in the broad meaning of the words might be called unfair, but to that "unfair competition" which has been closely associated with the misuse of trademarks, i.e., the passing off of one's goods as those of a competitor. It is clear, both from this statement of the intent and from a reading of the Act as a whole, that the primary purpose of the Act was to eliminate deceitful practices in interstate commerce involving the misuse of trademarks, but along with this it sought to eliminate other forms of misrepresentations which are of the same general character even though they do not involve any use of what can technically be called a trademark. . . .

This Court accordingly concludes that, as contended by the defendant, section 43(a) of the Lanham Act is limited in its scope and intent to merchandising practices equivalent to the misuse of trademarks, that is, the passing or "palming off" of one's goods as those of a competitor.

It is accordingly the opinion of the Court that the complaint in this case fails to allege and the evidence in the case fails to establish any violation of the Lanham Act and that no federal question jurisdiction would accordingly lie.

Case Questions

1. What role does the doctrine of stare decisis play in this case?
2. This discussion indicates that *Azoff* was decided in 1963, while this case is being decided thirteen years later in 1976. The case also makes it clear that other jurisdictions treat these cases differently. Why didn't the Supreme Court clarify this area of the law during this thirteen-year period?
3. Does this judge believe that the *Azoff,* decision was the correct one? If you think he does not agree with *Azoff* why do you think he followed it?

Consumers and Ads

Most of the law that gives rights to *consumers* (as opposed to administrative agencies or competitors) has evolved on the state level. The primary bodies of law affecting ads and consumers are the common law of contracts and the Uniform Commercial Code. Chapter 8 describes the elements that must be present before the law will conclude that a contract exists. These include offer, acceptance, consideration, capacity, and legality. Offer, acceptance, and consideration have great impact on many ads.

Offers

In general, a valid **offer** exists when you indicate an intent to contract by communicating all the essential information about the proposed transaction.

The law of offers is critically important when one advertises a product or service. If the advertisement is sufficiently detailed and specific—i.e., it contains *all* the essential information for a transaction—the law may treat it as an offer. If an ad constitutes an offer, anyone who reads or sees or hears it may, simply by accepting, create a contract, which binds the advertiser. And in some instances there may be more acceptances than there are products available. In these cases the advertiser may be liable to the party accepting for any financial injury. For example, a newspaper ad offering for sale a limited number of fur coats, described with drawings, for $1.00 each, "first come, first served" created an offer because it contained all the essential terms.

Catalogs containing detailed descriptions of the product and terms of sale, TV ads of specific cars offered for a specific cash price have a high potential for being offers. In contrast, an ad such as the following would not create an offer:

> Far-out four-bedroom, two-bath home at 121 Valley View Drive, San Fernando, California, $189,000 cash, first come, first served, call Wanda at 415–283–6671.

While this ad contains the same amount of information as the one for the fur coats, it does not contain all the essential terms to a transaction for the sale of a home. There is, for example, no mention of the nature of the title or of when a buyer would take possession. Thus, as the complexity of the transaction increases, so does the quantity of information needed to classify an ad as an offer.

Sometimes good ads must, for practical reasons, contain all the information necessary to create an offer. A catalog, such as the Penney's or Sears' catalogs, must contain all the transaction information or these ads won't do a good job of selling. Similarly, an ad for a subscription to *Time* magazine must identify the product *(Time),* the price (perhaps 85 cents per issue), and the subscription period (perhaps six months) so that all the information necessary for an offer is present. If any of the information were omitted so that there would be no offer, then the ad probably would not sell effectively. Advertisers have devised a variety of ways to sidestep the business risks of making public offers. Sometimes the ads state *"first come, first served";* sometimes they state *"offer limited to stock on hand."* Ads can also specify a time period for the life of the offer, such as "offer expires on December 1, 1988." In other situations, such as with magazine subscriptions, ads on postcards, and magazine inserts, the language selected by the advertiser creates a communication flowing *from* the consumer *to* the advertiser. Thus, a common *Time* clipout coupon states "Please send me 52 issues. . . ." There is also a place for the consumer's signature. While this advertisement communicates all the information necessary to create an offer, the language of the coupon creates an offer from the consumer to *Time* magazine. *Time* can then accept, reject, or ignore the consumer's offer.

Acceptances

This concept can be important to advertisers because contract law allows those who make offers to specify the time and method of acceptance. Generally, if one attempts to accept in a way different from the required method, the acceptance is invalid and no contract arises. Thus the time limitations on offers discussed above are valid because of the law of acceptance.

When offer and acceptance appear to exist, one party may still be able to withdraw from the transaction where there has been misrepresentations or fraud. Both require a misrepresentation about a material fact that is relied upon by the other party. In misrepresentation there need to be no *intent* to deceive. An innocent deception is sufficient. For fraud to occur, the deception must be intentional.

Consideration

This contract law doctrine is also an important concept for advertisers. The concept of **consideration** holds that there is generally no contract unless both parties get something of legal value out of the transaction. In the sale of a motorcycle, the buyer receives the bike, while the seller may receive a promise of $50 per month for ten months. These things have legal value, so the agreement is enforceable.

Often, advertisers wish to enter into transactions with consumers—for example, in promotional contests—*without* contracting. Thus they often state "send this boxtop *or a reasonable facsimile* to . . ." in the instructions to promotional games or contests. If it required the boxtop, then the advertiser would receive a legal benefit from the purchase of its products, so the transaction involving the contest could create a contract between participants and the promoter. Each participant might have the right to sue if the rules of the contest were not followed precisely. In contrast, by allowing participants to send the facsimiles, the promoter gives participants the ability to participate without directly benefiting the promoter in a strictly legal sense. If this path is chosen, then there is no consideration and no contract. This is because the law of consideration holds that if there is *any alternative* without legal value—such as the use of the facsimile—then there is no consideration and no contract. This is so even if the alternative that does create legal value is selected.

In other instances advertisers do desire to create legal value in promotional schemes. Thus it is very common to attach a value, such as "$\frac{1}{25}$ of one cent," to coupons. In some cases this tactic reflects a desire on the part of marketers to contract instead of making a gift. In most instances, however, the promoter's motive is to give the coupon a legal value so that its unauthorized reproduction will constitute a crime, often the crime of counterfeiting.

Warranty

This body of law is probably the most significant area of contract law affecting promotion. In general, warranty law is closely related to the Uniform Commercial Code. Thus, consumers are better able to assert warranty claims against promoters when the thing being promoted is a good rather than a service or realty.

Generally, a warranty is a specific statement relied upon by the buyer. Sometimes ads contain **warranty statements.** General statements or puffing do not create warranties. Thus an ad, or a statement by a salesperson stating "It is the finest car money can buy," is too general—mere puffing or sales talk. In contrast, the statements "This lawnmower is powered by a 3.2 horsepower engine'' or ''70 percent wool'' do create warranties. In addition to words, pictures and samples can create warranties. Thus when a consumer picks out carpeting for a house based on samples, there is a warranty that the actual carpet installed will be the same as the sample. Similarly, pictures in ads may create a warranty when the buyer relies on them.

All of these warranties are called *express* warranties because they are created by affirmative conduct in promoting a product. There is a very important *implied* warranty to which marketers must be very sensitive; it is the **warranty of merchantability** that is implied with the sale of every new good. This warranty promises that the goods will perform *reasonably*. This means that a lawnmower must cut grass reasonably well for a reasonable period of time without breaking down. In a promotional sleight of hand, many promoters give consumers a ''warranty plan'' that *eliminates* the warranty of merchantability and substitutes in its place such statements as ''30 days on labor and 60 on parts'' or ''12 months or 12,000 miles, whichever comes first.'' Generally these ''warranty plans'' are much less expensive to the seller than the warranty of merchantability. When such written warranties are given, they must be labeled as ''full warranties'' or as ''limited warranties.'' Chapter 23, Consumer Rights, describes this requirement in more detail.

Ethical Issues in the Regulation of Advertising

After studying the law of advertising, you should have a reasonable understanding of the way our society regulates truthtelling in business. Notice that there are clearly ''limits of the laws''; there are certain types of conduct that we probably judge to be wrong but which we cannot make illegal—often for practical reasons associated with enforceability. For example, how would the law determine whether or not an apartment is ''wonderful''? Because there are limits beyond which the legal system cannot go, there are often corresponding opportunities to engage in profitable business activities that are *legal,* but which many would judge to be morally *wrong*. Recall the example of the student who misunderstood the commuting time between the campus and the apartment. Would you have corrected his perception? Do your values about truthtelling require you to sacrifice legal profits in order to be completely forthright? The ethics questions at the end of the chapter afford you a chance to define your values about truthtelling in business.

The important concepts and terms in this chapter are listed below; page numbers have been provided for the key terms. By reading over each section you can assess your understanding of the chapter concepts and determine areas you may want to review.

Chapter Summary

1. Most of advertising law represents an attempt to invoke legal sanctions for violation of ethical beliefs about truthtelling.

2. Advertising law gives certain enforcement powers to governmental agencies, others to competitors, and still others to consumers.
3. The FTC challenges questionable advertising with the tests of *literal truth, total impression,* and *unfairness.*
4. The literal truth test is most often applied to statements about price, surveys, and demonstrations.
5. Even when an ad is literally true, if the total impression it creates deceives *some* consumers, it may be illegal.
6. Some advertising directed toward children has been attacked by the FTC under the unfairness doctrine.
7. Advertising claims about product characteristics must be justified by *prior substantiation.*
8. The FTC can require an "assurance of voluntary compliance" or it can issue a cease-and-desist order and fine those who violate such orders. It can also obtain restitution for consumers and require corrective advertising.
9. Corrective advertising is used as an FTC remedy when prior deceptive advertising is likely to have a continuing or "residual" effect on the beliefs of consumers.
10. The Food and Drug Administration has jurisdiction over the labeling of food and the safety and effectiveness of drugs and cosmetics.
11. Mail fraud involves use of the mails as part of a scheme to intentionally gain undue advantage by misrepresentation. Mail fraud is a crime.
12. Competitors can sometimes recover from an advertiser whose ad constitutes palming off, disparagement, or false advertising.
13. *False advertising* involves an untrue statement made by you about your business or product or service. In some jurisdictions, a competitor injured by that false advertisement can recover money damages in court.
14. Advertisement sometimes constitute offers to contract. But most advertisements do not contain enough information about the proposed transaction to constitute an offer.
15. *Misrepresentation* exists when you *unintentionally* indicate something untrue about a material fact and other parties reasonably rely on this to their injury.
16. *Fraud* involves an *intentional* misrepresentation of a material fact that others rely on to their injury.
17. The contract law concept of *consideration* can be used to alter the legal relations between advertisers and consumers.
18. Puffing and sales talk do not bind advertisers. These are *glittering generalities,* such as, "I promise, you are absolutely going to *love* this house!"
19. Warranty statements are concrete and specific. If an a advertisement contains a warranty statement and a consumer relies upon the warranty, it can become a term of the contract between the consumer and the seller.

Key Terms

- advertising substantiation 616
- affirmative disclosure 617
- cease-and-desist order 617
- consideration 627
- corrective advertising 617
- deceptive advertising 609
- false advertising 623
- literal truth deception 610
- mail fraud 621
- nutrition labeling 621
- offer 625
- palming off 622
- puffing 610
- total impression deception 610
- trade disparagement 623
- unfair methods of competition 609
- unfairness doctrine 616
- warranty of merchantability 628
- warranty statement 627

Questions on Ethics

1. You are aware that there is generally no legal liability for puffing in ads. Suppose you are considering using the following newspaper ad to help sell your used car:

   1982 Toyota—A truly fantastic car in great shape. Yours for less than blue book. Call 777–6787 after 6:00 P.M.

   Assume that you know your car is in poor mechanical condition. Does such an ad, in your opinion, constitute lying? If you believe it is lying, do you think it is justified? Would you use such an ad? Are the reasons for your decisions teleological (consequential) or deontological?
2. Suppose you have developed an inexpensive product that will protect linoleum floors while giving them a "newly waxed" look. After hiring the best marketing consultants available, you learn that the most effective way to advertise the product is to aim the ads at lonely housewives. These ads should create an aura for the product as an attractive masculine helpmate—Mr. Shine! The research on this theme reveals that such an ad campaign *would* sell the product but it *would not* make the target market feel less lonely.

   Does such an ad constitute lying? If you believe it is lying, do you think it is justified? Would you use such an ad? Why or why not?
3. Suppose you are a landlord showing an apartment to a prospective tenant in a building with a high vacancy rate. The student mentions that the apartment is attractive because it is only twenty minutes away from campus. You know that it is at least fifty minutes during the times when the student plans to commute.

   In your opinion, would it be a lie to remain silent, not correcting the student's misunderstanding? If you believe it is lying, is it justified? Would *you* remain silent? What is the ethical basis for your decision?

4. Suppose you hear an advertisement on the TV for a new car dealership some distance away from your home. The speaker indicates that "We offer the lowest prices in town. It's always worth it to drive the few extra miles to. . . ."

   Do you think this advertiser is bound by a moral duty not to create wrong impressions about the dealership's pricing policies? Do this dealer's moral and legal obligations overlap almost perfectly? If the dealership really doesn't sell cars cheaper, is it lying?
5. Suppose you are the manager of marketing for a diet cola. Your marketing research indicates that the purchase decision for this product is characterized by mental activity classified as "low involvement." Accordingly you devise a TV ad that is designed to attract viewer attention with young, thin, sexy women in bathing suits. The ad then tries to win purchases by creating the impression that if the viewer drinks the diet cola she too will become young, thin, and sexy. Your lawyer tells you that the ad is perfectly legal.

   Do you think advertisers have moral duties that are broader than legal duties? Is this ad telling the truth? Does this ad deceive? Are there ethical issues associated with this ad, aside from truthtelling?

Questions on Law

1. Singer Pat Boone made a commercial for Cooga Mooga, Inc. The ad extolled the benefits of a certain medication used to treat acne. In the commercial Boone indicated that he and his family used the medication. This representation was not true.

   Does such an endorsement fall within the category of puffing? What claims could be asserted by the FTC, competitors, or consumers? Which of these three is most likely to prevail against Cooga Mooga? *Cooga Mooga, Inc.,* 92 FTC. 310 (1978).
2. Suppose you manufactured pickup trucks and you wanted to demonstrate in TV ads their ruggedness by dropping them into view from a height of eight feet. This causes the windshields to crack. Accordingly, you order the windshield removed from the demonstration truck before it is dropped into view. Does this conduct subject your organization to any legal liability? To whom—the FTC, competitors, or consumers? Under what legal theories?
3. Suppose you sold watches and attached to each a price tag and then consistently discounted the prices of the watches. Would the price tags constitute deceptive advertising? False advertising? If there is deception, is it of the literal truth or total impression variety?
4. Anacin was advertised as a pain reliever superior to Tylenol for the relief of the pain associated with inflammation. Tylenol sued, claiming that consumers were likely to misunderstand the ad by concluding that Anacin is superior for relief of *general* pain. In fact, Anacin was not

superior in reducing general pain. To support its claim, Tylenol submitted survey data that demonstrated that consumers did perceive the ad as a claim of generalized superiority. What legal basis does Tylenol have for its suit? Is Tylenol's claim based on a literal truth or total impression theory? Is the defense of puffing available? *American Home Products Corp.* v. *Johnson & Johnson,* 577 F.2d 160 (2d Cir. 1978).

5. Montgomery Ward advertised rebuilt engines in newspapers. One part of these ads stated:

   > Montgomery Ward . . . [will] guarantee the engines for 90 days or 4,000 miles.

   The *written* guarantee stated more specifically:

   > FOR A PERIOD OF NINETY DAYS from date installed or four thousand miles (whichever occurs first) we warrant this rebuilt assembly for passenger car service against defects in material and factory workmanship provided our installation and operating instructions are followed. If this assembly is used in truck or commercial installation, it is warranted for thirty days only.
   >
   > Any part of this rebuilt assembly which under such conditions fails because of defective parts or factory workmanship during the period of warranty, may be exchanged for new parts without charge, provided old parts are returned. On such failures occurring within thirty days, we will also refund reasonable labor cost. After thirty days (on passenger cars) the warranty is limited to exchange of parts only.
   >
   > This warranty does not apply to any motor which has not been installed by Wards Authorized Installer, or customer does not return to Installer for the 500 mile checkup, or fails because of defects or inefficiency of parts or units (carburetor, air cleaner, fuel pump, etc.) not furnished with the motor. . . .
   >
   > This warranty is not valid unless the Certificate of Installation is properly filled in and returned to the Mail Order House or Retail Store from which motor was purchased.

   Is the language in the advertisement deceptive? If you think it is deceptive, does it violate the literal truth standard? Does this constitute false advertising? Do you think the *ad* would create a warranty differing from the written warranty? *Montgomery Ward* v. *FTC,* 379 F.2d 666 (7th Cir. 1967).

Suggested Readings

Bok, Sissela, *Lying: Moral Choice in Public and Private Life*. New York: Pantheon Books, 1978.

Gardner, "Deception in Advertising: A Conceptual Approach," *Journal of Marketing* 39 (1975).

Truth in Advertising: A Symposium of the Toronto School of Theology. Toronto, 1975.

5 Business and Consumers

23 Consumer Rights

In the framework of modern commercial life and business practices, [common law contract rules] cannot be applied on a strict, doctrinal basis. The conflicting interests of the buyer and seller must be evaluated realistically and justly, giving due weight to the social policy evinced by [sales law], the progressive decisions of the courts engaged in administering it, the mass production methods of manufacture and distribution to the public, and the bargaining position occupied by the ordinary consumer in such an economy.

—Henningsen *v.* Bloomfield Motors

LEARNING OBJECTIVES

After you have read this chapter, you should be able to:

1. Understand the judicial doctrines that may protect consumers who enter into common law contracts.
2. Understand commercial law consumer statutory protections.
3. Be familiar with the federal Magnuson-Moss Warranty Act.
4. Be familiar with federal statutory protection of consumers.

Business Decisions and the Law

The Case of the Detached Steering Wheel

Ten days after purchasing a new car, Mrs. Henningsen was driving when the steering wheel spun in her hands, and the car veered sharply to the right and crashed into a highway sign and a brick wall. As a result of the impact, the front of the car was so badly damaged that it was impossible to determine if any of the parts of the steering wheel mechanism or workmanship were defective or improper prior to the accident. The car manufacturer denied any legal liability for personal injuries suffered by Mrs. Henningsen, because it said that the car's written warranty limited its responsibility to repair or replacement of defective parts. Can Mrs. Henningsen recover damages for personal injury? See *Henningsen* v. *Bloomfield Motors*.

Introduction

The term *consumer protection* has many meanings, but it generally includes buyer-seller and lender-borrower relationships, with the buyers or borrowers being the consumers. The concept of consumer protection is based on the premise that, due to the nature of modern selling and moneylending relationships, buyers and borrowers need special help from the law to achieve equality of bargaining power with sellers and lenders.

As you have seen at various points throughout this book, traditional law assumed that parties to commercial transactions had equality of bargaining power. For example, if a colonial farmer wanted to buy a pot, he could bargain with a variety of sellers of pots; he did not have to buy from a particular potter. If the farmer made a bad bargain and the pot was defective, the law adopted the attitude of caveat emptor (let the buyer beware) and would not generally allow the buyer to rescind (take back) what had turned out to be a bad bargain. During the nineteenth century, the Industrial Revolution and the development of monopolies and oligopolies in many industries created circumstances in which many goods and services were only available from one or a few providers. Buyers and borrowers lost equality of bargaining power with sellers and lenders, and the doctrine of caveat emptor caused hardship to consumers, who were forced to buy or borrow on whatever terms the sellers and lenders were willing to give.

The purpose of consumer protection laws is to attempt to reestablish a real equality of bargaining power between purveyors and consumers of goods, money, and services. The development of consumer protection law is yet another example of the phenomenon so often discussed in this book in which dissatisfaction with business practices resulted in the passage of laws. The law corrects the perceived imbalance between purveyors and consumers in three ways: by development of common law doctrines in commercial law, by the passage of various state and federal laws, and by the issuance of administrative regulations. In this chapter, you will study these three types of legal protection of consumers.

Protection of the Consumer in Commercial Transactions

Common Law Legal Grounds

Over the years, the courts began to refuse to enforce certain types of contracts in special instances where it seemed unfair to do so. Some of these judicial doctrines formed the basis for statutes; others did not. The following circumstances will render contracts unenforceable: (1) lack of capacity of a party, (2) mutual mistake, (3) fraud, (4) duress or undue influence, (5) illegal contracts, and (6) contracts contrary to public policy.

Mentally incompetent or intoxicated persons and minors are said to *lack the capacity* to make a valid contract. Their contracts are generally voidable at their option. Chapter 9 discusses the concept of avoidance of contracts due to lack of capacity. That chapter also discusses the concept that a contract is void or may be rescinded when parties make a mistake about the nature of the subject matter or fundamental assumptions on which the entire contract was based.

A contract will be unenforceable if it is the product of fraud, duress, or undue influence. **Fraud** occurs when one person knowingly and willingly makes a false statement of a material fact to another person. For example, A needs money, so she tells B she will sell B a pair of skis and gets B to pay for the skis in advance of delivery. In fact, A never owned any skis and never had any intention of delivering skis to B. A is liable for the tort of fraud, and B can rescind the contract and get his money back. **Duress** consists of threats of harm. A contract entered into solely because of duress is not voluntary and is voidable. **Undue influence** exists when one person takes advantage of the special susceptibilities of another person. Generally, there is a requirement that some relationship of trust and confidence exist. A clear example of undue influence would be a person signing a will that leaves a large part of her estate to the attorney who drew up the will, to the exclusion of relatives. Some state courts have begun to adopt a concept of *innocent misrepresentation* as grounds for rescinding a contract. Innocent misrepresentation differs from fraud in that there is no specific intent to deceive a party to a contract. For example, suppose S sells B a house and assures B the house is structurally sound, but after B moves in, the house's foundation begins to collapse. S is not liable for fraud if he actually believed the house was sound when he made his statement, because he had no intent to defraud; however, he could be liable for innocent misrepresentation, since he did make the statement on which B relied to his detriment.

Some contracts may not be enforced by courts because they are *illegal* or *contrary to public policy*. A contract to pay off a gambling debt is illegal and unenforceable in almost every state. In some states, courts have refused to enforce on public policy grounds exculpatory clauses that absolve people from legal liability they would otherwise incur while providing a vital product. For example, if a tenant was injured when she fell through rotten wooden stairs that were the only method of entering and leaving an apartment building, a landlord in many states would not be allowed to avoid liability on the basis that the tenant had signed a lease forgiving the landlord in advance for injuries caused by the landlord's negligence.

The doctrine of **unconscionability** developed out of the general concept that some contracts are unenforceable because they are against public policy. This doctrine, which has been incorporated into the Uniform Commercial Code's sales article, allows courts to avoid or reform sales contract provisions that are extremely harsh to one of the parties. Two of the most well-known cases concerning unconscionability are *Williams* v. *Walker-Thomas Furniture Company*, presented here, and *Jones* v. *Star Credit Corporation*, presented in chapter 2. In *Jones*, reformation of a contract was allowed when a buyer agreed to undertake total payments of $1,235 (including interest payments) for a freezer with a cash value of about $300. The *Williams* case involved provisions for questionable payment procedures.

Williams v. Walker-Thomas Furniture Company

350 F.2d 445 (1965)

Facts

Appellee, Walker-Thomas Furniture Company, operates a retail furniture store in the District of Columbia. During the period from 1957 to 1962 each appellant in these cases purchased a number of household items from Walker-Thomas, for which payment was to be made in installments. The terms of each purchase were contained in a printed form contract that set forth the value of the purchased item and purported to lease the item to appellant for a stipulated monthly rent payment. The contract then provided, in substance, that title would remain in Walker-Thomas until the total of all the monthly payments made equaled the stated value of the item, at which time appellants could take title. In the event of a default in the payment of any monthly installment, Walker-Thomas could repossess the item.

The contract further provided that "the amount of each periodical installment payment to be made by [purchaser] to the Company under this present lease shall be inclusive of and not in addition to the amount of each installment payment to be made by [purchaser] under such prior leases, bills or accounts; and all payments now and hereafter made by [purchaser] shall be credited to pro rata on all outstanding leases, bills and accounts *due the Company by [purchaser] at the time each such payment is made." The effect of this rather obscure provision was to keep a balance due on every item purchased until the balance due on all items, whenever purchased, was liquidated. As a result, the debt incurred at the time of purchase of each item was secured by the right to repossess all the items previously purchased by the same purchaser, and each new item purchased automatically became subject to a security interest arising out of the previous dealings.*

On May 12, 1962, appellant Thorne purchased an item described as a Daveno, three tables, and two lamps, having total stated value of $391.10. Shortly thereafter, she defaulted on her monthly payments and appellee sought to replevy all the items purchased since the first transaction in 1958. Similarly, on April 17, 1962, appellant Williams bought a stereo set of stated value of $514.95. (At the time of this purchase her account showed a balance of $164 still owing from her prior purchases. The total of all the purchases made over the years in question came to $1,800. The total payments amounted to $1,400.) She defaulted shortly thereafter, and appellee sought to replevy all the items purchased since December 1957. The Court of General sessions granted judgment for appellee. The District of Columbia Court of Appeals affirmed.

Opinion

Circuit Judge J. Skelly Wright: We do not agree with the District of Columbia Court of Appeals that the court lacked the power to refuse enforcement to contracts found to be unconscionable. In other jurisdictions, it has been held as a matter of common law that unconscionable contracts are not enforceable. Since we have never adopted or rejected such a rule, the question here presented is actually one of first impression.

We hold that where the element of

unconscionability is present at the time a contract is made, the contract should not be enforced.

Unconscionability has generally been recognized to include an absence of meaningful choice on the part of one of the parties together with contract terms which are unreasonably favorable to the other party. Whether a meaningful choice is present in a particular case can only be determined by consideration of all the circumstances surrounding the transaction. In many cases the meaningfulness of the choice is negated by a gross inequality of bargaining power. The manner in which the contract was entered is also relevant to this consideration. Did each party to the contract, considering his obvious education or lack of it, have a reasonable opportunity to understand the terms of the contract, or were the important terms hidden in a maze of fine print and minimized by deceptive sale practices? Ordinarily, one who signs an agreement without full knowledge of its terms might be held to assume the risk that he has entered a one-sided bargain. But when a party of little bargaining power, and hence little real choice, signs a commercially unreasonable contract with little or no knowledge of its terms, it is hardly likely that his consent, or even an objective manifestation of his consent, was ever given to all the terms. In such a case the usual rule that the terms of the agreement are not to be questioned should be abandoned and the court should consider whether the terms of the contract are so unfair that enforcement should be withheld.

In determining reasonableness or fairness, the primary concern must be with the terms of the contract considered in light of the circumstances existing when the contract was made. The test is not simple, nor can it be mechanically applied. The terms are to be considered "in the light of the general commercial background and the commercial needs of the particular trade or case." Corbin suggests the test as being whether the terms are "so extreme as to appear unconscionable according to the mores and business practices of the time and place." We think this formulation correctly states the test to be applied in those cases where no meaningful choice was exercised upon entering the contract.

Because the trial court and the appellate court did not feel that enforcement could be refused, no findings were made on the possible unconscionability of the contracts in these cases. Since the record is not sufficient for our deciding the issue as a matter of law, the cases must be remanded to the trial court for further proceedings.

So ordered.

Case Questions

1. What were the provisions of the contract that the court found to be objectionable?
2. Why was the contract regarded by the court as being too unfair to enforce?
3. How do law and ethics overlap in the doctrine of unconscionability?

You should keep in mind that the doctrine of unconscionability is rarely applied by courts. It will not be used just because a consumer made a bad bargain and now wants to get out of it. It is only used in those few instances where the facts indicate that a seller took advantage of a buyer who did not understand he was being unfairly used or who did not have any real choice except to do business with the seller.

Another well-known case, *Henningsen* v. *Bloomfield Motors,* involving the relationship between the doctrine of unconscionability and warranty law, will be presented in the next section.

Commercial Law Statutory Protections

Consumers' interests are protected by a number of commercial law statutes. The Uniform Commercial Code (UCC) contains provisions for creating product warranties and gives consumers the right to reject or revoke acceptance of goods that do not conform to a sales contract. The federal Magnuson-Moss Warranty Act complements the UCC warranty provisions. Certain state and federal statutes give consumers the right to cancel contracts within a specified period of time after they are made. In this section we will discuss these commercial law provisions and how they protect consumers.

Warranty Laws

The Uniform Commercial Code

The Uniform Commercial Code, which has been adopted in every state except Louisiana, provides that sales of goods will result in the making of certain promises, or warranties, with respect to the goods. The two most important types of UCC warranties used by consumers are *express warranties* and *implied warranties*.

In order to create an **express warranty,** a seller must do or say something affirmative concerning the goods: he may make a description or other statement about the goods, he may make a promise about them, or he may show a sample or model of specific goods a buyer intends to purchase. For example, the following all create express warranties: (1) a statement that a product will be unharmed by two tons of pressure, (2) a catalog description or picture of a product, and (3) allowing a potential buyer to test a floor model. Once a seller has created an express warranty, if it was basic to the bargain, the buyer has a right to sue for breach of warranty if the goods fail to conform to the terms of the warranty. Ordinarily, the remedy for breach of warranty under the UCC is the recovery of monetary damages based on the difference between the actual value of the goods and their value if they had been as warranted. Oral express warranties are allowed under the UCC, but it is much easier to prove the existence of written warranties.

Implied warranties are created automatically whenever a sale of goods takes place; the seller does not have to do or say anything specific in order to create them. There are two types of implied warranties under the UCC: the warranty of merchantability and the warranty of fitness for a particular purpose. The **warranty of merchantability** is only made by sellers who are merchants—that is, sellers regularly engaged in selling the types of goods that are the subject matter of the sale. This warranty has several meanings under the UCC, but generally means that goods are of fair, average quality and are reasonably fit for ordinary purposes of goods of this type. The **warranty of fitness for a particular purpose** is made by all sellers, whether or not they are merchants. It promises that the goods will be reasonably fit for the particular purpose for which they are being purchased, if the seller has reason to know of the buyer's particular purpose in buying the goods, and if the buyer relies on the seller's expertise in selecting the goods.

The inclusion of warranties in the UCC, which first appeared in the 1950s and was generally adopted throughout the United States in the 1960s, created an important improvement in the ability of consumers to sue for damages if the products they purchased were defective. In addition to giving buyers new grounds to sue (a subject that is also discussed in chapter 25 on product liability), the UCC also expanded consumers' ability to sue by abolishing the common law notion of *privity* under which a buyer could only sue her immediate seller. The UCC abolished the privity requirement, and although different states have adopted different versions of the UCC, in all UCC states, any seller in a product's distributive chain (including manufacturers, wholesalers, and retailers) may be sued by a buyer, anyone in her household, or her guests.

The Uniform Commercial Code limits the rights of consumers to recover for breaches of warranty by allowing sellers to *disclaim* warranty liability. In order to limit liability successfully, the seller must comply exactly with the terms of the UCC, since courts tend not to favor disclaimers. The UCC provides that express warranties may be disclaimed by reasonable words or conduct; courts have tended not to allow merchant sellers to disclaim express warranty liability unless the disclaimer is clear, specific, and in writing. The implied warranty of merchantability may be disclaimed under the UCC by mentioning "merchantability," and, if in writing, the disclaimer must be conspicuous; the implied warranty of fitness for a particular purpose must be written and conspicuous. Notwithstanding the provisions just mentioned, the UCC further provides that implied warranties may be excluded by use of such language as "as is" or "with all faults"; by examination or refusal to examine goods (to the extent of excluding liability for obvious defects); or by course of dealing or trade usage. Courts have tended to allow "as is" disclaimers only for nonmerchant sellers.

The doctrine of unconscionability, discussed earlier, creates a limit on the rights of sellers to disclaim warranties under the UCC. The following was decided by the New Jersey Supreme Court in 1960 before New Jersey adopted the UCC. This case, which refused enforcement of a disclaimer limiting liability for personal injury caused by a defective automobile, was the basis for UCC section 2–719(3), which provides that "limitation of consequential damages for injury to the person in the case of consumer goods is prima facie unconscionable."

Henningsen v. Bloomfield Motors, Inc.

161 A.2d 69 (N.J. 1960)

Facts

Plaintiff Claus H. Henningsen purchased a Plymouth automobile, manufactured by defendant Chrysler Corporation, from defendant Bloomfield Motors, Inc. His wife, plaintiff Helen Henningsen, was injured while driving it and instituted suit against both defendants to recover damages on account of her injuries. The complaint was predicated upon breach of express and implied warranties. At the trial the case was submitted to the jury for determination on the issues of implied warranty of merchantability. Verdicts were returned against both defendants and in favor of the plaintiffs. Defendants appealed and plaintiffs cross-appealed from the dismissal of their negligence claim. The matter was certified by this court prior to consideration in the Appellate Division.

Opinion

J. Francis: The purchase order (which Mr. Henningsen signed when he agreed to buy the car) was a printed form of one page. The smallest type on the page appears in the two paragraphs, one of two and one-quarter lines and the second of one and one-half lines, on which great stress is laid by the defense in the case. These two paragraphs are the least legible and the most difficult to read in the instrument, but they are most important in the evaluation of the rights of the contesting parties. They do not attract attention and there is nothing about the format which would draw the reader's eye to them. In fact, a studied and concentrated effort would have to be made to read them. Deemphasis seems the motive rather than emphasis. . . .

The testimony of Claus Henningsen justifies the conclusion that he did not read the two fine print paragraphs referring to the back of the purchase contract. And it is uncontradicted that no one made any reference to them, or called them to his attention. With respect to the matter appearing on the back, it is likewise uncontradicted that he did not read it and that no one called it to his attention.

In the seventh paragraph, about two-thirds of the way down the page, the warranty, which is the focal point of the case, is set forth. It is as follows:

> 7. It is expressly agreed that there are no warranties, express or implied, made by either the dealer or the manufacturer on the motor vehicle, chassis, or parts furnished hereunder except as follows. "The manufacturer warrants each new motor vehicle (including original equipment placed thereon by the manufacturer except tires), chassis or parts manufactured by it to be free from defects in material or workmanship under normal use and service. Its obligation under this warranty being limited to making good at its factory any part or parts thereof which shall, within ninety (90) days after delivery of such vehicle to *the original purchaser* or before such vehicle has been driven, 4,000 miles, whichever event shall first occur, be returned to it with transportation charges prepaid and which its examination shall disclose to its satisfaction to have been thus defective; *this warranty being expressly in lieu of all other warranties expressed or implied, and all other obligations or liabilities on its part,* and it neither assumes nor authorizes any other person to assume for it any other liability in connection with the sale of its vehicles.***" (Emphasis ours.)

. . . The new Plymouth was turned over to the Henningsens on May 9, 1955. Thereafter, it was used for short trips on paved streets about the town. It had no servicing and no mishaps of any kind before the event of May 19. That day, Mrs. Henningsen drove to Asbury Park. On the way down and in returning the car performed in normal fashion until the accident occurred. She was proceeding north on Route 36 in Highlands, New Jersey, at 20–22 miles per hour. . . . Suddenly she heard a loud noise "from the bottom, by the hood." It "felt as if something cracked." The steering wheel spun in her hands; the car veered sharply to the right and crashed into a highway sign and a brick wall. As a result of the impact, the front of the car was so badly damaged that it was impossible to determine if any of the parts of the steering wheel mechanism or workmanship or assembly were defective or improper prior to the accident. The condition was such that the collision insurance carrier, after inspection, declared the vehicle a total loss. It had 468 miles on the speedometer at the time.

The insurance carrier's inspector and appraiser of damaged cars, with 11 years of experience, advanced the opinion, based on the history and his examination, that something definitely went "wrong from the steering wheel down to the front wheels" and that the untoward happening must have been due to mechanical defect or failure.

In the ordinary case of sale of goods by description an implied warranty of merchantability is an integral part of the transaction. Of course such sales, whether oral or written, may be accompanied by an express warranty.

The Uniform Sales Act codified, extended and liberalized the common law of sales. The motivation in part was to ameliorate the harsh doctrine of *caveat emptor,* and in some measure to impose a reciprocal obligation on the seller to beware. The transcendent value of the legislation, particularly with respect to implied warranties, rests in the fact that obligations on the part of the seller were imposed by operation of law, and did not depend for their existence upon express agreement of the parties. And of tremendous significance in a rapidly expanding commercial society was the recognition of the right to recover damages on account of personal injuries arising from a breach of warranty. The particular importance of this advance resides in the fact that under such circumstances strict liability is imposed upon the maker or seller of the product. Recovery of damages does not depend upon proof of negligence or knowledge of the defect.

As the Sales Act and its liberal interpretation by the courts threw this protective cloak about the buyer, the decisions in various jurisdictions revealed beyond doubt that many manufacturers took steps to avoid these ever increasing warranty obligations. Realizing that the act governed the relationship of buyer and seller, they undertook to withdraw from actual and direct contractual contact with the buyer.

The terms of the warranty are a sad commentary upon the automobile manufacturers' marketing practices. Warranties developed in the law in the interest of and to protect the ordinary consumer who cannot be expected to have the knowledge or capacity or even the opportunity to make adequate inspection of mechanical instrumentalities, like automobiles, and to decide for himself whether they are reasonably fit for the designed purpose. But the ingenuity of the Automobile Manufacturers Association, by means of its standardized form, has metamorphosed the warranty into a device to limit the maker's liability.

. . . In this instance, after reciting that defective parts will be replaced at the factory, the alleged agreement relied upon by Chrysler provides that the manufacturer's "obligation under this warranty" is limited to that undertaking; further, that such remedy is "in lieu of all other warranties, express or implied, and all other obligations or liabilities on its part." The contention has been raised that such language bars any claim for personal injuries which may emanate from a breach of the warranty.

Judicial notice may be taken of the fact that automobile manufacturers, including Chrysler Corporation, undertake large scale advertising programs over television, radio, in newspapers, magazines and all media of communication in order to persuade the public to buy their products. As has been observed above, a number of jurisdictions, conscious of modern marketing practices, have declared that when a manufacturer engages in advertising in order to bring his goods and their quality to the attention of the public and thus to create consumer demand, the representations made constitute an express warranty running directly to a buyer who purchases in reliance thereon.

In the light of these matters, what effect should be given to the express warranty in question which seeks to limit the manufacturer's liability to replacement of defective parts, and which disclaims all other warranties, express or implied? In assessing its significance we must keep in mind the general principle that, in the absence of fraud, one who does not choose to read a contract before signing it, cannot later relieve himself of its burdens. And in applying that principle, the basic tenet of freedom of competent parties to contract is a factor of importance. But in the framework of modern commercial life and business practices, such rules cannot be applied on a strict, doctrinal basis. The conflicting interests of the buyer and seller must be evaluated realistically and justly, giving due weight to the social policy evinced by the Uniform Sales Act, the progressive decisions of the courts engaged in administering it, the mass production methods of manufacture and distribution to the public, and the bargaining position occupied by the ordinary consumer in such an economy. This history of the law shows that legal doctrines, as first expounded, often prove to be inadequate under the impact of later experience. In such case, the need for justice has stimulated the necessary qualifications of adjustments.

In these times, an automobile is almost as much a servant of convenience for the ordinary person as a household utensil. For a multitude of other persons it is a necessity. Crowded highways and filled parking lots are a commonplace of our existence. There is no need to look any farther than the daily newspaper to be convinced that when an automobile is defective, it has great potentiality for harm.

What influence should these circumstances have on the restrictive effect of Chrysler's express warranty in the framework of the purchase contract? As we have said, warranties originated in the law to safeguard the buyer and not to limit the liability of the seller or manufacturer. It seems obvious in this instance that the motive was to avoid the warranty obligations which are normally incidental to such sales. The language gave little and withdrew much. In return for the delusive remedy of replacement of defective parts at the factory, the buyer is said to have accepted the exclusion of the marker's liability for personal injuries arising from the breach of the warranty, and to have agreed to the elimination of any other express or implied warranty. An instinctively felt sense of justice cries out against such a sharp bargain.

The warranty before us is a standardized form designed for mass use. It is imposed upon the automobile consumer. He takes it or leaves it, and he must take it to buy an automobile. No bargaining is engaged in with respect to it. In fact, the dealer through whom it comes to the buyer is without authority to alter it; his function is ministerial—simply to deliver it. The form warranty is not only standard with Chrysler but, as mentioned above, it is the uniform warranty of the Automobile Manufacturers Association.

The gross inequality of bargaining position occupied by the consumer in the automobile industry is thus apparent. There is no competition among the car makers in the area of the express warranty. Where can the buyer go to negotiate for better protection? Such control and limitation of his remedies are inimical to the public welfare and, at the very least, call for great care by the courts to avoid injustice through application of strict common-law principles of freedom of contract. Because there is no competition among the motor vehicle manufacturers with respect to the scope of protection guaranteed to the buyer, there is no incentive on their part to stimulate good will in that field of public relations. Thus, there is lacking a factor existing in more competitive fields, one which tends to guarantee the safe construction of the article sold. Since all competitors operate in the same way, the urge to be careful is not so pressing.

Can it be said that an ordinary layman would realize what he was relinquishing in return for what he was being granted? Any ordinary layman of reasonable intelligence, looking at the phraseology, might well conclude that Chrysler was agreeing to replace defective parts and perhaps replace anything that went wrong because of defective workmanship during the first 90 days or 4,000 miles of operation, but that he would not be entitled to a new car. It is not unreasonable to believe that the entire scheme being conveyed was a proposed remedy for physical deficiencies in the car. *In the context* of this warranty, only the abandonment of all sense of justice would permit us to hold that, as a matter of law, the phrase "its obligation under this warranty being limited to making good at its factory any part or parts thereof" signifies to an ordinary reasonable person that he is relinquishing any personal injury claim that might flow from the use of a defective automobile.

For the reasons set forth above, we conclude that the disclaimer of an implied warranty of merchantability by the dealer, as well as the attempted elimination of all obligations other than replacement of defective parts, are violative of public policy and void. Under all of the circumstances outlined above, the judgments in favor of the plaintiffs and against the defendants are affirmed.

Case Questions

1. What policy reasons did the court give for deciding to hold the disclaimer void?
2. What warranties were given in this sale that would be operative once the disclaimer was declared void?
3. This case is one of the most often-cited examples of a court using its power to transform an ethical norm into a legal one. The decision had the effect of significantly increasing the automobile manufacturer's cost of doing business. What ethical principles does this decision embody?

The Federal Magnuson-Moss Warranty Act

While states' enactment of the Uniform Commercial Code gave consumers many new rights regarding recovery for breach of warranty, as you can see, the disclaimer provisions often have the effect of negating the consumers' warranty rights. In an attempt to insure that consumers would have warranty rights, Congress passed the **Magnuson-Moss Warranty Act,** which took effect in 1975. Note that the Magnuson-Moss Act does not supercede the UCC, but complements it. For example, the act does not provide for the creation of implied warranties (as does the UCC), but it does provide that implied warranties cannot be disclaimed if a written warranty is given.

The Magnuson-Moss Act does not *require* sellers to give warranties; however, if a warranty is given, it must contain certain provisions and be in a certain form. The act only applies to sales of consumer goods (those normally used for family, household, or personal use). A seller who gives a written warranty must designate it as being "limited" or "full." In either written warranty, the products covered and the terms of the warranty must be stated in clear and understandable language, and the procedures a consumer should take in order to enforce the warranty must be clearly stated.

If a seller gives a full warranty, the so-called anti-lemon provision comes into effect. Under this provision, if a product does not live up to the terms of the warranty, the seller must repair it free of charge; if the seller cannot repair the product to the buyer's (good faith) satisfaction after reasonable efforts, the buyer has an option of obtaining a refund of the purchase price or replacement goods. The act allows sellers to establish informal settlement procedures to handle consumer complaints. The effect of the Magnuson-Moss Act has been that some sellers have stopped giving written express warranties at all. More noticeably, despite initial congressional expectations, most sellers have chosen not to give full warranties in order to avoid anti-lemon obligations.

In the 1980s, many states passed "Lemon Law" statutes concerning the sale of new automobiles. These laws gave consumers certain rights if new cars they purchased proved defective. The following case concerns the interpretation of Virginia's lemon law statute and its relationship to the federal Magnuson-Moss Warranty Act.

Wolf v. Ford Motor Company

829 F.2d 1277 (4th Cir. 1987)

Opinion

Circuit Judge Sprouse: In this diversity action, Fred F. Wolf appeals from the district court's dismissal of his common law fraud claim against Ford Motor Company and its denial of his request for attorneys' fees on his successful claim against Ford under the Virginia "Lemon Law." We affirm.

In July 1985, Wolf purchased a new Ford automobile from a Lincoln-Mercury dealer in Warrenton, Virginia. The written warranty issued by Ford provided that the dealer would repair or replace defective parts during the warranty period. It also provided that in case of a warranty dispute, Wolf could utilize the procedures of the Ford Consumer Appeals Board (FCAB), which was described as a "cost-free, independent, third-party, dispute settlement mechanism available to Ford Motor Company product owners." Wolf experienced difficulty with the car and, after he failed to reach a satisfactory solution with the dealer, submitted a complaint to the FCAB. The FCAB, however, concluded that Wolf had not complied with the Virginia "Lemon Law" and denied him relief. Wolf then brought this diversity action in district court.

Wolf's action contained two counts. In Count I, he asked for rescission of his purchase of the Ford automobile, refund of the purchase price, and expenses—including attorneys' fees—under the Virginia "Lemon Law." In Count II, Wolf sought to recover compensatory and punitive damages based on Ford's allegedly fraudulent representation that the FCAB was an independent and impartial apparatus for resolving disputes between Ford and its customers. The district court dismissed Count II at the beginning of the trial holding, in effect, that the fraud cause of action premised on Virginia law was preempted by a provision of the Magnuson-Moss Act and regulations issued pursuant to the Act. Wolf's claim under the "Lemon Law" proceeded to trial, and the jury returned a verdict in his favor. The court, however, denied Wolf's request for attorneys' fees.

The Magnuson-Moss Act regulates written warranties on consumer products distributed in interstate commerce. It provides that, subject to certain statutory requirements, an injured consumer can seek damages in a civil action for warranty violations. One of the requirements relates to informal dispute settlement mechanisms such as the consumer appeals board involved in this case. Although the Act does not require the establishment of such boards, it encourages warrantors, including automobile manufacturers, to do so. If a warrantor establishes such a board and incorporates a written requirement within the warranty that a consumer first resort to the procedures, the consumer must utilize the procedures prior to bringing the statutory action provided by the Act.

Wolf utilized the FCAB, the dispute settlement mechanism Ford established under the auspices of the Act. After his unsuccessful experience with it, however, he did not institute an action authorized by Magnuson-Moss. Instead, Wolf brought this two-prong diversity action grounded on Virginia's "Lemon Law" and common law fraud.

The district court dismissed Wolf's fraud count because "it would require the fact-finder to determine, under the guise of a fraud claim, whether the Ford Consumer Appeals Board has complied with FTC Rule 703, and whether the said appeals board is fair and impartial." Although not couched specifically in preemption terms, the district court's holding was grounded on the preemption doctrine, which emanates from the Supremacy Clause of the United States Constitution.

Here, Congress has not explicitly preempted any state laws affecting private dispute settlement boards. Congress' intent to preempt state regulation, however, can be inferred both from the pervasive nature of the federal regulatory scheme and from the conflict that would result if Wolf's fraud claim were allowed.

In the first place, the Magnuson-Moss Act's endorsement of private dispute settlement mechanisms to resolve warranty claims, coupled with its mandate that the Federal Trade Commission prescribe minimum requirements for such mechanisms, evince a congressional intent to reserve to the federal regulatory body the authority to supervise whether the mechanisms are created and operated fairly. The preemptive design of the FTC regulations is even more obvious. Pursuant to the Act's mandate, the FTC promulgated regulations governing private dispute settlement mechanisms and established minimum requirements for their operation. The FTC regulations are extensive and address all facets of the mechanisms' operation. They leave no room for state regulation.

Moreover, allowing consumers to challenge the operation of dispute settlement boards through state fraud actions would conflict with enforcement of the FTC regulations. The Act grants the FTC the authority, and the obligation upon written complaint, to investigate a dispute settlement procedure to determine if it is in compliance with the statutory and regulatory requirements. Upon complaint, the FTC "shall, review the bona fide operation of any dispute settlement procedure." If the mechanism is not in compliance, the Commission can take any remedial action authorized under the Act, including injunction proceedings.

Wolf seeks to test whether the FCAB was independent and unbiased under Virginia's common law fraud standard. The FTC, however, has promulgated detailed regulations to ensure the independent nature of private dispute settlement mechanisms. The Magnuson-Moss Act provides for oversight by the FTC to ensure that a mechanism is in compliance with the regulations. To permit consumers to test the bona fide nature and validity of private dispute settlement mechanisms, such as the FCAB, under the law of each state would frustrate completely the goal of national uniformity painstakingly designed by federal statute and regulation. The district court, therefore correctly dismissed Wolf's fraud claim.

Wolf also contends that the district court erred in denying him attorneys' fees in his claim under Virginia's "Lemon Law." The statute provides that the consumer may recover "[m]ileage, expenses, and reasonable loss of use necessitated by attempts to conform such motor vehicle to the express warranty." The district court interpreted this provision to contemplate expenses such as towing fees and repair costs, not attorneys' fees, and refused to infer that the Virginia legislature intended to include attorneys' fees as recoverable expenses. We agree.

For the above reasons, the judgment of the district court is affirmed.

Case Questions

1. What policy reasons did the court give for saying that federal law pre-empted state law?
2. Why do you think the drafters of Magnuson-Moss mandated use of informal settlement procedures?

Buyer's Right to Reject Goods or Revoke Acceptance under the Uniform Commercial Code

The Uniform Commercial Code allows buyers under certain circumstances to reject goods when they are initially tendered under the terms of a sales contract, and under other circumstances, to revoke their acceptance of goods. The buyer's right to reject goods is governed by what is often called the *perfect tender rule:* a buyer may reject goods if they fail in any way to conform to the terms of the sales contract. The perfect tender rule may be applied if the goods do not conform to the terms of the sales contract in quantity or quality, or if their delivery is improper (e.g., late). Violation of the perfect tender rule gives the buyer an absolute option to do any of the following: (a) accept all of the goods, (b) reject all of the goods, or (c) reject part and accept part. For example, suppose a buyer contracts to buy four black chairs, with delivery to occur by May 1. If the delivery is late, even by one day, the buyer does not have to take the chairs. Suppose the chairs arrive on May 1, but three are black and one is brown; the buyer can reject *all* of the chairs, because the seller's tender of delivery did not conform *in every way* to the specifications of the sales contract. At his option, instead of rejecting all of the chairs, the buyer could accept one of the four chairs, whether black or brown. While the perfect tender rule may seem harsh at times to a seller, it has a basic consumer protection purpose—to prevent buyers from being forced to accept goods that are fairly similar to, but not exactly, what they ordered.

Even if a buyer accepts goods, she may later be able to revoke her acceptance if the goods do not conform to the terms of the sales contract. The buyer has the right to revoke if there is a substantial impairment in the value of the goods to the buyer, and if she accepted the goods either (a) on the reasonable assumption that the nonconformity would be cured and it has not been, or (b) without discovery of the nonconformity if her acceptance was reasonably induced either by the difficulty of discovery before acceptance or by the seller's assurances. Even if a buyer has a right to revoke her acceptance, she will not be able to do so unless she revokes within a reasonable time after she discovers or should have discovered the defect.

Buyers' Statutory Rights to Cancel Contracts

Federal and state statutes and Federal Trade Commission regulations give consumers the right to cancel contracts in certain cases. Some forty states have passed statutes creating a three-day "cooling off" period when contracts are signed in a consumer's home as the result of a door-to-door solicitation. There is generally a statutory exception for emergencies where the consumer requests the seller of goods or services to begin performance without delay and the seller makes a substantial beginning on performing the contract. Many state statutes allow sellers to impose reasonable cancellation fees in credit sales. The Federal Trade Commission has also adopted a regulation (under section 5 of the Federal Trade Commission Act) that makes it a deceptive trade practice for door-to-door sales people to fail to give a consumer three days in which to cancel a home solicitation sale. This FTC regulation prohibits imposing a cancellation fee on the consumer. In the event of a conflict between the FTC regulation and a state statute, the regulation provides that whichever provision is more beneficial to the consumer will be applied.

The federal Truth-in-Lending Act (which will be discussed more fully in a later section) gives consumers the right in real estate transactions to cancel a contract to borrow money or receive improvements on real property when the loan is secured by a second (or subsequent) mortgage on the borrower's principal place of residence. This right to cancel runs for three days from the delivery of all material disclosures required under the act. If a borrower gives timely notice of cancellation, generally the parties must restore anything of value they gave to each other. For example, a lender would return any down payment he had received from a borrower, and a real estate owner would have to turn over any property of a creditor he had previously received.

The Federal Trade Commission Holder in Due Course Regulation

A very significant development in consumer protection law was the issuance by the Federal Trade Commission of a regulation that became effective in 1976 and changed the law of negotiable instruments under article 3 of the Uniform Commercial Code. This regulation changed the *holder in due course* doctrine under the UCC as it applies in consumer transactions (transactions in which natural persons acquire goods or services for personal, family, or household use).

Let us first determine how the **holder in due course** doctrine is applied and then examine how the FTC regulation changes it. Suppose that Joe Jones wants to buy a new deluxe refrigerator costing $900 from Ace Appliance Company. Joe does not want to pay cash for the refrigerator or put it on a credit card. He decides to finance his purchase by making a down payment of $300 and signing a negotiable promissory note for the remaining $600 (with interest). The named payee on the note is Ace Appliance, and the note calls for Joe to make installment payments of $25 per month until the note is paid off. Ace does not want to hold the note for a long period of time while receiving only $25 a month, because it needs a lump sum of money to go out and purchase a new refrigerator to replenish its inventory. Therefore, in return for immediate cash, Ace will almost certainly endorse the note to a commercial lending institution, First National Bank, which will now be the holder of the note. After Ace endorses the note to First National, Joe will be legally required to pay the $25 monthly installments to the bank. If First National paid value for the note in good faith and took it without notice of any claim or defense on the note, it would be what the UCC calls a *holder in due course (HDC)*.

Being a holder in due course is very significant, legally speaking, because almost all legal claims and defenses are *not* good against a holder in due course, including the defense of failure of consideration (of which breach of warranty is one example). Suppose that Ace delivers the refrigerator to Joe, that it stops working right away and that Ace either cannot or will not fix it, even though Ace is legally obligated to do so. While Joe and Ace are disputing who is responsible for fixing the refrigerator, Joe begins getting requests from First National to make his $25 monthly payments. Does Joe have to pay First National, even though he has a legal claim or defense that would be good against Ace? The answer, prior to the FTC regulation, was yes, Joe *would* have to pay First National because the defense of failure of consideration (or breach of warranty) is *not* good against a holder in due course (such as First National).

The FTC regulation changes the results in any consumer transaction such as Joe's that occurred after 1976. This regulation requires that any consumer credit contract contain a notice that any legal rights that a buyer has against a seller are also good against any holder of the contract. Now, Joe would be legally entitled to refuse to pay First National as long as he had a claim or defense on the note, even if First National was a holder in due course. The direct benefit of this regulation to consumers is obvious. However, there is also an indirect benefit: since financial institutions know they will not be paid while a consumer has a valid claim or defense, the institutions may lend their support to attempts to settle disputes between sellers and consumers. You should note that the FTC only applies where the buyer is using consumer goods; it does not apply to commercial buyers.

Federal Statutory Protection of Consumers

Federal Trade Commission Power under Section 5 of the Federal Trade Commission Act

The **Federal Trade Commission Act,** passed in 1914, was adopted primarily as an antitrust statute. While the act remains important in antitrust law, since the

1950s it has been used as a vehicle for much consumer protection activity not directly associated with antitrust. One section of the FTC Act that has been used extensively in consumer protection law is section 5, which gives the Federal Trade Commission authority "to prevent persons, partnerships or corporations from using unfair methods of competition in or affecting commerce and unfair or deceptive acts or practices in or affecting commerce." Section 5's consumer protection uses have centered on attempts to correct specific abuses connected with the sale of consumer goods and deceptive advertising. The use of the FTC Act as an antitrust statute is discussed in chapter 18 on antitrust law and in chapter 22 on advertising, both of which discuss the FTC's use of section 5. In this chapter, we will examine some of the important areas in which the FTC's power under section 5 has been used to protect consumers from specific types of abuses. You should note that the extension of the FTC's powers under section 5, aided by the passage in 1975 of the Magnuson-Moss Warranty-Federal Trade Commission Improvement Act, is another example of how laws are passed to accommodate concerns of society.

You have already seen in a preceding section of this chapter how the FTC adopted a regulation providing for a cooling-off period in contracts signed as a result of a door-to-door sale. Other specific examples of how section 5 is used include issuance of regulations concerning mail-order merchandise and bait-and-switch tactics in salesroom sales.

Consumer problems regarding mail-order merchandise may be divided into two categories: those involving unsolicited merchandise and those involving solicited merchandise. The controlling law concerning unsolicited merchandise is actually not the Federal Trade Commission Act, but the **Federal Postal Reorganization Act,** which provides that a person who is purposefully sent unsolicited merchandise is not under any legal obligation either to return it or pay for it. This law illustrates the difference between law and morality, for individuals might feel a moral obligation to return the merchandise or to pay for it, especially if they intended to use it.

The FTC has passed regulations concerning prompt delivery of customer-solicited merchandise. These rules prohibit solicitation of mail-order sales unless the seller reasonably expects to be able to ship goods within thirty days after receipt of an order. The seller who finds he cannot ship within thirty days must notify the buyer and give the buyer the right to cancel the order. Magazine subscription sales (after the first delivery) and C.O.D. (collect on delivery) sales are exempted from the regulation. You should note that, under article 2 of the Uniform Commercial Code, C.O.D. sales are only legally enforceable if the buyer agrees to a C.O.D. sale when the sales contract is made, and payment under a C.O.D. contract does not constitute acceptance of the goods, so the goods can be rejected after receipt and payment.

One sales practice that the FTC has aggressively tried to eliminate is using bait-and-switch techniques. This practice consists of luring a prospective customer into a sales establishment by advertising a particular product at a low price ("baiting") and then either knowingly not having an adequate amount of the product on hand or pressuring the customer into buying a more expensive item ("switching"). FTC regulations prohibit these bait-and-switch techniques.

In 1969–70, the American Bar Association criticized the FTC's consumer protection efforts. In response, the FTC adopted an aggressive consumer protection stance, creating such requirements as advertising substantiation and corrective advertising, which were discussed in chapter 22. By 1980, the FTC's activities had created a reaction; Congress adopted the **Federal Trade Commission Improvements Act,** which provides for congressional veto of FTC regulations. Once the FTC adopts a final regulation, following the rulemaking process described in chapter 5, the regulation does not become effective for ninety days. During that time, the houses of Congress can reject the regulation by a joint resolution. A well-known example of the exercise of this veto power occurred in 1981 when Congress vetoed an FTC regulation requiring used car dealers to put stickers on used cars containing information about warranties and listing any known material facts about the mechanical condition of the cars. You should note that in 1983 the Supreme Court overruled the congressional veto provision of this FTC regulation.

In 1985, the FTC's new Used Motor Vehicle Rule went into effect. This rule requires dealers to tell buyers who must pay for repairs after the sale of a used car and also requires them to place specific disclosures on the side window of a car offered for sale. These disclosures include a statement of the terms of any warranty offered with the car, a suggestion that the consumer get all promises about the car in writing, and a suggestion that the buyer get a mechanical inspection of the car. The rule makes it a deceptive practice for the dealer to misrepresent the mechanical condition of the car or to misrepresent the terms or existence of any warranty on the car. Note that the 1985 rule (unlike the 1981 rule that it replaced) does not require a dealer to list mechanical defects known by the dealer to exist.

The Consumer Product Safety Commission

The federal **Consumer Product Safety Commission (CPSC)** was created in 1972, primarily to establish safety standards for consumer products and to study the incidence of injuries caused by consumer products. If a particular consumer product does not meet the specifications of the CPSC standard, the manufacturer can be fined or imprisoned for up to a year. If a nonconforming product presents an unreasonable risk of several personal injury, its distribution can be banned by a federal court at the CPSC's request.

One method the CPSC uses to determine whether new safety standards are needed or whether a product should be banned is the National Electronic Injury Surveillance System (NEISS), a computer system that gathers data on product-caused injuries from hospitals around the country. The CPSC also has the power to inspect records of manufacturers to determine whether issuance of new safety standards or banning of a product is necessary.

The Electronic Fund Transfer Act and Consumer Access to Bank Deposits

It has been possible for a long time to transfer monetary funds electronically by debiting one account and crediting another. Financial institutions use this system extensively to transfer value between themselves, and they favor its use with their customers because it is more efficient (and less costly) than handling cash and checks by hand. Although predictions began as early as the 1960s that the United States would become a "cashless society," consumers proved reluctant to accept electronic fund transfer, partly because legal liability and rights related to its use were uncertain. With the strong urging of the banking industry, Congress passed the **Electronic Fund Transfer Act** in 1978. This act establishes legal rules regarding use of the most common types of electronic fund transfers (EFT): use of automated teller machines (ATMs), telephone transfers of funds, automatic deposits and withdrawals, and use of debit cards (in which use of a plastic card that looks like a credit card results in the automatic debiting of a person's bank account).

The most important legal aspect of the EFT Act is that it establishes limits on the liability of persons who use EFT, especially those who have EFT cards that are lost or stolen. Under the act, the liability of the holder of a debit card (which can be used at an ATM or otherwise) is limited as follows: if no use of a lost or stolen card occurs before the loss is reported, the card holder has no liability; if the loss is reported within two business days after it is discovered, the holder's liability is limited to $50; if the report is not made within the two business days, liability is raised to a maximum of $500; and, finally, if a holder does not report unauthorized use of her card within sixty days of receiving a statement that shows unauthorized use, she could have unlimited liability on the card.

Another aspect of the EFT Act is the rights it gives consumers concerning error resolution. Before the passage of the act, if a dispute arose regarding an alleged improper use of EFT (for example, if a consumer claimed his debit card had been illegally used, resulting in improper charges to his bank account), a bank could simply freeze the customer's account for as long as it pleased. Under the act, a bank has ten days to investigate an alleged error, and it must correct any error within one business day after it is discovered.

Since the passage of the EFT Act, use of EFT has grown rapidly. One business policy that has produced controversy is a requirement by certain banks that customers with small accounts (in some cities a "small" account can contain as much as $5,000) must use ATMs and cannot do business with a live teller.

In 1988, Congress passed the Expedited Funds Availability Act, which created deadlines on how long financial institutions could hold customers' funds from deposited checks without allowing the customers access to the money. This law was enacted in response to the banking practice of holding monies from deposited checks for up to three weeks without allowing the depositor access to the funds. The act (and federal regulations enacted pursuant to it) specifies various time limits on how long a financial institution can wait before allowing a customer access to funds from deposited checks. The time limits are determined by the nature of the deposit, and the type of check if the funds were deposited by check. Some of the most important time limits on allowing depositors access to their money are: same business day (date of deposit) withdrawals are allowed for such electronic transfers as social security benefits and direct payroll payments, and for checks drawn on the depository bank; the next business day after the date of deposit, withdrawals are permitted for government checks, and local employer payroll checks; for other kinds of checks, a customer can withdraw up to $100 on the first business day after deposit, with the balance of the funds being available anywhere from the next business day to a week later, depending on the place of origin of the check. You should note that a "business day" does not include Saturdays, Sundays, and federal holidays. Banks are allowed to disregard these withdrawal rules if they have reasonable cause to believe that certain checks will not be paid. Also, there are longer time limits if the withdrawals are from newly opened accounts.

Credit Regulation

Since World War II, the United States economy has become based on the granting and use of credit. Therefore, a person who wishes to function in a viable economic manner must have access to credit, whether the purpose is to obtain a mortgage, a car loan, or a credit card. The use of credit grew tremendously during the 1950s, but there were few laws (other than laws forbidding the charging of usurious interest) governing how credit should be granted or what could be done with credit information. To remedy consumer discontent with certain aspects of business credit practices, a number of federal laws were passed in the 1960s and '70s. Many states also passed laws that complement the federal credit laws. In this section we will discuss some of the most important federal credit regulation statutes: the Equal Credit Opportunity Act, the Truth-in-Lending Act, the Fair Credit Billing Act, and the Fair Credit Reporting Act.

The Equal Credit Opportunity Act

The **Equal Credit Opportunity Act (ECOA),** passed in 1974, prohibits discrimination on the basis of sex, marital status, race, color, age, religion, national origin, or receipt of welfare by any business that extends credit (including lending institutions, retail establishments, and credit card companies). One of the primary purposes of the ECOA was to assist women in obtaining credit. Therefore, the ECOA specifically provides that a woman may request that credit be extended in her name alone, without regard to marital status. In determining eligibility for credit, the creditor must consider income from alimony, child support, or welfare payments. If both spouses in a married couple use a charge account or credit card, information on the accounts must be reported to third parties (such as credit reporting agencies, which will be discussed later), in the names of both spouses.

The ECOA requires a creditor to notify an applicant of its decision on a credit application within thirty days of receiving a completed application. If an application is rejected, specific reasons for the rejection must be given. The ECOA can be enforced by various government agencies. In addition, an individual who sues may recover actual damages (including damages for mental distress), punitive damages of up to $10,000, legal costs, and attorneys' fees.

Truth-in-Lending Act

The **Truth-in-Lending Act (TILA)** was the first credit regulation statute passed by Congress. Originally adopted in 1968, it has been amended several times, including amendments that became effective in 1982. The TILA applies to consumer transactions for less than $25,000 and to all purchases secured by real property when credit is extended to natural persons primarily for family, household, personal, or agricultural use. Financial institutions and businesses who extend credit (including even such entities as hospitals) are subject to the TILA. The Federal Reserve Board is the agency charged with issuing regulations interpreting the TILA, and these regulations are incorporated in what is known as *Regulation Z.*

The TILA is a *disclosure statute;* its primary purpose is to give consumers information they can use in deciding whether to enter into a particular credit transaction. The two most important facts that must be disclosed under TILA are the amount of finance charges and the annual percentage rate (APR). The TILA requirements (as interpreted by Regulation Z) for disclosure of finance charges and the APR are very complicated. Some of the most important components of the finance charge are interest, any fees (including loan fees or points), and any service transactions or carrying charges. The calculation of the APR can be very complex, but the Federal Reserve Board has issued Regulation Z Annual Percentage Rate Tables that are usually used to determine the APR, once the total amount financed (including the finance charge) and the amount and duration of monthly payments have been agreed upon by the lender and borrower. It is important to note that the TILA does not set a limit on the amount of finance charges or the interest rates, although state usury laws or other statutes may do so; the only purpose of the TILA is to let the consumer *know,* but not regulate, what he is getting into. So that TILA disclosures will attract attention, they must be printed, typed, or clearly written on the credit document, and the words *finance charge* and *annual percentage rate* must stand out clearly.

The TILA mandates disclosures other than just the APR and finance charges. The exact disclosures required depend on whether a consumer is applying for closed-end or open-end credit. Closed-end credit transactions are basically "one-shot deals"—for example, purchase of a car or a refrigerator. In open-end transactions, a series of credit extensions is contemplated—for example, frequent use of a credit card. In closed-end transactions, disclosure of such information as the amount financed or credited as a trade-in is given at the beginning of the credit arrangement. In open-end transactions, initial disclosure at the beginning of the credit arrangement and periodic subsequent disclosures (usually in monthly statements) are required, including such information as the unpaid balance on which a finance charge was calculated, any payments or charges made by the consumer since a previous statement, and a statement of the consumer's rights under the Fair Credit Billing Act, which is discussed below.

Credit Card Transactions

Possibly the single most important type of credit mechanism used today is the credit card, which involves open-end credit. The Truth-in-Lending Act governs the holder's liability for unauthorized use of a credit card, and limits that liability to a $50 maximum, if the card is used in an unauthorized manner before the holder reports it lost or stolen. If the holder reports the card lost before it is used or at a time when the unauthorized use amounts to less than $50, he will be liable only for the amount for which the card was used to that point. If the holder contributed to the misuse of the credit card, for example, by giving the card to a "friend" who used it in an unauthorized manner, the holder's liability is unlimited.

If a credit card holder becomes involved in a dispute with a credit card company regarding payments or charges, the holder's rights are governed by the Fair Credit Billing Act. The following is a criminal case involving the question of what constitutes illegal use of a credit card. You should note that this case would have been clearer if it had occurred after passage of the federal Credit Card Fraud Act of 1984 and the Fraud by Wire Statute.

United States v. Fatima Bice-Bey

701 F.2d 1086 (4th Cir. 1983)

Opinion

Circuit Judge Ervin: Fatimah Bice-Bey appeals her conviction for violation of 15 U.S.C. § 1644(a). A jury found her guilty of two counts of credit card fraud after a trial that, she contends, was marred by numerous errors. In addition, Bice-Bey advances a reading of the statute that would absolve her of criminal liability under it. We find no prejudicial error in her trial and, although the issue is close, cannot agree with her interpretation of the statute. We affirm her conviction.

During December of 1981, Oak Park Electronics, a Raleigh firm, received a number of very similar telephone orders for electronic equipment. The orders were all charged to credit card numbers and were requested to be shipped by Federal Express overnight to the New York area. After the seventh such order, for almost $5,000 in merchandise, was received on December 28 from a person identifying herself as "Jane Johnson," Oak Park contacted the FBI, which arranged for subsequent telephone orders from New York to be recorded. On December 29, "Johnson" called to confirm her order; the conversation was taped.

On December 30, a man identifying himself as "Joe Johnson" attempted to place an order for over $2,000 in video equipment, to be sent to the address in Manhattan given two days earlier by "Jane Johnson." When informed that his order exceeded the limits on the credit card accounts he proffered, the man abruptly hung up. Oak Park immediately received another call from a woman who identified herself as "Jane Johnson," the December 28 customer and the wife of "Joe Johnson." She placed a smaller order using the same credit card number proferred on December 28 and by "Joe Johnson" in the earlier December 30 call.

Later in the day on December 30, FBI agents posing as Federal Express employees delivered the December 28 order to the designated address, Apartment B-1, 38 Edgecombe Avenue, Manhattan. Bice-Bey accepted delivery, although she stated that she was not "Johnson" and signed the Federal Express form with the name "Cadabra." The agents then arrested Bice-Bey and William Simmons, the resident of Apartment B-1.

Bice-Bey was indicted by a grand jury for two counts of credit card fraud, based on the December 28 order, and one count of conspiracy to engage in credit card fraud. Simmons also was indicted for these offenses, but the charges were later dismissed, and a superseding indictment against Bice-Bey only was filed.

At the trial, the government's witnesses identified "Jane Johnson's" voice on the tape-recorded December 30 telephone call as that of Bice-Bey. A bank employee testified that the credit card numbers used on December 28 by "Jane Johnson" were in fact those of a Suzanne Matthews and an Edward Bernstein, and that all of the charges on the orders made prior to that date were charged back to Oak Park because the cardholders denied making the charges. Bernstein specifically testified that he had never lost or loaned his credit card and had never authorized anyone to use his number to order anything from Oak Park. Bice-Bey testified that she did not know either Bernstein or Matthews. The district court also permitted the introduction of a polygraph examination to which Bice-Bey had agreed. The polygraph examiner testified that in his opinion Bice-Bey's answers to questions concerning her involvement in the credit card orders indicated deception.

Bice-Bey's trial defense was that her participation in the credit card transactions was limited to accepting the package on December 30, and that her actions then were made on behalf of someone else without knowledge of any illegality.

We must reject Bice-Bey's contention that the government's evidence cannot support the jury's guilty verdict on count one of the indictment. That count charged Bice-Bey with obtaining goods worth over $1,000 through fraudulent use of a VISA card issued to Suzanne Matthews of New York City. Although Edward Bernstein, holder of the Master Card Bice-Bey was charged with using by count two, testified that he did not authorize Bice-Bey to use his card, Matthews did not testify. The government argues that the evidence indicating that Bice-Bey used the Matthews card under a false name ("Jane Johnson") permitted the jury to infer unauthorized use of the card. Furthermore, Bice-Bey herself testified that she did not know Suzanne Matthews, and that she had no authorization to use anyone else's credit cards, admissions which permit a rational fact finder to conclude beyond reasonable doubt that if Bice-Bey used Matthews' card, she did so without Matthews' permission. Given our narrow scope of review for sufficiency of the evidence, this court should not disturb the jury's verdict on this ground.

Section 1644(a) of Title 15 of the United States Code imposes criminal liability on any person who

> knowingly in a transaction affecting interstate or foreign commerce, uses or attempts or conspires to use any counterfeit, fictitious, altered, forged, lost, stolen, or fraudulently obtained credit card to obtain money, goods, services, or anything else of value which within any one-year period has a value aggregating $1,000 or more.

Bice-Bey contends that she could not be convicted under this statute because the government failed utterly to show that she made any use whatsoever of a credit card—as opposed to a credit card number—or that she obtained the numbers by theft or fraud rather than in some lawful manner. Because her conduct does not come literally within the statutory language, she asserts that the statute does not reach her alleged activities.

As Bice-Bey points out, it *is* difficult to fit her actions within the statute's wording. The government did not claim that she obtained possession by fraud or theft of the credit cards, the account numbers of which she allegedly utilized in placing orders with Oak Park Electronics. Nor did the government seek to prove that the cards had been lost or stolen. Indeed, the holder of one of those cards testified that the card remained within his control at all relevant times. *A fortiori,* Bice-Bey made no use of a plastic credit card which was "counterfeit, fictitious, altered [or] forged."

Bice-Bey derives additional comfort from the definition given "credit card" in 15 U.S.C. § 1602(k) (1982):

> The term "credit card" means any card, plate, coupon book or other credit device existing for the purpose of obtaining money, property, labor, or services on credit.

This provision makes it clear, in her view, that section 1644 is concerned with the misappropriation and misuse of the plastic card itself and not of the credit account number to which the card witnesses. Her reading of the section, furthermore, has been adopted by the Ninth Circuit in *United States* v. *Callihan* (1982).

This argument is not without merit. We are conscious of the fundamental rule that criminal statutes are to be construed strictly and that we must not extend by "interpretation" the outer limits on criminal liability set by Congress. But we are mindful also of our obligation not to defeat the congressional purpose in creating a federal crime.

In this case we believe that Bice-Bey's suggested reading of the statute is overliteralistic. It is just as possible to go astray by being a fundamentalist about the letter of statutory language as by being too liberal in construing it. The core element of a "credit card" is the account number, not the piece of plastic. As this case illustrates, the "credit card" can be used over the telephone without the seller ever seeing the plastic card itself. The credit numbers Bice-Bey used were not hers and she had no authorization to use them. If she obtained them by ascertaining secretly the numbers belonging to Matthews and Bernstein, she was in effect stealing or fraudulently obtaining the essential element of the cards. In any event, by representing credit card numbers belonging to other persons as credit accounts belonging to "Jane Johnson," Bice-Bey was using a fictitious "credit device" in violation of the statute. To hold otherwise would be, in our view, to defeat the plain intent on Congress in enacting this statute.

We find no reversible error in the conduct of Bice-Bey's trial. Furthermore, although the question is close, and perhaps needs resolution by a higher tribunal, we disagree with Bice-Bey's reading of 15 U.S.C. § 1644(a) and hold that the government's evidence permitted the jury to find her liable under the statute. Bice-Bey's conviction, therefore, is affirmed.

Case Question

1. What other kinds of problems have use of "electronic" credit created?
2. Was the court giving credit to the letter or the spirit of the law?

Fair Credit Billing Act (FCBA)

The **Fair Credit Billing Act (FCBA),** which applies to all credit card issuers and creditors that require payment of a finance charge, is primarily designed to give consumers certain legal rights regarding billing error resolution. The FCBA requires that creditors disclose what the customers' rights and responsibilities are and the procedure for correcting errors.

In order to exercise FCBA rights, the consumer must notify the creditor *in writing* of any alleged billing error within sixty days of receipt of a billing statement. Once the creditor has received notice of a dispute, it must act to verify the charges or to correct an error within two billing cycles (or ninety days, whichever is less). A creditor cannot act to collect the debt, close the consumer's account, or make an unfavorable report to a credit reporting agency while the error resolution process is ongoing. If the creditor concludes it made no error and the consumer still refuses to pay, it may act to collect the debt, but in reporting to a credit reporting agency that the consumer's account is delinquent, the creditor must note that the debt is disputed.

Fair Credit Reporting Act (FCRA)

Almost anyone who has ever been extended credit has a credit history on file with a credit bureau (or credit reporting agency). This credit history may be supplied to potential creditors, insurance companies, and potential employers. Credit reports often contain not only information concerning a consumer's payment habits on debts, but also more personal information about his character or lifestyle garnered through interviews with various individuals. Much of the latter information, of course, amounts to no more than hearsay or opinion, and can be inaccurate or unfair because it may come from prejudiced parties.

The purpose of the **Fair Credit Reporting Act (FCRA),** originally passed in 1970, is to ensure that information contained in a person's credit history is accurate. The FCRA requires a credit reporting agency to maintain reasonable procedures to ensure the accuracy of its consumer reports. If a person is rejected for credit because of an adverse credit report, he has the right to be informed of the name and address of the consumer reporting agency that supplied the information. The consumer then has the right (within sixty days) to examine the files of that agency to determine the accuracy of the information. If the consumer believes the information is inaccurate, he can request a reinvestigation of it. Even if the agency refuses to change the contents of its files after reinvestigation, the consumer can still file a brief written statement of his version of the dispute, which becomes a permanent part of his file. If a consumer reporting agency is requested by an employer or insurer to conduct an investigative report, in which information is solicited from individuals concerning the consumer's lifestyle and reputation, the consumer has the right to be informed of the request within three days after it is made.

A violation of the FCRA is considered a violation of section 5 of the Federal Trade Commission Act. The FTC can enforce the FCRA, as can individuals whose rights have been violated. The FCRA carries both civil and criminal penalties.

Other Federal Consumer Protection Statutes

The statutory law we have discussed in this chapter, while substantial, is not all-inclusive. Two very important federal consumer protection statutes that are discussed in chapter 24 on debtor-creditor relations are the Fair Debt Collection Practices Act and the federal Bankruptcy Act.

Ethical Issues in Consumer Rights

As you can see from the chronology of the development of consumer law as discussed in this chapter, the 1960s and '70s was the "era of the consumer." Beginning in the late 1970s and during the 1980s, a feeling began to grow that the old philosophy of caveat emptor (let the buyer or consumer beware) had been replaced by the concept of caveat venditor (let the seller or money provider beware), and that further extension of consumer protection was unnecessary. Clear examples of this trend not to widen the scope of consumer protection laws were Congress' passing of the FTC Improvements Act, which attempted to give Congress veto power over FTC regulations, and Congress' refusal to create a federal Department of Consumer Protection. The tendency to pass laws to regulate the provider-consumer relationship further seems to have diminished, but there are still many ethical issues that remain.

You have seen that there are limits to how much information a seller is legally required to give a prospective buyer about the subject matter of a purchase. What ethical duties should a seller of a used car with potential mechanical difficulties or the seller of an older home with hidden structural problems have?

Neither the Uniform Commercial Code nor the federal Magnuson-Moss Warranty Act *requires* a seller of goods to make express warranties. Is a seller under an ethical duty to make such warranties?

As discussed previously, some big-city banks have begun requiring that customers with "small" accounts (which may be as large as $5,000) transact business with an automated teller machine instead of a live teller. This requirement is legal; is it ethical?

The evolution of consumer law often found business opposing proposed statutes or administrative regulations for which there was widespread public support. Business' opposition to these proposals was often based on a belief that the economic costs of the proposals outweighed their benefits to society. This opposition, however, was interpreted by some as being anticonsumer. A study of this area of the law clearly illustrates that if business is not perceived as being voluntarily responsive to society's demands, society will attempt to force responsiveness by passing laws.

The important concepts and terms in this chapter are listed below; page numbers have been provided for the key terms. By reading over each section you can assess your understanding of the chapter concepts and determine areas you may want to review.

Chapter Summary

1. The term *consumer protection* generally refers to the protection of consumers' bargaining power in buyer-seller and lender-borrower relationships.
2. The common law adopted the attitude of caveat emptor (let the buyer beware) in consumer transactions.
3. Common law doctrines that a consumer might be able to use to get out of an unfair contract include lack of capacity, mutual mistake, fraud, duress, and illegal or unconscionable contracts.
4. Under the Uniform Commercial Code, a buyer of goods may be able to enforce warranties against a seller or may be able to reject or revoke acceptance of goods.
5. The federal Magnuson-Moss Warranty Act prescribes the form in which warranties must be given.

6. Among federal statutes and administrative regulations that give buyers of goods legal rights against sellers are the Federal Trade Commission Act, the FTC's holder in due course rule, and the Federal Postal Reorganization Act.
7. The federal Consumer Product Safety Commission helps prevent the sale of dangerous goods, and the federal Electronic Fund Transfer Act gives rights to EFT users.
8. Among the most important federal statutes regulating the borrower-lender relationship and the extension of credit are the Equal Credit Opportunity Act, the Truth-in-Lending Act, the Fair Credit Billing Act, and the Fair Credit Reporting Act.

Key Terms

Consumer Product Safety Commission 650
duress 636
Electronic Fund Transfer Act 651
Equal Credit Opportunity Act 652
express warranty 639
Fair Credit Billing Act 656
Fair Credit Reporting Act 657
Federal Postal Reorganization Act 649
Federal Trade Commission Act 648
Federal Trade Commission Improvements Act 650
fraud 636
holder in due course 647
implied warranty 639
Magnuson-Moss Warranty Act 644
Truth-in-Lending Act 653
unconscionability 636
undue influence 636
warranty of fitness for a particular purpose 639
warranty of merchantability 639

Questions on Ethics

1. Mark is selling his house without using the services of a realtor. He knows his roof leaks, but when he shows the house to prospective buyers, he does not mention the leak, and no buyer has inquired about roof leaks. Is Mark ethically bound to disclose the leaky roof problem? Is he ethically bound to fix the roof?
2. Is there anything ethically wrong with a bank limiting the right of a customer to transact business with a live teller, requiring the customer to use an automated teller machine instead?
3. Is it ethical for sellers to refuse to give full warranties in order to avoid the antilemon provisions of the Magnuson-Moss Warranty Act?

4. It has been charged that some real estate agents "steer" customers to neighborhoods that an agent feels will suit the ethnic and social background of the customer, rather than showing a customer all homes in what the customer has stated is her price range. Is this "steering" ethical?
5. Certain companies have been calling people to tell them that they have been awarded a prize. The "winners" are then asked to verify the caller's information by giving out their credit card number. Later, the winners either receive something different from or something much less valuable than what they thought that they had won, but their credit cards are charged a large amount. While there have been legal cases brought against such companies, the outcome may be problematic because the winners did receive something. Even if such practices are legal, are they ethical?

Questions on Law

1. Emma applies for credit and is notified she was turned down. Emma doesn't know it, but her credit record has an untrue statement from a former employer, whose sexual advances she spurned, that she is a "deadbeat." What are Emma's rights?
2. A retail store advertised that it was selling eyeglasses for $7.50 a pair. The FTC discovered that of 1,400 pairs of glasses sold by the store, fewer than ten were sold for a price of $7.50 (excluding tax). The FTC sued the store for illegal bait-and-switch tactics. What result? *Tashof* v. *FTC,* 437 F.2d 707 (D.C. Cir. 1970).
3. Spiegel, a catalog retailer with its main business offices located in Chicago, made it a practice to sue delinquent debtors in Illinois courts. The FTC sued Spiegel, alleging that such suits, filed where many debtors had no hope of being able to respond, constituted an unfair and deceptive trade practice under section 5 of the FTC Act. What result? *Spiegel, Inc.* v. *FTC,* 540 F.2d 287 (7th Cir. 1976).
4. John Gilbert's daughter Ann charged $1,166.22 worth of goods on her father's Visa card. John refused to pay the credit card bill on the grounds that the charges were unauthorized. Does John have to pay Visa? *Fifth Third Bank/Visa* v. *Gilbert,* 478 N.E. 2d 1324 (Ohio 1984).
5. Szajna purchased a Pontiac Ventura in 1976. After the car developed transmission problems, Szajna discovered that the "Pontiac" had a Chevette transmission, which he characterized as being inferior to a Pontiac transmission. Szajna sued for breach of express warranty because the car did not have standard Pontiac parts. Will he recover? *Szajna* v. *General Motors Corporation,* 503 N.E. 2d 760 (Ill. 1986).

Suggested Readings

Barringer and Roberts, "The Credit Card Fraud Act of 1984: Clarification, or Further Confusion, of the Law of Credit Card Fraud?" 24 *American Business Law Journal* 449 (1986).

Kegley and Hiller, " "Emerging" Lemon Car Laws," 24 *American Business Law Journal* 87 (1986).

Zollers, "The Power of the Consumer Product Safety Commission to Levy Civil Penalties," 22 *American Business Law Journal* 551 (1985).

24 Debtor-Creditor Relations

[T]he primary purpose of the bankruptcy act is to relieve the honest debtor from the weight of oppressive indebtedness and permit him or her to start afresh.

—Local Loan Co. *v.* Hunt, *292 U.S. 234 (1934)*

LEARNING OBJECTIVES

After you have read this chapter, you should be able to:

1. Explain the social objective served and the ethical issues involved in the law of bankruptcy.
2. Recognize a bulk sale transfer and understand the reason for procedural notice to creditors.
3. Distinguish a wage earner's plan from a business reorganization under the Bankruptcy Reform Act.
4. Explain and understand what is meant by a secured transaction and how and why it is perfected.

Business Decisions and the Law

Debtor-Creditor Relations

Elizabeth Dayton Dovydenas, heiress to a retailing fortune, became a member of the Lenox, Massachusetts-based fundamentalist group, The Bible Speaks (TBS). Its founder, Pastor Carl H. Stevens, took an immediate interest in Dovydenas, simultaneously developing grandiose plans for both his ministry and family.

Through the exertion of undue influence over Dovydenas, found the court, Stevens convinced her to give up over $6 million of her personal fortune. He accomplished this by telling her that "giving money to the church was her primary mission on earth," and that "her family and attorneys were motivated by Satan." Pastor Stevens quickly spent all the money plus more.

Dovydenas "gradually came to her senses about Stevens" and sought return of the gifts that she made to the church. When the court found TBS owed the money to Dovydenas, she thereby became a creditor of TBS—and it became the debtor. Without cash, TBS was forced to sell its assets to satisfy the claims against it. Pastor Stevens lost all that he had built and acquired because he abused his fiduciary obligations.

The court ordered, among other things, the sale of his luxury Palm Beach condominium purchased with church funds, and auction of TBS's jewel—the Lenox campus. The prime real estate is located in the Berkshire mountain resort area and includes turn-of-the-century estate homes as well as TV broadcasting facilities. And who should be the high bidder for the church's real estate but none other than Elizabeth Dayton Dovydenas.

Introduction

In our economy, where credit is readily available to most individuals and business associations, it is inevitable that some debtors will be unable to pay their debts when due. In such instances, substantial debts could require a lifetime (and more!) to pay. Managing a family or business in a permanently insolvent status can lead to serious social and economic problems. We function in a legal environment where creditors have rights to pursue aggressively the collection of their claims, providing they do so within statutory and judicial constraints. The law of bankruptcy allows an honest, although negligent, debtor complete discharge of debts at the expense of an equally honest creditor. Providing the debtor has not engaged in fraudulent activity, the creditors may simply not be paid. Many students find it ethically indefensible for an individual or a business to be legally excused from paying a just debt at the expense of a creditor for *any* reason. Some feel this type of legal environment encourages irresponsible financial planning and reckless behavior beyond legitimate business risk taking. But the bankruptcy policy has been justified by allowing only an honest individual or business to be granted relief. Although most bankruptcies are declared by individuals, the business community accounts for the greater amount of financial losses.

Chapter 13 on business organizations explained the creation, managerial structure, exposure to liability, and operation of various types of business ventures. This chapter will explain what happens when business organizations buy and sell inventory on credit. Customers who are granted credit sometimes overextend themselves; this may lead to default, and the business creditors then begin collection procedures. Of course, debtors and creditors can be either individual consumers or business associations. This chapter will explain the debt collection process as it takes place both out of court (extrajudicial) and within the court system (judicial), including the law of bankruptcy. As you read this chapter, remember that very few businesses and individuals are fortunate enough to function without debt obligations. It is not being in debt that causes legal problems, but the inability to make payments when they are due.

Extrajudicial Collection Process

The common law provides little protection to the insolvent debtor. Creditors have the right to pursue the collection of debts aggressively, and in doing so they realize that a polite **dunning letter** demanding payment on an overdue debt will probably be ignored. Under the common law, courts allow creditors to pursue the collection of debts providing that the process is reasonable. An overzealous creditor may call or write to the debtor's employer or telephone the debtor at almost any hour. In many states, debtors may sue creditors for *intentional infliction of mental distress* if the emotional stress they cause is severe. Some courts require that mental distress be accompanied by a physical injury. Therefore, it is difficult for a debtor to prevail under this theory against an aggressive creditor.

Debtors may also sue creditors for *invasion of the right of privacy*. For example, a department store that published a list of its customers in default would be invading a privacy right. However, a personal letter informing the debtor's employer that a debt is overdue is usually not an invasion of a debtor's privacy, because the employer is considered to have a rightful interest in the employee's debts. In response to the social harm caused by unreasonable and overzealous creditors, Congress has enacted remedial legislation.

Fair Debt Collection Practices Act of 1977

In 1977, Congress enacted the Fair Debt Collection Practices Act (FDCPA), which took effect on March 15, 1977. The FDCPA does not apply to an individual or business attempting to collect its own debts, but rather to collection agencies or third parties who regularly collect the debts of others. Under the act, a debt collector must send a written notice stating the amount of the debt, the name of the creditor, and the debtor's right to contest the accuracy of the debt within five days after the debt collector has first communicated with the debtor. Debtors who dispute such debts may request verification of the debts within thirty days after they have received written notice from the debt collector.

Collection attempts by the debt collector must not be abusive, deceptive, misleading, or unfair. For example, debt collectors may not do any of the following: repeatedly use the telephone to disturb the debtor; publish a list of claims the debtor refuses to pay (they may, however, notify a credit bureau); use threats of violence to a debtor, his property, or his reputation; deposit a postdated check before the date on the check; make the debtor accept collect calls by misrepresenting facts or intentions; contact the debtor by postcard; place anything on an envelope other than the debt collector's name and address; or threaten to take the debtor's property unless there is a present right to do so.

All communication with the debtor must cease when the collector (1) receives a letter from the debtor requesting the collector to desist; (2) receives a written refusal to pay; or (3) is informed that the debtor is represented by an attorney.

Violation of the act subjects the debt collector to civil liability resulting in actual damages, additional damages up to $1,000 for intentional violations, and attorney's fees. If a debtor sues a debt collector in bad faith for the purpose of harassment, the court may allow attorney's fees to the debt collector.

A debt collector has two defenses when sued by a debtor for violating the act: that the violation was not intentional and resulted from a bona fide clerical error, or that the violation was based on a good faith conformity with a Federal Trade Commission advisory opinion.

The congressional response to collection abuses illustrates how the law can constrain an overzealous debt collector. The Federal Trade Commission (FTC) will investigate abuses of the FDCPA when notified by a debtor. Businesses throughout the country use the services of debt collectors; the act establishes a social policy that demands reasonable and fair collection practices. The act only applies when a creditor or a creditor's attorney turns over delinquent accounts to a debt collector, and some consider this a serious shortcoming of the law.

In 1986 attorneys lost their exemption under the FDCPA. Congress amended the act to include attorneys or law firms whose primary business is debt collection. Hence, attorneys who regularly collect debts for their clients must follow the statute or they will incur liability exposure for private litigation brought by debtors whose rights have been violated under the FDCPA.

Judicial Collection Process

Creditors who are unsuccessful in collecting a debt through a dunning letter and/or telephone calls must pursue a judicial remedy. Many states allow the prejudgment **attachment** of a debtor's selected assets. A prejudgment attachment is a legal process used to seize a debtor's property in order to ensure satisfaction of the debt when the judgment is later attained. A creditor must first file a complaint and a bond stating that the creditor (plaintiff) will pay any costs and damages sustained by the debtor (defendant) if the lawsuit is not justified. Generally, the debtor (defendant) must be granted advance notice of the attachment and the opportunity to be heard in court before the attachment is made.

The following landmark Supreme Court case involved a wage garnishment (attachment) that occurred without notice to the debtor.

Sniadach v. Family Finance Corp.

395 U.S. 337 (1969)

Facts

Family Finance Corp., plaintiff, instituted a garnishment action against Sniadach as defendant and Miller Harris Instrument Co., her employer, as garnishee. The complaint alleged a claim of $420 on a promissory note. The garnishee filed its answer, stating that it had wages of $63.18 under its control earned by Sniadach and unpaid, and that it would pay one-half to Sniadach as a subsistence allowance and hold the other half subject to the order of the court.

Sniadach moved that the garnishment proceedings be dismissed for failure to satisfy the due process requirements of the Fourteenth Amendment. The Wisconsin Supreme Court sustained the lower state court in approving the procedure.

The Wisconsin statute gave a plaintiff ten days in which to serve the summons and complaint on the defendant after service on the garnishee. Sniadach claimed that the Wisconsin garnishment procedure violated that due process required by the Fourteenth Amendment, in that notice and an opportunity to be heard were not given before the seizure of the wages.

Opinion

Judge Douglas: In this case the sole question is whether there has been a taking of property without that procedural due process that is required by the Fourteenth Amendment.

. . . [T]he right to be heard has little reality or worth unless one is informed that the matter is pending and can choose for himself whether to appear or default, acquiesce or contest. . . . In the context of this case the question is whether the interim freezing of the wages without a chance to be heard violates procedural due process.

We deal here with wages—a specialized type of property presenting distinct problems in our economic system. We turn then to the nature of that property and problems of procedural due process.

A prejudgment garnishment of the Wisconsin type is a taking which may impose tremendous hardship on wage earners with families to support. The result is that a prejudgment garnishment of the Wisconsin type may as a practical matter drive a wage-earning family to the wall. Where the taking of one's property is so obvious, it needs no extended argument to conclude that absent notice and a prior hearing this prejudgment garnishment procedure violates the fundamental principles of due process.

Case Questions

1. The U.S. Supreme Court in this case found that the Wisconsin statute violated the Due Process Clause of the Fourteenth Amendment by permitting a garnishment *before* a judgment was obtained against the debtor. Does the state legislature have the power to enact laws governing creditor's rights before a court reviews the statute?
2. What social purpose is served by giving an employee notice and a hearing, the fundamental principles of due process, before garnishing wages?
3. Assuming the debt is owed, is it right for a wage earner to argue at a court hearing that her wages should not be attached?

Notice that in this case the garnishment was brought against a third party (the employer) who owed a debt (wages) to the debtor (the employee). For example, if C sued D to collect a debt owed, and determined that D worked for X Company, C may garnish D's wages from X Company. When C obtains judgment against D, the judgment could be satisfied by D's wages being held by X Company. The same process of garnishment can be brought against the debtor's bank, holding his checking and/or savings account for the benefit of the creditor. Upon obtaining judgment, the creditor can receive the proceeds in the debtor's bank account. Some states allow a garnishment only *after* a judgment is received against a debtor.

Secured Transactions

Some creditors have an agreement with their debtors reserving special rights in the debtor's personal property in the event of default. They function in a legal environment governed by state statutory law that is based on article 9 of the Uniform Commercial Code. Creditors are always more inclined to grant a loan or sell merchandise on credit when the transaction is *secured* by **repossession** rights—the right to take back the merchandise if payments are not made.

Assume you bought an expensive stereo system on credit from a retailer under a secured sales contract. The retailer will require you to sign a statement called a **security agreement** (see figure 24.1), which gives him the right to repossess the stereo in the event of default. In such an agreement, you are the *debtor,* the retailer as creditor is the *secured party,* and the stereo is the *collateral.*

Perfecting a Security Interest

A creditor will be concerned about other creditors claiming an interest in the same collateral secured by the agreement. The written security agreement signed by the debtor and describing the collateral has the legal effect of attaching a **lien** on the property, a financial claim against the value of the property. The next step is to *perfect* the security agreement. This is an automatic process when a debtor who purchased consumer goods (i.e., goods used or bought for use primarily for personal, family, or household purposes) gave the creditor a **purchase money security interest,** which is an interest in the collateral retained by the seller to secure its price. However, this automatic perfection of a purchase money security interest in consumer goods will not protect the secured party creditor (the seller) against a subsequent purchaser who bought the goods with no knowledge of the security interest.

In the illustration in which you bought a stereo, what would happen to the retailer's interest in the stereo if you sold it to another party who had no knowledge of the retailer's interest? In the event a judgment was obtained against you for money owed to another creditor, may that creditor attach the stereo to satisfy his claim? If you declared personal bankruptcy, may the trustee in bankruptcy sell the stereo system and divide the proceeds equally among all of your creditors? If you default on your secured sales contract the retailer will attempt to repossess the stereo and satisfy the debt by selling the stereo to someone else. However, with respect to the retailer's priority over other credi-

Figure 24.1 Security Agreement between Seller and Buyer of Consumer Goods

Security Agreement Between Seller and Buyer of Consumer Goods
(Conditional Sale Type)

This agreement made this ________ day of ________ , 19 ______ , by and between ____________________

____ (Seller)

of ____________________ (Street Address) ____________________ (City, County and State)

hereinafter referred to as "seller," and ____________________ (Buyer)

of ____________________ (Street Address) ____________________ (City, County and State)

hereinafter referred to as "buyer," said address being buyer's place of residence.

Buyer, for a valuable consideration, receipt of which is hereby acknowledged, does hereby purchase and grant to seller a security interest pursuant to the Uniform Commercial Code the following described property:

together with all similar collateral hereafter acquired, all replacements thereof and all accessories, parts and equipment now and hereafter affixed thereto or used in connection therewith, which property is hereinafter collectively referred to as "goods," and is located or will be located at ____________________ (Location Address).

Proceeds of collateral are also covered; however, such shall not be construed to mean that the seller consents to any sale of such collateral.

Cash Price of Goods		$ ________
Less: Down payment in cash	$ ________	________
Allowance for ________ traded in	________	________
Unpaid cash price balance		________
Insurance (Type of Coverage)		________
Finance charge		________
Time balance		________

Buyer and any co-signers of this contract promise to pay the time balance at ____________ in ____________ equal (except the last, which may be unequal) monthly installments of ____________ dollars ($ ____________) beginning on ____________ (Date).

If Buyer defaults in the payment of any installment, buyer shall immediately pay seller, in addition to all amounts then due hereunder, a late charge calculated at the rate of 5 cents for each dollar of installment so in default. Until all installments and all other amounts due hereunder have been paid, seller shall retain title to and a security interest in the goods.

The property covered hereby (is not or is not to be) (is or is to be) so affixed or related to realty as to become a part thereof, and that if it is to be so affixed, it will be affixed to the following described realty: ________ . If the chief place of business of the buyer is other than that shown as buyer's residence, such chief place of business is at ________ .

Buyer warrants, covenants and agrees that:
The property is or is to be used by Buyer primarily [*check 1, 2 or 3*]:

☐ 1. In business;
☐ 2. For personal, family or household purposes;
☐ 3. In farming operations.

The rights and privileges of seller under this agreement shall inure to the benefit of its successors and assigns. All covenants, representations, warranties and agreements of buyer contained in this agreement are joint and several if buyer is more than one and shall bind buyer's personal representatives, heirs, successors and assigns. If any provision of this agreement shall for any reason be held to be invalid or unenforceable, such invalidity or unenforceability shall not affect any other provision hereof, but this agreement shall be construed as if such invalid or unenforceable provision had never been contained herein.

This Agreement is subject to the additional provisions set forth on the reverse side hereof, the same being incorporated herein by reference.

____________________________ ____________________________ (Buyer)

By ____________________________ (Seller) ____________________________ (Buyer)

Reprinted with permission from Herbert Lemelman's *Massachusetts Practice*, Volume 27. Copyright © 1984 by West Publishing Co.

tors, what must he do to protect his interest in the secured property? The law of secured transaction requires a creditor to *perfect* his security interest in order to protect the collateral from other creditors. There are four common methods of perfecting a security interest:

1. *Filing a financing statement.* A **financing statement** is a document that states the names and addresses of the creditor and the debtor and describes the secured property. It must be signed by the debtor. (See figure 24.2.) State law and the nature of the collateral will determine where the financing statement must be filed. Most are filed at the city hall where the debtor lives (if consumer goods) or operates a place of business (if inventory or equipment), and with the secretary of state. The effect of this filing by the secured party is to give *constructive notice* to other creditors that the personal property described in the financing statement is collateral for an outstanding (unpaid) loan with the secured party listed on the statement.

   Other creditors of the same debtor are bound by this statement even if they have no knowledge of it, because the law imputes knowledge once the document is properly filed. Hence, before personal property is purchased or accepted as collateral for a loan, the buyer or creditor should make a search in the appropriate filing place to determine if a financing statement has been filed for that personal property. Such a statement will place subsequent creditors in a subordinate position to the secured party.
2. *The creditor taking physical possession of the pledged goods without filing.* Perfection by the creditor's possessing the property—as when a debtor gives a bank possession of stocks and bonds as collateral for securing a loan—was known under the common law as a *pledge*. The security interest is perfected from the time possession is taken and continues so long as the creditor retains possession. A creditor can also maintain possession of equipment and inventory by sending its agent to the debtor's business to take control of the collateral, or by informing (with the debtor's consent) a warehouse company holding the collateral of the creditor's security interest in the debtor's property.
3. *Automatic perfection of financed consumer goods.* Products that are purchased to be used primarily for personal, family, or household purposes are consumer goods. They are often purchased on an installment basis, with the seller retaining a security interest in the goods. The seller's purchase money interest is perfected when the buyer signs the security agreement. Filing of a financing statement is not required under the UCC because the tremendous number of such transactions would make the cost and inconvenience of filing impractical. Hence, the seller, as a secured party, would have a priority interest over a subsequent creditor or trustee in bankruptcy who claimed an interest in the same consumer goods. However, someone who buys the goods from the debtor for his own personal use, who pays their full

Figure 24.2 Financing Statement

This FINANCING STATEMENT is presented to a filing officer for filing pursuant to the Uniform Commercial Code. | 3 Maturity date (if any):

Debtor(s) (Last Name First) and address(es)	2 Secured Party(ies) and address(es)	For Filing Officer (Date, Time, Number, and Filing Office)
Dan's Cafeteria, Inc. 240 Washington Street Marlboro, Mass.	SECURITY NATIONAL BANK 447 CENTRE ST. MARLBORO, MASSACHUSETTS	

4 This financing statement covers the following types (or items) of property:

All Furniture, Fixtures, Equipment with related accessories and attachments, etc. and Inventory, now on hand and hereafter acquired.

Record Owner of Realty:

Installed: 240 Washington St., Marlboro, Mass.

Frances N. Smith and James F. Smith
Trustee for Calvin F. Smith
Valley Road
Sunrise Valley, New York

Check ☒ if covered: ☒ Proceeds of Collateral are also covered ☐ Products of Collateral are also covered No. of additional sheets presented:

Filed with: Registry of Deeds, Commonwealth of Mass. and City of Marlboro

Dan's CAFETERIA, INC. SECURITY NATIONAL BANK

By: /s/ Daniel F. Conti By: /s/ Frank T. Newton, Assistant Cashier

Signature(s) of Debtor(s) Signature(s) of Secured Party(ies)

Filing Office: Copy — Alphabetical

This form of financing statement is approved by the Secretary of State.

STANDARD FORM — UNIFORM COMMERCIAL CODE — FORM UCC-2

Reprinted with permission from Herbert Lemelman's *Massachusetts Practice,* Volume 27. Copyright © 1984 by West Publishing Co.

value, and who has no knowledge of the creditor's security interest takes the goods free of the security interest. Hence, sellers who extend credit on expensive consumer goods often file a financing statement to protect their interest against such a possibility.

4. *Automobile certificate of title.* In most states the ownership of an automobile is evidenced by a document called a certificate of title. If the automobile is financed by a secured transaction, the creditor's security interest is perfected by a reference to it on the certificate of title.

Default by the Debtor

The security agreement signed by the debtor and the secured creditor generally defines the grounds for default. For example, failure of the debtor to insure the property, bankruptcy of the debtor, or the creditor's reasonable belief that payment is uncertain could authorize the creditor to repossess the collateral. If the security agreement is silent with respect to the basis for default, default will occur immediately on the debtor's failure to pay when due. If you failed to make the monthly payments on your car, the law authorizes the bank (secured party) to take possession of the car (collateral) without judicial process, providing there is no "breach of the peace."

Debtor's Right to Redemption

Redemption occurs when a debtor regains the property by paying the entire balance due as well as any expenses reasonably incurred by the secured party in repossessing, holding, and preparing the property for sale. If the property is going to be sold, the secured party must give to the debtor reasonable notice of the time, place, and terms of the sale. This allows the debtor to be present at the redemption sale to ensure that the sale is commercially reasonable. If it is not, and the sale proceeds are insufficient to satisfy the debt, the debtor is liable for the remaining amount. Of course, if the sale produces an amount greater than the amount owed, the secured party must account to the debtor for any surplus. Keep in mind that the law of secured transaction in article 9 of the Uniform Commercial Code applies to personal property, not real property, which is governed by the state law of mortgages.

The court in the following case required that the secured party give notice to the debtor of the intended sale of the repossessed goods as a prerequisite to the debtor's duty to show that a redemption sale was substantially below the fair market value of the goods.

Hemken v. First National Bank of Litchfield

394 N.E.2d 868, Ill. (1979)

Facts

Willard and Marilyn Hemken brought suit to recover damages for the failure of the First National Bank of Litchfield and Werner Motor Company to provide them with a notice of the intended sale of a repossessed 1971 GMC Astro tractor.

Hemken purchased a used tractor from the defendant on March 8, 1974, for a total deferred payment price of $18,280.52. Defendant, Werner Motor Company, then assigned the contract to the First National Bank of Litchfield with full recourse.

Sometime during August 1976 plaintiff was in default on the contract, which then had an outstanding balance of $7,389.22. The bank made demand for the collateral and then contacted the defendant, Werner Motor Company, who picked up the tractor and paid the total amount due on the contract.

The repossessed tractor was later sold to another dealer for the sum of $7,150.

It was undisputed that no notice of intent to sell was sent to plaintiff prior to the sale of this tractor.

Opinion

Judge Mills: The actions of a secured party in defendant's situation are governed by Article 9 of the Uniform Commercial Code. Absent certain enumerated circumstances, section 9–504 of the

Code requires a repossessing secured party to give the debtor reasonable notification of the intended sale or disposition of the repossessed collateral. This requirement is necessary to protect the debtor's right to redeem the collateral by tendering fulfillment of all obligations prior to the secured party's disposition of the collateral in a commercially reasonable manner.

When a secured party has failed to proceed in accordance with the Code provisions regulating disposition of repossessed collateral, the debtor may recover any loss caused by the failure. Although the trial court found that the defendant had breached its duty to give notice, it nevertheless denied plaintiff's claim for damages. The court gave these reasons for this ruling: (1) Plaintiff's failure to show a sale substantially below fair market value; (2) his failure to prove the cost of fuel, maintenance and repairs; and (3) his failure to show that he was ready, willing and able to perform. We disagree with this reasoning.

Although plaintiff may have failed to show that the price for which the tractor was sold was commercially unreasonable, the question of liability of the defendant is still unresolved. Article 9 of the Uniform Commercial Code creates a procedure which allows a secured party to dispose of repossessed collateral. To avoid liability, the secured party's right to sell must be exercised in compliance with the Code's procedure:

STEP ONE of the process requires the secured party to give reasonable notice of the intended sale to the debtor.

STEP TWO mandates that the sale then be conducted in a commercially reasonable manner which includes method, manner, time, place and terms.

Failure to take *either* of the required steps subjects the secured party to liability for any damages incurred by the debtor as a result of the omission.

Here, defendant omitted step one and is liable for the consequent harm.

Section 9–506 of the Uniform Commercial Code gives a debtor in default an opportunity to redeem by tendering fulfillment of all obligations. The defendant argues that since no actual tender was made there was no duty to delay the sale of the repossessed merchandise. Such an interpretation does violence to the provisions of the Code. A secured party does not have an unrestricted right to sell repossessed collateral. In situations such as the one at bench the secured party must give notice and conduct the sale in a commercially reasonable manner. The debtor's right to redeem may be exercised anytime prior to the disposition of the collateral by the secured party in compliance with section 9–504. That has not occurred in this case and the defendant breached a duty which it owed to the plaintiff. Defendant's argument would require tender prior to the duty to give notice and is clearly contrary to the procedure which has been adopted by our legislature.

Case Questions

1. What social purpose is served by giving a debtor in default the right to redeem repossessed property?
2. Should a debtor be required to prove that the collateral was sold at a price below its fair market value *before* he can recover under the notice rule?
3. The court in this case stated "a secured party does not have an unrestricted right to sell repossessed collateral." What legal restrictions are placed on that right?

Secured transactions, governed by article 9 of the Uniform Commercial Code, form the basis of credit usage in our economy. The legal process established by this code features a well-balanced system of rights and duties for both creditor and debtor. With credit, many people can achieve a standard of living beyond what their incomes would otherwise allow. Business associations that rely upon debt financing could not function without secured transactions.

Financing Realty

Most buyers of realty do not have enough cash to pay the full purchase price. So buyers usually borrow part of the price. Lenders want to be very certain they will be repaid. So they almost always require that the borrower give the lender the legal power, if loan payments are not made as promised, to force the sale of the property and collect the debt from the proceeds. The three major instruments of finance used to protect lenders in this way are the mortgage, the trust deed, and the land sale contract.

Mortgages

In the past, mortgages were the most common instrument for financing the purchase of realty. Generally the buyer gives a mortgage to a lender such as the bank or savings and loan association. The mortgage gives the lender the legal right, in the event loan payments are not made as promised, to file suit in court to foreclose (or cut off) the buyer's ownership rights in the property. After the suit is initiated and the judge hears the evidence, he can issue a decree of foreclosure. After the decree is issued, the lender can request a sheriff's sale, at which the property will be auctioned off to the highest bidder.

Trust Deeds

With this method of financing, the buyer first obtains the deed from the seller. The buyer then gives a trust deed to a trustee. The trustee holds the trust deed on behalf of the lender. The trust deed contains language that allows the *trustee* to sell the property if the buyer defaults on the loan payments. Note that a court order is not required to cause the sale, and that it is a sale conducted by the trustee rather than the sheriff.

Land Sale Contracts

This instrument is sometimes called the Contract of Sale, or Conditional Sale Contract. With a land sale contract, the lender—who is often also the seller—keeps the deed until all the contracted payments have been made. Then the lender must deliver a deed.

The land sale contract gives the buyer the right to occupy the realty and treat it as his own. The law refers to the buyer under a land sale contract as the equitable owner, even though he has not yet received the deed.

If the buyer defaults, the lender may have him removed from the property in about the same way a landlord evicts a tenant who has not paid the rent. While this may involve a lawsuit, it is sometimes concluded more rapidly than either a mortgage foreclosure or a sale by trustee.

Individuals and businesses that overextend their ability to pay their debts may become hopelessly insolvent. Our legal system provides relief for such parties by the declaration of bankruptcy.

Bankruptcy Reform Act and the Bankruptcy Amendments of 1984

The most common form of debtor relief is a **discharge** of debts from a federal bankruptcy court. Such a discharge is a release of the debtor by the bankruptcy court from all or most of the debts. The United States Constitution provides in article 1, section 8, clause 4, "The Congress shall have power to establish . . . uniform laws on the subject of bankruptcies throughout the United States." From 1800 on, Congress has enacted, amended, and repealed various bankruptcy acts. In 1978 Congress passed the Bankruptcy Reform Act, which became effective on October 1, 1979. On July 10, 1984, President Reagan signed new legislation known as the Bankruptcy Amendments and Federal Judgeship Act of 1984.

The Bankruptcy Reform Act applies to all states; individual states do not have the authority to enact bankruptcy laws. Hence, if you were going to voluntarily declare bankruptcy, the governing law would be the Bankruptcy Reform Act as amended in 1984. In contrast to your voluntary petition, your creditors can also file a bankruptcy petition against you; the latter type is called an **involuntary bankruptcy petition.**

As a creditor, you may file an involuntary petition if your debtor has twelve or more creditors and you are one of three or more whose unsecured claims together total at least $5,000. For example, you discover your debtor has eleven other creditors. You and two other creditors file a bankruptcy petition against the debtor. You are owed $1,000, creditor X is owed $1,000, and creditor Y $3,000. If the debtor has fewer than twelve unsecured creditors, the petition may be filed by one or more creditors whose total claims amount to at least $5,000. In either a voluntary or involuntary case, the filing of the petition prevents the creditors from pursuing other creditors' rights, such as the enforcement of a lien, repossession of goods, wage attachments, or judgments against the debtor. This has the effect of directing the activities of all concerned creditors to the same federal bankruptcy case. A debtor who is injured by a creditor's *willful* violation of the *automatic stay* that suspends creditor's rights outside of the bankruptcy proceedings may sue the creditor for damages, including costs, attorney fees, and possibly punitive damages.

As a debtor in a bankruptcy proceeding, you may have to appear and testify at a meeting of the creditors and answer any of their questions under oath. Your creditors will generally file a **proof of claim** that lists the money owed to them (see figure 24.3). A trustee-in-bankruptcy, appointed by the bankruptcy judge, will collect your property (called your *estate*), set apart your exempt property, liquidate your nonexempt property, investigate your financial status, and make a final report to the bankruptcy judge.

Note that some of your property can be exempt from liquidation in a bankruptcy proceeding. A debtor may assert exemptions listed in the federal bankruptcy statute or may claim the exemptions available under the state law where the debtor lives, unless state law has precluded a debtor's use of the federal

Figure 24.3 Proof of Claim

United States Bankruptcy Court
FOR THE DISTRICT OF KANSAS
AT KANSAS CITY, KS.

IN RE: James H. Brinton, Jr.
533 Mission Road
Prairie Village, Ks.
66207

Case No.: 85-B22546

PROOF OF CLAIM

1. This proof is made for the claimant named below by the undersigned individual who resides at 622 W. 59th St., Mission, Kansas 66212 and who also states that he is duly authorized to make this claim on behalf of the claimant, which is:

[XX] **An Individual** [ ] **A Partnership** [ ] **A Corporation** [ ] **Other**

(INDICATE THE STATE OF INCORPORATION, NAME OF PARTNERS, OR SUCH OTHER DESCRIPTION OF THE CLAIMANT AS MAY BE APPROPRIATE)

2. The post office address of the claimant and the address to which all notices to this claimant should be addressed is

If name or address, as printed, is not correct please indicate correct name and address to which checks and notices should be delivered.

John's Tire and Wheel Center
622 W. 59th St.,
Mission, Ks. 66212

SAMPLE

3. The debtor was, at the time of the filing of the petition initiating this case, and still is indebted (or liable) to this claimant, (excluding all unmatured interest) in the sum of **$** 422.37

4. The consideration for this debt (or ground of liability) is as follows:

Purchase of Tires and Battery

5. (If the claim is founded on writing) The writing on which this claim is founded (or a duplicate thereof) is attached hereto (or cannot be attached for the reason set forth in the statement attached hereto).

Service Order # 22516, copy is attached.

6. (If appropriate) This claim is founded on an open account which became (or will become) due on April 24, 1985 as shown by the itemized statement attached hereto. Unless it is attached hereto or its absence is explained in an attached statement, no note or other negotiable instrument has been received for the account or any part of it.

7. No judgment has been rendered on the claim except

None

8. The amount of all payments on this claim has been credited and deducted for the purpose of making this proof of claim.

9. This claim is not subject to any set-off or counter-claim except

None

10. No security interest is held for this claim except

[If security interest in property of the debtor is claimed]. The security interest is claimed under the writing referred to in Paragraph 5 hereof [or under a separate writing which (or a duplicate of which) is attached hereto, or under a separate writing which cannot be attached hereto for the reason set forth in the statement attached hereto]. Evidence of perfection of such security interest is also attached hereto.

11. This claim is a general unsecured claim, except to the extent that the security interest, if any, described in paragraph 10 is sufficient to satisfy the claim. (If priority is claimed, state the amount and the basis thereof.) Claim is unsecured.

12. If this claim is for salaries, wages, commissions or employee benefits entitled to priority as permitted by §507(a) 3 and/or §507(a) (4) of the Bankruptcy Code, indicate the dates and the nature of the services performed, the rates of compensation and claimants Social Security number.

SSN

FILE CLAIM WITH THE CLERK OF THE BANKRUPTCY COURT AT:

BANKRUPTCY COURT FOR THE DISTRICT OF KANSAS
U.S. COURTHOUSE AND POST OFFICE BLDG.
212 7TH AVE.
KANSAS CITY, KANSAS 66205

Dated 7/15/85

Signed John Wesley Harlin
(Name of individual, agent, officer, or partner signing this claim)

Penalty For Presenting Fraudulent Claim

Fine of not more than $5000 or imprisonment for not more than 5 years or both -- Title 18, U.S.C. Par 152.

3/80

Courtesy Electronic Processing, Inc., Shawnee Mission, Kansas.

exemptions. The 1984 Bankruptcy Amendments require a husband and wife who jointly file for bankruptcy to elect the same federal or state exemptions. Exempt property under federal law includes: (1) one motor vehicle up to $1,200 in value; (2) professional books and tools of the debtor's trade up to $750 in value; (3) up to $500 in jewelry; (4) household furnishings, clothing, appliances, books, or musical instruments held for personal, family, or household use up to $200 in value for each item, the aggregate total of all items not to exceed $4,000; (5) the debtor's equity in his residence up to a maximum interest of $7,500 (under the 1984 amendments there is a $3,750 limit on any unused portion of the amount claimed for a homestead exemption); (6) prescribed health aids; (7) alimony and support payments and pension and profit-sharing plans if they are reasonably necessary for the support of the debtor; (8) life insurance proceeds payable from a person of whom the debtor was a dependent; (9) a payment of up to $7,500 that was awarded in a personal injury claim; and (10) social security benefits, unemployment compensation, and veteran's and disability benefits.

Your nonexempt property will be distributed in accordance with the following priorities: the payment of administrative expenses and legal fees, followed by payment of your various unsecured claims. You will then be issued a discharge from the bankruptcy court, which has the effect of releasing you from all debts. Even after a discharge, certain debts must still be paid by the debtor. These include: (1) taxes due because the debtor filed a fraudulent tax return or failed to file a tax return; (2) debts incurred by providing false financial statements reasonably relied upon by creditors; (3) alimony or child support debts; (4) debts owed to creditors whose names were not given to the court by the debtor; (5) debts resulting from breach of a fiduciary duty; and (6) debts owed to the government, including educational loans, except in cases in which payment would create an undue hardship for the debtor.

The 1984 amendments created a rebuttable presumption that consumer debt for luxury goods or services of more than $500, when it is incurred within forty days of the order of relief, cannot be discharged. This provision will prevent a debtor from incurring consumer debts just before filing a bankruptcy petition and then having those debts discharged. The amendments also deny a bankruptcy discharge for debts arising from a judgment based on damages caused by drunken driving.

A discharge will also not be allowed under any of the following circumstances: (1) property is transferred, destroyed, or concealed within one year before the petition of bankruptcy is filed so that the debtor can defraud creditors; (2) the debtor conceals, destroys, or falsifies information related to her financial condition; (3) the debtor makes a false claim or oath or withholds recorded information from officials; (4) the debtor fails to explain satisfactorily a loss of assets; (5) the debtor refuses to obey a lawful court order; (6) the debtor has been granted a discharge in a prior bankruptcy case within the past six years; and (7) the debtor is a corporation or a partnership that must proceed under Chapter 11 or liquidate in accordance with state corporate law. (We will discuss item 7 in more detail later.) Notice that the public policy established by the Bankruptcy Act and its amendments protects an honest aggrieved debtor and not a fraudulent party.

The bankruptcy court in the following case found that an undue hardship would be imposed upon the debtor unless an educational loan was discharged.

In re Lawson

10 B.R. 477 (1981)

Facts

This case came on to be heard on April 21, 1981, on plaintiff's complaint to determine dischargeability of defendant's debt to it. The complaint alleged that a discharge does not discharge an individual debtor from any debt to a nonprofit institution of higher education for an educational loan, unless excepting such debtor from discharge will impose an undue hardship on the debtor and the debtor's dependents.

Opinion

Bankruptcy Judge Ralph H. Kelley: The complaint alleges that "defendant's obligation arises from a national direct student loan made by plaintiff to defendant as evidenced by a promissory note. The loan to defendant was for an educational loan."

The defendant filed an answer admitting the allegations of the complaint. She would show that to allow this debt to be nondischargeable would impose an undue hardship on the debtor. She would show that she is in fact still a student and that she has no income or earnings, and that to deny a discharge to this debt would be an undue hardship upon her and her family.

The court finds that debtor dropped out of college because she was unable to pay all costs incident to her education. For a while she tried to work as a waitress. She was not married, became pregnant, and returned home to her parents. She gets no child support. She has lived with her parents for the past two years.

With the help of CETA she has been able to graduate from Walker County Technical School with a Licensed Practical Nurse Diploma. It took 13 months of study to obtain the diploma.

Upon becoming licensed by the state, she hopes to work in a local hospital with an hourly income of $4.57. If she works a full week, or 40 hours, she will have a gross income of $728 per month.

The bankruptcy schedules list debts in the amount of $54,931.23. This includes a large claim for damages as a result of an automobile accident. The plaintiff is the only creditor as of this date who has filed a complaint seeking to have its indebtedness excepted from discharge.

In 1976 the Congress passed the Educational Amendments which restricted a discharge in bankruptcy. The restriction was designed to remedy an abuse by students who, immediately upon graduation, would file bankruptcy to secure a discharge of educational loans. These students often had no other indebtedness and could easily pay their debts from future wages.

In the present case the debtor did not file bankruptcy only to secure a discharge from her educational loans. The debtor has been unemployed and attending school for most of the last two years. She has had no regular wages or income. Her present prospects offer only enough money to barely maintain her and her two year old child.

The court concludes that, under these circumstances, requiring the debtor to repay the debt to the plaintiff would impose upon her an undue hardship. In passing the Educational Amendments of 1976 and including these amendments in the Bankruptcy Reform Act of 1978, Congress intended to correct an abuse. It did not intend to deprive those who have truly fallen on hard times of the "fresh start" policy of the new Bankruptcy Code.

Case Questions

1. Congress passed the Educational Amendments of 1976 and included them in the Bankruptcy Reform Act of 1978, restricting a discharge in bankruptcy for educational loans. To what extent does this law assist or hinder students from obtaining educational loans?
2. Do you agree that educational loans should be discharged if the debtor can show an "undue hardship"? Explain.
3. What social purpose is served by the "fresh start" policy of the new bankruptcy code? Can you give an ethical argument to justify it, or do you find a discharge in bankruptcy morally indefensible?

Wage Earner's Plan under Chapter 13

In order to avoid a straight bankruptcy, a debtor (including a sole proprietor) may file a voluntary petition, providing that he has regular income (hence the term **wage earner's plan**), unsecured debts of *less* than $100,000, and secured debts of *less* than $350,000. The debtor's future earnings and income are turned over to the control of a trustee, who provides for payment of claims on a *deferred* basis not to exceed three years, unless the bankruptcy court approves a longer period not to exceed five years. A Chapter 13 plan may provide for less than full payment for certain unsecured claims. Creditors have a right to object to the plan at a **confirmation hearing.**

Under the 1984 amendments, the court cannot approve a wage earner's plan over the objection of the trustee of any unsecured creditor unless the value of the property to be distributed under the plan is at least equal to the amount of the claim *or* all of the debtor's projected disposable income to be received during the three-year plan period will be applied to making payments. The bankruptcy court may grant a hardship discharge to a debtor if the debtor's failure to complete the plan was due to circumstances beyond his control, *and* the value of the payments made to each creditor at least equals what that creditor would have received under an ordinary liquidation proceeding, *and* modification of the plan is not "practicable."

If the plan is approved and the debtor pays as promised, he will be discharged of the debts. A wage earner's plan is not available to corporations or partnerships.

Business Reorganization under Chapter 11

A corporation or partnership may file a voluntary bankruptcy petition, or its creditors may force a business into bankruptcy by filing an involuntary petition. In either case, the debtor is obligated to file a list of creditors. The bankruptcy court then appoints a *committee of creditors* who investigate the debtor's financial condition and may request the appointment of a trustee.

The debtor corporation will generally continue in business as a *debtor in possession* unless a trustee is appointed by the court in the case of fraud, dishonesty, mismanagement, or incompetence. The debtor corporation must then file a **Chapter 11 plan,** which provides for distributions to creditors and continuation of the business. The plan may require the company to borrow money from outsiders or sell its corporate assets. The Chapter 11 plan often offers the creditors stock in the company rather than cash. So long as adequate disclosure is given to creditors and stockholders whose rights are affected, the bankruptcy court does not review the merits of the plan but only reviews the information provided to ensure that the creditors' and stockholders' acceptance is based on an informed judgment. The bankruptcy court will hold a confirmation hearing on the Chapter 11 plan after giving notice to all creditors allowing them to raise objections. After confirmation, the debtor corporation and its creditors are bound by the plan, which allows the "recognized corporation" to continue in business.

Bulk Sale Transfer

Suppose you were a manufacturer who sold component parts to computer companies. In order to compete and maintain a high volume of sales, your company must generally sell the parts on credit. You probably would insist upon a secured transaction that was perfected by filing a financing statement to protect your interest in the collateral. This would give you repossession rights over the materials sold in the event of the buyer's insolvency. However, if a sale of the goods by your customer is made in *bulk*—that is, the entire inventory or a major part of it is sold at once at once—and the sale occurs not in the ordinary course of business but rather as a complete sellout to a buyer of your customer's computer business, article 6 of the Uniform Commercial Code applies. This is known as a **bulk sale transfer** and is defined in the code as "any transfer in bulk and not in the ordinary course of the transferor's business of a major part of the materials, supplies, merchandise or other inventory of an enterprise."

Article 6 imposes performance obligations on both the seller of the inventory and/or supplies (called the transferor) and the buyer (the transferee). The *buyer* of the materials must do the following: (1) demand from the seller a list of the seller's business creditors and a schedule of the property sold to the business; and (2) at least ten days before the sale or payment, whichever occurs first, the buyer must give notice of the sale, by personal delivery or registered mail, to the seller's creditors. If the buyer does not give notice to the seller's creditors, the sale is *ineffective*. The effect of this notice is to alert you as a creditor that the materials sold to your customer are being resold as part of a major sale of the customer's business. This allows you to contact the potential buyer and arrange for payment in full or agreeable credit terms.

Note carefully the legal environment created by this statute. The burden of compliance with the performance obligations are on the *buyer*. An ineffective sale allows the creditors to recover the inventory sold or divide the sales proceeds. The assumption is that an unethical seller would probably pocket the money and move to parts unknown, preventing recourse by the creditors.

Hence, the buyer of a major part of a seller's inventory who does not comply with the Bulk Sales Transfer Act proceeds at great risk, which is precisely the purpose of the statute.

The court in the following case held that the defendant did not violate the bulk sales law because there was no bulk transfer of inventory.

H.L.C Imports Corp. v. M & L Siegel, Inc.

413 N.Y.S.2d 605 (New York 1979)

Facts

The defendant, M & L Siegel, Inc., rented and operated a selling booth in a jewelry exchange on 47th Street in Manhattan. It had purchased diamonds on credit from the plaintiff for $3,110.95. While the debt was still outstanding, M & L Siegel, Inc., vacated the booth and sold to the defendant some office furniture, six file cabinets, two safes, a scale, an adding machine, and a jewelry stretching machine. The sale further included customers' lists, jewelry catalogs, and the right of the defendant to use the same telephone number. The lease for the booth was not assigned. However, the defendant entered into a new lease with the landlord and proceeded to do business at the same booth, M & L Siegel, Inc.'s principal disappeared, and a default judgment for the $3,110.95 remained unsatisfied.

Because plaintiff was not notified of this sale, it claimed it was entitled to relief under the Bulk Sales Act to hold the defendant, as a transferee, liable for M & L Siegel, Inc.'s debt. The defendant argued that it was not subject to the provisions of the act because there was not a transfer of the debtor's bulk inventory as required by the statute.

Opinion

Judge Burton S. Sherman: The Act defines a bulk transfer as "any transfer in bulk and not in the ordinary course of the transferor's business of a major part of the materials, supplies, merchandise or other inventory . . . of an enterprise subject to this Article." An enterprise is one "whose principal business is the sale of merchandise from stock." And, inventory is defined as goods "held for sale." Clearly, M & L Siegel, Inc. was in the business of selling jewelry and diamonds, and the sale of its office furniture and equipment was not a bulk transfer of its inventory. Nor did the sale of catalogues, customers' lists and a telephone listing constitute a bulk transfer. While these items, as well as such other intangible assets as a corporate name or good will, might have great economic value, they do not constitute inventory within the statutory definition. They were not goods held for sale. At best they would be considered equipment because the Act provides that transferred goods not included in the definitions of inventory "shall be considered equipment." However, a transfer of a substantial part of an enterprise's equipment is only subject to the Bulk Sales Act, "if it is made in connection with a bulk transfer of inventory." This is not the fact in this case. Since there was no bulk transfer of inventory the defendant did not violate the provisions of the Bulk Sales Law and the action should be dismissed.

Case Questions

1. The defendant sold office furniture, jewelry catalogs, customer lists, telephone lists, six file cabinets, two safes, a scale, an adding machine, and a jewelry stretching machine, but not its inventory, namely, jewelry and diamonds. Hence, the court held that it was not necessary to give notice to the plaintiff (creditor). Can you offer a reason for amending the Bulk Sales Tranfer Act to include the sale of equipment?
2. What social purpose is served by protecting a buyer of equipment, as in this case, from being held liable for the seller's inventory debts?
3. Was the buyer of the equipment ethically obligated to obtain assurance that the *inventory* was paid for?

Suretyship and Guaranty

Suretyship

Businesses and individuals cannot always obtain credit on their own financial strength. In such an instance it may be necessary to rely on a surety, a party who will promise the creditor primary responsibility for the debtor's obligation. **Suretyship** is the written contract between the surety and the creditor that allows the creditor to demand immediate payment from the surety upon the principal debtor's default. The creditor may proceed directly against the surety without attempting to first collect the money owed from the debtor, because the surety is primarily liable for the debt.

Creditors under a suretyship will discharge a surety from liability if they execute any material changes in the written contract with the debtor without first obtaining the consent of the surety. A creditor will also discharge a surety by releasing a debtor from the suretyship contract, or by rejecting payment from a debtor who pays or offers to pay the amount due. The only defenses available to a surety in a suit by the creditor are those of the debtor. For example, a creditor's fraud or misrepresentations made to the debtor may be used by the surety to avoid liability under the suretyship contract.

Guaranty

Similar to the suretyship contract, a *guaranty* makes the **guarantor** responsible for the debtor's obligation. However, in the case of a guaranty, the creditor must first attempt to collect from the debtor; hence the guarantor is *secondarily liable* and must pay only if the debtor refuses to do so. The guarantor of an *absolute guaranty* promises to perform the obligation upon the debtor's default. For example, a promissory note may be signed by the debtor followed by the words "I guarantee payment in full of this obligation, signed Barbara Curtin." The debtor must first default before the guaranty is enforceable. Under a *conditional guaranty,* the guarantor will pay only if the creditor is unable to collect payment from the debtor. The creditor must first bring a suit against the debtor, obtain a judgment, and notify the guarantor of his inability to collect the amount due.

Ethical Issues in Debtor-Creditor Relations

In this chapter we have discussed a relationship between individuals and business associations that allows people to enjoy goods and services before they are paid for in full. Within prudent limits, debt financing has contributed to our economic well-being. As stated at the outset of this chapter, it is not the debtor-creditor relationship that causes legal and social problems, but rather the inability to make payments when they become due.

The very nature of debt financing anticipates an ability to repay on time.

Countless events, sometimes beyond the control of the debtor, may interfere with the payback plan—ill health, an unexpected layoff, an economic recession.

The ethical dimension of the relationship asks the question, at what point does the projected risk of defaulting on the debt exceed the reasonable likelihood that it will be paid off? For instance, a graduate MBA student may anticipate a starting salary sufficient to meet payments on a $30,000 educational loan. Would that same student be morally justified in borrowing twice that amount to purchase a new car and other luxury items while attending grad school? Would the creditor be acting ethically in allowing such a loan, knowing that it exceeded conventional borrowing standards? From the debtor's and creditor's points of view, the ethical issue is, does the loan applicant honestly and reasonably have the ability to pay back the amount borrowed? Today most creditors will insist upon collateral to secure a loan. In a secured transaction, upon default, the creditor may repossess the property. Is a creditor ethically justified in making a loan on the basis of secured collateral without considering the applicant's financial ability to repay the loan from earnings?

Once the loan has been extended and the debtor defaults, what ethical issues are involved in the collection of the debt or relief of the debtor through bankruptcy? For instance, if the goods that you purchased on credit are repossessed and sold at a redemption sale, but the income from the sale does not completely pay off the debt, is the creditor ethically justified in collecting the balance due from you when you no longer have the use of the goods? Some states no longer allow a creditor to sue on a deficiency balance due. Is it morally right, even with a court's permission, to attach the wages of a debtor whose family relies on that income?

The founding fathers included a provision in the Constitution allowing Congress to establish uniform bankruptcy laws. The public policy of relieving the honest debtor from the weight of oppressive indebtedness and permitting him or her to start afresh is part of our constitutional heritage. Does such a policy encourage dishonesty or unjustifiable risk-taking? When an individual or business receives a discharge and creditors are not paid, who ultimately bears that cost? If the debt is a deductible tax expense, the answer is other taxpayers.

While you review this chapter, consider the business ethics implications of each debtor-creditor relationship and the effect on society when they exceed prudent limits.

The important concepts and terms in this chapter are listed below; page numbers have been provided for the key terms. By reading over each section you can assess your understanding of the chapter concepts and determine areas you may want to review.

Chapter Summary

1. The Fair Debt Collection Practices Act of 1977 applies to collection agencies or third persons who regularly collect the debts of others.

Under the act, a debt collector must not be abusive, deceptive, misleading, or unfair. Violation of the act subjects the debt collector to damages and attorney's fees.

2. A secured transaction is an agreement between a debtor and creditor reserving special repossession rights in the debtor's property in the event of default. To ensure that they have these special rights in secured property, creditors must perfect their interest. A debtor may redeem the repossessed property by paying the balance due plus expenses.
3. The Bankruptcy Reform Act is a federal law that applies to all states. Three or more creditors whose unsecured claims against a debtor total at least $5,000 may file an involuntary petition if the debtor has twelve or more creditors. If there are fewer than twelve creditors, the petition may be filed by one or more creditors whose total claims amount to at least $5,000.
4. A debtor in a bankruptcy proceeding may have to appear and testify at a meeting of the creditors, each of whom generally file a proof of claim listing the money owed to them. A trustee-in-bankruptcy is appointed by the bankruptcy judge to collect the debtor's assets (the estate), set apart the debtor's exempt property, liquidate the nonexempt property, and make a final report to the bankruptcy judge.
5. A wage earner's plan under Chapter 13 allows an individual debtor, including a sole proprietor, to file a voluntary petition to avoid a straight bankruptcy, providing that he or she has *regular income* and unsecured debts of less than $100,000 and secured debts of less than $350,000. A wage earner's plan may provide for less than full payment for certain unsecured claims.
6. A business reorganization under Chapter 11 allows a corporation or partnership to file a voluntary bankruptcy petition and continue in business as a debtor in possession. After filing the petition, the debtor files a Chapter 11 plan that may alter the rights of creditors. The bankruptcy court will hold a confirmation hearing on the plan, allowing creditors to raise objections to it. After the hearing, the debtor and creditors are bound by the plan, which allows the reorganized corporation to continue in business.
7. The social objective served by the bankruptcy law is to allow an *honest* debtor, as an individual or a business association, to be resolved of its debts and, with a fresh start, to pursue a constructive contribution to society.
8. A bulk sale transfer is a transfer, not in the ordinary course of the transferor's business, of a major part of the materials, supplies, merchandise, or other inventory of an enterprise. The buyer of the materials must demand from the seller a list of the seller's business creditors and must give them timely notice of the sale. Failure to do so results in an ineffective sale, which allows the creditors to recover the inventory sold or divide the sale proceeds.
9. A surety is a party primarily liable to the creditor for the debtor's

obligations. The creditor may proceed directly against the surety without attempting to first collect the money owed from the debtor.

10. A guarantor is a party secondarily liable for the debts of another and must pay the creditor only if the debtor refuses to do so.

Key Terms

attachment 665
bulk sale transfer 679
Chapter 11 plan 679
confirmation hearing 678
discharge 674
dunning letter 664
financing statement 669
guarantor 681
involuntary bankruptcy petition 674
lien 667
proof of claim 674
purchase money security interest 667
redemption 671
repossession 667
security agreement 667
suretyship 681
wage earner's plan 678

Questions on Ethics

1. Assume that your company is owed a number of outstanding consumer debts. You suggest they be sent out to a collection agency, but your boss refuses because of the restrictions of the Fair Debt Collection Practices Act that apply to outside debt collectors. How would you persuade your boss that your company should also follow the collection practices prescribed by the act? Review the restraints on collection procedures under the act and make ethical arguments for them. Suppose your boss is not interested in anything but collecting the debts, regardless of the means used. How do you feel about a boss who determines your ethical values?
2. The law of secured transactions requires the secured party to give notice to the debtor of the intended sale of repossessed goods. Why does our legal system do this? What ethical value is served by informing the debtor of the sale? Why should a secured party have to sell the repossessed collateral in a commercially reasonable manner, which includes method, time, place, and sales price? Are you able to identify the moral values in this legal obligation?
3. Suppose your boss, anxious to collect an outstanding company debt, asks you to write a personal letter to the debtor's employer. You decide to call the debtor first and are informed that this information may prevent him from being promoted. Do you have a legal right to inform the debtor's employer of his outstanding debt? Would you try to assess

the ethical values involved, assuming you may legally inform the employer?

4. What image comes to mind when you read or hear the words *debtor* and *creditor?* Do you have an image of each that causes you to feel that one is more important than the other, one more moral, one more ethical? How much has our legal environment contributed to the creation of that image?
5. Under our state legal system, a creditor who perfects a security interest is given priority over one with an unperfected security interest. If a debtor owes the same amount to three creditors, and one creditor perfects her security interest by filing a financing statement before the others, she will be paid first if the debtor's property has to be sold, even if there are not enough funds to pay the remaining creditors. Is that system of "racing to perfect the security interest" ethically fair?

Questions on Law

1. D, a debtor, has no accumulated wealth; he recently obtained a divorce and his wife got everything. He lives with his parents and pays them $60 per month room and board. He is unemployed and has made several unsuccessful attempts to obtain a job. He does not have a car. He completed three years of college. He receives a $90 per week unemployment benefit. He owes $4,039 plus interest on several educational loans. His total unsecured debt, minus the educational loans, is over $13,000. Is this a sufficient case of "undue hardship" to allow a bankruptcy discharge of the educational loan? Explain your answer. *Matter of Hemmon,* 7 B.C. 63 (1980).
2. In 1971 Raymond Lee borrowed $500 in the form of a National Direct Student Loan to help defray his expenses for attendance at City College, which is part of City University of New York (CUNY). In 1973 Mr. Lee withdrew from school after completing 32 credit hours and began to repay the loan. In 1975, after having paid all but $107 of the loan, Mr. Lee lost his job. He gained employment six months later, but in the interim period of unemployment, he incurred debts of several thousand dollars. In February 1978, Mr. Lee filed a bankruptcy petition, listing liabilities of over $2,000, including the outstanding balance on his student loan. In May 1978, Mr. Lee received a discharge in bankruptcy of all dischargeable debts listed in his petition, including the balance of the City College loan. In June 1978, Mr. Lee was accepted as a B.A. candidate at New York Theological Institute. The Institute agreed to give Mr. Lee advanced standing for the 32 credits he had completed at City College, provided that Mr. Lee produce a transcript of the course work he had completed. Pursuant to CUNY's policy of denying transcripts to individuals who have defaulted on payment of student

loans obtained from CUNY notwithstanding their discharge in bankruptcy, Mr. Lee was advised that his record would not be released. Mr. Lee, the plaintiff, seeks to enjoin the defendant's policy on the ground that it violates the Supremacy Clause, art. VI, cl. 2 of the United States Constitution, and the Equal Protection and Due Process clauses of the Fourteenth Amendment. Decide. *Lee* v. *Board of Higher Ed. in City of New York,* 1 B.R. 781 (1979).

3. Harry Alton is deeply in debt and has decided to file for bankruptcy. He has the following debts: (1) \$800 owed to his landlord for rent due, (2) \$2,000 in alimony payments, (3) \$10,000 on his MasterCard charge account, (4) \$12,000 on an educational loan, (5) \$3,000 owed to the bank for a personal loan, and (6) \$3,000 on federal personal income tax for income that he never reported. If Harry is granted a discharge in bankruptcy, will any of these debts still have to be paid? How would your answer be affected if Harry was granted a discharge in a bankruptcy petition filed five years ago?
4. Jesse McDonald sold the entire inventory of his business to Karen Blackburn for \$150,000. Jesse's twelve business creditors, who were owed a total of \$80,000, were never notified of the sale. Karen was unaware of this and never asked about Jesse's debts. Karen is using the inventory in her own store. What are the rights of Jesse's creditors?
5. Declaring personal bankruptcy is a relatively simple and inexpensive procedure. Because it is fairly common, it has become a rather acceptable thing to do for a person seriously in debt. Some take the position that a discharge of an \$8,000 debt due to a large bank is not a serious thing. Would you file for bankruptcy upon discovering an inability to pay off your debts? What are the alternatives for a debtor?

Suggested Readings

Fisher, "Access to Fair Credit Reports: Current Practices and Proposed Legislation," 19 *American Business Law Journal* 9 (1981).

Fox, "New Hope for Harassed Consumers: The Federal Fair Debt Collection Practices Act of 1977," 18 *American Business Law Journal* 1 (1980).

Huffmire, "Repossession without Judicial Process: What Lies Ahead?" 15 *American Business Law Journal* 319 (1978).

25 Product Liability

[There is] a strong and growing tendency, where there is blame on neither side, to ask, in view of the exigencies of social justice, who can best bear the loss and hence to shift the loss by creating liability where there has been no fault.

—Roscoe Pound

■ LEARNING OBJECTIVES

After you have read this chapter, you should be able to:

1. Understand the law's historic attitude of caveat emptor and privity of contract requirements and why this attitude has been abandoned by the courts.
2. Know the three basic legal theories (negligence, breach of warranty, and strict liability in tort) used in product liability cases today.
3. Be familiar with the concept of market share liability.
4. Know what statutes of limitations and statutes of repose are and the difference between them.

Business Decisions and the Law

The High Cost of Design Defect

Uloth was working on a garbage collection truck. He jumped onto the loading sill at the back of the truck while the trash compactor was operating, and the descending panel of the compactor caught his left foot and dragged it into the hopper, resulting in loss of the foot. Uloth sued the manufacturer of the garbage truck, claiming that it was negligent in its design. Will Uloth recover from the manufacturer under the theory of design defect? See *Uloth v. City Tank Corporation*.

Introduction to Product Liability Law

One area of the law that has undergone tremendous growth and change since the 1960s is *product liability*. Product liability has a broad meaning and encompasses legal actions based on allegations of negligence, breach of warranty under the Uniform Commercial Code, and the concept of strict liability in tort. The basic theory of product liability cases is that sellers may be liable to persons injured by products. An unusual feature of product liability law is that it is almost all common law, and until recently very little legislation in the area had been passed. The question of the extent to which sellers of goods should be liable for injuries caused by their products is one of the most controversial in business law today. In this chapter, you will be introduced to the circumstances under which a seller is liable for injuries caused by products, and you will examine some of the current trends in this important and rapidly changing field.

Legal Background

As we pointed out in chapter 23 on consumer law, under the Uniform Commercial Code, the view of the common law into the twentieth century was summed up in the phrase *caveat emptor* (let the buyer beware). Caveat emptor applied with a vengeance if a buyer was injured by a defective product. In order to recover, the injured buyer had to prove a specific act of *negligence* by the seller that directly resulted in the buyer's injury. Suppose that in the 1800s Ben Buyer bought an oil lamp and on its first use it exploded, even though Ben had followed the instructions. Unless Ben could show the exact cause of the explosion (a defective wick, a defective base, etc.), he could not recover for any injuries caused by the explosion. Furthermore, even if the exact cause of the explosion were known, the only person who had a right to sue for injury caused by the explosion would be the buyer of the product, Ben. If members of Ben's family were injured, they could not recover monetary damages for their injuries directly, although Ben might be able to recover if he had to pay their medical or nursing bills.

The premise of caveat emptor and the doctrine of privity were that risks of product use were allocated on the basis of freedom of contract. In other words, if someone voluntarily purchased a product, there was always a chance something could go wrong and he could be injured by it; a purchaser, in effect, assumed a risk of injury *unless* he could show that the seller had been specifically negligent (i.e., breached a specific duty). Between an "innocent" (non-negligent) seller and an ''innocent'' (nonnegligent) buyer, the buyer bore the risk of loss from injuries caused by products. Some of the reasons given for this policy were that no one can insure that another person will not be injured, and the buyer could always have chosen not to buy the product or to buy a competing product.

In the past hundred years, the allocation of risk has been changed in such a way that it is often said that the rule of law in product liability today is not caveat emptor but ***caveat venditor*** (let the seller beware). The premise of modern product liability law is that the risk of loss for injuries caused by products should not fall on the ''innocent'' buyer, even if the buyer cannot prove exactly what characteristic of the product caused his injury.

This shift in the law represents a rethinking of the role of business in society. Today, through the development of new legal doctrines of product liability, business is being required to absorb much of the costs of both damage to the environment and product-related injuries. In the rest of this section you will study the manner in which the allocation of risk in product injury cases changed as the law developed. You will see how and why the common law requirement of *privity* between buyer and seller have been abolished. Then you will study the three legal bases for product liability recovery today: *negligence, breach of warranty,* and *strict liability in tort.*

Privity Requirements and Product-Liability Law

The common law required that parties to a lawsuit for injuries caused by a product have **privity**—that is, a direct contractual relationship with each other. Usually this requirement meant that the only plaintiff who could sue for damages was the original buyer of the product, and he could only sue the person who sold him the product, not the product's manufacturer, even if the defect in the product was caused by a manufacturing error. In 1916, in *MacPherson* v. *Buick Motor Company,* the eminent jurist Benjamin Cardozo began the erosion of the common-law doctrine of privity when he allowed the buyer of an automobile to sue a car manufacturer for injuries.

MacPherson v. Buick Motor Company

217 N.Y. 382, 111 N.E. 1050 (1916)

Facts

The defendant was a manufacturer of automobiles. It sold an automobile to a retail dealer. The retail dealer resold to the plaintiff. While the plaintiff was in the car it suddenly collapsed. He was thrown out and injured. One of the wheels was made of defective wood, and its spokes crumbled into fragments. The wheel was not made by the defendant; it was bought from another manufacturer. There is evidence, however, that its defects could have been discovered by reasonable inspection, and that inspection was omitted. The charge is one, not of fraud, but of negligence.

Opinion

Judge Cardozo: The question to be determined is whether the defendant owed a duty of care and vigilance to any one but the immediate purchaser. . . . If the nature of a thing is such that it is reasonably certain to place life and limb in peril when negligently made, it is then a thing of danger. Its nature gives warning of the consequences to be expected. If to the element of danger there is added knowledge that the thing will be used by persons other than the purchaser, and used without new tests, then, irrespective of contract, the manufacturer of this thing of danger is under a duty to make it carefully. That is as far as we are required to go for the decision of this case. There must be knowledge of a danger, not merely possible, but probable. It is possible to use almost anything in a way that will make it dangerous if defective. That is not enough to charge the manufacturer with a duty independent of his contract. Whether a given thing is dangerous may be sometimes a question for the court and sometimes a question for the jury. There must also be knowledge that in the usual course of events the danger will be shared by others than the buyer. In such circumstances, the presence of a known danger, attendant upon a known use, makes vigilance a duty. We have put aside the notion that the duty to safeguard life and limb, when the consequences of negligence may be foreseen, grows out of contract and nothing else. *We have put the source of the obligation where it ought to be. We have put its source in the law.* [Emphasis added.]

From this survey of the decisions, there thus emerges a definition of the duty of a manufacturer which enables us to measure this defendant's liability. Beyond all question, the nature of an automobile gives warning of probable danger if its construction is defective. This automobile was designed to go 50 miles an hour. Unless its wheels were sound and strong, injury was almost certain. It was as much a thing of danger as a defective engine for a railroad. The defendant knew the danger. It knew also that the car would be used by persons other than the buyer. This was apparent from its size; there were seats for three persons. Precedents drawn from the days of travel by stagecoach do not fit the conditions of travel today. The principle that the danger must be imminent does not change, but the things subject to the principle do change. They are whatever the needs of life in a developing civilization require them to be.

(The judgment, for the plaintiff buyer, is affirmed.)

Case Questions

1. Why did the court hold that the manufacturer should be liable to the injured buyer?
2. Why did the court reject the common-law privity of contract notion that a buyer could only sue his immediate seller, which would be the car retailer in this case?
3. This case represents a direct departure from all previous law in the area. This decision is in effect a change in norms as they had previously existed. What moral principles was the judge espousing when he commented, "We have put the source of the obligation where it ought to be. We have put its source in the law"?

In the *MacPherson* case, the court concluded that it was in the best interest of society for a manufacturer to be liable to the ultimate buyer of goods, even if the manufacturer and the buyer did not have a direct contractual relationship. The court, therefore, changed the law by abolishing the doctrine of privity in order to make the law better serve the needs of society. Over a period of years, the states gradually followed the reasoning of the *MacPherson* case and abolished the requirement of privity in cases based on negligence, so that today no state uses that doctrine in product liability negligence cases.

When the Uniform Commercial Code was drafted in 1954, it contained provisions limiting the doctrine of privity as it applied to lawsuits based on allegations of *breach of warranty*. The UCC was adopted by all the states (except

Louisiana) in the 1960s, so that today lack of privity is no longer a complete defense in a product-liability case based on beach of warranty. You should note, however (as was discussed in chapter 23), that different states have adopted different versions of the antiprivity provision of the UCC: over half the states limit recovery for breach of warranty to a product buyer or someone in his family or household or his guests, while many states allow recovery by anyone who might reasonably be expected to be affected by the goods.

The third and last theory of modern product-liability law (besides negligence and breach of warranty) is **strict liability in tort.** The concept of strict liability, which developed in the 1960s, has no place for the principle of privity. Under this concept, any seller in a distributive chain (whether manufacturer, wholesaler, or retailer) is liable to any person who is injured by a defective, unreasonably dangerous product, without regard to whether the plaintiff is a buyer of the product or has a personal relationship with the buyer.

Theories of Product Liability

Today, unless a state law places all suits for injuries caused by products into a single statutory cause of action, there are three legal theories that may be used in a product liability suit: negligence, breach of warranty, and strict liability in tort. As you have seen, early common-law product-liability cases were based on allegations of sellers' negligence; the concept of breach of warranty developed in the 1950s and strict liability in tort in the 1960s. In this section, we will examine each of these three legal theories and discuss the nature of proof necessary for recovery under each as well as current issues of interest connected with each theory.

Product Liability Based on Negligence

What Is Negligence?

The tort action of **negligence** is one of the oldest causes of action in civil common law. Negligence consists of a breach of a legal duty by one person that foreseeably exposes the interests of another to an unreasonable risk of harm. The tort of negligence is based on the principle that in order for society to function in an orderly fashion, it is necessary for everyone to conform to society's norms. For example, if a motorist fails to stop for a stop sign, he has breached his duty of care as imposed by traffic laws. This duty was created by society in order to prevent injuries. If the motorist's running the sign results in injury to a pedestrian or to the driver of another car who was lawfully in the intersection, he has breached his duty of care and will be liable for money damages to the injured parties for commission of the tort of negligence.

The major requirements for recovery for the tort of negligence are that the plaintiff must prove that (1) a duty existed, (2) a breach of the duty occurred in a specific way, (3) the injury caused by the breach of the duty was foreseeable, and (4) the breach of the duty was the proximate cause of the plaintiff's injury. Before we discuss these specific requirements of plaintiff's proof, which are often referred to as *elements,* it may be helpful to you to point out that the tort of negligence is perhaps the most common basis of litigation in our court system today. Some of the most common types of cases in which negligence is alleged are automobile accident cases, professional malpractice cases (especially medical malpractice), and product-liability cases. Although the common thread binding together these different types of cases may be difficult to see at first, the basic premise in all of them is breach of a duty and resulting injury, whether it is failure to obey traffic laws, failure to adhere to standards of a profession in dealing with patients or clients, or failure to make a product that is reasonably safe for its intended use.

The difficulty of proving breach of a duty varies depending on the nature of the case. Courts have developed some doctrines to help plaintiffs to meet this proof requirement. It has long been accepted that an action that violates a statute constitutes what is known as *negligence per se,* and proof of that violation generally shows the required breach of a duty. Proving how the breach of a duty occurred may not be difficult in some types of negligence cases, but it has caused difficulty in some product liability cases, especially when the product was destroyed when the plaintiff's injury occurred. This problem of proving the exact cause of the plaintiff's injury, and proving that this cause resulted from a defendant's lack of care, has been overcome in many cases by use of the doctrine of *res ipsa loquitur* and the development of an alternative tort action based on the concept of strict liability. These concepts will be discussed in the next section.

The concepts of foreseeability and proximate cause are conceptually difficult and intricate. Basically, they require that a defendant's breach of a duty directly cause an injury and that the nature of the injury be something that a reasonable person might expect. For example, suppose that while A is using his electric lawnmower as a hedge trimmer, a sharp stick is thrown through the air and injures the eye of N, A's neighbor. Is the lawnmower manufacturer liable for N's injuries for not installing more safety equipment on its lawnmowers? The answer is clearly no, because a reasonable person would not foresee that a lawnmower would be used as a hedge trimmer, and lack of safety equipment could not be said to be the direct cause of N's injuries (improper use of the mower by A was the direct cause). Proof of the elements of negligence in product liability cases has produced certain special problems for plaintiffs, some of which we will now examine.

The Doctrine of *Res Ipsa Loquitur*

As was pointed out earlier, one problem that can prevent an injured plaintiff from recovering in a product liability case is the requirement that the plaintiff prove the exact cause of his injury. Often the product that causes the injury is destroyed or changed in character by the event in which the plaintiff is hurt. For example, a plaintiff might be injured in a car crash that he alleges was caused by improperly manufactured brakes. Suppose the brakes were twisted and consumed by fire in the crash. The plaintiff can testify that when he put his foot on the brake pedal, the brakes did not hold, but at common law he would be required to prove specifically what aspect of the braking system failed, which he could not do in this situation.

Especially since the 1940s, a legal doctrine has developed that assists plaintiffs in proving negligence. This doctrine is known as ***res ipsa loquitur* (RIL),** "the thing speaks for itself." The basic premise of RIL is that some events just do not occur except in the presence of negligence, and that it may sometimes be appropriate to waive to a certain extent the requirement that a plaintiff prove the exact cause of an injury. The only purpose of *res ipsa loquitur* is to allow a plaintiff to "get to a jury" on the question of the existence of negligence on the part of the defendant. In the past, if a plaintiff could not prove the exact cause of an injury, a judge would often direct a verdict in favor of the defendant, and the plaintiff would not even get a chance to let the jury decide whether negligence was present. (For a discussion of directed verdicts, see chapter 3.)

The doctrine of *res ipsa loquitur* states that a plaintiff who proves all of the following three elements will be legally entitled to have a jury decide whether a defendant was negligent: (1) the event that injured the plaintiff ordinarily does not occur except when negligence is present, (2) the instrumentality that caused the accident was under the sole control of the defendant, and (3) the plaintiff was not contributorily negligent. To use the same example discussed a moment ago, the plaintiff could get to the jury in the case of the allegedly defective brakes by showing: (1) ordinarily brakes work to slow a car when pressure is applied to the brake pedal, (2) the brakes had not been adjusted or undergone any change since leaving the control of the manufacturer and/or retailer, and (3) the plaintiff had not engaged in any activity that would make the brakes defective (like tampering or improper maintenance). The jury could then decide whether the defendant was negligent and whether the plaintiff was entitled to a recovery. Due to its nature, increased use of RIL has not meant that more plaintiffs recover in negligence cases, but it has meant that more plaintiffs have a chance of recovering.

Design Defect as Negligence

Throughout most of the history of product liability and in most product-liability cases today, the basic theory upon which plaintiffs rely in suing for negligence is that goods were improperly manufactured—that is, that they did not function as they were intended to. In our faulty brakes example, the allegation of the plaintiff was that brakes *failed*. Especially since the 1970s, plaintiffs have often alleged in product-liability cases that a manufacturer was negligent in his *design* of a product. These plaintiffs argue that the finished product may have met the manufacturer's specifications, but the specifications were inadequate, and the manufacturer was negligent by not changing the design of the product to keep from exposing potential users to an unreasonable risk of harm. For example, assume the manufacturer of a piece of machinery that punches holes into metal sheets designs the machine with no guard to protect the machine operator from having his hand accidentally "punched." If the operator is injured by the machine, he could sue on the theory that it was foreseeable that someone could accidentally put his hand into the machine and cause injury to himself, and that the manufacturer was, therefore, negligent in not designing the machine in a manner that would prevent this accident from happening.

The problem with such **design-defect** cases, from a manufacturer's point of view, is that a jury may use *ex post facto* (after the fact) analysis in deciding what types of injuries could have been prevented by design modifications. To address the problem raised by design-defect cases, many states have begun to allow what is known as **state-of-the-art defenses.** This term embodies several different concepts. A state-of-the-art design could be one that meets all governmental requirements at the date of manufacture, or it could be one that is commonly used in a particular industry, or it could be the best design technologically and/or economically feasible at the time the product was designed and manufactured. Allowing negligence cases to be litigated on a theory of design defect represents a policy decision by the courts to use the law to ensure product user safety, even at the expense (in one form or another) of increased producer costs. Allowance of a state-of-the-art defense, on the other hand, recognizes that there is a limit to the precautions a manufacturer can reasonably be expected to take in designing products.

Breach of the Duty to Warn as Negligence

It is now well established that a manufacturer or other seller may be liable for negligence if it fails to *warn* of potential hazards associated with product use. In fulfilling its **duty to warn,** the seller must not only include instructions for proper use (e.g., DO NOT EXPOSE TO WATER), but it appears it must also anticipate foreseeable misuse of the product and make specific warnings to attempt to forestall such misuse (e.g., THIS PRODUCT CONTAINS SMALL PARTS. KEEP OUT OF THE REACH OF CHILDREN). As you will see in the following case, however, even if a warning is made, it may not protect the manufacturer from liability. While many sellers have been found negligent for breach of the duty to warn, you should keep in mind that in duty to warn and also in design-defect cases, the requirement of foreseeability of injury may limit a defendant's liability. The following case concerns the issues of design-defect liability and the legal effect of warnings.

Uloth v. City Tank Corp.

384 N.E.2d 1188 (Mass. 1978)

Opinion

Judge Abrams: Uloth was injured while working on the Loadmaster 316, a refuse body designed and manufactured by City Tank and Old Dominion. The refuse body had been installed on a used truck chassis supplied by Uloth's employer, the town of Amesbury, and was used for collecting trash. . . . On the day of the accident one of the regular crew members of the Loadmaster 316 became ill, and Uloth volunteered to fill in for him. The laborer working with Uloth had been on the job for one week, and Uloth was given the responsibility for operating the hydraulic packing unit on the back of the truck.

Uloth operated the lever once without incident. Then, ten minutes after starting work, Uloth signalled the driver to put the truck in neutral and activate the switches in the cab. When this was done, Uloth operated the lever on the side of the truck and lit a cigarette. When he heard the engine noise increase and saw the truck move a little, Uloth assumed that the truck was about to move ahead, and leaped onto the rear step of the truck. He lost his balance, his left foot went toward the loading sill, and the descending panel caught his left foot and dragged it into the trash hopper. Uloth's foot was severed from his leg.

City Tank and Old Dominion argues that the judge erred in denying their motions for directed verdicts and for judgments notwithstanding the verdicts on the issue of design negligence. They assert that, in order to establish design negligence, Uloth had to prove that the Loadmaster 316 did not function as intended. They contend that the Loadmaster 316 functioned precisely as intended, and therefore, as a matter of law, was not negligently designed. City Tank and Old Dominion read *Schaeffer* v. *General Motors Corp*. . . . (1977) as compelling such a result.

We do not read Schaeffer as establishing a rule that a product which functions as intended may not be negligently designed. A designer has a duty "to design the machine with reasonable care. . . ." In Schaeffer, the "testimony of the plaintiff's expert did not raise an issue of fact regarding a design defect making the differential unsafe for its intended use." Schaeffer did not offer proof that the differential could have been designed to perform the same function in a safer fashion. In this case Uloth did present evidence of several design changes which would have reduced the danger of the Loadmaster 316 without significant reduction in the efficiency of the machine; thus Schaeffer does not govern the outcome of Uloth's case.

In our view the focus in design negligence cases is not on how the product is meant to function, but on whether the product is designed with reasonable care to eliminate avoidable dangers. We reject the suggestion that we adopt a rule that design negligence turns solely on whether a product functions as intended. Such a rule would mean that there would be no liability for negligent design of a product which functioned as intended but which was designed in a fashion more dangerous than need be. Liability, however, would be imposed on a designer who tried to reduce the risk by designing and using safety features which for some reason did not function as intended. Such a rule would discourage designers from attempting to reduce the hazards from machinery. We do not think such a rule is a practical solution to the problems posed by design negligence in product liability cases.

City Tank and Old Dominion next argue that a designer's primary obligation is to warn of the dangers of his product. They assert that a designer may reasonably expect a user to heed a warning and avoid injury. Moreover, they claim that there is no duty to warn of an obvious danger, for there is adequate warning implicit in the obviousness of the danger. City Tank and Old Dominion point out that the dangers of the shear point on the Loadmaster 316 were obvious, and that the jury found they did not negligently fail to warn of the dangers of the machine. Thus, they conclude that the judge should have granted their motions for directed verdicts or judgments notwithstanding the verdicts. City Tank and Old Dominion ask us to adopt a rule that there can be no negligent design if the danger is obvious or if adequate warnings are given.

An adequate warning may reduce the likelihood of injury to the user of a product in some cases. We decline, however, to adopt any rule which permits a manufacturer or designer to discharge its total responsibility to workers by simple warning of the dangers of a product. Whether or not adequate warnings are given is a factor to be considered on the issue of negligence, but warnings cannot absolve the manufacturer or designer of all responsibility for the safety of the product. However, in some circumstances a warning may not reduce the likelihood of injury. For example, where the danger is obvious, a warning may be superfluous. A designer may have no duty to warn of such dangers.

Moreover, a user may not have a real alternative to using a dangerous product, as where a worker must either work on a dangerous machine or leave his job. Further, a warning is not effective in eliminating injuries due to instinctual reactions, momentary inadvertence or forgetfulness on the part of a worker. One of the primary purposes of safety devices is to guard against such foreseeable situations.

Balanced against the somewhat limited effectiveness of warnings is the designer's ability to anticipate and protect against possible injuries. If a slight change in design would prevent serious, perhaps fatal injury, the designer may not avoid liability by simply warning of the possible injury. We think that in such a case the burden to prevent needless injury is best placed on the designer or manufacturer rather than on the individual user of a product. "In today's world, it is often only the manufacturer who can fairly be said to know and to understand when an article is suitably designed and safely made for its intended purpose. . . . A casting of increased responsibility upon the manufacturer, who stands in a superior position to recognize and cure defects, for improper conduct in the placement of finished products into the channels of commerce furthers the public interest."

We reject any inflexible rule that negligent design of an obviously dangerous product precludes finding a manufacturer or a designer liable. "The manufacturer of the obviously defective product ought not to escape because the product was obviously a bad one. The law, we think, ought to discourage misdesign rather than encouraging it in its obvious form."

In sum, the judge correctly denied City Tank and Old Dominion's motions for directed verdicts. We decline to hold that there can be no negligence in design if the product performs as intended, or if there are warnings found to be adequate, or if the dangers are obvious. We hold that these factors should be considered by a jury in evaluating a claim of design negligence. But there is a case for the jury if the plaintiff can show an available design modification which would reduce the risk without undue cost or interference with the performance of the machinery.

Judgment affirmed.

Case Questions

1. Why did the court find liability based on design defect?
2. Why were warnings not sufficient to insulate the manufacturer from liability?
3. Do you think the result would have been different if redesign was ruinously expensive?

Defenses to Product-Liability Negligence Actions

In addition to the state-of-the-art defense just discussed, two other common-law defenses that are often used in product-liability actions are contributory negligence and assumption of the risk.

Contributory negligence occurs when a person's actions contribute to the likelihood that he will be injured by another's negligence. For example, use of a product by a member of a **specially susceptible class** may produce an injury, but if the person knew that use of the product might produce some injury to himself, he could be said to have contributed to his own injury. For example, suppose that Irma Jones, who knows she is allergic to strawberries (therefore susceptible to an injury), buys some Strawberry Essence shampoo. Irma knows, based on past experience, there might be a risk she will break out with a rash if the shampoo contains real strawberry extract, but she decides to take the chance. Her reaction to the shampoo is so severe that she gets a rash all over her face, resulting in such a swelling of her eyelids that she cannot see for a week. Since Irma knew about a possible allergic reaction, she can be said to have been *contributorily negligent*. Courts have generally been unwilling to allow the defense of contributory negligence to bar plaintiff recovery when the amount of the plaintiff's contributory negligence seems small in comparison to the amount of the defendant's negligence and the extent of the plaintiff's injuries.

Assumption of the risk occurs when a person knows an action is dangerous, but does it anyway. One particularly difficult area involving assumption of the risk in product-liability cases involves misuse of the product. Suppose a product's instructions carry a warning that the product must be cleaned after every use. If a person used the product repeatedly without cleaning, he could be said to have assumed a risk of injury. However, in product-liability cases there is often a reluctance to accept assumption of the risk as a defense, especially if the scope of the injury was severe and seemed to go beyond what was reasonably foreseeable.

One reason that both contributory negligence and assumption of the risk have been looked on with disfavor by many courts is that, at common law, these two defenses were a complete bar to recovery by the plaintiff. Today, a growing number of courts are using the doctrine of **comparative negligence** in assessing the liability of parties in a negligence suit. Under comparative negligence, which is used most frequently in automobile accident cases, the relative negligence of the parties is assessed and the plaintiff's award is reduced by the amount of his contributory negligence (or the amount to which he assumed the risk). The policy that the doctrine of comparative negligence embodies is that if a person was injured mostly through the fault of another, the injured party should not be totally barred from recovery.

Product Liability Based on Breach of Warranty

Article 2 of the Uniform Commercial Code, concerning sales of goods, establishes that when goods are sold, certain guarantees or promises (warranties) may be made about the goods. Warranties are discussed at length in chapter 23, so in this chapter only an overview of warranty law as it relates to injuries caused by products will be presented.

Creation of Warranty Liability under Article 2 of the Uniform Commercial Code and the Federal Magnuson-Moss Warranty Act

Under the Uniform Commercial Code, there are two types of warranties that may be the basis for a product-liability suit, express and implied. An **express warranty** is created when a seller describes goods, makes a promise or affirmation about them, or shows a sample or model of them. A seller does not have to make an express warranty, and unless he acts in one of the three ways mentioned, no express warranty is created under the UCC. The federal Magnuson-Moss Warranty Act also does not require creation of express warranties, although it does mandate that they be in a certain form if they are given.

There are two types of **implied warranties** under the UCC: warranty of merchantability and warranty of fitness for a particular purpose. These two warranties are said to be *implied* because the seller does not have to do or say anything to create them; they are created by operation of law whenever a sale occurs. The **warranty of merchantability** is only made by a merchant seller, not a casual seller who ordinarily does not deal in goods of the type he is selling. Basically, this warranty applies if the goods are of fair, average quality and are reasonably fit for ordinary purposes. The **warranty of fitness for a particular purpose** is created when a buyer relies on the expertise of the seller in deciding to purchase goods. In order for this warranty to apply, the seller must know of the buyer's particular purpose in purchasing the goods, and it must be reasonable for the buyer to rely on the seller's "expertise," but the seller does not have to be a merchant.

The federal Magnuson-Moss Warranty Act does not mandate the creation of either express or implied warranties; it assumes they will be created (if at all) under the UCC. The Magnuson-Moss Warranty Act provides for creation of "full" or "limited" warranties, at the seller's option. Perhaps the most important provisions of the Act concern the circumstances under which product warranty liability can be disclaimed, a subject that will be discussed in the next section.

Disclaimers of Warranties and Product Liability

One of the most troubling aspects of the Uniform Commercial Code from a consumer standpoint has been that it is possible for a seller to *disclaim* (destroy or limit) warranty liability. A very important provision of the UCC that has been of great benefit to plaintiffs in product-liability cases is Section 2–719(3), which provides that consequential damages may not be limited or excluded if that limitation is unconscionable (against public policy). The code's drafters have followed the principle adopted in *Henningsen* v. *Bloomfield Motors,* which is presented in chapter 23, or consumer law, that limitation on recovery for personal injuries caused by products under warranty is unconscionable and unenforceable. The *Henningsen* case, was decided by the New Jersey Supreme Court in 1960, before New Jersey adopted the UCC. This case, which refused enforcement of a disclaimer limiting liability for personal injury caused by a defective automobile, was the basis for UCC Section 2–719(3).

The Magnuson-Moss Warranty Act adopts the UCC rule regarding the unconscionability of personal injury disclaimers. Magnuson-Moss also supersedes the UCC by making it more difficult for sellers to disclaim warranties, especially implied warranties. Under Magnuson-Moss, if a seller elects to give a full warranty, he cannot disclaim implied warranties; and if a seller elects to give a limited warranty; he may limit the duration of implied warranties to the term (time period) of any express warranties if the seller is permitted to do so by state law.

The existence of warranties has been a great boon to injured product users, because the user does not have to show specifically what aspect of the product caused the injury, as he does in negligence actions. However, due to the fact that no warranty or only a limited warranty may be given when a product is sold, and due to the fact that some types of consequential damages (other than personal injury) may be excluded, a party cannot always rely on a legal action for breach of warranty to obtain damages for personal injuries caused by defective products.

Product Liability Based on Strict Liability in Tort

Background

In the 1916 case of *MacPherson* v. *Buick Motor Company,* presented earlier, Justice Cardozo based the rejection of the privity requirement in product-liability cases on acknowledgment of the changing "needs of life in a developing civilization." The development of the concept of strict liability in tort in product-liability cases is an example of how the courts changed the law to make it responsive to what the courts viewed as the changing needs of society regarding use of manufactured products. The concept of strict liability in tort is not new; it has been applied to cases involving food and drink sales since the Middle Ages, and to cases involving blasting since the nineteenth century. "Strict liability" is sometimes referred to as "liability without fault," because in strict-liability tort cases, unlike those involving the tort of negligence, a plaintiff does not have to prove the specific cause of an injury. You will remember the example from the section on negligence of the car with the allegedly defective brakes: unless the plaintiff could use the doctrine of *res ipsa loquitur,* he would generally have to prove that the brakes were defective and prove how they were defective in order to recover damages for injuries. The concept of strict liability in tort relieves the plaintiff from the requirement of proving exactly how his injury occurred; thus, the plaintiff does not have to prove the defendant's "fault."

The development of the concept of strict liability in tort in product-liability cases is unusual in the history of the law because, unlike the development of many other legal doctrines, it is possible to pinpoint exactly when the doctrine took its modern form. This concept was first enunciated by the California Supreme Court in 1963 in the case of *Greenman* v. *Yuba Power Products, Inc.*, and it was spelled out in its present form in 1965 when the American Law Institute adopted section 402A of the Second Restatement of Torts. The basis of the *Greenman* decision, presented here, is a policy judgment that between an "innocent" injured product user and the product seller, it is the seller who should bear the monetary loss caused by the injury. The *Greenman* case was used by the principal drafter of the Second Restatement of Torts, Dean William Prosser, as the basis for including in the restatement section 402A, which defines the requirements for proof of strict liability in tort in product liability cases.

Greenman v. Yuba Power Products, Inc.

Supreme Court of California, 59 Cal. 2d 57, 377 P.2d 897 (1963)

Facts

Plaintiff brought this action for damages against the retailer and the manufacturer of a Shopsmith, a combination power tool that could be used as a saw, drill, and wood lathe. He saw a Shopsmith demonstrated by the retailer and studied a brochure prepared by the manufacturer. He decided he wanted a Shopsmith for his home workshop, and his wife bought and gave him one for Christmas in 1955. In 1957 he bought the necessary attachments to use the Shopsmith as a lathe for turning a large piece of wood he wished to make into a chalice. After he had worked on the piece of wood several times without difficulty, it suddenly flew out of the machine and struck him on the forehead, inflicting serious injuries. About ten and one-half months later, he gave the retailer and the manufacturer written notice of claimed breaches of warranties and filed a complaint against them alleging such breaches and negligence.

Opinion

Judge Traynor: A manufacturer is strictly liable in tort when an article he places on the market, knowing that it is to be used without inspection for defects, proves to have a defect that causes injury to a human being. Recognized first in the case of unwholesome food products, such liability has now been extended to a variety of other products that create as great or greater hazards if defective.

We need not recanvass the reasons for imposing strict liability on the manufacturer. The purpose of such liability is to insure that the costs of injuries resulting from defective products are borne by the manufacturers that put such products on the market rather than by the injured persons who are powerless to protect themselves. Sales warranties serve this purpose fitfully at best. In the present case, for example, plaintiff was able to plead and prove an express warranty only because he read and relied on the representations of the Shopsmith's ruggedness contained in the manufacturer's brochure. Implicit in the machine's presence on the market, however, was a representation that it would safely do the jobs for which it was built. Under these circumstances, it should not be controlling whether plaintiff selected the machine because of the statements in the brochure, or because of the machine's own appearance of excellence that belied the defect lurking beneath the surface, or because he merely assumed that it would safely do the jobs it was built to do. It should not be controlling whether the details of the sales from manufacturer to retailer and from retailer to plaintiff's wife were such that one or more of the implied warranties of the sales act arose. "The remedies of injured consumers ought not to be made to depend upon the intricacies of the law of sales." To establish the manufacturer's liability it was sufficient that plaintiff proved that he was injured while using the Shopsmith in a way it was intended to be used as a result of a defect in design and manufacture of which plaintiff was not aware that made the Shopsmith unsafe for its intended use.

The judgment for the plaintiff is affirmed.

Case Questions

1. When does the doctrine of strict liability in product-injury cases apply?
2. According to the court, what is the purpose for adopting the theory of strict liability?
3. This case is fundamentally concerned with risk allocation. What moral judgments does the court make concerning the question of who should fear the risk of financial loss in product-injury cases?

Strict Liability in Tort under Section 402A of the Second Restatement of Torts

Section 402A of the Second Restatement of Torts, which establishes strict liability in tort in product-liability cases, states:

> Sec. 402A (1) One who sells any product in a defective condition unreasonably dangerous to the user or consumer or to his property is subject to liability for physical harm thereby caused to the ultimate user or consumer, or to his property, if (a) the seller is engaged in the business of selling such a product, and (b) it is expected to and does reach the user or consumer without substantial change in the condition in which it is sold. (2) The rule stated in Subsection (1) applies although (a) the seller has exercised all possible care in the preparation and sale of his product, and (b) the user or consumer has not bought the product from or entered into any contractual relation with the seller.

As discussed earlier, the primary purpose of strict liability in tort is to dispense with the requirement that an injured product user establish specific fault on the part of a seller. That section 402A embodies Justice Traynor's *Greenman* rationale of risk allocation against the seller is made clear by section 402A's statement that the seller will be liable even if he has exercised all possible care in the preparation and sale of his product. Although a plaintiff does not have to prove specific fault under section 402A, there are certain requirements or elements that he must meet: it must be proven that (1) the product was in a defective condition when it left the seller's control, (2) the product was unreasonably dangerous, (3) the seller was a merchant (not a casual seller), and (4) there was no substantial change in the product between the time it left the defendant's control and its use by the consumer. We will discuss some of the more important legal points that have developed in applying section 402A. First, however, please note that the Second Restatement of Torts is not a federal or state statute, nor is it a recommended state statute like the Uniform Commercial Code. Section 402A has been adopted into the common law of the states by court decision. As of the late 1980s, only a tiny minority of state courts had completely refused to adopt section 402A.

The primary element a plaintiff must prove in a strict-liability case is that the product was in a defective condition when it left the control of the seller and that it did not undergo substantial change between the time it left the seller's control and the time it caused the plaintiff's injury. Just as you saw in the discussion on the tort of negligence, courts have held that a product can be *defective* under section 402A if it fails to work as it was supposed to or, in many cases, if it was designed improperly. Thus, a lawnmower whose blade comes off after only a few uses would obviously be defective, but so, in many states, would be a mower that did not have a guard to keep the person pushing the mower from coming in contact with the revolving blade.

The requirement that the product be unreasonably dangerous is distinct from the requirement that the product be defective. An illustration of the difference between the concepts of "defective" and "unreasonably dangerous" might be made in the case of an injury caused by a sliding glass door. Suppose that such a door has not been manufactured according to government or trade specifications, so that when P walks into it, it shatters and P is cut. In this case, since the door did not meet the state of the art, it is defective, and this defect made the door unreasonably dangerous. Suppose, however, that P walks into a door that meets all current safety requirements and it does not shatter, but P breaks her nose on impact. Can P recover? At least one state in a similar case has held that P cannot recover because the product was not defective (it did not shatter) and the court did not deem the danger to be unreasonable. The question of when a product is unreasonably dangerous presents special problems, because some products are by their nature dangerous—for example, a knife. Given that a knife is inherently dangerous, when will a seller be liable for injury caused by it? The answer in many cases has been that liability will be imposed in cases of injuries caused by inherently dangerous products only if the product is both defective and the danger is unreasonable for the type of product. A person who accidentally cut herself with a knife could not recover damages—unless the cut resulted from the blade separating from the handle due to a manufacturing defect.

Defenses to an Action Based on Strict Liability under Section 402A

Questions about the nature of defenses to a strict-liability action under section 402A have not been resolved by the courts at present. Of course, some defenses naturally arise from the failure of a plaintiff to prove the elements for recovery required under section 402A. For example, the plaintiff must prove that the defendant is a merchant, that is, one regularly engaged in selling goods, whether that seller is a manufacturer, wholesaler, or retailer.

Courts have seemed to be sympathetic to defenses based on obvious misuse of products in strict-liability cases, just as in negligence cases. However, as in negligence cases, a manufacturer who fails to warn potential users of foreseeable hazards, including foreseeable misuse of the product, cannot defend against a charge of strict liability by claiming the product was misused. As in negligence, there is also a problem with specially susceptible groups (e.g., allergic persons). Suits by specially susceptible persons have been successfully defended when the susceptible group was very small and the seller gave adequate warnings of potential hazards connected with use of the product by members of the special group. Concerning warnings, however, you should keep in mind that, unlike warranty law, a seller cannot disclaim and a buyer cannot waive her rights to sue under strict liability in tort.

A question that courts have had to face is whether the common-law defenses of contributory negligence and assumption of the risk are applicable in strict-liability cases. The comments to section 402A state that contributory negligence is not a defense to an action under strict liability in tort when such negligence consists merely of a failure to discover the defect in the product or to guard against the possibility of its existence. Irrespective of this statement, some states have allowed a defense of contributory negligence when the plaintiff misused the product. Courts have also allowed assumption-of-the-risk defenses in strict-liability cases in which the risk of use was obvious and the plaintiff knowingly and willingly assumed the risk. For example, if a person was using an electric power tool and noticed sparks coming from the electrical cord, but decided to use the tool while pulling it across a patio containing puddles of water, he could be said to have assumed the risk of electric shock. It should be noted that courts have tended to allow these common-law defenses only in states that have adopted (by statute of court decision) the comparative-negligence approach to apportioning damages in personal injury cases. In these states, contributory negligence and assumption of the risk are not automatically complete bars to recovery, as they were at common law, but their existence will affect the amount of the award an otherwise meritorious candidate will receive. For example, suppose a jury finds that a plaintiff suffered damages of $100,000 for injuries caused by a defective product, but that it also finds that if the plaintiff had not misused the product, his injuries would have been 30 percent less severe. Under a comparative-negligence approach, the plaintiff will be allowed to recover $70,000. Notice that if this same plaintiff had sued under the theory of negligence at common law, he would have recovered nothing, because contributory negligence was a complete defense; under a strict reading of section 402A, on the other hand, the plaintiff might be able to recover the full $100,000 (if using electric cords in the manner described could be interpreted as a mere failure to discover a defect in the product).

Trends in Product-Liability Law

The Product-Liability "Crisis"

With the adoption by states of the Uniform Commercial Code's warranty provisions in the 1960s and the Restatement of Torts concept of strict product liability in the late 1960s and early 1970s, the number of lawsuits filed to recover damages for product-related injuries increased, as did the size of the awards recovered by plaintiffs. By the mid-1970s, sellers began to complain more and more about the number of product-liability cases and especially about the significant increases in the liability premiums charged by insurance companies. These problems continued unabated and escalated during the 1980s. Some businesses felt that they could no longer afford the skyrocketing premiums and began to consider "going bare" (not having insurance). One of the major problems faced by business and insurance carriers has been that each state has different product-liability laws, so that a case with the same facts would produce different results if tried in different states. For example, as you have seen, some states allow defenses to strict liability in tort, some do not; some states make it easier to disclaim liability for implied warranties than others.

As is usually the case, dilemmas such as these produce societal responses, and, as you have seen throughout this book, a common tendency in the United States is to respond by changing the law. This phenomenon of legal response to a societal issue is occurring with regard to product liability. We will now discuss a recent trend in United States common law that extends the boundaries of product-liability law even further, and we will also discuss recent state and proposed federal action that could restrict or change this area of the law.

Before we begin our discussion of these recent legal developments, it should be noted that a controversy continues to exist over whether there is or ever has been a product-liability "crisis" for business. During the 1970s and early 1980s, there was surprisingly little data available on this very important question. A very interesting report was issued in 1982 by the Institute for Civil Justice of the Rand Corporation. This report resulted from a study of nearly twenty thousand civil cases that were tried in Cook County, Illinois, between 1959 and 1979. One of the types of civil cases on which data was collected in this study was product-liability cases.

The Rand study found that although there was a large increase in the number of product-liability cases filed during the period (146 percent), there was a similar overall increase in the number of all cases filed, and product-liability cases made up only about 6 percent of the total number of civil cases filed. Interestingly, the study indicated that most product liability case plaintiffs lost their cases, with the highest success rate (achieved at the end of the study period) being 38 percent. Of course, from a manufacturing and insurance industry standpoint, the number of cases filed is in one sense more critical than the number of cases lost, since businesses must bear the costs of defending a suit, whether they win or lose. The average damages award for successful product-liability plaintiffs increased 146 percent during the period, but the average award for all types of civil cases increased 136 percent. The one striking feature that was unique to product-liability cases in the Rand study was the *size* of the average damages award: during the entire study period, product-liability cases almost consistently maintained the highest average award of any type of civil case, and the actual amount of an average product-liability award was $377,000 between 1975 and 1979.

A 1987 article by the Research Director of the Institute for Civil Justice of the Rand Corporation generally confirmed the 1982 Rand findings. The product-liability cases were divided into two categories: what might be characterized as "routine" product-liability cases and what were referred to as "mass latent injury torts." Mass latent injury torts would include such cases as asbestos exposure and use of the Dalkon Shield interuterine device, both of which have been alleged to produce severe personal injury. A steady growth in the number of "routine" product-liability cases filed was observed in the 1987 article, with a notable increase in plaintiffs' chances of winning, and a sharp increase in the amount of damages awards recovered by successful plaintiffs. In the area of mass latent injury torts, the evidence indicated that the number of cases filed tended to explode once the problem was identified. For example, in 1981 there were 16,000 cases relating to asbestos exposure, and by 1986 there were over 30,000. Similarly, there were 7,500 Dalkon Shield cases in 1981, and by 1986 over 300,000 claims had been filed against the manufacturer of the Shield, who had filed for protection under the bankruptcy laws. The 1987 article indicated that fear of exposure to toxic substances might "create a deluge of litigation in future years."

The effect of product-liability litigation on business was discussed in publications by the Conference Board, a business organization. In 1987, a Conference Board survey of the nation's five hundred largest businesses showed that 25 percent had removed products or services from markets in response to increased corporate tort liability. A 1988 Conference Board report, "The Impact of Product Liability," cited various statistics informative on the business response to product-liability litigation: 40 percent of the chief executives surveyed said that the reality and threat of lawsuits against their products had a major impact on their operations; 36 percent said that they had dropped product lines because of the possibility of suits; 15 percent had laid off workers; and 8 percent said that they had closed down production facilities. Over half of the executives surveyed for the 1988 report said that the current United States liability system had a big impact on their ability to compete on world markets. In regards to the the number of product-liability suits filed in the United States, as opposed to foreign countries, Dow Chemical Company noted that while half of the company's annual sales were earned abroad, it was sued in 1987 on product-liability issues only 4 times in foreign countries, versus 456 suits in the United States. One notable exception to the dearth of foreign suits is the legal proceedings growing out of the worst product-liability disaster in history: the release of poisonous gas from a Union Carbide factory in Bhopal, India, in 1984, which resulted in over 3,300 deaths and injuries to tens of thousands. In 1989, Union Carbide agreed to an Indian court order in the case that provided for payment of $470 million in settlement of all claims.

Whether the changes in the business environment created by the increase in product-liability litigation and recoveries amounts to a "crisis" may well be a matter of speculation. However, an important response to the changes in this area was pressure by the business and insurance communities for legislative changes in product-liability laws, since, as previously noted, the majority of change in the area had come through judicial decisions. The most notable legislative changes as of the late 1980s have been through the passage of state product-liability or "tort reform" laws, which are discussed below.

Market Share Liability

Perhaps the most important development in product-liability law in recent years has been the creation of the concept of **market share liability:** the idea that if more than one manufacturer could have made the product that caused an injury, liability for that injury should be divided among the manufacturers according to the share of the market each held at the time the injury occurred. This concept originated in California and grew out of the so-called DES daughter phenomenon: many daughters of women who took the drug diethylstilbestrol (DES) while they were pregnant developed cancer upon reaching adulthood. The drug was on the market between 1947 and 1971. Remember it was not the mothers, but the daughters who developed the cancer, so that there was an average delay time of some twenty years between exposure to the harmful product and manifestation of the injury. In the late 1970s, when scientists began to make a causal connection between maternal ingestion of DES and cancer in the daughters, the daughters began filing suit against the manufacturers of DES, who included almost all of the major pharmaceutical producers in the country. The plaintiffs faced many obstacles to recovery, but the most important one is that under any of the three theories of product liability, the plaintiff must identify the seller. Although the daughters could prove that their mothers had taken DES, it was often impossible to prove specifically which manufacturer had produced the drug. The DES daughters were therefore unsuccessful in their early suits, until the California Supreme Court issued the following decision in *Sindell* v. *Abbott Laboratories*.

Sindell v. Abbott Laboratories

Supreme Court of California, 607 P.2d 924 (1980)

Facts

A separate cause of action alleged that defendants were jointly liable regardless of which particular brand of DES was ingested by plaintiff's mother because defendants collaborated in marketing, promoting, and testing the drug, relied upon each other's tests, and adhered to an industry-wide safety standard.

Opinion

Justice Mosk: . . . DES was produced from a common and mutually agreed upon formula as a fungible drug interchangeable with other brands of the same product; defendants knew or should have known that it was customary for doctors to prescribe the drug by its generic rather than its brand name and that pharmacists filled prescriptions from whatever brand of the drug happened to be in stock. . . .

Plaintiff seeks compensatory damages of $1 million and punitive damages of $10 million for herself. For the members of her class, she prays for equitable relief in the form of an order that defendants warn physicians and others of the danger of DES and the necessity of performing certain tests to determine the presence of disease caused by the drug, and that they establish free clinics in California to perform such tests. . . .

This case is but one of a number filed throughout the country seeking to hold drug manufacturers liable for injuries allegedly resulting from DES prescribed to the plaintiffs' mothers since 1947. According to a note in the *Fordham Law Review,* estimates of the number of women who took the drug during pregnancy range from 1½ million to 3 million. Hundreds, perhaps thousands, of the daughters of these women suffer from adenocarcinoma, and the incidence of vaginal adenosis among them is 30 to 90 percent. . . .

. . . Should we require that plaintiff identify the manufacturer which supplied the DES used by her mother or that all DES manufacturers be joined in the action, she would effectively be precluded from any recovery. As defendants candidly admit, there is little likelihood that all the manufacturers who made DES at the time in question are still in business or that they are subject to the jurisdiction of the California courts. There are, however, forceful arguments in favor of holding that plaintiff has a cause of action.

In our contemporary complex industrialized society, advances in science and technology create fungible goods which may harm consumers and which cannot be traced to any specific producer. The response of the courts can be either to adhere rigidly to prior doctrine, denying recovery to those injured by such products, or to fashion remedies to meet these changing needs. Just as Justice Traynor in his landmark concurring opinion in *Escola* v. *Coca Cola Bottling Company* (1944) . . ., recognized that in an era of mass production and complex marketing methods the traditional standard of negligence was insufficient to govern the obligations of manufacturer to consumer, so should we acknowledge that some adaptation of the rules of causation and liability may be appropriate in these recurring circumstances. . . .

The most persuasive reason for finding plaintiff states a cause of action is that . . . as between an innocent plaintiff and negligent defendants, the latter should bear the cost of the injury. . . .

From a broader policy standpoint, defendants are better able to bear the cost of injury resulting from the manufacture of a defective product. As was said by Justice Traynor in *Escola,* "[t]he cost of an injury and the loss of time or health may be an overwhelming misfortune to the person injured, and a needless one, for the risk of injury can be insured by the manufacturer and distributed among the public as a cost of doing business. . . ." The manufacturer is in the best position to discover and guard against defects in its products and to warn of harmful effects; thus, holding it liable for defects and failure to warn of harmful effects will provide an incentive to product safety. . . .

But we approach the issue of causation from a different perspective: we hold it to be reasonable in the present context to measure the likelihood that any of the defendants supplied the product which allegedly injured plaintiff by the percentage which the DES sold by each of them for the purpose of preventing miscarriage bears to the entire production of the drug sold by all for that purpose. Plaintiff asserts in her briefs that Eli Lilly and Company and five or six other companies produced 90 percent of the DES marketed. If at trial this is established to be the fact, then there is a corresponding likelihood that this comparative handful of producers manufactured the DES which caused plaintiff's injuries, and only a ten percent likelihood that the offending producer would escape liability.

If plaintiff joins in the action the manufacturers of a substantial share of the DES which her mother might have taken, the injustice of shifting the burden of proof to defendants to demonstrate that they could not have made the substance which injured plaintiff is significantly diminished. . . .

The presence in the action of a substantial share of the appropriate market also provides a ready means to apportion damages among the defendants. Each defendant will be held liable for the proportion of the judgment represented by its share of that market unless it demonstrates that it could not have made the product which caused plaintiff's injuries. In the present case, as we have seen, one DES manufacturer has dismissed from the action upon filing a declaration that it had not manufactured DES until after the plaintiff was born. . . .

Under this approach, each manufacturer's liability would approximate its responsibility for the injuries caused by its own products. . . .

[R]eversed.

Justice Richardson, Dissenting: I respectfully dissent. In these consolidated cases the majority adopts a wholly new theory which contains these ingredients: The plaintiffs were not alive at the time of the commission of the tortious acts. They sue a generation later. They are permitted to receive substantial damages from multiple defendants without any proof that any defendant caused or even probably caused plaintiff's injuries.

Although the majority purports to change only the required burden of proof by shifting it from plaintiffs to defendants, the effect of its holding is to guarantee that plaintiffs will prevail on the causation issue because defendants are no more capable of disproving factual causation than plaintiffs are of proving it. "Market share" liability thus represents a new high water mark in tort law. The ramifications seem almost limitless, a fact which prompted one recent commentator, in criticizing a substantially identical theory, to conclude that "Elimination of the burden of proof as to identification [of the manufacturer whose drug injured plaintiff] would impose a liability which would exceed absolute liability. . . ." In my view, the majority's departure from traditional tort doctrine is unwise. . . .

Case Questions

1. What is the theory of *market share liability?*
2. How are a plaintiff's damages allocated among defendants when the theory of market share liability is used?
3. The *Sindell* case is based on the premise that an innocent injured plaintiff should be able to recover from somebody. Is it ethical to subject a number of manufacturers to liability when it is likely that only one of them is liable?

Since the *Sindell* decision in 1980, a number of state and federal courts have found for DES daughter plaintiffs using a market share liability rationale, although a number of other courts have specifically rejected the market share liability theory. In 1988, in *Brown* v. *Superior Court,* the California Supreme Court refused to extend the market share theory to become joint and several liability. Under a joint and several liability theory, one DES manufacturer could be liable for the entire amount of the judgment in favor of a plaintiff, even though its market share at the time of the ingestion of DES was relatively small. The court reiterated its *Sindell* position that the manufacturer should be responsible only for the proportion of the judgment represented by its market share, and its overall liability for injuries caused by DES should approximate the injuries caused by the DES it manufactured. The court observed that imposition of joint and several liability among manufacturers in a market share action would frustrate *Sindell*'s goal of achieving a balance between the interests of DES plaintiffs and manufacturers of the drug. Also in *Brown,* the California Supreme Court refused to rule that each defendant's liability should be "inflated" in proportion to its market share in an amount sufficient to ensure that the plaintiff would recover the entire amount of the judgment.

As the dissent in *Sindell* points out, this concept is a revolutionary one in the law. It has always been fundamental in Anglo-American jurisprudence that no person can be legally liable for an act unless it is satisfactorily proven that he committed the act. Yet under *Sindell,* a company can be held liable for damages because it *might have* produced a drug that caused harm—because it had a share of the market for the product. The rationale on which the *Sindell* case was decided is the same one that developed throughout the history of product liability law beginning with *MacPherson* v. *Buick Motor Company:* that between an innocent plaintiff and negligent defendants, the defendants should bear the cost of injury. Thus, you can see that the study of the development of product-liability law is a study of the development of public policy and the manner in which society adjusts its formal norms to meet changing circumstances. Whether the concept of market share liability will be upheld in the DES cases or expanded into other cases is unclear at this writing, since it represents quite a departure from standard procedures for assessing legal liability.

State Statutes Regulating Product Liability

One of the main responses to a perceived product-liability crisis, which developed in the 1970s, was to begin lobbying for passage of statutes to provide statutory, as opposed to common-law (court) regulation of the product-liability area. Courts are generally bound to follow a constitutional statute in lieu of the common law if such a statute exists. Business has continued to advocate passage of state and federal laws in this area. In the latter half of the 1970s, many states began to pass various types of statutes regulating to some extent the conduct of product-liability cases in their courts. In the 1980s, focus shifted toward "tort reform" legislation, which limited recovery of damages to some extent in all types of tort actions, including personal injury and malpractice as well as product-liability cases. In this section we will examine some of these state laws, and in the next section we will examine proposed federal action.

One idea that has been adopted by many states is that of a **consolidated product-liability statute.** Without such a statute, plaintiffs in all states generally file suit alleging all three theories of product liability (negligence, breach of warranty, and strict liability). A problem that often arises is that slightly different procedural requirements must be met in order to allow a plaintiff a chance of recovery under each theory, the most important requirement being compliance with the appropriate statute of limitations. A **statute of limitations** establishes a maximum time for instituting a lawsuit. Tort and contract actions often have different statute of limitation periods. For example, a state may allow a buyer to sue for breach of warranty up to four years from the date of sale of a product, but allow only a two-year limitation for filing a lawsuit when the tort of negligence occurs. It is possible, therefore, that a plaintiff would have longer to sue in a product-liability case based on breach of warranty than on negligence, but the facts of that plaintiff's case might make it easier to recover under the negligence theory than under warranty. A consolidated statute-of-limitations statute establishes a single time limitation for suing for an injury caused by a product, no matter what theory of liability is used. Of course, not all states that have adopted a consolidated statute of limitations have adopted the same time limit.

One of the most important developments in state statutory regulation of product-liability actions is the enactment in many states of so-called **statutes of repose.** Statutes of repose set a time limit on the duration of a seller's liability for injury caused by products, with this limit generally beginning on the date the product was sold. The purpose of statutes of repose is to deal with the problem of "tail end" liability for "old" products. For example, many statutes of repose establish a presumption that a seller is no longer liable for injuries caused by a product ten years after it is sold. Statutes of repose are therefore different from statutes of limitations, because statutes of repose could leave an injured plaintiff without a legal remedy. Suppose a state has a ten-year statute of repose. If a person is injured eleven years after a product is sold, she probably cannot institute a lawsuit to recover damages, but if she is injured nine years after the sale, the statute of repose does not apply and under the usual statute of limitations, she would then have two years from the date of her injury to file suit.

The following case is a decision by the New Hampshire Supreme Court regarding the constitutionality of the New Hampshire consolidated product-liability statute.

Heath v. Sears, Roebuck & Co.

464 A.2d 288 (N.H.)

Opinion

Justice Douglas: The plaintiffs in these consolidated appeals challenge the constitutionality of RSA chapter 507-D, governing suits for injuries caused by defective products.

In case No. 82-170, Clifford Heath was using a Sears drive ratchet to tighten the lug-bolt nuts while changing a rear tire on a logging skidder. The direction-change lever on the ratchet head snapped in two and a piece of the lever struck him, causing the near total loss of sight in one eye. The lever previously had been removed and reattached, allegedly because the metal used by the manufacturer was not suitable for northern climates and contracted in extremely cold weather. The United States District Court for the District of New

Hampshire, where the complaint was filed, transferred two questions to us by certification under Supreme Court Rule 34: Whether a "foreseeable repair" is a "modification or alteration" within the meaning of RSA 507-D:3, and whether that statutory section violates the equal protection provisions of either the State or the Federal Constitution.

In case No. 82-203, Roger Kidder was injured and permanently disabled after an accident involving a crane manufactured in 1958. Writs were brought against two prior owners and sellers of the crane for failure to disclose certain defects. The case was dismissed below by the Superior Court, acting upon the recommendation of a Master, because of the twelve-year statute of limitations contained in RSA 507-D:2, II(a).

In case No. 82-275, Norman Mallet was severely injured when his hand was drawn into a vertical rotary cutting disc attached to a milling machine. Both his action and the separate loss of consortium action filed by his wife were dismissed by the Superior Court under the three-year limitation provision of RSA 507-D:2, I and :5. The plaintiffs challenge the three-year limitation as well as the "state of the art" defense set forth in RSA 507-D:4.

In case No. 82-314, Sears, Roebuck & Co., as a defendant in another products liability case not presently before this court, seeks indemnity against the White Rogers Division of Emerson Electric Co., alleging that the latter's defective gas control valve caused an explosion in a wall heater which injured a Hampton, New Hampshire resident. This case was dismissed by the Superior Court as not timely filed under RSA 507-D:2, III and :5.

In case No. 82-458, Charles Eastman, a New Hampshire resident, was injured in 1979 when a piece of a saw blade broke off and struck him in the eye. Because suit was filed more than twelve years after the Massachusetts manufacturer parted with control of the saw, the United States District Court for the District of New Hampshire transferred to us the question whether RSA 507-D:2, II(a) violates part one, article fourteen of the New Hampshire Constitution.

In case No. 82-485, Michael Welch was injured in an accident involving a Japanese motorcycle. His case was also transferred here by the Federal District Court for a determination of the constitutionality of the statute of limitations for products liability actions.

In case No. 82-497, William Cunningham, a paraplegic patient at the Veteran's Administration Hospital in Manchester, was sitting on a portable commode when it collapsed, causing his leg to fracture. Again, the case was transferred here by the Federal District Court to determine the constitutionality of RSA 507-D:2, I.

All of these cases were consolidated for oral argument, and briefs from amici were filed as well. After the above cases were argued orally, cases Nos. 83-053 and 83-093 were filed in this court and consolidated for decision, without briefs or oral argument.

In case No. 83-053, Ethel Holt suffered permanent injuries from an explosion and fire in a mobile home that had been purchased from Raiche Mobile Homes, Inc., in March 1968. The suit was filed in June 1982, alleging that a defective bottled-gas cooking system in the mobile home caused the explosion and fire. The case was dismissed by the Superior Court on the basis of the twelve-year limitation period provided in RSA 507-D:2, II(a), the constitutionality of which is being challenged on appeal.

Finally, in case No. 83-093, Francis Linehan was killed in December 1979 in an accident involving a forklift manufactured by Clark Equipment Corp. and a tractor-trailer manufactured by International Harvester Co. Wrongful death actions were filed in December 1981, within the two-year limitation period of RSA 556:11. Nevertheless, based on a Master's recommendation, the Superior Court dismissed the suits because they were instituted more than twelve years after the defendants parted with possession or control of their machines or sold them. The decedent's administrator argues that RSA 507-D:2, II(a) is unconstitutional.

I. THE EVOLUTION OF PRODUCTS LIABILITY LAW

The law of products liability is of relatively recent origin. It has been noted, in fact, that a scholarly commentator could remark as late as 1955 that " '[p]roducts liability does not rank as a term of art in the courts of law.' " Under Roman law at the time of Justinian, the vendor's liability turned upon whether he knew of the defect. By the thirteenth century in England, the growth of crafts in a feudal agricultural society led to concern in the law for "quality good after the fashion of the day."

The maxim "caveat emptor" first appeared in *Moore* v. *Hussey* (1601). For the next few centuries in this country and in England, the buyer had best beware. Even during the early years of this century, an action generally could not lie against a "remote" manufacturer with whom the buyer had not directly entered into a contract (lack of "privity"). W. Prosser, *Handbook of the Law of Torts.* Where privity existed, negligence was the standard for recovery for personal injuries.

The Industrial Revolution during the nineteenth century led to the products liability revolution in this century, which began when a Scotsman named Donald MacPherson was injured after a wheel fell off his new 1910 Buick automobile. His $5,000 verdict was appealed on the ground that, because MacPherson had bought the Buick from a dealer instead of from Buick Motor Company, he should not be allowed to sue the manufacturer with whom he did not stand in privity. In the famous opinion by Justice Cardozo, then of the New York Court of Appeals, the manufacturer who placed the item into the stream of commerce was held to be "responsible for the finished product." *MacPherson* v. *Buick Motor Co.* (1916).

In New Hampshire, we adopted the doctrine of strict liability in tort fourteen years ago in *Buttrick* v. *Arthur Lessard & Sons, Inc.* (1969).

The reasons for the evolution of the law in the area of products liability are many. We live in an era of national advertising and of nationwide distribution which can add or remove a product from our store shelves in a matter of days. Many of those nationally sold products contain chemical compounds and synthetics the side effects of which clearly cannot be anticipated. It is believed that if today's products are capable of causing illness or physical injury, the risk of liability is best borne by the companies that profited from their sale, rather than by the unfortunate individual consumers. *Buttrick* v. *Lessard, Greenman* v. *Yuba Power Products, Inc.* (1963).

As Justice Holmes noted, the life of the law is experience, and the modern experience with consumer products has been one of ever-improving technology and rising standards of living, but also of injury and death:

"Americans—20 million of them—are injured each year in the home as a result of incidents connected with consumer products. Of the total, 110,000 are permanently disabled and 30,000 are killed. A significant number could have been spared if more attention had been paid to hazard reduction. . . .

The exposure of consumers to unreasonable consumer product hazards is excessive by any standard of measurement." Deterrence is also a valid consideration; without the stimulus of plaintiffs' products liability actions, the incentive to improve products and make them safer would not exist.

The recent rise in products liability claims and lawsuits has resulted in a corresponding increase in insurance rates for those making or selling products. This, in turn, led our own legislature in 1978 to enact a "products liability" law in the interest of protecting manufacturers who, it was believed, were being unduly burdened by rapidly rising insurance rates. It is significant that, during debate, a number of legislators expressed skepticism about the fairness of a State products liability law and about its effectiveness in stabilizing insurance rates for New Hampshire manufacturers. This concern about the legislation's effectiveness was based on the fact that most products manufactured in New Hampshire are sold in other States, and on the belief that the high insurance premiums paid by in-State manufacturers were attributable to the proliferation of lawsuits in larger industrialized States.

In fact, in conjunction with the enactment of RSA chapter 507-D, the New Hampshire Legislature authorized the creation of a fifteen-member Commission to Study Product Injury Reparations (commission) for the purpose of evaluating the legislation's effect on products liability insurance rates. The legislature directed the commission to issue a final report by January 1, 1980, on the following matters: (1) the effectiveness of RSA chapter 507-D "in improving the availability and affordability of products liability insurance"; (2) "other existing laws and practices which bear on the availability and affordability of such insurance"; and (3) "such changes as may be necessary to increase availability and affordability of such insurance, while at the same time allowing just compensation to those suffering injury from products."

The commission issued its final report on December 21, 1979, finding that it was "very difficult to assess the impact of RSA 507-D on the problems of availability and affordability" of products liability insurance. At the time of the report, the commission found that the "panic" rise in manufacturers' insurance rates had ended *nationwide,* and not just in New Hampshire, thereby tending to show that the State legislation was not the cause of the stabilization of rates. In conclusion, the commission stated that "[t]he problems of product liability insurance affordability and availability have eased, but it seems unlikely that this relaxation is attributable to the enactment of RSA 507-D."

Against this background, we now turn to the specific challenges raised by these consolidated cases.

II. THE STATUTES OF LIMITATIONS FOR PRODUCTS LIABILITY ACTIONS.

The constitutional challenges in these cases focus principally upon the twelve-year "statute of repose" in RSA 507-D:2, II(a) and the three-year limitation provision of RSA 507-D:2, I. Generally, both federal and State courts recognize the power of legislative bodies to enact statutes of limitations which prescribe a reasonable time within which a party is permitted to bring suit for the recovery of his right. The United States Supreme Court has stated:

> It may be properly conceded that all statutes of limitation[s] must proceed on the idea that the party has full opportunity afforded him to try his right in the courts. A statute could not bar the existing rights of claimants without affording this opportunity; if it should do so, it would not be a statute of limitations, but an unlawful attempt to extinguish rights arbitrarily, whatever might be the purport of its provisions.

The concept of allowing a reasonable period of time for suit to be brought after the cause of action arises is not new in our law, for along with "substantive rights, the first settlers brought over the incidental rights of adequate remedy and convenient procedure." Thus, the "right to an adequate remedy [exists] for the infringement of a right derived from the unwritten law." When it came time to establish a post-revolution form of government, the first part of our Constitution was devoted to chronicling our inherent rights. Part one, article fourteen of the New Hampshire Constitution provides:

> Every subject of this state is *entitled to a certain remedy,* by having recourse to the laws, for *all injuries he may receive* in his person, property, or character; to obtain right and justice freely, without being obliged to purchase it; completely, and without any denial; promptly, and without delay; conformably to the laws. [Emphasis added.]

In an effort to facilitate the vindication of tort victims' rights, legislatures and courts have developed the "discovery" rule, under which a cause of action does not accrue until the plaintiff discovers or, in the exercise of reasonable diligence, should have discovered both the fact of his injury and the cause thereof (see *United States* v. *Kubrick,* 444 U.S. 111 [1979]). The rule is premised on "the manifest unfairness of foreclosing an injured person's cause of action before he has had even a reasonable opportunity to discover its existence."

Although the legislature's power is broad in determining how long a plaintiff may have to initiate a cause of action and when that limitation period begins to run, this power may not be exercised in an unconstitutional manner. In *Carson* v. *Maurer* (1980), we held that, although not a fundamental right, "the right to recover for personal injuries is . . . an important substantive right." Thus, the classifications there at issue were required to be "reasonable" and to "rest upon some ground of difference having a fair and substantial relation to the object of the legislation. . . ."

In *Carson,* we ruled that the legislature's extension of the discovery rule to some medical injury plaintiffs, while denying its applicability to others, constituted an impermissible discrimination between classes of plaintiffs. We therefore held that RSA chapter 507-C violated the equal protection provisions of our Constitution to the extent that it limited application of the rule to only a narrow class of medical-malpractice plaintiffs.

More recently, in *Henderson Clay Products, Inc.* v. *Edgar Wood & Associates, Inc.* (1982), we struck down RSA 508:4-b insofar as it precluded application of the discovery rule against architects, but allowed its application against materialmen and suppliers of labor. Relying upon *Carson,* we concluded:

> It is difficult to rationally permit a situation to exist whereby the supplier of labor and material has a liability exposure for a period of six years after the injury has been discovered or, in the exercise of due care, should have been discovered when, at the same time, the designers of the premises can be immunized from the liability before the cause of action even accrues or can be factually asserted.

Here, too, our standard of review is whether the statute-of-limitations provisions contained in RSA 507-D:2 are reasonable and are substantially related to the legislative objective or reducing products liability insurance rates.

RSA 507-D:2, II(a), the twelve-year "statute of repose," requires a products liability action to be brought not "later than 12 years after the manufacturer of the final product parted with its possession and control or sold it, whichever occurred last." The effect of this absolute limitation on suits against manufacturers is to nullify some causes of actions before they even arise. As compared with nonproducts liability causes of action, which generally must be brought within six years after they accrue, *whenever* that may be, *see* RSA 508:4, we hold that the twelve-year bar imposed by RSA 507-D:2, II(a) is neither reasonable nor substantially related to the object of the legislation.

The twelve-year limit is unreasonable because the mere purchase of pills produced by a drug manufacturer in California, or of a defective automobile made in Michigan, does not place the consumer on notice of a hidden defect injurious to his health or safety. When product defects lead to injury, our law has long provided for recovery without regard to when the substance or object was made or placed into the national or international stream of commerce. This is particularly important in cases where the injuries may not clearly manifest themselves until years later, such as the clear-cell adenocarcinomas found in the daughters of mothers who twenty or more years previously took a female estrogen pill commonly known as DES (diethylstilbestrol).

The unreasonableness inherent in a statute which eliminates a plaintiff's cause of action before the wrong may reasonably be discovered was noted by Judge Frank in his dissent in *Dincher* v. *Marlin Firearms Co.* (2d Cir.1952), in which he condemned the "Alice in Wonderland" effect of such a result:

> Except in topsy-turvy land, you can't die before you are conceived, or be divorced before ever you marry, or harvest a crop never planted, or burn down a house never built, or miss a train running on a non-existent railroad. For substantially similar reasons, it has always heretofore been accepted, as a sort of logical 'axiom,' that a statute of limitations does not begin to run against a cause of action before that cause of action exists, i.e., before a judicial remedy is available to a plaintiff.

Nor do we think that the twelve-year "statute of repose" is substantially related to a legitimate legislative object. As previously noted, the crisis in products liability insurance had abated nationwide independent of RSA chapter 507-D. Nonetheless, persons injured by defective products are deprived arbitrarily of a right to sue the manufacturers responsible for those defective products by virtue of a statute that has become entirely divorced from its underlying purpose. Cf. *Boucher* v. *Sayeed* (R.I.1983) (medical malpractice crisis existing at time of enactment but not at time of suit was insufficient basis to uphold statute against equal protection challenge). We do not believe that the legislature may constitutionally bar suits against manufacturers by products liability plaintiffs, as a class, twelve years after the manufacturer sold or parted with control of the product, while allowing other plaintiffs to recover for personal injuries not related to a defective product, at any time within six years after the cause of action accrues.

Our sister States of Alabama, Florida, and North Carolina have come to the same conclusion under similar provisions of their State Constitutions.

The plaintiffs also challenge the three-year statute of limitations established in RSA 507-D:2, I. This three-year period begins to run from the "time the injury is, or should, in the exercise of reasonable diligence, have been discovered by the plaintiff." As previously mentioned, personal actions generally must be brought within six years of the time they accrue, with the exception of libel or slander actions, to which a three-year limit applies. RSA 508:4 (Supp.1981). We do not think that merely because a manufactured product causes the injury, or because the cause of action is legislatively defined as a "product liability action," *see* RSA 507-D:1, I, a plaintiff's injury is therefore different from any other injury.

For instance, in the context of an automobile collision case, it makes no sense to say that for that part of an injury caused by another driver's alleged negligence a six-year statute applies while a product defect that may have been a factor in causing the harm to the plaintiff is subject to a three-year statute. Libel and slander were and are separate common-law torts which may reasonably be distinguished for statute of limitations purposes; however, there is no tort called "products liability."

For the reasons stated in our analysis of the twelve-year "statute of repose," we hold that RSA 507-D:2, I also denies products liability plaintiffs equal protection of the laws. This is not to say that the legislature could not constitutionally establish a statute of limitations of three years for all personal injury actions if it so desired. However, it may not constitutionally discriminate against one class of plaintiffs for the purpose of protecting manufacturers by means of a statute of limitations which is neither reasonable nor substantially related to a legitimate legislative object.

The last statute-of-limitations provision under attack in these cases, RSA 507-D:2, III, requires third-party claims in products liability cases to be initiated within ninety days of the end of the time periods set forth in paragraphs I and II of that section. To the extent that the statute of limitations for third-party actions is dependent upon RSA 507-D:2, I and II(a), which we have already ruled invalid, we further hold that RSA 507-D:2, III (Supp. 1979) is unconstitutional.

Although the validity of the remaining provisions of RSA 507-D:2 (Supp. 1979) has not been questioned in the cases before us, these provisions would appear to be subject to the same constitutional infirmity as the provisions actually challenged on appeal. Nor are the provisions of the section severable from one another, due to their interrelationship. Accordingly, we must void RSA 507-D:2 in its entirety.

III. MODIFICATION OR ALTERATION OF PRODUCTS.

Next, we turn to RSA 507-D:3, which provides that a "defendant may be held liable only for harm that would have occurred if the product had been used in its unaltered and unmodified condition and shall not be held liable for harm arising in any part from alteration and modification of the product by another." Alterations or modifications based on the manufacturer's specifications or instructions do not bar the plaintiff's cause of action.

The plaintiffs maintain that this section violates the equal protection provisions of our State Constitution in two respects. First, they argue that the challenged provision denies persons injured by modified or altered products the same right to recover for personal injuries that is available to other products liability plaintiffs. Second, they contend specifically that RSA 507-D:3 impermissibly distinguishes between persons injured as a result of product *modification* and persons injured as a result of product *misuse*. For the reasons stated below, we rule section three of the products liability statute to be unconstitutional.

Under our decision in *Thibault* v. *Sears, Roebuck & Co.* (1978), the parties to a products liability action are entitled to have the jury "*compare* the causal effect of the defect in the product or design with the affirmative defense of misconduct of the plaintiff and *allocate* the loss. . . ." RSA 507-D:3, however, provides that a defendant "shall not be held liable for harm arising *in any part* from alteration and modification of the product by another." This provision thus operates to establish an absolute defense in products liability cases where the modification or alteration of the product contributes in any way to the plaintiff's injury, regardless of the dangerousness of the product or the insignificance of the modification. Consequently, RSA 507-D:3 denies to persons injured by modified products the same right of apportionment and at least partial recovery provided to all other products liability plaintiffs in *Thibault.*

Moreover, RSA 507-D:3 distinguishes impermissibly between plaintiffs injured by *modified* products and plaintiffs injured by *misused* products. Under current New Hampshire law, a plaintiff may recover some percentage of his damages where his misuse of a product did not contribute more to the accident than did the manufacturer's conduct, and the misuse is found to have been foreseeable to the manufacturer. This holds true whether the product is misused by the plaintiff, see *Thibault* v. *Sears, Roebuck & Co.,* or by a third party. In contrast, RSA 507-D:3 by its own terms bars recovery altogether by plaintiffs whose "misconduct" takes the form of modification or alteration not in accordance with the manufacturer's specifications or instructions, irrespective of how foreseeable such a modification may have been.

The overall effect of RSA 507-D:3 is both arbitrary and inequitable. For example, the statute would totally bar recovery by the plaintiff in case No. 82-170, who was injured when using a *modified* Sears tool, simply because a modification contributed to the injury. Yet if the same plaintiff had received the identical injury as a result of actually *misusing* an *unmodified* wrench, he would be entitled to sue the manufacturer and have the jury consider the foreseeability of such misuse in the balance of comparative responsibility. As we noted in *Thibault,* the term "plaintiff's misconduct" includes, "where applicable, product misuse or abnormal use" as well as the older concept of "assumption of the risk" or "voluntarily and unreasonably proceeding to encounter a known danger." Obviously, whether modified or not by a plaintiff, a product may be misused or altered from its foreseeable use to such a degree as to absolve the manufacturer of liability. But these are questions of fact to be resolved by the trier of fact.

While RSA 507-D:3 may result in some slight benefit to manufacturers, such an effect is clearly outweighed by the severe restriction of plaintiffs' right to recover for injuries caused by modified or altered products. We conclude that RSA 507-D:3 denies equal protection of the laws under the New Hampshire Constitution and is therefore invalid.

IV. THE STATE OF THE ART DEFENSE.

RSA 507-D:4 codifies what is known in products liability law as the "state of the art" defense. Under this section of the statute, "it is an affirmative defense that the risks complained of by the plaintiff were not discoverable using prevailing research and scientific techniques under the state of the art and were not discoverable using procedures required by federal or state regulatory authorities charged with supervision or licensing of the product in question. Discoverability of risks shall be measured as of the time the manufacturer parted with possession and control of, or sold the product in question, whichever occurred last."

The plaintiffs have raised a general objection to this provision on equal protection grounds. One assertion raised by the plaintiffs is that RSA 507-D:4 codifies current industry practice as the standard by which "discoverability of risk" is to be measured. We find this contention to be without merit.

It has long been recognized that because entire industries may lag behind in the development of safer and technologically feasible alternatives, "custom and usage" is an unsound standard of liability. The legislative history of RSA 507-D:4 indicates the legislature's intent to reject mere compliance with current industry practice as a defense to liability. Instead, RSA 507-D:4 holds a defendant in a products liability action to the standard of technological feasibility at the time of sale or distribution.

In recent years, some courts have held manufacturers liable for defects which, at the time of sale, were "scientifically unknowable." See, e.g., *Beshada* v. *Johns-Manville Products Corp.* (1982). By imposing what amounts to "absolute" liability upon manufacturers, such judicial decisions sever the traditional connection between tort liability and fault. To hold Ford Motor Company to today's standard of scientific knowledge when determining liability for an injury caused by a Model T bought in 1921 appears to us to be clearly unreasonable.

We view a properly worded "state of the art" defense as being a rational means of addressing manufacturers' reasonable objection to application of modern legal concepts and scientific knowledge to products made decades ago. We therefore find it both reasonable and constitutionally permissible to raise an affirmative defense based upon "discoverability of risk" as measured by the "state of the art" at the time of distribution or sale.

We note that the standard enunciated in RSA 507-D:4 is consistent with our decision in *Thibault v. Sears, Roebuck & Co.,* as well as with the judicial actions of many of our sister States. As we stated in *Thibault,* "strict liability is not a no-fault system of compensation. The common-law principle that fault and responsibility are elements of our legal system applicable to corporations and individuals alike will not be undermined or abolished" solely by a concept of spreading of risk and cost in this State.

Despite the constitutional validity of RSA 507-D:4 viewed in isolation, the question of its severability from the portions of the products liability statute which have been stricken, remains. Indeed, the plaintiffs have asserted that if we find enough of RSA chapter 507-D to be unconstitutional, we should follow our decision in *Carson v. Maurer* and strike down the statute in its entirety. We agree.

In *Carson,* we addressed the severability of the unconstitutional provisions of RSA chapter 507-C, the medical-malpractice statute, from the remainder of that statute. We stated that we were "not sure that the remaining provisions of RSA ch. 507-C would have been enacted without the rest." Accordingly, the entire statute was stricken.

Here, too, we are not sure whether the legislature would have enacted a "state of the art" defense in the absence of all of the unconstitutional provisions of the products liability statute. We must therefore leave that question to the legislature. Because we have stricken the remainder of the substantive sections of the statute, we void the entire chapter.

In light of our holding that RSA chapter 507-D is void in its entirety, the plaintiffs' argument that the retrospective application of the chapter under RSA 507-D:5 is unconstitutional is moot.

Nos. 82-203, 82-275, 82-314, 83-053, and 83-093 are reversed and remanded; Nos. 82-170, 82-458, 82-485, and 82-497 are remanded to the United States District Court.

All concurred.

Case Questions

1. Why did the court invalidate the New Hampshire statute of repose?
2. Why did the court accept in general the statutory "state-of-the-art" defense?

During the mid-1980s, many of the same business and insurance groups that had advocated passage of product-liability statutes began to urge adoption of broader "tort reform" statutes. These laws would apply to all kinds of tort actions, including personal injury and malpractice claims, as well as product liability. The two most common features of these tort reform proposals were limitations on the recovery of damages for such nonphysical or nonmonetary losses as pain and suffering and mental distress, and abolition of the concept of joint and several liability in the payment of tort judgments. The abolition of the concept of joint and several liability would prevent one defendant (tortfeasor) from having to pay the entire judgment in a case, even though his actions were not the primary cause of the plaintiff's injury. As of the end of the 1980s, a number of states had enacted some form of tort reform legislation, and the legality of these statutes had generally been upheld by the courts.

While business has pushed hard for enactment of consolidated product-liability statutes and statutes of repose, such laws have not proven to be a panacea, because not all states have adopted them and their provisions differ among the states that have. The federal government has studied the problems created by the development of product-liability law since the 1970s, and legislation on the subject has been regularly introduced in Congress. However, as of the late 1980s, no comprehensive controlling federal legislation had been enacted.

Federal Action in Product-Liability Law

The federal government's role in dealings with product-liability issues has been fairly limited. There is one federal agency, the Consumer Product Safety Commission, which deals with one aspect of the problem, and two federal task forces have studied the issues raised in this area.

The Consumer Product Safety Commission

The federal *Consumer Product Safety Commission (CPSC)* was created in 1972, primarily to establish safety standards for consumer products and to study the incidence of injuries caused by consumer products. If a particular consumer product does not meet the specifications of the CPSC standard, the manufacturer can be fined or imprisoned for up to one year. If a nonconforming product presents an unreasonable risk of severe personal injury, its distribution can be banned by a federal court at the CPSC's request.

One method the CPSC uses to determine whether new safety standards are needed or whether a product should be banned is the National Electronic Injury Surveillance System (NEISS), a computer system that gathers data on product-caused injuries from hospitals around the country. The CPSC also has the power to inspect records of manufacturers to determine whether issuance of new safety standards or banning of a product is necessary.

Federal Consideration of Product-Liability Issues

The Interagency Task Force on Product Liability was established in 1976 to investigate product liability (remember this was the time when many perceived a "crisis") and to recommend whether Congress should enact laws in this area. After exhaustive study, the Interagency Task Force published the model **Uniform Product Liability Act (UPLA)** in the Federal Register in late 1978. The UPLA is recommended legislation that was meant to be adopted by the states, as the Uniform Commercial Code has been. However, by the time the UPLA became widely disseminated in 1979, most states that had passed any laws in the product-liability area had already enacted statutes, and no state had adopted the UPLA in its entirety. However, as we have noted, some of the main provisions of the UPLA have been adopted by many states, including creation of a consolidated product-liability cause of action, passage of a statute of repose with complementary statute of limitations, and adoption of state-of-the-art or adequate-warning defenses to product-liability suits.

Probably one reason more states have not adopted the UPLA is that the state legislatures are waiting to see if Congress will adopt a federal law that might largely preempt any laws the state might pass. In the 1980s, business and insurance groups have focused on attempting to gain passage of a federal product-liability act, since there is now a perception that almost any federal act would create a uniformity and predictability in the area that would in turn produce a cost savings to industry. Over the past few years, a number of different laws have been proposed in each session of Congress, so it is difficult to make generalizations about what a federal act might do. However, these proposals have tended to incorporate the provisions of the UPLA.

In 1985, the United States Attorney General established a Tort Policy Working Group to study the causes, extent, and policy implications of the "current crisis" in insurance availability and affordability. The report of this group, issued in 1986, documented the difficulties with obtaining affordable insurance, which continued unabated into the 1980s. The group concluded that a major panacea for this problem was so-called tort reform, which could include such actions as eliminating joint and several liability in cases where defendants did not act in concert, limiting such noneconomic damages as pain and suffering to a "fair and reasonable" amount, and providing for periodic instead of lump-sum payments of damages for future medical care or lost income. The group felt that both state and federal legislative action was called for in this area. In the last half of the 1980s, states began adopting a number of tort reform measures similar to the ones suggested by the Tort Policy Working Group.

In 1988, the federal General Accounting Office submitted a briefing report to the Chairperson of the House of Representatives' Subcommittee on Commerce, Consumer Protection and Competitiveness of the Committee on Energy and Commerce, entitled "Product Liability: Extent of 'Litigation Explosion' in Federal Courts Questioned." The GAO found that from 1976 to 1986, the largest annual growth in federal court filings unrelated to asbestos, the Dalkon Shield, and Bendectin occurred between 1979 and 1981, with increases of 18 percent in 1979, 11 percent in 1980, and 17 percent in 1981. From 1976 through 1981, these filings increased at a faster rate than civil filings in general. Since 1981, however, product-liability filings unrelated to those three products were found to have grown at about the same rate as civil filings in general. The GAO report observed that the data seemed inconsistent with the contention that there was a rapidly accelerating growth in federal product-liability filings across a wide range of products. In addition, the data did not shed light on the reasons for the observed growth in filings, nor did it provide a basis for determining whether society is excessively litigious. The GAO concluded that the data did not indicate the extent to which the stated goals of providing equitable outcomes and deterring wrongdoing are fulfilled by the current tort system or would be fulfilled by reforming the current system.

Ethical Issues in Product Liability

Due to the nature of its development, product-liability law, more than any other type of law in the environment of business area, is public policy law. The courts have undertaken to balance the various interests of business' need to make a profit and compete successfully, consumers' need for safe, economical products, and society's need to insure that injured persons will be recompensed as much as possible by the persons responsible for their injuries, in order to avoid their becoming a financial burden on society. Legislatures are grappling with the question of how to balance these interests; they are also debating whether it is appropriate to take the development of this area of the law away from the courts.

In developing various legal theories to deal with issues raised in product-liability cases, the courts have injected the law into areas that were once regarded as purely ethical. There are now legal answers to such ethical questions as, Should manufacturers make their products as safe as possible? and Should sellers warn potential users of possible, but remote, consequences of their product's use?

There remain not only unanswered legal questions, but also unanswered ethical questions in the area of product liability. A few of these are:

Is it in the best interests of society for sellers to be liable to the extent they are now for injuries caused by products?

Is the theory of market share liability ethical? Is it in keeping with the general policy of tort law that people cannot be held legally liable for actions unless it can be proven that they committed the actions?

One result of the development of what business people consider pro-plaintiff product liability law is that manufacturers have hesitated to introduce new products until they are as sure as possible that the products are safe. While this hesitancy is understandable, and perhaps even commendable, in some cases it has delayed introduction of drugs and other products that might be beneficial to society. And in some cases American manufacturers who hesitate to introduce new products could lose sales to foreign manufacturers entering the American market.

The legal and ethical issues involved in the area of product liability are so complex that it should be some time before society is able to sort them out.

The important concepts and terms in this chapter are listed below; page numbers have been provided for the key terms. By reading over each section you can assess your understanding of the chapter concepts and determine areas you may want to review.

Chapter Summary

1. The common law adopted an approach of caveat emptor (let the buyer beware) in the area of product liability and, under the doctrine of privity

of contract, stated that only the buyer of a product could sue the person who sold him the product. Those who used but had not purchased the product could not sue, and buyers could not sue manufacturers who did not sell them the products directly.

2. A person injured by a product today can use one or more of these three legal theories to recover damages: negligence, breach of warranty, and strict liability in tort.
3. In order to recover under the tort of negligence, a plaintiff must prove that: (1) a duty to him existed, (2) a breach of that duty occurred in a specific way, (3) the injury caused by the breach was foreseeable, and (4) the breach of the duty was the proximate cause of the plaintiff's injury.
4. Under the Uniform Commercial Code, a plaintiff who was injured by a product may be able to recover for breach of warranty if she can show a breach of an express or implied warranty.
5. The concept of strict liability in tort is embodied in section 402A of the Second Restatement of Torts, which provides that a commercial seller who sells any product that is in a defective condition and is unreasonably dangerous to the user is liable for physical injury caused by the product if the product does not undergo change before it reaches the consumer.
6. Some courts have adopted a theory of market share liability, under which a plaintiff who cannot show which defendant manufactured a product that caused the seller injury can recover against any manufacturer whose product might have caused the seller's injury.
7. Many states have passed "consolidated" product-liability statutes, which incorporate the three common law product-liability theories into one statutory cause of action. These consolidated statutes often contain a statute of repose, which establishes a specific time limit (usually dating from the time of sale of the product) within which the manufacturer is subject to lawsuits for injuries caused by the product. In the 1980s, states began to pass tort reform statutes as a response to the difficulties of obtaining insurance.

Key Terms

assumption of the risk 697
caveat venditor 689
comparative negligence 697
consolidated product-liability statute 708
contributory negligence 696
design defect 694
duty to warn 694
express warranty 697
implied warranty 697
market share liability 705
negligence 691
privity 689
res ipsa loquitur 693
section 402A 700

specially susceptible class 696
state-of-the-art defenses 694
statute of limitations 709
statute of repose 709
strict liability in tort 691
Uniform Product Liability Act 717
warranty of fitness for a particular purpose 698
warranty of merchantability 697

Questions on Ethics

1. Acme Pharmaceuticals' research scientists believe that they have discovered a cure for certain types of cancer. Some of Acme's scientists want to do more test on animals before undertaking the procedures required by law for administering experimental drugs to humans. Others argue that the drug could save many lives and that its discovery should be disclosed right away. What ethical issues are involved in Acme's deciding whether to wait or go ahead with disclosure?
2. Beta Chemical Company manufactures pesticides, among other products. Some of Beta's pesticides are prohibited by law from being marketed in the United States because of evidence that they kill such desirable wildlife as birds, bees, and fish, in addition to insect pests. Beta manufactures the pesticide in the United States and then markets it to third world countries that are too poor to have the sophisticated government testing procedures used in the United Stated to determine if a pesticide is safe. Sale of the pesticides in these countries is perfectly legal, and indeed there has been some evidence that their use has contributed to preventing famine in some countries using them. Is it ethical for Beta to sell these pesticides abroad?
3. The state-of-the-art defense in product-liability cases means that a manufacturer adhered to government safety standards and the safety standards commonly used in the industry in manufacturing goods. Suppose a manufacturer discovers a method to make his product even safer than it would be if it met only government and industry standards, but this new method will make his product more expensive than other products on the market. Is the manufacturer ethically required to make the product safer?
4. During the middle to late 1980s, two automobile manufacturers, one German and one Japanese, came under criticism for allegedly dangerous defects in their cars. The German car was alleged to tend to accelerate suddenly out of control, and the Japanese car was alleged to be dangerously unstable and subject to rollovers. In both cases, the manufacturers initially denied that there was a problem with the cars. Was it ethical to deny that a problems existed at a time when the evidence indicated that members of the public could be endangered by the cars' defects?
5. Even though there is much evidence that smoking may cause cancer,

cigarette manufacturers continue to sell their products. The manufacturers argue that the cigarettes carry warning labels, so that anyone who smokes assumes the risk that health problems could result from the habit. Is it ethical for the manufacturers to market products that may be hazardous to health?

Questions on Law

1. After vaccination with Tri-Immunol, a form of diphtheria-pertussis-tetanus vaccine, the plaintiff became paralyzed. Plaintiff sued the manufacturer of the vaccine, Lederle Laboratories, on the theory that Lederle was negligent in not developing a safer form of the vaccine. Will Toner, the plaintiff, win? *Toner* v. *Lederle Laboratories,* US Supreme Court, No. 87-1151, 3-7-88.
2. Plaintiff Clois Osburn, a cowboy, developed leukemia from repeatedly administering chloramphenicol to calves. He claimed the manufacturer of the drug was liable to him for breach of a duty to warn about the danger caused by exposure to the drug. Will Osburn recover? *Osburn* v. *Anchor Laboratories, Inc.,* 825 F.2d 908 (5th Cir. 1987).
3. Elizabeth Ellsworth was wearing her nightgown inside out when it caught fire when it came too close to a burner on her electric stove. The manufacturer asserted as one defense that it was not liable for her injuries because she misused the product by wearing the nightgown inside out. Is she liable for misuse of product? *Ellsworth* v. *Sherne Lingerie, Inc.,* 495 A.2d 348 (Md. Ct. App. 1985).
4. A victim who was shot with a "Saturday-Night Special" handgun during a robbery sued the gun's manufacturer under a theory of strict liability in tort. The plaintiff argued that the manufacturer knew or should have known, that such weapons were principally used in criminal activity. Will the plaintiff recover? *Kelley* v. *R. G. Industries,* 497 A.2d 1143 (Md. Ct. App. 1985).
5. A two-month-old infant was given an oral polio vaccine, which caused him to develop a severe case of polio and left him paralyzed and dependent on a respirator. His parents sued the vaccine manufacturer, but also sued the National Institutes of Health's Division of Biologic Standards (DBS) under the Federal Tort Claims Act for approval of the vaccine lot. May the DBS be sued for approving the vaccine? *Berkovitz* v. *United States,* U.S. Supreme Court, No. 87-498, 6-13-88.

Suggested Readings

Bixby, "Judicial Interpretation of the Magnuson-Moss Warranty Act," 22 *American Business Law Journal* 125 (1984).

Liebman, "The Manufacturer's Responsibility to Warn Product Users of Unknowable Dangers," 21 *American Business Law Journal* 403 (1984).

Razook, "The Ultimate Purchaser's and Remote Seller's Guide through the Code Defenses in Product Economic Loss Cases," 23 *American Business Law Journal* 86 (1985).

6 International Business Law

26 International Business Law

International law is part of our law, and must be ascertained and administered by our courts of justice of appropriate jurisdiction, as often as questions of right depending upon it are duly presented for their determination.

—*Mr. Justice Grey,* The Paquete Habana, *175 U.S. 677 (1900)*

■ LEARNING OBJECTIVES

After you have read this chapter, you should be able to:

1. Understand and explain how companies in the United States legally engage in international business transactions.
2. Explain the act of state doctrine and its relationship to international business.
3. Explain the significance of the Foreign Sovereign Immunities Act of 1976 and its relationship to international business transactions.
4. Understand the ethical and social consequences of the Foreign Corrupt Practices Act.

Business Decisions and the Law

Disneyland International

Five years ago that symbol of American culture—Disneyland—opened its gates for business in Tokyo, Japan. Disneyland International entered into a private joint venture with Japanese firms that financed and built the theme park. For designing the park and advising on its operations, Disney receives shares of admission receipts as well as sales. Its Japanese partners, in turn, are responsible for the park's operations.

Tokyo Disneyland's reception has been phenomenal by all accounts. The Japanese have a longstanding affinity with all things Disney; indeed Emperor Hirohito occasionally wore a Mickey Mouse watch. Experts estimate over eleven million guests will visit the park, which is a near copy of the American version and even sports English as the first language.

The Disney adventure has not stopped in Tokyo. Next to be built is a theme park just outside of Paris, France. This European version is slated to open in 1992 and is the product of another joint venture in which Disney owns 17 percent of the business and controls management.

The French government added a public aspect to the joint venture by involving itself in an effort to win the park from other bidding nations. The government granted such expensive concessions as subway extensions, highway access routes, and reduced amusement taxes. In return, Disney agreed to tailor attractions to the European culture and to use French as the first language at Paris Disneyland.

The success of the two American Disney amusement parks has catapulted the company into the international business arena, necessitating an understanding of foreign markets and cultures, government regulations, and the process of forming international joint venturer.

This chapter will discuss the nature of a joint venture, various international law statutes and legal doctrines that affect multinational business transactions. Nations have become so interdependent that our survival requires an understanding of international law. The legal environment of international law is continually evolving as national needs change in such areas as technology, economics, and energy. International law is a composite of treaties, custom, and to a lesser extent, international judicial decisions. Countries are unlikely to adopt legal precedents set by other nations, since they are not bound to follow them.

Managers of a company about to engage in an international business transaction should be aware of the laws that will affect their dealings. A transnational contract should be formulated that specifies under which court the agreement will be governed in the event judicial resolution of a dispute is necessary. This is an important provision that should also provide for the choice of the substantive law to be applied (e.g., United States law or the foreign law). Selection of American law and courts to govern an international contract is not always possible. The courts will enforce a contract provision that agrees on the proper forum (court) and law to be applied, unless it was affected by fraud, undue influence, or is inconvenient to a party.

Throughout this chapter, keep in mind that multinational business transactions involve cross-cultural activity that often blurs the application of our ethical standards as we evaluate our operations in the light of foreign business conduct. For example, business practices in the Far East, although sometimes questionable to us, may be perfectly acceptable within that culture. Hence, a discerning system of business ethics is especially important in international transactions. Be aware of the foreign countries' economic, political, and social development as you assess the business ethics and legal issues presented in this chapter.

International Business Transactions Involving the Private Sector

Joint International Ventures

American multinational oil and automobile companies utilize the joint venture in their international transactions. A **joint venture** is an association of two or more parties—they may be individuals, partners, or corporations—who engage in business for a profit. For example, a Japanese company may export its computer technology to an American company for worldwide distribution. Investors (i.e., members of both companies) realize the enterprise will not succeed without a joint effort. Managerial control will be determined by stock owners with voting rights who elect directors. There will be both American and Japanese stockholders, and both American and Japanese directors will be corporate board members. A large multinational corporation could also form a subsidiary to function as a joint venture.

Multinational Affiliates in a Foreign Country

Assume that your company, Hi-Tech Inc., is a multinational computer company with affiliates authorized to do business in various countries of the world. In a business transaction, your Hi-Tech affiliate, Hi-Tech Italy, would act as a manufacturer and seller of your products to customers throughout Italy. Your affiliate would be organizationally structured like a small U.S. corporation, which in most cases would include staff legal counsel. Business transactions would be concluded by sales agreements that would address Italian law and contain terms and conditions peculiar to doing business in Italy. Any dispute over terms of the business transaction would be governed by Italian law and adjudicated in the Italian court system.

Multinational Corporations in the United States

Major differences occur among international transactions involving Hi-Tech Inc. with overseas customers. Ordinarily a team of Hi-Tech business representatives travels to the customer in its home office country. At that time the customer is presented with a standard Hi-Tech contract. The customer in turn presents Hi-Tech with its version of a purchase order covering its terms and conditions for purchase of equipment. These terms may address sales, rental or lease agreements, an installment purchase, or other method of financing equipment. Terms addressing title, risk of loss, patents, payments, warranty, intellectual property rights, inspection and acceptance, ***force majeure*** (i.e., excusable delays), etc., are discussed in detail and negotiated. Before this process takes place, the customer is qualified for creditworthiness. The Hi-Tech affiliate for that particular territory provides a credit check on the potential customer that is not unlike a Dun & Bradstreet report. Payment for goods delivered and accepted is usually in U.S. dollars and is provided through an irrevocable confirmed **letter of credit** at a bank of Hi-Tech's choice. A letter of credit is a promise by a bank to pay drafts drawn on it in accordance with its terms.

Equipment is usually shipped from the United States to the customer overseas, F.O.B. USA. Freight and custom charges are paid by the customer to allow the equipment to be delivered to its site. Equipment is installed by field engineers of the Hi-Tech affiliate, and an acceptance test is performed on the equipment and witnessed by the customer. A certificate of installation is signed by the customer and forwarded to the bank in the United States, and Hi-Tech is paid under the letter of credit. Should a dispute arise over such things as nonpayment or acceptability of the equipment, it would be governed by the conciliation and arbitration regulations of the International Chamber of Commerce; usually three arbitrators are appointed. The board of arbitrators ordinarily convenes in the capital city of the customer's country. The law of the customer's country prevails unless it has been agreed that the law of the United States will govern arbitration matters.

International Commercial Arbitration

Our example of Hi-Tech Inc. illustrates how a contract used in a transnational business venture often includes an arbitration clause in which the parties agree to be bound by the arbitrator's findings. This method of resolving disputes may avoid costly and time-consuming litigation. In addition to the International Chamber of Commerce, the United States has adopted the 1958 **United Nations Convention on the Recognition and Enforcement of Foreign Arbitral Awards,** whose purpose was stated by the Supreme Court in *Scherk* v. *Alberto-Culver Co.*, 417 U.S. 506, "to encourage the recognition and enforcement of commercial arbitration agreement in international contracts and to unify the standards by which agreements to arbitrate are observed and arbitral awards are enforced in the signatory countries." An arbitration award will be enforced by a member country and given the same legal effect as a judgment issued by the local court.

International Protection of Patents and Trademarks

The product you desire to market overseas may have a patent or trademark registered in the United States Patent Office in Washington, D.C. This is a valuable, legally protected property interest that you will want safeguarded in another country. However, an inventor is not granted international patent protection unless allowed by the foreign country where the product is being used.

Patent

If it is available, your U.S. company may desire to acquire patent registration in the foreign country. A **patent** is a property interest given by the federal government to an inventor to control the sale of the product. Many foreign countries have laws that protect the owners of patents. International treaties have been adopted that grant patent protection to its members. For example, the United States and twelve Latin American countries are members of the **Convention for the Protection of Inventions, Patents, Designs and Industrial Models.** The Patent Cooperation Treaty, signed by over twenty-five parties, including the United States, formed a union known as the **International Patent Cooperation Union** that deals in patent protection in several countries through one international filing of an application. It is administered by the International Bureau of the World Intellectual Property Organization at Geneva. And the European Economic Community Patent Convention, with sixteen member countries, makes a single patent valid in the European Common Market. Patent protection should always be among the first considerations when marketing a product abroad. A patent lawyer should be retained to register the patent and ensure its international protection.

Trademark

A **trademark** gives legal protection to a distinctive name and/or symbol to prevent others from using a confusingly similar device. May a foreign citizen who purchased a U.S. trademark and is using it in a foreign country be allowed the protection of American laws in a U.S. Court? Assume that X Corp. is an American franchise that sold its trademark to Z Co., a German corporation. Z Co. would have to register the mark in Germany to acquire trademark protection. However, if Z Co. is a licensee of X Corp., the American courts could give extraterritorial effect to the federal trademark law, the Lanham Act, providing the foreign activities have an effect on United States foreign commerce. The United States is not currently a party to a trademark treaty that would afford trademark protection through one international filing.

The World Intellectual Property Organization at Geneva administers the **Vienna Trademark Registration Treaty,** of which the United States is a member, and the **Madrid Agreement,** of which most European countries are members. These permit international filing of trademarks. International franchising must protect the trademark in the foreign country through the filing process.

International Transactions Involving the Public Sector

Act of State Doctrine

American investors may pursue a judicial remedy for an alleged wrong by a foreign company or government official in a United States court but be precluded from recovery because of the **act of state doctrine.** The act of state doctrine was clearly formulated by the United States Supreme Court in *Underhill* v. *Hernandez,* 168 U.S. 250, when it stated "Every sovereign state is bound to respect the independence of every other sovereign state, and the courts of one country will not sit in judgment on . . . the acts of the government of another done within its own territory." A judgment by a foreign court on executive decree issued by a government's ruler and an order by a foreign military commander acting within his authority have been held to be acts of state preventing redress in U.S. courts. Hence, although the foreign sovereign's act may violate United States law, the act of state doctrine may preclude challenging the act by a lawsuit in an American court. The act of state doctrine requires U.S. courts to apply the foreign law even though it may be contrary to the public policy of the court.

In the following case the government of Cuba, acting in Cuba, was not subject to U.S. laws. A Cuban corporation whose stock was owned by American investors was seized by the Cuban government. The court refused to inquire into the acts of the Cuban government even though they were denounced by the State Department as contrary to international law.

Banco Nacional de Cuba v. Sabbatino

376 U.S. 398 (1964)

Facts

In February and July 1960 respondent, Farr, Whitlock & Co., an American commodity broker, contracted to purchase Cuban sugar from a wholly owned subsidiary of Compania Azucarera Vertientes-Camuguey de Cuba (C.A.V.), a corporation organized under Cuban law whose capital stock was owned principally by United States residents. Farr, Whitlock agreed to pay for the sugar in New York upon presentation of the shipping documents and a sight draft.

On July 6, 1960, the Congress of the United States amended the Sugar Act of 1948 to permit a presidentially directed reduction of the sugar quota for Cuba. On the same day President Eisenhower exercised the granted power. The day of the congressional enactment the Cuban Council of Ministers adopted "Law No. 851," which characterized this reduction in the Cuban sugar quota as an act of "aggression, for political purposes" on the part of the United States, justifying the taking of countermeasures by Cuba. The law gave the Cuban president and prime minister discretionary power to nationalize by forced expropriation property or enterprises in which American nationals had an interest. Although a system of compensation was formally provided, the possibility of payment under it may well be deemed illusory. The U.S. State Department described the Cuban law as "manifestly in violation of those principles of international law which have long been accepted by the free countries of the West. It is in its essence discriminatory, arbitrary, and confiscatory."

The consent of the Cuban government was necessary before a ship carrying sugar of a named company could leave Cuban waters. In order to obtain this consent, Farr, Whitlock, on August 11, entered into contracts, identical to those it had made with C.A.V., with Banco Para el Comerico Exterior de Cuba, an instrumentality of the Cuban government.

Banco Exterior assigned the bills of lading to petitioner, also an instrumentality of the Cuban government, which instructed its agent in New York to deliver the bills and a sight draft in the sum of $175,250.69 to Farr, Whitlock in return for payment. Farr, Whitlock was served with an order of the New York Supreme Court, which had appointed Sabbatino as temporary receiver of C.A.V.'s New

York assets, enjoining it from taking any action in regard to the money claimed by C.A.V. that might result in its removal from the state. Following this, Farr, Whitlock, pursuant to court order, transferred the funds to Sabbatino, to abide the event of a judicial determination as to their ownership.

Petitioner then instituted this action in the Federal District Court for the Southern District of New York. Alleging conversion of the bills of lading, it sought to recover the proceeds thereof from Farr, Whitlock and to enjoin the receiver from exercising any dominion over such proceeds.

[The district court] . . . proceeding on the basis that a taking invalid under international law does not convey good title, found the Cuban expropriation decree to violate such law in three separate respects: It was motivated by a retaliatory and not a public purpose; it discriminated against American nationals; and it failed to provide adequate compensation.

The Supreme Court granted certiorari because the issues involved bear importantly on the conduct of the country's foreign relations and more particularly on the proper role of the judicial branch in this sensitive area. For reasons to follow the Court decided that the judgment must be reversed.

Opinion

Justice Harlan: That international law does not require application of the act of state doctrine is evidenced by the practices of nations. Most of the countries rendering decisions on the subject fail to follow the rule rigidly. The traditional view of international law is that it establishes substantive principles for determining whether one country has wronged another. Because of its peculiar nation-to-nation character, the usual method for an individual to seek relief is to exhaust local remedies and then repair to the executive authorities of his own state to persuade them to champion his claim in diplomacy or before an international tribunal. . . . [T]he public law of nations can hardly dictate to a country which is in theory wronged how to treat that wrong within its domestic borders.

The act of state doctrine does, however, have "constitutional" underpinnings. It arises out of the basic relationships between branches of government in a system of separation of powers. It concerns the competency of dissimilar institutions to make and implement particular kinds of decisions in the area of international relations. The doctrine as formulated in past decisions expresses the strong sense of the Judicial Branch that its engagement in the task of passing on the validity of foreign acts of state may hinder rather than further this country's pursuit of goals both for itself and for the community of nations as a whole in the international sphere.

There are few if any issues in international law today on which opinion seems to be so divided as the limitations on a state's power to expropriate the property of aliens. There is, of course, authority in international judicial and arbitral decisions, in the expressions of national governments, and among commentators for the view that a taking is improper under international law if it is not for a public purpose, is discriminatory, or is without provision for prompt, adequate, and effective compensation. However, Communist countries, although they have in fact provided a degree of compensation after diplomatic efforts, commonly recognize no obligation on the part of the taking country. Certain representatives of the newly independent and underdeveloped countries have questioned whether rules of state responsibility toward aliens can bind nations that have not consented to them and it is argued that the traditionally articulated standards governing expropriation of property reflect "imperialist" interests and are inappropriate to the circumstances of emergent states.

Respondents claim that the economic pressure resulting from the proposed exception to the act of state doctrine will materially add to the protection of United States investors. We are not convinced, even assuming the relevance of this contention. Expropriations take place for a variety of reasons, political and ideological as well as economic. When one considers the variety of means possessed by this country to make secure foreign investment, the persuasive or coercive effect of judicial invalidation of acts of expropriation dwindles in comparison. The newly independent states are in need of continuing foreign investment; the creation of a climate unfavorable to such investment by wholesale confiscations may well work to their long-run economic disadvantage. Foreign aid given to many of these countries provides a powerful lever in the hands of the political branches to censure fair treatment of United States nationals. Ultimately the sanctions of economic embargo and the freezing of assets in this country may be employed. Any country willing to brave any or all of these consequences is unlikely to be deterred by sporadic judicial decisions directly affecting only property brought to our shores. If the political branches are unwilling to exercise their ample powers to effect compensation, this reflects a judgment of the national interest which the judiciary would be ill-advised to undermine indirectly.

The judgment of the Court of Appeals is reversed and the case is remanded to the District Court for proceedings consistent with this opinion.

Case Questions

1. What is the international law on a state's power to expropriate the property of aliens?
2. Is it ever ethically justified for a country to confiscate the property of aliens?
3. Does a nation have an ethical responsibility to investors whose property has been expropriated that justifies an exception to the act of state doctrine?

In the following United States Supreme Court case the Court held the repudiation of a commercial debt by the Cuban government's instrumentality is not an act of state, and thus not immune from liability for the debt.

Alfred Dunhill of London, Inc. v. *Cuba*

425 U.S. 682 (1976)

Facts

Alfred Dunhill of London, Inc. (Dunhill), an exclusive men's shop, imported famed Havana cigars from Cuba. In 1960, the Cuban government confiscated the businesses of leading cigar manufacturers, which were organized under Cuban law and whose owners were Cuban. The Cuban government then appointed "interventors" to run the businesses.

The interventors continued to sell cigars to Dunhill and others, and to receive payment from these importers who assumed the interventors had the legal right to receive the money. The interventors also received from the importers payments relating back to pre-intervention shipments of cigars.

This litigation began when the former owners, most of whom fled to the United States, sued the importers, arguing inter alia, *that the interventors were wrongfully paid on accounts which belonged to the former owners.*

Based on the act of state doctrine, the district court concluded that the 1960 confiscation had full legal effect and awarded the interventors post-intervention profits. Pre-intervention profits, however, belonged to the former owners. The Court of Appeals agreed on the latter proposition, but viewed the interventor's repudiation of its obligation to repay money as an act of state not subject to question in American courts.

Opinion

Justice White: The issue in this case is whether the failure of respondents to return to petitioner Alfred Dunhill of London, Inc. (Dunhill), funds mistakenly paid by Dunhill for cigars that had been sold to Dunhill by certain expropriated Cuban cigar businesses was an "act of state" by Cuba precluding an affirmative judgment against . . . [Cuba].

The District Court and the Court of Appeals held that for purposes of this litigation interventors were not entitled to the preintervention accounts receivable by virtue of the 1960 confiscation. . . . We do not disturb [this conclusion]. . . .

If we assume . . . that the Cuban Government itself had purported to exercise sovereign power to confiscate the mistaken payments belonging to . . . foreign creditors and to repudiate interventors' adjudicated obligation to return those funds, we are nevertheless persuaded by the arguments . . . that the concept of an act of state should not be extended to include the repudiation of a purely commercial obligation owed by a foreign sovereign or by one of its commercial instrumentalities.

Distinguishing between the public and governmental acts of sovereign states on the one hand and their private and commercial acts on the other is not a novel approach.

When a state enters the market place seeking customers it divests itself of its *quasi* sovereignty *pro tanto,* and takes on the character of a trader. . . .

The major underpinning of the act of state doctrine is the policy of foreclosing court adjudications involving the legality of acts of foreign states on their own soil that might embarrass the Executive Branch of our Government in the conduct of our foreign relations.

[W]e are in no sense compelled to recognize as an act of state the purely commercial conduct of foreign governments in order to avoid embarrassing conflicts with the Executive Branch.

[T]he United States abandoned the absolute theory of sovereign immunity and embraced the restrictive view under which immunity in our courts should be granted only with respect to causes of action arising out of a foreign state's public or governmental actions and not with respect to those arising out of its commercial or proprietary actions.

Repudiation of a commercial debt cannot, consistent with this restrictive approach to sovereign immunity, be treated as an act of state; for if it were, foreign governments, by merely repudiating the debt before or after its adjudication, would enjoy an immunity which our Government would not extend them under prevailing sovereign immunity principles in this country.

Participation by foreign sovereigns in the international commercial market has increased substantially in recent years. The potential injury to private businessmen—and ultimately to international trade itself—from a system in which some of the participants in the international market are not subject to the rule of law has therefore increased correspondingly.

In their commercial capacities, foreign governments do not exercise powers peculiar to sovereigns. Instead, they exercise only those powers that can also be exercised by private citizens. Subjecting them in connection with such acts to the same rules of law that apply to private citizens is unlikely to touch very sharply on "national nerves."

[W]e hold that the mere assertion of sovereignty as a defense to a claim arising out of purely commercial acts by a foreign sovereign is no more effective if given the label "Act of State" than if it is given the label "sovereign immunity."

In describing the act of state doctrine in the past we have said that it "precludes the courts of this country from inquiring into the validity of the *public* acts a recognized foreign power committed within its own territory" and that it applies to "acts done within their own States, in the exercise of *governmental* authority." We decline to extend the act of state doctrine to acts committed by foreign sovereigns in the course of their purely commercial operations.

Case Questions

1. The act of state doctrine "precludes the courts of this country from inquiring into the validity of the public acts a recognized foreign power committed within its own territory . . . and it applies to acts done within their own states in the exercise of governmental authority." Why did the Court not apply this doctrine in this case?
2. When would the restrictive view of sovereign immunity apply?
3. Is it ethical for our judiciary to disregard the repudiation of a commercial debt by a foreign government?

The Foreign Sovereign Immunities Act of 1976

Assume that your company negotiated a contract for the sale of goods with a foreign corporation. The foreign corporation breached the contract, and your company pursued its claim in a United States court. Would the court have jurisdiction over the controversy? The **Foreign Sovereign Immunities Act** provides federal district courts with original jurisdiction, without regard to the amount of damages involved, in an action against a foreign state (e.g., a foreign corporation whose majority stockholder is a foreign country) unless the suit is barred by sovereign immunity. The act established the principle that "foreign states are immune from suits based on their public acts but not on their commercial or private acts." Hence, a foreign state comes within the jurisdiction of the American courts in any case "in which the action is based upon a commercial activity carried on in the United States by a foreign state, or elsewhere, if the act caused a direct effect in the United States."

The following case involves a New York–based multinational sales corporation that brought suit against a Romanian company represented in New York City through the Office of the Economic Counselor of the Romanian Embassy. The New York corporation sought to recover damages caused by the Romanian company's interference with a contract and wrongful interference with its trade and business. Notice the court's reasoning in finding that the Foreign Sovereign Immunities Act did not apply.

East Europe Domestic Intern. Sales Corp. v. Terra

467 F. Supp. 383 (1979)

Facts

Plaintiff, East Europe Domestic International Sales Corp. ("East Europe"), is a New York domestic international sales corporation and maintains its corporate headquarters and sole office in New York City.

On or about March 1, 1977, plaintiff entered into a contract with Vitrocim, a Romanian company, to purchase 20,000 metric tons of Portland cement at a price of $25.00 a metric ton. The contract was negotiated by plaintiff's President Robert Ross while on a trip to Bucharest, Romania, during the winter of 1977. As the date for delivery under the contract preceded the date of its execution, various changes in the contract were anticipated and needed. Plaintiff negotiated these changes with Vitrocim through the Office of the Economic Counselor of the Embassy of Romania in New York City and by telex communication. Vitrocim requested that the contract should be amended to include the requirement that a letter of credit "has to be received by Vitrocim not later than April 10, 1977."

Throughout March and early April 1977, plaintiff asserted that the world price of cement was rising. By telex dated March 24, 1977, plaintiff had its first contact with Terra. The telex read: "Kind Att Mr. Robert Ross—We have been informed that you bought 20,000 Mtons Romanian cement . . . from Messrs. Vitrocim, delivery in April 1977. We are ready to take over this quantity from you in same conditions as yours with Messrs. Vitrocim at a price of US Doll 26.10/Mton. Pls act very fast. Regards Terra 2C."

Plaintiff replied by return telex expressing its willingness to enter into a deal with Terra at a price of $27.00 a metric ton, provided that Terra establish an irrevocable, confirmed and transferable letter of credit in favor of Vitrocim by March 28, 1977, the letter of credit to be confirmed by Vitrocim. Terra was required to pay plaintiff the $2.00 a metric ton difference in price from the price under the Vitrocim contract by cabling $44,000.00 to John Foster at Chase Manhattan Bank in New York City.

After negotiating by telex over the next several days, plaintiff, Vitrocim, and Terra agreed on a price of $26.25 per metric ton with 40 cents of plaintiff's profit going to Vitrocim as commission. The three-way deal, however, ultimately fell through. Although Terra represented on at least two separate occasions that it had established a letter of credit in favor of Vitrocim, plaintiff repeatedly requested confirmation of this fact from Vitrocim.

On August 24, 1977, plaintiff filed its complaint naming Terra as the sole defendant. Plaintiff sought compensatory and punitive damages primarily on the theory that Terra and Vitrocim conspired to thwart performance of plaintiff's contract to enable both companies to take advantage of the rising world price of cement.

Opinion

District Judge Irving Ben Cooper: Plaintiff alleges that this Court has jurisdiction under the Foreign Sovereign Immunities Act of 1976. The Act codifies the principle of "restrictive" sovereign immunity in that, under international law, foreign states are immune from suits based on their public acts, but not on the commercial or private acts. Prior to the Act, the decision on whether an action was public or commercial was made by the executive branch. The Act now specifically enumerates those actions which may be termed commercial and grants the United States District Courts original jurisdiction over disputes involving them.

Section 1605(a)(2) of the Foreign Sovereign Immunities Act explicitly applies to the case before us:

> (a) a foreign state shall not be immune from the jurisdiction of courts of the United States or of the States in any case—(2) in which the action is based upon a commercial activity carried on in the United States in connection with a commercial activity of the foreign state elsewhere; or upon an act outside the territory of the United States in connection with a commercial activity of the foreign state elsewhere and that act causes a direct effect in the United States.

[The United States will have personal] jurisdiction over Terra . . . if we find that Terra either (1) conducts commercial activity in the United States; or (2) performed an act in the United States in connection with its commercial activity elsewhere or (3) acted outside the United States in connection with its commercial activity and that act caused a "direct effect in the United States."

We will deal with each of the three possible jurisdictional bases in turn.

1. Does Terra carry on commercial activity in the United States? Terra is a Romanian state-owned trading corporation. Its principal activities are export, import and re-export. Founded in 1970 on an experimental basis, Terra achieved permanent status in 1971. In examining Terra's activities in the United States since 1970 we must determine whether they are sufficiently "continuous and systematic" to satisfy the demands of due process. Apart from very few and scattered contracts, there is no evidence of systematic or continuous activity in the United States by Terra. The proof adduced by the parties shows that until August, 1977, when this suit was commenced, Terra had never: maintained an office in the United States; sent representatives or salesmen to the United States; entered into any contracts with United States companies either for the purchase or sale of goods; or engaged in any organized publicity in the United States.

We cannot find that Terra has "purposely availed itself of the privilege of conducting business in the United States."

2. Has Terra performed an act in the United States in connection with its commercial activity elsewhere? This portion of section 1605(a)(2)

"looks to conduct of the foreign state in the United States which relates either to a regular course of commercial conduct elsewhere or to a particular commercial transaction concluded or carried out in part elsewhere." We find no presence of Terra in the United States and, hence, no jurisdiction over Terra under this part of the clause.

3. Has Terra acted outside the United States in connection with its commercial activity and has that action caused a "direct effect in the United States"? This phrase requires us to examine defendant's contacts with the United States in connection with the specific transaction at issue.

The entire course of dealing between East Europe and Terra was by telex. It is undisputed that Terra initiated the transaction with its telex of March 24. Had the deal materialized, Terra would have paid East Europe by cabling funds to plaintiff's New York bank. The rest of the transaction is located in Romania. The cement was never supposed to leave Romania. Under plaintiff's contract with Vitrocim, the letter of credit to be established in favor of Vitrocim was to be payable in Bucharest.

4. We find that Terra's sole contacts with the United States in the course of the transaction in dispute are the telexes which comprise the negotiations between it and plaintiff. Although Terra made the initial communication, we find that the March 24 telex does not constitute activity having a "direct effect" in the marketplace of the United States; it is an insufficient factor upon which to confer jurisdiction.

5. East Europe claims that its injury in tort consists of damages occasioned by Terra's interference with its trade or business. Had Terra not represented that it had established the letter of credit, plaintiff asserts, the contract with Vitrocim would have been performed and plaintiff would have sold the cement to another customer. The alleged tortious activity took place outside the United States. The purported injury took place in the United States only because the plaintiff is domiciled or doing business here. This, too, is an insufficient contact for due process purposes.

Defendant has no other contacts with the United States besides negotiations. Plaintiff's complaint is dismissed.

Case Questions

1. The Foreign Sovereign Immunities Act provides "Under international law, states are not immune from the jurisdiction of foreign courts insofar as their *commercial* activities are concerned. . . ." A foreign state that is a party with the United States by international agreement is immune from the jurisdiction of the U.S. courts unless the commercial activity is carried on in the United States or outside the United States but causing a direct effect here. What were the court's reasons for finding that Terra did not carry on commercial activity in the United States and its business activity did not cause a direct effect in the United States?
2. Does the United States have an ethical obligation to foreign states to respect foreign acts performed within its own territory even at the expense of American investors?
3. Do you think Terra acted ethically in taking advantage of the rising world price of cement by delaying the necessary letter of credit?

The following case involves a suit originating in an American court between a foreign corporation and a foreign sovereign. The Dutch corporation argued that actions taken by the Federal Republic of Nigeria constituted an anticipatory breach of letter of credit. Upon surveying the law of foreign sovereign immunity, the Court concluded that the Act allows a foreign plaintiff to sue a foreign sovereign in the courts of the United States.

Verlinden B.V. v. Central Bank of Nigeria

461 U.S. 480 (1983)

Facts

The Federal Republic of Nigeria contracted with Verlinden B.V., a Dutch corporation, for it to provide Nigeria with 240,000 metric tons of cement. In return, Nigeria was to establish an irrevocable confirmed letter of credit. The complaint, however, alleged that Nigeria improperly established an unconfirmed letter of credit through a bank other than the one originally agreed to.

Verlinden then sued the Central Bank of Nigeria in United States district court and alleged an anticipatory breach of the letter of credit, basing jurisdiction under the Foreign Sovereign Immunities Act. The district court dismissed Verlinden's complaint, holding that the Central Bank was an instrumentality of the Republic of Nigeria, and as such, was entitled to sovereign immunity. Since none of the Act's sovereign immunity exceptions applied, Verlinden lacked both subject matter and personal jurisdiction. The Court of Appeals affirmed the dismissal of the complaint. Although it agreed with the district court that the Act permits actions by foreign plaintiffs, it held that Congress' expansion of jurisdiction under the Act to include suits by foreign plaintiffs against foreign sovereigns went beyond the bounds established by the Constitution.

Opinion

Chief Justice Burger: For more than a century and a half, the United States generally granted foreign sovereigns complete immunity from suit in the courts of this country. . . . [H]owever, foreign sovereign immunity is a matter of grace and comity on the part of the United States, and not a restriction imposed by the Constitution.

Until 1952, the State Department ordinarily requested immunity in all actions against friendly foreign sovereigns. But in the so-called Tate Letter, the State Department announced its adoption of the "restrictive" theory of foreign sovereign immunity. Under this theory, immunity is confined to suits involving the foreign sovereign's public acts, and does not extend to cases arising out of a foreign state's strictly commercial acts.

The restrictive theory was not initially enacted into law, however, and its application proved troublesome.

[S]overeign immunity determinations were made in two different branches, subject to a variety of factors, sometimes including diplomatic considerations. Not surprisingly, the governing standards were neither clear nor uniformly applied.

In 1976, Congress passed the Foreign Sovereign Immunities Act in order to free the Government from the case-by-case diplomatic pressures, to clarify the governing standards. . . . [T]he Act contains a comprehensive set of legal standards governing claims of immunity in every civil action against a foreign state or its political subdivisions, agencies, or instrumentalities.

[T]he Act codifies, as a matter of federal law, the restrictive theory of sovereign immunity. A foreign state is normally immune from the jurisdiction of federal and state courts, . . . subject to a set of exceptions. . . . Those exceptions include actions in which the foreign state has explicitly or impliedly waived its immunity, . . . and actions based upon commercial activities of the foreign sovereign carried on in the United States or causing a direct effect in the United States. . . . When one of these or the other specified exceptions applies, "the foreign state shall be liable in the same manner and to the same extent as a private individual under like circumstances. . . ."

The District Court and the Court of Appeals both held that the Foreign Sovereign Immunities Act purports to allow a foreign plaintiff to sue a foreign sovereign in the courts of the United States, provided the substantive requirements of the Act are satisfied. We agree. The Act contains no indication of any limitation based on the citizenship of the plaintiff.

The legislative history is less clear. . . .

Notwithstanding this reference to "our citizens," we conclude that, . . . the legislative history reveals an intent not to limit jurisdiction under the Act to actions brought by American citizens. . . . If an action satisfies the substantive standards of the Act, it may be brought in federal court regardless of the citizenship of the plaintiff.

We now turn to the . . . question . . . whether Congress exceeded the scope of Art. III of the Constitution by granting federal courts subject-matter jurisdiction over certain civil actions by foreign plaintiffs against foreign sovereigns where the rule of decision may be provided. . . .

We conclude, . . . that the "Arising Under" Clause of Art. III provides an appropriate basis for the statutory grant of subject-matter jurisdiction to actions by foreign plaintiffs under the Act.

A conclusion that the grant of jurisdiction in the Foreign Sovereign Immunities Act is consistent with the Constitution does not end the case. An action must not only satisfy Art. III but must also be supported by a statutory grant of subject-matter jurisdiction.

[This] entails an application of the substantive terms of the Act to determine whether one of the specified exceptions to immunity applies.

Case Questions

1. What is meant by the "restrictive" theory of foreign sovereign immunity?
2. Why is jurisdiction under the Act not limited to actions brought by American citizens?
3. Was it ethical for the Court to allow a foreign plaintiff to sue a foreign sovereign in the federal district court?

Antitrust Laws in International Transactions

The United States Supreme Court in *Northern Pac. Ry.* v. *United States,* 356 U.S. 1, has stated, "[Our antitrust laws are based] . . . on the premise that the unrestrained interaction of competitive forces will yield the best allocation of our economic resources, the lowest prices, the highest quality and the greatest material progress, while at the same time providing an environment conducive to the preservation of our democratic and social institutions." United States antitrust laws have been extraterritorially extended to protect export opportunities of American companies. The **Sherman Act,** for example, provides that every contract, combination, or conspiracy in unreasonable restraint of trade or commerce among the several states or with foreign nations is illegal. If Company X engages in illegal antitrust activity in a foreign country, U.S. courts will have jurisdiction if there is substantial effect on the interstate or foreign commerce of the United States.

The Export Trading Company Act of 1982

The federal **Export Trading Company Act** became law on 8 October 1982. The expressed purpose of the act is "to increase United States exports of products and services by encouraging more efficient . . . export trade services to United States producers and suppliers." Corporate disincentives to participate in export trade are generally based on the legal complexity of international transactions and the diminishing value of exported goods compared to those sold in the domestic market. Any attempt by the potential exporter to unreasonably restrain trade that has a substantial effect on U.S. commerce is an antitrust violation. In many cases, what legally constitutes an unreasonable restraint of trade and a substantial effect on U.S. commerce are difficult decisions. Hence, many potential exporters consider the uncertainties of antitrust laws and their treble damage liability to be beyond the range of a prudent business risk.

The Sherman Act prohibits, in part, business activity in unreasonable restraint of trade with foreign nations. The Clayton Act provides that "any person . . . injured in his business or property by reason of anything forbidden in the antitrust laws may sue . . . in any district court of the United States in which the defendant resides, or is found, or has an agent . . . and shall recover threefold the damages . . . sustained, and the cost of the suit, including a reasonable attorney's fee."

The Export Trading Company Act defines an export trading company as an individual, association, or organization operated for profit or nonprofit, doing business under the laws of the United States or any of its states and for the principal purposes of exporting goods or services produced in the United States. For example, a Massachusetts corporation organized for the purpose of exporting goods and/or services is an export trading company. In order to stimulate United States exporting, the act created the **Office of Export Trade** within the Department of Commerce to "promote and encourage to the greatest extent feasible the formation of export trade associations and export trading companies." An exporting company may contact the Office of Export Trade for information, advice, and referrals to producers of exportable goods and services who may be interested in a company offering export services. The secretary of commerce issues regulations implementing the act.

Once an export trading company (ETC) is organized, the financing and developing stages are enhanced under the act by encouraging the banking industry to extend credit to an ETC. Bank holding companies may own stock in an ETC and extend credit for up to 10 percent of its capital and surplus with approval of the Federal Reserve Board. A company's investment is limited to 5 percent of its own capital and surplus. The act amends the Federal Reserve Act by allowing its member banks to accept bills of exchange drawn on their accounts generated from export trading company transactions.

The act allows an ETC to file with the secretary of commerce an application describing its planned international business activity and requesting a **certificate of review.** A certificate of review is a document issued by the attorney general and the secretary of commerce conferring antitrust protection to the applicant for activity specified in the certificate. The attorney general will review the application and its possible antitrust violations. Notice of the application is then published in the *Federal Register.* A certificate of review is issued if the secretary of commerce and the attorney general agree that the export trade activity will not do any of the following:

1. result in either a substantial lessening of competition or restraint of trade within the United States or a substantial restraint of the export trade of any competitor of the applicant;
2. unreasonably affect prices within the United States of the goods or services of the class exported by the applicant;
3. constitute unfair methods of competition against competitors engaged in exporting goods or services of the class exported by the applicant;

4. include any act that might result in the sale or consumption of the applicant's goods or services within the United States;
5. include any act that may reasonably be expected to result in the sale for consumption or resale within the United States of the goods or services exported by the applicant.

The act provides for judicial review in the event that the certificate is denied. Upon issuance of the certificate of review, the ETC is granted protection from the antitrust laws for activity specified in the certificate. The act states, in part, "no criminal or civil action may be brought under the anti-trust laws against a person (ETC) to whom a certificate of review is issued . . . based on conduct which is specified in . . . [the] certificate issued." Hence, as long as the ETC transacts its international trade without violating the statutory prohibitions of the act, the certificate of review has the effect of providing antitrust immunity. Noncompliance with the certificate may subject the holder to a civil suit. However, so long as the ETC has a certificate of review, the treble damages of the Clayton Act are replaced by injunctive relief, actual damages, the cost of the suit, and reasonable attorney's fees. The act allows the ETC to be awarded the cost of defending the lawsuit, including a reasonable attorney's fee, if the court finds that the defendant's conduct does comply with the standards of the certificate of review.

The act amends the Sherman Act by providing it shall not apply to conduct involving export trade or commerce with foreign nations unless such conduct has a "direct, substantial and reasonably foreseeable effect" on domestic commerce and competition, giving rise to a legal claim. The reasonably foreseeable test may be compared to the business judgment rule that allows a director or officer to make an honest and rationally informed business decision that turns out to be wrong without being personally liable for its consequences. As long as the exporter did not foresee antitrust activity and acted with the care that an ordinary prudent exporter would be expected to exercise under similar circumstances, it will be protected from the unforeseen technical antitrust violations of the Sherman Act.

Marketing divisions of existing corporations and innovative entrepreneurs intending to penetrate foreign markets should be encouraged by the effect of the Export Trading Company Act. Potential antitrust violations may now be reviewed by the attorney general to ensure statutory compliance. Upon issuance of the certificate of review, the ETC is protected from the treble damages awarded under the Clayton Act. However, the application is published in the *Federal Register,* and competitors could easily take advantage of this information. An ETC could elect not to seek a certificate of review. However, violation of antitrust laws without a certificate of review will subject the ETC to treble damages. The Export Trading Company Act with its antitrust immunity is expected to provide American companies the incentives to develop our export potential and effectively compete in the international marketplace.

Foreign Corrupt Practices Act

The **Foreign Corrupt Practices Act** (FCPA) as amended in 1988 was discussed in chapter 13, "Forms of Business Organizations," and chapter 20, "Securities Regulations." You should read that material, because our explanation will now focus on the ethical and social consequences of the FCPA.

The act makes it a crime for American corporations to offer payments to officials of foreign governments for the purpose of retaining or obtaining business. The main objection to the act is that some foreign public officials now accept bribes from non-American businesses with a consequent loss of foreign trade to the United States. Some would argue that American multinational corporations have a fiduciary obligation to protect the shareholders' investment and provide job security to their employees, and hence that the act is not justified in prohibiting bribes in an environment where bribery is commonplace. Furthermore, the payment itself may not be a "bribe," since it is recognized by local custom in some countries and there is really no coercion of foreign officials.

Ethical arguments in support of the act recognize the federal government's moral obligation to protect the general welfare as paramount to private industry's concern to make a profit. The payment of a bribe does contribute to foreign corruption, and although bribery may be the norm, that does not make the practice right.

The European Economic Community

The 1957 Treaty of Rome economically integrated the Western European nations of Belgium, Denmark, France, the Federal Republic of Germany, Greece, Ireland, Italy, Luxembourg, and the Netherlands. Denmark, Ireland, and the United Kingdom became members in 1973. Collectively, they are referred to as the **European Economic Community (EEC)** or the Common Market. The purpose of the EEC is to encourage the free movement of workers, capital, and goods among members by imposing a custom tariff for outside countries and eliminating tariffs within the community. The EEC has the equivalent of its own legislature (the Commission), executive (the Council of Ministers), and judiciary (the Court of Justice).

The *Commission* is composed of members from each nation charged with the function of carrying out the Treaty of Rome by enacting EEC legislation that is presented to the Council of Ministers for adoption.

The *Council of Ministers* will act on proposals enacted by the Commission to coordinate the economic policies of the member nations in accordance with the Treaty of Rome.

The *Court of Justice* has jurisdiction over EEC disputes throughout the member nations. All member nations are subject to its findings.

Article 85 of the EEC is a policy statement on prohibited business practices considered incompatible with the Common Market. These include the fixing of prices, the control of production, markets, technical development, or investment, market-sharing or the sharing of sources of supply, placing members at a competitive disadvantage, and making the conclusion of a contract subject to the acceptance by the other party of additional obligations that according to commercial practices have no connection with the contract. Article 85 states that any agreements that violate this policy shall be null and void.

Article 86 enumerates business practices that constitute improper exploitation. Among these are the imposition of an unfair trading practice, the limitation of production, markets, or technical developments to the prejudice of consumers, placing parties undertaking equivalent engagements at a commercial disadvantage, and imposing contract terms that have no connection with the subject of the contract.

The Council of Ministers may review a proposed or existing business venture within the Common Market and rule on its applicability to article 85 and/or article 86. If there is no violation it will issue a *negative clearance*.

Articles 85 and 86 may have effect beyond the Common Market if an outside party owns a subsidiary company within the community and its conduct is attributable to the outside parent company. If the effect of the business transaction creates a competitive disadvantage to a company within the Common Market, articles 85 and 86 will apply. For example, Hi-Tech Italy, with its main office in New York but doing business in Italy, may be subject to articles 85 and 86 and be prevented from transacting business. Legal counsel should review the venture to assure compliance and, if appropriate, receive a negative clearance from the Council of Ministers.

The International Monetary Fund

In 1944 representatives of several nations met in Bretton Woods, New Hampshire, to discuss the needs of countries requesting foreign investment to stabilize their currency exchange rates and to improve their balance of payments after World War II. The need for a "world bank" to facilitate this process led to the development of the **International Monetary Fund (IMF)** (see figure 26.1).

Article 57 of the United Nations Charter authorized the International Monetary Fund as one of its specialized agencies by stating that "various specialized agencies, established by intergovernmental agreements . . . in economic . . . and related fields, shall be brought into relationship with the United Nations . . . [and] are hereinafter referred to as specialized agencies."

The International Monetary Fund consists of a board of governors that meets at least once a year, or more often by special session. Its powers are delegated to executive directors, who direct the IMF from their Washington, D.C., headquarters.

In the following case, Brazil had obtained the IMF's approval for restrictions on all payments involving foreign currencies. The government-controlled Bank of Brazil required all foreign currency to be surrendered to it at an official fixed rate of exchange. As the result of a private contract between a New York

Figure 26.1 Purposes of the International Monetary Fund

Art. I. The purposes of the International Monetary Fund are:

(i) To promote international monetary cooperation through a permanent institution which provides the machinery for consultation and collaboration on international monetary problems.

(ii) To facilitate the expansion and balanced growth of international trade, and to contribute thereby to the promotion and maintenance of high levels of employment and real income and to the development of the productive resources of all members as primary objectives of economic policy.

(iii) To promote exchange stability, to maintain orderly exchange arrangements among members, and to avoid competitive exchange depreciation.

(iv) To assist in the establishment of a multilateral system of payments in respect of current transactions between members and in the elimination of foreign exchange restrictions which hamper the growth of world trade.

(v) To give confidence to members by making the Fund's resources available to them under adequate safeguards, thus providing them with opportunity to correct maladjustments in their balance of payments without resorting to measures destructive of national or international prosperity.

(vi) In accordance with the above, to shorten the duration and lessen the degree of disequilibrium in the international balances of payments of members.

importer of coffee and a Brazilian exporter, the coffee was paid for with U.S. dollars directly to the Brazilian exporter; he sold these on the Brazilian currency black market at a rate in excess of the Brazilian government's official rate. In consideration for this agreement, the New York importer paid a lower rate for the coffee than the officially established minimum price for Brazilian coffee.

The government of Brazil sued the New York importer for damages for violating article VIII, section 2(b) of the International Monetary Fund Articles of Agreement, which states: "Exchange contracts which involve the currency of any member and which are contrary to the exchange control regulations of that member . . . shall be unenforceable in the territories of that member." Notice the court's reasoning in holding that the international law established by the members of the IMF does not impose obligations on individuals.

Banco do Brazil, S. v. A. C. Israel Commodity Co., Inc.

110 N.E.2d 235 (1963)

Facts

The plaintiff argues that respondent's participation in the violation of Brazilian exchange control laws affords a ground of recovery because of article VIII (S. 2. subd [b]) of the Bretton Woods Agreement, a multilateral treaty to which both this country and

Brazil are signatories. The section deals with "exchange contracts" that "involve" the "currency" of any member of the International Monetary Fund.

Opinion

Judge Burke: The sanction provided in subdivision (b) of section 2 is that contracts covered thereby are to be "unenforceable" in the territory of any member. The courts of no member should award any recovery for breach of an agreement in violation of the exchange controls of another member. . . . An obligation to withhold judicial assistance to secure the benefits of such contracts does not imply an obligation to impose tort penalties on those who have fully executed them.

From the viewpoint of the individuals involved, it must be remembered that the Bretton Woods Agreement relates to international law. It imposes obligations among and between States, not individuals. The fact that by virtue of the agreement New York must not "enforce" a contract between individuals which is contrary to the exchange controls of any member, imposes no obligation (under the law of the transaction—New York law) on such individuals not to enter into such contracts. While it does mean that they so agree at their peril inasmuch as they may not look to our courts for enforcement, this again is far from implying that one who so agrees commits a tort in New York for which he must respond in damages.

Lastly, and inseparable from the foregoing, there is a remedial consideration which bars recovery in this case. Plaintiff is an instrumentality of the Government of Brazil and is seeking, by use of an action for conspiracy to defraud, to enforce what is clearly a revenue law. Whatever may be the effect of the Bretton Woods Agreement in an action on "A contract made in a foreign country between citizens thereof and intended by them to be there performed" it is well established since the day of Lord Mansfield [*Holman* v. *Johnson,* 1 Cowp. 341, 98 E.R. 1120 (1775)] that one State does not enforce the revenue laws of another. Nothing in the Bretton Woods Agreement is to the contrary. In fact its use of the unenforcibility device for effectuation of its purposes impliedly concedes the unavailability of the more direct method of enforcement at the suit of the aggrieved government.

Case Questions

1. What was the court's reasoning for not finding for the plaintiff, although the exchange contract before the court violated the International Monetary Fund agreement?
2. Do you agree with the court that article VIII, section 2 of the IMF is "clearly a revenue law," and hence a tort action seeking damages for a conspiracy to defraud the Brazilian government is a bar to recovery in this case?
3. Do you think the private contract between the New York importer and the Brazilian exporter was unethical? Support your answer by explaining its effect on the parties involved.

International Taxes and Tax Havens

In an attempt to ensure that income from foreign corporations is reported to the Internal Revenue Service, a U.S. taxpayer who owns, directly or indirectly, 50 percent or more of a foreign corporation must report such items as receipts from and payments of compensation, commissions, rents, royalties, and dividends from such a corporation. The Tax Equity and Fiscal Responsibility Act of 1982 (TEFRA) imposes a penalty of $1,000 for each failure to furnish such information. **Tax treaties** are contracts between two countries for dividing taxes on international transactions between the country of the source of income and the country of residence of the recipient. They are used to prevent tax evasion in the two countries.

If the foreign country has no policy of taxing payments of income to nonresidents, it is referred to as a tax haven. Bermuda is an example of a tax haven. In the *United States* v. *Norman Johnson,* the defendant Johnson was chairman of the board of Lucey Products Company, a firm engaged in the sale of oil field pipe. Johnson organized two Bermudian corporations and concealed his stock ownership in each company. Lucey Products then sold oil field pipe below market price to the Bermuda corporations, which later sold the pipe to other companies at a substantial profit. The Bermudian corporations did not file corporate income tax returns in the United States or Bermuda. The profits were deposited in Bermudian banks in Lucey Products' checking accounts and were then withdrawn and used for the personal benefit of Johnson, who did not report the profit on his individual income tax return. Johnson was convicted and sentenced to a term of five years' imprisonment. The IRS is aggressively attempting to identify U.S. taxpayers who are establishing corporations and bank accounts in tax haven countries for the purpose of evading income tax.

International tax lawyers carefully examine the tax consequences of any proposed multinational business transaction.

The General Agreement on Tariffs and Trade

Various countries meeting in Geneva in 1947 recognized a postwar need to reduce trade obstacles. They adopted a document entitled the **General Agreement on Tariffs and Trade (GATT).** Its general purpose is to limit tariffs (i.e., import taxes on specific articles) and trade barriers on imported goods and thereby to encourage multinational trade and world economic development. For example, if the United States agreed with Japan to reduce tariffs on specific goods, it would have to allow the same reduction on tariffs to other less developed countries. In international business transactions involving the free market, as well as in centrally planned economics, it is important to discourage economic regionalism to maintain political stability in less developed countries. GATT's purpose is to encourage tariff reduction negotiations and world trade rather than regional trade.

Ethical Issues in International Business Law

American multinational corporations engaging in international business transactions owe a special duty to the foreign countries in which they operate. Is it ethical for a multinational to open a foreign plant in a third world nation and employ cheap nonunion laborers in a factory not subject to safety regulations? Some would argue that so long as the company employs people and reduces poverty, such a practice is ethically justified.

Multinationals in South Africa have been criticized for indirectly contributing to its political policy. South African law decrees racial segregation (apartheid), and blacks cannot vote or own property. Others claim it is ethically justified because multinationals strengthen the South African economy and this indirectly benefits its black citizens. Do you think it is ethical for United States firms to operate in South Africa?

Another area of ethical concern is related to international loans granted to third world countries. For instance, if Mexico ever went into bankruptcy, the effect on America's largest banks would be disastrous. Hence, in order to prevent Mexico from defaulting on its international loans, American banks working through the IMF made additional loans to Mexico on the condition that its government reduce spending on such programs as subsidies for the poor. Is this type of practice by the IMF ethically justified? Some would argue that the number of Mexicans crossing the Rio Grande into the United States is directly related to the austerity programs demanded by the IMF to ensure repayment of its loans. Does this practice bring about political instability? What alternatives would you recommend? Do you think ethical issues are relevant to international business transactions?

The important concepts and terms in this chapter are listed below; page numbers have been provided for the key terms. By reading over each section you can assess your understanding of the chapter concepts and determine areas you may want to review.

Chapter Summary

1. International law is a composite of treaties, custom, and international judicial decisions.
2. In addition to joining the International Chamber of Commerce, the United States has adopted the 1958 United Nations Convention on the Recognition and Enforcement of Foreign Arbitral Awards. An arbitration award will be enforced by the courts of a member country.
3. International treaties such as the Latin American Convention for the Protection of Inventions, Patents, Designs and Industrial Models and the International Patent Cooperation Union grant patent protection between member countries. Patent protection should always be obtained when dealing in international trade.
4. The act of state doctrine can require an American court to apply foreign law even though it may be contrary to American law.
5. The Foreign Sovereign Immunities Act establishes the principle of international law that foreign countries are immune from suits based on their public acts but *not on their commercial or private acts* that are carried on in the United States or outside the United States when those acts cause a direct effect in the United States.
6. The Export Trading Company Act authorizes the attorney general and the secretary of commerce to issue a certificate of review to an exporter, which provides the exporter with antitrust immunity.

7. The Foreign Corrupt Practices Act makes it a crime for American companies to offer payments to officials of foreign governments for the purpose of retaining or obtaining business.
8. The European Economic Community, also known as the Common Market, is comprised of Belgium, Denmark, France, the Federal Republic of Germany, Greece, Ireland, Italy, Luxembourg, the Netherlands, and the United Kingdom. The 1957 Treaty of Rome has economically integrated the member nations to encourage the free movement of labor, capital, and goods between them. The EEC has a Commission that enacts legislation, a Council of Ministers that acts on proposals enacted by the Commission, and a Court of Justice that has jurisdiction over member nation disputes.
9. The International Monetary Fund (IMF) is a specialized agency of the United Nations based in Washington, D.C. Its primary functions are to promote international monetary cooperation by consultation and collaboration on international monetary problems, to facilitate the growth of international trade and thereby promote high levels of employment, and to promote monetary exchange stability.
10. The General Agreement on Tariff and Trade (GATT) is an agreement by member countries to limit tariffs and trade barriers on imported goods and thereby encourage international trade.

Key Terms

act of state doctrine 730
article 85 742
article 86 743
certificate of review 740
Convention for the Protection of Inventions, Patents, Designs and Industrial Models 730
European Economic Community 742
Export Trading Company Act 739
force majeure 728
Foreign Corrupt Practices Act 742
Foreign Sovereign Immunities Act 735
General Agreement on Tariffs and Trade 746
International Monetary Fund 743
International Patent Cooperation Union 730
joint venture 728
letter of credit 729
Madrid Agreement 730
Office of Export Trade 740
patent 730
Sherman Act 739
tax treaties 745
trademark 730
United Nations Convention on the Recognition and Enforcement of Foreign Arbitral Awards 729
Vienna Trademark Registration Treaty 730

Questions on Ethics

1. Suppose you are a director of a joint international venture doing business with Japan. On the corporate board are American and Japanese directors. The company has an opportunity to sell its manufactured equipment to a third world country whose agent insists upon a $50,000.00 cash contribution before signing the contract. Some of the Japanese and American directors think this is an earned commission; you think it's a bribe that violates the Foreign Corrupt Practices Act. The cash contribution is a customary practice in doing business in this foreign country. Explain the difference between a bribe and a commission. Is this requested cash contribution a bribe or a commission? Are either or both ethical?
2. Assume a foreign company is doing business in the United States. In negotiating with that company you discover a valuable patent that is not registered in the U.S. Do you think it is ethically justified to use that patent because the foreign company failed to protect its interest prior to doing business in the U.S.?
3. Suppose you are a stockholder in a multinational corporation doing business in Nicaragua that was seized by the Nicaraguan government. The act of state doctrine may prevent your bringing a lawsuit against Nicaragua in an American court. Do you think it is ethical for our judiciary to refuse to protect American foreign investors in such a case?
4. Assume you are a bank officer working in the international division of an American bank. A third world country is seeking renewal of a substantial loan because of its deep recession and political instability. At a conference with other world bankers in the IMF headquarters in Washington, D.C., you are asked to vote for renewal only on the condition that the country promises to pay back the renewal at a high rate of interest and to stop all government subsidies. Discuss the ethical issues, both pro and con.
5. Suppose you are a director and majority shareholder of an export trading company as defined by the Export Trading Company Act. You are going to engage in international exporting and apply for a certificate of review from the attorney general's office. You know that your application will be published in the *Federal Register,* allowing competitors to take advantage of the information. Would it be ethical to withhold certain information on your application that you think would be helpful to your competition?

Questions on Law

1. Plaintiff, Montreal Trading Ltd., is a Canadian multinational commodities trading corporation that sued the defendant, Amox, Inc., and other United States potash-producing companies for treble damages

under the U.S. antitrust laws. Plaintiff alleges it is unable to sell potash to its customers because the defendants refuse to deal with plaintiff and defendants deliberately limited potash production to increase prices. Plaintiff has not sustained an injury in its business and cannot show that it could have resold any potash that it might have purchased. Is this a violation of our international antitrust laws? Judgment for whom? *Montreal Trading Ltd.* v. *Amox, Inc., et al.*, 661 F.2d 864 (1981).

2. Plaintiff, Taca International Airlines, a San Salvador corporation, brought this suit in a New York court for damages to its airplane caused by the negligence of defendant, Rolls-Royce of England, Ltd., a British corporation with a wholly owned subsidiary, Rolls-Royce, Inc., which sold and serviced the Canadian parent corporation's products in New York. Plaintiff served a summons on the New York subsidiary. Defendant, Rolls-Royce, Inc., brought a motion to dismiss the suit, alleging that service of a summons on its New York subsidiary is not service on Rolls-Royce of England, Ltd. Is service by plaintiff, a San Salvador corporation, on defendant, a subsidiary of a British parent corporation doing business in New York, sufficient service for the New York court to maintain jurisdiction? *Taca International Airlines* v. *Rolls-Royce of England, Ltd.* 204 N.E.2d 329 (N.Y. 1965).
3. Harry Blake, an American citizen, is employed as manager of Deutsch Frau, Ltd., a German retailer doing business in New York. Harry signed a contract not to compete with the company for three years after leaving its employment. The contract provided, "Any controversies arising out of this employment contract that cannot be negotiated by the parties shall be submitted to the International Chamber of Commerce in Bonn, Germany, and will be governed by German law." Harry left their employment and immediately opened a store directly competing with Deutsch Frau, Ltd. Harry wants the case tried in a New York court. May a New York court have jurisdiction over the controversy?
4. Nancy Wilson is the chief executive officer of Midwestern Audiometer, Inc., an Iowa corporation that holds a registered United States patent on a hearing aid. Her company wants to export the hearing aids to various European countries. Nancy asks you if her company's patent is protected overseas. Explain.
5. Tim Wood, an employee of IBM, was wrongfully detained by Venezuelan customs while on company business in Venezuela. As a direct result of this wrongful detention, Tim lost a valuable customer in Venezuela. Tim wants to sue the Venezuela customs official in an American court for damages. What doctrine may prevent him from recovering? Explain.

Suggested Readings

Friedman, Wolfgang G., Lissitzyn, Oliver J., and Pugh, Richard C. *Cases and Materials on International Law*. St. Paul: West, 1969.

Litka, Michael. *International Dimensions of the Legal Environment of Business*. Boston: PWS-Kent, 1988.

Wilson, Donald T. *International Business Transactions in a Nutshell* (Nutshell Series). St. Paul: West, 1981.

Appendix A
The Sherman Act (excerpts)

1. Trusts, etc., in restraint of trade illegal; penalty. Every contract, combination in the form of trust or otherwise, or conspiracy, in restraint of trade or commerce among the several States, or with foreign nations, is declared to be illegal. Every person who shall make any contract or engage in any combination or conspiracy declared by sections 1 to 7 of this title to be illegal shall be deemed guilty of a felony, and, on conviction thereof, shall be punished by fine not exceeding one million dollars if a corporation, or if any other person, one hundred thousand dollars, or by imprisonment not exceeding three years, or both said punishments, in the discretion of the court.

2. Monopolizing trade a felony; penalty. Every person who shall monopolize, or attempt to monopolize, or combine or conspire with any other person or persons, to monopolize any part of the trade or commerce among the several States, or with foreign nations, shall be deemed guilty of a felony, and, on conviction thereof, shall be punished by fine not exceeding one million dollars if a corporation, or, if any other person, one hundred thousand dollars, or by imprisonment not exceeding three years, or by both said punishments, in the discretion of the court.

Appendix B
The Federal Trade Commission Act (excerpts)

5. Unfair Methods of Competition Unlawful; Prevention by Commission—Declaration.
Declaration of unlawfulness; power to prohibit unfair practices.

(a)(1) Unfair methods of competition in or affecting commerce, and unfair or deceptive acts or practices in or affecting commerce, are declared unlawful. . . .

Penalty for violation of order, injunctions and other appropriate equitable relief.

(b) Any person, partnership, or corporation who violates an order of the Commission to cease and desist after it has become final, and while such order is in effect, shall forfeit and pay to the United States a civil penalty of not more than $5,000 for each violation, which shall accrue to the United States and may be recovered in a civil action brought by the Attorney General of the United States. Each separate violation of such an order shall be a separate offense, except that in the case of a violation through continuing failure or neglect to obey a final order of the Commission each day of continuance of such failure or neglect shall be deemed a separate offense.

Appendix C
The Robinson-Patman Act (excerpts)

2. Discrimination in Price, Services, or Facilities

(a) Price; selection of customers.

It shall be unlawful for any person engaged in commerce, in the course of such commerce, either directly or indirectly, to discriminate in price between different purchases of commodities of like grade and quality, where either or any of the purchasers involved in such discrimination are in commerce, where such commodities are sold for use, consumption, or resale within the United States or any Territory thereof or the District of Columbia or any insular possession or other place under the jurisdiction of the United States, and where the effect of such discrimination may be substantially to lessen competition or tend to create a monopoly in any line of commerce, or to injure, destroy, or prevent competition with any person who either grants or knowingly receives the benefit of such discrimination, or with customers of either of them: *Provided,* That nothing herein contained shall prevent differentials which make only due allowance for differences in the cost of manufacture, sale, or delivery resulting from the differing methods or quantities in which such commodities are to such purchasers sold or delivered: *Provided, however,* That the Federal Trade Commission may, after due investigation and hearing to all interested parties, fix and establish quantity limits, and revise the same as it finds necessary as to particular commodities or classes of commodities, where it finds that available purchasers in greater quantities are so few as to render differentials on account thereof unjustly discriminatory or promotive of monopoly in any line of commerce; and the foregoing shall then not be construed to permit differentials based on differences in quantities greater than those so fixed and established: *And provided further,* That nothing herein contained shall prevent persons engaged in selling goods, wares, or merchandise in commerce from selecting their own customers in bona fide transactions and not in restraint of trade: *And provided further,* That nothing herein contained shall prevent price changes from time to time where in response to changing conditions affecting the market for or the market-ability of the goods concerned, such as but not limited to actual or imminent deterioration of perishable goods, obsolescence of seasonal goods, distress sales under court process, or sales in good faith in discontinuance of business in the goods concerned.

(b) Burden of rebutting prima-facie case of discrimination.

Upon proof being made, at any hearing on a complaint under this section, that there has been discrimination in price or services or facilities furnished, the burden of rebutting the prima-facie case thus made by showing justification shall be upon the person charged with a violation of this section, and unless justification shall be affirmatively shown, the Commission is authorized to issue an order terminating the discrimination: *Provided, however,* That nothing herein contained shall prevent a seller rebutting the prima-facie case thus made by showing that his lower price or the furnishing of services or facilities to any purchaser or purchasers was made in good faith to meet an equally low price of a competitor, or the services or facilities furnished by a competitor.

(c) Payment or acceptance of commission, brokerage or other compensation.

It shall be unlawful for any person engaged in commerce, in the course of such commerce, to pay or grant, or to receive or accept, anything of value as a commission, brokerage, or other compensation, or any allowance of discount in lieu thereof, except for services rendered in connection with the sale or purchase of goods, wares, or merchandise, either to the other party to such transaction or to an agent, representative, or other intermediary therein where such intermediary is acting in fact for or in behalf, or is subject to the direct or indirect control, of any party to such transaction other than the person by whom such compensation is so granted or paid.

(d) Payment for services or facilities for processing or sale.

It shall be unlawful for any person engaged in commerce to pay or contract for the payment of anything of value to or for the benefit of a customer of such person in the course of such commerce as compensation or in consideration for any services or facilities furnished by or through such customer in connection with the processing, handling, sale, or offering for sale of any products or commodities manufactured, sold, or offered for sale by such person, unless such payment of consideration is available on proportionally equal terms to all other customers competing in the distribution of such products or commodities.

(e) Furnishing services or facilities for processing, handling, etc.

It shall be unlawful for any person to discriminate in favor of one purchaser against another purchaser or purchasers of a commodity bought for resale, with or without processing, by contracting to furnish or furnishing, or by contributing to the furnishing of, any services or facilities connected with the processing, handling, sale, or offering for sale of such commodity so purchased upon terms not accorded to all purchasers on proportionally equal terms.

(f) Knowingly inducing or receiving discriminatory price.

It shall be unlawful for any person engaged in commerce, in the course of such commerce, knowingly to induce or receive a discrimination in price which is prohibited by this section.

3. Discrimination in Rebates, Discounts, or Advertising Service Charges; Underselling in Particular Localities; Penalties.

It shall be unlawful for any person engaged in commerce, in the course of such commerce, to be a party to, or assist in, any transaction of sale, or contract to sell, which discriminates to his knowledge against competitors of the purchaser, in that, any discount, rebate, allowance, or advertising service charge is granted to the purchaser over and above any discount, rebate, allowance, or advertising service charge available at the time of such transaction to said competitors in respect of a sale of goods of like grade, quality, and quantity; to sell, or contract to sell, goods in any part of the United States at prices lower than those exacted by said person elsewhere in the United States for the purpose of destroying competition, or eliminating a competitor in such part of the United States; or, to sell, or contract to sell, goods at unreasonably low prices for the purpose of destroying competition or eliminating a competitor.

Any person violating any of the provisions of this section shall, upon conviction thereof, be fined not more than $5,000 or imprisoned not more than one year, or both.

Appendix D
The Clayton Act (excerpts)

3. Sale, etc., on Agreement Not To Use Goods of Competitor

It shall be unlawful for any person engaged in commerce, in the course of such commerce, to lease or make a sale or contract for sale of goods, wares, merchandise, machinery, supplies, or other commodities, whether patented or unpatented, for use, consumption, or resale within the United States or any Territory thereof or the District of Columbia or any insular possession or other place under the jurisdiction of the United States, or fix a price charged thereof, or discount from, or rebate upon, such price, on the condition, agreement, or understanding that the lessee or purchaser thereof shall not use or deal in the goods, wares, merchandise, machinery, supplies, or other commodities of a competitor or competitors of the lessor or seller, where the effect of such lease, sale, or contract for sale or such condition, agreement, or understanding may be to substantially lessen competition or tend to create a monopoly in any line of commerce.

6. Antitrust Laws Not Applicable to Labor Organizations

The labor of a human being is not a commodity or article of commerce. Nothing contained in the antitrust laws shall be construed to forbid the existence and operation of labor, agricultural, or horticultural organizations, instituted for the purposes of mutual help, and not having capital stock or conducted for profit, or to forbid or restrain individual members of such organizations from lawfully carrying out the legitimate objects thereof; nor shall such organizations, or the members thereof, be held or construed to be illegal combinations or conspiracies in restraint of trade, under the antitrust laws.

7. Acquisition by One Corporation of Stock of Another

No corporation engaged in commerce shall acquire, directly or indirectly, the whole or any part of the stock or other share capital and no corporation subject to the jurisdiction of the Federal Trade Commission shall acquire the whole or any part of the assets of another corporation engaged also in commerce, where in any line of commerce in any section of the country, the effect of such acquisition may be substantially to lessen competition, or to tend to create a monopoly.

No corporation shall acquire, directly or indirectly, the whole or any part of the stock or other share capital and no corporation subject to the jurisdiction of the Federal Trade Commission shall acquire the whole or any part of the assets of one or more corporations engaged in commerce, where in any line of commerce in any section of the country, the effect of such acquisition, of such stocks or assets, or of the use of such stock by the voting or granting of proxies or otherwise, may be substantially to lessen competition, or to tend to create a monopoly.

This section shall not apply to corporations purchasing such stock solely for investment and not using the same by voting or otherwise to bring about, or in attempting to bring about, the substantial lessening of competition. Nor shall anything contained in this section prevent a corporation engaged in commerce from causing the formation of subsidiary corporations for the actual carrying on of their immediate lawful business, or the natural and legitimate branches or extensions thereof, or from owning and holding all or part of the stock of such subsidiary corporations, when the effect of such formation is not to substantially lessen competition.

8. Interlocking Directorates and Officers

No person at the same time shall be a director in any two or more corporations, any one of which has capital, surplus, and undivided profits aggregating more than $1,000,000, engaged in whole or in part in commerce, other than banks, banking associations, trust companies, and common carriers subject to the Act to regulate commerce approved February fourth, eighteen hundred and eighty-seven, if such corporations are or shall have been theretofore, by virtue of their business and location or operation, competitors, so that the elimination of competition by agreement between them would constitute a violation of any of the provisions of any of the antitrust laws. The eligibility of a director under the foregoing provision shall be determined by the aggregate amount of the capital, surplus, and undivided profits, exclusive of dividends declared but not paid to stockholders, at the end of the fiscal year of said corporation next preceding the election of directors, and when a director has been elected in accordance with the provisions of this Act it shall be lawful for him to continue as such for one year thereafter.

Glossary

a

abstention a doctrine that courts use to decline to try or decide cases. p. 155

abuse of discretion a decision made by a public or administrative official without regard to legal requirements or the best interests of the public. p. 152

acceptance in contract law, manifesting and communicating a willingness to be bound according to the terms of an offer. p. 235

act of state doctrine a doctrine that holds that a sovereign state is obligated to consider the independence of another sovereign state and the courts of one country shall not judge the acts of the government of another committed within its own territory. p. 730

adaptation a test for the importance of a thing to the functioning of a structure which may cause that thing to be treated as real property. p. 176

adjudication in administrative law, the procedure whereby an administrative agency uses court-like procedures to decide cases. p. 128

administrative law the rules and regulations established by administrative agencies as opposed to law created by courts and legislators. p. 16

Administrative Procedure Act in administrative law, the statute that describes the procedures to be carried out by administrative agencies. p. 128

adverse possession transfer of ownership of realty that occurs when one publicly treats land as his own for a substantial period of time without opposition. p. 186

advertising substantiation a requirement that advertisers, at the request of the FTC, furnish tests, studies, or other data to support any claims made about product safety, performance, efficiency, quality, or comparative price. p. 616

affirmative action plan a document, required of all employers receiving federal money, in which the employers must establish goals and timetables for hiring minority employees. p. 419

affirmative disclosure a type of advertising whose remedial purpose is to instill new beliefs about a product. p. 617

Age Discrimination in Employment Act the federal statute that prohibits discrimination based on advanced age. p. 413

agency coupled with an interest occurs when an agent has a claim against the thing the agent is authorized to sell. For example, if a real estate agent had a claim against the owner of a parcel of land and was authorized by the owner to sell the land to earn money to pay the debt, this would be an agency coupled with an interest. p. 281

agent One authorized to alter, or assist in altering, the legal relations of another. p. 267

agreement in contract law, an agreement exists when a valid offer and acceptance exist. p. 225

American Arbitration Association an association that maintains expert arbitrators who are selected by parties to resolve their controversies. p. 63

annexation a refinement of the basic test of mobility whereby if something tangible is permanently attached to realty, then it is legally a part of the realty. p. 175

apparent authority exists when a principal acts toward a third party in a way that leads the third party to believe that someone possesses agency authority. p. 269

appellant the party to a lawsuit who initiates the appeal to overturn a lower court's decision. p. 17

appellate court a court that reviews the findings and procedures of a lower court. p. 69

arbitration a process of formally deciding disputes outside the court system by allowing persons called arbitrators to make the final decisions. pp. 63, 462

arm's length relationship legal relationship in which the law assumes that each party looks out for his own best interest. p. 266

articles 85 and 86 policy statements of the European Economic Community that describe prohibited business practices incompatible with the Common Market. Article 85 prohibits certain practices that create competitive disadvantages between members; Article 86 prohibits certain practices that constitute improper exploitation of a dominant position in the market. pp. 742, 743

articles of organization a formal document filed with the secretary of state's office that grants authorization to incorporate. p. 346

articles of partnership a written partnership agreement. p. 327

assignment a transfer of rights in a contract to one not originally a party to the contract. p. 253

assumption of the risk a situation that occurs when a person knows an action is dangerous and performs the action anyway. pp. 313, 370, 697

attachment a legal process used to seize a debtor's property to satisfy a debt. p. 665

audit committee a committee, comprised solely of directors who are independent of management, that reviews corporate financial statements and recommends the accounting firm to be employed as auditor. All companies listed on the New York Stock Exchange must have audit committees. p. 359

b

barriers to entry conditions that prohibit or discourage new entrants into a field of business. p. 34

best available technology economically achievable a standard for water pollution control that all dischargers of waste were required to comply with by 1987, according to the Clean Water Act. p. 589

best practicable control technology a standard for water pollution control that all dischargers of waste were required to meet by 1977, according to the Clean Water Act. p. 589

bilateral offer an offer that indicates it can be accepted with a promise. p. 231

bona fide occupational qualification an exception to Title VII of the 1964 Civil Rights Act that allows discrimination on the basis of sex, religion, or national origin by employers if this discrimination is reasonably necessary to the carrying out of the employer's business. BFOQs are not favored by the courts. p. 405

breach See *major breach, minor breach.*

bubble concept a regulatory policy that treats a factory's emissions as if they were encased in a single "bubble" and determines the factory's rate of compliance with air pollution standards by calculating the overall amount of pollution it generates, as opposed to calculating the amount generated by each source. p. 588

bulk sale transfer "any transfer in bulk and not in the ordinary course of the transferor's business of a major part of the materials, supplies, merchandise or other inventory of an enterprise." [Art. 6. UCC] p. 679

burden of proof proof in a civil case by a fair preponderance of the evidence. p. 77

business certificate a document filed in the city hall by a sole proprietor showing the business name and the sole proprietor's name and address. p. 327

business judgment rule under this rule, an officer or director will not be held personally liable for an honest and informed business judgment that turns out to be wrong. p. 351

business necessity test a standard that allows employers to discriminate in hiring on the basis of language or national origin if such factors would prevent an employee from properly carrying out the duties of the job. p. 403

business trust a legal device by which title to the trust property is held by trustees on behalf of the trust beneficiaries. p. 343

c

case law a law created when an appellate court issues a written opinion on a case. p. 16

categorical approach identifying frameworks—schemas—for analyzing ethical issues confronted by business managers. p. 54

caveat emptor "let the buyer beware"; the concept that the buyer bears the loss if there is anything defective in the goods he purchases. p. 119

caveat venditor "let the seller beware"; the premise of modern product liability law that the risk of loss for injuries caused by products should fall on the seller. p. 689

cease and desist order in advertising regulation, a type of injunction requiring that an advertising claim no longer be made. p. 617

certificate of review a document requested by an export trading company from the secretary of commerce stating that the secretary of commerce and the attorney general agree that the planned international activity is not an antitrust violation. p. 740

challenge for cause rejection of a prospective juror for a specific reason. p. 79

Chapter 11 plan a plan under which a corporation or partnership may file a voluntary bankruptcy petition, or its creditors may force the business into bankruptcy by filing an involuntary petition, and the debtor company is allowed to continue in business. p. 679

chattel personal property; tangible property that is mobile. p. 189

chip a device that processes electrical impulses through circuits of varying electrical characteristics. p. 203

civil law a set of laws, the violation of which subjects one to liability only to the person injured. p. 19

Civil Rights Act of 1866 a federal law that guarantees all citizens the rights under the law that are enjoyed by white persons. p. 418

class action action brought by a representative of a group who has the same questions of law and facts to be resolved as do the members of the group. p. 73

Clean Air Act the federal statute that mandates programs to obtain certain standards to limit the discharge of pollutants into the air. p. 585

Clean Water Act the federal statute that mandates certain standards to limit the discharge of pollutants into bodies of water. p. 589

closed shop a company that has agreed to hire only members of a particular union. This is now prohibited by federal statutes. p. 447

collective bargaining the process whereby employers bargain with union representatives concerning wages, hours, and other employment conditions. The result of this process is the collective bargaining agreement. p. 446

comity respect or deference; the doctrine upon which an administrative agency or a court defers to the actions or decisions of another court. p. 155

Commerce Clause the clause in the Constitution that gives Congress power to regulate commerce between the states. p. 96

commercial speech speech by businesses; commercial speech is protected by the First Amendment, but may sometimes be limited more than individual speech. p. 103

commingling mixing together the money or property of the agent and the principal. This conduct violates the fiduciary duty of accounting. p. 276

common law the law of England after Magna Carta. p. 7

community property a form of co-ownership only for married couples whereby property acquired during marriage is generally presumed to belong to both wife and husband. It has a modified right of survivorship. p. 181

comparable worth a concept that different jobs that require the same education and the same amount of physical effort to perform should yield the same salaries. p. 430

comparative negligence apportionment of liability between two parties who were both negligent. pp. 313, 697

compensatory money damages in contract law, recovery of the amount of your "bargain" in a contract from the breaching party. p. 259

complaint notification to a defendant describing the nature of the case and summoning him or her to appear and defend. p. 66

Comprehensive Environmental Response, Compensation and Liability Act the "Superfund" act, which provides for the identification and cleaning up of improperly disposed-of hazardous wastes. p. 598

condemnation a procedure by which a governmental agency takes title from an owner involuntarily on payment of reasonable compensation. p. 186

conditional estate ownership of realty that is conditional on some act or event. p. 177

confirmation hearing a hearing held by a bankruptcy court that allows creditors to object to a Chapter 11 plan. p. 678

conflict of interest a situation in which a director is a member of an interlocking board of directors or makes an undisclosed contract with a corporation with which she serves. p. 357

consequential money damages in contract law, recovery for injuries reasonably foreseeable (at the time of the contracting), which are caused by a breach. p. 259

consideration an act, promise, or forbearance, of legal value, given in a bargained-for exchange. pp. 225, 627

consolidated product liability statute a statute that creates one cause of action upon which a person injured by a faulty product may sue; it replaces the three common law theories of negligence, breach of warranty, and strict liability in tort. p. 708

constitutional law generally the supreme source of law as defined by a state or federal constitution. p. 8

Consumer Product Safety Commission the federal agency that establishes safety standards for consumer products and investigates allegations of the marketing of unsafe products. p. 650

Contract Clause a specific provision of the Constitution that guarantees to citizens the freedom to enter into contracts. p. 101

contractual duties obligations imposed on a party by a contract, pp. 225, 252

contractual rights the right, arising out of a contract, to receive a benefit from another party to the contract. pp. 225, 252

contributory negligence a condition that exists when an injured person contributes to her own injury. pp. 313, 370, 696

conventional wisdom beliefs that are common among most people but are not carefully thought through. p. 41

Convention for the Protection of Inventions, Patents, Designs and Industrial Models an association of United States and twelve Latin American countries that have an international treaty granting patent protection to members of the association. p. 730

conveyance the process of transferring the ownership of realty. p. 177

cooling-off period under the Labor Management Relations Act, the period of time that striking or soon-to-strike workers can be ordered back to work by the President of the United States. This can only be done if the threatened or actual strike will affect an entire industry, endangering national safety or health. p. 448

copyright protects the original work of authors, painters, sculptors, musicians, photographers, and others who produce works of artistic or intellectual merit. p. 195

corporate opportunity doctrine prohibits directors from using their position of trust with the stockholders to make a profit for themselves. p. 358

corporation a legal entity created by statute authorizing its officers, directors, and stockholders to carry on business. p. 346

corrective advertising remedial advertising whose purpose is to change or correct erroneous beliefs created by prior deceptive advertising. p. 617

counteroffer an indication by an offeree of a willingness to contract, but on terms different from those proposed by the offeror. p. 234

court of appeals a nonjury appellate court (usually comprised of three judges) that exercises intermediate jurisdiction in various judicial circuits. p. 70

court of original jurisdiction appropriate trial court where a case is first heard. p. 69

covenant not to compete an agreement between an employer and an employee that the employee will not compete with the employer in certain ways if the employment relationship ends. p. 393

criminal law a set of laws, the violation of which is an offense against society. p. 19

customary authority agency authority arising from the way certain transactions are usually handled. p. 272

d

damages a monetary award granted by a court to the plaintiff. p. 81

deceptive advertising exists if there is a representation, omission, or practice that is likely to mislead consumers acting reasonably under the circumstances, and the representation, omission, or practice is material. p. 609

decertification the removal of a union as the exclusive bargaining representative of a group of employees. This occurs after an election in which a majority of the employees vote against the particular union. p. 466

declaration of trust a written trust agreement. p. 343

default judgment a judgment rendered against a defendant who does not appear in court to defend the suit. p. 66

defendant the party being sued by the plaintiff. p. 17

delegation the process by which one constitutionally established branch of government gives part of its power to an administrative agency. Also, a transfer of duties under a contract to one not originally a party to the contract. pp. 120, 253

deliberation the jury's process of arriving at a verdict. p. 81

deontology a type of philosophy that attributes rightness or wrongness to each act without regard for consequences. pp. 24, 46

deposition a pretrial discovery process of testifying under oath. p. 76

design defect the concept that a manufacturer was negligent in designing a product. p. 694

disaffirmance, (right of) in contract law, a special right given those who lack contractual capacity. It allows them to return a non-necessary and receive back the thing exchanged for it under a contract. p. 250

discharge a document issued from a bankruptcy court releasing a debtor from most debts. p. 674

dissolution in partnership law, "a change in the relation of the partners caused by any partner ceasing to be associated in the carrying on . . . of the business." [UPA, Section 29]. p. 337

district courts trial courts that exercise original jurisdiction. p. 70

dual agency one who represents both the principal and the third party in a transaction. p. 275

due process a concept embodied in the Fifth and Fourteenth Amendments to the U.S. Constitution, meaning fundamental fairness and compliance with the basic rules for fair and orderly trials. p. 110

dunning letter a letter demanding payment on an overdue debt. p. 664

duress in contract law, the creation of fear, through a wrongful threat, to win assent to a contractual agreement. pp. 240, 636

duty of accounting a fiduciary duty that requires an agent to disclose to the principal the sources and use of all of the principal's money that the agent has controlled. p. 276

duty of confidentiality a fiduciary duty that requires that the agent not disclose information that the principal desires to keep confidential. p. 276

duty of loyalty and obedience the fiduciary obligation that agents owe their principals. It requires that the agent place the interests of the principal above the interests of all others. p. 275

duty of reasonable care and skill a fiduciary obligation that agents owe principals. It requires the agent to perform the agency actions with reasonable care and skill. p. 276

duty of reimbursement the obligation of a principal to repay the agent for expenses incurred for the benefit of the principal. p. 277

duty to warn the concept that a manufacturer has a duty to warn of possible hazards accompanying the use of a product. p. 694

e

easement irrevocable right to some limited use of another's realty. It is generally given for substantial periods of time. p. 183

egoism a self-centered type of consequential (teleological) ethics. p. 44

Electronic Fund Transfer Act a consumer protection law that establishes the rights of individuals in conjunction with the electronic transfer of funds. p. 651

employee one hired to do work under the direction of the employer for pay. p. 279

Employee Retirement Income Security Act the federal law that requires adequate pension funding by private employers and provides for vesting and portability of pension rights. p. 376

enabling legislation statutes that delegate specific authority to administrative agencies. p. 120

enumerated rights those rights specifically granted to individuals or states in the Constitution. p. 93

environmental impact statement a statement required by the National Environmental Policy Act to be made when any federal action may have an impact on the human environment. p. 582

Environmental Protection Agency the federal agency that oversees the enforcement of most federal environmental protection statues. p. 584

epistemology the study of the way persons obtain knowledge. p. 41

Equal Credit Opportunity Act the federal law that prohibits illegal discrimination in the granting of credit. p. 652

equal dignity rule a provision of the Statute of Frauds that requires that agency agreements be executed with the same degree of formality as the document the agent is authorized to execute. p. 271

Equal Employment Opportunity Commission the federal agency empowered to enforce most federal antidiscrimination statutes. p. 401

Equal Pay Act the federal statute that requires that men and women be paid the same wage for performing substantially similar work. p. 413

equal protection the concept embodied in the Fourteenth Amendment to the Constitution that persons in similar situations cannot be treated differently by the law. p. 111

estate in land a particular bundle of ownership owers in realty. p. 177

European Economic Community an economic alliance of the western European nations, sometimes referred to as the Common Market. p. 742

Exclusionary Rule a rule that prohibits evidence obtained in violation of the Fourth Amendment from being used to convict an accused person at trial. p. 108

executed contract a contract in which all the obligations have already been performed. p. 249

executive function in administrative law, the internal functions carried out by agencies. p. 127

Executive Order 11246 the executive order that requires most contractors with the federal government to engage in affirmative action to hire minorities, and to file affirmative action plans. p. 419

executory contract a contract in which none of the obligations have yet been performed. p. 249

exhaustion of administrative remedies the concept that an individual must go through all of the intra-agency appeals procedures of an administrative agency before that individual can appeal to a court. p. 148

ex parte injunction the order of an equity judge to do or to refrain from doing a particular act. It was widely used before the passage of the Norris-LaGuardia Act to restrict the power of unions to engage in strikes. p. 444

expert testimony testimony from an authority with special knowledge. p. 76

expert witness a qualified witness with special knowledge who may give an opinion in court. p. 76

Export Trading Company Act federal legislation enacted to increase United States exports of products and services. p. 739

express authority agency authority directly created by written or spoken words. p. 272

express warranty affirmative claim that a seller makes about the goods sold. pp. 639, 697

externalities costs or benefits that are not properly "accounted for" in a marketplace transaction. p. 34

f

Fair Credit Billing Act the federal law that grants to consumers certain rights regarding billing for purchases made on credit. p. 656

Fair Credit Reporting Act the federal law that gives consumers the right to examine their credit histories and requires credit reporting agencies to ensure the accuracy of their reports. p. 657

Fair Labor Standards Act the federal law that sets minimum wages and maximum hours of work and regulates child labor. p. 374

false advertising advertising that features untrue statements about the product or business. p. 623

featherbedding the union practice of making work for union members where none exists, so that money is exacted from an employer for services not performed. This is an unfair labor practice under the National Labor Relations act. p. 447

Federal Pesticides Control Act p. 600

Federal Postal Reorganization Act a federal statute that contains a section giving individuals the right to keep unsolicited merchandise that was not mailed to them by mistake. p. 649

Federal Rules of Civil Procedure rules governing procedures in the federal courts. p. 70

Federal Trade Commission Act the act that established the Federal Trade Commission; section 5 prohibits unfair and deceptive trade practices. p. 648

Federal Trade Commission Improvements Act a statute that provides for a congressional veto of FTC regulations. p. 650

fee simple absolute an estate with all the ownership powers allowed by law. p. 177

fellow servant doctrine a legal rule that holds an employer is not responsible for an injury that one employee does to another. p. 370

fiduciary duties the duties imposed by law on each agent. These include the duties of loyalty and obedience, reasonable care and skill, accounting, and confidentiality. p. 267

fiduciary relationship a relationship in which one (the fiduciary) is required by law to place the interests of another (the principal) above the interests of all others, including the fiduciary. p. 266

financing statement a document that states the names and addresses of a creditor and debtor, describes the secured property, and is signed by the debtor. p. 669

firm offer in contract law, a written and signed promise by a merchant to leave an offer for the purchase or sale of goods open for an agreed period of time up to three months. p. 233

fixtures things that were once personal property but have become real property. p. 175

force majeure excusable delays in an international business transaction. p. 728

Foreign Corrupt Practices Act federal legislation requiring corporations to comply with specific accounting standards and anti-bribery regulations. p. 742

Foreign Sovereign Immunities Act a law that provides that foreign states and countries are immune from suits based on their public act but not on their commercial or private acts. p. 735

fraud in contract law, a situation in which one party *intentionally* misrepresents a material fact that the other party relies on to his injury. pp. 239, 301, 636

Freedom of Information Act the federal law that gives citizens access to government information and prohibits secret government deliberations. p. 159

fruit of the poisonous tree doctrine a doctrine that prohibits information from being considered in a trial if that information was obtained as a result of an unconstitutional arrest, search, or seizure. p. 108

future interest an estate that usually grants the owner possession of the realty when a life or conditional estate terminates. p. 178

g

General Agreement on Tariffs and Trade an agreement by various countries to limit import tariffs and trade barriers and thereby encourage multinational trade. p. 746

general partnership an agreement between competent parties to combine their capital and/or services in a business and to share in the profits and losses. p. 327

the good the principal object toward which moral life is directed. p. 43

goods tangible personal property. p. 225

grant and acceptance of authority a communication of agency authority from the principal to the agent along with an indication by the agent of a willingness to perform the agency acts. p. 269

grievance a complaint (filed by a union, an employer, or an employee) in which a violation of a collective bargaining agreement is alleged. p. 462

guarantor a party secondarily liable for the debts of another. p. 681

h

Hazardous and Solid Waste Amendments of 1984 Act an amendment to the Solid Waste Disposal Act and the Resource Conservation and Recovery Act that strengthened and broadened the coverage of solid and hazardous waste disposal regulations. p. 597

hearing examiner in administrative law, a person who presides at an adjudicatory hearing and renders a verdict. p. 134

historical jurisprudence the school of jurisprudential thought that holds that law is an expression of the historical "spirit of the people." p. 5

holder in due course a person legally in possession of a negotiable instrument who has taken the instrument for value, in good faith, and without notice that the instrument is overdue, has been dishonored, or that there is a claim or defense against the instrument. p. 647

i

implied warranty a warranty that is created automatically upon the sale of goods, apart from any assertion by the seller. pp. 639, 697

incidental authority agency authority *implied* in the grant of express authority. p. 272

independent contractor one hired to accomplish a task, but who is not subject to control over how it is accomplished. p. 279

injunction a court order commanding a party to a lawsuit to cease certain conduct. p. 21

in rem jurisdiction property rights in land within the court's jurisdiction. p. 68

instructions to the jury directions that a judge gives to the jury explaining the law to be applied to the facts that the jury finds. p. 81

International Monetary Fund a specialized agency of the United Nations whose purpose is to resolve international monetary problems. p. 743

International Patent Cooperation Union a union of over twenty-five countries that deals in patent protection in those countries through one international filing of an application; it is administered by the International Bureau of the World Intellectual Property Organization at Geneva. p. 730

involuntary bankruptcy petition petition filed by creditors that causes a debtor to declare bankruptcy. p. 674

j

joint tenant co-owner of real estate with other joint tenants, each of whom has an equal interest in the property. Joint tenancy includes the right of survivorship, and any number can co-own as joint tenants. p. 181

joint venture an association of two or more parties who may be individuals, partners, or corporations engaged in business for a profit, often used in international business. p. 728

Judeo-Christian ethics the revelational ethic prescribed by the Old and New Testaments defining the appropriate relations among persons. p. 49

judicial review the process whereby a court reviews administrative agency action in order to insure that the action is legal and in compliance with the agency's enabling legislation. pp. 92, 148

jurisdiction in personam jurisdiction over the person of the defendant. p. 66

jurisprudence the study of the science or philosophy of law as distinguished from the study of only the rules of law. p. 4

jurisdiction over the subject matter a requirement that a court have jurisdiction over the matter being litigated. p. 65

jury a group of twelve people selected to hear a civil or criminal case and decide the facts. p. 79

k

Kantian ethics an ethical system based on the view that persons are autonomous moral entities who, by practical reasoning, give to themselves moral law. p. 46

l

laissez-faire "let (people) do (as they please)"; in business, the concept that a business should be free to do anything it pleases, as long as it does not break the law. p. 118

legal realism the idea that the American legal system is a good legal structure but that it can be corrupted when nonlegal factors influence legal decisions. p. 6

letter of credit a promise by a bank to pay drafts drawn on it in accordance with its terms. p. 729

license a written or oral right to come upon the realty of another for a very short period of time. p. 183

lien a financial claim against the value of any estate by a party other than the owner. pp. 183, 667

life estate ownership of realty for a time limited by the length of a life. p. 177

life of an offer a specified time period during which an offeree may accept an offer. p. 233

limited partnership a partnership formed by two or more persons having as members one or more general partners and one or more limited partners with limited liability. p. 338

literal truth deception deceptive advertising in which all of the statements made are technically true, but the total impression conveyed is misleading. p. 610

long-arm statutes state laws authorizing the courts to claim jurisdiction over parties outside the state. p. 67

m

Madrid Agreement an agreement among most European countries that permits international filing of trademarks. p. 730

Magnuson-Moss Warranty Act a federal statute that regulates the manner of giving warranties on products. p. 644

mail fraud exists when two elements are present: (1) the scheme to defraud others and (2) the use of the United States mail in the execution of the fraudulent scheme. p. 621

major breach a failure to perform a *major* contractual obligation. p. 257

manifest system a permit system for the use and disposal of hazardous wastes that involves labeling wastes that are created and documenting how they are disposed of. p. 596

market imperfections imperfections in the free enterprise or free market system. p. 34

market power a condition that exists when a firm ceases being a slave to the impersonal forces of the marketplace. p. 34

market share liability in product liability law, the concept that if more than one manufacturer could have caused an injury, liability to a plaintiff injured by a product should be divided according to the market shares held by the various manufacturers at the time the injury occurred. p. 705

meeting competition a defense to price discrimination in which the low price is justified by a good faith response to a competitor's equally low price.

mineral rights the right to dig or mine the earth beneath the surface of a parcel of land. p. 176

minor breach a failure to perform, or completely perform, a relatively minor contractual obligation. p. 257

misrepresentation in contract law, misrepresentation exists when one party *unintentionally* misleads another about a material fact related to their transaction. p. 238

mistake of law in contract law, a mistake of law exists when parties to an agreement misunderstand the law that applies to the transaction. Generally it is not a basis for avoiding a contract. p. 238

mitigation minimizing the extent of an injury; an obligation of someone who is injured by a breach of contract. p. 258

money damages See *damages*.

motion for class action certification a motion by a group of plaintiffs that their cases be united in a class action because the issues of the group are the same and there are too many persons in the group to make them individually appear in court. p. 73

mutual mistake of fact in contract law, a mistake that occurs when parties agree but they both share a wrong belief about the facts of a transaction. It is a basis for avoiding contractual liability. p. 238

n

National Environmental Policy Act a federal act that requires the filing of environmental impact statements for any proposed federal action that might significantly affect the environment. The Act established the Council on Environmental Quality. p. 581

natural law the school of jurisprudential thought that there are truths about what is right law that mankind can come to know, usually by the use of the reasoning mind. p. 4

necessaries things that a person lacking contractual capacity needs to maintain life and basic life style. p. 250

negligence voluntary conduct that foreseeably exposes the interests of another to an unreasonable risk of harm. pp. 307, 691

nonattainment areas areas not in compliance with EPA pollution control standards. p. 587

non-necessaries things that a person lacking contractual capacity *does not need* to maintain life and basic life style. p. 250

nutrition labeling description of ingredients on the label of a food product; required when nutrients are added to food. p. 621

o

Occupational Safety and Health Act the federal law that provides for the setting of standards in the workplace to protect employee safety and health. pp. 377, 600

offer in contract law, an offer must (1) manifest an intent to contract, (2) contain the essential and certain terms, (3) propose legal activities, and (4) be communicated to the offeree. pp. 227, 625

Office of Export Trade office of the Department of Commerce that promotes and encourages the formation of export trade associations and export trading companies. p. 740

offsets the concept that pollution from a new factory in a nonattainment area can be compensated for, or "offset," by reductions in the same type of pollutant by other factories in the area. p. 588

opening statement narration by plaintiff's lawyer on how he intends to prove the allegations in the complaint. p. 81

option a contract to leave an offer open for a specific period of time. p. 233

organizational meeting the first meeting of a corporation after approval of the articles of organization by the state. Bylaws are adopted and corporate elections held, among other activities. p. 347

p

palming off exists when one party creates an impression that its goods are the goods of a competitor. p. 622

partially disclosed principal one who acts through an agent when the third party knows that the agent represents someone else, but the third party does not know who the particular principal is. p. 280

partially executed contract a contract for which some, but not all, of the contractual obligations have been performed. p. 249

partnership by estoppel partnership liability that occurs when a nonpartner allows her name to be held out to the general public as a partner. p. 333

partnership property "all property originally brought into the partnership or subsequently acquired by purchase or otherwise." [UPA, Section 8] p. 336

patent the exclusive right to make, sell, and use a product or process for a period of seventeen years. This exclusive monopoly is granted by the government as an incentive and reward for the creation of ideas that are new, novel, and useful. pp. 193, 730

patent infringement an action that occurs when someone manufactures, sells, or uses a patented invention without authorization. p. 194

pattern and practices suit a lawsuit brought under Title VII of the 1964 Civil Rights Act, in which the plaintiff proves that an employer has engaged in a pattern or practice of illegal discrimination; the plaintiff does not have to prove specific instances of discrimination. p. 401

penumbral rights implied rights based on the Ninth and Tenth Amendments to the U.S. Constitution (nonenumerated rights). p. 93

peremptory challenge dismissal of a juror by either plaintiff's or defendant's attorney without a reason. p. 79

perspective an attribute of a philosophical good that answers the question of whose good—that of the decision maker (self) or that of others. p. 44

plaintiff the party who initiates a lawsuit. p. 17

pluralism a condition that exists when citizens embrace a variety of political, social, philosophical, and religious beliefs. p. 52

police power the ability of government to legislate for the public health, welfare, safety, and morals. pp. 102, 121

positive law jurisprudence the school of jurisprudential thought that holds that valid law is the end result of the lawmaking process of the legitimate governmental authority. p. 5

power of attorney a written grant of agency authority. p. 272

pre-emption in federal-state relations, the concept that where federal and state actions are in direct conflict, the federal action will have priority (the state action is void) p. 94

Pregnancy Discrimination Act the federal law that prohibits discrimination by employers based on pregnancy and prohibits discrimination in providing pregnancy benefits to workers or their spouses. p. 415

presumption of constitutionality a doctrine of judicial review that a statute or act of government is presumed to be constitutional unless it clearly infringes on a specific individual liberty. p. 89

pretrial conference a conference between parties to a lawsuit, the purpose of which is to narrow the issues and the area of dispute before the trial. p. 77

primary air quality standards general standards that outdoor air must meet to protect the public health. p. 585

primary jurisdiction the concept that, if both a court and an administrative agency have the power to hear a case as an initial matter, the agency should hear the case first. p. 158

principal a party who gives authority to an agent to alter, or assist in altering, the principal's legal relations. p. 267

Privacy Act the federal law that protects information about private citizens from general public scrutiny. p. 160

Privileges and Immunities Clause the section of the Constitution that provides that all citizens are entitled to the privileges and immunities guaranteed by a particular state to its own citizens. p. 95

privity at common law, the concept that the purchaser of a product could only sue the person who sold him the product. p. 689

procedural law the legal process that must be followed by the police, the parties to a trial, or a judge. p. 20

process patent a patent issued for a process that alters a substance to produce something new. p. 206

promissory estoppel a promise that causes reasonably foreseeable reliance by the promissee to her substantial injury if the promise is not kept. p. 241

proof of claim the claim filed by a creditor in a bankruptcy case. p. 674

public records doctrine the doctrine that a corporation, a large partnership, or a union cannot claim the Fifth Amendment privilege against self-incrimination for records required by law to be kept for a public purpose. p. 141

puffing expressions of personal opinion about intangible qualities of a product. p. 610

punitive damages awards unrelated to the victim's injuries that are designed to punish the wrongdoer. pp. 239, 259

purchase money security interest an interest in the collateral retained by the seller to secure its price. p. 667

q

quasi-judicial function the power of an administrative agency to function like a court in its adjudication procedures. p. 128

quitclaim deed a type of deed in which the words of conveyance state simply, "quitclaim," and which merely transfers the grantor's ownership, if any exists. p. 184

r

ratification in contract law, when one lacking capacity contracts, attains full capacity, then acts toward the contract as though he intends to be bound, he has ratified. In agency law, when a principal accepts and retains the benefits of a transaction negotiated by a purported agent who was not authorized to act in this manner for the principal. pp. 251, 269

realty land and things immovably attached to the land, such as buildings. p. 175

recording the process of filing a document related to realty with the county clerk, or recorder, or commissioner of documents. p. 187

redemption the debtor's right to pay off an obligation without losing repossessed property. p. 671

rejection the indication of a refusal, by words or conduct, to accept an offer. p. 234

remedies the aid that a court will give to a plaintiff who wins a lawsuit. p. 20

repossession a creditor's right to reclaim collateral because payments have not been made. p. 667

request for instructions request by attorneys asking the judge to instruct the jury in a certain fashion. p. 81

res ipsa loquitur "the thing speaks for itself"; in tort law, the concept that a plaintiff will be able to have a jury decide if negligence occurred if the plaintiff can show (1) the incident was one that ordinarily does not occur without the presence of negligence, (2) the defendant had control over the instrumentality that caused the plaintiff's injury, and (3) the plaintiff did not contribute to her own injury. pp. 312, 693

Resource Conservation and Recovery Act a statute that mandates how dangerous wastes can be used, transported, and disposed of. p. 592

respondent the one who "responds" to an appeal of a court decision and argues that the decision of the lower court was correct. p. 17

restitution in contract law, recovery of something you have given to someone because they have breached a contractual duty owed to you. p. 224

restrictive covenant a promise by the owner or by a former owner of land that limits the owner's use of the land in some way. p. 183

reverse discrimination a condition that exists when attempts to remedy the effect of past discrimination against members of minority groups results in discrimination against members of majority groups. p. 421

revocation in contract law, the withdrawal of an offer before it is accepted. p. 233

right of survivorship the right of surviving co-owners to have the interest of a deceased co-tenant in the property evenly divided among them. The right of survivorship is associated with joint tenancy, tenancy by entirety, and, with some modification, community property. p. 181

right to air space ownership of the air space above the surface of the land. p. 177

right-to-work law a state law that prohibits labor contracts between unions and employers from requiring union membership as a condition of employment. p. 447

ripeness the concept that a court will not hear a case or controversy until all the facts are known and the legal issues are fully developed. p. 152

rulemaking function the legislative procedure of administrative agencies that results in the adoption and issuance of regulations. p. 128

rules of evidence rules governing the admissibility of evidence at a trial. p. 78

s

scope of authority the range of acts of an agent that are authorized by the principal. p. 267

S corporation a small, closely held corporation that is taxed similarly to a partnership for corporate federal income tax purposes. p. 350

secondary air quality standards air pollution standards designed to protect the public interest in areas other than human health. p. 585

secondary boycott the refusal of a union to do business with a third party in order to force the third party to coerce another party (the real target of the union) to comply with the demands of the union. This is an unfair labor practice. p. 447

secondary meaning a shape or style or feature of a product that is arbitrary and nonfunctional, and which the general public comes to view as being associated with a particular product. p. 196

secret profits compensation received by an agent from an agency transaction when the compensation was not authorized by the principal. p. 275

section 402A a section of the Second Restatement of Torts that provides that commercial sellers will be liable for injuries caused by products that were in a defective condition and that were unreasonably dangerous. p. 700

security agreement an agreement that creates or provides for a secruity interest in goods that are purchased from a creditor. p. 667

security interest an interest acquired when any creditor establishes financial rights in personal property, analogous to those of a lien holder in realty. p. 192

service of process delivery of a complaint and summons to a defendant. p. 66

sexual harassment deliberate or repeated unsolicited verbal comments, gestures, or physical contact of a sexual nature that is unwelcome; any conduct of a sexual nature to which submission is made a term or condition of continued employment. p. 438

Sherman Act a federal law that prohibits every contract, combination, or conspiracy in restraint of trade or commerce. p. 739

Social Security a program established by the federal government to pay pensions to retired workers, disabled workers (in some cases), and the dependents of deceased workers. p. 376

Socratic dialog a process of examining philosophical generalizations by testing them against one's other beliefs. p. 42

Socratic knowledge an awareness of philosophical truth. p. 42

sole proprietorship a business that is owned and managed for a profit by one person. p. 325

solicitation of an additional offer in contract law, an action by which an offeree does not reject a first offer but induces the offeror to make a second offer on more favorable terms. p. 235

Solid Waste Disposal Act a federal statute that mandates the creation of standards for the disposal of solid wastes. p. 592

sovereign immunity a doctrine whereby the sovereign or government cannot be sued without its consent. p. 160

specially susceptible class a group of people that is more apt to be injured by a product than the average person. p. 696

specific performance in contract law, a decree by a judge commanding a party to do some act promised in the contract. pp. 21, 225, 260

standing the legal right to maintain a lawsuit; in order to have standing, an individual must have a personal stake in the outcome of a lawsuit. p. 149

stare decisis the doctrine that once case law is established, it must be followed by lower courts in other similar cases. p. 16

state of the art defense a manufacturer's defense in a product liability suit that the product met all applicable statutory safety standards, as well as the safety standards of the relevant industry. p. 694

Statute of Frauds a statute that defines when contracts should be placed in writing. p. 248

statute of limitations a law that fixes the time within which parties must take judicial action to enforce their rights or be barred from suing. p. 709

statute of repose a limit on the period of time a manufacturer of a product is exposed to liability for injuries caused by that product. p. 709

statutory law laws enacted by legislatures. p. 13

strict liability in tort a liability without the showing of fault or negligence by the party held responsible. p. 691

subpoena a writ issued by a court to compel a witness to appear and testify before the court. p. 134

subpoena duces tecum an order for a person to appear before a court or an administrative agency and to bring evidence. p. 134

substantial evidence rule a rule used in judicial review of administrative agency action, whereby a court will not overturn an agency decision if that decision is supported by substantial, probative, and relevant evidence on the record as a whole. p. 158

substantive laws the laws that define the conduct that constitutes a civil or criminal offense. p. 20

summary statement summarization by each attorney of evidence presented at a trial. p. 81

summons a notice from a court ordering a person to appear before that court. p. 66

Supremacy Clause the clause in the Constitution that declares that the Constitution and federal laws made in accordance with it are the supreme law of the land and binding on the states. p. 93

suretyship the written contract between the surety and the creditor allowing the creditor to demand immediate payment from the surety upon the debtor's default. p. 681

surface right the legal right to occupy the surface of a parcel of land. p. 176

t

takeover bid See *tender offer*.

tax treaties contracts between two countries for dividing taxes on international transactions between the country of the source of income and the country of residence of the recipient. p. 745

teleology a type of philosophy that judges the rightness or wrongness of conduct by its consequences. p. 24

tenancy by entirety a form of co-ownership only for married couples. It has the right to survivorship. p. 181

tenancy in common a form of co-ownership that permits any number of co-owners, with any interests, and without the right of survivorship. p. 180

tenancy by partnership a distinct statutory method for partners to hold partnership property, both real and personal. p. 336

termination in partnership law, the dissolution and winding up of partnership affairs. p. 337

test of the reasonable man in contract law, the legal test used to determine whether the offeror has manifested an *intention to contract*. It is an objective test based on an interpretation, by a judge or jury, of the offeror's conduct—in light of the particular facts and circumstances surrounding the conduct. p. 228

third party a party who deals through an agent in negotiations with a principal. p. 267

title ownership of tangible personal property. p. 190

Title VII of the 1964 Civil Rights Act the federal law that prohibits discrimination in hiring, firing, and promotion by most employers on account of race, color, religion, sex, or national origin. p. 400

total impression deception a type of deceptive advertising in which the total impression of the ad has the capacity to deceive consumers, even though its assertions are technically correct. p. 610

Toxic Substances Control Act a federal law that requires the listing and safe handling of toxic substances and prior government approval for using new substances. p. 598

trade disparagement occurs when someone makes a false statement about someone else's business or product. p. 623

trade fixtures the fixtures attached to real property by business tenants. p. 176

trademark a mark made on goods that distinguishes the marked goods from competing goods. pp. 196, 730

trade secret any secret formula, pattern, device, or compilation of information that is used in one's business, and which gives an advantage over competitors who do not know or use it. pp. 194, 292, 393

trial *de novo* a new trial; an appeals court may order a lower court to conduct a trial *de novo* if the appeals court finds an irregularity in the original lower court trial. p. 159

Truth in Lending Act the federal law that requires disclosure of interest payments and establishes liability for loss of credit cards. p. 653

u

unconscionability against public policy; unduly harsh and one-sided. p. 636

undisclosed principal one who acts through an agent when the third party is unaware that the agent represents someone else. p. 280

undue influence in contract law, the abuse of a special relationship, such as that between a lawyer and a client, to win assent to a contractual agreement. pp. 240, 636

unemployment compensation a state-administered program of payments to unemployed workers that is financed by a tax on employers. p. 375

unfair labor practices certain practices of employers or unions that are prohibited by either the National Labor Relations Act or state labor laws. Such practices are illegal because they use force (either economic, mental, or physical) to obtain a desired result, and the parties involved do not have equal bargaining power. p. 446

unfair methods of competition forms of competition between businesses that are unfair, such as deceptive advertising. p. 609

unfairness doctrine a doctrine administered by the Federal Trade Commission under which advertising that is deceptive or advertising aimed at children that encourages unsafe behavior is banned. p. 616

Uniform Arbitration Act a statute establishing arbitration procedures that has been adopted in twenty-three states and the District of Columbia. p. 63

Uniform Commercial Code (UCC) a body of state statutory law that is substantially the same in every state. It governs contracts for the sale of *goods,* but not realty or services. p. 225

Uniform Product Liability Act a model product liability act proposed by a federal interagency task force. Although it has not been adopted by the states, it has served as a guideline for proposed federal regulations. p. 717

union shop a workplace where the employment contract requires employees to join a union after they are hired. p. 447

unilateral offer an offer than indicates it can only be accepted by the performance of an act. p. 231

United Nations Convention on the Recognition and Enforcement of Foreign Arbitral Awards an organization whose purpose is to encourage the recognition and enforcement of commercial arbitration agreements in international contracts and to unify the standards by which agreements to arbitrate are observed and arbitral awards enforced in the signatory countries. p. 729

United States Supreme Court the nation's highest appellate court for federal and state cases; it consists of nine judges who sit in Washington, D.C. p. 71

utilitarianism the consequential approach according to which an action is morally good or "right" if it produces the greatest amount of good for the greatest number of people affected by the act. Conversely, an action is bad or "wrong" if it affects the majority adversely. p. 45

v

values general beliefs, perhaps even philosophical principles, that you have internalized. p. 54

venue location in which a court may legally function. p. 69

verdict judgment by a jury. p. 81

Vienna Trademark Registration Treaty a treaty that permits international filing of trademarks. p. 730

voir dire an examination of prospective jurors by attorneys and the judge before a trial to determine the attitude of each prospective juror about the case. p. 79

Volksgeist a consensus of opinion among the people of a nation. p. 5

w

wage earner's plan a bankruptcy court plan allowing a debtor with regular income to defer creditor's claims under court supervision. p. 678

warranty deed a type of deed whereby the words of conveyance in the deed indicate a promise made by the grantor to the grantee that the grantee will receive all the ownership rights described in the deed. p. 184

warranty of fitness for a particular purpose an implied warranty that promises that goods will be reasonably fit for the particular purpose for which they are being purchased. pp. 639, 698

warranty of merchantability a warranty, implied with the sale of every new product, promising that the product will perform reasonably. pp. 628, 639, 697

warranty statement generally a specific statement about a product, service, or transaction that the buyer relies upon. p. 627

water right the right to control water that is either on or beneath the surface of realty. p. 177

whistle blowing an employee's reporting an employer's illegal or unethical acts. p. 394

will the ability to act consistent with your own beliefs. p. 43

winding up in partnership law, a process that begins upon dissolution of a partnership caused by a change in a partner's relationship with the firm. p. 337

worker's compensation a program under which employers are required to make payments to employees who were injured while doing their jobs, regardless of negligence. p. 370

wrongful appropriation appropriation of trade secrets by competitors through such illegal means as bribery or coercion of employees. p. 195

y

yellow-dog contract an employment contract in which the employer requires the employee to promise not to join a union in order to retain employment. These contracts are illegal. p. 445

z

zoning ordinances enacted by municipalities to regulate land use. p. 581

Index